Fodor's

JAPAN

WELCOME TO JAPAN

Tradition and modernity share space in this island nation where ancient shrines bump up against skyscrapers. Castles and palaces whisper of history, and bullet trains shuttle you through spectacular landscapes to cities packed with world-class restaurants and shopping. From Tokyo's urban sprawl to the peacefulness of Kyoto, from boisterous Osaka nightlife to Hiroshima's contemplative spirit, Japan's big attractions never fail to dazzle first-time visitors. What keeps people coming back is astoundingly delicious food, a unique culture, and warm hospitality.

TOP REASONS TO GO

★ **Urban buzz:** Tokyo's skyscrapers, pedestrian throngs, clockwork trains, and nightlife.

★ **Food:** It's all here, from quick noodles to fresh sushi to delicate *kaiseki* cuisine.

★ **Festivals:** You can drop your inhibitions, pick up the sake, and dance in the street.

★ **Mt. Fuji:** The poster mountain for symmetrical, snowcapped peaks looms large.

★ **Shopping:** Craft markets, street stalls, trendy boutiques, flagship department stores.

★ **Serene spaces:** Temples, shrines, and traditional gardens offer room for reflection.

Fodor's JAPAN

Publisher: Amanda D'Acierno, *Senior Vice President*

Editorial: Arabella Bowen, *Editor in Chief;* Linda Cabasin, *Editorial Director*

Design: Tina Malaney, *Associate Art Director;* Chie Ushio, *Senior Designer;* Erica Cuoco, *Production Designer*

Photography: Jennifer Arnow, *Senior Photo Editor;* Mary Robnett, *Photo Researcher*

Production: Linda Schmidt, *Managing Editor;* Evangelos Vasilakis, *Associate Managing Editor;* Angela L. McLean, *Senior Production Manager*

Maps: Rebecca Baer, *Senior Map Editor;* Mark Stroud (Moon Street Cartography), David Lindroth, *Cartographers*

Sales: Jacqueline Lebow, *Sales Director*

Marketing & Publicity: Heather Dalton, *Marketing Director;* Katherine Punia, *Publicity Director*

Business & Operations: Susan Livingston, *Vice President, Strategic Business Planning;* Sue Daulton, *Vice President, Operations*

Fodors.com: Megan Bell, *Executive Director, Revenue & Business Development;* Yasmin Marinaro, *Senior Director, Marketing & Partnerships*

Copyright © 2016 by Fodor's Travel, a division of Penguin Random House LLC

Writers: Brett Bull, Judith Clancy, Jay Farris, Rob Goss, Misha Janette, Noriko Kitano, Robert Morel, Emma Parker, Annamarie Sasagawa, Chris Willson

Editors: Róisín Cameron (lead project editor), Alexis C. Kelly, Daniel Mangin, Amanda Sadlowski

Production Editor: Elyse Rozelle

22nd Edition

ISBN 978-1-101-87971-9

ISSN 0736-9956

SPECIAL SALES

This book is available at special discounts for bulk purchases for sales promotions or premiums. For more information, e-mail specialmarkets@penguinrandomhouse.com.

PRINTED IN THE UNITED STATES OF AMERICA

10 9 8 7 6 5 4 3 2 1

CONTENTS

Fodor's Features

Isolation and Engagement:
A History of Japan 46
A Taste of Japan 55
Shop Tokyo 209
Peerless Fuji 238
The Philosopher's Path:
Kyoto's Eastern Hills and
Temples 406
The Art of Monozukuri:
Traditional Japanese
Crafts 527
A Walk through Hiroshima's
Peace Memorial Park 562
The Henro: Shikoku's
88-Temple Pilgrimage 595

ABOUT THIS GUIDE

Fodor's Recommendations
Everything in this guide is worth doing—we don't cover what isn't—but exceptional sights, hotels, and restaurants are recognized with additional accolades. **Fodor's Choice** ★ indicates our top recommendations. Care to nominate a new place? Visit Fodors.com/contact-us.

Trip Costs
We list prices wherever possible to help you budget well. Hotel and restaurant price categories from **$** to **$$$$** are noted alongside each recommendation. For hotels, we include the lowest cost of a standard double room in high season. For restaurants, we cite the average price of a main course at dinner or, if dinner isn't served, at lunch. For attractions, we always list adult admission fees; discounts are usually available for children, students, and senior citizens.

Hotels
Our local writers vet every hotel to recommend the best overnights in each price category, from budget to expensive. Unless otherwise specified, you can expect private bath, phone, and TV in your room. For expanded hotel reviews, facilities, and deals visit Fodors.com.

Top Picks

★ **Fodor's Choice**

Listings

✉ Address
📨 Branch address
☎ Telephone
📠 Fax
🌐 Website
📧 E-mail
🎟 Admission fee
🕐 Open/closed times
[M] Subway
✥ Directions or Map coordinates

Hotels & Restaurants

🏨 Hotel
🛏 Number of rooms
🍽 Meal plans
🍴 Restaurant
✍ Reservations
👔 Dress code
▭ No credit cards
[$] Price

Other

⇨ See also
☞ Take note
⛳ Golf facilities

Restaurants
Unless we state otherwise, restaurants are open for lunch and dinner daily. We mention dress code only when there's a specific requirement and reservations only when they're essential or not accepted. To make restaurant reservations, visit Fodors.com.

Credit Cards
The hotels and restaurants in this guide typically accept credit cards. If not, we'll say so.

EUGENE FODOR

Hungarian-born Eugene Fodor (1905–91) began his travel career as an interpreter on a French cruise ship. The experience inspired him to write *On the Continent* (1936), the first guidebook to receive annual updates and discuss a country's way of life as well as its sights. Fodor later joined the U.S. Army and worked for the OSS in World War II. After the war, he kept up his intelligence work while expanding his guidebook series. During the Cold War, many guides were written by fellow agents who understood the value of insider information. Today's guides continue Fodor's legacy by providing travelers with timely coverage, insider tips, and cultural context.

EXPERIENCE JAPAN

WHAT'S WHERE

Numbers correspond to chapters.

3 **Tokyo.** Home to 10% of Japan's population, Tokyo would take a lifetime to fully explore. Rather than any coherent center there is a mosaic of colorful neighborhoods—Shibuya, Asakusa, Ginza, Tsukiji, Shinjuku, and dozens more—each with its own texture.

4 **Side Trips from Tokyo.** A quick train ride to Nikko or Kamakura will provide all your shrine and temple viewings. Hakone offers spectacular views of Mt. Fuji and numerous lakes. In Kamakura, the 37-foot Daibutsu—the Great Buddha—has sat for seven centuries, gazing inward.

5 **Nagoya, Ise-Shima, and the Kii Peninsula.** Ise Jingu (Grand Shrines of Ise)—the most important site in Japan's national religion—is found in Ise-Shima National Park. To the south, the Kii Peninsula has magnificent coastal scenery and fishing villages. Inland, the mountain monastery of Koya-san looms mythically with 120 temples.

6 **The Japan Alps and the North Chubu Coast.** Soaring mountains, slices of old Japan, famed lacquerware and superb hiking, skiing, and *onsen* soaking are found here. In Kanazawa is Kenroku

Garden, one of the three finest in the country.

7 Kyoto. Japan's ancient capital, Kyoto represents 12 centuries worth of history and tradition in its beautiful gardens, castles, museums, and nearly 2,000 temples and shrines—Kinkaku-ji and Kiyomizu-dera top most itineraries. Here you'll also see geisha and sample *kaiseki ryori*, an elegant meal.

8 The Kansai Region. Nara may not match Kyoto's abundance of sacred sites, but its expansive park and Great Buddha at Todaiji Temple are among Japan's finest. Osaka offers a mix of bright lights, as in the Dotombori entertainment area, and tradition, such as at Osaka-jo castle. Just minutes by train from Osaka is Kobe, where European and Japanese influences have long mingled.

9 Western Honshu. Mountains divide this region into an urban south and a rural north. Hiroshima is the modern stronghold, where the sobering remnants of the charred A-Bomb Dome testify to darker times. Offshore at Miyajima, the famous torii shrine gate appears to float on the water. In Okayama, Bizen masters craft the famous local pottery.

WHAT'S WHERE

10 Shikoku. Thanks to its isolation, this southern island has held on to its traditions and staved off the industry that blights parts of Japan. There's great hiking, dramatic scenery, some of the country's freshest seafood, and the can't-miss traditional dancing at the Awa Odori festival in Tokushima.

11 Kyushu. Rich in history and heavily reliant on the agriculture industry, lush Kyushu is the southernmost of Japan's four main islands. At Aso National Park you can look into the steaming caldera of Mt. Naka-dake, an active volcano. With its rolling hills and streetcars, Nagasaki is often called the San Francisco of Japan, a testament to the city's resurrection from the second atomic bomb.

12 Okinawa. Okinawa is known as the Hawaii of Japan. Relaxation and water sports are the main attractions of this archipelago, located some 700 km (435 miles) south of Kyushu. A paradise for snorkelers and scuba divers, the islands teem with reefs, canyons, and shelves of coral.

RUSSIA

Sea of Okhotsk

45°N

HOKKAIDO

Asahikawa
Kitami

Sapporo  14

Muroran Tomakomai
Kushiro

Hakodate

Aomori
Hirosaki Hachinohe

N i b o n – k a i
(S e a   o f   J a p a n)

13

Akita Morioka
Kakunodate
Sakata
Tsuruoka Yamagata
Sado
Island Niigata Sendai
Nagaoka Fukushima
Noto Iwaki
Peninsula
Kanazawa Nagano
Fukui
Gifu Mito
Kyoto Nagoya TOKYO
Tsu Shizuoka
Osaka Mt. Fuji Yokohama
Hamamatsu
Tokushima Nachi **JAPAN**
Shirahama

H O N S H U

40°N

35°N

T A I H E I Y O
O C E A N)
(P A C I F I C

Japan

30°N

140°E
145°E

13 **Tohoku.** Mt. Zao draws skiers, while tourists clamor for a look at the *juhyo*, snow-covered fir trees that resemble fairy-tale monsters. Sendai is a good base for trips to Mt. Zao and Matsushima, a bay studded with more than 250 pine tree-covered islands. Make time for the traditional town of Kakunodate and Japan's deepest lake, Tazawa-ko.

14 **Hokkaido.** Japan's northernmost island is also its last frontier. Glorious landscapes, hiking, and skiing adventures await. In February, the Sapporo Snow Festival dazzles with huge ice sculptures. To the south are the famous hot springs of Noboribetsu Onsen and Jigokudani (Valley of Hell), a volcanic crater that belches boiling water and sulfurous vapors.

JAPAN TODAY

Politics

After Prime Minister Junichiro Koizumi retired in 2006 following an enthusiastic spree of free-market economic reforms, Japan stumbled through seven years of political instability. Three prime ministers from the Liberal Democratic Party—Shinzo Abe, Yasuo Fukuda, and Taro Aso—came and went in quick succession without consolidating leadership. Fed up with LDP fecklessness, the Japanese public elected Yukio Hatoyama from the Democratic Party of Japan in 2009, turfing the LDP from power for the first time in decades. Unable to deliver on his big campaign promises, including a pledge to move the U.S. military base in Okinawa, Hatoyama resigned after less than a year in office. He passed the DPJ reigns to two short-lived successors who couldn't break through the political gridlock. Finally, elections in 2013 brought the LDP's Shinzo Abe back for another go at leading the country, and he agian won a majority in December 2014. This time, Abe promised an ambitious "Abenomics" economic development strategy while making no secret of his hope to amend Japan's pacifist constitution to allow the nation to maintain a standing army. Public reaction to the former has been enthusiastic; to the latter, ambivalent. An increasingly assertive China has many wondering if Japan should remove the constitutional constraints on its Self Defense Forces, but memories of World War II are fresh enough in collective memory to prompt second thoughts. At the core of this national debate and political maneuvering is the issue of how Japan sees itself: a bold nation actively shaping world affairs, or a peaceful middle power focused on growing an economy that assures the good life?

Arts and Culture

While its ever-changing cast of politicians was busy making speeches and promises, Japan's creative class was enjoying a boom of its own. The last two decades have seen exceptional creative output in Japan's fine arts, music, cinema, and architecture from Japanese artists such as novelist Haruki Murakami, animator Hayao Miyazaki, artist Takashi Murakami, fashion designer Rei Kawakubo, and architect Tadao Ando—though more than a few in this list would prefer to be known as artists, period, without the "Japanese" qualifier. Coinciding with a government push in the last decade to increase Japan's "soft power" or cultural influence around the globe, exports of anime and popular music have boomed. While Japan is the homeland of anime, in the world of teen-targeted pop music it has fierce competition from Korea's arsenal of bouncy boy bands and girl groups. As Japan's AKB48 goes head to head with Korea's Girls Generation in the global soft power arms race, a not unreasonable conversation is taking place in Japan's cultural policy circles about whether the candy-coated giddiness of Japanese pop music is really the face the nation wants to present to the world. What was wrong, ask the naysayers, with a nice, quiet tea ceremony and a spot of kabuki?

Green Japan

An island nation with limited natural resources, for much of its history Japan found ways to live within its energy means. Oil imports enabled by its postwar economic recovery as well as hydroelectric dams and nuclear power plants brought the country the energy it needed to power the Tokyo skyline, the Shinkansen, and the family sedan. When the nuclear reactors at Fukushima Daiichi

Power Plant began exploding after being swamped with tsunami water on March 11, 2011, however, that old Japanese reverence for nature came roaring back. Eco-consciousness, already making its way to the Japanese mainstream before 3/11, took center stage with government-promoted energy-saving measures and eco-friendly technology debuting across Japan. Japan's wholehearted drive to go green manifests in everything from Kyoto's electric city buses to the lightweight "cool biz" suits marketed to office workers so they'll use less air-conditioning. Although Japan still has 48 operational nuclear reactors, they were all shut down following the Fukushima disaster and as of late 2015 only the Sendai plant has been brought back.

Neighborly Relations

In person-to-person encounters with foreigners in temples, onsen, or city streets, the Japanese are gracious hosts. At the state level, though, Japan has been somewhat of a testy neighbor of late. Wartime trauma at the hands of the Japanese Imperial Army still smolders in social memory in Korea, China, and Taiwan—often deliberately stoked by politicians when it suits their needs—and Japan's political classes have been less than tactful about expressing their less-than-apologetic view on history. From annual visits by Japanese lawmakers to Tokyo's Yasukuni shrine, where 14 Class A war criminals are enshrined to then-Osaka mayor Toru Hashimoto's indelicate comment that the sexual slavery of Korean "comfort women" in World War II army brothels was "necessary," Japan's political class has not exactly gone out of its way of late to mend fences with the neighbors. Tensions flared with China in late 2012 over the Senkaku Islands, a chain of uninhabited Japan-administered islands near Taiwan that China also lays claim to, leading to the scrambling of Self Defense Forces fighter jets and massive anti-Japanese riots in China. It's a political tinderbox that the United States, bound to protect Japan under a defense alliance, watches carefully. Happily, Japan enjoys warm relations with Southeast Asia, partly due to decades of generous overseas development assistance.

Japan Tomorrow

It may be short of nurses to care for its aging population, but one occupation group Japan doesn't lack are would-be oracles making dire predictions for the nation's future. If you believe the media pundits, it's all a bit grim: Japan tomorrow will be a hapless nation of senior citizens on a bankrupt pension system, vainly trying to defend its territory from China, which, anyway, has already taken all the jobs. The likely truth is a bit brighter and a lot more global. Fast-expanding Asian markets and closer economic integration between Japan and its neighbors mean new opportunities for Japanese exporters. Japan's universities are aggressively recruiting talented students from around the world, hoping to nurture a global network of Japan-friendly future leaders. And while foreign residents of Japan are still less than 2% of the population, Japan made recent reforms to its immigration system, hoping to attract top talent to live and work in the country. The problems remain—an insufficiently funded social safety net, a dearth of stable career opportunities for young people, and one of the lowest birth rates in the world are just a few—but, as the nation's reaction to the 3/11 Tohoku disaster proved, Japan's resilience is nothing short of extraordinary.

JAPAN
TOP ATTRACTIONS

Mt. Fuji

(A) Mt. Fuji, the nation's highest peak, rises 12,388 feet. One of Japan's most famous symbols, the symmetrical Fuji-san inspires artists and commoners alike. The dormant volcano sits between Yamanashi and Shizuoka prefectures. During nice weather, it can be viewed from Tokyo and Yokohama. For a closer peek, climb it in summer or see it from the Shinkansen train between Tokyo and Osaka.

Imperial Palace East Gardens

(B) Open to the public, the gardens are all that remain of the former innermost circle of defense for Edo Castle, the residence of the Tokugawa Shogun between 1603 and 1867. The gardens are accessed by three gates: Hirakawa-mon, Ote-mon, and Kitahanebashi-mon. Sculpted, rolling greenery surround stone walls, moats, and guardhouses.

Grand Shrines of Ise

(C) Located in Mie Prefecture, the Ise Jingu Shrine is arguably Japan's most revered shrine complex. Often referred to simply as Jingu, or "The Shrine," it includes more than 100 small Shinto shrines and two main shrines, Naiku and Geku. Naiku, the Inner Shrine, houses the sun goddess Amaterasu omikami. The Outer Shrine, Geku, is home to the deity for industry and agriculture, Toyouke no omikami.

The Temples of Kyoto

(D) The former capital of Japan, Kyoto, is known for its grand, historic structures. Two of the famous Buddhist temples are the Ginkaku-ji (1474), the "Temple of the Silver Pavilion," which features the Kannon Hall and a rock-and-gravel Japanese garden, and Kinkaku-ji (1393), its golden sister that includes a gold-leaf adorned hall. Each is fronted by a spectacular lake.

Dotombori

(E) Osaka's liveliest entertainment area, Dotombori is a single street running along the Dotombori canal in the city's Namba district. It is filled with many small bars and restaurants. Be sure to sample the local specialty: *takoyaki* (battered octopus). Following large sporting events the street is at its most frenzied, with revelers sometimes diving into the canal.

Peace Memorial Park

(F) Hiroshima's Peace Memorial Park, dedicated to those killed following the atomic bomb attack, is the city's most famous tourist attraction. Inside is the Peace Memorial Museum, which provides a history of the bomb. Also in the park is the A-Bomb Dome (the former Prefectural Industrial Promotion Hall), whose curved roof stands partly intact and serves as a symbol of peace.

Koya-san

Deep in the mountains of Wakayama Prefecture, this mountain temple town is the holy site of Shingon Buddhism. Wandering priest Kobo Daishi founded Koya-san in the 9th century and his devotees have been following the esoteric practices of the sect ever since. A visit to the head temple, Kongobu-ji, and a stroll through the more than 100,000 tombs in Okuno-in graveyard put Japan—and life—in context.

Naoshima

This tiny island in the Seto Inland Sea has 0.02% of Tokyo's population but boasts contemporary art museums rivaling anything Tokyo has to offer. The Tadao Ando–designed Chichu Art Museum in particular, built into a hillside looking over the shimmering inland sea, is world-class.

TOP EXPERIENCES

Sumo

Sumo pits two extremely large athletes against one another in a ring (*dohyo*). A wrestler who breaches the ring's boundary or touches the ground with a body part (other than the sole of his foot) loses. Originally intended as entertainment for Shinto gods, single bouts usually last less than a minute. Tournaments, running 15 days, are held three times a year in Tokyo and once a year in Osaka, Nagoya, and Fukuoka. Novice wrestlers (*jonokuchi*) compete in the morning and top athletes (*yokozuna*) wrestle in the late afternoon. Crowds get pretty boisterous, especially for the later matches.

Ryokan

The *ryokan,* or traditional Japanese inn, offers rooms outfitted with Japanese-style interiors, such as tatami flooring and paper (*shoji*) blinds. For in-room tea service pillows and small tables make sitting very comfortable. Futons are rolled out onto the tatami at bedtime. Meals, often included in the room rate, are breakfast and dinner, both of which contain small Japanese dishes of various seafood and regional specialties.

Japanese Gardens

Gardens in the traditional Japanese style appear in parks, on castle grounds, and in front of shrines and temples. Featuring stone lanterns, rocks, ponds, a pavilion, and rolling hedges, many of the principles that influence Japanese garden design come from religion. Shintoism, Taoism, and Buddhism all stress the contemplation and re-creation of nature as part of the process of achieving understanding and enlightenment. Jisho-ji Garden and Nijo Castle Ninomaru Garden in Kyoto and Hamarikyu Gardens in Tokyo are some of Japan's more prominent gardens to visit.

Karaoke

Karaoke is a Japanese institution whose rabid popularity cannot be understated. Often used as an after-work recreation, the activity is enjoyed by millions and involves the singing of a popular song into a microphone as the instrumental track plays on the in-room sound system and its lyrics roll across a monitor. Rooms, referred to as karaoke boxes, can be rented by the hour and seat between 2 and 10 customers.

Baseball

Yakyu (baseball) is often said to epitomize the Japanese character. Players are subject to punishing preseason training regimes that test their stamina and will. In contrast to the American style of play, the sacrifice bunt is a routine tactic, often employed in the early innings. The prized quality of group harmony is evident as ballparks reverberate to repetitive theme songs created for each batter, with the fans of the Hiroshima Carp going through perhaps the most elaborate routines. Following the final out of the Japan Series, fans of the winner crowd into city streets for a night—or, if it's Osaka's Hanshin Tigers, jump from a bridge into a canal—and hit the victory sales at local stores that will follow.

Seafood and Sushi

As might be expected of a nation consisting of 3,000 islands, Japan is synonymous with the fruits of the sea. Sashimi and sushi have gained popularity with restaurant goers around the world, but it's hard to imagine some other so-called delicacies catching on. The northern island of Hokkaido boasts of the quality of its *uni* (sea urchin), while Akita Prefecture is famous for *shiokara* (raw squid intestines). Domestic tourism and television schedules are dominated by food, and city dwellers travel the length and breadth of the country on weekend excursions to taste regional specialties.

Depato

Department stores (*depato*) are towering palaces that cater to the whims of the kings and queens of global consumerism. From the ultrapolite elevator attendants to the expert package wrapper, the attention to detail is extraordinary. Established stores follow a convenient pattern in their layout. In the basement is an expansive array of elaborately presented food, ranging from handmade sweets to bento boxes. The first floor has cosmetics, and the next floors offer the latest in female fashion. Farther up you will find designer suits for men, ornate stationery, and refined home decorations. Finally, on the top floor, often with excellent urban views, is a restaurant area.

The Performing Arts

The performing arts date back hundreds of years but are still practiced in theaters across Japan. *Noh* is a minimalist dance drama where a masked actor performs stylized moves accompanied by instrumental music. Often in conjunction with Noh are *Kyogen* performances, which are comedic plays known for their down-to-earth humor. *Kabuki* is theater performed by adult males who also portray the female roles. Fans of puppet theater may enjoy a *Bunraku* performance, in which large puppets are manipulated to the accompaniment of narrators and stringed instruments.

Onsen

The Japanese share their country with more than 100 active volcanoes, and certainly make the most of one of the consequences: thermal hot springs. Japan has more than 6,700 onsen hot springs with facilities ranging from simple outdoor baths to lavish resort complexes. A soak in a Japanese onsen, be the facilities humble or grand, offers not only total relaxation but a chance to see the unguarded, playful side of Japanese society. Japan's top onsen include Hakone, where onsen ryokan have a long tradition of hospitality; the sulfurous waters of Kusatsu Onsen; the huge *dairotenburo* outdoor bath at Zao Onsen; and the ancient springs of Dogo Onsen.

Tea Ceremony

The tea ceremony, or *chanoyu* (the Way of Tea), is a precisely choreographed program that started more than 1,000 years ago with Buddhist monks. The ritual begins as the server prepares a cup of tea for the first guest. This process involves a strictly determined series of movements and actions, including the cleansing of each utensil to be used. One by one, the participants slurp up their bowl of tea and then eat a sweet confectionery served with it. In Tokyo, the teahouse at Hamarikyu Gardens offers a wonderful chance to enjoy this tradition.

Nightlife

Cocktails with pizzazz in a skyscraper's rooftop lounge or streetside sticks of skewered chicken, dreamy jazz or thumping techno beats—you'll find it all under urban Japan's neon-soaked night sky. Walking the bar-and-club crazy streets at night is a great way to discover a city's character, though the side of the city you'll see depends on whether you choose a sophisticated lounge, karaoke club, *izakaya,* nightclub, or jazz bar. Roppongi in Tokyo or Dotombori in Osaka have enough to keep all-night revelers going till dawn.

IF YOU LIKE

Architecture

The range of climates in Japan and the sweeping social changes over the centuries have left their trace in the country's architecture. It's all here, from temple design brought over from China in the 8th century to traditional thatched-roof farmhouses in the Japan Alps to the bold creativity of contemporary projects. If these walls could talk, they'd read you the entire social history of Japan.

Byodoin Temple, Kyoto. The Phoenix Hall at Byodoin is a beautiful example of 11th-century religious architecture. The temple garden is an attraction in its own right.

Hiroshima Peace Memorial Park, Hiroshima. Kenzo Tange, the father of modern Japanese architecture, took on the mammoth task of presenting wartime atrocity as a memorial to peace.

National Art Center, Tokyo. The glass and concrete curves of this Kisho Kurokawa–designed contemporary art museum marked a new wave in architectural creativity.

Shirakawa-go, Kanazawa. The preserved gassho-zukuri farmhouses in this mountain village testifies to the architectural ingenuity required to survive the region's bitter winters.

Garden Life

Gardens are an obsession in Japan. Many urban homes have a couple of topiary trees, and Buddhist temples nationwide have immaculately maintained grounds. The best Japanese gardens are like the canvasses of master painters, in which nature is ingeniously manipulated and represented in subtly rearranged forms. Some re-create entire landscapes in miniature, and are designed for viewing from one optimal position. Others skillfully integrate immense backdrops of mountains or forest, always managing to add to the innate beauty of the natural environment. Kyoto is home to Zen gardens, minimalist affairs of raked sand, moss, and meaningfully arranged rocks.

Imperial Palace East Garden, Tokyo. An oasis of tree-lined paths, rhododendrons, and water features that provides great views of the Imperial Palace buildings.

Kenrokuen, Kanazawa. Originally landscaped in 1676, 25-acre Kenrokuen looks good all year round thanks to a wide variety of seasonal plants and trees.

Koinzan Saiho-ji, Kyoto. The so-called Moss Temple has an extraordinary Zen garden, though entry is extremely pricey and requires advance permission.

Suizen-ji Koen, Kumamoto. Part of this garden re-creates the 53 stations of the old Tokaido post road that was immortalized by Hiroshiga Ando in a series of woodblock prints.

Outdoor Adventure

For many people modern Japan conjures images of the concrete, neon-lighted urban jungles of Kanto and Kansai. The country's wealth of natural attractions is easily overlooked, but outdoor enthusiasts will find their every whim catered to. In winter generous snowfall makes Hokkaido and Nagano ideal destinations for skiers and snowboarders. The Japan Alps mountain range that stretches along the north side of Honshu offers excellent hiking trails, and Shikoku is well suited to cyclists. To the south, Okinawa boasts tropical temperatures for much of the year, and its clear waters are excellent for scuba diving and snorkeling.

Kamikochi, Nagano. En route to this small mountain village you pass though some stunning scenery, and upon arrival a series of trails provides access to the upper reaches of the surrounding peaks.

Manta Scramble, Okinawa. From July to October divers can observe rarely seen manta rays feeding on plankton off the coast of Ishigaki Island.

Niseko, Hokkaido. Australians in the know head here by the tens of thousands each winter for arguably the best skiing in Japan.

Shikoku. The best way to enjoy this picturesque island in the Inland Sea is from the seat of a bicycle. Slow down to the local pace and spend time exploring unexpected diversions.

Holy Sites

Most modern Japanese would not express an affiliation with one religion, and both Shintoism and Buddhism play important roles in many people's lives. Shinto architecture, with the exception of Nikko's colorful shrines, tends to be plain and simple, like the style of the nation's most sacred site at Ise, emphasizing natural materials such as wood and thatch. Temples run the gamut from austere to gaudy, both in color and design. Kyoto boasts many of the finest examples of religious architecture, while in mountain areas the act of pilgrimage and supplication to the elements is almost as important as the shrines and temples themselves.

Ise Jingu, Mie Prefecture. Home of Shintoism, the national religion, the Grand Shrines of Ise are majestic thatched wooden buildings concealed in expansive forested grounds.

Kiyomizu-dera, Kyoto. The Golden Pavilion of Kinkaku-ji may feature on more postcards, but this temple's large-scale wood construction is stunning. The steep approach to Kiyomizu-dera is lined with hundreds of craft, souvenir, and food shops.

Senso-ji, Asakusa, Tokyo. Proof positive that even Japan's largest metropolis can preserve tradition. Senso-ji has a tangible Old Tokyo atmosphere from the first entrance gate, with its immense red lantern, through the narrow pedestrian streets to the huge incense burners of the temple.

Todai-ji, Nara. This temple's Daibutsu-den (Hall of the Great Buddha) is the largest wooden building in the world, and houses Japan's biggest Buddha figure, cast in bronze.

Quintessential Dining Experiences

You wouldn't think it to look at its slim inhabitants, but Japan is a nation passionate about food. Some of the offerings can catch you off guard (crab brain sushi, anyone?) but you won't find greater dedication to flavor and presentation anywhere else in the world. From Hokkaido crabs to Kyushu horse sashimi, each region has its own much-touted special dishes. Taste first, ask questions later.

Dotonbori River, Osaka. Osakans take eating delightfully seriously; this riverside nightlife district is the place to sample *okonomiyaki, takoyaki,* and *fugu* blowfish.

Koya-san, Wakayama. Staying in a temple in this mountain monastery town gives you the chance to try the subtle flavors and textures of *shojin ryori,* Buddhist vegetarian cuisine.

Tsukiji Fish Market, Tokyo. The world's largest wholesale fish and vegetable market is where to go for the freshest sushi breakfast you'll ever have (and never forget).

NEED TO KNOW

Sea of Japan

JAPAN

Tokyo

Pacific Ocean

AT A GLANCE

Capital: Tokyo

Population: 128,000,000

Currency: Yen

Money: ATMs are common in big cities, but many do not accept foreign-issued cards; cash is more widely used.

Language: Japanese

Country Code: 81

Emergencies: Ambulance and Fire: 119; Police: 110

Electricity: 100v/50 cycles in Eastern Japan; 100v/60 cycles in Western Japan; electrical plugs have two flat prongs

Time: 13 hours ahead of New York

Documents: Up to 90 days with valid passport for American citizens

Mobile Phones: 3F W-CDMA or 4G LTE

Major Mobile Companies: Docomo, SoftBank, KDDI

Official Tourism Guide for Japan: ⊕ www.japantravelinfo.com

GETTING AROUND

✈ **Air Travel:** Most international flights land at Narita or Haneda in Tokyo.

🚌 **Bus Travel:** Overnight buses are surprisingly luxurious and less expensive than trains.

🚗 **Car Travel:** You need an international driving permit (IDP) to drive in Japan. A car can be the best means for exploring rural areas, especially Kyushu and Hokkaido.

🚆 **Train Travel:** Japanese trains are efficient and convenient and run frequently and on schedule.

PLAN YOUR BUDGET

	HOTEL ROOM	MEAL	ATTRACTIONS
Low Budget	¥6,000	¥700	Imperial Palace, Tokyo: Free
Mid-Budget	¥17,000	¥3,000	National Museum, Tokyo: ¥620
High Budget	¥30,000	¥8,000	Kabuki theater single act: ¥2,000

WAYS TO SAVE

Go for ramen. Alternate your sashimi meals with heaping, hearty, bowls of ramen.

Book a capsule hotel. These have tiny, inexpensive rooms; they're called pod hotels in the West.

Get a JR Pass. A Japan Rail Pass can save you quite a bit of money.

Ask for discounts. Foreign visitors often get discounts to public museums and sights if you show your passport.

Take the slow train. If you have more time, skip the Shinkansen and travel by local trains.

Hassle Factor	Low. There are direct daily flights from the United States. Transportation from the airports and across Japan is easy to use, and trains and buses run frequently and on schedule.
3 days	See old and new Tokyo with a visit to buzzing Harajuku and tranquil Yoyogi Park, home to the Meiji Shrine.
1 week	Take your time in exploring Tokyo before hopping on the train to Kyoto. Unwind at the tranquil temples for which Kyoto is so well known. Day trips to urban Osaka and quaint Nara can be done easily by train.
2 weeks	After Tokyo, take a day trip to Nikko, then head to Nagoya and on to Takayama in the Japanese Alps. From there, go to Shirakawa-go. Wrap up in Osaka, Nara, and Kyoto.

WHEN TO GO

High Season: Japan's best seasons are spring and fall. To avoid crowds, be aware of when locals are on vacation: at these times,planes, trains, and hotels are booked far in advance, and many businesses are closed. Holiday periods include New Year's; Golden Week, which starts April 29; and mid-August.

Low Season: Summer brings the rainy season, with particularly heavy rains and stifling humidity in June and July. Avoid scorching July and August, unless you're visiting Hokkaido, where temperatures are more bearable.

Value Season: Winter can be chilly and overcast, but there's little snow in most areas and outside of the New Year's period, prices are low and hotels rarely fill up.

BIG EVENTS

February: Sapporo Snow Festival is a weeklong winter wonderland. ⊕ www.snowfes.com/english

Late March through April: Cherry blossom season sees trees across the country in gorgeous bloom. ⊕ www.mint.go.jp/category/eng

July: Gion Matsuri features enormous elaborate floats and parades, food stalls, and locals in traditional dress. ⊕ www.yasaka-jinja.or.jp

November: Tori no Ichi festival in Tokyo features specialty foods and the selling of a bamboo rake believed to bring good luck. ⊕ www.torinoichi.jp/english

READ THIS

■ *Memoirs of a Geisha,* Arthur Golden. Fictional life of a geisha before and after WWII.

■ *Kawaii!: Japan's Culture of Cute,* Manami Okazaki, Geoff Johnson. The history of "kawaii."

■ *Norwegian Wood,* Haruki Murakami. A man looks back on his student days in Tokyo.

WATCH THIS

■ *Lost in Translation.* Bill Murray and Scarlett Johansson share feelings of culture shock.

■ *Jiro Dreams of Sushi.* Touching documentary on 89-year-old sushi master Jiro Ono.

■ *My Neighbor Totoro.* Miyazaki's animated masterpiece, set in post–WWII Japan.

EAT THIS

■ *Ramen*: Wheat noodle in a meat-based broth.

■ *Sushi*: Raw fish atop cooked vinegared rice.

■ *Tamagoyaki*: Rolled omelet.

■ *Taiyaki*: A sweet fish-shape cake.

■ *Yakitori*: Any meat skewered and grilled

■ *Matcha*: Powdered green tea leaves whipped with water.

HOTEL AND RESTAURANT PLANNER

Making Reservations

The best way to book major chain hotels is through the company's website. The websites for smaller business hotels and ryokan usually lack English content online. Travel sites, such as **Rakuten** (⊕ *travel. rakuten.com*), Jalan (⊕ *www.jalan.net*), or JAPANiCAN (⊕ *www.japanican.com*) can assist booking these hotels. Making your Tokyo hotel reservation before you arrive is highly recommended. If you have not done so, head to a tourist office at the airport or major rail station for assistance.

Lodging Costs

Rates for the top foreign and domestic chains are generally in the ¥30,000–¥60,000 range (and could even go a bit higher). Business hotel rooms, with far fewer amenities, are available for under ¥20,000. A minshuku provides Japanese-style lodging and meals for roughly ¥8,000. A ryokan offers stays for between ¥10,000 and ¥30,000 that include meals and use of the onsen. Shoestring travelers head to hostels where a night's stay costs around ¥3,000. Capsule hotels are similarly priced.

Choosing the Right Hotel

Accommodations in Japan range from Japanese-style inns to large Western-style hotels, in all price categories. It's essential to book in advance if you're traveling during peak travel seasons and is recommended at other times.

The *ryokan,* a traditional Japanese inn, provides the most unique experience. Japanese-style interiors include tatami flooring, paper (shoji) blinds, a low table for tea service, and pillows. Futons that are rolled out in the evening serve as beds. Stays usually include traditional Japanese morning and evening meals, often with small seafood dishes and regional specialties. Lodges usually offer the use of an *onsen* (hot-spring bath), though many also have in-room showers.

Similar to the ryokan, but less expensive, *minshuku* are Japanese-style bed-and-breakfasts. Usually family-run, these inns feature Japanese-style rooms and meals. Baths (there are usually no in-room bathing options) are part of the shared public areas, which also include toilets.

Business hotels feature Western-style digs in basic, small rooms; these are ideal for one night and are usually close to major transportation hubs. Most major cities have high-end Western-style hotels with ritzy spas, fully equipped gyms, and some of Japan's better restaurants. Many are situated in high-rise buildings and provide fantastic views of the city's skyline.

The boutique hotel arrived late to Japan, but these quirky, trendy properties have taken hold. Earth tones, funky bathrooms, and curvy, chrome fixtures dominate at these hotels, which are priced just above business hotels. On the flip side, hostels are perfect for the budget conscious.

Capsule hotels—generally men-only—are the most spartan accommodations around, providing a chamber that you slide your body into laterally, much like a coffin. There are no frills here, but the price is right. Common areas with televisions and lockers for valuables and luggage come standard.

Types of Restaurants

The Japanese love to dine out and there is something for every taste and budget. Many restaurants specialize in just one kind of food. Ramen, soba (buckwheat noodles), and *udon* (thick, white-wheat noodles) restaurants are hard to beat for value and reliability. Choose between table and counter seats. To order, just choose the toppings for the broth.

Okonomiyaki-ya are no-frills eateries serving thick savory pancakes. Expect tables to be fitted with a hot plate as most often diners do the cooking themselves using their choice of ingredients to fill the okonomiyaki.

In the evening *akachochin*—red lantern restaurants, so called because these hang outside their doors—establishments are a safe, inexpensive bet. Customers sit at a counter space in an informal, convivial environment. *Robata* specialize in grilled foods and to order customers simply point at what they want grilled. *Oden-ya,* which serve a variety of slowly simmered meats and vegetables, have a similar atmosphere. Again, to order just point to your desired morsels. *Izakaya,* publike dens, have counter and table service and have more extensive menus.

High-end sushi restaurants, usually reserved for special occasions, are a breed apart. Expect a subdued atmosphere with wooden surfaces. Sit at the counter to get to see the *itamae* (sushi chef) in action. Point at the fish in the glass case to order or ask for *omakase*—or chef's choice. Standard sushi shops abound in major cities for those looking for a quick bite.

At tempura restaurants customers sit at the counter and enjoy the attention of their personal chef. Choose the course you desire (usually by how much you want to spend), which the chef will serve to you piece by piece.

Ryotei specialize in *kaiseki* (a formal multicourse meal). Expect to be greeted by kimono-clad waitresses who usher you to your private room. Leave your shoes and worries behind in the hallway, and enjoy this unforgettable experience. Those on a budget should visit at lunchtime, when many ryotei offer *kaiseki bento* at a fraction of the dinner price.

The regular bento, or Japanese box lunch of rice, fish or meat, and vegetable sides, is available everywhere. Sandwiches, sushi, and *onigiri* (rice balls with various fillings) are other popular to-go items.

Meals and Mealtimes

Office workers eat lunch from noon to 1, so eat later to avoid crowds. Most restaurants have lunchtime specials, which provide an opportunity for fine dining at a considerably lower price, until 2:30. Many restaurants close their doors between 3 and 5. Unless otherwise noted, the restaurants listed in this guide are open daily for lunch and dinner. For dinner at an upmarket establishment ask hotel staff to make reservations—this gives the management time to locate an English menu or staff with some language skills.

Paying

Credit cards are widely accepted in upmarket restaurants, but this isn't a given in more informal eateries. Check that your card will be accepted before sitting down.

Menus

In the more popular tourist areas English menus are often available, but if not most menus have photo illustrations and there is nearly always someone who can speak a little English. Many less expensive restaurants have plastic replicas of the dishes they serve, displayed in their front windows, so you can always point to what you want to eat if the language barrier is insurmountable.

TRANSPORTATION PLANNER

Getting Around by Train

Japan (and Tokyo in particular) has one of the world's best train and subway systems: trains are nearly always on time, have clean facilities, and provide a safe environment. But—it's complicated.

Shinkansen: The JR Shinkansen bullet trains travel up and down Honshu and into Kyushu. Tokyo Station is Tokyo's main hub, with lines heading north, south, and west. Other Shinkansen lines run to Nagano and Kanazawa, Niigata, Yamagata, and the Tohoku region.

Regional trains: About 70% of Japan's railways are owned by Japan Railways (JR Group), the other 30% are owned by private companies. Non-JR lines include Tokyu's Toyoko Line between Tokyo's Shibuya and Yokohama to the south. The main line of the Odakyu Company and Keio Inokashira Line use Shinjuku and Shibuya, respectively, as hubs to serve the west of Tokyo. For service to Saitama Prefecture, Tobu offers the Tojo Line, which leaves Tokyo from Ikebukuro Station. The most important JR-owned regional line in Tokyo is the Yamanote Line, which loops around the city, while its Sobu and Chuo lines cross that circle east to west; JR trains also travel to Tokyo Disneyland.

Subways: The easiest way to explore Tokyo is via subway. There are two subway companies: Tokyo Metro and Toei. Because these are separate entities, they have separate fares, and it's cheaper to stay with one company. At the outer edges of the subway networks, private companies operate the line. If you're going far afield, be prepared to pay an additional fare.

Tokyo monorail: Beginning at Hamamatsu-cho Station, the monorail provides the simplest access to Haneda Airport.

PURCHASING TICKETS

In Tokyo (and other major cities) basic fares (train or subway) are between ¥110 and ¥310. Tickets can be purchased from machines that take coins or cash near the gates. Maps above each machine—usually in Japanese and English—give destinations. ■**TIP→ If a station map is written only in Japanese, buy the lowest-priced ticket and adjust the fare on arrival.** Purchase tickets for Shinkansen lines and other long-distance regional lines that require a seat reservation at a ticket window.

JR Pass

Japan Railways offers the Japan Rail Pass, an affordable way to see the country. It can be used on all JR trains including the Shinkansen "bullet" trains—except for Nozomi trains on the Tokaido and Sanyo lines and Mizuho trains on the Kyushu Shinkansen. Hikari or Kodama trains and Sakura or Tsubame trains, however, serve these same respective routes and are included. The pass is also valid on local JR buses and on the JR ferry to Miyajima. Passes must be purchased at an authorized JR outlet outside of Japan before your trip and are available for 7-, 14-, or 21-day periods. Activate them on arrival at a major rail station or Narita airport. A first-class version allows access to the Shinkansen Lines' special Green Cars.

Tokyo-only Plans

Rechargeable debit cards **Suica** (from JR machines) or **PASMO** (from subway machines) can be used on all subways and trains. Tokyo also has some useful one-day passes including the **Tokunai Pass** for unlimited use of JR lines and the **Tokyo Free Kippu,** which also covers subways and buses.

HOW TO USE A TICKET MACHINE

Use the map above the ticket machine to determine how much money to put on your ticket. The numbers next to each stop indicate the price from your current station.

Follow direction in English on touch screen. Find the English option at the top of the screen.

Place coins in this slot.

Your ticket will pop out here.

Slide bills into the machine here.

⚠ You'll need your ticket to enter the train's boarding area as well as to exit the station.

JAPAN MADE EASY

What time of year is the best to travel to Japan?

For simple sightseeing in Tokyo and Kyoto, the pleasant weather in spring and fall cannot be beat. Also, in April, the cherry trees start to bloom in Kansai and the baseball season kicks off. In October, Tokyo is abuzz with its international film festival and numerous design events. Summer is hot and muggy nationwide, though August is also the peak of the festival and fireworks seasons. Winter means skiing in the mountains of Hokkaido and the Japan Alps, but New Year's is one of the three big travel periods—Obon in August and Golden Week in late April/early May are the other two—where the big cities empty as everyone heads for their ancestral homes, which makes travel generally more expensive and frantic.

Is free Wi-Fi readily available?

Japan is considered to be one of the most technologically advanced countries on the planet, but finding free wireless access to the Internet can be challenging. However, the number of free Wi-Fi hot spots is increasing, with Starbucks and 7-11 convenience stores both offering free access with registration. NTT-Flets also offers two weeks of free access at hot spots across Eastern Japan for foreign tourists; you need to pick up an access card in person in Tokyo. Wi2 also has an extensive network of Wi-Fi hot spots across the country and sells hourly, daily, or weekly access passes. You can also get online at *manga kissa* (comic-book coffee shops).

How do clothing sizes compare with Western countries?

For simple items, such as a T-shirt, the equivalent of a typical XL size may not exist, and even if it does it might be equivalent to an L size in the West. Women may be challenged finding designs that fit around both their hips and waist. The sizes for men's shoes will generally top out at 10½. The country's favorite clothing retailer, UNIQLO, usually stocks larger sizes, and foreign retailers like Gap and H&M are probably the most reliable options.

Can I get around easily if I don't read Japanese?

In major cities you will be fine. Public transportation maps, neighborhood maps, and street signs are written in Japanese and English, and most train stations will have staff who can speak some English. Taxi drivers in Japan's major cities are also used to foreign tourists and can speak basic English, but if you're trying to go somewhere that's not a major hotel or sightseeing spot it's better to show the address in Japanese. In rural areas, there's less English signage and fewer English speakers. If you're venturing into the countryside, purchase a bilingial road atlas.

How expensive is Japan?

Japan has a reputation for being very expensive, but things are not as they once were. Sure, that $10 cup of coffee does exist in Tokyo but so does the $3 version. In other words, do your homework. Buying a Japan Rail Pass can cut back on transportation costs. Book hotel rooms in advance online, and look for midweek discounts in tourist destinations. Spending time outside big cities like Tokyo will cut down on other common expenses.

MONEY-SAVING TIPS

Lodging

Big hotel chains can be expensive, but if you just need a comfortable place to sleep, try a business hotel. Usually near train stations in Japanese cities, these offer basic rooms at reasonable rates, often with weekend discounts. Likewise, if you're thinking of staying in a traditional ryokan, ask about discounts for midweek stays. Booking websites can have good rates, but if possible have a Japanese speaker check the hotel's Japanese website. You can often find the best rates there, often by booking far in advance or at the last minute. For more upscale hotels, have a Japan-based friend look for stockholder discount coupons at ticket reselling shops; these annual transferable vouchers issued to stockholders can get steep discounts at several major high-end chains.

Travel

If you're planning a multicity trip, a JR pass will probably save you money. You can use it not only on the Shinkansen, but, for a surcharge, on overnight trains, saving a night's accommodation. Long-distance buses are a surprisingly comfortable way to travel between cities, with many offering slippers, blankets, and private curtained-off sleeper seats, and Japanese overnight ferries, with tatami mat sleeping rooms and onboard baths, are also good value. In major cities, one-day subway passes are useful, and in smaller towns renting a bicycle is a budget-friendly way to explore.

Eating

Cheap eats abound in Japan. There are the usual fast-food chains, but other options include ramen noodles (a student favorite), *soba* or *udon* noodle stands, and take-out bento lunches from department store basement food halls. The latter are often marked down after 7 pm. Convenience stores sell bento boxes and quick snacks like *onigiri* rice balls or *nikuman* steamed meat buns. You can always head to the city hall cafeteria for a dirt-cheap lunch.

Shopping

Vintage kimonos are surprisingly cheap in Japan. At kimono resellers prices often start at ¥1,000. There are some used kimono shops in Asakusa in Tokyo and many in Kyoto. Antiques markets are a good place for interesting souvenirs. There's an antiques fair at Tokyo Forum on the first and third Sunday of the month, and a bustling antiques market at Kyoto's Toji temple on the 21st of every month. In department stores and electronics shops, ask about tax-free shopping for foreign visitors.

Sightseeing

Culture is also pleasantly cheap in Japan. At the country's many publicly funded museums and galleries, admission fees to regular exhibits are usually less than ¥800. Public gardens are also a bargain, usually at less than ¥300 for entry. Though major temples and shrines like Kyoto's Kiyomizu-dera and Kinkakuji charge an entry fee, they're the exception. Most temples and shrines in Japan are free and open to all. Another fun, cheap way to spend a day is visiting some of the hundreds of mini-museums on sometimes very obscure topics that dot this museum-loving nation. Run by volunteers passionate about, say, wooden hair combs or the history of stamps, these tiny museums usually charge less than ¥200 for entry—and you'll often get a private tour as the only guests.

JAPANESE ETIQUETTE

Many Japanese expect foreigners to behave differently and are tolerant of faux pas, but they are pleasantly surprised when people acknowledge and observe their customs. The easiest way to ingratiate yourself with the Japanese is to take time to learn and respect Japanese ways. ⇨ *For tips on dining etiquette, see A Taste of Japan in Chapter 2.*

General Tips

■ Bow on meeting someone.

■ Japanese will often point at their nose (not chest) when referring to themselves.

■ Pointing at someone is considered rude. To make reference to someone or something, wave your hand up and down in his or her direction.

■ Direct expression of opinions isn't encouraged. It's more common for people to gently suggest something.

■ Avoid physical contact. A slap on the back or hand on the shoulder would be uncomfortable for a Japanese person.

■ Avoid too much eye contact when speaking. Direct eye contact is a show of spite and rudeness.

At Someone's Home

■ Most entertaining is done in restaurants and bars; don't be offended if you're not invited to someone's home.

■ Should an invitation be extended, a small gift—perhaps a bottle of alcohol or box of sweets—should be presented.

■ At the entryway, remove your shoes and put on the provided slippers. Remove your slippers if you enter a room with tatami flooring (straw mats). Before entering the bathroom, remove your house slippers and switch to those found near the bathroom doorway.

■ Stick to neutral subjects in conversation. The weather doesn't have to be your only topic, but you should take care not to be too nosy.

■ It's not customary for Japanese businessmen to bring wives along. If you're traveling with your spouse, don't assume that an invitation includes both of you. If you want to bring your spouse, ask in a way that eliminates the need for a direct refusal.

In Business Meetings

■ For business meetings, *meishi* (business cards) are essential. Remember to place those you have received in front of you; don't shove them in your pocket. It's also good to have one side of your business card printed in Japanese.

■ Japanese position their employees based on rank within the company. Don't be surprised if the proceedings seem perfunctory—many major decisions were made behind the scenes before the meeting started.

■ Stick to last names and use the honorific -san after the name, as in Tanaka-san (Mr. or Mrs. Tanaka). Also, respect the hierarchy, and as much as possible address yourself to the most senior person in the room.

■ Many Japanese businessmen still don't know how to interact with Western businesswomen. Be patient, and, if the need arises, gently remind them that, professionally, you expect to be treated as any man would be.

■ There is a strict hierarchy determining who sits where at a table or in a taxi, or who stands where in an elevator. Generally, the spot farthest from the door is reserved for the group's senior-most member. When in doubt, wait for someone to gesture to your spot.

1

In Dressing

■ The Japanese tend to dress with care, eschewing sportswear or flip-flops for a slightly more formal look. Although foreigners are cut a lot of slack in the fashion department, you'll make a good first impression if you try for business casual: button-down shirts rather than T-shirts; loafers over sneakers.

■ Few restaurants have explicit dress codes, but a good rule of thumb is that if the place accepts dinner reservations, wear something that covers your knees, with a collar (men) and sleeves (women).

■ Sightseeing in Japan requires removing your shoes at temples, shrines, ryokan, and restaurant tatami rooms. Bring slip-ons, and wear your good socks.

■ Many facilities provide slippers to wear indoors, but if your feet are larger than a U.S. men's size 10 they won't fit. Bring a pair of thick socks.

At Lodgings and Ryokan

■ When you arrive at a minshuku or ryokan, put on the slippers that are provided and make your way to your room. Remember to remove your slippers before entering your room; never step on the tatami with shoes or slippers.

■ Before entering a thermal pool, make sure you wash and rinse off entirely before getting into the water. Do not get soap in the tub. Other guests will be using the same bathwater, so it is important to observe this custom. After your bath, change into the *yukata* (robe) provided in your room. Don't worry about walking around in it—other guests will be doing the same. ⇨ *For more tips on Ryokan behavior, see "The Ryokan" in Chapter 2.*

On Trains and Buses

■ For many in Japan, taking public transport is a brief chance to relax with their own thoughts. Keep your voice to a low murmur on trains and buses and don't make phone calls.

■ When riding the Shinkansen with large bags, duck to the side to let other passengers take their seats before you store your luggage. Stash bags on overhead shelves or behind the last seats in the car.

While Shopping

■ After entering a store, the staff will greet you with "*irasshaimase*," which is a welcoming phrase. A simple smile's an appropriate acknowledgment. After that, polite requests to view an item or try on a piece of clothing should be followed as anywhere in the West. Don't forget to take your shoes off before entering the fitting room. Bargaining is common at flea markets, but not so in conventional stores.

■ There's usually a plastic tray at the register for you to place your money or credit card. Your change and receipt, however, will be placed in your hand. It should be noted that many small shops do not accept credit cards.

Giving Gifts

■ Gift giving is a year-round national pastime, peaking during summer's *ochugen* and the year-end *oseibo* seasons. Common gifts between friends, family, and associates include elegantly wrapped packages of fruit, noodles, or beer.

■ On Valentine's Day women give men chocolate, but on White Day in March the roles are reversed.

■ For weddings and funerals, cash gifts are the norm. Convenience stores carry special envelopes in which the money (always crisp, new bills) should be inserted.

JAPAN WITH KIDS

PRACTICALITIES

At first glance, Japan might seem busy, bustling and all business, but it's actually a great destination to explore with kids. Transportation is quick and convenient, hotels and restaurants warmly accommodate children, and there is no shortage of attractions appealing to the younger set. Children are made much of here—they even have their own public holiday (May 5, Children's Day)—and giving your kids to explore the world and experience new things is seen as the hallmark of good parenting.

Accommodation

Children who don't need their own beds stay free at most Japanese hotels. At *ryokan*, small children who need neither futons nor meals stay free. There are small extra charges for older children who need their own futon or a special children's meal. Children's meals at some ryokan are kid-friendly feasts in themselves, and although adult meals are large enough to share, if you're traveling with little foodies it can be worth ordering special meals just for them.

Transportation

Children under 6 usually ride trains in Japan for free (though specifics vary by train company), and children 6 to 11 are half the adult fare. Japanese trains and station ticket gates are compact, so if you're using a stroller choose a foldable one that can fit through train doors and ticket gates. Most bullet trains and express trains have diaper change facilities (おむつ交換台 *omutsu kokan-dai*); ask the conductor to show you where they are. All rental car companies can provide rear- or front-facing car seats and booster seats, usually for around ¥1,000 per day. You can ride most public buses with strollers, as long as you use the designated stroller area (usually by the rear doors; look for a stroller logo).

Eating

Family restaurants in Japan will provide high chairs and booster seats, and Japanese-style restaurants usually have a tatami mat room with low tables that works well for families with small kids. Most restaurants in Japan welcome children and will provide small bowls and cutlery for kids to use. All family-style places have designated nonsmoking sections, but many nonfamily restaurants allow smoking throughout the restaurant, so check in advance if this is a concern.

Health and Safety

Japan is safe, but crowded, and the country's urban crowds can be especially unnerving for kids, In case you're separated in a crowd, it's a good idea to have kids carry a bilingual card with your contact information, hotel information, and basic details such as their name and nationality. Remind kids that if anyone does get lost, they can ask for help at the nearest police box (交番、*koban*), which is usually close to the train station. Japanese clinics and hospitals offer high-quality care, and many doctors speak at least basic English. If you call or visit a Japanese medical facility, you'll be asked early and often about your child's temperature, so carry a small centigrade thermometer with you just in case.

Other Tips

Most Japanese department stores and shopping centers have "baby rooms" complete with diaper change facilities, private nursing areas, and hot water for infant formula. Some also have diaper vending machines, baby scales, and free stroller rentals.

IN KYOTO

Though a full day touring Kyoto's staid temples and shrines can tire out little ones pretty quickly, there are lots of kid-friendly sites in this traditional city. Of Kyoto's traditional sites, **Nijo Castle**, with its lifelike mannequins reenacting life in this 17th-century shogun palace, is a good option for kids. The hundreds of vermillion gates at **Fushimi Inari Shrine** will also make an impression. Curious eaters will love the **Nishiki Food Market**. Kyoto is flat and its roads run in a grid pattern, making it a good spot for a family bike ride. Most bike rental companies in Kyoto rent bikes with child seats, and some also offer electric-assist models to ease the strain of pedaling an extra passenger.

IN TOKYO

In Tokyo, popular sights for toddlers and school-aged children include **Ueno Zoo**, and **Tokyo Disneyland. Shinjuku Gyoen Gardens** or **Yoyogi Park** are popular family picnic spots. Good options in Tokyo to introduce kids to traditional culture include the **Meiji Shrine** in Harajuku or **Senso-ji Temple** in Asakusa. The hands-on "culture experience" programs run by the Yanesen Tourist Information Center are a great chance for older kids to try traditional Japanese drumming or take a swordsmanship lesson. Daredevils will enjoy a ride on the Thunder Dolphin, the roller coaster at **Tokyo Dome** that soars and loops around city buildings. Kids must be eight or older and 51 inches or taller to ride. There are also gentler rides nearby for younger siblings.

IN OSAKA

Osakans love kids and are not shy about it, so traveling with kids in Osaka will involve lots of random conversations with friendly strangers. The **Osaka Aquarium Kaiyukan** is one of the world's largest, and is the top kid-friendly attraction in the city. **Osaka Castle** and **Osaka Castle Park** are also great spots to take in the city's history and enjoy a picnic. Near Osaka Station, the **Hep Five Ferris Wheel** offers good views of the city. The rides and attractions at **Universal Studios Japan** are also worth seeing.

FARTHER AFIELD

Although there are fewer English speakers in the Japanese countryside and smaller cities, a slower pace and fewer crowds make traveling in rural areas with kids a relaxing proposition. Some kid-friendly attractions in rural Japan include the **Muruto Dolphin Center** in Cape Muroto on Shikoku (a two-hour drive from Kochi), where, in summer, kids can swim with dolphins; and the **Asahiyama Zoo,** Japan's most-visited, in Hokkaido's Asahikawa City (90 minutes from Sapporo).

GREAT ITINERARIES

AN INTRODUCTION TO JAPAN

Like every other nation, Japan has some sights that are more famous than others. These sights tend to be in the major cities. The following itinerary covers the barest, surface-scratching minimum in modern Tokyo and glorious Nikko; the temples and shrines of Kamakura, the power center of Japan's first shogunate; the temples of classical Kyoto; and Nara, Japan's first permanent capital. Two weeks are obviously better than one in Japan. With more time you can visit Japan's mountainous areas, Osaka, Himeji, and Hiroshima.

Day 1: Arrival
Flights from the United States tend to land in the late afternoon, so you'll want to rest up and get to bed early on your arrival day.

Days 2 and 3: Tokyo
Visit the major Tokyo sights or shops that appeal to you (⇨ *Chapter 3*). Ginza, Ueno Koen's museums, Tsukiji, the Imperial Palace grounds, and Asakusa are all among the top areas to explore. Arrange to spend your evenings in one or two of the nighttime districts, such as Roppongi or Shinjuku, or try to see a Kabuki, Noh, or Bunraku performance.

Days 4 and 5: Side trips from Tokyo
Head to the picturesque Chusen-ji (temple) in Nikko either on your own or with a tour. Also make time to visit Kamakura, perhaps stopping in Yokohama on the way back (⇨ *Chapter 4*). These trips can all be done conveniently by train.

Days 6, 7, and 8: The Japan Alps
Nagano is 90 minutes from Tokyo by bullet train; from there it's 1–2½ hrs to the other destinations by train/bus.

Take the Shinkansen train to Nagano (90 minutes by bullet train) and visit Zenko-ji (temple). Continue by train to Matsumoto (1 hour) and visit Karasu-jo (the castle), the Japan Folklore Museum, and the Japan Ukiyo-e Museum. The next day travel via the mountain village of Kamikochi to Takayama (2 hours by bus), one of Japan's best-preserved traditional cities. Finally, on your third day head to the Asa-ichi (morning market); then see other Takayama sights—the farmhouses of Shirakawa-go village or the former samurai-controlled district of Kamisanno-machi—before taking a train via Toyama to Kanazawa in the late afternoon (2½ hours).

Days 9, 10, 11, and 12: Kanazawa, Kyoto, and Nara
Nara is one hour by train from Kyoto.

Kanazawa has also preserved many of its traditional buildings, and it is one of the country's finest cities. Take in what sights you can, perhaps the Kenroku Garden or the Naga-machi samurai district, before catching the late-afternoon train to Kyoto (a trip of about three hours), where you'll base yourself for a few days. In the morning, visit the sights in the eastern district (Higashiyama) in the afternoon and take in the Gion district in the evening. On your second full day in Kyoto, visit more eastern district sights as well as those in the western district. If you are in the city on the 25th of the month, don't miss Kitano Tenman-gu market. On your third day in Kyoto, cover Central Kyoto in the morning, and take a train to Nara in the afternoon to see the elegant temples, the Daibutsu (Great Buddha) of Nara Koen, and the famous deer. Return to Kyoto after dinner.

Day 13: Osaka and Kobe
Osaka is 30 minutes by train from Kyoto.

This morning, take the train to Osaka, a sprawling city of never-ending urban intrigue, where you should spend a few hours or the night. Drop your bags at your hotel (or send them onto Kobe), and hit the consumer electronics shops in the Den Den Town; check out Senri Expo Park, or head to the Osaka Museum of History. In the afternoon, move on to Kobe, which is only 20 minutes by train. It's a port city known for beef and an interest in all things foreign, dating from its days as a trading port. If the Hanshin Tigers are scheduled in the evening, don't miss a chance to catch a game at the historic Koshien Stadium, midway between Kobe and Osaka. Spend the night in either Kobe or Osaka.

Day 14: Himeji and Kurashiki
Himeji is one hour by train from Osaka; Okayama is one hour by train from Himeji.

Travel by train to Himeji (1 hour) to visit Himeji-jo, its remarkable castle. Continue on to Okayama (1 hour) and reach historic Kurashiki by early afternoon. In the historic Bikan area of the city, there are numerous museums.

TIPS

Not all trains in the Japan Alpine regions are operated by JR, so they may not be included in your JR Rail Pass.

Osaka and Kobe are close together, so if you want access to Osaka's nightlife, you can still stay there and be within each reach of Kobe and even Nara.

You can fly back to Tokyo from Hiroshima, but flights generally go only to Tokyo Haneda Airport. Since Haneda now has some international flights to the United States, this may be a viable option.

Day 15: Hiroshima
Hiroshima is 70 minutes by train from Kurashiki. Miyajima is one hour from Hiroshima by train and ferry.

Leave Kurashiki by train in time to reach Hiroshima for lunch. Visit the Peace Memorial Park and then take the train and ferry to Miyajima, with the glorious vermilion torii in the bay. If you are up for it, take the one-hour hike up Mt. Misen. Hiroshima is known for its *okonomiyaki* (a grilled pancake of egg, meat, and eggs). Give that a try before heading to your hotel for the night.

Day 16: Tokyo and Home

Tokyo is four hours from Hiroshima by train.

Return to Tokyo by Shinkansen train this morning, in time to reach Narita Airport in Tokyo for your flight home.

TOKYO IN 3 DAYS

Tokyo is a metropolis that confounds with its complexity: 35 million people occupy a greater metropolitan area that includes soaring towers of glass and steel, rolling expressways, numerous temples, parks, and mile after mile of concrete housing blocks. Since the end of World War II, the city has constantly reinvented itself. Few things have remained static other than Tokyo's preeminence as Japan's economic center.

Day 1: Tsukiji and Ginza

Start *very* early (around 5 am) with a visit to the **Fish Market** in the Tsukiji district to catch the lively tuna auctions and then have the finest, freshest sushi for breakfast at **Daiwa Sushi.** Take a morning stroll through **Ginza** to explore its fabled shops and *depato* (department stores). The skyscrapers of **Shiodome** are just down the street, in the direction of **Shimbashi.** Take a peek on the first floor of the **Shiodome Media Tower;** aerial photographs show Ginza as it was roughly 100 years ago—a network of canals. In the skyscrapers' shadows are the charming Hama Rikyu Tei-en Gardens, whose pathways and ponds are ideal for a late-afternoon stroll. In the evening, head back up toward Ginza and enjoy *yakitori* (grilled chicken) at one of the many small restaurants under the elevated railway lines in **Yurakucho.**

TIPS

The transit system in Tokyo is amazingly complex. Get a map that clearly defines the subways and rail lines.

The rainy season in June makes sightseeing very unpleasant. If you have a choice, it's best to avoid this time of year.

To reach Tokyo from Narita Airport requires more than an hour by train or bus. A taxi, however, is not any faster and much more expensive, around ¥25,000.

No matter what you do, Tokyo will require plenty of walking. Wearing comfortable shoes during all seasons is advisable.

Day 2: Asakusa and Ueno

Spend the morning at **Senso-ji** and adjacent **Asakusa Jinja** in Asakusa. If you're looking for souvenir gifts—sacred or secular—allow time and tote space for the abundant selection the local vendors along **Nakamise-dori** have to offer. A 10-minute walk west is **Kappabashi,** a street dedicated to outfitting restaurants and bars with dishes, cups, chopsticks, and even plastic food models. From there go to **Ueno** for an afternoon of museums, vistas, and historic sites, and take a break at **Ueno Park.** Keep in mind that in the evening the crowds in Asakusa are not as intrusive as during the day, and many of the major attractions, including the five-tier pagoda of Senso-ji, are brightly lighted. It's worth it to loop back to get a different view of the area and end the evening with dinner at one of Asakusa's *izakaya* (basically, a drinking den that serves food).

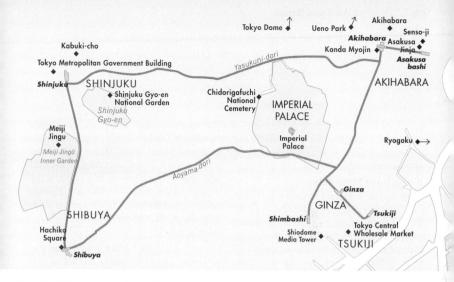

Day 3: Shibuya and Shinjuku

Start off at Shibuya's **Hachiko Square** and the famous "Scramble Crossing" intersection and hit nearby stores like Shibuya 109, which is crammed with teen fashion boutiques. Inside the station building is the once-lost masterpiece by avant-garde artist **Taro Okamoto**, *Myth of Tomorrow,* while towering over the east side of the station is the 34-story Shibuya Hikarie building, one of the latest redevelopments filled with shops, restaurants, and businesses to hit Tokyo. In the afternoon see the Shinto shrine, **Meiji Jingu,** and walk through the nearby Harajuku and **Omotesando** fashion districts. Spend the rest of the afternoon on the west side of **Shinjuku,** Tokyo's 21st-century model city; savor the view from the observation deck of architect Kenzo Tange's monumental **Tokyo Metropolitan Government Office;** and cap off the day visiting **Shinjuku Gyo-en National Garden.** For those seeking a bit of excitement, the red-light district of **Kabuki-cho,** just to the east of **JR Shinjuku Station,** comes alive once the sun goes down; Kabuki-cho and neighboring Golden Gai are full of good places to eat and drink.

TOKYO IN 5 DAYS

Add these two days onto the three-day itinerary.

Day 4: Akihabara and Imperial Palace

Spend the morning browsing in **Akihabara,** Tokyo's electronics quarter, and see the nearby Shinto shrine **Kanda Myojin.** In the afternoon, tour the **Imperial Palace** and the grounds surrounding it. The **Chidorigafuchi National Cemetery** has a wonderful park and a boat-rental facility—both great for unwinding. If the **Yomiuri Giants** are in town, catch a game at **Tokyo Dome** in the evening. If not, try a traditional hot spring bath or ride the roller coaster at LaQua amusement park next to Tokyo Dome.

Day 5: Get out of town to Kamakura

For a different perspective of Japan, spend a day out of Tokyo. Easily accessible by train is **Kamakura** the 13th-century military capital of the country. The **Great Buddha (Daibutsu)** of **Kotoku-in Temple** in nearby Hase is but one of many National Treasures of art and architecture in and around Kamakura. An early start will allow you to see most of the important sights in a full day and make it back to Tokyo by late evening. As Kamakura is one of the most popular of excursions from Tokyo, avoid the worst of the crowds by going on a weekday, but time it to avoid rush-hour commuting that peaks roughly at 8 am and just after 6 pm.

If You Have More Time

With a week or more, you can make Tokyo your base for side trips. After getting your fill of Tokyo, take a train out to **Yokohama,** with its scenic port and Chinatown. A bit farther away but still easily accessible by train is **Nikko,** where the founder of the Tokugawa Shogun dynasty is enshrined. The decadently designed Tosho-gu shrine complex is a monument unlike any other in Japan, and the picturesque **Lake Chuzenji** is in forests nearby. Two full days, with an overnight stay, would allow you an ideal, leisurely exploration of both.

HIGHLIGHTS OF KANSAI

Yes, Japan is a modern country with its skyscrapers, lightning-fast train service, and neon-lit entertainment areas. But it's also rich in history, culture, and tradition. Japan is perhaps most fascinating when you see these two faces at once: a 17th-century shrine sitting defiantly by a tower of steel and glass and a geisha chatting on a cell phone. This part of the Kansai region might be the best place to view this contrast.

Days 1–3: Kyoto

For many visitors **Kyoto** *is* Japan, and few leave disappointed. Wander in and out of temple precincts like **Ginkaku-ji,** spot geisha strolling about **Gion,** and dine on *kaiseki ryori,* an elegant culinary event that engages all the senses. Outside the city center, a day trip to hillside **Arashi-yama,** the gardens of the Katsura Rikyu, and the temple of Enryaku-ji atop **Hiei-zan** is a must. With nearly 2,000 temples and shrines, exquisite crafts, and serene gardens, Kyoto embodies traditional Japan.

For taking some with you, the **Kyoto Handicraft Center** stocks painted screens and traditional wear. Many restaurants serve dishes based on locally sourced ingredients. Embodying this spirit is the 400-hundred-year-old **Nishiki Market,** which includes roughly 100 mom-and-pop shops offering fish and vegetables.

Day 4: Nara

In the 8th century, Nara was the capital of Japan, and many cultural relics of that period, including some of the world's oldest wooden structures, still stand among forested hills and parkland. Be sure to visit Nara's 53-foot-high, 1,300-year-old bronze Daibutsu (Great Buddha) in **Todai-ji** temple and to make friends with the deer of **Nara Koen.** At the **Kofuku-ji** temple, the beautiful three- and five-story pagodas are worth a look. The **Nara National Museum** has numerous examples of Buddhist scrolls and sculpture.

Day 5: Koya-san

More than 100 temples belonging to the Shingon sect of Buddhism stand on one of Japan's holiest mountains, 48 km (30 miles) south of Osaka. Kobo Daishi established the original **Garan-ji** temple complex in AD 816. An exploration of the atmospheric cemetery of **Okuno-in** temple takes you past headstone art and 300-year-old cedar trees. But the temple's primary function is as the mausoleum for Daishi.

Day 6: Ise-Jingu

Ise-jingu (Grand Shrines of Ise), with their harmonious architecture and cypress-forest setting, provide one of Japan's most spiritual experiences. The Inner Shrine and Outer Shrine are roughly 6 km (4 miles) apart. In addition, there are 123 affiliated shrines in and around Ise City.

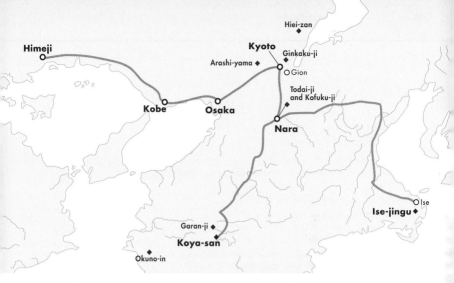

Day 7: Osaka

Although by no means picturesque, **Osaka** provides a taste of urban Japan outside the capital, along with a few traditional sights. The handsome castle **Osaka-jo** nestles among skyscrapers, and the neon of **Dotombori** flashes around the local Kabuki theater. Osakans are passionate about food, and you'll find some of the finest in the country here. The Hanshin Tigers have perhaps the most raucous fans in baseball, and the historic **Koshien Stadium** is the place to see them (and the Tigers) in action (though they play in the **Kyocera Osaka Dome** in August). The **Namba Grand Kagetsu Theatre** is a home to traditional *manzai* (stand-up) comedy and contemporary entertainment. Fans of electronics and the subculture will want to head to **Den Den Town,** which has shops selling consumer electronics and anime and manga products—much like Akihabara in Tokyo.

Day 8: Kobe

Kobe has recovered from the dark day in 1995 when it was struck by an earthquake that killed more than 5,000 people. The **Kobe Earthquake Memorial Museum** is dedicated to the event and its aftermath. Some of the first foreigners to live in Japan after the Meiji Restoration built homes in **Kitano-cho,** near the station, and the

TIPS

Kyoto is known for its traditional inns (ryokan). Book one for at least a night.

The bus network is the best way to get around in Kyoto. Buy an all-day pass. Renting a bicycle is also a good choice.

In Osaka, people stand on the right side of escalators (with the left being for those walking)—the opposite of the orientation used in Tokyo.

Koya-san and Ise-Jingu are best accessed by non-JR lines. A JR pass will save you money if you travel by Shinkansen beyond Kansai, but if you're flying in and out of Kansai, consider a Surutto (Thru) Kansai pass valid on most companies' trains and buses, or a JR West Kansai pass.

area retains a mix of architectural styles. The city will forever be associated with beef, but a trip to its **Chinatown** will reveal numerous Chinese delicacies. At an elevation of 931 meters, **Mt. Rokko** is accessible by cable car and features a museum and garden. On the way up the mountain take a look at Nunobiki Falls, considered one of Japan's most picturesque falls. The city has also recently added a "life-size" statue for **Tetsujin 28** (Gigantor), the robot in the popular manga and TV series.

Day 9: Himeji

The city's most famous sight, **Himeji-jo,** also known as the White Egret Castle (Shirasagi-jo), dominates the skyline. The castle takes only a few hours to see, and it's about a 15-minute walk (or a short bus ride) from the train station. Since Himeji is a short (50-minute) train ride from Kobe, it's a pleasant and unhurried day-trip destination for those based in Kobe (it's 15 minutes farther if you are based in Kyoto). However, the castle is shrouded by scaffolding and under renovation until mid-2016 (the interior of the main keep and other buildings in the site will be accessible during most of this period). If you get back early, use the rest of your day to buy last-minute souvenirs.

HIGHLIGHTS OF SOUTHERN JAPAN

South and west of Kyoto and Nara, Japan takes on a different feel. The farther you go, the more relaxed people become. Far from Japan's main islands, the stark divide between the tropical beaches of Okinawa and Honshu's concrete metropolises is reflected in a different culture and cuisine.

Day 1: Matsuyama

Start off in this castle town, Shikoku's largest city and home to several Shingon Buddhist pilgrimage temples and the ancient hot springs of **Dogo Onsen** (⇨ Chapter 10).

Days 2 and 3: Iya Valley

The **Iya Valley** may be slightly difficult to access, but it offers untouched, deep canyons, the best river rafting in Japan, and good walking trails. Despite its isolated

> **TIPS**
>
> Kurashiki udon noodles are famous around the country. Sample a bowl at least once.
>
> The best way to move around Hiroshima is through the city's streetcar network.
>
> For the crater Nakadake, the sulfurous gas emitted can make breathing difficult. A sign indicates the current levels.
>
> Typhoon season for Okinawa is July through September; a powerful typhoon can wreak havoc on vacation plans.

location, there are some fantastic lodging options here. (⇨ Chapter 10).

Day 4: Naoshima

Adjust to the even slower pace of Naoshima, spending a day at the world-class **Chichu Art Museum,** which integrates artworks into everyday locations, often with inspiring results and the **Benesse House Museum.**

Days 5 and 6: Hiroshima

A quick glance at the busy, attractive city of Hiroshima gives no clue to the events of August 6, 1945. Only the city's **Peace Memorial Park** (Heiwa Kinen Koen)—with its memorial museum and its **A-Bomb Dome** (Gembaku Domu), a twisted, half-shattered structural ruin—serves as a reminder of the atomic bomb. From Hiroshima, make a quick trip to the island of **Miyajima** to see the floating torii of **Itsukushima Jinja,** a shrine built on stilts above a tidal flat (⇨ Chapter 9).

Days 7 and 8: Yufuin and Mt. Aso

One of the locals' favorite pastimes is relaxing in an onsen, and in the artsy spa town of Yufuin, on the southernmost island of Kyushu, you can soak in mineral water or bubbling mud. Nearby, five volcanic cones create Japan's largest caldera at **Mt. Aso.** An immense 18 km (11 miles) by 24 km (15 miles), the stark volcanic peak contrasts vividly with the surrounding green hills. One crater, **Naka-dake,** is still active, and reaching it on foot or via cable car affords views of a bubbling, steaming lake.

Days 9 and 10: Okinawa

Check out cosmopolitan **Naha,** which gives a feel for how Okinawan culture and cuisine differ from those of "mainland" Japan. Explore the main island's many reminders of its tragic fate during World War II. Take a boat to one of the smaller **Kerama** islands to relax on unspoiled beaches. And to truly appreciate the beauty of the ocean, get into the water—there are plenty of scuba diving and snorkeling centers.

HIGHLIGHTS OF NORTHERN JAPAN

With 80% of Japan's surface covered by mountains, the country is a dream for hikers and lovers of the great outdoors. The wilds of Hokkaido, quietly impressive Tohoku, and the vertiginous Japan Alps reward exploration with spectacular scenery and experiences of traditional Japanese culture that have long since been lost from urban areas.

Days 1 and 2: Nagano

Nagano Prefecture, host of the 1998 Winter Olympics, is home to the backbone of the Japan Alps. Visit **Zenko-ji** temple in Nagano City before heading to the hot springs of **Yudanaka Onsen** or **Kusatsu.** In summer, try some day trekking in Hakuba.

TIPS

Be sure to bring plenty of warm clothes and a pair of boots suitable for walking in snow if traveling in winter. For summer, be prepared for mosquitoes.

A JR pass will be useful for this itinerary, if you take the Shinkansen from Tokyo to Nagano. Access from Sapporo back to Tokyo can be by air, sleeper train, or express train and Shinkansen.

For Hokkaido, take advantage of the abundant seafood, especially the crab; in Nagano, opt for the soba noodles. Don't miss locally brewed sake at every stop.

Day 3: Matsumoto

A one-hour train ride from Nagano, Matsumoto is home to the "Black Crow," Matsumoto Castle, as well as the fabulous Ukiyo-e Museum. Spend a day wandering the cafés and craft shops of this samurai town.

Days 4 and 5: Takayama

A bus ride over the mountains from Matsumoto brings you to Takayama, with an optional stop in summer at the alpine retreat of **Kamikochi.** You'll find traditional inns, ancient temples, mouthwatering Hida beef, a preserved historical district, and the gassho-zukuri thatched roof farmhouses in the memorable **Hida-no-Sato** folk museum.

Day 6: Shirakawago and Kanazawa

Between Takayama and Kanazawa lie the well-preserved farmhouses of Shirakawago, many of which are open to visitors for day visits or overnight stays. Continue on to the modern city of Kanazawa to visit serene **Kenrokuen** gardens and wander through the Nagamachi samurai district.

PLANNING YOUR TIME

Japan's most comfortable seasons are spring and fall. In spring the country is warm, with occasional showers, and flowers grace landscapes in both rural and urban areas. The first harbingers of spring are plum blossoms in early March; sakura (cherry blossoms) follow, beginning in Kyushu and usually arriving in Tokyo by mid-April.

Summer brings the rainy season, with particularly heavy rains and stifling humidity in June and July. Avoid July and August, unless you're visiting Hokkaido, where temperatures are more bearable. Fall relieves with clear blue skies and glorious foliage. A few surprise typhoons may occur in early fall, but the storms are usually as quick to leave.

Winter is gray and chilly, with little snow in most areas along the Pacific Ocean side of the country, where temperatures rarely fall below freezing. Hokkaido and the Japan Sea side of the country (facing Korea and Russia) are a different story, with heavy snowfalls in the winter months.

To avoid crowds, be aware of times when most Japanese are vacationing. Usually, Japanese vacation on the same holiday dates. As a result, airports, planes, trains, and hotels are booked far in advance. Many businesses, shops, and restaurants are closed during these holidays. Holiday periods include the few days before and after New Year's; Golden Week, which follows Showa Day (April 29); and mid-August at the time of the Obon festivals, when many Japanese return to their hometowns.

Days 7 and 8: Haguro-san

This mountain, the most accessible of the Dewa-san range, a trio of sacred mountains in Tohoku, is worth the trip not only for the lovely but rigorous climb (or bus trip) past cedars, waterfalls, and shrines but also for the thatched shrine at the top.

Days 9 and 10: Sapporo

A day's ride on the Shinkansen, an overnight ferry from Niigata, or a quick flight on low-cost carrier AirDo gets you to **Sapporo,** a pleasant and accessible city that serves as a good base for exploring the dramatic landscape of Hokkaido. Mountains encircle Sapporo, drawing Japanese and increasing numbers of Australian skiers in winter. Take day trips out to **Toya-ko** or **Shikotsu-ko,** picturesque lakes where you can boat or fish, and the excellent **Nibutani Ainu Culture Museum** for an insight into the island's original inhabitants.

ON THE CALENDAR

Matsuri (festivals) are very important to the Japanese, and around 30,000 are held throughout the year. Many of them originated in folk and religious rituals and date back hundreds of years.

Gala matsuri take place annually at Buddhist temples and Shinto shrines, and many are associated with the changing of the seasons or for honoring the spirits of the deceased. Most are free of charge and attract thousands of visitors as well as locals.

In most cases, matsuri are elaborated upon in the relevant chapters of this guide, especially when local history is involved. To find out specific matsuri dates, contact the Japan National Tourism Organization (⇨ *Visitor Information in Travel Smart*).

When national holidays fall on Sunday, they are celebrated on the following Monday. Museums and sights are often closed the days after these holidays.

WINTER January 1	**New Year's Day** is the "festival of festivals" for the Japanese. Some women dress in traditional kimonos, and many people visit shrines and hold family reunions. Although the day is solemn, streets are often decorated with pine twigs, plum branches, and bamboo stalks.
February	During the first half of the month, more than 300 pieces of ice sculpture, some huge, populate the **Sapporo Snow Festival,** bringing some 2 million people to the city to see them.
February 13–15	Akita (in Tohoku) City's **Namahage Sedo Festival** enacts in public a ritual from nearby Oga of threatening "good-for-nothings": men in demon masks carrying buckets and huge knives issue dire warnings to loafers.
SPRING April 29	**Showa Day.** The first day of **Golden Week**—when many Japanese take vacation, and hotels, trains, and attractions are booked solid—is *not* a good time to travel within Japan.
May 15	Dating back to the 6th century, the **Aoi Festival,** also known as the Hollyhock Festival, is the first of Kyoto's three most popular celebrations. An "imperial" procession of 300 courtiers starts from the Imperial Palace and makes its way to Shimogamo Shrine to pray for the prosperity of the city. Today's participants are local Kyotoites.

Mid-May	Another loud Tokyo blowout, the **Kanda Festival** is all about taking the Kanda shrine's gods out for some fresh air in their *mikoshi* (portable shrines)—not to mention drinking plenty of beer and having a great time on the weekend closest to May 15.
Late May	The **Sanja Festival,** held on the third weekend of May at Tokyo's Asakusa Jinja, is the city's biggest party. Men, often naked to the waist, carry palanquins through the streets amid revelers. Many of these bare bearers bear the tattoos of the Yakuza, Japan's Mafia.
SUMMER June	On Miyajima near Hiroshima, the lunar calendar determines the timing of three stately barges' crossing of the bay to the island's shrine for the **Kangen-sai Festival.**
July 16–17	The **Gion Festival,** which dates back to the 9th century, is perhaps Kyoto's most popular festival. Twenty-nine huge floats sail along downtown streets and make their way to Yasaka Shrine to thank the gods for protection from a pestilence that once ravaged the city.
July 24–25	Osaka's **Tenjin Festival** is a major event, with parades of floats and nighttime fireworks and processions of 100-plus lighted vessels on the city's canals.
August	The first week's dreamlike **Neputa Festival,** held in the Tohoku city of Hirosaki, finds nightly processions of floats, populated with illuminated paintings of faces from mythology, through the streets.
August 3–7	The **Nebuta Festival** in northern Tohoku's Aomori noisily celebrates an ancient battle victory with a nighttime parade of illuminated floats.
August 5–7	At Yamagata's **Hanagasa Festival,** in southern Tohoku, celebrants dance through the streets in local costume among floats. Food and drink are on hand for spectators.
August 6–8	Sendai's **Tanabata** celebrates two legendary astrological lovers with a theatrical rendition of their tale, and city residents decorate their streets and houses with colorful paper and bamboo streamers.
August 12–15	At Tokushima's **Awa Odori** festival, streets fill with local residents performing traditional Obon dances. The largest dance festival in Japan, things start off elegant but as the night

	goes on and drinks get downed, progress to enthusiastic if unpolished street dancing all over the city.
August 13–16	During the **Obon Festival,** a time of Buddhist ceremonies in honor of ancestors, many Japanese take off the entire week to travel to their hometowns—try to avoid travel on these days.
August 16	For the **Daimonji Gozan Okuribi,** huge bonfires in the shape of *kanji* characters illuminate five of the mountains that surround Kyoto. The most famous is the "Dai," meaning big, on the side of Mt. Daimonji in Higashiyama (Kyoto's eastern district). Dress in a cool *yukata* (cotton robe) and walk down to the banks of the Kamo-gawa to view this spectacular summer sight, or catch all five fires from the rooftop of your hotel downtown or a spot in Funaoka-yama or Yoshida-yama parks. There are *Bon* dances to honor the departed as well as the floating of lanterns in Arashiyama (the western district).
AUTUMN October 22	Kyoto's **Jidai Festival,** the Festival of Eras, features a colorful costume procession of fashions from the 8th through 19th century. The procession begins at the Imperial Palace and winds up at Heian Shrine. More than 2,000 Kyotoites voluntarily participate in this festival, which dates back to 1895. For the **Kurama Fire Festival,** at Kurama Shrine, there is a roaring bonfire and a rowdy portable shrine procession that makes its way through the narrow streets of the small village in the northern suburbs of Kyoto. If you catch a spark, it is believed to bring good luck.
WINTER December 23	**The Emperor's Birthday.** The Imperial Palace in Tokyo, which is usually off-limits to the public, opens its gates on this day. The only other day the public can enter the grounds is January 2.
Late December	City dwellers migrate to the countryside en masse for the **New Year** celebrations. Travel is *not* recommended.

DID YOU KNOW

Tokyo Tower, a knock-off of the Eiffel Tower, was built in the late 1950s to host TV transmitters as the city was trying to establish a new landmark in its skyline after the destruction of World War II.

ISOLATION AND ENGAGEMENT:
A HISTORY OF JAPAN   By Robert Morel

A century and a half after opening its shores to outsiders, Japan is still a mystery to many Westerners. Often misunderstood, Japan's history is much deeper than the stereotypes of samurai and geisha, overworked business-men, and anime. Its long tradition of retaining the old while embracing the new has captivated visitors for centuries.

Much of Japanese history has consisted of the ongoing tension between its seeming isolation from the rest of the world and a desire to be a part of it. During the Edo period, Japan was closed to foreigners for some 250 years. Yet while the country has always had a strong national identity, it has also had a rapacious appetite for all things foreign. Just 50 years after opening its borders, parts of Tokyo looked like London, and Japan had become a colo-nial power in Asia. Much earlier, the Japanese imported Buddhism, tea, and their first writing system from China.

In the 19th century, the country incor-porated Western architecture, technol-ogy, and government. More recently, the Japanese have absorbed Western fashion, music, and pop culture. Nev-ertheless, the country's history lives on in local traditions, festivals, temples, cities, music, and the arts.

Senso-ji Complex in Tokyo's Asakusa neighborhood

(top) Horyu-ji Inner Gate and pagoda, (bottom) Nihon Shoki, (right) Large Buddha statue at Todai-ji Temple

10,000 BC–AD 622

Ancient Japan

The first people in Japan were the hunters and fishers of the Jomon period, known for their pottery. In the following Yayoi period, hunting and fishing gave way to agriculture, as well as the introduction of rice farming and metalworking. Around AD 500 the Yamato tribe consolidated power in what is now the Kansai plain, with Yamato leaders claiming descent from the sun goddess Amaretsu and taking the title of emperor. Prince Shotoku promoted the spread of Buddhism from China and commissioned Horyu-ji Temple in Nara in 607.

- Horyu-ji Temple (Nara)
- National Museum (Tokyo)

710–784

Nara Period

As Japan's first permanent capital and urban center, Nara is often considered the birthplace of Japanese culture. Under the Emperor Shomu, who commissioned the Great Buddha at Todai-ji Temple, Buddhism rose to prominence. The first Japanese written histories, the *Kojiki* and *Nihon Shoki*, were compiled during this period, as was the *Manyoshu*, Japan's first collection of poetry. Since the country was the Eastern terminus of the Silk Road, Japan's royal family amassed an impressive collection of treasures from mainland Asia, many of which are still on display at Todai-ji Temple's Shoso-in.

- The Great Buddha at Todai-ji Temple (Nara)

794–1160

Heian Period

Partly to escape intrigues and the rising power of the Nara's Buddhist Priests, in 794 the Emperor Kammu moved the capital to Heian-kyo (now Kyoto). *Heian* translates roughly as "peace and tranquility," and during this time the Imperial court expanded its power throughout Japan. Inside the court, however, life was far from calm. This was a period of great courtly intrigue, and struggles for power between aristocrats, the powerful Fujiwara clan (the most powerful of Japan's four great noble families), and the new military class known as *bushi*. Though some emperors managed to maintain control of the court, the Heian period saw the

794–1160 The capital is moved from
Nara to Heian-kyo (now Kyoto)

1467–77 The Onin Wars initiate a
100-year period of civil war

1100　　　　1250　　　　1400　　　　1550

1

IN FOCUS ISOLATION AND ENGAGEMENT: A HISTORY OF JAPAN

(right) Zen Garden at
the Ryoan-ji Temple,
(top) Noh masks,
(bottom) Kyoto Imperial
Palace's wooden
orange gates.

slow rise of the military class, leading to a series of wars that established them as the ruling class until well into the 19th century. Considered Japan's great classical period, this was a time when courtly arts flourished. The new Japanese *kana* script gave rise to a boom in literature. Compiled in 990, Sei Shonagon's *Pillow Book* gave a window into courtly life, and Shibuki Murasaki's *Tale of Genji* is often regarded as the world's first classic novel. Japanese *waka* poetry experienced a revival, breeding the new forms of poetry such as *tanka* that are still in use today.

■ The Imperial Palace (Kyoto)

1185–1335 Kamakura Period

As the Imperial Court lost control, the Genpei War (1180–1185) resulted in the defeat of clans loyal to the emperor in Kyoto and the rise of a new government in Kamakura. Yoritomo Minamoto named himself *Sei-i Tai Shogun* and established the *Kamakura bakufu*, a spartan military government. During this time, Japan repelled two Mongol invasions, thanks to timely typhoons that were later dubbed *kamikaze*, or divine wind. In this militaristic climate, Zen Buddhism, with its focus on self-reliance and discipline, exploded in popularity.

■ Eihiji Temple (Fukushima)
■ Hachimangu Shrine and the Great Buddha (Kamakura)

1336–1568 Muromachi (Ashikaga) Period

The heyday of the samurai, the Muromachi period was one of near constant civil war. Feudal lords known as *daimyo* consolidated their power in local fiefdoms. Peasant rebellions and piracy were common. Nevertheless, trade flourished. The movement of armies required *daimyo* to build roads, while improved communications gave birth to many merchant and artisan guilds. Trade with China grew, and in 1543 Portugal began trading with Japan, introducing firearms and Christianity. Noh theater and the tea ceremony were founded, and Kyoto's most famous temples were built in this period.

■ Kinkaku-ji Temple (Kyoto)
■ Ryoan-ji Temple (Kyoto)

(left) Matsumoto Castle, (top) three wise monkeys at Toshogu shrine, (bottom) woodcut of Kabuki actor by Utagawa Toyokuni

National Unification (Momoyama Period)

1568–1600

In 1568 Oda Nobunaga, a lord from Owari in central Japan, marched on Kyoto and took the title of Shogun. He controlled the surrounding territories until his death in 1582, when his successor, Toyotomi Hideyoshi, became the new Shogun. After unifying much of central and western Japan, he attempted unsuccessful invasions of Korea before his death in 1598. In 1600 Tokugawa Ieyasu, a top general, defeated Hideyoshi's successor in the battle of Sekihagara.

- Osaka Castle (Osaka)
- Matsumoto Castle (Matsumoto)

Edo (Tokugawa) Period

1600–1867

The Edo period ushered in 250 years of relative stability and central control. After becoming Shogun, Ieyasu Tokugawa moved the capital to Edo (present-day Tokyo). A system of *daimyo*, lords beholden to the Shogun, was established along with a rigid class system and legal code of conduct. Although Japan cut off trade with the outside world, cities flourished. By the mid-18th century, Edo's population had grown to more than 1 million, and urban centers like Osaka and Kyoto had become densely populated. Despite such rapid growth, urban life in the Edo period was highly organized, with districts managed by neighborhood associations that have persisted (in a modified way) to the present day. Popular entertainment and arts arose to satisfy the thriving merchant and artisan classes. Kabuki, flashy and sensational, overtook Noh theater in popularity, and Japan's famed "floating world" (*ukio*), with its theaters, drinking houses, and geishas emerged. Sumo, long a Shinto tradition, became a professional sport. Much of what both Japanese and foreigners consider "Japanese culture" dates to this period. But by 1853, the Shogun's hold on power was growing tenuous.

- Toshogu (Nikko)
- Katsura Imperial Villa (Kyoto) Muhammad Ali Mosque

| 1853 U.S. Commodore Matthew Perry reopens Japan to foreign trade | 1868 Meiji Restoration begins | 1941 Japan attacks Pearl Harbor |

| 1800 | 1850 | 1900 | 1950 |

1

(top) Tokyo University, (left) wedding in Meiji Shrine, (bottom) A6M5 fighter plane at Yusyukan museum.

Meiji Period
1868–1912

The Tokugawa Shogunate's rigid class system and legal code proved to be its undoing. After U.S. Commodore Matthew Perry opened Japan to trade in March 1854, the following years were turbulent. In 1868, the last Shogun, Tokugawa Yoshinobu, ceded power to Emperor Meiji, and Japan began to modernize after 250 years of isolation. Adopting a weak parliamentary system from Germany, rulers moved quickly to develop national industry and universities. Victories over China and Russia also emboldened Japan.

- Tokyo University (Tokyo)
- Heian Shrine (Kyoto)
- Nara National Musuem (Nara)

Taisho Period
1912–1925

In the early 20th century, urban Japan was beginning to look a lot Europe and North America.
Fashion ranged from traditional *yukata* and kimono to zoot suits and bobbed hair. In 1923 the Great Kanto Earthquake and its resulting fires destroyed Yokohama and much of Tokyo. Although city planners saw this as an opportunity to modernize Tokyo's maze of streets, residents were quick to rebuild, ensuring that many neighborhood maps look much the same today as they did a century ago.

- Asakusa (Tokyo)
- The Shitamachi Museum (Tokyo)
- Meiji Shrine (Tokyo)

Wartime Japan
1926–1945

Although Japan was was increasingly liberal throughout the 1920s, the economic shocks of the 1930s helped the military gain greater control, resulting in crackdowns on left-leaning groups, the press, and dissidents. In 1931 Japan invaded Manchuria; in 1937 Japan captured Nanking, killing many civilians. Joining the Axis powers in 1936, Japan continued its expansion in Asia and in 1941 attacked Pearl Harbor. After the atomic bombings of Hiroshima and Nagasaki, the Emperor announced Japan's surrender on August 15, 1945.

- Hiroshima Peace Memorial Park (Hiroshima)
- Yasukuni Shrine Museum (Tokyo)

| 1964 Tokyo hosts the Summer Olympic games | 1989 Emperor Hirohito dies | 2006 Shinzo Abe elected as the country's youngest prime minister | 2009 Liberal Democratic Party loses power | 2012 LDP's Shinzo Abe re-elected as prime minister |

1970   **1990**   **2010**   **2030**

(top) 1964 Summer Olympics, Tokyo, (bottom) manga comic books, (right) Shinjuku, Tokyo

1945–1989 Postwar Japan and the Economic Miracle

The initial postwar years were hard on Japan. More than half of Japan's total urban area was in ruins, its industry in shambles, and food shortages common. Kyoto was the only major metropolitan area in the country that escaped widespread damage. Thanks to an educated, dedicated population and smart planning, however, Japan was soon on the road to recovery. A new democratic government was formed and universal suffrage extended to all adult men and women. Japan's famous "Peace Constitution" forbade the country from engaging in warfare. With cooperation from the government, old companies like Matsushita (Panasonic), Mitsubishi, and Toyota began exporting Japanese goods en masse, while upstarts like Honda pushed their way to the top. In 1964 Japan joined the Organization for Economic Cooperation and Development's group of "rich nations" and hosted the Tokyo Olympics. At the same time, anime began gaining popularity at the box office and on TV, with Osamu Tezuka's classic *Tetsuwan Atom* (*Astro Boy*) making a splash when it aired in 1963. In the 1970s and '80s Japan became as well known for its electronics as its cars, with Nintendo, Sony, and Panasonic becoming household names abroad.

- Showa-Kan (Takayama)
- National Stadium (Yoyogi Park)

1990–PRESENT From Goods to Culture

Unfortunately, much of Japan's rapid growth in the 1980s was unsustainable. By 1991 the bubble had burst, leading to 20 years of limited economic expansion. Japan avoided an economic crisis, and most people continued to lead comfortable, if somewhat simpler, lives. After decades of exporting goods, Japan has—particularly since 2000—become an exporter of culture in the form of animation, video games, and cuisine. Japan, famous for importing ideas, has begun to send its own culture to the world.

- Shinjuku, Harajuku, and Shibuya, (Tokyo)
- Akihabara (Tokyo)
- Manga Museum (Kyoto)

A JAPANESE CULTURE PRIMER

Updated by
Annamarie
Sasagawa

Something about Japanese culture must have led you to pick up this book and contemplate a trip to Japan. Perhaps it was a meal at your favorite sushi bar back home. It could have been the warm tones of an exquisite piece of Japanese pottery. Maybe it was a Japanese novel you read in translation—or a film. Whatever it was that sparked your interest, it's a good bet that something you find in this chapter will make your trip unforgettable.

There is a display of horsemanship called *yabusame* (now to be seen mainly at shrine festivals) in which a mounted archer, in medieval costume, challenges a narrow roped-off course lined at 260-foot intervals with small wooden targets on bamboo posts: the rider has to come down the course at full gallop, drop the reins, nock an arrow, aim and release, and take the reins again—with only seconds to set up again for the next target. Few archers manage a perfect score—but "for us," explains a yabusame official, "merely hitting the target is secondary."

Therein lies the key to understanding pretty nearly every expression of traditional Japanese culture: the passionate attention to *form* and *process*. The results are important, of course; otherwise the forms would be empty gestures. But equally important—perhaps more important—is *how you get there*. Not for nothing are so many of these disciplines, from the tea ceremony to calligraphy to the martial arts, presented to us as Ways; excellence in any one of them depends on *doing it the way it's supposed to be done*, according to traditions that may be centuries old. Philosophically, this is all about how rules can liberate: spend enough time and effort on the mastery of forms, and one day they leave the realm of conscious thought and become part of you. Not for nothing, either, are so many elements of Japanese culture rooted in the teachings of Zen Buddhism, about breaking free from the limits of the rational Self.

A TASTE OF JAPAN

By Aidan O'Connor

Get ready for an unparalleled eating adventure: from humble bowls of ramen to elaborate kaiseki feasts, a vast culinary universe awaits visitors to food-obsessed Japan.

Japan's food offerings are united by a few key philosophies. Presentation is paramount—a dedication to visual appeal means that colors and shapes are just as important as aromas, textures, and flavors. Details count—food is prepared with pride and care, and everything from a bowl's shape to a dish's finishing garnish carries meaning. Natural flavors shine through—seasonal ingredients star in minimally processed preparations, with condiments used to enhance flavors rather than mask them.

You'll find these culinary philosophies at all levels, from tiny noodle shops to lively robatayaki grills to elegant sushi restaurants. Here's what you need to know to make the most of your meals. As they say in Japan, *itadakimasho* (let's eat)!

Pressed sushi (oshizushi) and Japanese-style fried rice

THE JAPANESE MEAL

Breakfast (*asa-gohan*, literally "the morning rice") is typically eaten at home and features rice, fried fish, and miso soup. Lunch (*hiru-gohan*), mostly eaten out of the home at school or work, involves a bento lunch box of rice, grilled fish, vegetables, and pickles. The evening meal (*ban-gohan*) has the broadest range, from restaurant meals of sushi to traditional meals cooked at home.

For home-prepared meals, the basic formula consists of one soup and three dishes—a main dish of fish or meat and two vegetable side dishes. These are served together with rice, which is part of every meal. When entertaining guests, more dishes will be served. Classical Japanese cooking follows the principle of "fives." An ideal meal is thought to use five cooking methods—boiling, grilling, frying, steaming, and serving raw; incorporate five colors—black or purple, white, red or orange, yellow, and green; and feature five tastes—sweet, sour, salty, bitter, and *umami* (the Japanese are credited with discovering umami, or savoriness). Ingredient quality is key, as cooking techniques are intended to coax out an ingredient's maximum natural flavor.

Staple ingredients include seafood, which plays a leading role in Japanese cuisine, with dozens of species available,

Here are a few tips to help you fit in at the Japanese table:

■ Don't point or gesture with chopsticks.

■ Avoid lingering over communal dishes with your chopsticks while you decide what to take. Do not use the end you have been eating with to remove food from the dish—use the serving chopsticks provided or the thick end of your own chopsticks.

■ When not in use, place your chopsticks on the chopstick rest.

■ Never pass food from your chopsticks to someone else's or leave chopsticks standing in your rice bowl (it resembles incense sticks at a funeral).

■ There is no taboo against slurping your noodle soup, though women are generally less boisterous about it than men.

■ Pick up the soup bowl and drink directly from it. Take the fish or vegetables from it with your chopsticks. Return the lid to the soup bowl when you are finished eating. The rice bowl, too, is to be held in your free hand while you eat from it.

■ When drinking with a friend don't pour your own. Pour for the other person first. He will in turn pour yours.

■ Japanese don't pour sauce on their rice. Sauces are intended for dipping foods into it lightly.

■ It is still considered tacky to eat as you walk along a public street.

Pouring sake into a traditional Japanese cup

from familiar choices like *maguro* (tuna) and *ebi* (shrimp) to more exotic selections like *anago* (conger eel) and *fugu* (blowfish). Meat options include chicken, pork, beef, and—in rural areas—venison and wild boar. Then there is a huge variety of vegetables and fungi (both wild and cultivated) such as *renkon* (lotus root), *daikon* (white radish), and matsutake mushrooms. Finally there is the soy bean, eaten whole as edamame, or fermented in tofu or miso.

Condiments range from tangy *shiso* (a member of the mint family) to spicy wasabi and savory soy sauce.

SUSHI

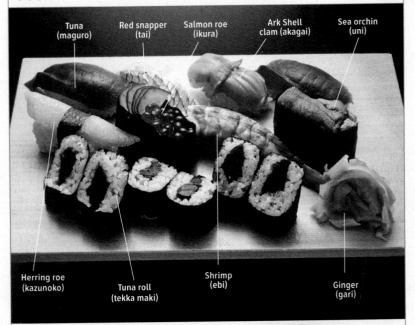

Tuna (maguro) — Red snapper (tai) — Salmon roe (ikura) — Ark Shell clam (akagai) — Sea orchin (uni)

Herring roe (kazunoko) — Tuna roll (tekka maki) — Shrimp (ebi) — Ginger (gari)

■ Sushi actually refers to anything, seafood or otherwise, served on or in vinegared rice. It is not raw fish. **Nigiri-zushi** (the sushi best known overseas) is actually a fairly recent development from Tokyo.

■ **Makizushi** is a sushi roll. These can be fat, elaborate rolls or simple sticks.

■ Other types of sushi include **chirashi-zushi** with fish and vegetables scattered artfully into the rice and, in Kyoto and Osaka, **oshizushi** in which preserved mackerel, among other fish, is pressed onto the rice. This is served in slices.

■ **Funazushi**, from around Lake Biwa near Kyoto, is perhaps the oldest type. The fish and rice are buried for six months. The rice is thrown away and the fish is eaten. This technique was historically used as a means of preserving protein. It is an acquired taste.

■ **Kaitenzushi** (conveyor belt sushi) outlets abound and are cheap. However, for the real

Hand-rolled sushi

experience, nothing matches a traditional sushi-ya.

■ Using your hands is acceptable. Dip the fish, not the rice, lightly in the soy.

■ The **beni-shoga** (pickled ginger) is a palate freshener. Nibble sparingly.

■ **Wasabi** may not be served with your sushi, as the chef often dabs a bit on the rice when making your sushi. If you want extra wasabi, ask for it.

■ Customers will often request **omakase** (tasting menu). The chef will then choose and serve the best fish, in the order he deems appropriate.

RAMEN

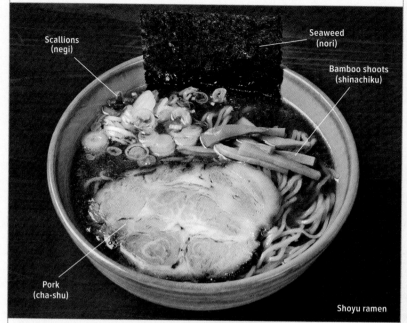

Scallions
(negi)

Seaweed
(nori)

Bamboo shoots
(shinachiku)

Pork
(cha-shu)

Shoyu ramen

■ Ramen is practically Japan's national dish. A ramen restaurant is never far away.

■ There are four main types: from the chilly north island of Hokkaido, there is **shio ramen** (salt ramen) and **miso ramen** (ramen in a miso broth). **Shoyu ramen** made with soy sauce is from Tokyo, while **tonkotsu ramen** (ramen in a white pork broth) is from Kyoto. Note that most ramen stocks contain meat or fish.

■ Each area has its own variation—corn and butter ramen in Sapporo; a stock made from pork and dried anchovies in northern Honshu; or Fukuoka's famed **Hakata ramen** with its milky tonkotsu broth and thin noodles with myriad toppings.

■ The reputation of a ramen restaurant depends on its stock, often a closely guarded secret.

■ Ramen is meant to be eaten with gusto. Slurping is normal.

■ Typical toppings include sliced roast pork, bean sprouts, boiled egg, **shinachiku** (fermented bamboo shoots), spring onion, **nori** (dried seaweed) and **kamaboko** (a fishcake made from white fish).

■ Beyond ramen, udon shops and soba shops also offer noodle dishes worth trying.

Miso ramen

Shio ramen

ROBATAYAKI

Grilled fish (tsukeba)

■ **Robata** means fireside, and the style of cooking is reminiscent of old-fashioned Japanese farmhouse meals cooked over a charcoal fire in an open hearth.

■ Robatayaki restaurants and izakaya taverns serving grilled foods can be found near any busy station.

■ It's easy to order at a robatayaki, because the selection of food to be grilled is lined up at the counter. Fish, meat, vegetables, tofu—take your pick.

■ Some popular choices are **yaki-zakana** (grilled fish), particularly **karei-shio-yaki** (salted and grilled flounder) and **asari saka-mushi** (clams simmered in sake).

■ Try the grilled Japanese **shiitake** (mushrooms), **ao-to** (green peppers), and the **hiyayakko** (chilled tofu sprinkled with bonito flakes, diced green onions, and soy sauce).

Matsutake mushroom

■ **O-tsukuri** (sashimi) and **katsuono tataki** (seared bonito) are very popular. The fish will vary according to the season.

■ Dipping sauces are concocted using soy, **dashi** (soup stock), and a hint of citrus such as yuzu.

■ Many robatayaki pride themselves on their wide selection of sake and shochu.

■ Most Japanese people will finish their meal with a rice dish.

TEMPURA

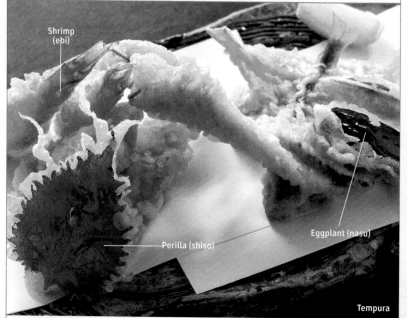

Shrimp (ebi)

Perilla (shiso)

Eggplant (nasu)

Tempura

■ Though tempura features in many busy eateries as part of a meal, it bears little resemblance to the exquisite morsels produced over the course of a full tempura meal at an intimate specialty restaurant.

■ The secret of good tempura lies in the quality of the ingredients, the freshness and temperature of the oil, and the lightness of the batter.

■ Good tempura is light and crispy, not crunchy like fried chicken.

■ Tempura is most often fried in soybean oil, but cottonseed or sesame oil also may be used.

■ Because only the freshest of ingredients will do, the menu changes with the season. Baby corn, green peppers, sweet potato, lotus root, shiitake mushrooms, and shiso leaves are the most common vegetables. In spring expect **sansai** (wild vegetables) picked that morning.

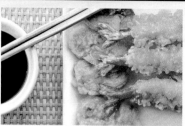

Shrimp Tempura with sweet potatoes

■ Prawns and white fish are also popular tempura items.

■ **Tsuyu** (dipping sauce) is made from dashi seasoned with soy and **mirin** (sweet rice wine). You may see a white mound of grated daikon on your plate. Add that to the tsuyu for a punch of flavor.

■ Alternatively, mixtures of salt and powdered green tea or salt and yuzu may be sprinkled on the tempura.

BENTO

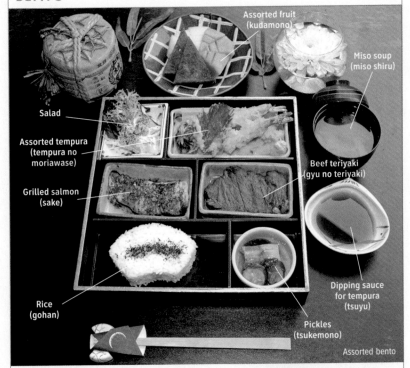

Assorted fruit
(kudamono)

Miso soup
(miso shiru)

Salad

Assorted tempura
(tempura no
moriawase)

Beef teriyaki
(gyu no teriyaki)

Grilled salmon
(sake)

Rice
(gohan)

Dipping sauce
for tempura
(tsuyu)

Pickles
(tsukemono)

Assorted bento

■ Bento boxes, the traditional Japanese box lunch, can be bought everywhere from the basement level of a luxurious department store to a convenience store.

■ A typical bento will contain rice, grilled fish, a selection of vegetable dishes, some pickles, and perhaps a wedge of orange or other fruit.

■ Every region has its **meibutsu**, or speciality dish. These are often showcased in lunch boxes available at stations or local stores.

■ Though the humble bento is usually relatively inexpensive, more ornate and intricate boxes featuring kaiseki dishes or sushi are often bought for special occasions.

■ The bento exists in an almost limitless number of variations according to the region and the season.

Bento lunch box

■ A bento is designed to be taken out and eaten on the move. They are perfect on long-distance train rides or for a picnic in the park.

BEVERAGES

Sake

■ There are more than 2,000 different brands of sake produced throughout Japan. It is often called rice wine but is actually made by a fermenting process that is more akin to beer-making. The result is a fantastically complex drink with an alcoholic content just above wine (15–17% alcohol). It is the drink of choice with sashimi and traditional Japanese food.

■ There are four main types of sake: **daiginjo, ginjo, junmai,** and **honjozo**. The first two are the most expensive and made from highly polished rice. The latter two, however, also pack flavor and character.

■ Like wine, sake can be sweet (*amakuchi*) or dry (*karakuchi*). Workaday sake may be drunk warm (*atsukan*) while the higher grades will be served chilled. Sake is the only drink that can be served at any temperature.

■ Another variety is **nama-zake**. This is unpasteurized sake and is prized for its fresh, zingy taste.

■ **Shochu** is a distilled spirit that is often 25% alcohol or more. Like vodka, it can be made from potato, sweet potato, wheat, millet, or rice. It is drunk straight, on the rocks, with water, or in cocktails.

■ Any good izakaya or robatayaki will stock a diverse selection of both sake and shochu, and staff will make recommendations.

■ Beer is, perhaps, the lubricant of choice for most social situations. Japanese beer is of a high standard and tends to be lager. It has a relatively high alcohol content at 5% or more. Recently there has been a boom in microbreweries.

JAPANESE FINE ARTS

What raises Japanese handicrafts to the level of fine arts? It is, one could argue, the standards set by the nation's *Ningen kokuho*: its Living National Treasures, who hand down these traditional skills from generation to generation.

(this page above) Japanese lacquerware; (opposite page upper right) a calligrapher at work; (opposite page bottom left) traditional Japanese papermaking

Legally speaking, these people are "Holders of Important Intangible Cultural Properties." A law, enacted in 1950, establishes two broad categories of Intangible Property. One comprises the performing arts: Kabuki, Noh, Bunraku puppet theater, and traditional music and dance. The other embraces a wide range of handicrafts, most of them in the various forms and styles of textiles, pottery, lacquerware, papermaking, wood carving, and metalworking—from all over the country. The tiny cohort of individuals and groups who exemplify these traditions at the highest levels (there are a maximum of 70 designees at any given time) receive an annual stipend; the money is intended not so much to support the title holders (Living National Treasures command very healthy sums for their work) as to help them attract and train apprentices, and thus keep the traditions alive.

CARRYING ON

Official sponsorship has proven itself a necessity in more than a few craft traditions. The weaving of *bashofu*, for example, a fabric from Okinawa, is on its way to becoming a lost art—unless the present Living National Treasure can encourage enough people to carry on with the craft. Papermaking, a cottage industry that once supported some 28,500 households nationwide, now supports only a few hundred.

LACQUERWARE

Japanese lacquerware has its origins in the Jomon period (10,000–300 BC), and by the Nara period (710–794) most of the techniques we recognize today, such as *maki-e* (literally, "sprinkled picture"), the use of gold or silver powder to underlay the lacquer, had been developed. The Edo period (1603–1868) saw the uses of lacquer extended to vessels and utensils for the newly prosperous merchant class.

The production of lacquerware starts with refining sap from the Japanese sumac (*urushi*). The lacquer is layered on basketry, wood, bamboo, metal, and even paper. The polished black and red surfaces may have inlays of mother-of-pearl or precious metals, creating motifs and designs of exquisite beauty and delicacy. Many regions in Japan are famous for their distinct lacquerware styles, among them Kyoto, Wajima, and Tsugaru. Hint: tableware with lacquer over plastic bases, rather than wood, are no less beautiful, but far less expensive.

PAPERMAKING

Washi, Japanese paper, can have a soft translucent quality that seems to belie its amazing strength and durability. It makes a splendid material for calligraphy and brush painting, and it can be fashioned into a wide variety of traditional decorative objects. The basic ingredient is the inner bark of the paper mulberry, but leaves, fiber threads, and even gold flake can be added in later stages for a dramatic effect. The raw mulberry branches are first steamed, then bleached in cold water or snow. The fibers are boiled with ash lye, rinsed, beaten into pulp, and soaked in a tank of starchy taro solution. A screen is dipped into the tank, pulled up, and rocked to drain the solution and cross-hatch the fibers. The wet sheets of paper are stacked to press out the excess liquid, then dried in the sun.

The best places to watch the papermaking process are Kurodani, near Kyoto; Mino, in central Japan; and Yame, near Kurume. Many are known for their unique washi products: Gifu for umbrellas and lanterns, Nagasaki for its distinctive kites, Nara for calligraphy paper.

CALLIGRAPHY

Calligraphy arrived in Japan around AD 500 with the sacred texts of Buddhism, written in *kanji* (Chinese ideograms). By 800, the *kana* syllabic alphabets of the Japanese language had also developed, and the writing of both kanji and kana with a brush, in india ink, had become an art form—a wedding of meaning and emotion that was (and still is) regarded as a revelation of the writer's individual character. The flow of the line from top to bottom, the balance of shapes and sizes, the thickness of the strokes, the

About 30 different styles of porcelain are made in Japan.

amount of ink on the brush: all contribute to the composition of the work. There are five main styles of calligraphy in Japan. Two are based on the Chinese: *tensho*, typically used for seal carving; and *reisho*, for the copying of sutras. Three are solely Japanese: *kaisho*, the block style often seen in wood carving; and the flowing *sosho* (cursive) and *gyosho* styles. Sosho is especially impressive—an expression of freedom and spontaneity that takes years of discipline to achieve; retouching and erasing is impossible.

CERAMICS

There are some 30 traditional styles of pottery in Japan, from unglazed stoneware to painted porcelain. Since the late 1600s, when Imari and Kakiemon porcelain were exported to Europe, the achievements of Japanese potters have delighted collectors.

Although the Japanese have been making pottery for some 12,000 years, the styles we know today were developed by Chinese and Korean craftsmen who immigrated (or were forcibly brought) to Japan in the 17th century. Some of

them discovered deposits of fine kaolin clay in northern Kyushu, and founded the tradition in that region of porcelains like Arita-yaki, with brilliantly colored enamel decoration over cobalt blue underglaze. Other porcelain wares include Tobe-yaki from Ehime Prefecture, Kutani-yaki from Ishikawa Prefecture, and Kiyomizu-yaki from Kyoto.

These apart, most Japanese pottery is stoneware—which has an earthier appeal, befitting the rougher texture of the clay. Stoneware from Mashiko, where celebrated potter Hamada Shoji (1894–1978) worked, is admired for its rustic brown, black, and white glazes, often applied in abstract patterns. Many regional potters use glazes on stoneware for coloristic effects, like the mottled, crusty Tokoname-yaki, with its red-iron clay. Other styles, among them the rough-surfaced Shigaraki-yaki made near Kyoto; the white or blue-white Hagi-yaki; and Bizen-yaki from Okayama Prefecture, are unglazed: their warm tones and textures are accidents of nature, achieved when the pieces take their colors from the firing process, in wood-burning through-draft kilns called *anagama* or *nobori-gama*, built on the slopes of hills. The effects depend on the choice of the wood the potter uses, where he places a particular piece in the kiln, and how he manipulates the heat, but the results are never predictable.

Main pottery towns include Hagi, Bizen, and Arita, but you can always find their products in Kyoto and Tokyo. If you do go on a pilgrimage, call ahead to local kilns and tourist organizations to verify that what you want to see will be open and to ask about sales. Recommended reading: *Inside Japanese Ceramics* by Richard L. Wilson.

TEXTILES

Run your fingers over a Japanese textile, and you touch the fabric of Japanese social history. As the caste system took shape under Buddhist and Confucian influences, it created separate populations of samurai, farmers, artisans, and merchants (in descending order). Rules and conventions emerged—enforced in the Edo period by strict sumptuary laws—about who could wear what, and on what occasions. Appearances identified people. One glance at a kimono, and you knew the wearer was a woman of middle age, the wife of a prosperous tradesman, on her way to the wedding of a family connection. Order was maintained. You were what you wore. Courtesans and actors, of course, could dress over the top; their roles gave them the license. And little by little, the merchants also found ways around the laws, to dress as befit their growing wealth and power. Evolving styles and techniques of making fabrics gave weavers and dyers and designers new opportunities to show their skills.

Western clothing follows the body line in a sculptural way; the kimono is meant as a one-size-fits-all garment in which gender matters, but size and shape are largely unimportant. Whatever the wearer's height or weight, a kimono is made from one bolt of cloth cut and stitched into panels that provide ample surface for decoration.

Regional styles proliferate. Kyoto's *Nishijin-ori* silk brocade is as sumptuous as a Japanese textile can be. Okinawa produces a variety of stunning fabrics; one, called *bashofu*, is made of plantain fiber threads, dyed and woven in intricate motifs, and feels like linen. Kyoto's and Tokyo's stencil dyeing techniques yield subtle, elegant geometric patterns and motifs from nature. Kanazawa's *Kaga yuzen* paste-resist dyeing on silk is famous for its flower and bird motifs, in elegant rainbow colors.

The used kimonos you often see in Kyoto or Tokyo flea markets can be bargains. Also look for lighter-weight *yukata* (robes), *obi* (sashes), or handkerchiefs from Arimatsu, near Nagoya, for example. Good introductions to these craft traditions can be seen at Kyoto's Fuzoku Hakubutsukan (Costume Museum) and Nishijin Orimono (Textile Center), and the Edo-period dress collection in Tokyo's National Museum.

Kaga yuzen textiles from Kanazawa exhibit a traditional flower motif

PERFORMING ARTS

Gorgeous costumes, sword fights and tearful reunions, acrobatics and magical transformations, spectacular makeup and masks, singing and dancing, ghosts and goblins, and star-crossed lovers: never let it be said that traditional Japanese culture is short on showmanship.

(this page above) A highly stylized Noh theater performance; (opposite page upper right) the Oshika Kabuki troupe; (opposite page bottom left) a Kabuki mannequin from the Edo-Tokyo Museum

The performing arts all have roots in continental Asia. Kabuki makeup as well as *gagaku* ceremonial court music and dance are Chinese-inspired; the four-string *biwa* shares a Silk Road ancestry with the Persian *oud*. Collectively, the theater traditions generate work for artisans—weavers and dyers, instrument makers, wood-carvers, and more—who make a special contribution of their own. Common features aside, the differences among them are astonishing. Kabuki is great showbiz, translatable and appreciable pretty much anywhere in the world. Gagaku is virtually inaccessible, even to the vast majority of the Japanese themselves. Most of an audience that will sit riveted by the graceful, suggestive movements of *buyo* (traditional dance) will fall asleep at a dance-recitation of Noh.

MASTER PERFORMERS

The performing arts also have National Treasures, but filling the 70 allotted slots is easier than in the fine arts. The worlds of Japanese theater are mainly in the grip of small oligarchies—"schools"—where traditions are passed down from father to son. Some of these master performers are 9th- and even 22nd-generation holders of hereditary family stage names and specializations.

KABUKI

Tradition has it that Kabuki was created around 1600 by an Izumo shrine maiden named Okuni; it was then performed by troupes of women, who were often available as well for prostitution (the authorities soon banned women from the stage as a threat to public order). Eventually Kabuki cleaned up its act and developed a professional role for female impersonators, who train for years to project a seductive, dazzling femininity. By the latter half of the 18th century it had become Everyman's theater par excellence—especially among the townspeople of bustling, hustling Edo. Kabuki had spectacle; it had pathos and tragedy; it had romance and social satire. It had legions of fans, who spent all day at the theater, shouting out the names of their favorite actors at the stirring moments in their favorite plays.

Kabuki flowered especially in the "floating world" of Edo's red-light entertainment district. The theater was a place to see and be seen, to catch the latest trends in music and fashion, where people of all classes came together under one roof—something that happened nowhere else in the city. Strict censorship laws were put in place and just as quickly circumvented by clever playwrights; Kabuki audiences could watch a *jidai-mono* (historical piece) set in the distant past, where the events and characters made

thinly veiled reference to troublesome contemporary events.

The Genroku era (1673–1841) was Kabuki's golden age, when the classic plays of Chikamatsu Monzaemon and Tsuruya Namboku were written, and most of the theatrical conventions and stage techniques we see today were honed to perfection. The *mie*, for example, is a dramatic pose the actor strikes at a certain moment in the play, to establish his character. The use of *kumadori* makeup, derived from Chinese opera and used to symbolize the essential elements of a character's nature, also dates to this period. The exaggerated facial lines of the kumadori, in vivid reds and blues and greens over a white rice-powder base, tell the audience at once that the wearer is a hero or villain, noble or arrogant, passionate or cold. To the Genroku also date revolving stages, trapdoors, and—most importantly—the *hanamichi*: a long, raised runway from the back of the theater, through the audience, to the main stage, where characters enter, exit, and strike their mie poses.

Kabuki traditions are passed down through generations in a small group of families; the roles and great stage names are hereditary. The repertoire does not really grow, but stars like Ichikawa Ennosuke and Bando Tamasaburo have developed unique performance styles that still draw audiences young and old.

The principal character in a Noh play wears a carved, wooden mask.

This ancient art now has a stylish home in the Kengo Kuma–designed Kabuki-za theater in Tokyo's Ginza district, which opened in 2013. Recommended reading: *The Kabuki Guide* by Masakatsu Gunji.

NOH

Noh is a dramatic tradition far older than Kabuki; it reached a point of formal perfection in the 14th century and survives virtually unchanged from that period. Where Kabuki was Everyman's theater, Noh developed for the most part under the patronage of the warrior class. It is dignified, ritualized, and symbolic. Many of the plays in the repertoire are drawn from classical literature or tales of the supernatural. The texts are richly poetic, and even the Japanese find them difficult to understand. (Don't despair: the major Noh theaters usually provide synopses of the plays in English.) The action—such as it is—develops at nearly glacial pace.

The principal character in a Noh play wears a carved wooden mask. Such is the skill of the actor, and the mysterious effect of the play, that the mask itself may appear expressionless until the actor "brings it to life," at which point the mask can express a considerable range of emotions. As in Kabuki, the various roles of the Noh repertoire all have specific costumes—robes of silk brocade with intricate patterns that are works of art in themselves. Noh is not a very "accessible" kind of theater: its language is archaic; its conventions are obscure; and its measured, stately pace can put even Japanese audiences to sleep.

More accessible is the *kyogen,* a short comic interlude traditionally performed between two Noh plays in a program. The pace is quicker, the costumes (based on actual dress of the medieval period) are simpler, and most kyogen do not use masks; the comedy depends on the satiric premise—a clever servant who gets the best of his master, for example—and the lively facial expressions of the actors.

Like Kabuki, Noh has a number of schools, the traditions of which developed as the exclusive property of hereditary families. The major schools have their own theaters in Tokyo and

Kyoto, with regular schedules of performances—but if you happen to be in Kyoto on June 1–2, don't miss the Takigi Noh: an outdoor performance given at night, by torchlight, in the precincts of the Heian Shrine. There are other torchlight performances as well in Tokyo, at the Meiji Shrine (early October) and Zojoji Temple (late May), and in Nara at the Kasuga Shrine (May).

BUNRAKU

The third major form of traditional Japanese drama is Bunraku puppet theater. Itinerant puppeteers were plying their trade in Japan as early as the 10th century; sometime in the late 16th century, a form of narrative ballad called *joruri*, performed to the accompaniment of a three-string banjolike instrument called the *shamisen,* was grafted onto their art, and Bunraku was born. The golden age of Bunraku came some 200 years later, when most of the great plays were written and the puppets themselves evolved to their present form, so expressive and intricate in their movements that they require three people acting in unison to manipulate them.

The puppets are about two-thirds human size and elaborately dressed in period costume; each one is made up of interchangeable parts—a head, shoulder piece, trunk, legs, and arms. The puppeteer called the *omozukai* controls the expression on the puppet's face and its right arm and hand. The *hidarizukai* controls the puppet's left arm and hand along with any props that it is carrying. The *ashizukai* moves the puppet's legs. The most difficult task belongs to the omozukai—a role it commonly takes some 30 years to master.

Creating the puppet heads is an art in itself, and today there are only a handful of carvers still working. As a rule, the heads are shaped and painted for specific figures—characters of different sex,

age, and personality—and fitted with elaborate wigs of human hair in various styles to indicate the puppet's social standing. Able to roll their eyes and lift their eyebrows, the puppets can achieve an amazing range of facial expression.

The chanters, who provide both the narration of the play and the voices of the puppets, deliver their lines in a kind of high-pitched croak from deep in the throat. The texts they recite are considered to be among the classics of Japanese dramatic literature; the great playwright Chikamatsu Monzaemon (1653–1725) wrote for both Bunraku and Kabuki, and the two dramatic forms often adapted works from each other.

The most important Bunraku troupe is the government-supported National Bunraku Theatre in Osaka, but there are amateur and semiprofessional companies throughout the country—the most active of them on Awaji Island, near Shikoku. Periodically there are also performances in Tokyo in the small hall of the National Theater.

Bunraku puppets are about two-thirds human size.

ONSEN AND BATHING

A chain of volcanic islands on the fiery Pacific Rim, Japan has developed a splendid subculture around one of the more manageable manifestations of this powerful resource: the *onsen* thermal spa.

(above) A lakeside rotenburo made from natural rocks; (opposite upper right) Gakenoyu Onsen in Nagano; (opposite bottom left) a spa in Shirahama Onsen

The benchmark Japanese weekend excursion—be it family outing, company retreat, or romantic getaway—is the hot spring resort. Fissured from end to end with volcanic cracks and crannies, the country positively wheezes with geothermal springs. Hot water gushes and sprays almost everywhere—but most especially in the mountains; there are hot springs in every prefecture, on every offshore island—even in cities built, incautiously, above the very fault lines themselves. And to all these superheated hollows flock the Japanese in endless enthusiasm, putting many thousands of people to work, catering to their needs; onsen are as nearly recession-proof an industry as the nation has. It's not too much to say that to understand the Japanese, to discover their innermost nature, you need to get naked with them a while in hot mineral water.

YUDEDAKO

The Japanese have a special term for that blissful state of total immersion: *yudedako*—literally "boiled octopus"—and Japanese people of all ages and both sexes will journey for miles to attain it. Getting boiled is a step on the road to sound health, good digestion, clear skin, marital harmony—to whatever it is that gives you a general sense of being at one with the universe.

If you're new to Japan, you might be astounded by the popularity of thermal baths. It can seem like the only way for a town to hope to bring in Japanese tourists is to have an onsen. Quite naturally, the Japanese have developed a subculture around one of the more relaxing side benefits of its geographic circumstances.

THE ONSEN EXPERIENCE

An *onsen* can refer to a particular region or subregion, like Yufuin in Oita Prefecture, Kinugawa in Tochigi, or Hakone in Kanagawa: a resort destination especially well endowed with thermal springs. Or it can mean more specifically a public bathhouse with a spring-fed pool, where you pay an admission fee and soak at your leisure. (At last count, there were some 6,700 of these nationwide.) Or it could mean a lodging—one of two basic varieties—with a spring of its own. One type is the *kanko* hotel: a mega-onsen with multiple baths, in grand pharaonic styles with mosaics and waterfalls, and banquet halls and dinner shows, as well as tatami guest rooms that sleep six— and, inevitably, discos and karaoke bars and souvenir shops. The other type is the onsen of everyone's dreams: the picture-perfect traditional inn, a ryokan of half a dozen rooms, nestled up somewhere in the mountains all by itself, with a spectacular view and a *rotenburo*—an outdoor pool—to enjoy it from.

THE ROTENBURO

Ah! the rotenburo! At smaller onsen, you can book the exquisitely crafted pool, with its stepping-stones and lanterns, and bamboo screens, for a private soak: an hour or so of the purest luxury, especially by moonlight. The rotenburo is a year-round indulgence; the view from the pool might be a mountainside white with cherry blossoms in spring, or a lakefront brilliant in the red and gold of maples in autumn, or—best of all, perhaps—a winter panorama, with the snow piled high on the pines and hedges that frame the landscape, to contemplate from your snug, steamy vantage point while you slowly wrinkle yourself like a prune. Be warned: whatever the season, you'll need to make reservations well in advance, for onsen accommodations of any sort. Japan has more than 3,000 registered spas; collectively, they draw nearly 140 million visitors a year, and hotel space is not easy to come by.

WHAT IS AN ONSEN?

By law, an onsen is only an onsen if the water comes out of the ground at a specified minimum temperature, and contains at least one of 19 designated minerals and chemical compounds—which makes for a wide range of choices. There are iron springs with red water; there are silky-smooth alkali springs; there are springs with radon and sulphur sodium bicarbonate; there are springs with water at a comfortable

Most onsen have single-sex bathing, a few have mixed bathing.

100°F (37.8°C), and springs so hot they have bath masters to make sure you stay only for three minutes and not a fatal second longer.

One reason many Westerners are reluctant to go bathing in Japan is the fact that you have to take all your clothes off. *In front of everyone else.* There is that issue—no getting around it: Japanese communal bathing is done in the buff—but that shouldn't deter you from the experience of a truly good thing. The bath is a great equalizer: in a sense the bath *is* Japan, in its unalloyed egalitarianism. Here, rank and title are stripped away: there is no way to tell if the body boiling beside you belongs to a captain of industry or his humble employee, to an ambassador, to a pauper, to a mendicant priest—and each bather offers the other an equal degree of respect and regard; no one ever behaves in a way that might spoil the enjoyment of any other bather; no one is embarrassed or causes embarrassment.

ONSEN ETIQUETTE

Another reason you might have for your reluctance is the worrisome conviction that bathing with a bunch of strangers comes with a raft of rules—rules all those strangers know from childhood, but at least one of which you're bound to break, to your everlasting horror and shame. "What if I drop the soap in the bath?" is a typical fear.

In fact, the pitfalls are not at all so awful. There certainly are protocols to follow, but it's a short list.

1. While there are still a few spas that keep alive the old custom of *konyoku* (mixed bathing), all of them have separate entrances for men and women, announced in Japanese characters on hangings over the doors. If in doubt, ask.

2. A word of warning: body tattoos, in Japan, are indelibly associated with the *yakuza*—organized crime families and their minions—and spas commonly refuse entry to tattooed visitors, to avoid upsetting their regular clientele. The rule is strictly enforced—and could extend to that little butterfly you got on

your shoulder when you were young and reckless. Put a bandage over it.

3. The first room you come to inside is the dressing room. It's almost always tatami-floored: take your shoes or slippers off in the entryway. The dressing room will have lockers for your keys and valuables, and rows of wicker or plastic baskets on shelves; pick one, and put your clothes in it. If you're staying overnight at an inn with a spa of its own, you'll find a cotton kimono called a *nemaki* in your room—you sleep in it, in lieu of pajamas—and a light quilted jacket called a *hanten*. Night or day, this is standard gear to wear from your room to the spa, anywhere else around the inn, and even for a stroll out of doors. Leave them in the basket.

The spa should provide—or you should bring—two towels: leave the bigger one in the basket, to dry off with, and take the smaller one with you next door, to the pools. (Holding this towel modestly over your nether parts is the accepted way of moving around in the spa.)

4. The pool area will have rows of washing stations along the walls: countertops with supplies of soap and shampoo, a mirror, taps and showerhead, a stool, and a bucket. Here's where you get clean—and that means *really* clean. Soap up, shower, scrub off every particle of the day's wear and tear. Take your time; use your wash towel. Leave no trace of soap. Then take your towel modestly to the pool.

You can bring the towel with you into the bath, but the onsen really would rather you didn't. Most people leave theirs at poolside or set them folded on top of their heads. (Another item of protocol: spas don't insist on bathing caps, but they do want you to keep your head above water.)

And that's all there is to it. Find a pleasant spot; soak in blissful silence, if you prefer (but not too long, if you're not used to it), or feel free to strike up a conversation with a fellow soaker: *atsui desu ne*—the local equivalent of "Hot enough for you?"—is a good start. The Japanese call their friendliest, most relaxing acquaintances *hadaka no o-tsukiai*: naked encounters.

Staying at a mega-onsen? Conviviality reigns in the pools of these establishments, with all sorts of amenities to help it along. At some inns, for example, you can order a small floating table for yourself and your fellow boilers, just big enough for a ceramic flask of sake or two, and a suitable number of cups. You get to warm your insides and outsides at the same time: how bad can that be?

When you've soaked to your heart's content, dry yourself off with your smaller towel and head back to the dressing room. Grab your larger towel from the basket, wrap it around yourself, and rest a bit until your body temperature drops back to normal. Get dressed and head out to the post-bath rest area to have a cold glass of water and lounge on the tatami mats before heading back out into the world.

You clean yourself thoroughly before setting foot in the onsen.

THE RYOKAN

You're likely to find Japanese hospitality polished, warm, and professional pretty much anywhere you stay—but nowhere more so than in a *ryokan*: a traditional inn.

(above) A traditional tatami-mat room in a ryokan; (opposite upper right) a ryokan meal served in myriad little dishes; (opposite bottom left) bedding for a ryokan, which is laid out nightly

Ryokans are typically one- or two-story wooden buildings where the guest rooms have tatami mat floors; the bedding—stowed by day in a closet—is rolled out at night. The rooms have hardly any furniture—perhaps one low dining table and cushions on the floor, a chest of drawers with a mirror, and a scroll painting or a flower arrangement in the *tokonoma* (alcove)—but every room in a proper ryokan will have windows with sliding paper screens looking out on an exquisite interior garden. Rates are per person and include the cost of breakfast and dinner. Some inns are reluctant to accept foreign guests: the assumption is that you don't know the language or the rules of ryokan etiquette. Call well ahead for reservations: better yet, have somebody Japanese make the call for you. The venerable, top-of-the-line ryokans expect even first-time Japanese guests to have introductions from a known and respected client.

COSTS

Ryokans of august lineage and exemplary service are expensive: expect to pay ¥30,000 or even ¥50,000 per person per night with two meals. There are plenty of lesser-priced ryokan in Japan, which start from ¥10,000 per person, including breakfast and dinner, though these may not have garden views. The Japan National Tourism Organization has a listing of some of the latter.

RYOKAN ETIQUETTE

Remove your shoes as you step up from the entryway of your ryokan, and change into slippers. A maid will escort you to your room. (It might take you two or three tries thereafter to find it on your own. Ryokans pride themselves on quiet and privacy, and the rooms are typically laid out in a labyrinth of corridors, where you're seldom aware of the presence of other guests.) Slippers come off at the door; on tatami, only socks/stockings or bare feet are acceptable. Relax first with a cup of green tea, and then head for the bath. In ryokans with thermal pools (not all have them), you can take to the waters pretty much anytime between 6 am and 11 pm; otherwise—unless you have in-room facilities—guests must stagger visits to the communal bath. The maid will make these arrangements. Be mindful of Japanese bathing rules *(Onsen and Bathing, above)*; wash and rinse off thoroughly before you get in the tub for a long hot soak. After your bath, change into a nemaki, the simple cotton kimono you'll find in your room, that doubles as sleepwear—or as standard garb for an informal stroll. These days, ryokans often have private baths, but especially in more venerable establishments (even those with astronomical rates), all facilities may be shared.

Ryokans don't have legions of staff, and will appreciate it if you observe

their routines and schedules. Guests are expected to arrive in the late afternoon and eat around 6. The front doors are usually locked at 10, so plan for early evenings. Breakfast is served around 8, and checkout is at 10.

FOOD

Not every inn that calls itself a ryokan offers breakfast and dinner. Indeed, some offer only breakfast; some inns have no meals at all. Seek out those that do; it's an important part of the experience. And while some ryokans will allow you to pay a lesser rate and skip dinner, why would you do that? Dinner—a feast of local specialties in beautiful dishes of all shapes and sizes—is sometimes served in your room. When you're finished, your maid will clear the table and lay out your futon bedding: a mattress filled with cotton wadding and (in winter) a heavy, thick comforter. In summer the comforter is replaced with a thinner quilt. In the morning the maid will clear away the futon and bring in your Japanese-style breakfast: grilled fish, miso soup, pickled vegetables, and rice. If you prefer, the staff will usually be able to come up with coffee and toast, not to mention a fried egg.

JAPANESE POP CULTURE

Step onto the streets of Shibuya—or brave the crowds of preening high-school fashionistas populating Harujuku's Takeshita-dori—and you'll get a crash course on Japanese pop culture that extends way beyond familiar exports like Hello Kitty and Godzilla. Japanese pop culture has long been a source of fascination—and sometimes bewilderment—for foreign visitors. New fashion styles, technology, and popular media evolve quickly here, and in something of a vacuum.

(top left) Manga is a Japan-wide obsession; (top right) distinctive manga style; (bottom right) matriarch of Japanese kawaii, Hello Kitty

That leads to a constant turnover of wholly unique, sometimes wacky trends you won't find anywhere outside Japan. Luckily, you don't have to go out of your way to explore Japan's popular obsessions. You can have an immersion experience just walking through neighborhoods like Shibuya, Shinjuku, Harujuku, and Akihabara.

DID YOU KNOW?

There are more than 5 million vending machines in Japan, making it the most dense population of machines, per capita, anywhere in the world. Here, automated machines sell everything from hot drinks to live lobsters. Some use facial recognition to verify age for tobacco and beer and even offer indecisive customers age-appropriate drink recommendations.

KAWAII

Kawaii, or "cute," isn't just a descriptor you'll hear coming out of the mouths of teenage girls, it's an aww-inducing aesthetic you'll see all over Tokyo; major airlines plaster depictions of adorable animation characters like Pikachu across the sides of their planes, and even at local police stations it's not unusual for a fluffy, stuffed-animal mascot to be on display. Duck into an arcade photo booth to take *purikura*—stickers pictures that let you choose your own kawaii background—or head to Sanrio Puroland, an entire theme park dedicated to cuteness.

J-POP IDOLS

The age of the boy band—or the girl band for that matter—is not over in Japan. "Idol" groups are hot. Over-the-top outfits, sugar-sweet synthesized beats, and love-professing lyrics (with the occasional English word thrown in) dominate the Japanese pop charts. AKB-48, one of Tokyo's hottest groups of idols, is 48 girls strong, and performs daily at its own theater complex in Akihabara. Beloved pop groups like all-male SMAP have been pumping out hits for more than 20 years.

ANIME AND MANGA

Peek over the shoulder of a comic-book-reading businessman and you'll quickly discover that, in Japan, cartoons aren't just kids' stuff. Animation (*anime*) and

comic books (*manga*) are extremely popular with readers both young and old. Comic book addicts, known as *otaku*, claim Tokyo's Akihabara as their home base. Though otaku can be translated as "nerd" or "obsessive," the term has been embraced by some. Former prime minister Taro Aso declared himself an otaku and confessed to reading 10 to 20 manga a week.

VIDEO GAMES

Japan is the cradle of the video game industry, and ever since the early 1970s it's been a dominant force in the gaming market. As companies like Namco gave way to Sega, Nintendo, and Sony, the gaming systems also continued to evolve and become more sophisticated. Like manga and anime, games enjoy a mainstream following. If you're a gamer, you'll be happy to find games that are unreleased in the United States alongside rebooted arcade classics like Legend of Zelda and Super Mario Bros.

BASEBALL IN JAPAN

Sumo may be the national sport, but without question, the most popular sport in Japan is baseball. It was first introduced in 1872 by Horace Wilson and has been popular ever since.

(above) Hanshin Tiger fans releasing balloons after the seventh inning; (opposite upper right) a night game at Yokohama Stadium; (opposite bottom left) players from the Japanese Little League

Each October, two major-league teams in the United States (or one major-league team from the United States and one major-league team from Canada) play the best of seven games to decide the World Series. But judging from the results of the World Baseball Classic (WBC) that Japan has won twice, any true world series of baseball would have to include Japan. While the Japanese professional-league season is shorter than its American counterpart (130–140 games versus 162 games), the major-league season's brevity is more than made up for by the company-league season, the university circuit, and the spring and summer high school tournaments. In addition, there are junior high school and elementary school leagues. Many municipalities and towns even have senior leagues for people over 60 years old. The game is played everywhere: from the southern islands of Okinawa to the northern tip of Hokkaido.

CATCHING A GAME

Even if you're not a baseball fan, you should try to take in a game on any level for the spectacle. Like the players, the fans come prepared. From team colors and fan paraphernalia to songs and boxed lunches, the Japanese fans have it down. The cheering starts with the first pitch and doesn't end until the last out. Wherever you go to see a game, you will be made to feel welcome and your interest or curiosity will be rewarded.

BASEBALL-DO

Martial arts in Japan (judo, kendo, kyudo) and many other activities including the tea ceremony (*chado*) and calligraphy (*shodo*) end in the suffix *do* (pronounced "doe" as in the female deer and meaning "way"). In Japan, baseball is also a *do*, an art rather than a sport. Of course, the Japanese watch baseball as they watch any sport, but in terms of their preparation and mental approach to the game, it is a do.

All of Japan's active arts require years of practice to achieve the level of intense concentration and mindlessness that mastery requires. The idea is that if you practice something long enough and hard enough, it will become pure reflex. Then you won't have to think about what to do and when to do it. You will just do it. Major players like Toritani and Sakamoto, Nishioka and Makajima play with a fluidity and grace that is beyond athleticism, exhibiting true mastery of the sport, and the result can be breathtaking.

SPRING AND SUMMER HIGH SCHOOL TOURNAMENTS

If you're fortunate enough to be in Japan in either March or August, you can attend the high school baseball tournament held annually at Koshien Stadium in Nishinomiya (near Osaka), the mecca of Japanese baseball. In what regard is high school baseball held?

Well, the pro team that normally plays at Koshien (the Hanshin Tigers) has to hit the road for two weeks in August to make way for the summer tournament. Both high school tournaments last about two weeks. Many of the star high school players go on to be standout players in both Japan and the United States. Both Boston Red Sox pitcher Koji Uehara and Miami Marlins star Ichiro Suzuki were star high school players.

TICKET PRICES

Tickets for a professional baseball game (the season runs from late March/early April to October) are a relatively good buy. At Koshien, home of the Hanshin Tigers, prices range from ¥1,900 for a seat in the outfield to ¥4,000 for a reserved seat on a lower level. When box seats are offered for sale, you can expect to pay around ¥6,000. Prices are similar at Tokyo Dome, where the Yomiuri Giants play.

Tickets for the high school baseball tournaments are even more affordable. Prices range from ¥500 for upper-reserved to ¥1,200 for lower-reserved to ¥1,600 for box seats. Seats in the bleachers are free throughout the tournaments.

Most other games (school, community, or company) are either free or, in the case of a championship game, require only a nominal fee.

JAPANESE MARTIAL ARTS

Take all that chop-socky stuff in the movies with a grain of salt: the Japanese martial arts are primarily about balance—mental, spiritual, and physical—and only incidentally about attack and self-defense.

(above) A practice kendo session; (opposite upper right) practicing aikido throws; (opposite bottom left) competitors at a judo tournament

Judo and karate are now as much icons of Japanese culture as anime or consumer electronics, and just as enthusiastically embraced abroad. Judo, karate, and aikido, all essentially 20th-century developments, have gone global; it would be hard to name a country anywhere without a network of *dojos* (martial arts academies or training halls) and local organizations, affiliates of the governing bodies in Japan, certifying students and holding competitions. Judo has been an Olympic sport for men since the 1964 games in Tokyo, and for women since 1988. An estimated 50 million people worldwide practice karate, in one or another of the eight different forms recognized by the World Union of Karate-do Federations. Aikido was first introduced abroad in the 1950s; the International Aikido Federation now has affiliates in 44 member nations. Korea and Taiwan have instruction programs in kendo (fencing) that begin at the secondary school level.

LEVELS

Levels of certification are as much a part of the martial arts as they are in other traditional disciplines—the difference being that marks of rank are clearly visible. Students progress from the 10th *kyu* level to the 1st, and then from 1st *dan* to 8th (or 10th, depending on the system or school). Beginners wear white belts, intermediates wear brown, dan holders wear black or black-and-red.

KYUDO: THE WAY OF THE BOW

Archery is the oldest of Japan's traditional martial arts, dating from the 12th century, when archers played an important role in the struggles for power among samurai clans. Today it is practiced as a sport and a spiritual discipline. The object is not just to hit the target (no mean feat), but to do so in proper form, releasing the arrow at the moment the mind is empty of all extraneous thought.

KENDO: THE WAY OF THE SWORD

Fencing was a mainstay of feudal Japan, but the roots of modern kendo date to the early 18th century, with the introduction of the *shinai*—a practice sword made of bamboo slats—and the distinctive armor (*bogu*) still in use to protect the specific target areas the fencer must strike to earn points in competition. Matches are noisy affairs; attacks must be executed with foot stamping and loud spirited shouts called *kiai.*

JUDO: THE GENTLE WAY

Dr. Kano Jigoro (1860–1938) was the proverbial 90-pound weakling as a teenager; to overcome his frailty, he immersed himself at the University of Tokyo in the martial arts, and over a period of years developed a reformed version of *jujutsu* on "scientific principles," which he finally codified in 1884. The *ju* of judo means "softness" or "gentleness"—a reference to its techniques of using one's opponent's strength against him—but belying the fact that this really is a rough-and-tumble contact sport.

KARATE: THE EMPTY HAND

Odd as it may sound, karate (literally: "the empty hand") doesn't quite qualify as a traditional Japanese martial art. Its origins are Chinese, but it was largely developed in the Ryukyu Kingdom (Okinawa before it was annexed), and didn't come to Japan proper until 1922. It lays stress on self-defense, spiritual and mental balance, and *kata*—formal, almost ritual sequences of movement. But it is as much about offense as defense: most of the movements end in a punch, a kick, or a strike with the knee or elbow.

AIKIDO: THE WAY OF HARMONY

The youngest of the Japanese martial arts was developed in the 1920s by Ueshiba Morihei (1883–1969), incorporating elements of both jujutsu and kendo, with much bigger doses of philosophy and spirituality. Aikido techniques consist largely of throws; the first thing a student learns is how to fall safely. Partner practice begins with a stylized strike or a punch; the intended receiver counters by getting out of the way, leading the attacker's momentum, pivoting into a throw or an arm/shoulder pin. The essential idea is to do no damage.

SUMO

This centuries-old national sport of Japan is not to be taken lightly—as anyone who has ever seen a sumo wrestler will testify.

(above) Two wrestlers battle in the ring; (opposite upper right) a wrestler in traditional dress outside the arena; (opposite bottom left) the ceremonial entrance of the tournament participants

Sheer mass, mind you, isn't necessarily the key to success—though it might seem that way. There are no weight limits or categories in sumo; contenders in the upper ranks average 350 pounds. But Chiyonofuji, one of the all-time great *yokozuna* (grand champions), who tipped the scales at a mere 280 pounds, regularly faced—and defeated—opponents who outweighed him by 200 pounds or more. That said, sumo wrestlers do spend a lot of their time just bulking up, consuming enormous quantities of a high-protein stew called *chanko nabe*, washed down with beer. Akebono, the first foreign-born yokozuna, weighed more than 500 pounds; current Grand Champion Hakuho, from Mongolia (the profusion of non-Japanese at the top of this most traditional of Japanese institutions is no small embarrassment to the Sumo Association), started his career at 160 pounds and doubled his weight in four years.

SUMO RULES

The official catalog of sumo techniques include 82 different ways of pushing, pulling, tripping, tossing, or slapping down your opponent, but the basic rules are exquisitely simple: Except for hitting below the belt (which is all a sumo wrestler wears) and striking with a closed fist, almost anything goes. Touch the sand with anything but the soles of your feet, or get forced out of the ring, and you lose.

SUMO HISTORY

The earliest written references to sumo date back to the year 712; for many centuries it was not so much a sport as a Shinto religious rite, associated with Imperial Court ceremonies. Its present form—with the raised clay *dohyo* (platform) and circle of rice straw bales to mark the ring, the ranking system, the referee and judges, the elaborate costumes and purification rituals—was largely developed in the 16th and early 17th centuries.

THE SUMO WORLD

Sumo is very much a closed world, hierarchical and formal. To compete in it, you must belong to a *heya* (stable) run by a retired wrestler who has purchased that right from the association. The stable master, or *oyakata*, is responsible for bringing in as many new wrestlers as the heya can accommodate, for their training (every stable has its own practice ring) and schooling in the elaborate etiquette of sumo, and for every facet of their daily lives. Youngsters recruited into the sport live in the stable dormitory, doing all the community chores and waiting on their seniors while they learn. When they rise high enough in tournament rankings, they acquire servant-apprentices of their own.

All the stables in the association—now some 50 in number—are in Tokyo. Most are clustered on both sides of the

Sumida River near the green-roofed *Kokugikan* (National Sumo Arena), in the areas called Asakusabashi and Ryogoku. Come early in the day, and you can peer through the windows of the heya to watch them practice; with luck—and good connections—you might even get invited in.

There are six official sumo tournaments throughout the year: three in Tokyo (January, May, and September); one each in Osaka (March), Nagoya (July), and Fukuoka (November). Wrestlers in the upper divisions fight 15 matches over 15 days. A few weeks before each tournament, a panel of judges and association *toshiyori* (elders) publish a table called a *banzuke*, which divides the 800-plus wrestlers into six ranks and two divisions, East and West, to determine who fights whom. Rankings are based on a wrestler's record in the previous tournament: win a majority of your matches and you go up in the next banzuke; lose a majority and you go down.

If you can't attend one of the Tokyo sumo tournaments, you may want to at least pay a short visit to the practice sessions (⇨ *Greater Tokyo in Chapter 3*). Sometimes tours can be arranged in advance.

THE GEISHA

The geisha—with her white makeup and Cupid's-bow red lip rouge, her hair ornaments, the rich brocade of her kimono—is as much an icon of Japan, instantly recognizable the world over, as Mt. Fuji itself.

(above) A traditional geisha performance in Kanazawa; (opposite upper right) geishas in Kyoto; (opposite bottom left) geishas on the streets of Kyoto

Gei stands for artistic accomplishment (*sha* simply means "person"), and a geisha must be a person of many talents. As a performer, she should have a lovely voice and a command of traditional dance, and play beautifully on an instrument like the *shamisen*. She must have a finely tuned aesthetic sense, and excel at the art of conversation. In short, she should be the ultimate party hostess and gracious companion. Geisha (or *geiko* in Kyoto dialect) begin their careers at a very young age, when they are accepted into an *okiya*, a sort of guildhall where they live and learn as *maiko* (apprentices). The okiya is a thoroughly matriarchal society; the owner/manager is called *o-kami-san*, who is addressed as *okaasan* ("mother"), to underscore the fact that the geishas have given up one family for another.

GEISHA LIFE

The okiya provides the apprentices with room and board, pays for their training and clothing (the latter a staggering expense), and oversees their daily lives. The maiko in turn do household chores; when they have become full-fledged geisha, they contribute a part of their income to the upkeep of the house and its all-female staff of teachers, dressers, and maids.

THE GEISHA BUSINESS

There are no free agents in the geisha world; to engage one for a party you need a referral. Geisha work almost exclusively at traditional inns (ryokan), restaurants (*ryotei*), and teahouses (*chaya*); the owners of one will contact an okiya with which they have a connection and make the engagement—providing, of course, that you've established yourself as a trustworthy client. That means you will understand and be prepared to pay the bill, when it shows up sometime later. Fees for a geisha's or maiko's time are measured in "sticks"—generally, one hour: the time it would take a stick of incense to burn down—and the okiya can really stick it to you. Bills are based on the number of guests at the party, and can run as high as ¥25,000 per person or more, for a two-hour engagement.

There were as many as 80,000 geisha in the 1920s; today there may be 1,000 left, most of them living and working in the Gion district of Kyoto; in Kanazawa; and in the Shimbashi, Akasaka, and Ginza districts of Tokyo. Fewer and fewer young Japanese women are willing to make the total commitment this closed world demands (even a geisha who opts to live independently will remain affiliated with her okiya for the rest of her career); fewer and fewer Japanese men

of means have the taste or inclination to entertain themselves or important guests in this elegant fashion. On the other hand, the profession—while it lasts—does provide considerable job security. A geisha is valued, not solely for her beauty, but for her artistic and social skills—and her absolute discretion (what she might see and hear, for example, at a party hosted by a political bigwig for his important business connections, could topple empires). A geisha with these accomplishments will still be in demand long after the bloom of youth has fled.

A geisha will establish a variety of relations with men. She will try to develop a roster of repeat clients, and may choose one among them as a patron, for financial support and—although she is by no means, as some people imagine, a prostitute—for sexual intimacy. When a geisha marries, most often to such a client, she leaves the profession.

THE TEA CEREMONY

The Way of Tea—in Japanese, *Cha-no-yu* or *Sado*—is more than a mere ceremonial occasion to have a cuppa: it is a profound spiritual and philosophical ritual. It's also a ritual you can experience easily and relatively inexpensively.

(above) Guests participating in a tea ceremony; (opposite upper right) a bowl of matcha green tea; (opposite bottom left) an outdoor garden tea ceremony

Tea came to Japan from China in the late 8th century, first as a medicinal plant; it was the Zen monks of the 12th century who started the practice of drinking tea for a refresher between meditation sessions. Rules and customs began to evolve regarding how to drink this precious beverage, and they coalesced in the Muromachi period of the 14th and 15th centuries as the earliest form of the Cha-no-yu. The Way of Tea developed an aesthetic of its own, rooted in the Zen sense of discipline, restraint, and simplicity: an aesthetic in which the most valued tea bowls, vessels, and utensils were humble, unadorned—and even imperfect. The choreographed steps and movements of the tea ceremony were devised to focus the appreciation—in Japanese, called *wabi*—for this subdued and quiet refinement.

THE TEA PAVILION

Contemplate a Japanese tea pavilion long enough, and you begin to see how much work and thought can go into the design of something so simple. A stone path through a garden, a thatched roof, a low doorway into a single room with a *tokonoma* (alcove) and tatami floor are barely big enough for the tea master and a few guests, and yet are a gateway to the infinite.

THE WAY OF TEA

The poet-priest Sen no Rikyu (1522–91) is the most revered figure in the history of Cha-no-yu. Three traditional schools of the tea ceremony, the Ura Senke, the Omote Senke, and the Mushakoji Senke—with some variations among them—maintain the forms and aesthetic principles he developed.

A full-scale formal tea ceremony, called a *chaji*, is like a drama in two acts, involving a multicourse *kaiseki* meal, two different kinds of powdered green tea, and an intermission—and can take as long as four hours to perform. Most ceremonies are less formal, confined to the serving of *usucha* ("thin tea") and a confection, for an intimate group; these are called *o-chakai*. Both forms demand a strictly determined, stately series of moves to be made by both guests and hosts.

Participants gather first in the *machiai*, a kind of waiting room or shelter in the garden, until they are invited to proceed to the teahouse. They remove their shoes, and enter the teahouse through a low doorway. It is customary to comment on the flower arrangement or scroll in the alcove. The guests sit in *seiza*, their legs tucked under them; the host enters from another small doorway, greets them, and carefully cleans the utensils: bowl, tea scoop, caddy, ladle, whisk. No matter that they are spotless already; cleaning them is part of the ritual.

When the tea is prepared, it is served first to the principal guest, who turns the bowl in the palm of his hand, drains it in three deep, careful sips, and returns it to the host. The other participants are served in turn. The guests comment on the presentation, and the ceremony is over; when they leave the pavilion, the host bows to them from the door.

You won't be expected to have the same mastery of the etiquette as a Japanese guest, but the right frame of mind will get you through, if you are invited to a tea ceremony. Make conversation that befits the serenity of the moment. (A well-known haiku poetess once said that what she learned most from Cha-no-yu was to think before she spoke.) Above all, pay close attention to the practiced movements of the host, and remember to praise the *wabi*—the understated beauty—of the utensils he or she has chosen.

Recommended reading: *The Book of Tea* by Okakura Kakuzo; *Cha-no-Yu: The Japanese Tea Ceremony* by A. L. Sadler.

JAPANESE GARDENS

Oases of calm and contemplation—and philosophical statements in their own right—Japanese gardens are quite unlike the arrangements of flowers, shrubs, and trees you find in the West.

(above) The garden of Hogon-in, Kyoto; (opposite upper right) the gardens of Kinkaku-ji, Kyoto; (opposite bottom left) Koishikawa Korakuen Garden, Tokyo

One key to understanding—and more fully enjoying—a Japanese garden is knowing that its design, like all traditional Japanese arts, emerged out of the country's unique mixture of religious and artistic ideas. From Shintoism comes the belief in the divinity or spirit that dwells in natural phenomena like mountains, trees, and stones. The influence of Taoism is reflected in the islands that serve as symbolic heavens for the souls of those who achieve perfect harmony. Buddhist gardens—especially Zen gardens, expressions of the "less is more" aesthetic of the warrior caste—evolved in medieval times as spaces for meditation and the path to enlightenment. The classic example from this period is the *karesansui* (dry landscape) style, a highly abstract composition of meticulously placed rocks and raked sand or gravel, sometimes with a single pruned tree, but with no water at all.

SHAKEI

Shakei ("borrowed landscape") is a way of extending the boundaries of the visual space by integrating a nearby attractive view—like a mountain or a sweeping temple roofline, for example—framing and echoing it with plantings of similar shape or color inside the garden itself. A middle ground, usually a hedge or a wall, blocks off any unwanted view and draws the background into the composition.

GARDEN DESIGN

Historically, the first garden designers in Japan were temple priests; the design concepts themselves were originally Chinese. Later, from the 16th century on, the most remarkable Japanese gardens were created by tea masters, who established a genre of their own for settings meant to deepen and refine the tea ceremony experience. Hence the *roji*: a garden path of stepping-stones from the waiting room to the teahouse itself, a transition from the ordinary world outside that prepares participants emotionally and mentally for the ceremony. Gradually, gardens moved out of the exclusive realm to which only nobles, wealthy merchants, and poets had access, and the increasingly affluent middle class began to demand professional designers. In the process, the elements of the garden became more elaborate, complex, and symbolic.

The "hide-and-reveal" principle, for example, dictates that there should be no point from which all of a garden is visible, that there must always be mystery and incompleteness in its changing perspectives: the garden *unfolds* as you walk from one view to another along the winding path. References to celebrated natural wonders and literary allusions, too, are frequently used design techniques. Mt. Fuji might be represented by a truncated cone of

stones; Ama-no-Hashidate, the famous pine-covered spit of land across Miyazu Bay, near Kyoto, might be rendered by a stone bridge; a lone tree might stand for a mighty forest. Abstract concepts and themes from myths and legends, readily understood by the Japanese, are similarly part of the garden vocabulary. The use of boulders in a streambed, for example, can represent life's surmountable difficulties; a pine tree can stand for strength and endurance; islands in a pond can evoke a faraway paradise.

Seasonal change is a highlight of the Japanese garden: the designer in effect choreographs the different plants that come into their glory at different times of year: cherry and plum blossoms and wisteria in spring; hydrangeas, peonies, and water lilies in summer; the spectacular reds and orange of the Japanese maple leaves in autumn. Even in winter, the snow clinging to the garden's bare bones makes an impressive sight. In change, there is permanence; in permanence, there is fluid movement—often represented in the garden with a water element: a pond or a flowing stream, or an abstraction of one in raked gravel or stone.

RELIGION IN JAPAN

Although both Buddhism and Shinto permeate Japanese society and life, most Japanese are blissfully unaware of the distinction between what is Shinto and what is Buddhist. A wedding is often a Shinto ceremony, while a funeral is a Buddhist rite.

(above) A Shinto shrine near Tokyo; (opposite upper right) a statue of Buddha at Todai-ji, Nara; (opposite bottom left) the gates at Futura-san Jinja, Nikko

There's a saying in Japan that you're Shinto at birth (marked with a Shinto ceremony), Christian when you marry (if you choose a Western-style wedding), and Buddhist when you die (honored with a Buddhist funeral). The Japanese take a utilitarian view of religion and use each as suits the occasion. One prays for success in life at a shrine and for the repose of a deceased family member at a temple. There is no thought given to the whys for this—these things simply are. The neighborhood shrine's annual *matsuri* is a time of giving thanks for prosperity and for blessing homes and local businesses. *O-mikoshi*, portable shrines for the gods, are enthusiastically carried around the district by young local men. Shouting and much sake drinking are part of the celebration. But it's a celebration first and foremost.

RELIGION IN NUMBERS

While most Japanese—some 90 million people out of some 128 million total—identify themselves as Buddhist, most also practice and believe in Shinto, even if they don't identify themselves as Shinto followers per se. The two religions overlap and even complement each other, even though most Japanese people would not consider themselves "religious."

2

SHINTO

Shinto—literally, "the way of the *kami* (god)"—is a form of animism or nature worship based on myth and rooted to the geography and holy places of the land. It's an ancient belief system, dating back perhaps as far as 500 BC, and is indigenous to Japan. The name is derived from a Chinese word, *shin tao,* coined in the 8th century AD, when divine origins were first ascribed to the royal Yamato family. Fog-enshrouded mountains, pairs of rocks, primeval forests, and geothermal activity are all manifestations of the *kami-sama* (honorable gods). For many Japanese, the Shinto aspect of their lives is simply the realm of the kami-sama and is not attached to a religious framework as it would be in the West. In that sense, the name describes more a way of thinking than a religion.

BUDDHISM

A Korean king gave a statue of Shaka—the first Buddha, Prince Gautama—to the Yamato Court in AD 538. The Soga clan adopted the foreign faith, using it as a vehicle to change the political order of the day. After battling for control of the country, they established themselves as political rulers, and Buddhism took permanent hold. Simultaneously, Japan sent its first ambassadors to China, inaugurating the importation of Chinese culture, writing, and religion into

Japan. By the 8th century, Buddhism was well established.

Japanese Buddhism developed in three waves. In the Heian period (794–1185), Esoteric Buddhism was introduced primarily by two priests, both of whom studied in China: Saicho and Kukai. Saicho established a temple on Mt. Hie near Kyoto, making it the most revered mountain in Japan after Mt. Fuji. Kukai established the Shingon sect of Esoteric Buddhism on Mt. Koya, south of Nara. In Japanese temple architecture, Esoteric Buddhism introduced the separation of the temple into an interior for the initiated and an outer laypersons' area.

Amidism (Pure Land) was the second wave, introduced by the monk Honen (1133–1212), and it flourished in the late 12th century until the introduction of Zen in 1185. Its adherents saw the world emerging from a period of darkness during which Buddhism had been in decline, and asserted that salvation was offered only to the believers in *Amida,* a Nyorai (Buddha) or enlightened being. Amidism's promise of salvation and its subsequent versions of heaven and hell earned it the appellation "Devil's Christianity" from visiting Christian missionaries in the 16th century.

In the Post-Heian period (1185 to the present) the influences of Nichiren and Zen Buddhist philosophies pushed Japanese Buddhism in new directions.

The Senso-ji Complex is the heart at soul of the Asakusa district of Tokyo.

Nichiren (1222–82) was a monk who insisted on the primacy of the Lotus Sutra, the supposed last and greatest sutra of Shaka. Zen Buddhism was attractive to the samurai class's ideals of discipline and worldly detachment and thus spread throughout Japan in the 12th century. It was later embraced as a nonintellectual path to enlightenment by those in search of a direct experience of the sublime. More recently, Zen has been adopted by a growing number of people in the West as a way to move beyond the subject/object duality that characterizes Western thought.

SHRINE AND STATE

While the modern Japanese constitution expressly calls for a separation of church and state, it hasn't always been this way. In fact, twice over the last 150 years, Shinto was the favored religion and the government used all of its influence to support it.

During the Meiji Restoration (1868), the emperor was made sovereign leader of Japan, and power that had been spread out among the shoguns was consolidated in the Imperial House. Shinto was favored over Buddhism for two reasons. First, according to Shinto, the members of the Imperial Family were direct descendants of the kami who had formed Japan. The second reason was more practical: many of the Buddhist temples were regional power bases that relied upon the shoguns for patronage. Relegating Buddhism to a minor religion with no official support would have a weakening effect on the shoguns, while the government could use Shinto shrines to strengthen its power base.

Indeed, Buddhism was actively suppressed. Temples were closed, priests were harassed, and priceless art was either destroyed or sold. The collections of Japanese art at the Museum of Fine Arts, Boston and the Freer Gallery in Washington, DC, were just two of the indirect beneficiaries of this policy.

During the Pacific War (the Japanese term for World War II), Shinto was again used by the military (with the complicity of the Imperial House) to justify an aggressive stance in Asia. (It should be noted that Kokuchukai Buddhism was also used to sanction the invasion of other countries.) The emperor was a god and therefore infallible. Since the Japanese people were essentially one family with the emperor at the head, they were a superior race that was meant to rule the lesser peoples of Asia.

Once ancestor worship was allied with worship of the emperor, the state became something worth dying for. So potent was this mix that General Douglas MacArthur identified state Shinto as one of the first things that had to be dismantled upon the surrender of Japan. The emperor could stay, but shrine and state had to go.

RELIGIOUS FESTIVALS

Although there are religious festivals and holy days observed throughout the year, the two biggest events in the Japanese religious calendar are New Year's (*Oshogatsu*) and *Obon*. New Year's is celebrated from January 1 to 3. Many people visit temples the night of December 31 to ring in the New Year or in the coming weeks. Temple bells are struck 108 times to symbolize ridding oneself of the 108 human sins. This practice is called *hatsumode*. Food stalls are set up close to the popular places, and the atmosphere is festive and joyous. Many draw fortune slips called *omikuji* to see what kind of a year the oracle has in store for them.

The other major religious event in the Japanese calendar is the Obon holiday, traditionally held from August 13 to 15. Obon is the Japanese festival of the dead when the spirits come back to visit the living. Most people observe the ritual by returning to their hometown or the home of their grandparents. Graves are cleaned and respects are paid to one's ancestors. Family ties are strengthened and renewed.

VISITING A BUDDHIST TEMPLE

The first thing to do when visiting a temple is to stop at the gate (called *mon* in Japanese), put your hands together, and bow. Once inside the gate, you should stop to wash your hands at the stone receptacle usually found immediately upon entering the temple grounds. Fill one of the ladles with water using your right hand and wash your left hand first. Then refill the ladle with water using your left hand and wash your right hand. Some people also pour water in their right hand to rinse their mouth, but this is not necessary.

After washing your hands, you can ring the temple bell if you choose.

Next, light a candle in front of the main altar of the temple and place it inside the glass cabinet. Then put your hands together and bow. You can also light three sticks of incense (lighting them together is customary) and put them in the large stone or brass stand. This action is also followed with a prayer and a bow. It is important to note, however, that while some people may light both a candle and three sticks of incense, others may just do one or the other. Some may skip this part entirely.

After you finish, you can proceed to the main altar, put your hands together, bow, and pray. Many people recite one of the Buddhist sutras.

A worshipper bows at the Meiji Shrine in the Shibuya District of Tokyo.

(Above) The massive torii (entrance gates) of the Meiji Shrine are over 40 feet tall.

If you'd like to have a closer look at the interior of the altar building, you can climb the steps and look inside. At this time, you can also throw a coin inside the wooden box on the top step as an offering, again putting your hands together and bowing.

Most temples have sub-altars dedicated to different Buddhist saints or deities, and you can repeat the candle, incense, and prayer steps observed at the main altar if you choose.

After praying at the main altar and/or sub-altar, you'll probably want to spend some time walking around the temple grounds. Most temples are incredibly beautiful places. Many have gardens and sculpture worthy of a visit in their own right.

Upon leaving the temple, you should stop at the gate, turn, put your hands together, and bow to give thanks.

VISITING A SHINTO SHRINE

Shrines, like temples, have gates, though they are called *torii* and are often painted bright orange. In terms of their appearance, torii look much like the mathematical symbol for pi.

As with the gates of temples, one enters and exits through the torii, bowing on the way in and again on the way out. However, when visiting a shrine one claps twice before bowing. This is to summon the kami. Once you have their attention, you clap twice again to pay them homage.

Inside the shrine, you wash your hands as you would at a temple (left hand and then right hand). You then proceed to the main altar, clap twice, and bow. In a shrine, clapping twice and bowing is often repeated, as there may be special trees, stones, and other holy objects situated throughout the grounds.

After you have finished visiting the shrine, you should turn around at the torii, clap twice, and bow upon leaving.

TOKYO

Visit Fodors.com for advice, updates, and bookings

WELCOME TO TOKYO

TOP REASONS TO GO

★ **Ultimate cityscape:** A skyline of neon-lit streets and vast high-rises awes the senses.

★ **Incredible eats:** From humble ramen to sumptuous sushi, Tokyo is foodie heaven.

★ **Green havens:** Pristine gardens and lush city-center parks soften the urban scene.

★ **Fashion-forward shops:** From Muji to Miyake, Tokyo is a playground for shopaholics.

★ **Contemporary art:** The Mori Art Museum caps a stunningly diverse scene.

★ **Sacred spaces:** Senso-ji Complex and Meiji Shrine offer spiritual retreats.

1 **Imperial Palace District.** This is the center of Tokyo, where Edo Castle once stood.

2 **Akihabara.** Akihabara is famed for its electronics stores, manga shops, video arcades, and cultish maid cafés.

3 **Ueno.** Ueno Park is home to three museums, a university of fine arts, and a zoo.

4 **Asakusa.** The sacred merges with the secular and ancient tradition with modernity in Asakusa. The area is home to Tokyo's oldest temple, Senso-ji.

5 **Tsukiji and Shiodome.** Tsukiji is home to what is purportedly the world's largest fish market. Its neighbor, Shiodome, is a massive development zone, with plenty of shops, hotels, and restaurants.

6 **Nihombashi, Ginza, and Marunouchi.** Nihombashi lays claim as the geographical and financial center of Tokyo. Slightly southwest is Ginza, where you'll find Tokyo's traditional high-end stores and equally expensive restaurants. On the other side of Tokyo Station, Marunouchi is home to plush retail and office complexes.

7 **Aoyama, Harajuku, and Shibuya.** Aoyama and Harajuku are chic neighborhoods saturated with shopping options. To the south is Shibuya, an urban teen's dream packed with people and hip shops.

8 **Roppongi.** With a rich and sometimes sordid history of catering to foreign nightlife, Roppongi now has the massive Roppongi Hills and Tokyo Midtown developments.

GETTING ORIENTED

Greater Tokyo incorporates 23 wards, 26 smaller cities, five towns, and eight villages—altogether sprawling 88 km (55 miles) from east to west and 24 km (15 miles) from north to south with a population of 35 million people. The wards alone enclose an area of 590 square km (228 square miles), which comprise the city center and house 8 million residents. Chiyoda-ku, Chuo-ku, Shinjuku-ku, and Minato-ku are the four central business districts.

9 Shinjuku. The train station here is supposedly the busiest in the world. And when the sun sets, the bars and clubs in the red-light area of Kabuki-cho come to life.

10 Greater Tokyo. Covering all of Tokyo plus large parts of its neighboring prefectures, the Greater Tokyo metropolitan area is home to destinations such as the ancient capital Kamakura and the port city of Yokohama.

TOKYO'S VENDING MACHINES AND CONVENIENCE STORES

With a brightly lighted convenience store on practically every corner and a few well-stocked vending machines in between, quick shopping is truly hassle-free in Tokyo—and with items ranging from novel to bizarre, an impulse buy can turn into a journey of discovery.

(top left) Ubiquitous vending machines provide fast, cheap drinks, snacks, and more; (top right) limited-edition potato chip flavors; (bottom right) convenience stores give a taste of Japanese culture.

While vending machines and convenience stores did not originate in Japan, their popularity in the country seems to have no limit. Today Japan has the world's highest density of vending machines per capita, with one machine for every 23 people. Those looking for a wider selection can head to one of the 40,000 or so convenience stores in the country. Canned drinks, both cold and hot, are the main staple of vending machines, but it is not uncommon to find ones with cigarettes, batteries, snacks, ice-cream cones, toiletries, fresh fruit, customized business cards, or even umbrellas. For North Americans used to convenience stores that sell little more than junk food and magazines, the Japanese equivalent can be a source of amazement, boasting everything from postal and courier services and digital photo printing to full hot meals.

DID YOU KNOW?

Vending machines hold a dizzying array of options from water and fruit juice to sugar-laden coffee, colas, and even alcohol. If you need a healthy snack, Dole installed banana dispensers around Shibuya train station, targeting hurried commuters with no time for breakfast. Need something like a quick change for work? Shinjuku Station even has machines selling white business shirts and ties.

VENDING MACHINES

If you visit Tokyo during the hot and humid summer months, you'll quickly understand why there is a machine selling cool drinks on every sidewalk. In winter, hot drinks warm both the stomach and hands. Popular drinks include Pocari Sweat, a noncarbonated sports drink with a mild grapefruit taste; Aquarius, a similar drink by Coca-Cola; and *Ito En*, a variety of cold green tea in plastic bottles. Machines sell beer and other alcoholic beverages, but you may want to avoid *shochu*, alcohol sold in glass jars or paper cartons—not only is it fairly strong at typically 20% ABV, but the variety sold in vending machines is usually of very low, throat-burning quality. Coffee—both hot and cold—comes in small cans. You'll see locals buy one, suck it down, and dispose of the can, all during the two-minute wait for the subway. Hot drinks have a red strip below them on the vending machine and cold drinks are marked with blue. If red Japanese text appears below an item, the machine is sold out. Edible items aren't the only things for sale, as shrines and temples use vending machines to sell *omikuji*, fortunes written on slips of paper.

CONVENIENCE STORES

The first convenience store opened in Japan in 1973, and like so many other imported concepts, the Japanese have embraced the *konbini*, turning it into something of their own. Beyond the usual products you might expect, Japanese convenience stores also carry *bento* (boxed meals), basic clothing items, and event tickets. Services available include digital photo printing, faxing, and utility bill payments. Convenience stores are actually a great option for a quick meal, including sandwiches, noodle dishes, fresh fruit, and a variety of salads. Peek into the freezer and Häagen-Dazs tempts you with flavors like matcha green tea. Near the cash register are hot food options, including fried chicken and steamed buns stuffed with meat or a sweet bean paste. Step into a 7-Eleven, Lawson, or Family Mart and see familiar brands with a Japanese twist such as salty watermelon Pepsi or soy sauce Pringles.

TOP BUYS

Japanese Pringles potato chips have come in flavors such as cheese and bacon and seaweed, and new surprising combinations are rolled out every season. Another international brand that often adds a local twist is Kit Kat, which in the past has released matcha green tea, wasabi, and passion fruit versions of its candy bars. New varieties of Kit Kat debut throughout the year, some only available in certain regions. If you are traveling with children, a fun purchase is *Ramune*, a carbonated drink sold in a glass bottle sealed with a glass marble held in place by the pressure of the gas—push the marble down with your thumb to break the seal. One convenience store treat you cannot leave Japan without trying at least once is *onigiri*, a triangular rice ball containing canned tuna with mayonnaise, pickled plum, or other fillings, and wrapped in sheets of dried seaweed.

Updated by
Brett Bull, Rob
Goss, Misha
Janette, Noriko
Kitano, and
Robert Morel

From the crush of the morning commute to the evening crowds flowing into shops, restaurants, and bars, Tokyo's image is that of a city that never stops and rarely slows down. It is all too often portrayed as a strange carousel of lights, sounds, and people set on fast-forward, but these days there is a greater focus on cultural development and quality of life.

For a time it seemed that Tokyo was becoming the city of the future—compact urban life, surrounded by high-tech skyscrapers, the world's densest rail system, and a 3-D network of highways overlapping and twisting above the city. Twenty years of gradual economic stagnation have cooled that vision, but if Tokyo no longer sees itself as the city of the future, it seems to have settled comfortably into being a city of the present.

While parts of the city such as Shibuya or Shinjuku's Kabuki-cho continue to overwhelm with a 24-hour cacophony of light, sound, and energy, other neighborhoods are surprisingly relaxed. In Ometesando and Aoyama, people are more likely to be sipping wine or coffee with friends at an outdoor café than downing beer and sake with coworkers in an *izakaya* (a bar that serves food). The people are as varied as their city. Residents of Aoyama may wear European fashion and drive fancy imports, but those residing in Asakusa prefer to be decidedly less flashy.

Even the landscape is varied. The city hosts some of the most unsightly sprawls of concrete housing—extending for miles in all directions—in the world, but offsetting all the concrete and glass is a wealth of green space in the form of parks, temple grounds, and traditional gardens.

Whether you're gazing at the glow of Tokyo's evening lights or the green expanse of its parks, this is a city of astonishing and intriguing beauty. If you're a foodie, artist, design lover, or cultural adventurer, then Tokyo, a city of inspiration and ideas, is for you.

PLANNING

WHEN TO GO

Spring and fall are the best times to visit. *Sakura* (cherry blossoms) begin blooming in Tokyo by early April, while fall has clear blue skies, albeit punctuated by the occasional typhoon. The short *tsuyu* (rainy season) in June brings humidity and rain that can linger into early July. July and August bring heat, mostly blue skies, and stifling humidity. Winter can be gray and chilly some days, mild and sunny others, with Tokyo and other areas along the coast receiving very little snow. Japanese vacation during three holiday periods: the few days before and after New Year's; Golden Week in early May; and the mid-August week for Obon. Travel's not advised during these times as plane and train tickets book up fast.

GETTING HERE AND AROUND

AIR TRAVEL

The major gateway to Japan is Tokyo's Narita Airport (NRT), 80 km (50 miles) northeast of the city. The Haneda Airport International Terminal also has flights to major international cities and is only 20 km (12 miles) south of central Tokyo. Most domestic flights to and from Tokyo are out of Haneda Airport.

Flying into Haneda provides visitors with quicker access to downtown Tokyo, which is a short monorail ride away. Stop by the currency exchange and Tourist Information Desk in the second-floor arrival lobby before taking a train into the city. There are also numerous jade-uniformed concierge staff on hand to help passengers with any questions.

Airport Information Haneda Airport (HND). ☎ *03/5757–8111* ⊕ *www.haneda-airport.com.* **Narita Airport (NRT).** ☎ *0476/34–8000* ⊕ *www.narita-airport.jp.*

GROUND TRANSPORTATION

Known as "The Gateway to Japan," Narita is about 90 minutes—dependent on city traffic—by taxi or bus from central Tokyo. The *Keisei Skyliner* and *Japan Railways NEX* are the easiest ways to get into the city.

Japan Railways trains stop at Narita Airport Terminals 1 and 2. The fastest and most comfortable is the Narita Limited Express (NEX). Trains from the airport go directly to the central Tokyo Station in just about an hour, then continue to Yokohama and Ofuna. Daily departures begin at 7:44 am; the last train is at 9:44 pm. In addition to regular seats, there is a first-class Green Car and private four-person compartments. All seats are reserved, and you need to reserve one for yourself in advance, as this train fills quickly.

Contacts The Access Narita. ⊕ *accessnarita.jp.* **Japan Railways.**
☎ *050/2016–1603 for JR East InfoLine* ⊕ *www.jreast.co.jp/e.* **Keisei Railway.**
☎ *03/3831–0131 for Ueno information counter, 0476/32–8505 at Narita Airport*
⊕ *www.keisei.co.jp/keisei/tetudou/skyliner/us.*

TAXI TRAVEL

Taxis are an expensive way of getting around cities in Japan, although nascent deregulation moves are easing the market a little. In Tokyo, for instance, the first 2 km (1 mile) cost ¥730 and it's ¥90 for every additional 400 yards. Between 10 pm and 5 am there is a 20% service charge on top of that. If possible, avoid using taxis during rush hours (7:30 am–9:30 am and 5 pm–7 pm).

TRAIN AND SUBWAY TRAVEL

Riding Japanese trains is one of the pleasures of travel in the country. Efficient and convenient, trains run frequently and on schedule. The Shinkansen (bullet train), one of the fastest trains in the world, connects major cities north and south of Tokyo. It is only slightly less expensive than flying, but is in many ways more convenient because train stations are more centrally located than airports (if you have a Japan Rail Pass, it's extremely affordable).

If you plan to travel by rail, get a Japan Rail Pass, which provides unlimited travel on Japan Railways (JR) trains (covering most destinations in Japan) but not on lines owned by other companies. For the Sanyo, Tokaido, and Kyushu Shinkansen lines, the pass is valid on any trains except the Nozomi and Mizuho, which stop infrequently. However, it is valid on all trains on the Yamagata, Tohoku, Joetsu, Akita, and Hokuriku Shinkansen lines.

The JR Pass is also valid on some local buses operated by Japan Railways, though not on the long-distance JR highway buses. You can make seat reservations without paying a fee on all trains that have reserved-seat coaches, usually long-distance trains. The Japan Rail Pass does not cover the cost of sleeping compartments on overnight trains (called blue trains).

You can purchase one-, two-, or three-week passes. A one-week pass is about as expensive as a regular round-trip ticket from Tokyo to Kyoto on the Shinkansen. You must obtain a rail pass voucher prior to arrival in Japan (you cannot buy them in Japan), and the pass must be used within three months of purchase. The pass is available only to people with tourist visas, as opposed to business, student, and diplomatic visas.

Tokyo Metro and Toei operate separate subway lines in Tokyo, with Tokyo Metro operating the majority of them. The companies charge separate fares—that is, a ticket from one company is not valid on a train operated by the other, so you want to complete a journey on lines operated by one company rather than switching. Some especially useful lines for visitors are the Ginza Line, which moves between Asakusa and Shibuya, and the Oedo and Marunouchi lines, which loop around the city center.

Basic train and subway fares within Tokyo are between ¥130 and ¥310, depending on how far you travel. Purchase tickets from machines that take coins or cash near the gates. Maps above each machine—usually in Japanese and English in central Tokyo—list destinations and fares. ■ TIP➔ Sometimes the station map will be written only in Japanese. In that case, buy the lowest-priced ticket and adjust the fare upon arrival.

Train Information **East Japan Railway Company.** ☎ *050/2016–1603* ⊕ *www. jreast.co.jp/e.* **Japan Rail Pass.** ⊕ *www.japanrailpass.net.*

VISITOR INFORMATION

The Japan National Tourism Organization (JNTO) has an office in Tokyo. The JNTO-affiliated International Tourism Center of Japan also has more than 140 counters/offices nationwide. Look for the sign showing a red question mark and the word "information" at train stations and city centers.

Contacts **Japan National Tourism Organization/Tokyo.** ⊠ *Tokyo* ☎ *03/3502–1461 in Japan, 212/757–5640 New York branch, 213/623–1952 Los Angeles branch* ⊕ *www.jnto.go.jp/eng.*

EXPLORING TOKYO

IMPERIAL PALACE DISTRICT 皇居近辺

The Imperial Palace district is the core of Japan's government. It is primarily comprised of the *Nagata-cho* (surrounding neighborhood), the Imperial Palace (*Kokyo-gaien*), the Diet (national parliament building), the prime minister's residence (*Kantei*), and the Supreme Court. The Imperial Palace and the Diet are both important for visitors to see, but the Supreme Court is rather nondescript. Unfortunately, the prime minister's residence is only viewable from afar, hidden behind fortified walls and trees.

The Imperial Palace was built by the order of Ieyasu Tokugawa, who chose the site for his castle in 1590. The castle had 99 gates (36 in the outer wall), 21 watchtowers (of which 3 are still standing), and 28 armories. The outer defenses stretched from present-day Shimbashi Station to Kanda. Completed in 1640 (and later expanded), it was at the time the largest castle in the world.

The Japanese Imperial Family resides in heavily blockaded sections of the palace grounds. Tours are conducted by reservation only, and restricted to designated outdoor sections, namely, the palace grounds and the East Gardens. While the East Gardens are open to visitors daily, the main grounds are open to the general public only twice a year, on January 2 and December 23 (the Emperor's birthday), when thousands of people assemble under the balcony to offer their good wishes to the Imperial Family.

ORIENTATION

The Imperial Palace is located in the heart of central Tokyo, and the city's other neighborhoods branch out from here. The palace, where the Imperial Family still resides, is surrounded by a moat that connects through canals to Tokyo Bay and Sumida River (Sumida-gawa) to the east.

PLANNING

Imperial Household Agency (宮内庁). The best way to discover the Imperial Palace is to take part in one of the free tours offered by the Imperial Household Agency. There are four different tours: Imperial Palace

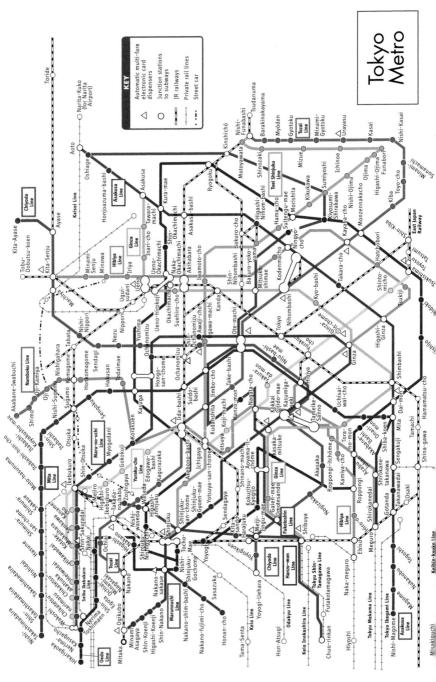

Grounds, the East Gardens (*Higashi Gyo-en*), Sannomaru Shozokan, and Gagaku Performance (autumn only). Tour registration is required a day in advance; hours change according to the season. ✉ *1-1 Chiyoda, Chiyoda-ku, Imperial Palace* ☎ *03/3213–1111* ⊕ *www.kunaicho.go.jp.*

If going on your own, allow at least an hour for the East Garden and Outer Garden. Visit Yasukuni Jinja after lunch and spend at least an hour there, taking half an hour each for the small Yushukan (at Yasukuni Jinja) and Kogeikan museums. The modern art museum requires a more leisurely visit.

GETTING HERE AND AROUND

The best way to get to the Imperial Palace is by subway. Take the Chiyoda Line to Nijubashimae Station (Exit 6) or the JR lines to Tokyo Station (Marunouchi Central Exit). There are three entrance gates—Ote-mon, Hirakawa-mon, and Kita-hane-bashi-mon. You can also easily get to any of the three from the Ote-machi or Takebashi subway stations.

TOP ATTRACTIONS

Fodor's Choice ★ **Imperial Palace East Garden** (皇居東御苑 *Kokyo Higashi Gyo-en*). Tokyo's most central yet most overlooked oasis of green and quiet is more a relaxed, spacious park than a traditional Japanese garden, making it a good picnic spot as well. Formerly part of the grounds of Edo Castle, it was claimed for the Imperial Family after the 1868 Meiji Restoration. Though most of the old castle was torn down or lost to fire, the stone foundations hint at the scale of the country's former seat of power.

The entrance to the East Garden is the Ote-mon, once the main gate of Ieyasu Tokugawa's castle. Here, you will come across the National Police Agency *dojo* (martial arts hall) and the Ote Rest House, where you can buy a simple map of the garden. The **Museum of the Imperial Collection** next door features rotating exhibits of imperial household treasures.

The **Hundred-Man Guardhouse** was once defended by four shifts of 100 soldiers each. Past it is the entrance to what was once the *ni-no-maru*, the "second circle" of the fortress. It's now a grove and garden. At the far end is the **Suwa Tea Pavilion**, an early-19th-century building relocated here from another part of the castle grounds.

The steep stone walls of the **hon-maru** (the "inner circle"), with the Moat of Swans below, dominate the west side of the garden. Halfway along is **Shio-mi-zaka**, which translates roughly as "Briny View Hill," so named because in the Edo period the ocean could be seen from here.

Head to the wooded paths around the garden's edges for shade, quiet, and benches to rest your weary feet. In the southwest corner is the Fujimi Yagura, the only surviving watchtower of the hon-maru; farther along the path, on the west side, is the **Fujimi Tamon,** one of the two remaining armories.

The odd-looking octagonal tower is the **Tokagakudo Concert Hall.** Its mosaic tile facade was built in honor of Empress Kojun in 1966. ✉ *1–1 Chiyoda, Chiyoda-ku, Imperial Palace* ☎ *03/3213–1111* 🎫 *Free* ☉ *Mar.–Apr. 14, Sept., and Oct., Tues.–Thurs. and weekends 9–4:30;*

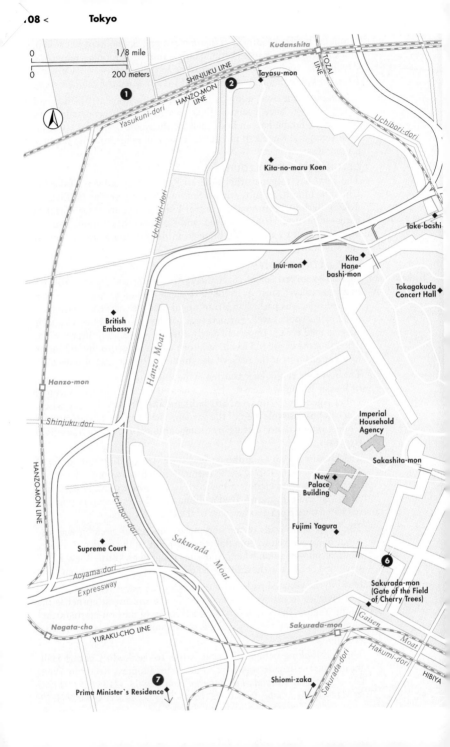

0
1/8 mile

0
200 meters

Kudanshita

SHINJUKU LINE

HANZO-MON LINE

1

2   Tayasu-mon

TOZAI LINE

Uchibori-dori

Yasukuni-dori

Kita-no-maru Koen

Take-bashi

Inui-mon

Kita
Hane-
bashi-mon

Tokagakuda
Concert Hall

British
Embassy

Uchibori-dori

Hanzo Moat

Hanzo-mon

Shinjuku-dori

HANZO-MON LINE

Imperial
Household
Agency

Sakashita-mon

New
Palace
Building

Uchibori-dori

Fujimi Yagura

Sakurada Moat

Supreme Court

Aoyama-dori

Expressway

6

Sakurada-mon
(Gate of the Field
of Cherry Trees)

Nagata-cho

YURAKU-CHO LINE

Sakurada-mon

Gaisen

Moat

Hakumi-dori

HIBIYA

7
Prime Minister's Residence

Shiomi-zaka

Sakurada-dori

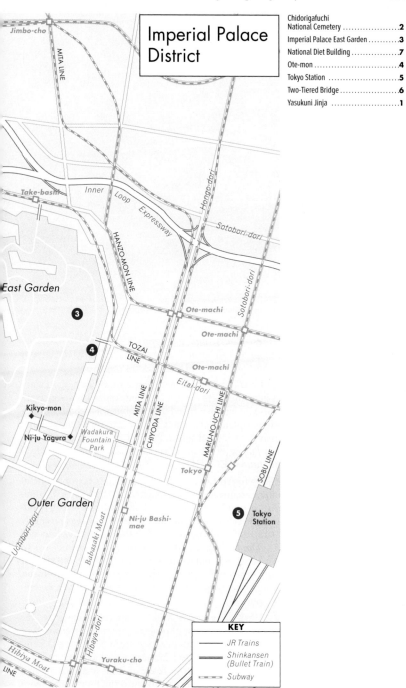

Imperial Palace District

3

Jimbo-cho

MITA LINE

Take-bashi

Inner Loop Expressway

HANZO-MON LINE

Hongo-dori

Sotobori-dori

Sotobori-dori

East Garden

❸

❹

TOZAI LINE

Ote-machi

Ote-machi

Ote-machi

Eitai-dori

MITA LINE

CHIYODA LINE

MARUNOUCHI LINE

SOBU LINE

Kikyo-mon

Ni-ju Yagura

Wadakura
Fountain
Park

Tokyo

❺ Tokyo
Station

Outer Garden

Ni-ju Bashi-
mae

Uchibori-dori

Babasaki Moat

Hibiya Moat

Hibiya-dori

Yuraku-cho

LINE

KEY

— JR Trains

═ Shinkansen
(Bullet Train)

╌╌ Subway

Once the site of the Imperial Palace's innermost defense circles, the East Garden now offers respite in a beautiful setting.

Apr. 15–Aug., Tues.–Thurs. and weekends 9–5; Nov.–Feb., Tues.–Thurs. and weekends 9–4 Ⓜ *Tozai, Marunouchi, and Chiyoda subway lines, Ote-machi Station (Exit C13B).*

Ote-mon (大手門 *Ote Gate*). The main entrance to the Imperial Palace East Garden was in former days the principal gate of Ieyasu Tokugawa's castle. Most of the gate was destroyed in 1945 but was rebuilt in 19__ based on the original plans. The outer part of the gate survived and offers an impressive entrance into the Palace's East Gardens. ✉ Chiyoda-ku, Imperial Palace Ⓜ *Tozai, Marunouchi, and Chiyoda subway lines, Ote-machi Station (Exit C10).*

Tokyo Station (東京駅 *Tokyo Eki*). This work of Kingo Tatsuno, one of Japan's first modern architects, was completed in 1914, with Tatsuno modeling his creation on the railway station of Amsterdam. The building lost its original top story in the air raids of 1945, but was promptly repaired. In the late 1990s, a plan to demolish the station was impeded by public outcry. The highlight is the historic and luxurious Tokyo Station Hotel, on the second and third floors. The area around the station is increasingly popular for dining, shopping, and entertainment. ✉ *1-9-1 Marunouchi, Chiyoda-ku, Marunouchi* Ⓜ *Marunouchi subway line and JR lines.*

Two-Tiered Bridge (二重橋 *Ni-ju-bashi*). Making a graceful arch across the moat, this bridge is surely the most photogenic spot on the grounds of the former Edo Castle. Mere mortals may pass through only on December 23 (the Emperor's birthday) and January 2 to pay their respects to the Imperial Family. The guards in front of their small, octagonal copper-roof sentry boxes change every hour on the hour—alas, wi nothing like the pomp and ceremony at Buckingham Palace. ⊠ *Chi-yoda-ku, Imperial Palace* Ⓜ *Chiyoda subway line, Ni-ju-bashi-mae Station (Exit 2).*

Yasukuni Jinja (靖国神社 *Shrine of Peace for the Nation*). Founded in 1869, this shrine is dedicated to approximately 2.5 million Japanese, Taiwanese, and Koreans who have died since then in war or military service. As the Japanese constitution expressly renounces both militarism and state sponsorship of religion, Yasukuni has been a center of stubborn political debate, particularly since 1978 when a shrine official added the names of several class-A war criminals to the list. Numerous prime ministers have visited the shrine since 1979, causing a political chill between Japan and its close neighbors, Korea and China, who suffered under Japanese colonialism. Despite all this, hundreds of thousands of Japanese come here every year, simply to pray for the repose of friends and relatives they have lost. These pilgrimages are most frenzied on August 15, the anniversary of the conclusion of World War II, when former soldiers and ultra-right-wing groups descend upon the shrine's grounds en masse.

The shrine is not one structure but a complex of buildings that include the **Main Hall** and the **Hall of Worship**—both built in the simple, unadorned style of the ancient Shinto shrines at Ise—and the **Yushukan,** a museum of documents and war memorabilia. Also here are a Noh theater and, in the far western corner, a sumo-wrestling ring. Sumo matches are held at Yasukuni in April, during the first of its three annual festivals. You can pick up a pamphlet and simplified map of the shrine, both in English, just inside the grounds.

Refurbished in 2002, the Yushukan presents Japan at its most ambivalent—if not unrepentant—about its more recent militaristic past. Critics charge that the newer exhibits glorify the nation's role in the Pacific War as a noble struggle for independence; certainly there's an agenda here that's hard to reconcile with Japan's firm postwar rejection of militarism as an instrument of national policy. Many Japanese visitors are moved by such displays as the last letters and photographs of young kamikaze pilots, while others find the Yushukan a cautionary, rather than uplifting, experience.

Although some of the exhibits have English labels and notes, the English is not very helpful; most objects, however, speak clearly enough for themselves. Rooms on the second floor house an especially fine collection of medieval swords and armor. Visiting on a Sunday offers a chance to forage at the flea market that runs from morning until sundown. ⊠ *3–1–1 Kudankita, Chiyoda-ku, Imperial Palace* ☎ *03/3261–8326* ⊕ *www.yasukuni.or.jp* ✈ *Shrine free, Yushukan ¥800* ⊙ *Grounds Mar.–Oct., daily 8:15–5; Nov.–Feb., daily 8:15–4; museum daily 9–4:30* Ⓜ *Hanzo-mon and Shinjuku subway lines, Kudanshita Station (Exit 1).*

WORTH NOTING

Chidorigafuchi National Cemetery (千鳥ヶ淵戦没者墓苑 *Chidorigafuchi Senbotsusha Boen*). High on the edge of the Imperial Palace moat, this cemetery holds the remains of thousands of unknown soldiers and is famous for its springtime cherry blossoms. The adjacent **Chidorigafuchi**

Stretch Your Legs

The venue of choice for runners is the **Imperial Palace Outer Garden**. At the west end of the park, Sakurada-mon's (Gate of the Field of Cherry Trees) small courtyard is the traditional starting point for the 5-km (3-mile) run around the palace—though you can join in anywhere along the route. Jogging around the palace is a ritual that begins as early as 6 am and goes on throughout the day, no matter what the weather. Almost everybody runs the course counterclockwise, but now and then you may spot someone going the opposite way.

Looking for a challenge? Japan hosts a number of marathons throughout the year and one of the most famous is the **Tokyo Marathon** (⊕ www. tokyo42195.org), which is held in February. Plan ahead if you're going to sign up, because the registration deadline is at the end of August of the previous year (most of the country's running events require signing up and qualifying far more in advance than their counterparts on other shores). The marathon starts at one of Tokyo's most prominent landmarks, the Tokyo Metropolitan Government Office in Shinjuku-ku, winds its way through the Imperial Palace, past the Tokyo Tower and Asakusa Kaminarimon Gate, and finishes at Tokyo Big Sight Exhibition Center in Koto Ward.

Boathouse rents out rowboats and pedal boats. Only a small part of the palace's outer moat is accessible, but a walk here makes for a refreshing 30 minutes. The entrance to the garden is near Yasukuni Jinja. ⊠ 2 San-ban-cho, Chiyoda-ku, Imperial Palace ☎ 03/3234–1948 ☜ Park free, boat rental ¥500 for 30 mins during regular season, ¥800 for 30 mins during cherry blossom season ⊙ Park daily sunrise–sunset; boathouse early Apr.–late Nov., Tues.–Sun. 11–5:30 Ⓜ Hanzo-mon and Shinjuku subway lines, Kudanshita Station (Exit 2).

National Diet Building (国会議事堂 Kokkai-Gijido). The Japanese parliament occupies a perfect example of post–World War II Japanese architecture; on a gloomy day it seems as if it might have sprung from the screen of a German Expressionist movie. Started in 1920, construction took 17 years to complete. Guided tours are available most days, but it's best to call ahead to confirm times. The prime minister's residence, Kantei, is across the street; you can try and get a glimpse of it, but it's quite hidden by walls and trees. ⊠ 1–7–1 Nagata-cho, Chiyoda-ku, Imperial Palace ☎ 03/5521–7445 ⊕ www.sangiin.go.jp ⊙ Weekdays 8–5 Ⓜ Marunouchi subway line, Kokkai-Gijido-mae Station (Exit 2).

AKIHABARA 秋葉原

Akihabara is techno-geek heaven. Also known as Akihabara Electric Town, or just Akiba, this district was once a dizzying collection of small, ultra-specialized electronics and computer shops, but has now become the center of Japan's anime, manga, and computer-focused *otaku* (nerd) culture.

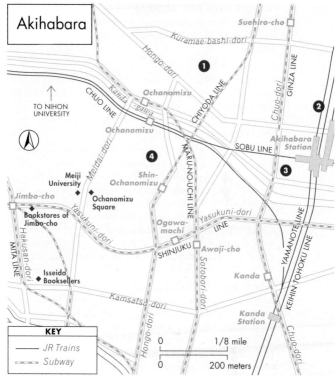

More recently, the area has gained mainstream appeal among shoppers and tourists, with large all-in-one electronics shops crowding out many of the smaller and unique stores. Even so, the area has stayed true to its roots. Venture off the main road to see the real Akiba, where maid cafés (where servers are, yes, dressed as maids and treat their customers as "masters and mistresses") mix with computer and hi-fi audio stores filled with dedicated fans searching for computer parts, rare comics, or techno-accessories they can't find anywhere else. For visitors, seeing the subculture and energy of Akiba is as much a draw as the shopping.

ORIENTATION

Akihabara is east of the Imperial Palace, right below Ueno and Asakusa. Akihabara Station is located north of Tokyo Station, on the JR Yamanote, Hibiya, and Tsukuba lines. It's right below Asakusa and Ueno districts.

PLANNING

Keep in mind that most stores in Akihabara do not open until 10 am. Weekends draw hordes of shoppers, especially on Sunday, when the four central blocks of Chuo-dori are closed to traffic and become a pedestrian mall.

GETTING HERE AND AROUND

Take the train to Akihabara Station on the JR Yamanote Line. Akihabara is a 20- to 30-minute ride from most hotels in Shinjuku or Minato-ku.

TOP ATTRACTIONS

Kanda Shrine (神田明神 *Kanda Myojin*). This shrine is said to have been founded in 730 in a village called Shibasaki, where the Ote-machi financial district stands today. The shrine itself was destroyed in the Great Kanto Earthquake of 1923, and the present buildings reproduce in concrete the style of 1616.

You will never be able to see every shrine in the city and the ones in Akihabara are of minor interest, unless you are around for the **Kanda Festival**—one of Tokyo's three great blowouts—in mid-May. (The other two are the Sanno Festival of Hie Jinja in Nagata-cho and the Sanja Festival of Asakusa Shrine.) Some of the smaller buildings you see as you come up the steps and walk around the Main Hall contain the *mikoshi*—the portable shrines that are featured during the festival. Kanda Myojin is on Kuramae-bashi-dori, about a five-minute walk west of the Suehiro-cho subway stop. ✉ *2–16–2 Soto-Kanda, Chiyoda-ku, Akihabara* ☎ *03/3254–0753* Ⓜ *Ginza subway line, Suehiro-cho Station (Exit 3)*.

Radio Kaikan (ラジオ会館). Eight floors featuring a variety of independent vendors selling mini-spy cameras, cell phones disguised as stun guns, manga comics, adult toys, gadgets, and oddball hobby supplies draw otaku, other shoppers, and visitors alike. And that's just the main building. Start browsing from the top floor and work your way down. There are two annexes across the street as well. ✉ *1–15–4 Soto-Kanda, Chiyoda-ku, Akihabara* ☎ *03/3251–3711 office* Ⓜ *JR Yamanote Line, Akihabara Station (Akihabara Electric Town Exit)*.

WORTH NOTING

Holy Resurrection Cathedral (ニコライ堂 *Nikolai-do*). It's curious that a Russian Orthodox cathedral was built in Tokyo's Electric Town, but it's a place to stop for a quick snapshot. Formally, this is the Holy Resurrection Cathedral, derived from its founder, St. Nikolai Kassatkin (1836–1912), a Russian missionary who came to Japan in 1861 and spent the rest of his life here. The building, planned by a Russian engineer and executed by a British architect, was completed in 1891. Heavily damaged in the earthquake of 1923, the cathedral was restored with a dome much more modest than the original. Even so, the cathedral endows this otherwise featureless part of the city with unexpected charm. ✉ *4–1–3 Surugadai, Chiyoda-ku, Akihabara* ☎ *03/3291–1885* Ⓜ *Chiyoda subway line, Shin-Ochanomizu Station (Exit B1)*.

Tokyo Anime Center (東京アニメセンター). As an information source and exhibitor of images and films, the center attracts tens of thousands of visitors each year. An on-site shop sells a wide range of anime goods that will satisfy even the most ardent of fans. ✉ *4F UDX Bldg., 4–14–1 Soto-Kanda, Chiyoda-ku, Akihabara* ☎ *03/5298–1188* ⊕ *www.animecenter. jp* ☉ *Tues.–Sun. 11–7* Ⓜ *JR Yamanote Line, Akihabara Station (Akihabara Electric Town Exit)*.

UENO 上野

Located in the heart of Ueno, JR Ueno Station is Tokyo's version of the Gare du Nord: the gateway to and from Japan's northeast provinces. Since its completion in 1883, the station has served as a terminus in the great migration to the city by villagers in pursuit of a better life.

Ueno was a place of prominence long before the coming of the railroad. After Ieyasu Tokugawa established his capital here in 1603, 36 subsidiary temples were erected surrounding the Main Hall, and the city of Edo itself expanded to the foot of the hill where the main gate of the Kan-ei-ji once stood. Some of the most important buildings in the temple complex have survived or have been restored and should not be missed.

ORIENTATION

Ueno, along with Asakusa, makes up the historical enclave of Tokyo. Though the Tokyo Sky Tree transmission tower can be seen from nearly all parts of these neighborhoods, traditional architecture and way of life are preserved here at the northeastern reaches of the city. If you are pressed for time all three areas can be explored in a single day, though if you want to visit Ueno's museums, it is best to devote an entire day to fully appreciate the area.

PLANNING

Ueno can be explored on one excursion or two: an afternoon of cultural browsing or a full day of cultural discoveries in one of the great centers of the city. Museums can get crowded later in the day, so it is a good idea to start at Ueno Station in the morning. ■TIP➔ Avoid Monday, when most of the museums are closed. In April, the cherry blossoms of Ueno Koen are glorious.

GETTING HERE AND AROUND

Ueno Station can be accessed by train on the Hibiya Line, Ginza Line, and JR Yamanote Line (Koen Entrance). Be sure to avoid rush hours in the morning (8–9) and evening (6–9) and bring plenty of cash for admission fees to museums and food for the day as finding an ATM may be challenging. Museums accept some major credit cards for admission and in their stores.

TOP ATTRACTIONS

Ame-ya Yoko-cho Market (アメヤ横丁). The sprawling stalls have become especially famous for the traditional prepared foods of the New Year, and, during the last few days of December, as many as half a million people crowd into the narrow alleys under the railroad tracks to stock up for the holiday. The market dates to World War II, when not much besides Ueno Station survived the bombings. Anyone who could make it here from the countryside with rice and other small supplies of food could sell them at exorbitant black-market prices. Sugar was a commodity that couldn't be found at any price in postwar Tokyo. Before long, there were hundreds of stalls in the black market selling various kinds of *ame* (confections), most made from sweet potatoes. These stalls gave the market its name, Ame-ya Yoko-cho (often shortened to Ameyoko), which means "Confectioners' Alley." Shortly before the Korean War,

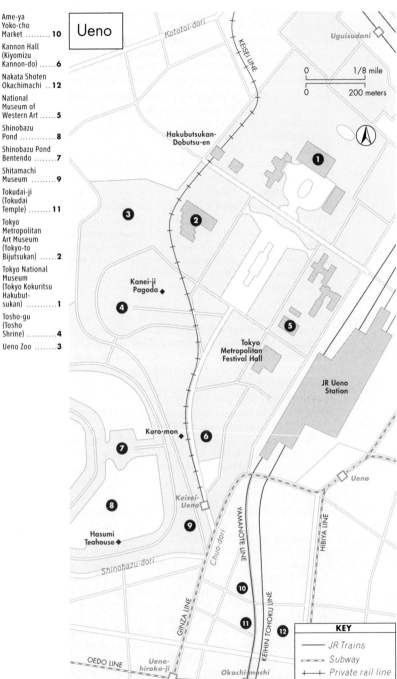

Ueno

the market was legalized, and soon the stalls were carrying watches, chocolate, ballpoint pens, blue jeans, and T-shirts that had somehow been "liberated" from American PXs. In years to come the merchants of Ameyoko diversified even further—to fine Swiss timepieces and fake designer luggage, cosmetics, jewelry, fresh fruit, and fish. For a break, the area also features numerous small restaurants specializing in raw slices of tuna over rice (*maguro-don*)—cheap, quick, and very good. ✉ *Ueno 4-chome, Taito-ku, Ueno* ⊗ *Most shops and stalls daily 10–7* Ⓜ *JR Ueno Station (Hiroko-ji Exit).*

Kannon Hall (清水観音堂 *Kiyomizu Kannon-do*). This National Treasure was a part of Abbot Tenkai's attempt to build a copy of Kyoto's magnificent Kiyomizu-dera in Ueno. His attempt was honorable, but failed to be as impressive as the original. The principal Buddhist image of worship here is the Senju Kannon (Thousand-Armed Goddess of Mercy). Another figure, however, receives greater homage. This is the Kosodate Kannon, who is believed to answer the prayers of women having difficulty conceiving children. If their prayers are answered, they return to Kiyomizu and leave a doll, as both an offering of thanks and a prayer for the child's health. In a ceremony held every September 25, the dolls that have accumulated during the year are burned in a bonfire. ✉ *1–29 Ueno Koen, Taito-ku, Ueno* ☎ *03/3821–4749* 🎫 *Free* ⊗ *Daily 7–5* Ⓜ *JR Ueno Station (Koen-guchi/Park Exit).*

FAMILY **Shinobazu Pond** (不忍池). When an inlet of Tokyo Bay receded around the 17th century, Shinobazu became a freshwater pond. Abbot Tenkai, founder of Kan-ei-ji on the hill above the pond, had an island made for Benzaiten, the goddess of the arts. Later improvements included a causeway to the island, embankments, and even a racecourse (1884–93). Today the pond is in three sections. The first, a wildlife sanctuary, is home to the city's locust flowers; this is the only place in Tokyo you can see them bloom from mid-June through August. Some 5,000 wild ducks migrate here from as far away as Siberia, sticking around from September to April. The second section, to the north, belongs to Ueno Zoo; the third, to the west, is a small lake for boating. In July, the Ueno *matsuri* (festival) features food stalls and music events in the small at the pond's edge. At the pond's southwestern corner, there is also a bandshell with various music events throughout the year. ✉ *Shinobazu-dori, Taito-ku* 🎫 *Free* Ⓜ *JR Ueno Station (Koen-guchi/Park Exit); Keisei private rail line, Keisei-Ueno Station (Higashi-guchi/East Exit).*

Shinobazu Pond Bentendo (不忍池弁財天). Perched in the middle of Shinobazu Pond, this shrine is dedicated to the goddess Benten, one of the Seven Gods of Good Luck that evolved from a combination of Indian, Chinese, and Japanese mythology. As matron goddess of the arts, she is depicted holding a lutelike musical instrument called a *biwa*. The shrine, built by Abbot Tenkai, was destroyed in the bombings of 1945; the present version, with its distinctive octagonal roof, is a faithful copy. You can rent rowboats and pedal boats at a nearby boathouse. ✉ *2–1 Ueno Koen, Taito-ku, Taito-ku* ☎ *03/3828–9502 boathouse* 🎫 *Rowboats ¥600 for 1 hr, pedal boats ¥600 for 30 mins, swan boats ¥700 for 30 mins* ⊗ *Boathouse daily 9–5* Ⓜ *JR Ueno Station (Koen-guchi/Park Exit); Keisei private rail line, Keisei-Ueno Station (Ikenohata Exit).*

The "ame" in Ame-ya Yoko-cho Market also means "American," referencing the many American products sold during the area's black market era.

Tokudai-ji (徳大寺 *Tokudai Temple*). This is a curiosity in a neighborhood of curiosities: a temple on the second floor of a supermarket. Two deities are worshipped here. One is the bodhisattva Jizo, and the act of washing this statue is believed to safeguard your health. The other is of the Indian goddess Marici, a daughter of Brahma; she is believed to help worshippers overcome difficulties and succeed in business. ⊠ *4–6–2 Ueno, Taitō-ku, Ueno* Ⓜ *JR Yamanote and Keihin-tohoku lines, Okachi-machi Station (Higashi-guchi/East Exit) or Ueno Station (Hiroko-ji Exit).*

Fodor's Choice
★ **Tokyo National Museum** (東京国立博物館 *Tokyo Kokuritsu Hakubutsu-kan*). This complex of four buildings grouped around a courtyard is one of the world's great repositories of East Asian art and archaeology. Altogether, the museum has some 87,000 objects in its permanent collection, with several thousand more on loan from shrines, temples, and private owners.

The Western-style building on the left (if you're standing at the main gate), with bronze cupolas, is the **Hyokeikan.** Built in 1909, it was devoted to archaeological exhibits; aside from the occasional special exhibition, the building is closed today. The larger **Heiseikan,** behind the Hyokeikan, was built to commemorate the wedding of crown prince Naruhito in 1993 and now houses Japanese archaeological exhibits. The second floor is used for special exhibitions.

In 1878, the 7th-century Horyu-ji (Horyu Temple) in Nara presented 319 works of art in its possession—sculpture, scrolls, masks, and other objects—to the Imperial Household. These were transferred to the National Museum in 2000 and now reside in the **Horyu-ji Homotsukan**

(Gallery of Horyu-ji Treasures), which was designed by Yoshio Taniguchi. There's a useful guide to the collection in English, and the exhibits are well explained. Don't miss the hall of carved wooden *gigaku* (Buddhist processional) masks.

The central building in the complex, the 1937 **Honkan,** houses Japanese art exclusively: paintings, calligraphy, sculpture, textiles, ceramics, swords, and armor. Also here are 84 objects designated by the government as National Treasures. The Honkan rotates the works on display several times during the year. It also hosts two special exhibitions annually (April and May or June, and October and November), which feature important collections from both Japanese and foreign museums. These, unfortunately, can be an ordeal to take in: the lighting in the Honkan is not particularly good, the explanations in English are sketchy at best, and the hordes of visitors make it impossible to linger over a work you especially want to study. The more attractive **Toyokan,** to the right of the Honkan, was completed in 1968 and recently renovated; it is devoted to the art and antiquities of China, Korea, Southeast Asia, India, the Middle East, and Egypt. ✉ *13–9 Ueno Koen, Taitō-ku, Ueno* ☎ *03/3822–1111* ⊕ *www.tnm.jp* ✉ *Regular exhibits ¥620, special exhibits ¥1,500* ☉ *Tues.–Sun. 9:30–5, times vary during special exhibitions* Ⓜ *JR Ueno Station (Koen-guchi/Park Exit).*

Fodor's Choice **Tosho-gu** (東照宮 *Tosho Shrine*). This shrine, built in 1627, is dedicated ★ to Ieyasu, the first Tokugawa shogun. It miraculously survived all major disasters that destroyed most of Tokyo's historical structures—the fires, the 1868 revolt, the 1923 earthquake, the 1945 bombings—making it one of the few early-Edo-period buildings left in Tokyo. The shrine and most of its art are designated National Treasures.

Two hundred *ishidoro* (stone lanterns) line the path from the stone entry arch to the shrine itself. One of them, just outside the arch to the left, and more than 18 feet high, is called *obaketoro* (ghost lantern). Legend has it that one night a samurai on guard duty slashed at a ghost (*obake*) that was believed to haunt the lantern. His sword was so strong, it left a nick in the stone, which can be seen today.

The first room inside the shrine is the **Hall of Worship;** the four paintings in gold on wooden panels are by Tan'yu, a member of the famous Kano family of artists, dating from the 15th century. Behind the Hall of Worship, connected by a passage called the *haiden,* is the sanctuary, where the spirit of Ieyasu is said to be enshrined.

The real glory of Tosho-gu is its so-called **Chinese Gate,** at the end of the building, and the fence on either side that has intricate carvings of birds, animals, fish, and shells of every description. The two long panels of the gate, with their dragons carved in relief, are attributed to Hidari Jingoro, a brilliant sculptor of the early Edo period whose real name is unknown (*hidari* means "left"; Jingoro was reportedly left-handed). ✉ *9–88 Ueno Koen, Taitō-ku, Ueno* ☎ *03/3822–3455* ✉ *¥200* ☉ *Daily 9–5* Ⓜ *JR Ueno Station (Koen-guchi/Park Exit).*

WORTH NOTING

Nakata Shoten Okachimachi (中田商店 御徒町店). This store probably has more shades of green than the average Tokyo park. Stuffed with cargo pants, camouflage jackets, military uniforms, and ammo boxes, Nakata Shoten is more about outfitting its customers in funky fashion than resurrecting Imperial militarism. The watches make interesting souvenirs. ⊠ *6–2–14 Ueno, Taitō-ku, Ueno* ☏ *03/3839–6866* ⊕ *www. nakatashoten.com* Ⓜ *JR lines, Okachi-machi Station (North Exit); Toei Oedo subway line, Ueno Okachi-machi Station (Exit A7).*

National Museum of Western Art (国立西洋美術館 *Kokuritsu Seiyo Bijutsukan*). Along with castings from the original molds of Rodin's *Gate of Hell, The Burghers of Calais,* and *The Thinker,* the wealthy businessman Matsukata Kojiro (1865–1950) acquired some 850 paintings, sketches, and prints by such masters as Renoir, Monet, Gauguin, van Gogh, Delacroix, and Cézanne. Matsukata kept the collection in Europe, but he left it to Japan in his will. The French government sent the artwork to Japan after World War II, and the collection opened to the public in 1959 in a building designed by Swiss-born architect Le Corbusier. Since then, the museum has diversified a bit; more recent acquisitions include works by Reubens, Tintoretto, El Greco, Max Ernst, and Jackson Pollock. The Seiyo is one of the best-organized, most pleasant museums to visit in Tokyo. ⊠ *7–7 Ueno Koen, Taito-ku, Ueno* ☏ *03/5777–8600* ⊕ *www.nmwa.go.jp* 💴 *¥430; additional fee for special exhibits* 🕙 *Tues.–Thurs. and weekends 9:30–5:30, Fri. 9:30–8* Ⓜ *JR Ueno Station (Koen-guchi/Park Exit).*

FAMILY **Shitamachi Museum** (下町風俗資料館 *Shitamachi Fuzoku Shiryokan*). Japanese society in the days of the Tokugawa shoguns was rigidly stratified. Some 80% of the city's land was allotted to the warrior class, temples, and shrines. The remaining 20%—between Ieyasu's fortifications on the west, and the Sumida-gawa on the east—was known as *shitamachi,* or "downtown" or the "lower town" (as it expanded, it came to include what today constitutes the Chuo, Taito, Sumida, and Koto wards). It was here that the common, hardworking, free-spending folk, who made up more than half the population, lived. The Shitamachi Museum preserves and exhibits what remained of that way of life as late as 1940.

The two main displays on the first floor are a merchant house and a tenement, intact with all their furnishings. This is a hands-on museum: you can take your shoes off and step up into the rooms. On the second floor are displays of toys, tools, and utensils donated, in most cases, by people who had grown up with them and used them all their lives. There are also photographs and video documentaries of craftspeople at work. Occasionally various traditional skills are demonstrated, and you're welcome to take part. This small but engaging museum makes great use of its space, and there are even volunteer guides (available starting at 10) who speak passable English. ⊠ *2–1 Ueno Koen, Taitō-ku, Ueno* ☏ *03/3823–7451* ⊕ *www.taitocity.net/taito/shitamachi* 💴 *¥300* 🕙 *Tues.–Sun. 9:30–4:30* Ⓜ *JR Ueno Station (Koen-guchi/Park Exit).*

Tokyo Metropolitan Art Museum (東京都美術館 *Tokyo-to Bijutsukan*). By far the most eclectic of Ueno's art museums, the Tokyo Metropolitan hosts large-scale exhibitions ranging from classic masterpieces to modern architecture. The museum's smaller galleries often play home to group exhibitions of painting, photography, calligraphy, sculpture, and nearly any other kind of art one can dream up. Many smaller exhibits are free. ⊠ *8–36 Ueno Koen, Taitō-ku, Ueno* ☎ *03/3823–6921* ⊕ *www.tobikan.jp* ✉ *Permanent collection free; fees vary for other exhibits (usually ¥800–¥1,400)* ⊙ *Daily 9:30–5; closed 1st and 3rd Mon. of month* Ⓜ *JR Ueno Station (Koen-guchi/Park Exit).*

FAMILY **Ueno Zoo** (上野動物園 *Ueno Dobutsuen*). The two main gardens of Japan's first zoo, built in 1882, host an exotic mix of more than 900 species of animals. The giant panda is the biggest draw, but the tigers from Sumatra, gorillas from the lowland swamp areas of western Africa, and numerous monkeys, some from Japan, make a visit to the East Garden worthwhile. The West Garden is highlighted by rhinos, zebras, and hippopotamuses, and a children's area. The process of the zoo's expansion somehow left within its confines the 120-foot, five-story Kan-ei-ji Pagoda. Built in 1631 and rebuilt after a fire in 1639, the building offers traditional Japanese tea ceremony services. ⊠ *9–83 Ueno Koen, Taitō-ku, Ueno* ☎ *03/3828–5171* ⊕ *www.tokyo-zoo.net/english/ueno* ✉ *¥600, free on Mar. 20, May 4, and Oct. 1* ⊙ *Tues.–Sun. 9:30–5* Ⓜ *JR Ueno Station (Koen-guchi/Park Exit).*

ASAKUSA 浅草

Cars make room for the rickshaw drivers who sometimes outpace the motorized traffic. On the neighborhood's backstreets, neo-French and Italian cafés mix with generations-old soba and tempura shops while customers in the latest fashions sit with those in traditional kimonos. Kaminari-mon, the gateway to Senso-ji—Tokyo's oldest temple—is a backdrop for artisans and small entrepreneurs, children and grandmothers, hipsters, hucksters, and priests. It is hard not to be swept away by the relaxed energy that pulses through the area. If you have any time to spend in Tokyo, make sure you devote at least a day to exploring Asakusa.

Historically, Asakusa has been the city's entertainment hub. The area blossomed when Ieyasu Tokugawa made Edo his capital, and it became the 14th-century city that never slept. For the next 300 years it was the wellspring of almost everything we associate with Japanese culture. In the mid-1600s, it became a pleasure quarter in its own right with stalls selling toys, souvenirs, and sweets; acrobats, jugglers, and strolling musicians; and sake shops and teahouses—where the waitresses often provided more than tea. Then, in 1841, the Kabuki theaters moved

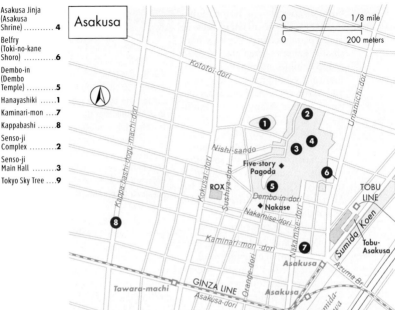

to Asakusa. The theaters were here for only a short time, but it was enough to establish Asakusa as *the* entertainment quarter of the city—a reputation it held unchallenged until World War II, when most of the area was destroyed.

After the war, development focused on areas to the west like Shinjuku and Shibuya. In a way, this saved Asakusa from becoming yet another neighborhood filled with neon, concrete, and glass instead mostly keeping to the same style of low buildings and tiny independent shops that existed before the war. Seven decades have certainly changed the neighborhood, but many of the smaller side streets retain the charm and feel of old Tokyo. Although the area has become dramatically more popular in recent years, tourists usually keep to the main streets and line up at the same restaurants around the Senso-ji Temple Complex. Venture a few minutes away from the temple area and the crowds thin out and souvenir shops give way to quiet storefronts selling traditional crafts. Although Senso-ji Temple is well worth seeing, taking the time to wander through the neighborhood gives you a hint of what it may have been like years ago.

ORIENTATION

Asakusa is a border city ward that separates central Tokyo from its suburban areas. It's a unique spiritual and commercial, tourist, and residential area, where locals walk their dogs on the Asakusa Jinja grounds or give offerings and pray at Kannon Temple. Asakusa is just east of Ueno and can be explored in a half day, whether you go straight from Ueno or on a separate excursion.

PLANNING

Unlike most of the other areas to explore on foot in Tokyo, Senso-ji is admirably compact. You can easily see the temple and explore the area surrounding it in a morning. The garden at Dembo-in is worth a half hour. If you decide to include Kappabashi, allow yourself an hour more for the tour. Some of the shopping arcades in this area are covered, but Asakusa is essentially an outdoor experience. Be prepared for rain in June and heat and humidity in July and August.

The Asakusa Tourist Information Center (Asakusa Bunka Kanko Center) is across the street from Kaminari-mon. English-speaking volunteers are on duty here daily 10–5 and will happily load you down with maps and brochures.

GETTING HERE AND AROUND

Getting here by subway from Ueno Station (Ginza Line, Ueno Station to Asakusa Station, ¥170) or taxi (approximately ¥1,000) is most convenient. Asakusa is the last stop (eastbound) on the Ginza Line.

Another way to get to Asakusa is by river-bus ferry from Hinode Pier, which stops at the southwest corner of Sumida Koen.

TOP ATTRACTIONS

Asakusa Jinja (浅草神社 *Asakusa Shrine*). Several structures in the famous Senso-ji shrine complex survived the bombings of 1945. The largest, to the right of the Main Hall, is this Shinto shrine to the Hikonuma brothers and their master, Naji-no-Nakamoto—the putative founders of Senso-ji. In Japan, Buddhism and Shintoism have enjoyed a comfortable coexistence since the former arrived from China in the 6th century. The shrine, built in 1649, is also known as Sanja Sama (Shrine of the Three Guardians). Near the entrance to Asakusa Shrine is another survivor of World War II: the original east gate to the temple grounds, **Nitenmon**, built in 1618 for a shrine to Ieyasu Tokugawa and designated by the government as an Important Cultural Property. ⊠ *2–3–1 Asakusa, Taitō-ku, Asakusa* ☎ *03/3844-1575* ⊕ *www.asakusajinja.jp*.

Belfry (時の鐘鐘楼 *Toki-no-kane Shoro*). The tiny hillock Benten-yama, with its shrine to the goddess of good fortune, is the site of this 17th-century belfry. The bell here used to toll the hours for the people of the district, and it was said that you could hear it anywhere within a radius of some 6 km (4 miles). The bell still sounds at 6 am every day, when the temple grounds open. It also rings on New Year's Eve—108 strokes in all, beginning just before midnight, to "ring out" the 108 sins and frailties of humankind and make a clean start for the coming year. Benten-yama and the belfry are at the beginning of the narrow street that parallels Nakamise-dori. ⊠ *Taitō-ku, Asakusa*.

Asakusa's heart and soul is the Senso-ji Complex, famous for its 17th-century Shinto shrine, Asakusa Shrine, well as its garden and the wild Sanja Festival in May.

Dembo-in (伝法院 *Dembo Temple*). Believed to have been made in t[?] 17th century by Kobori Enshu, the genius of Zen landscape design, t[?] garden of Dembo-in is part of the living quarters of the abbot of Senso[?] and the best-kept secret in Asakusa. The garden is usually empty a[?] always utterly serene, an island of privacy in a sea of pilgrims. Sprin[?] when the wisteria blooms, is the ideal time to be here.

A sign in English on Dembo-in-dori—you'll see it about 150 yards we[?] of the intersection with Naka-mise-dori—leads you to the entran[?] which is a side door to a large wooden gate. For permission to see t[?] abbot's garden, you must first apply at the temple administration buil[?] ing, between Hozo-mon and the Five-Story Pagoda, in the far corn[?] ⊠ *2–3–1 Asakusa, Taitō-ku, Asakusa* ☎ *03/3842–0181 for reservatio[?]* ⌨ *Free* ◷ *Daily 9–4; may be closed if abbot has guests* Ⓜ *Ginza subw[?] line, Asakusa Station (Exit 1/Kaminari-mon Exit).*

FAMILY **Hanayashiki** (花やしき). Dubbing itself "the old park with a smile[?] Tokyo's premier retro amusement park was established in 1853. Thi[?] Coney Island: a haunted house, Ferris wheel, and merry-go-round aw[?] the kids who will likely be a little tired of Asakusa's historic are[?] ⊠ *2–28–1 Asakusa, Taitō-ku, Asakusa* ☎ *03/3842–8780* ⊕ *ww[?] hanayashiki.net* ⌨ *¥900–¥2,200* ◷ *Daily 10–6, but check sched[?] for later closing times* Ⓜ *Ginza subway line, Asakusa Station (Exit [?] Kaminari-mon Exit).*

NEED A BREAK? **Nakase** (中清). Nakase is a lovely retreat from the overbearing crowds at the Senso-ji Complex. The building, which is 130 years old, lends a truly authentic Japanese experience: food is served in lacquerware bento boxe[?]

and there are an interior garden and a pond, which is filled with carp and goldfish. Across Orange-dori from the redbrick Asakusa Public Hall, Nakase is expensive, but the experience is worth it. ✉ *1–39–13 Asakusa, Taitō-ku, Asakusa* ☎ *03/3841–4015* ⊘ *Closed Thurs.* Ⓜ *Ginza subway line, Asakusa Station (Exit 1/Kaminari-mon Exit).*

Kaminari-mon (雷門 *Thunder God Gate*). The main entryway to Senso-ji's grounds towers above the ever-present throng of tourists and passing rickshaw drivers. With its huge red-paper lantern hanging in the center, this landmark of Asakusa is picture-perfect, provided you can find a clear shot. The original gate was destroyed by fire in 1865; the replica you see today was built after World War II. Traditionally, two fearsome guardian gods are installed in the alcoves of Buddhist temple gates to ward off evil spirits. The Thunder God (Kaminari-no-Kami) is on the left with the Wind God (Kaze-no-Kami) on the right. Want to buy some of Tokyo's most famous souvenirs? Stop at **Tokiwa-do,** the shop on the west side of the gate for *kaminari okoshi* (thunder crackers), made of rice, millet, sugar, and beans.

Kaminari-mon marks the southern extent of **Nakamise-dori,** the Street of Inside Shops. The area from Kaminari-mon to the inner gate of the temple was once composed of stalls leased to the townspeople who cleaned and swept the temple grounds. This is now kitsch-souvenir central, so be prepared to buy a few key chains, dolls, and snacks. ✉ *2–3–1 Asakusa, Taitō-ku, Asakusa* Ⓜ *Ginza subway line, Asakusa Station (Exit 1/Kaminari-mon Exit).*

Kappabashi (かっぱ橋). In the 19th century, according to local legend, a river ran through the present-day Kappabashi district. The surrounding area was poorly drained and was often flooded. A local shopkeeper began a project to improve the drainage, investing all his own money, but met with little success until a troupe of *kappa*—mischievous green water sprites—emerged from the river to help him. A more prosaic explanation for the name of the district points out that the lower-ranking retainers of the local lord used to earn extra money by making straw raincoats, also called *kappa,* that they spread to dry on the bridge.

Today, Kappabashi's more than 200 wholesale dealers sell everything the city's restaurant and bar trade could possibly need to do business, from paper supplies and steam tables to the main attraction, plastic food. ✉ *Nishi-Asakusa 1-chome and 2-chome, Taitō-ku, Asakusa* ⊘ *Most shops daily 9–6* Ⓜ *Ginza subway line, Tawara-machi Station (Exit 1).*

THE SANJA FESTIVAL

The Sanja Festival, held annually over the third weekend of May, is said to be the biggest, loudest, wildest party in Tokyo. Each of the areas in Asakusa has its own mikoshi, which, on the second day of the festival, are paraded through the streets of Asakusa to the shrine. Many of the "parishioners" take part naked to the waist, or with the sleeves of their tunics rolled up, to expose fantastic red-and-black tattoo patterns that sometimes cover their entire backs and shoulders. These are the markings of the Japanese underworld.

Senso-ji Complex. Even for travelers with little interest in history or temples, this complex in the heart and soul of Asakusa is without a doubt one of Tokyo's must-see sights. Come for its local and historical importance, its garden, its 17th-century Shinto shrine, and Tokyo's most famous festival: the wild Sanja Matsuri in May. The area also offers myriad interesting shops, winding backstreets, and an atmosphere unlike anywhere else in Tokyo. ⊠ *2–3–1 Asakusa, Taitō-ku, Asakusa* ☏ *03/3842–0181* ⊕ *www.senso-ji.jp* ☺ *Free* ☾ *Temple grounds daily 6–sunset* Ⓜ *Ginza subway line, Asakusa Station (Exit 1/Kaminari-mon Exit).*

Senso-ji Main Hall (浅草観音堂). Established in 645, the bright red Main Hall has long been the center of Asakusa, though what you see today is a faithful replica of the original that burned in the fire raids of 1945. It took 13 years to raise money for the restoration of the beloved Senso-ji, which is much more than a tourist attraction. Kabuki actors still come here before a new season of performances, and sumo wrestlers visit before a tournament to pay their respects. The large lanterns were donated by the geisha associations of Asakusa and nearby Yanagi-bashi. Most Japanese stop at the huge bronze incense burner, in front of the Main Hall, to bathe their hands and faces in the smoke—it's a charm to ward off illnesses—before climbing the stairs to offer their prayers.

Unlike in many other temples, however, part of the inside has a concrete floor, so you can come and go without removing your shoes. In this area hang Senso-ji's chief claims to artistic importance: a collection of 18th- and 19th-century votive paintings on wood. Plaques of this kind, called *ema*, are still offered to the gods at shrines and temples, but they are commonly simpler and smaller. The worshipper buys a little tablet of wood with the picture already painted on one side and inscribes a prayer on the other. The temple owns more than 50 of these works, which were removed to safety in 1945 to escape the air raids. Only eight of them, depicting scenes from Japanese history and mythology, are on display. A catalog of the collection is on sale in the hall, but the text is in Japanese only.

Lighting is poor in the Main Hall, and the actual works are difficult to see. One thing that visitors cannot see at all is the holy image of Kannon itself, which supposedly lies buried somewhere deep under the temple. Not even the priests of Senso-ji have ever seen it, and there is in fact no conclusive evidence that it actually exists.

Hozo-mon, the gate to the temple courtyard, is also a repository for sutras (Buddhist texts) and other treasures of Senso-ji. This gate, too, has its guardian gods; should either god decide to leave his post for a stroll, he can use the enormous pair of sandals hanging on the back wall—the gift of a Yamagata Prefecture village famous for its straw weaving. ⊠ *2–3–1 Asakusa, Taitō-ku, Asakusa* ⊕ *www.senso-ji.jp.*

Tokyo Sky Tree (スカイツリー). Opened in 2011 to mixed reviews, this 2,000-plus-foot-tall skyscraper has become a symbol of the ongoing revival of the eastern side of the city. When it opened, tickets to the observation decks were booked for months in advance and the tower, along with the adjacent Solamachi shopping complex, continues to draw shoppers and tourists to the area. On a clear day, the views from the 1,155-foot-high Tembo Deck observation area are impressive. For an extra fee, visitors can go to the Tembo Galleria, another 330 feet up. ⊠ *1-1-2 Oshiage, Sumida-ku, Asakusa* ⊕ *www.tokyo-skytree. jp/en* 🎫 *¥2,500 (plus ¥1,000 for top observation deck)* ⊙ *Daily 8 am–10 pm* Ⓜ *Tobu Skytree Line Skytree Station, Tobu Skytree Line Oshiage Station.*

TSUKIJI 築地 AND SHIODOME 汐留

Although it's best known today as the site of the largest wholesale fish market in the world, Tsukiji is also a reminder of the awesome disaster of the great fire of 1657.

In the space of two days, it killed more than 100,000 people and leveled almost 70% of Ieyasu Tokugawa's new capital. Ieyasu was not a man to be discouraged by mere catastrophe, however; he took it as an opportunity to plan an even bigger and better city, one that would incorporate the marshes east of his castle. Tsukiji, in fact, means "reclaimed land," and a substantial block of land it was, laboriously drained and filled, from present-day Ginza to the bay

Now a redeveloped business district, Shiodome (literally "where the tide stops") was once an area of saltwater flats where the Meiji government built the Tokyo terminal in 1872—the original Shimbashi Station—on Japan's first railway line. By 1997, long after the JR had run out of use for the land, an urban renewal plan for the area evolved, and the land was auctioned off. Among the buyers were Nippon Television and Dentsu, the largest advertising agency in Asia.

In 2002, Dentsu consolidated its scattered offices into the centerpiece of the Shiodome project: a 47-story tower and annex designed by Jean Nouvel. With the annex, known as the Caretta Shiodome, Dentsu created an "investment in community": a complex of cultural facilities, shops, and restaurants that has turned Shiodome into one of the most fashionable places in the city.

ORIENTATION
Shiodome is the southeastern transportation hub of central Tokyo while Tsukiji is a sushi-lover's dream. Perhaps getting up at 5 am to eat fish at the market isn't your idea of breakfast, but this is definitely an excellent place to taste the freshest sushi on Earth, located just east of Shiodome.

PLANNING
Tsukiji has few places to spend time *in*; getting from point to point, however, can consume most of a morning. The backstreet shops will probably require no more than an hour. Allow yourself about an hour to explore the fish market; if fish in all its diversity holds a special fascination for you, take two hours. Remember that in order to see the fish auction in action, you need to get to the market before 5:30 am; by 9 am the business of the market is largely finished for the day. Sushi and sashimi will be cheaper here than in other parts of Tokyo, with sushi sets at most sushi stalls costing between ¥1,000 to ¥2,100.

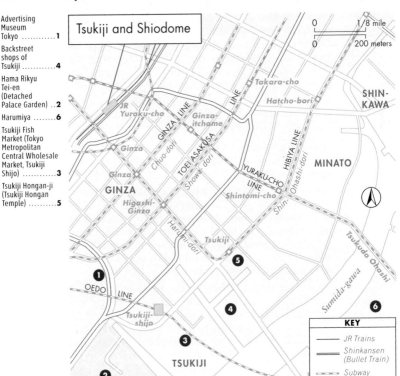

This part of the city can be brutally hot and muggy in August; during the O-bon holiday, in the middle of the month, Tsukiji is comparatively lifeless. Mid-April and early October are best for strolls in the Hama Rikyu Tei-en.

GETTING HERE AND AROUND

Shiodome is easily accessed by public transport: JR lines and Yurikamome Line at Shimbashi Station, Toei Oedo Line to Shiodome Station, and Asakusa Line and Ginza Line to Shimbashi Station. The connection station to the Yurikamome Monorail, a scenic ride that takes you to Odaiba in approximately 30 minutes, is also here. You can also get around quite easily on foot. There are elevated walkways that connect all the major buildings and subway and train stations. To visit the fish market, take the subway to Tsukiji Station, which will always be the more dependable and cost-efficient option.

TOP ATTRACTIONS

Advertising Museum Tokyo (アド・ミュージアム東京). The unique Japanese gift for graphic and commercial design comes into historical perspective in these exhibits featuring everything from 18th-century wood-block prints to contemporary fashion photographs and videos. The museum is maintained by a foundation established in honor of Hideo Yoshida, fourth president of the mammoth Dentsu Advertising Company, and includes a digital library of some 130,000 entries and articles on everything you ever wanted to know about hype. There are no explanatory panels in English—but this in itself is a testament to how well the visual vocabulary of consumer media can communicate across cultures. ✉ *B1F–B2F Caretta Shiodome, 1–8–2 Higashi-Shimbashi, Minato-ku, Shiodome* ☎ *03/6218–2500* ⊕ *www.admt.jp* ✉ *Free* ☉ *Tues.–Fri. 11–6:30, weekends 11–4:30* Ⓜ *Toei Oedo subway line, Shiodome Station (Exit 7); JR (Shiodome Exit) and Asakusa and Ginza lines (Exit 4), Shimbashi Station.*

3

Fodor's Choice
★ **Backstreet shops of Tsukiji** (築地6丁目). If you have time for only one market, this is the one to see. The three square blocks between the Tokyo Central Wholesale Market and Harumi-dori have scores of fishmongers, but also shops and restaurants. Stores sell pickles, tea, crackers and snacks, cutlery (what better place to pick up a professional sushi knife?), baskets, and kitchenware. Hole-in-the-wall sushi bars here have set menus ranging from ¥1,000 to ¥2,100; look for the plastic models of food in glass cases out front. The area includes the row of little counter restaurants, barely more than street stalls, under the arcade along the east side of Shin-Ohashi-dori, each with its specialty. If you haven't had breakfast by this point in your walk, stop for *maguro donburi*—a bowl of fresh raw tuna slices served over rice and garnished with bits of dried seaweed. Some 100 of the small retailers and restaurants in this area are members of the Tsukiji Meiten-kai (Association of Notable Shops) and promote themselves by selling illustrated maps of the area for ¥50; the maps are all in Japanese, but with proper frames they make great souvenirs. The Tsukiji fish market is slated to move to nearby Toyosu in November 2016, and it's unclear what will happen to these streets once the move occurs. Check the Tokyo tourism website before you visit. ✉ *Tsukiji 4-chome, Chūō-ku, Tsukiji* Ⓜ *Toei Oedo subway line, Tsukiji-shijo Station (Exit A1); Hibiya subway line, Tsukiji Station (Exit 1).*

Hama Rikyu Tei-en (浜離宮庭園 *Detached Palace Garden*). A tiny sanctuary of Japanese tradition and nature that's surrounded by towering glass buildings is a great place to relax or walk off a filling Tsukiji sushi breakfast. The land here was originally owned by the Owari branch of the Tokugawa family from Nagoya, and it extended to part of what is now the fish market. When a family member became shogun in 1709, his residence was turned into a palace—with pavilions, ornamental gardens, pine and cherry groves, and duck ponds. The garden became a public park in 1945, although a good portion of it is fenced off as a nature preserve. None of the original buildings have survived, but on the island in the large pond is a reproduction of the pavilion where former U.S. president Ulysses S. Grant and Mrs. Grant had an audience with the emperor Meiji in 1879. The building can now be rented for parties. The stone linings of the saltwater canal work and some of the bridges underwent a restoration project that was completed in 2009. The path to the left as you enter the garden leads to the "river bus" ferry landing, from which you can cruise up the Sumida-gawa to Asakusa. Note that you must pay the admission to the garden even if you're just using the ferry. ✉ *1–1 Hamarikyu–Teien,*

Cherry blossoms bloom at Hama Rikyu garden.

Chūō-ku, Shiodome ☎ *03/3541–0200* ✉ *¥300* ⊙ *Daily 9–4:30* Ⓜ *Toei Oedo subway line, Shiodome Station (Exit 8).*

Harumiya. As during the time of the samurai, cruising in a roof-topped boat, or *yakatabune*, is the perfect means to relax amid bursting fireworks or cherry blossoms. The charm remains intact: guests are treated like royalty and are entertained while floating on the gentle waves of the Sumida or Arakawa River. Hosts within the cabin serve multiple courses of tempura and sushi and pour beer and whiskey while the boats cruise past historic bridges and along the riverbanks that make up the bay front. When the *shoji* (paper blinds) are opened, panoramic views of the illuminated Tokyo nightscape are a sight to behold. Observation decks offer even better viewing opportunities. Boats accommodate groups of 20 to 350, and tours run day and night, year-round. Nighttime is the best time to take a ride, to see the spectacle of light that Tokyo becomes after dark. There are launch locations on the bay and the Arakawa River. ✉ *Harumi Josenba, 3-1 Harumi, Chuo-ku, Tsukiji* ☎ *03/3644–5445* ⊕ *www.harumiya.co.jp* ✉ *Around ¥10,000 per person for 2 hrs of touring* Ⓜ *Oedo subway line, Kachidoki Station (Exit A3).*

Fodor's Choice   **Tsukiji Fish Market** (中央卸売市場 *Tokyo Metropolitan Central Wholesale*
★   *Market, Tsukiji Shijo*). The world's biggest and busiest fish market was moved to from Nihonbashi to Tsukiji after the Great Kanto Earthquake of 1923, and part of it occupies the site of what was once Japan's first naval training academy. Today the market sprawls over some 54 acres of reclaimed land and employs approximately 15,000 people. Its warren of buildings houses about 1,200 vendors, supplying 90% of the seafood (and some of the vegetables, meat, and fruit) consumed in Tokyo

every day—some 2,000 metric tons of it. Most of the seafood sold in Tsukiji comes in by truck, arriving through the night from fishing ports all over the country. A big attraction for tourists is the early-morning tuna auction. Limited to 120 visitors a day, people line up in front of the Fish Information Center well before it opens at 5 am. The market is slated to move to nearby Toyosu in November 2016. Confirm its location and hours on the Tokyo tourism website before you visit. ✉ *5–2–1 Tsukiji, Chūō-ku* ☎ *03/3542–1111* ⊕ *www.tsukiji-market.or.jp* 🎟 *Free* ⊗ *Mon.–Sat. (except 2nd and 4th Wed. of month) 5 am–3 pm* Ⓜ *Toei Oedo subway line, Tsukiji-shijo Station (Exit A1); Hibiya subway line, Tsukiji Station (Exit 1).*

WORTH NOTING

Tsukiji Hongan-ji (築地本願寺 *Tsukiji Hongan Temple*). Disaster seemed to follow this temple, which is an outpost of Kyoto's Nishi Hongwan-ji. Since it was first located here in 1657, it was destroyed at least five times, and reconstruction in wood was finally abandoned after the Great Kanto Earthquake of 1923. The present stone building dates from 1935. It was designed by Chuta Ito, a pupil of Tokyo Station architect Tatsuno Kingo. Ito's other credits include the Meiji Shrine in Harajuku; he also lobbied for Japan's first law for the preservation of historic buildings. Ito traveled extensively in Asia; the evocations of classical Hindu architecture in the temple's domes and ornaments were his homage to India as the cradle of Buddhism. But with stained-glass windows and a pipe organ as well, the building is nothing if not eclectic. Talks in English are held on the third Saturday of the month at 5:30. ✉ *3–15–1 Tsukiji, Chūō-ku, Tsukiji* ☎ *03/3541–1131* ⊕ *www.tsukijihongwanji. jp* 🎟 *Free* ⊗ *Daily services at 7 am and 4 pm* Ⓜ *Hibiya subway line, Tsukiji Station (Exit 1).*

NIHOMBASHI 日本橋, GINZA 銀座, AND MARUNOUCHI 丸の内

Tokyo is a city of many centers. The municipal administrative center is in Shinjuku. The national government center is in Kasumigaseki while Nihombashi is the center of banking and finance.

When Ieyasu Tokugawa had the first bridge constructed at Nihombashi, he designated it the starting point for the five great roads leading out of his city, the point from which all distances were to be measured. His decree is still in force: the black pole on the present bridge, erected in 1911, is the Zero Kilometer marker for all the national highways and is considered the true center of Tokyo.

Long known as Tokyo's ritzy shopping district, Ginza was originally the city's banking district, and the district owes its name to the business of moneymaking: in 1912 Ieyasu Tokugawa relocated a plant making silver coins to a patch of reclaimed land west of his castle. The area soon came to be known informally as Ginza (Silver Mint). Today the neighborhood is still home to most of the country's major security companies, but it's best known as the place where high-end shopping first took root in Japan. Before the turn of the 20th century, Ginza was home to the great mercantile establishments that still define its character. The side streets of Ginza's Sukiya-bashi enclave also have many art galleries, where artists or groups pay for the gallery by the week, publicize their shows themselves, and in some cases even hang their own work.

As a neighborhood that is largely devoted to business, Marunouchi has stronger options for dining than sightseeing. It is home to the recently restored historic Tokyo Station, which is well worth a look.

Marunouchi lies west of Tokyo Station and extends between Hibiya Park and the Outer Garden of the Imperial Palace. In the late 19th century, Iwasaki Yanosuke, the second president of Mitsubishi Corporation, bought the land. Today it houses numerous office and retail complexes as well as the headquarters of various companies within the Mitsubishi group.

ORIENTATION

The combined areas of Marunouchi, Ginza, and Nihombashi are located beside the Imperial Palace district, to the southeast of central Tokyo. Marunouchi lies west of Tokyo Station and extends between Hibiya Park and the Outer Garden of the Imperial Palace.

PLANNING

Attack this area early in the morning but avoid rush hour (8–9) if you plan on taking the subway. None of the area's sites, with the possible exception of the Idemitsu Museum, should take you more than 45 minutes; the time you spend shopping is up to you. In summer start early or in the late afternoon, because by midday the heat and humidity can be brutal. On weekend afternoons (October–March, Saturday 3–5 and Sunday noon–5; April–September, Saturday 2–6 and Sunday noon–6), Chuo-dori is closed to traffic from Shimbashi to Kyo-bashi and becomes a pedestrian mall with tables and chairs set out along the street. Note that some museums and other sights in the area close Sunday.

GETTING HERE AND AROUND

To access Marunouchi, multiple north-south-running JR lines run between Tokyo and Yuraku-cho stations. The Yuraku-cho subway line, too, rolls through from Nagata-cho and Shin Kiba. To the east, the Ginza and Hibiya subway lines stop at Ginza Station. Slightly north is Nihombashi, which is also on the Ginza Line and only a few minutes from the bustling Ote-machi Station on the Tozai Line (¥170). By walking west from Yuraku-cho, Hibiya Park is reachable in five minutes. So is Ginza, in the opposite direction.

TOP ATTRACTIONS

Idemitsu Museum of Arts (出光美術館 *Idemitsu Bijutsukan*). The strength of the collection in these four spacious, well-designed rooms lies in the Tang- and Song-dynasty Chinese porcelain and in the Japanese ceramics—including works by Nonomura Ninsei and Ogata Kenzan. On display are masterpieces of Old Seto, Oribe, Old Kutani, Karatsu, and Kakiemon ware. The museum also houses outstanding examples of Zen painting and calligraphy, wood-block prints, and genre paintings of the Edo period. Of special interest to scholars is the resource collection of shards from virtually every pottery-making culture of the ancient world. The museum is on the ninth floor of the Teikoku Gekijo building, which looks down upon the lavish Imperial Garden. ⊠ *Teigeki Bldg. 9F, 3–1–1 Marunouchi, Chiyoda-ku, Marunouchi* ☎ *03/5777–8600*

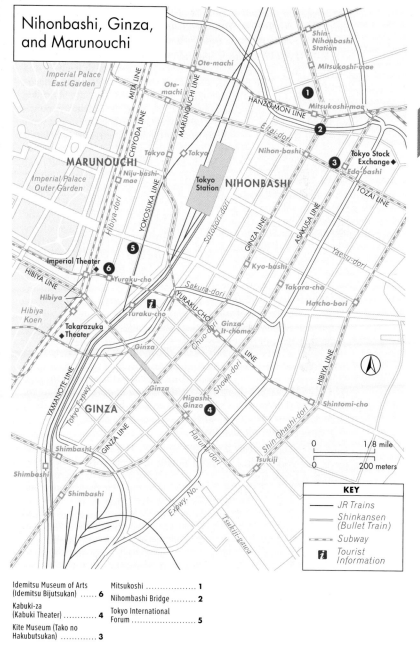

Nihonbashi, Ginza, and Marunouchi

Imperial Palace East Garden

Ote-machi

MITA LINE

Ote-machi

CHIYODA LINE

MARUNOUCHI LINE

HANZO-MON LINE

Shin-Nihonbashi Station

Mitsukoshi-mae

Mitsukoshi-mae ❶

❷

E-i-tai-dori

MARUNOUCHI

Tokyo

Tokyo

Nihon-bashi

YOKOSUKA LINE

Niju-bashi-mae

Hibiya-dori

Tokyo Station

NIHONBASHI

Tokyo Stock Exchange ◆

Edo-bashi

❸

TOZAI LINE

Imperial Palace Outer Garden

Satobori-dori

GINZA LINE

ASAKUSA LINE

Yaesu-dori

Imperial Theater ◆ ❻

HIBIYA LINE

Yuraku-cho

Kyo-bashi

Takara-cho

Hatcho-bori

Hibiya

Hibiya Koen

Yuraku-cho

YURAKU-CHO

Sakura-dori

Ginza-It-chome

Chuo-dori

Showa-dori

HIBIYA LINE

Takarazuka ◆ Theater

Ginza

LINE

Ginza

Ginza

YAMANOTE LINE

Tokyo Expwy.

GINZA

Higashi-Ginza ❹

Shintomi-cho

GINZA LINE

Haru-dori

Shin-Ohashi-dori

Shimbashi

Shimbashi

Tsukiji

Shimbashi

Shimbashi

Expwy. No. 1

Tsukiji-sanba

| 0 | | 1/8 mile |
| 0 | | 200 meters |

KEY	
———	JR Trains
═══	Shinkansen (Bullet Train)
┄┄┄	Subway
🛈	Tourist Information

⊕ *www.idemitsu.com/museum* ⊠ ¥1,000 ⊙ *Tues.–Thurs. and week-ends 10–5, Fri. 10–7* Ⓜ *Yurakucho subway line, Yurakucho Station (Exit B3); Yamanote Line, Yurakucho Station.*

Kabuki-za (*Kabuki Theater*). Soon after the Meiji Restoration and its enforced exile in Asakusa, Kabuki began to reestablish itself in this part of the city. The first Kabuki-za was built in 1889, with a European facade. In 1912 the Kabuki-za was taken over by the Shochiku theatrical management company, which replaced the old theater building in 1925; it was damaged during World War II but restored soon thereafter. The most recent iteration of the building retains its classic architecture—until one notices the looming office building coming out of the middle. The interior has been vastly improved, though. Tickets are sold only at the theater's ticket booth. Reservations by phone are recommended. If you want to see what all of the hype is about, this is the place to see a Kabuki show. For a short 15- to 30-minute sampling, get a single-act ticket; the final act usually provides the best spectacle. English Earphone Guides are available for a small fee and provide explanations and comments in English about the performance. ⊠ *4–12–15 Ginza, Chuo-ku, Ginza* ☎ *03/3545–6800* ⊕ *www. kabuki-bito.jp/eng* ⊠ ¥2,500–¥17,000 ⊙ *Box office daily 10–4, matinees 11–3:45, evening shows 4:30–9* Ⓜ *Hibiya or Asakusa subway line, Higashi-Ginza Station (Exit 3).*

Mitsukoshi (三越). Even if you don't plan to shop, this branch of Tokyo's first *depato* (department store), also called *hyakkaten* (hundred-kinds-of-goods emporium) merits a visit. Two bronze lions, modeled on those at London's Trafalgar Square, flank the main entrance and serve as one of Tokyo's best-known meeting places. Inside, a sublime statue of Magokoro, a Japanese goddess of sincerity, rises four stories through the store's central atrium. ⊠ *1–4–1 Nihombashi-muromachi, Chūō-ku, Nihombashi* ☎ *03/3241–3311* ⊕ *www.mitsukoshi.co.jp* ⊙ *Daily 10–7, basements until 8* Ⓜ *Ginza and Hanzo-mon subway lines, Mitsukoshi-mae Station (Exits A3 and A5).*

Tokyo International Forum (東京国際フォーラム). This postmodern masterpiece, the work of Uruguay-born American architect Raphael Viñoly, is the first major convention and art center of its kind in Tokyo. Viñoly's design was selected in a 1989 competition that drew nearly 400 entries from 50 countries. The plaza of the Forum is that rarest of Tokyo rarities: civilized open space. There's a long central courtyard with comfortable benches shaded by trees, the setting for an antiques flea market the first and third Sunday of each month. The Forum itself is actually two buildings. Transit fans should take a stroll up the catwalks to the top, which concludes with a view of the Tokyo Station JR lines. ⊠ *3–5–1 Marunouchi, Chiyoda-ku, Marunouchi* ☎ *03/5221–9000* ⊕ *www.t-i-forum.co.jp* Ⓜ *Yuraku-cho subway line, Yuraku-cho Station (Exit A-4B).*

WORTH NOTING

FAMILY **Kite Museum** (凧の博物館 *Tako no Hakubutsukan*). Kite flying is an old tradition in Japan. The collection here includes examples of every shape and variety from all over the country, hand-painted in brilliant colors

The Tokyo International Forum's glass atrium is the centerpiece of this arts- and culture-oriented building.

with figures of birds, geometric patterns, and motifs from Chinese and Japanese mythology. You can call ahead to arrange a kite-making workshop (in Japanese) for groups of children. ✉ *1–12–10 Nihombashi, Chūō-ku, Nihombashi* ☎ *03/3275–2704* ⊕ *www.taimeiken.co.jp/museum.html* ✉ *¥210* ☉ *Mon.–Sat. 11–5* Ⓜ *Tozai subway line, Nihombashi Station (Exit C5); JR Tokyo Station (Yaesu Exit)*.

Nihombashi Bridge (日本橋). Originally built in 1603, this was the starting point of Edo Japan's five major highways and the point from which all highway distances were measured. Even today one sees signs noting the distance to Nihombashi. Rebuilt in stone in 1911, the structure's graceful double arch, ornate lamps, and bronze Chinese lions and unicorns are unfortunately marred by an expressway running directly overhead. In the rush to relieve traffic congestion in preparation for the 1964 Olympics, city planners ignored the protestations of residents and preservation groups and pushed ahead with construction. ✉ *Nihombashi* Ⓜ *Tozai and Ginza subway lines, Nihombashi Station (Exits B5 and B6); Ginza and Hanzo-mon subway lines, Mitsukoshi-mae Station (Exits B5 and B6)*.

AOYAMA 青山, HARAJUKU 原宿, AND SHIBUYA 渋谷

As late as 1960, the area between the Meiji Shrine and the Aoyama Cemetery wasn't considered to be a very happening tourist hot spot; the municipal government zoned a chunk of it for low-cost public housing. The few young Japanese people in the area were either hanging around Washington Heights to practice their English or attending the

Methodist-founded Aoyama University, and sought entertainment farther south in Shibuya.

When Tokyo won its bid to host the 1964 Olympics, Washington Heights was turned over to the city for the construction of Olympic Village. Aoyama-dori, the avenue through the center of the area, was renovated and the Ginza and Hanzo-mon subway lines were built under it. Suddenly, Aoyama became attractive for its Western-style fashion houses, boutiques, and design studios. By the 1980s, the area had become one of the hippest parts of the city. Today, the low-cost public housing along Omotesando is long gone, replaced by the glass-and-marble emporia of *the* preeminent fashion houses of Europe: Louis Vuitton, Chanel, Armani, and Prada. Their showrooms here are cash cows of their worldwide empires. Superb shops, restaurants, and amusements in this area target a population of university students, wealthy socialites, young professionals, and people who like to see and be seen.

The heart of Tokyo's youth and street-fashion scene, Harajuku is home to a plethora of stores, boutiques, and cafés. But it isn't only a place for trendy teenagers; Omotesando Dori, the wide, tree-lined avenue leading through the neighborhood, is home to many high-fashion and designer brands. A walk through the neighborhood's winding backstreets also reveals a range of more sophisticated restaurants and cafés. Meanwhile Yoyogi Park and Meiji Shrine offer a respite from Tokyo's crowds and concrete, with a variety of museums and galleries that give a taste of Japanese art and history.

Once a small town on the road from Edo to Kamakura, it was only in the early 20th century that Harajuku started to become a central part of Tokyo. In 1919, the Meiji Shrine was unveiled and Omotesando Dori turned into the bustling boulevard it is today. These two additions brought more visitors, residents, and shops throughout the years. Like much of Tokyo, nearly all of Harajuku was destroyed in the bombings of 1945, with only Meiji Shrine remaining intact. After the war, Harajuku, along with nearby Aoyama, was home to an area called Washington Heights, which housed U.S. military soldiers and several shops catering to these Americans. After the occupation, the area received a boost as the central location of many events in the 1964 Tokyo Olympics.

One of Tokyo's busiest shopping and entertainment areas, Shibuya is a sometimes overwhelming mix of shops, restaurants, bars, and clubs. Shibuya Scramble is known as one of the world's busiest pedestrian crossings and nearly a tourist site in its own right. While most smaller shops tend to be youth-focused, the area's department stores, restaurants, and nightlife draw in people of all ages. Unlike many other parts of Tokyo, Shibuya offers little in way of museums, temples, or traditional culture, but more than makes up for it with its pure energy and atmosphere.

Shibuya gets its name from the samurai family who presided over the area in the 11th century; the family name Shibuya and the land was granted to a Heian Era general as a gift for thwarting an attack on the Imperial Palace in Kyoto. For the next six centuries, Shibuya remained a small hamlet of the city. With the opening of Shibuya Station in 1885, the area began to grow, taking off in the 1930s when it became a key terminal linking Tokyo and Yokohama. After being leveled in the war, Shibuya was quickly rebuilt and reestablished its reputation as an entertainment district. In the 1980s and '90s, it was the center of Tokyo's youth and fashion culture as well as the center of the technology industry.

ORIENTATION

Aoyama and Harajuku, west of the Imperial Palace and just north of Roppongi, are the trendsetting areas of youth culture and fashion. Aoyama and nearby Omotesando contain European fashion houses' flagship stores while Harajuku is the young, bohemian fashion district.

Shibuya, an entertainment district, is not as clean or sophisticated as Tokyo's other neighborhoods. Shops, cheap restaurants, karaoke lounges, bars, and nightclubs are everywhere.

PLANNING

Trying to explore Aoyama and Harajuku together will take a long time because there is a lot of area to cover. Ideally, spend an entire day here, allowing for plenty of time to browse the shops. You can see Meiji Shrine in less than an hour; the Nezu Museum and its gardens warrant a leisurely two-hour visit. The best way to enjoy this area is to explore the tiny shops, restaurants, and cafés in the backstreets.

Shibuya seems chaotic and intimidating at first, but it is fairly compact. You can easily cover it in about two hours. Be prepared for huge crowds: Shibuya crossing is one of the busiest intersections in the world and at one light change, hundreds rush to reach the other side. Unless you are shopping, no particular stop should occupy you for more than a half hour; allow an hour for the NHK Broadcasting Center if you decide to take the guided tour. Sunday is the best day to visit Shibuya and Yoyogi Koen, as it affords the best opportunity to observe Japan's younger generation.

GETTING HERE AND AROUND

Primary access to Shibuya is via the looping JR Yamanote Line, but the Fukutoshin subway line also goes north from Shibuya up through Shinjuku and onto Ikebukuro. Old standbys are the Hanzo-mon and Ginza lines, both of which stop in Omotesando Station (¥170). The Inokashira railway goes toward Kichijoji, home to Inokashira Park, and the Toyoko railway reaches Yokohama in about 30 minutes. Hachiko Exit will be swarmed with people. Just next to it is the "scramble crossing," which leads from the station to the area's concentration of restaurants and shops. Two bus stops provide service to Roppongi to the east and Meguro and Setagaya wards to the west. On Meiji-dori, Harajuku is walkable to the north in 15 minutes, and Ebisu takes about the same going south.

TOP ATTRACTIONS

Japanese Sword Museum (刀剣博物館 *Token Hakabutsukan*). It's said that in the late 16th century, before Japan closed its doors to the West, the Spanish tried to establish a trade here in weapons made from famous Toledo steel. The Japanese were politely uninterested; they had been making blades of incomparably better quality for more than 600 years. At one time there were some 200 schools of sword-making in Japan; swords were prized not only for their effectiveness in battle but for the beauty of the blades and fittings and as symbols of the higher spirituality of the warrior caste. There are few inheritors of this art today and the Sword Museum's mission is to maintain the knowledge and appreciation of sword-making. While the collection has swords made by famous craftsmen such as Nobufusa (a living cultural asset) and Sanekage (a famous 14th-century sword-maker), the focus here is on the swords as objects of beauty. The swords are individually displayed as works of art, giving visitors a chance to appreciate the detail, creativity, and skill involved in crafting

each one. ⊠ 4–25–10 Yoyogi, Shibuya-ku, Harajuku 🖀 03/3379–1386 ⊕ www.touken.or.jp 🖾 ¥600 ⊗ Tues.–Sun. 10–4:30 Ⓜ Odakyu private rail line, Sangu-bashi Station.

Fodor's Choice ★ **Meiji Shrine** (明治神宮 Meiji Jingu). This shrine honors the spirits of Emperor Meiji, who died in 1912, and Empress Shoken. It was established by a resolution of the Imperial Diet the year after the Emperor's death to commemorate his role in ending the long isolation of Japan under the Tokugawa Shogunate and setting the country on the road to modernization. Virtually destroyed in an air raid in 1945, it was rebuilt in 1958.

A wonderful spot for photos, the mammoth entrance gates (*torii*), rising 40 feet high, are made from 1,700-year-old cypress trees from Mt. Ari in Taiwan; the crosspieces are 56 feet long. Torii are meant to symbolize the separation of the everyday secular world from the spiritual world of the Shinto shrine. The buildings in the shrine complex, with their curving, green, copper roofs, are also made of cypress wood. The surrounding gardens have some 100,000 flowering shrubs and trees.

An annual festival at the shrine takes place on November 3, Emperor Meiji's birthday, which is a national holiday. On the festival and New Year's Day, as many as 1 million people come to offer prayers and pay their respects. Several other festivals and ceremonial events are held here throughout the year; check by phone or on the shrine website to see what's scheduled during your visit. Even on a normal weekend the shrine draws thousands of visitors, but this seldom disturbs its mood of quiet serenity.

The peaceful **Inner Garden** (Jingu Nai-en), where the irises are in full bloom in the latter half of June, is on the left as you walk in from the main gates, before you reach the shrine. Beyond the shrine is the **Treasure House,** a repository for the personal effects and clothes of Emperor and Empress Meiji—perhaps of less interest to foreign visitors than to the Japanese. ⊠ *1–1 Yoyogi-kamizono-cho, Shibuya, Harajuku* ☎ *03/3379–9222* ⊕ *www.meijijingu.or.jp* ◛ *Shrine free, Inner Garden ¥500, Treasure House ¥500* ◷ *Shrine daily sunrise–sunset; Inner Garden Mar.–Nov., daily 9–4; Treasure House daily 10–4; closed 3rd Fri. of month* Ⓜ *Chiyoda and Fukutoshin subway lines, Meiji-Jingu-mae Station; JR Yamanote Line, Harajuku Station (Exit 2).*

Myth of Tomorrow (明日の神話 *Ashita no Shinwa*). This once-lost mural by avant-garde artist Taro Okamoto has been restored and mounted inside Shibuya Station. Often compared to Picasso's *Guernica*, the 14 colorful panels depict the moment of an atomic bomb detonation. The painting was discovered in 2003 in Mexico City, where in the late '60s it was to be displayed in a hotel but was misplaced following the bankruptcy of the developer. Walk up to the Inokashira Line entrance; the mural is mounted along the hallway that overlooks Hachiko plaza. ⊠ *2 Dogenzaka, Shibuya-ku, Shibuya* Ⓜ *JR Shibuya Station (Hachikō Exit).*

NEED A BREAK? **Les Deux Magots** (デュ・マゴ・パリ). Sister of the famed Paris café, Les Deux Magots, on the Garden Floor of the Bunkamura complex, serves a good selection of beers and wines, sandwiches, salads, quiches, tarts, and coffee. There's a fine-arts bookstore next door, and the tables in the courtyard are perfect for people-watching. ⊠ *Bunka-mura, lower courtyard, 2–24–1 Dogen-zaka, Shibuya-ku* ☎ *03/3477–9124* ⊕ *www.bunkamura. co.jp* Ⓜ *JR Yamanote Line, Ginza and Hanzo-mon subway lines, and private rail lines; Shibuya Station (Exits 5 and 8 for Hanzo-mon subway line, Kitaguchi/North Exit for all others).*

Fodor's Choice ★ **Nezu Museum** (根津美術館 *Nezu Bijutsukan*). On view are traditional Japanese and Asian works of art owned by Meiji-period railroad magnate and politician Kaichiro Nezu. For the main building, architect Kengo Kuma designed an arched roof that rises two floors and extends roughly half a block through this upscale Minami Aoyama neighborhood. At any one time, the vast space houses a portion of the 7,000 works of calligraphy, paintings, sculptures, bronzes, and lacquerware that comprise the Nezu's collection. The museum is also home to one of Tokyo's finest gardens, featuring 5 acres of ponds, rolling paths, waterfalls, and teahouses. ⊠ *6–5–1 Minami-Aoyama, Minato-ku, Aoyama* ☎ *03/3400–2536* ⊕ *www.nezu-muse.or.jp* ◛ *¥1,200* ◷ *Tues.–Sun. 10–5* Ⓜ *Ginza and Hanzo-mon subway lines, Omotesando Station (Exit A5).*

Ukio-e Ota Memorial Museum of Art (太田記念美術館 *Ota Kinen Bijutsukan*). The gift of former Toho Mutual Life Insurance chairman Seizo Ota, this is probably the city's finest private collection of *ukiyo-e*, traditional Edo-period wood-block prints. Ukiyo-e (pictures of the floating world) flourished in the 18th and 19th centuries. The works on display are selected and changed periodically from the 12,000 prints

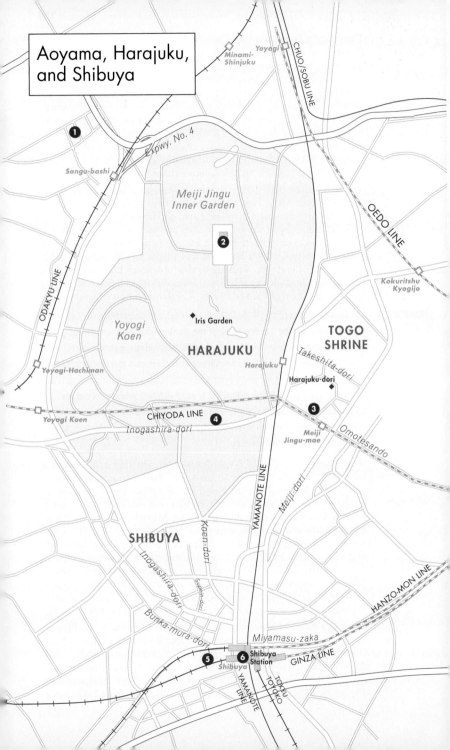

Aoyama, Harajuku, and Shibuya

3

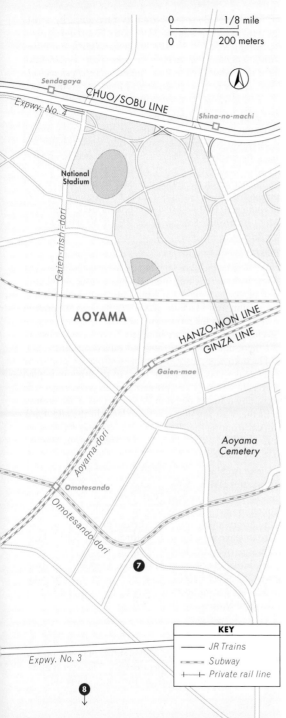

Sendagaya

CHUO/SOBU LINE

Expwy. No. 4

Shina-no-machi

National
Stadium

Gaien-nishi-dori

AOYAMA

HANZO-MON LINE

GINZA LINE

Gaien-mae

Aoyama-dori

Aoyama
Cemetery

Omotesando

Omotesando-dori

7

Expwy. No. 3

8

KEY	
——	*JR Trains*
▭▭▭	*Subway*
+——+	*Private rail line*

in the collection, which include some extremely rare work by artists such as Hiroshige, Hokusai, Sharaku, and Utamaro. ✉ *1–10–10 Jingu-mae, Shibuya-ku, Harajuku* ☎ *03/3403–0880* ⊕ *www.ukiyoe-ota-muse. jp* 🎫 *¥700–¥1,000, depending on exhibit* ☉ *Tues.–Sun. 10:30–5:30; closed a few days at the end of each month; call ahead or check website* Ⓜ *Chiyoda and Fukutoshin subway lines, Meiji-Jingu-mae Station (Exit 5); JR Yamanote Line, Harajuku Station (Omotesando Exit).*

FAMILY **Yoyogi Park** (代々木公園 *Yoyogi Koen*). This park is the perfect spot to have a picnic on a sunny day. On Sunday, people come to play music, practice martial arts, and ride bicycles on the bike path (rentals are available). From spring through fall there are events, concerts, and festivals most weekends. While the front half of the park makes for great people-watching, farther along the paths it is easy to find a quiet spot to slip away from the crowds of Harajuku. ✉ *2–1 Yoyogi-mizono-cho, Shibuya-ku, Harajuku* ☎ *03/3469–6081* Ⓜ *Chiyoda and Fukutoshin subway lines, Meiji-Jingu-mae Station (Exit 2); JR Yamanote Line, Harajuku Station (Omotesando Exit).*

WORTH NOTING

Statue of Hachiko (ハチ公像). Hachiko is the Japanese version of Lassie; he even starred in a few heart-wrenching films. Every morning, Hachiko's master, a professor at Tokyo University, would take the dog with him as far as Shibuya Station and Hachiko would go back to the station every evening to greet him on his return. In 1925 the professor died of a stroke. Every evening for the next seven years, Hachiko would go to Shibuya and wait there until the last train had pulled out of the station. When loyal Hachiko died, his story made headlines. A handsome bronze statute of Hachiko was installed in front of the station, funded by fans from all over the country. The present version is a replica—the original was melted down for its metal in World War II. This Shibuya landmark is one of the most popular meeting places in the city. Look for the green train car fronting the JR station; the statue is off the side, where everyone is standing. ✉ *2-1 Dogenzaka, Shibuya-ku, Shibuya* Ⓜ *JR Shibuya Station (Hachikō Exit).*

Tokyo Metropolitan Teien Art Museum (東京都庭園美術館). Once home to Japan's Prince Asaka, this lavish 1930s art-deco building hosts a range of fine arts exhibits throughout the year. With shows ranging from classic paintings to contemporary sculpture, it seems the exhibits are chosen for their ability to harmoniously mix with the building's lush interior. If you visit, be sure to leave time for a stroll through the Teien's Japanese Garden, which is particularly lovely when the leaves change in the fall or during cherry blossom season in April. ✉ *5–21–9 Shirokanedai, Minato-ku, Shibuya* ☎ *03/3443–0201* ⊕ *www.teien-art-museum.ne.jp* 🎫 *Usually ¥800–¥1,200, but varies by exhibit* Ⓜ *JR Yamanote Line or Toei Mita Line, Meguro Station (Central Exit).*

ROPPONGI 六本木

Roppongi, once known for its clubs, bars, and nightlife, has become one of Tokyo's major shopping, dining, and art districts. The area is abuzz with shoppers, tourists, and office workers throughout the day and evening. As the clock inches closer to the last train, the crowd changes to young clubbers and barhoppers staying out until sunrise.

For many travelers, the lure of the neighborhood is the shopping on offer in ritzy developments like Roppongi Hills and Tokyo Midtown. In addition, though, there's the three points of what's known as Art Triangle Roppongi—the National Art Center, Mori Art Museum, and Suntory Museum of Art. The neighborhood is also home to the Fujifilm Square photo gallery, 21_21 Design Sight, and many other art and cultural events.

ORIENTATION

Roppongi is located just east of Shibuya and Aoyama, and south of the Imperial Palace.

PLANNING

There are ATMs and currency-exchange services at Roppongi Hills and Tokyo Midtown shopping complexes, as well as family- and kid-friendly activities, such as small parks and sculptures.

Azabu Juban is a quick visit and a good place to sit in a café and people-watch. The best time to visit is in August, during the **Azabu Juban Summer Festival**, one of the biggest festivals in Minato-ku. The streets, which are closed to car traffic, are lined with food vendors selling delicious international fare and drinks. Everyone wears their nicest summer *yukatas* (robes) and watches live performances. Check the online *Minato Monthly* newsletter (⊕ *www.city.minato.tokyo.jp*) in August for a list of summer festivals.

GETTING HERE AND AROUND

The best way to get to Roppongi is by subway, and there are two lines that'll take you to Roppongi Station: the Hibiya Line, which takes you right into the complex of Roppongi Hills, or the Oedo Line, with exits convenient to Tokyo Midtown.

TOP ATTRACTIONS

Mori Art Museum (森美術館). Occupying the 52nd and 53rd floors of Mori Tower, this museum is one of the leading contemporary art showcases in Tokyo. The space is well designed (by American architect Richard Gluckman), intelligently curated, diverse in its media, and hospitable to big crowds. The nine galleries showcase exhibits that rotate every few months and tend to focus on leading contemporary art, architecture, fashion, design, and photography. ⊠ *6–10–1 Roppongi, Minato-ku, Roppongi* ☎ *03/5777–8600* ⊕ *mori.art.museum/eng* ☞ *Admission fee varies with exhibit* ☉ *Wed.–Mon. 10–10, Tues. 10–5* Ⓜ *Hibiya subway line, Roppongi Station (Exit 1C).*

National Art Center, Tokyo (国立新美術館). Tokyo's largest rotating exhibition space is home to major international modern and contemporary exhibits as well as smaller shows (usually free) and is worth visiting for the architecture alone. Architect Kisho Kurokawa's stunning facade shimmers in undulating waves of glass, and the bright exhibition space with its soaring ceilings feels a bit like being inside the set of a utopian sci-fi movie. The building houses seven exhibition areas; a library; a museum shop; and a restaurant, Brasserie Paul Bocuse Le Musée, offering fine French dishes. ⊠ *7–22–2 Roppongi, Minato-ku, Roppongi*

Roppongi

AKASAKA

❶

❷

Gaien-Higashi-Dori

Shuto-Expressway-No.3-Shibuyasen

Roppongi-Dori

Ⓜ Roppongi

ROPPONGI

Ⓜ Roppongi-
Itchome

Shuto Loop Line

Kamiyacho Ⓜ

❸

Azabu
Tunnel

Roppongi-Dori

Ⓜ Roppongi

Gaien-Higashi-Dori

Sakurada-Dori

❹

Imoarai-Zaka

Tori-Zaka

❺

Sakurada-Dori

Kurayami-Zaka

Azabu-
Juban
Ⓜ

Tanuki-Zaka

Daikoku-Zaka

Azabu-Ⓜ
Juban

Akabanebashi
Ⓜ

Shuto Loop Line

MOTOAZABU

Sendai-Zaka

Hinata-Zaka

Shuto-Expressway-No.2-Megurosen

Tsunanotebiki-Zaka

Tsuna-Zaka

Sakurada-Dori

MITA

0   1/4 mile

0   1/4 kilometer

KEY

═Ⓜ═ Metro lines

☎ *03/5777–8600* ⊕ *www.nact.jp* ✉ *Admission fee varies with exhibit* ⊙ *Mon., Wed., Thurs., and weekends 10–6; Fri. 10–8* Ⓜ *Toei Oedo and Hibiya lines, Roppongi Station (Exit 7).*

Suntory Museum of Art (サントリー美術館). Based on the principle of dividing profits three ways, Suntory, Japan's beverage giant, has committed a third of its profits to what it feels is its corporate and social responsibility to provide the public with art, education, and environmental conservation. The establishment of the Suntory Art Museum in 1961 was just one of the fruits of this initiative, and the museum's current home at Tokyo Midtown Galleria is a beautiful place to view some of Tokyo's finest fine art exhibitions. Past displays have included everything from works by Picasso and Toulouse-Lautrec to fine kimonos from the Edo period. ✉ *Tokyo Midtown Galleria, 3F, 9–7–4 Akasaka, Minato-ku, Roppongi* ☎ *03/3479–8600* ⊕ *www.suntory.com/sma* ✉ *Around ¥1,300 but varies by exhibit* ⊙ *Mon., Wed., Thurs., Sun. 10–6; Fri. and Sat. 10–8* Ⓜ *Toei Oedo Line, Roppongi Station; Hibiya Line, Roppongi Station (Exit 8).*

FAMILY **Tokyo Tower** (東京タワー). In 1958 Tokyo's fledgling TV networks needed a tall antenna array to transmit signals. Trying to emerge from the devastation of World War II, the nation's capital was also hungry for a landmark—a symbol for the aspirations of a city still without a skyline. The result was the 1,093-foot-high Tokyo Tower, an unabashed knockoff of Paris's Eiffel Tower, complete with great views of the city. The Main Observatory, set at 492 feet above ground, and the Special Observatory, up an additional 330 feet, quickly became major tourist attractions; they still draw many visitors a year, the vast majority of them Japanese youngsters on their first trip to the big city. A modest art gallery, the Guinness Book of World Records Museum Tokyo, and view-filled dining round out the tower's appeal as an amusement complex. ✉ *4–2–8 Shiba-Koen, Minato-ku, Roppongi* ☎ *03/3433–5111* ⊕ *www.tokyotower.co.jp* ✉ *Main Observatory ¥900, Special Observatory ¥700 extra* ⊙ *Tower daily 9 am–10:30 pm; museums and art gallery daily 10–9* Ⓜ *Hibiya subway line, Kamiyacho Station (Exit 2).*

WORTH NOTING

21_21 Design Sight. This low-slung building hosts rotating exhibitions focused on cutting-edge art and design. Designed by architect Tadao Ando, the subdued exterior belies the expansive and bright gallery space, where exhibits are often interactive and focus on presenting the world of design in an exciting and accessible light. ✉ *9–7–6 Akasaka, Minato-ku, Roppongi* ☎ *03/3475–2121* ⊕ *2121designsight.jp/ en* ✉ *¥1,000* ⊙ *Wed.–Mon. 11–8* Ⓜ *Hibiya subway line, Roppongi Station (Exit 6).*

SHINJUKU 新宿

If you love the grittiness and chaos of big cities, you're bound to love Shinjuku. Come here, and for the first time Tokyo begins to seem *real*: all the celebrated virtues of Japanese society—its safety and order, its grace and beauty, its cleanliness and civility—fray at the edges.

The Mori Art Museum curates temporary, contemporary art exhibits in a sky-high space.

To be fair, the area has been on the fringes of respectability for centuries. When Ieyasu, the first Tokugawa shogun, made Edo his capital, Shinjuku was at the junction of two important arteries leading into the city from the west. It became a thriving post station, where travelers would rest and refresh themselves for the last leg of their journey; the appeal of this suburban pit stop was its "teahouses," where the waitresses dispensed a good bit more than sympathy with the tea.

When the Tokugawa dynasty collapsed in 1868, 16-year-old Emperor Meiji moved his capital to Edo, renaming it Tokyo, and modern Shinjuku became the railhead connecting it to Japan's western provinces. It became a haunt for artists, writers, and students; in the 1930s Shinjuku was Tokyo's bohemian quarter. The area was virtually leveled during the firebombings of 1945—a blank slate on which developers could write, as Tokyo surged west after the war.

Now, by day the east side of Shinjuku Station is an astonishing concentration of retail stores, vertical malls, and discounters of every stripe and description. By night much of the activity shifts to the nearby red-light quarter of Kabuki-cho, which is an equally astonishing collection of bars and clubs, strip joints, hole-in-the-wall restaurants, *pachinko* parlors (an upright pinball game), and peep shows—just about anything that amuses, arouses, alters, or intoxicates is for sale. Recent crackdowns by police have limited this sort of adult activity but whatever you're after is probably still there if you know where to look.

ORIENTATION

By day, Shinjuku is a bustling center of business and government where office workers move in droves during rush hour. By night, people are inundated with flashing signs, and a darker side of Tokyo emerges, when hordes leave their offices to go out for drinks, food, and sometimes, sex. Perhaps this is a rougher side of town, but Shinjuku is a fascinating place to discover at night.

PLANNING

Every day three subways, seven railway lines, and more than 3 million commuters converge on Shinjuku Station, making this the city's busiest and most heavily populated commercial center. The hub at Shinjuku—a vast, interconnected complex of tracks and terminals, department stores and shops—divides the area into two distinctly different subcities, Nishi-Shinjuku (West Shinjuku) and Higashi-Shinjuku (East Shinjuku).

Plan at least a full day for Shinjuku if you want to see both the east and west sides. Subway rides can save you time and energy as you're exploring, but don't rule out walking. The Shinjuku Gyo-en National Garden is worth at least an hour, especially if you come in early April during *sakura* (cherry blossom) season. The Tokyo Metropolitan Government Office complex can take longer than you might expect as lines for the elevators to the observation decks are often excruciatingly long. Sunday, when shopping streets are closed to traffic, is the best time to tramp around Higashi-Shinjuku.

GETTING HERE AND AROUND

From Shibuya to the south and Ikebukuro to the north, the JR Yamanote Line is one of the more common ways to reach Shinjuku Station. The Saikyo Line travels the same path but less frequently. The Keio and Odakyu lines serve destinations to the west. Subway lines, like the Marunouchi, Shinjuku, and Toei Oedo, are best used to move to destinations in the center of the city, such as Ote-machi, Kudanshita, and Roppongi. On foot, Kabuki-cho is accessible in minutes to the east. For the forest of office-building skyscrapers, go through the underground passage to the west.

TOP ATTRACTIONS

Shinjuku Gyoen National Garden (新宿御苑). This lovely 150-acre park was once the estate of the powerful Naito family of feudal lords, who were among the most trusted retainers of the Tokugawa shoguns. After World War II, the grounds were finally opened to the public. It's a perfect place for leisurely walks: paths wind past ponds and bridges, artificial hills, thoughtfully placed stone lanterns, and more than 3,000 kinds of plants, shrubs, and trees. There are different gardens in Japanese, French, and English styles, as well as a greenhouse (the nation's first, built in 1885) filled with tropical plants. The best times to visit are April, when 75 different species of cherry trees—some 1,500 trees in all—are in bloom, and the first two weeks of November, during the chrysanthemum exhibition. ⊠ *11 Naito-machi, Shinjuku-ku, Shinjuku* ☎ *03/3350–0151* ⊠ *¥200* ☉ *Tues.–Sun. 9–4:30; also Mon. 9–4:30 in cherry-blossom season (late Mar.–early Apr.)* Ⓜ *Marunouchi subway line, Shinjuku Gyo-en-mae Station (Exit 1).*

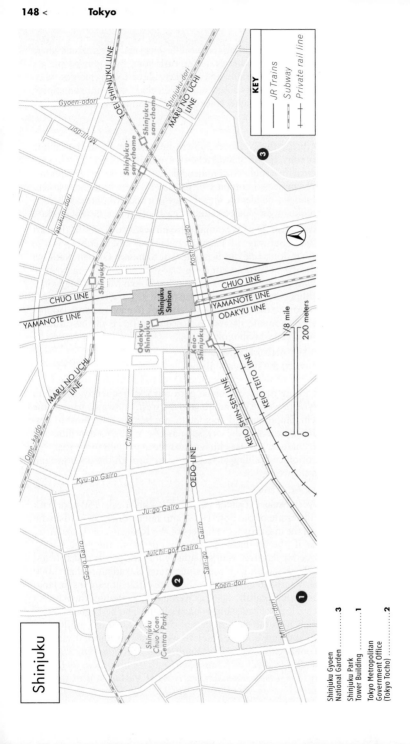

Shinjuku

KEY

——	JR Trains
‡‡‡	Subway
+++	Private rail line

TOEI SHINJUKU LINE

Gyoen-odori

Shinjuku-san-chome

Shinjuku-
san-chome

Meiji-dori

Yasukuni-dori

Shinjuku-dori

MARU NO UCHI
LINE

Koshu-kaido

CHUO LINE

Shinjuku

CHUO LINE

YAMANOTE LINE

YAMANOTE LINE

ODAKYU LINE

Shinjuku
Station

Odakyu-
Shinjuku

Keio-
Shinjuku

KEIO TEITO LINE

KEIO SHIN-SEN LINE

MARU NO UCHI
LINE

Ome-kaido

Chuo-dori

OEDO LINE

1/8 mile

200 meters

Kyu-go Gairo

Ju-go Gairo

Juichi-go Gairo

Go-go Gairo

San-go
Gairo

Koen-dori

Shinjuku
Chuo Koen
(Central Park)

Minami-dori

Shinjuku Park Tower Building (新宿パークタワー). Kenzo Tange's Shinjuku Park Tower has in some ways the most arrogant, hard-edged design of any of the skyscrapers in Nishi-Shinjuku, but it does provide any number of opportunities to rest and refuel. Some days there are free chamber-music concerts in the atrium. There are many international and Japanese restaurants to choose from in the building, and the sky-lighted bamboo garden of the Peak Lounge on the 41st floor of the Park Hyatt Hotel, part of the tower, was the set location of the Oscar-winning film *Lost in Translation.* ⊠ *3–7–1 Nishi-Shinjuku, Shinjuku* Ⓜ *JR Shinjuku Station (Nishi-guchi/West Exit).*

WORTH NOTING

Tokyo Metropolitan Government Office (東京都庁 *Tokyo Tocho*). Dominating the western Shinjuku skyline and built at a cost of ¥157 billion, this Kenzo Tange–designed, grandiose, city-hall complex is clearly meant to remind observers that Tokyo's annual budget is bigger than that of the average developing country. The late-20th-century complex consists of a main office building, an annex, the Metropolitan Assembly building, and a huge central courtyard, often the venue of open-air concerts and exhibitions. The building design has raised some debate: Tokyoites either love it or hate it. On a clear day, from the observation decks on the 45th floors of both towers (663 feet above ground), you can see all the way to Mt. Fuji and to the Boso Peninsula in Chiba Prefecture. Several other skyscrapers in the area have free observation floors—among them the Shinjuku Center Building and the Shinjuku Sumitomo Building—but city hall is the best of the lot. The Metropolitan Government website, incidentally, is an excellent source of information on sightseeing and current events in Tokyo. ⊠ *2–8–1 Nishi-Shinjuku, Shinjuku* ☎ *03/5321–1111* ⊕ *www.metro.tokyo.jp* ⊠ *Free* ☽ *South observation deck, daily 9:30–5:30; North observation deck, daily 9:30–10:30 pm* Ⓜ *ToeiOedo subway line, Tocho-mae Station (Exit A4).*

GREATER TOKYO

The size of the city and the diversity of its institutions make it impossible to fit all of Tokyo's interesting sights into neighborhoods. Plenty of worthy places—from Tokyo Disneyland to sumo stables to the old Oji district—fall outside the city's neighborhood repertoire. Yet no guide to Tokyo would be complete without them.

Central Tokyo is routinely described as a concrete haven, yet the Kasai Seaside Park offers numerous flora at the edge of Tokyo Bay. Tokyo has a few traditional areas remaining, but if the sport of sumo tickles your fancy, the largest collection of training stables is in the Ryogoku area. Two things make this working-class shitamachi neighborhood worth a special trip: this is the center of the world of sumo wrestling as well as the site of the extraordinary Edo-Tokyo Museum. Also outside the city center are some theme parks, like Tokyo Disneyland and Sanrio Puroland, whose numerous kitsch attractions celebrate Japan's love for all that is cute. Creatures from the sea abound at the Shinagawa Aquarium.

Among the bright lights of Kabuki-cho you may glimpse Yakuza members in the crowds of revelers.

ORIENTATION

Since they are so accessible, the central wards of Tokyo are often the focus for visitors. Of course, there is much more to discover in the city. The areas that lie to the west of Shibuya, south of Shinagawa, north of Ikebukuro, and east of Tokyo Station offer amusement parks, zoos, galleries, and museums.

PLANNING

For the amusement parks and zoos, visitors will want to plan to spend the entire day. The galleries and parks will only take a few hours. Be sure to plan ahead: some destinations can take over an hour to reach by train. Also keep in mind that the farther away from the city one moves the more spread out the city becomes, so plan on taking a taxi from the train station.

GETTING HERE AND AROUND

From central Tokyo, the city spreads out like the spokes of a wheel; various railways serve areas in all cardinal directions. For Chiba Prefecture, where Tokyo Disneyland is located, take Keiyo Line, which originates at Tokyo Station. Use the same line to access Kasai Seaside Park. Multiple JR lines and the Keihin Kyuko Line chug south from Shinagawa Station in the direction of Yokohama and to the Shinagawa Aquarium. The Keio Line, too, starts at Shinjuku Station; Sanrio Puroland is accessible from Tama Center Station on this line. The Namboku Line is a subway line that moves north through Komagome Station on the Yamanote Line before reaching the throwback town of Oji.

TOP ATTRACTIONS

Fodor's Choice ★ **Edo-Tokyo Museum.** From an open plaza on massive pillars an escalator takes you directly to the sixth floor—and back in time 300 years. You cross a replica of the Edo-period Nihombashi Bridge into a truly remarkable collection of dioramas, scale models, cutaway rooms, and even whole buildings: an intimate and convincing experience of everyday life in the capital of the Tokugawa shoguns. Equally elaborate are the fifth-floor re-creations of early modern Tokyo, the "enlightenment" of Japan's headlong embrace of the West, and the twin devastations of the Great Kanto Earthquake and World War II. If you only visit one non-art museum in Tokyo, make this it.

To get to the museum, leave Ryogoku Station by the West Exit, immediately turn right, and follow the signs. The moving sidewalk and the stairs bring you to the plaza on the third level; to request an English-speaking volunteer guide, use the entrance to the left of the stairs instead, and ask at the General Information counter in front of the first-floor Special Exhibition Gallery. ⊠ *1–4–1 Yokoami, Sumida-ku, Greater Tokyo* ☎ *03/3626–9974* ⊕ *www.edo-tokyo-museum.or.jp* 🎫 *¥600; additional fees for special exhibits* ☉ *Tues.–Fri. and Sun. 9:30–5:30, Sat. 9:30–7:30.*

Fodor's Choice ★ **Sengaku-ji** (泉岳寺 *Sengaku Temple*). In 1701, a young provincial baron named Asano Takumi-no-Kami attacked and seriously wounded a courtier named Yoshinaka Kira. Asano, for daring to draw his sword in the confines of Edo Castle, was ordered to commit suicide, so his family line was abolished and his fief confiscated. Forty-seven of Asano's loyal retainers vowed revenge; the death of their leader made them *ronin*—masterless samurai. On the night of December 14, 1702, Asano's ronin stormed Kira's villa in Edo, cut off his head, and brought it in triumph to Asano's tomb at Sengaku-ji, the family temple. The ronin were sentenced to commit suicide—which they accepted as the reward, not the price, of their honorable vendetta—and were buried in the temple graveyard with their lord.

Through the centuries this story has become a national epic and the last word on the subject of loyalty and sacrifice, celebrated in every medium from Kabuki to film. The temple still stands, and the graveyard is wreathed in smoke from the bundles of incense that visitors still lay reverently on the tombstones. There is a collection of weapons and other memorabilia from the event in the temple's small museum. One of the items derives from Kira's family desire to give him a proper burial. The law insisted this could not be done without his head, so they asked for it back. It was entrusted to the temple, and the priests wrote a receipt, which survives even now in the corner of a dusty glass case. "Item," it begins, "One head." ⊠ *2–11–1 Takanawa, Minato-ku, Greater Tokyo* ☎ *03/3441–5560* ⊕ *www.sengakuji.or.jp* 🎫 *Temple and grounds free, museum ¥200* ☉ *Temple Apr.–Sept., daily 7–6; Oct.–Mar., daily 7–5. Museum daily 9–4* Ⓜ *Asakusa subway line, Sengakuji Station (Exit A2).*

Sumo Museum. If you can't attend one of the Tokyo sumo tournaments, you may want to at least pay a short visit to this museum, in

A Mostly Naked Free-For-All

Sumo wrestling dates back some 1,500 years. Originally a religious rite performed at shrines to entertain the harvest gods, a match may seem like a fleshy free-for-all to the casual spectator, but to the trained eye, it's a refined battle. Two wrestlers square off in a dirt ring about 15 feet in diameter and charge straight at each other in nothing but silk loincloths. There are various techniques of pushing, gripping, and throwing, but the rules are simple: except for hitting below the belt, grabbing your opponent by the hair (which would certainly upset the hairdresser who accompanies every sumo ringside), or striking with a closed fist, almost anything goes. If you're thrown down or forced out of the ring, you lose. There are no weight divisions and a runt of merely 250 pounds can find himself facing an opponent twice his size.

You must belong to one of the roughly two dozen *heya* (stables) based in Tokyo to compete. Stables are run by retired wrestlers who have purchased the right from the Japan Sumo Association. Hierarchy and formality rule in the sumo world. Youngsters recruited into the sport live in the stable dormitory, do all the community chores, and wait on their seniors. When they rise high enough in tournament rankings, they acquire their own servant-apprentices.

Most of the stables are concentrated on both sides of the Sumida-gawa near the Kokugikan. Wander this area when the wrestlers are in town (January, May, and September) and you're more than likely to see some of them on the streets, in their wood clogs and kimonos. Come 7 am–11 am and you can peer through the doors and windows of the stables to watch them in practice sessions. One that offers tours is the **Michinoku Stable** (*1-18-7 Ryogoku*). Have a Japanese speaker complete the application form on the website in advance (⊕ *michinokubeya.com*) and you might be able to gain access.

When: Of the six Grand Sumo Tournaments (called *basho*) that take place during the year, Tokyo hosts three: in early January, mid-May, and mid-September. Matches go from early afternoon, when the novices wrestle, to the titanic clashes of the upper ranks at around 6 pm.

Where: Tournaments are held in the Kokugikan, the National Sumo Arena, in Ryogoku, a district in Sumida-ku also famed for its clothing shops and eateries that cater to sumo sizes and tastes. 1-3-28 Yokoami, Sumida-ku ☎ *03/3623-5111* ⊕ *www.sumo.or.jp* JR Sobu Line, Ryogoku Station (West Exit).

How: The most expensive seats, closest to the ring, are tatami-carpeted boxes for four people, called *sajiki*. The boxes are terribly cramped and cost ¥9,500–¥11,700 per person. Cheap seats start as low as ¥3,800 for advance sales, ¥2,200 for same-day box office sales for general admission seats. For same-day box office sales you should line up an hour before the tournament. You can also get tickets through Family Mart, Circle K Sunkus, and Lawson convenience stores.

the south wing of the arena. There are no explanations in English, but the museum's collection of sumo-related wood-block prints, paintings, and illustrated scrolls includes some outstanding examples of traditional Japanese fine art. ⊠ *1–3–28 Yokoami, Sumida-ku, Greater Tokyo* ☎ *03/3622–0366* ⊕ *www.sumo.or.jp* ⊡ *Free* ☉ *Weekdays 10–4:30.*

FAMILY **Tokyo Disneyland** (東京ディズニーランド). Mickey-san and his coterie of Disney characters entertain here at Tokyo Disneyland the same way they do in the California and Florida Disney parks. When the park was built in 1983 it was much smaller than its counterparts in the United States, but the construction in 2001 of the adjacent DisneySea and its seven "Ports of Call," all with different nautical themes and rides, added more than 100 acres to this multifaceted Magic Kingdom.

There are several types of admission tickets. Most people buy the One-Day Passport (¥6,900), which gives you unlimited access to the attractions and shows at one or the other of the two parks. See the park website for other ticketing options. You can buy tickets in advance from any local travel agency, such as the Japan Travel Bureau (JTB). ⊠ *1–1 Maihama, Urayasu, Greater Tokyo* ☎ *0570/00–8632* ⊕ *www.tokyodisneyresort.co.jp* ☉ *Disneyland, daily 9:30–6:30; Disney Sea, daily 10–10; seasonal closings in Dec. and Jan.* Ⓜ *JR Keiyo Line, Maihama Station.*

FAMILY **Tokyo Sea Life Park** (葛西臨海水族館). The three-story cylindrical complex of this aquarium houses more than 540 species of fish and other sea creatures within three different areas: "Voyagers of the Sea" ("Maguro no Kaiyu"), with migratory species; "Seas of the World" ("Sekai no Umi"), with species from foreign waters; and the "Sea of Tokyo" ("Tokyo no Umi"), devoted to the creatures of the bay and nearby waters. To get here, take the JR Keiyo Line local train from Tokyo Station to Kasai Rinkai Koen Station; the aquarium is a 10-minute walk from the South Exit. ⊠ *6–2–3 Rinkai-cho, Edogawa-ku, Greater Tokyo* ☎ *03/3869–5152* ⊕ *www.tokyo-zoo.net/english/kasai* ⊡ *¥700* ☉ *Thurs.–Tues. 9:30–5* Ⓜ *JR Keiyo Line, Kasai Rinkai Koen Station.*

WORTH NOTING

FAMILY **Sanrio Puroland** (サンリオピューロランド). As a theme park dedicated to the world's most famous white cat with no mouth—Hello Kitty, of course—Sanrio Puroland is effectively a shrine to the concept of cuteness. An all-day passport allows for unlimited use of multiple attractions, including three theaters, a boat ride, and the Kitty Lab, where guests are allowed to experiment with what exactly is "cute." Pens, packaged snacks, and plush toys are readily available so guests don't leave empty-handed. ⊠ *1–31 Ochiai, Tama-shi, Greater Tokyo* ☎ *042/339–1111* ⊕ *en.puroland.jp* ⊡ *¥3,300–¥3,800* ☉ *Mon.–Wed. and Fri. 10–5, summer until 6; weekends 10–8* Ⓜ *Keio Line, Tama Center Station.*

FAMILY **Shinagawa Aquarium** (品川水族館 *Shinagawa Suizokukan*). The fun part of this aquarium in southwestern Tokyo is walking through an underwater glass tunnel while some 450 species of fish swim around and above you. There are no pamphlets or explanation panels in English, however, and do your best to avoid Sunday, when the dolphin and sea lion shows draw crowds in impossible numbers. Take the local Keihin-Kyuko private rail line from Shinagawa to Omori-kaigan Station. Turn left as you exit the station and follow the ceramic fish on the sidewalk to the first traffic light; then turn right. ⊠ *3–2–1 Katsushima, Shinagawa-ku, Greater Tokyo* 🕾 *03/3762–3433* ⊕ *www.aquarium.gr.jp* 🎟 *¥1,300* ⊙ *Wed.–Mon. 10–5; dolphin and sea lion shows 3 times daily, on varying schedule* Ⓜ *Keihin Kyuko Line, Omori Kaigan Station.*

WHERE TO EAT

Tokyo is undoubtedly one of the most exciting dining cities in the world. Seasonal ingredients reign supreme here, and there's an emphasis on freshness—not surprising given raw seafood is the cornerstone of sushi. And though Tokyoites still stubbornly resist foreign concepts in many fields, the locals have embraced outside culinary styles with gusto.

While newer restaurants targeting younger diners strive for authenticity in everything from New York–style bagels to Neapolitan pizza, it is still not uncommon to see menus serving East-meets-West concoctions such as spaghetti topped with cod roe and shredded seaweed. That said, the city's best French and Italian establishments can hold their own on a global scale. Naturally, there's also excellent Japanese cuisine available throughout the city, ranging from the traditional to nouveau, which can be shockingly expensive.

That is not to imply that every meal in the city will drain your finances—the current rage is all about *"B-kyu gurume"* (B-class gourmet), restaurants that fill the gap between nationwide chains and fine cuisine, serving tasty Japanese and Asian food without the extra frills of tablecloths and lacquerware. All department stores and most skyscrapers have at least one floor of restaurants that are accessible, affordable, and reputable.

Asakusa is known for its tempura, and Tsukiji prides itself on its fresh sashimi, which is available in excellent quality throughout the city. Ramen is a passion for many locals, who travel across town or stand in line for an hour in order to sit at the counter of a shop rumored to have the perfect balance of noodles and broth. Even the neighborhood convenience stores will offer colorful salads, sandwiches, and a selection of beer and sake. There have been good and affordable Indian and Chinese restaurants in the city for decades. As a result of increased travel by the Japanese to more exotic locations, Thai, Vietnamese, and Turkish restaurants have popped up around the city. ■ **TIP→ When in doubt, note that Tokyo's top-rated international hotels also have some of the city's best places to eat and drink.**

Restaurant reviews are listed in alphabetical order within neighborhood. Use the coordinate (✛ B2) at the end of each listing to locate a site on the Where to Eat in Tokyo map.

	WHAT IT COSTS IN YEN			
	$	$$	$$$	$$$$
At Dinner	under ¥1,000	¥1,000–¥2,000	¥2,001–¥3,000	over ¥3,000

Prices in the reviews are the average cost of a main course at dinner or, if dinner is not served, at lunch.

AKIHABARA 神保町

$$ JAPANESE 🍴 **Kanda Matsuya** (神田まつや). Soba—thin buckwheat noodles often served chilled in summer and hot in winter—are available everywhere, even convenience stores. The family-run Matsuya serves authentic soba in a rustic atmosphere. A simple soba meal costs ¥650, or, for a bit more, get noodles topped with tempura or other goodies. [$] *Average main: ¥1000* ✉ *1–3 Kanda Sudacho, Chiyoda-ku* ☎ *03/3251–1556* 💳 *No credit cards* ⏲ *Closed Sun.* [M] *Marunouchi Line, Awajicho Station (Exit A3)* ✥ *F2.*

$$ JAPANESE 🍴 **Kanda Yabu Soba** (かんだやぶそば). Soba—thin noodles made from buckwheat flour and quickly dipped into a hot broth or cold dipping sauce—are the lighter cousin of udon. Because it can be eaten so quickly, soba is often sold at small stands in train stations, where it can be slurped down while waiting to change trains. The ever-popular Kanda Yabu Soba, located in a recently built but traditional building that replaced the original 130-year-old restaurant after a fire in 2013, is a great place to sit down and savor the dish—be that on tatami or at one of the tables. A basic soba meal costs just ¥670, but the *shun* (seasonal meal), which changes 10 times a year, is excellent and affordable. [$] *Average main: ¥1000* ✉ *2–10 Kanda Awajicho, Chiyoda-ku* ☎ *03/3251–0287* 💳 *No credit cards* [M] *JR and Marunouchi lines, Awajicho Station (Exit A3)* ✥ *F2.*

$$ AMERICAN FAMILY 🍴 **MLB Café Tokyo.** Located in the shadow of Tokyo Dome, the primary baseball stadium in Tokyo, this theme restaurant is filled with sports memorabilia, waitstaff dressed in baseball uniforms, and a menu with a lineup similar to a Hard Rock Cafe or TGI Fridays. This, or its sister branch near the Westin in Ebisu, is the perfect place for sports-loving kids. [$] *Average main: ¥2000* ✉ *1–3–61 Koraku, Bunkyo-ku* ☎ *03/5840–8905* 🌐 *www.mlbcafe.jp* [M] *JR Sobu and Toei Mita subway lines, Suidobashi Station (Exit A5)* ✥ *E1.*

UENO 上野

$$$$ JAPANESE 🍴 **Sasa-no-yuki** (笹の雪). In the heart of one of Tokyo's old working-class *shitamachi* (downtown) neighborhoods, Sasa-no-yuki has been serving meals based on homemade tofu for the past 325 years. The food is inspired in part by *shojin ryori* (Buddhist vegetarian cuisine), although not everything served is vegetarian. The basic set menu includes *ankake* (bean curd in sweet soy sauce), *uzumi* tofu (scrambled with rice and green tea), and *unsui* (a creamy tofu crepe filled with sea scallops, shrimp, and minced red pepper). For bigger appetites, there's also a 12-dish banquet (reservation required). There's both tatami and

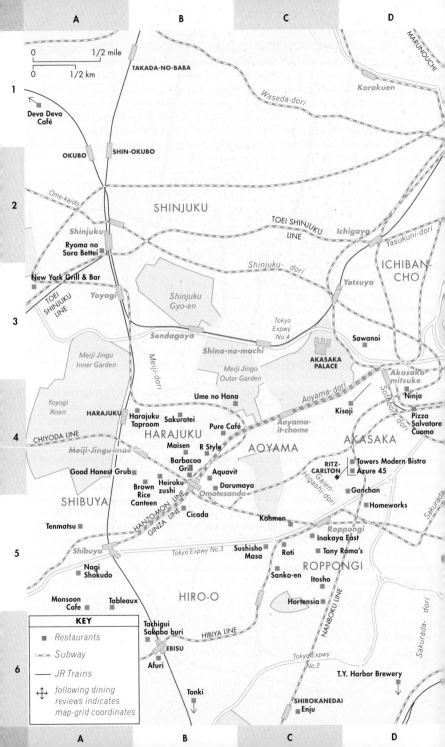

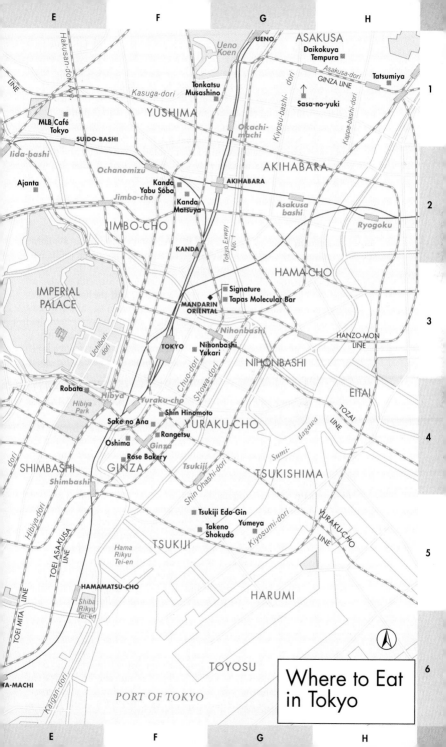

Where to Eat in Tokyo

table seating, and the dining room includes a view of the Japanese garden complete with an ornamental waterfall. Ⓢ *Average main: ¥4000* ✉ *2–15–10 Negishi, Ueno* ☎ *03/3873–1145* ⊙ *Closed Mon.* Ⓜ *JR Uguisudani Station (Kita-guchi/North Exit)* ✛ *G1.*

$$
JAPANESE

✕ **Tonkatsu Musashino** (とんかつ武蔵野). The deep-fried, breaded pork cutlets at this casual restaurant just south of Ueno Park's pond get rave reviews for good reason. They combine generous portions with melt-in-the-mouth tenderness, and for a great price. Set meals here are ¥1,200 and come with enough rice, miso soup, shredded cabbage, and pickles to loosen your belt a notch or two. Ⓢ *Average main: ¥1200* ✉ *2–8–1 Ueno, Ueno* ☎ *03/3831–1672* ⊙ *No dinner* ▭ *No credit cards* Ⓜ *JR Ueno Station* ✛ *G1.*

ASAKUSA 浅草

$$$
JAPANESE

✕ **Daikokuya Tempura** (大黒家天麩羅). Although tempura is available throughout the city, the Asakusa neighborhood prides itself on its battered, deep-fried seafood and vegetables. Daikokuya, in the center of Asakusa's historic district, is a point of pilgrimage for both locals and tourists. The specialty here is shrimp tempura, and the menu choices are simple—*tendon* is tempura shrimp served over rice, and the tempura meal includes rice, pickled vegetables, and miso soup. Famished diners can add additional pieces of tempura or side dishes such as sashimi for an additional fee, or opt for a multidish course (from ¥3,300 to ¥4,700). When the line of waiting customers outside is too long, head to the shop's annex (*bekkan*) just around the corner. Ⓢ *Average main: ¥2500* ✉ *1–38–10 Asakusa, Taitō-ku, Asakusa* ☎ *03/3844–1111* ⊕ *www.tempura.co.jp/english* ▭ *No credit cards* Ⓜ *Ginza and Asakusa subway lines, Asakusa Station* ✛ *H1.*

$$$
JAPANESE

✕ **Tatsumiya** (たつみ屋). Here's a restaurant that's run like a formal *ryotei* (traditional Japanese restaurant focused on luxury) but has the feel of a rough-cut *izakaya* (Japanese pub). Neither inaccessible nor outrageously expensive, Tatsumiya is adorned—nay, cluttered—with antique chests, braziers, clocks, lanterns, bowls, utensils, and craft work, some of it for sale. The evening meal is in the *kaiseki* style, meaning multiple courses are served; tradition demands that the meal include something raw, something boiled, something vinegary, and something grilled. The kaiseki dinner is served only until 8:30, and you must reserve ahead for it. Tatsumiya also serves a light lunch, plus a variety of *nabe* (one-pot seafood and vegetable stews, prepared at your table) until 10. The pork nabe is the house specialty. Ⓢ *Average main: ¥3000* ✉ *1–33–5 Asakusa, Taitō-ku, Asakusa* ☎ *03/3842–7373* ⊕ *www.kiwa-group. co.jp/restaurant/264* Ⓜ *Ginza and Asakusa subway lines, Asakusa Station (Exits 1 and 3)* ✛ *H1.*

TSUKIJI 築地

$$$
JAPANESE

✕ **Takeno Shokudo** (多け乃食堂). Just a stone's throw from the Tokyo fish market, Takeno Shokudo is a neighborhood restaurant that tends to fill up at noon with the market's wholesalers and auctioneers and personnel from the nearby Asahi newspaper offices. There's nothing here but the freshest and the best—big portions of it, at very reasonable prices. Sushi and sashimi are the staples, but there's also a wonderful *tendon* bowl for ¥1,000 with shrimp and eel tempura on rice. Prices are not posted because they vary with the costs that morning in the market. Reservations can only be made for large parties, or if you plan to dine before 6:30 pm. $ *Average main: ¥3000* ✉ *6–21–2 Tsukiji, Tsukiji* ☎ *03/3541–8698* 🖃 *No credit cards* 🕒 *Closed Sun.* Ⓜ *Hibiya subway line, Tsukiji Station (Exit 1); Oedo subway line, Tsukiji-shijo Station (Exit A1)* ✛ *F5.*

ORDER FOOD WITHOUT SPEAKING JAPANESE

English OK! (⊕ *www.englishok. jp*) lists restaurants where English is spoken so people with limited or no Japanese can order food without worrying about the language barrier. Before heading out, check the website for maps, sample menus, and printable coupons.

$$$$ ✕ **Tsukiji Edo-Gin** (築地江戸銀). In an area that teems with sushi bars,
SUSHI this one maintains its reputation as one of the best. Tsukiji Edo-Gin drapes generous slabs of fish over the vinegared rice rather than perching them demurely on top. The centerpiece of the main room is a huge tank where the day's ingredients swim about until required; it doesn't get any fresher than this. Set menus here are reasonable, especially for lunch, but a big appetite for specialties like sea urchin and *otoro* tuna can put a dent in your budget. $ *Average main: ¥4000* ✉ *4–5–1 Tsukiji, Tsukiji* ☎ *03/3543–4401* Ⓜ *Hibiya subway line, Tsukiji Station (Exit 1); Oedo subway line, Tsukiji-shijo Station (Exit A1)* ✛ *F5.*

$$ ✕ **Yumeya** (夢や). Not far from Tsukiji, Yumeya Tsukishima ("moon
JAPANESE island") is a large man-made island known as the birthplace of delicious *monjayaki*: a thin batter is mixed with shredded cabbage and other ingredients, fried on a griddle built into the table, and eaten directly from the grill with metal spatulas. The main street in Tsukishima is filled with dozens of monjayaki establishments, but Yumeya is one of the best, an obvious fact when you spot the line of waiting patrons. Tried-and-true monjayaki eaters make it themselves at the table, but it can be a tricky endeavor—you need to form a ring of dry ingredients on the grill and pour the batter into the middle. If you're not feeling confident, servers can also make it for you at your table. $ *Average main: ¥2000* ✉ *3–18–4 Tsukishima, Tsukiji* ☎ *03/3536–7870* 🕒 *Closed Mon and 3rd Tues. No lunch weekdays* Ⓜ *Oedo and Yuraku-cho subway lines, Tsukishima Station (Exit 7)* ✛ *G5.*

NIHOMBASHI 日本橋

$$$$ ✕ **Nihonbashi Yukari** (日本橋ゆかり). Anyone looking to experience
JAPANESE Japanese haute cuisine in a more relaxed atmosphere should look to
Fodor's Choice this *kappo*-style restaurant, where diners eat and order at the counter.
★ Third-generation chef—and 2002 Iron Chef champion—Kimio Nonaga displays his artistry in every element of Nihonbashi Yukari's menu. Dinner here is a multicourse affair, with each dish showcasing the freshness and quality of the seasonal ingredients. To witness him at work, and get the full *kappo* dining experience, be sure to request a counter

seat when making reservations. As a bonus, Nihonbashi Yukari also offers a lunch setting for around ¥3,500, which is unusual for this kind of restaurant. $ *Average main: ¥15000* ✉ *3–2–14 Nihonbashi, Chuo-ku* ☎ *03/3271–3436* ⊕ *www.nihonbashi-yukari.com* ⊘ *Closed Sun.* ⚑ *Reservations essential* ✛ *F3.*

$$$$
FRENCH
✗ **Signature** (シグネチャー). This elegant French restaurant on the 37th floor of the Mandarin Oriental Hotel has wonderful views of the Tokyo skyline as well an open kitchen, where diners can see the masterful chef Nicolas Boujéma and his staff at work. Boujéma has an impressive résumé, having worked in kitchens such as La Tour d'Argent, Le Balzac, and most recently with Pierre Gagnaire. And his cuisine does not disappoint. Inspired by Japanese kaiseki, the menu changes with the seasons. There is also a fine wine list here that includes biodynamic and organic selections. $ *Average main: ¥15000* ✉ *37F Mandarin Oriental Tokyo, 2–1–1 Nihonbashi, Chuo-ku* ☎ *03/3270–8188* ⊕ *www. mandarinoriental.com/tokyo/dining/signature* ⚑ *Reservations essential* Ⓜ *Ginza subway line, Mitsukoshi-mae Station (Exit A7)* ✛ *G3.*

$$$$
JAPANESE
✗ **Tapas Molecular Bar** (タパス モレキュラーバー). Occupying a mysterious place between traditional sushi counter, tapas bar, science lab, and magic show, this award-winning restaurant breaks new ground. In full view of diners, the team of chefs assemble a small parade of bite-size morsels in surprising texture and flavor combinations. There are only eight seats, and seatings are at 6 and 8:30 only (plus 1 pm on weekends), so reserve as early as possible. $ *Average main: ¥16000* ✉ *38F Mandarin Oriental Tokyo, 2–1–1 Nihonbashi, Chuo-ku* ☎ *03/3270–8188* ⊕ *www.mandarinoriental.com/tokyo/dining/molecular* ⚑ *Reservations essential* Ⓜ *Ginza subway line, Mitsukoshi-mae Station (Exit A7)* ✛ *G3.*

GINZA 銀座

$$$$
JAPANESE
✗ **Oshima** (大志満). The main draw at Oshima is sampling the *Kaga ryori* cooking of Kanazawa, a small city on the Sea of Japan known for its rich craft traditions. Waitresses dress the part in kimonos of Kanazawa's famous Yuzen dyed silk, and Kutani porcelain and Wajima lacquerware grace the exquisite table settings. As you'd expect from waterfront cuisine, seafood at Oshima is superb, but don't ignore the specialty of the house: a stew of duck and potatoes called *jibuni*. Kaiseki full-course meals are pricey (up to ¥12,960), but there's a reasonable lunchtime set menu for ¥2,700. $ *Average main: ¥9000* ✉ *9F Ginza Core Bldg., 5–8–20 Ginza, Chuo-ku* ☎ *03/3574–8080* Ⓜ *Ginza, Hibiya, and Marunouchi subway lines, Ginza Station (Exit A5)* ✛ *F4.*

$$$$
JAPANESE
✗ **Rangetsu** (らん月). Japan enjoys a special reputation for its lovingly raised, tender, marbled domestic beef, and if your budget can bear the weight, Rangetsu serves excellent dishes with this beef as a star ingredient. Try the signature shabu-shabu or sukiyaki course for a primer. For a blowout celebration, call ahead to reserve a private alcove, where you can cook for yourself, or have a kaiseki meal brought to your table by kimono-clad attendants. While dinner can damage the wallet, there is also a good variety of lunch sets available from ¥1,750. The location, opposite the Matsuya Department Store, is just as elegant as the restaurant itself. $ *Average main: ¥10000* ✉ *3–5–8*

Ginza, Chuo-ku ☎ *03/3567–1021* Ⓜ *Marunouchi and Ginza subway lines, Ginza Station (Exits A9 and A10)* ✛ *F4.*

$$$$
JAPANESE
Fodor's Choice
🥢 ◀ ★

✕ **Robata** (炉端). Old, funky, and more than a little cramped, Robata is a bit daunting at first. But fourth-generation chef-owner Takao Inoue holds forth here with an inspired version of Japanese home cooking. He's also a connoisseur of pottery and serves his food on pieces acquired at famous kilns all over the country. There's no menu; just tell Inoue-san (who speaks some English) how much you want to spend, and leave the rest to him. A meal at Robata—like the pottery—is simple to the eye but subtle and fulfilling. Typical dishes include steamed fish with vegetables, stews of beef or pork, and seafood salads. $ *Average main: ¥5000* ✉ *1–3–8 Yuraku-cho, Ginza* ☎ *03/3591–1905* ▭ *No credit cards* ☉ *Closed some Sun. each month. No lunch* Ⓜ *JR Yuraku-cho Station (Hibiya Exit); Hibiya, Chiyoda, and Mita subway lines, Hibiya Station (Exit A4)* ✛ *E4.*

$$
INTERNATIONAL

✕ **Rose Bakery** (ローズベーカリー). Satisfying the need for light, healthy food that is neither raw nor fried, this airy but rather nondescript bakery and café, which also has branches in Paris and London, serves up a tasty selection of salads, quiches, vegetables, and other deli-style dishes. Although the interior's rows of tables and blank white walls can feel a bit too much like a hip reinterpretation of a school cafeteria, Rose Bakery is a good bet for a quick lunch or pastry while out wandering the Ginza area. It's also good for breakfast (from 9 am), especially if you crave a full English. $ *Average main: ¥2000* ✉ *6–9–5 Ginza, Ginza Komatsu West Wing 7F, Chuo-ku* ☎ *03/5537–5038* ⊕ *www.rosebakery. jp* ▭ *No credit cards* ⟋ *Reservations not accepted* ✛ *F4.*

$$$$
JAPANESE

✕ **Sake no Ana** (酒の穴). With roughly 130 varieties of sake from all over Japan available by the carafe, Sake no Ana (literally, "the sake hole") does seem to feature a bottomless variety of the drink. The restaurant has its own sake sommelier, Sakamoto-san, who can help diners sort (or drink) through the restaurant's immense selection. Though most sake-specialty restaurants are open only for dinner, Sake no Ana is also open for lunch, good for those who want to space out their sampling of Japan's unofficial national drink. The food is classic izakaya fare, and at lunchtime there are hearty donburi dishes, large bowls of rice topped with seasonal sashimi or beef simmered in a sweet soy broth. $ *Average main: ¥5000* ✉ *3–5–8 Ginza, Chuo-ku* ☎ *03/3567–1133* ✛ *F4.*

$$$
JAPANESE
Fodor's Choice
★

✕ **Shin Hinomoto** (新日の基). Aka "Andy's," this izakaya is located directly under the tracks of the Yamanote Line, making the wooden interior shudder each time a train passes overhead. It's a favorite with local and foreign journalists, as the Foreign Correspondents Club is just across the street and is actually run by a Brit, Andy, who travels down the road to Tsukiji Market every morning to buy seafood. Don't miss the fresh sashimi and buttered scallops. It fills up very quickly, so call at least the day in advance to make a reservation. $ *Average main: ¥3000* ✉ *2–4–4 Yuraku-cho, Ginza* ☎ *03/3214–8021* ⊕ *www.andysfish.com/ shin-hinomoto* ▭ *No credit cards* ☉ *Closed Sun. No lunch* ⟋ *Reservations essential* Ⓜ *JR Yuraku-cho Station (Hibiya Exit); Hibiya, Chiyoda, and Mita subway lines, Hibiya Station (Exits A2 and A6)* ✛ *F4.*

AOYAMA 青山 AND AKASAKA 赤坂

$$ INDIAN 🍴 **Ajanta** (アジャンタ). In the mid-20th century, the founder of Ajanta came to Tokyo to study electrical engineering. He ended up changing careers and establishing what is today one of the oldest and best Indian restaurants in town. There's no decoration to speak of at this restaurant, which stays open until 2 am (Tuesday–Saturday). The emphasis instead is on the variety and intricacy of South Indian cooking—and none of its dressier rivals can match Ajanta's menu for sheer depth. The curries are hot to begin with, but you can order them even hotter. Try the *masala dosa* (a savory crepe), *keema* (minced beef), or mutton curry. A small boutique in one corner sells saris and imported Indian foodstuffs. [$] *Average main: ¥2000* ✉ *3–11 Niban-cho, Akasaka* ☎ *03/3264–6955* 🌐 *www.ajanta.com* 💳 *No credit cards* [M] *Yuraku-cho subway line, Koji-machi Station (Exit 5)* ✥ *E2.*

$ RAMEN 🍴 **Darumaya** (だるまや). The classic bowl of ramen is topped with slices of pork, but Darumaya, in the fashion district of Omotesando, has a slightly different take, topping its noodles with grilled vegetables. In the summertime be sure to order the *hiyashi soba*, a bowl of chilled noodles topped with vegetables and ham in a sesame dressing. Another shop specialty is the *tsukemen*, where the noodles and broth are served in separate bowls. Dip (don't drop) the ramen into the broth. Despite the focus on veggies, vegetarians should note, the soups and sauces are not meat-free. [$] *Average main: ¥850* ✉ *1F Murayama Bldg., 5–9–5 Minami-Aoyama, Minato-ku* ☎ *03/3499–6295* 💳 *No credit cards* 🕒 *Closed Sun. and 1st and 3rd Mon.* [M] *Ginza, Chiyoda, and Hanzo-mon subway lines, Omotesando Station (Exit B1)* ✥ *B4.*

$$$$ JAPANESE 🍴 **Kisoji** (木曽路). The specialty here is shabu-shabu: thin slices of beef cooked in boiling water at your table and dipped in sauce. Normally, despite the price, this is an informal, no-frills sort of meal. Kisoji, which has been serving the dish for more than 60 years, elevates the experience, with all the tasteful appointments of a traditional *ryotei*—private dining rooms with tatami seating (at a 10% surcharge), elegant little rock gardens, and alcoves with flower arrangements. There are branches in Ginza, Shimbashi, Shinjuku, and Ueno, as well. [$] *Average main: ¥6500* ✉ *3–10–4 Akasaka, 2nd fl., Minato-ku* ☎ *03/3588–0071* [M] *Ginza and Marunouchi subway lines, Akasaka-mitsuke Station (Belle Vie Akasaka Exit)* ✥ *D4.*

$$$$ JAPANESE FAMILY 🍴 **Ninja** (忍者). In keeping with the air of mystery you'd expect from a ninja-themed restaurant, a ninja-costumed waiter leads you through a dark underground maze to your table in an artificial cave. The menu has more than 100 choices, including some elaborate set courses that are extravagant in both proportion and price. Among the impressively presented dishes are "jack-in-the-box" seafood salad—a lacquerware box overflowing with seasonal seafood and garnished with mustard, avocado tartar, and miso paste—and the life-size bonsai-tree dessert made from cookies and green-tea ice cream. Magical tricks are performed at your table during dinner—it's slightly kitschy but entertaining nonetheless, especially for kids. [$] *Average main: ¥5000* ✉ *Akasaka Tokyu Plaza, 2–14–3 Nagata-cho, Minato-ku* ☎ *03/5157–3936* 🌐 *www.*

ninjaakasaka.com ⌨ *Reservations essential* Ⓜ *Ginza and Marunouchi subway lines, Akasaka-mitsuke Station (Tokyu Plaza Exit)* ✛ *D4.*

$$$
ITALIAN
FAMILY

✕ **Pizza Salvatore Cuomo** (ピッツァサルヴァトーレクオモ). Swing open the door to Pizza Salvatore Cuomo and you'll catch a rich aroma wafting from the wood-burning oven—the centerpiece of this homey, spacious restaurant. As with Cuomo's other branches around town, the chefs here adhere to traditional Neapolitan methods, while updating recipes with dough infused with spinach, herbs, and even squid ink. Lunch courses are filling, affordable (around ¥1,000), and quick. Though seating space is ample, expect a full house on weekdays. For dinner, classic antipasto dishes such as Caprese make for an authentic Italian meal. Branches are found throughout the city. Ⓢ *Average main: ¥2500* ✉ *Prudential Plaza Bldg., 2–13–10 Nagata-cho, Chiyoda-ku* ☎ *03/3500–5700* ⊕ *www.salvatore.jp* Ⓜ *Chiyoda and Marunouchi subway lines, Akasaka-mitsuke Station* ✛ *D4.*

$$
JAPANESE

✕ **Sawanoi** (澤乃井). The homemade udon noodles, served in a broth with seafood, vegetables, or chicken, make a perfect light meal or midnight snack. Try the *inaka* (country-style) udon, which has bonito, seaweed flakes, radish shavings, and a raw egg dropped into the hot broth to cook. For a heartier meal, chose the *tenkama* set: hot udon and shrimp tempura with a delicate soy-based sauce. A bit run-down, Sawanoi is one of the last remaining neighborhood shops in what is now an upscale business and entertainment district. (Dash up a short flight of stairs to get to the dining room.) It stays open until 3 am, and a menu is available in English. Ⓢ *Average main: ¥1000* ✉ *1F Shimpo Bldg., 3–7–13 Akasaka, Minato-ku* ☎ *03/3582–2080* ▭ *No credit cards* ⊘ *Closed Sun.* Ⓜ *Ginza and Marunouchi subway lines, Akasaka-mitsuke Station (Belle Vie Akasaka Exit)* ✛ *D3.*

$$$$
JAPANESE
Fodor'sChoice
★

✕ **Ume no Hana** (梅の花). The exclusive specialty here is tofu, prepared in more ways than you can imagine—boiled, steamed, stir-fried with minced crabmeat, served in a custard, or wrapped in thin layers around a delicate whitefish paste. Tofu is touted as the perfect high-protein, low-calorie health food; at Ume no Hana it's raised to the elegance of haute cuisine. Remove your shoes when you step up to the lovely central room. Latticed wood screens separate the tables, and private dining rooms with tatami seating are available. Prix fixe meals include a complimentary aperitif. Ume no Hana shops in Ueno and Ginza are also worth visiting. Ⓢ *Average main: ¥5000* ✉ *2F Aoyama M's Tower, 2–27–18 Minami-Aoyama, Minato-ku* ☎ *03/5412–0855* ⊕ *www.umenohana. co.jp* Ⓜ *Ginza Line, Gaien-mae Station (Exit 1A)* ✛ *C4.*

HARAJUKU 原宿

$$$$
SCANDINAVIAN

✕ **Aquavit** (アクアビット). If you'd like to take a detour from Tokyo's kaiseki- and sushi-centric fine dining, consider this unexpected alternative. One of a handful of authentic Swedish restaurants in Tokyo, Aquavit serves a reasonably priced prix fixe lunch and dinner. A great introduction to the cuisine is the herring sampler, which includes pickled and sweet varieties that change seasonally. Entrées like the dry-cured gravlax or the foie gras with shallot marmalade, fig, and elderflower continue the Scandinavian theme. But don't ask for the tab before sampling dessert in the form of scrumptious Swedish pancakes served with ginger confit, fresh cream, and raspberries. The ultraromantic dining room manages to be both inviting and modern, thanks to design and furniture by Fritz Hansen of Denmark. $ *Average main: ¥10000* ⊠ *1F Shimizu Bldg., 2–5–8 Kita-Aoyama, Minato-ku* ☎ *03/5413–3300* ⊕ *www.aquavit-japan.com* ⌣ *Reservations essential* Ⓜ *Ginza subway line, Gaien-mae Station (Exit 1B)* ✛ *B4.*

$$$$
BRAZILIAN

✕**Barbacoa Grill** (バルバッコアグリル). Carnivores flock here for the great-value, all-you-can-eat Brazilian grilled chicken and barbecued beef, which the efficient waiters keep bringing to your table on skewers until you tell them to stop. Those with lighter appetites can choose the less expensive salad buffet and *feijoada* (pork stew with black beans); both are bargains. Hardwood floors, lithographs of bull motifs, warm lighting, and salmon-color tablecloths provide the backdrop. The drink menu provides the chance to try a selection of Brazilian cocktails. Look for the entrance just off Omotesando-dori on the Harajuku 2-chome shopping street (on the north side of Omotesando-dori), about 50 yards down on the left. There's also a Barbacoa near Tokyo Station, as well as others in Roppongi, Shibuya, and Shinjuku. $ *Average main: ¥5400* ⊠ *4–3–24 Jingu-mae, Shibuya-ku* ☎ *03/3796–0571* ⊕ *www.barbacoa. jp/aoyama* Ⓜ *Ginza, Chiyoda, and Hanzo-mon subway lines, Omotesando Station (Exit A2)* ✛ *B4.*

$$
VEGETARIAN

✕**Brown Rice Canteen** (ブラウンライス 食堂). Run by Neal's Yard Remedies, this laid-back café has all-natural wooden interiors and natural produce on the menu. If shopping in Harajuku, it's a great place to stop for a tempeh burger, stuffed tofu pouch, or other vegetarian fare. $ *Average main: ¥1200* ⊠ *5–1–8 Jingu-mae, Shibuya-ku* ☎ *03/5778–5416* ⊕ *www.nealsyard.co.jp/brownrice* Ⓜ *Ginza and Hanzo-mon subway lines, Omotesando Station (Exit A1)* ✛ *B4.*

$$$$
MEDITERRANEAN
Fodor's Choice
★

✕**Cicada** (シカダ). Offering up high-end Mediterranean cuisine in an incredibly stylish setting, Cicada's resortlike atmosphere feels a world away from Ometosando's busy shopping streets. In the warmer months, the outdoor patio is especially relaxing. The menu ranges from Spanish tapas and Middle Eastern mezze to hearty grilled meats and seafood. An expansive wine list and craft beers complement the range of cuisine, and the outdoor bar makes a great spot for a nightcap. Though spacious, this popular restaurant fills up quickly, so dinner reservations are recommended. $ *Average main: ¥3500* ⊠ *5–7–28, Minami-Aoyama, Minato-ku* ☎ *03/6434–1255* ⊕ *www.tysons.jp/cicada* ✛ *B5.*

$$$
JAPANESE
Fodor's Choice
★

✕**Harajuku Taproom** (原宿タップルーム). Founded by American Bryan Baird in 2000, Baird Brewing has become one of the leaders in Japan's now booming craft beer movement, with a range of year-round brews, such as the hop-heavy Suruga Bay IPA, and creative seasonal beers that use local ingredients such as yuzu citrus and even wasabi. The Harajuku Taproom combines Baird's excellent lineup of microbrews with Japanese izakaya (pub) fare like yakitori (grilled chicken skewers), *gyoza* (dumplings), and curry rice. The Taproom's rotation of 15 beers on tap, plus two hand-pumped ales, as well as its quality food and friendly atmosphere make it a must for beer lovers and dispel any notion that all Japanese beers taste the same. There are other branches in Naka

Meguro and Yokohama. $ *Average main: ¥3000* ✉ *1–20–13, Jingumae, No Surrender Bldg. 2F, Shibuya-ku* ☎ *03/6438–0450* ⊕ *www.bairdbeer. com/en/tap/harajuku* 🗖 *No credit cards* ☉ *No lunch weekdays* ✛ *B4.*

$$ ✕ **Heiroku-zushi** (平禄寿司). Often, a meal of sushi is a costly indul-
SUSHI gence. The rock-bottom alternative is a *kaiten-zushi*, where it is liter-
FAMILY ally served assembly-line style: chefs inside the circular counter place a
constant supply of dishes on the revolving belt with plates color-coded
for price; just choose whatever takes your fancy as the sushi parades by.
A cheerful, bustling example of this genre is the Heiroku-zushi chain's
branch opposite Omotesando Hills; it's all about the fresh fish here
(and clearly not the design). When you're done, the server counts up
your plates and calculates your bill. Expect ¥130 for staples like tuna
and squid to ¥490 for delicacies like high-grade *toro* cuts of tuna and
sea urchin. $ *Average main: ¥2000* ✉ *5–8–5 Jingu-mae, Shibuya-ku*
☎ *03/3498–3968* Ⓜ *Ginza, Chiyoda, and Hanzo-mon subway lines,
Omotesando Station (Exit A1)* ✛ *B4.*

$$ ✕ **Maisen** (まい泉). Converted from a *sento* (public bathhouse), Maisen
JAPANESE still has the old high ceiling (built for ventilation) and the original signs
instructing bathers where to change, but now bouquets of seasonal
flowers transform the large, airy space into a pleasant dining room.
Maisen's specialty is the *tonkatsu* set: tender, juicy, deep-fried pork
cutlets served with a spicy sauce, shredded cabbage, miso soup, and
rice. Combine with sashimi, if feeling especially hungry. There is usually
a long line, but it moves quickly. Solo diners can jump the line to sit
at the counter. Those who want to keep their taste buds sharp should
try for the nonsmoking rooms upstairs. There's also a branch in Hikarie building in Shibuya. $ *Average main: ¥1800* ✉ *4–8–5 Jingu-mae,
Shibuya-ku* ☎ *03/3470–0071* 🗖 *No credit cards* Ⓜ *Ginza, Chiyoda,
and Hanzo-mon subway lines, Omotesando Station (Exit A2)* ✛ *B4.*

$$ ✕ **Pure Café** (ピュアカフェ). Stop along a backstreet in the upscale fash-
VEGETARIAN ion hub of Omotesando for a daily changing menu of salads, soups,
sandwiches, and other nutritious fare for breakfast, lunch, and din-
ner. $ *Average main: ¥2000* ✉ *5–5–21 Minami-Aoyama, Minato-ku*
☎ *03/5466–2611* ⊕ *www.pure-cafe.com* 🗖 *No credit cards* Ⓜ *Ginza
and Hanzo-mon subway lines, Omotesando Station (Exit B3)* ✛ *B4.*

$$ ✕ **R Style** (アールスタイル). Even in some of the swankiest restaurants,
JAPANESE Japanese *wagashi* (confectionaries) aren't up to par. To sample authentic
handmade wagashi while sipping green tea, head to this café in the fashionable Omotesando Hills mall. The main ingredients in wagashi are
adzuki beans, rice, and other grains sweetened slightly by sugarcane—
making these treats moderately healthy (at least compared with their
European counterparts). The intricate morsels of edible art are almost
too perfectly presented to eat—almost, but not quite. Try the *konomi*
(rice dumpling with adzuki conserve) or *koyomi* (bracken dumpling
with soy custard) set. $ *Average main: ¥1000* ✉ *3F Omotesando
Hills Main Bldg., 4–12–10 Jingu-mae, Shibuya-ku* ☎ *03/3423–1155*
⊕ *www.rstyle.co.jp* 🗖 *No credit cards* Ⓜ *Ginza, Chiyoda, and Hanzo-
mon subway lines, Omotesando Station (Exit A2); Chiyoda subway
line, Meiji-Jingu-mae (Harajuku) Station (Exit 5); JR Harajuku Station
(Omotesando Exit)* ✛ *B4.*

$$ JAPANESE

🍴 **Sakuratei** (さくら亭). Tucked away between the two buildings of the cutting-edge (yet very laid-back) Design Festa Gallery, Sakuratei also defies conventions—namely, that eating out doesn't mean you don't have to cook. At this do-it-yourself restaurant for *okonomiyaki* (a kind of savory pancake made with egg, meat, and vegetables), you choose ingredients and cook them on the *teppan* (grill). Okonomiyaki is generally easy to make, but flipping the pancake to cook the other side can be challenging—potentially messy but still fun. Fortunately, you're not expected to wash the dishes. Okonomiyaki literally means "as you like it," so experiment with your own recipe. But if you're feeling uninspired, you can always default to the house special, *sakurayaki* (with pork, squid, and onions) or *monjayaki* (a watered-down Tokyo variation of okonomiyaki from the Kanto region). [$] *Average main: ¥1500* ✉ *3–20–1 Jingu-mae, Shibuya-ku* ☎ *03/3479–0039* 🌐 *www.sakuratei.co.jp* 💳 *No credit cards* [M] *Chiyoda subway line, Meiji-Jingu-mae (Harajuku) Station (Exit 5)* ⊕ *B4.*

SHIBUYA 原宿

$ RAMEN

🍴 **Afuri** (阿夫利/あふり). Ramen is the quintessential Japanese fast food: thick Chinese noodles in a savory broth, with sliced leeks, grilled *chashu* (pork loin), and spinach in a bowl. Each neighborhood in Tokyo has its favorite, and in Ebisu the hands-down favorite is Afuri. Using the picture menu, choose your ramen by inserting coins into a ticket machine, find a seat, and hand over your ticket to the cooks, who prepare your ramen then and there. There's limited seating, and at lunch and dinner, the line of waiting customers extends down the street, but as expected, the ramen is worth it. [$] *Average main: ¥880* ✉ *1–1–7 Ebisu, Shibuya-ku* ☎ *03/5795–0750* 💳 *No credit cards* [M] *JR Yamanote Line (Nishi-guchi/West Exit) and Hibiya subway line (Exit 1), Ebisu Station* ⊕ *B6.*

$$ CAFÉ

🍴 **Good Honest Grub** (グッドオネストグラブ). This airy, laid-back restaurant has the feel of enjoying a home-cooked meal at a friend's house. Brunch is generously served 10:30–4 on weekends and national holidays, and includes Greek omelets, wraps, and perhaps the best eggs Benedict in town. True to its name, everything comes from the restaurant's own organic farm. [$] *Average main: ¥2000* ✉ *2–20–8 Higashi, Shibuya-ku* ☎ *03/3797–9877* 🌐 *www.goodhonestgrub.com* 💳 *No credit cards* 🕒 *No dinner* ✍ *Reservations not accepted* [M] *JR Yamanote, Shibuya Station (South Exit)* ⊕ *B4.*

$$ ASIAN

🍴 **Monsoon Cafe** (モンスーンカフェ). With a dozen locations (including Shinjuku and Omotesando), Monsoon Cafe meets the demand in Tokyo for "ethnic" food—which by local definition means spicy and primarily Southeast Asian. Complementing the eclectic Pan-Asian food are rattan furniture, brass tableware from Thailand, colorful papier-mâché parrots on gilded stands, Balinese carvings, and ceiling fans. Here, at the original Monsoon, the best seats in the house are on the balcony that runs around the four sides of the atrium-style central space. Try the satay (grilled, skewered cubes of meat) platter, steamed shrimp dumplings, or *nasi goreng* (Indonesian fried rice). [$] *Average main: ¥2000* ✉ *15–4 Hachiyama-cho, Shibuya-ku* ☎ *03/5489–3789*

CLOSE UP

What's a Vegetarian to Do?

Tokyo has had a reputation of being difficult for vegetarians, but as more Japanese opt to forgo meat, the number of truly vegetarian restaurants is rising. Organic produce has also become more in demand, and many nonvegetarian restaurants now serve organic meals that very often are vegetarian. The city's numerous Indian eateries are a safe bet, as are the handful of restaurants (such as Sasa-no-yuki in Ueno, which also serves nonvegetarian) that specialize in *shojin ryori*, traditional Zen vegetarian food that emphasizes natural flavors and fresh ingredients without using heavy spices or rich sauces. However, you should always inquire when making reservations at these restaurants, as some still use *dashi*, a stock made with smoked skipjack tuna and kelp. The variety and visual beauty of a full-course shojin ryori meal opens new dining dimensions to the vegetarian gourmet. *Goma-dofu*, or sesame-flavored bean curd, for example, is a tasty treat, as is *nasu-dengaku*, grilled eggplant covered with a sweet miso sauce.

Take note that a dish may be described as meat-free even if it contains fish, shrimp, or chicken. And one should assume that salads, pastas, and soups in nonvegetarian restaurants are garnished with ham or bacon.

Deva Deva Café (デヴァデヴァカフェ). Near the picturesque Inokashira Park, Deva Deva Café is an organic oasis. Don't be surprised to see pizza, burgers, and grilled chicken on the menu of this vegan restaurant. But don't worry—the pizza is made with soy cheese; the burgers are meat-free, made with chickpeas, veggies, and herbs; and the chicken is made from soy protein. ✉ *2-15-26 Kichijoji Honcho* ☎ *042/221-6220* 💳 *No credit cards* [M] *JR Chuo Line, Kichijoji Station (North Exit)* ✣ *A1.*

If you plan to stay in town long-term, check out **Alishan** 阿里山 (🌐 *www.alishan-organics.com*), a vegetarian mail-order specialist.

🌐 *www.monsoon-cafe.jp* [M] *Tokyu Toyoko private rail line, Daikan-yama Station (Kita-guchi/North Exit)* ✣ *A5.*

$$ VEGETARIAN 🍴 **Nagi Shokudo** (なぎ食堂). This small restaurant hidden away on a little side street a short walk from Shibuya Station has mismatched chairs and tables and a selection of books and magazines you can read over a vegan meal. The ¥1,200 prix fixe lunch includes a choice of three dishes, which change daily, rice, miso soup, and a drink. In the evening, it's a great place to enjoy a light dinner in an arty atmosphere. [$] *Average main: ¥2000* ✉ *15-10 Uguisudani-cho, Shibuya-ku* ☎ *050/1043-7751* 🌐 *nagishokudo.com* 💳 *No credit cards* ⏲ *Closed Sun. evenings and holidays* [M] *JR Yamanote Line, Shibuya Station (South Exit)* ✣ *A5.*

$$$$ ECLECTIC 🍴 **Tableaux** (タブロー). This restaurant may lay on more glitz than necessary—the mural in the bar depicts the fall of Pompeii, the banquettes are upholstered in red leather, and the walls are papered in antique gold—but the service is cordial and professional and the food, which is centered on Italian cuisine and U.S. steaks, is superb. The wine list is one of the most varied in town, with everything from affordable house

wines (¥1,000 per glass) to rarities that will set you back upward of ¥100,000 a bottle. [$] *Average main: ¥8000* ✉ *B1 Sunroser Daikanyama Bldg., 11–6 Sarugaku-cho, Shibuya-ku* ☎ *03/5489–2201* 🌐 *www.tableaux.jp* ⏲ *No lunch* 👔 *Jacket and tie* [M] *Tokyu Toyoko private rail line, Daikanyama Station (Kita-guchi/North Exit)* ⊕ *A5.*

$$$ JAPANESE

🍴 **Tachigui Sakaba buri** (立食酒場buri). "One cup" sake—a single serving of sake in what looks a bit like a small mason jar—is usually bottom-of-the-barrel convenience store swill. Buri, however, turns the concept on its head by offering tasty *ji-zake* (local sake) from around Japan in the one-cup style, pairing it with a range of tapas-like servings of sashimi, yakitori, salads, and prosciutto. They also have beer on tap. Just a five-minute walk from Ebisu Station, this casual, standing-only restaurant/bar fills up quickly on weekends, so it's best to stop in early if you want to grab a table. [$] *Average main: ¥3000* ✉ *1–14–1 Ebisu-Nishi, Shibuya-ku* ☎ *03/3496–7744* 💳 *No credit cards* ⊕ *B6.*

$$$ JAPANESE

🍴 **Tenmatsu** (天松). The best seats in the house at Tenmatsu, as in any tempura-*ya*, are at the counter, where your selections are taken straight from the oil and served immediately. At this vantage point, you also get to watch the chef in action, and the good-natured, hospitable chefs and staff add to the experience. Here you can rely on a set menu or order à la carte tempura delicacies like lotus root, shrimp, *unagi* (eel), and *kisu* (smelt). There is also a branch in Nihonbashi. [$] *Average main: ¥3000* ✉ *Tokyu Department Store, 9F, 2–24–1 Shibuya, Shibuya-ku* ☎ *03/3477–4584* 🌐 *www.tenmatsu.com* [M] *JR Yamanote Line, Shibuya Station; Ginza and Hanzo-mon subway lines, Shibuya Station (connected to the station)* ⊕ *A5.*

ROPPONGI 六本木

$$$$ FRENCH

🍴 **Azure 45** (アジュール フォーティーファイブ). French restaurants in Japan have the luxury of using Japanese beef, poultry, and fresh seafood as well as vegetables that are plentiful throughout the country. On the 45th floor of the Ritz-Carlton, the restaurant makes the most of this bounty, buying seafood not only from Tsukiji Market, but also at the local Kanazawa fish port for a broader range of delicacies. Prix fixe lunch courses (from ¥5,000) come with a choice of four or five dishes from a changing monthly menu. For dinner there is a chef's tasting menu, which is paired with wine selected by the hotel's sommelier. The dining room, decorated in soft beige, white, and black, and crowned with a city skyline view, provides the appropriate tony ambience. [$] *Average main: ¥15000* ✉ *Tokyo Midtown, 9–7–1 Akasaka, Minato-ku* ☎ *03/6434–8711* 🌐 *www.ritzcarlton.com* [M] *Hibiya subway line, Roppongi Station (Exit 4A); Toei Oedo Line, Roppongi Station (Exit 7)* ⊕ *D4.*

$$$$ JAPANESE Fodor's Choice ★

🍴 **Ganchan** (がんちゃん). Smoky, noisy, and cluttered, Ganchan is exactly what the Japanese expect of their yakitori joints—restaurants that specialize in bits of charcoal-broiled chicken and vegetables. The counter here seats barely 15, and you have to squeeze to get to the chairs in back. Festival masks, paper kites, lanterns, and greeting cards from celebrity patrons adorn the walls. The cooks yell at each other, fan the grill, and serve up enormous schooners of beer. Try the *tsukune* (balls of minced chicken) and the fresh asparagus wrapped in bacon. Otherwise opt for a mixed eight-skewer set that also comes with several small side dishes (¥2,625). The place stays open until 1:30 am (midnight on Sunday). $ *Average main: ¥4000* ✉ *6–8–23 Roppongi, Minato-ku* ☎ *03/3478–0092* ⊕ *r.gnavi.co.jp/g898300* ☉ *No lunch* Ⓜ *Hibiya subway line, Roppongi Station (Exit 1A)* ✛ *D5.*

$$
AMERICAN

✕ **Homeworks** (ホームワークス). Every so often, even on foreign shores, you've got to have a burger. When the urge strikes, the Swiss-and-bacon special at Homeworks is an incomparably better choice than anything you can get at one of the global chains. Hamburgers come in three sizes on white or wheat buns, with a variety of toppings. You also find hot teriyaki chicken sandwiches, pastrami sandwiches, and vegetarian options like a soybean veggie burger or a tofu sandwich. Desserts, alas, are so-so. With its hardwood banquettes and French doors open to the street in good weather, Homeworks is a pleasant place to linger over lunch. There are also branches in Hiro-o and Shinagawa. $ *Average main: ¥1500* ✉ *1F Vesta Bldg., 1–5–8 Azabu Juban, Minato-ku* ☎ *03/3405–9884* ⊕ *www.homeworks-1.com* Ⓜ *Namboku and Oedo subway lines, Azabu Juban Station (Exit 4)* ✛ *D5.*

$$$$
FRENCH

✕ **Hortensia** (オルタシア). French restaurants in Tokyo tend to have little in terms of variety, but this restaurant in trendy Azabu Juban is the exception to the rule. The prix fixe lunch allows diners to choose any four dishes on the menu, plus a dessert. For dinner, the varieté meal includes eight courses, each with the course's main ingredient meticulously prepared in two or three ways, such as a lobster claw served with mango confit and lobster meat paired with caviar. While the menu is playful, the dining room is serious, with oversized floral arrangements and black leather banquet seats facing the glass-encased floor-to-ceiling wine collection. The excellent wine list includes new entries from California, Oregon, and Washington in addition to old French standards. $ *Average main: ¥8800* ✉ *B1F NS Azabu Juban, 3–6–2 Azabu Juban, Minato-ku* ☎ *03/5419–8455* ⊕ *www.lahortensia.com/en* ✛ *C5.*

$$$$
JAPANESE
Fodor'sChoice
★

✕ **Inakaya East** (田舎屋東). The style here is *robatayaki*, a dining experience that segues into pure theater. Inside a large U-shape counter, two cooks in traditional garb sit on cushions behind a grill, with a cornucopia of food spread out in front of them: fresh vegetables, seafood, skewers of beef and chicken. You point to what you want, and your server shouts out the order. The cook in back plucks your selection up out of the pit, prepares it, and hands it across on an 8-foot wooden paddle. Inakaya is open from 5 pm and fills up fast after 7. If you can't get a seat here, there is now another branch, Inakaya West, on the other side of Roppongi Crossing. $ *Average main: ¥9000* ✉ *1F Reine Bldg., 5–3–4 Roppongi, Minato-ku* ☎ *03/3408–5040* ⊕ *www.roppongiinakaya.jp/en* ☉ *No lunch* ⌧ *Reservations not accepted* Ⓜ *Hibiya subway line, Roppongi Station (Exit 3)* ✛ *C5.*

$$$$
VEGETARIAN

✕ **Itosho** (いと正). At this Zen restaurant near Zenpuku temple, food arrives in a procession of 13 tiny dishes, each selected according to season, texture, and color. Dinner costs between ¥8,000 and ¥10,000, and reservations must be made at least two days in advance. $ *Average main: ¥10000* ✉ *3–4–7 Azabu Juban, Minato-ku* ☎ *03/3454–6538*

No credit cards ⟨ Reservations essential Ⓜ Namboku and Oedo subway lines, Azabu Juban Station (Exit 1) ✛ C5.

$$
RAMEN

✕ **Kohmen** (光麺). With a polished, stainless-steel-and-glass interior, this always-busy ramen shop may be usual, but the food is still completely authentic and tasty. Kohmen is known for its *tonkotsu* (pork bone) soup, and yelling "tonkotsu" over the counter gets you a basic bowl of soup with noodles topped with a slice of barbecued pork. Adding *zen bu no say* (with the works) gets you a side dish of hardboiled egg, vegetables, dried seaweed, and other goodies you dump over your soup before eating. Alternatively, opt for the *tsukemen* (where you dip the noodles into a separate broth) or a spicy, sesameheavy bowl of *tantanmen* noodles. Near Roppongi Crossing, Kohmen is open until at least 6 am, making it the perfect place to stop after a night in the neighborhood's entertainment district. There are 10 other branches around Tokyo, including 2 in Shinjuku and 1 in Ueno. Ⓢ *Average main: ¥1000* ✉ *7–14–3 Roppongi, Minato-ku* ☎ *03/6406–4565* No credit cards ✛ C5.

$$$
AMERICAN

✕ **Roti** (ロティ). Billing itself a "modern American brasserie," Roti takes pride in the creative use of simple, fresh ingredients fused with Eastern and Western elements. For an appetizer, try the falafel and char-grilled vegetables on flat bread, or shoestring french fries with white truffle oil and Parmigiano-Reggiano cheese. Don't neglect dessert: the espressochocolate tart is outrageously good. Other indulgences include some 60 California wines, microbrewed ales from the famed Rogue brewery in Oregon, and Cuban cigars. There is also a fantastic weekend brunch menu and a great-value kids set menu (¥900). The best seats in the house are, in fact, outside, at one of the dozen tables around the big glass pyramid on the terrace. Ⓢ *Average main: ¥3000* ✉ *1F Piramide Bldg., 6–6–9 Roppongi, Minato-ku* ☎ *03/5785–3671* ⊕ *www.roti.jp/en* Ⓜ *Hibiya subway line, Roppongi Station (Exit 1A); Toei Oedo Line, Roppongi Station (Exit 1A)* ✛ C5.

$$$$
KOREAN

✕ **Sanko-en** (三幸園). In a neighborhood thick with Korean-barbecue joints, Sanko-en stands out as the best of the lot. Korean barbecue is a smoky affair; you cook your own food, usually thin slices of beef and vegetables, on a gas grill at your table. The *karubi* (brisket), which is accompanied by a great salad, is the best choice on the menu. If you like kimchi (spicy pickled cabbage), Sanko-en's is considered by some to be the best in town. Customers from all over agree, including those from the South Korean embassy a few blocks away. And they line up at all hours (from 11:30 am to midnight) to get in. Ⓢ *Average main: ¥6000* ✉ *1–8–7 Azabu Juban, Minato-ku* ☎ *03/3585–6306* ⊗ *Closed Wed.* ⟨ *Reservations not accepted* Ⓜ *Namboku and Oedo subway lines, Azabu Juban Station (Exit 4)* ✛ C5.

$$$$
SUSHI

✕ **Sushisho Masa** (すし匠 まさ). Diners here need a dose of luck—there are only seven counter seats and reservations fill up fast. You also need a full wallet, as high-end sushi comes at a pretty price. But for the few that manage to cross those two hurdles, Sushiso Masa gives a sublime experience. The interior is unpretentious, putting the focus squarely on the gorgeous presentations for each course. But what really sets this apart from other upscale sushi spots is the extreme quality of the cuts of fish, and the garnishes that use incredibly rare ingredients, such as *zha cai* (pickled stem of the mustard plant). $ *Average main: ¥20000* ✉ *B1F Seven Nishi-Azabu Bldg., 4–1–15 Nishi-Azabu, Minato-ku* ☎ *03/3499–9178* 🕐 *Closed Mon. No lunch* 🍴 *Reservations essential* Ⓜ *Hibiya subway line, Roppongi Station (Exit 1B); Toei Oedo Line, Roppongi Station (Exit 1A)* ✛ *C5.*

$$$
AMERICAN
FAMILY

✕ **Tony Roma's** (トニーローマ). If your kids flee in terror when a plate of sushi is placed in front of them, you may want to take them for a taste of home at this American chain world-famous for its barbecued ribs. Started in Miami in the 1970s, this casual place serves kid-sized (and much larger) portions of ribs, burgers, chicken strips, and fried shrimp. There's another branch in the Hanzomon area. $ *Average main: ¥3000* ✉ *5–4–20 Roppongi, Minato-ku* ☎ *03/3408–2748* ⊕ *www.tonyromas. jp/en* 🕐 *No lunch weekdays* Ⓜ *Hibiya subway line, Roppongi Station (Exit 3); Toei Oedo Line, Roppongi Station (Exit 3)* ✛ *C5.*

$$$$
AMERICAN

✕ **Towers Modern Bistro** (タワーズグリル.). When you're looking for a break from all the ramen, tempura, and yakitori, this restaurant on the 45th floor of the Ritz-Carlton Hotel serves a mix of international flavors that range from American to Southeast Asian to Mediterranean. A prix fixe lunch includes a choice of three items from a seasonally changing menu, and there are dinners with three, four, and five courses. A plush brunch (¥7,000) is also available weekends and holidays. Best of all, the dining room overlooks a panorama of the Tokyo Sky Tree and Tokyo Tower, which is where the eatery gets its name. $ *Average main: ¥11000* ✉ *Tokyo Midtown, 9–7–1 Akasaka, Minato-ku* ☎ *03/6434–8711* ⊕ *www.ritzcarlton.com* Ⓜ *Hibiya subway line, Roppongi Station (Exit 4A); Toei Oedo Line, Roppongi Station (Exit 7)* ✛ *D4.*

SHINJUKU 新宿

$$$$
INTERNATIONAL
Fodor's Choice
★

✕ **New York Grill & Bar** (ニューヨーク グリル＆バー). The Park Hyatt's 52nd-floor bar and restaurant may have come to international fame thanks to Sofia Coppola's *Lost in Translation*, but expats and locals have long known that it's one of the most elegant places to take in Tokyo's nighttime cityscape over a steak or cocktail. The restaurant menu showcases excellent steaks and grilled seafood in the evening, and has one of the city's best lunch buffets during the day. If the restaurant is out of your budget, come instead to the bar when it opens (before a ¥2,200 cover charge is added to your bill) and enjoy a drink as the sun sets over the city. The cover charge for the bar starts at 8 pm every day but Sunday, when it starts at 7 pm. $ *Average main: ¥20000* ✉ *Park Hyatt Tokyo, 52nd fl., 3–7–1 Nishi-Shinjuku, Shinjuku-ku* ☎ *03/5322–3458* ⊕ *www.tokyo.park.hyatt.com* 🍴 *Reservations essential* ✛ *A3.*

$$$$
JAPANESE

✕ **Ryoma no Sora Bettei** (龍馬の空別邸). Tokyoites love unique dining experiences and their own history—they can revel in both in this eatery, which is a tribute to Ryoma Sakamoto, a young hero who died while helping overthrow the feudal Tokugawa Shogunate in the 1860s. When you enter from the ultramodern streets of Shinjuku, slide off your shoes, stash them in a wooden locker, and walk by a statue of the sword-wielding Sakamoto as you step into the Japan of the past. You can sit in the main dining hall, which resembles a bustling historic inn,

3

or you can phone ahead to reserve a private tatami-mat dining room. The cuisine also harkens back to the traditional rural cooking, popular before Japan opened up to the West. The house specialty is *seiro-mushi*, a bamboo box filled with carefully arranged seafood, poultry, or meat, steamed over a pot, served piping hot, and quickly shared with everyone at the table. [$] *Average main: ¥4000* ✉ *B2 141 Shinjuku Bldg., 1–4–2 Nishi-Shinjuku, Shinjuku-ku* ☎ *03/3347–2207* ⏲ *No lunch* [M] *JR Shinjuku Station (Nishi-guchi/West Exit)* ✥ *A2.*

GREATER TOKYO

$$$$ JAPANESE Fodor's Choice ★

🍴 **Enju** (槐樹). The grand exterior and pristine banquet rooms are somewhat uninviting and overly formal at this upscale restaurant in the quiet surroundings of Shirokanedai (five minutes by taxi from Shinagawa), but the tables overlooking the 300-year-old Japanese garden provide a tranquil backdrop for an unforgettable meal. Yes, the views are stunning, but it's the food that draws locals and visitors again and again. Among the costly, seasonally changing prix fixe dinners are kaiseki, shabu-shabu, sukiyaki, and tempura, and there's also a buffet dinner. Go in the afternoon for more affordable options, such as the set sushi lunch (¥2,200) and green tea service (¥1,200). For more casual dining, the organic-focused Café Thrush, in the same complex, has an open-air terrace with a stunning view of the garden. [$] *Average main: ¥10000* ✉ *1–1–1 Shirokanedai, Minato-ku* ☎ *03/3443–3125* 🌐 *www.happo-en.com/restaurant/enju* ✍ *Reservations essential* [M] *Mita and Namboku subway lines, Shirokanedai Station (Exit 2)* ✥ *C6.*

$$ JAPANESE

🍴 **Tonki** (とんき). A family joint, with Formica-top tables, Tonki is a success that never went conglomerate or added frills to what it does best: deep-fried pork cutlets, soup, raw-cabbage salad, rice, pickles, and tea. That's the standard course, and almost everybody orders it, with good reason—it's utterly delicious. Just listen to customers in line as they put in their usual orders while a server comes around to take it. Then go ahead and join in; the wait is only about 10 minutes, but the line continues every night until the place closes at 10:45. [$] *Average main: ¥1900* ✉ *1–1–2 Shimo-Meguro, Meguro-ku* ☎ *03/3491–9928* 💳 *No credit cards* ⏲ *Closed Tues. and 3rd Mon. of month. No lunch* [M] *JR Yamanote and Namboku subway lines, Meguro Station (Nishi-guchi/West Exit)* ✥ *B6.*

$$$$ ECLECTIC

🍴 **T. Y. Harbor Brewery** (T.Y.ハーバーブルワリーレストラン). A converted warehouse on the waterfront houses this restaurant, a Tokyo hot spot for private parties. Chef David Chiddo refined his signature California-Thai cuisine at some of the best restaurants in Los Angeles and now incorporates Japanese twists into some of the dishes here. Don't miss his Thai-style red curry chicken skewers, or the shrimp cocktail with *yuzu kosho* mayonaisse. True to its name, T. Y. Harbor brews six of its own year-round beers (plus seasonal specials) in a tank that reaches all the way to the 46-foot-high ceiling. The best seats in the house are on the bay-side deck, open from May to October. Reservations are a good idea on weekends. [$] *Average main: ¥4000* ✉ *2–1–3 Higashi-Shinagawa, Shinagawa-ku* ☎ *03/5479–4555* 🌐 *www.tysons.jp/tyharbor* [M] *Tokyo Monorail or Rinkai Line, Ten-nozu Isle Station (Exit B)* ✥ *D6.*

WHERE TO STAY

Japan may have experienced more than two decades of stagnation following the collapse of the asset-inflated "bubble" economy of the late '90s, but one wouldn't know it from the steadily increasing number of high-end hotels throughout the metropolis. As land prices subsequently fell, Tokyo's developers seized the chance to construct centrally located skyscrapers. Oftentimes hotels from international brands were installed on the upper floors of these glimmering towers. This boom has complemented the spare-no-expense approach taken by many of the domestic hoteliers a decade earlier, when soaring atriums, elaborate concierge floors, and oceans of marble were all the rage. The result: Tokyo's present luxury accommodations rival those of any big city in the world.

Are there bargains to be had? Absolutely, but you'll have to do your homework, which has become an easier task with Tokyo set to host the Olympic Games in 2020, as operators are now increasingly aware of the foreign traveler on a budget. Lower-profile business and hotels are decent bets for singles or couples who do not need a lot of space, and, in addition to hostels, exchanges, and rentals, the budget-conscious traveler can utilize plenty of Japanese accommodations: *ryokan, minshuku,* "capsule" hotels, homes, and temples.

A number of boutique hotels—typified by small rooms, utilitarian concepts, and quirky, stylish elements—have popped up in Tokyo. Modern room furnishings of neutral hues are prevalent, but so are such Japanese touches as paper lanterns and tatami flooring. Reception areas are simple spaces bathed in dim lights and surrounded by earth-tone wall panels. Given that these accommodations often contain only a few floors, their locations are likely not easy to find. But when priced at around ¥20,000 a night, they can offer some of the best bargains in a city known for being incredibly expensive.

Hotel reviews have been shortened. For full information, visit Fodors.com. Use the coordinate (⊕ B2) at the end of each listing to locate a site on the Where to Stay in Tokyo map.

	WHAT IT COSTS IN YEN			
	$	$$	$$$	$$$$
Hotels	under ¥15,000	¥15,000–¥30,000	¥30,001–¥45,000	over ¥45,000

Prices in the reviews are the lowest cost of a standard double room in high season.

IMPERIAL PALACE 皇居近辺

$$$$ HOTEL Fodor's Choice ★ 🏨 **Aman Tokyo** (アマン東京). Mixing modern design with Japanese aesthetics, the Aman Tokyo is more than a hotel; it is an experience in the center of the city. **Pros:** immaculate; blend of Japanese aesthetics and modernity; wonderful views. **Cons:** expensive. [$] *Rooms from: ¥90000* ✉ *The Otemachi Tower, 1–5–6 Otemachi, Chiyoda-ku* ☎ *03/5224–3333* 🌐 *www.amanresorts.com* 🛏 *52 guest rooms, 32 suites* 🍴 *No*

meals Ⓜ *Hanzomon, Chiyoda, Tozai, and Marunouchi subway lin* *Otemachi Station (Exits C11 and C8)* ✚ *F3.*

$$$ 🏨 **Imperial Hotel** (帝国ホテル). Though not as fashionable or as spar
HOTEL ing-new as its neighbor, the Peninsula, the venerable Imperial can't beat for traditional elegance. **Pros:** an old Japanese hotel with a lc history; great service; large rooms. **Cons:** layout can be confusing; so rooms have dated interiors. Ⓢ *Rooms from: ¥31000* ✉ *1–1–1 Uc saiwai-cho, Chiyoda-ku* ☎ *03/3504–1111* ⊕ *www.imperialhotel.co* 🛏 *875 rooms, 56 suites* ❌No meals Ⓜ *Hibiya subway line, Hib Station (Exit 5)* ✚ *E4.*

$$$ 🏨 **Palace Hotel Tokyo** (パレスホテル東京). This hotel has a handsor
HOTEL refined look that sets the stage for a luxury experience. **Pros:** gr
Fodor'sChoice location; tasteful design; wonderful service; complimentary in-ro
★ Wi-Fi. **Cons:** on the pricey side; charge to use the pool. Ⓢ *Roo from: ¥45000* ✉ *1–1–1 Marunouchi, Chiyoda-ku* ☎ *03/3211–52* ⊕ *www.en.palacehoteltokyo.com* 🛏 *278 guest rooms, 12 suites* ❌ meals Ⓜ *Chiyoda, Tozai, Hanzomon subway lines, Otemachi Stati (Exit C13)* ✚ *F3.*

$$$$ 🏨 **The Peninsula Tokyo** (ザ・ペニンシュラ東京). From the staff in ca
HOTEL and sharp suits, often assisting guests from a Rolls-Royce shuttling and from Narita, to the shimmering gold glow emitting from the ▮ floors, the 24-floor Peninsula Tokyo exudes elegance and grace. **Pr** first-class room interiors; luxurious details; wonderful spa; great s vice. **Cons:** high prices; public areas can be crowded. Ⓢ *Rooms fro ¥52000* ✉ *1–8–1 Yuraku-cho, Chiyoda-ku* ☎ *03/6270–2888* ⊕ *ww peninsula.com* 🛏 *267 rooms, 47 suites* ❌No meals Ⓜ *JR Yaman Line, Yuraku-cho Station (Hibiya-guchi/Hibiya Exit); Mita, Chiyo and Hibiya subway lines, Hibiya Station (Exits A6 and A7)* ✚ *F4.*

AKIHABARA 秋葉原

$ 🏨 **Hotel Niwa Tokyo** (庭のホテル 東京). Traditional and contempora
HOTEL elements come together to make the Niwa Tokyo a prized little boutiq hotel in the middle of the city. **Pros:** affordable; quiet area; central loc tion; charming Japanese touches. **Cons:** small rooms; finding entrance a bit challenging. Ⓢ *Rooms from: ¥11000* ✉ *1–1–16 Misaki-cho, C yoda-ku* ☎ *03/3293–0028* ⊕ *www.hotelniwa.jp* 🛏 *238 rooms* ❌? meals Ⓜ *JR Chuo or Sobu lines, Suido-bashi Station (East Exit); M subway line, Suido-bashi Station (Exit A1)* ✚ *E2.*

$$ 🏨 **Tokyo Dome Hotel** (東京ドームホテル). Next to the city's most popul
HOTEL sports facility, the Tokyo Dome Hotel has a great location for spo
FAMILY fans at a comfortable price. **Pros:** convenient location; solid valu great for kids. **Cons:** no gym; in-room amenities are limited. Ⓢ *Roor from: ¥17000* ✉ *1–3–61 Koraku, Bunkyo-ku* ☎ *03/5805–2111* ⊕ *ww tokyodome-hotels.co.jp/e* 🛏 *978 guest rooms, 28 suites* ❌No mea Ⓜ *JR lines, Suidobashi Station (East Exit); Namboku and Marunou subway lines, Korakuen Station* ✚ *E1.*

UENO 上野

$ ⚏ **Ryokan Katsutaro** (旅館勝太郎). Established four decades ago, this
B&B/INN small, simple, economical inn is a 5-minute walk from the entrance to
Ueno Koen (Ueno Park) and a 10-minute walk from the Tokyo National
Museum. **Pros:** a traditional and unique Japanese experience; reasonably priced room rates; free Wi-Fi. **Cons:** no breakfast served; small
baths; some rooms have shared Japanese baths. Ⓢ *Rooms from: ¥10000*
✉ *4–16–8 Ikenohata, Taito-ku* ☎ *03/3821–9808* ⊕ *www.katsutaro.com*
⤳ *8 Japanese-style rooms, 4 with bath* ⑂ *No meals* Ⓜ *Chiyoda subway
line, Nezu Station (Exit 2)* ✛ *F1.*

$ ⚏ **Sawanoya Ryokan** (澤の屋旅館). The shitamachi sub-area of Ueno is
B&B/INN known for its down-to-earth friendliness, which you get in full mea-
sure at Sawanoya. **Pros:** traditional Japanese experience; affordable
rates; friendly management. **Cons:** rooms somewhat small; a bit of a
hike to the subway station; must book well in advance; many rooms
share Japanese baths. Ⓢ *Rooms from: ¥10000* ✉ *2–3–11 Yanaka, Taito-
ku* ☎ *03/3822–2251* ⊕ *www.sawanoya.com* ⤳ *10 rooms, 2 with bath*
⑂ *No meals* Ⓜ *Chiyoda subway line, Nezu Station (Exit 1)* ✛ *F1.*

ASAKUSA 浅草

$$ ⚏ **Asakusa View Hotel** (浅草ビューホテル). The box-shape Asakusa View
HOTEL is the largest Western-style hotel in the traditional Asakusa area. **Pros:**
FAMILY affordable; located in a historic temple area; free in-room Wi-Fi. **Cons:**
room interiors generally basic; not near central Tokyo; only one key
provided per room. Ⓢ *Rooms from: ¥16000* ✉ *3–17–1 Nishi-Asakusa,
Asakusa* ☎ *03/3847–1111* ⊕ *www.viewhotels.co.jp/asakusa* ⤳ *323
rooms, 3 suites* ⑂ *No meals* Ⓜ *Ginza subway line, Tawara-machi Sta-
tion (Exit 3)* ✛ *H1.*

$$ ⚏ **The Gate Hotel Kaminarimon** (ザ・ゲートホテル雷門). This relative new-
HOTEL comer to the historic Asakusa area presents a certain stylish flair, start-
Fodor's Choice ing from the entrance, where an elevator whisks you up 13 floors to the
★ beautiful, glass-walled lobby. **Pros:** historic area; surrounded with great
dining options; lovely views. **Cons:** rooms small by Western standards;
not exactly a central location; can be crowded on weekends. Ⓢ *Rooms
from: ¥16000* ✉ *2–16–11 Kaminarimon, Taito-ku* ☎ *03/5826–3877*
⊕ *www.gate-hotel.jp* ⤳ *134 guest rooms, 3 suites* ⑂ *No meals* Ⓜ *Ginza
and Asakusa subway lines, Asakusa Station (Exit 2)* ✛ *H1.*

$$ ⚏ **Ryokan Asakusa Shigetsu** (旅館浅草 指月). Just off Nakamise-dori
B&B/INN and inside the Senso-ji grounds, this small inn, with both Japanese-
and Western-style rooms, could not be better located for a visit to
the temple. **Pros:** affordable rooms; located in a historic temple area;
close to subway station. **Cons:** not convenient to central Tokyo; some
guests may feel uncomfortable with futon beds and communal Japa-
nese bathing. Ⓢ *Rooms from: ¥16000* ✉ *1–31–11 Asakusa, Asakusa*
☎ *03/3843–2345* ⊕ *www.shigetsu.com/e/index.html* ⤳ *15 Japanese-
style rooms, 6 Western-style rooms* ⑂ *No meals* Ⓜ *Ginza subway line,
Asakusa Station (Exit 1/Kaminari-mon Exit)* ✛ *H1.*

3

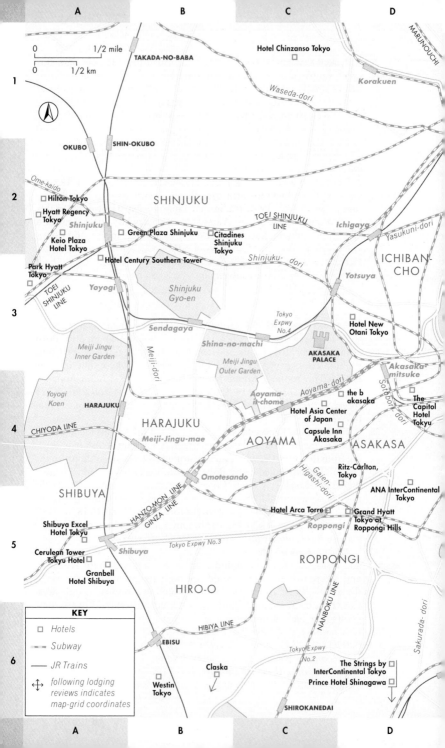

A

0 ——— 1/2 mile
0 ——— 1/2 km

1

TAKADA-NO-BABA

OKUBO SHIN-OKUBO

Ome-kaido

2

SHINJUKU

□ Hilton Tokyo

□ Hyatt Regency Tokyo

Shinjuku

□ Keio Plaza Hotel Tokyo

□ Green Plaza Shinjuku

□ Citadines Shinjuku Tokyo

TOEI SHINJUKU LINE

□ Hotel Century Southern Tower

Shinjuku-dori

□ Park Hyatt Tokyo

TOEI SHINJUKU LINE

Yoyogi

Shinjuku Gyo-en

3

Sendagaya

Shina-no-machi

Meiji Jingu Inner Garden

Meiji-dori

Meiji Jingu Outer Garden

Yoyogi Koen

HARAJUKU

CHIYODA LINE

4

HARAJUKU

Meiji-Jingu-mae

AOYAMA

Aoyama-it-chome

Aoyama-dori

□ the b akasaka

□ Hotel Asia Center of Japan

□ Capsule Inn Akasaka

ASAKASA

SHIBUYA

Omotesando

HANZO-MON LINE

GINZA LINE

Gaien-Higashi-dori

Ritz-Carlton, Tokyo □

□ ANA InterContinental Tokyo

□ Shibuya Excel Hotel Tokyu

□ Hotel Arca Torre

□ Grand Hyatt Tokyo at Roppongi Hills

5

□ Cerulean Tower Tokyu Hotel

Shibuya

Tokyo Expwy No.3

Roppongi

ROPPONGI

□ Granbell Hotel Shibuya

HIRO-O

NANBORU LINE

KEY

□ *Hotels*

┅ *Subway*

── *JR Trains*

↔ *following lodging reviews indicates map-grid coordinates*

HIBIYA LINE

6

EBISU

Claska □

Tokyo Expwy No.2

□ The Strings by InterContinental Tokyo

□ Westin Tokyo

□ Prince Hotel Shinagawa

SHIROKANEDAI

A   **B**   **C**   **D**

Waseda-dori

MARUNOUCHI

□ Hotel Chinzanso Tokyo

Korakuen

Ichigaya

Yasukuni-dori

ICHIBAN-CHO

Yotsuya

Tokyo Expwy No.4

□ Hotel New Otani Tokyo

AKASAKA PALACE

Akasaka-mitsuke

Sotobori-dori

□ The Capitol Hotel Tokyu

Sakurada-dori

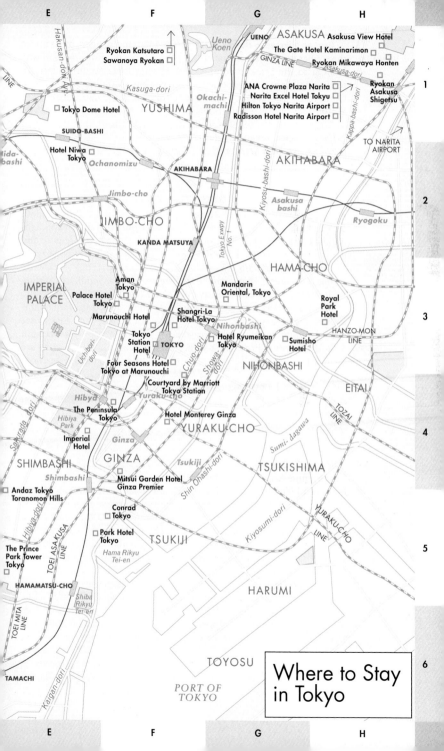

Where to Stay in Tokyo

$ B&B/INN 🏨 **Ryokan Mikawaya Honten** (旅館三河屋本店). In the heart of Asakusa, this concrete ryokan is just behind the Kaminari-mon, the gateway leading to the Senso-ji complex. **Pros:** affordable accommodations; traditional Japanese experience; interesting shopping in the area. **Cons:** futons and tatami might not be suitable for those accustomed to Western-style beds; small rooms; friendly staff struggles with English. [$] *Rooms from: ¥9700* ✉ *1–30–12 Asakusa, Asakusa* ☎ *03/3841–8954* 🌐 *www.asakusamikawaya.com* 🛏 *15 rooms* 🍴 *No meals* [M] *Ginza subway line, Asakusa Station (Exit 1/Kaminari-mon Exit)* ✣ *H1.*

SHIODOME 汐留

$$$$ HOTEL 🏨 **Conrad Tokyo** (コンラッド東京). The Conrad, part of the Hilton family, welcomes you to the space age with a Japanese twist. **Pros:** modern design; fantastic bay view; fine restaurants. **Cons:** very expensive; finding the entrance to the elevator is troublesome; charge to use pool and gym. [$] *Rooms from: ¥50000* ✉ *1–9–1 Higashi-Shimbashi, Minato-ku, Shiodome* ☎ *03/6388–8000* 🌐 *www.conradtokyo.co.jp* 🛏 *222 rooms, 68 suites* 🍴 *No meals* [M] *JR Yamanote Line, Shimbashi Station (Shiodome Exit); Oedo subway line, Shiodome Station (Exit 9)* ✣ *F5.*

$$ HOTEL Fodor's Choice ★ 🏨 **Park Hotel Tokyo** (パークホテル東京). Comfortable beds, large bathrooms, and sweeping panoramas of Tokyo or the bay—it's easy to see why the guest rooms of this reasonably priced "artist" hotel remain a tourist favorite. **Pros:** great value; guest rooms and public areas are stylish; excellent concierge service. **Cons:** small rooms; few in-room frills; no pool or gym. [$] *Rooms from: ¥17000* ✉ *1–7–1 Higashi Shimbashi, Minato-ku* ☎ *03/6252–1111* 🌐 *www.parkhoteltokyo.com* 🛏 *272 rooms, 1 suite* 🍴 *No meals* [M] *JR Yamanote Line, Shimbashi Station (Shiodome Exit); Oedo subway line, Shiodome Station (Exit 10)* ✣ *E5.*

NIHOMBASHI 日本橋

$$$$ HOTEL Fodor's Choice ★ 🏨 **Mandarin Oriental, Tokyo** (マンダリン オリエンタル 東京). Occupying the top nine floors of the glistening Nihombashi Mitsui Tower, this hotel is a blend of harmony and outright modernity. **Pros:** wonderful spa and concierge service; nice city views; attractive room interiors. **Cons:** pricey; quiet area on the weekends; no pool. [$] *Rooms from: ¥50000* ✉ *2–1–1 Nihombashi Muromachi, Chuo-ku* ☎ *03/3270–8800* 🌐 *www.mandarinoriental.com/tokyo* 🛏 *157 rooms, 21 suites* 🍴 *No meals* [M] *Ginza and Hanzo-mon subway lines, Mitsukoshi-mae Station (Exit A7)* ✣ *G3.*

$$ HOTEL 🏨 **Royal Park Hotel** (ロイヤルパークホテル). A passageway connects this hotel to the Tokyo City Air Terminal, where you can easily catch a bus to Narita Airport, making the Royal Park a great one-night stopover option. **Pros:** convenient airport access; nice lobby; warm, friendly service. **Cons:** not located near downtown; immediate area deserted on weekends. [$] *Rooms from: ¥18000* ✉ *2–1–1 Nihombashi, Kakigara-cho, Chuo-ku* ☎ *03/3667–1111* 🌐 *www.rph.co.jp* 🛏 *398 rooms, 9 suites* 🍴 *No meals* [M] *Hanzo-mon subway line, Suitengu-mae Station (Exit 4)* ✣ *H3.*

$ 🏨 **Sumisho Hotel** (住庄ほてる). Set in a down-to-earth, friendly neigh-

HOTEL borhood, this hotel is popular with budget-minded foreign visitors who prefer to stay near the small Japanese restaurants and bars of the Ningyo-cho area of Nihombashi. **Pros:** nicely priced; friendly staff; neighborhood restaurants and pubs have great food for a good price. **Cons:** small rooms and baths; not particularly stylish; quiet area on weekends. $ *Rooms from: ¥8000* ✉ *9–14 Nihombashi-Kobunacho, Chuo-ku* ☎ *03/3661–4603* ⊕ *www.sumisho-hotel.co.jp* 🛏 *83 rooms* 🍴 *No meals* Ⓜ *Hibiya and Asakusa subway lines, Ningyo-cho Station (Exit A5)* ✛ *G3.*

3

GINZA 銀座

$ 🏨 **Hotel Monterey Ginza** (ホテルモントレー銀座). Yes, the faux-stone exte-

HOTEL rior that attempts to replicate 20th-century Europe is a bit cheesy, but the Monterey remains a bargain in the middle of Ginza. **Pros:** multiple shopping choices in area; central location; reasonable prices considering the area. **Cons:** design lacks elegance; rooms are a tad small and a bit outdated; in-hotel dining options are limited. $ *Rooms from: ¥10000* ✉ *1–10–18 Ginza, Chuo-ku* ☎ *03/3544–7111* ⊕ *www.hotelmonterey. co.jp/ginza* 🛏 *224 rooms* 🍴 *No meals* Ⓜ *Ginza subway line, Ginza Station (Exit A13)* ✛ *F4.*

$$ 🏨 **Mitsui Garden Hotel Ginza Premier** (三井ガーデンホテル銀座プレミア).

HOTEL A winning combination—chic and reasonable—this hotel occupies the top of the 38-floor Nihonbashi Mitsui Tower at the edge of bustling Ginza. **Pros:** affordable; sharp design; convenient location; plenty of nearby shopping. **Cons:** small rooms; in-hotel restaurant a tad pricey; geared toward business rather than leisure travelers. $ *Rooms from: ¥19000* ✉ *8–13–1 Ginza, Chūō-ku, Ginza* ☎ *03/3543–1131* ⊕ *www. gardenhotels.co.jp/eng/ginzapremier* 🛏 *361 rooms* 🍴 *No meals* Ⓜ *Ginza subway line, Ginza Station (Exit A3) or JR Shimbashi Station (Ginza Exit)* ✛ *F4.*

MARUNOUCHI 丸の内

$$$ 🏨 **Courtyard by Marriott Tokyo Station** (コートヤード・バイ・マリオット 東京

HOTEL ステーション). Situated on the first four floors of the sleek Kyobashi Trust Tower, the Courtyard by Marriott is a convenient option for business travelers. **Pros:** convenient; many nearby dining options; attentive staff. **Cons:** small rooms; closet space limited. $ *Rooms from: ¥32000* ✉ *2–1–3 Kyobashi, Chuo-ku* ☎ *03/5488–3923* ⊕ *www.cytokyo.com* 🛏 *150 guest rooms* 🍴 *No meals* Ⓜ *Ginza subway line, Kyobashi Station (Exit 1); JR lines, Tokyo Station (Yaesu Exit)* ✛ *F4.*

$$$$ 🏨 **Four Seasons Hotel Tokyo at Marunouchi** (フォーシーズンズホテル丸の内

HOTEL 東京). A departure from the typical grand scale of most Four Seasons

Fodor's Choice properties, the Marunouchi branch, set within the glistening Pacific

★ Century Place, has the feel of a boutique hotel. **Pros:** supreme luxury; convenient airport access; central location; helpful, English-speaking staff. **Cons:** high priced; the only views are those of nearby Tokyo Station. $ *Rooms from: ¥50000* ✉ *1–11–1 Marunouchi, Chiyoda-ku*

☎ *03/5222–7222* 🌐 *www.fourseasons.com/marunouchi* 🛏 *48 rooms, 9 suites* 🍴 *No meals* [M] *JR Tokyo Station (Yaesu South Exit)* ✣ *F3.*

$$ HOTEL Fodor's Choice ★ 🏨 **Hotel Ryumeikan Tokyo** (ホテル龍名館東京). One of the most affordable hotels near Tokyo Station (a mere three-minute walk away), the Ryumeikan is a great option for the business traveler or those making side trips outside the city. **Pros:** great, convenient location; wonderful restaurant; English-speaking staff. **Cons:** busy area during the week; rooms can feel small. [$] *Rooms from: ¥19000* ✉ *1–3–22 Yaesu, Chuo-ku* ☎ *03/3271–0971* 🌐 *www.ryumeikan-tokyo.jp/english* 🛏 *134 guest rooms, 1 suite* 🍴 *No meals* [M] *JR Tokyo Station (Yaesu North Exit)* ✣ *F3.*

$$ HOTEL 🏨 **Marunouchi Hotel** (丸ノ内ホテル). Convenience is one reason to choose the Marunouchi Hotel, occupying the upper 11 floors of the Marunouchi Oazo Building and joining Tokyo Station via an underground walkway. **Pros:** convenient airport access; central location; helpful concierge. **Cons:** designed for business travelers; rooms are smallish; limited dining choices. [$] *Rooms from: ¥24000* ✉ *1–6–3 Marunouchi, Chiyoda-ku* ☎ *03/3217–1111* 🌐 *www.marunouchi-hotel.co.jp* 🛏 *204 rooms, 1 suite* 🍴 *No meals* [M] *JR Tokyo Station (Marunouchi North Exit)* ✣ *F3.*

$$$$ HOTEL 🏨 **Shangri-La Hotel Tokyo** (シャングリ・ラ ホテル 東京). The Shangri-La Hotel Tokyo, which opened in 2009, boasts high-end luxury, lavish interiors, and superb views of Tokyo Bay and the cityscape from the top 11 floors of Marunouchi Trust Tower Main, a 37-floor building conveniently located near Tokyo Station. **Pros:** convenient location; lavish service. **Cons:** pricey; located in a business district; entrance might be hard to find. [$] *Rooms from: ¥51000* ✉ *Marunouchi Trust Tower Main, 1–8–3 Marunouchi, Chiyoda-ku* ☎ *03/6739–7888* 🌐 *www.shangri-la.com* 🛏 *184 rooms, 16 suites* 🍴 *No meals* [M] *JR Tokyo Station (Yaesu North Exit)* ✣ *F3.*

$$$ HOTEL 🏨 **Tokyo Station Hotel** (東京ステーションホテル). Convenience and nostalgia come together at this hotel, located inside the busy Tokyo train station, a grand building that recently refurbished its redbrick exterior. **Pros:** convenient location; easy access to shopping; lovely, historic setting; helpful English-speaking staff. **Cons:** rooms on the small side; views from some rooms limited. [$] *Rooms from: ¥45000* ✉ *1–9–1 Marunouchi, Chiyoda-ku* ☎ *03/5220–1111* 🌐 *www.tokyostationhotel.jp* 🛏 *145 guest rooms, 5 suites* 🍴 *No meals* [M] *JR Line, Tokyo Station (South Exit)* ✣ *F3.*

AOYAMA 青山 AND AKASAKA 赤坂

$$$ HOTEL 🏨 **ANA InterContinental Tokyo** (インターコンチネンタルホテル東京 *ANA*). With a central location and modest pricing, the ANA is a great choice for the business traveler, and its ziggurat-atrium points to the heyday of the power lunch: the mid-1980s. **Pros:** great concierge; wonderful city views; spacious lobby. **Cons:** charge for in-room Internet; room bathrooms a bit small. [$] *Rooms from: ¥31000* ✉ *1–12–33 Akasaka, Minato-ku* ☎ *03/3505–1111* 🌐 *www.anaintercontinental-tokyo.jp* 🛏 *801 rooms, 43 suites* 🍴 *No meals* [M] *Ginza and Namboku subway lines, Tameike-Sanno Station (Exit 13); Namboku subway line, Roppongi-itchome Station (Exit 3)* ✣ *D4.*

$$$$ 🏨 **Andaz Tokyo Toranomon Hills** (アンダーズ東京). In 2014, Hyatt brought
HOTEL its high-end boutique brand Andaz to the Toranomon Hills complex
Fodor's Choice with great fanfare. **Pros:** great bar; amazing views; huge bathrooms.
★ **Cons:** finding entrance can be troublesome; expensive. Ⓢ *Rooms from:*
¥49000 ✉ *1–23–4 Toranomon, Minato-ku* ☎ *03/6830–1234* ⊕ *www.*
tokyo.andaz.hyatt.jp ➥ *156 guest rooms, 8 suites* ⏐⊙⏐ *No meals* Ⓜ *Ginza*
subway line, Toranomon Station (Exit 1) ✛ *E5.*

$ 🏨 **the b akasaka** (ザ・ビー赤坂). Part of a boutique chain that promotes
HOTEL its ability to deliver the five *b*s—bed, breakfast, balance, business, and
benefits—the b akasaka is a simple, stylish option with great value. **Pros:**
near large entertainment area; affordable. **Cons:** difficult to find; single
rooms can feel confining. Ⓢ *Rooms from: ¥14000* ✉ *7–6–13 Akasaka,*
Minato-ku ☎ *03/3586–0811* ⊕ *www.theb-hotels.com* ➥ *156 rooms*
⏐⊙⏐ *No meals* Ⓜ *Chiyoda subway line, Akasaka Station (Exit 3B)* ✛ *D4.*

$$$ 🏨 **The Capitol Hotel Tokyu** (ザ・キャピトルホテル東急). Everything old
HOTEL is new again: the Capitol, once a boxy 29-floor commercial complex
Fodor's Choice designed by architect Kengo Kuma and run by Hilton, has a long his-
★ tory that includes hosting The Beatles. **Pros:** convenient location; beau-
tiful and spacious pool; no charge for Wi-Fi throughout hotel. **Cons:**
pricey; government district might not appeal to tourists. Ⓢ *Rooms from:*
¥33000 ✉ *2–10–3 Nagata-cho, Minato-ku* ☎ *03/3503–0109* ⊕ *www.*
capitolhoteltokyu.com ➥ *238 rooms, 13 suites* ⏐⊙⏐ *No meals* Ⓜ *Ginza*
and Namboku subway lines, Tameike-Sanno Station (Exit 5) ✛ *D4.*

$ 🏨 **Capsule Inn Akasaka** (かぷせるイン赤坂). Travelers looking for a
HOTEL budget option—or adventurous souls wanting a full-immersion expe-
rience—seek out the Capsule Inn. After changing out of your clothes
(for which lockers are provided), bathing in the communal bath, and
donning your yukata, you locate your accommodations, one of the
chambers stacked on each floor not unlike pet carriers at a kennel. **Pros:**
Wi-Fi; convenient location; unique experience. **Cons:** not for the claus-
trophobic; few services; women not allowed. Ⓢ *Rooms from: ¥3500*
✉ *6–14–1 Akasaka, Minato-ku* ☎ *03/3588–1811* ⊕ *www.marroad.jp/*
capsule ➥ *201 capsules* ⏐⊙⏐ *No meals* Ⓜ *Chiyoda subway line, Akasaka*
Station (Exit 6) ✛ *D4.*

$$ 🏨 **Hotel New Otani Tokyo** (ホテルニューオータニ東京). A bustling com-
HOTEL plex in the center of Tokyo—restaurants and shopping arcades beneath
the sixth-floor lobby swarm with crowds—the New Otani can feel frantic, but its best feature, a spectacular 10-acre Japanese garden, readily
visible from the appropriately named Garden Lounge, helps guests find
sanctuary. **Pros:** beautiful garden; first-rate concierge; outdoor pool.
Cons: complex layout could be off-putting; public areas a bit dated.
Ⓢ *Rooms from: ¥20000* ✉ *4–1 Kioi-cho, Chiyoda-ku* ☎ *03/3265–1111*
⊕ *www.newotanihotels.com/tokyo* ➥ *1,418 rooms, 61 suites* ⏐⊙⏐ *No*
meals Ⓜ *Ginza and Marunouchi subway lines, Akasaka-mitsuke Sta-*
tion (Exit 7) ✛ *D3.*

SHIBUYA 渋谷

$$$ 🏨 **Cerulean Tower Tokyu Hotel** (セルリアンタワー東急ホテル). Perched on
HOTEL a slope above Shibuya's chaos, the Cerulean Tower has a cavernous yet
bustling lobby filled with plenty of attentive, English-speaking staffers.

3

Pros: friendly, attentive service; great city views; convenient location. **Cons:** pricey rates; Shibuya is one of Tokyo's more crowded areas; building fronts a very busy street. Ⓢ *Rooms from: ¥31000* ✉ *26–1 Sakuragaoka-cho, Shibuya-ku* ☎ *03/3476–3000* ⊕ *www.ceruleantower-hotel.com* ⤳ *402 rooms, 9 suites* ⦿*No meals* Ⓜ *JR Shibuya Station (South Exit)* ✛ *A5.*

$ ⌂ **Granbell Hotel Shibuya** (渋谷グランベルホテル). Location, location, HOTEL location—that's the Granbell, and with a minimalist pop-art style to boot. **Pros:** reasonable rates; great location; funky, fun design; free Wi-Fi throughout property. **Cons:** small rooms; neighborhood can be noisy; difficult to find hotel entrance. Ⓢ *Rooms from: ¥14000* ✉ *15–17 Sakuragaoka–cho, Shibuya-ku* ☎ *03/5457–2681* ⊕ *www.granbellhotel. jp* ⤳ *98 rooms, 7 suites* ⦿*No meals* Ⓜ *JR Shibuya Station (West Exit)* ✛ *A5.*

$$ ⌂ **Shibuya Excel Hotel Tokyu** (渋谷エクセル東急). The key to this unre-HOTEL markable but very convenient hotel within the towering Mark City complex is access: local shopping and cheap dining options are aplenty, Shinjuku is a five-minute train ride to the north, and the Narita Express departs from nearby Shibuya Station frequently each morning. **Pros:** affordable; convenient location; friendly staff. **Cons:** small, uninspired rooms; crowds in the area can be intimidating. Ⓢ *Rooms from: ¥24000* ✉ *1–12–2 Dogenzaka, Shibuya-ku* ☎ *03/5457–0109* ⊕ *shibuya-e. tokyuhotels.com* ⤳ *407 rooms, 1 suite* ⦿*No meals* Ⓜ *JR Shibuya Station (Hachiko Exit)* ✛ *A5.*

ROPPONGI 六本木

$$$$ ⌂ **Grand Hyatt Tokyo at Roppongi Hills** (グランドハイアット東京). Japa-HOTEL nese refinement and a contemporary design come together perfectly at the Grand Hyatt—a tasteful and well-appointed hotel in the middle of Roppongi, one of Tokyo's top entertainment areas. **Pros:** great spa; wide range of restaurants; stunning rooms. **Cons:** pricey; easy to get lost in the building's complicated layout. Ⓢ *Rooms from: ¥50000* ✉ *6–10–3 Roppongi, Minato-ku, Roppongi* ☎ *03/4333–1234* ⊕ *www. tokyo.grand.hyatt.com* ⤳ *359 rooms, 28 suites* ⦿*No meals* Ⓜ *Hibiya subway line, Roppongi Station (Exit 1A); Oedo subway line, Roppongi Station (Exit 3)* ✛ *D5.*

$$ ⌂ **Hotel Arca Torre** (ホテルアルカトーレ). Sitting on a coveted location in HOTEL the heart of one of Tokyo's premier nightlife quarters, this European-inspired hotel is just a few minutes' walk from the Tokyo Midtown and Roppongi Hills shopping-and-entertainment complexes. **Pros:** affordable; convenient access to nightlife; free Wi-Fi. **Cons:** no room service; no closets; small rooms; neighborhood's bars and clubs make the area noisy. Ⓢ *Rooms from: ¥15000* ✉ *6–1–23 Roppongi, Minato-ku, Roppongi* ☎ *03/3404–5111* ⊕ *www.arktower.co.jp/arcatorre* ⤳ *76 rooms* ⦿*No meals* Ⓜ *Hibiya and Oedo subway lines, Roppongi Station (Exit 3)* ✛ *C5.*

$ ⌂ **Hotel Asia Center of Japan** (ホテルアジア会館). Established mainly for HOTEL Asian students and travelers on limited budgets, these accommodations have become popular due to their good value and easy access (a 15-minute walk) to the nightlife of Roppongi. **Pros:** affordable; great area for those who love the nightlife; free Wi-Fi. **Cons:** just one restaurant; no room service; small rooms. $ *Rooms from: ¥12000* ⊠ *8–10–32 Aka-saka, Minato-ku, Roppongi* ☎ *03/3402–6111* ⊕ *www.asiacenter.or.jp* ⤸ *173 rooms* ⦶ *No meals* Ⓜ *Ginza and Hanzo-mon subway lines, Aoyama-itchome Station (Exit 4)* ✛ *C4.*

$$ 🏨 **The Prince Park Tower Tokyo** (ザ・プリンス パークタワー東京). The sur-
HOTEL rounding parkland and the absence of any adjacent buildings make
FAMILY the Park Tower a peaceful retreat in the middle of the city. **Pros:** park nearby; well-stocked convenience store on first floor; fun extras like a bowling alley and pool. **Cons:** a tad isolated; extra fee for pool and fitness center; few dining options in immediate area. $ *Rooms from: ¥18000* ⊠ *4–8–1 Shiba-koen, Minato-ku* ☎ *03/5400–1111* ⊕ *www. princehotels.com/en/parktower* ⤸ *580 rooms, 23 suites* ⦶ *No meals* Ⓜ *Oedo subway line, Akabanebashi Station (Akabanebashi Exit)* ✛ *E5.*

$$$$ 🏨 **The Ritz-Carlton, Tokyo** (ザ・リッツ・カールトン東京). Installed in the
HOTEL top floors of the 53-story Midtown Tower, the Ritz-Carlton provides
Fodor's Choice Tokyo's most luxurious accommodations squarely in the middle of the
★ city. **Pros:** great views of Tokyo; romantic setting; convenient access to nightlife; stunning rooms loaded with luxurious goodies. **Cons:** high prices; immediate area is somewhat grungy. $ *Rooms from: ¥51000* ⊠ *9–7–1 Akasaka, Minato-ku* ☎ *03/3423–8000* ⊕ *www.ritzcarlton.com* ⤸ *212 rooms, 36 suites* ⦶ *No meals* Ⓜ *Hibiya subway line, Roppongi Station (Exit 4); Oedo subway line, Roppongi Station (Exit 7)* ✛ *D4.*

SHINJUKU 新宿

$$ 🏨 **Citadines Shinjuku Tokyo** (シタディーン新宿). Part hotel, part serviced
HOTEL apartments catering to short- or long-term travelers, the Citadines Shin-juku is a sunny venue of superb value. **Pros:** away from the congestion of Shinjuku Station; sizable rooms; very clean; cheerful design. **Cons:** a little difficult to find; dining options limited on the premises. $ *Rooms from: ¥16000* ⊠ *1–28–13 Shinjuku, Shinjuku-ku* ☎ *03/5379–7208* ⊕ *www.citadines.jp* ⤸ *160 apartments* ⦶ *No meals* Ⓜ *Marunouchi subway line, Shinjuku Gyoemmae Station (Exit 2)* ✛ *B2.*

$ 🏨 **Green Plaza Shinjuku** (グリーンプラザ新宿). Budget travelers in Shin-
HOTEL juku willing to throw claustrophobia to the wind can settle in for a night at the Green Plaza, a capsule hotel in the entertainment dis-trict of Kabuki-cho. **Pros:** a top choice for a capsule hotel as it's fairly priced; convenient location; public bath area has mineral baths and saunas. **Cons:** small and limited accommodations; noisy neighborhood. $ *Rooms from: ¥4500* ⊠ *1–29–2 Kabuki-cho, Shinjuku-ku* ☎ *03/3207–5411* ⊕ *www.hgpshinjuku.jp* ⊟ *No credit cards* ⤸ *660 capsules (630 for men, 30 for women)* ⦶ *No meals* Ⓜ *Shinjuku Station (Higashi-guchi/East Exit)* ✛ *A2.*

$$ 🏨 **Hilton Tokyo** (ヒルトン東京). A short walk from the megalithic Tokyo
HOTEL Metropolitan Government Office, the Hilton is a particular favorite of Western business travelers. **Pros:** great gym; convenient location; free shuttle to Shinjuku Station. **Cons:** hotel lobby can get busy; res-taurants are pricey. $ *Rooms from: ¥26000* ⊠ *6–6–2 Nishi-Shinjuku, Shinjuku-ku* ☎ *03/3344–5111* ⊕ *www3.hilton.com* ⤸ *683 rooms, 128*

suites ❐No meals Ⓜ *Shinjuku Station (Nishi-guchi/West Exit); Marunouchi subway line, Nishi-Shinjuku Station (Exit C8); Oedo subway line, Tocho-mae Station (all exits)* ✛ *A2.*

$$ Ⓣ **Hotel Century Southern Tower** (小田急ホテルセンチュリーサザンタワー).
HOTEL   The sparse offerings at the Century (i.e., no room or bell service, empty refrigerators) are more than compensated for by the hotel's reasonable prices and wonderful location atop the 35-floor Odakyu Southern Tower, minutes by foot from Shinjuku Station. **Pros:** affordable; convenient location; great views; simple but tasteful rooms. **Cons:** room amenities are basic; no room service or pool. Ⓢ *Rooms from: ¥19000* ✉ *2–2–1 Yoyogi, Shibuya-ku* ☎ *03/5354–0111* ⊕ *www. southerntower.co.jp* ✍ *375 rooms* ❐No meals Ⓜ *Shinjuku Station (Minami-guchi/South Exit); Oedo and Shinjuku subway lines, Shinjuku Station (Exit A1)* ✛ *A3.*

$$ Ⓣ **Hyatt Regency Tokyo** (ハイアットリージェンシー 東京). Set amid Shinjuku's
HOTEL   skyscrapers, this hotel has the trademark Hyatt atrium-style lobby: seven stories high, with open-glass elevators soaring upward and three huge chandeliers suspended from above. **Pros:** friendly staff; affordable room rates; spacious rooms. **Cons:** rather generic exteriors and common areas; restaurant options are limited outside hotel. Ⓢ *Rooms from: ¥23000* ✉ *2–7–2 Nishi-Shinjuku, Shinjuku-ku* ☎ *03/3348–1234* ⊕ *tokyo.regency.hyatt.com* ✍ *726 rooms, 18 suites* ❐No meals Ⓜ *Marunouchi subway line, Nishi-Shinjuku Station (Exit C8); Oedo subway line, Tocho-mae Station (all exits)* ✛ *A2.*

$$ Ⓣ **Keio Plaza Hotel Tokyo** (京王プラザホテル). Composed of two cereal-
HOTEL   box-shape towers, this hotel has a reputation as a business destination that serves its guests with a classic touch. **Pros:** nice pools; affordable nightly rates; convenient location. **Cons:** bland exteriors and common areas; restaurant options outside hotel limited; crowded if there are conventions or large groups in residence. Ⓢ *Rooms from: ¥18000* ✉ *2–2–1 Nishi-Shinjuku, Shinjuku-ku* ☎ *03/3344–0111* ⊕ *www.keioplaza.com* ✍ *1,414 rooms, 22 suites* ❐No meals Ⓜ *Shinjuku Station (Nishi-guchi/West Exit)* ✛ *A2.*

$$$$ Ⓣ **Park Hyatt Tokyo** (パークハイアット東京). Sofia Coppola's classic film
HOTEL   *Lost in Translation* was a love letter to this hotel, and when the ele-
Fodor's Choice vator inside the sleek, Kenzo Tange–designed Shinjuku Park Tower
★   whisks you to the atrium lounge with a panorama of Shinjuku through floor-to-ceiling windows, you may feel smitten as well. **Pros:** city icon that stays relevant; wonderful room interiors; great skyline views; top-class restaurants. **Cons:** pricey; somewhat remote; taxi is best way to get to Shinjuku Station. Ⓢ *Rooms from: ¥52000* ✉ *3–7–1–2 Nishi-Shinjuku, Shinjuku-ku* ☎ *03/5322–1234* ⊕ *www.tokyo.park. hyatt.com* ✍ *154 rooms, 23 suites* ❐No meals Ⓜ *JR Shinjuku Station (Nishi-guchi/West Exit)* ✛ *A3.*

GREATER TOKYO

$$ Ⓣ **Claska** (クラスカ). Hip, modern, and utterly Japanese, the Claska
HOTEL   provides a premier boutique hotel experience. **Pros:** stylish Japanese aesthetics in a modern setting; great staff; cool gift shop. **Cons:** five minutes by taxi from Meguro Station; dining options in immediate area are

DID YOU KNOW?

In the 1970s the first major skyscraper construction began in Shinjuku, a then undeveloped tract of land at the city's edge. Today the neighborhood is considered the new city center, with its collection of malls and government buildings, as well as one of the world's busiest train stations. The Gyoen National Garden provides a calm space to recover from the densely packed, bustling crowds.

limited; often fully booked. [$] *Rooms from: ¥21000* ⊠ *1–3–18 Chuo-cho, Meguro-ku* ☎ *03/3719–8121* ⊕ *www.claska.com* ⊅ *15 rooms, 3 suites* |⊙| *No meals* [M] *Toyoko Line, Gakugeidaigaku Station (Higashi-guchi/East Exit); 5 mins by taxi from JR Meguro Station* ⊹ *B6.*

$$$
HOTEL

⌂ **Hotel Chinzanso Tokyo** (ホテル椿山荘東京). Set inside a 17-acre garden, the elegant and European Hotel Chinzanso is a sheltered haven in Tokyo's busy metropolis and a former estate of an imperial prince. **Pros:** gorgeous, sprawling grounds; huge bathrooms; glamorous pool. **Cons:** limited dining options in immediate area; isolated location; room interiors a tad dated. [$] *Rooms from: ¥32000* ⊠ *2–10–8 Sekiguchi, Bunkyo-ku* ☎ *03/3943–1111* ⊕ *www.hotel-chinzanso-tokyo.com* ⊅ *219 rooms, 41 suites* |⊙| *No meals* [M] *Yuraku-cho subway line, Edogawa-bashi Station (Exit 1A)* ⊹ *C1.*

$$
HOTEL
FAMILY

⌂ **Prince Hotel Shinagawa** (品川プリンスホテル). Just a three-minute walk from JR Shinagawa Station, the Prince is a sprawling complex that's part hotel (with four towers) and part entertainment village, featuring everything from a bowling alley to tennis courts to a 10-screen movie theater. **Pros:** affordable rates; multiple entertainment choices, including a bowling alley and an IMAX theater; nice view of Tokyo Bay from lounge. **Cons:** complicated layout; crowded on weekends; rooms can be small. [$] *Rooms from: ¥16000* ⊠ *4–10–30 Takanawa, Minato-ku* ☎ *03/3440–1111* ⊕ *www.princehotels.com/en/shinagawa* ⊅ *3,331 rooms* |⊙| *No meals* [M] *JR Yamanote Line, Shinagawa Station (Nishi-guchi/West Exit)* ⊹ *D6.*

$$$
HOTEL

⌂ **The Strings by InterContinental Tokyo** (ストリングスホテル東京インターコンチネンタル). Beautifully blending modernity with traditional Japanese aesthetics, the Strings is one of Shinagawa's top-tier hotels. **Pros:** great lobby; convenient location; nice view of the Tokyo skyline. **Cons:** expensive rates; finding elevator entrance can be challenging; no pool or spa. [$] *Rooms from: ¥31000* ⊠ *2–16–1 Konan, Minato-ku, Shinagawa-ku* ☎ *03/5783–1111* ⊕ *www.intercontinental-strings.jp* ⊅ *206 rooms, 6 suites* |⊙| *No meals* [M] *JR Yamanote Line, Shinagawa Station (Konan Exit)* ⊹ *D6.*

$$
HOTEL

⌂ **Westin Tokyo** (ウェスティンホテル東京). In the Yebisu Garden Place development, the Westin provides easy access to Mitsukoshi department store, the Tokyo Metropolitan Museum of Photography, the elegant Ebisu Garden concert hall, and the Taillevent-Robuchon restaurant (in a full-scale reproduction of a Louis XV château). **Pros:**"Heavenly Beds"; large rooms; great concierge. **Cons:** walk from station is more than 10 minutes; rooms can feel stuffy to some; charge for Internet. [$] *Rooms from: ¥28000* ⊠ *1–4 Mita 1-chome, Meguro-ku* ☎ *03/5423–7000* ⊕ *www.westin-tokyo.co.jp* ⊅ *418 rooms, 20 suites* |⊙| *No meals* [M] *JR Yamanote Line and Hibiya subway line, Ebisu Station (Higashi-guchi/East Exit)* ⊹ *B6.*

NEAR NARITA AIRPORT

Transportation between Narita Airport and Tokyo proper takes at least an hour and a half. In heavy traffic, a limousine bus or taxi ride, which could set you back ¥30,000, can stretch to two hours or more. A sensible strategy for visitors with early-morning flights home would be to spend the night before at one of the hotels near the airport, all of which have courtesy shuttles to the departure terminals; these hotels are also a boon to visitors en route elsewhere with layovers in Narita. Many of them have soundproof rooms to block out the noise of the airplanes.

$ **ANA Crowne Plaza Narita** (ANAクラウンプラザホテル成田). With its
HOTEL brass-and-marble detail in the lobby, this hotel replicates the grand style of other hotels in the ANA chain. **Pros:** convenient location; pleasant staff; airport shuttle. **Cons:** small rooms; charge to use pool; in-house restaurants are the only dining options in the area. **$** *Rooms from: ¥14000* ⊠ *68 Hori-no-uchi, Chiba-ken, Narita* ☎ *0476/33–1311, 0120/029–501 toll-free* ⊕ *www.anacrowneplaza-narita.jp* ➴ *389 rooms, 7 suites* ◎| *No meals* ✛ *H1.*

$$ **Hilton Tokyo Narita Airport** (ヒルトン成田). Given its proximity to the
HOTEL airport (a 10-minute drive), this C-shape hotel is a reasonable choice for a one-night visit. **Pros:** reasonably priced rooms; spacious lobby; airport shuttle. **Cons:** charge to use the pool and gym; common areas a bit worn; in-room Wi-Fi is not free. **$** *Rooms from: ¥15000* ⊠ *456 Kosuge, Chiba-ken, Narita* ☎ *0476/33–1121* ⊕ *www.hilton.com* ➴ *537 rooms, 11 suites* ◎| *No meals* ✛ *H1.*

$ **Narita Excel Hotel Tokyu** (成田エクセル東急). Airline crews rolling their
HOTEL bags through the lobby are a common sight at the Excel, a hotel with reasonable prices and friendly service. **Pros:** nice concierge; view of runway from bar; nice Japanese garden. **Cons:** small bathrooms; no outside dining options in immediate area. **$** *Rooms from: ¥9000* ⊠ *31 Oyama, Chiba-ken, Narita* ☎ *0476/33–0109* ⊕ *narita.tokyuhotels.com* ➴ *704 rooms, 2 suites* ◎| *No meals* ✛ *H1.*

$ **Radisson Hotel Narita Airport** (ラディソンホテル成田). Set on 28 spa-
HOTEL cious, green acres, this modern hotel feels somewhat like a resort, with massive indoor and outdoor pools. **Pros:** reasonably priced rooms; high-quality bathroom toiletries by Shiseido; nice-size rooms; airport shuttle available. **Cons:** a 15-minute drive by car to the airport; no outside restaurants in the immediate area. **$** *Rooms from: ¥9000* ⊠ *650–35 Nanae, Chiba-ken, Tomisato* ☎ *0476/93–1234* ⊕ *www.radissonnarita. jp* ➴ *488 rooms, 2 suites* ◎| *No meals* ✛ *H1.*

NIGHTLIFE AND PERFORMING ARTS

Tokyo's rich cultural history entwines itself with an influx of foreign influences, so Tokyoites get the best of both worlds. An astonishing variety of dance and music, both classical and popular and much of it Western, can be found in Tokyo, alongside the must-see traditional Japanese arts of Kabuki, Noh, and Bunraku.

Meanwhile, sheer diversity of nightlife in Tokyo is breathtaking. Rickety street stands sit yards away from luxury hotels, and wallet-crunching hostess clubs can be found next to cheap and raucous rock bars. Whatever your style, you'll find yourself in good company if you venture out after dark.

Metropolis, a free English-language weekly magazine, and *Weekend Scene,* published for free by *The Japan Times on Friday,* have up-to-date listings of what's going on in the city; they are available at hotels, book and music stores, some restaurants and cafés, and other locations. *The Japan News* also has entertainment features and listings in the Friday edition.

Ticket Pia. If your hotel can't help you with concert and performance bookings, call Ticket Pia or visit their shops around Tokyo, including two at Narita Airport. Beware, though, that except at the airport and Asakusa Culture Tourist Information Center, few people speak English here. Note that credit cards issued overseas are often not accepted, so bring cash. ⊠ *2–18–9 Kaminarimon, Taito-ku* ☎ *0570/02–9111, 03/5774–5200 customer service center.*

PERFORMING ARTS

The city is a proving ground for local talent and a magnet for orchestras and concert soloists from all over the world. Tokyo also has modern theater—in somewhat limited choices, to be sure, unless you can follow dialogue in Japanese, but Western repertory companies can always find receptive audiences here for plays in English. And it doesn't take long for a hit show from New York or London to open. Musicals such as *Mamma Mia!* have found enormous popularity here—although the protagonists speak Japanese.

Among about 10 professional dance troupes in Japan, the best known are the New National Ballet, which usually performs at the New National Theater, and the K-Ballet Company and the Tokyo Ballet, both of which stage performances at the Bunka Kaikan in Ueno and Orchard Hall of the Bunkamura complex in Shibuya. Tokyo has plenty of venues for opera, and few groups to perform in them, so touring companies like the Metropolitan, the Bolshoi, Sadler's Wells, and the Bayerische Staatsoper find Tokyo a very compelling venue—as well they might when even seats at ¥30,000 or more sell out far in advance.

Tokyo movie theaters screen a broad range of films—everything from big Asian hits to American blockbusters and Oscar nominees. The diversity brought by smaller distributors and an increased appetite for Korean, Middle Eastern, South American, and Aussie cinema have helped develop vibrant small theaters that cater to art-house fans. New multiplexes have also brought new screens to the capital, providing a more comfortable film-going experience than some of the older Japanese theaters.

FILM

Bunkamura. This complex has two movie theaters that tend to screen French and foreign films; a concert, opera, and classic ballet auditorium (Orchard Hall); a performance space (Theater Cocoona, often used for ballet and other dance); a gallery; and a museum. ⊠ *2–24–1 Dogenzaka* ☎ *03/3477–9111* ⊕ *www.bunkamura.co.jp* Ⓜ *JR Yamanote Line, Ginza and Hanzo-mon subway lines, and private rail lines, Shibuya Station (Exit 3A).*

Eurospace. One of the best venues for art-house films in Japan screens independent European and Asian hits and small-scale Japanese movies.

Directors and actors often appear on the stage, greeting fans on opening days. Occasionally Japanese films run with English subtitles. ⊠ *3F Kinohaus, 1–5 Maruyama-cho* ☎ *03/3461–0211* ⊕ *www.eurospace. co.jp* Ⓜ *JR, Ginza subway lines, Shibuya Station (Hachiko Exit).*

TOHO Cinemas Chanter. This three-screen cinema complex shows many European and American films by independent producers but also showcases fine work by filmmakers from Asia and the Middle East. ⊠ *1–2–2 Yuraku-cho, Chiyoda-ku* ☎ *03/6868–5001* ⊕ *www.tohotheater.jp/ theater/034/institution04.html* Ⓜ *Hibiya, Chiyoda, and Mita subway lines, Hibiya Station (Exit A5).*

FAMILY **TOHO Cinemas Roppongi Hills.** This complex provides good comfort along with its nine screens, and about 2,100 seats that include "First-Class" VIP seats. It also has an extra-large screen and MediaMation MX4D technology. It's the principal venue for the Tokyo International Film Festival held each fall. There are plenty of bars in the area for post-movie discussions. Late shows screen on weekends. ⊠ *Keyakizaka Complex, 6–10–2 Roppongi, Minato-ku* ☎ *03/6868–5024* ⊕ *www. tohotheater.jp/theater/009/access.html* ✉ *Regular theater ¥1,800, premier theater ¥4,800* Ⓜ *Hibiya and Oedo subway lines, Roppongi Station (Roppongi Hills Exit).*

MODERN THEATER

Takarazuka. Japan's all-female theater troupe was founded in the Osaka suburb of Takarazuka in 1913 and has been going strong ever since. Today it has not one but five companies, one of which has a permanent home in Tokyo at the 2,069-seat Takarazuka Theater. Where else but at the Takarazuka could you see *Gone With the Wind,* sung in Japanese, with a young woman in a mustache and a frock coat playing Rhett Butler? Same-day tickets are sold at the box office at either 9:30 am or 10 am for later shows. Advance tickets are available through ticketing agencies and the theater's website. Any remaining tickets are sold at the theater box office. ⊠ *1–1–3 Yuraku-cho, Chiyoda-ku* ☎ *03/5251–2001* ⊕ *kageki.hankyu.co.jp/english* ✉ *¥2,500–¥8,800* Ⓜ *JR Yamanote Line, Yuraku-cho Station (Hibiya Exit); Hibiya subway line, Hibiya Station (Exit A5); Chiyoda and Mita subway lines, Hibiya Station (Exit A13).*

FAMILY **Tokyo Dome.** A 45,852-seat sports arena, the dome also hosts big-name Japanese pop acts as well as the occasional international star. ⊠ *1–3– 61 Koraku, Bunkyō-ku* ☎ *03/5800–9999* ⊕ *www.tokyo-dome.co.jp/e* Ⓜ *Marunouchi and Namboku subway lines, Koraku-en Station (Exit 2); Mita subway line, Suido-bashi Station (Exit A5); JR Suido-bashi Station (Nishi-guchi/West Exit).*

MUSIC

New National Theater and Tokyo Opera City Concert Hall. With its 1,632-seat main auditorium, this venue nourishes Japan's fledgling efforts to make a name for itself in the world of opera. The Opera City Concert Hall has a massive pipe organ and hosts a free concert on Friday from 11:45 to 12:30, as well as visiting orchestras and performers. Ballet and large-scale operatic productions such as *Carmen* draw crowds at the New National Theater's Opera House, while the Pit and Playhouse theaters showcase dance and more-intimate dramatic works. The complex also includes an art gallery. ✉ *3–20–2 Nishi-Shinjuku, Shin-juku* ☎ *03/5353–0788, 03/5353–9999 ticket center* ⊕ *www.operacity. jp/en* ✉ *¥3,000–¥21,000* Ⓜ *Keio Shin-sen private rail line, Hatsudai Station (Higashi-guchi/East Exit)*.

NHK Hall. The home base for the Japan Broadcasting Corporation's NHK Symphony Orchestra, known as N-Kyo, is probably the auditorium most familiar to Japanese lovers of classical music, as performances here are routinely rebroadcast on the national TV station. The concerts also sometimes take place in adjoining Suntory Hall. ✉ *2–2–1 Jinnan* ☎ *03/3465–1751, 03/3465–1780 for N-Kyo* ⊕ *www.nhk-sc.or.jp/nhk_hall* Ⓜ *JR Yamanote Line, Harajuku Station (Exit Omotesando-guchi)*.

Suntory Hall. This lavishly appointed concert auditorium in the Ark Hills complex has probably the best acoustics in the city, and its great location allows theatergoers to extend their evening out: there's an abundance of great restaurants and bars nearby. ✉ *1–13–1 Akasaka, Minato-ku, Roppongi* ☎ *03/3505–1001* ⊕ *www.suntory.com/culture-sports/suntoryhall* Ⓜ *Ginza subway line, Tameike-Sanno Station (Exit 13); Namboku subway line, Roppongi-Ichome Station (Exit 3)*.

Tokyo Metropolitan Festival Hall (*Tokyo Bunka Kaikan*). In the 1960s and '70s this hall was one of the city's premier showcases for classical ballet, orchestral music, and visiting soloists. It still gets major bookings. ✉ *5–45 Ueno Koen, Taitō-ku* ☎ *03/3828–2111* ⊕ *www.t-bunka.jp/en* Ⓜ *JR Yamanote Line, Ueno Station (Koen-guchi/Park Exit)*.

PERFORMING ARTS CENTERS

Bunkyo Civic Hall. This three-story, city-run performance hall showcases classical music and ballet, opera, dance, and drama. Visitors might be especially interested in performances of local interest featuring puppets, wind music, and Japanese Kabuki dance. ✉ *1–16–21 Kasuga, Bunkyō-ku* ☎ *03/5803–1100, 03/5803–1111 tickets only* ⊕ *bunkyo-civichall.jp* Ⓜ *Marunouchi and Nanboku subway lines, Kourakuen Station (Exit 5)*.

Tokyo Opera City (東京オペラシティ). This mixed-use office and entertainment complex is home to the New National Theater, Tokyo (Shin Kokuritsu Gekijo Tokyo), consisting of the 1,814-seat Opera House, the 1,010-seat Playhouse, and an intimate performance space called the Pit, with seating for up to 438. Architect Helmut Jacoby's design for this building, with its reflecting pools, galleries, and granite planes of wall, deserves real plaudits.

Its east side consists of a 54-story office tower flanked by a sunken garden and art gallery on one side and a concert hall on the other. The museum focuses rather narrowly on post–World War II Japanese abstract painting, with its 3,000-piece Terada Collection. The 1,632-seat concert hall is arguably the most impressive classical-music venue in Tokyo, with tiers of polished-oak panels, and excellent acoustics despite the venue's daring vertical design. ✉ *3–20–2 Nishi-Shinjuku, Shinjuku* ☎ *03/5353–0788 concert hall, 03/5351–3011 New National Theater* ⊕ *www.tokyooperacity.co.jp* Ⓜ *Keio Shinsen Line, Hatsudai Station (Higashi-guchi/East Exit)*.

TRADITIONAL THEATER

KABUKI

FAMILY **Kabuki-za.** This legendary theater opened in 1889 was rebuilt after an earthquake in 1923, air raids in 1945, and again a few years ago. The new theater retains the original style and architecture and includes a *hanamichi* (runway) passing diagonally through the audience to a revolving stage, which looks out to 1,800 seats. Depending on programs, matinees usually begin at 11 and end at 3:30; evening performances start at 4:30 and end at 9. You can buy an unreserved ticket that allows you to see one act of a play from the topmost gallery. Bring binoculars—the gallery is very far from the stage. You might also want to rent an earphone set to follow the play in English. ⊠ *4–12–15 Ginza, Chūō-ku* ☎ *03/3545–6800* ⊕ *www.kabuki-bito.jp/eng* ⧆ *Reserved seats ¥4,000–¥20,000, topmost gallery ¥500–¥2,000* Ⓜ *Hibiya and Asakusa subway lines, Higashi-Ginza Station (station directly connected to the theater).*

National Theater (国立劇場 *Kokuritsu Gekijo*). Architect Hiroyuki Iwamoto's winning entry in the design competition for the National Theater building (1966) is a rendition in concrete of the ancient *azekura* (storehouse) style, invoking the 8th-century Shosoin Imperial Repository in Nara. The large hall seats 1,610 and presents primarily Kabuki theater, ancient court music, and dance. The small hall seats 590 and is used mainly for *bunraku* puppet theater and traditional music. Performances are in Japanese, but English-translation headsets are available for many shows. Debut performances, called *kao-mise*, are worth watching to catch the stars of the next generation. Tickets can be reserved until the day of the performance by calling the theater box office between 10 and 6. ⊠ *4–4–1 Hayabusa-cho, Chiyoda-ku, Imperial Palace* ☎ *03/3265–7411* ⊕ *www.ntj.jac.go.jp* ⧆ *Varies depending on performance* Ⓜ *Hanzo-mon subway line, Hanzo-mon Station (Exit 1).*

Shimbashi Enbujo. Dating to 1925, this theater was built for the geisha of the Shimbashi quarter to present their spring and autumn performances of traditional music and dance. This is the top spot in Tokyo to see the nation's favorite traditional performing art. The theater is also the home of "Super Kabuki," a faster, jazzier modern version. Seats commonly run ¥3,000–¥16,500, and there's no gallery. ⊠ *6–18–2 Ginza, Chūō-ku* ☎ *03/3541–2600* ⊕ *www.shochiku.co.jp/play/enbujyo* Ⓜ *Hibiya and Asakusa subway lines, Higashi-Ginza Station (Exit 6).*

NOH

FAMILY **National Noh Theater.** One of the few public halls to host Noh performances, this theater provides basic English-language summaries of the plots at performances. Individual screens placed in front of each seat also give an English translation. ⊠ *4–18–1 Sendagaya, Shibuya* ☎ *03/3423–1331, 03/3230–3000 reservations* ⊕ *www.ntj.jac.go.jp/ nou.html* ⧆ *¥2,700–¥6,700* Ⓜ *JR Chuo Line, Sendagaya Station (Minami-guchi/South Exit); Oedo subway line, Kokuritsu-Kyogijo Station (Exit A4).*

NIGHTLIFE

Most bars and clubs in the main entertainment districts have printed price lists, often in English. Drinks generally cost ¥700–¥1,200, although some small exclusive bars and clubs will set you back a lot more. Be wary of establishments without visible price lists. Hostess clubs and small backstreet bars known as "snacks" or "pubs" can be particularly treacherous territory for the unprepared. That drink you've just ordered could set you back a reasonable ¥1,000; you might, on the other hand, have wandered unknowingly into a place that charges you ¥30,000 up front for a whole bottle—and slaps a ¥20,000 cover charge on top. If the bar has hostesses, it's often unclear what the companionship of one will cost you, but as an unfamiliar face, you can bet it will cost you a lot. Ignore the persuasive shills on the streets of Roppongi and Kabuki-cho, who will try to hook you into their establishment. There is, of course, plenty of safe ground: hotel lounges, jazz clubs, and the rapidly expanding Irish pub scene are pretty much the way they are anywhere else. But elsewhere it's best to follow the old adage: if you have to ask how much it costs, you probably can't afford it.

Major nightlife districts include Aoyama, Ginza, Harajuku, Roppongi, Shibuya, and Shinjuku, and each has a unique atmosphere, clientele, and price level.

ASAKUSA 浅草

BARS

Fodor's Choice ★ **Kamiya Bar.** Tokyo's oldest Western-style bar hasn't had a face-lift for decades (the main building is registered as a tangible cultural property) and that's part of what draws so many drinkers to this bright, noisy venue. The other major attraction is the Denki Bran, a delicious but hangover-inducing liquor (comprising gin, red wine, brandy, and curaçao) that was invented here about 100 years ago and is now stocked by bars throughout Japan. ⊠ *1–1–1 Asakusa, Taitō-ku, Asakusa* ☎ *03/3841–5400* ☉ *Closed Tues.* Ⓜ *Asakusa and Ginza subway lines, Asakusa Station (Exit 3 and A5).*

FAMILY **Top of Tree.** Perched on the top of the Soramachi complex, this bar-restaurant attracts locals and tourists for overwhelming, breathtaking views of Tokyo Sky Tree. Signature drinks include Amaou-brand strawberry cocktails. The music's mostly jazz, and spacious and cushy seats, with sprawling views of Tokyo through the oversized glass windows and ceiling, make you want to linger. ⊠ *31F Soramachi, Tokyo Skytree Town, 1–1–2 Oshiage, Sumida-ku, Asakusa* ☎ *03/5809–7377.*

BEER HALLS AND PUBS

World Beer Museum. As the name suggests, beers from around the world are for sale, including 300 kinds in bottles and 20 more on tap. The large outdoor terrace with low-key downtown views is quiet and pleasant. The English-speaking German staff, when available, can help you choose the right beer. ⊠ *7F Soramachi, Tokyo Skytree Town, 1–1–2 Oshiage, Sumida-ku, Asakusa* ☎ *03/5610–2648* ⊕ *www.world-liquor-importers.co.jp/en/index.html.*

CLOSE UP

The Red Lights of Kabuki-cho

Tokyo has more than its fair share of red-light districts, but the leader of the pack is unquestionably Kabuki-cho, located just north of Shinjuku Station. The land was once a swamp, although its current name refers to an aborted post–World War II effort to bring culture to the area in the form of a landmark Kabuki theater. Nowadays, most of the entertainment is of the insalubrious kind, with strip clubs, love hotels, host and hostess clubs, and thinly disguised brothels all luridly advertising their presence.

The area's also home to throngs of Japanese and Chinese gangsters, giving rise to its image domestically as a danger zone. But in truth, Kabuki-cho poses little risk even to the solo traveler. The sheer volume of people in the area each night, combined with a prominent security-camera presence, means that crime stays mostly indoors.

Despite its sordid reputation, Kabuki-cho does have attractions beyond the red lights. There are eateries galore ranging from chain diners to designer restaurants.

GINZA 銀座

BARS

Peter. Like most of Tokyo's high-end hotels, the Peninsula has a high-rise bar. But unlike many staid hotel bars, this 24th-floor spot with a forest of chrome trees, designed by Yabu Pushelberg, is lots of fun. ⊠ *24F Peninsula Tokyo, 1–8–1 Yuraku-cho, Chiyoda-ku, Ginza* ☎ *03/6270–2763* ⊕ *tokyo.peninsula.com/en/fine-dining/peter-lounge-bar* Ⓜ *Hibiya and Mita subway lines, Hibiya Station (Exit A6).*

Star Bar. It's often said that Ginza has all the best bars, and Star Bar may be the best of the lot. Owner and bartender Hisashi Kishi is the president of the Japan Bartenders Association, and his attention to detail in the narrow, dark, and calm room is staggering. ⊠ *B1, 1–5–13 Ginza, Chūō-ku, Ginza* ☎ *03/3535–8005* ⊕ *starbar.jp/english.shtml* Ⓜ *JR Yamanote Line, Yuraku-cho Station (Kyobashi Exit).*

BEER HALLS AND PUBS

FAMILY **Ginza Lion.** This bar, in business since 1899 and occupying the same stately Chuo-dori location since 1934, is remarkably inexpensive for one of Tokyo's toniest addresses. Ginza shoppers and office workers alike drop by for beer and ballast—anything from Japanese-style fried chicken to spaghetti. Beers start at ¥600. ⊠ *7–9–20 Ginza, Chūō-ku, Ginza* ☎ *03/3571–2590, 0120/84–8136 for customer service center* ⊕ *www.ginzalion.jp* Ⓜ *Ginza, Hibiya, and Marunouchi subway lines, Ginza Station (Exit A3).*

MARUNOUCHI 丸の内

JAZZ CLUBS

Cotton Club. In these intimate and luxurious surroundings you can listen to not only jazz but also a diverse range of music: soul, R&B, J-pop, and world music. The club has such an excellent sound system that musicians such as Ron Carter record here. Fine French cuisine lures music lovers for special nights out and important business entertaining. ⊠ *2F Tokia, 2–7–3 Marunouchi, Chiyoda-ku, Marunouchi* ☎ *03/3215–1555* ⊕ *www.cottonclubjapan.co.jp/en* Ⓜ *JR and subway lines, Tokyo Station, directly connected to the Tokia bldg.*

AOYAMA 青山

BARS

Radio. Koji Ozaki is the closest thing Tokyo has to a superstar bartender. This demure septuagenarian, who still works one week per month, has been crafting cocktails for half a century, and he's known for both his perfectionism and creativity. Ozaki designed not only the bar he works behind, but the glasses he serves his creations in (some of the best in the city). All bartenders arrange the bar's flowers. You need to dress up (avoid short pants or flip-flops by all means), and remember, this is a place for quiet relaxation. ⊠ *3–10–34 Minami-Aoyama, Aoyama* ☎ *03/3402–2668* ⊕ *www.bar-radio.com* ☉ *Closed Sun. and holidays* Ⓜ *Chiyoda, Ginza, and Hanzomon subway lines, Omotesando Station (Exit A4).*

Two Rooms. Aoyama's dressed-up drinkers hang out on the stylish terrace. Drinks are big, pricey, and modern—think martinis in multiple fresh fruit flavors such as kiwi. The terrace overlooking Shinjuku area is particularly comfortable in spring and summer. ⊠ *5F AO Bldg., 3–11–7 Kita-Aoyama, Aoyama* ☎ *03/3498–0002* ⊕ *www.tworooms. jp* Ⓜ *Chiyoda, Ginza, and Hanzomon subway lines, Omotesando Station (Exit B2).*

DANCE CLUBS

Le Baron de Paris. The Tokyo branch of the Paris and New York club is partly owned by superstar designer Marc Newson and as you might expect, draws a fashionable crowd of fashion designers, models, editors, stylists, and actors. Expect an eclectic mix of nostalgic and modern party music from the '80s plus hip-pop, disco, and rock. ⊠ *B1, 3–8–40 Minami-Aoyama, Minato-ku, Aoyama* ☎ *03/3408–3665* ⊕ *www. lebaron.jp/en* Ⓜ *Chiyoda, Ginza, and Hanzomon subway lines, Omotesando Station (Exit A4/A3).*

JAZZ CLUBS

Blue Note Tokyo. This premier live jazz venue isn't for everyone: prices are high, sets short, and patrons packed in tight, sometimes sharing a table with strangers. But if you want to catch Pat Metheny and Natalie Cole in a relatively small venue, this is the place. Expect to pay upward of ¥11,000 to see major acts. ⊠ *Raika Bldg., 6–3–16 Minami-Aoyama, Minato-ku, Aoyama* ☎ *03/5485–0088* ⊕ *www.bluenote.co.jp* Ⓜ *Chiyoda, Ginza, and Hanzo-mon subway lines, Omotesando Station (Exit A5).*

HARAJUKU 原宿

BARS

Harajuku Taproom. Expat Bryan Baird runs an acclaimed microbrewery in a Shuzenji area of Izu, and he serves his range of brews in this casual and friendly place, along with decent and inexpensive Japanese-style pub grub such as *yakitori* (chicken skewers). ⊠ *2F No Surrender Bldg., 1–20–13 Jingu-mae, Shibuya* ☎ *03/6438–0450* ⊕ *bairdbeer.com/en.*

Montoak. Positioned halfway down the prestigious shopping street Omotesando-dori, within spitting distance of such fashion giants as Gucci, Louis Vuitton, and Tod's, this hip restaurant-bar is a great place to rest after testing the limits of your credit card. With smoky floor-to-ceiling windows and cushy armchairs, the place attracts a hipper-than-thou clientele and young fashionistas. The bar food consists of proscuitto, salads, cheese plates, and the like. ⊠ *6–1–9 Jingu-mae, Shibuya* ☏ *03/5468–5928* ⊕ *www.montoak.com* Ⓜ *Chiyoda subway line, Meiji-Jingu-mae Station (Exit 4).*

SHIBUYA 渋谷

BARS

Akaoni. The emphasis here is *nama*, unrefined, unpasteurized sake. About 80 kinds from 60 brewing companies are available daily. You may want to sample this unique beverage while in Tokyo, since you won't find it at home: nama is short-lived, too delicate and fresh to transport or export, so it's not widely available overseas. You can accompany your choice with authentic Japanese fare, served here as small bites. Reservations are necessary. ⊠ *2–15–3 Sangenjaya, Shibuya* ☏ *03/3410–9918* ⊕ *www.akaoni39.com* Ⓜ *Denenchofu-sen and Tokyu Setagaya lines, Sagenjaya Station.*

BEER HALLS AND PUBS

What the Dickens. This spacious pub in the Ebisu feels like "grandma's house" and more authentically British than many of its rivals, thanks partly to a menu of traditional pub grub, including hearty pies. Using aged logs, the second floor feels like a nice tree house. The place hosts regular live music (funk, folk, jazz, rock, reggae—anything goes here) and other events, so it can be very loud, particularly on Friday and Saturday. ⊠ *4F Roob 6 Bldg., 1–13–3 Ebisu-Nishi, Shibuya* ☏ *03/3780–2099* ⊕ *www.whatthedickens.jp* ☾ *Closed Mon.* Ⓜ *Hibiya subway line, Ebisu Station (Nishi-guchi/West Exit).*

DANCE CLUBS

Shelter. An ever-popular, long-running venue attracts everyone from their late teens to early forties. This is a great place to catch promising local rock bands. Admission runs ¥2,000–¥4,000. ⊠ *B1F, Senda Bldg., 2–6–10 Kitazawa, Setagaya-ku, Shibuya* ☏ *03/3466–7430* ⊕ *www.loft-prj.co.jp/SHELTER* Ⓜ *Keio Inokashira, Odakyu private rail lines, Shimo-Kitazawa Station (South Exit).*

Womb. Well-known techno and break-beat DJs make a point of stopping by this Shibuya überclub on their way through town. The turntable talent, local and international, and four floors of dance and lounge space make Womb Tokyo's most consistently rewarding club experience. Drawing adults from their late twenties to forties, the place gets packed sometimes after 1 in the morning. Entry costs around ¥3,500. ⊠ *2–16 Maruyama-cho, Shibuya* ☏ *03/5459–0039* ⊕ *www.womb.co.jp* Ⓜ *JR Yamanote Line, Ginza and Hanzo-mon subway lines, Shibuya Station (Hachiko Exit for JR and Ginza, Exit 3A for Hanzo-mon).*

Tokyo-Style Nightlife

Tokyo has a variety of nightlife options, so don't limit yourself to your hotel bar in the evenings. Spend some time relaxing the way the locals do at izakaya, karaoke, and live houses—three unique forms of contemporary Japanese entertainment.

IZAKAYA

Izakaya (literally "drinking places") are Japanese pubs that can be found throughout Tokyo. If you're in the mood for elegant decor and sedate surroundings, look elsewhere; these drinking dens are often noisy, bright, and smoky. But for a taste of authentic Japanese-style socializing, a visit to an izakaya is a must—this is where young people start their nights out, office workers gather on their way home, and students take a break to grab a cheap meal and a drink.

Typically, izakaya have a full lineup of cocktails, a good selection of sake, draft beer, and lots of cheap, greasy Japanese and Western food; rarely does anything cost more than ¥1,000. Picture menus make ordering easy, and because most cocktails retain their Western names, communicating drink preferences shouldn't be difficult.

KARAOKE

In buttoned-down, socially conservative Japan, karaoke is one of the safety valves. Employees, employers, teenage romancers, and good friends all drop their guard when there's a microphone in hand. The phenomenon started in the 1970s when cabaret singer Daisuke Inoue made a coin-operated machine that played his songs on tape so that his fans could sing along. Unfortunately for Inoue, he neglected to patent his creation, thereby failing to cash in as karaoke became one of Japan's favorite pastimes. Nowadays it's the finale of many an office outing, a cheap daytime activity for teens, and a surprisingly popular destination for dates.

Unlike most karaoke bars in the United States, in Japan the singing usually takes place in the seclusion of private rooms that can accommodate groups. Basic hourly charges vary and are almost always higher on weekends, but are usually less than ¥1,000. Most establishments have a large selection of English songs, stay open late, and serve inexpensive food and drink, which you order via a telephone on the wall. Finding a venue around one of the major entertainment hubs is easy—there will be plenty of young touts eager to escort you to their employer. And unlike with most other touts in the city, you won't end up broke by following them.

LIVE HOUSES

Tokyo has numerous small music clubs known as "live houses." These range from the very basic to miniclub venues, and they showcase the best emerging talent on the local scene. Many of the best live houses can be found in the Kichijoji and Koenji areas, although they are tucked away in basements citywide. The music could be gypsy jazz one night and thrash metal the next, so it's worth doing a little research before you turn up. Cover charges vary depending on who's performing but are typically ¥3,000–¥5,000.

IZAKAYA

Tatemichiya. The concrete walls are adorned with rock musicians' autobiographies and posters of the Sex Pistols and Ramones, who also provide the sound track. Artist Yoshitomo Nara shows up here, so if you're lucky, you can drink with him and watch him draw on the walls. ✉ *B1, 30–8 Sarugaku-cho, Shibuya* ☎ *03/5459–3431* Ⓜ *Tokyu Toyoko Line, Daikanyama Station.*

KARAOKE

Shibuya Shidax Village Club. Next to the corporate headquarters of Shidax, Japan's largest karaoke chain, this facility has 80 private karaoke rooms and a restaurant. Weekday rates run about ¥620 per hour and double on weekends and holidays. ✉ *1–12–13 Jinnan, Shibuya* ☎ *03/3461–9356* ⊕ *www.shidax.co.jp/sc/index.html* Ⓜ *JR, Ginza, and Hanzo-mon subway lines, Shibuya Station (Hachiko Exit).*

Smash Hits. If karaoke just isn't karaoke for you without drunken strangers to sing to, this expat favorite is the place to be. It has about 50,000 international songs, including about 28,000 English, Spanish, and French choices, and a central performance stage. The ¥3,500 cover charge gets you two drinks. ✉ *B1F M2 Bldg., 5–2–26 Hiro-o, Shibuya* ☎ *03/3444–0432* ⊕ *www.smashhits.jp* ⊘ *Closed Sun. and Mon.* Ⓜ *Hibiya Line, Hiroo Station (Exit B2).*

ROPPONGI 六本木

BARS

Agave. In this authentic Mexican cantina, your palate will be tempted by a choice of more than 400 kinds of tequilas and mescals—making this the world's largest selection. Most of the varieties here aren't available anywhere else in Japan, so the steep prices may be worth paying. Foods are mostly Mexican appetizers. ✉ *B1 Clover Bldg., 7–15–10 Roppongi, Minato-ku, Roppongi* ☎ *03/3497–0229* ⊕ *agave. jp* ⊘ *Closed Sun. and holiday Mon.* Ⓜ *Hibiya and Oedo subway lines, Roppongi Station (Exit 3).*

JAZZ CLUBS

Billboard Live Tokyo. With everything from rock and J-pop to soul and funk, this three-story joint makes one of the best food-and-live music experiences in Tokyo, all with panoramic views of Roppongi. Patrons love this venue partly because they're so close to performers like George Clinton, Dicky Betts, and Gen Hoshino; they often end up on the stage dancing and singing or shaking hands. Shows usually kick off at 7 and 9:30 pm on weekdays, 6 and 9 pm on Saturday and 4:30 and 7:30 pm on Sunday. ✉ *4F Tokyo Midtown Garden Terr., 9–7–4 Akasaka, Minato-ku, Roppongi* ☎ *03/3405–1133.*

KARAOKE

Pasela Resort Roppongi. This 10-story entertainment complex on the main Roppongi drag of Gaien-Higashi-dori has seven floors of karaoke rooms, some Bali-themed, with more than 10,000 foreign-song titles. Both large and small groups can be accommodated. A Mexican-theme darts bar and a restaurant are also on-site. Rates run ¥500–¥1,300 per hour. ✉ *4F–10F, 5–16–3 Roppongi, Minato-ku, Roppongi*

☎ *0120/911–086* ⊕ *www.pasela.co.jp* Ⓜ *Hibiya and Oedo subway lines, Roppongi Station (Exit 4A).*

MUSIC

Akasaka Blitz. Eclectic performances at this artsy music venue range from Japanese rock to Korean and Japanese pop to *visual-kei* (visual-style) groups, who wear elaborate makeup and stage costumes. ⊠ *Akasaka Sacas, 5–3–2 Akasaka, Minato-ku* ☎ *03/3584–8811* ⊕ *www.tbs.co.jp/blitz* Ⓜ *Chiyoda subway line, Akasaka Station.*

FAMILY **Kioi Hall.** Behind Hotel New Otani stands this relatively small concert venue, which showcases both performances of Western classical music, such as piano and violin recitals, and Japanese works, including *shaku-hachi* flute music. It hosts programs for families to learn how to play such traditional Japanese instruments. ⊠ *6–5 Kioi-cho, Chiyoda-ku* ☎ *03/3237–0061* ⊕ *www.kioi-hall.or.jp* Ⓜ *JR, Marunouchi and Nan-boku subway lines, Yotsuya Station (Koujimachi Exit); Yurakucho subway line, Koujimachi Station (Exit 2).*

SHINJUKU 新宿

BARS

Donzoko. This venerable bar claims to be Shinjuku's oldest—established in 1951—and has hosted Yukio Mishima and Akira Kurosawa among many other luminaries. It's also one of several bars that claim to have invented the popular *chu-hai* cocktail (*shochu* with juice and soda). The vibrant atmosphere feels more like a pub, and the four floors are almost always packed. ⊠ *3–10–2 Shinjuku, Shinjuku* ☎ *03/3354–7749* ⊕ *www.donzoko.co.jp* Ⓜ *Marunouchi and Shinjuku subway lines, Shinjuku-san-chome Station (Exit C3).*

Fodor's Choice **New York Bar.** Even before *Lost in Translation* introduced the Park
★ Hyatt's signature lounge to filmgoers worldwide, New York Bar was a local Tokyo favorite. All the style you would expect of one of the city's top hotels combined with superior views of Shinjuku's skyscrapers and neon-lighted streets make this one of the city's premier nighttime venues. The quality of the jazz and service equals that of the view. With the largest selection of U.S. wines in Japan, drinks start at ¥1,200, and there's a cover charge of ¥2,200 after 8 pm (7 pm on Sunday). Local jazz bands play on Sunday. ⊠ *52F Park Hyatt Hotel, 3–7–1–2 Nishi-Shinjuku, Shinjuku* ☎ *03/5322–1234* ⊕ *tokyo.park.hyatt.jp/en/hotel/dining/NewYorkBar.html* Ⓜ *JR Shinjuku Station (West Exit for the shuttle bus service, South Exit for walk-in).*

GAY BARS

Aiiro Cafe. Almost every great gay night out begins at this welcoming street-corner pub with a large red shrine gate, where the patrons spill out onto the street. This is the perfect place to put back a few cocktails, meet new people, and get a feeling for where to go next. The crowd is mixed and very foreigner-friendly. ⊠ *2–18–1 Shinjuku, Shinjuku* ☎ *03/6273–0740* ⊕ *aliving.net/english.html.*

ArcH. The spacious basement joint hosts a wide range of events for gays and lesbians every night. The events include thirtysomething nights and underwear-only nights. Cover charge depends on the event. ⊠ *B1 Casa Verde, 2–11–2 Shinjuku, Shinjuku* ☎ *03/6380–6966* ⊕ *aliving.net.*

Kabukicho, in Shinjuku, is a brightly lit hub for bars, pachinko parlors, and restaurants, as well as tattooed Yakuza.

Arty Farty. Cheap and cheesy, Arty Farty is a fun club, complete with a ministage and stripper pole. Those with aversions to Kylie or Madonna need not bother. The crowd is mixed and foreigner-friendly. ✉ *2F Kyu-tei Bldg., 2–11–7 Shinjuku, Shinjuku* ☎ *03/5362–9720* ⊕ *www.arty-farty.net.*

Dragon Men. Despite the name, Tokyo's swankiest gay lounge also welcomes women. The neon-lighted space would look right at home in New York or Paris. ✉ *1F Stork Nagasaki, 2–11–4 Shinjuku, Shinjuku* ☎ *03/3341–0606* Ⓜ *Marunouchi subway line, Shinjuku-san-chome Station.*

GB. This men-only club carries a whiff of the old days when things were less mainstream. Video monitors show contemporary music hits. On weekends the place is packed with rather quiet and reserved gentlemen, mostly in their thirties and forties, and cruising via strategically placed mirrors. Women are welcome, too. ✉ *B1 Shinjuku Plaza Bldg., 2–12–3 Shinjuku, Shinjuku* ☎ *03/3352–8972* ⊕ *www.gb-tokyo.com/index.php/en* ⊙ *Closed Mon.* Ⓜ *Marunouchi subway line, Shinjuku-san-chome Station.*

Gold Finger. This relaxed bar for "women who love women" is a cozy den of vintage lamps and cafélike ambience. Men are welcome on Friday; Saturdays are women-only. ✉ *Hayashi Bldg., 2–12–11 Shinjuku, Shinjuku* ☎ *03/6383–4649* ⊕ *www.goldfingerparty.com* ⊙ *Closed Tues. and Wed.* Ⓜ *Marunouchi subway line, Shinjuku-san-chome Station.*

Hot House. This could very well be the world's smallest jazz club. An evening here is like listening to live jazz in your living room. Live acts are trios at most, with no space for a full set of drums or amplifiers.

TOKYO'S GAY BARS

Gay culture is a little different in Japan than it is in the West. Though the gay presence on TV is increasing, most gay life still takes place well under the radar. Even so, there's less prejudice than you might experience elsewhere. People are more likely to be baffled than offended by gay couples, and some hotels may "not compute" that a same-sex couple would like a double bed. But with a little digging you'll find a scene more vibrant than you—or many Tokyoites—might expect. The city's primary LGBT hub is Ni-chome in the Shinjuku district (take the Shinjuku or Marunouchi subway line to Shinjuku-Sanchome Station; Exit C7). Ni-chome is sometimes likened to its more notorious neighbor Kabuki-cho, and the name is also spoken in hushed tones and accompanied by raised eyebrows. Ni-chome, however, is more subtle in its approach. Gay and gay-friendly establishments can be found sprinkled in other areas, too, among them Shibuya, Asakusa, Ueno, and, surprisingly, Shinbashi, where a cluster of gay bars near Shinbashi Station are cheek-by-jowl with establishments that cater to hard-drinking businessmen out for a night on the town.

Simple, homemade Japanese cooking (free of charge) helps make this a truly intimate experience. With 10 seats and no standing allowed, reservations are recommended. Entry costs ¥3,500–¥4,500. ☒ *B1 Liberal Takadanobaba, 3–23–5 Takadanobaba, Shinjuku* ☎ *03/3367–1233* Ⓜ *JR Takadanobaba Station (Waseda Exit).*

Intro. This small basement jazz joint is home to one of the best jazz experiences in Tokyo, with a Saturday "12-hour jam session" that stretches until 5 am. Live sessions run throughout the week except Monday and Friday, when the regulars enjoy listening to the owner's extensive vinyl and CD collection. Italian food is available. ☒ *B1 NT Bldg., 2–14–8 Takadanobaba, Shinjuku* ☎ *03/3200–4396* Ⓜ *JR Takadanobaba Station (Waseda Exit).*

Shinjuku Pit Inn. Most major jazz musicians have played at least once in this classic Tokyo club. The veteran club stages mostly mainstream fare with the odd foray into the avant-garde. The emphasis here is strictly on jazz—and the place resembles a small concert hall. Entry runs ¥1,400–¥5,000. ☒ *B1 Accord Shinjuku Bldg., 2–12–4 Shinjuku, Shinjuku* ☎ *03/3354–2024* ⊕ *www.pit-inn.com/index_e.html* Ⓜ *Marunouchi subway line, Shinjuku-san-chome Station.*

GREATER TOKYO

BARS

Kuri. Specializing in seasonal sake, this little bar serves about 100 varieties from around 40 breweries. Food is limited to appetizers that include salted squid, pickled cheese, and sea urchin. Dim lighting creates a nice mood, and the staff is happy to help you choose the right sake. Note that the surrounding Shinbashi district is a popular nighttime hangout for businessmen, so don't be surprised to encounter wandering hordes of inebriated accountants on the streets. ☒ *2F Sakurai Bldg., 3–19–4 Shinbashi, Minato-ku, Greater Tokyo* ☎ *03/3438–3375* ☉ *Closed Sun.*

BEER HALLS AND PUBS

Craft Beer Market. This craft beer specialist serves nearly 30 Japanese beers on tap, with regional variations from around the country, at reasonable prices. The wide selection of foods includes roast chicken and carpaccio. This loftlike space with plenty of elbow room will make you comfortable, as will the easygoing ambience. A drink menu is available in English. ✉ *1F Sumitomo-shoji Jinbochobil, 2–11–15 Jinbocho, Kanda, Chiyoda-ku, Greater Tokyo* ☎ *03/6272–5652* ⊕ *www.craftbeermarket.jp/store_jimbo.html* ☾ *Closed Sun.*

Popeye. Of the staggering 70 beers on tap here, 70% are top-quality Japanese microbrews, from pilsners to IPAs to barley wines. The owner is one of Japan's leading authorities on beer, and his passion is reflected in the quality of the brews. The convivial, sports-bar-like atmosphere attracts a mature clientele, making this a great option for a post-sumo spot. The menu includes chicken ale stew, beer cake, and beer ice cream. ✉ *2–18–7 Ryogoku, Sumida-ku, Greater Tokyo* ☎ *03/3633–2120* ⊕ *www.40beersontap.com* ☾ *Closed Sun.* Ⓜ *JR Ryogoku Station (West Exit).*

DANCE CLUBS

Ageha. This massive, bay-side Ageha is probably the Japan's largest club venue with the city's best sound system and most diverse musical lineup. The arena hosts well-known house and techno DJs, the bar plays hip-hop, a summer-only swimming-pool area has everything from reggae to break beats, and inside a chill-out tent "Box," there's usually ambient or trance music according to programs. Because of its far-flung location and enormous capacity, Ageha can look like either a throbbing party or an embarrassingly empty hall, depending on the caliber of the DJ. Free buses to Ageha depart about every half hour or 45 minutes between midnight and 4 am from a stop opposite the Shibuya police station on Roppongi-dori, a one-minute walk from Shibuya Station (there are also return buses about every half hour or 45 minutes from midnight to 5 am). For gay nights, shuttles also depart from Shibuya. Entry costs around ¥3,500. ✉ *2–2–10 Shin-Kiba, Kōtō-ku, Greater Tokyo* ☎ *03/5534–2525* ⊕ *www.ageha.com* Ⓜ *Yuraku-cho subway line, Shin-Kiba Station.*

LIVE MUSIC

Manda-la 2. Relaxed, quiet, and intimate, this local favorite in the bustling western suburb of Kichijoji attracts an eclectic group of performers. Cover charges range from ¥2,200 to ¥3,300. ✉ *2–8–6 Kichijoji-Minami-cho, Musashino* ☎ *0422/42–1579* Ⓜ *Keio Inokashira private rail line, JR Chuo and JR Sobu lines, Kichijoji Station (Koen-guchi/Park Exit and South Exit).*

Showboat. A small, basic venue in western Tokyo that's been going strong for more than a decade, Showboat attracts semiprofessional and professional performers. Entry runs ¥2,000–¥5,000. ✉ *B1 Oak Hill Koenji, 3–17–2 Koenji Kita, Suginami-ku, Greater Tokyo* ☎ *03/3337–5745* ⊕ *showboat1993.wix.com/showboat1993* Ⓜ *JR Sobu and JR Chuo lines, Koenji Station (Kita-guchi/North Exit).*

CLOSE UP

All That Tokyo Jazz

The Tokyo jazz scene is one of the world's best, far surpassing that of Paris and New York with its number of venues playing traditional, swing, bossa nova, rhythm and blues, and free jazz. Though popular in Japan before World War II, jazz really took hold of the city after U.S. forces introduced Charlie Parker and Thelonius Monk in the late 1940s. The genre had been banned in wartime Japan as an American vice, but even at the height of the war, fans were able to listen to their favorite artists on Voice of America radio. In the 1960s Japan experienced a boom in all areas of the arts, and jazz was no exception. Since then, the Japanese scene has steadily bloomed, with several local stars—such as Sadao Watanabe in the 1960s and contemporary favorites Keiko Lee and Hiromi Uehara—gaining global attention.

Today there are more than 120 bars and clubs that host live music, plus hundreds that play recorded jazz. Shinjuku, Takadanobaba, and Kichijoji are the city's jazz enclaves. Famous international acts regularly appear at big-name clubs such as the Blue Note, but the smaller, lesser-known joints usually have more atmosphere. With such a large jazz scene, there's an incredible diversity to enjoy, from Louis Armstrong tribute acts to fully improvised free jazz—sometimes on successive nights at the same venue.

If you time your visit right, you can listen to great jazz at one of the city's more than 20 annual festivals dedicated to this adopted musical form. The festivals vary in size and coverage, but two to check out are the Tokyo Jazz Festival and the Asagaya Jazz Street Festival.

SHOPPING

Tokyo is Japan's showcase. The crazy clothing styles, obscure electronics, and new games found here are capable of setting trends for the rest of the country—and perhaps the rest of Asia, and even Europe and America.

Part of the Tokyo shopping experience is simply to observe, and on Saturday especially, in districts like the Ginza and Shinjuku, you will notice that the Japanese approach to shopping can be nothing short of feverish. You'll probably want to resist the urge to join in the fray, especially since many of the wildly trendy clothes and accessories for sale will already be "uncool" by the time you get home. But shopping in Tokyo can also be an exercise in elegance and refinement, especially if you shop for items that are Japanese-made for Japanese people and sold in stores that don't cater to tourists. With brilliantly applied color, balance of form, and superb workmanship, crafts items can be exquisite and well worth the price you'll pay—and some can be quite expensive.

Note the care taken with items after you purchase them, especially in department stores and boutiques. Goods will be wrapped, wrapped again, bagged, and sealed. Sure, the packaging can be excessive—does anybody really need three plastic bags for one croissant?—but such a focus on presentation has deep roots in Japanese culture.

This focus on presentation also influences salespeople who are invariably helpful and polite. In the larger stores they greet you with a bow when you arrive, and many of them speak at least enough English to help you find what you're looking for. There's a saying in Japan: *o-kyaku-sama wa kami-sama,* "the customer is a god"—and since the competition for your business is fierce, people do take it to heart.

Horror stories abound about prices in Japan—and some of them are true. Yes, European labels can cost a fortune here, but did you really travel all the way to Tokyo to buy an outfit that would be cheaper in the designer mall at home? True, a gift-wrapped melon from a department-store gourmet counter can cost $150. But you can enjoy gawking even if you don't want to spend like that. And if you shop around, you can find plenty of gifts and souvenirs at fair prices.

Japan has finally embraced the use of credit cards, although some smaller mom-and-pop shops may still take cash only. So when you go souvenir hunting, be prepared with a decent amount of cash; Tokyo's low crime rates make this a low-risk proposition. The dishonor associated with theft is so strong, in fact, that it's considered bad form to conspicuously count change in front of cashiers.

Japan has an across-the-board 8% value-added tax (V.A.T.) imposed on luxury goods. This tax can be avoided at some duty-free shops in the city (don't forget to bring your passport). It's also waived in the duty-free shops at the international airports, but because these places tend to have higher profit margins, your tax savings there are likely to be offset by the higher markups.

Stores in Tokyo generally open at 10 or 11 am and close at 8 or 9 pm.

AKIHABARA 神保町

ANTIQUES

Yasukuni Jinja (靖国神社 *Yasukuni Shrine*). Most Sundays, from sunrise to sunset, antiques-hunters can search and explore this flea market, which boasts 30–50 booths run by professional collectors. It's located within the controversial Yasukuni Jinja grounds, so when you're finished shopping, stroll through the shrine that pays respect to dead Japanese soldiers. ✉ *3–1–1 Kudan-Kita, Chiyoda-ku* ☎ *03/3261–8326* ⊕ *www.yasukuni.or.jp/english/index.html* Ⓜ *Hanzo-mon and Shinjuku subway lines, Kudanshita Station (Exit 1).*

DOLLS

Kyugetsu (九月). In business for more than a century, Kyugetsu sells every kind of doll imaginable, from the East and the West. ✉ *1–20–4 Yanagi-bashi, Taitō-ku* ☎ *03/5687–5176* ⊕ *www.kyugetsu.com/e/index.html* Ⓜ *Asakusa subway line, JR Sobu Line, Asakusa-bashi Station (Exit A3).*

ELECTRONICS

LAOX (ソフマップ). One of the big Akihabara department stores, LAOX has several locations and the largest and most comprehensive selection in the district, with four buildings. The seven-story main branch is duty-free, with three floors dedicated to electronic gadgets, such as lightweight vacuum cleaners and eco-friendly humidifiers, that come with English instruction booklets. English-speaking staff members are on call. LAOX has annexes—one exclusively for musical instruments, another for duty-free appliances—and outlets in Ginza, Odaiba and Narita Airport. This is a good place to find the latest in digital cameras, watches, and games. ✉ *1–2–9 Soto-Kanda, Chiyoda-ku, Akihabara* ☎ *03/3253–7111* ⊕ *www.laox.co.jp* Ⓜ *JR Yamanote Line, Akihabara Station (Electric Town Exit).*

Sofmap (ソフマップ). One Akihabara retailer that actually benefited from the bursting of Japan's economic bubble in the early '90s is this electronics chain, once known as a used-PC and software chain with a heavy presence in Tokyo. Now its multiple branches also sell all sorts of new electronics, music, and mobile phones. Most are open daily until 8. ✉ *4–1–1 Soto-Kanda, Chiyoda-ku, Akihabara* ☎ *03/3253–1111* Ⓜ *JR Yamanote Line, Akihabara Station (Electric Town Exit).*

PAPER

Origami House (おりがみ会館 *Origami Kaikan*). There's more than just shopping for paper goods at this mini-tower dedicated to the art of folding, open since 1885. You can also tour a papermaking workshop and learn the art of origami in the shop's gallery. ✉ *1–7–14 Yushima, Bunkyo-ku, Akihabara* ☎ *03/3811–4025* ⊕ *www.origamihouse.jp* ☽ *Closed Sun.* Ⓜ *JR Chuo and Sobu lines, Ochanomizu Station (West Exit); Chiyoda subway line, Yushima Station (Exit 5).*

UENO 上野

SHOPPING STREETS AND ARCADES

Ameyoko Market (アメヤ横丁). Everything from fresh fish to cheap import clothing is for sale at this bustling warren of side streets between Okachi-machi and Ueno stations. In the days leading up to New Year's, the area turns into mosh-pit mayhem as shoppers fight for fish and snacks to serve over the holidays. The official name of the market is Ameya-Yoko-cho but is almost always shortened to Ameyoko. ✉ *Ueno 6-chome, Taitō-ku* Ⓜ *JR Ueno Station (Hiroko-ji Exit), JR Okachi-machi Station (Exit A7).*

SPECIALITY COMBS

Jusan-ya (十三や). A samurai who couldn't support himself as a feudal retainer launched this business selling handmade boxwood combs in 1736. It has been in the same family ever since. Jusan-ya is on Shinobazu-dori, a few doors west of its intersection with Chuo-dori in Ueno. ✉ *2–12–21 Ueno, Taitō-ku* ☎ *03/3831–3238* ⊕ *www.kyoto-wel.com/shop/S81004* ☽ *Closed Sun.* Ⓜ *Ginza subway line, Ueno Hiroko-ji Station (Exit 3); JR Yamanote Line, Ueno Station (Shinobazu Exit).*

ASAKUSA 浅草

FOOD

Kawahara Shoten (川原商店). The brightly colored bulk packages of rice crackers, shrimp-flavored chips, and other Japanese snacks sold here make offbeat gifts. ✉ 3–9–2 *Nishi-Asakusa, Taitō-ku, Asakusa* ☎ 03/3842–0841 ⊙ *Closed Sun.* Ⓜ *Ginza subway line, Asakusa Station (Exit 1).*

Tokiwa-do (常盤堂). Come here to buy some of Tokyo's most famous souvenirs: *kaminari okoshi* (thunder crackers), made of rice, millet, sugar, and beans. The shop is on the west side of Asakusa's Thunder God Gate, the Kaminari-mon entrance to Senso-ji, and you can watch as they make them in front of you. ✉ *1–3–2 Asakusa, Taitō-ku, Asakusa* ☎ 03/3841–5656 ⊕ *www.tokiwado.tokyo* Ⓜ *Ginza subway line, Asakusa Station (Exit 1).*

Tsubaya Knives (つば屋包丁店). This shop's remarkable selection of high-quality cutlery for professionals is designed for every imaginable use, as the art of food presentation in Japan requires a great variety of cutting implements. The best of these carry the Traditional Craft Association seal: hand-forged tools of tempered blue steel, set in handles banded with deer horn to keep the wood from splitting. Be prepared to pay the premium for these items. A cleaver just for slicing soba can cost as much as ¥50,000. ✉ *3–7–2 Nishi-Asakusa, Taito-ku, Asakusa* ☎ 03/3845–2005 Ⓜ *Ginza subway line, Asakusa (Exit 1).*

SHOPPING STREETS AND ARCADES

Nakamise Market (仲見世通り *Nakamise-dori*). This narrow street is heaven for those seeking out traditional knickknacks and souvenirs. It is just as lively as it was when it was established in the Edo period, although now shops sells cheap sushi key chains and T-shirts alongside traditional hairpieces and silk screens. The entrance is marked by the giant red lantern at the Kaminari-mon, and ends at the grounds of the Senso-ji Complex. ✉ *Asakusa 1-chome, Taito-ku* ☎ 03/3844–3350 Ⓜ *Ginza subway line, Asakusa Station (Exit 1).*

Nishi-Sando Arcade (西参道商店街 *Nishi-Sando Shoten-gai*). Kimono and *yukata* (cotton kimono) fabrics, traditional accessories, swords, and festival costumes at very reasonable prices are all for sale at this Asakusa arcade. It runs east of the area's movie theaters, between Rok-ku and the Senso-ji Complex. ✉ *Asakusa 2-chome, Taito-ku* Ⓜ *Ginza subway line, Asakusa Station (Exit 1).*

SWORDS AND KNIVES

Ichiryo-ya Hirakawa (一両屋平川). This small, cluttered souvenir shop in the Nishi-Sando arcade carries antique swords and reproductions and has some English-speaking salesclerks. ✉ *2–7–13 Asakusa, Taitō-ku, Asakusa* ☎ 03/3843–0052 ⊙ *Closed Thurs.* Ⓜ *Ginza subway line, Asakusa Station (Exit 1) or Tawara-machi Station (Exit 3).*

TRADITIONAL WARES

Fuji-ya (ふじ屋). Master textile creator Keiji Kawakami is an expert on the hundreds of traditional towel motifs that have come down from the Edo period: geometric patterns, plants and animals, and scenes from

Kabuki plays and festivals. His cotton *tenugui* (teh- *noo*-goo-ee) hand towels are collector's items, often framed instead of used as towels. When Kawakami feels he has made enough of one pattern of his own design, he destroys the stencil. The shop is near the corner of Dembo-in Dori, on the street that runs parallel behind Naka-mise dori. ⊠ *2–2–15 Asakusa, Taitō-ku, Asakusa* ☎ *03/3841–2283* ☉ *Closed Thurs.* Ⓜ *Ginza subway line, Asakusa Station (Exit 1).*

Hyaku-suke (百助). This is the last place in Tokyo to carry government-approved skin cleanser made from powdered nightingale droppings. Ladies of the Edo period—especially the geisha—swore by the cleanser. These days this 300-year-old-plus cosmetics shop sells little of the nightingale powder, but its theatrical makeup for Kabuki actors, geisha, and traditional weddings—as well as unique items like seaweed shampoo, camellia oil, and handcrafted combs and cosmetic brushes—makes it a worthy addition to your Asakusa shopping itinerary. ⊠ *2–2–14 Asakusa, Taitō-ku, Asakusa* ☎ *03/3841–7058* ☉ *Closed Tues.* Ⓜ *Ginza subway line, Asakusa Station (Exit 6).*

FAMILY **Maizuru** (まいづる). This perennial tourist favorite manufactures the plastic food that's displayed outside almost every Tokyo restaurant. Ersatz sushi, noodles, and even beer cost just a few thousand yen. You can buy tiny plastic key holders and earrings, or splurge on a whole Pacific lobster, perfect in coloration and detail down to the tiniest spines on its legs. ⊠ *1–5–17 Nishi-Asakusa, Taitō-ku, Asakusa* ☎ *03/3843–1686* Ⓜ *Ginza subway line, Asakusa Station (Exit 6).*

Naka-ya (中屋). If you want to equip yourself for the neighborhood's annual Sanja Festival in May, this is the place to come for traditional costumes. Best buys here are *sashiko hanten;*, which are thick, woven firemen's jackets; and *happi* coats, cotton tunics printed in bright colors with Japanese characters. Some items are available in children's sizes. ⊠ *2–2–12 Asakusa, Taitō-ku, Asakusa* ☎ *03/3841–7877* ⊕ *www.nakaya.co.jp* Ⓜ *Ginza subway line, Asakusa Station (Exit 6).*

Soi Interior & Style Design. The selection of lacquerware, ceramics, and antiques sold at this Kappabashi shop is modest, but Soi displays the items in a primitivist setting of stone walls and wooden floor planks, with up-tempo jazz in the background. ⊠ *3–25–11 Nishi-Asakusa, Taitō-ku, Asakusa* ☎ *03/3843–7200* ⊕ *www.soi-2.jp* Ⓜ *Ginza subway line, Asakusa Station (Exit 6).*

NIHOMBASHI 日本橋

BOOKS

Yaesu Book Center (八重洲ブックセンター). English-language paperbacks, art books, and calendars are available on the seventh floor of this celebrated bookstore. ⊠ *2–5–1 Yaesu, Chūō-ku, Marunouchi* ☎ *03/3281–0811* Ⓜ *JR Yamanote Line, Tokyo Station (Yaesu South Exit 5).*

DEPARTMENT STORES

Fodor's Choice **Mitsukoshi** (三越). Founded in 1673 as a dry-goods store, Mitsukoshi
★ later played one of the leading roles in introducing Western merchandise to Japan. It has retained its image of quality and excellence, with

a particularly strong representation of Western fashion designers. The store also stocks fine traditional Japanese goods—don't miss the art gallery and the crafts area on the sixth floor. With its own subway stop, bronze lions at the entrance, and an atrium sculpture of the Japanese goddess Magokoro, this flagship store merits a visit even if you're not planning on buying anything. ⊠ *1–4–1 Nihombashi Muro-machi, Chūō-ku, Nihombashi* ☎ *03/3241–3311* Ⓜ *Ginza and Hanzo-mon subway lines, Mitsukoshi-mae Station (Exits A3 and A5).*

FOOD

Yamamoto Seaweed (山元海苔店 *Yamamoto Noriten*). The Japanese are resourceful in their uses of products from the sea. Nori, the paper-thin dried seaweed used to wrap maki sushi and *onigiri* (rice balls), is the specialty here. If you plan to bring some home with you, buy unroasted nori and toast it yourself at home; the flavor will be far better than that of the preroasted sheets. ⊠ *1–6–3 Nihombashi Muro-machi, Chūō-ku, Nihombashi* ☎ *03/3241–0290* ⊕ *www.yamamoto-noriten.co.jp/english* Ⓜ *Hanzo-mon and Ginza subway lines, Mitsukoshi-mae Station (Exit A1).*

MALLS AND SHOPPING CENTERS

Coredo (コレド). Unlike other big stores in the Nihombashi area, this sparkling mall feels contemporary thanks to an open layout and extensive use of glass. Neighboring it are three more new glittery towers: Coredo Muromachi 1, 2, and 3, which fuse traditional housewares stores with modern fashion boutiques. The in-house Nihombashi Tourist Center runs workshops on everything from dressing like a Geisha to cooking food. ⊠ *1–4–1 Nihombashi, Chūō-ku, Nihombashi* ☎ *03/3242–0010* ⊕ *31urban.jp/en/index.html* Ⓜ *Ginza, Tozai, and Asakusa subway lines, Nihombashi Station (Exit B12).*

PAPER

Ozu Washi (小津和紙). This shop, which was opened in the 17th century, has one of the largest *washi* showrooms in the city and its own gallery of antique papers. Best to check ahead of time, but they sometimes have classes for just ¥500 on how to make your own washi paper. ⊠ *3–6–2 Nihombashi-Honcho, Chūō-ku, Nihombashi* ☎ *03/3662–1184* ⊕ *www.ozuwashi.net/english* ⊙ *Closed Sun.* Ⓜ *Ginza and Hanzo-mon subway lines, Mitsukoshi-mae Station (Exit A4).*

SWORDS AND KNIVES

Kiya Blades (木屋刃物 *kiya hamono*). Workers shape and hone blades in one corner of this shop, which carries cutlery, pocketknives, saws, and more. Scissors with handles in the shape of Japanese cranes are among the many unique gift items sold here, and custom-made knives are available, too. Kiya is located in the Coredo Muro-machi complex. ⊠ *2–2–1 Nihombashi-Muromachi, Chuo-ku, Nihombashi* ☎ *03/3241–0110* ⊕ *www.kiya-hamono.co.jp* Ⓜ *Ginza subway line, Mitsukoshi-mae Station (Exit A6).*

GINZA 銀座

CLOTHING

Fodor's Choice ★ **Dover Street Market.** This multistory fashion playhouse is a shrine to exclusives, one-offs, and other hard-to-find pieces from luxury brands all over the world. Curated by Comme des Garçons, the selection may leave all but the most dedicated fashion fans scratching their heads, but the unique interior sculptures and rooftop shrine with Japanese garden alone warrant a visit. ⊠ *6–9–5 Ginza, Chūo-ku, Ginza* ☎ *03/6228–5080* ⊕ *ginza.doverstreetmarket.com* Ⓜ *Ginza, Hibiya, and Marunouchi subway lines, Ginza Station (Exit A2).*

FAMILY **Uniqlo** (ユニクロ). Customers can wrap themselves in simple, low-price items from the company's own brand. This 12-story location is the world's largest, and sells men's, women's, and children's clothing right on the main Ginza drag. ⊠ *6–9–5 Ginza, Chuo-ku, Ginza* ☎ *03/6252–5181* Ⓜ *Ginza, Hibiya, and Marunouchi subway lines, Ginza Station (Exit A2).*

DEPARTMENT STORES

Fodor's Choice ★ **Matsuya** (松屋). On the fourth floor, this gleaming department store houses an excellent selection of Japanese fashion, including Issey Miyake and Yohji Yamamoto. The European-designer boutiques on the second floor are particularly popular with Tokyo's brand-obsessed shoppers. The rooftop terrace is a welcome respite for the weary. ⊠ *3–6–1 Ginza, Chūo-ku, Ginza* ☎ *03/3567–1211* ⊕ *www.matsuya. com/visitor/en* Ⓜ *Ginza, Marunouchi, and Hibiya subway lines, Ginza Station (Exit A12).*

Mitsukoshi (三越). The Ginza branch of Japan's first department-store chain has been open since 1930 and remains the largest department store in the area, with a sprawling grass-covered terrace on the ninth floor that provides a respite from the shopping bustle. On the third floor is an area called "Le Place" that sells only local designer fashion, and the two basement floors have an impressive selection of delicacies. ⊠ *4–6–16 Ginza, Chūo-ku, Ginza* ☎ *03/3562–1111* ⊕ *mitsukoshi.mistore. jp.e.bm.bp.transer.com/store/ginza/index.html* Ⓜ *Ginza, Marunouchi, and Hibiya subway lines, Ginza Station (Exits A6, A7, and A8).*

FAMILY
Fodor's Choice ★ **Muji** (無印良品). This chain sells generically branded housewares and clothing at reasonable prices. At the massive Ginza store is a large selection of furniture, appliances, bedding, and clothes for the whole family, all in the signature Bauhaus-inspired simplified designs. If you're a bit overwhelmed by the options, relax at the dining area that boasts— what else?—Muji meals. ⊠ *3–8–3 Marunouchi, Chiyoda-ku, Ginza* ☎ *03/5208–8241* Ⓜ *JR Yamanote Line, Yuraku-cho subway line, Yuraku-cho Station (JR Kyobashi Exit, subway Exit D9).*

Wako (和光). This grand old department store is well known for its high-end watches, glassware, and jewelry, as well as having some of the most sophisticated window displays in town. The clock atop the curved 1930s-era building is illuminated at night, making it one of Tokyo's more recognized landmarks. ⊠ *4–5–11 Ginza, Chūo-ku,*

Continued on page 217

 # SHOP TOKYO

(*) By Misha Janette

Tokyo, the most retail-dense city in the world, lures even the most reluctant shoppers with promises of every product imaginable. Travel back in time at department and specialty stores selling traditional ceramics and lacquerware, or leap into the future in Akihabara and other gadget-oriented neighborhoods. Fashionistas watch trends in Harajuku morph before their eyes, while those with more highbrow sensibilities browse the jewelry at stalwarts like Mikimoto.

Each Tokyo neighborhood has its own specialty, style, mood, and type of customer. Local production still thrives in the city's backstreets despite an influx of global chains and mega-corporations. Keep in mind, however, that nearly all of the locally produced goods will cost a pretty penny; the Japanese are meticulous in design and quality, and tend to prefer small-scale production to large output. Here in Tokyo you will find that one-offs and limited-edition items are often the norm rather than the exception.

For clothing, sizing is still the biggest roadblock to really getting the most from Tokyo boutiques. But with the abundance of quirky trends sometimes it's enough just to window-shop.

Above: Shoppers mill around the entrance to Tokyo's Louis Vuitton.

WHAT TO BUY

MANGA

Manga, or Japanese comic books, have had an incredible influence on pop culture around the world. The inherently Japanese-style illustrations are fun to look at, and the simple language is great for studying. Book-Off, a well-known used manga chain, sells comics at rock-bottom prices, sometimes ¥100 each.

INNERWEAR

The Japanese are known for their electronics, but did you know their textile and fiber industry is also one of the most advanced in the world? The sweat-repelling, heat-conducting, UBAV/UVB-blocking and aloe-vera dispensing underthings available at Tokyo department stores are probably already in every Japanese person's top drawer at home.

FLAVORED SNACKS

Japan is the land of limited-edition products, and every season brings new, adventurous flavors in finite quantities. All it takes is a trip to the local convenience store to find melon- or Sakura-flavored Kit-Kat bars, or sweet Mont Blanc-flavored Pepsi. We dare you to try them.

PHONE ACCESSORIES

Cell phones and their accoutrement have become a fashion statement all their own. Phone straps, small plastic models that hang from one's phone, are the most popular. They come in all forms, from Asahi beer bottles to Hello Kitty dolls. There are also matching plastic "no peek" sheets that prevent others from spying on your phone's screen.

HOUSEWARES

Tokyoites appreciate fine design, and this passion is reflected in the exuberance of the city's *zakka* shops—retailers that sell small housewares. The Daikanyama and Aoyama areas positively brim with these stores, but trendy zakka can be found throughout the city. Handmade combs, chopsticks, and towels are other uniquely Japanese treasures to consider picking up while in Tokyo.

RECORDS

Tokyo's small specialty music stores are a real treat: local music and imports from around the world are usually available on both vinyl and CD. Out-of-print or obscure vinyl editions can run well over ¥10,000, but collectors will find the condition of the jackets to be unmatched.

SOCKS

As it's customary in Japanese houses to remove one's shoes, socks are more than mere padding between foot and shoe. It's no surprise, then, that the selection of socks goes well beyond black and white. Stripes, polka-dots, Japanese scenery, and monograms are just some of the depictions you'll find at the high-end sock boutiques. The complicated weaving techniques mean they will also cost more than the average cotton pair.

SAKE SETS

Sake is a big deal here, and the type of sake presented to another can make or break business deals and friendships. Better than just a bottle are the gift sets that include the short sake glasses and oversized bottles in beautiful packaging fit for royalty.

JEWELRY

Japan has always been known for its craftsmen who possess the ability to create finely detailed work. Jewelry is no exception, especially when cultured pearls are used. Pearls, which have become something of a national symbol, are not inexpensive, but they are much cheaper in Japan than elsewhere.

WASHLETTE TOILET SEATS

It may seem ludicrous, but the Japanese "washlette" toilet seat is perhaps the best innovation of this millennium. The seats are heated, come with deodorizers, and may even play music to mask any "rude" sounds. Even better, some can be retrofitted to old toilets—just be sure to check your seat measurements before leaving home.

CHARCOAL

Japanese women have been using charcoal, or *takesumi*, in their beauty routines for centuries, believing it cleans out the pores and moisturizes the skin. Charcoal-infused formulas are used in soaps, cleansers, cremes, and masques, and often are naturally colored pitch-black like squid ink.

FOLK CRAFTS

Japanese folk crafts, called *mingei*—among them bamboo vases and baskets, fabrics, paper boxes, dolls, and toys—achieve a unique beauty in their simple and sturdy designs. Be aware, however, that simple does not mean cheap. Long hours of labor go into these objects, and every year there are fewer craftspeople left, producing their work in smaller and smaller quantities. Include these items in your budget ahead of time: The best—worth every cent—can be fairly expensive.

EXPERIENCING JAPANESE DEPATO

The impressive architecture at the Prada flagship matches the designer wares inside.

A visit to a Japanese *depato* (department store) is the perfect Cliff's Notes introduction to Japanese culture. Impeccable service combines with the best luxury brands, gourmet food, and traditional goods—all displayed as enticing eye candy.

These large complexes are found around major train stations and are often owned by the conglomerate rail companies who make their profit when visitors take the train to shop there. The stores themselves commonly have travel agencies, theaters, and art galleries on the premises, as well as reasonably priced and strategically placed restaurants and cafés.

ARRIVE EARLY
The best way to get the full experience is to arrive just as the store is opening. Err on the early side: Tokyo's department stores are exacting in their opening times. White-gloved ladies and gents bow to waiting customers when the doors open on the hour. Early birds snatch up limited-edition food and goods before they sell out. There's never a dearth of reasons to come: local celebrity appearances, designer Q&A sessions, and fairs.

ANATOMY OF A DEPATO
The first floors typically house cosmetics, handbags, and shoes, with the next few floors up going to luxury import brands. On many a top floor you'll find gift packages containing Japan's best-loved brands of sake, rice crackers, and other foods. Department stores also typically devote one floor to traditional Japanese crafts, including ceramics, paintings, and lacquerware.

Don't miss the *depachika* (food departments) on the basement levels, where an overwhelming selection of expensive Japanese and Western delicacies are wrapped with the utmost care. More affordable versions come packed deli-style to be taken home for lunch or dinner.

Shibuya's depato attract trendsetters.

BEST DEPATO FOR...

Most department stores are similar and house the same brands. But some have distinctive characteristics.

The Trendy Dresser: Seibu in Shibuya and Ikebukuro is known for its collection of fashion-forward tenants.

Emerging Designers: Isetan in Shinjuku oozes style and has ample space on the fourth floor dedicated to up-and-coming designers.

Gifts: Shinjuku's Takashimaya is the place to buy souvenirs for discerning friends back home.

Traditional Crafts: Mitsukoshi in Nihombashi will leave those looking for a bit of Old Japan wide-eyed.

Depato interiors are often dramatic.

TIPS FOR DEPATO SHOPPING

■ Major department stores accept credit cards and provide shipping services.

■ It's important to remember that, unlike most of the Western world, goods must be purchased in the department where they were found. This goes for nearly every multilevel shop in Japan.

■ Nowadays, most salesclerks speak some English. If you're having communication difficulties, someone will always come to the rescue.

■ On the first floor you'll invariably find a general information booth with maps of the store in English.

■ Some department stores close one or two days a month. To be on the safe side, call ahead.

FASHIONABLE TOKYO

The Japanese fashion scene has gone through many changes since Yohji Yamamoto's solemn, deconstructed garments and Rei Kawakubo's Comme des Garçons clothing lines challenged norms in the 1980s. While these designers and their ilk are still revered, it's Tokyo's street fashion that keeps the city on the world's radar.

Clockwise from top left: An orange-haired Harajuku Girl; manga-influenced street fashion; Sailor Moon-inspired Harajuku girls.

Thanks to Gwen Stefani's "Harajuku Girls" and Quentin Tarantino's *Kill Bill*, images of the Gothic Lolita—a fashion subculture typified by a Victorian porcelain-doll look punctuated by dark makeup and macabre accessories—have seeped into Western popular culture. New subcultures, or "tribes," like the Harajuku Girls emerge, take hold in Tokyo, and evolve (or get thrown aside) with blazing speed. The "forest girl" tribe's aesthetic draws from sources such as the American prairie and traditional German attire in loose layers, often in organic and vintage materials. The "skirt boys" are among the mens' tribes. These cool boys stomp around in boots and skirts that Japanese menswear designers have been favoring on the runway in recent years.

Japanese fashion continues to awe and inspire; international designers come to Tokyo for ideas. This means you might already be wearing something from Tokyo without even knowing it!

SIZING UP JAPANESE SIZES

Japanese garments, even if they are not a troublesome and common "one-size-fits-all," run considerably smaller than American items. The female aesthetic tends to favor loose and roomy shapes so is far more forgiving than the menswear, which is often cut impossibly small and tight.

Shibuya brands often carry items in nothing more than an arbitrary "one-size-only" on the racks that may not fit many Westerners at all. Many designers, in deference to the growing foreign market, are starting to offer larger sizes. The internationally recognized brands, department stores, and bigger boutiques, including Opening Ceremony in Shibuya, are the best bets for finding a range of sizes.

Shoes tend to run small, often stopping at 27 cm (U.S. size 9) for men and 24 cm (U.S. size 8) for women. What's more, Japanese shoes are often made a little wider than their Western counterparts.

Above: Harajuku Girls wear dramatic costume-like outfits.

A TALE OF TWO NEIGHBORHOOD STYLES

You don't need to be an industry insider attending Japan's Fashion Week shows to get a sense of Tokyo's multiple styles; you just need to stroll the neighborhoods where every sidewalk is a catwalk.

Japanese street fashion begins and ends along the maze-like backstreets of **Harajuku**, referred to as "Ura-Hara." You'll find many of Tokyo's most popular and promising up-and-coming brands' boutiques, although it might take sharp eyes to spot the often-obstructed store signs. Tokyo's youngest shoppers come for the newest fashions and to show off their costume-like vestments. Visit on a Sunday to see them in full regalia. If the throngs of tweens prove too much, there are other incredible street-fashion shopping areas. Shimokitazawa and Koenji are known for their used-clothing shops and a young fashion scene that's just as lively as that of Harajuku.

For a different take, go to **Shibuya**, where women and men have cultivated a distinctive fashion and lifestyle. The so-called Shibuya style is vivid, brash, and hyper, and comes with its own idols, models, and magazines. Malls such as 109, which is the center of this movement's universe, dedicate their retail space wholly to this world.

More than 50,000 people, including many visitors to Tokyo, attend the biannual **Tokyo Girls Collection**, daylong events of Shibuya-style fashion shows and musical performances by pop big acts. JTB offers full package tours around the event starting at ¥8,000 per person.

FIVE EMERGING DESIGNERS

Limi Feu: Limi, Yohji Yamamoto's daughter, takes a hint from him in her loose, monotone, punk attire, but injects it with a cool, feminine touch. ⊕ www.limifeu.com

Matohu: This unisex brand creates looks based on traditional and colorful Japanese clothing, namely robes, by incorporating ancient dye and weaving techniques into 21st-century designs. ⊕ www.matohu.com/en

N. Hoolywood: Daisuke Obana's menswear line has been on the top of Japanese editors' lists since 2002. He adds contemporary design elements to used clothing, and his attire tends to be loose and casual. ⊕ www.n-hoolywood.com

Phenomenon: This is one of the most exciting menswear brands to come out since A Bathing Ape. Expect a combo of hip-hop, 80s, and bespoke tailoring with pitch-perfect styling. ⊕ www.phenomenon.tv

Somarta: This brand is known for its intricate, seamless knitwear and other experimental textiles developed using Japanese technology. The menswear line called Molfic follows the same innovative ethos in its seasonless designs. ⊕ www.somarta.jp

Top to bottom: Limi Feu, N. Hoolywood, Somarta

CLOSE UP

Shopping in Kappabashi

A wholesale-restaurant-supply district might not sound like a promising shopping destination, but Kappabashi, about a 10-minute walk west of the temples and pagodas of Asakusa, is worth a look. Ceramics, cutlery, cookware, folding lanterns, and even kimonos can all be found here, along with the kitschy plastic food models that appear in restaurant windows throughout Japan. The best strategy is to stroll up and down the 1-km (½-mile) length of Kappabashi-dogu-machi-dori and visit any shop that looks interesting. Most stores here emphasize function over charm, but some manage to stand out for their stylish spaces as well. Most Kappabashi shops are open until 5:30; some close Sunday. To get here, take the Ginza subway line to Tawara-machi Station.

3

Ginza ☎ *03/3562–2111* ⊕ *www.wako.co.jp* Ⓜ *Ginza, Marunouchi, and Hibiya subway lines, Ginza Station (Exits A9 and A10).*

ELECTRONICS

Apple Store. Like its counterparts in cities around the world, this very stylish showroom displays the newest models from Apple's line of computer products. The Genius Bar on the second floor provides consulting services should you need to resuscitate a comatose iPad or MacBook while traveling. ✉ *3–5–12 Ginza, Chūō-ku, Ginza* ☎ *03/5159–8200* ⊕ *www.apple.com/jp/retail/ginza* Ⓜ *Ginza, Hibiya, and Marunouchi subway lines, Ginza Station (Exit A13).*

FAMILY **Sony Building** (ソニービル). Test-drive the latest Sony gadgets at this retail and entertainment space in the heart of Ginza. The first- to fourth-floor showrooms allow parents to fiddle with digital cameras and computers from Japan's electronics leader, while kids can enjoy interactive displays of electric trains and weight-sensitive musical stairs. The Opus theater on the eighth floor shows movie trailers on a super-high-definition 4K screen and hosts games and events to coincide with movie releases. Take a break by browsing the Internet for free or at one of the cafés or pubs on the floors above the showroom. ✉ *5–3–1 Ginza, Chūō-ku, Ginza* ☎ *03/3573–2371* ⊕ *www.sonybuilding.jp/e* Ⓜ *JR Yamanote Line, Yuraku-cho Station (Ginza Exit); Ginza, Hibiya, and Marunouchi subway lines, Ginza Station (Exit B9).*

Sukiya Camera (スキヤカメラ). The cramped Nikon House branch of this two-store operation features so many Nikons—old and new, digital and film—that it could double as a museum to the brand. Plenty of lenses and flashes are available as well. ✉ *4–2–13 Ginza, Chūō-ku, Ginza* ☎ *03/3561–6000* Ⓜ *JR Yamanote Line, Yuraku-cho Station (Ginza Exit); Ginza, Hibiya, and Marunouchi subway lines, Ginza Station (Exit B10).*

JEWELRY

Ginza Tanaka (銀座田中). One of the finest jewelers in Japan was founded in 1892. The store specializes in precious metals and diamond jewelry. It also sells a wide variety of art objects in gold, like those found

CLOSE UP

The Power of Tea

Green tea is ubiquitous in Japan. But did you know that besides being something of a national drink, it's also good for you? Green tea contains antioxidants twice as powerful as those in red wine; these help reduce high blood pressure, lower blood sugar, and fight cancer. A heightened immune system and lower cholesterol are other benefits attributed to this beverage.

Whether drinking green tea for its healing properties, good taste, or as a manner of habit, you'll have plenty of choices in Japan. Pay attention to tea varietals, which are graded by the quality and parts of the plant used, because price and quality runs the spectrum within these categories. For the very best Japanese green tea, take a trip to the Uji region of Kyoto.

Bancha (common tea). This second-harvest variety ripens between summer and fall, producing leaves larger than those of sencha and a weaker-tasting tea.

Genmai (brown rice tea). This is a mixture, usually in equal parts, of green tea and roasted brown rice.

Genmaicha (popcorn tea). This is a blend of bancha and genmai teas.

Gyokuro (jewel dew). Derived from a grade of green tea called *tencha* (divine tea), the name comes from the light-green color the tea develops when brewed. Gyokuro is grown in the shade, an essential condition to develop just this type and grade.

Hojicha (panfried tea). A panfried or oven-roasted green tea.

Kabusecha (covered tea). Similar to gyokuro, kabusecha leaves are grown in the shade, though for a shorter period, giving it a refined flavor.

Kukicha (stalk tea). A tea made from stalks by harvesting one bud and three leaves.

Matcha (rubbed tea). Most often used in the tea ceremony, matcha is a high-quality, hard-to-find powdered green tea. It has a thick, paintlike consistency when mixed with hot water. It is also a popular flavor of ice cream and other sweets in Japan.

Sencha (roasted tea). This is the green tea you are most likely to try at the local noodle or bento shop. Its leaves are grown under direct sunlight, giving it a different flavor from cousins like gyokuro.

---

on Buddhist altars. ⊠ *1–7–7 Ginza, Chūō-ku, Ginza* ☎ *03/5561–0491* ⊕ *www.ginzatanaka.co.jp/en* Ⓜ *Yuraku-cho subway line, Ginza 1-chome Station (Exit 7).*

Fodor's Choice **Mikimoto.** Kokichi Mikimoto created his technique for cultured pearls
★ in 1893. Since then his name has been associated with the best quality in the industry. Mikimoto's tower in Ginza is a boutique devoted to nature's ready-made gems; the building, like the pearls it holds, dazzles visitors with a facade that resembles Swiss cheese. ⊠ *2–4–12 Ginza, Chūō-ku, Ginza* ☎ *03/3562–3130* ⊕ *www.mikimoto.com* Ⓜ *Ginza, Hibiya, and Marunouchi subway lines, Ginza Station (Exit C8).*

Tasaki Pearls (田崎). Tasaki sells pearls at slightly lower prices than Mikimoto. The brand opened this glittery flagship tower in Ginza that moved them from the old guard into the contemporary big leagues.

There's a large collection of pearl and gem items, from costume to bridal and fine jewelry. On the fifth floor is an event space that holds numerous art exhibits. ⊠ *5–7–5 Ginza, Chūō-ku, Ginza* ☎ *03/3289–1111* ⊕ *www.tasaki.co.jp* Ⓜ *Ginza, Hibiya, and Marunouchi subway lines, Ginza Station (Exit A2).*

KIMONO

Tansu-ya (たんす屋). This small but pleasant Ginza shop has attractive used kimonos, yukata, and other traditional clothing in many fabrics, colors, and patterns. The helpful staff can acquaint you with the somewhat complicated method of putting on the garments. There are tax-free locations scattered throughout the city, including Shibuya, Asakusa, Aoyama, and Shibuya. ⊠ *3–4–5 Ginza, Chūō-ku, Ginza* ☎ *03/3561–8529* ⊕ *tansuya.jp* Ⓜ *Ginza, Hibiya, and Marunouchi subway lines, Ginza Station (Exit A13).*

PAPER

Itoya (伊東屋). Completely remodeled in 2015, this huge paper emporium is brimming with locally crafted and imported stationery, much of which is designed to translate traditional motifs onto contemporary office tools. ⊠ *2–7–15 Ginza, Chūō-ku, Ginza* ☎ *03/3561–8311* ⊕ *www.ito-ya.co.jp* Ⓜ *Ginza, Hibiya, and Marunouchi subway lines, Ginza Station (Exit A13).*

Kyukyodo (鳩居堂). Kyukyodo has been in business since 1663—and in this spacious Ginza location since 1880—selling wonderful handmade Japanese papers, paper products, incense, brushes, and other materials for calligraphy. ⊠ *5–7–4 Ginza, Chūō-ku, Ginza* ☎ *03/3571–4429* ⊕ *www.kyukyodo.co.jp* Ⓜ *Ginza, Hibiya, and Marunouchi subway lines, Ginza Station (Exit A2).*

SHOPPING STREETS AND ARCADES

International Shopping Arcade (インターナショナルアーケード). A ragtag collection of shops holds a range of goods, including cameras, electronics, pearls, and kimonos in a retro passageway. The shops are duty-free, and most of the sales staff speaks decent English. If you listen carefully you'll hear the rumble of cars passing above on the freeway that forms the roof of the building. ⊠ *1–7–23 Uchisaiwai-cho, Chiyoda-ku, Ginza* Ⓜ *Chiyoda and Hibiya subway lines, Hibiya Station (Exit A13).*

SWORDS AND KNIVES

Fodor's Choice ★ **Nippon Token** (日本刀剣 *Japan Sword*). Wannabe samurai can learn how to tell their *toshin* (blades) from their *tsuka* (sword handles) with help from the English-speaking staff at this small shop, which has been open since the Meiji era (1868–1912). Items that range from a circa-1390 samurai sword to inexpensive or decorative reproductions allow you to take a trip back in time. ⊠ *3–8–1 Toranomon, Minato-ku, Ginza* ☎ *03/3434–4321* ⊕ *www.japansword.co.jp* ⊗ *Closed Sun.* Ⓜ *Hibiya and Ginza subway lines, Tora-no-mon Station (Exit 2).*

Token Shibata (刀剣柴田). This tiny, threadbare shop incongruously situated near Ginza's glittering department stores sells expensive well-worn antique swords. They can also sharpen your blade for you, if you happen to be packing while traveling. ✉ *5–6–8 Ginza, Chūō-ku, Ginza* ☎ *03/3573–2801* ◷ *Closed Sun.* Ⓜ *Ginza, Hibiya, and Marunouchi subway lines, Ginza Station (Exit A1).*

MARUNOUCHI 丸の内

BOOKS

FAMILY **Maruzen** (丸善書店). In this flagship branch of the Maruzen chain in the Oazo building, there are English titles on the fourth floor as well as art books; the store also hosts occasional art exhibits. ✉ *1–6–4 Marunouchi, Chiyoda-ku* ☎ *03/5288–8881* ⊕ *www.maruzen.co.jp* Ⓜ *JR Yamanote Line, Tokyo Station (North Exit); Tozai subway line, Otemachi Station (Exit B2C).*

HOUSEWARES

Pass the Baton (パスザバトン). *Zakka* is what the Japanese call small knickknacks and gifts, and this eccentric store is brimming with zakka from the coffers of local fashion designers, artists, magazine editors, celebrities, and other stylish Tokyo denizens. The carefully curated goods are fixed up and resold, with an option to give a portion of the profit to charity. It is tucked inside the Brick Square complex, next to an English rose garden. ✉ *2–6–1 Marunouchi, Chiyoda-ku* ☎ *03/6269–9555* ⊕ *www.pass-the-baton.com* Ⓜ *Marunouchi subway line, Tokyo Station (Marunouchi Bldg. Exit); JR Yamanote Line, Tokyo Station (Marunouchi Minami-guchi/South Exit).*

MALLS AND SHOPPING CENTERS

Marunouchi Buildings (丸の内ビル). Bringing some much-needed retail dazzle to the area are these six shopping, office, and dining megacomplexes called Marunocuhi, Shin-marunouchi, Oazu, Iiyo, Brick Square, and Tokia. Highlights include the fifth-floor open terrace on the Marunouchi building, with its view of Tokyo Station, and Bricksquare, which has its own oasislike European garden on the ground floor to rest in between bouts of shopping at the luxury and everyday boutiques. ✉ *2–4–1 Marunouchi, Chiyoda-ku, Marunouchi* ☎ *03/5218–5100* ⊕ *www.marunouchi.com/e* Ⓜ *Marunouchi subway line, Tokyo Station (Marunouchi Bldg. Exit); JR Yamanote Line, Tokyo Station (Marunouchi Minami-guchi/South Exit).*

AOYAMA 青山

ANTIQUES

Fuji-Torii (富士鳥居). An English-speaking staff, a central Omotesando location, and antiques ranging from ceramics to swords are the big draws at this shop, in business since 1948. In particular, Fuji-Torii has an excellent selection of folding screens, lacquerware, painted glassware, and *ukiyo-e* (wood-block prints). You can also pick up contemporary gifts, such as reading glasses with frames wrapped in traditional fabric. ✉ *6–1–10 Jingu-mae, Shibuya-ku, Aoyama* ☎ *03/3400–2777* ⊕ *www.fuji-torii.com* ◷ *Closed Tues. and 3rd Mon. of every month* Ⓜ *Chiyoda and Fukutoshin subway lines, Meiji-Jingu-mae Station (Exit 4).*

Komingei Morita (古民芸もりた *Traditional Crafts Morita*). Antiques and new *mingei* (Japanese folk crafts) are on display alongside a large stock of textiles from throughout Asia. An easy-to-transport gift would be *furoshiki*, which is rather inexpensive wood-blocked cloth used as decorative covers in daily life. ⊠ *5–12–2 Minami-Aoyama, Minato-ku, Aoyama* ☎ *03/3407–4466* ⊕ *www.aoyama-omotesandou.com/global/english.html* Ⓜ *Ginza, Chiyoda, and Hanzo-mon subway lines, Omotesando Station (Exit B1).*

CERAMICS

Tsutaya Kakichaki (つたや花器茶器 *Tsutaya Ikebana and Tea*). Ikebana (flower arrangement) and *sado* (tea ceremony) goods are the only items sold at this shop, but they come in such stunning variety that a visit is definitely worthwhile. Colorful vases in surprising shapes and traditional ceramic tea sets make unique souvenirs. ⊠ *5–10–5 Minami-Aoyama, Minato-ku, Aoyama* ☎ *03/3400–3815* Ⓜ *Ginza, Chiyoda, and Hanzo-mon subway lines, Omotesando Station (Exit B1).*

CLOTHING

Bapexclusive Aoyama. Since the late 1990s, no brand has been more coveted by Harajuku scenesters than the BATHING APE label (shortened to BAPE) founded by DJ–fashion designer NIGO. At the height of the craze, hopefuls would line up outside NIGO's well-hidden boutiques for the chance to plop down ¥7,000 for a T-shirt festooned with a simian visage or *Planet of the Apes* quote. BAPE has since gone aboveground, with the brand expanding across the globe. You can see what the fuss is all about in this spacious two-story shop with an upstairs conveyor belt of sneakers that is always a draw. ⊠ *5–5–8 Minami-Aoyama, Minato-ku, Aoyama* ☎ *03/3407–2145* ⊕ *www.bape.com* Ⓜ *Ginza and Hanzo-mon subway lines, Omotesando Station (Exit A5).*

Fodor's Choice ★ **Comme des Garçons** (コムデギャルソン). Sinuous low walls snake through Comme des Garçons founder Rei Kawakubo's flagship store, a minimalist labyrinth that houses the designer's signature clothes, shoes, and accessories. Staff members do their best to ignore you, but that's no reason to stay away from one of Tokyo's funkiest retail spaces. ⊠ *5–2–1 Minami-Aoyama, Minato-ku, Aoyama* ☎ *03/3406–3951* ⊕ *www.comme-des-garcons.com* Ⓜ *Ginza, Chiyoda, and Hanzo-mon subway lines, Omotesando Station (Exit A5).*

Fodor's Choice ★ **Issey Miyake** (イッセイミヤケ). The otherworldly creations of internationally renowned brand Issey Miyake are on display at his flagship store in Aoyama, which carries the full Paris line. Keep walking on the same street away from Omotesando Station and also find a string of other Miyake stores just a stone's throw away, including Issey Miyake Men and Pleats Please. At the end of the street is the Reality Lab with a barrage of Miyake's most experimental lines like BaoBao, In-Ei, and incredible origamilike clothing. ⊠ *3–18–11 Minami-Aoyama, Minato-ku, Aoyama* ☎ *03/3423–1408* ⊕ *www.isseymiyake.com* Ⓜ *Ginza, Chiyoda, and Hanzo-mon subway lines, Omotesando Station (Exit A4).*

Fodor's Choice ★ **Prada.** This fashion "epicenter," designed by Herzog & de Meuron, is one of the most buzzed-about architectural wonders in the city. Its facade is made up of a mosaic of green glass "bubble" windows:

alternating convex and concave panels create distorted reflections of the surrounding area. Many world-renowned, nearby boutiques have tried to replicate the significant impact the Prada building has had on the Omotesando, but none have been unable to match this tower. Most visitors opt for a photo in front of the cavelike entrance that leads into the basement floor. ✉ *5–2–6 Minami-Aoyama, Minato-ku, Aoyama* ☎ *03/6418–0400* Ⓜ *Ginza, Chiyoda, and Hanzo-mon subway lines, Omotesando Station (Exit A5).*

Undercover (アンダーカバー). This stark shop houses Paris darling Jun Takahashi's cult clothing. Racks of men's and women's punkish duds sit under a ceiling made of a sea of thousands of hanging lightbulbs. ✉ *5–3–18 Minami-Aoyama, Minato-ku, Aoyama* ☎ *03/3407–1232* ⊕ *www.undercoverism.com* Ⓜ *Ginza, Chiyoda, and Hanzo-mon subway lines, Omotesando Station (Exit A5).*

CRAFTS

Oriental Bazaar (オリエンタルバザー). The three floors of this popular tourist destination are packed with just about anything you could want as a traditional Japanese handicraft souvenir: painted screens, pottery, chopsticks, dolls, and more, all at very reasonable prices. ✉ *5–9–13 Jingu-mae, Shibuya-ku, Aoyama* ☎ *03/3400–3933* ⊕ *www.orientalbazaar.co.jp* ☾ *Closed Thurs.* Ⓜ *Chiyoda and Fukutoshin subway lines, Meiji-Jingu-mae Station (Exit 4).*

FOOD

FAMILY

Fodor's Choice

★

Ginza Natsuno (銀座夏野). This two-story boutique sells an incredible range of chopsticks, from traditional to pop motifs, and wooden to crystal-encrusted sticks that can be personalized. Children's chopsticks and dishes are housed in their own boutique behind it, but it's a must-see no matter your age. ✉ *4–2–17 Jingu-mae, Aoyama* ☎ *03/3403–6033* ⊕ *www.e-ohashi.com* Ⓜ *Ginza, Chiyoda, and Hanzo-mon subway lines, Omotesando Station (Exit A2).*

HOUSEWARES

Sempre (センプレ). Playful, colorful, and bright describe both the products and the space of this Kotto-dori housewares dealer. Among the great finds here are interesting tableware, glassware, lamps, and jewelry. ✉ *5–13–3 Minami-Aoyama, Minato-ku, Aoyama* ☎ *03/5464–5655* ⊕ *www.sempre.jp* Ⓜ *Ginza, Chiyoda, and Hanzo-mon subway lines, Omotesando Station (Exit B1).*

KIMONO

Gallery Kawano (ギャラリー川野). Kawano sells kimonos and kimono fabric in a variety of patterns. A satchel made of crepe fabric called *kinchaku* is the bag traditionally held when wearing a kimono, and cute little patchwork ones here make a unique find. ✉ *4–4–9 Jingu-mae, Shibuya-ku, Aoyama* ☎ *03/3470–3305* ⊕ *gallery-kawano.com* Ⓜ *Ginza, Chiyoda, and Hanzo-mon subway lines, Omotesando Station (Exit A2).*

MALLS AND SHOPPING CENTERS

Glassarea (グラッセリア). Virtually defining Aoyama elegance is this small cobblestone shopping center, which draws well-heeled young professionals to its handful of fashion boutiques, spa, and a specialty store of Japanese crafts from Fukui Prefecture. ⊠ *5–4–41 Minami-Aoyama, Minato-ku, Aoyama* ☎ *03/5778–4450* ⊕ *www.glassarea.com* Ⓜ *Ginza, Chiyoda, and Hanzo-mon subway lines, Omotesando Station (Exit B1).*

Gyre (ジャイル). Near the Harajuku end of Omotesando, this mall houses luxury-brand shops such as Chanel and Maison Martin Margiela, three concept shops by Comme des Garçons, and one of only two Museum of Modern Art Design Stores outside New York City. ⊠ *5–10–1 Jingu-mae, Shibuya-ku, Harajuku* ☎ *03/5400–5801* ⊕ *gyre-omotesando.com* Ⓜ *Chiyoda and Fukutoshin subway lines, Meiji-Jingu-mae Station (Exit 4).*

Omotesando Hills (表参道ヒルズ). Architect Tadao Ando's adventure in concrete is also one of Tokyo's monuments to shopping. Despised and adored with equal zeal, the controversial project demolished the charming yet antiquated Dojunkai Aoyama Apartments along Omotesando Avenue. Six wedge-shape floors include some brand-name heavy hitters (Saint Laurent and Harry Winston) and a wide range of smaller stores whose shelves showcase mid- to high-end shoes and bags. It's worth a stroll to see the latest in Japanese haute couture, and restaurants and cafés can also be found here—but beware of long lines. ⊠ *4–12–10 Jingu-mae, Shibuya-ku, Aoyama* ☎ *03/3497–0310* ⊕ *www.omotesandohills.com* Ⓜ *Hanzo-mon, Ginza, and Chiyoda subway lines, Omotesando Station (Exit A2), Chiyoda and Fukutoshin subway lines, Meiji-Jingumae Station (Exit 4).*

HARAJUKU 原宿

CLOTHING

6% Doki Doki. If there's one shop that is the epitome of crazy, *kawaii* (cute) Harajuku fashion, it's this pastel dollhouselike shop on the second floor of a nondescript building. The acid-color tutus and glittery accessories are part of a style called "kawaii anarchy" and may be the most unique shopping experience in Tokyo. The colorful shopgirls alone are an attraction, and if asked nicely they will happily pose for photos. ⊠ *4–28–16 Jingu-mae, Shibuya-ku, Harajuku* ☎ *03/3479–6116* ⊕ *www.dokidoki6.com* Ⓜ *Chiyoda and Fukutoshin subway lines, Meiji-Jingu-mae Station (Exit 5).*

Fodor's Choice ★ **Beams** (ビームス). Harajuku features a cluster of no fewer than 10 Beams stores that provide Japan's younger men and women with extremely hip threads. With branches ranging from street wear to high-end import brands, as well as a record store, uniform gallery, funky "from Tokyo" souvenir shop that sells anime figurines, and one that sells manga alongside designer-made T-shirts inspired by comic books, shopping here ensures that you or your kids will be properly stocked with the coolest wares from the city. ⊠ *3–24–7 Jingu-mae, Shibuya-ku, Harajuku* ☎ *03/3470–3947* ⊕ *www.beams.co.jp* Ⓜ *JR Harajuku*

Station (Takeshita-Dori Exit); Chiyoda and Fukutoshin subway lines, Meiji-Jingu-mae Station (Exit 5).

MALLS AND SHOPPING CENTERS

Laforet (ラフォーレ). This mall is so earnest about staying on the tip of Harajuku fashion trends that it changes out stores every six months. While shop genres vary, from Gothic Lolita to bohemian chic, they all target fashion-conscious teenagers. Rumor has it that many of the West's top fashion designers still come here to look for inspiration for their next collections. ✉ *1–11–6 Jingu-mae, Shibuya-ku, Harajuku* ☎ *03/3475–0411* ⊕ *www.laforet.ne.jp/en* Ⓜ *Chiyoda and Fukutoshin subway lines, Meiji-Jingu-mae Station (Exit 5).*

SHIBUYA 渋谷

BOOKS

Daikanyama T-Site. This oasis within the metropolis is a calming respite with a Zen garden, trendy terrace eatery, gallery, and, of course, the main business, a shop selling books, music, and videos with a focus on art and design. Almost all of the 30,000 books here can be taken to the lounge to read, as can a large selection of foreign magazines. Many locals come here to be seen, bringing along their lapdogs dressed in designer duds from the store's pet boutique. ✉ *17–5 Sarugaku-cho, Meguro-ku, Shibuya* ☎ *03/3770–2525* ⊕ *tsite.jp/daikanyama/* Ⓜ *Tokyu Toyoko Line, Daikanyama Station (Central Exit).*

CLOTHING

Harcoza (ハルコ座). This is one of those "only in Tokyo" shops, with a quirky selection of clothing and accessories such as a bonsai tree watch and rings made of solidified croissants and desserts. Even the changing room is a statement: it's a replicated stage for Japanese idols of the '70s and '80s, replete with a disco ball. ✉ *2–15–9 Ebisu-nishi, Shibuya* ☎ *03/6416–0725* ⊕ *www.harcoza.com* ☾ *Closed Tues.* Ⓜ *Tokyu Toyoko Line, Daikanyama Station (West Exit).*

Journal Standard (ジャーナルスタンダード). This is not a chain dedicated to outfitting office workers in shirts and ties. In fact, this branch is frequented by young couples looking for the season's *it* fashions, with the signature JS uber-casual aesthetic. The neighboring boutiques follow in the same vein, so take a stroll down the street as well. ✉ *1–5–6 Jinnan, Shibuya* ☎ *03/5457–0700* ⊕ *journal-standard.jp* Ⓜ *JR Yamanote Line, Ginza, Fukutoshin, and Hanzo-mon subway lines, Shibuya Station (Hachiko Exit for JR, Exits 6 and 7 for subways).*

HOUSEWARES

Tokyu Hands (東急ハンズ). This chain carries a wide and varied assortment of goods, including hobby and crafts materials, art supplies, and knitting and sewing materials, as well as jewelry, household goods, stationery, even cosmetics. There's a new café and exhibit space on the seventh floor with an ever-changing selection of small goods from local artisans for sale. It's not unusual to see Japanese hobbyists spending an entire afternoon browsing in here. ✉ *12–18 Udagawa-cho, Shibuya* ☎ *03/5489–5111* ⊕ *www.tokyu-hands.co.jp/foreign.html* Ⓜ *JR*

Yamanote Line, Ginza, Fukutoshin, and Hanzo-mon subway lines, Shibuya Station (Hachiko Exit for JR, Exits 6 and 7 for subway).

Zero First Design. Kyu-Yamate-dori at Daikanyama is a well-known hub of interior goods stores, and this one is full of unique and modern pieces from both local and international designers. ✉ *2–3–1 Aobadai, Meguro-ku, Shibuya* ☎ *03/5489–6101* ⊕ *01st.com* Ⓜ *Tokyu Toyoko Line, Daikanyama Station (Komazawa-dori Exit).*

JEWELRY AND ACCESSORIES

B Jirushi Yoshida. This Beams boutique's main draw is the limited-edition Porter bag for men and women, plus other collaborations of savvy daily goods, including brands such as Monocle, Wonderwall, and Wacko Maria. ✉ *2F, 19–6 Sarugakucho, Shibuya* ☎ *03/5428–5952* ⊕ *www.bjirushi.com* Ⓜ *Tokyu Toyoko Line, Daikanyama Station (Komazawa-dori Exit).*

LACQUERWARE

Fodor's Choice
★

Yamada Heiando (山田平安堂). With a spacious, airy layout and lovely lacquerware goods, this fashionable shop is a must for souvenir hunters—and anyone else who appreciates fine design. Rice bowls, sushi trays, *bento* lunch boxes, *hashioki* (chopstick rests), and jewelry cases come in traditional blacks and reds, as well as patterns both subtle and bold. Prices are fair—many items cost less than ¥10,000—but these are the kinds of goods for which devotees of Japanese craftsmanship would be willing to pay a lot. ✉ *Hillside Terr. G Block #202, 18–12 Sarugakucho, Shibuya* ☎ *03/3464–5541* ⊕ *www.heiando1919.com* Ⓜ *Tokyu Toyoko Line, Daikanyama Station (Komazawa-dori Exit).*

MALLS AND SHOPPING CENTERS

Parco (渋谷パルコ). These vertical malls filled with small retail shops and boutiques are all within walking distance of one another in the commercial heart of Shibuya. Parco Part 1 caters to a young crowd and stocks many trendy "it" brands from the local runways, though Comme des Garçons Black and the curiously conceptual Pyaruco are less expensive options. Part 3 also sells a mixture of casual fashion and hip interior goods that won't break the bank. ✉ *15–1 Udagawa-cho, Shibuya* ☎ *03/3464–5111* ⊕ *www.parco.co.jp/customer* Ⓜ *Ginza, Fukutoshin, and Hanzo-mon subway lines, Shibuya Station (Exits 6 and 7).*

Shibuya 109. This nine-floor outlet is a teenage girl's dream, especially if they follow the *gyaru* tribe, a particularly gaudy and brash fashion genre born in Shibuya. The place is filled with small stores whose merchandise screams kitsch and trend. Here, the fashionable sales assistants are the stars, and their popularity in this mall can make them media superstars. On weekends, dance concerts and fashion shows are often staged at the front entrance. ✉ *2–29–1 Dogenzaka, Shibuya* ☎ *03/3477–5111* ⊕ *www.shibuya109.jp/en* Ⓜ *JR Yamanote Line, Ginza, Fukutoshin, and Hanzo-mon subway lines, Shibuya Station (Hachiko Exit for JR, Exit 3A for subway lines).*

MUSIC

Manhattan Records (マンハッタンレコード). The hottest hip-hop, reggae, house, and R&B vinyl can be found here, and a DJ booth pumps out the jams from the center of the room. Don't expect a lot of advice from the

Gothic styles influence the striking outfits worn by Harajuku Girls.

staff—no one can hear you over the throbbing tunes. ✉ *10–1 Udagawa-cho, Shibuya* ☎ *03/3477–7166* ⊕ *manhattanrecords.jp* Ⓜ *JR Yamanote Line, Ginza, Fukutoshin, and Hanzo-mon subway lines, Shibuya Station (Hachiko Exit for JR, Exits 6 and 7 for subway).*

Tower Records (タワーレコード). This huge emporium carries one of the most diverse selections of CDs and DVDs in the world. Take a rest at the café after visiting the second floor, which houses books, with a large selection of English-language publications. ✉ *1–22–14 Jinnan, Shibuya* ☎ *03/3496–3661* ⊕ *tower.jp/store/kanto/shibuya* Ⓜ *JR Yamanote Line, Hanzo-mon, Fukutoshin, and Ginza subway lines, Shibuya Station (Hachiko Exit for JR, Exit 7 for subway).*

TOYS

FAMILY
Fodor's Choice
★

Kiddy Land (キディランド). The Omotesando landmark commonly regarded as Tokyo's best toy store carries the cutest and most kitschy of everyday goods that draw in even the most hardened of souls. This is the leader in making or breaking the popularity of the myriad character goods that Japan spits out seasonally. Like caterpillars with salaryman faces, some of the items may be odd or surprising, but they're never boring. ✉ *6–1–9 Jingu-mae, Shibuya-ku, Harajuku* ☎ *03/3409–3431* ⊕ *www.kiddyland.co.jp/en/stores.html* Ⓜ *JR Yamanote Line, Harajuku Station (Omotesando Exit); Chiyoda and Fukutoshin subway lines, Meiji-Jingu-mae Station (Exit 4).*

ROPPONGI 六本木

CERAMICS

Savoir Vivre (サボアービブレ). In the swanky Axis Building, this store sells contemporary and antique tea sets, cups, bowls, and glassware. ⊠ *3F Axis Bldg., 5–17–1 Roppongi, Minato-ku, Roppongi* ☎ *03/3585–7365* ⊕ *savoir-vivre.co.jp* ⊗ *Closed Wed.* Ⓜ *Hibiya and Oedo subway lines, Roppongi Station (Exit 3).*

CLOTHING

Restir (レスティアー). Next to the Midtown Tokyo complex, this is possibly the most exclusive and fashion-forward boutique in the city. It's made up of a cluster of stores, from luxury stores for men and women to a surf and activewear store, a café, and another store dedicated to high-end lifestyle gadgets like headphones, toy cameras, and stylish mobile peripherals. ⊠ *9–6–17 Akasaka, Minato-ku, Roppongi* ☎ *03/5413–3708* ⊕ *restir-holdings.com/section/index.html* Ⓜ *Hibiya and Oedo subway lines, Roppongi Station (Exit 8); Chiyoda subway line, Nogizaka Station (Exit 3).*

MALLS AND SHOPPING CENTERS

Axis (アクシス). Classy and cutting-edge furniture, electronics, fabrics, ceramics, and books are sold at this multistory design center on the main Roppongi drag of Gaien-Higashi-dori. Savoir Vivre has an excellent selection of ceramics, and automobile-philes love the Garage shop for its array of accessories for high-end cars. On the fourth floor, the JIDA Gallery shows the best of what's current in Japanese industrial design. ⊠ *5–17–1 Roppongi, Minato-ku, Roppongi* ☎ *03/3587–2781* ⊕ *www.axisinc.co.jp* ⊗ *Closed Sun.* Ⓜ *Hibiya and Oedo subway lines, Roppongi Station (Exit 3); Namboku subway line, Roppongi Itchome Station (Exit 1).*

FAMILY **Roppongi Hills** (六本木ヒルズ). You could easily spend a whole day exploring the retail areas of this minicity, a complex of shops, restaurants, residential and commercial towers, a nine-screen cineplex, the Grand Hyatt Tokyo hotel, and the Mori Art Museum—all wrapped around the TV Asahi studios and sprawled out in five zones located between the Roppongi intersection and Azabu Juban. The shops here emphasize eye-catching design and chichi brands. The world's only Alexander McQueen accessories store, modern kimono brand Jotaro Saito, and Estnation, with its often-occurring pop-up shops, are good destinations. Finding a particular shop, however, can be a hassle given the building's Escher-like layout. To navigate, go to the information center to retrieve a floor guide with color-coded maps in English; most of the staff members speak English as well. ⊠ *6–10–1 Roppongi, Minato-ku, Roppongi* ☎ *03/6406–6000* ⊕ *www.roppongihills.com* Ⓜ *Hibiya and Oedo subway lines, Roppongi Station (Roppongi Hills Exit).*

Tokyo Midtown (東京ミッドタウン). This huge complex is an architectural statement with sweeping glass roofs and a large walkable garden in the back. The airy, open spaces house exclusive boutiques, hotels, and a concentration of cafés by the world's top pâtissiers on the first few floors. ⊠ *9–7–3 Akasaka, Minato-ku, Roppongi* ☎ *03/3475–3100*

⊕ *www.tokyo-midtown.com/en* Ⓜ *Hibiya and Oedo subway lines, Roppongi Station (Exit 8); Chiyoda subway line, Nogizaka Station (Exit 3).*

SHINJUKU 新宿

BOOKS

Kinokuniya (紀伊国屋). This mammoth bookstore, an annex of Takashimaya, devotes most of its sixth floor to English titles, with an excellent selection of travel guides, magazines, and books on Japan. ✉ *Takashimaya Times Sq., 5–24–2 Sendagaya, Shibuya-ku, Shinjuku* ☎ *03/5361–3301* ⊕ *www.kinokuniya.co.jp* Ⓜ *JR Yamanote Line, Shinjuku Station (Minami-guchi/South Exit); Fukutoshin subway line, Shinjuku Sanchome Station (Exit E8).*

CLOTHING

Don Quixote (ドンキホーテ). This 24-hour discount store has chains all around the country. The generally tight quarters aren't recommended for those with claustrophobia, but bargain-hunters love the costumes, odd cosmetics, family-size bags of Japanese snacks, and used luxury handbags and watches. It's all haphazardly stacked from the floor to the ceiling. ✉ *1–16–5 Kabuki-cho, Shinjuku-ku, Shinjuku* ☎ *03/5291–9211* ⊕ *www.donki.com* Ⓜ *Marunouchi, Oedo, and Shinjuku subway lines, JR Yamanote Line, Keio and Odakyu lines, Shinjuku Station (Higashi-guchi/East Exit).*

CRAFTS

Bingo-ya (備後屋). This tasteful four-floor shop allows you to complete your souvenir shopping in one place. The store carries traditional handicrafts—including ceramics, toys, lacquerware, Noh masks, fabrics, and lots more—from all over Japan. ✉ *10–6 Wakamatsu-cho, Shinjuku-ku, Shinjuku* ☎ *03/3202–8778* ⊕ *www.quasar.nu/bingoya* ◷ *Tues.–Sun. 10–7* ◷ *Closed Mon. and every 3rd weekend of the month* Ⓜ *Oedo subway line, Wakamatsu Kawada Station (Kawada Exit).*

DEPARTMENT STORES

Isetan (伊勢丹). Established in 1886, "The Bergdorf's of Tokyo" is known for its high-end fashions both local and foreign, including a selection of larger sizes not found in most Tokyo stores. The second and third floors have champagne bars and snazzy store design that rival the world's best shops, making this one of the most pleasant shopping experiences in Tokyo, or anywhere, for that matter. The basement food court, which includes both traditional and modern prepared cuisine, is one of the city's largest in a department store. ✉ *3–14–1 Shinjuku, Shinjuku-ku, Shinjuku* ☎ *03/3225–2514* ⊕ *isetan.mistore.jp/store/shinjuku* Ⓜ *JR Yamanote Line, Marunouchi subway line, Shinjuku Station (Higashi-guchi/East Exit for JR, Exits B2, B3, B4, and B5 for subway line).*

Fodor's Choice
★

Marui O1O1 (O1O1 マルイ). Easily recognized by its red-and-white "O1" logo, Marui burst onto the department store scene in the 1980s by introducing an in-store credit card—one of the first stores in Japan to do so. The four Marui buildings—Marui Honkan, Marui Annex, Marui One, and Marui Mens—comprise the largest department store in the area by a large margin. Women flock to the stores in search of petite clothing, and you can find the largest concentration of Gothic and Lolita clothing in the city at the Annex. ✉ *3–30–13 Shinjuku, Shinjuku-ku, Shinjuku* ☎ *03/3354–0101* ⊕ *www.0101.co.jp/stores/language/en* Ⓜ *JR Yamanote Line, Shinjuku Station (Higashi-guchi/East Exit); Marunouchi, Shinjuku, and Fukutoshin subway lines, Shinjuku San-chome Station (Exit A1).*

Seibu (西武デパート池袋本店). Even Japanese customers have been known to get lost in this mammoth department store; the main branch is in Ikebukuro, a bustling neighborhood just north of Shinjuku. Seibu has an excellent selection of household goods, from furniture to lacquerware and quirky interior design pieces in its stand-alone Loft shops (which you'll find throughout the city next to Seibu branches, or occasionally in the department store itself). ✉ *1–28–1 Minami Ikebukuro, Toshima-ku, Shinjuku* ☎ *03/3981–8569* ⊕ *www.sogo-seibu.jp.e.ld.hp.transer.com/foreign/en/ikebukuro/index.html* Ⓜ *JR Yamanote Line, Marunouchi, Fukutoshin, and Yurakucho subway lines, Ikebukuro Station (Minami-guchi/South Exit); Seibu Ikebukuro Line, Seibu Ikebukuro Station (Seibu Department Store Exit); Tobu Tojo Line, Tobu Ikebukuro Station (Minami-guchi/South Exit).*

Takashimaya (高島屋). In Japanese, *taka* means "high"—a fitting word for this store, which is beloved for its superior quality and prestige. Gift-givers all over Japan seek out this department store; a present that comes in a Takashimaya bag makes a statement regardless of what's inside. Like most department stores each floor is dedicated to stores with similar price points, but here the north half is for women and south for men, so couples and families can shop on the same floors. The basement-level food court carries every gastronomic delight imaginable, from Japanese crackers and Miyazaki beef to one of the largest gourmet dessert courts in the city. The annexes boast a large-scale Tokyu Hands and Kinokuniya bookstore as well. ✉ *Takashimaya Times Sq., 5–24–2 Sendagaya, Shibuya-ku, Shinjuku* ☎ *03/5361–1111* ⊕ *www.takashimaya.co.jp* Ⓜ *JR Yamanote Line, Shinjuku Station (Minami-guchi/South Exit); Fukutoshin subway line, Shinjuku San-chome Station (Exit E8).*

ELECTRONICS

Yodobashi Camera (ヨドバシカメラ). This discount-electronics superstore near Shinjuku Station carries a selection comparable to that of Akihabara's big boys. It is made up of a number of annexes, including a watch, hobby, and professional camera building, that together span several blocks. ✉ *1–11–1 Nishi-Shinjuku, Shinjuku-ku, Shinjuku* ☎ *03/3346–1010* ⊕ *www.yodobashi.com* Ⓜ *Marunouchi, Shinjuku, and Oedo subway lines, JR Yamanote Line, Keio and Odakyu lines, Shinjuku Station (Nishi-guchi/West Exit).*

MUSIC

Fodor's Choice ★ **Disk Union** (ディスクユニオン). Vinyl junkies rejoice. The Shinjuku flagship of this chain sells Latin, rock, and indie at 33 rpm. Be sure to grab a store flyer that lists all of the branches, since each specializes in one music genre. Oh, and for digital folk, CDs are available, too. ✉ *3–31–4*

Shinjuku, Shinjuku-ku, Shinjuku ☎ *03/5919–4565* ⊕ *diskunion.net*
Ⓜ *Marunouchi, Oedo, and Shinjuku subway lines, JR Yamanote Line,*
Keio and Odakyu lines, Shinjuku Station (Higashi-guchi/East Exit).

PAPER

Kami-no-Takamura (紙のたかむら). Specialists in washi and other papers
printed in traditional Japanese designs, this shop also carries brushes,
inkstones, and other tools for calligraphy. At the entrance is a gallery
showcasing seasonal traditional stationery and the work of local artists.
✉ *1–1–2 Higashi-Ikebukuro, Toshima-ku, Shinjuku* ☎ *03/3971–7111*
⊕ *www.wagami-takamura.com* Ⓜ *JR Yamanote Line, Marunouchi and*
Fukutoshin subway lines, Ikebukuro Station (East Exit for JR, Exit
35 for subway).

SIDE TRIPS
FROM TOKYO

SIDE TRIPS FROM TOKYO

TOP REASONS TO GO

★ **Peer at Fuji:**
Climb Japan's tallest mountain or catch a glimpse of it from Fuji-Hakone-Izu National Park.

★ **Escape into rustic Japan:**
The endless modernity of Tokyo seems worlds away in Nikko, where the Tosho-gu area shrines and temples transport you centuries back into the country's past and the Kegon Falls just transport you.

★ **Get into a Zen-like state:**
Kita-Kamakura is home to two preeminent Zen temples, Engaku and Kencho. In Hase, gaze on the Great Buddha or explore inside the giant statue.

★ **Go to China without boarding a plane:**
In Yokohama, a port city, sample authentic Chinese goods, spices, and crafts in Chinatown. For a bit of whimsy and a great view, ride Yokohama's Ferris wheel.

1 Fuji-Hakone-Izu National Park and Mt. Fuji. Fuji-Hakone-Izu National Park lies southwest of Tokyo. Its chief attraction, of course, is Mt. Fuji. South of it, the Izu Peninsula projects out into the Pacific, with Suruga Bay to the west and Sagami Bay to the east. The beaches and rugged shoreline of Izu and its numerous hot-springs inns and resorts make the region a favorite destination for the Japanese.

2 Nikko. Nikko is not simply the site of the Tokugawa Shrine but also of a national park, Nikko Kokuritsu Koen, on the heights above it. The centerpiece of the park is Chuzenji-ko, a deep lake some 21 km (13 miles) around, and the 318-foot-high Kegon Falls, Japan's most famous waterfall.

3 Kamakura. Kamakura is an ancient city—the birthplace, one could argue, of the samurai way of life. Minamoto no Yoritomo, the country's first shogun, chose this site, with its rugged hills and narrow passes, as the seat of his military government. The warrior elite took much of their ideology—and their aesthetics—from Zen Buddhism, endowing splendid temples that still exist today.

4 Yokohama. Yokohama is Japan's largest port and has an international character that rivals—if not surpasses—that of Tokyo. Its waterfront park and its ambitious Minato Mirai bay-side development project draw visitors from all over the world.

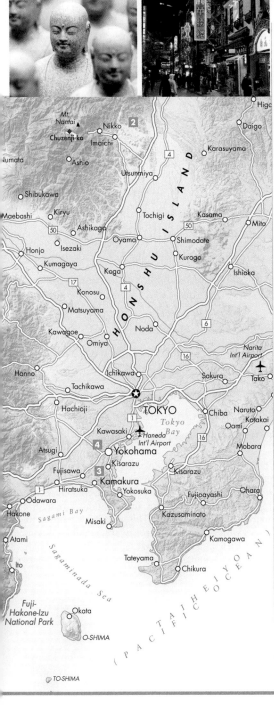

HONSHU ISLAND

Higa
Daigo
Nikko
Mt. Nantai
Chuzenji-ko
Imaichi
Karasuyama
Iumata
Ashio
Utsunmiya
Shibukawa
Kiryu
Tochigi
Kasama
Maebashi
Ashikaga
Oyama
Shimodate
Mito
Honjo
Isezaki
Kurogo
Kumagaya
Koga
Ishioka
Konosu
Matsuyama
Noda
Kawagoe
Omiya
Narita Int'l Airport
Hanno
Ichikawa
Sakura
Tako
Tachikawa
Hachioji
TOKYO
Chiba
Naruto
Kawasaki
Haneda Int'l Airport
Tokyo Bay
Oami
Katakai
Atsugi
Yokohama
Mobara
Fujisawa
Kisarazu
Kisarazu
Hiratsuka
Kamakura
Fujioayashi
Ohara
Odawara
Yokosuka
Kazusaminato
Hakone
Misaki
Kamogawa
Atami
Tateyama
Ito
Chikura
Sagami Bay
Sagaminada Sea
Fuji-Hakone-Izu National Park
Okata
O-SHIMA
TO-SHIMA
(P A C T A I H E I Y O C E A N)

GETTING ORIENTED

Kamakura and Yokohama are close enough to Tokyo to provide ideal day trips, and as it's unlikely that you'll stay overnight in either city, no accommodations are listed for them. Nikko is something of a toss-up: you can easily see Tosho-gu and be back in Tokyo by evening. But when the weather turns glorious in spring or autumn, why not spend some time in the national park, staying overnight at Chuzenji and returning to the city the next day? Mt. Fuji and Hakone, on the other hand—and especially the Izu Peninsula—are pure resort destinations. Staying overnight is an intrinsic part of the experience, and it makes little sense to go without hotel reservations confirmed in advance.

Updated by
Robert Morel

As diverse and exciting as the neighborhoods of Tokyo are, a short day trip or overnight away from the city offers a refreshingly different perspective on Japan. The city is a great base for numerous day trips, including visits to the iconic Fuji-san (Mt. Fuji) in Fuji-Hakone-Izu National Park, one of Japan's most popular resort areas; Nikko, a popular vacation destination for Tokyo residents and the home of Tosho-gu, the astonishing shrine to the first Tokugawa shogun Ieyasu; the ancient city of Kamakura, which has great historical and cultural sights; and Yokohama, a port city with an international character all its own—it's home to the country's largest Chinatown.

One caveat: the term "national park" does not quite mean what it does elsewhere in the world. In Japan, pristine grandeur is hard to come by; there are few places in this country where intrepid hikers can go to contemplate the beauty of nature for very long in solitude. If a thing's worth seeing, it's worth developing. This worldview tends to fill Japan's national parks with bus caravans, ropeways, gondolas, scenic overlooks with coin-fed telescopes, signs that tell you where you may or may not walk, fried-noodle joints and vending machines, and shacks full of kitschy souvenirs. That's true of Nikko, and it's true as well of Fuji-Hakone-Izu National Park.

PLANNING

RESTAURANTS

The local specialty in Nikko is a soybean-based concoction known as *yuba* (tofu skin); dozens of restaurants in Nikko serve it in a variety of dishes you might not have believed possible for so prosaic an ingredient. Other local favorites are *soba* (buckwheat) and *udon* (wheat-flour) noodles—both inexpensive, filling, and tasty options for lunch.

Three things about Kamakura make it a good place to dine. It's on the ocean (properly speaking, on Sagami Bay), which means that fresh seafood is everywhere; it's a major tourist stop; and it has long been a prestigious place to live among Japan's worldly and well-to-do (many successful writers, artists, and intellectuals call Kamakura home). On a day trip from Tokyo, you can feel confident picking a place for lunch almost at random.

Yokohama, as befits a city of more than 3 million people, lacks little in the way of food: from quick-fix lunch counters to elegant dining rooms, you'll find almost every imaginable cuisine. Your best bet is Chinatown—Japan's largest Chinese community—with more than 100 restaurants representing every regional style. If you fancy Italian, Indian, or even Scandinavian, this international port is still guaranteed to provide an eminently satisfying meal.

HOTELS

In both Nikko and the Fuji-Hakone-Izu area, there are modern, Western-style hotels that operate in a fairly standard international style. More common, however, are the traditional *ryokan* (inns). The main difference between these lodging options is that Western-style hotels are situated in prime tourist locations whereas ryokans stick strictly to Japanese-style rooms and are found in less touristy locations. The undisputed pleasure of a ryokan is to return to it at the end of a hard day of sightseeing, luxuriate for an hour in a hot bath with your own garden view, put on the *yukata* (cotton kimono) provided for you (remember to close your right side first and then the left), and sit down to a catered private dinner party. There's little point to staying at a Western-style hotel: these places do most of their business with big, boisterous tour groups; the turnover is ruthless; and the cost is way out of proportion to the service they provide.

The price categories listed here are for double occupancy, but you'll find that most normally quote per-person rates, which include breakfast and dinner. Remember to stipulate whether you want a Japanese or Western breakfast. If you don't want dinner at your hotel, it's usually possible to renegotiate the price, but the management will not be happy about it; the two meals are a fixture of their business. The typical ryokan takes great pride in its cuisine, usually with good reason: the evening meal is an elaborate affair of 10 or more different dishes, based on the fresh produce and specialties of the region, served to you—nay, *orchestrated*—in your room on a wonderful variety of trays and tableware designed to celebrate the season. *Hotel reviews have been shortened. For full information, visit Fodors.com.*

WHAT IT COSTS IN YEN			
$	**$$**	**$$$**	**$$$$**
Restaurants	Under ¥1,000	¥1,000–¥2,000	¥2,001–¥3,000	Over ¥3,000
Hotels	Under ¥12,000	¥12,000–¥18,000	¥18,001–¥22,000	Over ¥22,000

Restaurant prices are the average cost of a main course at dinner, or if dinner is not served, at lunch. Hotel prices are the lowest cost of a standard double room in high season.

FUJI-HAKONE-IZU NATIONAL PARK
富士箱根伊豆国立公園

This region, southwest of Tokyo between Suruga and Sagami bays, is one of Japan's most popular resort areas. The main attraction, of course, is Mt. Fuji, a dormant volcano—it last erupted in 1707—rising to a height of 12,388 feet. The mountain is truly beautiful; utterly captivating in the ways it can change in different light and from different perspectives. Its symmetry and majesty have been immortalized by poets and artists for centuries. Keep in mind that in spring and summer, Mt. Fuji often hides behind a blanket of clouds—worth noting if seeing the mountain is an important part of your trip.

Apart from Mt. Fuji itself, each of the three areas of the park—the Izu Peninsula, Hakone and environs, and the Five Lakes—has its own unique appeal. The Izu Peninsula is popular for its beaches and scenically rugged coastline. Hakone has mountains, volcanic landscapes, and lake cruises, plus *onsen* (hot springs) of its own. The Five Lakes form a recreational area with some of the best views of Mt. Fuji. And in each of these areas there are monuments to Japan's past.

Although it's possible to make a grand tour of all three areas at one time, most people make each of them a separate excursion from Tokyo.

Trains serve you well in traveling to major points anywhere in the northern areas of the national-park region and down the eastern coast of the Izu Peninsula. For the west coast and central mountains of Izu, there are no train connections; unless you are intrepid enough to rent a car, the only way to get around is by bus.

Especially in summer and fall, most towns and resorts have local visitor information centers. Few of them have staff members who speak fluent English, but you can still pick up local maps and pamphlets, as well as information on low-cost inns, pensions, and guesthouses.

FUJI-SAN (MT. FUJI) 富士山

Fodor's Choice ★ Mt. Fuji is the crown jewel of the national park. There are six routes to the summit of the 12,388-foot-high mountain but only two, both accessible by bus, are recommended: from Go-gome (Fifth Station), on the north side, and from Shin-Go-gome (New Fifth Station), on the south.

Continued on page 246

Fuji-Hakone-Izu National Park

Mt. Kanayama
Lake Kawaguchi
Lake Shoji
Lake Sai
Fuji-Yoshida
Fuji-Q Highland
Lake Motosu
Fuji Go-ko
Mt. Tenja
Lake Yamanaka

F U J I   G O K O

52

Fuji-san (Mt. Fuji)

Fuji-Hakone-Izu National Park

Matsuda
Kozu

Gotemba

Hakone Ropeway
Gora
Miyanoshita
Odawara
Owaku-dani
Togendai
Soun-zan (Mt. Soun)
Hakone

52

Mt. Ashitaka

Lake Ashi

Sagami Bay

Fuji
Susono

Kanbara
Hara
Mishima
MOA Museum of Art

1

Numazu
Nirayama
Oyu Geyser
Atami
Atami Plum Garden
Kinomiya Station
Izu-Nagaoka
Hatsu-Shima
Mita

Suruga Bay

Heda
Shuzenji
Usami
Ito

Ikeda 20th Century Art Museum
Komuro-san Koen
Toi
Tsukigase
Izu Cactus Park

Fuji-Hakone-Izu National Park

Kamo
Mt. Amagi

Sagaminada Sea

Izu Peninsula
Atagawa

Dogashima
Matsuzaki
Mizukuri
Kawazu

Hofuku-ji
Shimoda
Ryosen-ji
Yumi-ga-hama

Iro-zaki (Iro Point)

0   5 mi
0   5 km

KEY
Shinkansen (Bullet Trains)
JR Trains or Private Trains
Cable Car
Beaches

PEERLESS FUJI

by Peter MacMillan

Climbing Mt. Fuji

Mount Fuji greets hikers who arrive at its summit just before dawn with the *go-raiko,* or the Honorable Coming of the Light. The reflection of this light shimmers across the sky just before the sun first appears, giving the extraordinary sunrise a mystical feel. Fuji-san's early morning magic is just one of the characteristics of the mountain that has captured the collective imagination of the Japanese, along with its snowy peak, spiritual meaning, and propensity to hide behind clouds. The close-to-perfectly symmetrical cone is an object to conquer physically and to admire from afar.

Japan is more than 70% mountainous, and Fuji is its tallest mountain. It appears in literature, art, and culture from the highest level to the most ordinary in countless ways. In a word, Fuji is ubiquitous.

Since ancient times Mt. Fuji has been an object of worship for both Shinto and Buddhist practitioners. Shrines devoted to Konohana-Sakuya Hime, Mt. Fuji's goddess, dot the trails. So sacred is Fuji that the mountaintop torii gate at the Okumiya of Sengen Taisha Shrine (though at Fuji's foot, the shrine also encompasses the mountain above the 8th station) states that this is the greatest mountain in the world. Typically the gate would provide the shrine's name. Here, the torii defines not the shrine but the sacred space of the mountain.

Rising to 12,385 feet (3,776 meters) Mt. Fuji is an active volcano, but the last eruption was in 1707. Located on the boundaries of Shizuoka and Yamanashi prefectures, the mountain is an easy day trip west of Tokyo, and on clear days you can see the peak from the city. In season, hikers clamber to the peak, but it is gazing upon Fuji that truly inspires awe and wonder. No visit to Japan would be complete without at least a glimpse of this beautiful icon.

(top left) Mt. Fuji's famous morning light draws visitors, (top right) the summit is often surrounded by clouds, (bottom right) the trails are rocky and rugged at tiimes.

THE SYMBOLISM OF FUJI-SAN

ARTISTIC FUJI

Mt. Fuji is one of the world's most painted and photographed mountains. But rising above all the visual depictions are Katsushika Hokusai's *Thirty-six Views of Mt. Fuji* and his *One Hundred Views of Mt. Fuji*. The latter is a stunning work and considered his masterpiece. However, the *Thirty-Six Views* is more famous because the images were printed in full color, while the *One Hundred Views* was printed in monochrome black and gray. His *Great Wave off Kanagawa* is one of the most famous prints in the history of art.

Hokusai believed that his depictions would get better and better as he got older, and they did; his *One Hundred*

Views was completed when he was 75. He was also obsessed with achieving immortality. In creating the *One Hundred Views of Mt. Fuji*, a mountain always associated with immortality, he hoped to achieve his own. History proved him right.

LITERARY FUJI

There are thousands of literary works related to Fuji, including traditional and modern poems, haiku, Noh dramas, novels, and plays. In the Man'yoshu, 8th-century poet Yamabe no Akahito famously extolled Fuji: "When I sail out/on the Bay of Tago/every where's white-/Look! Snow's piling up/on the peak of Fuji." Matsuo Basho, in another well known poem, wrote about not being able to see the mountain: "How lovely and intriguing!/ Covered in drifting fog,/ the day I could not see Fuji." There are many times of the year when Fuji hides behind the clouds, so don't be disappointed if you miss it. Like the great haiku poet, see the mountain in the eye of your heart.

(top) Katsushika Hokusai's *Red Fuji*, (bottom) *Great Wave off Kanagawa* by Katsushika Hokusai

SEE FUJI-SAN FROM AFAR

Like the poets and artists who have found inspiration in gazing at Fuji-san, you, too, can catch a glimpse of the snow-capped cone on the horizon. On a clear day, most likely in winter when the air is dry and the clouds lift, the following experiences provide some of the best Fuji views.

SEE FUJI

Atop Tokyo. Visit the Tokyo City View observation promenade on the 52nd floor of the Mori Tower in Roppongi. You can walk all around this circular building and take in the spectacular views of Tokyo and, when the weather is fine, Fuji. While you're here, don't miss the sky-high Mori Art Museum, a contemporary art space on the 52nd and 53rd floors. The evening view of the city is also splendid, but Fuji will be slumbering under the blanket of nightfall.

From Hakone. Part of Fuji-Hakone-Izu National Park, the same park Fuji calls home, and an easy day trip from Tokyo, Hakone is a playground of hiking trails, small art museums, an onsen, and more. Head to the beautiful gar-

den at Hakone Detached Palace for scenic views of Fuji-san. Early morning and late evening will provide the best chance for clear skies.

Speeding out of town. The classic view of Fuji is from the Shinkansen traveling from Tokyo to Kyoto. Some of the world's fastest transportation technology hums beneath you when, suddenly, the world's most beautiful and sacred mountain appears on the left. This striking combination of the ancient and cutting-edge is at the heart of understanding Japan. Make sure not to fall asleep!

(top) Shinkansen speeding past Fuji, (bottom) Fuji from inside Hakone National Park i

CLIMBING FUJI-SAN
FROM KAWAGUCHIKO TRAIL

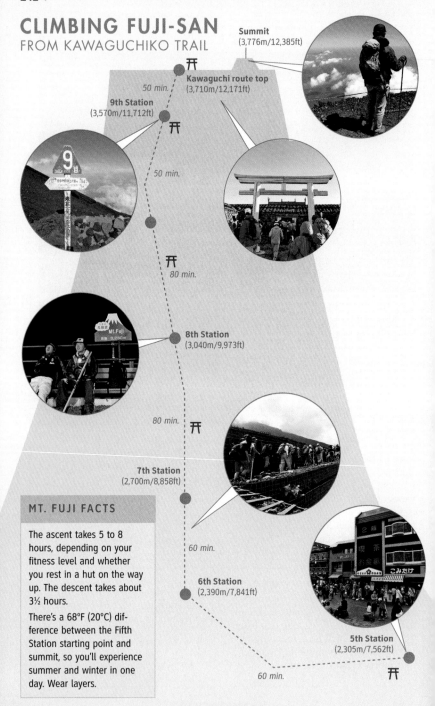

Summit
(3,776m/12,385ft)

Kawaguchi route top
(3,710m/12,171ft)

50 min.

9th Station
(3,570m/11,712ft)

50 min.

80 min.

8th Station
(3,040m/9,973ft)

80 min.

7th Station
(2,700m/8,858ft)

60 min.

6th Station
(2,390m/7,841ft)

5th Station
(2,305m/7,562ft)

60 min.

MT. FUJI FACTS

The ascent takes 5 to 8 hours, depending on your fitness level and whether you rest in a hut on the way up. The descent takes about 3½ hours.

There's a 68°F (20°C) difference between the Fifth Station starting point and summit, so you'll experience summer and winter in one day. Wear layers.

A photographer capturing view from Mt. Fuji

Although many Japanese like to climb Mt. Fuji once in their lives, there's a saying in Japanese that only a fool would climb it twice. You, too, can make a once-in-a-lifetime climb during the mountain's official open season from July through August. Unless you're an experienced hiker, do not attempt to make the climb at another time of year.

TRAIL CONDITIONS

Except for the occasional cobblestone path, the routes are unpaved and at times steep, especially toward the top. Near the end of the climb there are some rope banisters to steady yourself, but for the most part you'll have to rely on your own balance.

Fuji draws huge crowds in season, so expect a lot of company on your hike. The throngs grow thicker in August during the school break and reach their peak during the holiday Obon week in mid-August; it gets so crowded that hikers have to queue up at certain passes. Trails are less crowded overnight. Go during the week and in July for the lightest crowds (though the weather is less reliable). Or accept the crowds and enjoy the friendships that spring up among strangers on the trails.

TRAILS OVERVIEW

If you're in good health you should be able to climb from the base to the summit. That said, the air is thin, and it can be humbling to struggle for oxygen while some 83-year-

old Japanese grandmother blithely leaves you in her dust (it happens).

Most visitors take buses as far as the Fifth Station and hike to the top from there (⇨ See Mt. Fuji listing in this chapter for more information on buses). The paved roads end at this halfway point.

Four routes lead to Mt. Fuji's summit—the **Kawaguchiko, Subashiri, Gotemba,** and **Fujinomiya**—and each has a corresponding Fifth Station that serves as the transfer point between bus and foot. Depending on which trail you choose, the ascent takes between 5 and 10 hours. Fujinomiya is closest to the summit; Gotemba is the farthest.

We recommend Kawaguchiko (Fuji-Yoshida) Trail in Yamanashi, as its many first-aid centers and lodging facilities (huts) ensure that you can enjoy the climb. ■ TIP➔ Those interested in experiencing Fuji's religious and spiritual aspects should walk this trail from the mountain's foot. Along the way are small shrines

that lead to the torii gate at the top, which signifies Fuji's sacred status. While the food and cleanliness standards at mountain huts are subpar, they provide valuable rest spots and even more valuable camaraderie and good will among travelers.

AT THE TOP

Once you reach the top of Mt. Fuji, you can walk along the ridge of the volcano. A torii gate declares that Fuji is the greatest mountain in the world. It also marks the entrance to the **Fuji-san Honmiya Sengen Taisha Shrine** (at the foot of the mountain near the Kawaguchiko Trail is the shrine's other facility). Inside the shrine, head to the post office where you can mail letters and postcards with a special Mt. Fuji stamp. There's also a chalet at the top for those captivated enough to stay the night.

NIGHT HIKES

The most spectacular way to hike Mt. Fuji is to time the climb so that you arrive at sunrise. Not only is the light famously enchanting, but the sky is also more likely to be clear, allowing for views back to Tokyo. Those who choose this have a few options. Start from the Kawaguchiko Fifth Station on the Kawaguchi Trail around 10 PM (or later, depending on the sunrise time) and hike through the night, arriving at the summit between 4:30 and 5 AM, just as the sun begins to rise. A better alternative is to begin in the afternoon or evening and hike to the Seventh or Eighth Station, spend a few hours resting there, and then depart very early in the morning to see the sun rise. ■TIP→ **The trail isn't lit at night, so bring a headlamp to illuminate the way. Avoid carrying flashlights, though, as it is important to keep your hands free in case of a fall.**

COMMEMORATE YOUR VISIT

Purchase a walking stick at the base of Mt. Fuji and, as you climb, have it branded at each station. By the time you reach the top you'll have the perfect souvenir to mark your achievement.

(top) First glimpse of the go-raiko, (bottom) Mt. Fuji at dawn

Walking sticks for sale

DID YOU KNOW?

Although earlier meanings of the word *Fuji* include "peer-less," and "immortal one," the current way of writing Fuji implies "wealthy persons of military status." The mountain called *fuji-san* (not *fuji-yama*) in Japanese.

GETTING HERE AND AROUND

Take one of the daily buses directly to Go-gome from Tokyo; they run July through August and leave from Shinjuku Station. The journey takes about two hours and 40 minutes from Shinjuku and costs ¥2,600. Reservations are required; book seats through the Fuji Kyuko Highway Bus Reservation Center, the Keio Highway Bus Reservation Center, the Japan Travel Bureau (which should have English-speaking staff), or any major travel agency.

Although the buses are more affordable and convenient, if you need to return from Mt. Fuji to Tokyo by train, take an hour-long bus ride from Shin-Go-gome to Gotemba (¥1,500). From Gotemba take the JR Tokaido and Gotemba lines to Tokyo Station (¥1,940), or take the JR Asagiri express train from Gotemba to Shinjuku station (¥2,810).

ESSENTIALS

Buses from Tokyo Fuji Kyuko Highway Bus Reservation Center. ☎ *03/5376–2222* ⊕ *highway-buses.jp/fuji.* **JTB Sunrise Tours.** ☎ *03/5796–5454* ⊕ *www.jtb-sunrisetours.jp.* **Keio Highway Bus Reservation Center.** ☎ *03/5376–2222* ⊕ *highway-buses.jp.* **Tokai Bus Company** (東海バス). ☎ *0557/36–1112 main office, 0558/22–2514 Shimoda Information Center.*

EXPLORING

Fuji-san (Mt. Fuji). ⊠ *Fuji-Hakone-Izu National Park* ⊕ *www.fujisan-climb.jp* ⊗ *Official hiking season: July 1–Aug. 26* ⇨ *For more information, see the highlighted listing in this chapter.*

IZU PENINSULA 伊豆半島

Izu is defined by its dramatic rugged coastline, beaches, and onsen (hot springs).

GETTING HERE AND AROUND

Having your own car makes sense only for touring the Izu Peninsula, and only then if you're prepared to cope with less-than-ideal road conditions, lots of traffic (especially on holiday weekends), and the paucity of road markers in English. It takes some effort—but exploring the peninsula *is* a lot easier by car than by public transportation. From Tokyo take the Tomei Expressway as far as Oi-matsuda (about 84 km [52 miles]); then pick up Routes 255 and 135 to Atami (approximately 28 km [17 miles]). From Atami drive another 55 km (34 miles) or so down the east coast of the Izu Peninsula to Shimoda.

■ TIP➔ **One way to save yourself some trouble is to book a car through the Nippon or Toyota rental agency in Tokyo and arrange to pick it up at the Shimoda branch.** You can then simply take a train to Shimoda and use it as a base. From Shimoda you can drive back up the coast to Kawazu (35 minutes) and then to Shuzenji (30 minutes). It is possible to drop off the car in Tokyo, but only at specific branches, so visit your rental-car company's website or call them in advance.

Once you are on the Izu Peninsula itself, sightseeing excursions by boat are available from several picturesque small ports. From Dogashima, you can take the Dogashima Marine short (20 minutes, ¥1,200) or long (50 minutes, ¥2,300) tours of Izu's rugged west coast.

The Fuji Kyuko company operates a daily ferry to Hatsu-shima from Atami (25 minutes, ¥2,400 round-trip) and another to the island from Ito (23 minutes, ¥1,200 one-way). Izukyu Marine offers a 40-minute tour (¥1,400) by boat from Shimoda to the coastal rock formations at Iro-zaki.

JTB Sunrise Tours operates a tour to Hakone, including a cruise across Lake Ashi and a trip on the gondola over Owaku-dani (¥15,000 includes lunch and return to Tokyo by Shinkansen; ¥12,000 includes lunch and return to Tokyo by bus). ■ TIP→ These tours are an economical way to see the main sights all in one day and are ideal for travelers with limited time. Sunrise tours depart daily from Tokyo's Hamamatsu-cho Bus Terminal and some major hotels.

Trains are by far the easiest and fastest ways to get to the Izu Peninsula and the rest of the Fuji-Hakone-Izu National Park area. The gateway station of Atami is well served by comfortable express trains from Tokyo, on both JR and private railway lines. These in turn connect to local trains and buses that can get you anywhere in the region you want to go. Call the JR Higashi-Nihon Info Line (10–6 daily, except December 31–January 3) for assistance in English.

The *Kodama* Shinkansen from JR Tokyo Station to Atami costs ¥4,190 and takes 45 minutes; JR (Japan Railways) passes are valid. The JR local from Atami to Ito takes 25 minutes and costs ¥320. Ito and Atami are also served by the JR Odoriko Super Express (not a Shinkansen train) also departing from Tokyo Station; check the schedule display board for the correct platform. The Tokyo–Ito run takes 1¾ hours and costs ¥4,190; you can also use a JR Pass. The privately owned Izukyu Railways, on which JR Passes are not valid, makes the Ito–Shimoda run in one hour for ¥1,620.

The Izu–Hakone Railway Line runs from Tokyo to Mishima (one hour, 36 minutes; ¥4,090), with a change at Mishima for Shuzenji (31 minutes, ¥500); this is the cheapest option if you don't have a JR Pass. With a JR Pass, a Shinkansen–Izu Line combination saves about 35 minutes and is the cheapest option. The Tokyo–Mishima Shinkansen leg (62 minutes) costs ¥4,400; the Mishima–Shuzenji Izu Line leg (31 minutes) costs ¥500.

ESSENTIALS

Rental-Car Contacts Nippon Rent-a-Car. ☎ 03/3485–7196 ⊕ www.nipponrentacar.co.jp. **Toyota Rent-a-Car.** ☎ 0800/7000–815 toll-free in Japan; English operator available, 03/5954–8020 international ⊕ rent.toyota.co.jp/eng.

Tour Contacts Dogashima Marine (堂ヶ島マリン). ☎ 0558/52–0013 ⊕ www.izudougasima-yuransen.com. **Fuji Kyuko** (富士急行). ☎ 0557/81–0541 ⊕ www.fujikyu.co.jp/en/. **Izukyu Marine** (伊豆急マリン). ☎ 0558/22–1151.

Tourist Information Atami City Tourist Association. ✉ Shinsui Park, 2018-8 Nagisa-cho, Atami ☎ 0557/85–2222. **Shimoda Tourist Association** (伊豆下田観光ガイド). ✉ 1-4-27 Shimoda, Shimoda ☎ 0558/22–1531 ⊕ www.shimoda-city.info.

CLOSE UP

A Healing Headache

While earthquakes are an annoying, everyday fact of life in Japan, they also provide one of the country's greatest delights: thermal baths. Wherever there are volcanic mountains—and there are a lot—you're sure to find springs of hot water, called *onsen*, which are rich in all sorts of restorative minerals. Any place where lots of spas have tapped these sources is an *onsen chiiki* (hot-springs resort area). The Izu Peninsula is particularly rich in onsen. It has, in fact, one-fifth of the 2,300-odd officially recognized hot springs in Japan.

Spas take many forms, but the ne plus ultra is that small secluded Japanese mountain inn with a *rotemburo* (an open-air mineral-spring pool). For guests only, these pools are usually in a screened-off nook with a panoramic view. A room in one of these inns on a weekend or in high season should be booked months in advance. (High season is late December to early January, late April to early May, the second and third weeks of August, and the second and third weeks of October.) More typical is the large resort hotel, geared mainly to groups, with one or more large indoor mineral baths of its own. Where whole towns and villages have developed to exploit a local supply of hot water, there will be several of these large hotels, an assortment of smaller inns, and probably a few modest public bathhouses, with no accommodations, where you just pay an entrance fee for a soak of whatever length you wish.

Train Information Izukyu Corporation (伊豆急). ☎ *0557/53–1115 main office, 0558/22–3202 Izukyu Shimoda Station* ⊕ *www.izukyu.co.jp.* **JR Higashi-Nihon Info Line** (JR東日本お問い合わせ先 *JR East Info Line*). ☎ *050/2016–1603 English info line.* **Odakyu Sightseeing Service Center.** ✉ *Shinjuku Station 1F, Odakyu Railway West Exit* ☎ *03/5321–7887* ⊕ *www.odakyu.jp/english/center.*

ATAMI 熱海

100 km (60 miles) southwest of Tokyo Station.

The gateway to the Izu Peninsula is Atami. Most Japanese travelers make it no farther into the peninsula than this town on Sagami Bay, so Atami itself has a fair number of hotels and traditional inns.

When you arrive, collect a map from the **Atami Tourist Information Office** at the train station.

GETTING HERE AND AROUND

From JR Tokyo Station, take the Tokaido Line to Atami, which is the last stop (one hour, 34 minutes, ¥1,990) or the Kodama Shinkansen (49 minutes, ¥4,190).

EXPLORING

Atami Plum Garden (熱海梅園 *Atami Bai-en*). The best time to visit the garden is in late January or early February, when its 850 trees bloom. If you do visit, also stop by the small shrine that's in the shadow of an enormous old camphor tree. The shrine is more than 1,000 years old and is popular with people who are asking the gods for help with alcoholism. The tree is more than 2,000 years old and has been designated a

National Monument. It's believed that if you walk around the tree once, another year will be added to your life. Atami Bai-en is always open to the public and is 15 minutes by bus from Atami or an eight-minute walk from Kinomiya Station, the next stop south of Atami served by local trains. ✉ *8–11 Baien-cho* ☎ *0557/85–2222* 🎫 *Free.*

Hatsu-shima (初島). If you have the time and the inclination for a beach picnic, it's worth taking the 25-minute high-speed ferry (round-trip ¥2,400) from the pier. There are five departures daily between 7:30 and 5:20 from both Atami and Ito, though the times vary by season. You can easily walk around the island, which is only 4 km (2½ miles) in circumference, in less than two hours. Use of the **Picnic Garden** (open daily 10–3) is free. ✉ *Atami Port, 6–11 Wadahama Minamicho* ☎ *0557/81–0541 ferry* 🌐 *www.hatsushima.jp.*

MOA Museum of Art (美術館 *MOA Bijutsukan*). This museum houses the private collection of the messianic religious leader Mokichi Okada (1882–1955), who founded a movement called the Sekai Kyusei Kyo (Religion for the Salvation of the World). He also acquired more than 3,000 works of art; some are from the Asuka period (6th and 7th centuries). Among these works are several particularly fine *ukiyo-e* (Edo-era wood-block prints) and ceramics. On a hill above the station and set in a garden full of old plum trees and azaleas, the museum also affords a sweeping view over Atami and the bay. ✉ *26–2 Momoyama* ☎ *0557/84–2511* 🌐 *www.moaart.or.jp/en* 🎫 *¥1,600* ⏲ *Fri.–Wed. 9:30–4:30.*

Oyu Geyser (大湯間欠泉 *Oyu Kanketsusen*). Located just a 15-minute walk southeast from Atami Station, the geyser used to gush on schedule once every 24 hours but stopped after the Great Kanto Earthquake of 1923. Not happy with this, the local chamber of commerce rigged a pump to raise the geyser every five minutes. ✉ *3 Kamijuku-cho.*

WHERE TO STAY

$$$$ B&B/INN 🏨 **Atami Taikanso** (熱海大観荘). The views of the sea must have been the inspiration for Yokoyama Taikan, the Japanese artist who once owned this villa that is now a traditional Japanese inn with exquisite furnishings and individualized service. **Pros:** seaside rooms have beautiful views. **Cons:** eating dinner may take most of your evening. [$] *Rooms from: ¥45000* ✉ *7–1 Hayashigaoka-cho* ☎ *0557/81–8137* 🛏 *44 Japanese-style rooms with bath* 🍴 *Some meals.*

$$$$ HOTEL 🏨 **Hotel Micuras.** Style, comfort, ocean views, and natural hot springs make this hotel one of Atami's best. **Pros:** stylish, modern. **Cons:** lacks the history or charm of a traditional inn. [$] *Rooms from: ¥40,000* ✉ *3–19 Higashikaigan-cho* ☎ *0577/86–111* 🌐 *www.micuras.jp* 🛏 *62 rooms (55 ocean-view, 7 mountain-view)* 🍴 *No meals.*

ITO 伊東

16 km (10 miles) south of Atami.

There are some 800 thermal springs in the resort area surrounding Ito. These springs—and the beautiful, rocky, indented coastline nearby—remain the resort's major attractions, although there are plenty of interesting sights here. Some 150 hotels and inns serve the area.

Ito traces its history of associations with the West to 1604, when William Adams (1564–1620), the Englishman whose adventures served as the basis for James Clavell's novel *Shogun,* came ashore.

Four years earlier Adams had beached his disabled Dutch vessel, *De Liefde,* on the shores of the southwestern island of Kyushu and become the first Englishman to set foot on Japan. The authorities, believing that he and his men were Portuguese pirates, put Adams in prison, but he was eventually befriended by the shogun Ieyasu Tokugawa, who brought him to Edo (present-day Tokyo) and granted him an estate. Ieyasu appointed Adams his adviser on foreign affairs. The English castaway taught mathematics, geography, gunnery, and navigation to shogunate officials and in 1604 was ordered to build an 80-ton Western-style ship. Pleased with this venture, Ieyasu ordered the construction of a larger oceangoing vessel. These two ships were built at Ito, where Adams lived from 1605 to 1610.

This history was largely forgotten until British Commonwealth occupation forces began coming to Ito for rest and recuperation after World War II. Adams's memory was revived, and since then the Anjin Festival (the Japanese gave Adams the name *anjin,* which means "pilot") has been held in his honor every August. A monument to the Englishman stands at the mouth of the river.

GETTING HERE AND AROUND

From JR Tokyo Station or Shinagawa Station, take the Tokaido Line (two hours, 15 minutes, ¥2,210) or the Super Odoriko Express (one hour, 40 minutes, ¥4,190) to Ito Station.

ESSENTIALS

Visitor Information Ito Tourist Association (伊東観光協会 *Ito Kanko Kyoukai*). ✉ *1-8-3 Yukawa* ☎ *0557/37–6105* ⊕ *itospa.com/ito-city-english-tour-guide.*

EXPLORING

Ikeda 20th-Century Art Museum (池田20世紀美術館 *Ikeda 20-Seiki Bijutsukan*). The museum, which overlooks Lake Ippeki, houses works by Picasso, Dalí, Chagall, and Matisse, plus a number of wood-block prints. The museum is a 15-minute walk northwest from Izu Cactus Park. ✉ *614 Totari* ☎ *0557/45–2211* 🎟 *¥1,000* ⊙ *Thurs.–Tues. 10–4:30.*

Izu Cactus Park (伊豆シャボテン公園 *Izu Shaboten Koen*). The park consists of a series of pyramidal greenhouses that contain 5,000 kinds of cacti from around the world. At the base of Komuro-san (Mt. Komuro), the park is 20 minutes south of Ito Station by bus. ✉ *1317–13 Futo* ☎ *0557/51–1111* 🎟 *¥2,300* ⊙ *Mar.–Oct., daily 9–5; Nov.–Feb., daily 9–4.*

Komuro-san Koen (小室山公園 *Mt. Komuro Park*). Some 3,000 cherry trees of 35 varieties bloom at various times throughout the year. You can take a cable car to the top of the mountain, which has a lovely view of the sea below. The park is about 20 minutes south of Ito Station by bus. ✉ *1428 Komuro-cho* ☎ *0557/37–6105* 🎟 *Free; round-trip cable car to mountaintop ¥500* ⊙ *Daily 9–4.*

WHERE TO STAY

$$$$ B&B/INN **Hanafubuki** (花吹雪). This traditional Japanese inn, which is located in the Jogasaki forest, has modern, comfortable rooms, but still retains classic elements like tatami mats, sliding screen doors, and *chabudai* (low dining tables) with *zabuton* (cushion seating). **Pros:** an authentic Japanese experience. **Cons:** meals are available to nonguests, so the dining room can be a bit crowded. [$] *Rooms from: ¥45,000* ✉ *1041 Yawatano Isomichi* ☎ *0557/54–1550* 🌐 *www.hanafubuki.co.jp* 🛏 *12 Japanese-style rooms with bath, 2 Western-style rooms with bath, 3 family rooms with bath* 🍴 *Some meals.*

$$$$ HOTEL **Hatoya Sun Hotel** (ホテルサンハトヤ). A scenic coastline provides a backdrop for traditional-style lodgings and such amenities as open-air hot springs that look out to the ocean and mountains beyond. **Pros:** live entertainment at dinner. **Cons:** a lot of guests with children make this a bit noisy. [$] *Rooms from: ¥40,000* ✉ *572–12 Yukawa Tateiwa* ☎ *0557/36–4126* 🛏 *187 Japanese-style rooms with bath, 3 Western-style rooms with bath, 1 mixed Western-Japanese-style room with bath* 🍴 *Some meals.*

EN ROUTE **Atagawa.** South of Ito the coastal scenery is lovely—each sweep around a headland reveals another picturesque sight of a rocky, indented shoreline. There are several spa towns en route to Shimoda. Higashi-Izu (East Izu) has numerous hot-springs resorts, of which Atagawa is the most fashionable. South of Atagawa is **Kawazu,** a place of relative quiet and solitude, with pools in the forested mountainside and waterfalls plunging through lush greenery. ✉ *Ito.*

SHIMODA 下田

35 km (22 miles) south of Ito city.

Of all the resort towns south of Ito along Izu's eastern coast, none can match the distinction of Shimoda. The town's encounter with the West began when Commodore Matthew Perry anchored his fleet of black ships off the coast here in 1853. To commemorate the event, the three-day Black Ship Festival (Kurofune Matsuri) is held here every year in mid-May. Shimoda was also the site, in 1856, of the first American consulate.

The **Shimoda Tourist Office,** in front of the station, has the easiest of the local English itineraries to follow. The 2½-km (1½-mile) tour covers most major sights. On request, the tourist office will also help you find local accommodations.

GETTING HERE AND AROUND

From JR Shinagawa Station, take the Tokaido Line to Atami, change to the Ito Line, and take it to the final stop, Izukyu Shimoda Station (three hours, 45 minutes, ¥3,883).

ESSENTIALS

Shimoda Tourist Office. ✉ *1–1 Sotogaoka* ☎ *0558/22–1531.*

EXPLORING

Hofuku-ji (宝福寺). The first American consul to Japan was New York businessman Townsend Harris. Soon after his arrival in Shimoda, Harris asked the Japanese authorities to provide him with a female servant; they sent him a young girl named Okichi Saito, who was engaged to be married. The arrangement brought her a new name, Tojin (the Foreigner's) Okichi, much disgrace, and a tragic end. When Harris sent her away, she tried, but failed, to rejoin her former lover. The shame brought upon her for working and living with a Westerner and the pain of losing the love of her life drove Okichi to drown herself in 1892. Her tale is recounted in Rei Kimura's biographical novel *Butterfly in the Wind* and inspired Puccini's *Madame Butterfly*, although some skeptics say the story is more gossip than fact. Hofuku-ji was Okichi's family temple. The museum annex displays a life-size image of her, and just behind the temple is her grave—where incense is still kept burning in her memory. The grave of her lover, Tsurumatsu, is at Toden-ji, a temple about midway between Hofuku-ji and Shimoda Station. ✉ *18–26–1 Shimoda* ☎ *0558/22–0960* 🎫 *¥300* 🕐 *Daily 8–5.*

Ryosen-ji (了仙寺). This is the temple in which the negotiations took place that led to the United States–Japan Treaty of Amity and Commerce of 1858. The **Treasure Hall** (Homotsu-den) contains more than 300 original artifacts relating to Commodore Perry and the "black ships" that opened Japan to the West. ✉ *3–12–12 Shimoda* ☎ *0558/22–0657* 🌐 *www.izu.co.jp/~ryosenji* 🎫 *Treasure Hall ¥500* 🕐 *Daily 8:30–5.*

OFF THE BEATEN PATH

Yumi-ga-hama (弓ケ浜). If you love the sun, make sure you stop at Yumi-ga-hama. It's one of the nicest sandy beaches on the whole Izu Peninsula. Although the water is usually warm enough to swim from June, the crowds come out during Japan's beach season in July and August. The bus from Shimoda Station stops here before continuing to Irozaki, the last stop on the route. **Amenities:** food and drink (July and August); lifeguards (July and August); toilets; parking. **Best for:** swimming (June–August); solitude (September–June). ✉ *Shimoda* ✥ *11 km (7 miles) southwest of Shimoda, just south of highway 136.*

WHERE TO STAY

$ B&B/INN 🏨 **Pension Sakuraya** (ペンション桜家). The best lodgings at this family-run inn just a few minutes' walk from Shimoda's main beach are the Japanese-style corner rooms, which have nice views of the hills surrounding Shimoda. **Pros:** very homey atmosphere. **Cons:** rooms are a bit cramped. [$] *Rooms from: ¥10000* ✉ *2584–20 Shira-hama* ☎ *0558/23–4470* 🌐 *izu-sakuraya.jp/english* 🛏 *4 Western-style rooms with bath, 5 Japanese-style rooms without bath* 🍴 *Some meals.*

$$$$ HOTEL 🏨 **Shimoda Prince Hotel** (下田プリンスホテル). At this modern V-shape resort hotel that faces the Pacific, the decor is more functional than aesthetic, but a white-sand beach is just steps away, and there's a panoramic view of the ocean from the picture windows in the dining room. **Pros:** an excellent view of the sea; one of the best hotels in town. **Cons:** restaurants are on the pricey side. [$] *Rooms from: ¥32000* ✉ *1547–1 Shira-hama* ☎ *0558/22–2111* 🌐 *www.princehotels.com* 🛏 *70 Western-style rooms with bath, 6 Japanese-style rooms with bath* 🍴 *Some meals.*

$$$$ HOTEL 🏨 **Shimoda Tokyu Hotel** (下田東急ホテル). Perched just above the bay, the Shimoda Tokyu has impressive views of the Pacific from one side (where rooms cost about 10% more) and mountains from the other. **Pros:** nice views of the ocean. **Cons:** restaurants are expensive for Tokyo standards. [$] *Rooms from: ¥40000* ✉ *5–12–1 Shimoda* ☎ *0558/22–2411*

🌐 shimoda.tokyuhotels.com 🛏 107 Western-style rooms with bath, 8 Japanese-style rooms with bath 🍴 Breakfast.

DOGASHIMA 堂ヶ島

16 km (10 miles) northeast of Mishima.

The sea has eroded the coastal rock formations into fantastic shapes near the little port town of Dogashima, including a tombolo, or a narrow band of sand, that connects the mainland to a small peninsula with a scenic park.

GETTING HERE AND AROUND

Dogashima is not directly accessible by train but buses run from Shinjuku and Tokyo Stations. From Tokyo Station, take the JR Shinkansen to Mishima (44 minutes, ¥3,890), change to the Izu Hakone Line to Shuzenji (35 minutes, ¥500), and take the Tokai bus to the Dogashima stop. There is also an express Tokai Bus, Minami Izu Line, which takes you from Shimoda Station to Dogashima (55 minutes).

TOURS

Dogashima Marine Sightseeing Boat. Sightseeing boats from Dogashima Pier make 20-minute runs to see the rocks (¥1,200). In an excess of kindness, a recorded loudspeaker—which you can safely ignore—recites the name of every rock you pass on the trip. *☎ 0558/52–0013 🌐 www.izudougasima-yuransen.com.*

WHERE TO STAY

$$$$ HOTEL **Dogashima New Ginsui** (堂ヶ島ニュー銀水). Perched above the water and a secluded beach, every Japanese-style guest room overlooks the sea. **Pros:** by far the best luxury resort on Izu's west coast; stunning views; concierge. **Cons:** a bit far from sightseeing spots. *[$] Rooms from: ¥46000 ✉ 2977–1 Nishina, Nishi-Izu-cho ☎ 0558/52–2211 🌐 www.dougashima-newginsui.jp 🛏 121 Japanese-style rooms with bath 🍴 Some meals.*

SHUZENJI 修善寺

25 km (15 miles) south of Mishima by Izu-Hakone Railway.

Shuzenji—a hot-springs resort in the center of the peninsula, along the valley of the Katsura-gawa (Katsura River)—enjoys a certain historical notoriety as the place where the second Kamakura shogun, Minamoto no Yoriie, was assassinated in the early 13th century. Don't judge the town by the area around the station; most of the hotels and hot springs are 2 km (1 mile) to the west.

GETTING HERE AND AROUND

The train is by far the easiest way to get to Shuzenji. The JR Tokaido Line runs from Tokyo to Mishima (two hours, 10 minutes, ¥2,270), with a change at Mishima for Shuzenji (31 minutes, ¥510); this is the cheapest option if you don't have a JR Pass. With a JR Pass, a Kodama Shinkansen–Izu Line combination saves an hour. The Tokyo–Mishima Shinkansen leg (62 minutes) costs ¥4,520; the Mishima–Shuzenji Izu Line leg (31 minutes) costs ¥510.

CLOSE UP

Ryokan Etiquette

Guests are expected to arrive at ryokan in the late afternoon. When you do, put on the slippers that are provided and a maid will escort you to your room. Remember to remove your slippers before entering your room; never step on the tatami (straw mats) with shoes or slippers. Each room will be simply decorated—one small, low table, cushions on the tatami, and a scroll on the wall—which will probably be shoji (sliding paper-paneled walls).

In ryokan with thermal pools, you can take to the waters anytime, although the pool doors are usually locked from 11 pm to 6 am. In ryokan without thermal baths or private baths in guest rooms, visits must be staggered. Typically the maid will ask what time you would like to bathe and fit you into a schedule. Make sure you wash and rinse off entirely before getting into the bath. Do not get soap in the tub. Other guests will be using the same bathwater, so it is important to observe this custom. After your bath, change into the yukata provided in your room. Don't worry about walking around in it—other guests will be doing the same.

Dinner is served around 6. At the larger, newer ryokan, meals will be in the dining room; at smaller, more personal ryokan, it is served in your room. When you are finished, a maid will clear away the dishes and lay out your futon. In Japan *futon* means bedding, and this consists of a thin cotton mattress and a heavy, thick comforter, which is replaced with a thinner quilt in summer. The small, hard pillow is filled with grain. Some of the less expensive ryokan (under ¥7,000 per person) have become slightly lackadaisical in changing the quilt cover with each new guest; in as inoffensive a way as possible, feel free to complain—just don't shame the proprietor. Around 8 am, a maid will gently wake you, clear away the futon, and bring in your Japanese-style breakfast, which will probably consist of fish, pickled vegetables, and rice. If this isn't appealing, politely ask if it's possible to have coffee and toast. Checkout is at 10 am.

Make sure you call or email as far in advance as possible for a room—inns are not always willing to accept foreign guests because of language and cultural barriers. It is nearly impossible to get a room in July or August. Many top-level ryokan require new guests to have introductions and references from a respected client of the inn to get a room; this goes for new Japanese guests, too. On the other hand, inns that do accept foreigners without introduction sometimes treat them as cash cows, which means they might give you cursory service and a lesser room. If you don't speak Japanese, try to have a Japanese speaker reserve a room for you.

WHERE TO STAY

$$$$ B&B/INN **Goyokan** (五葉館). This family-run ryokan on Shuzenji's main street has rooms that look out on the Katsura-gawa, plus gorgeous stone-lined (for men) and wood-lined (for women) indoor hot springs. **Pros:** unique, modern take on a ryokan. **Cons:** lacks cozy feel of a true ryokan. [$] *Rooms from: ¥32000* ✉ *765–2 Shuzenji-cho* ☎ *0558/72–2066* 🌐 *www.goyokan.co.jp* 🛏 *11 Japanese-style rooms without bath* 🍴 *Breakfast.*

$$$$
B&B/INN 🏠 **Kyorai-An Matsushiro-kan** (去来庵 松城館). Although this small fam-ily-owned inn is nothing fancy, the owners make you feel like a guest in their home. **Pros:** nice shared hot-spring bath. **Cons:** rather dated design throughout. Ⓢ *Rooms from: ¥34000 ⊠ 55 Kona, Izunokuni ☎ 055/948–0072 ⊟ No credit cards 🛏 16 Japanese-style rooms, 14 with bath* ⑩ *Some meals.*

$$$$
B&B/INN 🏠 **Ochiairou Murakami** (落合楼村上). This traditional ryokan was built in the Showa period, and though it has been renovated and modern-ized, the main wooden structure remains true to its original design, with spacious and comfortable rooms that look out into the gardens. **Pros:** free pickup from Yugashima bus terminal; lovely garden on the grounds. **Cons:** rather expensive. Ⓢ *Rooms from: ¥38000 ⊠ 1887–1 Yugashima, Izu ☎ 055/885–0014 🛏 15 Japanese-style rooms with bath* ⑩ *Some meals.*

$$$$
B&B/INN 🏠 **Ryokan Sanyoso** (旅館三養荘). At the former villa of the Iwasaki fam-ily, founders of the Mitsubishi conglomerate, museum-quality antiques furnish the rooms. The best rooms have traditional baths made of fra-grant cypress wood and overlook exquisite little private gardens. **Pros:** authentic ryokan and furnishings; Japanese bath available; as luxuri-ous and beautiful a place as you'll find on the Izu Peninsula. **Cons:** most expensive ryokan in the area. Ⓢ *Rooms from: ¥60000 ⊠ 270 Mamanoue, Izunokuni ☎ 055/947–1111 ⊕ www.princehotels.com/en/sanyo-so 🛏 3 Western-style, 30 Japanese-style, and 7 mixed Western-Japanese-style rooms with bath* ⑩ *Some meals.*

HAKONE 箱根

The national park and resort area of Hakone is a popular day trip from Tokyo and a good place for a close-up view of Mt. Fuji (assuming the mountain is not swathed in clouds, as often happens in summer). ■TIP→ **On summer weekends it often seems as though all of Tokyo has come out to Hakone with you. Expect long lines at cable cars and traffic jams everywhere.**

TIMING

You can cover the best of Hakone in a one-day trip out of Tokyo, but if you want to try the curative powers of the thermal waters or do some hiking, then stay overnight. Two of the best areas are around the old hot-springs resort of Miyanoshita and the western side of Koma-ga-take-san (Mt. Koma-ga-take).

GETTING HERE AND AROUND

The typical Hakone route, outlined here, may sound complex, but this is in fact one excursion from Tokyo so well defined that you really can't get lost—no more so, at least, than any of the thousands of Japanese tourists ahead of and behind you. The first leg of the journey is from Odawara or Hakone-Yumoto by train and cable car through the moun-tains to Togendai, on the north shore of Ashi-no-ko (Lake Ashi). The long way around, from Odawara to Togendai by bus, takes about an hour—in heavy traffic, an hour and a half. The trip over the mountains, on the other hand, takes about two hours. Credit the difference to the Hakone Tozan Tetsudo Line—possibly the slowest train you'll ever ride.

Using three switchbacks to inch its way up the side of the mountain, the train takes 54 minutes to travel the 16 km (10 miles) from Odawara to Gora (38 minutes from Hakone-Yumoto). The steeper it gets, the grander the view.

Trains do not stop at any station en route for any length of time, but they do run frequently enough to allow you to disembark, visit a sight, and catch another train.

Within the Hakone area, buses run every 15 to 30 minutes from Hakone-machi to Hakone-Yumoto Station on the private Odakyu Line (40 minutes, ¥960), and Odawara Station (one hour, ¥1,180), where you can take either the Odakyu Romance Car back to Shinjuku Station or a JR Shinkansen to Tokyo Station.

Hakone Sightseeing Cruise. This ride is free with your Hakone Free Pass; otherwise, buy a ticket (¥1,480 round-trip) at the office in the terminal. A few ships of conventional design ply Lake Ashi; the rest are astonishingly corny Disney knockoffs. One, for example, is rigged like a 17th-century warship. ⊠ *181 Hakone, Ashigarashimo District* ☎ *0460/83–6325* ⊕ *www.hakone-kankosen.co.jp* ⊠ *¥1,840 round-trip (without Hakone Free Pass)* ☉ *Summer, 40-min intervals; winter, 50-min intervals. Mar.–Nov., daily 9:30–5; Dec.–Feb., daily 9:30–4.*

Odakyu Sightseeing Service Center. Many places in Hakone accept the Hakone Free Pass. It's valid for three days and issued by the privately owned Odakyu Railways. The pass covers the train fare to Hakone and allows you to use any mode of transportation, including the Hakone Tozan Cable Car, the Hakone Ropeway, and the Hakone Cruise Boat. In addition to transportation, Free Pass holders get discounts at museums such as the Hakone Museum of Art, restaurants, and shops. The list of participants is pretty extensive and it always changes, so it's a good idea to check out the website for a complete list of participating companies and terms and conditions.

The Hakone Free Pass (¥5,640) and the Fuji-Hakone Pass (¥7,400) can be purchased at the Odakyu Sightseeing Service Center inside JR Shinjuku Station in Tokyo, near the West Exit, or by credit card over the phone. Allow a couple of days for delivery to your hotel. If you have a JR Pass, it's cheaper to take a Kodama Shinkansen from Tokyo Station to Odawara and buy the Hakone Free Pass there (¥4,500) for travel within the Hakone region only. ⊠ *JR Shinjuku Station, 3–8 Shinjuku, near the West Exit* ☎ *03/5321–7887* ⊕ *www.odakyu.jp.*

ESSENTIALS

Tourist Information Hakone Tourist Association (箱根観光協会 *Hakone Kanko Kyoukai*). ⊠ *698 Yumoto, Hakone* ☎ *0460/85–7177* ⊕ *www.hakone.or.jp/en.*

EXPLORING

TOP ATTRACTIONS

Fodor's Choice ★

Hakone Kowakien Yunessun (箱根小涌園 ユネッサン). This complex on the hills overlooking Hakone has more than the average onsen. In addition to all the water-based attractions, there is a shopping mall modeled on a European outdoor market, swimsuit rental shop, massage salon, and game center. The park is divided into two main zones, called Yunessun

CLOSE UP

The Road to the Shogun

In days gone by, the town of Hakone was on the Tokaido, the main highway between the imperial court in Kyoto and the shogunate in Edo (present-day Tokyo). The road was the only feasible passage through this mountainous country, which made it an ideal place for a checkpoint to control traffic. The Tokugawa Shogunate built the Hakone-machi here in 1618; its most important function was to monitor the *daimyo* (feudal lords) passing through—to keep track, above all, of weapons coming into Edo, and womenfolk coming out.

When Ieyasu Tokugawa came to power, Japan had been through nearly 100 years of bloody struggle among rival coalitions of daimyo. Ieyasu emerged supreme because some of his opponents had switched sides at the last minute, in the Battle of Sekigahara in 1600. The shogun was justifiably paranoid about his "loyal" barons—especially those in the outlying domains—so he required the daimyo to live in Edo for periods of time every two years. When they did return to their own lands, they had to leave their wives behind in Edo, hostages to their good behavior. A noble lady coming through the Hakone Sekisho without an official pass, in short, was a case of treason.

The checkpoint served the Tokugawa dynasty well for 250 years. It was demolished only when the shogunate fell, in the Meiji Restoration of 1868. An exact replica, with an exhibition hall of period costumes and weapons, was built as a tourist attraction in 1965.

and Mori no Yu ("Forest Bath"). In the Yunessun side, you need to wear a swimsuit, and can visit somewhat tacky re-creations of Turkish and ancient Roman baths. You can also take a dip in coffee, green tea, sake, or red wine. It is all a bit corny, but fun. Younger visitors enjoy the waterslides on "Rodeo Mountain." In the more secluded Mori no Yu side, you can go au naturel in a variety of indoor and outdoor, single-sex baths. When signing in at reception, get a waterproof digital wristband that allows you to pay for lockers and drink machines within the complex. ⊠ *1297 Ninotaira Hakone-machi, Ashigarashimo-gun* ☎ *0460/82–4126* ⊕ *www.yunessun.com* ⬚ *Yunessun zone ¥2,900, Mori no Yu zone ¥1,900, both for ¥4,100* ☉ *Mar.–Oct., Yunessun daily 9–7, Mori no Yu daily 11–9; Nov.–Feb., Yunessun daily 9–6, Mori no Yu daily 11–9.*

Hakone Open-Air Museum (箱根彫刻の森美術館 *Hakone Chokoku-no-mori Bijutsukan*). Only a few minutes' walk from the Miyanoshita Station (directions are posted in English), the museum houses an astonishing collection of 19th- and 20th-century Western and Japanese sculpture, most of it on display in a spacious, handsome garden. There are works here by Rodin, Moore, Arp, Calder, Giacometti, Takashi Shimizu, and Kotaro Takamura. One section of the garden is devoted to Emilio Greco. Inside are works by Picasso, Léger, and Manzo, among others. ⊠ *1121 Ni-no-taira* ☎ *0460/82–1161* ⊕ *www.hakone-oam.or.jp* ⬚ *¥1,600* ☉ *Mar.–Nov., daily 9–5; Dec.–Feb., daily 9–4.*

Hakone Ropeway. At the cable-car terminus of Soun-zan, a gondola called the Hakone Ropeway swings up over a ridge and crosses the valley called **Owaku-dani,** also known as "Great Boiling Valley," on its way to Togendai. The landscape here is desolate, with sulfurous billows of steam escaping through holes from some inferno deep in the earth—yet another reminder that Japan is a chain of volcanic islands. At the top of the ridge is one of the two stations where you can leave the gondola. From here, a ¾-km (½-mile) walking course wanders among the sulfur pits in the valley. Just below the station is a restaurant; the food here is truly terrible, but on a clear day the view of Mt. Fuji is perfect. Remember that if you get off the gondola at any stage, you—and others in the same situation—will have to wait for someone to make space on a later gondola before you can continue down to Togendai and Ashi-no-ko (but the gondolas come by every minute). ⊠ *1–15–1 Shiroyama, Odawara* ☎ *0460/32–2205* 💰 *¥1,510 round-trip Sounzan Station to Owakudani Station* ⊗ *Mar.–Nov., daily 8:45–5:15; Dec.–Feb., daily 9:15–4:15.*

Miyanoshita (宮ノ下). The first stop on the train route from Hakone-Yumoto, this is a small but very pleasant and popular resort. As well as hot springs, this village has antiques shops along its main road and several hiking routes up the ¾-km- (½-mile-) tall Mt. Sengen. If you get to the top, you'll be rewarded with a great view of the gorge. ⊠ *Hakone.*

WORTH NOTING

Ashi-no-ko (芦ノ湖 *Lake Ashi*). From Owaku-dani, the descent by gondola to Togendai on the shore of Lake Ashi takes 25 minutes. There's no reason to linger at Togendai; it's only a terminus for buses to Hakone-Yumoto and Odawara and to the resort villages in the northern part of Hakone. Head straight for the pier, a few minutes' walk down the hill, where boats set out on the lake for Hakone-machi. With still water and good weather, you'll get a breathtaking reflection of the mountains in the waters of the lake as you go. ⊠ *Hakone.*

Gora (強羅). This small town is at the end of the train line from Odawara and at the lower end of the Hakone Tozan Cable Car. It's a good jumping-off point for hiking and exploring. Ignore the little restaurants and souvenir stands here: get off the train as quickly as you can and make a dash for the cable car at the other end of the station. If you let the rest of the passengers get there before you, and perhaps a tour bus or two, you may stand 45 minutes in line. ⊠ *Hakone.*

Hakone Museum of Art (箱根美≠術館 *Hakone Bijutsukan*). A sister institution to the MOA Museum of Art in Atami, Hakone Museum of Art is at the second stop of the Hakone Tozan Cable Car. The museum, which consists of two buildings set in a garden, houses a modest collection of porcelain and ceramics from China, Korea, and Japan. ⊠ *1300 Gora* ☎ *0460/2–2623* ⊕ *www.moaart.or.jp/hakone* 💰 *¥900* ⊗ *Apr.–Nov., Fri.–Wed. 9:30–4:30; Dec.–Mar., Fri.–Wed. 9:30–4.*

Hakone Sekisho (箱根町). This barrier, a checkpoint on the road with a guardhouse and lookout tower, was built in 1618 to inspect incoming and outgoing traffic until it was demolished during the Meiji Restoration of 1868. An exact replica was built as a tourist attraction in 1965

Passengers floating over the Owaku-dani valley on the Hakone Ropeway can see Fuji looming—on a clear day, of course.

and is only a few minutes' walk from the pier, along the lakeshore in the direction of Moto-Hakone. ✉ *1 Hakone-machi* ☎ *0460/83–6635* 🎫 *¥500* 🕐 *Mar.–Nov., daily 9–5; Dec.–Feb., daily 9–4:30, last entry 30 mins before closing.*

Soun-zan (早雲山 *Mt. Soun*). The Hakone Tozan Cable Car travels from Gora to Soun-zan, departing every 20 minutes; it takes 10 minutes (¥410; free with the Hakone Free Pass) to get to the top. It provides a good launch for an ideal day of hiking. There are four stops en route, and you can get off and reboard the cable car at any of them if you've paid the full fare. ✉ *Hakone.*

WHERE TO STAY

$$$$ HOTEL 🏨 **Fujiya Hotel** (富士屋ホテル). Built in 1878, this Western-style hotel with modern additions is showing signs of age, but that somehow adds to its charm. **Pros:** wonderful, friendly service. **Cons:** rooms and bath design are rather dated. [$] *Rooms from: ¥50000* ✉ *359 Miyanoshita, Hakone-machi* ☎ *0460/82–2211* 🌐 *www.fujiyahotel.jp* 🛏 *149 Western-style rooms with bath* 🍴 *Some meals.*

$ HOTEL 🏨 **Fuji-Hakone Guest House** (富士箱根ゲストハウス). This small, family-run Japanese inn has simple tatami rooms with the bare essentials. **Pros:** friendly staff; inexpensive rates. **Cons:** difficult to access from nearest transportation, especially at night. [$] *Rooms from: ¥10000* ✉ *912 Sengoku-hara (103 Moto-Hakone for Moto-Hakone Guest House), Hakone-machi* ☎ *0460/84–6577 Fuji-Hakone, 0460/83–7880 Moto-Hakone* 🌐 *fujihakone.com/en* 🛏 *14 Japanese-style rooms without bath in Fuji-Hakone, 5 Japanese-style rooms without bath in Moto-Hakone* 🍴 *Some meals.*

WHAT THE . . . ?

No, your eyes are not playing tricks on you. Those are in fact local entrepreneurs boiling eggs in the sulfur pits in Owaku-dani. Locals make a passable living selling the eggs, which turn black, to tourists at exorbitant prices. A popular myth suggests that eating one of these eggs can extend your life by seven years.

$$$$ B&B/INN 🏨 **Gora Tensui** (強羅天翠). Upon entering this cross between a luxury Western-style hotel and traditional inn, guests remove their shoes and socks, sit at a counter bar with their tired feet resting in the hot-mineral-spring bath under the bar, and enjoy a tea or beer as they check in. **Pros:** four rooms have a private onsen on a terrace. **Cons:** no Japanese food in the restaurant. [$] *Rooms from: ¥50000* ✉ *1320–276 Gora, Ashigarashimo-gun* ☎ *0460/86–1411* 🌐 *www.gora-tensui.com* 🛏 *10 Western-style rooms, 7 Japanese-style rooms, all with bath* 🍴 *Some meals.*

$$$$ HOTEL 🏨 **Hakone Prince Hotel Ashinoko** (箱根プリンスホテル芦ノ湖). You have a choice of hotel rooms or cozy cottages at this resort complex, with the lake in front and the mountains of Koma-ga-take in back. **Pros:** lovely quaint cottages surrounded by nature. **Cons:** a bit remote from sightseeing spots; popular with groups and business conferences. [$] *Rooms from: ¥50000* ✉ *144 Moto-Hakone, Hakone-machi* ☎ *0460/83–1111* 🌐 *www.princehotels.com* 🛏 *142 Western-style rooms with bath, 116 Western-style cottages with bath* 🍴 *Breakfast.*

$$ B&B/INN 🏨 **Lodge Fujimien** (ロッジ富士見苑). This traditional ryokan, complete with an on-site onsen, has all the trimmings of an expensive ryokan, for a fraction of the price. **Pros:** affordable rates; convenient location. **Cons:** occasional overcrowding. [$] *Rooms from: ¥12000* ✉ *1245 Sengoku-hara* ☎ *0460/84–8675* 🌐 *www.fujimien.com* 💳 *No credit cards* 🛏 *21 Japanese-style rooms with bath, 5 Western-style rooms with bath* 🍴 *Some meals.*

FUJI GO-KO (FUJI FIVE LAKES) 富士五湖

To the north of Mt. Fuji, the Fuji Go-ko area affords an unbeatable view of the mountain on clear days and makes the best base for a climb to the summit. With its various outdoor activities, such as skating and fishing in winter and boating and hiking in summer, this is a popular resort area for families and business conferences.

The five lakes are, from the east, Yamanaka-ko, Kawaguchi-ko, Sai-ko, Shoji-ko, and Motosu-ko. Yamanaka and Kawaguchi are the largest and most developed as resort areas, with Kawaguchi more or less the centerpiece of the group.

TIMING

You can visit this area on a day trip from Tokyo, but unless you want to spend most of it on buses and trains, plan on staying overnight.

GETTING HERE AND AROUND

Direct bus service runs daily from Shinjuku Station in Tokyo to Lake Kawaguchi every hour between 7:10 am and 11:20 pm. Buses go from Kawaguchi-ko Station to Go-gome (the fifth station on the climb up

Mt. Fuji) in about an hour; there are eight departures a day until the climbing season (July and August) starts, when there are 15 departures or more, depending on demand. The cost is ¥1,750.

The transportation hub, as well as one of the major resort areas in the Fuji Five Lakes area, is Kawaguchi-ko. Getting there from Tokyo requires a change of trains at Otsuki. The JR Chuo Line Kaiji and Azusa express trains leave Shinjuku Station for Otsuki on the half hour from 7 am to 8 pm (more frequently in the morning) and take approximately one hour. At Otsuki, change to the private Fuji-Kyuko Line for Kawaguchi-ko, which takes another 50 minutes. The total traveling time is about two hours, and you can use your JR Pass as far as Otsuki; otherwise, the fare is ¥1,490. The Otsuki–Kawaguchi-ko leg costs ¥1,140.

The Holiday Kaisoku Fuji train, available on weekends and national holidays, has direct express service from Shinjuku, leaving at 8:14 and arriving at Kawaguchi-ko Station at 10:26. Coming back, you have a choice of late-afternoon departures from Kawaguchi-ko that arrive at Shinjuku in the early evening. Check the express timetables before you go; you can also call either the JR Higashi-Nihon Info Line or Fuji-kyuuko Kawaguchi-ko Station for train information.

ESSENTIALS

Visitor Information Fuji-Kawaguchiko Tourist Association
(富士河口湖観光協会 *Fuji Kawaguci-ko Kanko Kyoukai*). ✉ *364–1 Funatsu, Fujikawaguchiko-machi, Minami-Tsuru-gun* ☎ *0555/72–6700* ⊕ *www.fujisan.ne.jp.*

EXPLORING

FAMILY **Fuji-Q Highland** (富士急ハイランド). The largest of the recreational facilities at Lake Kawaguchi has an impressive assortment of rides, roller coasters, and other amusements, but it's probably not worth a visit unless you have children in tow. In winter there's superb skating here, with Mt. Fuji for a backdrop. Fuji-kyu Highland is about 15 minutes' walk east from Kawaguchi-ko Station. In addition to the entry fee, there are charges for various attractions, so it's best to get the one-day free pass. ✉ *5–6–1 Shin Nishihara, Fujiyoshida* ☎ *0555/23–2111* ⊕ *www. fujiq.jp/en* 🎫 *1-day free pass ¥5,200, entrance only ¥1,400* ⊙ *Weekdays 9–5, weekends 9–8.*

Lake Kawaguchi (河口湖 *Kawaguchi-ko*). A 5- to 10-minute walk from Kawaguchi-ko Station, this is the most developed of the five lakes. It's ringed with weekend retreats and vacation lodges—many of them maintained by companies and universities for their employees. Excursion boats depart from a pier here on 30-minute tours of the lake. The promise, not always fulfilled, is to have two views of Mt. Fuji: one of the mountain itself and the other inverted in its reflection on the water.

Lake Motosu (本栖湖 *Motosu-ko*). Lake Motosu is the farthest west of the five lakes. It's also the deepest and clearest of the Fuji Go-ko. It takes about 50 minutes to get here by bus.

Lake Sai (西湖 *Sai-ko*). Between Lakes Shoji and Kawaguchi, Lake Sai is the third-largest lake of the Fuji Go-ko, with only moderate development. From the western shore there is an especially good view of Mt. Fuji. Near

Sai-ko there are two natural caves, an ice cave and a wind cave. You can either take a bus or walk to them.

Lake Shoji (精進湖 *Shoji-ko*). Many consider Lake Shoji, the smallest of the lakes, to be the prettiest. There are still remnants of lava flow jutting out from the water, which locals perch upon while fishing. The Shoji Trail leads from Lake Shoji to Mt. Fuji's fifth station through Aoki-ga-hara (Sea of Trees). This forest has an underlying magnetic lava field that makes compasses go haywire. Be prepared with a good trail map before taking this hike.

THE SHOJI TRIANGLE

The Aoki-ga-hara Jukai (Sea of Trees) seems to hold a morbid fascination for the Japanese. Many people go into Aoki-ga-hara every year and never come out, some of them on purpose. If you're planning to climb Mt. Fuji from this trail, go with a guide.

Lake Yamanaka (山中湖 *Yamanaka-ko*). The largest lake of the Fuji Go-ko, Yamanaka is 35 minutes by bus to the southeast of Kawaguchi. It's also the closest lake to the popular trail up Mt. Fuji that starts at Go-gome, and many climbers use this resort area as a base.

Mt. Tenjo (天上山 *Tenjo-san*). From the shore of Lake Kawaguchi (near the pier) the Kachikachi Ropeway quickly brings you to the top of the 3,622-foot-tall mountain. From the observatory here the whole of Lake Kawaguchi lies before you, and beyond the lake is a classic view of Mt. Fuji. ✉ *1163–1 Azagawa, Fuji-Kawaguchiko-machi* ☎ *0555/72–0363 Ropeway* 🌐 *www.kachikachiyama-ropeway.com* 🎟 *Round-trip ¥700, one-way ¥400* 🕒 *Daily Mar.–Nov. 9–5; Dec.–Feb, 9–4:30 (every 5 mins).*

WHERE TO STAY

$$$$ HOTEL 🏨 **Fuji View Hotel** (富士ビューホテル). Accommodations are a little threadbare but comfortable and right on the lakefront, and the terrace lounge affords fine views of the lake and of Mt. Fuji beyond. **Pros:** comparatively inexpensive lodgings. **Cons:** rooms are rather small. [$] *Rooms from: ¥34000* ✉ *511 Katsuyama-mura, Fuji-Kawaguchiko-machi* ☎ *0555/83–2211* 🌐 *www.fujiview.jp* 🛏 *40 Western-style rooms with bath, 30 Japanese-style rooms with bath* 🍴 *Some meals.*

$$$$ HOTEL 🏨 **Hotel Mount Fuji** (富士山ホテル). This is the best resort hotel on Lake Yamanaka, with European-style rooms and all the facilities for a recreational holiday, including on-site game and karaoke rooms and a nature walk on the grounds. **Pros:** comfortable rooms; many activities on the hotel grounds. **Cons:** one of the more expensive options in the area; convenient location and large banquet halls make it a favorite among tour groups. [$] *Rooms from: ¥30000* ✉ *1360–83 Yamanaka, Yamanaka-ko-mura* ☎ *0555/62–2111* 🌐 *mountfujihotels.jp* 🛏 *150 Western-style rooms with bath, 1 Japanese-style room with bath* 🍴 *Some meals.*

$ B&B/INN 🏨 **Inn Fujitomita** (旅館ふじとみた). One of the closest lodging options to the Mt. Fuji hiking trails is not much to look at from the outside, but the interior is spacious and homey. **Pros:** spacious rooms; pleasant surrounding grounds. **Cons:** very crowded during climbing season. [$] *Rooms from: ¥10000* ✉ *3235 Shibokusa, Oshinomura, Minami-Tsuru-gun* ☎ *0555/84–3359* 🌐 *www.tim.hi-ho.ne.jp/innfuji* 💳 *No credit cards* 🛏 *9 Japanese-style rooms, 2 with bath* 🍴 *Some meals.*

NIKKO 日光

130 km (81 miles) north of Tokyo.

"Think nothing is splendid," asserts an old Japanese proverb, "until you have seen Nikko." Nikko, which means "sunlight," is a popular vacation spot for the Japanese, for good reason: its gorgeous sights include a breathtaking waterfall and one of the country's best-known shrines. In addition, Nikko combines the rustic charm of a countryside village (complete with wild monkeys that have the run of the place) with a convenient location not far from Tokyo.

> **THE UBIQUITOUS TORII**
>
> Wondering what those gatelike structures are with two posts and two crosspieces? They are torii and are used as gateways to Japanese Shinto temples.

4

GETTING HERE AND AROUND

The limited express train of the Tobu Railway has two direct connections from Tokyo to Nikko every morning, starting at 7:30 am from Tobu Asakusa Station, a minute's walk from the last stop on Tokyo's Ginza subway line (one hour, 48 minutes, ¥2,800) with additional trains on weekends, holidays, and in high season. All seats are reserved. Bookings are not accepted over the phone and can be bought only at Asakusa Station. During summer, fall, and weekends, buy tickets a few days in advance. Alternatively, the rapid train takes only a bit longer at half the price and requires no reservations (two hours, 10 minutes, ¥1,360). If you're visiting Nikko on a day trip, note that the last return train is at 7:43 pm, requiring a quick and easy change at Shimo-Imaichi, and arrives at Asakusa at 9:35 pm. If you have a JR Pass, use JR (Japan Railways) service, which connects Tokyo and Nikko, from Ueno Station. Take the Tohoku–Honsen Line limited express to Utsunomiya (about 1½ hours) and transfer to the train for JR Nikko Station (45 minutes). The earliest departure from Ueno is at 5:10 am; the last connection back leaves Nikko at 9:02 pm and brings you into Ueno at 11:38 pm. (If you're not using the JR Pass, the one-way fare costs ¥2,590.)

More expensive, but faster, is taking the Shinkansen to Utsunomiya and changing for the JR train to Nikko Station; the one-way fare, including the surcharge for the express, is ¥5,370. The first train leaves Tokyo Station at 6:04 am (or Ueno at 6:10) and takes about 1 hour, 30 minutes to Nikko. To return, take the 9:46 pm train from Nikko to Utsunomiya and catch the last Shinkansen back at 10:38 pm.

It's possible, but unwise, to travel by car from Tokyo to Nikko. The trip takes at least three hours, and merely getting from central Tokyo to the toll-road system can be a nightmare. Coming back, especially on a Saturday or Sunday evening, is even worse.

Buses and taxis can take you from Nikko to the village of Chuzenji and nearby Lake Chuzenji; one-way cab fare from Tobu Nikko Station to Chuzenji is about ¥7,000. ■**TIP→ There is no bus service between Tokyo and Nikko.** Local buses leave Tobu Nikko Station for Lake Chuzenji, stopping just above the entrance to Tosho-gu, approximately every 30 minutes from 6:15 am until 7:01 pm. The fare to Chuzenji is ¥1,150, and the ride takes about 40 minutes. The last return bus from the lake leaves at 7:39 pm, arriving back at Tobu Nikko Station at 9:17 pm.

VISITOR INFORMATION

You can do a lot of preplanning for your visit to Nikko with a stop at the Japan National Tourist Organization office in Tokyo, where the helpful English-speaking staff will ply you with pamphlets and field your questions about things to see and do. Closer to the source is the Tourist Information and Hospitality Center in Nikko itself, about halfway up the main street of town between the railway stations and Tosho-gu, on the left; don't expect too much in the way of help in English, but the center does have a good array of English information about local restaurants and shops, registers of inns and hotels, and mapped-out walking tours.

ESSENTIALS

Tourist Information Nikko Tourist Information Center (日光観光案内所). ✉ *591 Gokou-machi* ☎ *0288/54–2496.*

EXPLORING

The town of Nikko is essentially one long avenue—Sugi Namiki (Cryptomeria Avenue)—extending for about 2 km (1 mile) from the railway stations to Tosho-gu. You can easily walk to most places within town. Tourist inns and shops line the street, and if you have time, you might want to make this a leisurely stroll. The antiques shops along the way may turn up interesting—but expensive—pieces like armor fittings, hibachi, pottery, and dolls. The souvenir shops here sell ample selections of local wood carvings.

TOSHO-GU 東照宮

Fodor's Choice ★   The Tosho-gu area encompasses three UNESCO World Heritage sites—Tosho-gu Shrine, Futarasan Shrine, and Rinnoji Temple. These are known as *nisha-ichiji* (two shrines and one temple) and are Nikko's main draw. Signs and maps clearly mark a recommended route that will allow you to see all the major sights, which are within walking distance of each other. You should plan for half a day to explore the area.

A multiple-entry ticket is the best way to see the Tosho-gu precincts. The ¥1,300 pass gets you entrance to Rinno-ji (Rinno Temple), the Taiyu-in Mausoleum, and Futara-san Jinja (Futara-san Shrine); for an extra ¥400 you can also see the Sleeping Cat and Ieyasu's tomb at Taiyu-in (separate fees are charged for admission to other sights). There are two places to purchase the multiple-entry ticket: one is at the entrance to Rinno Temple, in the corner of the parking lot, at the top of the path called the Higashi-sando (East Approach) that begins across the highway from the Sacred Bridge; the other is at the entrance to Tosho-gu, at the top of the broad Omote-sando (Central Approach), which begins about 100 yards farther west.

CLOSE UP

Ieyasu's Legacy

In 1600, Ieyasu Tokugawa (1543–1616) won a battle at a place in the mountains of south-central Japan called Seki-ga-hara that left him the undisputed ruler of the archipelago. He died 16 years later, but the Tokugawa Shogunate would last another 252 years.

The founder of such a dynasty required a fitting resting place. Ieyasu (ee-eh- *ya*-su) had provided for one in his will: a mausoleum at Nikko, in a forest of tall cedars, where a religious center had been founded more than eight centuries earlier. The year after his death, in accordance with Buddhist custom, he was given a *kaimyo*—an honorific name to bear in the afterlife. Thenceforth, he was Tosho-Daigongen: the Great Incarnation Who Illuminates the East. The Imperial Court at Kyoto declared him a god, and his remains were taken in a procession of great pomp and ceremony to be enshrined at Nikko.

The dynasty he left behind was enormously rich. Ieyasu's personal fief, on the Kanto Plain, was worth 2.5 million *koku* of rice. One koku, in monetary terms, was equivalent to the cost of keeping one retainer in the necessities of life for a year. The shogunate itself, however, was still an uncertainty. It had only recently taken control after more than a century of civil war. The founder's tomb had a political purpose: to inspire awe and to make manifest the power of the Tokugawas. It was Ieyasu's legacy, a statement of his family's right to rule.

Tosho-gu was built by his grandson, the third shogun, Iemitsu (it was Iemitsu who established the policy of national isolation, which closed the doors of Japan to the outside world for more than 200 years). The mausoleum and shrine required the labor of 15,000 people for two years (1634–36). Craftsmen and artists of the first rank were assembled from all over the country. Every surface was carved and painted and lacquered in the most intricate detail imaginable. Tosho-gu shimmers with the reflections of 2,489,000 sheets of gold leaf. Roof beams and rafter ends with dragon heads, lions, and elephants in bas-relief; friezes of phoenixes, wild ducks, and monkeys; inlaid pillars and red-lacquer corridors: Tosho-gu is everything a 17th-century warlord would consider gorgeous, and the inspiration is very Chinese.

TOP ATTRACTIONS

Futara-san Jinja (二荒山神社 *Futara-san Shrine*). Nikko's holy ground is far older than the Tokugawa dynasty, in whose honor it was improved upon. Founded in 782, Futara-san Jinja (Futura-san Shrine) is a peaceful contrast to the more elaborate Toshogu Shrine. Futara-san actually has three locations: the Main Shrine at Tosho-gu; the Chugu-shi (Middle Shrine), at Chuzenji-ko; and the Okumiya (Inner Shrine), on top of Mt. Nantai.

The bronze torii at the entrance to the shrine leads to the gilded and elaborately carved **Kara-mon** (Chinese Gate); beyond it is the **Hai-den,** the shrine's oratory. The Hai-den, too, is richly carved and decorated, with a dragon-covered ceiling. The Chinese lions on the panels at the rear are by two distinguished painters of the Kano school. From the oratory of the Taiyu-in a connecting passage leads to the **Hon-den** (Sanctum)—the present version of which dates from 1619. Designated a National Treasure, it houses a gilded and lacquered Buddhist altar some 9 feet high, decorated with paintings of animals, birds, and flowers, in which resides the object of all this veneration: a seated wooden figure of Iemitsu himself. ⊠ *Take the avenue to the left as you're standing before the stone torii at Tosho-gu and follow it to the end, 2307 Sannai* ⊑ *Shrine only ¥200, multiple-entry ticket (includes Rinno Temple and Taiyu-in Mausoleum) ¥1,300* ⊗ *Apr.–Oct., daily 8–5; Nov.–Mar., daily 9–4.*

> ## SEEKING YOUR FORTUNE?
>
> Make sure you visit **Gohoten-do**, in the northeast corner of Rinno Temple, behind the Sanbutsu-do. Three of the Seven Gods of Good Fortune, derived from Chinese folk mythology, are enshrined here. These three Buddhist deities are Daikoku-ten and Bishamon-ten, who bring wealth and good harvests, and Benzai-ten, patroness of music and the arts.

Rinno-ji (輪王寺 *Rinno Temple*). This temple belongs to the Tendai sect of Buddhism, the head temple of which is Enryaku-ji, on Mt. Hiei near Kyoto. The main hall of Rinno Temple, called the **Sanbutsu-do,** is the largest single building at Tosho-gu; it enshrines an image of Amida Nyorai, the Buddha of the Western Paradise, flanked on the right by Senju (Thousand-Armed) Kannon, the goddess of mercy, and on the left by Bato-Kannon, regarded as the protector of animals. These three images are lacquered in gold and date from the early part of the 17th century. The original Sanbutsu-do is said to have been built in 848 by the priest Ennin (794–864), also known as Jikaku-Daishi. The present building dates from 1648.

In the southwest corner of the Rinno Temple compound, behind the abbot's residence, is an especially fine Japanese garden called **Shoyo-en,** created in 1815 and thoughtfully designed to present a different perspective of its rocks, ponds, and flowering plants from every turn on its path. To the right of the entrance to the garden is the Homotsu-den (Treasure Hall) of Rinno Temple, a museum with a collection of some 6,000 works of lacquerware, painting, and Buddhist sculpture. The museum is rather small, and only a few of the pieces in the collection—many of them designated National Treasures and Important Cultural Properties—are on display at any given time. ⊠ *2300 Yamauchi* ☎ *0288/54–0531* ⊑ *Taiyu-in Mausoleum and Futara-san Shrine ¥1,300, Shoyo-en and Homotsu-den ¥400* ⊗ *Apr.–Oct., daily 8–5, last entry at 4; Nov.–Mar., daily 8–4, last entry at 3.*

Taiyu-in Mausoleum (大猷院廟). This grandiose building is the resting place of the third Tokugawa shogun, Iemitsu (1604–51), who imposed a policy of national isolation on Japan that was to last more than 200 years. Iemitsu, one suspects, had it in mind to upstage his illustrious grandfather; he marked the approach to his own tomb with no fewer than six different decorative gates. The first is another Nio-mon—a Gate of the Deva Kings—like the one at Tosho-gu. The dragon painted on the ceiling is by Yasunobu Kano. A flight of stone steps leads from

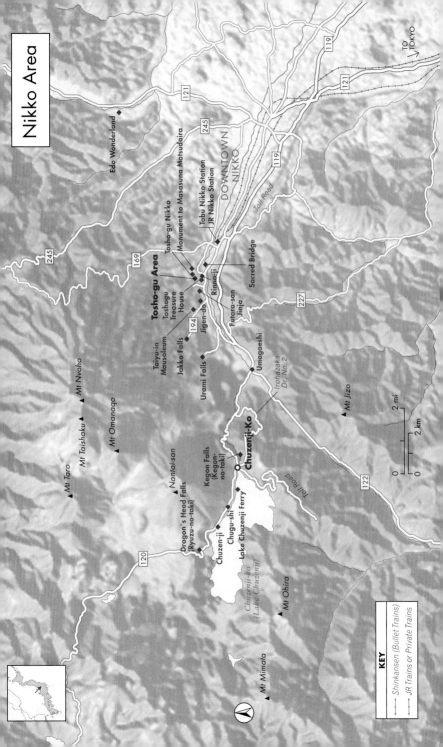

Nikko Area

Mt Taro

Mt Taishaku ▲

Mt Nyoho ▲

Mt Omanago ▲

Dragon's Head Falls
(Ryuzu-no-taki)

Nantai-san ▲

Chuzen-ji

Chugu-shi
Lake Chuzenji Ferry

Kegon Falls
(Kegon-no-taki)

Chuzenji-Ko

Chuzenji-ko
(Lake Chuzenji)

Mt Ohira ▲

Mt Mimata ▲

Urami Falls

Jakko Falls

Taiyu-in
Mausoleum

Tosho-gu Area

Toshogu
Treasure
House

Jigen-do

Rinno-ji

Futara-san
Jinja

Tosho-gu Nikko
Monument to Masasuna Matsudaira

Sacred Bridge

DOWNTOWN
NIKKO

Tobu Nikko Station
JR Nikko Station

Umagaeshi

Irohazaka
Dr. No. 2

Mt Jizo ▲

Toll Road

Edo Wonderland

TO
TOKYO

Toll Road

169

194

245

121

119

121

119

227

245

120

122

KEY

→ Shinkansen (Bullet Trains)

→ JR Trains or Private Trains

0   2 mi

0   2 km

The gold-leaf detailing at Rinno Ji complements the gold on the three famed Buddhas in Sanbutsudoh Hall.

here to the second gate, the Niten-mon, a two-story structure protected front and back by carved and painted images of guardian gods. Beyond it, two more flights of steps lead to the middle courtyard. As you climb the last steps to Iemitsu's shrine, you'll pass a bell tower on the right and a drum tower on the left; directly ahead is the third gate, the remarkable **Yasha-mon,** so named for the figures of *yasha* (she-demons) in the four niches. This structure is also known as the Peony Gate (Botan-mon) for the carvings that decorate it.

As you exit the shrine, on the west side, you come to the fifth gate: the **Koka-mon,** built in the style of the late Ming dynasty of China. The gate is normally closed, but from here another flight of stone steps leads to the sixth and last gate—the cast copper **Inuki-mon,** inscribed with characters in Sanskrit—and Iemitsu's tomb. ⊠ *2300 Sannai* ✉ *¥1,300, includes admission to Rinno Temple and Futara-san Shrine* ⊙ *Apr.–Oct., daily 8–5; Nov.–Mar., daily 8–4.*

Fodor's Choice
★ **Tosho-gu Nikko** (東照宮). With its riot of colors and carvings, inlaid pillars, red-lacquer corridors, and extensive use of gold leaf, this 17th-century shrine to Ieyasu Tokugawa is one of the most elaborately decorated shrines in Japan.

The **Hon-den (Main Hall)** of Tosho-gu is the ultimate purpose of the shrine. You approach it from the rows of lockers at the far end of the enclosure; here you remove and store your shoes, step up into the shrine, and follow a winding corridor to the Oratory (Hai-den)—the anteroom, resplendent in its lacquered pillars, carved friezes, and coffered ceilings bedecked with dragons. Over the lintels are paintings by Tosa Mitsuoki (1617–91) of the 36 great poets of the Heian period, with their poems in the calligraphy of Emperor Go-Mizunoo. Deeper yet, at the back of the Oratory, is the Inner Chamber (Nai-jin)—repository of the Sacred Mirror that represents the spirit of the deity enshrined here. The hall is enclosed by a wall of painted and carved panel screens; opposite the right-hand corner of the wall, facing the shrine, is the **Kito-den,** a hall where annual prayers were once offered for the peace of the nation.

Behind the Inner Chamber is the Innermost Chamber (Nai-Nai-jin). No visitors come this far. Here, in the very heart of Tosho-gu, is the gold-lacquer shrine where the spirit of Ieyasu resides—along with two other deities, whom the Tokugawas later decided were fit companions. One was Toyotomi Hideyoshi, Ieyasu's mentor and liege lord in the long wars of unification at the end of the 16th century. The other was Minamoto no Yoritomo, brilliant military tactician and founder of the earlier (12th-century) Kamakura Shogunate (Ieyasu claimed Yoritomo for an ancestor).

Between the Goma-do and the Kagura-den (a hall where ceremonial dances are performed to honor the gods) is a passage to the Sakashita-mon (Gate at the Foot of the Hill). Above the gateway is another famous symbol of Tosho-gu, the Sleeping Cat—a small panel said to have been carved by Hidari Jingoro (Jingoro the Left-handed), a late-16th-century master carpenter and sculptor credited with important contributions to numerous Tokugawa-period temples, shrines, and palaces. A separate admission charge (¥520) is levied to go beyond the Sleeping Cat, up the flight of 200 stone steps through a forest of cryptomeria to **Ieyasu's tomb.** The climb is worth it for the view of the Yomei-mon and Kara-mon from above; the tomb itself is unimpressive.

The centerpiece of Tosho-gu is the **Yomei-mon** (Gate of Sunlight), at the top of the second flight of stone steps. A designated National Treasure, it's also called the **Higurashi-mon** (Twilight Gate)—implying that you could gape at its richness of detail all day, until sunset. And rich it is indeed: 36 feet high and dazzling white, the gate has 12 columns, beams, and roof brackets carved with dragons, lions, clouds, peonies, Chinese sages, and demigods, painted vivid hues of red, blue, green, and gold. On one of the central columns, there are two carved tigers; the natural grain of the wood is used to bring out the "fur." As you enter the Yomei-mon, there are galleries running east and west for some 700 feet; their paneled fences are also carved and painted with nature motifs.

The portable shrines that appear in the Tosho-gu Festival, held yearly on May 17–18, are kept in the **Shinyo-sha,** a storeroom to the left as you come through the Twilight Gate into the heart of the shrine. The paintings on the ceiling, of *tennin* (Buddhist angels) playing harps, are by Tan-yu Kano (1602–74).

Mere mortals may not pass through the Chinese Gate (Kara-mon), which is the "official" entrance to the Tosho-gu inner shrine. Like its counterpart, the Yomei-mon, on the opposite side of the courtyard, the Kara-mon is a National Treasure—and, like the Yomei-mon, is carved and painted in elaborate detail with dragons and other auspicious figures. ⊠ *2301 Sannai* ☎ *0288/54–0560* 🖱 *Free* ◷ *Apr.–Oct., daily 9–5; Nov.–Mar., daily 9–4.*

Tosho-gu honors Ieyasu Tokugawa, the first shogun and founder of Tokyo.

OFF THE
BEATEN
PATH
Located on the northern shore of peaceful Yunoko (Lake Yuno), these isolated **hot springs** were once a popular destination for 14th-century aristocrats. Today, the area is still known for its hot springs—being able to soak in an onsen (hot springs) all year long, even when temperatures drop below zero, will always be a major plus—but they are now controlled by separate resorts. Besides the healing and relaxing effects of the baths, visitors come for the hiking trails, fishing, camping, skiing, bird-watching, and mountain-climbing opportunities. ■**TIP→ Try to avoid the fall season, as it's peak visitor time and there are always delays.** You can get to the Yumoto onsen by taking the Tobu Operated Buses, which leave Tobu Nikko and JR Nikko stations. There are one or two services an hour, depending on the time of day. A one-way trip from central Nikko takes about 80 minutes and costs ¥1,700.

WORTH NOTING

FAMILY **Edo Wonderland** (日光江戸村 *Nikko Edo Mura*). Edo Wonderland, a living-history theme park a short taxi ride from downtown, re-creates an 18th-century Japanese village. The complex includes sculpted gardens with waterfalls and ponds and 22 vintage buildings, where actors in traditional dress stage martial arts exhibitions, historical theatrical performances, and comedy acts. You can even observe Japanese tea ceremony rituals in gorgeous tatami-floor houses, as well as people dressed as geisha and samurai. Strolling stuffed animal characters and acrobatic ninjas keep kids happy. Nikko Edo Mura has one large restaurant and 15 small food stalls serving period cuisine like *yakisoba* (fried soba) and *dango* (dumplings). ✉ *470–20 Karakura* ☎ *0288/77–1777* ⊕ *www.edowonderland.net* ✍ *¥4,700 unlimited day pass* *includes rides and shows ⊗ Mid-Mar.–Nov., daily 9–5; Dec.–mid-Mar., daily 9:30–4.*

Monument to Masasuna Matsudaira (松平正綱の杉並木寄進碑). Opposite the Sacred Bridge, at the east entrance to the grounds of Tosho-gu, this monument pays tribute to one of the two feudal lords charged with the construction of Tosho-gu. Matsudaira's great contribution was the planting of the wonderful cryptomeria trees (Japanese cedars) surrounding the shrine and along all the approaches to it. The project took 20 years, from 1628 to 1648, and the result was some 36 km (22 miles) of cedar-lined avenues—planted with more than 15,000

trees in all. Fire and time have taken their toll, but thousands of these trees still stand in the shrine precincts, creating a setting of solemn majesty the buildings alone could never have achieved. Thousands more line Route 119 east of Nikko on the way to Shimo-Imaichi. ✉ *Moritomo.*

Sacred Bridge (神橋 *Shinkyo*). Built in 1636 for shoguns and imperial messengers visiting the shrine, the original bridge was destroyed in a flood; the present red-lacquer wooden structure dates to 1907. Buses leaving from either railway station at Nikko go straight up the main street to the bridge, opposite the first of the main entrances to Tosho-gu. The Sacred Bridge is just to the left of a modern bridge, where the road curves and crosses the Daiya-gawa (Daiya River). ✉ *2307 Sannai* ⊗ *Apr.–Oct., daily 9–5; Nov.–Mar., daily 9–4.*

Toshogu Treasure House (宝物館 *Homotsu-kan*). An unhurried visit to the precincts of Tosho-gu should definitely include the Treasure House, as it contains a collection of antiquities from its various shrines and temples. From the west gate of Rinno Temple, turn left off Omote-sando, just below the pagoda, onto the cedar-lined avenue to Futara-san Jinja. A minute's walk brings you to the museum, on the left. ✉ *2280 Sannai* ☎ *0288/54–2558* 🖃 *¥500* ⊗ *Apr.–Oct., daily 9–5; Nov.–Mar., daily 9–4.*

CHUZENJI-KO 中禅寺湖

More than 3,900 feet above sea level, at the base of the volcano known as Nantai-san, is Chuzenji-ko (Lake Chuzenji), renowned for its clean waters and fresh air. People come to boat and fish on the lake and to enjoy the surrounding scenic woodlands, waterfalls, and hills.

TOP ATTRACTIONS

Fodor's Choice
★

Kegon Falls (華厳滝 *Kegon-no-taki*). More than anything else, the country's most famous falls are what draw the crowds of Japanese visitors to Chuzenji. Fed by the eastward flow of the lake, the falls drop 318 feet into a rugged gorge; an elevator takes you to an observation platform at the bottom. The volume of water over the falls is carefully regulated, but it's especially impressive after a summer rain or a typhoon. In winter the falls do not freeze completely but form a beautiful cascade of icicles. The elevator is just a few minutes' walk east from the bus stop at Chuzenji village, downhill and off to the right at the far end of the parking lot. ⊠ *2479–2 Chugushi* ☎ *0288/55–0030* 🛗 *Elevator* ¥*550* ⊗ *Daily 8–5.*

NEED A BREAK?   **Ryuzu-no-taki Chaya** (竜頭滝茶屋). Take a breather at this charming, but rustic, tea shop near the waterfalls. Enjoy a cup of green tea, a light meal, or Japanese sweets like rice cakes boiled with vegetables and dango (sweet dumplings) while you gaze at the falling waters. ⊠ *2485 Chugushi* ☎ *0288/55–0157.*

THREE LITTLE MONKEYS

While in the Sacred Stable, make sure to look at the second panel from the left. The three monkeys, commonly known as "Hear no evil, Speak no evil, See no evil," have become something of a Nikko trademark; the image has been reproduced on plaques, bags, and souvenirs. While the phrase's true origins are uncertain, scholars and legend suggest it originated from this shrine as a visual interpretation of the religious phrase, "If we do not hear, see, or speak evil, we ourselves shall be spared all evil." As for the monkeys, it's been said that a Chinese Buddhist monk introduced the image to Japan in the 8th century.

Lake Chuzenji Ferry (中禅寺湖機船 *Chuzenjiko Kisen*). Explore Lake Chuzenji on chartered 60-minute boat rides. ⊠ *2478–21 Chugushi* ☎ *0288/55–0360* 🛥 ¥*150–*¥*1,500 depending on route* ⊗ *Dec.–Mar., daily 9:30–3:30.*

Urami Falls (裏見滝 *Urami-no-taki*). A poetic description says it all and still holds true: "the water," wrote the great 17th-century poet Basho, "seemed to take a flying leap and drop a hundred feet from the top of a cave into a green pool surrounded by a thousand rocks. One was supposed to inch one's way into the cave and enjoy the falls from behind." The falls and the gorge are striking—but you should make the climb only if you have good hiking shoes and are willing to get wet in the process. ⊠ *The steep climb to the cave begins at the Arasawa bus stop, with a turn to the right off the Chuzenji road.*

WORTH NOTING

Chugu-shi (中宮祠). A subshrine of the Futara-san Shrine at Tosho-gu, this is the major religious center on the north side of Lake Chuzenji, about 1½ km (1 miles) west of the village. The Homotsu-den (Treasure House) contains an interesting historical collection, including swords, lacquerware, and medieval shrine palanquins. ⊠ *Nikko* 🛗 *Homotsu-Den* ¥*300; Shrine free* ⊗ *Apr.–Oct., daily 8–5; Nov.–Mar., daily 9–4.*

Chuzen-ji (中禅寺 *Chuzen Temple*). A subtemple of Rinno Temple, at Tosho-gu, the principal object of worship here is the **Tachi-ki Kannon,** a 17-foot-tall standing statue of the Buddhist goddess of mercy, said to have been carved more than 1,000 years ago by the priest Shodo from the living trunk of a single Judas tree. The bus trip from Nikko to the national park area ends at Chuzenji village, which shares its name with the temple established here in 784. ⊠ *2578*

The three monkeys, who "hear no evil, speak no evil, see no evil," perch on the paneling of Tosho-gu's Sacred Stable.

Chugushi ✛ *1½ km (1 mile) south of Chugu-shi village along the eastern shore of the lake* 🎫 *¥500* 🕐 *Apr.–Oct., daily 8–5; Mar. and Nov., daily 8–4; Dec.–Feb., daily 8–3:30.*

Dragon's Head Falls (竜頭滝 *Ryuzu-no-taki*). If you've budgeted an extra day for Nikko, you might want to consider a walk around the lake. A paved road along the north shore extends for about 8 km (5 miles), one-third of the whole distance, as far as the "beach" at Shobu-ga-hama. Here, where the road branches off to the north for Senjogahara, are the lovely cascades of Dragon's Head Falls. To the left is a steep footpath that continues around the lake to Senju-ga-hama and then to a campsite at Asegata. The path is well marked but can get rough in places. From Asegata it's less than an hour's walk back to Chuzenji village. ✉ *Nikko.*

Jakko Falls (寂光滝 *Jakko-no-taki*). Falling water is one of the special charms of the Nikko National Park area; people going by bus or car from Tosho-gu to Lake Chuzenji often stop off en route to see these falls, which descend in a series of seven terraced stages, forming a sheet of water about 100 feet high. About 1 km (½ mile) from the shrine precincts, at the Tamozawa bus stop, a narrow road to the right leads to an uphill walk of some 3 km (2 miles) to the falls. ✉ *Nikko.*

Umagaeshi (馬返し). In the old days, the road became too rough for horse riding, so riders had to alight and proceed on foot; the lake is 4,165 feet above sea level. From Umagaeshi the bus climbs a one-way toll road up the pass; the old road has been widened and is used for the traffic coming down. The two roads are full of steep hairpin turns, and on a clear day the view up and down the valley is magnificent—especially from the halfway point at **Akechi-daira** (Akechi Plain), from which you can see the summit of **Nantai-san** (Mt. Nantai), reaching 8,149 feet. Hiking season lasts from May through mid-October; if you push it, you can make the ascent in about four hours. Wild monkeys make their homes in these mountains, and they've learned the convenience of mooching from visitors along the route. Be careful—they have a way of not taking no for an answer. Do not give in to the temptation to give them food—they will never leave you alone if you do. ✉ *About 10 km (6 miles) from Tobu Station in Nikko, or 8 km (5 miles) from Tosho-gu.*

FEELING ADVENTUROUS?

Akechi-daira Ropeway (明智平ロープウェイ). If you want to avoid the hairpin turns, try the ropeway that runs from Akechi-daira Station directly to the Akechi-daira lookout. It takes three minutes and the panoramic views of Nikko and Kegon Falls are priceless. ✉ *703 Hosomachi* ☎ *0288/55–0331* 🎫 *¥400* 🕑 *Apr.–Oct., daily 8:30–4; Nov.–Mar., daily 9–3.*

WHERE TO EAT

DOWNTOWN NIKKO

$$$$ JAPANESE FUSION 🍴 **Gyoshintei** (堯心亭). This is the only restaurant in Nikko devoted to *shojin ryori,* the Buddhist-temple vegetarian fare that evolved centuries ago into haute cuisine. Gyoshintei is decorated in the style of a *ryotei* (traditional inn), with all-tatami seating. It differs from a ryotei in that it has one large, open space where many guests are served at once, rather than a number of rooms for private dining. Dinner is served until 7. [$] *Average main: ¥4000* ✉ *2339–1 Sannai* ☎ *0288/53–3751* 🕑 *Closed Thurs.*

$$$$ JAPANESE 🍴 **Masudaya** (ゆば亭ますだや). Masudaya started out as a sake maker more than a century ago, but for four generations now, it has been the town's best-known restaurant. The specialty is yuba, which the chefs transform, with the help of local vegetables and fresh fish, into sumptuous high cuisine. The building is traditional, with a lovely interior garden; but meals here are prix fixe, and the assembly-line-style service detracts from the ambience. [$] *Average main: ¥5000* ✉ *439–2 Ishiya-machi* ☎ *0288/54–2151* 🕑 *Closed Thurs. No dinner* ✍ *Reservations essential.*

$$$$ EUROPEAN 🍴 **Meiji-no-Yakata** (明治の館). Not far from the east entrance to Rinno Temple, Meiji-no-Yakata is an elegant 19th-century Western-style stone house, originally built as a summer retreat for an American diplomat. The food, too, is Western-style; specialties of the house include fresh rainbow trout from Lake Chuzenji, roast lamb with pepper sauce, and melt-in-your-mouth filet mignon made from local Tochigi beef. High ceilings, hardwood floors, and an air of informality make this a very pleasant place to dine. [$] *Average main: ¥5000* ✉ *2339–1 Sannai* ☎ *0288/53–3751* 💳 *No credit cards.*

$$$$ JAPANESE 🍴 **Sawamoto** (澤本). Charcoal-broiled *unagi* (eel) is an acquired taste, and there's no better place in Nikko to acquire it than at this small and unpretentious place with only five plain-wood tables. Service can be lukewarm, but Sawamoto is reliable for a light lunch or dinner of unagi on a bed of rice, served in an elegant lacquered box. Eel is considered

DID YOU KNOW?

The 320-foot-high Kegon Falls draws visitors from all over Japan and the world. The spectacular sight near Lake Chuzenji is also home to 12 other waterfalls. Behind and next to Kegon, these falls drip out of cracks in the volcano, Nantai-san. Try to spot a few of them once you've taken in Kegon's grandeur.

a stamina builder: just right for the weary visitor on a hot summer day. $ *Average main: ¥4000* ⊠ *1037 Kamihatsuishi-machi* ☏ *0288/54–0163* ⊗ *No dinner.*

CHUZENJI-KO

$$$ ✕ **Nantai** (なんたい). The low tables, antiques, and pillows scattered
JAPANESE on tatami flooring make visitors feel like they're dining in a traditional Japanese living room. Try the Nikko specialty, yuba (tofu skin), which comes with the *nabe* (hot pot) for dinner. It's the quintessential winter family meal. The seafood here is fresh and both the trout and salmon are recommended. Each meal comes with rice, pickles, and selected side dishes like soy-stewed vegetables, tempura, udon, and a dessert. $ *Average main: ¥3000* ⊠ *2478–4 Chugushi* ☏ *0288/55–0201.*

WHERE TO STAY

DOWNTOWN NIKKO

$$$$ ▥ **Nikko Kanaya Hotel** (日光金谷ホテル). This family-run operation is a
RESORT little worn around the edges after a century of operation, but it still has the best location in town—across the street from Tosho-gu—and the main building is a delightful, rambling Victorian structure that has hosted royalty and other important personages from around the world. **Pros:** spacious; staff is better at giving area information than the tourist office. **Cons:** rooms rather pricey; very touristy: daytime visitors browse through the old building and its gift shops. $ *Rooms from: ¥30000* ⊠ *1300 Kami Hatsuishi-machi* ☏ *0288/54–0001* ⊕ *www.kanayahotel. co.jp/english/nikko/index.html* ⟿ *70 rooms with bath* ⦿ *Breakfast.*

$$$$ ▥ **Nikko Lakeside Hotel** (日光レイクサイドホテル). In the village of
HOTEL Chuzenji at the foot of the lake, the Nikko Lakeside has no particular character, but the views are good and the transportation connections (to buses and excursion boats) are ideal. **Pros:** close to lake and hot-spring baths. **Cons:** room design a bit dated. $ *Rooms from: ¥24000* ⊠ *2482 Chugu-shi* ☏ *0288/55–0321* ⊕ *www.tobuhotel.co.jp/nikkolake/ en* ⟿ *100 rooms with bath* ⦿ *Some meals.*

$ ▥ **Turtle Inn Nikko** (タートルイン日光). Modest, cost-conscious Western-
HOTEL and Japanese-style accommodations come with or without a private bath. **Pros:** cozy atmosphere; English-speaking staff. **Cons:** rooms a bit on the small side. $ *Rooms from: ¥10000* ⊠ *2–16 Takumi-cho* ☏ *0288/53– 3168* ⊕ *www.turtle-nikko.com* ▭ *No credit cards* ⟿ *7 Western-style rooms, 3 with bath; 5 Japanese-style rooms without bath* ⦿ *No meals.*

CHUZENJI-KO

$$$$ ▥ **Chuzenji Kanaya** (中禅寺金谷ホテル). Pastel colors decorate the sim-
RESORT ple, tasteful rooms of this outpost of the Nikko Kanaya on the road from the village to Shobu-ga-hama, and floor-to-ceiling windows over-look the lake or grounds. **Pros:** relaxing resort feel; spacious rooms. **Cons:** the most expensive hotel in the area. $ *Rooms from: ¥54000* ⊠ *2482 Chugu-shi* ☏ *0288/51–0001* ⊕ *www.kanayahotel.co.jp/english/ chuzenji/index.html* ⟿ *60 rooms, 54 with bath* ⦿ *Some meals.*

KAMAKURA 鎌倉

40 km (25 miles) southwest of Tokyo

As a religious center, Kamakura presents an extraordinary legacy. Most of its temples and shrines are in settings of remarkable beauty; many are designated National Treasures. If you can afford the time for only one day trip from Tokyo, you should probably spend it here.

For the aristocrats of the Heian-era Japan (794–1185), life was defined by the Imperial Court in Kyoto. Who in their right mind would venture elsewhere? In Kyoto there was grace and beauty and poignant affairs of the heart; everything beyond was howling wilderness. By the 12th century two clans—the Taira (*ta*-ee-ra) and the Minamoto, themselves both offshoots of the imperial line—had come to dominate the affairs of the court and were at each other's throats in a struggle for supremacy. The rivalry between the two clans became an all-out war, and by 1185 the Minamoto were masters of all Japan. Yoritomo no Minamoto forced the Imperial Court to name him shogun; he was now de facto and de jure the military head of state. The emperor was left as a figurehead in Kyoto, and the little fishing village of Kamakura, a superb natural fortress surrounded on three sides by hills and guarded on the fourth by the sea, became—and for 141 years remained—the seat of Japan's first shogunal government.

After 1333, when the center of power returned to Kyoto, Kamakura reverted to being a sleepy backwater town on the edge of the sea. After World War II, it began to develop as a residential area for the well-to-do. Though the religious past is much in evidence, nothing secular survives from the shogunal days; there wasn't much there to begin with. The warriors of Kamakura had little use for courtiers, or their palaces and gardened villas; the shogunate's name for itself, in fact, was the Bakufu—literally, the "tent government."

GETTING HERE AND AROUND

A bus from Kamakura Station (Sign 5) travels to most of the temples and shrines in the downtown Kamakura area, with stops at most access roads to the temples and shrines. However, you may want to walk out as far as Hokoku-ji and take the bus back; it's easier to recognize the end of the line than any of the stops in between. You can also go by taxi to Hokoku-ji—any cabdriver knows the way—and walk the last leg in reverse.

Bus companies in Kamakura don't conduct guided English tours. However, if your time is limited or you don't want to do a lot of walking, the Japanese tours hit the major attractions. These tours depart from Kamakura Station eight times daily, starting at 9 am; the last tour leaves at 1 pm. Purchase tickets at the bus office to the right of the station.

The KSGG Club Volunteer Guides has a free guide service. Arrangements must be made in advance through the group's website.

JTB Sunrise Tours runs daily English-language trips from Tokyo to Kamakura; these tours are often combined with trips to Hakone. You can book through, and arrange to be picked up at, any of the major hotels. Check to make sure that the tour covers everything you want to see, as many include little more than a passing view of the Great Buddha in Hase. Given how easy it is to get around—most sights are within walking distance of each other, and others are short bus or train rides apart—you're better off seeing Kamakura on your own.

TIMING TIP

If your time is limited, you may want to visit only Engaku Temple and Tokei Temple in Kita-Kamakura before riding the train one stop to Kamakura. If not, follow the main road all the way to Tsuru-ga-oka Hachiman-gu and visit four additional temples en route.

Traveling by train is by far the best way to get to Kamakura. Trains run from Tokyo Station (and Shimbashi Station) every 10 to 15 minutes during the day. The trip takes 56 minutes to Kita-Kamakura and one hour to Kamakura. Take the JR Yokosuka Line from Track 1 downstairs in Tokyo Station (Track 1 upstairs is on a different line and does not go to Kamakura). The cost is ¥800 to Kita-Kamakura, ¥920 to Kamakura (or use your JR Pass). It's now also possible to take a train from Shinjuku, Shibuya, or Ebisu to Kamakura on the Shonan-Shinjuku Line, but these trains depart less frequently than those departing from Tokyo Station. Local train service connects Kita-Kamakura, Kamakura, Hase, and Enoshima.

To return to Tokyo from Enoshima, take a train to Shinjuku on the Odakyu Line. There are 11 express trains daily from here on weekdays, between 8:38 am and 8:45 pm; 9 trains daily on weekends and national holidays, between 8:39 am and 8:46 pm; and even more in summer. The express takes about 70 minutes and costs ¥1,250. Or you can retrace your steps to Kamakura and take the JR Yokosuka Line to Tokyo Station.

VISITOR INFORMATION
Both Kamakura and Enoshima have their own tourist associations, although it can be problematic getting help in English over the phone. Your best bet is the Kamakura Station Tourist Information Center, which has a useful collection of brochures and maps. And since Kamakura is in Kanagawa Prefecture, visitors heading here from Yokohama can preplan their excursion at the Kanagawa Prefectural Tourist Association office in the Silk Center, on the Yamashita Park promenade.

ESSENTIALS
Tour Contacts KSGG Club Volunteer Guides. ⊕ *www.ksgg.org.*

Tourist Information **Fujisawa City Tourist Association.** ☎ *0466/22–4141* ⊕ *www.fujisawa-kanko.jp.* **Kamakura Station Tourist Information Center.** ⊠ *1-1-1 Komachi* ☎ *0467/22-3350.* **Kamakura Tourist Association** (鎌倉観光協会 *Kamakura Kanko Kyoukai*). ⊠ *1-12 Onarimachi* ☎ *0467/23-3050* ⊕ *kamakura-info.jp.* **Kanagawa Prefectural Tourist Association.** ☎ *045/681-0007* ⊕ *www.kanagawa-kankou.or.jp.*

EXPLORING

There are three principal areas in Kamakura, and you can easily get from one to another by train. From Tokyo head first to Kita-Kamakura for most of the important Zen temples, including Engaku-ji (Engaku Temple) and Kencho-ji (Kencho Temple). The second area is downtown Kamakura, with its shops and museums and the venerated shrine Tsuru-ga-oka Hachiman-gu. The third is Hase, a 10-minute train ride southwest from Kamakura on the Enoden Line. Hase's main attractions are the great bronze figure of the Amida Buddha, at Kotoku-in, and the Kannon Hall of Hase-dera. There's a lot to see in Kamakura, and even to hit just the highlights takes you most of a busy day.

KITA-KAMAKURA 北鎌倉

Hierarchies were important to the Kamakura Shogunate. In the 14th century it established a ranking system called Go-zan (literally, "Five Mountains") for the Zen Buddhist monasteries under its official sponsorship. These are clustered in the Kita-Kamakura district.

TOP ATTRACTIONS

Engaku-ji (円覚寺 *Engaku Temple*). The largest of the Zen monasteries in Kamakura, Engaku-ji (Engaku Temple) was founded in 1282 and ranks second in the Five Mountains hierarchy. Here, prayers were to be offered regularly for the prosperity and well-being of the government; Engaku Temple's special role was to pray for the souls of those who died resisting the Mongol invasions in 1274 and 1281. The temple complex currently holds 18 buildings, but once contained as many as 50. Often damaged in fires and earthquakes, it has been completely restored.

Engaku Temple belongs to the Rinzai sect of Zen Buddhism. Introduced into Japan from China at the beginning of the Kamakura period (1192–1333), the ideas of Zen were quickly embraced by the emerging warrior class. The samurai especially admired the Rinzai sect, with its emphasis on the ascetic life as a path to self-transcendence. The monks of Engaku Temple played an important role as advisers to the shogunate in matters spiritual, artistic, and political.

Among the National Treasures at Engaku Temple is the **Hall of the Holy Relic of Buddha** (Shari-den), with its remarkable Chinese-inspired thatched roof. Built in 1282, it was destroyed by fire in 1558 but rebuilt in its original form soon after, in 1563. The hall is said to enshrine a tooth of the Gautama Buddha himself, but it's not on display. In fact, except for the first three days of the New Year, you won't be able to go any farther into the hall than the main gate. Such is the case, alas, with much of the Engaku Temple complex: this is still a functioning monastic center, and many of its most impressive buildings are not open to the public. The accessible National Treasure at Engaku Temple is the **Great Bell** (Kosho), on the hilltop on the southeast side of the complex. The bell—Kamakura's most famous—was cast in 1301 and stands 8 feet tall. It's rung only on special occasions, such as New Year's Eve. Reaching the bell requires a trek up a long staircase, but once you've made it to the top you can enjoy tea and traditional Japanese sweets at a small outdoor café. The views of the entire temple grounds and surrounding cedar forest from here are tremendous.

The two buildings open to the public at Engaku Temple are the **Butsu-nichi-an,** which has a long ceremonial hall where you can enjoy *sado* (Japanese tea ceremony), and the **Obai-in.** The latter is the mausoleum of the last three regents of the Kamakura Shogunate: Tokimune Hojo, who led the defense of Japan against the Mongol invasions; his son Sadatoki; and his grandson Takatoki. Off to the side of the mausoleum is a quiet garden with apricot trees, which bloom in February. As you exit Kita-Kamakura Station, you'll see the stairway to Engaku Temple just in front of you. ⊠ *409 Yama-no-uchi, Kita-Kamakura* ☎ *0467/22–0478* 🎫 *¥300* 🕙 *Nov.–Mar., daily 8–4; Apr.–Oct., daily 8–5.*

Enno-ji (円応寺 *Enno Temple*). In the feudal period, Japan acquired from China a belief in Enma, the lord of hell, who, with his court attendants, judged the souls of the departed and determined their destination in the afterlife. Kamakura's otherwise undistinguished Enno-ji (Enno Temple) houses some remarkable statues of these judges—as grim and merciless a court as you're ever likely to confront. To see them is enough to put you on your best behavior, at least for the rest of your excursion. Enno Temple is a minute's walk or so from Kencho Temple, on the opposite (south) side of the main road to Kamakura. ⊠ *1543 Yama-no-uchi, Kita-Kamakura* ☎ *0467/25–1095* 🎫 *¥200* 🕙 *Mar.–Nov., daily 9–4; Dec.–Feb., daily 9–3.*

Kencho-ji (建長寺 *Kencho Temple*). Founded in 1250, Kencho-ji (Kencho Temple) was the foremost of Kamakura's five great Zen temples, and it lays claim to being the oldest Zen temple in all of Japan. It was modeled on one of the great Chinese monasteries of the time and built for a distinguished Zen master who had just arrived from China. Over the centuries, fires and other disasters have taken their toll on Kencho-ji, and although many buildings have been authentically reconstructed, the temple complex today is half its original size. Near the Main Gate (San-mon) is a bronze bell cast in 1255; it's the temple's most important treasure. The Main Gate and the Lecture Hall (Hatto) are the only two structures to have survived the devastating Great Kanto Earthquake of 1923. Like Engaku-ji, Kencho-ji is a functioning temple of the Rinzai sect, where novices train and laypeople can come to take part in Zen meditation. Nearly hidden at the back of the temple is a long stairway and hiking trail that leads to Zuisen-ji, another of Kamakura's major temples. The hike takes about 90 minutes. ⊠ *8 Yama-no-uchi* ✚ *The entrance to Kencho Temple is about halfway along the main road from Kita-Kamakura Station to Tsuru-ga-oka Hachiman-gu, on the left* ☎ *0467/22–0981* ⊕ *www.kenchoji.com* 🎫 *¥300* 🕙 *Daily 8:30–4:30.*

Tokei-ji (東慶寺 *Tokei Temple*). A Zen temple of the Rinzai sect, Tokei-ji holds special significance for the study of feminism in medieval Japan. More popularly known as the Enkiri-dera, or Divorce Temple, it was founded in 1285 by the widow of the Hojo regent Tokimune as a refuge for the victims of unhappy marriages. Under the shogunate, a husband of the warrior class could obtain a divorce simply by sending his wife back to her family. Not so for the wife: no matter what cruel and unusual treatment her husband meted out, she was stuck with him. If she ran away, however, and managed to reach Tokei Temple without being caught, she could receive sanctuary at the temple and remain there

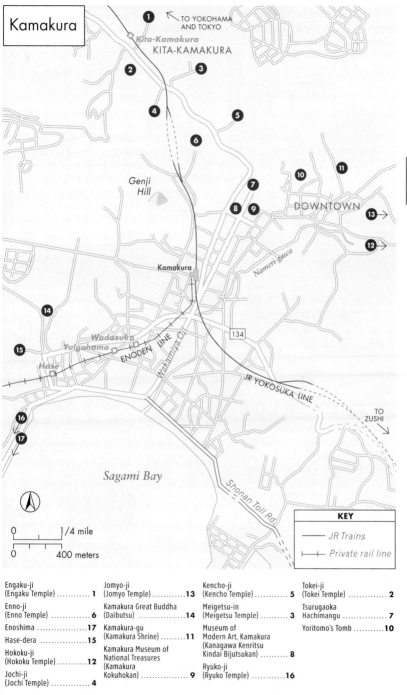

Kamakura

TO YOKOHAMA
AND TOKYO

Kita-Kamakura
KITA-KAMAKURA

Genji
Hill

DOWNTOWN

Kamakura

Nameri-gawa

134

Wadazuka

Yuigahama

ENODEN LINE

Wakamiya Oji

Hase

JR YOKOSUKA LINE

TO
ZUSHI

Sagami Bay

Shonan Toll Rd.

0 ___ 1/4 mile
0 ___ 400 meters

KEY

—— *JR Trains*

+—+ *Private rail line*

4

Engaku-ji
(Engaku Temple) **1**

Enno-ji
(Enno Temple) **6**

Enoshima **17**

Hase-dera **15**

Hokoku-ji
(Hokoku Temple) **12**

Jochi-ji
(Jochi Temple) **4**

Jomyo-ji
(Jomyo Temple) **13**

Kamakura Great Buddha
(Daibutsu) **14**

Kamakura-gu
(Kamakura Shrine) **11**

Kamakura Museum of
National Treasures
(Kamakura
Kokuhokan) **9**

Kencho-ji
(Kencho Temple) **5**

Meigetsu-in
(Meigetsu Temple) **3**

Museum of
Modern Art, Kamakura
(Kanagawa Kenritsu
Kindai Bijutsukan) **8**

Ryuko-ji
(Ryuko Temple) **16**

Tokei-ji
(Tokei Temple) **2**

Tsurugaoka
Hachimangu **7**

Yoritomo's Tomb **10**

as a nun. After three years (later reduced to two), she was officially declared divorced. The temple survived as a convent through the Meiji Restoration of 1868. The last abbess died in 1902; her headstone is in the cemetery behind the temple, beneath the plum trees that blossom in February. Tokei Temple was later reestablished as a monastery.

The **Matsugaoka Hozo** (Treasure House) of Tokei Temple displays several Kamakura-period wooden Buddhas, ink paintings, scrolls, and works of calligraphy, some of which have been designated by the government as Important Cultural Objects. The library, called the Matsugaoka Bunko, was established in memory of the great Zen scholar D. T. Suzuki (1870–1966).

Tokei Temple is on the southwest side of the JR tracks (the side opposite Engaku Temple), less than a five-minute walk south from the station on the main road to Kamakura (Route 21—the Kamakura Kaido), on the right. ⊠ *1367 Yama-no-uchi, Kita-Kamakura* ☎ *0467/22–1663* ⊕ *www. tokeiji.com* ☑ *Tokei Temple ¥200, Matsugaoka Hozo additional ¥400* ⊙ *Tokei Temple: Apr.–Oct., daily 8:30–5; Nov.–Mar., daily 8:30–4. Matsugaoka Treasure House: Mon.–Thurs. 9:30–3:30.*

WORTH NOTING

Jochi-ji (浄智寺 *Jochi Temple*). In the Five Mountains hierarchy, Jochi-ji (Jochi Temple) was ranked fourth. The buildings now in the complex are reconstructions; the Great Kanto Earthquake of 1923 destroyed the originals. The garden here is exquisite. Jochi-ji is on the south side of the railway tracks, a few minutes' walk farther southwest of Tokei-ji in the direction of Kamakura. ⊠ *1402 Yama-no-uchi, Kita-Kamakura* ⊹ *Turn right off the main road (Rte. 21) and cross over a small bridge; a flight of moss-covered steps leads up to the temple* ☎ *0467/22–3943* ☑ *¥200* ⊙ *Daily 9–4:30.*

Meigetsu-in (明月院 *Meigetsu Temple*). This temple is also known as Aji-sai-dera (the hydrangeas temple), and when the flowers bloom in June, it becomes one of the most popular places in Kamakura. The gardens transform into a sea of color—pink, white, and blue—and visitors can number in the thousands. A typical Kamakura light rain shouldn't deter you; it only showcases this incredible floral display to its best advantage. Meigetsu-in features Kamakura's largest *yagura* (a tomb cavity enclosing a mural) on which 16 images of Buddha are carved. ⊠ *189 Yama-no-uchi, Kita-Kamakura* ⊹ *To reach Meigetsu-in from Tokei-ji, walk along Route 21 toward Kamakura for about 20 minutes until you cross the railway tracks; take the immediate left turn onto the narrow side street that doubles back along the tracks. This street bends to the right and follows the course of a little stream called the Meigetsu-gawa to the temple gate* ☎ *0467/24–3437* ☑ *¥300* ⊙ *Nov.–May and July–Oct., daily 9–4; June, daily 8:30–5.*

DOWNTOWN KAMAKURA 鎌倉市

Downtown Kamakura is a good place to stop for lunch and shopping. Restaurants and shops selling local crafts, especially the carved and lacquered woodwork called Kamakura-bori, abound on Wakamiya Oji and the street parallel to it, Komachi-dori.

When the first Kamakura shogun, Minamoto no Yoritomo, learned he was about to have an heir, he had the tutelary shrine of his family moved to Kamakura from nearby Yui-ga-hama and ordered a stately avenue to be built through the center of his capital from the shrine to the sea. Along this avenue would travel the procession that brought his son—if there were a son—to be presented to the gods. Yoritomo's consort did indeed bear him a son, Yoriie (yo- *ree*-ee-eh), in 1182; Yoriie was brought in great pomp to the shrine and then consecrated to his place in the shogunal succession. Alas, the blessing of the gods did Yoriie little good. He was barely 18 when Yoritomo died, and the regency established by his mother's family, the Hojo, kept him virtually powerless until 1203, when he was banished and eventually assassinated. The Minamoto were never to hold power again, but Yoriie's memory lives on in the street that his father built for him: Wakamiya Oji, "the Avenue of the Young Prince."

TOP ATTRACTIONS

Hokoku-ji (報国寺 *Hokoku Temple*). Visitors to Kamakura tend to overlook this lovely little Zen temple of the Rinzai sect that was built in 1334, but it's worth a look. Over the years it had fallen into disrepair and neglect, until an enterprising priest took over, cleaned up the gardens, and began promoting the temple for meditation sessions, calligraphy exhibitions, and tea ceremony. Behind the main hall are a thick grove of bamboo and a small tea pavilion—a restful oasis and a fine place to go for *matcha* (green tea). The temple is about 2 km (1 mile) east on Route 204 from the main entrance to Tsuru-ga-oka Hachiman-gu; turn right at the traffic light by the Hokoku Temple Iriguchi bus stop and walk about three minutes south to the gate. ✉ *2–7–4 Jomyo-ji* ☎ *0467/22–0762* ⊕ *www.hokokuji.or.jp* 🎫 *¥200, tea ceremony ¥500* ⊘ *Daily 9–4.*

Tsurugaoka Hachimangu (鶴岡八幡宮 *Minamoto Shrine*). This shrine is dedicated to the legendary emperor Ojin, his wife, and his mother, from whom Minamoto no Yoritomo claimed descent. At the entrance, the small, steeply arched, vermilion **Taiko-bashi** (Drum Bridge) crosses a stream between two lotus ponds. The ponds were made to Yoritomo's specifications. His wife, Masako, suggested placing islands in each. In the larger **Genji Pond,** to the right, filled with white lotus flowers, she placed three islands. Genji was another name for clan, and three is an auspicious number. In the smaller **Heike Pond,** to the left, she put four islands. Heike (*heh*-ee-keh) was another name for the rival Taira clan, which the Minamoto had destroyed, and four—homophonous in Japanese with the word for "death"—is very unlucky indeed.

On the far side of the Drum Bridge is the **Mai-den.** This hall is the setting for a story of the Minamoto celebrated in Noh and Kabuki theater. Beyond the Mai-den, a flight of steps leads to the shrine's Hon-do (Main Hall). To the left of these steps is a ginkgo tree that—according to legend—was witness to a murder that ended the Minamoto line in 1219. From behind this tree, a priest named Kugyo leapt out and beheaded his uncle, the 26-year-old Sanetomo, Yoritomo's second son and the last Minamoto shogun. The priest was quickly apprehended, but Sanetomo's head was never found. As at all other Shinto shrines,

An Ancient Soap Opera

Once a year, during the Spring Festival (early or mid-April, when the cherry trees are in bloom), the Mai-den hall at Tsuru-ga-oka Hachiman-gu is used to stage a heartrending drama about Minamoto no Yoritomo's brother, Yoshitsune. Although Yoritomo was the tactical genius behind the downfall of the Taira clan and the establishment of the Kamakura Shogunate in the late 12th century, it was his dashing half brother who actually defeated the Taira in battle. In so doing, Yoshitsune won the admiration of many, and Yoritomo came to believe that his sibling had ambitions of his own. Despite Yoshitsune's declaration of allegiance, Yoritomo had him exiled and sent assassins to have him killed. Yoshitsune spent his life fleeing from one place to another until, at the age of 30, he was betrayed in his last refuge and took his own life.

Earlier in his exile, Yoshitsune's lover, the dancer Shizuka Gozen, had been captured and brought to Yoritomo and his wife, Masako. They commanded her to dance for them as a kind of penance. Instead she danced for Yoshitsune. Yoritomo was furious, and only Masako's influence kept him from ordering her death. When he discovered, however, that Shizuka was carrying Yoshitsune's child, he ordered that if the child were a boy, he was to be killed. A boy was born. Some versions of the legend have it that the child was slain; others say he was placed in a cradle, like Moses, and cast adrift in the reeds.

the Hon-do is unadorned; the building itself, an 1828 reconstruction, is not particularly noteworthy. ✉ *2–1–31 Yuki-no-shita* ✛ *To reach Tsuru-ga-oka Hachiman-gu from the east side of Kamakura Station, cross the plaza, turn left, and walk north along Wakamiya Oji. Straight ahead is the first of three arches leading to the shrine, and the shrine itself is at the far end of the street* ☎ *0467/22–0315* 💲 *Free* ⊙ *Daily 9–4.*

Yoritomo's tomb (頼朝の墓). The man who put Kamakura on the map, so to speak, chose not to leave it when he died: it's only a short walk from Tsuru-ga-oka Hachiman-gu to the tomb of the man responsible for its construction, Minamoto no Yoritomo. If you've already been to Nikko and have seen how a later dynasty of shoguns sought to glorify its own memories, you may be surprised at the simplicity of Yoritomo's tomb. ✉ *2–5–2 Nishimi-kaido* ✛ *Exit Tsuru-ga-oka Hachiman-gu, turn left and then left again, and follow the small road up to Yoritomo's tomb* 💲 *Free* ⊙ *Daily 9–4.*

WORTH NOTING

Jomyo-ji (浄明寺 *Jomyo Temple*). Founded in 1188, this is one of the Five Mountains Zen monasteries. Though this modest single-story monastery belonging to the Rinzai sect lacks the grandeur and scale of the Engaku and Kencho, it still merits the status of an Important Cultural Property. It is nestled inside an immaculate garden that is particularly beautiful in spring, when the cherry trees bloom. A tea ceremony with Japanese green tea takes place in this lovely setting. The monastery's only distinctive features are its green roof and the statues of Shaka Nyorai and Amida Nyorai, who represent truth and enlightenment, in the main hall. ⊠ *3–8–31 Jomyo-ji* ✛ *From Hokoku-ji, cross the main street (Route 204) that brought you the mile or so from Tsuru-ga-oka Hachiman-gu, and take the first narrow street north. The monastery is about 100 yards from the corner* ☏ *0467/22–2818* ✉ *Jomyo Temple* ¥100, tea ceremony ¥500 ⊘ Daily 9–4.

Kamakura-gu (鎌倉宮 *Kamakura Shrine*). This Shinto shrine was built after the Meiji Restoration of 1868 and was dedicated to Prince Morinaga (1308–36), the first son of Emperor Go-Daigo. When Go-Daigo overthrew the Kamakura Shogunate and restored Japan to direct imperial rule, Morinaga—who had been in the priesthood—was appointed supreme commander of his father's forces. The prince lived in turbulent times and died young: when the Ashikaga clan in turn overthrew Go-Daigo's government, Morinaga was taken into exile, held prisoner in a cave behind the present site of Kamakura Shrine, and eventually beheaded. The **Homotsu-den** (Treasure House), on the northwest corner of the grounds, next to the shrine's administrative office, is of interest mainly for its collection of paintings depicting the life of Prince Morinaga. ⊠ *154 Nikaido* ✛ *From Yoritomo's tomb walk to Route 204 and turn left; at the next traffic light, a narrow street on the left leads off at an angle to the shrine, about 5 minutes' walk west* ☏ *0467/22–0318* ✉ *Kamakura Shrine free, Treasure House ¥300* ⊘ *Daily 9–4.*

Kamakura Museum of National Treasures (鎌倉国宝館 *Kamakura Kokuhokan*). This museum was built in 1928 as a repository for many of the most important objects belonging to the shrines and temples in the area; many of these are designated Important Cultural Properties. Located along the east side of the Tsuru-ga-oka Hachiman-gu shrine precincts, the museum has an especially fine collection of devotional and portrait sculpture in wood from the Kamakura and Muromachi periods; the portrait pieces may be among the most expressive and interesting in all of classical Japanese art. ⊠ *2–1–1 Yuki-no-shita* ☏ *0467/22–0753* ✉ ¥400 ⊘ Tues.–Sun. 9–4.

The Museum of Modern Art, Kamakura (神奈川県立美術館 *Kanagawa Kenritsu Kindai Bijutsukan*). On the north side of the Heike Pond at Tsuru-ga-oka Hachiman-gu, this museum houses a collection of Japanese oil paintings and watercolors, wood-block prints, and sculpture. ⊠ *2–1–53 Yuki-no-shita* ☏ *0467/22–5000* ⊕ *www.moma.pref. kanagawa.jp* ✉ ¥900–¥1,200, depending on exhibition ⊘ Tues.–Sun. 9:30–4:30.

HASE 長谷

On hydrangea-clad hillsides just outside downtown Kamakura are two of the town's main attractions, the Great Buddha and Hase-dera Temple.

TOP ATTRACTIONS

Fodor'sChoice
★

Hase-dera (長谷寺). The only temple in Kamakura facing the sea, this is one of the most beautiful, and saddest, places of pilgrimage in the city. On a landing partway up the stone steps that lead to the temple grounds are hundreds of small stone images of Jizo, one of the bodhisattvas in the Buddhist pantheon. Jizo is the savior of children, particularly the souls of the stillborn, aborted, and miscarried; the mothers of these children dress the statues of Jizo in bright red bibs and leave them small offerings of food, heartbreakingly touching acts of prayer.

The **Kannon Hall** (Kannon-do) at Hase-dera enshrines the largest carved-wood statue in Japan: the votive figure of Juichimen Kannon, the 11-headed goddess of mercy. Standing 30 feet tall, the goddess bears a crown of 10 smaller heads, symbolizing her ability to search out in all directions for those in need of her compassion. No one knows for certain when the figure was carved. According to the temple records, a monk named Tokudo Shonin carved two images of the Juichimen Kannon from a huge laurel tree in 721. One was consecrated to the Hase-dera in present-day Nara Prefecture; the other was thrown into the sea in order to go wherever the sea decided that there were souls in need, and that image washed up on shore near Kamakura. Much later, in 1342, Takauji Ashikaga—the first of the 15 Ashikaga shoguns who followed the Kamakura era—had the statue covered with gold leaf.

The **Amida Hall** of Hase-dera enshrines the image of a seated Amida Buddha, who presides over the Western Paradise of the Pure Land. Minamoto no Yoritomo ordered the creation of this statue when he reached the age of 42; popular Japanese belief, adopted from China, holds that your 42nd year is particularly unlucky. Yoritomo's act of piety earned him another 11 years—he was 53 when he was thrown by a horse and died of his injuries. The Buddha is popularly known as the *yakuyoke* (good-luck) Amida, and many visitors—especially students facing entrance exams—make a point of coming here to pray. To the left of the main halls is a small restaurant where you can buy good-luck candy and admire the view of Kamakura Beach and Sagami Bay. ✉ *3–11–2 Hase ✢ From Hase Station, walk north about 5 minutes on the main street (Rte. 32) toward Kotoku-in and the Great Buddha, and look for a signpost to the temple on a side street to the left* ☎ *0467/22–6300* ⊕ *www.hasedera.jp* ✉ *¥300* ⊙ *Mar.–Sept., daily 8–5:30; Oct.–Feb., daily 8–4:30.*

NEED A BREAK? **Kaiko-an** (海光庵). A spacious tearoom inside the temple grounds offers dango (sweet rice dumplings on a stick), green tea, and sweets. Rest your feet, grab a table by the windows, and take in the breathtaking views of the ocean. ✉ *3–11–2 Hase, Hase* ☎ *0467/22–6300.*

Fodor's Choice **Kamakura Great Buddha** (鎌倉大仏 *Kamakura Daibutsu*). The single biggest attraction in Hase is the Great Buddha—sharing the honors with Mt. Fuji, perhaps, as the quintessential picture-postcard image of Japan. The statue of the compassionate Amida Buddha sits cross-legged in the temple courtyard, the drapery of his robes flowing in lines reminiscent of the sculpture of ancient Greece, his expression profoundly serene. The 37-foot bronze figure was cast in 1292, three centuries before Europeans reached Japan; the concept of the classical Greek lines in the Buddha's robe must have come over the Silk Route through China during the time of Alexander the Great. The casting was probably first conceived in 1180, by Minamoto no Yoritomo, who wanted a statue to rival the enormous Daibutsu in Nara. Until 1495 the Amida Buddha was housed in a wooden temple, which washed away in a great tidal

wave. Since then the loving Buddha has stood exposed, facing the cold winters and hot summers, for more than five centuries.

It may seem sacrilegious to walk inside the Great Buddha, but for ¥20 you can enter the figure from a doorway in the right side and explore his stomach, with a stairway that leads up to two windows in his back, offering a stunning view of the temple grounds (open until 4:15 pm). To reach Kotoku-in and the Great Buddha, take the Enoden Line from the west side of JR Kamakura Station three stops to Hase. From the East Exit, turn right and walk north about 10 minutes on the main street (Route 32). ⊠ *4–2–28 Hase* ☎ *0467/22–0703* ⊕ *www.kotoku-in. jp* ☑ *¥200* ⊙ *Apr.–Sept., daily 7–6; Oct.–Mar., daily 7–5:30.*

Ryuko-ji (龍口寺 *Ryuko Temple*). The Kamakura story would not be complete without the tale of Nichiren (1222–82), the monk who founded the only native Japanese sect of Buddhism and is honored here. Nichiren's rejection of both Zen and Jodo (Pure Land) teachings brought him into conflict with the Kamakura Shogunate, and the Hojo regents sent him into exile on the Izu Peninsula in 1261. Later allowed to return, he continued to preach his own interpretation of the Lotus Sutra—and to assert the "blasphemy" of other Buddhist sects, a stance that finally persuaded the Hojo regency, in 1271, to condemn him to death. The execution was to take place on a hill to the south of Hase. As the executioner swung his sword, legend has it that a lightning bolt struck the blade and snapped it in two. Taken aback, the executioner sat down to collect his wits, and a messenger was sent back to Kamakura to report the event. On his way he met another messenger, who was carrying a writ from the Hojo regents commuting Nichiren's sentence to exile on the island of Sado-ga-shima.

Followers of Nichiren built Ryuko Temple in 1337, on the hill where he was to be executed, marking his miraculous deliverance from the headsman. There are other Nichiren temples closer to Kamakura—Myohon-ji and Ankokuron-ji, for example. But Ryuko has not only the typical Nichiren-style main hall, with gold tassels hanging from its roof, but also a beautiful pagoda, built in 1904. ⊠ *3–13–37 Katase, Fujisawa* ✛ *Take the Enoden train line west from Hase to Enoshima—a short, scenic ride that cuts through the hills surrounding Kamakura to the shore. From Enoshima Station walk about 100 yards east, keeping the train tracks on your right* ☎ *0466/25–7357* ☑ *Free* ⊙ *Daily 6–4.*

OFF THE BEATEN PATH

Enoshima (江ノ島). The Sagami Bay shore in this area has some of the closest beaches to Tokyo, and in the hot, humid summer months it seems as though all of the city's teeming millions pour onto these beaches in search of a vacant patch of rather dirty gray sand. Pass up this mob scene and press on instead to Enoshima. The island is only 4 km (2½ miles) around, with a hill in the middle. Partway up the hill is a shrine where the local fisherfolk used to pray for a bountiful catch—before it became a tourist attraction. Once upon a time it was quite a hike up to the shrine; now there's a series of escalators, flanked by the inevitable stalls selling souvenirs and snacks. The island has several cafés and restaurants, and on clear days some of them have spectacular views of Mt. Fuji and the Izu Peninsula. To reach the causeway from Enoshima

Hase-dera, in Kamakura, is dedicated to unborn children. The beautiful temple faces the sea.

Station to the island, walk south from the station for about 3 km (2 miles), keeping the Katase-gawa (Katase River) on your right. To return to Tokyo from Enoshima, take a train to Shinjuku on the Odakyu line. From the island walk back across the causeway and take the second bridge over the Katase-gawa. Within five minutes you'll come to Katase-Enoshima Station. Or you can retrace your steps to Kamakura and take the JR Yokosuka Line to Tokyo Station. ✉ *Kamakura.*

WHERE TO EAT

KITA-KAMAKURA

$$$$ JAPANESE

🍴 **Hachinoki Kita-Kamakura-ten** (鉢の木北鎌倉店). Traditional shojin ryori (the vegetarian cuisine of Zen monasteries) is served in this old Japanese house on the Kamakura Kaido (Route 21) near the entrance to Jochi Temple. The seating is mainly in tatami rooms with beautiful antique wood furnishings. If you prefer table seating, visit the annex building. Allow plenty of time; this is not a meal to be hurried through. [$] *Average main: ¥3500* ✉ *350 Yama-no-uchi, Kita-Kamakura* ☎ *0467/23–3723* ⏲ *Closed Wed.*

$$$ JAPANESE FUSION

🍴 **Kyorai-an** (去来庵). A traditional Japanese structure houses this restaurant known for its excellent Western-style beef stew. Also on the menu are pasta dishes, rice bouillon, homemade cheesecake, and wine produced in the Kita-Kamakura wine region. Half the seats are on tatami mats and half are at tables, but all look out on a peaceful patch of greenery. Kyorai-an is on the main road from Kita-Kamakura to Kamakura on the left side; it's about halfway between Meigetsu Temple and Kencho Temple, up a winding flight of stone steps. [$] *Average* main: ¥2500 ⌧157 *Yamanou-chi* ☏0467/24–9835 ⊟ *No credit cards* ⊘ *Closed Fri. No dinner Mon.–Thurs.*

DOWNTOWN KAMAKURA

$ ✕ **Bergfeld** (ベルグフェルド). If you
CAFÉ need to take a break during your walking tour of Kamakura, you may want to stop by this quaint café and bakery. It serves German cakes and cookies that are surprisingly authentic—the baker trained in Germany. There are a few small tables outside, and cozy tables inside where you can enjoy coffee and cakes before resuming your tour. Many Japanese who visit from other parts of the country bring back the bakery's butter cookies as souvenirs. Ⓢ *Average main: ¥700* ⌧3–9–24 *Yukinoshita* ☏0467/24–2706 ⊟ *No credit cards* ⊘ *Closed Tues. and 3rd Thurs. of the month.*

$$ ✕ **Kaisen Misaki-ko** (海鮮三崎港). This *kaiten-zushi* (sushi served on a
SUSHI conveyor belt that lets you pick the dishes you want) restaurant serves eye-poppingly large fish portions that hang over the edge of their plates. All the standard sushi creations, including tuna, shrimp, and egg, are prepared here. As in any kaiten-zushi joint, simply stack up your empty dishes to the side. When you are ready to leave, the dishes will be counted and you will be charged accordingly. The restaurant is on the right side of the road just as you enter Komachi-dori from the East Exit of Kamakura Station. Ⓢ *Average main: ¥1500* ⌧1–7–1 *Komachi* ☏0467/22–6228 ⊟ *No credit cards.*

HASE

$$$$ ✕ **Kaiserro** (華正樓). This establishment, in an old Japanese house, serves
CHINESE the best Chinese food in the city. The dining-room windows look out on a small, restful garden. Make sure you plan for a stop here on your way to or from the Great Buddha at Kotoku-in. Ⓢ *Average main: ¥8000* ⌧3–1–14 *Hase* ☏0467/22–0280 ⌂ *Reservations essential.*

THE POWER OF THE JAPANESE BLADE

In the corner of the enclosure where the Chinese Gate and Sanctum are found, an antique bronze lantern stands some 7 feet high. Legend has it that the lantern would assume the shape of a goblin at night; the deep nicks in the bronze were inflicted by swordsmen of the Edo period—on guard duty, perhaps, startled into action by a flickering shape in the dark. This proves, if not the existence of goblins, the incredible cutting power of the Japanese blade, a peerlessly forged weapon.

YOKOHAMA 横浜

20 km (12½ miles) southwest of Tokyo

In 1853, a fleet of four American warships under Commodore Matthew Perry sailed into the bay of Tokyo (then Edo) and presented the reluctant Japanese with the demands of the U.S. government for the opening of diplomatic and commercial relations. The following year Perry returned and first set foot on Japanese soil at Yokohama—then a small fishing village on the mudflats of Tokyo bay.

Two years later New York businessman Townsend Harris became America's first diplomatic representative to Japan. In 1858 he was finally able to negotiate a commercial treaty between the two countries; part of the deal designated four locations—one of them Yokohama—as treaty ports. In 1859 the shogunate created a special settlement in Yokohama for the growing community of merchants, traders, missionaries, and other assorted adventurers drawn to this exotic new land of opportunity.

The foreigners (predominantly Chinese and British, plus a few French, Americans, and Dutch) were confined here to a guarded compound about 5 square km (2 square miles)—placed, in effect, in isolation—but not for long. Within a few short years the shogunal government collapsed, and Japan began to modernize. Western ideas were welcomed, as were Western goods, and the little treaty port became Japan's principal gateway to the outside world. In 1872 Japan's first railway was built, linking Yokohama and Tokyo. In 1889 Yokohama became a city; by then the population had grown to some 120,000. As the city prospered, so did the international community and by the early 1900s Yokohama was the busiest and most modern center of international trade in all of East Asia.

Then Yokohama came tumbling down. On September 1, 1923, the Great Kanto Earthquake devastated the city. The ensuing fires destroyed some 60,000 homes and took more than 40,000 lives. During the six years it took to rebuild the city, many foreign businesses took up quarters elsewhere, primarily in Kobe and Osaka, and did not return.

Over the next 20 years Yokohama continued to grow as an industrial center—until May 29, 1945, when in a span of four hours, some 500 American B-29 bombers leveled nearly half the city and left more than half a million people homeless. When the war ended, what remained became—in effect—the center of the Allied occupation. General Douglas MacArthur set up headquarters here, briefly, before moving to Tokyo; the entire port facility and about a quarter of the city remained in the hands of the U.S. military throughout the 1950s.

By the 1970s Yokohama was once more rising from the debris; in 1978 it surpassed Osaka as the nation's second-largest city, and the population is now inching up to the 3.5-million mark. Boosted by Japan's postwar economic miracle, Yokohama has extended its urban sprawl north to Tokyo and south to Kamakura—in the process creating a whole new subcenter around the Shinkansen Station at Shin-Yokohama.

The development of air travel and the competition from other ports have changed the city's role in Japan's economy. The great liners that once docked at Yokohama's piers are now but a memory, kept alive by a museum ship and the occasional visit of a luxury vessel on a Pacific cruise. Modern Yokohama thrives instead in its industrial, commercial, and service sectors—and a large percentage of its people commute to work in Tokyo. Is Yokohama worth a visit? Not, one could argue, at the expense of Nikko or Kamakura. But the waterfront is fun and the museums are excellent.

GETTING HERE AND AROUND

From Narita Airport, a direct limousine-bus service departs once or twice an hour between 7:05 am and 10:25 pm for Yokohama City Air Terminal (YCAT). YCAT is a five-minute taxi ride from Yokohama Station. JR Narita Express trains going on from Tokyo to Yokohama leave the airport every hour from 7:44 am to 9:44 pm. The fare is ¥4,290 (¥5,830 for the first-class Green Car coaches). Or you can take the limousine-bus service from Narita to Tokyo Station and continue on to Yokohama by train. Either way, the journey takes more than two hours—closer to three, if traffic is heavy.

The Airport Limousine Information Desk phone number provides information in English daily 9 to 6; you can also get timetables on its website. For information in English on Narita Express trains, call the JR Higashi-Nihon Info Line, available daily 10 to 6.

Most of the things to see in Yokohama are within easy walking distance of a JR or subway station, but this city is so much more negotiable than Tokyo that exploring by bus is a viable alternative. The city map available in the visitor centers in Yokohama has most major bus routes marked on it, and the important stops on the tourist routes are announced in English. The fixed fare is ¥210. One-day passes are also available for ¥600. Contact the Sightseeing Information Office at Yokohama Station (JR, East Exit) for more information and ticket purchases.

One subway line connects Azamino, Shin-Yokohama, Yokohama, Totsuka, and Shonandai. The basic fare is ¥200. One-day passes are also available for ¥740. The Minato Mirai Line, a spur of the Tokyu Toyoko Line, runs from Yokohama Station to all the major points of interest, including Minato Mirai, Chinatown, Yamashita Park, Motomachi, and Basha-michi. The fare is ¥180–¥200, and one-day unlimited-ride passes are available for ¥450. On weekends Yokohama has the 1-Day Green Family Pass, allowing up to five members of the same family to travel on all city buses for ¥1,000 in total.

There are taxi stands at all the train stations, and you can always flag a cab on the street. ■TIP➔ **Vacant taxis show a red light in the windshield.** The basic fare is ¥730 for the first 2 km (1 mile), then ¥80 for every additional 350 meters (0.2 mile). Traffic is heavy in downtown Yokohama, however, and it's often faster to walk.

JR trains from Tokyo Station leave approximately every 10 minutes, depending on the time of day. Take the Yokosuka, the Tokaido, or the Keihin Tohoku Line to Yokohama Station (the Yokosuka and Tokaido lines take 30 minutes; the Keihin Tohoku Line takes 40 minutes and cost ¥470). From there the Keihin Tohoku Line (Platform 3) goes on to Kannai and Ishikawa-cho, Yokohama's business and downtown areas. If you're going directly to downtown Yokohama from Tokyo, the blue commuter trains of the Keihin Tohoku Line are best.

The private Tokyu Toyoko Line, which runs from Shibuya Station in Tokyo directly to Yokohama Station, is a good alternative if you leave from the western part of Tokyo. ■TIP➔ **The term "private" is** important because it means that the train does not belong to JR and is not a subway line. If you have a JR Pass, you'll have to buy a separate ticket. Depending on which Tokyu Toyoko Line you catch—the Limited Express, Semi Express, or Local—the trip takes between 25 and 44 minutes and costs ¥270.

Yokohama Station is the hub that links all the train lines and connects them with the city's subway and bus services. Kannai and Ishikawa-cho are the two downtown stations, both on the Keihin Tohoku Line; trains leave Yokohama Station every two to five minutes from Platform 3. From Sakuragi-cho, Kannai, or Ishikawa-cho, most of Yokohama's points of interest are within easy walking distance; the one notable exception is Sankei-en, which you reach via the JR Keihin Tohoku Line to Negishi Station and then a local bus.

VISITOR INFORMATION
The Yokohama Tourist Office, in the central passageway of Yokohama Station, is open daily 9 to 7 (closed December 28–January 3). The head office of the Yokohama Convention & Visitors Bureau, open weekdays 9 to 5 (except national holidays and December 29–January 3), is in the Sangyo Boeki Center Building, across from Yamashita Koen.

ESSENTIALS
Airport Transportation Airport Limousine Information Desk. ☎ *03/3665–7220* ⊕ *www.limousinebus.co.jp.*

EXPLORING

Large as Yokohama is, the central area is very negotiable. As with any other port city, much of what it has to offer centers on the water-front—in this case, on the west side of Tokyo Bay. The downtown area is called Kannai (literally, "within the checkpoint"); this is where the international community was originally confined by the shogunate. Though the center of interest has expanded to include the waterfront and Ishikawa-cho, to the south, Kannai remains the heart of town.

Think of that heart as two adjacent areas. One is the old district of Kannai, bounded by Basha-michi on the northwest and Nippon-odori on the southeast, the Keihin Tohoku Line tracks on the southwest, and the waterfront on the northeast. This area contains the business offices of modern Yokohama. The other area extends southeast from Nippon-odori to the Moto-machi shopping street and the International Cemetery, bordered by Yamashita Koen and the waterfront to the northeast; in the center is Chinatown, with Ishikawa-cho Station to the southwest. This is the most interesting part of town for tourists. ■**TIP→ Whether you're coming from Tokyo, Nagoya, or Kamakura, make Ishikawa-cho Station your starting point. Take the South Exit from the station and head in the direction of the waterfront.**

CENTRAL YOKOHAMA 横浜市街
TOP ATTRACTIONS
Basha-michi (馬車道). Running southwest from Shinko Pier to Kannai is Basha-michi, which literally translates into "Horse-Carriage Street." The street was so named in the 19th century, when it was widened to

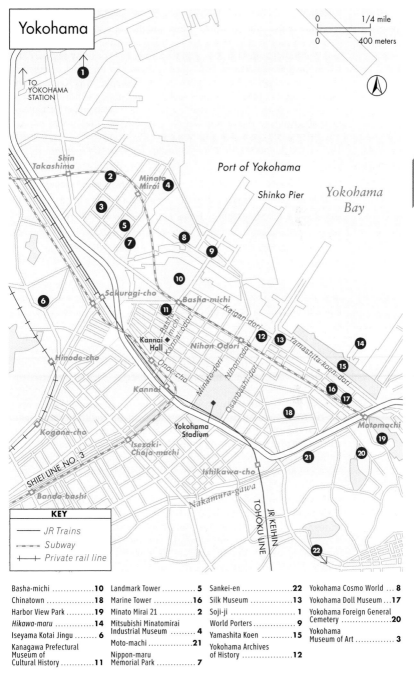

accommodate the horse-drawn carriages of the city's new European residents. This redbrick thoroughfare and the streets parallel to it have been restored to evoke that past, with faux-antique telephone booths and imitation gas lamps. Here you'll find some of the most elegant coffee shops, patisseries, and boutiques in town. On the block northeast of Kannai Station, as you walk toward the waterfront, is **Kannai Hall** (look for the red-orange abstract sculpture in front), a handsome venue for chamber music, Noh, classical recitals, and occasional performances by such groups as the Peking Opera. If you're planning to stay late in Yokohama, you might want to check out the listings. ⊠ *Naka-ku* Ⓜ *JR Line, Kannai Station; Minato Mirai Line, Basha-michi Station.*

NEED A BREAK?

Keyuca Café and Sweets. Japanese pâtissiers excel at making exquisite European sweets, occasionally giving them a new twist with Japanese ingredients such as sweet bean paste. This elegant café is a good place to taste these skills while taking a break from your walking tour. The cappuccino is excellent, and there's a daily changing menu of bagel sandwiches and other light fare. ⊠ *B1 Queen's East, 2–3–2 Minato-Mirai, Nishi-ku* ☎ *045/640–1361.*

Chinatown (中華街 *Chuka-gai*). The largest Chinese settlement in Japan—and easily the city's most popular tourist attraction—Yokohama's Chinatown draws more than 18 million visitors a year. Its narrow streets and alleys are lined with some 350 shops selling foodstuffs, herbal medicines, cookware, toys and ornaments, and clothing and accessories. If China exports it, you'll find it here. Wonderful exotic aromas waft from the spice shops. Even better aromas drift from the quarter's 160-odd restaurants, which serve every major style of Chinese cuisine: this is the best place for lunch in Yokohama. Chinatown is a 10-minute walk southeast of Kannai Station. When you get to Yokohama Stadium, turn left and cut through the municipal park to the top of Nihon-odori. Then take a right, and enter Chinatown through the Gembu-mon (North Gate), which leads to the dazzling red-and-gold, 50-foot-high Zenrin-mon (Good Neighbor Gate). ⊠ *Naka-ku* Ⓜ *JR Line, Ishikawa-cho Station; Minato Mirai Line, Motomachi-Chukagai Station.*

Harbor View Park (港の見える丘公園 *Minato-no-Mieru-Oka Koen*). The park—a major landmark in this part of the city, known, appropriately enough, as the Bluff (*yamate*)—was once the barracks of the British forces in Yokohama. Come here for spectacular nighttime views of the waterfront, the floodlit gardens of Yamashita Park, and the Bay Bridge. Foreigners were first allowed to build here in 1867, and it has been prime real estate ever since—an enclave of consulates, churches, international schools, private clubs, and palatial Western-style homes. ⊠ *Naka-ku* Ⓜ *JR Line, Ishikawa-cho Station; Minato Mirai Line, Motomachi-Chukagai Station.*

Hikawa-maru (氷川丸). Moored on the waterfront, more or less in the middle of Yamashita Park, is the *Hikawa-maru*. The ocean liner was built in 1929 by Yokohama Dock Co. and launched on September 30, 1929. For 31 years, she shuttled passengers between Yokohama

Get a taste of China in Japan with a visit to the restaurants and shops of Yokohama's Chinatown.

and Seattle, Washington, making a total of 238 trips. A tour of the ship evokes the time when Yokohama was a great port of call for the transpacific liners. The ship has a French restaurant, and in summer there's a beer garden on the upper deck. ⊠ *Yamashita-koen, Naka-ku* ☎ *045/641–4362* 🎫 *¥500* ⏰ *Apr.–June, Sept., and Oct., daily 9:30–7; July and Aug., daily 9:30–7:30; Nov.–Mar., daily 9:30–6:30* Ⓜ *JR Line, Ishikawa-cho Station; Minato Mirai Line, Motomachi-Chukagai Station.*

Silk Museum (シルク博物館 *Shiruku Hakubutsukan*). From the opening of its borders to the beginning of the 20th century, silk was Japan's most sought-after export and nearly all of it went through Yokohama. The museum, which pays tribute to this period, houses an extensive collection of silk fabrics and an informative exhibit on the silk-making process. People on staff are very happy to answer questions. In the same building, on the first floor, are the main offices of the Yokohama International Tourist Association and the Kanagawa Prefectural Tourist Association. The museum is at the northwestern end of the Yamashita Park promenade, on the second floor of the Silk Center Building. ⊠ *1 Yamashita-cho, Naka-ku* ☎ *045/641–0841* 🌐 *www.silkmuseum.or.jp* 🎫 *¥500* ⏰ *Tues.–Sun. 9–4* Ⓜ *Minato Mirai Line, Nihon Odori Station (Exit 3).*

WORTH NOTING

Kanagawa Prefectural Museum of Cultural History (神奈川県立歴史博物館 *Kanagawa Kenritsu Rekishi Hakubutsukan*). One of the few buildings in Yokohama to have survived both the Great Kanto Earthquake of 1923 and World War II, the museum is a few blocks north of Kannai

Station on Basha-michi. Most exhibits here have no explanations in English, but the galleries on the third floor showcase some remarkable medieval wooden sculptures (including one of the first Kamakura shogun, Minamoto no Yoritomo), hanging scrolls, portraits, and armor. The exhibits of prehistory and of Yokohama in the early modern period are of much less interest. ⌧ *5–60 Minami Naka-dori, Naka-ku* ☎ *045/201–0926* ⊕ *ch.kanagawa-museum.jp* ▧ *¥300, special exhibits ¥800* ☾ *Tues.–Sun. 9:30–4:30; closed last Tues. of month and the day after a national holiday* Ⓜ *JR Line, Kannai Station (Exit 8).*

Marine Tower (マリンタワー). For an older generation of Yokohama residents, the 348-foot-high decagonal tower, which opened in 1961, was the city's landmark structure; civic pride prevented them from admitting that it falls lamentably short of an architectural masterpiece. The tower has a navigational beacon at the 338-foot level and purports to be the tallest lighthouse in the world. At the 328-foot level, an observation gallery provides 360-degree views of the harbor and the city, and on clear days in autumn or winter, you can often see Mt. Fuji in the distance. Marine Tower is in the middle of the second block northwest from the end of Yamashita Park, on the left side of the promenade. ⌧ *15 Yamashita-cho, Naka-ku* ☎ *045/641–7838* ⊕ *www.marinetower. jp* ▧ *¥750* ☾ *Daily 10–10* Ⓜ *JR Line, Ishikawa-cho Station; Minato Mirai Line, Motomachi-Chukagai Station.*

Moto-machi (元町). Within a block of Ishikawa-cho Station is the beginning of this street, which follows the course of the Nakamura-gawa (Nakamura River) to the harbor where the Japanese set up shop 100 years ago to serve the foreigners living in Kannai. The street is now lined with smart boutiques and jewelry stores that cater to fashionable young Japanese consumers. ⌧ *Naka-ku* Ⓜ *JR Line, Ishikawa-cho Station; Minato Mirai Line, Motomachi-Chukagai Station.*

Yamashita Koen (山下公園 *Yamashita Park*). This park is perhaps the only positive legacy of the Great Kanto Earthquake of 1923. The debris of the warehouses and other buildings that once stood here were swept away, and the area was made into a 17-acre oasis of green along the waterfront. The fountain, representing the Guardian of the Water, was presented to Yokohama by San Diego, California, one of its sister cities. ⌧ *279 Yamashita-cho, Naka-ku* ✛ *From Harbor View Park, walk northwest through neighboring French Hill Park and cross the walkway over Moto-machi. Turn right on the other side and walk one block down toward the bay to Yamashita-Koen-dori, the promenade along the park* Ⓜ *JR Line, Ishikawa-cho Station; Minato Mirai Line, Motomachi-Chukagai Station.*

Yokohama Archives of History (横浜開港資料館 *Yokohama Kaiko Shiryokan*). Within the archives, housed in what was once the British Consulate, are some 140,000 items recording the history of Yokohama since the opening of the port to international trade in the mid-19th century. Across the street is a monument to the U.S.–Japanese Friendship Treaty. ⌧ *3 Nihon-odori, Naka-ku* ✛ *To get here from the Silk Center Building, at the end of the Yamashita Park promenade, walk west to the corner of Nihon-odori; the archives are on the left* ☎ *045/201–2100* ⊕ *www.*

kaikou.city.yokohama.jp/en ⌧*¥200* ⊙ *Tues.–Sun. 9:30–5* Ⓜ *Minato Mirai Line, Nihon-odori Station.*

FAMILY **Yokohama Doll Museum** (横浜人形の家 *Yokohama Ningyo-no-ie*). This museum houses a collection of roughly 3,500 dolls from all over the world. In Japanese tradition, dolls are less to play with than to display—either in religious folk customs or as the embodiment of some spiritual quality. Japanese visitors to this museum never seem to outgrow their affection for the Western dolls on display here, to which they tend to assign the role of timeless "ambassadors of goodwill" from other cultures. The museum is worth a quick visit, with or without a child in tow. It's just across from the southeast end of Yamashita Park, on the left side of the promenade. ⌧ *18 Yamashita-cho, Naka-ku* ☎ *045/671–9361* ⊕ *www.doll-museum.jp* ⌧ *¥400* ⊙ *Tues.–Sun., 9:30–5* Ⓜ *JR Line, Ishikawa-cho Station; Minato Mirai Line, Motomachi-Chukagai Station.*

Yokohama Foreign General Cemetery (横浜山手外国人墓地 *Yokohama Yamate Gaikokujin Bochi*). This Yokohama landmark is a reminder of the port city's heritage. It was established in 1854 with a grant of land from the shogunate; the first foreigners to be buried here were Russian sailors assassinated by xenophobes in the early days of the settlement. Most of the 4,500 graves on this hillside are English and American, and about 120 are of the Japanese wives of foreigners; the inscriptions on the crosses and headstones attest to some 40 different nationalities whose citizens lived and died in Yokohama. ⌧ *96 Yamate-cho, Naka-ku* ⚓ *From Moto-machi Plaza, it's a short walk to the north end of the cemetery* ⊕ *www.yfgc-japan.com* ⊙ *No entry after 4 pm* Ⓜ *JR Line, Ishikawa-cho Station; Minato Mirai Line, Motomachi-Chukagai Station.*

AROUND YOKOHAMA
TOP ATTRACTIONS

Iseyama Kotai Jingu (伊勢山皇大神宮 *Iseyama Kotai Shrine*). A branch of the nation's revered Grand Shrines of Ise, this is the most important Shinto shrine in Yokohama—but it's worth a visit only if you've seen most everything else in town. ⌧ *64 Miyazaki-cho, Nishi-ku* ⚓ *The shrine is a 10-minute walk west of Sakuragi-cho Station* ☎ *045/241–1122* ⌧ *Free* ⊙ *Daily 9–7* Ⓜ *JR Line, Sakuragi-cho Station; Minato Mirai Line, Minato Mirai Station.*

FAMILY **Landmark Tower** (ランドマークタワー). Although no longer Japan's tallest building—that title now goes to Osaka's brand-new Abeno Harukas— this 70-story tower in Yokohama's Minato Mirai is the tallest in Greater Tokyo. The observation deck on the 69th floor has a spectacular view of the city, especially at night; you reach it via a high-speed elevator that carries you up at an ear-popping 45 kph (28 mph). The complex's **Dockyard Garden,** built in 1896, is a restored dry dock with stepped sides of massive stone blocks. The long, narrow floor of the dock, with its water cascade at one end, makes a wonderful year-round open-air venue for concerts and other events; in summer (July–mid-August), the beer garden installed here is a perfect refuge from the heat. The Yokohama Royal Park Hotel occupies the top 20 stories of the building,

Landmark Tower and the Ferris wheel create a lovely skyline along Yokohama Bay.

and the courtyard on the northeast side connects to **Queen's Square,** a huge atrium-style vertical mall with dozens of shops (mainly for clothing and accessories) and restaurants. ✉ *2–2–1 Minato Mirai, Nishi-ku* ☎ *045/222–5015* ⊕ *www.yokohama-landmark.jp* ✉ *Elevator to observation deck ¥1,000* ☉ *Daily 10–9* Ⓜ *JR Line, Sakuragi-cho Station; Minato Mirai Line, Minato Mirai Station.*

Minato Mirai 21 (みなとみらい21). If you want to see Yokohama urban development at its most self-assertive, then this is a must. The aim of this project, launched in the mid-1980s, was to turn some three-quarters of a square mile of waterfront property, lying east of the JR Negishi Line railroad tracks between the Yokohama and Sakuragi-cho stations, into a model "city of the future." As a hotel, business, international exhibition, and conference center, it's a smashing success. ✉ *Nishi-ku* ⊕ *www.minatomirai21.com* Ⓜ *JR Line, Sakuragi-cho Station; Minato Mirai Line, Minato Mirai Station.*

Sankei-en (三溪園). Opened to the public in 1906, this was once the estate and gardens of Tomitaro Hara (1868–1939), one of Yokohama's wealthiest men, who made his money as a silk merchant before becoming a patron of the arts. On the extensive grounds of the estate he created is a kind of open-air museum of traditional Japanese architecture, some of which was brought here from Kamakura and the western part of the country. Especially noteworthy is **Rinshun-kaku,** a villa built for the Tokugawa clan in 1649. There's also a tea pavilion, Choshu-kaku, built by the third Tokugawa shogun, Iemitsu. Other buildings include a small temple transported from Kyoto's famed Daitoku-ji and a farmhouse from the Gifu district in the Japan Alps (around Takayama). ✉ *58–1*

Honmoku San-no-tani, Naka-ku ☎ *045/621–0634* ⊕ *www.sankeien. or.jp* ⌧ *Inner garden ¥500* ⊙ *Inner garden: daily 9–4. Outer garden and farmhouse: daily 9–4:30* Ⓜ *JR Keihin Tohoku Line to Negishi Station and a local bus (number 58, 99, or 101) bound for Honmoku; Yokohama Station (East Exit) and take the bus (number 8 or 148) to Honmoku Sankei-en Mae (the trip takes about 35 mins).*

WORTH NOTING

FAMILY **Mitsubishi Minatomirai Industrial Museum.** Filling galleries on the first floor of the Landmark Tower are rocket engines, power plants, a submarine, various gadgets, and displays that simulate piloting helicopters—great fun for kids. ⌧ *3-3–1 Minato Mirai, Nishi-ku* ⌧ *¥500* ⊙ *Wed.–Mon. 10–5* Ⓜ *JR Line, Sakuragi-cho Station; Minato Mirai Line, Minato Mirai Station.*

Nippon-maru Memorial Park (日本丸メモリアルパーク). The centerpiece of the park, which is on the east side of Minato Mirai 21, where the O-oka-gawa (O-oka River) flows into the bay, is the *Nippon-maru,* a full-rigged three-masted ship popularly called the "Swan of the Pacific." Built in 1930, it served as a training vessel. The *Nippon-maru* is now retired, but it's an occasional participant in tall-ships festivals and is open for guided tours. Adjacent to the ship is the **Yokohama Port Museum,** a two-story collection of ship models, displays, and archival materials that celebrate the achievements of the Port of Yokohama from its earliest days to the present. ⌧ *2–1–1 Minato Mirai, Nishi-ku* ☎ *045/221–0280* ⊕ *www.nippon-maru.or.jp* ⌧ *¥600* ⊙ *Tues.–Sun. 10–5* Ⓜ *JR Line, Sakuragi-cho Station; Minato Mirai Line, Minato Mirai Station.*

World Porters (ワールドポーターズ). This shopping center, on the opposite side of Yokohama Cosmo World, is notable chiefly for its restaurants that overlook the Minato Mirai area. Try arriving at sunset; the spectacular view of twinkling lights and the Landmark Tower, the Ferris wheel, and hotels occasionally include Mt. Fuji in the background. Walking away from the waterfront area from World Porters leads to **Aka Renga** (Redbrick Warehouses), two more shopping-and-entertainment facilities. ⌧ *2–2–1 Shinko, Naka-ku* ☎ *045/222–2121* ⊕ *www. yim.co.jp* ⌧ *Free* ⊙ *Daily 10–9, restaurants 10 am–11 pm* Ⓜ *JR Line, Sakuragi-cho Station; Minato Mirai Line, Minato Mirai Station.*

FAMILY **Yokohama Cosmo World** (よこはまコスモワールド). This amusement-park complex claims—among its 30 or so rides and attractions—the world's largest water-chute ride, four stories high. The Ferris wheel towers over Yokohama. The park is west of Minato Mirai and Queen's Square, on both sides of the river. ⌧ *2–8–1 Shinko, Naka-ku* ☎ *045/641–6591* ⌧ *Park free, rides ¥300–¥700 each* ⊙ *Mid-Mar.–Nov., weekdays 11–9,* *weekends 11–10; Dec.–mid-Mar., weekdays 11–8, weekends 11–9* Ⓜ *JR Line, Sakuragi-cho Station; Minato Mirai Line, Minato Mirai Station.*

Yokohama Museum of Art (横浜美術館 *Yokohama Bijutsukan*). Designed by Kenzo Tange and housed at Minato Mirai 21, the museum has 5,000 works in its permanent collection. Visitors will see paintings by both Western and Japanese artists, including Cézanne, Picasso, Braque, Klee, Kandinsky, Ryusei Kishida, and Taikan Yokoyama. ✉ *3–4–1 Minato Mirai, Nishi-ku* ☎ *045/221–0300* ⊕ *yokohama.art.museum/ eng* 🎟 *¥500, ¥1,000–¥1,500 for special exhibits* ◷ *Mon.–Wed. and weekends 10–5:30* Ⓜ *JR Line, Sakuragi-cho Station; Minato Mirai Line, Minato Mirai Station.*

OFF THE BEATEN PATH

Soji-ji (総持寺). One of the two major centers of the Soto sect of Zen Buddhism, Soji-ji, in Yokohama's Tsurumi ward, was founded in 1321. The center was moved here from Ishikawa, on the Noto Peninsula (on the Sea of Japan, north of Kanazawa), after a fire in the 19th century. There's also a Soji-ji monastic complex at Eihei-ji in Fukui Prefecture. The Yokohama Soji-ji is one of the largest and busiest Buddhist institutions in Japan, with more than 200 monks and novices in residence. The 14th-century patron of Soji-ji was the emperor Go-Daigo, who overthrew the Kamakura Shogunate; the emperor is buried here, but his mausoleum is off-limits to visitors. However, you can see the **Buddha Hall,** the **Main Hall,** and the **Treasure House.** ✉ *2–1–1 Tsurumi, Tsurumi-ku* ⛟ *Take the JR Keihin Tohoku Line 2 stops from Sakuragi-cho to Tsurumi. From the station walk 5 mins south (back toward Yokohama), passing Tsurumi University on your right. Look out for the stone lanterns that mark the entrance to the temple complex* ☎ *045/581–6021* 🎟 *¥300* ◷ *Daily dawn–dusk; Treasure House Tues.–Sun. 10–4.*

WHERE TO EAT

$$$$
SEAFOOD

✕ **Aichiya** (愛知屋). The "house of Aichi Prefecture" specializes in dishes of crab shipped in from Aichi. The merchandise is displayed in its pre-prepared state in cases and tanks at the front of the restaurant. There is crab soup, grilled crab, stewed crab, crab salad, and so on. A fall and winter course boasts *fugu* (blowfish), a delicacy that must be prepared by licensed experts, so as to avoid allowing the fish's poisonous organs to seep into the meat. Ⓢ *Average main: ¥6000* ✉ *2–17–6 Minamisaiwai, Nishi-ku* ☎ *045/251–4163* ◷ *Closed Mon. No lunch.*

$$$$
JAPANESE

✕ **Chano-ma** (茶の間). This stylish eatery serves modern Japanese cuisine that you enjoy while lounging on bedlike seats as a house DJ spins tunes. Make sure you try the miso sirloin steak or grilled scallops with tasty citron sauce drizzled on top, served with a salad. It gets crowded here on the weekends, so come early to avoid a long wait. Try coming at lunchtime and you can take advantage of the set-lunch special. Ⓢ *Average main: ¥3500* ✉ *3F Red Brick Warehouse Bldg. 2, 1–1–2 Shinkou, Naka-ku* ☎ *045/650–8228* Ⓜ *Minato Mirai Line, Basha-michi Station; JR Negishi Line, Sakuragi-cho and Kannai stations.*

$$$$
CHINESE

✕ **Kaseiro** (華正樓). Surprisingly, Chinese food can be hit-or-miss in Japan, but not at Kaseiro. This elegant restaurant, with red carpets and gold-tone walls, is the best of its kind in the city, serving authentic Beijing cuisine, including, of course, Peking Duck and shark-fin soup. The consistently delicious dishes, combined with the fact that both the owner and chef are from Beijing, make this restaurant a well-known favorite among locals and travelers alike. $ *Average main: ¥10000* ⊠ *186 Yamashita-cho, Chinatown, Naka-ku* ☎ *045/681–2918* 🏛 *Jacket and tie.*

$$$$
JAPANESE

✕ **Motomachi Bairin** (元町梅林). The area of Motomachi is known as the wealthy, posh part of Yokohama; restaurants here tend to be exclusive and expensive, though the service and quality justify the price. This restaurant is an old-style Japanese house complete with a Japanese garden and five private tatami rooms. For a real feast, try the 27-course banquet that includes traditional Japanese delicacies such as sashimi, shiitake mushrooms, and chicken in white sauce; deep-fried burdock; and broiled sea bream. $ *Average main: ¥12000* ⊠ *1–55 Motomachi, Naka-ku* ☎ *045/662–2215* ⊗ *Closed Mon.* 🗠 *Reservations essential.*

$$$$
JAPANESE

✕ **Rinka-en** (隣花苑). If you visit the gardens of Sankei-en, you might want to have lunch or dinner at this traditional country restaurant, which serves kaiseki-style cuisine. The owner is the granddaughter of Hara Tomitaro, who donated the gardens to the city. $ *Average main: ¥7000* ⊠ *52–1 Honmoku San-no-tani, Naka-ku* ☎ *045/621–0318* 🖃 *No credit cards* ⊗ *Closed Wed. and Aug.* 🗠 *Reservations essential* 🏛 *Jacket and tie.*

$$$$
ITALIAN

✕ **Roma Statione** (ローマステーション). Opened more than 40 years ago, this popular venue between Chinatown and Yamashita Park is Yokohama's source for Italian food. The owner, whose father studied cooking in Italy before returning home, is also the head chef and has continued using the original recipes. The house specialty is seafood: the spaghetti *vongole* (with clam sauce) is particularly good, as is the spaghetti *pescatora* and the seafood pizza. An added bonus is the impressive selection of Italian wines. $ *Average main: ¥3500* ⊠ *26 Yamashita-cho, Naka-ku* ☎ *045/681–1818* Ⓜ *Minato Mirai Line, Motomachi-Chukagai Station (Exit 1).*

$$$$
SCANDINAVIAN

✕ **Scandia** (スカンディア). This Scandinavian restaurant near the Silk Center and the business district is known for its smorgasbord. It's popular for business lunches as well as for dinner. Scandia stays open until midnight, later than many other restaurants in the area. Expect dishes like steak tartare, marinated herring, and fried eel, and plenty of rye bread. While dinner is pricey, lunches are a relative bargain. $ *Average main: ¥9000* ⊠ *1–1 Kaigan-dori, Naka-ku* ☎ *045/201–2262* 🖃 *No credit cards.*

$$$$
STEAKHOUSE

✕ **Serina Romanchaya** (瀬里奈 浪漫茶屋). The hallmarks of this restaurant are *ishiyaki* steak, which is grilled on a hot stone, and shabu-shabu—thin slices of beef cooked in boiling water at your table and dipped in one of several sauces; choose from sesame, vinegar, or soy. Fresh vegetables, noodles, and tofu are also dipped into the seasoned broth for a filling yet healthful meal. $ *Average main: ¥10000* ⊠ *B1 Shin-Kannai Bldg., 4–45–1 Sumiyoshi-cho, Naka-ku* ☎ *045/681–2727.*

$$$$

ITALIAN

FAMILY

✕ **Yokohama Cheese Cafe** (横浜チーズカフェ). This is a cozy and inviting casual Italian restaurant, whose interior looks like an Italian country home. There are candles on the tables and an open kitchen where diners can watch the cooks making pizza. On the menu: 18 kinds of Napoli-style wood-fire–baked pizzas, 20 kinds of pastas, fondue, and other dishes that include—you guessed it—cheese. The set-course menus are reasonable, filling, and recommended. ⓢ *Average main: ¥3500* ✉ *2–1–10 Kitasaiwai, Nishi-ku* ☎ *045/290–5656* ⊗ *No lunch* Ⓜ *JR Yokohama Station.*

NAGOYA, ISE-SHIMA, AND THE KII PENINSULA

WELCOME TO NAGOYA, ISE-SHIMA, AND THE KII PENINSULA

TOP REASONS TO GO

★ **The shrines:** The Grand Shrines of Ise, rebuilt every two decades for the last 1,500 years, are the most sacred in Japan.

★ **Shopping:** Nagoya's Noritake is one of the world's largest porcelain makers. Seto, Tajimi, and Tokoname produce ceramics, Arimatsu tie-dyed fabrics, Gifu paper lanterns and umbrellas, and Seki samurai swords.

★ **Japan at work and play:** Tour the factories of Toyota and Noritake. See the sumo tournament in July, watch a Chunichi Dragons baseball game or take in a Grampus soccer match.

★ **Fish from the bird's mouth:** In *ukai*, cormorants snatch *ayu* (sweetfish) from the water, but rings around the birds' necks prevent them from swallowing their catch, which is taken by fishermen.

★ **Japan's modernization:** Meiji-mura holds more than 60 original Meiji-era buildings (1868–1912)—including the foyer of Frank Lloyd Wright's Imperial Hotel—that were reconstructed here.

1 Nagoya. An ancient transport, business, and cultural hub, Nagoya combines the best of old and contemporary Japan. To the north, along the edge of the Gifu and Nagano mountains, are cormorant fishing and craft centers.

2 Ise-Shima National Park. Many people get no farther than the shrines at Ise, but just to the south is a world of bays ringed by fishing villages and oyster farms.

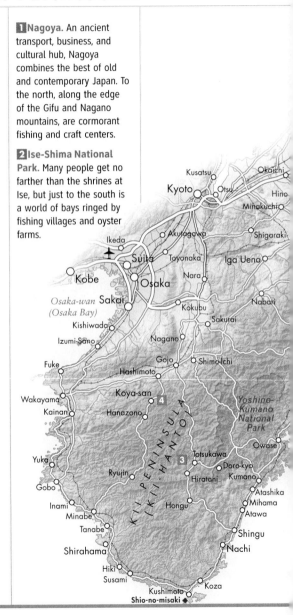

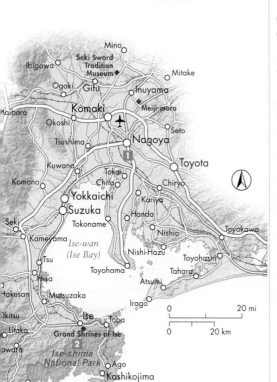

Mino
Seki Sword
Tradition
Museum
Ibigawa
Mitake
Ogaki
Gifu
Inuyama
Komaki
Meiji-mura
aibara
Okoshi
Seto
Tsushima
Nagoya
Kuwana
Toyota
Tokai
Komono
Chita
Chiryo
Yokkaichi
Kariya
Suzuka
Handa
Seki
Tokoname
Toyokawa
Kameyama
Nishio
Ise-wan
Nishi-Hazu
(Ise Bay)
Toyohashi
Tsu
Toyohama
Tahara
Hisa
Atsumi
lakusan
Matsuzaka
Irago
0   20 mi
)kitsu
Ise
Toba
Litaka
Grand Shrines of Ise
0   20 km
awara
Ise-shima
National Park
Ago
Kashikojima
Kowa
Ago-wan
(Ago Bay)
Kii-nagashima

GETTING ORIENTED

Nagoya is between Tokyo and Kyoto, and we recommend spending a couple of days exploring the sights. The city serves as a jumping-off point for traveling south to Ise-Shima and southwest to the Kii Peninsula and Koya-san. Nagoya is on a wide plain in the main urban and industrial corridor that runs along the south side of Honshu from Tokyo as far west as Kobe. The mountains of the southern Japan Alps rise just north and east of the city, and to the southwest is the lush Kii Peninsula.

5

3 Kii Peninsula. Traveling southwest and inland on the Kii Peninsula, time slows down, with few roads and only one coastal railway line. The peninsula rewards patient explorers with beautiful wilderness and the shrines of the Kumano Kodo pilgrimage road.

4 Koya-san. Headquarters of the 1,200-year-old Shingon Buddhist sect, this small, isolated mountain town, dotted by 117 temples, is a calm and spiritual retreat. Koya-san also has overnight temple accommodation.

TOYOTA: NAGOYA'S MAINSTAY

It may sound like the kind of activity reserved for only the most dedicated of motorheads, but you don't need to be into cars to be awed by the Toyota museum and plant tour.

(This page above) Workers assembling a car in a Toyota plant; (opposite page upper right) the Prius assembly line at Toyota's Tsutsumi Plant; (opposite page bottom left) finished cars roll off the assembly line.

Few things in Japan are as ubiquitous as Toyota. Working men drive Toyota trucks, families get about in its station wagons, and executives are rarely seen in anything other than a Toyota luxury sedan or limo. Even the Emperor gets driven about in one of the Aiichi automaker's creations—a custom-made, $500,000 Toyota Century Royal. Though the company has had its troubles in recent years—most notably with a succession of unfortunate recalls —in Japan, Toyota is still synonymous with quality and innovation. And it's not hard to see why if you head to Toyota City (yes, a city named after the company) for a tour of one of Toyota's high-tech car plants.

WHAT'S IN A NAME?

Although the motor company was founded by Kiichiro Toyoda and early models were branded with his surname, Toyoda soon decided to drop the "da" for a "ta," and the Toyota brand was born. The reason? Firstly, "ta" sounds clearer, but more importantly, when written in katakana Toyota (トヨタ) uses 8 brush strokes, a number considered to be fortuitous. Toyoda (トヨダ) uses 10.

TOURING TOYOTA

For many the quintessential Japanese company, Toyota was a prominent figure in Japan's remarkable postwar recovery. Its success has in large part been attributed to its pioneering and integrated approach to production and management—the Toyota Production System—based around "just-in-time" production and *jidoka* (automation with a human touch). With the former, Toyota makes only what is needed, when it is needed. The latter is Toyota's way of building quality control into each stage of the production process—as you'll hear on the tour, each worker on the Toyota production line has the power to bring the entire line to a halt if they discover a defect.

The tour itself, in the company of an English-speaking guide and up to 40 other visitors, starts at 11 am with a quick bus trip to one of three nearby plants—the Motomachi Plant, where Toyota makes its Crown, Mark X, and Estima models; the Takaoka Plant, where the Corolla and iQ models are produced; or the Tsutsumi Plant, which rolls out Camry, Premio, and Prius autos. Whichever plant you end up at, the first stop, the welding shop, is designed to wow. It's a blur of machinery and sparks as state-of-the-art robots apply more than 90% of the more than

3,000 welding spots it takes to secure almost 400 different parts to each car.

After that, it's briefly back on the bus and off to the main part of the two-hour tour—an hour walking above the sprawling assembly shop, watching the workers below rapidly attaching parts as the cars flow ceaselessly along the production line. All the while, against a backdrop of beeps, flashing lights, and noisy air jet blasts, the guide reels off an astonishing list of facts and figures: almost 40,000 boxes of parts pass through each factory daily; a single car needs almost 30,000 parts; and around 300 cars roll off the line a day at each plant.

TOURING DETAILS

You need to be at the Kaikan (Exhibition Hall) by 10:30 am to sign in for the 11 am tour, which gives ample time to explore the museum's slick exhibits on environmentally friendly technology, motor sports, and safety—try the Driving Safety Simulator to test out Toyota's latest safety measures. You'll also be able to get hands-on with the latest Toyota and Lexus models, catch a quick musical performance given by Toyota's partner robot, and see a demonstration of the futuristic i-unit, a single-passenger concept vehicle that's been designed to operate on the motorway, in pedestrian zones, and even indoors.

5

Updated by
Rob Goss

Nagoya punches well above its weight. The present-day industries of Japan's fourth-largest city are a corollary to its *monozukuri* (art of making things) culture. This is manifested in the efficiency of Toyota's production lines, but traditional crafts including ceramics, tie-dyeing, and knife making are still very much alive. The Greater Nagoya area's GDP accounts for more than 5% of the country's total GDP, but this economic prowess is matched by a capacity to pleasantly surprise any visitor.

Nagoya purrs along contentedly, burdened neither by a second-city complex nor by hordes of tourists, and it has an agreeable small-town atmosphere. A substantial immigrant population, by Japanese standards, includes many South Americans working in local factories and provides international flavor to the city's food and entertainment choices.

On arrival, you will first notice the twin white skyscrapers sprouting from the ultramodern station, almost a city in itself. An extensive network of underground shopping malls stretches out in all directions below the wide, clean streets around Nagoya Station and in downtown Sakae. Above ground are huge department stores and international fashion boutiques. The even taller building opposite the station is the headquarters of the sales division of auto-making giant Toyota, the driving force of the local economy.

Within two hours' drive of the city are the revered Grand Shrines of Ise, Japan's most important Shinto site, and to the south are the quiet fishing villages of Ise-Shima National Park. Southwest of Nagoya, on the untamed Kii Peninsula, steep-walled gorges and forested headlands give way to pristine bays, and fine sandy beaches await in Shirahama. Inland is the remarkable mountain temple town of Koya-san. Add to this some memorable *matsuri* (festivals), and this corner of Japan becomes far more than just another stop on the Shinkansen train.

⇨ *See the glossary at the end of this book for definitions of the common Japanese words and suffixes used in this chapter.*

PLANNING

WHEN TO GO

Spring is the most popular season, especially early April when cherry trees bloom. Nagoya gets extremely hot and humid in July and August, but in autumn the trees turn color under blue skies. Sea breezes make coastal areas bearable in summer. Cold winds blow into Nagoya from the ski grounds to the north in winter, but Wakayama Prefecture remains mild. The weather can be changeable along the coastline of Ise-Shima, and the area is occasionally hit hard by typhoons. If you're heading inland on the Kii Peninsula be prepared for hilly terrain.

GETTING HERE AND AROUND

In Nagoya subways are the easiest way to get around. Outside the city the extensive rail network will take you to most places of interest, although buses may be necessary on the remote Kii Peninsula.

AIR TRAVEL

Nagoya's compact, user-friendly Chubu Centrair International Airport (referred to locally as just "Centrair") serves overseas flights and is a hub for domestic travel. Many major airlines have offices in downtown Nagoya, 45 km (28 miles) northeast of the airport, including Japan Airlines (JAL) and All Nippon Airways (ANA), both of which fly from Nagoya to most major Japanese cities. The Meitetsu Airport Limited Express train makes the 28-minute run between Centrair and Nagoya Station for ¥1,230. This price includes a seat-reservation fee.

Airline Contacts All Nippon Airways. ☎ 0120/029–709 ⊕ www.ana.co.jp.
Japan Airlines. ☎ 0120/747–222 ⊕ www.ar.jal.com.

Airport Contacts Chubu Centrair International Airport (中部国際空港 Chubu Kokusai Kuko). ⊠ 1–1 Centrair, Matsusaka ☎ 0569/38–1195 daily 6:40 am–10 pm ⊕ www.centrair.jp. **Meitetsu Airport Limited Express** (空港 Kuko-sen). ☎ 052/582–5151 weekdays 8 am–7 pm, weekends 8 am–6 pm ⊕ www.meitetsu.co.jp.

BUS TRAVEL

Highway buses operated by JR and Meitetsu connect Nagoya with major cities, including Tokyo and Kyoto. The fare is half that of the Shinkansen trains, but the journey takes three times longer.

City buses crisscross Nagoya, running either north–south or east–west. The basic fare is ¥210—pay when you get on the bus. A one-day bus pass costs ¥600, and a combination bus/subway pass costs ¥850.

Detailed information on bus travel can be collected at the Tourist Information Office in the center of Nagoya Station, and day- and combination-passes are available at ticket machines in bus terminals and subway stations.

Bus Contacts JR Tokai Bus (JR東海バス). ☎ 052/563–0489. **Meitetsu Highway Bus** (名鉄バス). ☎ 052/582–0489 ⊕ www.meitetsu.co.jp. **Nagoya City Transportation Bureau** (名古屋市交通局 Nagoya-shi Kotsukyoku). ☎ 052/522–0111.

CLOSE UP

Festivals

Nagoya and the surrounding cities host a wide variety of matsuri (festivals) throughout the year. Running the gamut from chaotic to tranquil and beautiful to bizarre, these events bring the culture and traditions of the area to life in ways that castles, museums, and temples cannot. Whenever you visit check with the Tourist Information Center or Nagoya International Center for upcoming festivals. All the events that follow are free.

FEBRUARY

Hadaka (Naked) Festival. For 1,200 years, thousands of men aged 23 and 42 (unlucky ages in Japan) have braved the winter cold wearing nothing but *fundoshi* (loincloths). Their goal, in an event that regularly results in serious injury to participants, is to touch the *shin otoko* (the one truly "naked man") and transmit their bad spirits to him before he reaches Konomiya shrine and submits to cleansing rituals. Eagerness to achieve this task often leads to stampedes, but the crowds of more than 100,000 are well protected from harm. The festival is held in the first half of February, on the second day of the new lunar year—contact Nagoya City Tourist Information Center in JR Nagoya Station for details. Konomiya Station is 15 minutes north of Nagoya on the Meitetsu Gifu Line, and the shrine is a 10-minute walk from the station.

MARCH

Honen Festival. The 1,500-year-old Tagata-jinja in Komaki is home to one of Japan's male fertility festivals. On March 15 large crowds gather to watch and take pictures of a 6-foot, 885-pound *owasegata* (phallus) being carried between two shrines and

offered to the *kami* (god) for peace and a good harvest. The festival starts at 10 am and climaxes with face-size "lucky" rice cakes being tossed into the crowd just before 4 pm. Visitors who get hungry before then will find plenty of street stalls selling phallic snacks, including chocolate-coated bananas. The closest station is Tagata-jinja-mae on the Meitetsu Komaki Line. Change at Inuyama if you are traveling from Nagoya. The train takes one hour.

JULY

Owari Tsushima Tenno Festival. The main feature of this charming, low-key event is five wood-and-straw boats decorated with 365 paper lanterns (for the days of the year) arranged into a circular shape and 12 more (representing the months) hanging from a mast. The 500-year-old festival occurs over two days on the fourth weekend in July. Haunting traditional music accompanies the boats as they drift around the river and the lanterns and fireworks reflect in the water. Tsushima is 25 minutes west of Nagoya on the Meitetsu Bisai Line. Follow the crowds west from the station for about 15 minutes to the shrine and festival area.

AUGUST

Domannaka. More than 20,000 dancers in troupes of up to 150 each arrive from all over Japan to take over Nagoya's public spaces. Started in 1999, this energetic festival has rapidly gained popularity. It mixes hip-hop beats with spiced-up traditional dance moves and colorful costumes. Domannaka takes place over a weekend in late August.

CAR TRAVEL

The journey on the two-lane expressway from Tokyo to Nagoya takes about 5 hours; from Kyoto allow 2½ hours. Major highways also connect Nagoya to Nagano, Takayama, Kanazawa, and Nara. Japanese highways are jam-prone, with holiday season traffic jams out of Tokyo sometimes reaching 100 km (60 miles) in length. Signage is confusing, so be sure to get a car with satellite navigation or a good road map.

Wide main streets make Nagoya relatively easy to navigate. Road signs in the city often point to places out of town, however, so a detailed map is advised.

TRAIN TRAVEL

Frequent bullet trains run between Tokyo and Nagoya. The ride takes 1 hour, 48 minutes on the *Hikari* Shinkansen and 2½ hours on the slower *Kodama* Shinkansen, and costs ¥10,880. The trip west to Kyoto takes 40 to 50 minutes, and Shin-Osaka is about 1 hour. JR Passes are not accepted on the faster *Nozomi* Shinkansen, which does the journey from Tokyo in 1 hour, 41 minutes and costs ¥11,090. Less-expensive Limited Express trains proceed from Nagoya into and across the Japan Alps—to Takayama, Toyama, Matsumoto, and Nagano.

RESTAURANTS

Restaurants in Nagoya and on the peninsulas are slightly less expensive than in Tokyo. Your cheapest options are the noodle shops, *donburi* (rice bowl) chains, and *kaiten* (revolving) sushi and curry houses. Nagoya's coffee shops are also known for their cheaper-than-usual morning sets, where for not much more than the price of a regular cup of coffee you will also get some toast, a sandwich, or bacon and eggs. Franchised restaurants often have English alongside Japanese on their menus, but don't expect the staff to know more than a few words.

HOTELS

Nagoya's lodging ranges from *ryokan* (traditional Japanese inns) and efficient business hotels to large luxury palaces. At Koya-san, temple accommodation is a fascinating experience. Furnishings in temples are spartan but sufficient, and the food is strictly vegetarian. You will probably be invited to attend the early-morning prayer service and fire ceremonies—an experience well worth getting up for. In addition to holidays, hotels can be busy in October and November owing to conferences held in Nagoya and autumn foliage outside the city. The large hotels in downtown Nagoya have English-speaking staff, but it's advisable to ask at the Tourist Information Center to make reservations for you outside the city.

Hotel reviews have been shortened. For full information, visit Fodors. com. For a short course on accommodations in Japan, see Accommodations in Travel Smart.

WHAT IT COSTS IN YEN			
$	**$$**	**$$$**	**$$$$**
Restaurants	under ¥1,000	¥1,000–¥2,000	¥2,001–¥3,000	over ¥3,000
Hotels	under ¥12,000	¥12,000–¥18,000	¥18,001–¥22,000	over ¥22,000

Restaurant prices are the average cost of a main course at dinner or, if dinner is not served, at lunch. Hotel prices are the lowest cost of a standard double room in high season.

VISITOR INFORMATION

The **Nagoya International Center** is a wise stop on any Nagoya itinerary. Multilingual staff have a wealth of information on Nagoya and the surrounding area, and the center publishes a monthly newsletter, "Nagoya Calendar," which gives up-to-date advice, information, and event listings in English. It is one stop from JR Nagoya Station on the Sakura-dori subway line or a seven-minute walk through the underground walkway that follows the line.

Contacts Nagoya International Center (名古屋国際センター *Nagoya Kokusai Senta*). ✉ 1–47–1 Nagono, Nagoya ☎ 052/581–0100 ⊕ www.nic-nagoya.or.jp/en.

NAGOYA 名古屋

366 km (227 miles) southwest of Tokyo, 190 km (118 miles) east of Osaka, 148 km (92 miles) east of Kyoto.

In 1612, shogun Ieyasu Tokugawa established Nagoya by permitting his ninth son to build a castle here. Industry and merchant houses sprang up in the shadow of this magnificent fortress, as did pleasure quarters for samurai. Supported by taxing the rich harvests of the surrounding Nobi plain, the Tokugawa family used the castle as its power center for the next 250 years.

After the Meiji Restoration in 1868, when Japan began trade with the West in earnest, Nagoya developed rapidly. When the harbor opened to international shipping in 1907, Nagoya's industrial growth accelerated, and by the 1930s it was supporting Japanese expansionism in China with munitions and aircraft. This choice of industry was Nagoya's downfall; very little of the city was left standing after World War II.

Less than two months after the war, ambitious and extensive reconstruction plans were laid, and Nagoya began its remarkable comeback as an industrial metropolis. Planners laid down a grid system, with wide avenues intersecting at right angles. Hisaya-odori, a broad avenue with a park in its 328-foot-wide median, bisects the city. At Nagoya's center is an imposing 590-foot-high television tower (useful for getting your bearings). Nagoya-jo is north of the tower, Atsuta Jingu to the south, Higashiyama-koen east, and the JR Station west. The Sakae subway station serves as the center of the downtown commercial area. Today Nagoya is home to 2.3 million people living in a 326-square-km (126-square-mile) area.

GETTING HERE AND AROUND

AIR TRAVEL International flights from major airlines arrive at Nagoya's Chubu Centrair International Airport, and frequent bullet trains make it easy to access Nagoya from Tokyo, Osaka, and Kyoto.

BUS TRAVEL The golden **Nagoya Sightseeing Route Bus,** known to locals as the *Meguru*, provides cheap tours of the city. The service runs Tuesday through Sunday on a loop from Nagoya Station, via Noritake Garden, Nagoya-jo, the Tokugawa Art Museum, and Sakae. A single ticket is ¥210, while a hop-on, hop-off ticket for the day, which can be bought on the bus, costs ¥500 and includes discounts of 10% to 20% on most major attractions. The buses run once or twice hourly on weekdays, two or three times per hour on weekends, but don't run on Monday when many attractions are closed.

Bus Contacts Nagoya Sightseeing Route Bus (メーグル *Me-guru*). ☎ *052/521–8990* ⊕ *www.nagoya-info.jp/en/routebus.*

TAXI TRAVEL Taxis are parked at all major stations and hotels. Elsewhere it is still far easier to wave one down on the street than to call one of the Japanese-speaking reservation numbers. The initial fare is ¥500. A ride from Nagoya Station to Nagoya-jo costs about ¥1,200. For English-speaking taxi service and charters, try MK Taxi.

Taxi Contacts MK Taxi Nagoya (名古屋MKタクシー). ✉ *Nagoya* ☎ *052/912–5489* ⊕ *www.mktaxi-japan.com.*

TRAIN AND SUBWAY TRAVEL All Nagoya's stations have bilingual maps, and many trains have English announcements. The Higashiyama Line snakes from the west into JR Nagoya Station and then goes due east, cutting through the city center at Sakae. The Meijo Line runs in a loop, passing through the city center at downtown Sakae. A spur line, the Meito, connects Kanayama to Nagoya Port. The Tsurumai Line runs north–south through the city, then turns from the JR Station to Sakae to cross the city center. A fourth line, the Sakura-dori, cuts through the city center from the JR Station, paralleling the east–west section of the Higashiyama Line. The basic fare is ¥200. A one-day pass for Nagoya's subways costs ¥740, while a combination bus/subway pass is ¥850 on weekdays and ¥600 (Weekend Eco Pass) on weekends or national holidays. All the passes can be bought at station ticket machines.

Nagoya's subway system is user-friendly, with signs and announcements in English, and it can get you to almost all places of interest in the city.

The JR trains are the easiest for jumping on and off, but they do not serve all destinations. Meitetsu and Kintetsu stations are lacking in English signage, though Meitetsu prints a handy English-language guide to their network with instructions on how to purchase tickets. You can pick up a copy at Meitetsu Nagoya Station or Chubu Centrair International Airport.

JR Nagoya Station is like a small city, with a variety of shops in, under, and around the station complex. The main **Nagoya City Tourist Information Center** is in the station's central concourse. English-speaking staff can supply sightseeing information, subway maps, and details of upcoming events. Smaller information centers are in three other parts of the city—Sakae, Kanayama, and Nagoya Port.

Train Contacts JR Nagoya Station (名古屋駅 *Nagoya Eki*). ⊠ *1–1–4 Meieki* ☎ *050/3772–3910 daily 6 am–midnight* ⊕ *www.jr-central.co.jp.*

VISITOR INFORMATION
Information Centers
Kanayama Tourist Information Center (名古屋市金山観光案内所 *Nagoya-Shi Kanayama Kankou Annaijyo*). ⊠ *17–18–1 Kanayama, North Exit of Kanayama Station, Naka-ku* ☎ *052/323–0161.* **Nagoya City Tourist Information Center** (名古屋市名古屋駅観光案内所 *Nagoya-Shi Nagoya-Eki Kankou Annaijyo*). ⊠ *1–4–1 Meieki, , Nagoya Station, Nakamura-ku* ☎ *052/541–4301.* **Nagoya Port Tourist Information Center** (名古屋港総合案内所 *Nagoya-ko Sougou Annaijyo*). ⊠ *1–9 Minato-cho , next to Nagoya-ko subway station, Minato-ku* ☎ *052/654–7000.* **Sakae Tourist Information Center** (オアシス21iセンター *Oashisu Niju-ichi Ai Sentaa*). ⊠ *Oasis 21 Bus Station and Shopping Center, 1–1–1 Higashi-sakura, Higashi-ku* ☎ *052/963–5252.*

ESSENTIALS
Emergency Contacts Kokusai Central Clinic. ⊠ *Nagoya International Center Bldg., 1–47–1 Nagono* ☎ *052/561–0633.* **Nagoya Medical Center.** ⊠ *4–1–1 Sannomaru, Naka-ku* ☎ *052/951–1111.*

Shipping DHL. ⊠ *Nagoya Central Service Point, 2–127 Osu, Minato-ku* ☎ *0120/39–2580* ⊕ *www.dhl.co.jp/en.html.* **Federal Express.** ⊠ *Asaikosan 7, 1–9–57 Chitose, Atsuta-ku* ☎ *0120/00–3200* ⊕ *www.fedex.com.* **Nagoya Central Post Office** (名古屋中央郵便局名古屋駅前分室 *Nagoya Chuo Yubin-kyoku Nagoya-Ekimae Bunshitsu*). ⊠ *Central Nagoya Ekimae Bunshitsu, 4–23–13 Nakamura, Nakamura-ku* ☎ *052/564–2103* ⊕ *www.post.japanpost.jp/english.*

EXPLORING

TOP ATTRACTIONS
Tokugawa Art Museum (徳川美術館 *Tokugawa Bijutsukan*). The seldom-displayed 12th-century hand scrolls of *The Tale of Genji,* widely recognized as the world's first novel, are housed here. Even when the scrolls are not available, beautiful relics of the lifestyle of the aristocratic samurai class—including swords and armor, tea-ceremony artifacts, Noh masks, clothing, and furnishings—fascinate visitors. If you're visiting specifically to see the scrolls, check out the Hosa Library rooms, which house an incredible collection of other ancient scrolls and texts (some 110,000 in all), some dating to the 8th century. If you've got time, it's worth paying an additional ¥150 for entry to the adjacent **Tokuga-waen** 徳川園, an attractive Japanese garden modeled in the Edo style. Tokugawa Art Museum is a 10-minute walk south of Ozone Station, which is on the Meijo subway line and the JR Chuo Line. It's also served by the Me-guru bus, which gives a ¥200 discount on admission for bus pass holders. ⊠ *1017 Tokugawa-cho, Higashi-ku* ☎ *052/935–6262* ⊕ *www.tokugawa-art-museum.jp* ⌸ *¥1,200* ⊙ *Museum early Jan.–mid-Dec., Tues.–Sun. 10–5; garden Tues.–Sun. 9:30–5:30.*

Fodor's Choice ★ **Toyota Plant Tour** (トヨタ工場見学 *Toyota Kojo Migaku*). Dropping in at an automobile factory might not be everyone's idea of holiday fun, but a

The Tokugawa Art Museum in Nagoya owns the original 12th-century scrolls for *The Tale of Genji*.

Toyota Plant Tour makes all those dry books about *kaizen* (improvement) and the Japanese postwar economic miracle come to life. The tour starts at the **Toyota Kaikan** トヨタ会館 (Toyota Exhibition Hall), with impressive exhibits on environmentally friendly technology, safety, and motor sports. Then a bus whisks you to one of several giant factories in the vicinity, where a guide takes you around the main welding and assembly shops—hives of modern manufacturing activity where man and machine operate as one. English guides are available for the two-hour tour. The Kaikan is about 90 minutes from Nagoya Station. Take the JR Tokaido Line Rapid service to Okazaki Station, then the Aichi Kanjo local service to Mikawa-Toyota Station, from where it's a 15-minute walk or 5-minute taxi to the Kaikan. At Okazaki, be sure to get on one of the front two carriages of the Aichi Kanjo Line; only these carriages go as far as Toyota-Mikawa. ■ TIP➔ Reserve tours at least two weeks in advance, and arrive a half hour early. ⊠ *Toyota Kaikan, 1 Toyota-cho, Toyota-cho* ☏ *0565/29–3345* ⊕ *www.toyota.co.jp/en/about_toyota/facility/toyota_kaikan* ⊠ *Free* ☉ *Mon.–Sat. 9:30–5; tours available weekdays.*

WORTH NOTING

Arimatsu-Narumi Shibori Kaikan (有松鳴海絞会館 *Arimatsu Tie-Dyeing Museum*). Traditional *shibori* (tie-dyed cotton) has been produced in this area for more than 400 years. At the Arimatsu-Narumi Tie-Dyeing Museum, you can learn about the history of the dyeing technique and see demonstrations of the production process. The museum sells samples of the cloth, which features striking white designs on the deepest indigo, as well as clothing, tablecloths, and other items. You can also try making your own tie-dyed souvenirs at one of the regular workshops, which require a reservation and cost upward of ¥1,080. Arimatsu Station is 25 minutes south of Nagoya on the Meitetsu Nagoya Line. ✉ *3008 Arimatsu, Arimatsu-cho, Midori-ku* ☎ *052/621–0111* 🌐 *www.shibori-kaikan.com* 🎫 *¥300* ⏲ *Apr.–Nov., daily 9:30–5; Dec.–Mar., Thurs.–Tues. 9:30–5.*

Atsuta Jingu (熱田神宮 *Atsuta Shrine*). A shrine has stood at the site of Atsuta Jingu for 1,700 years. After Ise, this is the country's most important Shinto shrine. The **Homotsukan** 宝物館 (Treasure House) is reputed to house one of the Emperor's three imperial regalia—the Kusanagi-no-Tsurugi (Grass-Mowing Sword)—and although it is never on public display, there are many other worthy artifacts to see. Nestled among 1,000-year-old trees, making it easy to spot from the train, the shrine is an oasis of tradition in the midst of modern industrialism. Dozens of major festivals and religious events are held here each year. From Meitetsu Nagoya Station take the Meitetsu Nagoya Line south to Jingumae Station. The shrine is across the road from the West Exit. ✉ *1–1–1 Jingu, Atsuta-ku* ☎ *052/671–4151* 🌐 *www.atsutajingu.or.jp/en/intro* 🎫 *Shrine free, Treasure House ¥300* ⏲ *Daily 9–4:30; closed last Wed. of month and following Thurs.*

FAMILY **Nagoya City Science Museum** (名古屋市科学館 *Nagoya-shi Kagakukan*). Given a major makeover in 2011, the seven-story Nagoya City Science Museum is packed with fun, hands-on attractions designed to teach kids of all ages about science. The highlights are a planetarium—Japan's biggest—and several visually impressive "labs" where you can experience a tornado, learn about electricity, or feel the Arctic cold. ✉ *17–1–2 Sakae, Naka-ku* ☎ *052/201–4486* 🌐 *www.ncsm.city.nagoya.jp* 🎫 *Museum only ¥400; museum and planetarium ¥800* ⏲ *Tues.–Sun. 9:30–5.*

Nagoya-jo (名古屋城 *Nagoya Castle*). This castle is notable for its size and for the pair of gold-plated dolphins—one male, one female—mounted atop the *donjon* (principal keep). Built on land artificially raised from the flat Nagoya plain, the castle is protected by vast stone walls and two picturesque moats. The current castle is a 1959 reconstruction of the 1612 original, and an elevator whisks you between floors. Between the entrance and the top floor, which has 360-degree views of modern-day Nagoya, are five floors of exhibits. On the third floor is an evocative re-creation of Edo-era streets, complete with sound effects. The fifth floor has several hands-on exhibits, including a full-scale replica of the 2,673-pound female dolphin that you can clamber all over. Inside the east gate a traditional teahouse built of *hinoki* (Japanese cypress) stands in the otherwise unspectacular **Ninomaru Tei-en** 二の丸庭園 (Ninomaru Gardens), where you can break for green tea for ¥500. Also on the grounds is the site of the once **Honmaru Palace**, which is undergoing a rebuild ready for unveiling in 2018; you can tour the construction site (except Tuesday and Thursday) for a close-up look at traditional Japanese construction methods and craftsmanship. Nagoya-jo's east gate is one block north of the Shiyakusho 市役所 (City Hall) subway station. ✉ *Honmaru, 1–1 Honmaru, Nishi-ku* ☎ *052/231–1700* 🌐 *www.nagoyajo.city.nagoya.jp* 🎫 *¥500* ⏲ *Daily 9–4:30.*

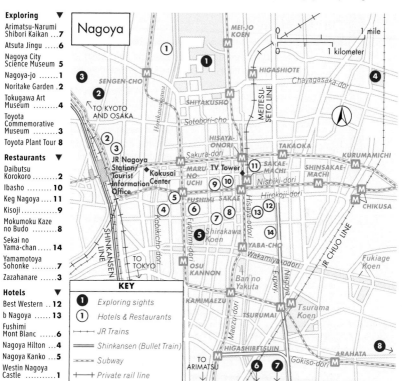

Noritake Garden (ノリタケの森 *Noritake-no-Mori*). Delicate colors and intricate hand-painted designs characterize the china of Noritake, one of the world's largest manufacturers of porcelain. Its garden complex includes a craft center—effectively a mini-factory where workers demonstrate the 15-step manufacturing process from modeling to glazing to hand painting. You can even paint a design and transfer it to a piece of china. Workshops run 10 am to 4 pm and cost from ¥1,800 plus the price of shipping your piece once it has been fired (only plates can be shipped overseas). The upper floors house a small museum displaying "Old Noritake" works with art nouveau and art deco influences. A free Welcome Center shows the diverse industrial applications of ceramics, from circuit boards to racing helmets. There's the odd bargain to be found in the outlet section of the company shop. Noritake Garden is a 15-minute walk north of JR Nagoya Station or 5 minutes from the Kamejima subway station, and can easily be combined with a trip to the nearby Toyota Commemorative Museum. ✉ *3–1–36 Noritake-Shinmachi, Nishi-ku* ☏ *052/561–7114* ⊕ *www.noritake.co.jp/eng/mori* ✄ *¥500; ¥800 includes Toyota Commemorative Museum* ⊙ *Tues.–Sun. 10–5.*

FAMILY **Toyota Commemorative Museum of Industry and Technology** (産業技術記念館 *Sangyo-gijutsu Kinenkan*). Housed in the distinctive brick buildings of the company's original factory, this museum is dedicated to the rise of

CLOSE UP

On the Menu

Nagoya cuisine is considered hearty, and is famous for its *aka miso* (red miso). Dishes featuring this sticky, sweet paste include *misonikomi udon*, thick noodles cooked in an earthenware pot of miso soup with chicken, egg, wood mushrooms, and green onions (you may want the chili pepper served on the side); *hitsumabushi*, chopped eel cooked in miso; and calorie-laden *miso katsu*, pork cutlet with miso-flavored sauce.

Other local specialties include *kishimen*, velvety smooth flat white noodles; *tebasaki*, deep-fried (sometimes spicy) chicken wings; and *uiro*, a sweet cake made of rice powder and sugar, eaten during the tea ceremony. The highly prized *ko-chin* is a specially fattened and extremely tender kind of chicken.

Nagoya's most famous company. Toyota's textile-industry origins are explored in the first of two immense halls, with an amazing selection of looms illustrating the evolution of spinning and weaving technologies over the last 200 years. The second, even larger hall focuses on the company's move into auto manufacturing, with exhibits including the Model AA, Toyota's first mass-production automobile. In the Technoland zone, kids can try out a wind tunnel, play with water and air jets, and test out mini electric cars. The museum is a 20-minute walk north of JR Nagoya Station or 3 minutes from JR Sako Station. ⊠ *4–1–35 Noritake-Shinmachi, Nishi-ku* ☎ *052/551–6115* ⊕ *www.tcmit.org* ✉ ¥*500;* ¥*800 includes Noritake Garden* ⊙ *Tues.–Sun. 9:30–5.*

WHERE TO EAT

Nagoya Station and Sakae have the highest concentrations of restaurants.

$$$$
JAPANESE
✕ **Daibutsu Korokoro** (大仏ころころ). This traditional restaurant has several twists, the main one being the decor. Modern Japanese restaurants should all look like this—dark wood, discreet lighting, and a maze of private dining rooms. A 9½-foot-tall bronze Buddha sits in the center. If anything, the fancy trappings slightly overshadow the food and drink, which includes decent sashimi sets and some inventive tofu dishes, as well as a small but good selection of *shochu* and sake. To make ordering easier, and if you're feeling hungry, consider the ¥4,300 Daibutsu Kaiseki course, which comes with nine dishes (including sashimi and tempura) as well as 90 minutes of all-you-can-drink alcohol (beer, sake, cocktails) and soft drinks. $ *Average main: ¥4000* ⊠ *B1 Kuwayama Bldg., 2–45–19 Meieki, Nakamura-ku* ☎ *052/581–9130* ⊙ *No lunch.*

$$$
JAPANESE
✕ **Ibasho** (いば昇). This fabulous old wooden restaurant serves a Nagoya specialty, *hitsumabushi* (chopped eel smothered in miso sauce and served on rice), which fills the restaurant with a mouthwatering, grilled-charcoal aroma. Some of the seating is at low tables on raised tatami-mat flooring, though there are also rustic tables and chairs overlooking a small Japanese garden. As for the benefits of a night

at Ibasho, locals say eating eel is not only good for curing summer fatigue but also for building up stamina for certain bedroom activities. ■ **TIP→ An English menu is available and it's cash only.** [$] *Average main: ¥2800* ✉ *3–13–22 Nishiki, Naka-ku* ☎ *052/951–1166* 🌐 *www.ibashou.jp* 💳 *No credit cards* 🕒 *Closed Sun. and the 2nd and 3rd Mon. of each month.*

$$$ ECLECTIC 🍴 **Keg Nagoya** (ケグナゴヤ). The focus of this laid-back eatery near Hisaya Odori Station is craft beer, with 13 taps pouring a frequently changing lineup of Japan's best microbrews (look for brands like Baird and Shiga Kogen). You can pair your choice with a good selection of pizzas and more inventive dishes like pork marinated in ale. The only drawback, as with all of Japan's craft pubs, is price: not-quite-pints start at ¥1,050 (a half is ¥680). ■ **TIP→ The whole pub is smoke-free, which is still quite uncommon in Japan.** [$] *Average main: ¥3000* ✉ *10–13–1 Higashisakura, Higashi-ku* ☎ *052/971–8211.*

$$$$ JAPANESE 🍴 **Kisoji** (木曽路). Come here for reasonably priced *shabu-shabu*—thinly sliced beef and vegetables that you boil in broth in the center of your table and then dip into various sauces before eating. Set courses run from ¥4,800 to ¥10,000. Sukiyaki courses and decent sushi and sashimi sets are also available. There are Western-style tables and chairs, but waitresses wear kimonos and serve with all the attention and poise you would expect in a traditional Japanese restaurant. ■ **TIP→ There are half a dozen other branches around Nagoya, including one in Sakae.** [$] *Average main: ¥7000* ✉ *3–20–15 Nishiki, Naka-ku* ☎ *052/951–3755.*

$$ JAPANESE 🍴 **Mokumoku Kaze no Budo** (モクモク風の葡萄). In a perfect world, all school and office canteens would be a bit more like this. For ¥2,300 (¥1,800 at lunchtime) you get all you can eat from a generously stocked buffet of healthy vegetable, fish, and meat dishes, plus drinks and dessert, all made from locally sourced produce. There are also all-you-can-drink options that include organic wine and local beer (from ¥1,050). It is on the seventh floor of La Chic mall in Sakae. [$] *Average main: ¥2000* ✉ *7F La Chic, 3–6–1 Sakae, Naka-ku* ☎ *052/241–0909.*

$$ JAPANESE 🍴 **Sekai no Yama-chan** (世界の山ちゃん). Pepper-coated *tebasaki* (deep-fried chicken wings) are the specialty at the main branch of Nagoya's best-known izakaya chain, though you can also order sashimi and other favorites. With most dishes costing around ¥400 to ¥500, the prices are affordable. This no-frills place mixes traditional and Western-style seating, and the atmosphere is lively. To avoid the worst of the cigarette smoke that will inevitably be coming from other tables, ask for a seat in the small nonsmoking area. [$] *Average main: ¥2000* ✉ *4–9–6 Sakae, Naka-ku* ☎ *052/242–1342* 🕒 *No lunch.*

$$ JAPANESE 🍴 **Yamamotoya Sohonke** (山本屋総本家). *M isonikomi udon* (noodles in a miso-based broth with green onions and mushrooms) dominates the menu at this simple, almost rustic restaurant. A big, steaming bowl of this hearty, cold-chasing specialty starts at ¥976. Pay a little extra to top it off with something like a raw egg, or opt for a side dish like yakitori chicken. [$] *Average main: ¥1000* ✉ *3–12–19 Sakae, Naka-ku* ☎ *052/241–5617* 💳 *No credit cards.*

5

$$$$ ✕ **Zazahanare** (座座はなれ). Head to this plush traditional izakaya near
JAPANESE Nagoya Station for a variety of local flavors that include Nagoya favorites *tebasaki* (chicken wings), *hitsumabushi* (char-grilled eel), *kishimen*
noodles, and miso-coated pork cutlets. To make ordering easy, consider
the ¥4,000 Nagoya *meibutsu* set, which includes a little of everything
listed above. Also on the menu is a good selection of sake, as well as
more common izakaya fare such as tofu and sashimi. Most seating is
at dark wooden tables on tatami mats in the large main dining hall, but
there are also some intimate private rooms available. $ *Average main:*
¥4000 ✉ *3–13–13 Mieki, Nakamura-ku* ☎ *052/562–9995* ⊕ *www.*
zazahanare.com.

WHERE TO STAY

Nagoya's hotels are concentrated in three major areas: the district
around JR Nagoya Station, downtown Fushimi and Sakae, and the
Nagoya-jo area.

$$ ⊞ **Best Western Hotel Nagoya** (ベストウェスタンホテル名古屋). Bridging
HOTEL the gap between straightforward business hotels and top-of-the-line
lodgings, this hotel garners good reviews from Japanese travelers. **Pros:**
convenient location for shoppers and party animals; good discounts
with online booking. **Cons:** budget travelers will find cheaper rooms
elsewhere; has limited facilities for the price. $ *Rooms from: ¥13300*
✉ *4–6–1 Sakae, Naka-ku* ☎ *052/263–3411* ⊕ *www.nagoya.bwhotels.*
jp ⤢ *140 rooms* ⦿ *Breakfast.*

$ ⊞ **b Nagoya.** The Nagoya branch of this relatively new, but growing
HOTEL business hotel chain combines an excellent central location in Sakae
(on Hisaya-odori) with good value rates. **Pros:** good discounts book-
ing online; good rates on singles for solo travelers. **Cons:** can get a bit
noisy; rooms will be too compact for some. $ *Rooms from: ¥7900*
✉ *4–15–23 Sakae, Naka-ku* ☎ *052/264–1732* ⊕ *www.theb-hotels.com*
⤢ *219 rooms* ⦿ *Breakfast.*

$ ⊞ **Fushimi Mont Blanc Hotel** (伏見モンブランホテル). Centrally located
HOTEL and affordably priced, this business hotel is a good alternative when
you're looking to save a few yen. **Pros:** inexpensive rates; good front
desk service; less than 10 minutes from central Sakae. **Cons:** rooms feel
a little claustrophobic; can be noisy at times. $ *Rooms from: ¥7800*
✉ *2–2–26 Sakae, Naka-ku* ☎ *052/232–1121* ⊕ *www.montblanc-hotel.*
co.jp ⤢ *145 rooms* ⦿ *No meals.*

$$$$ ⊞ **Nagoya Hilton** (ヒルトン名古屋). This large business hotel, albeit slightly
HOTEL expensive, always gets good guest reviews for service and location and it's
a reliable option in Nagoya. **Pros:** attentive and flexible staff; convenient
location; excellent restaurants. **Cons:** Internet costs extra; slightly better
rooms available elsewhere for a comparable fee, but rooms are being
renovated. $ *Rooms from: ¥23000* ✉ *1–3–3 Sakae, Naka-ku* ☎ *052/212–*
1111 ⊕ *www.hilton.com* ⤢ *434 rooms, 16 suites* ⦿ *Breakfast.*

$$$$ ⊞ **Nagoya Kanko Hotel** (名古屋観光ホテル). The Imperial Family is
HOTEL among those served by the city's oldest hotel, which is also a haunt for
Fodor's Choice celebrities in search of a little privacy. **Pros:** exceptional service; free
★ parking; great central location. **Cons:** the old-fashioned elegance won't

be to everyone's taste; the atmosphere could feel too formal. $ *Rooms from:* ¥24000 ✉ *1–19–30 Nishiki, Naka-ku* ☎ *052/231–7711* ⊕ *www. nagoyakankohotel.co.jp* ⇄ *375 rooms, 7 suites* ⦿ *Breakfast.*

$$$$ 🖼 **The Westin Nagoya Castle** (ウェスティンナゴヤキャッスルホテル).
HOTEL Perched on the edge of Nagoya Castle's moat, this hotel has a more relaxed atmosphere than some of the other places in the center of the city and your room might overlook the beautiful white fortress, which is illuminated at night. **Pros:** close to the castle; early check-in is perfect for sightseers; good facilities and restaurants. **Cons:** inconvenient for everywhere except the castle; in a quiet part of town. $ *Rooms from:* ¥28000 ✉ *3–19 Hinokuchi-cho, Nishi-ku* ☎ *052/521–2121* ⊕ *www. castle.co.jp/wnc* ⇄ *191 rooms, 5 suites* ⦿ *Some meals.*

NIGHTLIFE

Sakae has a high concentration of bars and clubs appealing to pleasure seekers of all stripes. Most of the good bars are to be found in the narrow streets to the southwest of the Sakae subway station and in the immediate vicinity of the TV tower. Avoid a "snack" establishment (a kind of hostess club) unless you've got money to burn on overpriced drinks and female company.

Nagoya attracts international DJs, although you might have to head out on a weekday night to catch the biggest names. Expect to pay between ¥1,500 and ¥2,500 for admission (usually including a couple of drinks).

Elephant's Nest. Close to Exit 5 of the Fushimi subway station, this popular English pub has Guinness on tap, frequent challenges on the dartboards, and live soccer on the telly. The food, including traditional fish-and-chips, is okay. Happy hour is 5:30 to 7. ✉ *1–4–3 Sakae, Naka-ku* ☎ *052/232–4360.*

iD Café. A young crowd gathers at this wild, five-floor club, where the music ranges from techno and trance to reggae and hip-hop. Admission ranges from ¥1,500 to ¥2,000, depending on the event, and typically includes one or two free drinks. ✉ *Mitsukoshi Bldg., 3–1–15 Sakae, Naka-ku* ☎ *052/251–0382* ⊕ *www.idcafe.info.*

Marumikanko Building (丸美観光ビル). Two of the city's best clubs can be found in this building, two blocks south of Hirokoji-dori. Café Domina, in the basement, leans toward more abstract and bass-heavy fare. Club JB's, also in the basement, is a stronghold for house and techno. ✉ *4–3–15 Sakae, Naka-ku.*

SPORTS

In Nagoya you will find Japanese sports fans just as entertaining as the action on the field. Ask at Tourist Information about upcoming events and where to buy tickets.

BASEBALL

The Chunichi Dragons play home games at the 40,500-capacity Nagoya Dome. Two leagues of six teams make up Japanese professional baseball, and the Dragons have won the Central League pennant eight times and the Japan Series twice. In recent years the team is in a groove, reaching the Japan Series in 2004 and 2006 before finally winning it—for the first time since 1954—in 2007. They came close again in 2010 and 2011, losing both Japan Series in game seven. Fans here are a bit different—they sing well-drilled songs for each of the batters on their own team, but sit in stony silence when the opposing team is at bat. The season runs from late March to October, and tickets for the upper-tier "Panorama" seats start at ¥1,500, rising to ¥5,800 for those behind home plate. Other than when a big team such as the Yomiuri Giants or Hanshin Tigers is in town, tickets are usually available at the stadium.

SOCCER

The remarkably loyal fans who turn up in the thousands to cheer on Nagoya Grampus finally had something to cheer about in 2010, as the team romped to a first J-League Division One title. Until then, Grampus had a reputation as perennial underachievers, always seeming to hang around mid-table in J-League 1—despite having had star players such as Gary Lineker and Dragan Stojkovic (now the head coach)—and managing a couple of Emperor's Cup wins in the 1990s. However, despite being runners-up in 2011, mid-table mediocrity has once again returned. From March to December they play half their home games in Nagoya at the 20,000-seat Mizuho Stadium, where the running track dissipates the atmosphere, and half at the futuristic 45,000-seat Toyota Stadium, which also hosts some national team games. Tickets on game day range in price from ¥2,300 to ¥7,200

SUMO

Nagoya Grand Sumo Tournament (大相撲名古屋場所 *Oozumou Nagoya Basho*). In mid-July, Nagoya's Aichi Prefectural Gymnasium hosts one of the three sumo tournaments held outside Tokyo each year. The arena holds 8,000 people, and you are almost guaranteed a good view of the *dohyo* (ring). Tickets, which start at ¥3,500, are often available on the day of the tournament, but it's better to book ahead. The venue is a two-minute walk from Exit 7 of the Shiyakusho subway station. ⊠ *Aichi Prefectural Gymnasium, 1–1 Ninomaru, Naka-ku* ☏ *052/971–2516* ⊕ *www.sumo.or.jp.*

SOUTH GIFU-KEN

Old Japan resonates in the foothills of the Hida Sanmyaku 飛騨山脈 (*Hida Mountains*), just north of Nagoya. Ancient customs and crafts, such as cormorant fishing and umbrella-, lantern-, pottery-, and sword making, are still practiced, and the nation's oldest castle, Inuyama-jo, has seen it all for almost 500 years. Gifu is the main center of *ukai* (cormorant fishing). Inuyama also offers the fishing experience, and it boasts a superior castle and, in Meiji-mura, an outstanding museum.

GIFU 岐阜

30 km (18 miles) northwest of Nagoya.

Gifu's main attraction is its 1,300-year tradition of *ukai* fishing, which uses live birds to catch fish in the river. The city center spreads several blocks north from the JR and Meitetsu stations. Extensive rebuilding after World War II didn't create the prettiest place, but there is plenty going on. *Wagasa* (oiled paper umbrellas) are handmade in small family-owned shops, and *chochin* (paper lanterns) and lacquered *uchiwa* fans are also produced locally. If you are interested in seeing these items being made, ask Tourist Information for workshops that allow visitors.

Between May 11 and October 15, you can watch cormorant fishing from the banks of the river just east of Nagara Bridge at around 7:30 pm each evening. Or you can buy a ticket on one of about 130 boats, each carrying between 10 and 30 spectators. Allow two hours for an ukai outing—an hour and a half to eat and drink (bring your own food if you haven't arranged for dinner) and a half hour to watch the fishing. The ¥3,400 boat trips depart at 6:15 pm and 6:45 pm nightly; reservations, made through the Gifu City Cormorant Fishing Sightseeing Office or the Tourist Information Center, are essential. There's no fishing on the autumn full moon.

GETTING HERE AND AROUND
Gifu is a 20-minute ride on the JR Tokaido Line (¥470) or 30-minute ride on the Meitetsu Nagoya Line (¥550) from Nagoya. Gifu Park, in and around which most of the main attractions are centered, is 15 minutes by bus (numbers N32, N80, or N86) or 30 minutes on foot north from JR Gifu Station.

A city Tourist Information Office is on the second floor of the train station, just outside the ticket gates.

ESSENTIALS
Gifu City Cormorant Fishing Boat Office (岐阜市鵜飼観覧船事務所 *Gifu-shi Ukai Kanransen Jimusho*). ⊠ *2–1 Minato-machi* ☎ *058/262–0104.*

Gifu Tourist Information Office (岐阜市観光案内所 *Gifu-shi Kankou Annai-jyo*). ⊠ *JR Gifu Station, 1–10–1 Hashimoto-cho* ☎ *058/262–4415* ⊕ *travel.kankou-gifu.jp* ☙ *Dec.–Feb., daily 9–6; Mar.–Nov., daily 9–7.*

EXPLORING
FAMILY **Gifu City Museum of History** (岐阜市歴史博物館 *Gifu-shi Rekishi Hakubut-sukan*). In Gifu Park, five minutes south of the cable-car station, sits this well-presented hands-on-museum. On the second floor you can dress up in traditional clothing and play old Japanese games such as *bansu-goroku* (similar to backgammon). ⊠ *2–18–1 Omiya-cho* ☎ *058/265–0010* ☙ *¥300* ☙ *Tues.–Sun. 9–5.*

Gifu-jo (岐阜城 *Gifu Castle*). This castle, perched dramatically on top of Mt. Kinka, overlooks the city center and Nagara River. It's especially attractive when it's illuminated at night and when the mountain changes color in the fall. The current building dates from 1951; the 16th-century structure was destroyed by an 1891 earthquake. A cable-car ride up from Gifu Park (¥1,080 round-trip) gets you to the castle in 10 minutes, or you can walk the 2.3-km (1.5-mile) path to the 1,079-foot summit in about an hour. Take bus N32, N80, or N86 to Gifu Park (15 minutes, ¥210). ⊠ *Omiya-cho* ☎ *058/263–4853* ☙ *¥210* ☙ *Mar. 16–May 11, daily 9–5:30; May 12–Oct. 16, daily 8:30–5:30; Oct. 17–Mar. 15, daily 9:30–4:30.*

Nagara River Ukai Museum (長良川うかいミュージアム *Nagaragawa Ukai Myujiamu*). Learn about the history of *ukai* fishing, in which fishermen use live cormorants to catch river fish, and the lives of the odd-looking birds at the center of it, at this smart museum alongside the Nagara River. It's near the Ryokan Sugiyama, a six-minute walk from the Ukai-ya bus stop. ✉ *51–2 Nagara* ☎ *058/210–1555* 🌐 *ukaimuseum.jp* 🎫 *¥500* 🕘 *May–mid-Oct., daily 9–7; mid-Oct.–Apr., Wed.–Mon. 9–5.*

FAMILY **Nawa Insect Museum** (名和昆虫博物館 *Nawa Konchu Hakubutsukan*). Located in Gifu Park, this small museum houses disturbingly large beetles, colorful butterflies, and other bugs. It's ideal for kids into gross creepy-crawlies. ✉ *2–18 Omiya-cho* ☎ *058/263–0038* 🎫 *¥500* 🕘 *Mar.–Nov., Fri.–Tues. 10–5; Dec.–Feb., Fri.–Mon. 9–5.*

OFF THE BEATEN PATH

Seki Sword Tradition Museum (関鍛冶伝承館 *Seki Kaji Denshokan*). Seki has a 700-year-old sword-manufacturing heritage, and you'll appreciate the artistry and skill of Japanese sword smiths at this museum. Three types of metal are used to form blades, which are forged multiple times and then beaten into shape with a hammer. Demonstrations are held on January 2 and the first Sunday of March, April, June, and November. Special displays occur during the Seki Cutlery Festival the second weekend of October. Seki is 30 minutes northeast of Gifu via the Meitetsu Minomachi Line. ✉ *9–1 Minamikasuga-cho, Seki* ☎ *0575/23–3825* 🎫 *¥200* 🕘 *Wed.–Mon. 9–4:30.*

Shoho-ji (正法寺 *Shoho Temple*). This small temple is rather run-down, but it houses Japan's third-largest Buddha, which you can often view with no other visitors in sight. This imposing incarnation of Shaka Nyorai (Great Buddha) is 45 feet tall and constructed of pasted-together paper *sutra* (prayers) coated with clay and stucco and then lacquered and gilded; it took 38 years to complete. From Gifu Park, walk two blocks south. ✉ *8 Daibutsu-cho* ☎ *058/264–2760* 🎫 *¥200* 🕘 *Daily 9–5.*

WHERE TO EAT AND STAY

$$ JAPANESE 🍴 **U no Iori U** (鵜の庵鵜). Cormorants strut around the Japanese garden outside this café, where the specialty is *ayu* (sweetfish). The owner boasts of upholding the 1,300-year-old local ukai tradition, and the ayu are prepared every way imaginable. Most popular are *ayu-zosui*, a rice porridge, and *ayu-no-narezushi*, a kind of reverse sushi with the ayu stuffed full of rice. It is 1½ blocks west of Ryokan Sugiyama. [$] *Average main: ¥1500* ✉ *94–10 Naka-Ukai, Nagara* ☎ *058/232–2839* 💳 *No credit cards* 🕘 *Closed 2nd and 4th Sun., 1st, 3rd, and 5th Mon. No dinner.*

$ HOTEL 🏨 **Hotel Resol Gifu** (ホテルリソル岐阜). Situated one block north of JR Gifu Station, this conveniently located hotel comes with larger-than-average Western-style rooms and some of the best views in Gifu. **Pros:** spacious rooms; lovely views; close to station. **Cons:** often booked up well in advance; rather bland modern interiors. [$] *Rooms from: ¥6800* ✉ *5–8 Nagazumi-cho* ☎ *058/262–9269* 🌐 *www.resol-gifu.com* 🛏 *119 rooms* 🍽 *Breakfast.*

$$$$ B&B/INN 🏨 **Ryokan Sugiyama** (旅館すぎ山). Across the Nagara River from Gifu Castle, Ryoken Sugiyama is a tasteful blend of traditional and modern. **Pros:** good food; ideally positioned for ukai watchers; good deals on

Nighttime cormorant fishing (called *ukai* 鵜飼) is a top attraction in Gifu.

weekends. **Cons:** not cheap as meals are included; decor a little threadbare in places. [$] *Rooms from: ¥32000* ✉ *73–1 Nagara* ☎ *058/231–0161* 🌐 *www.gifu-sugiyama.com* 🛏 *45 rooms* 🍴 *Some meals.*

INUYAMA 犬山

22 km (14 miles) east of Gifu, 32 km (20 miles) north of Nagoya.

Inuyama sits along the Kiso River, on the border between Aichi and Gifu prefectures. A historically strategic site, the city changed hands several times during the Edo period. You can see cormorant fishing here from June 1 to October 15; tickets are available from major hotels for ¥2,600 to ¥5,000.

GETTING HERE AND AROUND

Access Inuyama on the Meitetsu Kakamigahara Line via Gifu or on the Meitetsu Inuyama Line via Nagoya. A good way to see the Kiso-gawa is on a tame raft. To travel the hour-long, 13-km (8-mile) river trip, take the very brief trip on the Meitetsu Inuyama Line from Inuyama to Inuyama Koen. Several companies, including Kisogawa Ukai, offer trips between March 10 and November 11. Call the Tourist Information Office in the station for information on traveling the river and fishing.

Contacts Inuyama Tourist Information Office (犬山観光案内所 *Inuyama Kankou Annaijyo*). ✉ *Inuyama Station, 14 Inuyama-fujimi-cho* ☎ *0568/61–6000* 🌐 *ml.inuyama.gr.jp.* **Kisogawa Ukai.** ☎ *0574/28–2727* 🌐 *www.kisogawa-ukai.jp.*

EXPLORING

Inuyama-jo (犬山城 *Inuyama Castle*). Inuyama's most famous sight is Inuyama Castle, also known as Hakutei-jo (White Emperor Castle). Built in 1537, it is the oldest of the 12 original castles in Japan. The exceedingly pretty castle stands amid carefully tended grounds on a bluff overlooking the Kiso River. Climb up the creaky staircases to the top floor for a great view of the river, city, and surrounding hills. The gift shops at the foot of the castle hill are good for browsing. From Inuyama-Yuen Eki, walk southwest along the river for 15 minutes. ✉ *65–2 Kita-koken* ☎ *0568/61–1711* 🌐 *inuyama-castle.jp* 🎫 *¥550* 🕒 *Daily 9–4:30.*

Jo-an Teahouse (茶室如庵 *Chashitsu Jo-an*). In Uraku-en, a traditional garden attached to the grounds of the Meitetsu Inuyama Hotel, sits the Jo-an Teahouse. The teahouse was constructed in Kyoto in 1618 and moved to its present site in 1971. Admission to the garden is pricey, so it's worth paying an extra ¥600 to be served green tea in the traditional style. Uraku-en is less than ½ km (¼ mile) from Inuyama-jo, behind the Meitetsu Inuyama Hotel. ✉ *1 Gomon-saki* ☎ *0568/61–4608* 🎫 *¥1,000* 🕒 *Mar.–mid-July and Sept.–Dec., daily 9–5; Jan.–Feb., daily 9–4; mid-July–Aug., daily 9–6.*

Fodor's Choice ★ **Meiji-mura Museum** (明治村 *Hakubutsukan Meiji-mura*). Considered one of Japan's best museums, Meiji-mura has more than 60 buildings originally constructed during the Meiji era (1868–1912), when Japan ended its policy of isolationism and swiftly industrialized. The best way to experience the exhibits is to wander about, stopping at things that catch your eye. There's an English pamphlet to help guide you. If you get tired of walking, hop on a tram originally from Kyoto, a steam train from Yokohama, and an old village bus; a ¥1,200 pass covers all three. Among the exhibits are a surprisingly beautiful octagonal wood prison from Kanazawa, a Kabuki theater from Osaka that hosts occasional performances, and the former homes of renowned writers Soseki Natsume and Lafcadio Hearn. The lobby of legendary American architect Frank Lloyd Wright's Imperial Hotel, where Charlie Chaplin and Marilyn Monroe were once guests, is arguably the highlight. It opened on the day of the Great Kanto Earthquake in 1923, 11 years after the death of Emperor Meiji, and though it is not strictly a Meiji-era building, its sense of grandeur and history are truly unique. Buses run from Inuyama Station to Meiji-mura two to three times an hour from 9 to 4. The ride takes 20 minutes and costs ¥420. ✉ *1 Uchiyama* ☎ *0568/67–0314* 🌐 *www.meijimura.com* 🎫 *¥1,600* 🕒 *Mar.–Oct., daily 9:30–5; Nov.–Dec., daily 9:30–4; Jan.–Feb, Tues.–Sun. 9:30–4.*

WHERE TO STAY

$$ HOTEL 🏨 **Meitetsu Inuyama Hotel** (名鉄犬山ホテル). On the south bank of the Kiso River, this hotel has winning views of the castle and the surrounding hills. **Pros:** convenient for accessing local sights; excellent on-site hot-spring baths; great views. **Cons:** younger travelers are likely to feel a little out of place; room and restaurant interiors are fairly characterless. [$] *Rooms from: ¥13500* ✉ *107–1 Kita-koken* ☎ *0568/61–2211,* 🌐 *www.m-inuyama-h.co.jp* 🛏 *92 Western-style rooms, 34 Japanese-style rooms* 🍴 *Some meals.*

HIKING

Tsugao-san (継鹿尾山 *Mount Tsugao*). To get here, start on the riverside trail at the base of Inuyama Castle. Follow the paved trail east past the best-avoided Monkey Park, then north to Jakko Temple (built in AD 654), where the maples blaze in fall. Along the route are good views of the foothills stretching north from the banks of the Kiso-gawa. You can climb Tsugao-san or continue northeast to Obora Pond and southeast to Zenjino Station, where you can catch the Meitetsu Hiromi Line two stops back to Inuyama Station. The train passes through Zenjino at least three times an hour. From Inuyama-jo to Zenjino Station is an 8-km (5-mile) hike. Allow 2½ hours from the castle to the top of Tsugao-san; add another hour if you continue to Zenjino via Obora Pond. ⊠ *Inuyama.*

IGA UENO 伊賀上野

95 km (59 miles) southwest of Nagoya, 67 km (42 miles) east of Kyoto, 39 km (24 miles) east of Nara, 88 km (55 miles) east of Osaka.

This small city halfway between Nagoya and Nara has some interesting claims to fame. Noted haiku poet Matsuo Basho was born here in the 1640s, and it was home to one of Japan's leading ninja schools. Iga Ueno is accessible from Nagoya, Kyoto, Nara, and Osaka on JR lines.

EXPLORING

FAMILY **Iga-Ryu Ninja Museum** (伊賀流忍者博物館 *Iga Ryu Ninja Hakubutsukan*). The Iga-Ryu school of *ninjutsu* (ninja arts) was one of the top two training centers for Japan's ancient spies and assassins in the 14th century. At the ninja residence, a guide in traditional dress explains how they were always prepared for attack. The hidden doors and secret passages are ingenious, but it can't have been a relaxed existence. Energetic demonstrations of ninja weapons like throwing stars, swords, daggers, and sickles are fun, and for an extra fee you can try out the throwing star (¥200) or even dress up as a ninja (¥1,000). One special exhibit gives you some background on ninja history and techniques, while another displays the disguises and encryption used here, as well as the inventive tools that enabled them to walk on water and scale sheer walls. The museum is in Ueno Park, a 10-minute walk up the hill from Uenoshi Station. ⊠ *117–13–1 Ueno Marunouchi* ☎ *0595/23–0311* ⊕ *www. iganinja.jp/en* ☑ *¥756* ⊙ *Daily 9–5; times and days for demonstrations of weapons vary, so check website.*

Iga Ueno-jo (伊賀上野城 *Iga Ueno Castle*). This castle stands today because of one man's determination and wealth. The first castle built here was destroyed by a rainstorm in 1612, before it was completed. More than 300 years later, local resident Katsu Kawasaki financed a replica that sits atop vertiginous 98-foot stone walls—be careful when it's windy. Kawasaki also paid for the Haiku Poetry Master's Pavilion, built in memory of Japan's famous wandering poet, Matsuo Basho, which stands near the castle in Ueno Park. ⊠ *106 Ueno-marunouchi* ☎ *0595/21–3148* ☑ *¥500* ⊙ *Daily 9–5.*

ISE-SHIMA NATIONAL PARK 伊勢志摩国立公園 (ISE-SHIMA KOKURITSU KOEN)

Hanging like a fin underneath central Honshu, Ise-Shima is a scenic and sacred counterweight to Japan's overbuilt industrial corridor. Ise-Shima National Park, which holds the supremely venerated shrines of Ise Jingu, extends east from Ise to Toba (the center of the pearl industry), and south to the indented coastline and pine-clad islands near Kashikojima. The bottom hook of the peninsula, around to Goza via Daio, has some of the prettiest coves on the Ago Bay, each one home to oyster nets and small groups of fishing boats.

ISE 伊勢

107 km (66 miles) south of Nagoya, 158 km (98 miles) east of Kyoto, 127 km (79 miles) east of Nara, 143 km (89 miles) east of Osaka.

When you step off the train, you may feel that Ise is a drab city, but hidden in two forests of towering cedar trees are the most important and impressive Shinto shrines in Japan. Indeed, the city's income comes mainly from the pilgrims who visit Geku 外宮 and Naiku 内宮, the Outer and Inner shrines, respectively. Near the Inner Shrine you'll find an array of shops hawking souvenirs to the busloads of tourists and a few spots to eat such local specialties as *Ise udon* (udon noodles with a thick broth) and *akafuku* (sweet rice cakes). The busiest times at Ise Jingu are during the Grand Festival, held over a weekend in mid-October every year, when crowds gather to see the pageantry, and on New Year's Eve and Day, when hundreds of thousands come to pray for good fortune.

GETTING HERE AND AROUND

Ise can be reached from Kyoto, Nara, and Osaka by the JR and Kintetsu lines, with the latter's Limited Express service from Nagoya being the fastest option. The city has two stations five minutes apart, Ise-Shi (JR and Kintetsu) and Uji-Yamada (Kintetsu only). From either station it's a 10-minute walk through town to the Outer Shrine. A frequent shuttle bus makes the 6-km (4-mile) trip between Geku and Naiku; a bus also goes directly from the Inner Shrine to Uji-Yamada Station.

You can arrange a full-day tour to Ise and the Mikimoto Pearl Island at Toba from Nagoya (¥28,800) through JTB Sunrise Tours, although visiting just Ise from Nagoya by yourself is fairly straightforward.

Ise Tourist Information Center is across the street from the Outer Shrine, and has information about both Ise and the surrounding area.

Contacts Ise Tourist Information Center (伊勢市観光案内所 *Ise-shi Kankou Annaijyo*). ✉ *14–6 Honmachi* ☎ *0596/23–3323* ⊕ *www.ise-kanko.jp.* **JTB Sunrise Tours Central Japan.** ☎ *052/211–3065* ⊕ *www.jtb-sunrisetours.jp.*

EXPLORING

Fodor'sChoice ★ **Geku** (外宮). Deep in a park of ancient Japanese cedars, Geku, dating from AD 477, is dedicated to Toyouke Omikami, goddess of agriculture. Its buildings are simple, predating the influx of 6th-century Chinese and

Korean influence. It's made from unpainted hinoki (cypress), with a closely cropped thatched roof. You can see very little of the exterior of Geku—only its roof and glimpses of its walls—and none of the interior. Four fences surround the shrine, and only the Imperial Family and their envoys may enter. Geku is a 5-minute walk southwest of Ise-Shi Station or a 10-minute walk west of Uji-Yamada Station. ⊠ *279 Toyokawa-machi* ⊕ *www.isejingu.or.jp/english* ✉ *Free* ☉ *Daily sunrise–sunset.*

Fodor's Choice **Ise Jingu** (伊勢神宮 *Grand Shrines of Ise*). These shrines are rebuilt every
★ 20 years, in accordance with Shinto tradition. To begin a new generational cycle, exact replicas of the previous halls are erected with new wood, using the same centuries-old methods, on adjacent sites. The old buildings are then dismantled. The main halls you see now—the 62nd set—were completed in 2013 at an estimated cost of more than ¥5.5 billion. For the Japanese, importance is found in the form of the buildings; the vintage of the materials is of little concern. You cannot enter any of the buildings, but the tantalizing glimpses of the main halls that you catch while walking the grounds add to the mystique of the site. Both Grand Shrines exhibit a natural harmony that the more-contrived buildings in later Japanese architecture do not. ⊠ *Ise* ⊕ *www.isejingu.or.jp/english* ✉ *Free* ☉ *Daily sunrise–sunset.*

Fodor's Choice **Naiku** (内宮). The even more venerated **Naiku** is 6 km (4 miles) south-
★ west of Geku. Naiku is said to be where the Yata-no-Kagami (Sacred Mirror) is kept, one of the three sacred treasures of the imperial regalia. The shrine, reputed to date from 4 BC, also houses the spirit of the sun goddess Amaterasu, who Japanese mythology says was born of the left eye of Izanagi, one of the first two gods to inhabit the earth. According to legend, Amaterasu was the great-great-grandmother of the first mortal emperor of Japan, Jimmu. Thus, she is revered as the country's ancestral goddess-mother and guardian deity. The Inner Shrine's architecture is simple. If you did not know its origin, you might call it classically modern. The use of unpainted cypress causes Naiku to blend into the ancient forest encircling it. To get to Naiku, take Bus 51 or 55 from Uji-Yamada Station or in front of Geku to the Naiku-mae bus stop, which is right in front of the shrine. The ride takes about 20 minutes. ⊠ *1 Uji-kan-machi* ⊕ *www.isejingu.or.jp/english* ✉ *Free* ☉ *Daily sunrise–sunset.*

WHERE TO EAT AND STAY

$$$$ ✕ **Izakaya Toramaru** (虎丸). This traditional restaurant doesn't open on
JAPANESE days when there's not a delivery of fresh fish, which tells you how seriously the cooks take their food. Though it has a fairly diverse menu, the main draw here is the expertly prepared sashimi, served in haphazardly shaped pottery dishes. Ask the staff to recommend a libation from the extensive selection of Japanese sake and shochu. Izakaya Toramaru is housed in a replica warehouse two blocks east of Hoshide-kan. $ *Average main: ¥4000* ⊠ *2-13-6 Kawasaki* ☎ *0596/22–9298* ▭ *No credit cards* ☉ *Closed Thurs. No lunch.*

$$$$ ✕ **Restaurant Wadakin** (和田金). If you love beef, make a pilgrimage to
JAPANESE Matsusaka, one express train stop north of Ise. Wadakin claims to be the originator of Matsusaka beef's fame; the cattle are raised with loving care on the restaurant's farm out in the countryside. Sukiyaki or the

The Grand Shrine of Ise is rebuilt every 20 years, in accordance with the Shinto tradition.

chef's steak dinner will satisfy your cravings. Advance reservations are highly recommended. [$] *Average main: ¥12000* ✉ *1878 Naka-machi, Matsusaka* ☎ *0598/21–1188* 🌐 *e-wadakin.co.jp* 🕒 *Daily 11:30–8* 🕒 *Closed 4th Tues. of month and 1st Tues. in Dec.*

$ B&B/INN 🏨 **Hoshide-kan.** Almost a century old, this traditional inn has wood-decorated tatami rooms and narrow, squeaking corridors. **Pros:** foreigner friendly; good location; charming building. **Cons:** area is quiet after dark; at the mercy of the elements in summer and winter; shared bathing facilities. [$] *Rooms from: ¥11500* ✉ *2–15–2 Kawasaki* ☎ *0596/28–2377* 🌐 *www.hoshidekan.jp* 🛏 *10 Japanese-style rooms with shared bath* 🍴 *Some meals.*

KASHIKOJIMA 賢島

25 km (16 miles) south of Toba, 145 km (90 miles) south of Nagoya.

GETTING HERE AND AROUND

Kashikojima can be reached on the Kintetsu Line from Toba (¥470; 39 minutes) or Nagoya (¥3,580; just over 2 hours) or by bus from Toba. It's possible to follow the coast from Kashikojima to the Kii Peninsula, but there is no train, and in many places the road cuts inland, making the journey long and tedious. From Kashikojima or Toba you are better off taking the Kintetsu Line back to Ise to change to the JR Sangu Line and travel to Taki, where you can take the JR Kisei Line south to the Kii Peninsula.

EXPLORING

The jagged coastline at Ago-wan (Ago Bay), with calm waters and countless hidden coves, presents a dramatic final view of the Ise Peninsula. The best approach to Kashikojima is to catch a bus to Goza, the tip of the headland, and ride a ferry back across the bay. From the boat you'll get a close-up look at the hundreds of floating wooden rafts from which the pearl-bearing oysters are suspended.

Daio (大王). Tucked behind a promontory, this fishing village is an interesting stop on the journey around the headland. At a small fish market you can sample fresh squid, mackerel, and other seafood. Standing above the village is **Daiozaki todai** 大王崎灯台, a 72-feet tall lighthouse built in 1927 that's open to visitors daily from 9 to 4. Admission is ¥200. To reach this towering white structure, walk up the narrow street lined with fish stalls and pearl souvenir shops at the back of the harbor. ✉ *Kashikojima* 🌐 *www.daiozaki.com.*

5

WHERE TO STAY

$ B&B/INN 🏨 **Daioso** (大王荘). Staying at this small, family-run ryokan next to the harbor in Daio allows you to enjoy the peaceful evening after the tourists have left and witness the early-morning activity of the fishermen. **Pros:** reasonably priced; on the harbor; good if you like fish. **Cons:** some spoken Japanese essential; Western-style rooms are drab. [$] *Rooms from: ¥9200* ✉ *244 Namigiri, Shima-gun* ☎ *0599/72–1234* 🛏 *3 Western-style rooms, 4 Japanese-style rooms, 2 with bath* 🍴 *Some meals.*

$ B&B/INN 🏨 **Ishiyama-so** (石山荘). On tiny Yokoyama Island, this small inn has painted its name in large letters on the red roof. **Pros:** idyllic setting; doesn't get much more remote than this. **Cons:** no frills; limited dining options; no private baths. [$] *Rooms from: ¥6480* ✉ *Ago-cho, Yokoyama-jima* ☎ *0599/52–1527* 💳 *No credit cards* 🛏 *2 Western-style rooms, 4 Japanese-style rooms, all with shared bath* 🍴 *Some meals.*

KII PENINSULA 紀伊半島 (KII HANTO)

Beyond Ise-Shima, the Kii Peninsula has magnificent marine scenery, coastal fishing villages, beach resorts, and the temple mountain of Koya-san. Wakayama Prefecture, which constitutes much of the Kii Peninsula, has a population of only 1 million, and life here moves at a relaxed pace. From Shingu you can reach all three great shrines of the Kumano Kodo pilgrimage route. Nearby Yoshino-Kumano National Park has pristine gorges, holy mountains, and another ancient Buddhist site at Yoshino-san, where gorgeous hillside sakura flower in early April.

SHINGU 新宮

138 km (86 miles) southwest of Taki, 231 km (144 miles) southwest of Nagoya.

Shingu is home to one of the three great shrines of the Kumano Kodo, **Hayatama-taisha** 速玉大社, which sits at the mouth of the Kumano River.

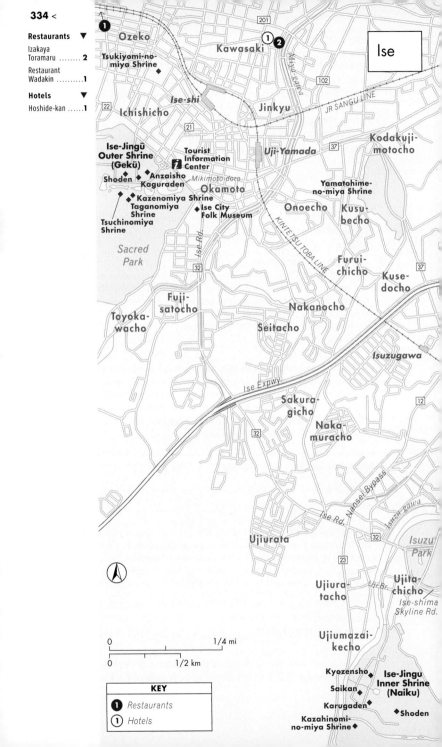

Restaurants ▼

Izakaya
Toramaru 2

Restaurant
Wadakin 1

Hotels ▼

Hoshide-kan 1

Ise

Ozeko

Kawasaki

Tsukiyomi-no-
miya Shrine

Ise-shi

Ichishicho

Jinkyu

JR SANGU LINE

Kodakuji-
motocho

Ise-Jingū
Outer Shrine
(Gekū)

Tourist
Information
Center

Uji-Yamada

Shoden   Anzaisho
Kaguraden   Mikimoto-doro

Okamoto

Yamatohime-
no-miya Shrine

Kazenomiya Shrine
Taganomiya
Shrine
Tsuchinomiya
Shrine

Ise City
Folk Museum

Onoecho

Kusu-
becho

Sacred
Park

Ise Rd.

KINTETSU TOBA LINE

Furui-
chicho

Kuse-
docho

Fuji-
satocho

Nakanocho

Toyoka-
wacho

Seitacho

Isuzugawa

Ise Expwy

Sakura-
gicho

Naka-
muracho

Ise Rd.   Nansei Bypass

Isuzu Kawa

Isuzu
Park

Ujiurata

Ujiura-
tacho

Uji Br.

Ujita-
chicho

Ise-shima
Skyline Rd.

Ujiumazai-
kecho

0 _____ 1/4 mi

0 _____ 1/2 km

Kyozensho
Saikan

Ise-Jingu
Inner Shrine
(Naiku)

Karugaden

Shoden

Kazahinomi-
no-miya Shrine

KEY

❶ *Restaurants*

① *Hotels*

The Pearl Divers

At Toba, before Kokichi Mikimoto (1858–1954) perfected a method for cultivating pearls here in 1893, *Ama,* or female divers (women were believed to have bigger lungs), would dive all day, bringing up a thousand oysters, but they wouldn't necessarily find a valuable pearl. Pearl oysters are now farmed, and the famous female divers are a dying breed. On the outlying islands, however, women do still dive for abalone, octopus, and edible seaweed.

The quickest and cheapest way to get from Ise to Toba is a 17-minute ride on the JR Line for ¥230. Pick up English-language maps from the Toba Tourist Information Center, just outside the station.

Toba Tourist Information Center. Outside Exit 1 of Kintetsu Toba Station, you'll find an English map of the main attractions. ☎ *0599/25–2844* ⊕ *tobakanko.jp* ⊙ *Daily 9–5:30.*

Mikimoto Pearl Museum (ミキモト真珠博物館 *Mikimoto Shinju no Hakubutsukan*). This museum on Pearl Island, 500 yards southeast rom Toba Station, explores the history of pearl diving in Japan. ⊠ *1–7–1 Toba, Toba* ☎ *0599/25–2028* ⊕ *www. mikimoto-pearl-museum.co.jp* ☎ *¥1,500* ⊙ *Daily at least 9–4:30.*

GETTING HERE AND AROUND

You can reach Shingu by JR Limited Express from Taki or Nagoya. The Shingu Tourist Association Information Center is to the left as you exit the station.

ESSENTIALS

Visitor Information Shingu Tourist Association Information Center (新宮市観光協会 *Shinguu-shi Kankou Kyoukai*). ⊠ *Shingu Station, 2–1–1 Jofuku* ☎ *0735/22–2840* ⊕ *kumano-shingu.com.*

EXPLORING

One of the few north–south roads penetrating the Kii Peninsula begins in town and continues inland to Nara by way of Doro-kyo (Doro Gorge). A drive on this winding, steep, narrow road, especially on a bus, warrants motion-sickness pills. The mossy canyon walls outside your window and the rushing water far below inspire wonder, but frequent sharp curves provide plenty of anxiety. Continue north on the road past Doro-kyo to reach **Hongu** 本宮 shrine, which has attractive wooden architecture and a thatched roof.

Hayatama-taisha (速玉大社 *Hayatama Shrine*). Although the buildings here are modern re-creations, this great shrine is said to have been located here since at least the 12th century, and is steeped in much Shinto mythology. A sacred stone found here was said to have once carried three Shinto deities to Earth. ⊠ *1 Shingu* ⊕ *kumanohayatama. jp* ⊙ *Daily 9–4:30.*

WHERE TO STAY

$ HOTEL **Shingu UI Hotel** (新宮ユーアイホテル). Better than the average business hotel, this place with fair-size Western- and Japanese-style rooms is a good option if you're staying overnight in Shingu. **Pros:** convenient base for day-trippers; decent service; good range of rooms. **Cons:** perfunctory decor; showing its age. [$] *Rooms from: ¥10500* ✉ *3–12 Inosawa* ☎ *0735/22–6611* 🌐 *www.ui-hotel.co.jp* 🛏 *82 rooms* 🍴 *Some meals.*

DORO-KYO 瀞峡

20 km (12 miles) north of Shingu.

The wide ocean views of the coastal journey to Shingu give way to gorges and mountainsides of a deep mossy green when you pass through the tunnel five minutes north of the city. Up the Kumano River, the walls of the steep-sided Doro-kyo rise above you. Farther up, sheer 150-foot cliffs tower over the Kumano-gawa. Tours of the gorge depart from Shingu Station and can be booked through the Shingu Tourist Association Information Center (¥4,800), which is located at Shingu Station. A bus goes as far as Shiko (40 minutes), and then a flat-bottom, fan-driven boat travels an hour upriver to Doro-hatcho and back again. Outside seats on the boats are the best.

NACHI 那智

13 km (8 miles) southwest of Shingu.

Reputed to be 1,400 years old, this is perhaps the most impressive of the Kumano Kodo shrines.

GETTING HERE AND AROUND

Nachi can be reached by hourly JR services via Shingu. The trip takes 17 minutes and costs ¥240. From Nachi Station, a 16-minute bus ride (¥480) gets you to the shrine and waterfall.

EXPLORING

Nachi Taisha (那智大社). The shrine overlooks **Nachi-no-taki** 那智の滝, the highest waterfall in Japan, which drops 430 feet into a rocky river. At the bus stop near the falls, a large *torii* (gate) marks the start of a short path that leads to a paved clearing near the foot of the falls. A 15-minute climb up the mossy stone path opposite the souvenir shops is the temple and its small museum. You can ride an elevator to the top of the bright red pagoda for an on-high view of the waterfall. Next to the shrine is the 1587 Buddhist temple **Seiganto-ji** 青岸度時, starting point for a 33-temple Kannon pilgrimage through western Honshu. Many visitors walk here from a point several kilometers away on the road to Nachi Station. The temple grounds offer mountain views to the southwest. ✉ *1 Nachi-san, Nachi-Katsuura-cho* 🎫 *Shrine free, elevator ¥300, museum ¥200* 🕒 *Shrine: daily 7–5; museum: daily 8:30–4:30.*

Shio-no-misaki (潮岬). About 8 km (5 miles) from Kushimoto, this is Honshu's southernmost point. Stationed high above the rocky cliffs is a white lighthouse that unfortunately closes before sunset. Adjacent to the lighthouse is a good spot for picnics and walking on the cliff paths.

The beach looks inviting, but sharp rocks and strong currents make swimming a bad idea. ⊠ *Nachi* 🖃 *¥200* 🕓 *Lighthouse: daily 9–4.*

SHIRAHAMA 白浜

82 km (51 miles) west of Nachi, 178 km (111 miles) south of Osaka.

Rounding the peninsula 54 km (34 miles) northwest of Shio-no-misaki, Shirahama is a small headland famous for its pure white-sand beach. If you're wondering why it looks and feels so different from the other beaches, it's because this sand is imported from Australia. Hot springs are dotted along the beach and around the cape. The climate, which allows beach days even in winter, makes Shirahama an inviting base for exploring the area. While it can be intolerably busy in July and August, it is otherwise pretty laid-back. JR trains from Nachi and Osaka run to Shirahama. A 17-minute bus ride from the train station gets you to the beachside town.

EXPLORING

Sakino-yu Onsen (崎の湯温泉 *Sakino-yu Hot Spring*). Soak in this open-air hollow among the wave-beaten rocks facing the Pacific Ocean, where it's said that emperors Saimei (594–661) and Mommu (683–707) once bathed. It's at the south end of the main beach, below Hotel Seamore. ⊠ *Shirahama* 🖃 *¥420* 🕓 *July and Aug., Thurs.–Tues. 7–7; Apr.–June, Sept., Thurs.–Tues. 8–6; Oct.–Mar., Thurs.–Tues. 8–5.*

Shirara-yu Onsen (白良湯温泉 *Shirara-yu Hot Spring*). At the north end of the beach, locals come and go all day to bathe and chat. The baths overlook the beach and ocean from the second floor of this old wooden building, and on the first floor is an open lounge area. You can rent or buy towels, but bring your own toiletries. ⊠ *Shriahama* 🖃 *¥420* 🕓 *Wed.–Mon. 7 am–11 pm, Tues. noon–11.*

KOYA-SAN 高野山

63 km (39 miles) east of Wakayama, 64 km (40 miles) southeast of Osaka.

This World Heritage Site is the headquarters of the Shingon sect of Buddhism, founded by Kukai, also known as Kobo Daishi, in AD 816.

GETTING HERE AND AROUND

If you approach Koya-san by cutting across the Yoshino-Kumano National Park by bus from Shingu or Hongu on Route 168, get off the bus at Gojo and backtrack one station on the JR Line to Hashimoto; then take the Nankai Line. If you are coming from Osaka, take the Nankai Line from Namba Station, which sometimes requires a change of train at Hashimoto Station.

By rail, the last leg of the trip is a five-minute cable-car ride (¥390) from Gokuraku-bashi Station. JR Passes are not valid for the cable car. The lift deposits you at the top of 3,000-foot Koya-san, where you can pick up a map and hop on a bus to the main attractions, which are about 2½ km (1½ miles) from the station and 4 km (2½ miles) from each other on opposite sides of town. Two buses leave the station when the cable

Koya-san is a World Heritage Site and the headquarters of the Shingon sect of Buddhism.

car arrives, which is every 20 or 30 minutes. One goes to Okuno-in Cemetery, on the east end of the main road, and the other goes to the Dai-mon, to the west. The main Koya-san Tourist Association office, at the intersection in the center of town, can be reached by either bus for ¥300. The staff here can arrange volunteer English-speaking guides to take visitors to Koya-san's main sights, and they also have audio guides (¥500) and maps available that are handy for self-guided tours of the town.

ESSENTIALS

Visitor Information **Koya-san Tourist Association** (高野山観光協会 *Koyasan Kankou Kyoukai*). ⊠ *600 Koya-san, Koya-cho* ☎ *0736/56–2616* ⊕ *eng.shukubo.net.*

EXPLORING

Dai-mon (大門 *Great Gate*). Every year a million visitors pass through Koya-san's Great Gate to enter the great complex of 117 temples and monasteries. Traveling to Koya-san takes you through mountain wilderness, but the town itself is sheltered and self-contained. The main buildings are imposing, while the minor temples are in a wide range of styles and colors, each offering small-scale beauty in its decor or garden. Monks, pilgrims, and tourists mingle in the main street, the sneaker-wearing, motorcycle-riding monks often appearing the least pious of all. ⊠ *249 Koya-san, Koya-cho.*

Danjo Garan (壇上伽藍 *Sacred Precinct*). The most striking of Danjo Garan's outsize halls is the 147-feet tall Kompon-daito (Great Stupa). This red pagoda with an interior of brightly colored beams contains five large seated gold Buddhas. Last rebuilt in 1937, the two-story structure has an unusual style and rich vermilion color. From Kongobu-ji, walk down the temple's main stairs and take the road to the right of the parking lot in front of you; in less than five minutes you will reach Danjo Garan itself. ✉ *152 Koya-san, Koya-cho* 💳 *¥200 to enter the Kompon-daito* ◷ *Daily 8:30–5.*

Kongobu-ji (金剛峯寺 *Kongobu-ji Temple*). On the southwestern side of Koya-san, Kongobu-ji is the chief temple of Shingon Buddhism. It was first built in 1592 as the family temple of Hideyoshi Toyotomi, and rebuilt in 1861 to become the main temple of the Koya-san community. The screen-door artwork and landscaped rock garden, the largest in Japan, are both well worth the admission fee. ✉ *132 Koya-san, Koya-cho* 💳 *¥500* ◷ *Daily 8:30–5.*

5

Fodor's Choice
★ **Okuno-in** (奥の院 *Okuno-in Cemetery*). If time is limited, head for this memorial park first. Many Japanese make pilgrimages to the mausoleum of Kobo Daishi or pay their respects to their ancestors buried here. Arrive early in the morning, before the groups take over, or even better, at dusk, when it gets wonderfully spooky.

Exploring this cemetery is like peeking into a lost and mysterious realm. Incense hangs in the air, and you can almost feel the millions of prayers said here clinging to the gnarled branches of 300-year-old cedar trees reaching into the sky. The old-growth forest is a rarity in Japan, and among the trees are buried some of the country's most prominent families, their graves marked by mossy pagodas and red-robed bodhisattvas.

You can reach Okuno-in by way of the 2½-km (1½-mile) main walkway, which is lined with more than 100,000 tombs, monuments, and statues. The lane enters the cemetery at Ichi-no-hashi-guchi; follow the main street straight east from the town center for 15 minutes to find this small bridge at the edge of the forest.

The path from Okuno-in-mae ends at the refined **Toro-do** (Lantern Hall), named after its 11,000 lanterns. Two fires burn in this hall; one has reportedly been alight since 1016, the other since 1088. Behind the hall is the mausoleum of Kobo Daishi. The hall and the mausoleum altar are extremely beautiful, with subtle lighting and soft gold coloring. ✉ *550 Koya-san, Koya-cho* 💳 *Free* ◷ *Daily 6–5:30.*

Reihokan (霊宝館 *Treasure Hall*). Here you'll find a collection of more than 5,000 well-preserved Buddhist relics, some dating back 1,000 years. The New Wing houses themed exhibitions of sculpture, painting, and artifacts. The Old Wing (confusingly marked "Exit") has a permanent exhibition of Buddha and bodhisattva figures and calligraphic scrolls. The museum sits across the road from the Danjo Garan. ✉ *306*

Koya-san, Ito-gun ☎ *0736/56–2029* 🎟 *¥600* 🕐 *May–Oct., daily 8:30–5:30; Nov.–Apr., daily 8:30–5.*

WHERE TO STAY

Koya-san has no modern hotels; however, 52 of the temples offer Japanese-style accommodations—tatami floors, futon mattresses, and traditional Japanese shared baths. You eat the same food as the priests. Dinner and breakfast is *shojin ryori,* vegetarian cuisine that uses locally made tofu and seasonal vegetables. Prices start from ¥9,500 per person, including meals. All the temples are open to foreign guests, but only half will cater to non-Japanese speakers. An advance reservation is strongly advisable, especially in October and November, when crowds come for the autumn leaves, and the August holidays. Arrangements can be made through Koya-san Tourist Association, the Nankai Railway Company office in Namba Station (Osaka), and the Japan Travel Bureau in most Japanese cities.

$$$ 🏨 **Eko-in** (恵光院). This friendly temple, close to Okuno-in, is where
B&B/INN you can take part in morning prayers and observe the morning fire ceremony. **Pros:** good vegetarian food; very welcoming to foreigners; can book direct online in English. **Cons:** some single rooms have no locks; if you neighbor smokes, you will smell it. [$] *Rooms from: ¥20000* ✉ *497 Koya-san, Ito-gun* ☎ *0736/56–2514* 🛏 *37 rooms* 🍴 *Some meals.*

6

THE JAPAN ALPS
AND THE NORTH
CHUBU COAST

Visit Fodors.com for advice, updates, and bookings

WELCOME TO
THE JAPAN ALPS AND
THE NORTH CHUBU COAST

TOP REASONS
TO GO

★ **Onsen:** The salty, calcium-rich waters of coastal thermal spas and iron- and sulfur-heavy springs in the mountains make your skin smooth, your bones strong, and set your mind at ease.

★ **Hiking:** The Japan Alps offer staggering views and a serious workout. Trails wind through peaks and ridges, and summer brings wildflowers to the highland slopes and valleys.

★ **Skiing:** The resorts around Nagano attract outdoor enthusiasts, particularly on weekends. Shiga Kogen, near Yudanaka, and Happo-o-ne, near Hakuba, are among the best areas.

★ **Feudal Japan:** Visit the former samurai quarters in Kanazawa's Naga-machi section. Matsumoto Castle evokes the history of a strictly hierarchical society.

★ **Folk art:** Kanazawa is renowned for dyed silk and pottery, while Matsumoto has excellent wood craftsmanship. Lacquer is a specialty of the Noto Peninsula.

1 The Japan Alps. The Alps are divided into three ranges: the northern Hida Mountains, the central Kiso range, and the southern Alps. The northern region is the most popular for hiking and skiing and is easily accessed from Matsumoto or Nagano. The jagged snowcapped peaks interspersed with high basins reach elevations of 9,850 feet. Mostly forested, they are covered with alpine flora in the warmer months. Hot springs are scattered throughout this volcanic region.

GETTING ORIENTED

The label "Japan Alps" does not refer to a defined political region; it's a name for the mountains in Chubu, the middle district. Chubu encompasses nine prefectures in the heart of Honshu, three of which—Gifu, Nagano, and Yamanashi—make up the central highlands. Between the Alps and the Sea of Japan is a narrow coastal belt known as Hokuriku, comprised of Kanazawa, Fukui, and the rugged coastline of the Noto Peninsula. Heavy snowfall in winter and hot summers make this region ideal for growing rice. Niigata and Sado Island form the northeastern coast.

6

2 Kanazawa and the North Chubu Coast. Ishikawa Prefecture stretches long and narrow from north to south; thus the topographies of the Noto Peninsula and the Ishikawa's southern Kaga region are significantly different. Kanazawa, the administrative, economic, and cultural center of Kaga, is also renowned for traditional crafts. The Noto Peninsula has both rugged cliffs on its northern Sea of Japan side and calmer bays in the south.

GASSHO-ZUKURI FARMHOUSES

It's tempting to think of traditional domestic architecture in Japan, with its paper windows and tatami mats and sliding screens as, well, insubstantial. The moment you see a gassho-zukuri farmhouse, that temptation will disappear.

(This page above) A Doboruku Matsuri procession; (opposite page upper right) a snowy winter in Shirokawa-go; (opposite page bottom left) gassho-zukuri farmhouses in Shirakawa-go

The term *gassho-zukuri* in Japanese means "praying hands." As hands come together, fingertips touching, in Buddhist observance, so lie the sloping, gable roofs of these remarkable farmhouses, watertight layers of reed thatching 3 feet thick or more, over massive wooden beams, set at a steep 60-degree angle to keep the snow from piling up. The mountain forests of Gifu and Toyama prefectures in the Japan Alps, where most of these houses survive, get some of the heaviest snow falls in Japan—12 feet of it, from November through March, is not uncommon—and no less a roof would do. The houses, four and sometimes five stories high, are usually built on a north–south axis, so the angle offers the least resistance to the winter wind. They are a masterfully practical architectural adaptation to challenging weather conditions, but they also have a certain beauty.

STRONGLY BUILT

Gassho-zukuri houses represent one of the crowning achievements of traditional Japanese carpentry. Astonishingly, these houses were built without nails, pegs, or brackets. Complex joinery, ropes, and strips of hazel wood hold the beams together, the joints tightened with small wedges, typically with no diagonal bracing. They are flexible enough to withstand winter storms and even earthquakes.

A PRACTICAL HOUSE

Like most traditional farmhouses, the gassho-zukuri was a living and working space for one, two, or even four generations of an immediate and extended family and their hired help—often 30 people or more—under the one pitched roof. Sleeping quarters were on the first and second floors; in the medieval period, the ground floor was also used for the making of niter (for gunpowder) in summer—tribute paid to the feudal lord in lieu of taxes—and *washi* (Japanese paper) in winter. The triangular top stories were reserved for silkworm cultivation. Stables were connected to the living space, so no one had to go outdoors during the long, cold winter months—except, alas, to the outhouse.

In the center of the huge open room on the main floor was—and still is—the *irori,* a charcoal fire pit with a huge wooden pot hook suspended over it for cooking. In winter, it was the only source of heat in the house; the higher your standing in the family, the closer you got to sit by the fire. The hearth sent billows of smoke upward to cure meats and dry food set on a metal grill suspended from the ceiling; the rising heat also kept the precious silkworms warm. Centuries of smoke would darken the walls and beams of the house, giving them as well a protective coating against insects, but the smoke takes its toll on the thatching, which has to be replaced every 30 or 40 years. When there's a roof to be done, the whole community pitches in, like an Amish barn-raising, laying some 20 truckloads of new reeds in two or three days.

SEEING THE GASSHO-ZUKURI TODAY

At one time, it was estimated that there were more than 1,800 of these extraordinary farmhouses in the mountain villages of central Japan, between the castle towns of Nagoya and Kanazawa, many dating back to the 17th century. Today, only some 150 remain—the largest number of them in the villages of Shirakawa-go and Takayama on the border of Toyama and Gifu prefectures, which together were declared a UNESCO World Heritage Site in 1959. Access to them is by no means easy, but since the 1990s these villages have become increasingly popular tourist destinations, especially for domestic travelers; many of the houses in Ogi-machi village have been converted to *minshuku* (guesthouses) to accommodate visitors to this area. Another group of gassho-zukuri farmhouses can be found in Hida no Sato (Hida Folk Village), an open-air historical museum in the Gifu city of Takayama.

6

Updated by Annamarie Sasagawa

No trip to Japan is complete without spending a few days in this central alpine region. Until the 20th century brought highways and railways to central Japan, villages here were largely isolated from the rest of the country. Unique traditions still linger in this region of snow-topped mountains, coastal cliffs, open-air hot springs, and superb hiking and skiing.

Come here for traditional architecture in towns like Tsumago and Magome, or to wander around thatch-roofed farmhouses in Takayama and Shirakawa-go village. Visit Buddhist temples such as Fukui's Eihei-ji, a major Zen center, Nagano's Zenko-ji, and Kanazawa's Nichiren Myoryu-ji (locally called Ninja-dera or the temple of the Ninja).

Central Japan is justly famous for its festivals. Takayama's biannual town festival draws crowds from all over the country. Sado Island parties for days on end during its annual Earth Celebration, hosted by taiko drum group Kodo, and the tiny town of Nanao on the Noto Peninsula lets it all hang out during its riotous Seihakusai festival. When they're not dancing in the streets, local craftspeople produce some of Japan's best ceramics, pottery, dyed silk, wood carvings, and lacquerware.

Escape summer city heat by trekking in the Japan Alps or strolling through the car-free alpine village of Kamikochi. When the winter snows start to fall, ski fields in Nagano and Niigata offer endless fresh powder, and the many hot springs and sake breweries in the region are a weary snowbunny's dream.

Food lovers should head to the Hokuriku coastline, where Ishikawa, Toyama, and Niigata prefectures meet the Sea of Japan. The cold winters and abundant rainfall make this one of Japan's major rice-producing regions, and where there's rice there's sake. The locally brewed sake pairs perfectly with sashimi straight from the ocean.

See the glossary at the end of this book for definitions of the common Japanese words and suffixes used in this chapter.

PLANNING

WHEN TO GO

Temperatures vary widely from the coastal areas to the mountains. Hikers should bring warm clothes even in summer. Cherry-blossom season in April is beautiful; May, June, and September are when transportation is safe and reliable, and not too crowded. At the height of summer, from mid-July to the end of August, the Alps and coastal regions are the prime getaway for those fleeing the stagnant heat of urban Japan—expect throngs of tourists and lofty prices. The skiing season peaks over Christmas and New Year's. Winter's heavy snows make driving around the Alps difficult or impossible, and only a few buses and trains run per day. It's fine if you're sticking to the major cities, but unless you've got skiing to do, and a direct train to get there, winter is not ideal for exploring the countryside.

PLANNING YOUR TIME

A quick loop of the major towns and destinations—the Alps, the Noto Peninsula, the Chubu Coast, and Sado Island—takes more than a week. To enjoy the unique scenery and culture of the region, it is best to choose two or three cities as sightseeing hubs. In the Alps region, frequent trains run north and south through the mountain valleys, while cutting across the mountains east to west and visiting smaller towns requires more planning. Local tourist offices can supply you with detailed bus and train information for the surrounding area.

GETTING HERE AND AROUND

Travel in the Alps is largely restricted to the valleys and river gorges that run north and south. The only east–west route is through the mountains, between Matsumoto and Takayama. It's easier to go along the coast and through the foothills of Fukui, Ishikawa, Toyama, and Niigata, except in winter when Fukui gets hit with furious blizzards. In Noto-hanto, buses and trains can be relied on for trips to key places.

AIR TRAVEL

The major airport in the area is Komatsu Kuko in Kanazawa, although there are daily flights from Fukuoka, Osaka, and Sapporo to Matsumoto and Toyama for those wanting to reach the Alps quickly. Since the opening of Noto Airport in Wajima, you can reach the Noto Peninsula in one hour from Tokyo. Chubu International Airport (Centrair) near Nagoya has frequent domestic and international flights.

BUS AND TRAIN TRAVEL

Whether to take the bus or the train isn't usually a choice, because there is often only one form of public transportation to the place you're going. Not all train lines in Nagano Prefecture are JR, so budget in additional charges if you are traveling on a JR pass.

Shinkansen service has effectively shortened the distance to the Alps from the east: the trip on the Nagano Shinkansen takes about 90 minutes. With the opening of the Hokuriku Shinkansen line extension in 2015, it's now possible to take a Shinkansen directly from Tokyo to Kanazawa in 2½ hours. From Kyoto and Nagoya the Alps are three hours away on the Hokuriku and Takayama lines. Unless you are coming from Niigata, you will need to approach Takayama from the south, taking the Shinkansen to Nagoya Station and changing there to an express train JR.

CAR TRAVEL

To really explore the area, rent a car in Kanazawa or Toyama to make the loop of the Noto Peninsula at your own pace. Another good driving route is between Kanazawa and Takayama via Shirakawa-go.

An economy-size car costs about ¥8,000 per day or ¥50,000 per week. Reserve the car in a city like Kanazawa, Nagano, or Matsumoto, or before you leave Tokyo, Nagoya, or Kyoto—not many people speak English in rural Japan. Tollways are convenient but expensive and less scenic than the many beautiful national roads in the region.

In winter certain roads through the central Japan Alps are closed, and the road into Kamikochi is inaccessible from November through April.

RESTAURANTS

Traditional Japanese *ryotei* specialize in seasonal delicacies while casual eateries serve delicious home-style cooking and regional dishes. Western fare is easy to come by, especially in larger cities like Kanazawa, which is famed for the local Kaga cuisine.

HOTELS

Accommodations run the gamut from Japanese-style inns to large, modern hotels. *Ryokan* and *minshuku* (guesthouses) serve traditional Japanese food, and usually highlight regional specialties. Hotels in the bigger cities have a variety of Western and Japanese restaurants. Japanese inns mostly include two meals in the room rate. In summer, it's advisable to book as far in advance as possible.

Most hotels have high-speed Internet connections in the rooms or an Internet terminal for guest use, but ryokan rarely do. Hotel lobbies and areas around train and bus stations often have free Wi-Fi access.

Hotel reviews have been shortened. For full information, visit Fodors.com.

WHAT IT COSTS IN YEN				
	$	**$$**	**$$$**	**$$$$**
Restaurants	under ¥1,000	¥1,000–¥2,000	¥2,001–¥3,000	over ¥3,000
Hotels	under ¥12,000	¥12,000–¥18,000	¥18,001–¥22,000	over ¥22,000

Restaurant prices are the average cost of a main course at dinner or, if dinner is not served, at lunch. Hotel prices are the lowest cost of a standard double room in high season.

VISITOR INFORMATION

Offices of the JR Travel Information Center and Japan Travel Bureau are at major train stations. They can help you book local tours, hotel reservations, and travel tickets. You shouldn't assume English will be spoken, but someone usually speaks sufficiently well for your basic needs. Where public transportation is infrequent, such as the Noto-hanto and Sado-ga-shima, local tours are available; however, the guides speak only Japanese.

CLOSE UP

On the Menu

Every microregion in Japan's alpine region has its specialties and unique style of preparing seafood from the Sea of Japan. Vitamin-rich seaweed such as *wakame* or *kombu* is a common ingredient, sometimes served in miso soup with tiny *shijimi* clams.

In **Toyama** spring brings tiny purple-hue baby firefly squid (*hotaru-ika*) to the menu, which are boiled in soy sauce or sake and eaten whole with a tart mustard-miso sauce. Try the seasonal *ama-ebi* (sweet shrimp) and *masu-zushi* (thinly sliced trout sushi that's been pressed flat). In winter, crabs abound, including the red, long-legged *beni-zuwaigani.*

Speaking of crabs, **Fukui** has huge (some 28 inches leg to leg) *echizen-gani* crabs. When boiled with a little salt and dipped in rice vinegar, they're pure heaven. In both Fukui and Ishikawa, restaurants serve *echizen-soba* (homemade buckwheat noodles with mountain vegetables) with sesame oil and bean paste for dipping.

The seafood-based *Kaga-ryori* (Kaga cuisine) is common to **Kanazawa and Noto-hanto**. *Tai* (sea bream) is topped with mountain fern brackens, greens, and mushrooms. At Wajima's early-morning fish market near the tip of Noto-hanto and at Kanazawa's *omi-cho* market you have your choice of everything from abalone to seaweed, and nearby restaurants will cook it for you.

In **Niigata Prefecture** try *noppei-jiru,* a hot (or cold) soup with *sato-imo* (a type of sweet potato) as its base, and mushrooms, salmon, and a few other local ingredients. It goes well with hot rice and grilled fish. *Wappa-meshi* is steamed rice garnished with local ingredients, especially wild vegetables,

chicken, fish, and shellfish. In autumn try *kiku-no-ohitashi,* a side dish of chrysanthemum petals marinated in vinegar. Like other prefectures on the Sea of Japan, Niigata has outstanding fish in winter—*buri* (yellowtail), flatfish, sole, oysters, abalone, and shrimp. A local specialty is *namban ebi,* raw shrimp dipped in soy sauce and wasabi. It's butter-tender and especially sweet on Sado-ga-shima. Also on Sado-ga-shima, take advantage of the excellent wakame dishes and *sazae-no-tsuboyaki* (wreath shellfish) broiled in their shells with a soy or miso sauce.

The area around **Matsumoto** is known for its wasabi and chilled *zarusoba* (buckwheat noodles), a refreshing meal on a hot day, especially with a cold glass of locally brewed sake. Eel steamed inside rice wrapped in bamboo leaves is also popular.

Sansai soba (buckwheat noodles with mountain vegetables) and *sansai-ryori* (wild vegetables and mushrooms in soups or tempura) are specialties in the mountainous areas of **Takayama and Nagano**. Local river fish like *ayu* (smelt) or *iwana* (char) are grilled on a spit with *shoyu* (soy sauce) or salt. *Hoba miso* is a dark, slightly sweet type of miso roasted on a large magnolia leaf.

Nagano is also famous for *ba-sashi* (raw horse meat), *sakura nabe* (horse-meat stew cooked in an earthenware pot), and boiled baby bees. The former two are still very popular; as for the latter, even locals admit they're something of an acquired taste.

6

Local Festivals

Takayama's spring and fall festivals (April 14 and 15 and October 9 and 10) transform the usually quiet town into a rowdy, colorful party, culminating in a musical parade of intricately carved and decorated *yatai* (floats) and puppets. Flags and draperies adorn local houses, and at night the yatai are hung with lanterns. Book rooms well ahead and expect inflated prices. April's Sanno Matsuri is slightly bigger than October's Hachi-man Matsuri.

During Kanazawa's Hyaku-man-goku Matsuri (early June) parades of people dressed in ancient Kaga costumes march through the city to the sound of folk music. Torchlit Noh theater performances, ladder-top acrobatics by Kaga firemen, and singing and dancing in parks create a contagious atmosphere of merrymaking.

Of the *many* festivals on the Noto-hanto, the most impressive are Nanao's Seihakusai festival, a 400-year-old tradition during which a trio of 30-ton wooden *Hikiyama* (Towering Mountain) floats are hauled around the city streets by locals, held May 3–5, and Issaki Hoto Matsuri, held the first Saturday of August.

THE JAPAN ALPS

The Japan Alps cover a region known as Shinshu, between the north and south coasts of the Chubu area. There are 10 peaks above 9,800 feet that attract both skiers and hikers, but the region also has many parks and forests for less-strenuous nature exploring.

Roads and railways through the Japan Alps follow the valleys. This greatly lengthens trips such as the three-hour Matsumoto–Takayama ride. Route maps for Shinkansen and JR lines are at any train station or bookstore. Some routes only have a few trains a day. The last train or bus may leave as early as 7 pm.

Buses are not as convenient as trains, but some scenic routes are recommended. Any bus station, always located near the train station, has maps and schedules. The local tourist information office—also in or near the train station—will help you decipher timetables and fares.

KARUIZAWA 軽井沢

145 km (90 miles) northwest of Tokyo, 72 km (45 miles) southeast of Nagano.

When Archdeacon A.C. Shaw, an English prelate, built his summer villa here in 1886 at the foot of Mt. Asama in southeastern Nagano Prefecture, he sparked the interest of fashionable, affluent Tokyoites, who soon made it their preferred summer destination. Some became patrons of the arts, which led to the opening of galleries and art museums. Pamphlets on current exhibitions are at the tourist office.

Emperor Akihito met the Empress Michiko on a tennis court here in the 1950s. Two decades later John Lennon and Yoko Ono lolled at her family's *besso* (summer house) and the Monpei Hotel. In Kyu-Karuizawa, near the Karuizawa train station, more than 500 branches of trendy boutiques sell the same goods as their flagship stores in Tokyo.

GETTING HERE AND AROUND

Coming from Tokyo, Karuizawa is a nice stop en route to the hot-spring towns of Kusatsu and Yudanaka or Matsumoto and Kamikochi. The town itself is easy to explore by foot, taxi, or bicycle. Naka-Karuizawa Station, one stop (five minutes) away on the Shinano Tetsudo Line, is a gateway to Shiraito and Ryugaeshi waterfalls, the Yacho wild bird sanctuary, and hiking trails. ■ TIP➔ Karuizawa is very crowded from mid-July to late August, so book your accommodations well in advance.

VISITOR INFORMATION

Contact **Karuizawa Tourist Information Service.** ⊠ *JR Karuizawa Station, Karuizawa-eki* ☎ *0267/42–5538.*

EXPLORING

Shiraito-no-taki and Ryugaeshi-no-taki (白糸の滝と竜返しの滝 *Shiraito and Ryugaeshi Waterfalls*). Hiking paths get crowded during the tourist season, but these waterfalls make a good afternoon excursion in the off-season. To get to the trailhead at Mine-no-Chaya, take the bus from Karuizawa Station. The ride takes about 25 minutes. From the trailhead it's about a one-hour hike to Shiraito. You can take the bus back to Karuizawa Station from here or continue on to the Ryugaeshi falls (90 minutes). From the falls, it's a 15-minute walk to the bus stop and a 20-minute bus ride back to Karuizawa. ⊠ *Shiraito-no-taki.*

View of Asama-yama from Usui Pass (碓氷峠から見た浅間山 *Mt. Asama*). This active volcano of more than 8,000 feet threatens to put an end to the whole "Highlands Ginza" below. For a view of the glorious Asama-san in its entirety, head to the observation platform at **Usui-toge** (Usui Pass). You can also see neighboring Myogi-san, as well as the whole Yatsugatake, a range of eight volcanic peaks. Walk northeast along shop-filled Karuizawa Ginza street to the end, past Nite-bashi, and follow the trail through an evergreen forest to the pass. A lovely view justifies the 1½-hour walk. Two to three buses leave per hour if you want a ride back. ⊠ *Mt. Asama.*

Yacho-no-mori (野鳥の森 *Wild Bird Forest*). This sanctuary is home to some 120 bird species, including the Japanese white-eye. You can watch from two observation huts along a 2½-km (1½-mile) forest course. To get here from Karuizawa Station, take a free shuttle bus bound for the "Hoshino area," or take the local Seibu Koden bus. Get off at the Tombo no Yu stop and walk about one minute to the park. You can wander around on your own, or book an English guided eco-tour. ■ TIP➔ Try to book at least a week on advance for English tours. ⊠ *Nagakura Hoshino, Karuizawa-cho* ☎ *0267/45–7777* ⊕ *picchio.co. jp/eng.*

6

WHERE TO EAT

$$ ✕ **Kastanie** (カスターニエ). The tiled bar and wooden tables topped with red-and-white-checked linens are as inviting as the staff of this terraced restaurant a few blocks north of the Karuizawa Station. Most dishes are seasonal, but try the grilled vegetable spaghetti and the salmon and Camembert pizza. Meat plates include herb-seasoned grilled chicken or sizzling rib-roast steak. Look for the sign hanging from the second floor. $ *Average main: ¥1500* ✉ *2–3–2 Karuizawa Higashi* ☎ *0267/42–3081* ☾ *Closed Tues.*

MEDITERRANEAN
FAMILY

NAGANO AND ENVIRONS 長野とその周辺

217 km (135 miles) northwest of Tokyo, 72 km (45 miles) northwest of Karuizawa, 249 km (155 miles) northeast of Nagoya.

Nagano Prefecture is called the "Roof of Japan," home to the northern, central, and southern Japan Alps and six national parks that offer year-round recreational activities. Active volcanoes include Mt. Asama on the border between Nagano and Gunma prefectures and Mt. Ontake in Nagano Prefecture, which is a destination for religious pilgrims.

GETTING HERE AND AROUND

Nagano is 97 minutes from Tokyo Station by Shinkansen, 40 minutes from Karuizawa by Shinkansen, and three hours from Nagoya by JR Limited Express. It's a convenient base for visiting some of the surrounding onsen and mountains, though you can easily see the main sights around Zenko-ji in half a day.

VISITOR INFORMATION

You'll find tourist information offices in Kusatsu, Nagano, and Yamanouchi.

Contacts Kusatsu Information Center. ✉ *3–9 Kusatsu-machi, Kusatsu* ☎ *0279/88–0800* ⊕ *www.kusatsu-onsen.ne.jp.* **Nagano Tourist Office.** ✉ *692–2 Habashita, Minami Nagano, Nagano* ☎ *026/234–7165* ⊕ *www.go-nagano. net.* **Yamanouchi Information Center.** ✉ *Yamanouchi-machi, 2987–1 Hirao, Yamanouchi-machi* ☎ *0269/33–2138* ⊕ *www.info-yamanouchi.net.*

NAGANO 長野

Rimmed by mountains, Nagano has been a temple town since the founding of Zenko-ji in the 7th century. Before the 1998 Winter Olympics, a new Shinkansen line was built connecting Tokyo and Nagano, and new highways were added to handle the car and bus traffic. Suddenly the fairly inaccessible Alps region was opened to visitors. Tourism peaks in winter when the fresh powder on Nagano's ski hills and its abundant natural hot spring baths draws crowds, but a second boom follows in summer when the mountains open for alpine hiking.

EXPLORING

Zenko-ji (善光寺 *Zenko Temple*). Nagano's unusual temple is the final destination each year for millions of religious pilgrims. Since the 7th century, this nonsectarian Buddhist temple has accepted believers of all faiths and admitted women when other temples forbade it. Each morning the head priest (*Tendai sect*) and head priestess (*Jodo sect*) hold a joint service to pray for the prosperity of the assembled pilgrims (usually

Zenko-ji is a nonsectarian Buddhist temple that accepts believers of all faiths.

on tour packages). Line up outside to be blessed by the priest, who taps his rosary on each head. You then pass the incense burner, waving the smoke over yourself for good fortune and health. Inside, rub the worn wooden statue of the ancient doctor Binzuru (Pindola Bharadvaja in Sanskrit) for relief of aches and pains. A faithful disciple of Buddha, Binzuru is famous for stories of his miraculous powers and ability to fly. After the service, descend into the pitch-black tunnel in the basement to find the iron latch on the wall—seizing it is said to bring enlightenment.

The temple is a 3-km (2-mile) walk from the station, or you can arrange a taxi through your hotel the night before. The starting time for the morning service ranges from 5:30 to 7 am, depending on the season, a minute later or earlier each day. From 8:35 you can hop on the Gururin-go bus for the 10-minute trip (¥150) to the temple gate. ⊠ *4–9–1 Motoyoshi, Nagano* ☎ *026/234–3591* ⊕ *www.zenkoji.jp* ⊠ *¥500* ⊗ *Temple open 24 hrs.*

YUDANAKA ONSEN AND SHIBU ONSEN 湯田中温泉 渋温泉

Northwest of Nagano, these historic hot-spring towns are the gateway to the Shiga Kogen Plateau ski area, known for its alpine skiing and snowboarding. Yudanaka and Shibu are worthwhile destinations, especially if you like watching monkeys take a bath. One of the nine hot springs between Yudanaka and Shibu is favored by the monkeys, and in recent years this has become something of a tourist destination. Both towns are considerably developed, but Shibu has managed to preserve the atmosphere of a traditional hot-spring town. Steam still drifts up from the thermally heated springs, and in the evenings you'll see hotel guests wandering through town in robes and sandals trying out the many town-run baths. Yudanaka is the last stop on the Nagano Dentetsu Line; the trip from Nagano takes 40 minutes and costs ¥1,230.

EXPLORING

Jigoku-dani Yaen Koen (地獄谷野猿公苑 *Jigoku-dani Monkey Park*). When snow is on the ground, the Japanese white macaques (Asian monkeys) that make their home here are a big draw, as are their bathing habits. To be on the safe side, don't feed or touch them—or look them in the eye. The train goes as far as Yudanaka; from there, take a taxi or bus to Kanbayashi Onsen, from which it is a 40-minute walk. There is also a direct bus to Kanbayashi Onsen from Nagano Station. Although winter is the best time to see the bathing apes, there are usually some in the onsen in other seasons. Wear good shoes as the path can get muddy, and leave heavy luggage at your hotel or in your car. ✉ *6845 Yamanouchi-machi, Shimotakai-gun, Nagano* ☎ *0269/33–4279* ⊕ *www.jigokudani-yaenkoen.co.jp* 🎟 *¥500* ⏱ *Apr.–Oct., daily 8:30–5; Nov.–Mar., daily 9–4:30.*

KUSATSU 草津

The highly touted hot springs at Kusatsu contain sulfur, iron, aluminum, and even trace amounts of arsenic. Just inside the border of Gunma Prefecture, the springs can be reached between April and November by a bus route across the Shiga Kogen ski area from Yudanaka, or year-round from Karuizawa. Every minute the *yu-batake* (hot springs field) gushes over 1,000 gallons of boiling water, which is cooled in seven long wooden boxes and sent to more than 130 guesthouses in the village. The field is beautifully lighted at night.

EXPLORING

Netsu-no-yu (熱の湯 *Fever Bath*). This is the often unbearably hot public bath next door to the *yu-batake* (hot springs field). You can't actually bathe here, but you can watch one of several daily *yumomi* shows in which locals churn the waters with long wooden planks until they reach a comfortable temperature. You can also sign up for a Yumomi Experience and try churning the waters yourself. It's about 20 minutes of churning and fairly tiring, but you'll be enthusiastically encouraged by local yumomi pros. ✉ *414 Kusatsu-cho, Nagano* ☎ *0279/88–3613* 🎟 *Yumomi Show: ¥500; Yumomi Experience: ¥250* ⏱ *Shows: 9:30, 10, 10:30, 3:30, 4, and 4:30. Yumomi experiences: Sept.–Apr., weekends 11:30–2; May–Aug., daily 11:30–2.*

Sai-no-Kawara Dai-Rotenburo (西の河原大露天風呂 *Sai-no-Kawara Open-Air Bath*). For a soak in the open air, try this expansive bath at the western end of Kusatsu village, which has pleasing scenery by day and lots of stars by night. Known for its milky waters, the bath can hold up to 100 people at a time. It's a 15-minute walk west from the Kusatsu bus terminal. ✉ *521–3 Kusatsu-machi, Nagano* ☎ *0279/88–6167* 🎟 *¥500* ⏱ *Apr.–Nov., daily 7 am–8 pm; Dec.–Mar., daily 9 am–8 pm.*

WHERE TO EAT AND STAY

$$$$
ITALIAN
✕ **Fujiya Gohonjin** (藤屋御本陣). This stately building just outside the gates of the Zenko Temple combines a bar, lounge, café, and fantastic Italian restaurant. The rather formal modern dining room offers prix fixe or à la carte options, mainly Italian with high-quality local

ingredients, and an extensive wine list. The bar and lounge serve up light meals in stately surroundings, while the café is a good place to relax after an afternoon of exploring the region. For dinner, reservations are recommended. $ *Average main: ¥5000* ⊠ *80 Daimon-cho, Nagano* ☏ *026/232–1241* ⊘ *No lunch weekends.*

$$
JAPANESE

✕ **Restaurant Sakura** (さくら). Seasonal delights like pungent Matsutake mushrooms are packed into the *bento* (box lunches) at this eatery, which has an open-air terrace and a glass-walled interior. A few blocks southwest of Zenko-ji, it's attached to the sake factory and warehouses of the famous distiller Yoshinoya. From 9 to 5 you can tour for free, ending with a sampling of fresh sake. $ *Average main: ¥2000* ⊠ *941 Nishinomon-cho, Nagano* ☏ *026/237–5000* ⊟ *No credit cards* ⊘ *Closed 4th Wed. of each month. Last order for dinner is 8 pm.*

$$
HOTEL

🏨 **Nagano Sunroute Hotel** (ホテルサンルート長野). A coffee table and two easy chairs are squeezed into each compact Western-style room here, which is all you need if you're en route to other Alps destinations. **Pros:** convenient location next to the station; friendly staff eager to assist foreign visitors. **Cons:** small rooms for the price; nondescript decor. $ *Rooms from: ¥16000* ⊠ *1356 Suehiro-cho, Nagano* ☏ *026/228–2222* ⊕ *www.sunroutehotel.jp/nagano* ⇌ *143 rooms* ❑ *No meals.*

$$$$
B&B/INN

Fodor'sChoice
★

🏨 **Ryokan Kanaguya.** Before it was upstaged by the bathing monkeys, Kanaguya Ryokan, the town's oldest and grandest traditional inn, was Shibu Onsen's main draw. **Pros:** attentive service; historical building; rooftop outdoor bath. **Cons:** few rooms with attached baths; no credit cards accepted; limited English ability. $ *Rooms from: ¥36000* ⊠ *2202 Hirao, Shibu Onsen, Nagano* ☏ *0269/33–3131* ⊕ *www.kanaguya.com* ⊟ *No credit cards* ⇌ *29 rooms* ❑ *Some meals* ☞ *Phone reservations need to be made by a Japanese speaker.*

$
B&B/INN

🏨 **Uotoshi Ryokan** (魚敏旅館). This small ryokan in the steamy village of Yudanaka has a *hinoki* (cypress) bathtub that's continually fed by the hot springs. **Pros:** the chance to try your hand at Japanese archery is a rare treat; quirky owners offer genuine local hospitality. **Cons:** somewhat out of the way; no rooms with bath. $ *Rooms from: ¥9000* ⊠ *2563 Sano, Yamanouchi-machi, Shimo-Takai-gun* ☏ *0269/33–1215* ⊕ *www.avis.ne.jp/~miyasaka* ⊟ *No credit cards* ⇌ *8 rooms without bath* ❑ *Breakfast.*

MATSUMOTO 松本

64 km (40 miles) southwest of Nagano, 282 km (175 miles) northwest of Tokyo, 185 km (115 miles) northeast of Nagoya.

Snowcapped peaks surround the old castle town of Matsumoto, where the air is cool and dry on the alpine plateau. More interesting and picturesque than Nagano, this gateway to the northern Alps is one of the best bases for exploring the area. Full of good cafés and restaurants, Matsumoto is also a center for traditional crafts including *tensan*, fabric woven from silk taken from wild silkworms; Matsumoto *shiki* or lacquerware; and Azumino glass. Old merchant houses stand along Nakamachi Street, south of the castle. Several influential educators,

6

Matsumoto-jo is also called "Crow Castle" because of its black walls.

lawyers, and writers from this city have impacted Japan's sociopolitical system in the past.

Though it only takes a day to visit the main sights in town, Matsumoto's restaurants, cafés, and relaxed atmosphere make it a hard place to leave. It is worth staying a night or two to visit the outlying museums and hot springs. Matsumoto is also a good base to visit Kamikochi to the west, or the post towns of Magome and Tsumago to the south.

GETTING HERE AND AROUND

Fuji Dream Airlines (FDA), code-sharing with Japan Airlines, has daily flights among Matsumoto, Fukuoka, and Sapporo. Trains are also available: Matsumoto is 1 hour from Nagano on JR Shinonoi Line, 2 hours from Tokyo Shinjuku Station on JR Chuo Line "Azusa" express, and 2¼ hours from Nagoya on JR Chuo Line's "Wide View Shinano" express. By bus it's 3¼ hours east of Takayama.

Contact Fuji Dream Airlines (フジドリームエアラインズ). ☎ *0570/55-0489* ⊕ *www.fujidream.co.jp.*

VISITOR INFORMATION

Matsumoto is compact, so grab a map at the Tourist Information Center at the JR Station and head for the old part of town near the Chitose-bashi Bridge at the end of Hon-machi-dori. Alternatively, Matsumoto's Town Sneaker shuttle bus (¥150–¥190) stops at the main sights, and the tourist office can direct you to one of the many locations lending free bicycles.

Contact Matsumoto Tourist Information Center. ⊠ *3–7 Marunoichi* ☎ *0263/32-2814* ⊕ *welcome.city.matsumoto.nagano.jp.*

EXPLORING

OLD TOWN

Kyu Kaichi Gakkou (旧開智学校 *Kaichi School Museum*). Built in 1873, the former Kaichi Primary School houses more than 80,000 educational artifacts from the Meiji Restoration, when education was to become the unifying tool for the rapid modernization of postfeudal Japan. The displays in the former classrooms include wall charts (used prior to the introduction of textbooks) and 19th-century desks and writing slates. The building was used as a school until 1960. Its bizarre style reflects the architecture of the period: a mishmash of diverse Occidental elements fashioned from Japanese materials. A big, fancy cupola sits atop the shingled roof; the white walls made of mortar are dotted with red, slatted windows; and the front door, hidden in the shadow of the blue, grandiose balcony, is protected by a skillfully carved dragon. ⊠ *2–4–12 Kaichi* ☎ *0263/32–5725* 🎫 *¥300* ⊘ *Tues.–Sun. 9–5.*

Matsumoto-jo (松本城 *Matsumoto Castle*). Nicknamed Crow Castle for its black walls, this local landmark began as a small fortress with moats in 1504. It was remodeled into its current three-turreted form between 1592 and 1614, just as Japan became a consolidated nation under a central government. The civil wars ended and the peaceful Edo era (1603–1868) began, rendering medieval castles obsolete. Its late construction explains why the 95-foot-tall *tenshukaku* (inner tower) is the oldest surviving tower in Japan—no battles were ever fought here. Exhibits on each floor break up the challenging climb up very steep stairs. If you hunker down to look through rectangular openings (broad enough to scan for potential enemies) on the sixth floor, you'll have a gorgeous view of the surrounding mountains. In the southwest corner of the castle grounds, which bloom in spring with cherry trees, azaleas, and wisteria, the **Nihon Minzoku Shiryokan** (Japan Folklore Museum) exhibits samurai clothing and centuries-old agricultural implements.

At the end of July there is a *taiko* (Japanese drum) festival, and on November 3 the Matsumoto Castle Festival features a samurai parade. In January an ice-sculpture exhibition is held in the museum's park. The castle is a 20-minute walk from the station. ⊠ *4–1 Marunouchi* ☎ *0263/32–2902 for castle, 0263/32–0133 for museum* 🎫 *Castle and museum ¥610* ⊘ *Daily 8:30–5.*

NEED A BREAK?

Old Rock. Two blocks before the Chitose-bashi Bridge, this Japanese version of a traditional British pub serves fish-and-chips, pizza, and, in a case of fusion cuisine done right, *wagyu* beef stewed in a Guinness-based sauce. Kilkenny, Boddingtons, Stella Artois, and local Karuizawa beer are on draft. It's close to Parco department store, between the station and castle. ⊠ *2-3-20 Chuo* ☎ *0263/38-0069.*

WEST OF THE STATION

Two of the city's best museums are west of the JR Station. It's too far to walk, and there's no bus. You can take the Kamikochi train (on the private Matsumoto Dentetsu Line) four stops to Oniwa Station and walk 15 minutes. The museums can be hard to find though, so the ¥2,000 taxi ride, albeit expensive, is recommended.

Matsumoto Rekishi no Sato (松本市歴史の里 *Matsumoto History Village*). Next to the Ukiyo-e Museum is Japan's oldest wooden courthouse. Displays pertain to the history of law enforcement from the feudal period to the modern era. ⊠ *2196–01 Shimadachi* ☎ *0263/47–4515* 🖅 *¥400* 🕙 *Tues.–Sun. 9–4:30.*

Nihon Ukiyoe Hakubutsukan (日本浮世絵博物館 *Japan Wood-Block Print Museum*). The museum is devoted to the lively, colorful, and widely popular *ukiyo-e* wood-block prints of Edo-period artists. Highlights include Hiroshige's scenes of the Tokaido (the main trading route through Honshu in feudal Japan), Hokusai's views of Mt. Fuji, and Sharaku's Kabuki actors. Based on the enormous holdings of the wealthy Sakai family, the museum's 100,000 pieces (displays rotate every three months) include some of Japan's finest prints and represent the largest collection of its kind in the world. ⊠ *2206–1 Shimadachi, Shinkiri* ☎ *0263/47–4440* ⊕ *www.japan-ukiyoe-museum.com* 🖅 *¥1,200* 🕙 *Tues.–Sun. 10–5.*

AROUND MATSUMOTO 松本の周辺

The local train to the Daio horseradish farm and the Rokuzan Art Museum journeys through vibrant green fields, apple orchards, and miles of rice paddies.

Daio Wasabi Nojo (大王わさび農場 *Daio Wasabi Farm*). At the country's largest wasabi farm, the green horseradish roots are cultivated in flat gravel beds irrigated by melted snow from the Alps. The chilly mineral water is ideal for the durable wasabi. You should try some of the farm's products, which range from wasabi cheese to wasabi chocolate and wasabi ice cream (sounds bad, tastes pretty good). You can pickle your own horseradish in one of the 20-minute workshops (¥1,030). The closest train station is Hotaka, 10 stops (one on the express) north along the JR Oito Line from Matsumoto Station. To reach the farm from Hotaka Station, take a 40-minute walk along a path (the station attendant will direct you), rent a bike, or hop in a taxi for about ¥1,300. ⊠ *1692 Hotaka, Azumino-shi* ☎ *0263/82–8112* 🖅 *Free* 🕙 *Mar.–Oct., daily 9–5:20; Nov.–Feb., daily 9–4:30.*

Rokuzan Bijutsukan (碌山美術館 *Rokuzan Art Museum*). This museum displays the work of Rokuzan Ogiwara, a sculptor who was influenced by Auguste Rodin and pioneered modern sculptural styles in Japan. He is especially known for his female figures in repose and male figures in heroic poses. This ivy-covered brick building with a stunning bell tower is in Hotaka, 10 stops north of Matsumoto Station on the JR Oito Line. From Hotaka Station it's a 10-minute walk to the museum. ⊠ *5095–1 Oaza-hotaka, Azumino-shi* ☎ *0263/82–2094* 🖅 *¥700* 🕙 *Mar.–Oct., daily 9–5:10; Nov.–Feb., daily 9–4:10; between Nov. and Apr., closed Mon. and day after public holidays.*

WHERE TO EAT

$$$
JAPANESE
Fodor's Choice
★

✕ **Kura** (蔵). For a surprisingly small number of yen you can feast in this 90-year-old Meiji-era warehouse in the center of town. Kura serves a large assortment of sushi and traditional dishes: the *aji tataki* (horse-mackerel sashimi) and tempura are particularly tasty. The stoic owner expertly prepares your meal, but should his wife spot you relishing the food, you're in for some disarming hospitality—she has an arsenal of potent *ji-zake* (locally brewed sake) and a heart of gold. From the station, take a left onto Koen-dori. Take a left after the Parco department store, and you'll see the restaurant's whitewashed facade and curved black eaves on the left. $ *Average main: ¥2500* ⊠ *1–10–22 Chuo* ☎ *0263/33–6444* ▭ *No credit cards* ⊘ *Closed Wed.*

$$ ✕ **Yakitori Yume-ya** (焼き鳥夢屋). With a retro vibe, Yume-ya specializes
JAPANESE in old-style *yakitori* (skewered, grilled meat and vegetables). Cozy up to the narrow counter for food and drinks, or sit outside during the warmer months. Little English is spoken by the staff, but the cooks are happy to explain the menu with exaggerated gestures. The *negima* chicken and leek skewers are particularly good. $ *Average main: ¥1000* ⊠ *Showa Yokocho Bldg., 1–13–11 Chuo* ☎ *0263/33–8430* ▭ *No credit cards* ⊘ *Closed Sun. No lunch.*

WHERE TO STAY

$$$ ⊺ **Hotel Buena Vista** (ホテルブエナビスタ). One of Matsumoto's most
HOTEL elegant lodgings, the Buena Vista has a glowing marble lobby, a hip coffeehouse, a chic café-bar, and three restaurants, including one on the penthouse level known for its French cuisine and skyline views. **Pros:** large rooms; good location; upper floors have great views. **Cons:** buffet dinner is pricey; can be busy with weddings and meetings. $ *Rooms from: ¥22000* ⊠ *1–2–1 Hon-jo* ☎ *0263/37–0111* ⊕ *www.buena-vista. co.jp* ⤳ *200 rooms* ⦿ *No meals.*

$$ ⊺ **Hotel New Station** (ホテルニューステーション). Although business
HOTEL hotels are often cold, this one warms things up with a cheerful staff and a lively restaurant that serves freshwater *iwana* (char)—an area specialty. **Pros:** inexpensive rates; excellent staff; near the station. **Cons:** small rooms. $ *Rooms from: ¥13000* ⊠ *1–1–11 Chuo* ☎ *0263/35–3850* ⊕ *www.hotel-ns.co.jp* ⤳ *95 rooms* ⦿ *Breakfast.*

NIGHTLIFE

Eonta (エオンタ). This jazz bar has been popular with locals since the 1970s. Playing whatever he feels like from his 1,000-plus CDs, the owner has what is probably the best set of speakers in the Japan Alps. Sit at the bar or on the corner sofas and choose from the extensive list of cocktails. Eonta is in a quasi-dilapidated two-story building a few blocks southeast of the castle. ⊠ *9–7 Ote 4-chome* ☎ *0263/33–0505* ⊘ *Closed Wed.*

HAKUBA 白馬

64 km (40 miles) north of Matsumoto, 48 km (30 miles) northwest of Nagano.

In the northwestern part of Nagano Prefecture, Hakuba Village lies beneath the magnificent Hakuba Range, the best of the northern Japan Alps. Hakuba means "white horse," because the main peak, Mt. Shirouma-dake (9,617 feet), resembles a horse. This is an all-year resort area for trekking, skiing, and climbing around the 9,500-foot mountains among rare alpine flora, insects, and wildlife. Gondola and chairlifts carry you up to ridges with panoramic views. More than 850 lodging facilities serve the 3.7 million annual visitors. Olympic alpine runs and ski jumps await winter sports fans, and summer visitors can still find snow, especially in the Grand Snowy Gorge.

Because the main attractions of Hakuba are hiking and skiing in the mountains, plan to stay at least two days to take advantage of the surroundings. The ski season in Hakuba runs from December to the first week of May. The hiking season is late June until the end of September, though the trails can be crowded in August. In July the mountains are covered in fields of wildflowers, making for a spectacular sight.

GETTING HERE AND AROUND

Both the JR Limited Express and the JR Oito Line run from Matsumoto to Hakuba. From Nagano the bus will take about an hour.

VISITOR INFORMATION

The Hakuba Village Office of Tourism, to the right as you exit the train station, provides basic maps (mostly in Japanese). Near the Alpico bus terminal and Happo bus stop is the Happo-o-ne Tourism Association, which can help you reserve a hotel room (for the peak summer and winter seasons, you should book in advance). Run by a Canadian and Japanese couple, Evergreen Outdoor Center offers a variety of outdoor tours year-round. It is also a good place to get information on outdoor activities in the Hakuba area.

Contacts **Evergreen Outdoor Center.** ⊠ *Kokusai Lodge, 4377 Hokujou, Hakuba Village* ☎ *0261/72–5150* ⊕ *www.evergreen-hakuba.com.* **Hakuba Village Office of Tourism.** ⊠ *6141–4 Hakuba-machi, Kita-anbo-gun* ☎ *0261/72–5000* ⊕ *www.hakubavalley.jp.* **Happo-o-ne Tourism Association.** ⊠ *5734–1 Kitajo-happo, Hakuba-mura* ☎ *0261/72–3066.*

EXPLORING

Happo-o-ne Ski Resort (八方尾根スキー場). Hakuba itself is one of Japan's best ski destinations, famous for powder snow, clear weather, and miles of tracks. The Happo-o-ne (also written Happo One but pronounced "oh-ney") resort is the best in town, and hosted several events for the 1998 Nagano Winter Olympics. Japan's first parallel jumping hills were constructed here with critical points of 393 feet and 295 feet, and each has a scaffold structure for the in-run and landing slope. The Champion and Panorama courses have starting points of an altitude of 5,510 feet, with separate courses for men (vertical drop 2,755 feet) and women (vertical drop 2,555 feet). The downhill course for super-giant slalom starts lower. This ridge stretches to the east from Mt. Karamatsu (8,843 feet), with breathtaking views, if the mist doesn't roll in. Almost all the runs here are intermediate level, with the rest split between beginner and advanced.

Happo-o-ne also has some great summer hiking, though the high elevation means that even in summer a sweater or light jacket may be needed. You can reach the hiking area via three connecting gondolas (5 minutes to Happo Gondola Station, then 8 minutes to Usagidaira, then an additional 10 minutes by alpine lift). From here the jewel-like Happo Pond is a 6-km (4-mile) hike. For more-ambitious hikers, three more hours gets you to the top of Mt. Karamatsu-dake.

To get from the center of town to Happo-o-ne, it's a five-minute, 3-km (2-mile) bus ride from Hakuba to Happo Information Center, and then a 15-minute walk through the resort of Swiss-like chalets and hotels to the gondola station. **Facilities:** 13 trails, 494 acres; 3,513-foot vertical drop; 32 lifts ✉ *5734–1 Hokujo Happo, Kitaajimi-gun, Hakuba Village* ☎ *0261/72–3150* 🌐 *www.happo-one.jp* 🎫 *Lift ticket ¥5,000.*

Shirouma-dake (白馬岳 *Mt. Shirouma*). Hiking at the bottom of Dais-ekkei (Big Snow) Gorge, which extends for 3½ km (2 miles), requires warm clothes even in midsummer, when temperatures can dip below freezing. More than 100 types of alpine flowers grace the nearby fields in summer. From the trailhead at Sarukura Village (reached by a 30-minute bus ride from Hakuba Station), the hike through the forest takes 1 hour 45 minutes. If you're luck, you may spot a snow grouse, a protected species in Japan. For climbers who want to scale Mt. Shirouma, which takes six hours to the top (two huts are on the way for overnight stays), proper equipment is necessary. ✉ *Shirouma Mountain* 🌐 *www.hakuba-sanso.co.jp.*

Tsugaike Shizen-en (栂池自然園 *Tsugaike Nature Park*). This marshland dazzles with a wide variety of rare alpine flora from early June to late October and is graced with gold and crimson leaves from September to October. It's a three-hour walk to take in the entire park. The best way to get here is to take a bus (25 minutes) from Otari Station, two stops from Hakuba, and then a gondola up to the alpine park. ✉ *131 Naka Otani-bei, Kita-Azumi-gun district, Otari-mura* ☎ *0261/82–2233* 🎫 *Park entry: ¥300 Gondola: ¥3,600 return, ¥1,920 one-way* 🕒 *Mid-May–early Nov., daily 8–4:20; extended summer hrs.*

Yari Onsen (鑓温泉). The trail from Sarukura to Yarigatake—a hike of three hours—leads to the area's highest outdoor hot spring, Yari Onsen. It's part of a lodge, but you can pay ¥500 to use the onsen. The lodge is open from mid-July to the end of September. Sarukura is a 40-minute bus ride from Hakuba Station. Crampons can be rented in Hakuba Village. ✉ *Hakuba Village* ☎ *0261/72–2002* 🌐 *www.hakuba-sanso.co.jp* 🎫 *¥500.*

WHERE TO STAY

$ B&B/INN 🏠 **Pension Noichigo** (野いちご). A five-minute walk (or ski) from the Happo-o-ne lift, the family-run Noichigo feels more like a European guesthouse than a Japanese inn. **Pros:** excellent location for hiking and skiing; friendly and knowledgeable owners; artsy vibe. **Cons:** fewer luxury amenities than larger hotels. [$] *Rooms from: ¥10500* ✉ *4869 Wadano-no-mori, Wadano* ☎ *0261/72–4707* 🌐 *www.janis.or.jp/users/noichigo/top_page_english.html* 🛏 *6 rooms* 🍴 *Some meals.*

KISO VALLEY 木曾谷(木曾路)

89 km (55 miles) south of Matsumoto.

This deep and narrow valley is cut by the Kiso River and walled in by the central Alps to the east and the northern Alps to the west. From

Hakuba Village, at the foot of the Hakuba Range of mountains, is green in spring and summer and a major skiing center in winter.

1603 to 1867 the area was called Nakasendo (center highway), because it connected western Japan and Kyoto to Edo (present-day Tokyo).

After the Tokaido highway was built along the Pacific coast and the Chuo train line was constructed to connect Nagoya and Niigata, the 11 once-bustling post villages, where travelers and traders once stopped to refresh themselves and share news, became ghost towns. Two villages, Tsumago and Magome, have benefited from efforts to retain the memory of these old settlements. Traditional houses have been restored along the sloping stone streets and power lines have been buried underground. Walking through these historical areas, you can almost imagine life centuries ago, when the rustic shops were stocked with supplies for travelers instead of the traditional crafts now offered for sale.

EN ROUTE

You can hike the **old trade route** between Magome and Tsumago. The full 500-km (310-mile) post road connecting Tokyo and Kyoto was constructed during the 8th century. Hiking the section between Magome and Tsumago is a hilly three-hour trip. At points the road becomes a dirt pathway winding through forests of cedar past small shrines and a pair of waterfalls. There's a daily baggage delivery service between the two towns (¥500 per bag) from mid-March to the beginning of December. It's available during the rest of the year for a flat rate of ¥3,000 for up to six bags. Make arrangements at tourist information offices.

GETTING HERE AND AROUND

The central valley town of Nagiso is one hour south of Matsumoto on the JR Chuo Line. Tsumago is a 10-minute bus ride (¥300) from JR Nagiso Station. Magome is closer to JR Nakatsugawa Station, which is 12 minutes south on the same line. Both towns are served by buses from the Nagiso and Nakatsugawa stations, so you can take a bus to one village and return from the other. Local buses between Magome and Tsumago are infrequent. A taxi costs about ¥3,000. To get to Takayama, take the JR Chuo Line from Nakatsugawa or Nagiso to Tajimi, change to a local JR Takayama Line train to Mina-Ota, then an express train to Takayama (total four hours). There are also infrequent buses from Nakatsugawa to Gero, 45 minutes from Takayama by express train. There are also direct highway buses from Magome to Tokyo's Shinjuku Station (4½ hours).

VISITOR INFORMATION

The staff at Magome Tourist Information Office—in the village center along the old post road—can help you reserve a hotel room. The Tsumago Tourist Information Office, in the center of town, has the same services as the Magome tourist office.

Contacts Magome Tourist Information Office. ✉ *4300-1 Magome, Nakatsugawa* ☎ *0573/69–2336.* **Tsumago Tourist Information Office.** ✉ *2159–2 Nagiso-machi, Kiso-gun* ☎ *0264/57–3123.*

WHERE TO STAY

$ B&B/INN **Hatago Matsushiro-ya** (旅籠松代屋). This small ryokan has welcomed guests since 1804. **Pros:** traditional setting; beautiful building; some English is spoken. **Cons:** no private bath or toilets; paper walls mean little privacy. [$] *Rooms from: ¥11000* ✉ *807 Azuma-Terashita, Minami-Nagiso-machi, Kiso-gun* ☎ *0264/57–3022* 💳 *No credit cards* 🕒 *Closed some Wed.* 🛏 *7 Japanese-style rooms without bath* 🍴 *Some meals.*

$$$ B&B/INN **Onyado Daikichi** (御宿大吉). The windows in all six tatami rooms of this minshuku face the wooded valley. **Pros:** lovely views; traditional setting; tasty food. **Cons:** no private baths; no nearby restaurants. [$] *Rooms from: ¥19000* ✉ *Tsumago, Nagiso-machi, Kiso-gun* ☎ *0264/57–2595* 🌐 *www17.plala.or.jp/daikiti/english.html* 💳 *No credit cards* 🛏 *6 Japanese-style rooms without bath* 🍴 *Some meals.*

KAMIKOCHI 上高地

48 km (30 miles) west of Matsumoto, 64 km (40 miles) east of Takayama.

The incomparably scenic route from Matsumoto to Takayama winds over the mountains and through Chubu-Sangaku National Park (Chubu-Sangaku Kokuritsu Koen) via Kamikochi. Entry to the village is only possible after the last week of April or the first week of May, when plows have removed the almost 30 feet of winter snow. If you spend the night in Kamikochi, which is surrounded by virgin forests of birch, larch, and hemlock, consider renting a rowboat at Taisho-ike (Taisho Pond) for the spectacular view of the snow-covered peaks.

Unless you plan to do some serious hiking, Kamikochi is best done as a day trip from Takayama or Matsumoto. Plan to arrive in the morning, though, as it is worth spending the entire day here.

GETTING HERE AND AROUND

No cars are allowed in Kamikochi. Take the Matsumoto Electric Railway from Matsumoto Station to Shin-Shimashima, the last stop. The ride takes 30 minutes and departs once or twice an hour. At

Shin-Shimashima Station, cross the road for the bus to Naka-no-yu and Kamikochi (¥1,950, or ¥2,450 for a bus-and-train combo ticket). There are also buses from Matsumoto to Kamikochi, departing twice daily when the road is open (late April–November; ¥2450), as well as direct highway buses from Nagano, Tokyo, Kyoto, and Osaka run by the Alpico bus company To get here from Takayama, take a bus to Hirayu Onsen (one hour; ¥1,570) and change to another bus for Kamikochi (25 minutes; ¥1,160). There are some direct buses in summer from Takayama.

VISITOR INFORMATION

Up-to-date bus and road information is available at the Matsumoto and Takayama tourist offices. Kamikochi is where the trails for some of the most famed alpine ascents begin; favorite peaks are Mt. Yariga-take and Mt. Hotaka-dake. Most maps are in Japanese, but some English information is available from tourist information offices. Planning in advance is essential; climbs range from a few days to a week, and the trails can be crowded in summer.

WHERE TO STAY

Hotels and ryokan here close from mid-November to late April.

$$$$
HOTEL
Fodor's Choice
★

🏨 **Imperial Hotel** (上高地帝国ホテル). This rustic alpine lodge is owned by Tokyo's legendary Imperial Hotel, and the service is so exemplary because the staff is borrowed from that establishment for the summer. **Pros:** luxurious accommodations; professional staff; beautiful architecture. **Cons:** more expensive than other lodgings in the area. Ⓢ *Rooms from: ¥34000* ✉ *Azumi-kamikochi, Matsumoto* ☎ *0263/95–2006, 03/3592–8001 Nov.–Mar., 212/692–9001 in U.S.* ⊕ *www.imperialhotel. co.jp* ↳ *75 rooms* ⊙ *Some meals.*

$$$$
HOTEL

🏨 **Taisho-ike Hotel** (大正池ホテル). This small mountain resort is perched on the rim of the brilliant-blue Taisho Pond. **Pros:** lovely views; comfortable Western-style rooms. **Cons:** Japanese-style rooms aren't recommended; bit of a walk from the center of Kamikochi. Ⓢ *Rooms from: ¥34000* ✉ *Azumi-kamikochi, Matsumoto* ☎ *0263/95–2301* ⊕ *www. taisyoike.co.jp* ↳ *21 Western-style rooms, 6 Japanese-style rooms* ⊙ *Some meals.*

SPORTS AND THE OUTDOORS
HIKING

As you approach Kamikochi, the valley opens onto a row of towering mountains: Oku-Hotaka-san is the highest, at 10,466 feet. Mae-Hotaka-san, at 10,138 feet, is on the left. To the right is 9,544-foot Nishi-Hotaka-san. The icy waters of the Azusa-gawa flow from the small Taisho Pond at the southeast entrance to the basin.

There are many hiking trails in the river valley around Kamikochi. One easy three-hour walk east starts at **Kappabashi** 河童橋, a small suspension bridge over the crystal clear Azusa-gawa, a few minutes northeast of the bus terminal. Along the way is a stone sculpture of the British explorer Reverend Walter Weston, the first foreigner to ascend these mountains. Continuing on the south side of the river, the trail cuts through a pasture to rejoin the river at Myoshin Bridge. Cross here to reach Myoshin-ike (Myoshin Pond). At the edge of the pond

Traditional houses have been restored along Magome's sloping streets.

sits the small Hotaka Jinja Kappabashi (Water Sprite Bridge). To see the beautiful **Taisho-ike** 大正池, head southeast from Kappabashi for a 20-minute walk. You can rent a boat (¥800 per half hour), or continue 90 minutes farther east to **Tokusawa** 徳沢, an area with camping grounds and great mountain views.

TAKAYAMA 高山

267 km (166 miles) north of Nagoya, 80 km (50 miles) north of Matsumoto.

Originally called Hida, Takayama is a tranquil town whose rustic charms are the result of hundreds of years of peaceful isolation in the Hida Mountains. Downtown, shops and restaurants mingle with museums and inns along rows of traditional wood-lattice buildings. A peculiar-looking ball of cedar leaves suspended outside a storefront indicates a drinking establishment or brewery. Nicknamed "Little Kyoto," Takayama has fewer crowds and wider streets, not to mention fresh mountain air and gorgeous scenery.

Takayama's hugely popular festivals, spring's Sanno Matsuri (April 14 and 15) and the smaller autumn Hachi-man Matsuri (October 9 and 10), draw hundreds of thousands of spectators for parades of floats. Hotels are booked solid during Matsuri time, so if you plan to join the festivities, make reservations several months in advance.

GETTING HERE AND AROUND

Takayama has connections north to Toyama by JR train (four departures daily). The regular train takes about two hours (with up to an hour waiting for connections) and costs ¥1,620, and the express Wide View Hida train takes 1 hour 40 minutes and costs ¥2,480. You can transfer to the Hokuriku Shinkansen at Toyama Station to go back to Tokyo, or west to Kanazawa and the Noto-hanto. It's easy to get to Takayama by bus from Matsumoto for ¥3,190. A highly recommended detour to Kamikochi—available May through early November—increases the fare to ¥6,260.

Laid out in a compact grid, Takayama can be explored on foot or bicycle. Several shops rent bikes; ask at the tourist information office for details.

VISITOR INFORMATION

The Hida Tourist Information Office, in front of the JR Station, is open from April to October, daily 8:30–6:30; and from November to March, daily 8:30–5. The English-speaking staff provides maps and helps with accommodations, both in town and in the surrounding mountains.

Contact Hida Tourist Information Office. ⊠ *Eki-mae* ☎ *0577/32–5328* ⊕ *www.hida.jp/english.*

EXPLORING

TOP ATTRACTIONS

Fodor's Choice ★ **Hida no Sato** (飛騨の里 *Hida Folk Village*). These traditional farmhouses, dating from the Edo era, were transplanted from all over the region. Many of the houses are A-frames with thatch roofs called *gassho-zukuri* (praying hands). A dozen of the buildings are "private houses" displaying folk artifacts like tableware and weaving tools. Another five houses are folk-craft workshops, with demonstrations of *ichii ittobori* (wood carving), *Hida-nuri* (Hida lacquering), and other traditional regional arts. It's possible to walk here from Takayama Station, but the roads are busy. It's better to buy a combination bus/folk village ticket at the bus station next to Takayama Station. ⊠ *1–590 Kami-Okamoto-cho, Gifu* ☎ *0577/34–4711* ⊕ *www.hidanosato-tpo.jp/english12.htm* ⟟ *¥700; ¥900 for combination bus/village ticket* ⊗ *Daily 8:30–5.*

Takayama Jinya (高山陣屋 *Historical Government House*). This rare collection of stately buildings housed the 25 officials of the Tokugawa Shogunate who administered the Hida region for 176 years. Highlights include an original storehouse (1606), which held city taxes in sacks of rice, a torture chamber (curiously translated as the "law court"), and samurai barracks. Free guided tours in English are available on request and take 30 to 50 minutes. Fruit, vegetables, and local crafts are sold at the nearby **Jinya-mae Asa-ichi** morning market, open until noon. From the JR Station, head east on Hirokoji-dori for a few blocks to the old section of town. Before the bridge, which crosses the small Miya-gawa, turn right, pass another bridge, and the Takayama Jinya is on your right. ⊠ *1–5 Hachiken-machi* ☎ *0577/32–0643* ⟟ *¥430* ⊗ *Mar.–Oct., daily 8:45–5 (Aug., 8:45–6); Nov.–Feb., daily 8:45–4:30.*

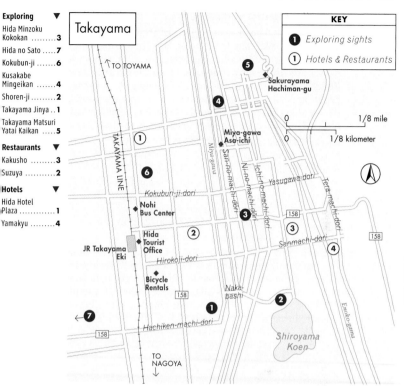

Takayama

Takayama Matsuri Yatai Kaikan (高山祭屋台会館 *Takayama Float Exhibition Hall*). This community center displays four of the 11th-, 17th-, and 18th-century *yatai* (festival floats) used in Takayama's famous Sanno and Hachi-man festivals. More than two centuries ago Japan was ravaged by the bubonic plague, and yatai were built and paraded through the streets to appease the gods. Because this seemed to work, locals built bigger, more elaborate yatai to prevent further outbreaks. The delicately etched wooden panels, carved wooden lion-head masks for dances, and elaborate tapestries are remarkable. Technical wizardry is also involved, as each yatai contains puppets, controlled by rods and wires, that perform amazing, gymnast-like feats. ✉ *178 Sakura-machi* ☎ *0577/32–5100* 💴 *¥820* ⊙ *Mar.–Nov., daily 8:30–5; Dec.–Feb., daily 9–4:30.*

WORTH NOTING

Hida Minzoku Kokokan (飛騨民俗考古館 *Hida Archaeology Museum*). This mansion once belonged to a physician who served the local *daimyo* (feudal lord). It has mysterious eccentricities—hanging ceilings, secret windows, and hidden passages—all of which suggest ninja associations. Displays include wall hangings, weaving machines, and other Hida regional items. ✉ *82 Kamisanno-machi* ☎ *0577/32–1980* 💴 *¥500* ⊙ *Mar.–Oct., daily 9–5; Nov.–Feb., daily 10–4.*

Kokubun-ji (飛騨国分寺 *Kokubun Temple*). The city's oldest temple, dating from 1588, houses many objects of art, including a precious sword used by the Heike clan. In the Main Hall (built in 1615) sits a figure of Yakushi Nyorai, a Buddha who eases those struggling with illness. In front of the three-story pagoda is a wooden statue of another esoteric Buddhist figure, Kannon Bosatsu, who vowed to hear the voices of all people and immediately grant salvation to those who suffer. The ginkgo tree standing beside the pagoda is believed to be more than 1,200 years old. ✉ *1–83 Sowa-machi* ☎ *0577/32–1395* 🎫 *¥300* 🕒 *Daily 9–4.*

Kusakabe Mingeikan (日下部民芸館 *Kusakabe Folk Craft Museum*). This museum is in a house from the 1880s that belonged to the Kusakabe family—wealthy traders of the Edo period. This national treasure served as a residence and warehouse, where the handsome interior, with heavy, polished beams and an earthy barren floor, provides an appropriate setting for Hida folk crafts such as lacquered bowls and wood carvings. ✉ *1–52 Ojin-machi* ☎ *0577/32–0072* 🎫 *¥500* 🕒 *Mar.–Nov., daily 9–4:30; Dec.–Feb., Wed.–Mon. 9–4.*

Shoren-ji (照蓮寺 *Shoren Temple*). The main hall of Shoren-ji in Shiroyama Koen (Shiroyama Park) was built in 1504. It was moved here in 1961 from its original site in Shirakawa-go, right before the area was flooded by the Miboro Dam. Beautifully carved, allegedly from the wood of a single cedar tree, this temple is an excellent example of classic Muromachi-period architecture. The temple sits on a hill surrounded by gardens, and you can see the Takayama skyline and the park below. ✉ *Shiroyama Koen* ☎ *0577/32–2052* 🎫 *¥200 admission to main hall* 🕒 *Daily 8:30–5.*

WHERE TO EAT AND STAY

$$$$ JAPANESE Fodor's Choice ★

🍴 **Kakusho** (角正). This restaurant is famous for its vegetarian *shojin* (temple food), which it serves up in a 200-year-old building south of the Higashiyama temple area. Specialties include *sansai ryori,* light dishes of mountain vegetables soaked in a rich miso paste and served atop a roasted magnolia leaf called *hoba-miso*. Set menus change with the seasons but can include salt-grilled river fish, crispy tempura, handmade soba noodles, or tofu chilled in ice-cold Takayama water. The English-speaking owner, Sumitake-san, can translate for you while her mother tells you all about Takayama history. From Miya-gawa, head east on the Sanmachi-dori, crossing four side streets (including the one running along the river). Walk up the hill, and take a left at the top. There is no English sign out front, but a white *noren* (hanging cloth) hangs in the entrance way of this Edo-era house. You need to book in advance and might want to dress up a bit. Ask for a private tatami room overlooking the garden. [$] *Average main: ¥12000* ✉ *2-98 Babacho-dori* ☎ *0577/32–0174* ☞ *Reservations recommended.*

$$ JAPANESE

🍴 **Suzuya** (寿々や). This restaurant's recipes have been passed down over several generations—the house specialty is the superb and inexpensive *sansai-ryori,* time-honored mountain cuisine. Suzuya is in a traditional Hida-style house, and the wood-beamed dining room has an intimate feel. There's an English menu, and the staff is used to serving foreign guests. From the station, turn onto Kokubunji-dori and take a right after five blocks. Lunch is served until 3 pm, and dinner begins at 5. Try to go during off-hours to avoid tour groups. $ *Average main: ¥1600* ⊠ *24 Hanakawa-cho* ☎ *0577/32–2484* ▭ *No credit cards* ☾ *Closed Tues.*

$$$$

HOTEL

⌂ **Hida Hotel Plaza** (ひだホテルプラザ). The best international-style hotel in town, the Hida Hotel Plaza exudes a old-style ambience. **Pros:** luxurious furnishings; central location; rooftop hot spring. **Cons:** lacks the personal touch of many area ryokan and inns; can be crowded with weddings and parties. $ *Rooms from: ¥30000* ⊠ *2–60 Hanaoka-cho* ☎ *0577/33–4600* ⊕ *www.hida-hotelplaza.co.jp* ↩ *133 Western-style rooms, 92 Japanese-style rooms, 1 suite* ⏀ *No meals.*

$$

B&B/INN

⌂ **Yamakyu** (山久). Antiques-filled nooks with chairs and coffee tables become cozy lounges in this old Tera-machi minshuku. **Pros:** warm atmosphere; excellent food; relaxing bath. **Cons:** early-to-bed curfew means less freedom; some private toilets but no private baths. $ *Rooms from: ¥12000* ⊠ *58 Tensho-ji-machi* ☎ *0577/32–3756* ↩ *20 Japanese-style rooms without bath* ⏀ *Some meals.*

NIGHTLIFE

Nightlife in sleepy Takayama revolves around locally produced beer and sake. Try one of the many small Japanese-style bars, or *izakaya*, that line the streets to the north of Kokubunji Street.

Red Hill (レッドヒル). Two blocks east and one block south of City Hall you'll find this bar, popular with the foreign locals. ⊠ *2-24 Sowa-cho* ☎ *0577/33–8139.*

6

SHIRAKAWA-GO 白川郷

80 km (50 miles) northwest of Takayama.

It's speculated that the Shirawaka-go area—and particularly Ogi-machi, an Edo-era hamlet deep within—was originally populated by survivors of the powerful Taira family, who were nearly killed off in the 12th century by the rival Genji family. The majority of the residents living here still inhabit gassho-zukuri houses. Their shape and materials enable the houses to withstand the heavy regional snow, and in summer the straw keeps the houses cool. Household activities center on the *irori* (open hearth), which sends smoke up through the timbers and thatch roof. Meats and fish are preserved (usually on a metal shelf suspended above the hearth) by the ascending smoke, which also prevents insects and vermin from taking up residence in the straw.

Shirakawa-go makes for a good day trip from Kanazawa or Takayama, or as a stop on the way to either. Several of the old houses are now minshuku, making Ogi-machi village a relaxing place to stay overnight.

GETTING HERE AND AROUND

It's more convenient to drive to Shirakawa-go and Ogi, but it's possible to get there by public transportation. A bus departs from Nagoya at 9 am daily, taking three hours and costing ¥3,600. There are also eight buses a day between Shirakawa-go and Kanazawa (1 hour 15 minutes; ¥1,850). Some routes require advance seat reservations, which you can do at tourist offices. From Takayama, buses go year-round four to six times daily for ¥2,470 one-way, ¥4,420 round-trip.

VISITOR INFORMATION

Many old houses in Ogi-machi village function as minshuku. To stay in one, make reservations through the Ogi-machi Tourist Office, open daily 9–5. It's next to the Gassho-shuraku bus stop in the center of town.

Contact Shirakawa-go Tourist Association. ✉ *2495-3 Ogi-machi, Shirakawa-mura, Ogi-machi* ☎ *0576/96–1013.*

EXPLORING

Fodor's Choice
★

Shirakawa-go Gassho-zukuri Village (白川郷合掌造り村). Opposite Ogi-machi, on the banks of the Sho-gawa, this open-air museum has 25 traditional gassho-zukuri farmhouses. The houses were transplanted from four villages that fell prey to the Miboro Dam, built upriver in 1972. Over the years a colony of artisans has established itself in the village. You can watch them creating folk crafts like weaving, pottery, woodwork, and hand-dyeing in a few of the preserved houses. Many of the products are for sale. ■ TIP➔ Keep in mind that individual houses do close irregularly. ✉ *Ogi-machi, Shirakawa mura, Ono-gun, Ogi-machi* ☎ *0576/96–1231* ✐ *¥600 for museum; ¥300 per house* ☉ *Mar.–Nov., daily 8:40–5; Dec.–Feb., Fri.–Wed. 9–4.*

KANAZAWA AND THE NORTH CHUBU COAST 金沢と北陸の海岸

The center of culture and commerce in the Hokuriku region, Kanazawa ranks among Japan's best-loved cities. To the east are snowcapped mountains, including the revered (and hikeable) Haku-san. To the north stretches the clawlike peninsula of the Noto-hanto, where lush rolling hills and rice fields meet scenic coastlines. Farther north along the Sea of Japan are the hardworking industrial capitals of Toyama and Niigata, and offshore the secluded Sado Island.

KANAZAWA 金沢

225 km (140 miles) northeast of Kyoto, 257 km (160 miles) north of Nagoya, 153 km (95 miles) northwest of Takayama, 343 km (213 miles) southwest of Niigata.

Twenty-first-century Kanazawa presents an extraordinary union of unblemished Old Japan and a modern, trendsetting city. More than 300 years of history have been preserved in the earthen walls and flowing canals of Naga-machi, the former samurai quarter west of downtown; the cluster of Buddhist temples in Tera-machi on the southern bank of the Sai-gawa River; and the wooden facades of the former geisha district, located north of the Asano-gawa River. Modern art, fashion, music, and international dining thrive in the downtown core of Korinbo, and in the shopping districts of Tate-machi and Kata-machi. The Japan Sea provides great seafood and a somewhat dreary climate. Fortunately, cold, gray, and wet weather is offset by friendly people and only adds to the sad, romantic air of the city.

In the feudal times of the Edo period, the prime rice-growing areas around Kanazawa (known then as the province of Kaga) made the ruling Maeda clan the second wealthiest in the country. Harvests came in at more than *hyaku-man-goku* (1 million *koku*, the Edo-period unit of measurement based on how much rice would feed one person for a year). This wealth funded various cultural pursuits such as silk dyeing, ceramics, and the production of gold-leaf and lacquerware products.

This prosperity did not pass unnoticed. The fear of attack by the Edo daimyo inspired the Maeda lords to construct one of the country's most massive castles amid a mazelike network of narrow, winding lanes that make the approach difficult and an invasion nearly impossible. These defensive tactics paid off, and Kanazawa enjoyed 300 years of peace and prosperity. Nevertheless, seven fires over the centuries reduced the once-mighty Kanazawa-jo to just the remaining castle walls and a single, impressive gate.

Between sightseeing, shopping, and sampling Kanazawa's many restaurants and cafés, it is worth staying here a couple of nights. Though the atmosphere of the city changes with each season, it is an excellent place to visit any time of the year.

GETTING HERE AND AROUND

Kanazawa became much easier to access from Tokyo with the opening of the Hokuriku Shinkansen in 2015. The trip now takes 2 hours 30 minutes. By train, Kanazawa is 2 hours from Kyoto; 3 hours from Nagoya; 2½ hours from Takayama (requiring a change to the Shinkansen at Toyama); and 3 hours from Niigata. The three-hour direct bus between Kanazawa and Takayama is also an option; there are two daily, and the cost is ¥3,000 one-way.

Ideal for tourists, the city's *shu-yu basu* (loop bus) departs every 15 minutes from 8:30 am to 9 pm from Gate 0 of Kanazawa Station's East Exit, and delivers you to the major tourist sites. Stops are announced in English and displayed on a digital board at the front of the bus. A single ride costs ¥200; the day pass is ¥500. You can purchase the pass from the Hokutetsu bus ticket office in front of Kanazawa Station.

Kanazawa is a good place to rent a car to explore the Noto-hanto and other parts of the Japan Sea coast. The area around the station is where you'll find all the major car rental companies.

VISITOR INFORMATION

The Kanazawa Information Office has two desks at the train station and staff that will help you find accommodations. An English speaker is on duty from 10 am to 6 pm from the Kanazawa Goodwill Guide Network, which offers free guide and interpreting services.

Contact Kanazawa Information Office. ⊠ *1–1 Kinoshinbo-machi* ☎ *076/232–6200.*

EXPLORING

TOP ATTRACTIONS

Buke Yashiki Ato Nomura-ke (武家屋敷跡 野村家 *Nomura Samurai House*). This elegant house in Naga-machi was rebuilt more than 100 years ago by an industrialist named Nomura. Visit the Jodan-no-ma drawing room made of cypress, with elaborate designs in rosewood and ebony. Then pass through the sliding doors, adorned with the paintings

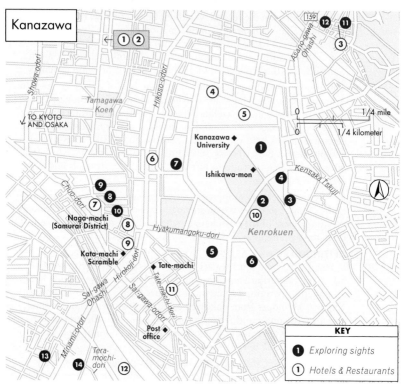

Kanazawa

KEY

❶ Exploring sights

① Hotels & Restaurants

of Sasaki Senkai of the illustrious Kano School, to a wooden veranda. Rest your feet here, and take in the stunning little garden with weathered lanterns among pine and maple trees, and various shrubs and bonsai. Stepping stones lead to a pond dotted with moss-covered rocks and brilliant orange-flecked carp. In the upstairs tearoom you can enjoy a bird's-eye view of the gardens and a cup of *macha* (green tea) for ¥300. ⊠ *1–3–32 Naga-machi* ☎ *076/221–3553* ✉ *¥550* ⊙ *Apr.–Sept., daily 8:30–5:30; Oct.–Mar., daily 8:30–4:30.*

Fodor's Choice
★
Gyokusen-en (玉泉園 *Gyokusen Garden*). This tiny garden was built by Kim Yeocheol, who later became Naokata Wakita when he married into the ruling Kanazawa family. Yeocheol was the son of a Korean captive brought to Japan in the late 16th century. He became a wealthy merchant, using his fortune to build this quiet getaway. The garden's intimate tranquillity stems from the imaginative and subtle arrangement of moss, maple trees, and small stepping stones by the pond. Two waterfalls that gracefully form the Chinese character for *mizu* (water) feed the pond. The garden is markedly different from the bold strokes of Kenroku Garden. You can have tea here for ¥600. ⊠ *8–3 Kosho-machi* ☎ *076/221–0181* ✉ *¥700* ⊙ *Thurs.–Sun. 10:30 am–sunset.*

Kenroku-en (兼六園 *Six Attributes Garden*). Across the street from the Kanazawa Castle is the largest of the three most famous landscaped gardens in the country (the other two are Mito's Kairaku Garden and Okayama's Koraku Garden). The Maeda lord Tsunanori began construction of Kenrokuen in 1676, and by the early 1880s it had become 25 sprawling acres of skillfully wrought bridges and fountains, ponds, and waterfalls. The garden changes with the seasons: spring brings cherry blossoms; brilliant azaleas foretell the arrival of summer; autumn paints the maples deep yellow and red; and in winter the pine trees are strung with long ropes, tied from trunk to bough, for protection against heavy snowfalls. Kenrokuen means "Garden of Six Qualities" (*ken-roku* means "integrated six"). The garden was so named because it exhibited the six superior characteristics judged necessary by the Chinese Sung Dynasty for the perfect garden: spaciousness, artistic merit, majesty, abundant water, extensive views, and seclusion. Despite the promise of its last attribute, the gardens attract a mad stampede of visitors—herded by megaphone—during cherry-blossom season (mid-April) and Golden Week (late April and early May). Early morning is the most sensible time for a visit, when the grounds are a little more peaceful and relaxing. ⊠ *1 Kenroku-cho* ☎ *076/234–3800* ⊕ *www.pref. ishikawa.jp/siro-niwa/english/top.html* ✉ *¥310* ⊙ *Mar.–mid-Oct., daily 7–6; mid-Oct.–Feb., daily 8–5.*

Fodor's Choice
★
Myoryu-ji (妙立寺 *Myoryu Temple*). On the south side of the Sai-gawa is the intriguing and mysterious Myoryu-ji. Its popular name, Ninja-dera (Temple of the Ninja), suggests it was a clandestine training center for martial-arts masters who crept around in the dead of night armed with *shuriken* (star-shape blades). In fact, the temple was built to provide an escape route for the daimyo in case of invasion. Ninja-dera was built by Toshitsune in 1643, when the Tokugawa Shogunate was stealthily knocking off local warlords and eliminating competition. At first glance, it appears a modest yet handsome two-story structure. Inside,

6

The intimate Gyokusen Garden is one of the most impressive sights in Kanazawa.

however, you find 29 staircases, seven levels, myriad secret passageways and trapdoors, a tunnel to the castle hidden beneath the well in the kitchen, and even a *seppuku* room, where the lord could perform an emergency ritual suicide. Unfortunately (or fortunately, considering all the booby traps), visitors are not permitted to explore the hidden lair alone. You must join a Japanese-language tour and follow along with your English pamphlet. Reservations are necessary, but can be made on the day of your visit. ✉ *1–2–12 No-machi* ☎ *076/241–0888* 💴 *¥800* 🕐 *Mar.–Nov., daily 9–4:30; Dec.–Feb., daily 9–4.*

Naga-machi (長町 *Samurai District*). Behind the modern Korinbo 109 shopping center, Seseragi-dori leads to the samurai district where the Maeda clan lived. Narrow, snaking streets are lined with golden adobe walls footed with large stones and topped with black tiles. ✉ *Nagamachi.*

21 Seiki Bijutsukan (金沢21世紀美術館 *21st Century Museum of Contemporary Art*). This circular building was created to entwine a museum's architecture with the art exhibits, and for exhibition designers to take cues from the architecture. Transparent walls and scattered galleries encourage visitors to choose their own route. Previous exhibitions have included a Gerhard Richter retrospective, a video installation by Mathew Barney, and the work of Japanese photographer Araki Nobuyoshi. The building itself it a sight worth seeing, and the free, public terraces and plazas are a perfect place to stroll and relax. It's south of Kanazawa Park, next to City Hall. ✉ *1–2–1 Hirosaka* ☎ *076/220–2800* 🌐 *www.kanazawa21.jp/en* 💴 *Varies by exhibition*

🕐 *Museum: Tues.–Thurs. and Sun. 10–6, Fri. and Sat. 10–8; public areas daily 9 am–10 pm.*

WORTH NOTING

Higashi Chaya Machi (ひがし茶屋街 *Eastern Pleasure Quarter*). The high-class entertainment district of Edo-period Kanazawa was near the Asano-gawa. Now the pleasures are limited to viewing quaint old geisha houses recognizable by their wood-slat facades and latticed windows. Many have become tearooms, restaurants, or minshuku. If you are lucky, you might see a geisha scuttling to an appointment. Take the JR bus from Kanazawa Station (¥200) to Hachira-cho, just before the Asano-gawa Ohashi. Cross the bridge and walk northeast into the quarter. ✉ *Higashi no Kurawa.*

Ishikawa-ken Kanko Bussankan (石川県観光物産館 *Ishikawa Prefectural Products Center*). Near Gyokusen Garden, the center serves as a place where you can both buy traditional crafts from the region and see demonstrations of Yuzen dyeing, pottery, and lacquerware production. You can also try your hand at carving a personal seal or painting a wooden doll at regularly scheduled workshops. ✉ *2–20 Kenroku-cho* ☎ *076/222–7788* 💴 *Free* 🕐 *Nov.–July, daily 10–6; Aug.–Oct., Wed.–Mon. 9–6.*

Ishikawa Kenritsu Bijutsukan (石川県立美術館 *Ishikawa Prefectural Art Museum*). Come here to see the country's best permanent collection of *Kutani-yaki* (colorful overglaze-painted porcelain), dyed fabrics, and old Japanese paintings. ✉ *2–1 Dewa-machi, southwest of Kenrokuen* ☎ *076/231–7580* ⊕ *www.ishibi.pref.ishikawa.jp/english/index.html* 💴 *¥360* 🕐 *Daily 9:30–6.*

Kanazawa Castle Park (金沢城公園). Though most of the castle is a reproduction, the original Ishikawa-mon (Ishikawa Gate) remains intact—its thick mossy stone base is topped with curving black eaves and white lead roof tiles. The tiles could be melted down and molded into ammunition in case of a prolonged siege. To reach the castle, take any bus (¥200) from Gate 11 at the bus terminal outside the JR Station or walk 30 minutes. ✉ *1–1 Marunouchi* ☎ *076/234–3800* ⊕ *www.pref. ishikawa.jp/siro-niwa/english/access.html* 💴 *Free* 🕐 *Mar.–mid-Oct., daily 7–6; mid-Oct.–Feb., daily 8–5.*

Kutani Kosen Gama (九谷光仙窯 *Kutani Pottery Kiln*). You can watch artisans making the local Kutani pottery, which is noted for its vibrant color schemes, at this spot dating from 1870. ✉ *5–3–3 No-machi* ☎ *076/241–0902* 💴 *Free* 🕐 *Mon.–Sat. 9–noon and 1–5, Sun. 9–noon.*

Nagamachi Yuzenkan (長町友禅館 *Saihitsuan Yuzen Silk Center*). A few houses have been carefully restored in the samurai district, including the Saihitsuan Yuzen Silk Center, where you can watch demonstrations of Yuzen silk painting—a centuries-old technique in which intricate floral designs with delicate white outlines are meticulously painted onto silk used for kimonos—and, of course, buy the products. It's behind the Tokyu Hotel, five blocks southwest of Oyama Jinja. ✉ *2–6–16 Naga-machi* ☎ *076/264–2811* ⊕ *www.kagayuzen-club.co.jp/english* 💴 *¥350* 🕐 *Daily 9–4:30.*

Oyama Jinja (尾山神社 *Oyama Shrine*). Built in 1599, Oyama Jinja was dedicated to Lord Toshiie Maeda, the founder of the Maeda clan. The shrine's unusual three-story gate, **Shin-mon,** was completed in 1875. Previously located atop Mt. Utatsu, the square arch and its stained-glass windows were believed to once function as a lighthouse, guiding ships in from the Japan Sea to the Kanaiwa Port, 6 km (4 miles) northwest. You're free to walk around the shrine. ✉ *11–1 Oyama-cho* ☎ *076/231–7210* 🎫 *Free.*

Shima-ke (志摩家 *Shima House*). Constructed in the early 19th century, this elegant former geisha house is now a museum of Kanazawa geisha culture. ✉ *1–13–21 Higashi-yama* ☎ *076/252–5675* 🌐 *www.ochaya-shima.com* 🎫 *¥500* ⏲ *Daily 9–6.*

WHERE TO EAT

$$$ JAPANESE 🍴 **Fumuroya** (不室屋). Not far from the Omi-Cho market, this shop specializes in *ofu,* or wheat gluten. Its adjacent restaurant offers a ¥2,500 set lunch of *jibu ni,* a stew made with chicken (instead of the usual duck), wheat gluten, and shiitake mushrooms. Lunch is served from 11:30 to 2; after that, coffee is served until about 5. [$] *Average main: ¥2500* ✉ *2–3–1 Owari-cho* ☎ *076/224–2886* ⏲ *No dinner* ✍ *Reservations essential.*

$$$ JAPANESE 🍴 **Itaru** (いたる). Slip into Itaru for a taste of good Kaga-ryori local specialties, including stewed Kanazawa pork, mackerel from the Noto Peninsula, and fresh sashimi from the Sea of Japan. Dinner here costs a bit, but it's a real Kanazawa dining experience. Although the staff speaks little English, there are English menus to help you out. For a sampling of the region's cuisine, try the seasonal set meal and wash it down with local sake. Watching the cooks behind the counter adds to the overall dining experience. [$] *Average main: ¥3000* ✉ *2–7–5 Katamachi* ☎ *0762/24–4156* 💳 *No credit cards* ⏲ *Closed Sun. No lunch.*

$$$$ JAPANESE 🍴 **Kincharyo** (加賀料理 金茶寮). As the seasons change, so do the menu options at this showplace in the Kanazawa Tokyu Hotel. With its graceful curve, the lacquered countertop of the sushi bar is beautiful. In spring your meal may include *hotaru-ika* (firefly squid) and *iidako* (baby octopus) no larger than your thumbnail. The lunch bento box costs ¥2,000 to ¥3,800. Pris fixe *kaiseki* (a traditional Japanese dinner) courses will set you back ¥7,000 to ¥10,000. [$] *Average main: ¥5000* ✉ *3F Kanazawa Tokyu Hotel, 2–1–1 Korinbo* ☎ *076/263–5511.*

$ INDONESIAN 🍴 **Legian** (レギャン). You might be surprised to find a funky Balinese eatery alongside the Sai-gawa River, but the *gado-gado* (vegetables in a spicy sauce), *nasi goreng* (Indonesian-style fried rice), or chicken *satay* (grilled on a skewer, with peanut sauce) prove that it's the real deal. Indonesian beer and mango ice cream are also available. After dinner the atmosphere gets quite lively, as the place stays open past midnight during the week and until 4:30 am on weekends. From Katamachi Scramble (the area's central intersection), turn right just before Sai-gawa Bridge, and follow the narrow lane along the river. [$] *Average main: ¥800* ✉ *2–31–30 Kata-machi* ☎ *076/262–6510* 💳 *No credit cards* ⏲ *No lunch.*

$$$ JAPANESE 🍴 **Miyoshian** (三芳庵). At this place in the renowned Kenroku Garden, excellent fish and vegetable dishes have been carefully prepared for

nearly 100 years. The prices are still reasonable—a multicourse meal is less than ¥3,000. In the annex, macha tea is served with Japanese pastries from Morihachi, a confectioner with a 360-year history. Ⓢ *Average main: ¥3000* ⊠ *1–1 Kenroku-cho* ☎ *076/221–0127* ▭ *No credit cards* ☽ *Usually closed Wed., but sometimes closed Tues. or Thurs. instead. No dinner.*

$
CAFÉ JAPANESE
✕ **Noda-ya** (野田屋). Slip into this little shop for a scoop of delicious *macha sofuto kurumu* (green tea ice cream) or a cup of tea. You can relax in the little garden in the rear or on benches out front. At the far end of the Tate-machi shopping street, the heavenly scent of roasting green tea leaves wafts out the door. The café is open daily 9 to 7:30. Ⓢ *Average main: ¥1000* ⊠ *3 Tate-machi* ☎ *076/221–0982* ▭ *No credit cards.*

$$$$
JAPANESE
✕ **Sugi no I** (杉の井). On the south bank of the Sai-gawa River close to the Sakura-bashi Bridge, this elegant restaurant serves Kaga specialties like duck stew with wheat gluten and *gori no tsukuda ni,* tiny soy-simmered river fish. Kutani china, Oribe pottery, and lacquerware provide the perfect canvas for these culinary works of art. Dinner in a private room overlooking the garden is a splurge, but worth it. In traditional Japanese style, the meal finishes with rice, pickles, and soup; in autumn the broth is clear with herbs and a shrimp dumpling. Full-course dinners start at ¥15,000; the ¥3675 "Ladies' Course," which anyone can order, is a more reasonably priced option. Lunch bento boxes are ¥3,800. It's a fancy place, so you'll want to dress up a bit. Ⓢ *Average main: ¥15000* ⊠ *3–11 Kyokawa-machi* ☎ *0762/43–2288* ✎ *Reservations essential.*

WHERE TO STAY

$$
HOTEL
🏨 **APA Hotel Eki-mae** (アパホテル金沢駅前). This hotel is so close to the JR Station it's practically inside it. **Pros:** convenient to train station; classy atmosphere; comfortable rooms. **Cons:** a 30-minute walk from the sights and nightlife of Kata-machi; neutral color scheme in rooms somewhat boring. Ⓢ *Rooms from: ¥16000* ⊠ *1–9–28 Hiroka* ☎ *076/231–8111* ⊕ *www.apahotel.com* ⟿ *456 rooms* ⦿ *Some meals.*

$$$$
HOTEL
🏨 **Hotel Nikko Kanazawa** (ホテル日光金沢). This 30-story hotel's exotic lobby is more reminiscent of Singapore than Japan, with tropical plants, cherry-oak slatted doors, and colonial-style furniture. **Pros:** near the train station; spacious rooms; great views. **Cons:** it's a long walk to Kata-machi's sights and nightlife; extra fee to use the gym and pool. Ⓢ *Rooms from: ¥40000* ⊠ *2–15–1 Hon-machi* ☎ *076/234–1111* ⊕ *www.hnkanazawa.jp* ⟿ *250 rooms, 4 suites* ⦿ *Some meals.*

$$$$
HOTEL
🏨 **Kanazawa New Grand Hotel** (金沢ニューグランドホテル). Stepping into this hotel's sleek black-and-cream marble lobby is a refreshing break from the dreary concrete of the city's main drag. **Pros:** convenient location; lovely views; restaurant serves some of the city's best contemporary French cuisine. **Cons:** few interesting places in the immediate vicinity; rooms could use an update. Ⓢ *Rooms from: ¥26000* ⊠ *4–1 Minami-cho* ☎ *076/233–1311* ⊕ *www.new-grand.co.jp* ⟿ *100 Western-style rooms, 2 Japanese-style rooms, 2 suites* ⦿ *Breakfast.*

$$$
B&B/INN
🏨 **Nakayasu Ryokan** (中安旅館). Just north of Kenroku Garden, this family-run ryokan dates from 1920. **Pros:** helpful staff; reasonable rates; free bicycles. **Cons:** some rooms have shared baths; somewhat tired-looking lobby. Ⓢ *Rooms from: ¥20000* ⊠ *23 Jukken-machi*

6

☎ *076/232–2228* ⊕ *nakayasu-ryokan.co.jp* ▭ *No credit cards* ↪ *21 Japanese-style rooms* ⧫ *Some meals.*

$ ⊡ **Yogetsu** (陽月). In a century-old geisha house in the Eastern Pleasure
B&B/INN Quarter, Yogetsu is a small, stylish minshuku. **Pros:** quiet location; charming atmosphere; lovely owner. **Cons:** fewer amenities than major hotels; not much English spoken. $ *Rooms from:* ¥*11000* ⊠ *1–13–22 Higashiyama* ☎ *076/252–0497* ▭ *No credit cards* ↪ *5 Japanese-style rooms without bath* ⧫ *Breakfast.*

NIGHTLIFE

All-night fun can be found in the center of town. ■ TIP→ Be warned: Many bars and night spots don't take credit cards.

Pole-Pole. Pronounced "po-ray po-ray," this reggae bar is run by the same jolly owner as the restaurant Legian, which sits next door. If you want to sit, arrive before midnight. The two dark, cramped rooms get so full that the crowd spills out into the hallway. Pole-Pole is open until 5 am every night except Sunday. ⊠ *2–31–30 Kata-machi* ☎ *076/260–1138* ☾ *Closed Sun.*

FUKUI 福井

80 km (50 miles) southwest of Kanazawa, 177 km (110 miles) north of Nagoya.

Fukui, the capital city of the small eponymous prefecture on the Sea of Japan, doesn't have much to draw foreign visitors beyond amazing seafood and remarkably friendly local residents, but it's a convenient transfer point or overnight stop if you're visiting Eiheiji Temple.

GETTING HERE AND AROUND

The city is 50 minutes by JR express train from Kanazawa, 1 hour 20 minutes by JR express from Kyoto, and 1 hour 45 minutes from Nagoya by Shinkansen and express train with a transfer at Maibara.

EXPLORING

Eihei-ji Temple (永平寺). One of the two headquarters of Soto Zen, the Eihei-ji Temple sits 19 km (12 miles) southeast of Fukui. Founded in 1244, the extensive complex of 70 temple buildings is spread out on a hillside surrounded by hinoki and *sugi* (cedar) trees more than 100 feet tall, some as old as the original wooden structures. This temple offers a rare glimpse into the daily practice of the 200 or so monks (and a few nuns) in training. They are called *unsui,* or cloud water, the traditional name for monks wandering in search of a teacher. The rigorous training has remained unchanged since the 13th-century monk Eihei Dogen started this monastery. Each monk has one tatami mat to eat, sleep, and meditate on, and these are lined in rows on raised platforms in a communal room. All activities, including cleaning out the incense tray, are considered to be meditations, so visitors are expected to dress modestly and explore in silence. With at least one month's notice, visitors affiliated with Soto Zen organizations can lodge at the temple (¥8,000 a night, including two meals). The easiest way to get to Eihei-ji from Fukui is by train to Eihei-ji Guchi Station and by bus from there to the temple. ⊠ *5–15 Shibi Eiheiji-cho, Yoshida-gun* ☎ *0776/63–3102* ⊴¥*500* ☾ *Daily 8–5.*

Eihei-ji, southeast of Fukui, is one of two headquarters of the Soto Zen school of Buddhism.

WHERE TO STAY

$$ HOTEL **Hotel Fujita Fukui** (ホテルフジタ福井). Across from Fukui Castle, Hotel Fujita Fukui has the amenities of a luxury hotel at prices that won't empty your wallet. **Pros:** good rates; helpful staff; many dining options. **Cons:** can be crowded during conventions; small rooms. $ *Rooms from: ¥14000* ✉ *3–12–20 Ote* ☎ *0776/27–8811* 🌐 *fukui.hotel-fujita.jp* 🛏 *354 rooms* 🍴 *No meals.*

NOTO-HANTO (NOTO PENINSULA) 能登半島

Thought to be named after an *Ainu* (indigenous Japanese) word for "nose," the Noto-hanto, a national park, juts out into the Sea of Japan and shelters the bays of both Nanao and Toyama. Steep, densely forested hills line the eroded west coast, which is wind- and wave-blasted in winter and ruggedly beautiful in other seasons. The eastern shoreline is lapped by calmer waters and has stunning views of Tate-yama (Mt. Tate), the Hida Mountains, and even of some of Nagano's alpine peaks more than 105 km (70 miles) away.

A quick sightseeing circuit of the Noto-hanto, from Hakui to Nanao, can be done in six to eight hours, but to absorb the peninsula's remarkable scenery, stay two or three days, stopping in Wajima and at one of the minshuku along the coast; arrangements can be made through tourist information offices in Kanazawa, Nanao, or Wajima.

This region is well known for its festivals. Seihakusai festival, a 400-year-old tradition held May 3 to 5 in Nano, is essentially three days of nonstop partying. Huge (26-foot) 10-ton floats resembling ships called deka-yama (big mountains) are paraded through the streets. At midnight the floats become miniature Kabuki stages for dance performances by costumed children.

GETTING HERE AND AROUND

You can fly to Noto Airport from Tokyo (two daily flights with ANA) and take the "Furusato Taxi" shuttle bus to nearby towns. There is semi-regular bus service around the peninsula, but the best way to get around is by car. Driving from Kanazawa is easiest, but you can also take the train to Wakura Station and pick up a rental car from Nissan Rent-a-Car there. You can also combine train and bus trips or guided tours, which can be arranged in Kanazawa.

Rental Car Contact Nissan Rent-a-Car. ⊠ *14–27 Yube, Ishisaki-machi, Nanao* ☎ *0767/62–0323.*

Visitor Information Wajima Tourist Office. ⊠ *20–1–8 Kawai-machi, Wajima* ☎ *0768/22–1503.*

EXPLORING

TOP ATTRACTIONS

Noto Seacoast (能登金剛 *Noto-Kongo*). Although inland buses will get you around faster, the coastal route is recommended for its scenic value. The 16-km (10-mile) stretch between Fuku-ura and Sekinohana, known as the Noto Seacoast, has fantastic wind- and wave-eroded rocks, from craggy towers to partly submerged checkerboard-pattern platforms. Among the best is Gan-mon, a rock cut through the center by water. Gan-mon is about 45 minutes north of Hakui and is a stop on tour-bus routes. ⊠ *Noto Seacoast.*

Wajima Lacquerware Hall (輪島漆器会館 *Shikki Kaikan*). To observe the traditional lacquerware manufacturing process, visit Wajima Lacquerware Hall. The production of a single piece involves more than 20 steps, from wood preparation and linen reinforcement to the application of layers of lacquer, carefully dried and polished between coats. The museum was fully renovated in 2015, and is in the center of town on the north side of Route 249, near the New Bridge. ⊠ *24–55 Kawaimachi, Wajima* ☎ *0768/22–2155* 🎟 *¥300* ⊙ *Daily 8:30–5.*

Wajima Morning Market (朝市 *Asa Ichi*). At the tip of the peninsula, the fishing village of Wajima is known for its gorgeous lacquerware. A good place to purchase some good pieces is the Wajima Morning Market, held daily except for the second and fourth Wednesday of each month. You can also buy seafood, fruit, vegetables, and local crafts from elderly women wearing indigo *monpei* (field pants). Almost anyone can point you in the right direction. ⊠ *Asa-ichi dori, Kawai-cho, Wajima* ☎ *0768/22–7653* ⊙ *Daily 8–noon. Closed 2nd and 4th Wed. of month.*

WORTH NOTING

Mitsuke-jima (見附島 *Mitsuke Island*). Just south of the village of Suzu is a dramatic offshore rock formation called Mitsuke-jima, a huge wedge of rock topped with lush vegetation, connected to the shore with a pebbly path popular with lovers. It is said that Buddhist priest Kobo Daishi gave it the nickname of *Gunkan-jima*, or Battleship Island, because it resembles a warship sailing to attack. ✉ *Mitsuke-Jima, Suzu.*

Myojo-ji Temple (妙成寺). This seldom-visited but well-tended temple complex sits a few miles north of the town of Hakui on the bus route from Kanazawa. The temple, founded in 1294 and belonging to the Nichiren sect of Buddhism, has a five-story pagoda dating from the 1600s. A large, colorful Buddha statue sits inside a squat wooden building. The influence of mainland Asia is visible in the gargantuan, wooden guardian deities. It's a 10-minute walk to the temple from the nearest bus stop. ✉ *1 Yo Taki-dani-machi, Hakui* ☎ *0767/27–1226* 🎫 *¥500* 🕓 *Apr.–Oct., daily 8–5; Nov.–Mar., daily 8–4:30.*

Soji-ji Souin (總持寺相院 *Soji-ji Temple*). The Zen temple complex at Monzen once served as the Soto sect's headquarters. Though a fire destroyed most of the buildings in 1818 and the sect moved its headquarters to Yokohama in 1911, this is still an important training temple. Strolling paths traverse the lush grounds, where you can see some spectacular red maples and an elaborately carved gate. As at the Eihei-ji Temple in Fukui, lay practitioners may stay here for ¥6,500 (although the temple hesitates to accept lone female travelers because room doors don't lock). To get here, take a bus to Soji-ji Souin Mae bus stop. ✉ *1–18 Monzen, Monzen-cho* ☎ *0768/42–0005* 🎫 *¥400* 🕓 *Daily 8–5.*

6

NEED A BREAK?

Shin-puku (神ぷく). Various sashimi and sushi combinations are reasonably priced at this small but beautiful sushi bar close to the post office in Wajima. With the post office on your right, walk two blocks down Route 249. It's on your right just after the road takes a slight diagonal turn. ✉ ***1–41–23 Kawai-cho, Wajima*** ☎ ***0768/22–8133*** 🕓 ***Daily 11:30–2 and 6:30–10.***

Takaoka City (高岡). The southern gateway to the Noto Peninsula, Takaoka is mostly known for its traditions of copper-, bronze-, and iron-smithing, and remains a major bell-casting center. No wonder it has one of Japan's three oldest Daibutsu (Great Buddha) statue. The Takaoka Daibutsu is made entirely of bronze. A short walk from the station is Zuiryu-ji, a delightful Zen temple. A sprawling park, Kojo-koen, is particularly stunning in autumn, with its red-and-silver maples. ✉ *Toyama.*

WHERE TO STAY

$$ B&B/INN 🏨 **Fukasan** (深三). Near the morning market and the harbor, this two-story wooden minshuku is furnished with locally made crafts. **Pros:** excellent location for visiting the morning market; traditional atmosphere; friendly staff. **Cons:** fewer amenities than a larger hotel; no en suite baths. [$] *Rooms from: ¥18000* ✉ *4–4 Kawai-machi, Wajima* ☎ *0768/22–9933* 💳 *No credit cards* 🛏 *4 Japanese rooms, without en suite baths* 🍴 *Some meals.*

$$ HOTEL 🏨 **Mawaki Po-re Po-re** (真脇ポーレポーレ). Built into a hillock, this little hotel has great views of the sea and surrounding hills. **Pros:** great views; quiet atmosphere; close to mineral baths. **Cons:** somewhat out of the way. [$] *Rooms from: ¥13000* ✉ *19–110 Aza-Mawaki, Noto-cho, Housu-gun* ☎ *0768/62–4700* 🛏 *6 Western-style rooms, 5 Japanese-style rooms* 🍴 *Breakfast.*

The Kurobe Gorge Railway operates from April through November through the deepest valley in Japan.

$$$ **Shunran Village** (春欄の里). More than 47 traditional houses in this
B&B/INN farming village at the end of the peninsula have been turned into min-
FAMILY shuku, giving you the chance to experience rural life. **Pros:** welcom-
ing staff; some English spoken; rare chance to experience rural life.
Cons: access difficult without a car; no hotel-style amenities. $ *Rooms
from: ¥20000* ✉ *16–9 Miya-chi, Noto-cho, Hosu-gun* ☎ *0768/76–0021*
✉ *shunran@shunran.info* ➴ *4 rooms* ᴼ *Some meals.*

TOYAMA 富山

*18 km (11 miles) southeast of Takaoka, 61 km (38 miles) east of
Kanazawa, 282 km (175 miles) north of Kyoto.*

Busy, industrial Toyama is beautified by Toyama-joshi Koen (Toyama
Castle Park), a spread of greenery with a reconstructed version of the
original 1532 castle. Toyama Bay is the habitat of the glowing hotaru
ika, or firefly squid. Their spawning grounds stretch for 15 km (9 miles)
along the coast from Uozu to the right bank of Toyama City's Jouganji
River and about 1½ km (¾ mile) from shore. From March until June,
their spawning season, the females gather close to the seabed and come
to the surface from dusk until midnight. From the early morning until
dawn the sea magically glows from the squids' photophores, blue-white
light-producing organs that attract their prey. This phenomenon has
been designated a Special Natural Monument. Sightseeing boats pro-
vide close-up views.

GETTING HERE AND AROUND

All Nippon Airways has five flights daily between Tokyo and Toyama. Toyama is 30 minutes from Takaoka by JR local, one hour from Kanazawa by JR Limited Express, and three and four hours north of Kyoto and Nagoya, respectively, by JR. Toyama has a network of street-cars that can take you to most destinations within town.

Visitor Information Toyama Tourist Information Office. ☎ 076/444–3200 ⊕ *foreign.info-toyama.com/en/.*

EXPLORING

Kurobe Gorge Railway (黒部峡谷鉄道 *Kurobe Keikoku Tetsudo*). Running along the deepest valley in Japan, the open-air Kurobe Gorge Railway takes you on a 90-minute ride past gushing springs and waterfalls. You might even see wild monkeys or a *serow*, a type of mountain goat. One of the best views is from the 128-foot-high bridge called Atobiki-kyo. Bring a windbreaker, even in summer, as it's a cold and damp ride. Kuronagi Onsen, Kanetsuri Onsen, and Meiken Onsen are three of the hot springs along the trolley route. You can get off at any of them and enjoy a soak. ⊠ *11 Kurobe Keikoku-guchi, Kurobe City* ☎ *0765/62–1011 for reservations only* ⊕ *www.kurotetu.co.jp/en* ☑ *¥1,710 one-way* ⊙ *Mid-Apr.–late-Nov., daily (exact departures vary by date).*

6

NIIGATA 新潟

155 miles northeast of Toyama, 205 mi northwest of Tokyo.

The coast between Kurobe and Niigata is flat and not so interesting. Two towns along the way, Naoetsu and Teradomari, serve as ferry ports to Ogi and Akadomari, respectively, on Sado-ga-shima. From Niigata ferries go to Sado-ga-shima and even Hokkaido. In the skiing season people fly into Niigata before traveling by train to the northern Alps for quick access to ski resorts.

GETTING HERE AND AROUND

Niigata is 3 hours from Toyama on the JR Hokuriku Line, and 2 hours, 15 minutes from Tokyo by Shinkansen. Niigata serves as a transfer point en route to Sado-ga-shima.

VISITOR INFORMATION

There are tourist information centers at both the Bandai-guchi and Minami-guchi exits of Niigata Station. Staff there can provide English maps and information on sights in the city, including restaurant infor-mation. On Sado Island, Niigata Kotsu Information center is found to the left of the Ryotsu bus terminal and offers tours of Sado-ga-shima covering Skyline Drive, where public buses don't run. Tours, from May to November, depart daily from Ryotsu and cost ¥6,440. You'll also find city maps, ferry schedules, and help finding a hotel there.

Contact Niigata Visitors and Convention Bureau. ⊠ *6–894–1 Nishibori Maedori Chuo-ku, Chuo-ku* ☎ *025/223–8181* ⊕ *www.nvcb.or.jp/travelguide/en/.*

EXPLORING

Northern Culture Museum (北方文化博物館 *Hoppo Bunka Keikan*). On the banks of the Agano River on the Kamabara Plain, the museum is a 40-minute bus ride from Niigata Station. This former estate was established in the Edo period by the Ito family, which, by the 1930s, was the largest landowner in the Kaetsu area, with 8,352 acres of paddy fields, 2,500 acres of forest, and 78 overseers who controlled no fewer than 2,800 tenants. The family also owned about 60 warehouses, which stored 1,800 tons of rice every autumn. Ito Mansion, built in 1887, was their home for generations until the Land Reform Act of 1946, which compelled landowners to sell off their paddy land holdings above 7.5 acres. Their mansion with its valuable art collection became this museum, which has two restaurants and coffee shops. The house has 65 rooms, a special art gallery, gardens, a tearoom, and an annex for study called "Sanrakutei" where everything—pillars, furniture, and even tatami mats—is triangular or diamond-shape.

The garden is laid out in the traditional style of the Kamakura and Muromachi periods (14th–15th century). Its five teahouses are in different parts of the garden (two of them built later), and numerous natural rocks—mostly from Kyoto—are artistically arranged around the pond. At Niigata ask the Tourist Information office to point you in the direction of the right bus, which takes 40 minutes. A taxi takes 25 minutes. ✉ *2–15–25 Somi* ☎ *025/385–2001* 🎟 *¥800* 🕘 *Apr.–Nov., daily 9–5; Dec.–Mar., daily 9–4:30.*

WHERE TO EAT AND STAY

$$ JAPANESE 🍴 **Inaka-ya** (田舎家). The specialty here, *wappa-meshi* (rice steamed in a wooden box with toppings of salmon, chicken, or crab), makes an inexpensive and excellent lunch. The *yanagi karei hitohoshi-yaki* (grilled flounder), *nodo-kuro shioyaki* (grilled local whitefish), and *buri teriyaki* (yellowtail) will make your mouth water. Inaka-ya, which closes between lunch and dinner from 2 to 5, is found in the heart of Furu-machi, the local eating and drinking district. [$] *Average main: ¥1500* ✉ *1457 Kyuban-cho, Furu-machi-dori* ☎ *025/223–1266.*

$$$ SUSHI 🍴 **Marui** (丸伊). Here you'll find all kinds of fresh fish, some of which are found only in the Sea of Japan. For easy ordering, choose the tokujo nigiri set meal (¥3,000 for 10 pieces) and a chilled bottle of the local Kitayuki sake. Then glance at what your neighbors have ordered and ask for what looks good. You can't go wrong with the freshest abalone, sea urchin, and squid in town; try the *nodo-guro* (sea bass) or the *bai-gai,* delightfully called the "Japanese babylon" in English. Marui closes during mid-afternoon. It's one block off the Furu-machi arcade. [$] *Average main: ¥3000* ✉ *8–1411 Higashibori-dori* ☎ *025/228–0101.*

$$ HOTEL 🏨 **Hotel Mets Niigata** (ホテルメッツ新潟). Opened in 2013, this sleek hotel offers spotless, if cramped, rooms at reasonable rates. **Pros:** great location; near train station; close to shopping and dining. **Cons:** rooms are small; station area can be noisy at night. [$] *Rooms from: ¥12000* ✉ *1–96–47 Hanazono Chuo-ku* ☎ *025/246–2100* 🌐 *www.jrhotelgroup.com/eng/hotel/eng167.htm* 🛏 *197 rooms* 🍽 *Breakfast.*

$$$ HOTEL 🏨 **Okura Hotel Niigata** (ホテルオークラ新潟). On the Shinano River, this sophisticated hotel offers views of the water from many of its rooms.

Pros: city views; excellent service; good location. **Cons:** pricey for what you get; can be crowded with wedding and conference guests. $\boxed{\$}$ *Rooms from:* ¥20000 ⊠ *6–53 Kawabata-cho Chuo-ku* ☎ *025/224–6111, 0120/10–0120 toll-free in Japan* ⊕ *www.okura-niigata.co.jp* ⇩ *263 Western-style rooms, 2 Japanese-style rooms* ⦿ *Breakfast.*

SADO ISLAND (SADO-GA-SHIMA) 佐渡島

84 km (52 miles) west of Niigata.

Sado is known as much for its unblemished natural beauty as for its melancholy history. Revolutionary intellectuals, such as the Buddhist monk Nichiren, were banished to Sado to endure harsh exile as punishment for treason. When gold was discovered on Sado during the Edo period (1603–1868), the homeless and poverty-stricken were sent to Sado to work as forced laborers in the mines. This long history of hardship has left a tradition of soulful ballads and folk dances. Even the bamboo grown on the island is said to be the best for making *shakuhachi,* the flutes that accompany the mournful music.

May through September is the best time to visit Sado. In January and February the weather is bitterly cold, and at other times storms can prevent sea and air crossings. Although the island is Japan's fifth largest, it's still relatively small, at 530 square km (331 square miles). Two parallel mountain chains running along the northern and southern coasts are split by a wide plain, and it is here that the island's cities are found. Despite the more than 1 million tourists who visit the island each year (more than 10 times the number of inhabitants), the pace is slow.

Sado's usual port of entry is **Ryotsu** 両津, the island's largest township. The town's center runs between Kamo-ko (Kamo Lake) and the coast, with most of the hotels and ryokan on the shore of the lake. Kamo-ko is connected to the sea by a small inlet running through the middle of town. Ryotsu's Ebisu quarter has the island's largest concentration of restaurants and bars. Give yourself at least two days to take advantage of the beauty of Sado Island. For music lovers, the Kodo Earth Celebration in mid-August is not to be missed.

GETTING HERE AND AROUND

Sado Kisen has two main ferry routes, both with regular ferry and hydrofoil service. From Niigata to Ryotsu the journey takes 2½ hours, with six or seven crossings a day; the one-way fare is ¥2,380 to ¥6,640, depending on what class you choose. The jetfoil (¥6,390 one-way) takes one hour, with 10 or 11 crossings daily in summer, three in winter. Bus No. 17 or 18, leaving from in front of the JR Niigata Station, takes 15 minutes (¥210) to reach the dock.

There is a fast car ferry running between the town of Ogi on Sado and Naoetsu, a smaller city two hours by express train south of Niigata. One-way fares start from ¥3780.

Depending on the season, one to three ferries sail between Teradomari (a port between Niigata and Naoetsu) and Akadomari, taking one hour. The fare is ¥2,830. The port is five minutes on foot from the Teradomari

The main attraction in Ogi, on Sado Island, is a trip on a traditional *taraibune* fishing boat.

bus station, and 10 minutes by bus from the JR train station (take the Teradomari-ko bus).

Frequent bus service is available between major towns on Sado-ga-shima. The scenic 90-minute bus ride from Ryotsu to Aikawa departs every 30 minutes and costs ¥740. There is also a sightseeing taxi offering three, four, or five-hour tours of the island for a flat rate.

From late April to late November, Sado Bus also operates several sightseeing bus routes taking in the island's best sights. Day tickets cost ¥3,300 to ¥7,000, depending on the route. It's an efficient way to see the island, but these buses have a magnetic attraction to souvenir shops. The best compromise is to use the tour bus for the mountain skyline drive, "Golden Road B" course (¥7,000), then rent a bike or car, or hire a taxi to explore on your own. You can make bus-tour reservations directly with the Niigata Kotsu Regular Sightseeing Bus Center.

Ferry Contact Sado Kisen Ferries. ⊠ *353 Ryotsu Minato, Sado-shi* ☎ *0570/200–310.*

Tour Information Niigata Kotsu Regular Sightseeing Bus Center. ⊠ *1–6–1 Bandai, Niigata* ☎ *0259/52–3200.*

Visitor Information Sado Tourism Association. ⊠ *Ryotsu Port, Terminal Bldg., 353 Ryotsu-minato, Sado-shi* ☎ *0259/27–5000* ⊕ *www.visitsado.com/en.* **Senkaku Bay Tourism.** ⊠ *432 Tassha, Sado-shi* ☎ *0259/75–2221.*

EXPLORING

The simplest way to explore Sado is to take the bus from Ryotsu west to Aikawa. Before gold was discovered here in 1601 it was a town of 10,000 people. The population swelled to 100,000 before the gold was exhausted. Now it's back to a tenth that size.

Ogi (小木). This tiny port town on Sado's southwest coast is famous for *taraibune,* tublike boats used for fishing. You can rent one (¥500 for 10 minutes), and with a single oar paddle your way around the harbor. Taraibune can also be found in the village of Shukunegi on the Sawasaki coast, where the water is dotted with rocky islets and the shore is covered with rock lilies in summer. ⊠ *Ogi Machi, Sado-shi.*

Osado Skyline Drive (大佐渡スカイライン). The island's most scenic route is Osado Skyline Drive, which snakes across the mountains from Ryotsu to Aikawa. You must take either a tour bus from Ryotsu or a taxi from Aikawa to Chiguse, where you can catch a bus for the return trip. (You can do the route in reverse as well.) It's particularly beautiful in autumn foliage season. ⊠ *Sado Skyline Rd., Sado-shi.*

Sado Gold Mine (佐渡金山 *Sado Kinzan*). This mine was once the most productive in Japan, producing gold, silver, and copper for the Tokugawa shogunate. After closing in the late 1980s, it has been preserved as a historical museum. Part of the mine's 325 km (250 miles) of underground tunnels, some running as deep as 1,969 feet, are open to the public. Down in the depths, robots illustrate how Edo-period slaves worked in the mine and the appalling conditions they endured. The mine is a tough 40-minute uphill walk or a 5-minute taxi ride (about ¥900) from the bus stop at Aikawa. Three daily Nana-Ura Kaigan buses let you off at the Sado-Kinzan-mae bus stop. ⊠ *1305 Shimo-Aikawa, Sado-shi* ☎ *0259/74–2389* ✉ *¥1,400* ⊙ *Apr.–Oct., daily 8–5:30; Nov.– Mar., daily 8–5 (last entry for tours at 3 pm).*

Senkaku Bay (尖閣湾 *Senkaku Bay*). Glass-bottomed boats operate sightseeing cruises around Senakaku Bay, offering views of the fantastic, sea-eroded rock formations and 60-foot cliffs. You get off the boat at Senkaku-wan Ageshima Yuen (Senkaku Bay Park), where you can picnic, stroll, and gaze at the varied rock formations offshore. From the park, return by bus from the pier to Aikawa. To reach the bay, take a 15-minute bus ride from Aikawa to Senkaku-wan Ageshima Yuen Mae bus stop, where you catch boats for the 40-minute sightseeing cruise. The one-way cruise boat runs mid-March to late November. It's also possible to enter the park without taking a cruise. ⊠ *432 Tassha* ✉ *Boats ¥1,100; park entry ¥550.*

Shukunegi (宿根木). Once known for building small wooden ships to traverse the waters between Sado and Honshu, laid-back Shukunegi is a great place to see traditional buildings that date back more than a century. From Ogi, you can reach Shukunegi by bus or by bike. If renting a bike in Ogi, ask for an electric assist model to help power you up the steep hills between the two towns. ⊠ *Shukunegi.*

6

WHERE TO EAT AND STAY

You can make hotel reservations at the information counters of Sado Kisen ship company at Niigata Port or Ryotsu Port.

$$ JAPANESE 🍴 **Uoharu** (魚春). A short drive from the ferry terminal in Ogi, this three-story building has a fish shop on the ground level and a restaurant upstairs. Choose from among the fish displayed on ice or try one of the excellent set lunches that include sashimi, *awabi* (abalone steak), or *sazae* (sea urchin). The restaurant owners sometimes take unscheduled days off, so call in advance to make sure they're open. [$] *Average main: ¥2000* ✉ *415–1 Ogi-machi, Ogi* ☎ *0259/86–2085* 💳 *No credit cards.*

$$$ B&B/INN 🏨 **Hotel Oosado** (ホテル大佐渡). Perched on a cliff overlooking the Sea of Japan, this resort offers ocean views, an open-air hot spring pool, and comfortable Japanese- or Western-style rooms. **Pros:** delicious meals; ocean views; peaceful location. **Cons:** not much sightseeing nearby; Western-style rooms are uninspiring. [$] *Rooms from: ¥20000* ✉ *288–2 Kabuse Aikawa, Sado-shi* ☎ *0259/74–3300* 🌐 *www.oosado.com* 🛏 *74 rooms.*

$$$$ HOTEL 🏨 **Sado Royal Hotel Mancho** (ホテル万長). The best hotel on the island's west coast, the Sado Royal caters mostly to Japanese tourists. **Pros:** excellent views in clear weather; friendly staff. **Cons:** no English spoken; dismal views on rainy days. [$] *Rooms from: ¥24000* ✉ *58 Orito, Aikawa-orito* ☎ *0259/74–3221* 🛏 *74 rooms* 🍽 *Some meals.*

KYOTO

WELCOME TO KYOTO

TOP REASONS TO GO

★ **Architecture:** Despite modernization, about 27,000 traditional houses still grace the Kyoto cityscape. The preservation districts include Sannen-zaka, Gion Shin-bashi, the sake brewing district in Fushimi, and the canal street leading to Kamigamo Jinja.

★ **Gardens:** Chinese-influenced gardens symbolize paradise on Earth. The *karesansui* (rock gardens) of Zen temples signify the quest for wholeness; the most famous of these is at Ryoan-ji.

★ **Crafts:** There's no short-age of art and antiques shops; secondhand kimonos are a bargain; and ceramics, lacquerware, and woven bamboo make great souvenirs.

★ **Living culture:** With their opulent kimonos, hair ornaments, and artistic skills, the professional dancers and perform-ers known as geisha are revered as an embodiment of Japanese culture.

★ **Festivals:** Kyoto is known for its elaborate fes-tivals, many of which occur between May and October.

1 Eastern Kyoto. Higashiyama, as eastern Kyoto is known, abounds with temples and shrines. The Gion shopping and entertainment neighborhood is also here.

2 Central Kyoto. Here are the majority of the hotels, the business district, and the Kiyamachi entertainment area. The Karasuma subway line runs north–south through central Kyoto.

3 Southern Kyoto. The area south of Kyoto Station contains several gems, including the unforgettable Fushimi-Inari Taisha shrine. The tea-producing city of Uji shares a border with Kyoto.

GETTING ORIENTED

Central Kyoto is fairly compact and easily navigable. Its grid layout, originally modeled on Xi'an, in China, makes this Japan's most rational urban space. Broad avenues running east–west are numbered, provides an opportunity to practice your Japanese. Counting to eight—*ichi, ni, san, shi, go, roku, shichi, hachi*—names most of the main arteries: Ichijo-dori, Nijo-dori, Sanjo-dori, and so on. Several important avenues don't follow this system, notably Oike-dori, running in front of city hall, and Marutamachi-dori and Imadegawa-dori, on the northern and southern sides of the Imperial Palace. Streets running north–south aren't numbered, but sights are clustered around a few main thoroughfares. Karasuma-dori bisects Kyoto Station in the middle of the city. East of the Kamogawa River, Higashiyama holds many popular sights, all connected by the congested Higashi-oji-dori.

4 **Western Kyoto.** Though not as dense with sights as eastern Kyoto, this neighborhood includes many temples and gardens.

5 **Arashiyama.** Just outside the city, the exquisite Katsura Imperial Villa, the lovely Tenryu-ji Temple, and beautiful riverside parks are in Arashiyama.

6 **Northern Kyoto.** Far from the city center, the main attractions of northern Kyoto are the Buddhist enclave Enryaku-ji atop Mt. Hiei, and the charming countryside of Ohara.

Updated by
Judith Clancy

The astonishing number of temples, shrines, and palaces that adorn the city make Kyoto's architecture its most famous feature worldwide. Japan's capital for more than 1,000 years, Kyoto was the center not only of politics, but religion, philosophy, art, culture, and cuisine. All of Japan's refined cultural arts blossomed from seeds planted here, including the tea ceremony, Kabuki theater, Zen, and Tantric Buddhism.

Breathtaking sights are everywhere, though some places truly stand out, among them Kyoto's great temples, such as Kiyomizu-dera in the city's eastern mountains, and the forest-cloaked Fushimi-Inari Taisha, a shrine pathway through a miles-long chain of towering vermilion gates. Visitors also flock to cultural hubs like the Museum of Traditional Crafts, which showcases the city's artisanal legacy, and Sanjusangen-do, with its 1,000 golden statues of Kannon.

Kyoto residents have a fierce sense of propriety about nearly everything, ranging from good table manners to family pedigree. This subtle yet strict code has some notorious consequences for locals—who are not considered true Kyotoites unless they can trace their lineage back four generations—but certain benefits for visitors. Wear out your welcome in a Kyoto home and they are likely to offer you tea as a signal that your time is up. The refined and symbolic Kyoto mind-set, however, insists that nothing made here should be of less than exquisite craftsmanship and stellar design. This philosophy means that whether browsing for gifts in a handkerchief shop, sightseeing at a local temple, or sitting down to a 12-course dinner, whatever you encounter is likely to be top-notch. As a visitor here you're a guest of the city, and Kyoto will make sure you leave with wonderful memories.

PLANNING

With hundreds of temples and shrines and several former imperial and shogun residences, Kyoto offers a lot to see. Don't run yourself ragged trying to take in everything—even many locals have trouble finding the time to experience all the history and culture here. Balance a morning at temples or museums with an afternoon in traditional shops, and a morning at the market with the rest of the day in Arashiyama or at one of the imperial villas. Visit at least one of the mountaintop temple complexes, such as Enryaku-ji on Hiei-zan, Daigo-ji, or Ohara. Remember that you must apply in advance (anywhere from one to several days) to visit attractions that require permits, such as the Imperial Palace, the imperial villas Katsura Rikyu and Shugaku-in, and Koinzan Saiho-ji.

WHEN TO GO

Cherry-blossom time in spring (usually the first week of April) and the glorious autumn foliage in early November are remarkable, though the city can become extremely crowded and very expensive. Except for the depths of winter, the rainy season in June, and the peak of summer heat in late July and August, Kyoto's climate is mild enough to make sightseeing pleasant the rest of the year. In the high season (April, May, and from September to November) the large numbers of visitors can make accommodations scarce.

PLANNING YOUR TIME

It would take several days minimum just to take in Kyoto's highlights, more if you want to bask in the serenity of the city's temples and gardens. You could easily spend a day each in Ohara and Arashiyama and walking along the Philosopher's Path. Nijo Castle takes about an hour to visit because its grounds are so large; otherwise, a half hour to 45 minutes at most sights is enough for most people. Walking around the old Imperial Palace and park is a nice one-hour stroll. The main part of Gion is easily done in half an hour because so much of its architecture can only be seen from the outside and not toured.

GETTING HERE AND AROUND

Kyoto has an excellent public transportation system, so getting around the city is a snap. Buses are frequent and reliable, though the thick crowds can make riding them somewhat claustrophobic. JR trains and five private light-rails and subways service the city, and are especially useful for reaching outlying sights and making day trips to nearby cities.

AIR TRAVEL

International and some domestic flights land at Kansai International Airport, near Osaka. Osaka's Itami Airport handles all regional flights. To get to downtown Kyoto from Kansai, take the JR Haruka Limited Express, a train that departs every half hour (75 minutes; ¥3,490). From Itami, buses depart approximately every 20 minutes between 8:10 am and 9:20 pm (from 55 to 90 minutes; from ¥1,280 to ¥1,370). MK Taxi offers shuttle buses from both Kansai (¥3,500) and Itami (¥2,300); reserve in advance.

BUS TRAVEL

Buses in Kyoto are quick, reliable, and punctual. Bus 100 and Bus 101 connect all the major sightseeing spots. Pick up route maps at the Kyoto Tourist Information Center.

Within the city the fare is ¥230, which you pay when getting off the bus; outside the city limits the fare varies according to distance. Several special transportation passes are available, including a one-day city bus pass for ¥500, valid for use inside the inner-city area; one-day (¥1,200) or two-day (¥2,000) passes that cover travel on city buses, the subway, and private Kyoto Line buses; and the *torafika kyo* pass, which provides ¥3,300 worth of transport via city bus or subway for ¥3,000. Passes are sold at travel agencies, bus terminals, and information centers in Kyoto Station. ■**TIP→ Trips to Uji, Ohara, and other outlying areas are not included in the one-day all-you-can-ride pass.**

SUBWAY TRAVEL

Kyoto has a 28-station subway system. The Karasuma Line runs north to south from Kokusai Kaikan to Takeda. The Tozai Line runs between Uzumasa Tenjingawa in the west and Roku-jizo in the east. Purchase tickets at the vending machines in stations before boarding. Fares begin at ¥210 and increase with distance traveled. Service runs from 5:30 am to 11:30 pm. First and last train times are posted at the entrance of each station.

TAXI TRAVEL

Taxis are readily available in Kyoto. Fares for smaller-size cabs start at ¥640 for the first 2 km (1 mile), with ¥100 added for each additional 500 meters (1,640 feet). Many taxi companies provide guided tours of the city, priced per hour or per route. MK Taxi runs tours starting at ¥18,000 for three hours. There are fixed fares for some sightseeing services that start and end at Kyoto Station. A 7½-hour tour of the city's major sights will cost in the region of ¥26,000 with any of the 17 taxi companies, including MK Taxi and Yasaka Taxi.

Contacts Keihan Taxi. ⊠ *Kyoto-shi* ☎ *0120/113–103, 075/622–4000.* **MK Taxi.** ⊠ *Kyoto-shi* ☎ *075/778–4141* ⊕ *www.mk-group.co.jp/kyoto.* **Yasaka Taxi.** ⊠ *Kyoto-shi* ☎ *075/842–1214* ⊕ *www.yasaka.jp/english.*

TRAIN TRAVEL

Frequent Shinkansen trains run between Tokyo and Kyoto, taking 2 hours and 40 minutes. The return reserved fare is ¥15,960. JR train service between Osaka and Kyoto costs ¥540 and takes 30 minutes; trains connecting with Shin-Osaka take 15 minutes and also cost ¥540. Keihan and Hankyu lines express trains take 40 minutes and cost between ¥390 and ¥460. They depart every 15 minutes from Osaka's Yodoyabashi and Umeda stations.

For travel to Kyoto's northern reaches, change from the Keihan subway line to the Eizan Railway by transferring at Imadegawa-dori/Demachi-Yanagi Station. The Eizan has two lines, the Kurama Line, running north to Kurama, and the Eizan Line, running northeast to Yase. The Hankyu Line, which, within Kyoto, runs west as far as the Katsura Imperial Villa, connects with the subway at Karasuma Station. From

Shijo-Omiya Station, the Keifuku Arashiyama Line runs to western Kyoto. JR also runs to western Kyoto on the San-in Main Line.

RESTAURANTS

Attuned to subtle seasonal changes, Kyoto cuisine emphasizes freshness and contrast. From the finest *ryotei* (high-class Japanese restaurants) to the smallest *izakaya* (pub), the distinctive elements of gracious hospitality, subtle flavors, and attention to decor create an experience that engages all the senses. Both elaborate establishments and casual shops usually offer set menus at lunchtime, at a considerably lower price than at dinner. Although the finest traditional *kaiseki ryori* (the elaborate, multicourse meal) is often costly, this experience is highly recommended at least once during your visit to Japan.

If you find yourself with an unintelligible menu, ask for the *o-makase,* or chef's recommendation and you can specify your budget in some instances. The custom of dining early, from 6 pm until 8 pm, still endures in very traditional restaurants, but many restaurants are open until 10 or 11 pm. If possible, let the hotel staff make reservations for you. For more formal restaurants try to book at least two days in advance; bookings are often not accepted for the following day if called in after 4 pm. Keep in mind that not all restaurants accept credit cards.

WHAT IT COSTS IN YEN			
$	**$$**	**$$$**	**$$$$**
At Dinner under ¥1,000	¥1,000–¥2,000	¥2,001–¥3,000	over ¥3,000

Restaurant prices are the average cost of a main course at dinner or, if dinner is not served, at lunch.

HOTELS

No other Japanese city can compete with Kyoto for style and grace. For the ultimate experience of Kyoto hospitality, stay in a *ryokan,* a traditional Japanese inn. Though often costly, a night in a ryokan guarantees you beautiful traditional Japanese surroundings, excellent service, and two elegant meals (breakfast and dinner) in most cases. But you don't have to limit yourself to the traditional. Kyoto is a tourist city, so accommodations range from luxurious hotels to small guesthouses. Service in this city is impeccable. The information desks are well stocked, and concierges or guest-relations managers are often available in the lobby to respond to your needs.

Hotel reviews have been shortened. For full information, visit Fodors.com.

WHAT IT COSTS IN YEN			
$	**$$**	**$$$**	**$$$$**
For 2 People under ¥12,000	¥12,000–¥18,000	¥18,001–¥22,000	over ¥22,000

Hotel prices are the lowest cost of a standard double room in high season.

TOURS

Doi Taxi Tours. Former U.S. President Bill Clinton is among the past customers of the extremely popular Mr. Doi, whose English is nearly perfect. Mr. Doi will take care of everything as you travel with him in comfort and style in his seven-seater, Wi-Fi-enabled van. Contact him directly or have your hotel concierge do so. ⊠ *Kyoto-shi* ☎ *090/9596–5546* ⊕ *www.kyoto-doitaxi.com* 🖃 *From ¥6,100.*

Esprit Travel. This respected U.S.-based outfit creates deluxe culture-oriented private package tours that include encounters with artists, craftspeople, landscape designers, and other artisans and contributors to Japanese culture. On these tours you might visit places not generally open to the public. Esprit also arranges custom itineraries. ⊠ *Kyoto-shi* ☎ *800/377–7481* ⊕ *www.espritttravel.com* 🖃 *From $5,250.*

JTB Sunrise Tours. JTB's half-day morning and afternoon deluxe coach tours highlight major city attractions. ⊠ *Kyoto-shi* ☎ *075/341–1413* ⊕ *www.japanican.com/tours* 🖃 *From ¥4,500.*

Kyoto Sights and Nights. Peter MacIntosh of Kyoto Sights and Nights is a seasoned guide whose late-afternoon 90-minute walking tour of the geisha areas provides insight into the mysterious world of the female entertainers known as geisha. ⊠ *Kyoto-shi* ☎ *090/5169–1654* ⊕ *www. kyotosightsandnights.com/walking.html* 🖃 *From ¥3,000.*

Kyoto-Tokyo Private Tours. Ian Roepke, a consultant to the *Kyoto Visitor's Guide,* operates this company that provides customized half- and full-day tours based on clients' preferences. You can focus on popular highlights, off-the-beaten path sights and restaurants, or a little of each. ⊠ *Kyoto-shi* ☎ *090/5895–8425* ⊕ *www.kyoto-tokyo-private-tours.com* 🖃 *From ¥43,500.*

WaRaiDo Guide Networks. The five-hour Walk in Kyoto Talk in English daytime tour is this company's flagship offering. The walk, which starts at Kyoto JR Station, takes in a temple, Shinto shrines, former geisha areas, and artisans' workshops, with a final stop for dessert and tea. The company's guides also conduct a 100-minute nighttime tour of the Gion geisha district. ⊠ *Kyoto-shi* ☎ *075/622–6803* ⊕ *www.waraido. com/walking* 🖃 *Daytime tour ¥2,000, nighttime tour ¥1,000* ⊗ *No tours Dec.–Feb.* Ⓜ *Kyoto JR Station.*

Windows to Japan. A Kyoto-based company, Windows crafts custom tours to places all over the country based on clients' interests and wishes. The tours aim to provide a "window" into Japanese culture and society. ⊠ *Kyoto, Sakyo-ku, Konoe-dho, Yase 723–12–2, Kyoto-shi* ☎ *075/601–1253* ⊕ *www.windowstojapan.com* 🖃 *Call for prices.*

VISITOR INFORMATION

One of the city's best resources, the Kyoto Tourist Information Center, is on the second floor of Kyoto Station. Heading away from the tracks, take the escalator up one flight; the information desk is next to the entrance of Isetan Department Store. The office publishes pamphlets with five self-guided walking tours, including maps. The tours range in length from about 40 to 80 minutes. The office is open daily 8:30 to 7 year-round, and there's Wi-Fi access. To get the lay of the land, pick up an up-to-date bus map, a tourist map, and a copy of the free monthly

Kyoto Visitor's Guide, which contains invaluable information on restaurants, hotels, and festivals and fairs.

Visitors require special permission from the Imperial Household Agency to visit three sights in Kyoto: Kyoto Imperial Palace, Katsura Imperial Villa, and Shugaku-in Imperial Villa. It's best to obtain permission at least a few days in advance, but the permission to visit the Imperial Palace can often be obtained for a same-day visit by stopping in at the agency's office in the northwest corner of the Imperial Palace's park; you can also apply online.

A good general-information resource for tourists, the Kyoto International Community House has a library on-site and can arrange home visits and lessons in calligraphy, the tea ceremony, and Japanese.

Contacts Imperial Household Agency. ⊠ *3 Kyoto Gyoen-nai, Kamigyo-ku* ⊹ *5-min walk from Karasuma-Imadegawa subway station* ☎ *075/211–1215* ⊕ *sankan.kunaicho.go.jp/english.* **Kyoto International Community House.** ⊠ *2–1 Torii-cho, Awata-guchi, Sakyo-ku* ⊹ *7-min walk from Keage subway* ☎ *075/752–3010* ⊕ *www.kcif.or.jp/HP/kaikan/top/en.* **Kyoto Tourist Information Center.** ⊠ *JR Kyoto Station, Karasuma-dori, Shimogyo-ku* ⊹ *Upper level, next to Isetan Department Store entrance* ☎ *075/343–6655.* **Kyoto Visitor's Guide.** ⊠ *Kyoto-shi* ⊕ *www.kyotoguide.com.*

EXPLORING

EASTERN KYOTO

East of the Kamogawa River, in the neighborhoods known as Higashi-yama (literally, Eastern Mountain) and Okazaki, are some of Kyoto's most dazzling shrines and temples, stretching from solemn Sanjusangen-do in the south to the elegant Ginkaku-ji in the north. The cobbled streets of the Gion district are mysterious during the day, and even more so at night.

GETTING AROUND

Subway lines crisscross eastern Kyoto, making them a great way to get around. Maps detailing the extensive bus network are available at tourist information centers. Buses run on major roads like Shichijo-dori, Shijo-dori, and Higashi-oji-dori. But the best way to explore these neighborhoods is on foot. Starting from anywhere, you can't walk 10 minutes in any direction without encountering a landmark.

TOP ATTRACTIONS

Eikan-do (永観堂 *View of Eternity Hall*). Next to the Nanzen-ji temple complex, Eikan-do was built after the original temple, dating from 855, was destroyed in the 15th century. Visitors come throughout the year to see the image of Amida Buddha statue, which represents the time when Eikan paused in his prayers and the Buddha turned his head to encourage him to continue. The temple draws the most visitors in autumn, when people come to see the colorful foliage, and in November, when there's an excellent display of painted doors. ⊠ *48 Eikando-cho, Higashiyama-ku* ⊹ *South end of Philosopher's Walk*

A Brief History of Kyoto

Although Kyoto was Japan's capital for more than 10 centuries, the real center of political power was often elsewhere, be it Kamakura (1192–1333) or Edo (1603–1868). Until 710 Japan's capital moved with the accession of each new emperor. When it was decided that this expense was too great, Nara was chosen as the permanent capital. This experiment lasted 74 years, during which Buddhists rallied for, and achieved, tremendous political power. In an effort to thwart them, Emperor Kammu moved the capital to Nagaoka for a decade and then, in 794, to Kyoto.

Until the end of the 12th century, the city flourished under imperial rule. The city's nobility, known as "cloud dwellers," cultivated an extraordinary culture of refinement called *miyabi.* But when imperial power waned, the city saw the rise of the samurai class, employed to protect the noble families' interests. Ensuing clashes between various clans led to the Gempei War (1180–85), from which the samurai emerged victorious. The *bushido,* or warrior spirit, found a counterpart in the minimalism of Zen Buddhism's austerity. The past luxury of miyabi was replaced with Zen's respect for frugality and discipline.

This period also brought devastating civil wars. Because the various feuding clans needed the Emperor's support to claim legitimacy, Kyoto, as imperial capital, became the stage for bitter struggles. The Onin Civil War (1467–77) was particularly devastating for Kyoto. Two feudal lords, Yamana and Hosokawa, disputed who should succeed the reigning shogun. Yamana camped in the western part of the city with 90,000 troops, and Hosokawa settled in the eastern part with 100,000 troops. Central Kyoto was the battlefield, and many of the city's buildings were destroyed.

Ieyasu Tokugawa, founder of the Tokugawa shogunate, eventually moved the country's political center to Edo. Kyoto remained the imperial capital, and the first three Tokugawa shoguns paid homage to the city by restoring old temples and building new villas in the early 1700s. Much of what you see in Kyoto dates from this period. When Emperor Meiji was restored to power in the late 1860s his capital and Imperial Court were moved to Tokyo. Commerce flourished, though, and Kyoto continued as the center of traditional culture.

7

☎ *075/761–0007* ⊕ *www.eikando.or.jp* ✉ *Nov. ¥1,000; Dec.–Oct. ¥600* ⊗ *Nov., daily 9–9; Dec.–Oct., daily 9–4.*

Fodor'sChoice
★ **Ginkaku-ji** (銀閣寺 *Temple of the Silver Pavilion*). A UNESCO World Heritage Site, the Temple of the Silver Pavilion was intended to impress the courtly world with its opulence, but the current structure is an exercise in elegance and restraint. Yoshimasa Ashikaga spent years constructing his retirement villa in a conspicuous homage to his grandfather's Golden Pavilion on the west side of town. The shogun wanted the large hall here to be wrapped in silver leaf, but during construction in the 1470s a tumultuous war and government unrest left the clan bereft of funds. Today, an elaborate entryway of stone, bamboo, and hedge lead into a modest compound of buildings giving way to extensive

gardens. The Silver Pavilion, which stares down at its reflection in the water, sits among the rolling moss-covered hillsides, dark pools, and an enormous dry garden, called the Sea of Sand. ⊠ *1 Ginkaku-ji-cho, Sakyo-ku* ✛ *From Kyoto Station take Bus 5, 11, or 17 to Ginkaku-ji-michi stop* ☎ *075/771–5725* 💴 *¥500* ⊙ *Mid-Mar.–Nov., daily 8:30–5; Dec.–mid-Mar., daily 9–4:30.*

Heian Jingu (平安神宮 *Heian Shrine*). The massive vermilion *torii* gate of Heian Jingu is one of Kyoto's best-known symbols. Built in the 1890s to commemorate the 1,100th anniversary of Kyoto's founding, Heian Jingu pays homage to the two emperors who bookend the city's era of national prominence: Kammu, who brought the imperial throne here in 794, and Komei, whose reign ending in 1866 saw the sun set on Kyoto's days as the capital. An assertion of Kyoto's unfaded splendor, Heian Jingu was built as a slightly smaller replica of the Imperial Palace, destroyed in 1227. The architecture reveals China's strong influence on the early Japanese court. The gate, the biggest in Japan, is particularly impressive, as are the three elaborate gardens behind the main shrine, conceived by the master designer Ogawa Jihei, which draw on Kyoto's landscaping origins. The complex makes a wonderful backdrop for several annual events, most famously the brazier-lighted plays of Takigi Noh Drama every June 1 and 2, and the Jidai Costume Festival on October 22. ⊠ *Okazakinishi Tenno-cho, Sakyo-ku* ✛ *3-min walk from Bus 5, 32, or 100 to Heian Jingu stop; 7-min walk from Tozai subway station of Higashiyama; 10-min walk from Keihan train station at Sanjo-dori* ☎ *075/761–0221* 💴 *Gardens ¥800* ⊙ *Mid-Mar.–Aug., daily 8:30–5:30; Sept., Oct., and early Mar., daily 8:30–5; Nov.–Feb., daily 8:30–5:40.*

Fodor's Choice **Kiyomizu-dera** (清水寺). Pilgrims have climbed Higashiyama's stone-
★ inlaid streets to this historic mountainside temple, a UNESCO World Heritage Site, for centuries. Kiyomizu-dera's tremendous gates and pagodas are marvels to behold. The main hall's huge veranda, jutting out over the forested valley, is one of the city's quintessential images. Immense timbers support the large deck and gracefully angular cypress-shingle roof. Finding the courage to set out on a daring new adventure is often likened to "taking a leap from the veranda of Kiyomizu."

The temple was founded in 780, but the buildings you see today date from 1633. Two huge temple guardians man the gateway, and the first sight is of people trying to lift the heavy iron staves and geta clogs, supposedly used by the warrior Benkei. The interior of the temple has been darkened by the ages. Visitors may pass along the area behind the main altar, a metaphoric journey into the soul; in the dark passageway below the temple, quietly follow a chain of thick wooden beads to an ancient tablet carved with the Sanskrit rune for heart. Away from the main hall, the quirky Jishu Shrine is dedicated to Okuni Nushi-no-mikoto, a deity considered to be a powerful matchmaker. Many young people visit the shrine to seek help in finding their life partners. They try to walk between two stones placed 59 feet apart, with their eyes closed. It's said that love will materialize for anyone who can walk in a straight line between the two.

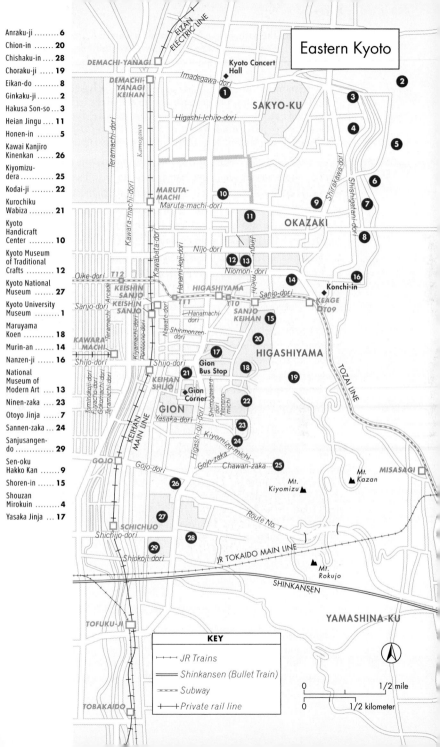

Eastern Kyoto

KEY

- ···|··· JR Trains
- ─── Shinkansen (Bullet Train)
- ▭▭▭ Subway
- ─┼─ Private rail line

0 ———— 1/2 mile

0 ———— 1/2 kilometer

Farther down the path, the Sound of Feathers waterfall funnels down in three perfect streams before a raised platform. You can catch some of its water by using one of the long-handled silver cups; drinking from the falls supposedly helps with health, longevity, and academic success. If you need more to fortify you, enjoy some noodles, shaved iced, hot tea, or cold beer (depending on the season) from one of the old stalls below the trellised balcony. ✉ *1 Kiyomizu, Higashiyama-ku* ✚ *Bus 100 or 206 to Gojo-zaka or Kiyomizu-michi, walk uphill 10 mins* ☎ *075/551–1234* ⊕ *www.kiyomizudera.or.jp/lang/01.html* 🖃 *¥300* ⊘ *Daily 6–6.*

NEED A BREAK?

Bunnosuke Jaya (文の助茶屋). On the road to Kiyomizu-dera, a wooden archway plastered with *senja-fuda* (name cards pilgrims affix on the entryways to shrines and temples) is the entry to this charming courtyard teahouse that opened in 1910. The specialties here are *amazake*, a sweet, nonalcoholic sake often served hot with a touch of ginger, and *warabimo-chi* rice cakes. The interior is adorned with an eclectic collection of kites and folk dolls. ✉ *373 Yasaka Uemachi Shimogawara-dori, Higashi-iru, Higashiyama-ku* ☎ *075/561–1972* ⊘ *Closed Wed.*

Kurochiku Wabiza (くろちく倭美坐). Fine traditional crafts, including reasonably priced dolls, ceramics, lacquerware, prints, incense, textiles, and bonsai, can be found at this center. ✉ *Gion Kurochiku Bldg., 275 Gion-machi Kitagawa, Higashiyama-ku* ✚ *From Kyoto Station, take any bus that stops at Gion on Shijo-dori* ☎ *075/541–1196* ⊕ *www. kurochiku.co.jp/wabiza* ⊘ *Daily 10–7.*

Murin-an (無隣庵庭園 *Murin Garden*). Ogawa Jihei (1860–1932), a leading landscape architect of the Meiji period, departed from tradition in developing this late-19th-century garden whose rolling expanses of English-style lawn represent the first use of this type of ground cover within a Japanese garden. The blending of Western and Japanese influences can also be detected in some of the architecture and interiors of this estate, once part of Nanzen-ji, that was commissioned by Arimoto Yamagata, twice Japan's prime minister in the late 19th century. The paths of Murin-an, a small but classic Meiji stroll garden, meander along converging streams and past a three-tier waterfall. The garden's southern section is almost always in shadow, creating wonderful contrasts. ✉ *31 Nanzenji-Kusakawa-cho, Sakyo-ku* ☎ *075/752–0203* 🖃 *¥600* ⊘ *Daily 9–4:30.*

Nanzen-ji (南禅寺 *Nanzen Temple*). Several magnificent temples share this corner of the forested foothills between Heian Jingu and Ginkaku-ji, but with its historic gatehouse the most prominent is Nanzen-ji. A short distance away are Nanzen-in, a subtemple noted for its garden's serene beauty, and Kochi-in, a subtemple, which also has a noteworthy garden.

As happened with Ginkaku-ji, the villa of Nanzen-ji was turned into a temple upon the death of its owner, Emperor Kameyama (1249–1305). By the 14th century this had become the most powerful Zen temple in Japan, which spurred the Tendai monks to destroy it. During the

Ginkaku-ji (Temple of the Silver Pavilion) was built in the late 15th century as a retirement villa for Shogun Yoshimasa Ashikaga.

15th-century Onin Civil War the buildings were again demolished. Some were reconstructed during the 16th century.

Nanzen-ji has again become one of Kyoto's most important Rinzai Zen temple complexes, and monks are still trained here. Entrance is through the enormous 1628 **Sanmon** (Triple Gate), the classic "gateless" gate of Zen Buddhism that symbolizes entrance into the most sacred part of the temple precincts. After ascending, visitors have a view of the city beyond and the statue of Goemon Ishikawa. In 1594 this Robin Hood–style outlaw tried but failed to kill the *daimyo* (feudal lord) Toyotomi Hideyoshi. He hid in this gate until his capture, after which he was boiled to death in a cauldron of oil, thus lending his name to the old traditional rounded iron bathtubs once popular in Japan. His story is still enacted in many Kabuki plays.

On your way to see the major subtemples and gardens within the complex, don't overlook Nanzen-ji's other attractions. The **Hojo** (Abbots' Quarters) is a National Treasure. Inside, screens with impressive 16th-century paintings divide the chambers. Eitoku Kano (1543–90) painted these wall panels of the Twenty-Four Paragons of Filial Piety and Hermits. Outside, Enshu Kobori (1579–1647) is responsible for what's commonly known as the Leaping Tiger Garden, an excellent example of a dry rock-and-sand garden. The large rocks are grouped with clipped azaleas, maples, pines, and moss, all positioned against a plain white well behind the raked gravel expanse. The greenery effectively connects the garden with the lush forested hillside beyond. Visible in the complex's southeastern section is an arched redbrick aqueduct from the 1890s, with the waters of Lake Biwa, in the next prefecture, still flowing

CLOSE UP

The Geisha of Gion

Japan's traditional and modern worlds intersect where Shijo-dori crosses Hanami-koji-dori in the district of Gion. To the south, stone streets lead past wood-fronted teahouses displaying red paper lanterns; on the north side of Shijo-dori are high-rises filled with bars. Eastward is Yasaka Jinja's commanding orange-and-white arched gate; westward are the city's best department stores.

Gion remains Kyoto's center for high culture such as Kabuki theater, but perhaps more famous to foreign visitors is the world of the geisha, referred to as *geiko* in Kyoto, brought into the spotlight in recent decades by the novel and subsequent film *Memoirs of a Geisha.* Wandering around Hanami-koji-dori at dinner time you might see *maiko-san* and *geiko san*, the modern equivalents of apprentice and senior geisha, on their way to appointments at exclusive teahouses behind curtained doorways.

The practiced gait of these women and their gorgeous apparel marks them as the most refined and talented in the traditional performing arts. The spring and autumn dance revues entertain hundreds of admirers. Several restaurants and inns can arrange for private parties to have a maiko-san or geiko-san sing and dance while you dine.

---

along it. The canopy of trees here, which keeps this favorite picture-taking spot cool, stands as a reminder of the city's awakening to new technology that changed residents' lives. Boring through the mountain allowed supplies as well as water to flow more easily into the city.

Nanzen-in. This subtemple's east-facing garden has recently been renovated into a contemplative one with a pathway of diamond-shaped stones resting on moss-covered ground. Farther back is a large stroll garden with bridges over the tree-shaded, koi-stocked pond. A small building back here with a curving Chinese-style roof is a memorial to Emperor Kameyama. (☎ *075/771–0365* ⊕ *www.nanzen.com.* ✉*¥300.* ☼ *Daily 8:40–4.*)

Konchi-in. Recognized by aficionados around the world as one of Japan's finest gardens, Konchi-in was first established in the 15th century. It was moved inside Nanzen-ji's temple complex in 1605 and landscaped by designer Enshu Kobori several decades later. The elaborate black-lacquered gate, reminiscent of Nikko, is a shrine dedicated to Tokugawa Ieyasu, the shogun whose clan ruled Japan for centuries. The garden is one of Japan's finest examples of a classic tortoise-and-crane design, representing longevity and wisdom. It's also the most authentic example of Kobori's work. Konchi-in is before Nanzen-ji's main entrance, slightly southwest of the Sanmon Gate. (☎ *075/771–3511* ✉*¥400.* ☼ *Daily 8:30–5)* ✉ *Nanzenji, Sakyo-ku* ☎ *075/771–0365* ⊕ *www.nanzen.com* ✉ *Abbotts' Quarters ¥500, Gate ¥500* ☼ *Mar.–Nov., daily 8:40–5; Dec.–Feb., daily 8:40–4:30.*

NEED A BREAK?

Taian-en (大安苑). Within the Nanzen-ji temple complex is a restaurant designed by Ogawa Jihei 11th, a renowned Showa designer whose predecessor Ogawa Jihei 7th conceived the garden at Heian Jingu. A gnarled red pine stands as the centerpiece of the restaurant's garden. Multicourse *kaiseki* meals (¥10,000) are available in this beautiful setting. Bento box lunches (¥3,500) and boiled tofu (¥1,800) are served in a tatami room. On the second floor is Ankoan, a Japanese-style café that serves coffee, tea, and alcoholic beverages. Desserts cost ¥800. ⊠ *Nanzenji-Kusakawa-machi 81, Sakyo-ku* 🕾 *075/752-4333* ⊕ *www.taianen.com/taian/taian.html.*

Fodor's Choice ★

Sanjusangen-do (三十三間堂 *Sanjusangen Hall*). This 400-foot-long hall preserves 1,001 golden, graceful Buddhist images, one of the world's most magnificent collections of wooden statuary. Enthroned in the hall's center is a seated thousand-armed Kannon (enlightened being) crowned with 10 tiny heads. Tankei, a noted sculptor of the Kamakura period (1192–1333), carved the statue. In the corridor behind it are 30 other images, carved by the members of the same school of sculptors, that include the mythological birdlike beings called Garuda, the holy man Basusenin, and the gods of wind and thunder. The name of the hall refers to the 33 spaces between the 34 pillars that make up its length. ⊠ *657 Sanjusangen-do Mawari-cho, Higashiyama-ku* ✛ *From Kyoto Station, take Bus 206, 208, or 100 to Sanjusangen-do-mae stop; temple is to south, east of Hyatt Regency* ⊕ *sanjusangendo.jp* 🎟 *¥600* ⊙ *Apr.– mid-Nov., daily 8–5; mid-Nov.–Mar., daily 9–4.*

OFF THE BEATEN PATH

Sannen-zaka and Ninen-zaka (三年坂と二年坂). With their ancient stone paths and traditional wooden buildings, these two winding streets are the finest extant examples of Old Kyoto—the area is one of four historic preservation districts in the city. Shops along the way sell crafts such as pottery, dolls, and bamboo baskets. ⊠ *Higashiyama-ku* ✛ *7-min walk uphill from bus stop at Higashi-oji and Gojo.*

Yasaka Jinja (八坂神社 *Yasaka Shrine*). Stone stairs lead up through the vermilion-and-white gate of Kyoto's central shrine, which plays an essential role in the city's fiscal good fortune. In addition to the good-luck charms people flock here to buy, you will see the names of the city's biggest stores and companies marking the lanterns hanging from the main hall's eaves, each of the corporate sponsors seeking financial favor as well. The shrine, just off Higashi-oji-dori, was built in the 7th century above an underground lake to ensure that the god who resided in the east—the blue water dragon—received the fresh water needed to ensure healthy Earth energy. The original enshrined Shinto deity, Susano-no-mikoto, later came to be associated with the Buddhist spirit Gozu Ten-no, a protector against pestilence and the god of prosperity. Also known as the Gion Shrine, Yasaka hosts the Gion Festival, a monthlong event that takes place in July. The festival started in 869 as a religious ritual to rid the city of a terrible plague that originated in Kyoto and swiftly spread all over Japan. The grounds of Yasaka Shrine are filled with revelers during cherry-blossom season, usually in early April. ⊠ *625 Gion-machi, Kitagawa, Higashiyama-ku* ✛ *From Kyoto*

Continued on page 412

7

THE PHILOSOPHER'S PATH

哲学の道

A STROLL THROUGH KYOTO'S EASTERN HILLS AND TEMPLES

by
Christal Whelan

"If my heart can become pure and simple, like that of a child, I think there probably can be no greater happiness." —Kitaro Nishida

Tucked away in the lush foothills of the Eastern Mountains of Kyoto, the Philosopher's Path winds along a canal lined with cherry trees and through a quiet residential neighborhood. With notable Buddhist temples, imperial tombs, Shinto shrines, and quaint shops, the route has become one of the city's most popular walking courses.

Although it traverses an area rich in antiquity, the Philosopher's Path is a modern promenade, receiving its name in the early Showa era (1926–1989) after its counterpart in Heidelberg. Later, the path became associated with the legacy of the philosopher Kitaro Nishida (1870–1945), renowned for his synthesis of Eastern and Western thought, who walked the path daily. Today many follow in Nishida's footsteps along the canal and likewise bear witness to the drama of the changing seasons. Flanked by two bridges—the Nyakaou-ji and Ginkaku-ji—and a Zen temple at both extremes, this mile offers a perfect balance of Japanese history, culture, cuisine, art, and devotion to nature all within a single walk.

(opposite) The Philosopher's Path, (top) Tea house on the Philosopher's Path

7

IN FOCUS: THE PHILOSOPHER'S PATH

Ginkaku-ji

THE ROUTE (NORTH TO SOUTH)

If you decide to follow this route from south to north, simply reverse the walk.

Begin your morning at **Ginkaku-ji**, the Silver Pavilion. Although it was once the aesthetic and cultural center of a nation, fires over the years have ravaged the complex and left only two original buildings, both now National Treasures—the Kannon-den and the Toku-do. These graceful structures are thatched with layers of thin cypress shingles. On the apex of the Kannon-den a bronze phoenix stands perched prophetically, and the paper windows shimmer with reflections from the rippling pond below. Exquisite dry sand and classical stroll gardens are by Soami, a master landscape designer of the medieval period. The road away from Gin-

kaju-ji, down an incline, leads to the Philosopher's Path on the left. If you're in need of some fortification, detour a few hundred meters away to the pert **Noa Noa** café which serves coffee drinks, pizzas, and sturdier pasta dishes.

Heading south, the outdoor chapel at **Shounzan Mirokuin** is dedicated to the bodhisattva Jizo, who protects children and those in dire straits. This temple belongs to Shugendo, a fusion of mountain veneration, Shinto, and Japanese Tantric Buddhism (here, Tendai). Normally closed, the temple opens to the public on August 28, from 1 to 3 pm, when the ascetic practitioners called *yamabushi* hold a religious procession that culminates in a *saito-goma*, or outdoor fire ceremony.

Follow the path markers and cross the bridge to **Honen-in Temple.** The thatched entrance gate and the temple grounds are the highlights here since the temple interior is closed to the public most of the year. To the right of

the entry is a building used for contemporary year-round art exhibitions. Honen-in, built in the late 17th century, is named for the founder of the Jodo sect of Buddhism, who chose the site during the 13th century, when he also arranged to have the temple of **Anraku-ji**, to the south, constructed to honor four believers who died tragically.

The temple runs Café Momiji on its premises and hosts the popular *kabocha kuyo*, a service conducted since 1790 in honor of pumpkin-squash (July 25, 9–3).

The nearby **Otoyo Jinja** is an ancient Shinto shrine that serves as the guardian for the people living in the nearby neighborhoods. Otoyo holds

Sen-oku Museum

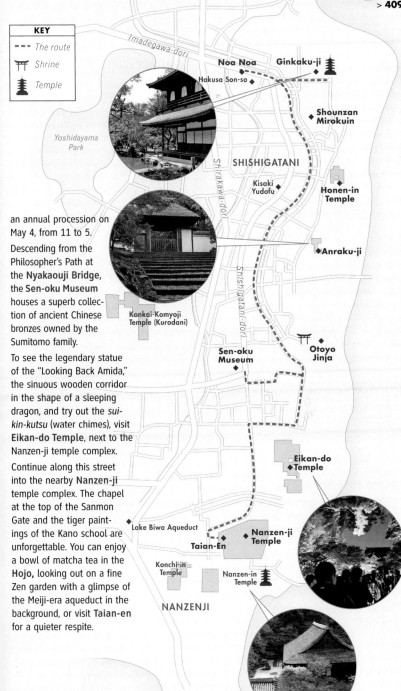

KEY
- - - *The route*
⛩ *Shrine*
🏯 *Temple*

Imadegawa-dori

Noa Noa

Ginkaku-ji

Hakusa Son-so

Yoshidayama Park

Shounzan Mirokuin

Shirakawa-dori

SHISHIGATANI

Kisaki Yudofu

Honen-in Temple

an annual procession on May 4, from 11 to 5.

Descending from the Philosopher's Path at the **Nyakaouji Bridge**, the **Sen-oku Museum** houses a superb collection of ancient Chinese bronzes owned by the Sumitomo family.

Anraku-ji

Konkai-Komyoji Temple (Kurodani)

Shishigatani-dori

To see the legendary statue of the "Looking Back Amida," the sinuous wooden corridor in the shape of a sleeping dragon, and try out the *sui-kin-kutsu* (water chimes), visit **Eikan-do Temple**, next to the Nanzen-ji temple complex.

Sen-oku Museum

Otoyo Jinja

Continue along this street into the nearby **Nanzen-ji** temple complex. The chapel at the top of the Sanmon Gate and the tiger paintings of the Kano school are unforgettable. You can enjoy a bowl of matcha tea in the **Hojo,** looking out on a fine Zen garden with a glimpse of the Meiji-era aqueduct in the background, or visit **Taian-en** for a quieter respite.

Eikan-do Temple

Lake Biwa Aqueduct

Taian-En

Nanzen-ji Temple

Konchi-in Temple

Nanzen-in Temple

NANZENJI

THE PATH IN ALL SEASONS

In the **spring**, the eruption of cherry blossoms transforms the Philosopher's Path into a heavenly pink.

With the **summer** comes fireflies, flourishes of hydrangea, bird song, cicada cries, and murmur of water tumbling over rocks.

The **autumn** gives way to a palette of yellows, oranges, and the deep red of the Japanese maple.

In **winter** snows blanket the Philosopher's Path.

SEASONAL EVENTS

Go-san Okuribi (Sending off ceremony on five mountains): August 16

Kabocha Kuyo (Anraku-ji): July 25, 9–3

Saito goma (Mirokuin): August 28, 1–3

Otoyo gyoretsu (Otoyo Jinja): May 4, 11–5

Eikando (Light Up): Nov. 6–30, 5:30–9, evening autumn foliage viewing

(top left) Spring cherry blossoms; (top right) summer strolling; (bottom left) Ginkaku-ji in winter; (bottom right) the fall Eikando festival

PRACTICAL INFO

GETTING THERE

You can begin your walk at either end of the pathway—Ginkaku-ji or Nanzen-ji. If you choose Nanzen-ji, take the subway (Tozai line) from Sanjo-Keikan and get off at Keage, or catch Bus 5 from Kyoto Station to Nazen-ji Eikando-mae. From either, it is a 10-minute walk. To start from Ginkaku-ji, catch Bus 17, 5, or 100 and get off at Ginkaku-ji-mae. An easy walk up Imadegawa to Ginkaku-ji-michi leads into the temple.

TIMING

With no stops along the way, the entire course takes just under an hour. But if you stop at the suggested points of interest, allow three hours or more. You can begin at any time, but should bear in mind that Gingaku-ji closes at 4:30 or 5 depending on the season. A visit to Ginkaku-ji is probably best done as early as possible (it opens at 8:30 am) to beat the crowds at one of Kyoto's most frequented temples.

FUEL UP

If you begin the walk at Gingaku-ji, then you will wind up at Taian-en for either lunch or dinner, depending on what hour you set out. The trip from north to south allows you to end up sipping from a frothy bowl of green tea in Nanzen-ji's **Hojo,** or Abbots' Quarters, or sitting down to a traditional bento lunch or a multicourse meal at Taian-en. A trip in the reverse (from Nanzen-ji to Ginkaku-ji) can conclude with dinner at either **Kisaki Yudofu,** or for a more sumptuous *kaiseki* feast, try the teahouse at the **Hakusa Son-so** (down the hill from Ginkaju-ji) in its garden (reservations required).

SHUIN-CHO

From whichever end you do start, be sure to pick up a *shuin-cho* at your starting temple (¥1,300). These small, cloth-covered books have thick, blank sheets for collecting ink stamps and calligraphic signatures from each temple you visit. There is a nominal fee for these signatures, but they're worth every yen for such an authentic souvenir of Japan's ancient capital.

Creation of a dry landscape garden, or *karesansui,* at Honen-in temple

Station take Bus 206 or 100 to Gion bus stop; shrine is 1-min walk east from stops on Higashi-oji and Shijo-dori ⊕ *www.yasaka-jinja.or.jp* 🎫 *Free* ☉ *Daily 24 hrs.*

WORTH NOTING

Anraku-ji (安楽寺 *Anraku Temple*). This small temple in the foothills of Higashiyama dates back to the 12th century, when the priest Honen began to preach a novel means of salvation accessible to anyone, the recitation of the name of Amida Buddha *(nenbutsu)*. Two of Honen's disciples, Anraku and Juren, preached this new, at the time heretical, faith in the countryside outside the usual surveillance. Two ladies in the Imperial Court, Matsumushi and Suzumushi, who were also said to be concubines of Emperor Go-Toba (1180–1239), inspired by the teachings, became nuns. Convinced that the monks had seduced the two ladies, the Emperor had the monks seized and beheaded. The court ladies then took their own lives in response, and Honen was exiled as a heretic. When he was finally permitted to return to Kyoto in 1212, the now elderly priest had Anraku-ji built to honor his faithful disciples and their two converts. The tombs of all four are on the temple grounds. The shrine is open in spring to showcase its gorgeous azaleas and in autumn for its vivid maples. ✉ *Shishigatani, Goshonodan-cho 21, Sakyo-ku* ☎ *075/771–5360* ⊕ *anrakuji-kyoto.com/information* 🎫 *¥500* ☉ *Daily 9:30–5 in spring and autumn.*

Chion-in (知恩院 *Chion Temple*). The headquarters of the Jodo sect of Buddhism, Chion-in is impressive enough to have been cast in the film *The Last Samurai* as a stand-in for Edo Castle. Everything here is on a massive scale. The imposing tiered gateway is the largest in the country, and the bell inside the temple grounds, cast in 1633, is the heaviest in Japan, requiring 17 monks to ring it. If you're in Kyoto over New Year's you can hear it being struck 108 times to release believers from the 108 worldly desires of the old year. The bell may not be struck again until the previous sound has ceased, so it takes more than an hour to ring in the new year. The event is nationally televised.

The extensive temple buildings contain many artworks, along with simpler pleasures such as the exposed *uguisu-bari* (nightingale floor)—floor planks that "chirp" when trod upon, alerting residents of potential intruders. There are two halls, the greater and lesser, connected via corridors with gardens between.

The temple is adjacent to Maruyama Park. As with most Kyoto temples, Chion-in's history includes a litany of fires and earthquakes. Most of the buildings you see date from the early 1600s. ✉ *400 Rinka-cho, Higashiyama-ku* ✈ *From Kyoto Station take Bus 206 to Gion stop* ⊕ *www.chion-in.or.jp/e* 🎫 *¥500* ☉ *Daily 9–4.*

Chishaku-in (智積院 *Chishaku Temple*). The lush garden of Chishaku-in and paintings by Tohaku Hasegawa and his son Kyuzo make a visit to this temple a memorable experience. A small museum exhibits works by father and son that are among the finest of the Momoyama period (1573–1615). The elder Hasegawa (1539–1610) painted exclusively for Zen temples in his later years, with masterpieces ranging from lyrical monochrome ink creations to bolder, more colorful works such as the gold-backed images of cherry, maple, pine, and plum trees exhibited here, and ones of autumn grasses. A mountain in China reputedly inspired the design of the temple's hilly garden, whose pond was sculpted to look like a river. The pond is stocked with colorful carp. Equally colorful when they're in bloom are the mounds of sculpted camellia and azalea bushes. ⊠ *964 Higashi-kawaramachi, Higashi-oji Nanajo-sagaru, Higashiyama-ku* ✛ *From Kyoto Station take Bus 206 or 208 to Higashiyama-Shichijo stop; temple is at southern junction of Shichijo-dori and Higashi-oji-dori* ⊕ *www.chisan.or.jp* 💬 *¥500* ☾ *Daily 9–4.*

Choraku-ji (長楽寺 *Choraku Temple*). A procession of stone lanterns lines the steep stairway to this tiny temple founded in the early 9th century by Emperor Kammu with the priest Saicho. In 1185, after the Minamoto clan's defeat of the Taira clan in the Genpei War, the last survivor found refuge here, a circumstance depicted in the epic *The Tale of the Keike.* Within the temple, note the 11-headed statue of Kannon, evocative of the deity's Indian origins. Another structure houses precious items: ancient scrolls, remnants of a child emperor's clothing, and Buddhist images. ⊠ *Maruyama Park, 626 Maruyama-cho, Higashiyama-ku* ✛ *Far eastern section of park* 💬 *¥500* ☾ *Fri.–Wed. 9–5.*

Hakusa Son-so (白沙村荘庭園 *The Inn of White Sand*). A century-old villa with a large stroll garden, this was once the home of the painter Kansetsu Hashimoto (1883–1945). Combining influences from various Japanese periods and drawing inspiration from Chinese imagery, Hashimoto created a unique style of painting. A new museum contains many of Hashimoto's sketches and paintings, as well as works by his Chinese and Japanese contemporaries and an enthralling collection of Greek and Persian pottery. An exquisite stone garden and a teahouse are also open to the public. If you book at least two days in advance, it's possible to experience a complete tea ceremony. Adjacent to the estate is the Noa Noa café, which serves light casual fare from ¥1,500. ⊠ *37 Ishibashi-cho, east of Imadegawa and Ginkaku-ji intersection, Higashiyama-ku* ✛ *From Kyoto Station take Bus 5 or 100 to Ginkaku-ji-michi stop and walk east along canal* ☏ *075/751–0446* ⊕ *www.hakusasonso.jp* 💬 *¥1,000* ☾ *Daily 10–5; last entry at 4:30.*

Honen-in (法然院 *Honen Temple*). South of Ginkaku Temple on the Philosopher's Path lie the serene grounds of a once rural temple. Tall spindly bush camellia and slender maple trees form a canopy over the long entry path. Inside the temple's thatched gateway, two long regular mounds of sand are formed into shapes symbolizing the changing seasons. While strolling through the verdant garden, you may notice the tombs of several notables, including novelist Junichiro Tanizaki (1886–1965), economist Hajime Kawakami (1879–1946), and artist Heihachiro Fukuda (1892–1974).

The temple, built in 1680, is on a site chosen in the 13th century by Honen, founder of the populist Jodo sect of Buddhism. This is a training temple. Year-round, monks place 25 flowers before the Amida Buddha statue in the main hall, representing the 25 bodhisattvas who accompany the Buddha to receive the souls of the newly deceased.

Five Kyoto Gardens Not to Miss

CLOSE UP

To know Kyoto is to know its gardens, which at their best express an admirable quest for beauty, harmony, and discreet joy. Below are five exquisite examples not to be missed.

DAITOKU-JI
This Zen temple complex shelters some of Kyoto's finest contemplative gardens, most notably the rock-and-gravel garden at the subtemple Daisen-in.

HEIAN JINGU SHRINE
In conceiving the stroll garden at this late-19th-century shrine honoring Kyoto's founding, designer Ogawa Jihei took inspiration from some of the city's original 1,200-year-old gardens.

KOINZAN SAIHO-JI
More than a hundred varieties of moss carpet the one-of-a-kind two-level garden at this appropriately named landmark, the Moss Temple.

KONCHI-IN
Of all the gardens in Japan, the one at this subtemple of Nanzen-ji most closely resembles the designs of Kobori Enshu, a famous 17th-century landscape gardener.

RYOAN-JI
The world's most renowned Zen dry rock garden continues to intrigue scholars and visitors alike for the subtle message of its meticulous design.

✉ *Shishigatani-Goshonodan-cho, Sakyo-ku* ☎ *075/771–2420* 🎫 *Free* ◷ *Daily 6–4.*

Kawai Kanjiro Kinenkan (河井寛次郎記念館 *Kawai Kanjiro Memorial House*). The house and workshop of prolific potter Kanjiro Kawai (1890–1966) has been transformed into a museum showcasing his distinctive works. The asymmetrical vases, bowls, and pots on display represent only a fraction of his output of this leading light of the *Mingei* (folk art) movement of the 1920s. Besides the intriguing workshop and enormous kiln preserved in an inner courtyard, there is residence itself, an old country farmhouse Kaiwai had moved to this location. A little hard to find, this compound is along a small street one block west of Higashi-oji-dori and two blocks south of Gojo-dori. ✉ *569 Kanei-cho, Gojo-zaka, Higashiyama-ku* ⊹ *20-min walk from Kyoto Station, or take Bus 100 or 206 to Gojo-zaka, walk west on Gojo-dori, and take first left* ☎ *075/561–3585* 🎫 *¥900* ◷ *Tues.–Sun. 10–5. Closed briefly in mid-Aug. and at New Year.*

Kodai-ji (高台寺 *Kodai Temple*). On a quiet stone-inlaid street in the Eastern Hills district, Kodai-ji is a jewel of a Momoyama-era temple complex. A koi pond figures in the beautifully tended garden, whose teahouses sit elegantly on higher ground. Many of the splendid paintings and friezes inside the temple buildings were relocated from Fushimi Castle, parts of which were used to construct Kodai-ji in the early 1600s, most notably the sinuous covered walkway. A back lacquer altar filled with tiny images is a masterpiece of that craft.

The temple was a memorial to Toyotomi Hideyoshi (1537–98), a powerful warrior and political leader, commissioned by his wife Nene (1548–1624). The road in front of the temple is called Nene-no-michi in her honor. On the hills overlooking the main temple, which dates to 1912, are teahouses designed by a pupil of the tea master Sen-no-Rikyu; they are identifiable by their umbrella-shape bamboo ceilings, thatched roofs, and large circular windows. Evening illumination in April, November, and December is popular among locals and visitors. ⊠ *Shimogawara-cho, Higashiyama-ku* ✛ *From Kyoto Station, take Bus 206 (Bus 207 from Shijo-Kawaramachi Station) to Higashiyama-Yasui stop and walk east 5 min* ☎ *075/561–9966* ⊕ *www.kodaiji.com/e_index.html* 🎫 *¥600* ⏱ *Daily 9–5.*

Kyoto Handicraft Center (京都ハンディクラフトセンター *Kyoto Handicraft Center*). This center has served visitors and residents for decades with its huge selection of crafts and art, both new and old. Various vendors sell dolls, kimonos, pottery, swords, wood-block prints, and pearls, and you'll find one of the best collections of English-language books on Japan. The prices are reasonable in this duty-free commercial center that's also great just for browsing. Regular demonstrations of traditional craft techniques and hands-on workshops (reservation required before 5 pm) make this place tourist-oriented, though not a tourist trap. Everything is of high quality. ⊠ *21 Entomi-cho Shogo-in, north side of Marutamachi-dori, north of Heian Jingu, Sakyo-ku* ✛ *Bus 202 or 206 to Kumano Jinja-mae, or Bus 5, 32, 46, or 100 to Kyoto Kaikan Bijutsukan-mae* ☎ *075/761–7000* ⊕ *www.kyotohandicraftcenter.com/?lang=en* 🎫 *Free* ⏱ *Daily 10–7.*

Kyoto Museum of Traditional Crafts (京都伝統産業ふれあい館 *Kyoto Fureaikan*). This museum on the Miyako Messe exhibition hall's basement level is devoted to the finely made crafts for which Kyoto is famous. Bamboo tea utensils, lacquerware, Buddhist imagery, and fine silk textiles, including kimonos, are among the traditional craft objects on display. Artisans are invited to create their works at the museum to help visitors comprehend the remarkable skill required to master a craft, and well-made videos further illustrate the point. At the museum's shop, you can purchase pieces similar to those on display. ⊠ *Miyako Messe Kyoto International Exhibition Hall, 9–1 Seishoji-cho, B-1F, Okazaki, Sakyo-ku* ✛ *Museum is on south side of Nijo-dori, opposite Kyoto Kaikan Concert Hall* ☎ *075/762–2670* 🎫 *Free* ⏱ *Tues.–Sun. 9–5.*

Kyoto National Museum (京都国立博物館 *Kokuritsu Hakubutsukan*). The national museum is one of three established in the late 19th century (the others are in Tokyo and Nara) to preserve Japanese antiquities and traditional culture. The original 1897 redbrick French Renaissance–style building is still in use, these days for special exhibitions, but in 2014 an angular limestone, steel, and glass structure designed by Yoshio Taniguchi became the much-praised home of the permanent collection. The architect's other commissions include the Gallery of Horyuji Treasures at the Tokyo National Museum, Tokyo Sea Life Park, and the 2004 redesign of New York City's Museum of Modern Art.

Calligraphy, textiles and costumes, lacquerware, metalwork, and sculpture are exhibited on the first floor. Paintings are on the second floor, the strengths being religious and secular Japanese painting, works from China, and medieval ink and Momoyama-Edo painting. Archaeological relics and ceramics fill the third floor. The labels are in English and Japanese, and audio guides are available for a fee. ✉ *527 Chaya-machi, at corner of Shichijo-dori and Higashi-oji-dori, Higashiyama-ku* ✚ *From Kyoto Station take Bus 206 or 208 to Sanjusangen-do-mae stop* ☎ *075/541–1151* ⊕ *www.kyohaku.go.jp* ✑ *¥520 (admission varies with exhibitions), ¥500 for audio guide* ⊙ *Early Jan.–late Dec., Tues.–Sun. 9:30–5; sometimes closed for exhibition installation.*

FAMILY **Kyoto University Museum** (京都大学総合博物館). The university's small natural history museum displays ancient stone coffins, fossils, and many other artifacts. A two-story exhibition is devoted to the school's Primate Research Institute, world-famous for its investigations of human and nonhuman primates. ✉ *Sakyo Ku, Yoshida Cho, beside university campus, east side of Higashi-oji, south of Imadegawa-dori, Kyoto-shi* ✚ *3-min walk from Imadegawa and Higashi-oji bus stops* ☎ *075/753–3272* ⊕ *www.museum.kyoto-u.ac.jp* ✑ *¥400* ⊙ *Wed.–Sun. 9:30–4:30.*

Maruyama Koen (円山公園 *Maruyama Park*). A gift to the city in 1886, this well-attended park lies just north of the also popular Yasaka Shrine. Crowds flow through, locals stop to people-watch, vendors supply visitors with beverages, and musicians occasionally entertain passersby. Visitation spikes as the new year dawns, when many people gather to hear the gigantic bell of Chion-in rung at midnight; and during cherry-blossom season, when the sky turns pink with those overhead boughs. ✉ *Higashiyama-ku* ✚ *From Kyoto Station take Bus 206 to Higashiyama stop at Shijo-dori.*

National Museum of Modern Art (京都国立近代美術館 *Kindai Bijutsukan*). Architect Fumihiko Maki, whose recent commissions include the Aga Khan Museum in Toronto (2014) and 4 World Trade Center in New York City (2013), designed Museum of Modern Art's 1986 steel, glass, and reinforced concrete structure. The museum is known for its collection of modern Japanese paintings, with an emphasis on the artistic movements in the Kansai region. The museum's other important holdings include ceramic treasures by Kanjiro Kawai, Rosanjin Kitaoji, Shoji Hamada, and others. ✉ *Enshoji-cho, on west side of Jingu-michi, south of Heian Jingu, Sakyo-ku* ✚ *Take Bus 5 or 100 to Kyoto Kaikan Bijustsukan-mae* ☎ *075/761–4111* ⊕ *www.momak.go.jp* ✑ *Admission fee changes with exhibition* ⊙ *Tues.–Sun. 9:30–4:30.*

Otoyo Jinja (大豊神社 *Otoyo Shrine*). Dating from 887, this very small shrine is best known for its "guardian rats." Most shrines have pairs of Koma-inu, mythical dogs, but Otoyo is unique in this regard, and very popular during the Year of the Rat. As with the canine twosomes, one rat's mouth is open, and the other's is closed. The main halls enshrine Sukunahikona-no-mikoto, the Japanese god of medicine; Emperor Ojin, Japan's 15th emperor; and Sugawara Michizane (845–903), a Heian-era poet and politician. The grounds are resplendent with several varieties of camellia. Otoyo Jinja is considered the guardian shrine for people who live in the adjacent neighborhoods of Shishigatani, Honenin, and Nanzenji. ✉ *Shishigatani, Miyanomae-machi Kanyuchi, Sakyo-ku* ☎ *075/771–1351* ✑ *Free* ⊙ *Daily 9–5.*

Sen-oku Hakko Kan (泉屋博古館 *Sumitomo Collection*). The very fine Sen-oku Hakko Kan museum exhibits ancient Chinese bronzes collected over three decades by Kichizaemon Sumitomo (1865–1926), the 15th head of the family behind the 400-year-old Sumitomo Corporation. Following the collapse of Qing Dynasty in 1912, many of China's treasures appeared in foreign markets, enabling Kichizaemon to amass the largest collection outside China. The museum's strongest suits are objects crafted during the Shang and Zhou periods (1600–221 BC), though the holdings include more recent items such as ritual implements, musical instruments, mirrors, bells, and calligraphy. The museum closes in winter and when new exhibitions are being installed, so call or check website before coming. ⊠ *24 Miyanomae-cho, Shishigatani, Sakyo-ku* ✛ *Take Bus 93, 203, or 204 to Higashi-Tenno-cho stop and walk 5 mins* ☎ *075/771–6411* ⊕ *www.sen-oku.or.jp/kyoto* ⌑*¥800* ⊗ *Mid-Mar.–mid-July and early-Sept.–late-Nov., Tues.–Sun. 10:30–5 and Mon. national holidays (and then closed Tues.); open at other times for special exhibitions.*

Shoren-in (青蓮院 *Shoren-in Temple*). Large 800-year-old camphor trees flank the entrance path to this Tendai sect temple. Although the present main hall dates from 1895, its interior sliding doors and screens are the work of the 16th-century painter Motonobu Kano, known for combining Chinese ink techniques and Japanese ornamental styles. The painting of a blue Fudo Myo-o, a Buddhist deity, is a copy of the 900-year-old National Treasure now kept in the Kyoto National Museum. Shoren-in served as a temporary imperial palace during the 18th century. Its stroll gardens and delicate interior architecture represent fine examples of staggered *tokonoma* (alcove) shelves and covered corridors leading to other buildings. In fall and spring the temple is lighted up from 6 pm to 10 pm. ⊠ *69–1 Sanjobo-cho, Awataguchi, Higashiyama-ku* ✛ *From Kyoto Station take Bus 206 to the Higashiyama-Sanjo stop* ☎ *075/561–2345* ⊕ *www.shorenin.com/english* ⌑*¥500* ⊗ *Daily 9–4:30.*

Shouzan Mirokuin (祥雲山弥勒院 *Shouzan Chapel*). Set on the mountainside of Philosopher's Walk is the small shrine of Shiawase no Jizo (Joyful Jizo), with an image of the Buddhist figure holding a child on his left arm and a pilgrim's staff in his right hand. Similar images of the protector of children and the guardian of travelers can be found throughout the city, often clothed by devotees in colored bibs and caps. Jizo is beloved by Kyoto's citizens—fresh bouquets of flowers are dutifully set in the shrines twice a month. The image of *Dainichi Nyorai,* or the Cosmic Buddha, in the building beside the Jizo shrine, is attended to by mountain priests who announce their presence by blowing a conch shell, one of which rests on a low table, and by wearing deerskin aprons, much like the deerskin draped over another low table. ⊠ *Jodoji Minamida-cho 29, Sakyo-ku* ☎ *075/771–2277* ⌑ *Free* ⊗ *Daily.*

CENTRAL KYOTO

The two major sights in central Kyoto are the opulent Nijo Castle and the more modest Imperial Palace. Visiting the latter requires permission, and you must join a guided tour. Central Kyoto is a big shopping destination: west of the Kamogawa to Karasuma-dori and on the north–south axis between Shijo-dori and Oike-dori, there are department stores, specialty shops, and restaurants. The walk (from 20 to 30 minutes) down Sanjo-dori from the south end of Nijo Castle to eastern Kyoto is loaded with tea- and coffeehouses, international cuisine, high-end boutiques, and museums.

GETTING AROUND

Buses and several subway lines service all of central Kyoto's sights, but taxis may be a cost-neutral and easy way for groups of three or four to get around the central and eastern parts of the city. Farther-away areas like Arashiyama and Fushimi are best accessed by train.

TOP ATTRACTIONS

Higashi-Hongan-ji (東本願寺 *Eastern Temple of the Initial Vow*). The high walls, immense wooden gates, and enormous roof of the Otani headquarters of the Jodo Shinshu sect of Buddhism are sufficiently impressive to convince some newcomers they're looking at the Imperial Palace. In the current complex, largely an 1895 reconstruction, the cavernous **Hondo** (Main Hall), also called the **Amida-do**, the second-largest wooden structure in Japan, dwarfs everything else. During the temple's construction, female devotees offered their hair, which was woven into strong, thick ropes used to set heavy timbers into place. A coiled length of one of these *kezuna* is within a glass case in a passageway between the Amida-do and the **Daishi-do**, a double-roof structure notable for its graceful curving lines. ⊠ *Karasuma Shichijo-agaru, Shimogyo-ku* ✛ *From Kyoto Station walk 5 mins north on Karasuma-dori* ☎ *075/371–9181* ⊕ *www.higashihonganji.or.jp* ☐ *Free* ⊙ *Mar.–Oct., daily 5:50–5:30; Nov.–Feb., daily 6:20–4:30.*

Kyoto Kokusai Manga Museum (京都国際マンガミュージアム *Kyoto International Manga Museum*). Many famous artists have signed the walls near at this bilingual museum that claims to have the world's largest collection of manga materials. Most international visitors likely associate manga with Tokyo, but Kyoto is a significant hub for the stylized comic books thanks to its rich traditions and universities specializing in the visual arts. The main permanent installation answers the question "What is Manga?" and temporary exhibitions probe topics such as depictions of war in the comics. The museum's approximately 300,000 artifacts include items from outside Japan and early examples of the genre. The shelves of the Wall of Manga hold 50,000 publications you can peruse on-site. ⊠ *Karasuma-Oike, Nakagyo-ku* ✛ *Karasuma or Tozai subway to Karasuma Oike Station, or Kyoto Bus 61, 62, or 63, or Kyoto City Bus 15, 51, or 61 to Karasuma Oike stop* ☎ *075/254–7414* ⊕ *www.kyotomm.jp* ☐ *¥800* ⊙ *Thurs.–Tues. 10–6 (last admission 5:30); on wks with Wed. holidays, open Wed. and closed Thurs.; sometimes closed at other times.*

Fodor's Choice ★   **Nijo-jo** (二条城 *Nijo Castle*). Another of Kyoto's World Heritage Sites, this castle whose construction began in 1603 is a grandiose and unequivocal statement of power by Ieyasu, the first Tokugawa shogun. In the early Edo period, the shogun stripped all power from Kyoto's Imperial Court by consolidating a new military and political center

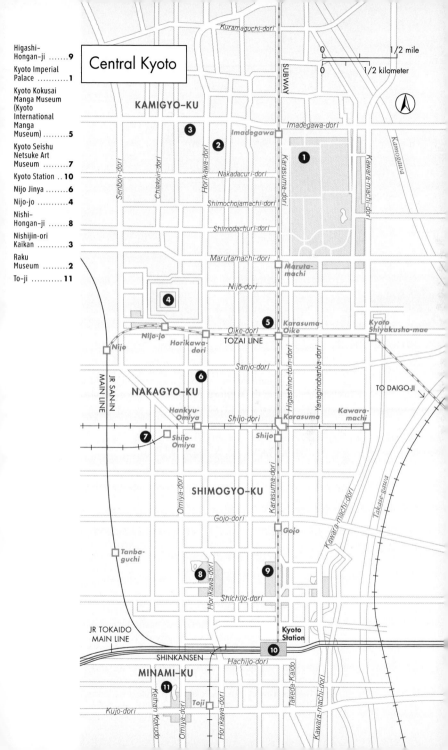

Nijo-jo was constructed in 1603 as the residence of Ieyasu Tokugawa, the founder of the shogunate.

at his far-off fortress in Tokyo. Nijo-jo's moat and towering walls are intimidating enough, but once inside, a second moat and defensive wall assert the power of the warlord. What seems a second line of defense has less to do with defending the castle than reinforcing the structure's social statement: access to the inner sanctum depended on a visitor's status within the shogunate's hierarchy. Once inside, a guest was as much a hostage as a guest, a point surely driven home by the castle's ingenious nightingale floors, which "chirp" as people walk across them, revealing their movements. If you look under the balcony while strolling the garden, you can observe how the mechanism behind this architectural feature works.

The Tokugawa shoguns were rarely in Kyoto. Ieyasu stayed in the castle three times, and the second shogun stayed twice, including the time in 1626 when Emperor Gomizuno-o was granted an audience. After that, for the next 224 years, no Tokugawa shogun visited Kyoto, and the castle fell into disrepair. Only when the Tokugawa shogunate was under pressure from a failing economy did the 14th shogun, Tokugawa Iemochi (1846–66), come to Kyoto to confer with the Emperor. The 15th and last Tokugawa shogun, Yoshinobu, famously returned power to the Emperor in 1867, the central event of the Meiji Restoration. Since 1939, the castle has belonged to the city of Kyoto, and considerable restoration has taken place.

You can explore Nijo-jo at your own pace, and handy audio guides provide explanations of what you are seeing. Entry is through the impressive **Kara-mon gate**, whose sharp angles were intended to slow an attack. The path from the Kara-mon leads to the **Ni-no-maru Palace,** whose five buildings are divided into various smaller chambers. The costumed mannequins inside the central hall are displayed as their real-life counterparts might have reacted at the moment of the Tokugawa shogunate's demise. Following this, governmental power returned to the reigning Emperor. The impressive garden was created by landscape designer Enshu Kobori shortly before Emperor Gomizuno-o's visit in 1626. Crane- and tortoise-shape islands symbolize strength and longevity. ⊠ *Horikawa Nishi-iru, Nijo-dori, Nakagyo-ku* ✛ *3-min walk from Karasuma Oike subway station, or Bus 9, 12, 50, or 101 to Nijo-jo-mae* ☎ *075/841–0096* 💴 *¥600* ☯ *Daily 8:45–5; last entry at 4.*

Nishi-Hongan-ji (西本願寺 *Western Temple of the Original Vow*). The interior of this enormous World Heritage Site has 1,000 *tatami* mats in its main hall, and as the headquarters for the Jodo Shinshu sect of Buddhism has a similar number of followers. The compound contains many fine examples of 16th-century Momoyama architecture. Among the most renowned of these is a gate on the south side. Elaborately carved in fascinating detail, it is called *Higureshi-no-mon* (All the Day Long Gate) because one could stand and look at its depictions of mythical and real animals, birds, and flowers for hours.

Founded in 1272, the sect gained great popularity by appealing to the masses in making paradise accessible by reciting a simple incantation. As with all Jodo Shinshu temples, the main altar is the image of Amida Buddha, surrounded by vases of graceful gold-painted lotus and a canopy of hanging gold ornaments, all which seem to glow in the darkened hall. Some of the Buddhist images belonging to this temple are now housed in the **Ryukoku Museum,** across the street on the east side of Horikawa. A re-creation of the murals in Chinese cave paintings have been replicated via photographs in the museum.

Several buildings can be entered if permission is granted that takes from a week to a month to obtain (visit website for details). One of them, the **Hiunkaku Pavilion,** a graceful three-storied structure built in 1587, was once the residence of the warlord Toyotomi Hideyoshi and was moved here. The morning service, which takes place daily at 6 am, provides a good opportunity to observe or participate. ⊠ *Gakurin-cho, Higashi-nakasuji, Rokujo-sagaru, on Horikawa-dori, a block north of Shichijo-dori, Shimogyo-ku* ✛ *5-min walk north of Kyoto Station* ☎ *075/371–5181* ⊕ *www.hongwanji.or.jp/english* 💴 *Free* ☯ *Nov.–Feb., daily 5:30–5; Mar., Apr., Sept., and Oct., daily 5:30–5:30; May–Aug., daily 5:30 am–6 pm.*

To-ji (東寺 *East Temple*). Famous for its towering pagoda, the most prominent one visible when entering the city, the temple of To-ji was established by imperial edict in 796 and called the East Temple. Farther west was Sai-ji, the West Temple, but receiving no special patronage it was long ago destroyed. To-ji, on the other hand, was assigned to the priest Kukai (774–835), also known as Kobo Daishi, a major figure in Japanese Buddhism whose accomplishments include founding the Shingon sect in the early 9th century and establishing the 88-temple pilgrimage on the island of Shikoku.

TOYOTOMI HIDEYOSHI: THE WARLORD WHO UNIFIED JAPAN

Toyotomi Hideyoshi (1536–98) ranks among Japan's most fascinating leaders. During the late 16th century, the country was strife-ridden, with various warriors fighting for supremacy. Nobunaga Oda partially succeeded, but he was ambushed and died. Hideyoshi, his foot soldier, completed the job. Hideyoshi's tastes for the arts brought him into contact with the famous tea master Sen no Rikyu. Both men practiced that art diligently, transforming it to one of the most subtle and sophisticated forms of entertainment in Japan. The son of a commoner, of tiny stature with the uncomely appearance of a monkey—his nickname was Saru-san (Mr. Monkey)—Hideyoshi was responsible for realigning the streets of Kyoto, surrounding the city with an earthen embankment to defend it, and later, constructing a castle in Fushimi. He spent extravagantly building temples, shrines, and palaces. In his declining years, he attempted to conquer Korea and beyond with unfortunate results, but his accomplishments, including bringing peace to Japan after decades of civil war, overshadow his late-in-life missteps.

Fires and battles during the 16th century destroyed the temple buildings, but many were rebuilt, including in 1603 the **Kon-do** (Main Hall), which blends Chinese and Japanese elements. The one building that has managed to survive the ravages of war since it was built in 1491 is the **Ko-do** (Lecture Hall). Inside this hall are 15 original statues of Buddhist gods, forming a mandala, that are considered masterpieces of the Heian era (750–1150). There's a daily morning service at 6 am in the Daishi-do with devotional chanting.

On the 21st of each month, a market known locally as Kobo-san after Kobo Daishi is held. Used and old kimonos, fans, furniture, potted plants, oriental medicine, kitchen utensils, and many other items can be found at bargain prices. A little patience and a pencil and paper to write down your desired price will make the venture an enjoyable one. A smaller antiques market is held on the first Sunday of the month. ✉ *1 Kujo-cho, Minami-ku* ✥ *15-min walk southwest of Kyoto Station, or take Kintetsu subway additional one stop; Bus 207 also serves To-ji* ☎ *075/691–3325* ⊕ *www.toji.or.jp/en* ✉ *¥500 main buildings, other parts free* ⊗ *Mar. 20–Sept. 19, daily 8:30–5:30; Sept. 20–Mar. 19, daily 8:30–4:30.*

WORTH NOTING

Kyoto Imperial Palace (京都御所 *Kyoto Gosho*). Although it tops many tourists' list of must-see sights, the former Imperial Palace often leaves them disappointed because visitors may not enter any of the buildings on the subdued hour-long tour. The original building burned down in 1788, as did some of its replacements. The present structure dates from 1855. The garden, however, is a revelation, the work of a century of master landscapers. Its noteworthy facets include the stone shoreline of the pond, the graceful bridges, and the magnificent trees and flower selection.

To see the palace, you must receive permission from the Imperial Household Agency. You can usually arrange a same-day visit by showing your passport at the office, in the park's northwest corner, but you can also apply there earlier or make a request online. Guided tours in English begin inside the imperial park at the Seishomon entrance. ⊠ *Kunaicho, Kyoto Gyoen-nai, Kamigyo-ku* ✛ *For palace, 10-min walk from Nijubashi-mae or Otemachi subway; for Imperial Household Agency, 5-min walk southeast from Imadegawa/Karasuma subway station* ☎ *075/211–1215* ⊕ *sankan.kunaicho.go.jp* ☞ *Free* ☉ *Tours weekdays 10 and 2; office weekdays 8:45–noon and 1–5.*

Kyoto Seishu Netsuke Art Museum (清宗根付館). Netsuke are miniature carvings of wood, ivory, and stone traditionally used as toggles of tobacco cases or just as ornamentation. This museum is within an former samurai's estate. The architecture and garden alone make this a worthwhile visit, but the collection of netsuke is fascinating as well. ⊠ *Nakagyo-ku, Mibukayougosho-cho 46, Kyoto-shi* ✛ *5-min walk south from Shijo Mibu bus stop, 10-min walk from Hankyu subway Shijo Omiya Station* ☎ *075/802–7000* ⊕ *www.netsukekan.jp/en* ☞ *¥1,000* ☉ *Tues. 10–5, last admittance 4:30.*

Kyoto Station (京都駅 *Kyoto-eki*). This massive steel-and-glass train station, hailed by some as an architectural masterpiece and derided by many Kyotoites for failing to convey their beloved city's genteel spirit, is more than just the city's central point of arrival and departure: the station, designed by Tokyoite Hiroshi Hara and completed in 1997, houses dozens of shops and restaurants and offers great views of the city from the 12th floor. If you have the time, ride the escalators from the concourse floor up to the open roof, a journey Hara says he choreographed to replicate ascending from a valley floor. Excellent ramen shops cluster on the 10th level. ⊠ *137 Karasuma-dori Shiokoji-sagaru, Shimogyo-ku* ⊕ *www.kyoto-station-building.co.jp/english.*

Nijo Jinya (二条陣屋 *Nijo Encampment*). A short walk south of Nijo-jo, this 17th-century merchant house saw later service as an inn for traveling *daimyo* (feudal lords). A warren of rooms, Nijo Jinya is crammed with built-in safeguards against attack, including hidden staircases, secret passageways, and hallways too narrow to allow the wielding of a sword. The house is again a family residence, so visitation is limited and only on one-hour tours that require reservations at least a day ahead. The tours are in Japanese, but you can arrange for an interpreter on the house's website. ⊠ *137 Sanbo Omiya-cho, 2 blocks south of Nijo Castle, Nagakyo-ku* ✛ *Take Bus 9, 12, 50, or 101 to Horikawa Oike and walk west 5 mins* ☎ *075/841–0972* ⊕ *nijyojinya.net/English.html* ☞ *¥1,050* ☉ *Tours Thurs.–Tues. 10–6.*

Nishijin-ori Kaikan (西陣会館 *Nishijin-ori Textile Center*). The sound of looms and spinning machines adds a subtle rhythm to the narrow streets of the Nishijin district, a longtime center of weaving and dyeing in northwestern Kyoto. The textile center here was established to showcase the skills of the local artisans. In hands-on lessons you can weave your own garment: for ¥1,800 you'll learn something and get a great souvenir. Reserve ahead and you can try on various different kimonos, rent one for a night on the town, or even buy one (¥10,000). On the second floor are weavers at work and items for sale, and artisans work at their crafts on the third floor. Several times a day, kimono-clad models appear in the latest seasonal designs during 15-minute shows. ✉ *Horikawai-Imadegawa-Minami-Iru, Kamigyo-ku* ✛ *Take Bus 9, 12, 51, 101, or 59 to Horikawa-Imadegawa stop* ☎ *075/451–9231* ⊕ *www. nishijin.or.jp* ⌦ *Free* ⊙ *Daily 9–5.*

Raku Museum (樂美術館). Serious collectors of tea-ceremony utensils are likely to have a raku bowl in their collections. The Raku Museum displays more than 1,000 bowls and containers of subtle beauty embodying the Japanese aesthetic terms of *wabi* and *sabi*, which refer to understated elegance and mature beauty. Raku refers to a low-temperature firing technique that yields a ceramic that is soft to the touch. Raku is the family name with a long history of creating pleasing tea utensils for the shogun's use. ✉ *84 Aburakoji, Nakadachi-uri agaru, east of Horikawa-dori, 3 blocks south of Imadegawa-dori, Kamigyo-ku* ✛ *Take Karasuma subway to Imadegawa Station or Bus 9 or 12 to Ichi-jo-modori-bashi* ☎ *075/414–0304* ⊕ *www.raku-yaki.or.jp/e/museum* ⌦ *Around ¥900 (fee varies, depending on exhibition)* ⊙ *Tues.–Sun. 10–4.*

SOUTHERN KYOTO

The most interesting southern Kyoto sights are three religious structures: Byodo-in, Fushimi-Inari Taisha, and Tofuku-ji. A World Heritage Site, Byodo-in is a 40-minute train ride south of Kyoto in Uji, whose other religious sites include Kosho-ji, a quiet Zen temple, and Ujigamijinja, another World Heritage Site. Uji is one of Japan's major tea-producing districts, as evident by all the tea shops lining the streets. Stop in and sample this fine green tea brewed at a temperature guaranteed to enhance its flavor. The Tourist Information Center has maps in English. Both Fushimi-Inari Taisha and the Temple Daigo-ji in southern Kyoto are on mountains with trails to explore.

GETTING AROUND

The temples and shrines in southern Kyoto are far from one another, so traveling time can eat into your day. If you visit Tofuku-ji, consider combining it with a visit to Fushimi-Inari Taisha, farther south. Uji City can easily take the thorough traveler an entire day, too. To get to Uji, take the JR Nara Line or the Keihan Line to Uji Station.

TOP ATTRACTIONS

Fodor's Choice ★

Byodo-in (平等院 *Temple of Equality*). In 1083, the Fujiwara no Yorimichi, a member of a very powerful clan, built this villa, a World Heritage Site whose image graces the face of ¥10 coins. The main building, the **Amida-do**, is known as the Phoenix Hall owing to the sweep of its curved roofline. A large statue of Amida Buddha, compassionate and benevolent, sits in repose as he views those below him. Small mounted images of *bosatsu* (enlightened beings) drift through clouds, playing instruments and dancing, an 11th-century image of paradise. The landscaped garden and pond reflect Amida's paradise. A video in the museum takes viewers back a millennium to demonstrate what the original bright colors would have looked like. Other

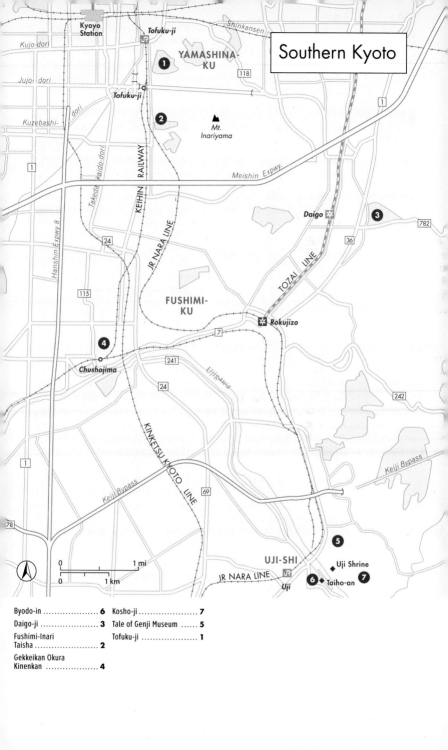

Southern Kyoto

Kyoyo Station
Tofuku-ji
Shinkansen
Kujo-dori
YAMASHINA-KU
118
Jujo-dori
Mt. Inariyama
Tofuku-ji
Kuzebashi-
1
Meishin Expwy.
Daigo
782
3
36
Hanshin Expwy 8
Takeda Kaido-dori
KEIHIN RAILWAY
JR NARA LINE
24
115
FUSHIMI-KU
TOZAI LINE
Rokujizo
7
Chushojima
241
24
Ujigawa
242
KINKETSU KYOTO LINE
Keiji Bypass
69
Keiji Bypass
78
UJI-SHI
5
1
JR NARA LINE
Uji Shrine
Uji
Taiho-an
7
6

0 —— 1 mi
0 —— 1 km

small images of the 52 small wooden *kuyo* or reverent *bosatsu* have been put on display here. ⊠ *116 Ujirenge, Uji-shi* ✚ *12-min walk east toward river from Uji Station* ☎ *0774/21–2861* 🎫 *¥600; additional ¥300 for Phoenix Hall* 🕐 *Phoenix Hall daily 9:30–4:10; garden daily 8:30–5:30; museum daily 9–5.*

Taiho-an (対鳳庵). Uji is renowned throughout Japan for its excellent tea, and this teahouse along the picturesque banks of the Uji River is a fine place to enjoy a cup of the green variety with a seasonal Japanese sweet. To experience a full tea ceremony, you must book it in advance. ⊠ *1–5 Ujitogawa, Uji* ☎ *0774/23–3334* 🕐 *Daily 10–4 (closed wk of New Year holiday).*

Fodor'sChoice
★

Fushimi-Inari Taisha (伏見稲荷大社 *Fushimi Inari Shrine*). This shrine's thousands of red gates may well be the quintessential image of Japan. The gates line the path up the mountainside, parted at irregular intervals by shrines, altars, mausoleums, and hundreds of foxes in stone and bronze. This is the central headquarters for 40,000 shrines nationally that pay tribute to Inari, the god of rice, sake, and prosperity. As Japan's economic focus shifted from agriculture to other businesses, Inari was adopted as the patron deity of any kind of entrepreneurial venture—the gates in the path are donated by businesses from around the country seeking a blessing. Walking the whole circuit takes about two hours, a bit longer if you stop at the shops selling snacks along the way. Hikers can continue up the path and follow it along the Higashiyama Range and into central Kyoto. ⊠ *68 Fukakusa Yabu-no-uchi-cho, Fushimi-ku* ✚ *Take JR Nara Line to Inari Station or Keihan Railway to Fushimi-Inari Station* 🎫 *Free* 🕐 *Daily sunrise–sunset.*

Gekkeikan Okura Kinenkan (月桂冠大倉記念館 *Gekkeikan Okura Sake Museum*). Not far from the Fushimi-Inari Shrine lies a district of high-wall sake breweries and warehouses, some dating to the early Edo era—Gekkeikan, founded in 1637, is one of the oldest and best known. Its museum displays many artifacts connected to the brewing process. The admission fee includes a tasting and small bottle of sake or plum wine. Fushimi is noted for its pure springs. If your water bottle is empty, fill it up at the on-site well. ⊠ *247 Minamihama-cho, Fushimi-ku* ✚ *5-min walk from Keihan Line's Chushojima Station, 10-min walk from Kintetsu Kyoto Line's Momoyama Goryo-mae Station* ☎ *075/623–2056* ⊕ *www.gekkeikan.co.jp/english/products/museum* 🎫 *¥300* 🕐 *Daily 9:30–4:30.*

Tale of Genji Museum (源氏物語). *The Tale of Genji* is an 11th-century literary masterpiece that depicts the life of an imperial prince. The final chapters, set in the Uji region, are commonly referred to as the Uji-Jujo, or the Ten Uji Chapters. The museum offers a glimpse into this classic epic through life-size displays, colorful murals, and interesting related videos, as well as temporary seasonal exhibits. ⊠ *45–26 Uji-Higashi-uchi, Uji* ✚ *Take Keihan-Uji train to Uji Station and walk east 8 mins* ☎ *774/39–9300* ⊕ *www.uji-genji.jp/en* 🎫 *¥500* 🕐 *Tues.–Sun. 9–4:30.*

WORTH NOTING

Daigo-ji (醍醐寺 *Daigo Temple*). Goju-no-to, the five-story main pagoda of the Daigo-ji temple complex, dates from 951 and is reputed to be the oldest existing structure in Kyoto. Daigo-ji, which includes many subtemples, was founded in 874 in the Eastern Mountains foothills in what is now the southeastern suburb of Yamashina Ward. Many of the smaller temples, along with the pagoda, can be found on the lower, entry level, with more up a long stone stairway that takes 45 minutes to ascend.

By the late 16th century the Daigo-ji enclave had begun to decline in importance, and its buildings showed signs of neglect. The warlord Toyotomi Hideyoshi paid a visit when the cherry trees were in bloom, and their beauty so delighted him that he ordered the complex restored. Among the notable subtemples is **Sanbo-in**, a 1598 reconstruction commissioned by Hideyoshi of a temple built here in 1115. The present structure has a Momoyama-period thatched roof; displayed inside are colorful, gold-leaf paintings of Chinese village scenes. The adjacent multistone garden combines elements of a *chisen-kaiyu* (stroll garden with a pond) and a *karesansui* (dry garden). Visitors cannot stroll the main garden, but a newer one to the left of the entrance can be entered.

Daigo-ji holds the Daigo-ichi, a monthly bazaar on the 29th with food and clothing stalls that line the temple walkways. ✉ *22 Higashi Oji-cho, Fushimi-ku* ✛ *Take Tozai subway to Daigo Station and walk 10 mins* ☎ *075/571–0002* ⊕ *www.daigoji.or.jp/guide_fee_e.html* ✆ *¥600 for lower level; ¥600 for upper level; ¥1,500 includes Sanbo-in, whole complex, and museum* ⊙ *Mar.–Nov., daily 9–4:30; Dec.–Feb., daily 9–3:30 (upper level closes early in winter).*

Kosho-ji (興聖寺 *Kosho Temple*). One of the few Soto sect Zen temples in Kyoto, Kosho-ji was founded in the 13th century in Kyoto, where it remained until it burned down four centuries later. The temple was rebuilt in Uji in the 17th century from timber provided by the Tokugawa Shogun, and it has remained unchanged ever since. The Chinese influence is evident in the architecture and dolphin finials gracing the roof. Kosho-ji, across the river from Byodo-in and upriver from Uji-gami Shrine, is popular in spring for its azaleas and in autumn for its maple trees. Walk a ways on the loop trail to the right of the temple for a view of Uji City. ✉ *2–7–1 Yamad, Uji* ☎ *0774/21–2040* ✆ *Free* ⊙ *Daily 9–4.*

Tofuku-ji (東福寺 *Tofuku Temple*). The immense Sanmon Gate at the west entrance of Tofuku-ji, a Rinzai Zen temple, is the oldest gate in Japan and one of three approaches to this medieval complex of 24 temples. Modeled after its counterpart at Todai-ji, in Nara, the 72-foot-high gate was destroyed several times over the years by fire. The gate was disassembled and reconstructed in 1978. Entry is not permitted through the gate, but you can observe it up close.

Tofuku-ji was established in 1236 and ranks, along with Myoshin-ji and Daitoku-ji, among the most important temples in Kyoto. Arranged around the main hall are four contrasting gardens (separate admission), both dry gravel and landscaped, including a stroll garden. The "Heavenly Way Bridge" that spans a maple-filled ravine is one of Kyoto's most popular autumn viewing spots. The gardens in the Hojo (Abbot's Quarters), completed in 1939, were the first large-scale commission of Shigemori Mirei, a famous garden designer. ✉ *15–777 Hon-machi, Higashiyama-ku* ✛ *Take Bus 208 from Kyoto Station to Tofuku-ji stop and walk 12 mins, or JR Nara or Keihan train to Tofuku-ji Station and walk southeast 15 mins* ☎ *075/561–0087* ⊕ *www.tofukuji.jp/english* ⌨ *¥400 temple; ¥400 gardens* ⊙ *Daily 9–4.*

WESTERN KYOTO

Western Kyoto's most iconic sights are the opulent golden temple at Kinkaku-ji and the dazzling rock garden at Ryoan-ji, but the city's western precincts are filled with remarkable religious architecture. The sprawling temple complexes Daitoku-ji and Myoshin-ji are well worth a visit, as is the blossom-covered Kitano Tenman-gu, which hosts a fabulous market each month.

GETTING AROUND

The sights in the northern and western parts of this area can be reached easily using city buses. For the Katsura Imperial Villa, rail is best; and to reach Koinzan Saiho-ji, you can take Bus 29 from Karasuma Shijo.

TOP ATTRACTIONS

Fodor's Choice ★ **Kinkaku-ji** (金閣寺 *Temple of the Golden Pavilion*). Possibly the world's most ostentatious retirement cottage, the magnificent gold-sheathed Kinkaku-ji was commissioned by Shogun Yoshimitsu Ashikaga (1358–1409). He erected the villa in 1393 in anticipation of the time when he would retire from active politics to manage the affairs of state through the new shogun, his 10-year-old son. On Yoshimitsu's death, his son followed his father's wishes and converted the villa into a temple. The grounds were designed in a stroll-garden style favored by 11th-century aristocrats.

> ### HIDDEN CHRISTIANS
>
> Japan's so-called Hidden Christians are descended from early converts to Christianity as introduced to Japan in 1549 by the Spanish Jesuit missionary Francis Xavier. Christianity initially flourished under the warlord Oda Nobunaga, but after his death edicts outlawed the religion in 1614 and 1640. Churches were burned, Christians were executed (or exiled), and a system to ferret out remaining Christians was instituted. An estimated 150,000 Christians went underground at this time, only beginning to reemerge in the Meiji period.

The current temple was reconstructed in the 1950s after a monk set fire to the standing structure. The monk's internal conflict is the focus of Yukio Mishima's 1956 famous novel *Temple of the Golden Pavilion*, published the year after construction had finished. Corresponding to Yoshimitsu's original vision, the top two stories are coated with gold leaf, a spectacular sight when reflected in the pond's still waters. Kinkaku-ji is one of 17 Kyoto-area locations collectively designated a UNESCO World Heritage Site. ✉ *1 Kinkaku-ji-cho, Kita-ku* ✛ *Take Bus 12, 59, 101, 102, 204, or 205 to Kinkaku-ji-mae* ⊕ *www.shokoku-ji.jp/top.php* ⌨ *¥400* ⊙ *Daily 9–5.*

Kinkaku-ji was burned down in 1950 and was rebuilt in 1955; its top two stories were covered in gold leaf.

Kitano Tenman-gu (北野天満宮 *Kitano Tenman-gu Shrine*). A shrine of major importance to the city, Kitano Tenman-gu is famous for the hundreds of plum trees on its grounds. It is also well known to students, who come to ask the gods' help in passing exams. On the 25th of every month, Tenjin-san, streets around the shrine turn into a huge market. Treasures, old and new, food, bonsai, gadgets, and other items delight throngs of shoppers. ⊠ *Imakoji-agaru, Onmae-dori, Kamigyo-ku* ✛ *Take Bus 50, 101, or 201 to Kitano Tenman-gu-mae* ⊕ *kitanotenmangu.or.jp/english* 🎫 *Free; Treasure House: ¥300* 🕙 *Daily 9–5.*

Myoshin-ji (妙心寺 *Myoshin Temple*). A Zen temple complex with 47 subtemples, Myoshin-ji contains many valuable treasures. One of them, a painting of a coiling, writhing dragon by Tan'yu (1602–74), a major artist of the Kano school of painting, graces the ceiling of the main temple's Hatto lecture hall. The dragon, a revered animal in Asia, symbolizes might and success. You can apply at the hall for a 20-minute tour of it and the temple's bathhouse, where after scraping off the grime loosened by the heat and steam, monks rinsed off with buckets of water that flowed down the slanted floors.

Japan's oldest bell is in daily use in Myoshin-ji, having tolled out the hour for meditation since 698. Shunko-in, one of the 47 subtemples, has a Hidden Christian bell. Made in Portugal in 1577, the bell was placed in Nanban-ji Church, Kyoto's first Christian church. Established in 1576, the church was the center of Catholic missionary activity until eligious persecution brought about its destruction in 1587. ⊠ *1 Hanazono Myoshinji-cho, Ukyo-ku* ✛ *Take Bus 61, 62, or 63 to Myoshin-ji-mae stop, or JR Sagano train to Hanazono-cho*

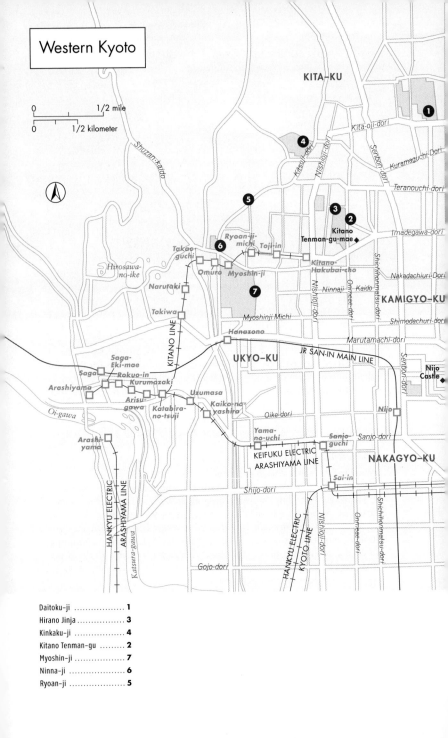

Western Kyoto

KITA-KU

KAMIGYO-KU

UKYO-KU

NAKAGYO-KU

0   1/2 mile
0   1/2 kilometer

Shuzan-kaido

Kita-oji-dori

Kuramaguchi-Dori

Teranouchi-dori

Kirasui-dori

Nishioji-dori

Senbon-dori

Imadegawa-dori

Kitano Tenman-gu-mae

Kitano-Hakubai-cho

Nakadachiuri-Dori

Shichihonmatsu-dori

Ninnaji   Kaido

Onmeee-dori

Shimodachuri-dori

Nishioji-dori

Ryoan-ji-michi   Toji-in

Takao-guchi

Omuro   Myoshin-ji

Narutaki

Tokiwa

Myoshinji Michi

Hirosawa-no-ike

Hanazono

Marutamachi-dori

KITANO LINE

JR SAN-IN MAIN LINE

Nijo Castle

Saga-Eki-mae

Saga   Rokuo-in

Kurumazaki

Arashiyama

Arisu-gawa

Katabira-no-tsuji

Uzumasa

Kaiko-no-yashiro

Oike-dori

Nijo

Sanjo-guchi

Sanjo-dori

Oi-gawa

Yama-no-uchi

KEIFUKU ELECTRIC
ARASHIYAMA LINE

Arashi-yama

Shijo-dori

Sai-in

Senbon-dori

Shichihonmatsu-dori

HANKYU ELECTRIC ARASHIYAMA LINE

Katsura-gawa

HANKYU ELECTRIC
KYOTO LINE

Nishioji-dori

Onmeee-dori

Gojo-dori

☎ *075/461–5226* ⊕ *www.myoshinji.or.jp/english* 🎫 *¥500* ⊗ *Nov.– Mar., daily 9:10–3:40; Apr.–Oct., daily 9:10–4:40.*

Ninna-ji (仁和寺 *Ninna Temple*). Immense images of temple guardians are enclosed on both sides of the massive gate here. With a five-tier pagoda at its center, Ninna-ji has grounds filled with late-blooming cherry trees that attract crowds every May. Emperor Omuro's palace stood on this site in the late 9th century, but the buildings you see today were constructed in the 17th century. The Hon-do (Main Hall), moved here from the Imperial Palace, is the home of the Omura School of Ikebana. A miniature version of Shikoku island's 88-temple pilgrimage wends it way up the mountain behind the complex. The walk takes about an hour. Ninna-ji, a World Heritage Site, is a 10-minute walk west of Ryoan-ji and a 5-minute walk northwest of Myoshin-ji's north gate. ⊠ *33 Ouchi Omuro, Ukyo-ku* ✛ *Take Bus 26 or 59 to Omuro-ninna-ji, or JR Sagano train to Hanazono-cho* ☎ *075/461–1155* ⊕ *www.ninnaji.or.jp/multilingual_info.html* 🎫 *¥500* ⊗ *Daily 9–5.*

Fodor's Choice **Ryoan-ji** (龍安寺 *Ryoan Temple*). The arrangement of stones amid the
★ raked sand of this temple's rock garden is appropriately solemn for a national treasure and World Heritage Site. The simple composition, a photograph in many schoolchildren's textbooks, can be viewed as a contemplative oasis or a riddle to challenge the mind. From any single vantage point, only 14 of the 15 stones can be seen. In the Buddhist tradition, the number 15 signifies completion, and the garden's message is interpreted by many to be that completion is not possible in this world. As mystical as the experience is for some visitors, first-timers may find themselves mystified at the garden's fame. This is a setting that changes with every viewing, reflecting the maturity of the onlooker as years pass. The stroll garden beyond the temple building remains much as it was originally designed in the 11th century. ⊠ *13 Goryoshita-cho, Ryoan-ji, Ukyo-ku* ✛ *Take Bus 50 or 55 to Ritsumeikan-daigaku-mae stop, Bus 59 to Ryoan-ji-mae stop, or Keifuku Kitano train to Ryoanjimichi* ☎ *075/463–2216* ⊕ *www.ryoanji.jp/smph/eng* 🎫 *¥500* ⊗ *Mar.–Nov., daily 8–5; Dec.–Feb., daily 8:30–4:30.*

WORTH NOTING

Daitoku-ji (大徳寺 *Daitoku Temple*). This major temple complex of the Rinzai sect of Zen Buddhism dates from 1319, but fires during the Onin Civil War destroyed it in 1468. Most buildings now here were erected under the patronage of the warlord Toyotomi Hideyoshi in the late 16th century. The four subtemples below are open to visitors much of the year, and several others are open during the spring and autumn.

Daisen-in is best known for its Muromachi-era garden, attributed to Soko Kogaku (1465–1548). The rock-and-gravel garden depicts the flow of life in the movement of a river, swirling around rocks, over a waterfall, and finally into an ocean of nothingness.

Ryogen-in has five small gardens of gravel, stone, and moss. The Ah-Un garden includes a stone with ripples emanating from it, symbolizing the cycle of life, from the "ah" sound said at birth to the "un" said at death, encompassing all in between.

Koto-in is famous for its long, maple tree–lined approach and the single stone lantern central to the main moss-carpeted garden.

Zuiho-in has Hidden Christian roots. Its rock garden suggests an abstract cross; a statue of Mary is supposedly buried under the stone lantern in an adjacent garden. ✉ *53 Murasakino Daitokuji-cho, Kita-ku* ✛ *Take Karasuma subway to Kita-oji Station and walk west 15 mins, or take Bus 12, 204, 206, and others west on Kitaoji-dori to Daitokuji-mae stop* ☎ *075/491–0019* 🖱 *Free to grounds; subtemples ¥350–¥400 each* ☉ *Daily; temple hrs vary, most open at least 9–4:30.*

NEED A BREAK?

Ichiwa and Kazariya (いち和. かざりや). Ichiwa and Kazariya have been serving tea and *aburi mochi*—charcoal-grilled and skewered rice-flour cakes dipped in sweet miso sauce—for centuries. You can enjoy the treats under the eaves of 17th-century houses as you watch visitors proceeding to and from the Imamiya Shrine. Ichiwa and Kazariya are just outside the shrine's eastern gate, northwest of Daitoku-ji. ✉ *69 Murasakino Imamiya-cho, Kita-ku* ☎ *075/492–6852* ☉ *Thurs.–Tues. 10–5.*

Hirano Jinja (平野神社 *Hirano Shrine*). The gorgeous cherry blossoms at this modest shrine near Kinkaku-ji have been the focus of an annual spring festival since 985. The pale pink petals contrast with vermilion lanterns lining the lanes of the Heian-style complex. The shrine was brought here from Nagaoka, the country's capital after Nara and before Kyoto. The four buildings open for touring date from the 17th century. Installed next to a 400-year-old camphor tree is a huge magnetic boulder from Iwate Prefecture, chosen for the power it is said to contain. ✉ *Miyamoto-cho 1, Hirano, Kita-ku* ✛ *Take Bus 50, 52, or 100 to Kitano Tenmongu-mae stop and walk north 10 mins* ☎ *075/461–4450* 🖱 *Free* ☉ *Daily 6–5.*

ARASHIYAMA

Beyond the city is the semirural hillside area of Arashiyama, which lies along and above the banks of the Oi-gawa (the local name for the Katsura-gawa as it courses through this area). The pleasure of Arashiyama, the westernmost part of Kyoto, is the same as it has been for centuries. The gentle foothills of the mountains, covered with cherry and maple trees, are splendid. The sights are spaced apart, connected by a pathway that meanders along the hillside, through fields and a peaceful bamboo grove, and past several craft shops and restaurants. It's no wonder that the aristocracy of feudal Japan came here to escape famine, riots, and political intrigue.

GETTING AROUND

The easiest ways to get to Arashiyama are by the JR San-in Main Line from Kyoto Station to Saga Station, or via the Keifuku Electric Railway to Arashiyama Station, which is just south of Saga Station. You can also take the scenic truck train, a fine way to view the river gorge.

The Katsura Imperial Villa includes Japan's oldest surviving stroll garden, which dates to the 17th century.

TOP ATTRACTIONS

Fodor's Choice ★ **Adashino Nembutsu-ji** (化野念仏寺 *Adashino Nembutsu-ji Temple*). The most unusual feature of this temple is its cemetery, where about 8,000 stone images stand, a solemn sea of silent mourners. The statues honor the many nameless dead who fell victim to the tumult of pre-Edo Japan and were abandoned in the outskirts of the city, burned here in mass pyres. On August 23 and 24, a ceremony called Sento-kuyo is held here, with more than 1,000 candles lighted for the peaceful repose of these spirits. Whatever time of year you visit, the quiet repose of the multitude of images will make a lasting impression. The temple's main hall, built in 1712, contains an arresting statue of Amida Buddha carved by the Kamakura-era sculptor Tankei. ⊠ *17 Adashino-cho, Saga-toriimoto, Ukyo-ku* ✛ *Take Bus 72 from Kyoto Station to Arashiyama Toriimoto, or walk 20 mins from Saga Arashiyama JR Station* ☎ *075/861–2221* 🎫 *¥500* ⊗ *Mar.–Nov., daily 9–4:30; Dec.–Feb., daily 9–4.*

Bamboo Forest (竹林). A narrow path through dense patches of bamboo—thick, with straight, smooth green stems—gives most who pass through it a feeling of composure and tranquillity. The wind, clacking the stems and rustling the leaves, provides the sound track. Though bamboo has treelike qualities, it is actually a grass that grows throughout the country. Its springtime shoots are a culinary treat. ⊠ *Ukyo-ku* ✛ *Short walk from Saga-Arashiyama train station on road to Okochi Sansoa.*

Fodor's Choice ★ **Katsura Imperial Villa** (桂離宮 *Katsura Rikyu*). Considered the epitome of beauty, culture, landscape, and architecture, the Imperial Villa is highly regarded here and abroad. The landscape architect Enshu Kobori (1579–1647) employed aesthetic gardening concepts founded on *shin-gyo-so* (formal, semiformal, informal) principles that imbue every pathway with a special beauty. Kobori incorporated horticultural references to famous Japanese literature, including *The Tale of Genji,* and natural sites.

Built in the 17th century for Prince Toshihito, brother of Emperor Go-yozei, Katsura is in southwestern Kyoto near the western bank of the Katsura River. Bridges constructed from earth, stone, and wood connect five islets in the pond, some moss covered, softened by the ages yet as fresh as rain.

The villa is fairly remote from other historical sites. Allow several hours for a visit, for which you must secure permission from the Imperial Household Agency in Kyoto or by filling out and submitting a form on the agency's website. ⊠ *Katsura Rikyu Shimizu-cho, Ukyo-ku* ☏ *075/211–1215* ⊕ *sankan.kunaicho.go.jp/english/guide/katsura.html* 🎫 *Free* ☉ *Weekdays 9–3:30.*

Fodor's Choice ★ **Koinzan Saiho-ji** (供隠山西芳寺 *Moss Temple*). The monks who run this temple and garden complex require visitors to perform a task upon arrival to prepare them to appreciate fully the alternative realm they are entering. After sitting quietly, you're given an inkstone, a brush, and a sheet of tracing paper covering a *shakyo*, or sutra, you are encouraged to trace. The exercise complete, you may enter the grounds, with a calm and perhaps awakened spirit, and stroll at your leisure.

The inspiration for the temple's name becomes apparent as you observe the gently swirling greens and blues the 120 varieties of moss create throughout the garden. Designed by the monk Suso Soseki (1275–1351), the garden was a forerunner of later contemplative Zen gardens. This garden, designed on two levels surrounding a pond shaped like the Chinese character for heart, represents Jodo, the western paradise of Buddhism. Permission is required to visit Koinzan Saiho-ji. The simplest ways to arrange a visit are to ask your hotel's concierge, contact the Kyoto Tourist Information Center, or apply directly by mail. It's best to apply at least a month ahead, however, as the limited spaces fill up quickly. ⊠ *56 Jingatani-cho, Matsuo, Nishi-kyo-ku* ⊹ *Take Hankyu train from Arashiyama to Matsuo Station; buses from JR Station stop here* ☏ *075/391–3631* 🎫 *¥3,000* ☉ *Daily 9–5 with advance permission only.*

Fodor's Choice ★ **Koryu-ji** (広隆寺 *Koryu Temple*). One of Kyoto's oldest temples, Koryu-ji was founded in 622 by Kawakatsu Hata in memory of Prince Shotoku (572–621). Shotoku ruled during an era before the founding of Kyoto. When the capital was to be moved from Nara, the Hata clan was living in this area and invited the present Emperor to build a new capital on their lands. Prince Shotoku was the first powerful advocate of Buddhism after it was introduced to Japan in 552 and based his government on its dictates.

In the **Hatto** (Lecture Hall) of the main temple stand three statues, each a National Treasure. The central statue, a seated Buddha, is flanked by the figures of the Thousand-armed Kannon and Fukukenjaku-Kannon. In the **Taishi-do** (Prince Hall) is a wooden statue of Prince Shotoku,

Arashiyama

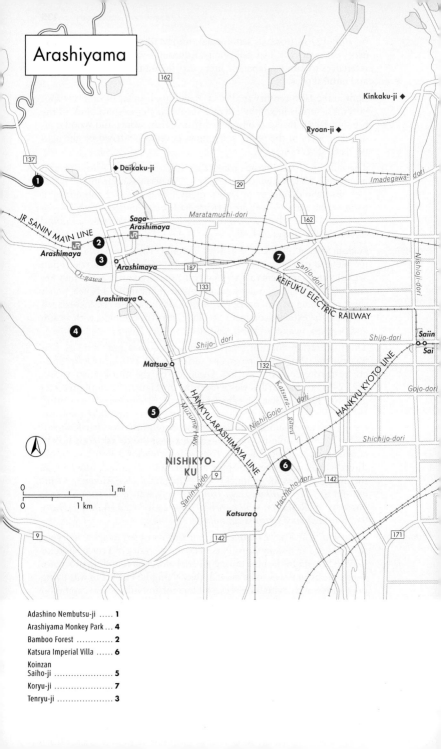

162

Kinkaku-ji ◆

Ryoan-ji ◆

137

◆ Daikaku-ji

29

Imadegawa- dori

JR SANIN MAIN LINE

Saga-
Arashimaya
JR

Maratamuchi-dori

162

Arashimaya

JR

2

7

Sano-dori

Oi-gawa

3

Arashimaya

187

KEIFUKU ELECTRIC
RAILWAY

Nishioji-dori

133

Arashimaya ○

4

Shijo- dori

Shijo-dori

Saiin
Sai

Matsuo ○

132

HANKYU KYOTO LINE

Gojo-dori

HANKYU ARASHIMAYA LINE

Muzume Hwy.

Nishi-Gojo-
dori

Katsura-
gawa

5

Shichijo-dori

NISHIKYO-
KU

9

6

142

Sanin-kaido

Katsura ○

142

171

N

| 0 | | | 1 , mi |
| 0 | | 1 km | |

Koinzan

thought to have been carved by him personally. Another statue of Shotoku here is believed to depict him at age 16, when it was carved.

The most famous of the Buddhist images in the **Reiho-den** (Treasure House) is the statue of Miroku Bosatsu, who, according to Buddhist belief, is destined to appear on Earth in the far-off future to save those unable to achieve enlightenment. Japan's first registered National Treasure, this exquisite wooden statue is thought to date from the 6th or 7th century. This may be the most captivating, ethereal Buddhist image in Kyoto. The epitome of serenity, the image's gentle face is one of the finest examples of 6th-century wooden carving in the world. Other images represent a progression of the carving techniques for which Japan is renowned. ⊠ *Hachioka-cho, Uzumasa, Ukyo-ku* ✛ *From Kyoto Station take JR San-in Main Line train to Hanazono Station and board Bus 61. From Shijo-Omiya Station in central Kyoto, take Keifuku Electric Arashiyama train to Uzumasa Station. From central or western Kyoto, take Bus 61, 62, or 63 to Uzumasa-koryuji-mae stop* ☎ *075/861–1461* 🎫 *¥700* ☯ *Mar.–Nov., daily 9–5; Dec.–Feb., daily 9–4:30.*

Fodor's Choice
★

Tenryu-ji (天龍寺 *Temple of the Heavenly Dragon*). This temple is well named. In the 14th century, Emperor Go-Daigo, who had brought an end to the Kamakura shogunate, was forced from his throne by Takauji Ashikaga. After Go-Daigo died, Takauji had twinges of conscience. That's when Priest Muso Soseki had a dream in which a golden dragon rose from the nearby Oi-gawa. He told the shogun about his dream and interpreted it to mean the spirit of Go-Daigo was not at peace. Worried about this ill omen, Takauji completed Tenryu-ji in 1339 on the same spot where Go-Daigo had his favorite villa. Apparently the late emperor's spirit was appeased. Construction took several years and was partly financed by a trading mission to China, which brought back treasures of the Ming Dynasty.

In the **Hatto** (Lecture Hall), where today's monks meditate, a huge "cloud dragon" is painted on the ceiling. The temple was often ravaged by fire, and the current buildings are as recent as 1900; the painting of the dragon was rendered by Shonen Suzuki, a 20th-century artist.

The **Sogenchi garden**, which dates from the 14th century, is one of Kyoto's most noteworthy gardens. Muso Soseki, an influential Zen monk and garden designer, created the garden to resemble Mt. Horai in China, the mythological home of the Immortals. It is famed for its arrangement of vertical stones embanking the large pond and as one of the first gardens to use "borrowed scenery," incorporating the mountains in the distance into the design of the garden. Now a World Heritage Site, the temple and its grounds are well attended by many admirers.

If you visit Tenryu-ji at lunchtime, consider dining at **Shigetsu**, within the temple precinct. The price for lunch in the large dining area overlooking a garden begins at ¥3,500, which includes admission to the garden. Although you won't partake in the monk's daily helping of gruel, a salted plum, and pickled radishes, you will try vegetarian Zen cuisine at its tastiest. The *tenzo*, a monk trained to prepare Zen cuisine, creates a multicourse meal that achieves the harmony of the six basic flavors—bitter, sour, sweet, salty, light, and hot—attributes necessary to balance body and mind. Reservations are required. ✉ *68 Susuki-no-bamba-cho, Saga-Tenryu-ji, Ukyo-ku* ⊹ *From Kyoto Station take JR San-in Main Line train to Saga Station and walk west 12 mins. From Shijo-Omiya Station in central Kyoto take Keifuku Dentetsu-Arashiyama train to Arashiyama Station and walk west 5 mins. Or take Bus 61, 72, or 83 to Arashiyama Tenryu-ji-mae stop* ☎ *075/881–1235* ⊕ *www.tenryuji. com/en* ✆ *Garden only ¥500; garden and buildings ¥600; cloud-dragon painting ¥500* ☿ *Garden and buildings Apr.–Oct., daily 8:30–5:30; Nov.–Mar., daily 8:30–5; cloud painting weekends, holidays, and occasionally other times; lunch by reservation only.*

WORTH NOTING

FAMILY **Arashiyama Monkey Park** (磐田山自然遊園地 *Arashiyama Monkey Park*). The tables are turned at this primate reserve where humans enter a cage while the resident monkeys roam free—except when clinging to the cage's fencing to grab peanuts offered by visitors. Scientists at Kyoto University's Primate Research Institute track the movement of these macaques, the most northern monkeys in the world. The trek to the cage takes 20 minutes up a steep paved path. Look for entrance at the southern end of the Togetsukyo Bridge. ✉ *Genrokuyama-cho, 8 Arashiyama, Nishikyo-ku* ⊕ *www.kmpi.co.jp/english* ✆ *¥550.*

NORTHERN KYOTO

The mountain, Hiei-zan, and the Ohara region are the focal points in the northern suburbs of Kyoto. For several centuries Ohara was a sleepy Kyoto backwater surrounded by mountains. Although it's catching up with the times, it retains a feeling of Old Japan. Hiei-zan is a fount of Kyoto history. On its flanks the priest Saicho founded Enryaku-ji in the 8th century and with it the vital Tendai sect of Buddhism. It's an essential Kyoto sight, and walking on forested slopes among its 70-odd temples is a good reason to make the trek to Hiei-zan.

GETTING AROUND

The sights in northern Kyoto are spread out and must be reached by a combination of train, bus, and cable car. It's best to make this a day trip to allow some time to explore Ohara and Hiei-zan. If you're booked on a tour to the Shugaku-in Imperial Villa on the same day, then you'll probably only have time to explore one or the other.

TOP ATTRACTIONS

Fodor'sChoice **Enryaku-ji** (*Enryaku Temple*). This temple complex, a World Heritage ★ Site, is as majestic as the mountain where it is located. Mt. Hiei has a long and entangled history with the capital, an involved and intriguing involvement with the court and the stronghold of warrior monks it became. More than a millennium ago, the priest Dengyo-Daishi (767–822), also known as Saicho, was given imperial permission to build a temple to protect the city against misfortune it was believed would emanate from the northeast. The temple grew in wealth and power and became a training place for monks-turned-warriors to force the Imperial Court to accede to its leaders' demands. The power accrued over the centuries lasting until Nobunaga Oda, the general who helped

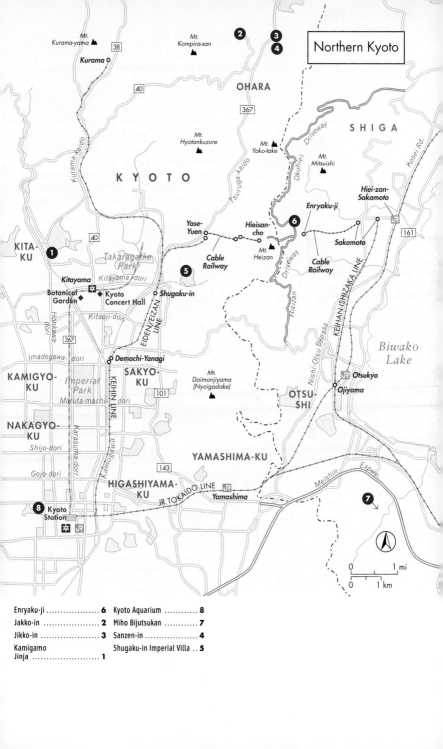

Northern Kyoto

OHARA

SHIGA

Mt. Kurama-yama

Kurama

Mt. Kompira-san

Mt. Hyotankuzure

Mt. Yoko-take

Mt. Mitsuishi

Okuhiei Driveway

Kosei Rd.

KYOTO

Tsuruga-kaido

Kurama-kaido

Hiei-zan-Sakamoto

Enryaku-ji

Yase-Yuen

Hieisan-cho

Sakamoto

KITA-KU

Takaragaike Park

Cable Railway

Mt. Heizan

Cable Railway

Hiezan Driveway

Kitayama

Kitayama-dori

Kyoto Concert Hall

Shugaku-in

Botanical Garden

Honkawa-dori

Kitaoji-dori

EIDEN/EIZAN LINE

KEIHAN-ISHIZAKA LINE

161

Biwako Lake

KAMIGYO-KU

Imadegawa-dori

Demachi-Yanagi

SAKYO-KU

Imperial Park

Maruta-machi-dori

101

Mt. Daimonjiyama (Nyoigadake)

Kamogawa

KEIHIN LINE

OTSU-SHI

Otsukyo

Ojiyama

Nishi-Otsu Bypass

NAKAGYO-KU

Shijo-dori

Karasuma-dori

YAMASHIMA-KU

Gojo-dori

143

HIGASHIYAMA-KU

Meishin Expwy

Yamashima

JR TOKAIDO LINE

Kyoto Station

0 ___ 1 mi

0 ___ 1 km

unify Japan and ended more than a century of civil strife, destroyed the complex in 1571.

The current temple is divided into three complexes—Todo, Saito, and Yokawa—that date from the 17th century. The **Kompon Chu-do hall** in Todo has a massive copper roof in the *irimoya-zukuri* layered style. Its dark, cavernous interior conveys the mysticism for which the Tendai sect is known. Giant pillars and a coffered ceiling shelter the central altar, which is surrounded by religious images. You can kneel with worshippers on a dais above the shadowy recess containing the smaller altars, an arrangement that looks upon the enshrined deities. The interior, darkened by the smoke of centuries of lighted candles, conveys a sense of spirituality even among nonbelievers. Each of the ornate oil lanterns hanging before the altar represents a stage of enlightenment. Near the main hall, a mausoleum contains the remains of Saicho.

Saito is a 25-minute walk from Todo along a stairway lined with stone lanterns. The ancient wooden temple in the Yokawa complex has been replaced with a concrete structure, dimming some of its allure, though like Todo and Saito it remains remarkable for its longevity and active religious rites. ⊠ *Enryaku-ji, 4220 Sakamoto-hon-machi, Otsu* ⊹ *To access cable car to base of temple, take JR Kosei train to Eizan Station, Keihan train to Hiei-zan Sakamoto Station, or Eiden/Eizan train from Demachi-Yanagi Station to Yase-Yuen Station; Kyoto Buses 16, 17, and 18 also run to Yase-Yuen* ☎ *077/578–0001* ⊕ *www.hieizan.or.jp/_att/ english.pdf* ☞ *¥800, cable car ¥550* ⊗ *Mar.–Nov., daily 8:30–4:30; Dec.–Feb., daily 9–4.*

Jikko-in (実光院 *Jikko Temple*). Smaller than other nearby temples, this one is less visited and quieter. A gong has been placed its humble-looking entrance for visitors to strike before stepping down inside. The garden for viewing is small and delicate; there's a larger stroll garden as well. Within the Main Hall are 36 portraits of Chinese poets by members of the Kano School. Near Sanzen-in, Jikko-in is easily combined with a visit to that temple. ⊠ *187 Ohara Shorin'in-cho, Sakyo-ku* ⊹ *From Kyoto Station take Kyoto Line Bus 17 or 18 for 90 mins to Ohara stop and walk northeast 7 mins* ☎ *075/744–2537* ☞ *¥800 for entrance and a bowl of green tea* ⊗ *Daily 9–4:30.*

Kamigamo Jinja (上賀茂神社 *Kamigamo Shrine*). The approach at one of Kyoto's oldest and most stately shrines takes visitors along a path in the middle of an expanse of lawn and through the red *torii* gate. That same path is the scene of horse racing on May 5 and the approach of the imperial messenger of the Hollyhock Festival on May 15 as he reports the events of the court to the resident gods.

At this favorite place for weddings, visitors may be pleasantly surprised to see one taking place in the inner shrine. The grounds are vast, with smaller shrines and a stream into which believers write their wishes on pieces of kimono-shaped paper and set them afloat. In recent years, the shrine has become the setting for a torch-lit Noh drama play on the evening of July 1. On other days, families spread out their picnic blankets on the lawn or in shadier spots and enjoy the day. ⊠ *339 Motoyama, Kamigamo, Kita-ku* ⊹ *Bus 9 to Kamigamojinja-mae or*

*Kamigamo Misono-bashi stop, or from Kyoto Station take Karasuma
subway to Kitayama Station and walk north 25 mins* ☏ *075/781–0011*
⊕ *www.kamigamojinja.jp/english* 🖃 *Free* ☉ *Open 24 hrs.*

Sanzen-in (三千院 *Sanzen Temple*). Set in the rural village of Ohara,
northeast of the city, this Tendai sect temple was founded by the priest
Dengyo-Daishi (767–822), also known as Saicho. The approach is
up steep stone steps and onto the temple grounds. Tall cypress trees
admit spots of sunlight onto the moss-and fern ground cover. The most
famous building, constructed in 985, houses a huge image of Amida
Buddha. On either side are images of Seishi and Kannon. The convex
ceiling is painted with scenes of paradise, but with the passing of the
centuries, these paintings of the descent of Amida, accompanied by 25
bodhisattvas, to welcome the believer are fading. Famed for its maples,
the temple draws its largest crowds in autumn, but the grounds north
of the main buildings have been planted with hundreds of hydrangea
bushes, in bloom throughout June. ✉ *540 Ohara Raigoin-cho, Sakyo-
ku* ✛ *From Kyoto Station take Kyoto Line Bus 17 or 18 north, or
subway to Kokusai Station and board Bus 1 or 17* ☏ *075/744–2531*
⊕ *www.sanzenin.or.jp* 🖃 *¥700* ☉ *Mar.–Nov., daily 8:30–5; Dec.–Feb.,
daily 8:30–4:30.*

WORTH NOTING

Jakko-in (寂光院 *Jakko Temple*). The small and beloved nunnery was
completely rebuilt in 2005 after a devastating fire, but its history is
almost as old as the city. Rival clans had their final battle in 1185,
taking the lives of all except Kenreimon-in, the 29-year-old mother of
the 8-year-old emperor Antoku. Kenreimon-in returned to the capital
and eventually this remote place to spend her days in prayer. Years
passed until a visit by a retired emperor who was moved to write a
poem about her harsh existence as embodied by the gnarled remains
of a cherry tree on the ground. Jakko-in is on the west, or opposite
side of the valley from Sanzen-in. The steep stairway approaching the
nunnery evokes the solitude Kenreimon-in and the other nuns who
lived here endured. ✉ *676 Oharakusao-cho, Sakyo-ku* ✛ *From Kyoto
Station take Kyoto Line Bus 17 or 18 (90-min ride), or subway to
Kokusai Station and board Kyoto Bus 6 or 17; walk is about 20 mins*
☏ *075/744–3341* ⊕ *www.jakkoin.jp* 🖃 *¥600* ☉ *Mar.–Nov., daily 9–5;
Dec.–Feb., daily 9–4:30.*

FAMILY **Kyoto Aquarium** (京都水族館). Inspired by the multitude of rivers that
flow into the Kyoto basin, this landlocked city opened an aquarium to
display Kyoto's native salamander, a large specimen that dwells deep
in forest streams. Holding 500 tons of water, the main pool is truly one
of a kind. A horseshoe-shape pool gives you the illusion that you're
swimming with sea lions. The penguins and dolphin stadium are also
popular. ✉ *Umekoji Park, 35–1 Kankijicho, Shimogyo-ku* ✛ *15-min
walk west of Kyoto Station* ☏ *075/354–3130* ⊕ *www.kyoto-aquarium.
com/en/index.html* 🖃 *¥2,050* ☉ *Daily 10–8.*

Miho Bijutsukan (ミホミュージアム *Miho Museum*). The phenomenal
architecture and impressive collection of Japanese tea-ceremony

Sanzen-in, a temple of the Tendai Buddhist sect, faces east, not south, as is the case with most Buddhist temples.

artifacts and antiquities from the west, China, and the Middle East make a visit to this museum in Shiga Prefecture well worth the hour-long journey from Kyoto. Three-quarters of the museum, which opened in 1997, is underground, with skylights illuminating the displays. The grounds are extensively and beautifully landscaped and well incorporated into architect I.M. Pei's design. The Japanese collection is housed in a wing separate from the antiquities. ✉ *300 Momodani, Shiga-ken, Shigariki* ✚ *From Kyoto Station take JR Tokaido train to Ishiyama Station, then Teisan Line bus for 50 mins* ☏ *0748/82–3411* ⊕ *www.miho.jp* 🎟 *¥1,100* 🕐 *Mar.–mid-Dec., Tues.–Sun. 10–5; last entry at 4.*

Shugaku-in Imperial Villa (修学院離宮 *Shugaku-in Rikyu*). The Imperial Villa was in active use until about 100 years ago when it became part of the Imperial Household Agency, thereby requiring permission to enter. The grounds are extensive, and masterpieces of gardening. The maples and cherries are especially pretty in their seasons, but year-round the Imperial retreat is an essay in the respect the Japanese have for nature. The goal wasn't to have gold and diamonds decorating their lives, but well-trimmed pine trees, painted wooden doors, and stone-strew pathways.

You can apply for permission to visit the villa online or at the Kyoto office of the Imperial Household Agency—if you haven't applied before your arrival in Kyoto, your hotel concierge can also assist you. Visitors are asked to arrive, identification ready, 10 minutes prior to the appointed tour time. Although the approximately 80-minute tours are in Japanese, free English-language audio guides are available.

Be aware that the route involves some steep inclines. ✉ *Yabusoe Shugaku-in, Sakyo-ku* ⊕ *From Kyoto Station take Bus 5 (about 1 hr) to Shugakuin-rikyu-michi stop and walk east 15 mins, or Keifuku Eizan train from Demachi-Yanagi Station to Shugakuin Station and walk northeast 20 mins* ☎ *075/211–1215* 🌐 *sankan.kunaicho.go.jp* 🎫 *Free* 🕒 *Weekdays 9–3.*

WHERE TO EAT

EASTERN KYOTO

$ JAPANESE

🍴 **Gion Kappa Nawate** (祇園かっぱ縄手). In contrast to the expensive restaurants favored by tourists, residents seek out just-plain-folks places like this fun one. It's a late-night izakaya specializing in *robata-yaki,* which is to say it's a casual bar-restaurant with a charcoal grill and great selection of meat, poultry, and vegetable dishes. Here it's common to order several dishes to share. If no tables are available, find a seat at the long counter. The restaurant is two blocks north of Shijo-dori in the heart of Gion. Everything here is ¥390, even the drinks. The friendly men who work here enjoy using their broken English with tourists. [$] *Average main: ¥390* ✉ *Sueyoshi-cho, Nawate-dori Shijo-agaru, Higashiyama-ku* ☎ *075/531–1112* 💳 *No credit cards* 🕒 *No lunch.*

$$$ JAPANESE

🍴 **Izama** (居様). Patrons enter this restaurant through a dark blue curtain on the east side of Shinmachi-dori. The design inside is pure contemporary, minimalist and sleek. The chef emphasizes Kyoto vegetables in many of the dishes. Because Izama is the restaurant attached to the Mitsui Garden Hotel-Shinmachi, three meals a day are served, and at reasonable prices. Breakfast, Japanese and Western-style buffets, starts at 6:30 am. [$] *Average main: ¥2800* ✉ *Mitsui Garden Hotel-Shinmachi, Rokkaku-dori Nakagyo-ku, east side of Shinmachi-dori, Kyoto-shi* ☎ *075/251–2500* 🌐 *kyoto-izama-web.com.*

$$$$ JAPANESE Fodor's Choice ★

🍴 **Kikunoi** (菊乃井). The care lavished on every aspect of dining is unparalleled here, thanks to the conscientious attention of Kikunoi's owner, Yoshihiro Murata, a world-renowned chef and authority on Kyoto cuisine. A lifetime study of French and Japanese cooking, a commitment to using the finest local ingredients, and a playful creative sense make every meal hum with flavor. Once seated in a private dining room, you are brought a small *sakizuke,* or appetizer, the first of a multicourse meal, all of whose selections are seasonal and decided by the chef. Each is exquisitely presented and unfailingly delicious. Dishes like cedar-smoked barracuda fillets, citrus-infused matsutake mushroom soup, or sashimi served on chrysanthemum petals keenly accord to the nuances of each new season. This restaurant is on the northern edge of Kodai-ji Temple. Evening courses start at ¥15,500, lunches at ¥4,200. [$] *Average main: ¥15500* ✉ *Yasakatoriimae-sagaru, Shimokawara-dori, 459 Shimokawara-cho, Higashiyama-ku* ☎ *075/561–0015* 🌐 *kikunoi.jp/english/store* ✍ *Reservations essential.*

$$$$ JAPANESE

🍴 **Kikusui** (菊水). Near Nanzen-ji Temple, Kikusui serves elegant *kaiseki ryori* (traditional cuisine) with an aristocratic flair. Dine on tatami mats at low tables or at table-and-chair seating, all overlooking an elegant

CLOSE UP

On the Menu

Compared with the style of cooking elsewhere in Japan, *Kyoto-ryori* (Kyoto cuisine) is lighter and more delicate, stressing the natural flavor of seasonal ingredients over enhancement with heavy sauces and broths. *O-banzai* (Kyoto home cooking) is served at many restaurants at reasonable prices. The freshness and quality of the ingredients is paramount, and chefs carefully handpick only the best. *Sosaku ryori* (creative cuisine) is becoming popular as chefs find inspiration in other cultures while retaining light and subtle flavors.

Kyoto is also the home of *shojin ryori*, the Zen vegetarian-style cooking best sampled on the grounds of one of the city's Zen temples, such as Tenryu-ji in Arashiyama. Local delicacies like *fu* (glutinous wheat cakes) and *yuba* (soy-milk skimmings) have found their way into the mainstream of Kyoto ryori, but were originally devised to provide protein in the traditional Buddhist diet.

For a reasonably priced alternative to the kaiseki ryori (the elaborate, multicourse, often expensive meal), the *kaiseki bento* (box lunch) served by many ryotei is a good place to start. Box lunches are so popular in Kyoto that restaurants compete to make their bento unique, exquisite, and delicious.

Japanese garden. The subtle flavors of the set menus are embellished by the setting, where in spring a canopy of pink and white cherry blossoms accents a meal, and in autumn the fiery red and orange maples highlight the warm flavors. *Kyo-no-aji*, smaller versions of kaiseki ryori served for lunch, make it possible for you to savor Kikusui's elegant setting and fine cuisine for ¥5,000. This restaurant seats 200, yet the serene garden view makes it feels cozy and intimate. $ *Average main: ¥12000* ✉ *31 Fukui-cho, Nanzen-ji, Sakyo-ku* ☎ *075/771–4101* ⊕ *kyoto-kikusui.com* ⌕ *Reservations essential.*

$$$ ✗ **Kisaki Yudofu** (喜さ起京湯どうふ). Tempura and tofu hot pots cooked
JAPANESE at the table are staples at this attractive two-story restaurant along the tree-lined Philosopher's Path. Try the *Kisaki nabe,* which includes pork, chicken, beef, chrysanthemum leaf, shiitake mushrooms, and spinach. Though like some nabe some dishes include meat, this is essentially a tofu house whose cuisine is centered on fresh vegetables, including plenty of pickles and seaweed. The hospitable, English-speaking owner, Emiko, will cater to special requests. $ *Average main: ¥2500* ✉ *19–173 Minamida-cho, Jodoji, Sakyo-ku* ☎ *075/751–7406* ⊕ *kyotokisaki.web. fc2.com/english.html* ▭ *No credit cards* ⊘ *Closed Wed.*

$$$$ ✗ **Minoko** (美濃幸). Rooms connected by charming wooden passages
JAPANESE look out onto this restaurant's expansive garden, and tables are set with simple but sumptuous decorations. The decor sets the scene for a delicious, if not overly daring, *kaiseki ryori* (multicourse) meal. The attention to quality here is unfailing. Inquire about the *ko-cha-shitsu,* or "small tearoom" that is perfect for a romantic dinner for two. $ *Average main: ¥13000* ✉ *480 Kiyoi-cho, Shimogowara-dori, Gion, Higashiyama-ku* ✛ *Short walk south of Shijo-dori on west side*

of Hanami-koji ☎ *075/561–0328* ⊙ *Closed irregularly a few times a month* ⌂ *Reservations essential.*

$$ ✕ **Omen** (おめん). The country-style exterior of this popular noodle shop
JAPANESE near the Philosopher's Path echoes the hearty fare served within. *Men*
means noodles; the *O* is honorific, appropriately so. The ingredients
are served separately with a small bowl of fresh sesame seeds for you
to sprinkle as liberally as you like. You can dine on stools at the coun-
ter, chairs at tables, or tatami mats. Reservations are accepted only on
weekdays. Ⓢ *Average main: ¥1950* ⊠ *74 Ishi-bashi-cho, Jodoji, Sakyo-*
ku ✛ *North side of Shishigatani-dori a little east of Ginkaku-ji-michi*
☎ *075/771–8994* ⊕ *omen.co.jp* ⊙ *Closed Thurs.*

$ ✕ **Rakusho** (洛匠). Here's a good spot to take a tea-and-sweets break
JAPANESE while wandering the stone-laid streets of the Gion district. The house
specialty is *warabimochi*, made from *yomogi* (steamed and pounded
rice and mugwort). The sweet, which has a gelatinlike consistency, is
served on a heap of golden *kinako*, toasted and powdered soybeans. The
restaurant also serves ice cream along with other Japanese sweets. Ⓢ *Av-*
erage main: ¥980 ⊠ *Kodai-ji Kitamon-mae-dori, 516 Washio-cho, at*
northern end Nene-no-michi, Higashiyama-ku ☎ *075/561–6892* ▭ *No*
credit cards ⌂ *Reservations not accepted.*

$ ✕ **Ramen Santouka** (らーめん山頭火). Inspired by the classic food movie
JAPANESE *Tampopo* (1985), directed by Kyoto-born Juzo Itami, this ramen
shop's soups are well made and satisfying. The restaurant, part of
a chain from Hokkaido, is well located, even offering a view of
a rock garden. Ⓢ *Average main: ¥950* ⊠ *137 Yamato-oji-dori, Sanjo-*
sagaru Higashigawa, Daikokucho, Higashiyama-ku ☎ *075/532–1335*
⊕ *santouka.co.jp.*

$$$$ ✕ **Tozentei** (陶然亭). Among the antiques stores and kimono shops on
JAPANESE Shinmonzen-dori, Tozentei emphasizes to-the-letter traditional Japa-
nese cooking. The meals here, made with only local produce, are old-
school enough to please a shogun. Grumpy gray windows frame this
intimate hideaway that fits only 14. Lunch is less pricey than dinner.
Ⓢ *Average main: ¥10000* ⊠ *Nishmonzen Yamato-oji-dori Higashi-iru,*
Higashiyama-ku ☎ *075/561–8024* ⊙ *Closed Sun. and Mon.* ⌂ *Reser-*
vations essential.

$$$$ ✕ **Yagenbori** (やげんぼり). Kimono-clad waitresses serve fine traditional
JAPANESE fare inside this three-story, 130-year-old teahouse south of a tiny bridge
that spans the Shirakawa River in Gion. Original paintings by Clif-
ton Karhu, renowned wood-block artist, provide a visual treat that
matches the culinary ones. On the à la carte menu, don't miss the *hoba*
miso, bean paste with mushrooms and green onions. It's wrapped in a
giant oak leaf and grilled at your table. The mini-kaiseki lunch costs
¥3,300. Ⓢ *Average main: ¥8000* ⊠ *Sueyoshi-cho, Kiridoshi-kado, Gion,*
Higashiyama-ku ☎ *075/551–3331* ⊕ *yagenbori.co.jp.*

$ ✕ **Yojiya Café** (よーじやカフェ). This treasure of a café just off the Phi-
CAFÉ losopher's Path is inside a traditional house that overlooks a low-lying
garden with a pond and a miniature bridge. A tatami room with soft
cushions for seating is arranged to maximize the view. Yojiya's specialty
is desserts that blend traditional Japanese flavors and Western ones.
Try a dessert set to get a good sense of what's on offer, and enjoy the

7

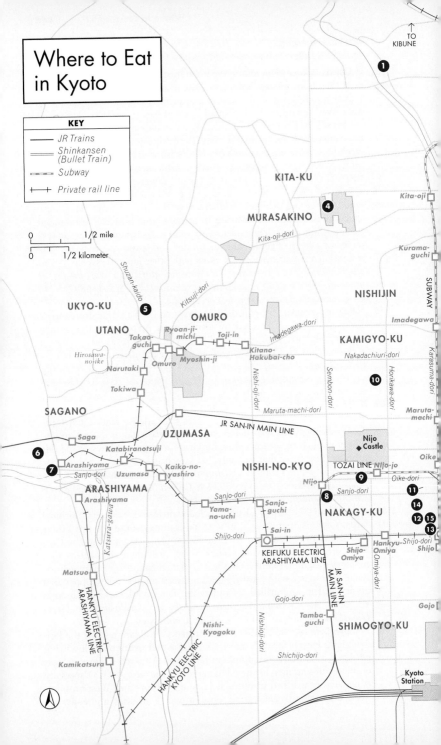

7

intricate designs and pictures swirled into the foamy top of your "green tea cappuccino" or other drink. The food is served not at tables but on small black-lacquer trays. If natural cosmetics interest you, have a look at the elegant shop in the garden's rear. $ *Average main: ¥980* ✉ *Honenin-cho 15, Shishigatani, Sakyo-ku* ☎ *075/754–0017* ▭ *No credit cards* ☾ *No dinner.*

CENTRAL KYOTO

$$ ✕ **Baan Rim Naam** (バーン｡リムナーム). The two well-trained Thai chefs
THAI   here prepare several dozen of their country's dishes at very reasonable prices. Spicy green papaya salad, hot-and-sour prawn soup with rice noodles, and green curry with chicken are all on the menu—there's a version in English—and vegetarian dishes are served. The restaurant is on the Kamo River, so the view, especially in good weather on the outdoor terrace, is as splendid as the food and friendly service. $ *Average main: ¥1200* ✉ *Kiyamachi-dori, Higashi-iru, Shijo Minami, Kyoto-shi* ✛ *2 blocks south of Shijo-dori on east (river) side of Kiyamachi-dori* ☎ *075/352–3823* ⊕ *www.rimnaam.com/english_page.html* ☾ *Closed Mon..*

$$$ ✕ **Ca' Del Viale** (カデルヴィアーレ). The signature dish at this well-
ITALIAN   regarded trattoria is handmade pasta topped with a flavorful tomato sauce. Carefully selected organic vegetables and fine Italian ham are among the antipasti stars. Entrées that might include tender pork steaks or grilled fish in orange-infused balsamic vinegar are uniformly excellent, and the decadent desserts are a great way to finish a meal: the lychee mousse alone is worth the visit. Savoring your multicourse meal on the terrace is a delight in this trendy, bustling area of town. $ *Average main: ¥2800* ✉ *Senbon, Sanjo Nishi-iru, Kitagawa Nakagyo-ku, Nakagyo-ku* ☎ *075/812–2366* ⊕ *www.watanabechef.com/ca-del-viale* ☾ *Closed Mon.* ⌲ *Reservations essential.*

$$ ✕ **Café Bibliotic HELLO!** (カフェビブリオテックハロー). Leafy banana trees
CAFÉ   visible from several blocks away mark this airy two-story town-house café that's especially popular at night with young people. Attached is an art gallery. Lunch options that include sandwiches, rice dishes, and curries change regularly. All go well with Moroccan chai or imaginative seasonal smoothies like one with strawberry, mint, and ginger. Among the desserts are mango and coconut cream and French toast with candied almonds. While waiting for your meal you can browse the wall of books. The café is a 10- to 15-minute walk from either the Oike or Marutamachi subways stations. $ *Average main: ¥1500* ✉ *Nijo-dori Yanaginobana, Higashi-iru, Haremeicho 650, Nakagyo-ku* ✛ *North side of Nijo-dori, east of Yanaginobanba-dori* ☎ *075/231–8625* ⊕ *cafe-hello.jp* ▭ *No credit cards* ☾ *Closed Mon.*

$ ✕ **Café Indépendants.** A great backpacker hangout, this café is especially
CAFÉ   popular midday, when a devoted clientele of students and artists comes for the cheap, bountiful plate lunches (including curries, salads, and soups), friendly service, live music, and convivial atmosphere. The setting is the former Mainichi Newspaper Building, with its brick-and-plaster basement, colorful mosaic tiles, and exposed masonry. If the

scene here is too frenetic for you, head up to the pleasant **Cafe Chocolat,** on the second floor. [$] *Average main: ¥980* ⊠ *1928 Bldg., Sanjo-dori and Gokomachi-dori, Nakagyo-ku* ⊹ *Southeast corner, 1 block west of Teramachi shopping arcade* ☎ *075/255–4312* ⊟ *No credit cards* ⌂ *Reservations not accepted.*

$$$
JAPANESE

✕ **Ganko Nijyoen** (がんこ高瀬川). The estate of a former prime minister has been turned into a *kaiseki* (multicourse-meal) restaurant, and the stroll garden by landscape artist Ogawa Jihei ensures wonderful views by day or night. The century-old traditional structure, between the Kamo and Takase rivers, suits the delicate tasting courses served by kimono-clad women. Sushi and shabu-shabu are among the specialties here. The sunken seating and low chairs in tatami rooms make for comfortable dining. [$] *Average main: ¥3000* ⊠ *Kyoto, Nakagyo-ku, Kiyamachi-dori, Nijo sagaru, Kyoto-shi* ⊹ *On Kiyamachi-dori just south of Nijo-dori* ☎ *075/223–3456.*

$$$$
JAPANESE
Fodor's Choice
★

✕ **Giro Giro Hitoshina** (枝魯枝魯ひとしな). Popular Giro Giro has a lively atmosphere, excellent food, and great Takase-gawa River location. Sit at the counter to watch the busy chefs, many of whom have studied at the owner's Paris location, or grab a table upstairs. The set menu changes monthly to showcase seasonal ingredients. The chef's style has been described as "punk kaiseki ryori" cuisine; what this means is that you can have a multicourse, kaiseki-style menu without the strict convention. Expect an elaborate *hassun* (appetizer) tray followed by seven more courses. You will be hard-pressed to find a better high-end value than these meals that usually cost less than ¥5,000. Giro Giro is easiest to find by walking the narrow lane along the Takase-gawa; look for the glow of the massive window a few blocks north of Gojo-dori. [$] *Average main: ¥4500* ⊠ *420–7 Nanba-cho, Nishi Kiya-machi-dori, Higashigawa, Matsubarashita, Shimogyo-ku* ☎ *075/343–7070* ⊙ *No lunch* ⌂ *Reservations essential.*

$$$$
INDIAN

✕ **Kerala** (ケララ). Imported spices and very fresh vegetables are the secrets to this second-floor Indian restaurant's success. Dishes may not be as spicy as you would expect, but the spinach, lamb, and chickpea curries—also the tandoori chicken—are deeply flavorful. The house special chicken Kerala curry is the most popular dish. The evening set courses are reasonably priced, though lunch is a better value. The furnishings are on the tatty side. [$] *Average main: ¥3500* ⊠ *Kawaramachi-dori Sanjo-agaru Nishigawa, Nakagyo-ku* ⊹ *Opposite Kyoto Royal Hotel & Spa* ☎ *075/251–0141.*

$$
JAPANESE

✕ **Kyo-machiya Suishin** (京町家すいしん). Not far from Gion Kaburenjo Theatre, a black-and-white latticed storefront with a lantern above the door conceals a vegetable lover's paradise. The dining area is raised with sunken seating, allowing customers to view the busy chefs in the open kitchen. For a survey of typical Kyoto dishes, opt for the *Fushimi* menu or the more-extensive *Gosho* menu. The cooks here bring out the flavors of local organic vegetables, fish, and meats with a conspicuously restrained hand, creating flavors so light they seem to float in your mouth. Suishin, meaning "drunken heart," is a popular chain with other branches around the city. [$] *Average main: ¥1400* ⊠ *181 Zaimoku-cho,*

Ponto-cho, Nakagyo-ku ☎ *075/221–8596* ⊕ *kyomachiya-suishin.jp* 🖃 *No credit cards.*

$$$
CHINESE FUSION

✕ **Louran** (楼蘭). Exquisite Chinese fare is presented French-style at a wooded resort in Kyoto's northwestern quadrant. The chefs focus on the cuisines of four regions—Szechuan, Guangdong, Shanghai, and Beijing—and the meals are served graciously in dining areas decorated with black carved Chinese furnishings. The eclectic offerings include spicy Szechuan-style buckwheat noodles, dim sum shrimp and pork dumplings, minced duck wrapped in lettuce leaves, and Beijing duck, The grounds, a former kimono magnate's estate, are well landscaped for strolling. $ *Average main: ¥2100* ⊠ *Shozan Resort Kyoto, Kita Ku, Gentaku Ishi cho 27, Kyoto-shi* ✛ *15-min taxi ride from Kitaoji subway station or 20-min walk from Gentaku-mae bus stop on Kitaoji* ☎ *075/491–5101.*

$
CAFÉ

✕ **Maeda Coffee** (前田明倫店). The lively café occupies a classroom in a former elementary school the city converted into an arts center. Maeda serves simple fare, an assortment of beverages, and some innovative desserts. With its creaky wooden classroom floors and the artworks of many university students and local artist groups the arts complex is heavy on atmosphere. $ *Average main: ¥950* ⊠ *Kyoto, Nakagyo Ku, Muromachi-dori, north of Nishikikoji-dori, Kyoto-shi* ✛ *5-min walk from Karasuma-Shijo intersection* ☎ *075/221–2224* ⊙ *Closed Mon.* ⌲ *Reservations not accepted* 🖃 *No credit cards.*

$$$$
JAPANESE
Fodor's Choice
★

✕ **Mankamero** (萬亀楼). Since 1722, Mankamero's specialty has been *yusoku ryori*, cuisine intended for members of the Imperial Court. Every step of the meal is incredibly elaborate, down to the ceremonially dressed chef who prepares your dishes using specially made utensils. A dramatic if oddly named course is the "dismembered fish," in which each part of a single fish is prepared and served on pedestal trays. The prices reflect the aristocratic experience—from ¥10,000 to ¥30,000 per person for the full repertoire. A wonderful *take-kago* (bamboo box) lunch set for ¥6,325 contains a series of steamed surprises. Mankamero is on the west side of Inokuma-dori north of Demizu-dori. Look for the blue-tile roof. $ *Average main: ¥20000* ⊠ *387 Ebisu-cho, Kamigyo-ku* ☎ *075/441–5020* ⌲ *Reservations essential.*

$$$$
JAPANESE
Fodor's Choice
★

✕ **Manzaratei Nishiki** (まんざら亭). The unpretentious vibe, the sense of adventure, and the superb cuisine—Japanese-based, with European and other Asian influences—have made Manzaratei a local favorite. Depending on the season, the ample menu includes handmade soba, oven-roasted chicken, or spring rolls with citrusy *ponzu* dressing. Outdoor dining in warm months and counter seating on both floors of the two-story town house facilitate mingling with other patrons; for a more intimate experience, ask for a table upstairs under the eaves. An English menu is available. $ *Average main: ¥3500* ⊠ *Karasuma Nishiki-koji, 317 Nishi-iru, Nakagyo Ku, Uradeyama-cho* ✛ *A block north of Shijo-dori and Karasuma-dori intersection* ☎ *075/257–5748* ⊕ *manzara.co.jp/nishiki/cuisine.html* ⊙ *No lunch* ⌲ *Reservations essential.*

$$$$

JAPANESE ✕**Mishima-tei** (三嶋亭). Five generations of chefs have preserved the delicious sukiyaki recipe prepared since 1873 at this restaurant that was among the nation's first to serve beef. A kimono-clad attendant will serve and assist with the dishes cooked at your table. The beef dishes include sukiyaki, shabu-shabu, and oil yaki. All beef is of the highest quality and price, as shoppers buying from the associated shop nearby can attest. The ¥6,000 Mini Course belies its name in terms of quantity. $ *Average main: ¥6000* ✉ *Teramachi, Sanjo-sagaru, Higashi-iru, 405 Sakuranomachi, Nakagyo-ku* ✛ *South of Sanjo-dori at southeast entrance to Teramachi arcade* ☎ *075/221–0003* ⊕ *mishima-tei.co.jp* ⊘ *Closed Wed.* ⌂ *Reservations essential.*

$$

JAPANESE ✕**Omen Nippon** (おめん Nippon). This branch of the famed soba noodle shop is convenient to the downtown shopping area, just across the river from Gion. It's a perfect place to drop in for a lunch of udon noodle soup with a liberal sprinkling of sesame seeds. $ *Average main: ¥1500* ✉ *171–1 Kashiwaya-cho, Nakagyo-ku* ✛ *North side of Shiji-dori a little west of Ponto-cho* ☎ *075/253–0377* ⊕ *www.omen.co.jp* ⊘ *Closed Thurs.* ⌂ *Reservations not accepted.*

$$$$

JAPANESE ✕**Ponto-cho Robin** (先斗町魯ビン). An adventurous menu sets this restaurant inside a 150-year-old town house apart from its competition. The chef here goes to the market daily and improvises based on what's fresh. Charcoal-colored walls, wooden staircases, and a great view of the Kamo River provide an elegant setting for dishes like sea urchin in wasabi broth, grilled river fish, and the ever-popular *kami-nabe*, a hot pot made of treated paper and cooked on an open flame at your table: it's mesmerizing *and* tasty. Deck seating is an option during the summer. $ *Average main: ¥7000* ✉ *137–4 Wakamatsu-cho, Ponto-cho, Nakagyo-ku* ☎ *075/222–8200 direct line, 050/5869–4426 reservation line* ⊕ *www.robin-kyoto.com* ⌂ *Reservations essential.*

$$$$

FRENCH ✕**Restaurant Ogawa** (レストラン おがわ). The best in Kyoto-style nouvelle cuisine is served in this intimate spot across from the Takasegawa Canal. Dishes depend on the chef's whims as much as on what's in season, but the menu might include buttery, risottolike rice pilaf topped with delicate sea urchin; duck meat and foie gras in bite-size portions; and hors d'oeuvres such as oyster gratin, crab-and-scallop stew, and wild mushroom tempura. The fruit and vegetable salads are exceptional, and for dessert there's a take-all-you-want dessert tray with tarts, tortes, and pastries. With notice the chef will even grant special-order requests. $ *Average main: ¥10260* ✉ *Kiyamachi Oike-agaru Higashi-iru, Nakagyo-ku* ☎ *075/256–2203* ⊕ *r-ogawa.com* ⊘ *Closed Tues.* ⌂ *Reservations essential.*

$$$$

JAPANESE ✕**Shinsen-en Heihachi** (神泉苑平八). South of Nijo Castle, this touristy restaurant is on the grounds of the remaining garden of the original Imperial Palace. The 1,200-year-old Sacred Spring Garden dates from 794, when the Emperor Kammu established Kyoto as the nation's capital. The charming shrine, placid pond, and vermilion bridge are all that remain. You can dine with a view of the pond while you enjoy an ultrathick udon noodle hot pot and listen to taiko drummers perform. Lunch courses beginning at ¥3,800 are a better deal than the ¥8,400-and-up dinners. There are not many à la carte options, but single items start at a more affordable ¥950. $ *Average main: ¥8000* ✉ *167 Monzen-cho, Nakagyo-ku* ☎ *075/841–0811* ⊕ *www.heihachi-web.com/english.html.*

$$
KOREAN
Fodor's Choice
★

✕ **Somushi Tea House** (素夢子 古茶家). Dark-wood furnishings create a provocative and intimate environment for sampling the bountiful brews at Kyoto's top Korean teahouse. Unlike Japanese and Chinese teas, which pull flavor from leaves or powder, the house favorites here are brewed full of berries, spices, and herbs. The intense aromas are complemented by a menu of vegetable stews, stuffed fritters, and innovative versions of Korean staples like organic *bibimbap* (a rice bowl topped with various ingredients). Reserve ahead to sample the Gozen menu, with nine bronze pots filled with royal cuisine good enough to leave you wishing you were an ancient Seoul nobleman. Seating is in a cozy private room at the back, on cushions at floor-level tables, or at the sturdy wooden counter with a better chance to chat with the convivial proprietors. The restaurant closes at 8 pm, with the last order taken at 7 pm. $ *Average main: ¥1800* ✉ *Karasuma Sanjo Nishi-iru, 73 Mikura-cho, Nakagyo-ku* ☎ *075/253–1456* ☉ *Closed Wed.*

$$$$
JAPANESE

✕ **Yoshikawa** (吉川). Adjacent to an inn of the same name, Yoshikawa serves full-course kaiseki ryori lunches and dinners. The beautifully presented meal includes soup, vegetables, grilled or baked fish, and a light, crisp tempura that is the house specialty. Roasted duck is available for those who don't eat raw fish. Tempura dinners include 13 pieces of fried fish, meat, and vegetables. A special shabu-shabu set is offered to hotel guests, and a visit by a maiko or geiko can be arranged by the hotel staff. The establishment boasts a breathtaking Enshu-style landscaped garden that greatly complements this truly elegant experience. $ *Average main: ¥12500* ✉ *Tomino-koji, Oike-sagaru, Nakagyo-ku* ☎ *075/221–5544* ⊕ *kyoto-yoshikawa.co.jp* ☉ *Closed Sun.* ⌂ *Reservations essential.*

$$$
CHINESE

✕ **Zezekan Pocchiri** (膳處漢 ぽっちり). A Taisho-era kimono business office and home was meticulously renovated into this restaurant whose Chinese cuisine is prepared as though it were Japanese. The street-side former office is furnished with Chinese tables and chairs and *tatami* rooms with low tables and cushion seating; some of the areas have views of the well-groomed inner-courtyard garden. The restaurant derives its name the wall in the bar displaying ornate *pocchiri* clasps used by maiko-san as decoration on the front of their obi (kimono sashes). Lunch is a Japanese-style bento but with Chinese food. Dinner may be tofu dishes, chicken stews, and delicately flavored sea bream. For ¥11,000 you can order a meal inspired by Imperial Court cuisine, featuring savory Peking duck and seasonal delicacies such as spiny lobster and crab stew. $ *Average main: ¥3000* ✉ *Nishiki-koji, Muromachi-Nishi-iru, 283–2 Tenjinyama-cho, Nakagyo-ku* ☎ *075/257–5766* ⌂ *Reservations essential.*

ARASHIYAMA

$$
JAPANESE

✕ **Arashiyama Yoshimura** (嵐山よしむら). This old-style soba noodle shop two blocks south of Tenryu-ji Temple sits right in the thick of things and has a splendid view of the river. Feel free to relax on a cushion and face the river while you recharge before visiting your next temple. The tempura comes highly recommended. An English menu is available. $ *Average main: ¥1500* ⊠ *Sagatenryuji, 3 Susukinobabacho, Ukyo-ku* ☎ *075/863–5700* ▭ *No credit cards* ☉ *No dinner.*

$$$$ ✕ **Sagano** (嵯峨野). Amid Arashiyama's lush bamboo forests, this quiet
JAPANESE   retreat offers a fine example of hot-pot tofu *yudofu* cooking. The set meal includes delicacies such as *abura-age* (fried tofu with black sesame seeds), tempura vegetables and shrimp, and Kyoto's famous Morita tofu. The service is leisurely and elegant, and most tables have garden views. Both floor and chair seating are available. The owner is an enthusiast of the bamboo *shakuhachi* flute. Its dulcet tones accompany meals. $ *Average main: ¥3800* ⊠ *45 Susuki-no-bamba-cho, Saga, Tenryu-ji, Ukyo-ku* ☎ *075/871–6946* ☉ *Closed 4th Wed. and Thurs. in July.*

NORTHERN KYOTO

$$ ✕ **In The Green.** This combination trattoria, pizzeria, and café in a con-
CAFÉ   temporary glass, metal, and wood space borders the northern side of the Kyoto Botanical Gardens. Both the location and the food make it popular, so it is wise to make a reservation by phone or in person and see the gardens first. The chefs fire up thin-crust Neapolitan-style pizzas in a tile-covered wood-fired oven, and simple fish and meat dishes are also on the daily-changing menu. $ *Average main: ¥1300* ⊠ *Kyoto, Kita Ku, Kyoto Shokubutsu-en mae, Kitayama-dori, Kyoto-shi* ⊹ *3-min walk from Kitayama subway station* ☎ *075/706–8740* ⊕ *www.inthegreen.jp.*

$$$$ ✕ **Izusen** (泉仙). Vegetarian cuisine plays a part in all major Kyoto
JAPANESE   temples, and one of the most scenic restaurants in which to sample it is in the southwestern section of Daitoku-ji. The monastic *shojin ryori* cuisine here is served in luminous red-lacquer bowls at low tables in the temple garden (beware the mosquitoes in summer) or inside if the weather is inclement. Another branch of Izusen outside the east (main) gate serves the same excellent cuisine but has table-and-chair seating. Set meals cost between ¥3,800 and ¥8,000. $ *Average main: ¥3800* ⊠ *4 Daitoku-ji-cho, Murasakino, Kita-ku* ☎ *075/491–6665 Inside Izusen, 075/491–6161 outside east gate* ☉ *Closed during New Year's holiday.*

$$$$ ✕ **Ristorante Azekura** (リストランテ愛染倉). The huge darkened beams
ITALIAN   and white plastered walls of the former farmhouse this Italian res-taurant occupies create a sophisticated rustic atmosphere, known as *wabi*, the Japanese love. A kimono merchant moved the structure here from Nara a generation ago. The set menu changes with the season and sometimes the month, but from simpler pasta courses to more elaborate meat and fish dishes, the food is always fresh, flavorful, and skillfully presented. $ *Average main: ¥9000* ⊠ *30 Okamoto-cho, Kamigamo, Kita-ku* ⊹ *10-min walk from Kamigamo shrine, 20-min walk from Kitayama subway station, or take taxi* ☎ *075/701–0162* ⊕ *www.azekurakankou.co.jp/ristorante/index.html* ☉ *Closed Mon.* ⚐ *Reservations essential.*

$$$$ ✕ **Yamabana Heihachi-Jaya** (山花 平八茶屋). Along one of the centuries-
JAPANESE   old exit roads from the city into the mountains, this roadside inn is

beloved for its full-course kaiseki ryori dinners, duck hot pots, boar stew, and boxed lunches with mountain potatoes and barley rice. There were seven roads that led out of the city, and wayside inns such as Yamabana Heihachi-Jaya provided travelers with food and respite before the long trek ahead. On the bank of the Takano River, it is one of the more picturesque examples. [$] *Average main: ¥15000* ✉ *8–1 Kawagishi-cho, Yamabana, Sakyo-ku* ☎ *075/781–5008* 🌐 *www.heihachi.co.jp/english* ⏲ *Closed Wed.* ✍ *Reservations essential.*

WHERE TO STAY

EASTERN KYOTO

$$$$ B&B/INN FAMILY 🏨 **Gion Hatanaka** (祇園 畑中). South of Yasaka Jinja, this elegantly appointed *ryokan* (traditional Japanese inn) is near Maruyama Park close to the green foothills of the Eastern Mountains and nearby temples. **Pros:** great location; elegant; comfortable rooms; very professional staff. **Cons:** basic amenities. [$] *Rooms from: ¥27000* ✉ *Minami-monmae, Gion, Higashiyama-ku* ☎ *075/541–5315* 🌐 *www.thehatanaka.co.jp* 🛏 *21 Japanese-style rooms* 🍴 *Some meals.*

$$$$ HOTEL Fodor's Choice ★ 🏨 **Hyatt Regency Kyoto** (ハイアットリージェンシー京都). Directly opposite the Kyoto National Museum and next to the famous Sanjusangen-do Temple, this is one of Kyoto's premier hotels. **Pros:** great location; multilingual staff; extravagant breakfast. **Cons:** plain facade. [$] *Rooms from: ¥25000* ✉ *644–2 Sanjusangen-do-mawari, Higashiyama-ku* ☎ *075/541–1234* 🌐 *kyoto.regency.hyatt.com* 🛏 *185 rooms, 4 suites* 🍴 *No meals.*

$$ HOTEL 🏨 **Kyomachiya-Ryokan-Sakura Honganji** (京町屋旅館さくら本願寺). Traditional architecture and attractive *tatami* rooms, baths included, are among the draws at this popular property in Honganji's quiet temple area. **Pros:** traditional architecture; courteous multilingual staff; "Japan" feel. **Cons:** small rooms. [$] *Rooms from: ¥15000* ✉ *Shimogyoku, Hanayacho sagaru, Kyoto-shi* ✣ *10-min walk from Kyoto Station* ☎ *075/343–0003* 🌐 *www.kyoto-ryokan-sakura.com* 🛏 *30 rooms* 🍴 *No meals.*

$$$$ HOTEL Fodor's Choice ★ 🏨 **The Ritz-Carlton.** Along the scenic Kamo River with views of the Eastern Mountains, the Ritz-Carlton provides world-class luxury in a Japanese milieu, with subtle lighting, artistic ornamentation, and a renovated century-old estate used for dining. **Pros:** fabulous views from river-facing rooms; world-class service; luxurious decor. **Cons:** very expensive. [$] *Rooms from: ¥70000* ✉ *Kamogawa Nijo-Ohashi Hotori, Nagagyo ku, Kyoto-shi* ☎ *075/746–5555* 🌐 *www.ritzcarlton.com/kyoto* 🛏 *79 rooms, 55 suites* 🍴 *No meals.*

$$$ HOTEL FAMILY 🏨 **Westin Miyako Hotel** (ウェティン都ホテル). At the foot of the Philosopher's Path and near the temple and shrine-filled Okazaki area, the Westin Miyako is only minutes from major attractions. **Pros:** quiet area; helpful concierge; free transfer from Kyoto Station. **Cons:** not within walking distance of downtown; some facilities dated. [$] *Rooms from: ¥20000* ✉ *Sanjo-Keage, Higashiyama-ku*

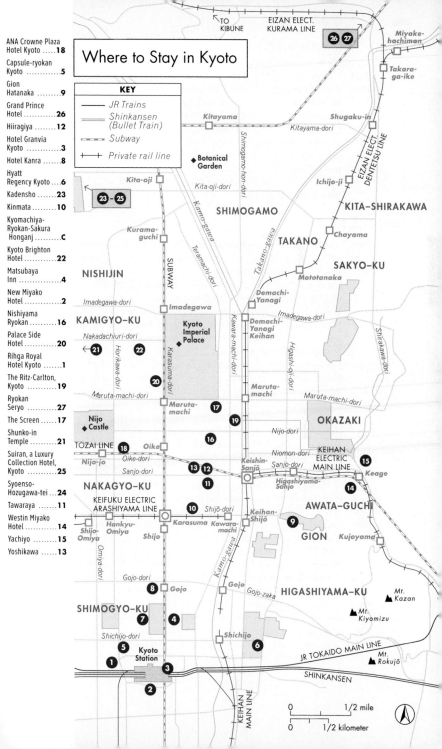

☎ *075/771–7111* 🌐 *www.miyakohotels.ne.jp/westinkyoto/english* 🛏 *320 rooms* 🍴 *No meals.*

$$$$ B&B/INN 🏨 **Yachiyo** (八千代). A traditional ryokan , Yachiyo is in a quiet, verdant part of town close to the Heian Jingu Shrine and the National Museum of Modern Art. The place feels very "Japanese," and what it lacks in big-hotel amenities it makes up for in atmosphere. **Pros:** rooms with garden views; quiet surroundings; Western breakfast option. **Cons:** not all rooms have garden views; some rooms share baths; staff's English-language skills are spotty; public areas and some rooms look careworn. [$] *Rooms from: ¥24000* ✉ *34 Nanzenji-Fukuchi-cho, Sakyo-ku* ☎ *075/771–4148* 🌐 *www.ryokan-yachiyo.com* 💳 🛏 *25 rooms, 20 with bath* 🍴 *Some meals.*

CENTRAL KYOTO

$$$ HOTEL 🏨 **ANA Crowne Plaza Hotel Kyoto** (京都全日空ホテル). Some of the rooms at this Western-style chain property have great views of Nijo Castle, which sits directly across the street. **Pros:** ideal location; English-speaking concierge; Nijo Castle views; expected amenities; popular rooftop beer garden. **Cons:** dated room decor; gym and sauna cost extra; Western chain-property feel. [$] *Rooms from: ¥18000* ✉ *Nijo-jo-mae, Horikawa-dori, Nakagyo-ku, Nakagyo-ku* ☎ *075/231–1155* 🌐 *www.anacpkyoto.com* 🛏 *303 rooms* 🍴 *No meals.*

$ B&B/INN 🏨 **Capsule-ryokan Kyoto** (カプセル旅館). Too late for the last train home, many an exhausted businessman has checked into a capsule hotel, crawled into the capsule-shaped sleeping unit, and fallen fast asleep: Kyoto doesn't have many of these lodgings, but one entrepreneur decided that tourists might like the experience. **Pros:** unique experience; inexpensive; staff speaks fluent English; convenient to public transit. **Cons:** not much space. [$] *Rooms from: ¥4000* ✉ *204 Tsuchihashi-cho, Shimogyo-ku, Kyoto, Kyoto-shi* ✥ *5-min walk from Kyoto Station* ☎ *075/344–1510* 🌐 *www.capsule-ryokan-kyoto.com* 🛏 *18 capsules* 🍴 *No meals.*

$$$$ B&B/INN Fodor's Choice ★ 🏨 **Hiiragiya** (柊家旅館). Founded in 1818 to accommodate provincial lords visiting the capital, this elegant inn is well known for its restrained and subtle beauty. **Pros:** excellent location; historic and elegant; multilingual staff; holly-infused soaps and bath oils. **Cons:** inflexible meal plans; on a busy street. [$] *Rooms from: ¥40000* ✉ *Nakahakusan-cho, Fuyacho-Anekoji-agaru, Nakagyo-ku* ☎ *075/221–1136* 🌐 *www.hiiragiya.co.jp* 🛏 *28 Japanese-style rooms* 🍴 *Some meals.*

$$$$ HOTEL FAMILY Fodor's Choice ★ 🏨 **Hotel Granvia Kyoto** (ホテルグランヴィア京都). Located at Kyoto Station, the hotel is noteworthy for its good service and fusion of ultramodern design and traditional Japanese style. **Pros:** good location; interesting architecture; amenities-laden. **Cons:** charge for pool and gym; main entrance is up a narrow escalator. [$] *Rooms from: ¥25000* ✉ *Kyoto Station, Karasuma-dori, Shimogyo-ku* ☎ *075/344–8888* 🌐 *www.granvia-kyoto.co.jp/e/index.html* 🛏 *535 rooms* 🍴 *No meals.*

$$$$ HOTEL
🏨 **Hotel Kanra** (ホテルカンラ京都). This chic downtown pied-à-terre successfully combines traditional ryokan elements—sliding paper screens, tatami rooms—with some unexpected boutique-hotel touches like the contemporary room design and the lobby aromas that change with the season (citrus when it's cool outside, mint when it's warm). **Pros:** contemporary room design; excellent restaurant with reasonable prices; near subway; on-site electric-bicycle rental. **Cons:** smallest rooms may be too snug for some; not close to the best restaurants and shopping. [$] *Rooms from: ¥30000* ✉ *Kyoto, Shimogyo-ku, Rokujo-sagaru, Kyoto-shi* ✥ *2-min walk from Gojo subway station* ☎ *075/344–3815* 🌐 *www.hotelkanra.jp* 🛏 *29 rooms* 🍴 *No meals.*

$$$$ B&B/INN
🏨 **Kinmata** (斤又). Only a few hundred feet from Kyoto's main street of Shijo-dori, the Kinmata has retained its historic character and appeal despite the garish evolution of the surrounding area: stepping into the incense-tinged entranceway to your quiet *tatami* room slows the pulse and calms the spirit. **Pros:** antique furnishings; great location; welcoming atmosphere. **Cons:** unofficial midnight curfew; shared bath requires patrons to reserve a bathing time; books up fast (it's best to email to reserve a room). [$] *Rooms from: ¥45000* ✉ *Gokomachi Shijo Agaru, Nakagyo-ku* ☎ *075/221–1039* 🌐 *www.kinmata.com* 🛏 *7 Japanese-style rooms with shared bath* 🍴 *Some meals.*

$$$ HOTEL FAMILY Fodor's Choice ★
🏨 **Kyoto Brighton Hotel** (京都ブライトンホテル). One of the city's best hotels, the Kyoto Brighton has an elegant design, and its staff displays a thorough dedication to gracious, efficient hospitality. **Pros:** conscientious staff; free concerts on summer evenings; noteworthy restaurants. **Cons:** expensive; a bit far from Kyoto Station. [$] *Rooms from: ¥20000* ✉ *Nakadachiuri, Shin-machi-dori, Kamigyo-ku* ☎ *075/441–4411, 800/223–6800 in U.S.* 🌐 *www.kyotobrighton.com* 🛏 *183 rooms, 2 suites* 🍴 *No meals.*

$$ B&B/INN
🏨 **Matsubaya Inn** (松葉家旅館). This unpretentious ryokan welcomed its first guest, a monk from the nearby Higashi-Hongan-ji Temple, in 1884. **Pros:** friendly staff; tasty breakfast. **Cons:** bland rooms; thin walls; staff speaks little English. [$] *Rooms from: ¥17,000* ✉ *Kamijuzuya-machi-dori, Higashi Nito-in, Nishi-iru, Shimogyo-ku* ☎ *075/351–3727* 🌐 *www.matsubayainn.com/top_e.html* 🛏 *8 Japanese-style rooms, 7 with bath* 🍴 *No meals.*

$$ HOTEL FAMILY
🏨 **New Miyako Hotel** (新都ホテル). Directly south of Kyoto Station, the hotel is more convenient than glamorous. **Pros:** next to Kyoto Station; pleasant staff. **Cons:** slightly stuffy decor; showing its age. [$] *Rooms from: ¥13000* ✉ *17 Nishi-Kujoin-cho, Minami-ku* ☎ *075/661–7111* 🌐 *www.miyakohotels.ne.jp/newmiyako/english* 🛏 *988 rooms* 🍴 *No meals.*

$$ B&B/INN
🏨 **Nishiyama Ryokan** (西山旅館). In a neighborhood with many traditional buildings, this ryokan that's an easy distance from the city center has a welcoming staff and serves delightful *kaiseki* (multicourse) meals. **Pros:** helpful concierge; flexible meal plans; good food; welcoming staff. **Cons:** basic hotel feel; shared bathrooms. [$] *Rooms from: ¥17000* ✉ *Gokomachi-dori, Nijo-sagaru, Nakagyo-ku* ☎ *075/222–1166* 🌐 *www.ryokan-kyoto.com* 🛏 *34 Japanese-style rooms, 1 Western-style room, all with shared bath* 🍴 *Some meals.*

$ 🛏 **Palace Side Hotel** (パレスサイドホテル). Adjacent to the Imperial
HOTEL   Palace and its park, this reasonably priced hotel has extended-stay
FAMILY rates. **Pros:** reasonable rates; central location; free Japanese lessons.
Cons: major wear and tear; cramped rooms. ⓢ *Rooms from: ¥10200*
✉ *Karasuma-dori, Shimo-dachiuri-agaru, Kamigyo-ku ✚ 7-min walk
from Imadegawa or Marutamachi subway station* ☎ *075/415–8887*
⊕ *www.palacesidehotel.co.jp/english_site* ⇗ *120 rooms* ⦿ *No meals.*

$$$ 🛏 **Rihga Royal Hotel Kyoto** (リーガロイヤルホテル京都). One of Kyoto's
HOTEL   major hotels, recognized for its excellent service and restaurants, the
FAMILY Rihga Royal is a five-minute walk from Kyoto Station, making it an
especially fine choice for those with early train connections. **Pros:** close
to Kyoto Station; excellent restaurants. **Cons:** extra charge for pool
and sauna; near a busy and noisy intersection. ⓢ *Rooms from: ¥20000*
✉ *1 Taimatsucho, Shiokoji-sagaru, Higashi Horikawa-dori, Shimogyo-
ku* ☎ *075/341–1121, 800/877–7107 in U.S.* ⊕ *www.rihga.com/kyoto*
⇗ *494 rooms* ⦿ *No meals.*

$$$ 🛏 **The Screen** (ザスクリーン). Its chic interiors have enabled this boutique
HOTEL   hotel near the Imperial Palace to gain a foothold in this competitive
market. **Pros:** individually designed suites; convenient location; close to
shops; most guests feel pampered here. **Cons:** minimalist style does not
appeal to everyone; not much English spoken. ⓢ *Rooms from: ¥20000*
✉ *640–1 Shimogoryomae-cho, Nakagyo-ku* ☎ *075/252–1113* ⊕ *www.
screen-hotel.jp* ▭ ⇗ *13 suites* ⦿ *No meals.*

$$$$ 🛏 **Tawaraya** (俵屋). Founded by the Okazaki family more than 300
B&B/INN   years ago and now run by the 11th generation, this hotel is justly
Fodor's Choice celebrated for its hospitality, sumptuous but subdued decor, impec-
★   cable service, and splendid gardens. **Pros:** excellent reputation; proud
heritage; impeccable service; superb antiques. **Cons:** extremely expensive; must reserve dinner a day in advance; no online reservations.
ⓢ *Rooms from: ¥50000* ✉ *Fuyacho-Aneyakoji-agaru, Nakahaku-
san-cho, Nakagyo-ku* ☎ *075/211–5566* ⇗ *18 Japanese-style rooms*
⦿ *Some meals.*

$$$$ 🛏 **Yoshikawa** (吉川). This traditional inn is within walking distance of
B&B/INN   the downtown shopping area. **Pros:** indoor garden; fine food; driver
Fodor's Choice available; near downtown shopping. **Cons:** expensive; fixed meal times.
★   ⓢ *Rooms from: ¥30000* ✉ *Tomino-koji, Oike-sagaru, Nakagyo-ku*
☎ *075/221–5544* ⊕ *kyoto-yoshikawa.co.jp/en* ⇗ *9 Japanese-style
rooms* ⦿ *Some meals.*

WESTERN KYOTO

$ 🛏 **Shunko-in Temple.** Visiting Kyoto's temples conveys a sense of the
B&B/INN city's spiritual side, but staying in one is a more intimate way of experiencing an aspect of monastic life. **Pros:** insider tour; plenty of atmosphere. **Cons:** no meal service; books up fast. ⓢ *Rooms from: ¥5500*
✉ *42 Myoshinji-cho, Hanazono, Ukyo-ku* ☎ *075/462–5488* ⊕ *www.
shunkoin.com* ▭ *No credit cards* ⇗ *6 Japanese-style rooms, 2 with
bath* ⦿ *No meals.*

$$$$ 🛏 **Syoenso-Hozugawa-tei** (松園荘保津川亭). Some rooms at this hillside
B&B/INN hot-springs resort outside Kyoto proper have their own *rotemburo*

(outdoor hot tub) overlooking a private garden. **Pros:** healthful hot springs; private baths; mountain views. **Cons:** far from city center; expensive; little English spoken. [$] *Rooms from: ¥26000* ✉ *Yunohana-onsen, 1–4 Hiedanocho, Ashinoyama, Kameoka City* ☎ *0771/22–0903* 🌐 *www.syoenso.com* 💳 🛏 *56 Japanese-style rooms, all with shared bath* 🍴 *Breakfast; Some meals.*

ARASHIYAMA

$$$$ HOTEL 🏨 **Kadensho** (花伝抄). If the beauty of Arashiyama inspires you to spend the night in the area, consider this resort whose draws include its kimono-clad staff, modern amenities, full-course meals, and spacious hot springs. **Pros:** good food; private baths; modern interior; short walk to monkey park. **Cons:** staff doesn't speak much English; neighborhood shops close by 7 pm. [$] *Rooms from: ¥35000* ✉ *5–4 Arashiyama Nishi-ichikawacho, Nishikyo-ku* ☎ *075/863–0489* 🌐 *www.japanican.com/en/hotel/detail/6240017* 🛏 *100 rooms* 🍴 *Some meals.*

$$$$ HOTEL 🏨 **Suiran, a Luxury Collection Hotel, Kyoto.** The original wooden structure of an industrialist's traditional estate was renovated into the river-view dining room of this woodsy hotel, one of the Starwood chain's upscale properties. **Pros:** quiet, restful setting; exquisite dining facilities. **Cons:** expensive; may feel too isolated for some guests. [$] *Rooms from: ¥60000* ✉ *12 Susukinobaba-cho, Saga-Tenryuji, Ukyo-ku, Kyoto-shi* ☎ *075/872–0101* 🌐 *www.suirankyoto.com/en* 🛏 *33 rooms (14 Japanese style), 6 suites* 🍴 *No meals.*

NORTHERN KYOTO

$$ HOTEL FAMILY 🏨 **Grand Prince Hotel** (グランドプリンスホテル京都). Directly across from the Kyoto International Conference Hall, nestled in a forest setting, the Prince Hotel will make you feel like visiting royalty. **Pros:** excellent breakfast; responsive staff; near conference hall. **Cons:** in far northern part of the city; dated decor; expensive meals. [$] *Rooms from: ¥17500* ✉ *Takaraga-ike, 1092–2 Hataedacho, Iwakura, Sakyo-ku* ☎ *075/712–1111, 800/542–8686 in U.S.* 🌐 *www.princehotels.com/en/kyoto* 🛏 *309 rooms* 🍴 *Breakfast.*

$$$$ B&B/INN 🏨 **Ryokan Seryo** (芹生). A bit of a miniature miracle, the Ryokan Seryo is in the semi-rural village of Ohara, near the Sanzen-in Temple. **Pros:** peaceful atmosphere; great food; rejuvenating hot springs. **Cons:** far from downtown; communal hot spring is open to the public during business hours. [$] *Rooms from: ¥47000* ✉ *22 Shorinin-cho, Ohara, Sakyo-ku* ☎ *075/744–2301* 🌐 *www.seryo.co.jp* 🛏 *7 Japanese-style rooms, 1 Western-style room* 🍴 *Some meals.*

NIGHTLIFE AND PERFORMING ARTS

PERFORMING ARTS

Kyoto is known for its traditional performances—particularly dance and Noh theater. All dialogue is in Japanese, but sometimes there are synopses available. From time to time international musicians play the intimate venues. The most convenient source for information is your hotel concierge or guest-relations manager, who may even have a few tickets on hand. For further information on Kyoto's arts scene check the music and theater sections of the monthly magazine *Kansai Scene,* at bookshops for ¥300; you can also find information on the website ⊕ *www.kansaiscene.com.* Another source is the *Kyoto Visitor's Guide (see Visitor Information, above),* which devotes a few pages to "This Month's Theater." Look at the festival listings for temple and shrine performances. It's available free from the Kyoto Tourist Information Center on the ninth floor of the Kyoto Station Building; the staff can also provide you with information.

CONCERTS

EASTERN KYOTO

Kyoto Concert Hall (京都コンサトハール). The architect Isozaki Araki designed this complex that has a huge round glass facade and a spiral entrance walkway up to the 1,839-seat Main Hall, the home of the Kyoto Symphony Orchestra. Visiting orchestras and artists, including excellent ones unknown outside Asia, also perform here and in the 514-seat Ensemble Hall. Ask your concierge for a schedule. There's a restaurant on the ground floor. ⊠ *Kyoto, Sakyo-Ku, Shimogamo, Hangi-cho 1-26, Kyoto-shi* ✛ *5-min walk from Kitayama subway station* ☎ *075/711–3231* ⊕ *www.kyoto-ongeibun.jp/kyotoconcerthall_e* 🎫 *From ¥5,000.*

SEASONAL DANCES AND TRADITIONAL PERFORMANCES

In the **Miyako Odori** in April and the **Kamogawa Odori** in May and October, geisha and maiko dances and songs pay tribute to the seasonal splendor of spring and fall. The stage settings are spectacular. Year-round, other traditional arts are performed.

EASTERN KYOTO

Fodor's Choice ★ **Gion Corner Theater** (ギオンコーナ). This theater's 50-minute performances sample five traditional disciplines: *gagaku* (court music), *kyomai* (Kyoto-style dance), *bunraku* (puppet theater), *kyogen* (comic drama), and *kot o* (Japanese harp). The theater is old, the seats aren't comfortable, and this is definitely a tourist trap, but it's also only place to see these performing arts most of year. The admission price is a bargain considering the number of talented artists involved. ⊠ *Yasaka Hall, 570–2 Gion-machi Minamigawa, Higashiyama-ku* ✛ *5-min walk from Shijo-Gion bus stop or Hankyu Kawaramachi or Keihan Shijo train station* ☎ *075/561–1119* ⊕ *www.kyoto-gioncorner.com/global/en.html* 🎫 *¥3,150* 🕐 *Mar.–Nov., nightly at 6 and 7; Dec.–Feb., Fri., weekends, and holidays at 6 and 7.*

7

Gion Kobu Kaburenjo Theatre (祇園歌舞練場). In the same complex as Gion Corner, this theater is used for special performances, most notably the spring and fall dances by maiko and geiko. Kyotoites feel that the season has truly arrived with the announcement of these shows. ✉ *Gion Hanami-koji, Higashiyama-ku* ☎ *075/561–1115* 💴 *¥2,500– ¥4,800* 🕐 *www.miyako-odori.jp/english.*

CENTRAL KYOTO

Ponto-cho Kaburenjo Theater (先斗町歌舞伎練場). The maiko and geiko of the Ponto-cho district perform at this theater in spring and fall. Occasionally other dance performances are scheduled here. ✉ *Ponto-cho, Sanjo-sagaru, Nakagyo-ku* ☎ *075/221–2025* 💴 *¥2,000–¥4,000.*

KABUKI

Kabuki developed in the Edo era as a theatrical art with lavish costumes and sets and dynamic all-male performances. Though Kabuki is faster-paced than Noh, a single performance can easily take half a day. Devotees pack bentos to eat while watching shows. Kyoto hosts traveling Kabuki performances periodically; most of the troupes are based in Tokyo. Especially anticipated in Kyoto is the annual monthlong **Kaomise** (Face Showing) Kabuki Festival in December, featuring top Kabuki stars and introducing up-and-coming artists. Tickets cost between ¥5,500 and ¥27,000 and should be booked weeks in advance.

EASTERN KYOTO

Minami-za (南座). The renovated Minami-za theater, the oldest in Japan, hosts Kabuki performances most of the year. Even the mounted posters announcing the plays here are beautifully rendered. The typical Kabuki performance can last up to four hours; there are two shows daily. Box lunches are the choice meal during a play so that one does not miss anything. Front downstairs seats are often occupied by the who's who of the world of maiko and geiko. ✉ *Shijo Kamogawa, Higashiyama-ku* ✛ *Southeast side of Shijo and Kawabata-dori* ☎ *075/561–1155* 🌐 *www. shochiku.co.jp/play/minamiza.*

NOH

Kyoto is the home of Japan's most ancient form of traditional theater, Noh, which is more ritualistic and sophisticated than Kabuki. Some understanding of the plot of each play is necessary to enjoy a performance, an acquired taste that is generally slow-moving and solemnly chanted. The carved masks used by the main actors express a whole range of emotions, though the mask itself may appear expressionless until the actor "brings it to life." Noh performances are held year-round and tickets range in price from ¥3,000 to ¥13,000. Particularly memorable are outdoor Noh performances, especially **Takigi Noh,** held outdoors by firelight on the nights of June 1 and 2 in the precincts of the Heian Jingu. For more information about performances, contact the Kyoto Tourist Information Center.

EASTERN KYOTO

Kanze Kaikan Noh Theater (観世会館). This is one of Kyoto's oldest Noh schools. The libretto is all in Japanese, with only some information in English. ✉ *44 Enshoji-cho, Okazaki, Sakyo-ku* ☎ *075/771–6114* 🌐 *www.kyoto-kanze.jp* 💴 *¥2,000–¥6,000.*

The Saio-dai, an unmarried woman, represents the Emperor in the Aoi (Hollyhock) Matsuri, which takes place in mid-May.

CENTRAL KYOTO

Kongo Noh Theater (金剛能楽堂). This theater presenting performances of the Kongo school of Noh drama was moved to this location on the former estate of an aristocrat. The architecture is completely modern, but the garden—there's a view of it from the lobby—is completely traditional. English translations of the librettos are often available. ⊠ *Karasuma-dori, Ichijo-sagaru, Kamigyo-ku* ✢ *Just south of Imadegawa subway stop* ☎ *075/441–7222* 🎟 *¥3000–¥6000.*

THEATER

CENTRAL KYOTO

FAMILY **GEAR** (ギア). This nonverbal show incorporates mime, magic, break dancing, and dramatic lighting effects as its energetic actors play robots temporarily unstuck from their assembly line. The 1928 art deco–like architecture of the former Mainichi Newspaper building provides the set. ⊠ *Nakagyo-ku Sanjo-dori, Gokomachi-dori, Kyoto-shi* ✢ *3-min walk from Kawaramachi-Sanjo-dori bus stop* ☎ *075/254–6520* ⊕ *www.gear.ac/en* 🎟 *From ¥3,700* 🕐 *Fri., weekends, holidays, and 2nd and 4th Wed. of month at 2 pm and 7 pm.*

NIGHTLIFE

Though Kyoto's nightlife is more sedate than Osaka's, the areas around the old geisha quarters downtown thrive with nightclubs and bars. The Kiyamachi area along the small canal near Ponto-cho in central Kyoto is packed full of bars, restaurants, and a few dance clubs and is as close to a consolidated nightlife area as you'll get in Kyoto. It's full of small watering holes with red lanterns (indicating inexpensive places) or small neon signs in front. It's also fun to walk around the Gion in eastern Kyoto and Ponto-cho in central Kyoto to try to catch a glimpse of a geisha or maiko stealing down an alleyway on her way to or from an appointment.

BARS AND PUBS

EASTERN KYOTO

Gael Irish Pub (ゲールアイリッシュパブ). This pub entertains patrons with traditional music and sports on TV. If you want more than a drink, classic fish-and-chips, Irish stew, and beef-and-Guinness pie are served. The bilingual staff will put you at ease. ✉ *Kawabata-Shijo, 236 Otobiru, Nijuichiken-cho, Yamato-oji, 2nd fl., Higashiyama-ku* ☎ *075/525–0680* 🌐 *www.irishpubkyoto.com.*

CENTRAL KYOTO

A-Bar (エイバー). This wood-panel one-room izakaya pub doesn't look like much, but it regularly fills up with expats and locals. Visitors and regulars sit around the communal tables to swap stories and adventures. Watch out for flying bottle caps, though—the staff has a knack for popping open beer bottles with chopsticks. ✉ *Reiho Bulding, Nishi Kiyamachi-dori, Shijo-agaru, 2nd fl., Nakagyo-ku* ✥ *1 block west of Kiyamachi-dori* ☎ *075/213–2129* 🌐 *www.a-bar.net.*

Yoramu (ヨラム). An Israeli sake aficionado named Yoram stocks an extensive selection of the delicate rice wine, from unfiltered to aged, fruity to dry, all available by the glass. A tasting set of three kinds of sake starts at ¥1,200. The dishes on the menu have all been chosen to complement the libations. By day this cozy bar is a soba shop run by Yoram's partner. ✉ *Nakagyo-Ku, Higashinotoin, Nijo-dori, Higashi-iru, Nakagyo-ku* ✥ *South of Nijo-dori, east of Higashino-toin-dori* ☎ *075/213–1512* 🌐 *sakebar-yoramu.com/index_eng* ⏲ *Closed Sun.–Tues.*

MUSIC CLUBS

EASTERN KYOTO

Club Metro (クラブメトロ). Popular Metro frequently hosts famous DJs from Tokyo and abroad. The range of music played—experimental dance, hip-hop, reggae, disco, salsa, and more—is very broad. ✉ *Ebisu Bldg., 82 Shimotsutsumi-cho, Marutamachi-sagaru, Kawabata-dori, Sakyo-ku* ✥ *Near Keihan Station* ☎ *075/752–2787* 🌐 *www.metro.ne.jp.*

CENTRAL KYOTO

Café Independants (カフェエンデパンダン). Trestle tables line the graffiti-covered walls of this basement café and bar that hosts indie rock, jazz, and blues musicians. It's a good place to tap into Kyoto's underground music scene. In the evening, you can order simple plates to accompany your beer or wine. ✉ *1928 Bldg., Sanjo-dori and Gokomachi-dori, Nakagyo-ku* ✥ *Southeast corner, 1 block west of Teramachi shopping arcade* ☎ *075/255–4312.*

Le Club Jazz (ルクラブジャズ). Depending on the night you might hear jazz, blues, or soul at this club on the second floor of a trendy-looking building. The ¥2,000 cover charge on weekends includes two drinks.

Jam sessions often take place. ⊠ *Sanjo Arimoto Bldg., Teramachi and Sanjo-dori, 2nd fl., Kamigyo-ku* ✛ *Northwest corner* ☎ *075/211–5800.*

Taku Taku (ライブハウス磔磔). An enduring live-music venue that generally presents rock and blues acts, Taku Taku occasionally hosts well-known Japanese performers. You can find it in an old *kura*, or storehouse, in the backstreets southwest of the Takashimaya department store. ⊠ *Tominokoji-dori, Bukkoji-sagaru, Shimogyo-ku* ☎ *075/351–1321* 🎟 *Cover charge varies.*

UrBANGUILD. The atmosphere is very New-York-experimental-theater at this multidisciplinary venue for music, dance, video, and other performances about 20 nights a month. The cover charge includes a drink, and you can order snacks and light meals. ⊠ *New Kyoto Bldg., Nakagyo Ku, Kiyamachi, Sanjo Shita, 3rd fl., Kyoto-shi* ✛ *East side of Kiyamachi, 2 blocks south of Sanjo-dori; 5-min walk from bus stops on Kawaramachi Shijo or Sanjo* ☎ *075/212–1125* ⊕ 🎟 *¥3,000.*

SHOPPING

Most shops slide their doors open at 10, and many shopkeepers partake of the morning ritual of sweeping and watering the entrance to welcome the first customers. Traditional shops lock up at 6 or 7 in the evening. Stores often close sporadically once or twice a month (closings are irregular), so it helps to call in advance if you're making a special trip. On weekends, downtown can be very crowded.

A shopkeeper's traditional greeting to a customer is *o-ideyasu* (Kyoto-ben, the Kyoto dialect, for "honored to have you here"), voiced in the lilting Kyoto intonations with the required bowing of the head. When a customer makes a purchase, the shopkeeper will respond with *o-okini* ("thank you" in Kyoto-ben), a smile, and a bow. Take notice of the careful effort and adroitness with which purchases are wrapped; it's an art in itself.

Kyoto's *depato* (department stores) are small in comparison to their mammoth counterparts in Tokyo and Osaka. They still carry a wide range of goods and are great places for one-stop souvenir shopping. Wandering around the basement food halls is a good way to build up an appetite. Prices drop dramatically during end-of-season sales.

Kyoto has several popular seasonal fairs, from local area pottery sales to the national antiques fairs, usually held in May, June, and October. Several temple markets take place in Kyoto each month. These are great places to pick up bargain kimonos or unusual souvenirs. They're also some of the best spots for people-watching.

SHOPPING DISTRICTS

Kyoto is compact and relatively easy to navigate. Major shops line both sides of **Shijo-dori,** which runs east–west, and **Kawaramachi-dori,** which runs north–south. Concentrate on Shijo-dori between Yasaka Jinja and Karasuma Station as well as Kawaramachi-dori between Sanjo-dori and Shijo-dori. Some of modern Kyoto's shopping districts are near

Kyoto Station in central Kyoto. **Porta** ポルタ , under Kyoto Station, a sprawling subterranean arcade, contains more than 200 shops and restaurants. **Aeon Mall** イオンモール on the south side of Kyoto Station has the feel of a large Western mall.

Roads leading to **Kiyomizu-dera** run uphill, yet you may hardly notice the steepness for all of the alluring shops that line the way. Be sure to peek in for unique gifts. Food shops offer sample morsels, and tea shops serve complimentary cups of tea. **Shin-Kyogoku,** a covered arcade running between Teramachi-dori and Kawaramachi-dori, is another general-purpose shopping area with many souvenir shops.

> ## SHUINCHO
>
> The *shuincho* is a booklet usually no larger than 4 by 6 inches, usually covered with brocade, composed of blank sheets of heavyweight paper that continuously fold out. You can find them at gift stores or at temples for as little as ¥1,000. Use them to collect ink stamps from places you visit while in Japan. Stamps and stamp pads are ubiquitous in Japan—at sights, train stations, and some restaurants. Most stamps are given for free; at temples monks will write calligraphy over the stamp for a small fee.

EASTERN KYOTO
ART AND ANTIQUES

If you are looking for antiques in eastern Kyoto, **Nawate-dori,** in the Higashiyama-ku neighborhood between Shijo-dori and Sanjo-dori, is noted for fine antique textiles, ceramics, and paintings.

Shinmonzen-dori, also in Higashiyama-ku, is an unpretentious little street of two-story wooden buildings between Higashi-oji-dori and Hanami-koji-dori, just north of Gion. About a dozen and a half shops here specialize in scrolls, *netsuke* (small carved figures to attach to Japanese clothing), lacquerware, bronze, wood-block prints, paintings, and antiques. Shop with confidence, because shopkeepers are trustworthy and goods are authentic. Pick up a copy of the pamphlet *Shinmonzen Street Shopping Guide* from your hotel or from the Kyoto Tourist Information Center to learn more about them.

CERAMICS

Asahi-do (朝日堂). In the heart of the pottery district near Kiyomizu-dera, Asahi-do specializes in Kyoto-style hand-painted porcelain. It offers the widest selection of any pottery store in the area, and can arrange overseas shipping. ⊠ *1–280 Kiyomizu, Higashiyama-ku* ☎ *075/531–2181* ⊕ *www.asahido.co.jp/english* ⊗ *Daily 9–6.*

DOLLS

Ningyo were first used in Japan in the purification rites associated with the Doll Festival, an annual family-oriented event on March 3. Kyoto ningyo are made with fine detail and embellishment.

Ando Japanese Doll Shop (安藤人形店). The Ando brothers, Tadao and Tadahiko, hand-make dolls for the Imperial Court and individual families. The finest silk brocades adorn these *Hina* and *Ichimatsu* dolls, which have earned high praise and many awards over the years. ⊠ *Kamigyo Ku, Aburanokoji, Marutamachi-dori, agaru, Kyoto-shi* ✛ *Take Bus 9 to Horikawa/Marutamachi stop and walk 3 mins* ☎ *075/231–7466*

⊕ *www.ando-doll.com/english* ⊗ *May–Dec., Mon.–Sat. 9–6. Closed Sun., holidays, and 2nd Sat. of month.*

KIMONOS AND ACCESSORIES

Kasagen (かさ源). A thing of beauty more than utility in Japan, traditional umbrellas provide protection from the scorching sun and pelting rain. Since 1861, Kasagen has produced beautiful oiled-paper umbrellas that are guaranteed to last for years. ⊠ *284 Gion-machi, Kitagawa, Higashiyama-ku* ☎ *075/561–2832* ⊗ *Tues.–Sun. 10–7.*

RAAK. The *tenugui* hand towels sold by this shop have served many purposes through the centuries. In designs today that range from traditional to playful, the towels make wonderful scarves, napkins, bottle holders, and other items depending on how you twist and shape them. The colors and designs are so vibrant and eye-catching that framing one and hanging it as art is another possibility. This RAAK store is one of several in the city. ⊠ *Muromachi-dori, 358 Yakugyosha-cho, Anekoji Sagaru, Nakagyo-ku* ☎ *075/222–8870* ⊗ *Daily 11–7.*

LACQUERWARE

Zohiko Lacquerware (象彦京都寺町店). Kyoto's oldest and most renowned maker of lustrous lacquerware trays, tea ceremony utensils, calligraphy, boxes and other lacquer products was established in 1661. The showroom on Teramachi-dori has both contemporary and traditional specimens. ⊠ *Nakagyo-ku, Teramachi-dori, Nijo agaru, nishi-gawa, Nakagyo-ku, Kyoto-shi* ✢ *West side of Teramachi-dori, north of Nijo-dori; 10-min walk from Karasuma Oike subway station, 3-min walk from Kawaramachi Nijo bus stop* ☎ *075/229–6625* ⊕ *www.zohiko. co.jp/en/shop* ⊗ *Daily 10–6.*

TEMPLE MARKETS

Chion-ji Market (知恩寺). A market specializing in handmade goods and crafts is held here on the 15th of each month. Dolls, small carved wooden statues, fabric, ceramics, costume jewelry, and many other items are sold. Baked goods and other foods are available. ⊠ *Imadegawa and Higashioji-dori , northeast corner, opposite Kyoto University campus, Higashiyama-ku* ✢ *Take Bus 206 from Kyoto Station to Hyakumanben stop* ⊗ *15th of month, 9–4.*

CENTRAL KYOTO

ART AND ANTIQUES

Teramachi-dori, between Oike-dori and Marutamachi-dori in Nakagyo-ku, is known for antiques of all kinds and tea-ceremony utensils.

Gallery Utsuwa-kan (器館). Kyoto's hottest place to see contemporary arts and crafts—mostly ceramics but also glass—displays works on four floors. Though young, the artists represented already have established reputations. The gallery, whose name means "containers," is in just south of Daitoku-ji Temple. Packaging and shipping can be arranged. ⊠ *Kyoto Kita Ku, Murasakino Higashino Cho 20–17, Kyoto-shi* ✢ *Bus 204, 205, or 206 to Diatoku-ji-mae stop, or 1-min walk from temple* ☎ *075/491–3995* ⊕ *www.g-utsuwakan.com* ⊗ *Fri.–Wed. 11–7.*

CLOSE UP

Kyoto Crafts

Temples, shrines, and gardens can't be taken home with you. You can, however, pack up a few *omiyage* (mementos) for which this city is famous. The ancient craftspeople of Kyoto served the Imperial Court for more than 1,000 years, and the prefix *kyo-*before a craft is synonymous with fine craftsmanship.

DOLLS

Kyo-ningyo, exquisite display dolls, have been made in Kyoto since the 9th century. Constructed of wood coated with white shell paste and clothed in elaborate, miniature patterned-silk brocades, Kyoto dolls are considered the finest in Japan. Kyoto is also known for fine ceramic dolls and *Kyo-gangu,* its local varieties of folk toys.

FANS

Kyo-sensu are embellished folding fans used as accoutrements in Noh theater, tea ceremonies, and Japanese dance. They also have a practical use—to keep you cool. Unlike other Japanese crafts, which have their origin in Tang Dynasty China, the folding fan originated in Kyoto.

LACQUERWARE

Kyo-shikki refers to Kyoto lacquerware, which also has its roots in the 9th century. The making of lacquerware, adopted from the Chinese, is a delicate process requiring patience and skill. Finished lacquerware products range from furniture to spoons and bowls, which are carved from cypress, cedar, or horse-chestnut wood. These pieces have a brilliant luster; some designs are decorated with gold leaf and inlaid mother-of-pearl.

CERAMICS

Kyo-yaki is the general term applied to ceramics made in local kilns; the most popular ware is from Kyoto's Kiyomizu district. Often colorfully hand-painted in blue, red, and green on white, these elegantly shaped teacups, bowls, and vases are thrown on potters' wheels located in the Kiyomizu district and in Kiyomizu-danchi in Yamashina. Streets leading up to Kiyomizu-dera—Chawan-zaka, Sannen-zaka, and Ninen-zaka—are sprinkled with kyo-yaki shops.

SILK

Nishijin-ori is the weaving of silk. *Nishijin* refers to a Kyoto district producing the best silk textiles in all Japan, which are used to make kimonos. Walk along the narrow backstreets of Nishijin and listen to the persistently rhythmic looms. *Kyo-yuzen* is a paste-resist silk-dyeing technique developed by 17th-century dyer Yuzen Miyazaki. Fantastic designs are created on plain white silk pieces through the process of either *tegaki yuzen* (hand-painting) or *kata yuzen* (stenciling).

7

DEPARTMENT STORES

Daimaru Department Store (大丸). This large department store is known for high-quality merchandise—cosmetics, clothing, furniture, kitchen-wares, and other products that appeal to more expensive and conservative tastes. International shipping is available. An exhibition hall and several galleries are worth checking out, as are sections displaying traditional crafts. In the basement are prepared foods, breads, cakes, wine, and other edibles. ⊠ *Shijo-Karasuma, Shimogyo-ku* ✛ *1-min walk from Karasuma Station (Hankyu-Kyoto train), 2-min walk from Shijo Station (Karasuma subway)* ☎ *075/211–8111* ⊕ *www.daimaru.co.jp/ kyoto* ⊙ *Daily 10–7:30.*

Fujii Daimaru Department Store (藤井大丸). This store focuses on trendy fashions but caters to all ages. Many locals favor the basement food market for its reasonable prices and wine selection. ⊠ *Shijo-Teramachi, Shimogyo-ku* ✛ *2-min walk from Kawaramachi Station (Hankyu-Kyoto train), 5-min walk from Shijo Station (Karasuma subway)* ☎ *075/211–8181* ⊕ *www.fujiidaimaru.co.jp* ⊙ *Daily 10–8.*

Isetan (伊勢丹). The 13-story Isetan, in the Kyoto Station Building, is a branch of its Tokyo-based cousin. The feel here is slightly exclusive Tokyo. The store sells high-quality goods and has a well-attended exhibition hall. Many of the restaurants have city views. ⊠ *Kyoto Station Bldg., Karasuma-dori, Shimogyo-ku* ✛ *Kyoto Station Karasuma subway* ☎ *075/352–1111* ⊕ *kyoto.wjr-isetan.co.jp* ⊙ *Daily 10–7:30.*

Takashimaya Department Store (高島屋). Another of Kyoto's favorite department stores, Takashimaya specializes in luxury goods and designer fashions. You'll find an accommodating, English-speaking staff and a convenient money-exchange counter. The top floor has bargain merchandise, and another floor is filled with restaurants to revive the shop weary. The exhibition hall and galleries are also worth a visit, as is the basement gourmet food market. ⊠ *Shijo-Kawaramachi, Shimogyo-ku* ☎ *075/221–8811* ⊕ *www.takashimaya.co.jp/kyoto* ⊙ *Daily 10–7:30.*

FOLK CRAFTS

Kuraya Hashimoto (蔵屋橋元). One of Kyoto's best collections of antique and newly forged swords is fittingly located on a corner south of Nijo Castle. Authentic swords are not for sale, but sword paraphernalia and related items are on display. ⊠ *Nishihorikawa-dori, southeast corner of Nijo-jo, Nakagyo-ku* ☎ *075/811–4645* ⊕ *www.kurayahashimoto.com* ⊙ *Thurs.–Mon. 10–5:30.*

Ryushido (龍枝堂). One-room Ryushido sells exquisite paper products for calligraphers: paper of varying thicknesses, writing brushes, ink sticks, ink stones, and paperweights. The shop has a classic, artisanal feel. ⊠ *Nijo-agaru, Teramachi-dori, Kamigyo-ku* ☎ *075/252–4120* ⊙ *Sun. and holidays 9–6.*

Yamato Mingei-ten (やまと民芸店). The ceramics, glass, basketry, lacquerware, and other objects sold here are made with such artistry that only their utilitarian nature nudges them into the craft, as opposed to fine art, category. The owner keeps the prices reasonable so these beautiful things will be appreciated and used daily. ⊠ *Kawaramachi-dori, Takoyakushi-agaru, Nakagyo-ku* ☎ *075/221–2641* ⊙ *Wed.–Mon. 11–7.*

INCENSE

Kyukyodo (鳩居堂). In an attractive traditional building, this shop has been in business for 330 years, specializing in stationery, brushes for calligraphy, and incense, some of which (aloeswood) is more expensive than gold. ⊠ *Nakagyo-ku, Teramachi-dori, Oike sagaru, opposite*

Nishi-Hongan-ji-mae, Shimogyo-ku ✛ In covered shopping arcade of Teramachi ☎ 075/231–0510 ⊕ www.kyukyodo.com ☉ Mon.–Sat. 10–6.

KIMONOS AND ACCESSORIES

Shimmering new silk kimonos can cost more than ¥1,000,000—they are art objects, as well as couture—while equally stunning old silk kimonos can cost less than ¥3,000. You can find used kimonos at some local end-of-the-month temple markets.

Aizen Kobo (愛染工房). Fine handwoven and hand-dyed indigo textiles are this shop's specialty. The indigo plant is grown only in one place in Japan nowadays, and Aizen Kobo makes exclusive use of that product crafting cloth and garments in this rich deep-blue color. The owner dyes the cloth and his wife, Hisako Utsuki, designs. ✉ *Omiya Nishi-iru, Nakasuji-dori, Kamigyo-ku* ☎ *075/441–0355* ☉ *Daily 10–5:30.*

Miyawaki Baisen-an (宮杮脇賣扇庵). The famous fan shop Miyawaki Baisen-an has been in business since 1823, delighting customers not only with its fine collection of lacquered, scented, painted, and paper fans, but also with the old-world atmosphere of the shop itself. ✉ *Tominokoji Higashi-iru, Rokkaku-dori, Nakagyo-ku* ☎ *075/221–0181* ⊕ *www.baisenan.co.jp* ☉ *Daily 9–6.*

YAYA yufu (やや游風). Steps from Shijo subway station's Exit 5, this quaint kimono shop stocks original attire and antique accessories. Its English-speaking staff is kind and extremely knowledgeable. Your time spent trying on different items is sure to be a fun fashion experience. Many of the goods sold here are painstakingly tracked down at estate sales and flea markets. ✉ *319–3 Kamiyanagi-cho, Karasuma-higashi-iru, Bukkoji-dori, Shimogyo-ku* ☎ *075/341–8777* ☉ *Thurs.–Tues. noon–7.*

MARKETS

Nishiki-koji (錦小路). Kyoto's central food market is located elsewhere, but restaurateurs and housewives visit this long narrow street to select fresh produce and other foods. In recent years, the covered arcade has started to include souvenir shops in addition to tempting edibles. Ogling is fine. At some places you might be offered samples. If that happens, don't be shy. Have a taste. ✉ *Nishiki-koji-dori, Nakagyo-ku.*

NOVELTIES

FAMILY **Loft** (ロフト). This popular store, part of a national chain, has five floors with everything from beauty products to anime merchandise. Kids and teenagers love browsing here. There's much to catch the eye. ✉ *Kawaramachi-nishi, Takoyakushi-dori, Nakagyo-ku* ☎ *075/255–6210* ⊕ *www.loft.co.jp/shoplist/kyoto* ☉ *Daily 11–9.*

TEMPLE MARKETS

Kitano Tenman-gu (北野天満宮). On the 25th of each month, the streets around the shrine grounds overflow with all sorts of goods: used clothing and kimonos, food, plants, furniture, Buddhist images, dolls—just about everything you can imagine. Bargaining with a smile often brings good results. ✉ *Imakoji-agaru, Onmae-dori, Kamigyo-ku.*

To-ji (東寺). One of the two largest temple markets takes place on the 21st of each month. Vendors arrive early and set up by 7 or 8 am. Hundreds of stalls display fans, kimonos, antiques, potted plants, herbs, and newly designed clothing. Bring a pencil and paper to help you bargain down the price. The temple also hosts a smaller antiques market on the first Sunday of the month. ⊠ *1 Kujo-cho, Minami-ku.*

THE KANSAI REGION

WELCOME TO THE KANSAI REGION

TOP REASONS TO GO

★ **Architecture:** Skyscrapers share Osaka's 1,500-year-old skyline with 4th-century burial mounds, while Nara's wealth of classical temples, pagodas, and shrines are outstanding.

★ **Food:** Osaka has been known as Japan's kitchen since the 17th century. The region's tender, highly marbleized Kobe beef is world famous.

★ **Nada no Sake:** The sake breweries of Nada, in western Kobe, mineral-rich water and Yamada Nishiki rice, grown near Mt. Rokko.

★ **Shopping:** Locals in old wooden shops sell Nara's famous crafts, *sumi* (ink sticks) for calligraphy and ink painting, *Narasarashi* (fine handwoven, sun-bleached linen), and *akahadayaki* pottery.

★ **Todai-ji Temple Complex:** The complex in Kobe includes the Daibutsu-den, home to the monumental Great Buddha. The 8th-century San-gatsu-do houses Tenpyo-era statues.

1 **Osaka.** The people's eccentric friendliness in Japan's third-largest city plays against its rough-and-tumble urban background.

2 **Nara.** Visitors come for Nara's expansive parks and temples only to be enchanted by its rustic side streets and quiet sense of history.

3 **Kobe.** The city's relaxed cosmopolitan vibe blends into the waterfalls and *onsen* (thermal spas) of Arima.

GETTING ORIENTED

Osaka sits between Kobe to the west and Nara to the east and has the Kansai region's main international airport, which serves all three cities. Travel to either Kobe or Nara from Osaka takes about 30 minutes, and it's about an hour from Kobe to Nara, and vice versa. Kyoto is the other major tourist destination in the Kansai region, and it is covered separately.

8

NARA'S SACRED DEER

Of all the attractions in Nara, there is one that no visitor can miss. At some point, as you wander between temples, the city's sacred deer will come to inspect you. Cute they may be, just remember they are also wild animals, and coexistence with humans is not always trouble-free, neither for the deer nor their two-legged admirers.

(This page above) A deer nibbling the grass in Nara Koen; (opposite page upper right) feeding the deer; (opposite page bottom left) Nara's deer can be assertive.

Nara's deer have been part of the landscape of the city for as long as any of the temples, and they rival Todai-ji (with its Daibutsu, the famed statue of Buddha) as the favorite attraction for many tourists, Japanese especially. Red and flecked with white in summer, their coats turn gray in winter; today there are some 1,200 deer freely roaming around Nara Park and the surrounding hills. After such a long time cohabiting with humans they are, of course, only too familiar with us. And they are used to deference: traffic stops when they decide to cross the road, and they are likely to make their interest in being hand-fed known as soon as they approach you.

FEEDING THE DEER

Many tourists buy special biscuits, *shika senbei* (deer crackers), that are available at kiosks dotted around the park. The deer have learned how to appeal and cajole. Some will even bow their head meekly to request food. More often, however, they are not so demure and will jostle for that treat. As they can smell the crackers it is best not to hide them in a bag or pocket.

Normally, Nara's deer and humans get on harmlessly enough, but visitors should be wary of mothers in May and June, when they will be fiercely protective of their fawns. Likewise, young males can be unpredictable in the rutting season in fall.

THE LEGEND OF THE DEER

Legend has it that in AD 768 a white deer carried the deity Takemikazuchi-no-Mikoto, one of the first four deities of Kasuga Taisha, from a distant province called Hitachi (now known as Ibaraki, north of Tokyo) all the way to Nara. As a reward, the deer was hailed as divine—and would be forever untouchable. Ever since, the deer inhabiting the Kasuga hills, now part of Nara Park, were considered messengers of the gods and have been both protected and revered. In fact, it was only after World War II that the animals were stripped of their divine status, though they are no less cherished. In fact, they are designated as "national natural treasures" by the government, and punishment for harming them can be draconian. One hapless, would-be poacher found this out in 2010, when he tried to bag some illicit venison but ended up with a stretch in jail.

SHIKA NO TSUNOKIRI

Partly to protect visitors, but chiefly to stop the deer from hurting each other, there is an antler-cutting ceremony each

October. The *shika no tsunokiri* has changed little in 300 years. The bucks are chased into a special enclosure near Kasuga Taisha by *seko* (beaters) in traditional garb. The seko use *juji* (nets made of bamboo with rope), which they hurl at the animals, hook the antlers, and then pull the bucks in. A Shinto priest next gives each animal some purified water before sawing off its antlers. All males over four years face the same indignation. The fully grown antlers do not have nerves or veins, so they will not bleed and no lasting harm is done, but the bucks do not undergo the ordeal without a struggle.

SENTO-KUN

So popular are the deer with tourists that when Nara recently celebrated 1,300 years since its founding and was looking for a character that would embody everything about the city, the winning entry was *Sento-kun*. Looking suspiciously like an impish Buddha with antlers, he did not go down well with some of the city's more conservative figures who thought him disrespectful to the Buddha. Sento-kun has, however, proved enormously popular with visitors ever since and, if nothing else, is confirmation that Nara's deer are as big a draw as any of the magnificent temples or shrines.

SAKE, THE JAPANESE DRINK

Sake, or *nihonshu*, is the essential Japanese drink. Ranging in taste from fruity and bright to rich and mellow, there is a nihonshu for virtually every palette. Many sake breweries offer free tours and tastings to tourists.

(This page above) Assorted sake bottles, some decorated; (opposite page upper right) sake in its different varieties; (opposite page bottom left) sake from Hokkaido

Sake is brewed throughout Japan, and brewery tours are common. If you are in Kansai, you may want to visit one of the breweries in Nada, which accounts for more than a quarter of Japan's sake production. Thanks to a near-perfect combination of rice, water, brewing techniques, and its location next to the port of Kobe, Nada has been Japan's premier sake-brewing region since the 18th century. Many breweries offer tours in both Japanese and English, followed by free tastings and a chance to buy the hard-to-find sake produced there. Unfortunately, few breweries allow guests to enter the actual brewing area. To visit a brewery, call ahead for reservations since tours may only be available on certain days. If you don't have time for a brewery visit, most souvenir shops sell local sake. Just ask for *ji-zake* (local sake).

KOBE SHU-SHIN-KAN BREWERY

Kobe Shu-shin-kan Brewery (☎ 078/841–1121 ⊕ www.shushinkan.co.jp/guide/english.html), in business since 1751, is one of the few that opens its brew house to tours. Sake is brewed from October to March, but the rest of the year you can still see the facilities and learn about the process. To book a tour call the day before. There's also a shop (daily 10–6) and restaurant.

IMPORTANT SAKE TERMS

Like wine, nihonshu is nuanced and complex. It is officially separated into different grades depending on how much of the rice grain remains after polishing. Since the glutinous, low-protein inner cores of rice kernels produce the best sake, more polishing results in better sake. Anyone at a liquor store, souvenir shop, or restaurant should be able to give you further recommendations.

Dai-Ginjoshu 大吟醸酒

The highest grade of sake, *dai-ginjoshu* rice is polished so that only 50% of the grain remains. These sake are usually complex, light, and crisp. If you only try one nihonshu in Japan, make sure it is a dai-ginjoshu.

Ginjoshu 吟醸酒

The second-highest level sake, *ginjoshu* uses rice with 60% of the grain remaining. Ginjoshu usually has a clear, crisp flavor and slightly fruity bouquet.

Honjozoshu 本醸造酒

Honjozoshu rice is polished so that less than 70% of the grain remains. These sake are less complex than ginjoshu and dai-ginjoshu, but still light and fragrant. Quite affordable, they are an excellent companion to most Japanese food.

Futsushu 普通酒

Literally "normal sake," *futsushu* is the table wine of nihonshu. Some varieties

are quite tasty, while others are best avoided. Most hot sake, or *atsukan,* is this variety.

Junmaishu 純米酒

Junmaishu ("pure rice") indicates a sake that has been brewed using only white rice, pure water, and the fermenting agent *koji.* Not one of the four official grades of nihonshu, there are junmai honjozoshu (often called simply junmaishu), junmai ginjoshu, and junmai dai-ginjoshu. Junmai sake often has a mellow, smooth flavor.

Namazake 生酒

Bottled without aging, these unpasteurized sakes are known for their refreshing crispness. *Namazake* is only available for a short time after being brewed and must be refrigerated. While breweries release namazake at different times, spring is the most popular season.

Nigorizake にごり酒

Nigorizake is only slightly filtered, giving it a cloudy white appearance. Nigori sake has a heavier, sweeter taste than other sake.

Nihonshudo 日本酒度

This indicates whether a sake is sweet or dry. Dry sake has a positive number while sweet sake has a negative. For those new to nihonshudo, sake in the +/-5 range is some of the most popular.

8

Updated by
Robert Morel

Stretching from Mie Prefecture in the east to Hyogo Prefecture in the west, the Kansai region is both a snapshot of archetypal Japan and a showcase for the country's diversity. As home to Japan's capitals for nearly a millennium, Kansai is the undisputed seat of Japanese culture and tradition. It is the birthplace of Japan's traditional theater styles — Noh, Kabuki, and Bunraku — as well as the tea ceremony, Japanese Buddhism, and *ikebana* (flower arrangement). Thanks to Kobe and Osaka, it was also the heart of Japanese trade and industry until Tokyo surpassed it in the 1970s.

After the Kanto region around Tokyo, Kansai is Japan's most populous and economically important area. Most major companies have offices in Kansai and a few, like Panasonic and Nintendo, still have their headquarters in the region. Though much of the shipping and manufacturing industry has moved overseas, the cities of Kansai have responded by investing heavily in science, research, and technology businesses.

Because of its size and location, the geography of Kansai is as varied as the culture. The Kii Mountain range in southern Mie and Nara prefectures quickly gives way to the stunning rural coastline of Wakayama. Most of the region's population is concentrated around the four cities of Osaka, Kyoto, Kobe, and Nara, all in southern Kansai. Northern Kansai, including Lake Biwa and the Japan Sea coast, is quite rural. Thanks to the tempering effect of the inland sea, the climate of Kansai is generally mild, though summers are renowned for their humidity.

Kansai deserves its reputation as the culinary center of Japan. Whether it be delicate temple food in Kyoto and Nara, hearty Osaka fare, or Kobe's cosmopolitan fusion of Japanese and Western cuisines, no other region has such a range of local specialties. Kyoto may be the Kansai's main draw, but to sample the diversity of Japan's cities, make time to see Osaka, Kobe, and Nara. Within an hour's train ride, each city has its own unique culture, cuisine, and attractions. No other region of Japan produces such urban variety in such a small area.

Osaka's urban energy complements its offbeat fashions and reputation as Japan's culinary capital. For urban explorers, the side streets of Amerika-mura, Minami-horie, or Shin-Sekai offer countless surprises. Anime fans can visit Den Den Town for the latest games, anime goods, and "maid" cafés (where waitresses dress in French parlor maid uniforms).

In Kobe's East-meets-West cosmopolitan mix, travelers can wander Chinatown and have tea in a 19th-century European mansion before taking a cable car up Mt. Rokko for the romantic night view or a stay at Arima Onsen. For foodies, the city is home to Kobe beef and Japan's largest concentration of sake distilleries.

Nara is home to Japan's most famous World Heritage Site, where visitors can feed (or fend off) Nara Park's gregarious deer and see the stunning Todai-ji and Horyu-ji temples. The charming old houses of Nara-machi have become restaurants, galleries, and cafés—the perfect places to find souvenirs and sample local specialties like *nara-zuke* (vegetables pickled in sake).

Each city may not be for everyone, but to skip all three is to miss out on a chance to see some of Japan's most unique urban landscapes.

KANSAI REGION PLANNER

WHEN TO GO

Spring (March to May) and fall (September to November) are the best times to visit the Kansai region. The cherry blossoms flower mid-March to early April, and the autumn leaves are brightest late October to early November. Though summer (June to August) is very hot and sticky, winter is relatively balmy. There's an erratic rainy season, mostly in June.

PLANNING YOUR TIME

For many tourists, Osaka is a day trip, but it is also an excellent base for exploring the surrounding Kansai region—Kyoto, Nara, and Kobe are each 30 minutes away by train. Osaka is also the most convenient jumping-off point for a trip to the mountainside monasteries of Koya-san, two hours away on the Nankai private rail line.

Most visitors miss the best that Nara has to offer on a hurried day trip from Kyoto, Osaka, or Kobe. If time is an issue, the city is compact and well connected enough to explore all the temples and shrines in Nara Koen and spend a full morning or afternoon shopping and walking the streets of Nara-machi in one day. Spending a night in Nara gives you a chance to see a more traditional side of Kansai and to hit the main temples before the crowds arrive. Staying in Kobe means a chance to see the city's famous night panorama from the top of Mt. Rokko and a relaxing dinner at one of the many excellent restaurants overlooking the harbor.

The big attractions of Kobe can be covered in a day or two. Hit the Great Hanshin-Awaji Earthquake Museum and the Kobe City Museum in the morning. Follow this with a stroll around Kitano-cho and a café stop, and wind down the day at Harborland for dinner. On a second day head up Rokko-san and to the resort town of Arima, where you can soak in mineral hot springs and wander the quaint streets.

GETTING HERE AND AROUND

AIR TRAVEL

Many international carriers fly into Kansai International Airport (KIX) south of Osaka, which handles all of the Kansai region's international flights as well as connecting domestic flights to major Japanese cities. The airport, constructed on reclaimed land in Osaka Bay, is easy to navigate and is an interesting sight in its own right. Exiting customs on the first floor, you will find English-language tourist information and direct access to the limousine buses that run to many downtown hotels and destinations (roughly 60 minutes depending on the destination). Japan Airlines (JAL) and All Nippon Airways (ANA) have ongoing domestic flights to many major cities—Osaka is about 30 to 70 minutes away, Kobe about 40 minutes, and Nara about 90 minutes. Skymark offers good fares to major cities, and Peach Aviation, a Kansai-based discount carrier, offers inexpensive flights to many cities.

About half of domestic flights use Itami Airport, roughly 30 minutes northwest of Osaka. Travel to Kobe from Itami Airport takes about 40 minutes, 55 minutes to Nara.

Airport Contact Kansai International Airport (関西国際空港 *Kansai Kokusai Kuko*). ✉ *1–Banchi, Senshu-kuko Kita, Izumisano* ☎ *07/2455–2500* ⊕ *www. kansai-airport.or.jp/en/index.asp*.

BUS TRAVEL

There are a number of highway buses to Osaka from most cities in Japan, and from Osaka it's an easy trip to either Kobe or Nara. There are many bus companies, but JR Bus is one of the most popular.

Bus Contact JR West Bus. ✉ *1-3-23 Hokko* ☎ *06/6371–0111.*

TRAIN TRAVEL

Hikari Shinkansen trains from Tokyo Station to Shin-Osaka Station take about 3 hours and cost ¥14,250; the trip to Kobe from Tokyo takes 3½ hours and costs ¥14,900. The Nozomi Shinkansen trains cost a bit more and are about 30 minutes faster, but you can't use a JR Pass on these trains.

Nara can be reached from either Osaka or Kobe, but there are no direct trains from Tokyo. From Kintetsu's Osaka Namba Station, Nara is 42 minutes by Ordinary Express train (¥540), which leaves every 20 minutes. The JR Line rapid train from Tenno-ji Station takes 36 minutes and costs ¥470; from JR Namba it costs ¥560 and takes 50 minutes; from Osaka Station it takes one hour and costs ¥720.

From Kobe, take the JR Tokaido Line rapid train from San-no-miya Station to Osaka (around 25 minutes) and transfer to one of the trains listed here.

The Kansai Thru Pass offers unlimited travel on many private railways, subways, and buses and discounts at more than 350 tourist sites in Kansai. It can be a good choice for people doing a lot of sightseeing in all three cities, but at ¥4,000 for two days (¥5,200 for three) it is not a good value for visitors with JR Passes or those who plan to stay mostly in one city. Passes can be purchased at the main Tourist Information Centers in Osaka and Nara.

Train Contact Kansai Thru Pass (スッルッと関西 *Surutto Kansai*). ⊕ *www. surutto.com/tickets/kansai_thru_english.html.*

RESTAURANTS

Thanks to its history and unique culture, the Kansai region offers an unparalleled variety of Japanese cuisine. In addition to the local specialties of Osaka, Kobe, and Nara, Kansai has the same inexpensive chain restaurants as Tokyo and a good variety of international food. Outside tourist areas, restaurant staff may not speak English but often exhibit Kansai's signature friendliness, going out of their way to help.

HOTELS

Hotels in Kansai are slightly cheaper than those in Tokyo. Business hotels and international hotels comprise most of the lodging offerings in the larger cities, while *ryokan* (traditional inns) are common in more-rural destinations like Arima Onsen. Because of Kyoto's popularity during Golden Week (beginning of May), cherry-blossom season (mid-March to early April), and its autumn foliage (October and November), hotels in the surrounding cities are often booked solid. If you are traveling during one of these times, reserve a room early. Large international-chain hotels have English-speaking staff, but it's advisable to ask a tourist information center to make reservations for you outside the city.

Hotel reviews have been shortened. For full information, visit Fodors. com.

8

WHAT IT COSTS IN YEN			
$	$$	$$$	$$$$
Restaurants	under ¥1,000	¥1,000–¥2,000	¥2,001–¥3,000	over ¥3,000
Hotels	under ¥12,000	¥12,000–¥18,000	¥18,001–¥22,000	over ¥22,000

Restaurant prices are the average cost of a main course at dinner or, if dinner is not served, at lunch. Hotel prices are the lowest cost of a standard double room in high season.

VISITOR INFORMATION

There's a regional visitor information center in Kansai International Airport. Each city has its own visitor information centers as well.

Contact Kansai Tourist Information Center (観光の総合案内所 *Kanko no Sogo Annai-jo*). ⊠ *1F Passenger Terminal Bldg., Kansai International Airport, 1–Banchi, Senshu-kuko Kita, Izumisano.*

OSAKA

From Minami's neon-lighted Dotombori and historic Tenno-ji to the high-rise class and underground shopping labyrinths of Kita, Osaka is a city that pulses with its own unique rhythm. Though Osaka has no shortage of tourist sites, it is the city itself that is the greatest attraction. Home to some of Japan's best food, most unique fashions, and warmest locals, Osaka does not beg to be explored—it demands it. More than anywhere else in Japan, it rewards the impulsive turn down an interesting side street or the chat with a random stranger. People do not come here to see the city, they come to experience it.

Excluded from the formal circles of power and aristocratic culture in 16th-century Edo (Tokyo), Osaka took advantage of its position as Japan's trading center, developing its own art forms such as Bunraku puppet theater and Rakugo comic storytelling. It was in Osaka that feudal Japan's famed Floating World—the dining, theater, and pleasure district—was at its strongest and most inventive. Wealthy merchants and common laborers alike squandered fortunes on culinary delights, turning Osaka into "Japan's Kitchen," a moniker the city still has today. Though the city suffered a blow when the Meiji government canceled all of the samurai class's outstanding debts to the merchants, it was quick to recover. At the turn of the 20th century, it had become Japan's largest and most prosperous city, a center of commerce and manufacturing.

Today Osaka remains Japan's iconoclastic metropolis, refusing to fit Tokyo's norms and expectations. Unlike the hordes of Tokyo, Osakans are fiercely independent. As a contrast to the neon and concrete surroundings, the people of Osaka are known as Japan's friendliest and most outgoing. Ask someone on the street for directions in Tokyo and you are lucky to get so much as a glance. Ask someone in Osaka and you get a conversation.

The main areas of the city, Kita (north) and Minami (south), are divided by two rivers: the Dojima-gawa and the Tosabori-gawa. Between Kita and Minami is Naka-no-shima, an island and the municipal center of Osaka.

Kita (north of Chuo Dori) is Osaka's economic hub and contains Osaka's largest stations: JR Osaka and Hankyu Umeda. The area is crammed with shops, department stores, and restaurants. Nearby are a nightlife district, Kita-shinchi; Naka-no-shima and the Museum of Oriental Ceramics; Osaka-jo (Osaka Castle); and Osaka Koen (Osaka Park).

Restaurants, bars, department stores, and boutiques attract Osaka's youth to Minami (south Chuo Dori); theatergoers head to the National Bunraku Theatre and electronics-lovers to Den Den Town. For a glimpse of old Osaka, visit Tenno-ji Temple and Shin Sekai. The main stations are Namba, Shin-sai-bashi, Namba Nankai, and Tenno-ji. There's easy access to the Municipal Museum of Fine Art and Sumiyoshi Taisha (Sumiyoshi Grand Shrine).

The bay area, to the west of the city center, is home to the Osaka Aquarium and Universal Studios Japan. The Shinkansen stops at Shin-Osaka, three stops (about five minutes) north of Osaka Station on the Mido-suji subway line. To the north of Shin-Osaka is Senri Expo Park.

GETTING HERE AND AROUND

AIRPORT TRANSFERS
Frequent trains run from Kansai International Airport to Tenno-ji and Shin Osaka (JR Kansai Airport Express Haruka, 30 and 45 minutes), JR Kyo-bashi Station (Kansai Airport Rapid, 70 minutes), and the Nankai Namba Station (Nankai Rapid Limited Express, 30 minutes).

Buses from Itami Airport operate at intervals of 15 minutes to one hour (depending on your destination), daily 6 am to 9 pm, and take passengers to seven locations in Osaka: Shin-Osaka Station, Umeda, Namba (near the Nikko and Holiday Inn hotels), Ue-hon-machi, Abeno, Sakai-higashi, and Osaka Business Park (near the Hotel New Otani). Buses take 25 to 50 minutes, depending on the destination, and cost ¥520 to ¥650.

SUBWAY TRAVEL
Osaka's subway system is extensive and efficient, running from early morning until nearly midnight at intervals of three to five minutes. Fares are between ¥180 and ¥400 and are determined by the distance traveled. Mido-suji is the main line, which runs north–south and has stations at Shin-Osaka, Umeda (next to Osaka Station), Shin-sai-bashi, Namba, and Tenno-ji. The Osaka Visitors' Ticket (¥550) provides unlimited municipal transportation on subways, the New Tram (a tram line that runs to the port area), and city buses—at the commuter ticket machines in major subway stations and at the Japan Travel Bureau office in Osaka Station.

The JR Loop Line (Kanjo-sen) circles the city above ground and intersects with all subway lines. Fares range from ¥130 to ¥200, or you can use your JR Pass; these trains are not included in the day-pass price.

If you plan to do a lot of sightseeing the Osaka Amazing pass is an excellent deal. For ¥2,300 (one day) or ¥23,000 (two days) you get unlimited travel on all non-JR trains and buses, a coupon book, and free admission to many of Osaka's most popular sights like Osaka Castle, the Museum of Oriental Ceramics, and the Osaka Municipal Museum of Fine Art.

TAXI TRAVEL
You'll have no problem hailing taxis on the street or at taxi stands. (A red light in the lower left corner of the windshield indicates availability.) The problem is Osaka's heavy traffic. Fares are metered at ¥550 to ¥640 for the first 2 km (1 mile), plus ¥90 for each additional 300 meters. Few taxi drivers speak English, so it's advisable to have your destination written in Japanese characters to show to the driver. You don't need to tip, and many taxis now accept credit cards. Late at night, generally after midnight, there's a 20% surcharge. Expect to pay ¥1,500 for trips between Osaka Station and Shin-sai-bashi/Namba. For short distances, walking is recommended.

TRAIN STATION TRANSFERS
Shin-Osaka Station, on the north side of Shin-Yodo-gawa, is linked to the city center by the JR Kyoto Line and the Mido-suji subway line. On either line the ride, which takes 6 to 20 minutes depending on your mid-city destination, costs ¥180 to ¥230. A taxi from Shin-Osaka Station to central Osaka costs ¥1,500 to ¥2,700.

VISITOR INFORMATION

The main visitor information center is at JR Osaka Station. To get there from the Mido-suji Exit, turn right and walk about 50 yards. The office is beneath a pedestrian overpass, next to the city bus station. The

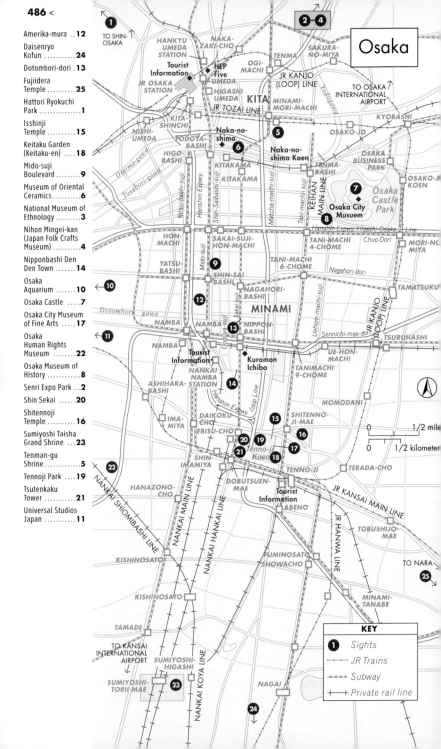

Osaka

KEY

- ① Sights
- ⊢——⊣ JR Trains
- ⊏⊐⊏⊐ Subway
- +——+ Private rail line

Shin-Osaka center is at the JR local line exit at Shin-Osaka Station. The Namba center is on the first floor of Namba Station. The Universal City center is a two-minute walk from JR Universal City Station. They are all open daily 8 to 8 (except Universal City which opens at 9) and closed December 31 to January 3.

Contacts Kansai Tourist Information Center Shinsaibashi. ⊠ *Tommy Hilfiger 3F, 2–5–1 Shinsaibashi-suji, Chuo-ku.*
Osaka Station Tourist Information Center (*Osaka-eki Kanko Annai-jo*). ⊠ *3–1–1 Umeda, JR Osaka Station, 1F, Kita-ku* ☎ *06/6345–2819.*
Osaka Visitors' Information Center Namba (難波駅観光案内所 *Namba-eki Kankou Annai-jo*). ⊠ *5–1–60 Namba, Chuo-ku.*
Shin-Osaka Tourist Information Center (新大阪観光案内所 *Shin Osaka Kanko Annai-jo*). ⊠ *JR Shin-Osaka Station, 3F, 5–16–1 Nishinakajima, Yodo-gawa-ku* ☎ *06/6305–3311.*

EXPLORING OSAKA

Most of Osaka's museums are closed Monday. One exception is Senri Expo Park, which closes (along with its museums) Wednesday. Museums stay open on Monday national holidays, closing the following day instead. Likewise, Senri Expo Park stays open on Wednesday holidays, closing Thursday instead.

KITA

Culture by day and glamour by night: Kita (north of Chuo Dori) is the place to come for the museums of Naka-no-shima, the city's deluxe department stores, and the chance to lose yourself (intentionally or not) in one of Japan's largest underground shopping labyrinths. At night take in the view from the Umeda Sky Building or the Ferris wheel at the HEP Five department store before you explore Osaka's upscale entertainment district, Kita-shinichi.

8

TOP ATTRACTIONS

Fodor'sChoice ★ **Museum of Oriental Ceramics** (大阪市立東洋陶磁美術館 *Osaka Shiritsu Toyo Toji Bijutsukan*). Located in Naka-no-shima Koen, Osaka's oldest park, the Museum of Oriental Ceramics houses more than 900 pieces of Chinese, Korean, and Japanese ceramics. Though only a fraction is on display at a given time, the collection is one of the finest in the world and includes 15 works designated as National Treasures or Important Cultural Properties. Those interested in art and ceramics should put this at the top of their must-see list. To get here take the Sakai-suji subway line to Kita-hama or the Midō-suji subway line to Yodoya-bashi and walk north across the Tosabori-gawa. ⊠ *1–1–26 Naka-no-shima* ☎ *06/6223–0055* ⊕ *www.moco.or.jp* ☒ *¥500* ⊗ *Tues.–Sun. 9:30–5.*

FAMILY
Fodor'sChoice ★ **Osaka Aquarium** (海遊館 *Kaiyukan*). This eye-catching red, gray, and blue building is Japan's best aquarium outside of Okinawa and one of the world's largest. More than 11,000 tons of water hold a multitude of sea creatures, including whale sharks, king penguins, giant spider crabs, jellyfish, and sea otters. You can stroll through 15 different environments, including the rivers and streams of Japanese and Ecuadorian forests, the icy waters around Antarctica, the dark depths of the Japan

Osaka's aquarium is one of the best in Japan and also one of the world's largest.

Sea, and the volcanically active Pacific Ring of Fire. The surrounding Tempozan Harbor Village also contains the Suntory Museum, cruises around Osaka Bay on a reproduction of the Santa María, and various shops and restaurants. There are often street performances outside on weekends. To get here, take the Chuo subway line to Osaka-ko Station; the aquarium is a five-minute walk northwest from the station. ⊠ *1–1 10 Kaigan-dori* ☎ *06/6576–5501* ⊕ *www.kaiyukan.com/language/eng* 🎫 *¥2,300* ⊗ *Tues.–Sun. 10–8; last entrance 1 hr before closing.*

Fodor's Choice **Osaka Castle** (大阪城 *Osaka-jo*). Osaka's most visible tourist attraction and symbol, Osaka Castle exemplifies the city's ability to change with the times. Originally built in the 1580s, what you see today is a five-story reconstruction completed in 1931. Instead of leaving a collection of steep wooden staircases and empty rooms, Osaka turned its castle into an elevator-equipped museum celebrating the history of its creator, Hideyoshi Toyotomi, the chief imperial minister to unite Japan.

For those more interested in aesthetics than artifacts, the eighth-floor *donjon* (tower) offers a stunning view of the urban landscape. Watching the sun set behind the skyscrapers is reason enough for a visit. The surrounding park makes for a relaxing break from the energy of the city as well. From Osaka-jo Koen-mae Station, it's about a 10-minute uphill walk to the castle. You can also take the Tani-machi subway line from Higashi-Umeda Station (just southeast of Osaka Station) to Tani-machi 4-chome Station. From here it's a 15-minute walk. ⊠ *1–1 Osaka-jo* ☎ *06/6941–3044* ⊕ *www.osakacastle.net* 🎫 *¥600* ⊗ *Sept.–mid-July, daily 9–5, last entry at 4:30; mid-July–Aug., daily 9–8, last entry at 7:30.*

Venice of the East

Despite changes in its political fortunes, Osaka developed as a trade center during the emerging Japanese (Yamato) nation, a role its waterways had destined it to play. Exchange wasn't limited to commerce. Buddhism and Chinese characters filtered into the fledgling Japanese society through Osaka to Nara, and from Nara to the rest of the country.

A MERCHANT CITY

By 1590 Hideyoshi Toyotomi (1536–98), the first *daimyo* (warlord) to unite Japan, had completed construction of Osaka Castle to protect his realm against the unruly clans of Kyoto. He designated Osaka a merchant city to consolidate his position. After Toyotomi died, Tokugawa Ieyasu's (1543–1616) forces defeated the Toyotomi legacy at the Battle of Sekigahara in 1600. Osaka's strategic importance was again short-lived, as Tokugawa moved the capital to Edo (now Tokyo) in 1603. Osaka grew rich supplying the new capital with rice, soy sauce, and sake as Edo transformed its agricultural land into city suburbs. All copper produced in Japan was exported through Osaka, and the National Rice Exchange was headquartered in Dojima, near Kita-shinchi: "70% of the nation's wealth comes from Osaka" was the catchphrase of the era. Some of Japan's business dynasties were founded during the economic boom of the 17th century, and they prevail today—Sumitomo, Konoike, and Mitsui among them.

"MANCHESTER OF THE EAST"

By the end of the Genroku Era (1688–1704) Osaka's barons were patronizing Bunraku puppetry and *Kamigata Kabuki* (comic Kabuki). Chikamatsu Monzaemon (1653–1724), writer of *The Forty-Seven Ronin,* penned the tragedies, which quickly became classics. Ihara Saikaku (1642–93) immortalized the city's merchants in the risqué *Life of an Amorous Man* and *The Great Mirror of Male Love.* When Tokyo became the official capital of Japan in 1868 there were fears that the "Venice of the East" would suffer. But expansion of the spinning and textile industries assured prosperity, and earned Osaka a new epithet—"Manchester of the East."

JAPAN'S MAIN PORT

As a consequence of the Great Kanto Earthquake in 1923, Osaka became Japan's main port and by 1926 the country's largest city. Chemical and heavy industries grew during World War I, and were prime targets for American bombers during World War II. Much of Osaka was flattened, and more than a third of the prefecture's 4.8 million people were left homeless. During the postwar years many Osaka companies moved their headquarters to Tokyo. Even so, Osaka was rebuilt and went on to host Asia's first World Expo in 1970. It has since fashioned itself as a city of cutting-edge technology, trendsetting, and a unique way of life. The Osaka City Government plans to revive the "Water City" appellation for Osaka, but for now the heritage of the city's waterways lives on in its place-names: *bashi* (bridge), *horie* (canal), and *semba* (dockyard).

8

WORTH NOTING

Hattori Ryokuchi Park (服部緑地公園 *Hattori Ryokuchi Koen*). Come for the park's open-air **Museum of Old Japanese Farmhouses** (Nihon Minka Shuraku Hakubutsukan), and wander about full-size traditional rural buildings such as the giant *gassho-zukuri* (thatch-roof) farmhouse from Gifu Prefecture. The park also has horseback-riding facilities, tennis courts, and an open-air stage that hosts concerts and other events in summer. There's even an outdoor Kabuki theater. An English-language pamphlet is available. Take the Mido-suji subway line from Umeda to Ryokuchi Koen Station. The park is a 10-minute walk away. ⊠ *1–1 Hattori Ryokuchi, Toyonaka* ☎ *06/6862–4946 park office, 06/6862–3137 museum* 🖂 *Park free, museum ¥500* ⊗ *Daily 9:30–5; last entry at 4:30.*

National Museum of Ethnology (国立民族学博物館 *Kokuritsu Minzokugaku Hakubutsukan*). The National Museum of Ethnology has informative displays about the Ainu (the original inhabitants of Hokkaido) and other cultures from around the world. Information sheets explaining the sections of the museum are available and supplement the English-language brochure included with admission. The museum is on the east side of the main road that runs north–south through Senri Expo Park. ⊠ *Senri Expo Park, Suita* ☎ *06/6876–2151* ⊕ *www.minpaku.ac.jp/english* 🖂 *¥420* ⊗ *Thurs.–Tues. 10–5; last entry at 4:30.*

Nihon Mingei-kan (日本民芸館 *Japan Folk Crafts Museum*). The exhibits of "beauty from day-to-day life" at this museum in Senri Expo Park explore the diversity and intricacy of Japanese handicrafts from Hokkaido to Okinawa. The cloth, wood, and bamboo items in simple displays evoke Japan's traditional past and make quite a contrast to Osaka's modernity. ⊠ *Senri Expo Park, 10–5 Bampaku Koen, Suita* ☎ *06/6877–1971* 🖂 *¥700* ⊗ *Thurs.–Tues. 10–5; last entry at 4:30.*

FAMILY

Fodor's Choice

★

Osaka Museum of History (大阪歴史博物館 *Osaka Rekishi Hakubutsukan*). Informative as it is enjoyable, the Osaka Museum of History immerses you in the city's history from pre-feudal times to the early 20th century. Full of life-size displays and hands-on activities, the museum does an excellent job of offering attractions for both children and adults. There are two paths through the exhibits, a "Highlight Course" (to get a hint of Osaka's past in less than an hour) and the "Complete Course" (for a fuller experience). The museum makes an excellent stop on the way to Osaka Castle. To get here take the Chuo or Tani-machi subway line to Tani-machi 4-Chome Station and take Exit 9 or 2. ⊠ *4–1–30 Otemae* ✢ *Chuo-ku* ☎ *06/6946–5728* ⊕ *www.mus-his.city.osaka.jp* 🖂 *¥600* ⊗ *Mon., Wed., Thurs., and weekends 9:30–5, Fri. 9:30–8.*

Senri Expo Park (万博公園 *Banpaku Koen*). Originally the site of Expo 1970, the garden-filled Senri Expo Park still draws visitors thanks to the presence of the National Museum of Ethnology, the Japan Folk Art Museum, and the enormous statue by Taro Okamoto called the *Tower of the Sun*. Located outside the city center, the park offers an interesting look at how Osaka has blossomed in the postwar years in the Expo'70 Pavilion. To get to the park, take the Mido-suji subway line to Senri-Chuo Station (20 minutes from Umeda); then take the monorail to Bampaku Koen-mae (10 minutes). ⊠ *Senri Expo Park,*

Osaka-jo, originally built in the 1580s and reconstructed in 1931, is on a hill above the Osaka-jo Koen-mae Station.

Suita City ☎ 06/6877–3339 ⊕ *www.expo70-park.jp* ✉ *Gardens ¥250 each; Expo'70 Pavilion ¥200* ☾ *Thurs.–Tues. 9:30–5.*

Tenman-gu Shrine (天満宮). This 10th-century shrine is the main site of the annual **Tenjin Matsuri**, held July 24 and 25, one of the largest and most enthusiastically celebrated festivals in Japan. Dozens of floats are paraded through the streets, and more than 100 vessels, lighted by lanterns, sail along the canals amid fireworks. The shrine is dedicated to Sugawara no Michizane, the Japanese patron of scholars. Sugawara was out of favor at court when he died in 903. Two years later plague and drought swept Japan—Sugawara was exacting revenge from the grave. To appease Sugawara's spirit he was deified as Tenjin-sama. He is enshrined at Tenman-gu. On the 5th, 15th, and 25th of each month students throughout Japan visit Tenman-gu shrines to pray for academic success. Tenman-gu is a short walk from either JR Tenman-gu Station or Minami-Mori-machi Station on the Tani-machi-suji subway line. ✉ *2–10 Higashitenma, Kita-ku, Kita-ku* ☎ 06/6353–0025 ✉ *Free* ☾ *Apr.–Sept., daily 5:30 am–sunset; Oct.–Mar., daily 6 am–sunset.*

FAMILY **Universal Studios Japan** (ユニバーサルスタジオジャパン). The 140-acre Universal Studios Japan combines the most popular rides and shows from Universal's Hollywood and Florida movie-studio theme parks with special attractions designed specifically for Japan. Popular attractions include those based on *Harry Potter, Spider-Man,* and *E.T.* The Japan-only Snoopy attraction appeals to the local infatuation with all things cute, as do the daily Hello Kitty parades. Restaurants and food outlets abound throughout the park, and the road from JR Universal City Station is lined with the likes of Hard Rock Cafe and Bubba Gump

Shrimp, local fast-food chain MOS Burger, and Ganko Sushi. Due to high demand on weekends and during holiday periods, tickets must be bought in advance at branches of Lawson convenience stores and larger JR stations. The park is easily reached by direct train from JR Osaka Station (about 20 minutes) or by changing to a shuttle train at JR Nishi-kujo Station on the Loop Line. ⊠ *2–1–33 Sakurajima, Kono-hana-ku, Konohana-ku* ☎ *06/6465–3000* ⊕ *www.usj.co.jp* ✐ *¥6,980* ⊙ *Daily 10–10.*

MINAMI

Tradition by day and neon by night, Minami is the place to come for Osaka history: Japan's oldest temple, a breathtaking collection of Japanese art in the Municipal Museum of Fine Art, and a mausoleum bigger than the pyramids. And then youth culture takes over: this is where future fashionistas forge the haute couture of tomorrow. Amid all this modernity are glimpses of an older Osaka in sites like Shin Sekai and Tenno-ji Temple.

TOP ATTRACTIONS

Amerika-mura (アメリカ村 *America Village*). Though it takes its name from the original shops that sold cheap American fashions and accessories, Ame-mura (*ah-meh moo-ra*), as it's called, is now a bustling district full of trendy clothing stores, record stores, bars, cafés, and clubs that cater to teenagers and young adults. Shops are densely packed, and it's virtually impossible to walk these streets on weekends. To see the variety of styles and fashions prevalent among urban youth, Ame-Mura is *the* place to go in Osaka. ⊠ *West side of Mido-suji, 6 blocks south of Shin-sai-bashi Station.*

Fodor's Choice ★ **Dotombori-dori** (道頓堀通り *Dotombori Street*). If you only have one night in Osaka, Dotombori-dori is the place to go. Once Osaka's old theater district, Dotombori-dori is now a neon-lighted pedestrian street filled with restaurants, shops, and the shouts of countless touts each proclaiming (usually falsely) that their restaurant is the only one worth visiting. Stop at Ebisu-bashi to watch street musicians attract crowds as spiky-haired twentysomethings practice the art of *nampa* (the elaborate, amusing, and uniquely Japanese method of chatting people up). Stroll along the riverfront walkways to avoid the crowds, or slip into Hozenji Yokocho Alley, two blocks south of Dotombori-dori, to splash water on the moss-covered statues at Hozenji Shrine or dine in any of the excellent restaurants hidden away on this quiet street. ⊠ *Dotombori-dori, Chuo-ku.*

Nipponbashi Den Den Town (でんでんタウン). All the latest video games, computers, cameras, phones, MP3 players, and other gadgets are on display here. Even if you are not in the market for electronics, a stroll through Den Den Town provides an interesting look at Japan's anime, video game, and computer subcultures. "Den Den" is derived from the word *denki*, which means electricity. ⊠ *2 blocks east of Namba Station, Naniwa-ku.*

Osaka City Museum of Fine Arts (大阪市立美術館 *Osaka Shiritsu Bijutsu-kan*). The building isn't too impressive, but the exceptional collection of 12th- to 14th-century classical Japanese art on the second floor is.

The Shinsaibashi district is one of Osaka's busiest shopping areas.

Other collections include the works of Edo-period artist Korin Ogata, more than 3,000 examples of modern lacquerware, and a collection of Chinese paintings and artifacts. Take the Loop Line or the Mido-suji subway line to Tenno-ji Station, or the Tani-machi subway to Shitenno-ji-mae. ⊠ *1–82 Chausuyama-cho, Tennoji-ku* ☎ *06/6771–4874* ⊕ *www. osaka-info.jp/en/facilities/cat/post_279.html* ⊠ *¥300, includes entry to Tenno-ji Park* ☉ *Tues.–Sun. 9:30–5; last entry at 4:30.*

Fodor's Choice **Shin Sekai** (新世界 *New World*). Stepping into Shin Sekai is a chance
★ to see the Osaka of a generation ago. Built in 1912, the neighborhood was meant to emulate New York and Paris (complete with its own Eiffel Tower). After the war, the area fell into neglect and became one of the few dangerous areas in Osaka. Over the past decade, Shin Sekai has cleaned up its act while retaining its retro feel. On weekends everyone lines up to try *kushi katsu*, or batter-fried meat and vegetables on skewers. Near Tenno-ji Park and Shitenno-ji Temple, Shin Sekai is an excellent afternoon or early evening stop. After dinner, visit Tsutenkaku Tower for lovely night views of Osaka. ⊠ *Ebisu-Higashi* ✚ *The easiest way to get to Shin Sekai is from Exit 2 of Dobutuenn-mae subway on Mido-suji Line. Cross street in direction of towering pachinko parlor, and walk through Jan Jan Yokocho, the covered shopping street that leads to Shin Sekai* ⊠ *Free.*

Shitennoji Temple (四天王寺 *Tennoji Temple*). Tenno-ji, as this temple is popularly known, is one of the most important historic sights in Osaka and the oldest temple in Japan. Founded in 593, it's been destroyed by fire many times. The last reconstruction of the five-story pagoda in 1965 has maintained the original design and adhered to the traditional mathematical alignment. What has managed to survive from earlier times is the 1294 stone *torii* (gate) that stands at the main entrance. (Interestingly enough, these are rarely used at Buddhist temples.)

The founder, Umayado no Mikoto (573–621), posthumously known as Prince Shotoku (Shotoku Taishi), is considered one of early Japan's most enlightened rulers. He was made regent over his aunt, Suiko, and set about instituting reforms and establishing Buddhism as the state religion. Buddhism had been introduced to Japan from China and Korea in the early 500s, but it was seen as a threat to the aristocracy, who claimed prestige and power based up their godlike ancestry. On the 21st of every month the temple hosts a flea market that sells antiques and baubles; go in the morning for a feeling of Old Japan. ⊠ *1–11–18 Shitenno-ji, Tenno-ji-ku* ✚ *Three train lines will take you near Shitenno-ji. The Tanimachi-suji subway line's Shitenno-ji-mae Station is closest to temple and temple park. Loop Line's Tenno-ji Station is several blocks south of temple. Mido-suji subway line also has a Tenno-ji stop, next to JR Station* ☎ *06/6771–0066* ✉ *¥300* ☉ *Apr.–Sept., daily 8:30–4:30; Oct.–Mar., daily 8:30–4.*

Sumiyoshi Taisha Grand Shrine (住吉大社). In a city of mariners it's no surprise that locals revere Sumiyoshi Taisha, dedicated to the guardian deity of sailors. According to legend, the shrine was founded by Empress Jingu in 211 to express her gratitude for her safe return from a voyage to Korea. Sumiyoshi Taisha is one of three shrines built prior to the arrival of Buddhism in Japan (the other two are Ise Jingu in Mie Prefecture and Izumo Taisha in Tottori Prefecture). According to Shinto custom, shrines were torn down and rebuilt at set intervals to the exact specifications of the original. Sumiyoshi was last replaced in 1810. Sumiyoshi is also famous for its *taiko-bashi* (arched bridge), given by Yodo-gimi, the consort of Hideyoshi Toyotomi, who bore him a son.

Every June 14 starting at 1 pm, a colorful rice-planting festival takes place here with traditional folk performances and processions. Sumiyoshi Matsuri, a large and lively festival, is held from July 30 to August 1. A crowd of rowdy young men carries a 2-ton portable shrine from Sumiyoshi Taisha to Yamato-gawa and back; this is followed by an all-night street bazaar. To reach the shrine, take the 20-minute ride south on the Nankai Main Line from Nankai Namba Station to Sumiyoshi Koen Station. ⊠ *2–9–89 Sumiyoshi, Sumiyoshi-ku* ☎ *06/6672–0753* ✉ *Free* ☉ *Apr.–Oct., daily 6–5; Nov.–Mar., daily 6:30–5.*

Fodor's Choice **Tennoji Park** (天王寺公園 *Tennoji Koen*). The best place to get away
★ from the noise and concrete of the city, this park contains not only the **Municipal Museum of Fine Art** and the garden of **Keitaku-en,** but also the **Tenno-ji Botanical Gardens** (Tenno-ji Shokubutsuen). Also within the park is a prehistoric burial mound, **Chausuyama Kofun,** that was the site of Tokugawa Ieyasu's camp during the siege of Osaka-jo in 1614–15. Visit in the morning or evening when the park is at its quietest. Take the Loop Line from Osaka Station to Tenno-ji Station. The park is on the left side of the road going north to Shitenno-ji. ⊠ *6–74 Chausuyama-cho, Tenno-ji-ku* ☎ *06/6771–8401* ✉ *¥150 park only, ¥300 with Municipal Museum of Fine Art* ☉ *Tues.–Sun. 9:30–4:30; last entry at 4.*

Tsutenkaku Tower (通天閣). Nearly every major city in Japan has its tower, and while they all offer lovely views, most are not much to look at themselves. Shin Sekai's Tsutenkaku breaks this trend by looking decidedly strange. Built in 1912 with the rest of Shin Sekai, the original tower merged Paris's Arc de Triomphe and Eiffel Tower into a single design. Though the original was dismantled to supply iron for Japan's war effort, it was designed and rebuilt in 1956. On the face of the tower is Japan's largest clock (changing color by the minute); the top displays different-color LED lights to indicate the weather. Charmingly gaudy, Tsutenkaku is considered one of the most authentic symbols of Osaka. The observation deck provides one of the city's best night views and a chance to meet Billiken, Shin Sekai's deity of "things as they ought to be." ⊠ *1–18–6 Ebisu Higashi* ☎ *06/6641–9555* ⊕ *www.tsutenkaku. co.jp* ⊡ *¥700* ☉ *Daily 9–9.*

WORTH NOTING

Daisenryo Kofun (仁徳天皇陵古墳 *Nintoku Mausoleum*). The 4th-century mausoleum of Emperor Nintoku is in the city of Sakai, southeast of Osaka. The mausoleum was built on an even larger scale than that of the pyramids of Egypt—archaeologists calculate that the central mound of this site covers 1.3 million square feet. Construction took more than 20 years and required a total workforce of about 800,000 laborers. Japan has been pushing hard to have the mausoleum declared a UNESCO World Heritage Site. Surrounding the Emperor's burial place are three moats and pine, cedar, and cypress trees. You can walk around the outer moat to get an idea of the size of the mausoleum and the grounds. From Tenno-ji Station, take the JR Hanwa Line to Mozu Station (a half-hour ride). From there the mausoleum is within a five-minute walk. ⊠ *7–1 Daisen-cho, Sakai-shi, Sakai-shi* ☎ *072/955–1115* ⊡ *Free* ☉ *Daily sunrise–sunset.*

Fujiidera Temple (藤井寺). An 8th-century statue of the 1,000-handed Kannon, the goddess of mercy, is this temple's main object of worship. The seated figure is the oldest Buddhist sculpture of its kind, and it's only on view on the 18th of each month. To get here, take the Mido-suji subway line to Tenno-ji Station, then transfer to the Kintetsu Minami–Osaka Line and take it to Fujii-dera Station. The temple is a few minutes away. ⊠ *1–16–21 Fujii-dera, Fujii-dera-shi* ☎ *0721/938–0005* ⊡ *Free, ¥300 to view Kannon statue* ☉ *Statue on view 18th of month.*

Isshinji Temple (一心寺 *Isshin-ji Temple*). The ultramodern gate and fierce guardian statues of Isshin-ji Temple are a stark contrast to the nearby Shitenno-ji Temple. Dating back to 1185, the temple is now known for its *Okotsubutsu*—a Buddha statue made of the cremated remains of more than 200,000 people laid to rest at Isshin-ji. Far from morbid, the statue is meant to reaffirm one's respect for the deceased and to turn them into an object of everyday worship. An Okutsubutsu is made every 10 years, the first in 1887. Though 12 Okutsubutsu have been made, due to a direct hit to the temple during World War II, only the six crafted after the war remain. To get here take the Sakisuji Subway to Ebisu Cho Station and walk east along Isshin-ji-mae. The temple is on the right soon after passing under the expressway. ⊠ *2–8–69 Osaka,*

8

Tennoji-ku ☏ *06/6771–0444* ⊕ *www.osaka-info.jp/en/facilities/cat22/ post_318.html* ✉ *Free* ☉ *Daily 9–5.*

Keitaku Garden (慶沢園 *Keitaku-en*). Jihei Ogawa, master gardener of the late Meiji period, spent 10 years working the late Lord Sumitomo's circular garden into a masterpiece. The woods surrounding the pond are a riot of color in spring, when the cherry blossoms and azaleas bloom. Keitaku-en is adjacent to Shiritsu Bijutsukan in Tenno-ji Koen. ✉ *108 Chausuyama-cho, Tennoji-ku, Tenno-ji-ku* ✉ *Free* ☉ *Tues.–Sun. 9:30–4:30; last entry at 4.*

Mido-suji Boulevard (御堂筋). Osaka's Champs Élysées, this ginko-tree-lined boulevard is Osaka's most elegant thoroughfare and home to its greatest concentration of department stores. To the east of Mido-suji is the Shin-sai-bashi-suji arcade, one of Osaka's best shopping and entertainment streets. If you're in town on the second Sunday in October, catch the annual Mido-suji Parade, with its colorful procession of floats and musicians. ✉ *Chuo-ku* ⊹ *The Shin-sai-bashi stop (Exit 7) on Mido-suji subway line is in heart of city's shopping districts.*

Osaka Human Rights Museum (リバティおおさか *Liberty Osaka*). In a country that often falls back on the myth of everyone living in egalitarian harmony, Liberty Osaka is one of the city's more unique sights. The museum delves into issues of discrimination in Japan based on ethnicity, gender, sexual orientation, and physical disabilities. In addition to an English-language audio guide and a 30-page booklet detailing the museum's contents, each section has a documentary video with English subtitles. The highly informed volunteer staff is happy to answer questions about the permanent and temporary exhibits. Although it's less centrally located than some of Osaka's other sights, Liberty Osaka is highly recommended for anyone interested in issues regarding discrimination. The museum is closed the fourth Friday of each month. To get here, take the JR Loop Line to Ashihara Station and walk south along the main road 656 yards. The museum will be on your right. ✉ *3–6–36 Naniwa-Nishi, Naniwa-ku, Naniwa-ku* ☏ *06/6561–5891* ⊕ *www.osaka-info.jp/en/facilities/cat/post_302.html* ✉ *¥500* ☉ *Wed.–Sun. 10–5.*

WHERE TO EAT

You can find a particularly broad range of Japanese food in Osaka, from the local snack foods, *okonomiyaki* (a thick pancake filled with cabbage and other ingredients) and *takoyaki* (tasty, grilled octopus in batter), to full *kaiseki* restaurants. The seafood from the Seto Inland Sea is always fresh, as is the tender beef used at the many Korean barbecue restaurants in Osaka's Korea Town, Tsuruhashi, located just outside the west exit of Tsuruhashi Station. It is also easy to find a variety of international cuisines throughout town.

Under Osaka Station is the Shin-Umeda Shokudogai—a maze of narrow alleys lined with *izakaya* (lively after-work drinking haunts). The beer and hot snacks comfort many an overworked person on the commute home.

CLOSE UP

On the Menu

Osakans are passionate about food. In fact, they coined the word *kuidaore*—to eat until you drop. They expect restaurants to use the freshest ingredients. For centuries the nearby Seto Inland Sea has allowed easy access to fresh seafood. Osakans continue to have discriminating palates and demand their money's worth.

Osakan cuisine is flavored with a soy sauce lighter in color and milder in flavor than the soy used in Tokyo. One local delicacy is *okonomiyaki,* something between a pancake and an omelet, filled with cabbage, mountain yams, pork, shrimp, and other ingredients. *Osaka-zushi* (Osaka-style sushi), made in wooden molds, has a distinctive square shape. *Unagi* (eel) remains a popular local dish; grilled unagi is eaten in summer for quick energy. *Fugu* (blowfish), served boiled or raw, is a winter delicacy. Osaka is also the home of *kappo-ryori,* intimate, counter-only eateries that serve only the freshest seasonal foods in a relaxed atmosphere.

The thick, white noodles known as *udon* are a Japanese staple, but Osakans are particularly fond of *kitsune* udon, a local dish (now popular throughout Japan) in which the noodles are served with fried tofu known as *abura-age.* Another Osaka invention is *takoyaki,* griddle dumplings with octopus, green onions, and ginger smothered in a delicious sauce. Sold by street vendors in Dotombori, these tasty snacks also appear at every festival and street market in Kansai. And for heavier fare, Osaka is famous for *kushi katsu,* skewered, deep-fried meat and vegetables. If you don't want to fall over, try to leave the table *hara-hachi bunme,* meaning 80% full.

8

For some energetic dining neonside, head to Dotombori-dori and Soemon-cho (pronounced *so*-eh-mon cho), two areas along Dotombori River packed with restaurants and bars. Kimono-clad *mama-sans* serve the city's expense-accounters at Kita-shinchi, in south Kita-ku, the city's most exclusive dining quarter.

KITA

$$$ JAPANESE 🍴 **Akashiya** (明石屋). It may look like a hole-in-the-wall from the outside, but this tiny restaurant serves up some of Osaka's finest *akashi-yaki,* a much fluffier and more delicate take on the city's famous grilled octopus. The staff is friendly and helpful. In addition to *akashi-yaki,* the shop also serves up excellent *gyoza* (fried meat-filled dumplings) and *ika-yaki* (grilled squid). It also carries a good selection of local sake. [$] *Average main: ¥2200* ✉ *Kita Shinichi Bldg. 1F, 1–3–23 Dojima, Kita-ku* ☎ *06/6341–3910* 🕓 *Closed Mon. No lunch.*

$$$ JAPANESE 🍴 **Bat-ten Yokato** (バッテンよかとお). In the basement of Kita-Shinichi's Aspa (Takagawa Umeda) Building, the hip, low-ceilinged Bat-ten Yokato serves up a wide selection of very good *yakitori* (skewered meat and vegetables) in a fun, cozy atmosphere. Sitting at the long bar, you can watch the cooks work and call out requests. In addition to the quality of the food, the fact that the staff is obviously having a good time makes this an excellent place to try one of the most popular foods in Japan. [$] *Average main: ¥3000* ✉ *Takagawa Umeda Bldg.,*

Akashiya **4**

Bat-ten
Yokato **3**

Hana Goyomi .. **10**

Kani Doraku **7**

Kigawa **9**

La Baie **2**

Mizuno **8**

Planet 3rd
Café and
Lounge **6**

Shunkoku
Shunsai **1**

Taqueria
La Fonda **5**

Yaekatsu **12**

Zuboraya **11**

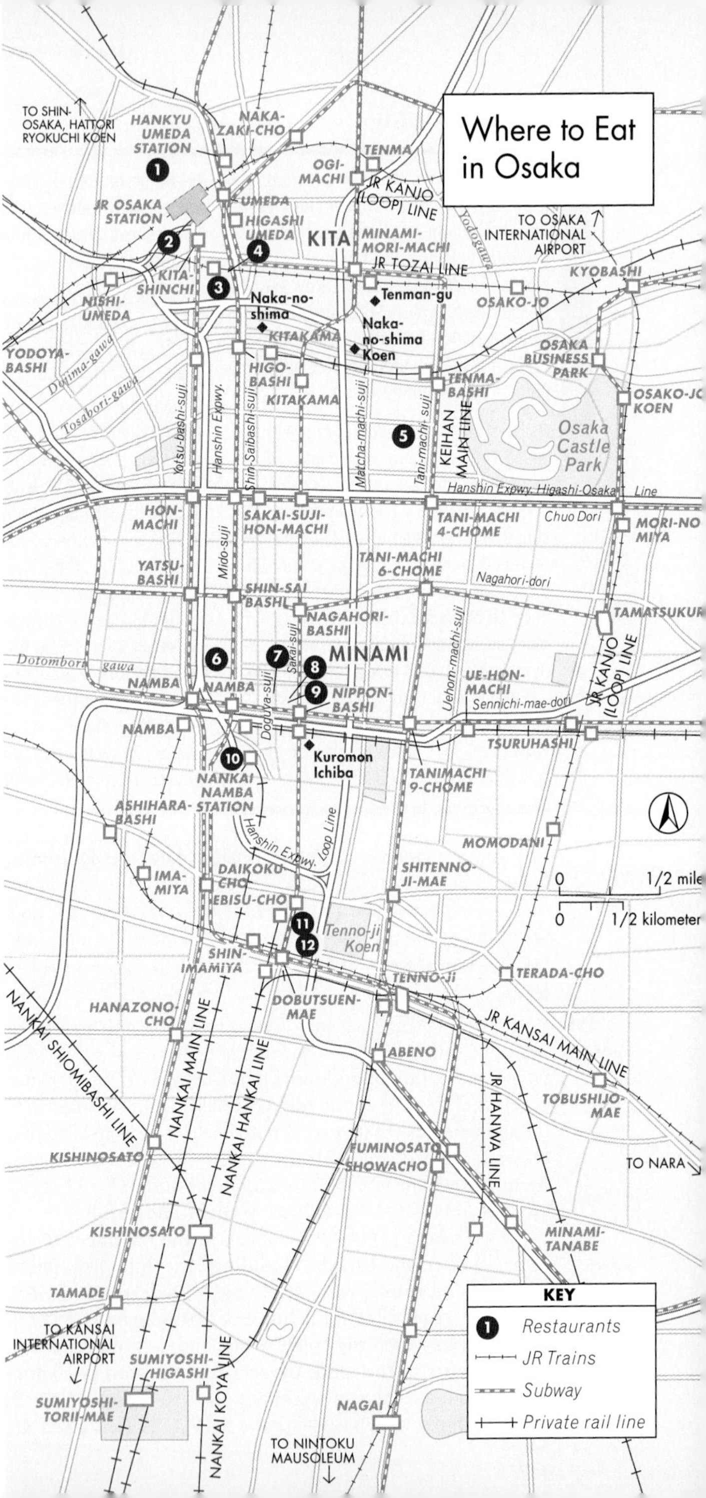

Where to Eat in Osaka

KEY

1. Restaurants
   JR Trains
   Subway
   Private rail line

B1F, 1–11–24 Kita-shinichi, Kita-ku, Chuo-ku ☏ *06/4799–7447* ▭ *No credit cards* ☿ *Closed Sun. No lunch* ⚃ *Reservations not accepted.*

$$$$ ✕**La Baie** (ラベ). The city's premier hotel restaurant serves extremely
FRENCH good French food. The elegant yet relaxed atmosphere, seasonal menus,
Fodor's Choice and extensive wine list make La Baie an excellent choice when you're
★ in the mood for European-style fare. With its high ceiling, 18th-century
paintings, and dark-wood accents, the interior is impressive and the service is impeccable. The weekday lunch courses are a good way to sample
some of the best French cuisine in Osaka. Ⓢ *Average main: ¥15000*
✉ *Ritz Carlton, 2–5–25 Umeda, Kita-ku* ☏ *06/6343–7020.*

$$$ ✕**Shunkoku Shunsai.** Osaka food, while delicious, can be on the heavy
ASIAN FUSION side. Shunkoku Shunsai (literally "seasonal grains, seasonal vegeta-
bles") more than lives up to its name. The healthy French-Japanese
fusion dishes are fresh and light but filling and the ¥1,155 lunch sets
are a good value. You can even see the vegetables growing next door at
it's City Farm indoor garden. Located in Grand Front Osaka (connected
to Osaka Station), it is also a good place for a meal on your way in or
out of the city. Ⓢ *Average main: ¥3000* ✉ *Grand Front Osaka North
Bldg. 6F, 4–1 Ofuku-cho, Kita-ku* ☏ *06/6359–3072* ▭ *No credit cards.*

MINAMI

$$$$ ✕**Hana Goyomi** (花暦). Dining at the Swissôtel's flagship restaurant is
JAPANESE an elegant escape from the crowds of Osaka. The seasonal kaiseki din-
ners are presented with exquisite attention to detail, bringing out the
flavor of each ingredient. The restaurant offers separate seating at the
sushi bar, tempura counter, and even four private rooms. Choose from
one of the seasonal set menus, or put your dinner in the hands of the
skilled chefs. The staff is also happy to serve Kobe beef from Minami,
the hotel's teppanyaki restaurant. Ⓢ *Average main: ¥10000* ✉ *Swissô-
tel, 5–1–60 Namba, Chuo-ku* ☏ *06/6646–5127* ⊕ *www.swissotel.com/
hotels/nankai-osaka.*

$$$$ ✕**Kani Doraku** (かに道楽). The most famous restaurant on Dotombori-
SEAFOOD dori—the enormous mechanical crab is a local landmark—Kani Doraku
has fine crab dishes at reasonable prices. The lunch set menu, with large
portions of crab, costs around ¥4,500; dinner costs around ¥5,000. If
you prefer a quick snack, a stand outside sells crab legs (¥500 for two).
An English-language menu is available. Reserve a table on weekends.
Ⓢ *Average main: ¥5000* ✉ *1–6–18 Dotombori* ☏ *06/6211–8975.*

$$$$ ✕**Kigawa** (喜川). There's no better place to try Osaka's *kappo-ryori* (a
JAPANESE more intimate, less formal version of *kaiseki-ryori*) than the restaurant
that started the trend. Chef and owner Osamu Ueno scours the markets
daily to find the best ingredients for dinner each evening. The menu here
is a constantly rotating selection of à la carte items, all superb. If you're
unsure about what to order, simply leave it up to the chef for a delight-
ful dinner. The restaurant has a relaxed atmosphere and friendly staff,
with counter seating and two private rooms for small groups. Ⓢ *Av-
erage main: ¥15000* ✉ *1–7–7 Dotonbori, Chuo-ku* ☏ *06/6211–3030*
☿ *Closed Mon.* ⚃ *Reservations essential.*

8

$$ JAPANESE Fodor's Choice ★ 🍴 **Mizuno** (美津の). If there is one food Osaka is known for, it is okonomiyaki. This dish, something between a savory pancake and an omelet, filled with cabbage, mountain yams, pork, shrimp, and other ingredients, is one of Osaka's must-try foods. Mizuno, opened in 1945, is one of the city's best and oldest places to try this hearty specialty. Mizuno's okonomiyaki are light and fluffy, using a variety of ingredients delivered from Osaka's Kuromon Market. Sitting at the long *teppan* counter grill you can watch as the chef whips up a hearty taste of Osaka before your eyes. Long lines form around lunch and dinnertime, but move rather quickly. [$] *Average main: ¥1500* ✉ *1–4–15 Dotombori, Chuo-ku* ☎ *06/6212–6360* 🌐 *www.mizuno-osaka.com* 💳 *No credit cards.*

$$ CAFÉ 🍴 **Planet 3rd Café and Lounge** (プラネットサード). A hip hangout on the fringe of Amerika-mura, Planet 3rd Café and Lounge is perfect for a quick snack or a full meal. The food is tasty—consisting mostly of sandwiches, curries, and sweets—and the atmosphere is cool and laid back. In the morning the café serves breakfast from 7 am. The computers at the front are free use for customers. [$] *Average main: ¥1500* ✉ *1–5–24 Nishi-Shin-sai-bashi, Chuo-ku, Chuo-ku* ☎ *06/6282–5277* 🌐 *www.cafecompany.co.jp* 💳 *No credit cards.*

$$ MEXICAN 🍴 **Taqueria La Fonda** (タケリア ラ フォンダ). Serving up some of the best Tex-Mex food in the city, this tiny taqueria is an excellent stop for travelers in need of some comfort food. The owner makes his own salsas and tortillas, and offers up some unique dishes like cactus tacos in addition to the standard Tex-Mex fare. While not the most central location, La Fonda is only a 10-minute walk from the west gate of Osaka Castle Park, making it a good choice for dinner after seeing the castle. [$] *Average main: ¥$1000* ✉ *2–2–14 Tokui-cho, Chuo-ku* ☎ *06/6943–5657* 💳 *No credit cards.*

$$ JAPANESE 🍴 **Yaekatsu** (八重勝). For a real taste of Osaka, line up for *kushi katsu* (skewered meats and vegetables) outside Shin Sekai's Yaekatsu. This no-frills, counter-only restaurant has the reputation of being one of Osaka's oldest and best places to get kushi katsu. At dinner the line stretches the length of the shop, so arrive early or be prepared to wait. Yaekatsu is in Shin Sekai's Jan Jan Yokocho shopping street. Coming from Dobutsuen-mae Station, the shop is halfway down the shopping street on your left. The sign is only in Japanese, so don't hesitate to ask someone where it is. [$] *Average main: ¥2000* ✉ *3–4–13 Ebisu-higashi, Naniwa-ku, Naniwa-ku* ☎ *06/6643–6332* 💳 *No credit cards* ⏲ *Closed Thurs.* ✍ *Reservations not accepted.*

$$$$ JAPANESE 🍴 **Zuboraya** (づぼらや). This is one of Osaka's best known *fugu* (blowfish) restaurants. There are now branches in other parts of town, but this location is the original. In addition to fugu sashimi, the store has *fugu nabe* (hot pot) and many other varieties. For less-adventurous diners, Zuboraya serves a range of Japanese foods, like sushi, tempura, and shabu-shabu. [$] *Average main: ¥5000* ✉ *2–5–5 Ebisu-higashi, Naniwa-ku, Naniwa-ku* ☎ *06/6633–5529.*

WHERE TO STAY

Osaka is known more as a business center than as a tourist destination, so hotel facilities are usually excellent, but their features are rarely distinctive, except at the high end of the scale. The city has modern accommodations for almost every taste. Choose accommodations based on location rather than amenities. Note that most hotels offer special rates much lower than the listed rack rates.

KITA

$$$$
HOTEL
ANA Crowne Plaza Osaka (大阪全日空ホテル). One of Osaka's most venerable deluxe hotels, the Crowne Plaza overlooks Naka-no-shima Park. **Pros:** centrally located; interesting architecture; cozy rooms. **Cons:** at least a 10-minute walk from heart of the Kita area. $ *Rooms from:* ¥25000 ✉ *1–3–1 Dojima-hama, Kita-ku* ☎ *06/6347–1112* ⊕ *www.anacrowneplaza-osaka.jp* ⌑ *493 rooms* ❚◯❙ *No meals.*

$$$$
HOTEL
Hilton Osaka. Glitz and glitter lure expense-accounters to the Hilton Osaka, in the heart of the business district, a typical Western-style hotel with endless marble and brass. **Pros:** deluxe and executive floors have stylish rooms; across from JR Osaka Station. **Cons:** little sets it apart from less expensive hotels. $ *Rooms from:* ¥50000 ✉ *1–8–8 Umeda, Kita-ku* ☎ *06/6347–7111* ⊕ *www3.hilton.com/en/index.html* ⌑ *525 rooms* ❚◯❙ *No meals.*

$$$$
HOTEL
Hotel New Otani Osaka (ホテルニューオータニ大阪). Indoor and outdoor pools, a rooftop garden, tennis courts, and a sparkling marble atrium make this hotel a popular choice for both Japanese and Western travelers. **Pros:** beautiful views; large rooms; many amenities. **Cons:** not as centrally located as other hotels. $ *Rooms from:* ¥35000 ✉ *1–4–1 Shiromi, Chuo-ku* ☎ *06/6941–1111* ⊕ *www.hotelnewotaniosaka.jp* ⌑ *525 rooms, 53 suites* ❚◯❙ *No meals.*

$$$$
HOTEL
Fodor's Choice
★
InterContinental Osaka (インターコンチネンタルホテル大阪). Since it opened in 2013, the InterContinental Osaka has been regarded as one of the city's top luxury hotels. **Pros:** excellent location next to Umeda Station; lovely views; everything's completely up-to-date. **Cons:** one of the most expensive hotels in the area. $ *Rooms from:* ¥40000 ✉ *3–60 Ofuka-cho, Kita-ku, Kita-ku* ☎ *06/6374–5700* ⊕ *www.intercontinental.com/osaka* ⌑ *272 rooms* ❚◯❙ *No meals.*

$$$$
HOTEL
Rihga Royal Hotel (リーガロイヤルホテル大阪). Built in the 1930s, the well-established Rihga Royal is where the royal family stays when visiting Osaka. **Pros:** the scale is impressive; amenities abound; imperial visits set it apart from similar hotels. **Cons:** less-than-convenient location requires taking the shuttle bus. $ *Rooms from:* ¥50000 ✉ *5–3–68 Naka-no-shima, Kita-ku, Kita-ku* ☎ *06/6448–1121* ⊕ *www.rihga.com* ⌑ *980 rooms, 53 suites* ❚◯❙ *No meals.*

$$$$
HOTEL
Fodor's Choice
★
The Ritz-Carlton, Osaka (リッツカールトン大阪). More intimate than the city's other luxury hotels, the Ritz-Carlton combines a homey atmosphere and European elegance. **Pros:** luxurious to the last detail; high-tech touches; stunning views. **Cons:** rates hit the stratosphere. $ *Rooms from:* ¥60000 ✉ *2–5–25 Umeda, Kita-ku, Kita-ku* ☎ *06/6343–7000* ⊕ *www.ritzcarlton.com* ⌑ *292 rooms* ❚◯❙ *No meals.*

8

ANA Crowne Plaza
Osaka **5**

Hearton Hotel
Shin-sai-bashi ..**13**

Hilton Osaka **3**

Hotel New
Otani Osaka **7**

Hotel Nikko
Osaka **12**

Hyatt Regency
Osaka **10**

InterContinental
Osaka **2**

Osaka Marriott
Miyako Hotel ...**16**

Rihga Royal
Hotel **6**

The Ritz-Carlton,
Osaka **4**

The St. Regis
Osaka **8**

Sheraton Miyako
Hotel Osaka **15**

Shin-Osaka
Washington
Hotel Plaza **1**

Superhotel Osaka
Umeda
Higo-bashi **9**

Swissôtel Nankai
Osaka **14**

Toyoko Inn
Shin-sai-bashi
Nishi **11**

Where to Stay in Osaka

TO SHIN-
OSAKA, HATTORI
RYOKUCHI KOEN

HANKYU
UMEDA
STATION

NAKA-
ZAKI-CHO

TENMA

OGI-
MACHI

JR OSAKA
STATION

UMEDA

HIGASHI
UMEDA

JR KANJO
(LOOP) LINE

TO OSAKA
INTERNATIONAL
AIRPORT

KITA-
SHINCHI

KITA

MINAMI-
MORI-MACHI

JR TOZAI LINE

KYOBASHI

NISHI-
UMEDA

Naka-no-
shima

Tenman-gu

OSAKO-JO

YODOYA-
BASHI

KITAKAMA

Naka-
no-shima
Koen

OSAKA
BUSINESS
PARK

OSAKO-
KOEN

HIGO-
BASHI

KITAKAMA

TENMA-
BASHI

Osaka
Castle
Park

HON-
MACHI

SAKAI-SUJI-
HON-MACHI

KEIHAN
MAIN LINE

Hanshin Expwy, Higashi-Osaka Line

TANI-MACHI
4-CHOME

Chuo Dori

MORI-N-
MIYA

YATSU-
BASHI

TANI-MACHI
6-CHOME

Nagahori-dori

SHIN-SAI
BASHI

NAGAHORI-
BASHI

MINAMI

TAMATSUKI

Dotombori-gawa

NAMBA

NAMBA

NIPPON-
BASHI

OSAKA
UEHONMACHI

Sennichi-mae-dori

TSURUHASHI

NAMBA

Kuromon
Ichiba

TANIMACHI
9-CHOME

NANKAI
NAMBA
STATION

ASHIHARA-
BASHI

IMA-
MIYA

DAIKOKU-
CHO

EBISU-CHO

Tenno-ji
Koen

SHITENNO-
JI-MAE

MOMODANI

0 ——— 1/2 mi

0 ——— 1/2 kilometer

SHIN-
IMAMIYA

DOBUTSUEN-
MAE

TENNO-JI

TERADA-CHO

HANAZONO-
CHO

ABENO

JR KANSAI MAIN LINE

TOBUSHIJO-
MAE

TO NARA

KISHINOSATO

YUMINOSATO

SHOWACHO

MINAMI-
TANABE

KISHINOSATO

TAMADE

TO KANSAI
INTERNATIONAL
AIRPORT

SUMIYOSHI-
HIGASHI

SUMIYOSHI-
TORII-MAE

NAGAI

TO NINTOKU
MAUSOLEUM

KEY

1 *Hotels*

+—+ *JR Trains*

::::: *Subway*

+—+ *Private rail line*

$$ HOTEL 🏨 **Shin-Osaka Washington Hotel Plaza** (新大阪ワシントンホテルプラザ). Part of a no-nonsense chain of business hotels, the Shin-Osaka Washington Hotel Plaza is the smartest of its kind. **Pros:** great location if you have an early train to catch; good value; nice restaurant. **Cons:** not very close to any sights or nightlife. [$] *Rooms from: ¥15000* ✉ *5–5–15 Nishi-Nakajima, Yodo-gawa-ku* ☎ *06/6303–8111* 🌐 *washington.jp/shinosaka/en* 🛏 *490 rooms* 🍴 *No meals.*

$ HOTEL 🏨 **Superhotel Osaka Umeda Higo-bashi** (スーパーホテル大阪梅田肥後橋). Part of the popular national chain of business hotels, this Superhotel Osaka sits in a quiet, leafy neighborhood five minutes south of Naka-no-shima. **Pros:** in a centrally located neighborhood; reasonably priced; breakfast is included. **Cons:** not much of interest within walking distance. [$] *Rooms from: ¥9500* ✉ *1–20–1 Edo-bori* ☎ *06/6448–9000* 🛏 *80 rooms* 🍴 *Breakfast.*

MINAMI

$ HOTEL 🏨 **Hearton Hotel Shin-sai-bashi** (ハートンホテル心斎橋). For travelers on a budget, the Hearton Hotel Shin-sai-bashi offers a good location and very reasonable rates. **Pros:** good location for shopping and nightlife; inexpensive rates. **Cons:** simple rooms; not many amenities. [$] *Rooms from: ¥10000* ✉ *1–5–24 Nishi-Shin-sai-bashi, Chuo-ku* ☎ *06/6251–3711* 🌐 *heartonhotel.com* 🛏 *302 rooms* 🍴 *No meals.*

$$$$ HOTEL 🏨 **Hotel Nikko Osaka** (ホテル日航大阪). A striking white tower in the colorful Shin-sai-bashi district, the Nikko is within easy reach of shopping meccas like Amerika-mura. **Pros:** excellent location near shopping and nightlife. **Cons:** pricier than many hotels of the same caliber. [$] *Rooms from: ¥35000* ✉ *1–3–3 Nishi-Shin-sai-bashi, Chuo-ku, Chuo-ku* ☎ *06/6244–1111* 🌐 *www.hno.co.jp* 🛏 *640 rooms, 5 suites* 🍴 *No meals.*

$$$$ HOTEL 🏨 **Hyatt Regency Osaka** (ハイアットリージェンシー大阪). If Universal Studios Japan is on your itinerary, the Hyatt is quite convenient to the area's most popular theme park. **Pros:** larger than average rooms; some nice views; located near Universal Studios. **Cons:** not a convenient location for experiencing the city. [$] *Rooms from: ¥30000* ✉ *1–13–11 Nanko-Kita, Suminoue-ku* ☎ *06/6612–1234* 🌐 *osaka.regency.hyatt.com* 🛏 *500 rooms, 7 suites* 🍴 *No meals.*

$$$$ HOTEL Fodor's Choice ★ 🏨 **Osaka Marriott Miyako Hotel** (大阪マリオット都ホテル). One of Osakas's most luxurious hotels looks out over the city from Japan's tallest building and has some of the best nighttime views of any hotel in the city. **Pros:** above Tennoji Station; floor-to-ceiling windows. **Cons:** not walking distance from the center of Osaka's shopping and nightlife. [$] *Rooms from: ¥42000* ✉ *1–1–43 Abenosuji, Abeno-ku* ☎ *06/6628–6111* 🌐 *www.marriott.com/hotels/travel/osamc-osaka-marriott-miyako-hotel* 🛏 *360 rooms.*

$$$ HOTEL 🏨 **Sheraton Miyako Hotel Osaka** (都ホテル大阪). An excellent base for exploring Osaka, the Miyako is also handy when you plan on taking day trips to Kyoto and Nara—the Kintetsu Ue-hon-machi Station next door offers quick access to both cities. **Pros:** excellent location; discounts for booking online; airport shuttle available. **Cons:** less luxurious than some of its rivals. [$] *Rooms from: ¥20000* ✉ *6–1–55 Ue-hon-machi,*

Tennoji-ku, Tenno-ji-ku ☎ *06/6773–1111, 06/6773–3322* 🌐 *www.miyakohotels.ne.jp/osaka* 🛏 *575 rooms, 2 suites* 🍴 *No meals.*

$$$$ HOTEL 🏨 **The St. Regis Osaka** (セントレジスホテル大阪). One of Osaka's top luxury hotels, the St. Regis offers an oasis of comfort just a short walk from the lights and excitement of Shinbashi and Namba, and a short train ride from many of the city's major sights. **Pros:** butler service; luxurious interiors ; real attention to detail. **Cons:** very expensive, especially by Osaka standards; Honmachi Station is not a convenient base for visiting other places in Kansai. [$] *Rooms from: ¥70000* ✉ *3–6–12 Honmachi, Chuo-ku* ☎ *06/6258–3333* 🌐 *www.starwoodhotels.com/stregis* 🛏 *160 rooms* 🍴 *No meals* [M] *Honmachi Station (Chuo, Mido-suji, or Yotsubashi Subway lines).*

$$$$ HOTEL Fodor's Choice ★ 🏨 **Swissôtel Nankai Osaka** (スイスホテル南海大阪). European-style furnishings and mellow contemporary art make the standard rooms at this high-end hotel some of the best in the city. **Pros:** best location in Osaka; luxurious rooms; at Nankai Namba Station. **Cons:** one of the most expensive hotels in the area. [$] *Rooms from: ¥50000* ✉ *5–1–60 Namba, Chuo-ku, Chuo-ku* ☎ *06/6646–1111* 🌐 *www.swissotel.com/osaka* 🛏 *548 rooms, 5 Western-style suites, 1 Japanese-style suite* 🍴 *No meals.*

$ HOTEL 🏨 **Toyoko Inn Shin-sai-bashi Nishi** (東横イン心斎橋西). Close to the laid-back cafés of Minami, the Toyoko Inn is a comfortable business hotel with rates that won't empty your wallet. **Pros:** inexpensive rates; located near the Minami hot spots. **Cons:** small rooms; few amenities. [$] *Rooms from: ¥9000* ✉ *1–9–22 Kita-horie, Nishi-ku, Nishi-ku* ☎ *06/6536–1045* 🌐 *www.toyoko-inn.com* 🛏 *144 rooms* 🍴 *Breakfast.*

NIGHTLIFE AND PERFORMING ARTS

NIGHTLIFE

Osaka has a lively nightlife scene, though it often revolves around eating and drinking. The Kita (North) area surrounds JR Umeda Station; and the Minami (South) area is between the Shin-sai-bashi and Namba districts and includes part of Chuo-ku (Central Ward). Many Japanese refer to Minami as being "for kids," but there are plenty of good restaurants and drinking spots for more-seasoned bon vivants. Osaka's hip young things hang out in Amerika-mura, in the southern part of Chuo-ku, with its innumerable bars and clubs. Kita draws a slightly more adult crowd, including businesspeople.

BARS

Café Absinthe (カフェアブセン). After browsing the fashions in Minami's boutiques, pop into Café Absinthe in neighboring Kita-horie for Mediterranean food and good music. Live performances usually start at around 9. The music and the crowd are very international and very laid-back. ✉ *1–2–27 Kita-horie, Nishi-ku* ☎ *06/6534–6635.*

JAZZ

Mr. Kelly's (ミスターケリーズ). This club on the ground floor of the Hotel Vista Prima Donna regularly features a jazz trio and a vocalist. Well-known acts also stop by for performances. The cover charge starts at

¥3,000. ✉ *Hotel Vista Prima Donna, 2–4–1 Sonezaki Shinchi, Kita-ku, Kita-ku* ☎ *06/6342–5821.*

ROCK AND ALTERNATIVE

Club Quattro (クラブクアトロ). Up-and-coming Japanese rock bands and popular Western bands play at this popular venue. The sound system is excellent. ✉ *Plaza Umeda 10F, 8–17 Taiyujicho, Kita-ku* ☎ *06/6311–8111.*

PERFORMING ARTS

BUNRAKU

National Bunraku Theatre (国際文楽劇場 *Kokusai Bunraku Gekijo*). Theater fans won't want to miss the chance to see a performance at Osaka's National Bunraku Theatre. Bunraku is not your average puppet show: the 3-foot-tall puppets each require a trio of handlers, and the stories, mostly originating in Osaka, contain all the drama and tension (if not the sword fights) of a good samurai drama. The National Bunraku Theatre is Japan's premier place to watch this 300-year-old art form. An "Earphone Guide" (¥650 rental) explains the action in English as the play unfolds. Performances are usually twice daily (late morning and late afternoon) on weekends. To get here, take the Sennichimae or Sakai-suji subway lines to Nippon-bashi Station and take Exit 7. The theater is just before you pass under the Hanshin Expressway. ✉ *1–12–10 Nippon-bashi, Chuo-ku, Chuo-ku* ☎ *06/6212–2531* ⊕ *www.ntj.jac. go.jp* ✉ *¥2,300–¥5,800.*

SPORTS

BASEBALL

Hanshin Tigers (阪神タイガース *Hanshin Taigasu*). The Orix Buffaloes are the local team, but it is the Hanshin Tigers from Nishi-no-miya, between Kobe and Osaka, that prompt excited fans to jump into the Dotombori River. The Tigers are based in historic Koshien Stadium near Kobe, but they play at the Saka Dome (Kyocera Domu Osaka) for the season opener and during the month of August. The Osaka Dome looks like a spaceship and has pleasing-to-the-eye curved edges in a city dominated by gray cubes. Tickets cost as little as ¥1,600. Buy them at the gate, at Lawson convenience stores, or by telephone from Ticket Pia. The dome is next to Osaka Domu-mae Chiyozaki subway station on the Nagahori Tsurumi-ryokuchi Line. ✉ *3–2–1 Chiozaki* ☎ *06/6586–0106 Ticket Pia.*

SOCCER

Gamba Osaka (ガンバ大阪). The Gamba Osaka soccer team plays at the Expo '70 Commemorative Stadium (Banpaku Kinen Kyogi-jo), located in the north part of the city. Access is via the Osaka Monorail to Koen Higashi-guchi Station. Tickets start at ¥1,500 for adults, and the season runs from March to November. ✉ *3–3 Senri Bampaku Koen* ☎ *06/6875–8111* ⊕ *www.gamba-osaka.net/en.*

SUMO

Osaka Prefectural Gymnasium (大阪府立体育会館 *Osaka Furitsu Taiiku-kan*). The sumo scene has become a hotbed of international rivalry as Bulgarians, Estonians, and some Russians with attitude have been edging the local talent out of the *basho* (ring). From the second Sunday through the fourth Sunday in March, one of Japan's six sumo tournaments takes place in Osaka. Most seats, known as *masu-seki*, are prebooked before the tournament begins, but standing-room tickets (¥1,000) and a limited number of seats (¥3,000) are available on the day of the event. The ticket office opens at 9 am, and you should get in line early. The stadium is a 10-minute walk from Namba Station. ⊠ *3–4–36 Namba-naka, Naniwa-ku, Naniwa-ku* ☎ *06/6631–0121.*

SHOPPING

As with everything else in Osaka, the city rewards shoppers with a sense of adventure. Though Osaka is full of shopping complexes, towering department stores, and brand-name shops, you must step away from the main streets and explore neighborhood shops and boutiques to find the best deals, newest electronics, and cutting-edge fashions. Osaka's miles of labyrinthine underground shopping complexes offer an escape from summer heat and are an experience in and of themselves. The network of tunnels and shops in underground Umeda is the most impressive (and confusing). Fortunately, signs and maps are plentiful and the information desk staff speaks English.

There are specialized wholesale areas throughout the city, and many have a few retail shops as well. One such area is **Doguya-suji**, just east of Nankai Namba Station and the Takashimaya department store. This street is lined with shops selling nothing but kitchen goods—all sorts of pots, pans, utensils, and glassware are piled to the rafters. Though most customers are in the restaurant trade, laypeople shop here, too. Feel free to wander around: there's no obligation to buy. A trip here could be combined with a visit to nearby **Den Den Town**, known for its electronic goods. Also in this neighborhood, east of the main entrance to Doguya-suji, is **Kuromon Ichiba**, the famous market district where chefs select the treats—fruits, vegetables, meat, and much more—cooked up at the city's restaurants that evening.

Though it is being slowly invaded by chain stores, Osaka's famed **Amerika-mura** is still a good place to find hip fashions. For original boutiques and cutting-edge styles, head to the streets of **Minami-semba** and **Minami-horie** to the west.

SHOPPING COMPLEXES AND MALLS

Hilton Plaza West and East have international brands like Max Mara, Dunhill, Chanel, and Ferragamo. Herbis Ent Plaza is a local high-end shopping complex connected to the Hilton Plaza West complex. These three shopping complexes are opposite Osaka Station.

Grand Front Osaka. This new shopping complex sits just outside of Umeda Station. With more than 266 shops, restaurants, and galleries as well as the InterContinental Hotel, this all-in-one complex is set to fulfill just about any shopping needs. Even if you aren't in the market for anything, the Panasonic showroom is worth a quick visit to see how Osaka's leading electronics manufacturer envisions life in the future. ⊠ *3–60 Ofukacho, Kita-ku* ☎ *06/6372–6300.*

NU Chayamachi. To the east of the Hankyu Grand Building is NU Chayamachi—a collection of small boutiques, both local and foreign, and some good cafés. ✉ *10–12 Chayamachi, Kita-ku, Kita-ku* ☎ *06/6373–7371* ⊕ *nu-chayama-chi.com.*

DEPARTMENT STORES

All major Japanese *depato* (department stores) are represented in Osaka. They're open 10 to 7, but usually close one day a month, on a Wednesday or Thursday.

> ### CRAFTS SHOPPING
>
> At one time famous for its traditional crafts—particularly *karaki-sashimono* (ornately carved furniture), fine Naniwa Suzu-ki pewterware, and *uchihamono* (Sakai cutlery)—Osaka lost much of its traditional industry during World War II. The simplest way to find Osakan crafts is to visit one of the major department stores.

Daimaru (大丸). The department stores around Osaka Station are "gourmet palaces," each with several floors of restaurants. Daimaru, an Osaka landmark, has one of the best selections. ✉ *1–7–1 Shin-sai-bashi-suji, Chuo-ku, Chuo-ku* ☎ *06/6343–1231.*

Hankyu (阪急百貨店). Headquartered in Osaka, Hankyu has 15 floors of shopping. Across the street is Hankyu Men's Osaka, which claims to have the country's largest selection of men's clothing. ✉ *8–7 Kakuta-cho, Kita-ku, Kita-ku* ☎ *06/6361–1381* ⊕ *www.hankyu-dept.co.jp/fl/english/honten/.*

Hanshin (阪神百貨店). The food hall in the basement of Hanshin department store is the city's best. ✉ *1–13–13 Umeda, Kita-ku* ☎ *06/6345–1201.*

HEP Five (ヘップファイブー). If you want to take a break from shopping, head to the roof of HEP Five, where you can take in great night views of the city from the enormous Ferris wheel for just ¥500 ✉ *5–15 Kakuda-cho, Kita-ku, Kita-ku* ☎ *06/6313–0501* ⊕ *www.hepfive.jp/* ✎ *Ferris wheel ¥500* ☉ *Daily 11–9.*

Takashimaya (株式会社髙島屋). One of the largest Japanese department store chains, Takashimaya has an impressive presence in Osaka. ✉ *5–1–5 Namba, Chuo-ku, Chuo-ku* ☎ *06/6631–1101* ⊕ *www.takashimaya.co.jp/osaka/store_information.*

ELECTRONICS

Although some Japanese electronic goods may be cheaper in the United States than in Japan, many electronics products are released on the Japanese market 6 to 12 months before they reach the West. The reason to buy in Japan is to find something you won't find elsewhere, not to find a bargain.

Yodobashi Camera (ヨドバシカメラ). Don't be put off by the name: this enormous electronics department store sells far more than just cameras. On the north side of JR Osaka Station, the store is impossible to miss. ✉ *1–1 Ofuka-cho, Kita-ku, Kita-ku* ☎ *06/4802–1010* ☉ *Daily 9:30–9.*

8

NARA

Nara is a place of synthesis, where Chinese art, religion, and architecture fused with Japanese language and Shinto traditions. The city was established in 710 and was then known as Heijo-Kyo (citadel of peace). Fujiwara-no-Fuhito, father-in-law of Emperor Mommu, was responsible for the city's creation. His grandson, the future Emperor Shomu, later graced the new capital with its wealth of temples, pagodas, and shrines.

Buddhism had come to Japan in the 6th century. Along with *kanji* (Chinese characters) and tea, it spread throughout the archipelago. Emperor Shomu hoped that making the new capital the center of Buddhism would unite the country and secure his position as head of an emergent nation state. The grandest of the Buddhist temples built in Nara during this era was Todai-ji, which Emperor Shomu intended as a nexus for all the temples of his realm. But after 84 years the citadel of peace fell victim to the very intrigue that the Emperor had tried to suppress. In 794, the capital moved to Kyoto and Nara lost prominence, as did the Kegon sect that still manages Todai-ji today.

Now Nara is a provincial city whose most obvious role is a historical one, and Todai-ji is a monument rather than a political stronghold. Nara is a site of renewal and reinvention that has overcome typhoons, fires, and wars to remain a city of superlatives. Its position in the national consciousness as the birthplace of modern Japanese culture is well secured.

With relatively flat roads, an abundance of greenery, and most of the major sights located within Nara Koen, by far the best way to see Nara is on foot. Even the quaint, traditional streets of Nara-machi are a 10-minute walk from Nara's two central stations. For people with less time, most of the main sites can be reached by bicycle, except for those along the eastern edge of the park, such as the San-gatsu-do, the Ni-gatsu-do, and Kasuga Taisha.

Almost at the center of the Japanese archipelago, Nara is on the Yamato plain, with Osaka to the west and Kyoto to the north. Much of what you'll come to Nara to see is in picturesque Nara Koen (Nara Park), which is a short distance east of the two main stations.

It was created out of wasteland in 1880 and sits east of the Kasuga Mountain and the cleared slopes of Wakakusa-yama, in a dense forest. The park is home to some 1,200 tame deer, the focus of much local lore and legend. The commercial shopping district is south of Kintetsu Nara Station, while Sanjo-dori, west of Nara Koen and Nara-machi, has the two main tourist shopping areas. Horyu-ji, Yakushi-ji, and Toshodai-ji, the major temples of western Nara, are all on one bus route or can be reached by JR train.

Nara-machi was the "new" area of Nara at the beginning of the Edo period (1603–1868). Today its lanes and alleys are still lined by old wooden houses with latticed windows and whitewashed walls. Many of these old houses have been converted into galleries, museums, and shops.

In Western Nara, Horyu-ji Temple has the oldest wooden structures in the world and is considered the apotheosis of classical Japanese architecture. Toshodai-ji Temple is where Ganjin, the first Buddhist monk to come to Japan from China, taught Japanese monks and legitimized the spread of Buddhism throughout the country.

GETTING HERE AND AROUND

AIRPORT TRANSFERS The hourly airport limousine bus from KIX takes 90 minutes and costs ¥2,050. From Itami, buses leave hourly, take 55 minutes, and cost ¥1,480.

BUS TRAVEL Two local bus routes circle the main sites (Todai-ji, Kasuga Taisha, and Shin-Yakushi-ji) in the central and eastern parts of the city: Bus 1 runs counterclockwise, and Bus 2 runs clockwise. Both stop at JR Nara Station and Kintetsu Nara Station and have a flat fare of ¥180. The city also offers one- and two-day bus passes ranging from ¥500 to ¥1,500 depending on area.

Bus 97 heads west to Horyu-ji (with stops at Toshodai-ji and Yakushi-ji), takes about 50 minutes, and costs ¥760; you can catch it in front of either station. Pick up a bus map at the Nara City Tourist Information Center.

TAXI TRAVEL For small groups, short taxi rides within Nara cost only slightly more than buses. Expect to pay about ¥1,000 to get to Kasuga Taisha from either of the main train stations.

TRAIN TRAVEL From Kyoto, the best option is the private Kintetsu Railway's trains, which run directly to Kintetsu Nara Station (45 minutes, ¥660). Three JR trains from Kyoto run every hour. The express takes 45 minutes (change at Yamato-Saidai-ji); the two locals take 70 minutes. All JR trains cost ¥710 without a JR Pass.

To get to Horyu-ji Temple in western Nara, take a JR Main Line train from JR Nara Station. The ride to Horyu-ji Station takes 11 minutes and costs ¥220.

Contacts JR Nara Station (JR奈良駅 *JR Nara-eki*). ⊠ *Sanjo-hon-cho* ☎ *0742/22–9821.* **Kintetsu Nara Station** (近鉄奈良駅 *Kintetsu Nara-eki*). ⊠ *29 Higashi-mukinaka-cho* ☎ *0742/24–4858.*

EXPLORING NARA

NARA KOEN 奈良公園

Nara Koen has the city's popular tourist sites. Even so, it is wide enough to accommodate thousands of giggling schoolchildren and other Japanese tourists, yet still feel spacious and quiet. Be warned that it is home to many divine messengers of god—the tame deer seen just about everywhere.

TOP ATTRACTIONS

Fodor's Choice
★ **Kasuga Taisha** (春日大社 *Kasuga Shrine*). Famous for the more than 2,000 stone *mantoro* (lanterns) that line its pathways, Kasuga Taisha is a monument to the Shinto tradition of worshipping nature. The lighting of the lanterns on three days of the year attracts large crowds that whisper with reverential excitement. February 3 is the Mantoro Festival,

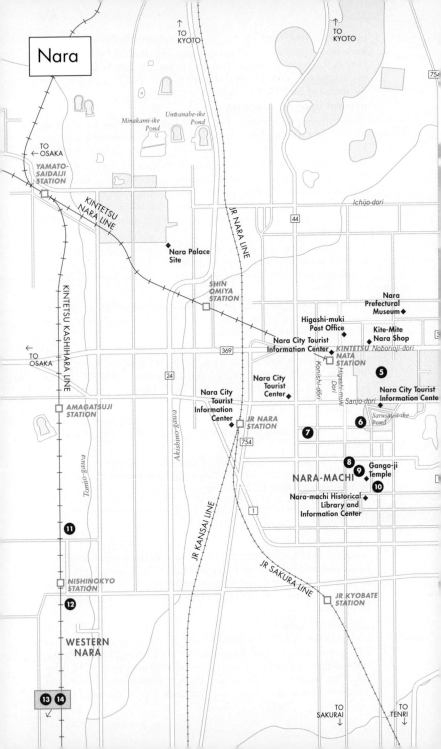

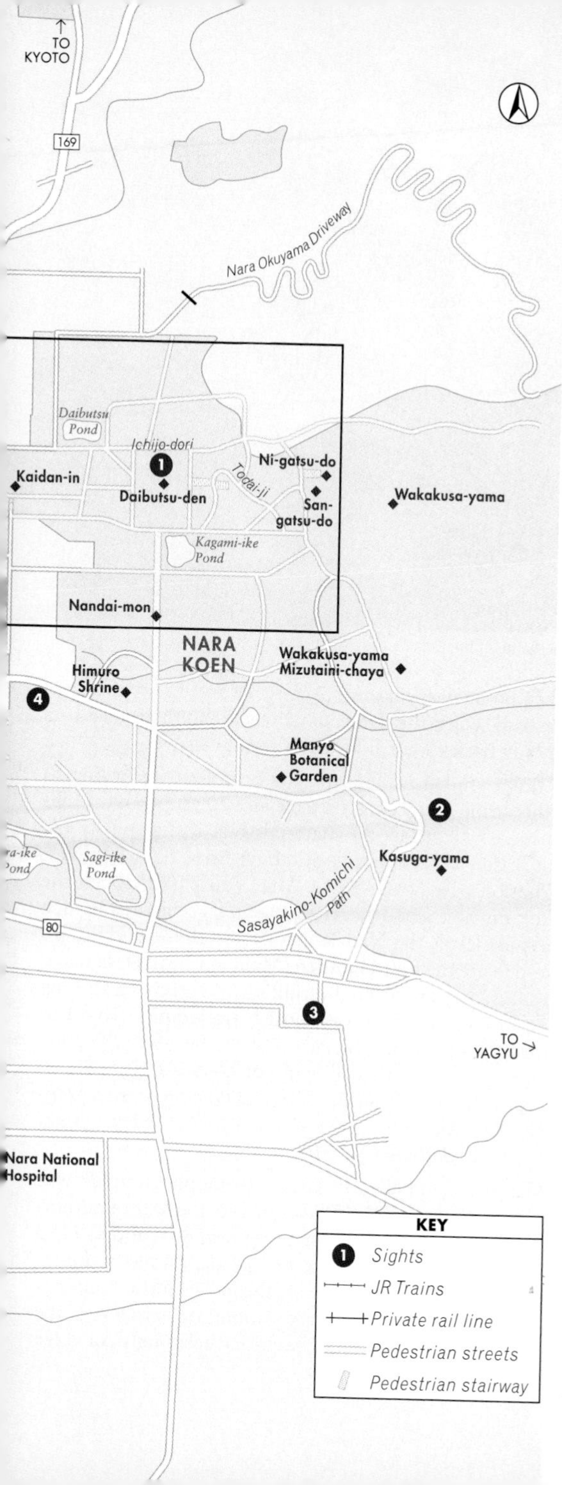

↑
TO
KYOTO

169

Nara Okuyama Driveway

Daibutsu
Pond

Ichijo-dori

Kaidan-in ◆

❶

Daibutsu-den ◆

Todai-ji

Ni-gatsu-do ◆

San-gatsu-do ◆

◆ **Wakakusa-yama**

Kagami-ike
Pond

Nandai-mon ◆

NARA KOEN

Himuro Shrine ◆

❹

Wakakusa-yama Mizutaini-chaya ◆

Manyo Botanical Garden ◆

❷

ra-ike
Pond

Sagi-ike
Pond

80

Kasuga-yama ◆

Sasayakino-Komichi Path

❸

TO →
YAGYU

Nara National Hospital

8

KEY

❶ *Sights*

├── *JR Trains*

+──+ *Private rail line*

─── *Pedestrian streets*

▯ *Pedestrian stairway*

Todai-ji's Daibatsu-den houses a 53-foot statue of the Buddha.

celebrating the beginning of spring, and August 14 and 15 are the Chugen Mantoro Festival, when the living show respect to their ancestors by lighting their way back to Earth for their annual visit.

Kasuga Taisha was founded in 768 and for centuries, according to Shinto custom, the shrine was reconstructed every 20 years on its original design—not merely to renew the materials but also to purify the site. It's said that Kasuga Taisha has been rebuilt more than 50 times; its current incarnation dates from 1893. After you pass through the orange *torii* (gate), the first wooden structure you'll see is the **Hai-den** (Offering Hall); to its left is the **Naorai-den** (Entertainment Hall). To the left of Naorai-den are the four **Hon-den** (Main Shrines). Designated as National Treasures, they are painted vermilion and green—a striking contrast to the dark wooden exterior of most Nara temples. To get to Kasuga Taisha from Nara Koen, walk east past the Five-Story Pagoda until you reach a torii. This path will lead you to the shrine. ⊠ *160 Kasuga-no-cho, Nara Koen* ☎ *0742/22–7788* 📧 *Free; main sanctuary ¥1,000; gardens ¥500* ⊙ *Museum daily 9–4; inner precincts Nov.–Mar., daily 7–4:30; Apr.–Oct., daily 6:30–5:30.*

Fodor's Choice **Todai-ji Temple** (東大寺). Completed in 752, this temple complex was
★ conceived by Emperor Shomu in the 8th century as the seat of authority for Buddhist Japan. An earthquake damaged it in 855, and in 1180 the temple was burned to the ground. Its reconstruction met a similar fate during the 16th-century civil wars. Only the most central buildings in the once sprawling complex exist today. Among the structures, the Daibutsu-den is the grandest, with huge beams that seemingly converge upward toward infinity.

The **Daibutsu-den** (Hall of the Great Buddha) is a rare example of monumentality in the land of the diminutive bonsai. The current Daibutsu-den was restored in 1709 at two-thirds its original scale. At 157 feet tall and 187 feet wide, it is the largest wooden structure in the world.

Inside the Daibutsu-den is the **Daibutsu**, a 53-foot bronze statue of the Buddha. His hand alone is the size of six tatami mats. The Daibutsu was originally commissioned by Emperor Shomu in 743 and completed six years later. A statue of this scale had never been cast before in Japan, and it was meant to serve as a symbol to unite the country. The Daibutsu was dedicated in 752 in a grand ceremony attended by the then-retired Emperor Shomu, the Imperial Court, and 10,000 priests and nuns. The current Daibutsu is an amalgamation of work done in three eras: the 8th, 12th, and 17th centuries.

A peaceful pebble garden in the courtyard of **Kaidan-in** belies the ferocious expressions of the Four Heavenly Guardian clay statues inside. Depicted in full armor and wielding weapons, they are an arresting sight. The current *kaidan-in*, a building where monks are ordained, dates from 1731. The Kaidan-in is in northwestern Nara Koen, west of the Daibutsu-den.

The soaring **Nandai-mon** (Great Southern Gate), the entrance to the temple complex, is supported by 18 large wooden pillars, each 62 feet high and nearly 3 1/3 feet in diameter. The original gate was destroyed in a typhoon in 962 and rebuilt in 1199. Two outer niches on either side of the gate contain fearsome wooden figures of Deva kings, who guard the great Buddha within. They are the work of master sculptor Unkei, of the Kamakura period (1185–1335). In the inner niches are a pair of stone *koma-inu* (Korean dogs), mythical guardians that ward off evil.

Named for a ritual that begins in February and culminates in the spectacular sparks and flames of the Omizu-tori festival in March, the **Ni-gatsu-do** (Second Month Temple) was founded in 752. It houses important images of the Buddha that are, alas, not on display. Still, its hilltop location and veranda afford a commanding view of Nara Koen. Behind the Ni-gatsu-do is a lovely rest area, where free water and cold tea are available daily from 9 to 4. Although no food is sold, it's a quiet spot to enjoy a picnic.

The **San-gatsu-do** (Third Month Temple), founded in 733, is the oldest original building in the Todai-ji complex. It takes its name from the *sutra* (Buddhist scripture) reading ceremonies held here in the third month of the ancient lunar calendar (present-day February to April). You can sit on benches covered with tatami mats and appreciate the 8th-century treasures that crowd the small room. The principal display is the lacquer statue of Fukukensaku Kannon, the goddess of mercy, whose diadem is encrusted with thousands of pearls and gemstones. The two clay *bosatsu* (bodhisattva) statues on either side of her, the Gakko (Moonlight) and the Nikko (Sunlight), are fine examples of the *Tenpyo* period (Nara period), the height of classical Japanese sculpture. The English pamphlet included with admission details all the statues in the San-gatsu-do.

The important temples and structures are close together; allow about three hours to see everything, allowing for time to feed the deer. ✉ *406–1 Zoushi-chou, Nara Koen* ✥ *To get to Todai-ji, board Bus 2 from JR Station or Kintetsu Nara Station and exit at Daibutsu-den. Cross street to path that leads to temple. You can also walk from Kintetsu Nara Station in about 15 mins by heading east on Noborioji-dori. In Nara Koen, turn left onto pedestrians-only street that leads to Todai-ji. A taxi from JR or Kintetsu Nara station costs about ¥1,000* ☎ *0742/22–5511* ✆ *¥500* 🕓 *Apr.–Sept., daily 7:30–5:30; Oct., daily 7:30–5; Nov.–Feb., daily 8–4:30; Mar., daily 8–5.*

NEED A BREAK?

Wakakusa-yama Mizutani-chaya (若草山水谷茶屋). At the foot of Wakakusa-yama and down some stone steps is a delightful old thatched-roof farmhouse. You can order simple noodle dishes (¥700 to ¥900) and *matcha* whisked green tea (¥650). Alternatively, enjoy a cold beer (¥500) under the canopy of maple trees. ✉ *30 Kasugano-cho, Nara Koen* ☎ *0742/22–0627* 🕓 *Thurs.–Tues. 10–4 (food served 11–2).*

WORTH NOTING

Kofuku-ji Temple (興福寺). The Kofuku-ji Temple's **Five-Story Pagoda** dominates the skyline. Built in 1426, it's an exact replica of the original pagoda that Empress Komyo built here in 730, which burned to the ground. At 164 feet, it is the second tallest in Japan, a few centimeters shorter than the pagoda at To-ji Temple in Kyoto. To the southwest of the Five-Story Pagoda, down a flight of steps, is the **Three-Story Pagoda.** Built in 1114, it is renowned for its graceful lines and fine proportions.

Although the Five-Story Pagoda is Kofuku-ji's most eye-catching building, the main attraction is the first-rate collection of Buddhist statues in the **Tokondo** (Great Eastern Hall). A reconstruction dating from the 15th century, the hall was built to speed the recovery of the ailing Empress Gensho. It is dominated by a statue of Yakushi Nyorai (Physician of the Soul) and is flanked by the Four Heavenly Kings and the Twelve Heavenly Generals. In contrast to the highly stylized and enlightened Yakushi Nyorai, the seated figure on the left is a statue of a mortal, Yuima Koji. A lay devotee of Buddhism, Yuima was respected for his eloquence but perhaps more revered for his belief that enlightenment could be accomplished through meditation even while mortal passions were indulged. Although Kofuku-ji Temple is no longer a religious mecca, you may see older Japanese writing on *ema* (votive plaques) left by pilgrims to ensure the happiness and safety of their families. The exquisite incense and the patina of the gold leaf on the drapery of the Yakushi Nyorai create a reflective experience.

The concrete-and-steel **Kokuhokan** (National Treasure House), north of Kofuku-ji, houses the largest and most varied collection of National Treasure sculpture and other works of art. The most famous is a statue of Ashura, one of the Buddha's eight protectors, with three heads and six arms.

Kofuku-ji is a 5-minute walk west of Nara Kokuritsu Hakubutsukan in the central part of Nara Koen, and it's an easy 15-minute walk from the JR Station or Kintetsu Nara Station. ✉ *48 Noborioji-cho*

CLOSE UP

Fire Festivals and Light-Ups in Nara

To light up doesn't mean to have a cigarette in Japan. In fact, most light-ups are at temples and shrines where, unlike most public spaces in Japan, smoking is banned. Here are the more dramatic illuminations on the Nara festival calendar.

JANUARY
Wakakusa-yama Yaki (Grass Burning Festival). On the night before the second Monday in January, 15 priests set Wakakusa-yama's dry grass afire while fireworks illuminate Kofuku-ji's Five-Story Pagoda in one of Japan's most photographed rituals. This rite is believed to commemorate the resolution of a boundary dispute between the monks and priests of Todai-ji and Kofuku-ji. The fireworks start at 5:50 and the grass fire is lighted at 6.

FEBRUARY
Mantoro (Lantern Festival). On February 3 the 2,000 stone and 1,000 bronze lanterns at Kasuga Taisha are lighted to mark the traditional end of winter called *setsubun*. It takes place between 6 pm and 8:30 pm.

MARCH
Shuni-e Omizutori (Water Drawing Festival). From March 1 to 14

priests circle the upper gallery of the Ni-gatsu-do (Second Month Hall) wielding 21-foot-long *taimatsu* (bamboo torches) weighing more than 160 pounds, while sparks fall on those below. Catching the embers burns out sins and wards off evil. This festival is more than 1,200 years old, a rite of repentance to the Eleven-Headed Kannon, an incarnation of the Goddess of Mercy. These evening events happen March 1 to 11 and 13, 7 to 7:20; March 12, 7:30 to 8:15; March 14, for five minutes from 6:30 to 6:35.

JULY–OCTOBER
Light-up Promenade. Sights including Yakushi-ji, Kofuku-ji, and Todai-ji are illuminated at night in July, August, September 7 to 10, and October 6 to 10.

AUGUST
Toka-e. From August 1 to 15 Nara Koen is aglow with more than 7,000 candles from 7 to 9:45 pm.

Chugen Mantoro (Mid-year Lantern Festival). For more than 800 years the thousands of lanterns at Kasuga Taisha have been lighted to guide ancestors back to Earth on their annual pilgrimage, in Obon on August 14 to 15 from 7 to 9:30 pm.

8

☎ *0742/22–7755* ⊕ *www.kohfukuji.com* ✉ *Great Eastern Hall* ¥300, *National Treasure House* ¥600 ☉ *Daily 9–5.*

Nara National Museum (奈良国立博物館 *Nara Kokuritsu Hakubutsukan*). One of the earliest examples of Western-style Meiji architecture, the Nara National Museum was completed in 1889 to much controversy over its decidedly non-Japanese design. True to Nara's reputation as the seat of Japanese culture, the museum houses sculpture from China, Korea, and Japan, though its collection focuses mainly on the Nara and Heian periods. The West Wing has paintings, calligraphy, ceramics, and archaeological artifacts from Japan, some dating back to the 10th-century BC. The East Wing is used for temporary exhibitions.

During the driest days of November, the Shoso-in Repository, behind the Todai-ji, displays some of its magnificent collection. ⊠ *50 Noboriojicho, Nara Koen* ☎ *0742/22–7771* ⊕ *www.narahaku.go.jp* ⎙ *¥500* ⊗ *Tues.–Sun. 9:30–5.*

Shin-Yakushi-ji Temple (新薬師寺). This temple was founded in 747 by Empress Komyo (701–760) in gratitude for the recovery of her sick husband, Emperor Shomu. Only the Main Hall, which houses many fine objects from the Nara period, remains. In the center of the hall is a wooden statue of Yakushi Nyorai, the Physician of the Soul. Surrounding this statue are 12 clay images of the Twelve Divine Generals who protected Yakushi. Eleven of these figures are originals. The generals stand in threatening poses, bearing spears, swords, and other weapons, and wear terrifying expressions. ⊠ *1352 Takabatake-cho, Nara Koen* ☎ *0742/22–3736* ⎙ *¥600* ⊗ *Daily 9–5.*

NARA-MACHI 奈良町

Nara-machi is a maze of lanes and alleys lined with old warehouses and *machiya* (traditional wooden houses) that have been converted into galleries, shops, and cafés. A lot of locals still live here, so the smell of grilled mackerel at lunchtime or roasted tea in the afternoon wafts through the air. Many of the old shops deal in Nara's renowned arts and crafts, such as akahadayaki pottery, ink, and linen. In recent years, Nara-machi has also become home to younger artisans with a contemporary take on the city's traditional crafts. A free map, available from any Nara City Tourism Information Office, guides you to the main shops, museums, and galleries, as do English signposts.

Remember that stores can close irregularly. From the southwest corner of Sarusawa-ike, with the pond notice board on your left, walk straight until you come to a main road, on the other side of which is the center of Nara-machi.

EXPLORING

Kai (界). Rooted in tradition, Kai houses a collection of shops with new takes on traditional Japanese arts and crafts. In addition to a café and gallery, Kai also serves as work and gallery space for various local artisans. With artists producing everything from paintings to wood carvings to glass jewelry, this is an excellent stop for unique souvenirs. ⊠ *12–1 Wakido-cho, Nara-machi* ☎ *0742/24–3056* ⊕ *www.kai. st* ⊗ *Tues.–Sun. 11–6.*

Kobaien (古梅園). Nara accounts for about 90% of Japan's sumi-ink production, and for 400 years Kobaien has made fine ink sticks for calligraphy and ink painting. More recently, some types of sumi-ink have been used for tattooing. ⊠ *7 Tsubai-cho, Nara-machi* ☎ *0742/23–2965* ⊗ *Weekdays 9–5.*

Koshi-no-ie (ならまち格子の家 *Lattice House*). This well-to-do merchant's house has been thoroughly restored, making it a quick trip through the Edo period. English pamphlets are available. ⊠ *44 Gangoji-cho, Nara-machi* ☎ *0742/23–4820* ⎙ *Free* ⊗ *Tues.–Sun. 9–5.*

Nara-machi Shiryokan (奈良町資料館 *Nara-machi Historical Library and Information Center*). So just what are those red cloth animals on pieces of rope outside houses in Nara? Called *migawarizaru* (substitute

Horyu-ji's wooden buildings are among the world's oldest.

monkeys), they are hung on the eaves of houses to ward off illness and accidents. There is a monkey for every member of a household ready to suffer illness and accidents in place of its owner. The migawarizaru are just one of the many traditions that have lived on in Nara-machi. The Nara-machi Shiryokan displays many other artifacts relating to the history of this neighborhood. ⊠ *14–2 Nishi Shinya-cho, Nara-machi* ☏ *0742/22–5509* ⏲ *Daily 10–4.*

Yu Nakagawa (遊中川). This shop specializes in handwoven, sun-bleached linens, a local specialty known as Nara *sarashi*. This shop sells *noren* (two-panel curtains businesses display when they are open), handbags, slippers, and other textiles incorporating traditional Nara motifs. ⊠ *31–1 Ganrin-in-cho, Nara-machi* ☏ *0742/22–1322* ⏲ *Daily 11–6:30.*

WESTERN NARA 奈良西部

Horyu-ji is home to some of the oldest wooden buildings in the world. Just east of Horyu-ji is Chugu-ji, with one of the finest sculptures in Japan, the 7th-century Miroku Bodhisattva. A short bus ride back toward Nara brings you to Yakushi-ji and Toshodai-ji temples, both religious and political centers during the Nara period. To visit all four temples in one day go to Horyu-ji by the JR Main Line first (Chugu-ji is a 10-minute walk from Horyu-ji) and proceed to Toshodai-ji and Yakushi-ji by bus.

TOP ATTRACTIONS

Fodor's Choice ★ **Horyu-ji Temple** (法隆寺). This temple is the jewel in the crown of classical Japanese architecture. In the morning, elderly locals on their way to work pray in front of the temple with intensity. Founded in 607 by Prince Shotoku (573–621), Horyu-ji's original wooden buildings are among the world's oldest. The first gate you pass through is the **Nandai-mon,** which was rebuilt in 1438 and is thus a relatively young 500 years old. The second gate, **Chu-mon** (Middle Gate), is the 607 original. Unlike most Japanese gates, which are supported by two pillars at the ends, central pillars support this gate. Note their entasis, or swelling at the center, an architectural feature from ancient Greece that traveled as far as Japan. Such columns are found in Japan only in the 7th-century structures of Nara.

After passing through the gates, you enter the temple's western precincts. The first building on the right is the **Kon-do** (Main Hall), a two-story reproduction of the original 7th-century hall, which displays Buddhist images and objects from as far back as the Asuka period (552–645). The Five-Story Pagoda to its left was disassembled in World War II to protect it from air raids, after which it was reconstructed with the same materials used in 607. Behind the pagoda is the **Daiko-do** (Lecture Hall), destroyed by fire and rebuilt in 990. Inside is a statue of Yakushi Nyorai (Physician of the Soul) carved from a camphor tree.

From the Daiko-do, walk past the Kon-do and Chu-mon; then turn left and walk past the pond on your right. You come to two concrete buildings known as the **Daihozo-den** (Great Treasure Hall), which display statues, sculptures, ancient Buddhist religious articles, and brocades. Of particular interest is a miniature shrine that belonged to Lady Tachibana, mother of Empress Komyo. The shrine is about 2½ feet high; the Buddha inside is about 20 inches tall. The **Todai-mon** (Great East Gate) opens onto Horyu-ji's eastern grounds. The octagonal **Yumedono** (Hall of Dreams) was so named because Prince Shotoku used to meditate in it.

To get here, take a JR Kansai Main Line train to Horyu-ji Station (¥210). The temple is a short shuttle ride or a 15-minute walk. Alternatively, Bus 52, 60, or 97 to Horyu-ji is a 50-minute ride from the JR Nara Station or Kintetsu Nara Station (¥760). The Horyu-ji-mae bus stop is in front of the temple. ✉ *1–1 Horyuji Sannai, Ikaruga-cho, Ikoma-gun, Western Nara* ☎ *0745/75–2555* ⊕ *www.horyuji.or.jp* 🎟 *¥1,000* ⊙ *Feb. 22–Nov. 3, daily 8–5; Nov. 4–Feb. 21, daily 8–4:30; last entry 30 mins before closing.*

WORTH NOTING

Chugu-ji Temple (中宮寺). This temple was originally the home of Prince Shotoku's mother in the 6th century and is now a Buddhist nunnery. It houses an amazing wooden statue of the Miroku Bodhisattva, the Buddha of the Future. His gentle countenance has been a famous image of hope since it was carved, sometime in the Asuka period (552–645). Chugu-ji is a few minutes' walk north of the Yumedono. ✉ *1–1–2 Horyu-j Kita, Ikaruga-cho, Ikoma-gun, Western Nara* ☎ *0745/75–2106* 🎟 *¥500* ⊙ *Daily 9–4.*

Toshodai-ji Temple (唐招提寺 *Toshodai Temple*). The main entrance to Toshodai Temple, which was built in 751, is called the Path of History, since in Nara's imperial days dignitaries and priests trod this route; today it is lined with clay-walled houses, tranquil gardens, and the occasional shop selling crafts.

BRINGING BUDDHISM TO JAPAN

Toshodai-ji Temple was built in 751 for Ganjin, a Chinese priest who traveled to Japan at the invitation of Emperor Shomu. At that time, Japanese monks had never received formal instruction from a Buddhist monk. The invitation was extended by two Japanese monks who had traveled to China in search of a Buddhist willing to undertake the arduous and perilous journey to Japan.

It seemed that Ganjin would never make it to Japan. On his first journey some of his disciples betrayed him. His second journey resulted in a shipwreck. During the third trip his ship was blown off course, and on his fourth trip government officials refused him permission to leave China. Before his next attempt, he contracted an eye disease that left him blind. He persevered, nonetheless, and finally reached Japan in 750. Ganjin shared his knowledge of Buddhism with his adopted country and served as a teacher to many Japanese abbots as well as Emperor Shomu. He is also remembered for bringing the first sampling of sugar to Japan. Every June 6, to commemorate his birthday, the Miei-do (Founder's Hall) in the back of the temple grounds displays a lacquer statue of Ganjin that dates from 763.

At the temple's entrance entasis pillars support the **Nandai-mon** (Great South Gate). Beyond the Nandai-mon is the **Kon-do** (Main Hall), a superb example of classical Nara architecture. It was restored in 2009. Inside the hall is a lacquer statue of Vairocana Buddha, the same incarnation of Buddha that is enshrined at Todai-ji. The halo surrounding him was originally covered with 1,000 Buddhas; now there are 864. In back of the Kon-do sits the **Daiko-do** (Lecture Hall), formerly an assembly hall of the Nara Imperial Court, the only remaining example of Nara palace architecture.

Toshodai-ji is a 10-minute walk from the rear gate of Yakushi-ji along the Path of History. From central Nara or Horyu-ji, take Bus 52 or 97 to the stop in front of Toshodai-ji. ⊠ *13–46 Gojo-cho, Western Nara* ☎ *0742/33–7900* 💴 *¥600* 🕐 *Daily 8:30–5.*

Yakushi-ji Temple (薬師寺). The two pagodas that tower over Yakushi Temple are an analogy of past and present Japan. Yakushi-ji's **East Pagoda** dates from 1285, and has such an interesting asymmetrical shape that it inspired Boston Museum of Fine Arts curator Ernest Fenollosa (1853–1908), an early Western specialist in Japanese art, to remark that it was as beautiful as "frozen music." Its simple, dark brown beams with white ends contrast starkly with its flashier, vermilion-painted 20th-century neighbor, the **West Tower,** built in 1981. For many, the new goes against the "imperfect, impermanent, and incomplete" principles of the old *wabi-sabi* aesthetic; but we think the contrast thrusts Yakushi-ji right into the 21st-century. Officially named one of the Seven Great Temples of Nara, Yakushi-ji was founded in 680 and moved to its current location in 718. From central Nara take either the Kintetsu Line train, changing at Yamato-Saidai-ji to Nishinokyo, or Bus 52 or 97 to Yakushi-ji; from Horyu-ji or Chugu-ji, take Bus 97 to Yakushi-ji-mae.

✉ 457 Nishinokyo-cho, Western Nara ☎ 0742/33–6001 🎫 ¥500–¥800, depending on event ⏲ Daily 8:30–5.

WHERE TO EAT

It's a sin to visit Nara and not have a kaiseki dinner (an aesthetically arranged 7- to 12-course set meal using the freshest ingredients) if you can afford the splurge. It's usually an evening meal, but most kaiseki restaurants serve mini-kaiseki at lunchtime for day-trippers that are considerably more affordable. Most traditional restaurants are small and have set courses. Nara retires early, and restaurants close around 10 pm, taking last orders around 9 pm. Small restaurants and *izakaya* (after-work drinking haunts that serve an array of small dishes and drinks) are dispersed throughout the two main shopping streets, Higashi-muki Dori (a pedestrian arcade) and Konishi-dori, close to Kintetsu Nara Station.

NARA KOEN AREA

$$ JAPANESE 🍴 **Aji-tei Yamazakiya** (味亭山崎屋). Pungent nara-zuke will lure you into this well-known shop and adjoining restaurant. Inside, white-capped prep cooks busily prepare packages of pickles that you can try with *cha-gayu* (green tea porridge) or a meal of crispy tempura. The set menus are on display, making ordering simple. This is a good place to escape the crowds on Higashi-muki Dori, the main shopping street. Nara Kintetsu Station and Nara Koen are within a five-minute walk. [$] *Average main: ¥2000 ✉ 5 Higashimuki-minamimachi ☎ 0742/22–8039 💳 No credit cards ⏲ Closed Mon.*

$$$$ JAPANESE 🍴 **Onjaku** (温石). Hidden down a quiet street just south of Ara-ike in Nara Koen is this intimate restaurant serving exquisitely presented traditional kaiseki meals. Within the faded wooden walls, a common architectural motif in Nara, you can sit at a rustic counter or in one of two serene tatami rooms. Choose from one of the two set meals. Both lunch and dinner here are short and served early (noon–1 for lunch, 6–7:30 for dinner). [$] *Average main: ¥15000 ✉ 1043 Takabatake-cho, Nara Koen ☎ 0742/26–4762 💳 No credit cards ⏲ Closed Tues. ✍ Reservations essential.*

$$$$ JAPANESE 🍴 **To-no-chaya** (塔の茶屋 *Tearoom of the Pagoda*). One of Nara's most distinctive meals is *cha-gayu* (green-tea-flavored rice porridge). During the day To-no-chaya serves this special dish with sashimi and vegetables, plus a few sweetened rice cakes for dessert. If you're coming for dinner, call ahead to enjoy cha-gayu. For lunch, opt for bento-box meals. The restaurant's name means "Tearoom of the Pagoda," for its views of the Kofuku Temple. [$] *Average main: ¥3500 ✉ 47 Noborioji-cho, Nara Koen ☎ 0742/22–4348 💳 No credit cards ⏲ Closed Tues.*

$$$$ JAPANESE 🍴 **Tsukihitei** (月日亭). Deep in the forest behind Kasuga Taisha, Tsukihitei has the perfect setting for a traditional kaiseki meal. From the walk up a wooded path to the tranquillity of your own tatami room, everything here is conducive to experiencing the beautiful presentation and delicate flavors—as Helen Keller did when she dined here in 1948. When reserving a table, enlist the help of a good Japanese speaker to select a set meal for you, and allow yourself to be regaled. The lunch

sets cost between ¥10,000 and ¥15,000, not exactly cheap, but cheaper than dinner. [$] *Average main: ¥25000* ✉ *158 Kasugano-cho, Nara Koen* ☎ *0742/26–2021* ✍ *Reservations essential.*

$$$$ JAPANESE 🍴 **Uma no Me** (馬の目). In a little 1920s farmhouse just north of Ara-ike pond in Nara Koen this delightful restaurant with dark beams and pottery-lined walls serves delicious home-style cooking. Everything is prepared from scratch. The ¥3,500 lunch course with fried fish, tofu, and seasonal vegetables is delightful. As there is only one set meal, ordering is no problem. [$] *Average main: ¥3500* ✉ *1158 Takabatake-cho, Nara Koen* ☎ *0742/23–7784* 💳 *No credit cards* ⏲ *Closed Thurs.* ✍ *Reservations essential.*

$$ JAPANESE 🍴 **Yanagi-ja-ya** (柳茶屋). Just past the Five-Story Pagoda, this longtime favorite is the place to try some *warabi mochi* for morning or afternoon tea. Delicious morsels made from warabi (bracken fern root) are tossed in soybean flour and sweetened with brown sugar syrup. At a second location in Nara Koen, at 49 Noborioji-cho, the unassuming exterior belies an elegant interior. You're transported to a bygone age in a secluded tatami room overlooking a garden where you'll be served simple bento meals of sashimi, stewed vegetables, and tofu in black-lacquer boxes. Lunch at this branch is more expensive, setting you back ¥4,000 to ¥6,000. [$] *Average main: ¥1000* ✉ *4–48 Noborioji-cho, Nara Koen* ☎ *0742/22–7560* 💳 *No credit cards* ⏲ *Closed Mon. No dinner* ✍ *Reservations essential.*

NARA-MACHI

$$$ JAPANESE 🍴 **Harishin** (はり新). This eatery's *kamitsumichi* bento box, with a selection of sashimi, fried shrimp, tofu, vegetables, and homemade plum liqueur, is a bargain for ¥2,900. Harishin is traditional and quite rustic. You sit in either a large tatami room overlooking a garden or around a large *irori* (hearth). [$] *Average main: ¥2900* ✉ *15 Nakashinya-cho, Nara-machi* ☎ *0742/22–2669* ⏲ *Closed Mon.*

$$$ SUSHI 🍴 **Hiraso** (平宗). At Hiraso you can try *kakinoha-zushi*, sushi wrapped in persimmon leaves. What's more, you can take it away in a nicely wrapped wooden box for a satisfying lunch in Nara Park. Another featured delicacy is *kakisuga*, dried persimmon dusted with *kudzu* (flour made from the East Asian kudzu vine) or arrowroot powder and cooked tempura style. Most set menus include green tea porridge, which is usually made with mushrooms or seasonal vegetables. Hiraso has tables and chairs, but the tatami alcoves are more intimate. [$] *Average main: ¥2500* ✉ *30–1 Imamikado-cho, Nara-machi* ☎ *0742/22–0866* ⏲ *Mon. takeout only.*

WHERE TO STAY

Nara has accommodations in every style and price range. Since most people treat the city as a day-trip destination, at night the quiet streets are the domain of Nara's residents. Hotels in central Nara around the main railway stations are often noisier than those closer to Nara Koen and in Nara-machi. In spring and autumn and at peak holiday periods, rooms are hard to find on weekend nights. Book well in advance if you plan to travel to Nara during these times.

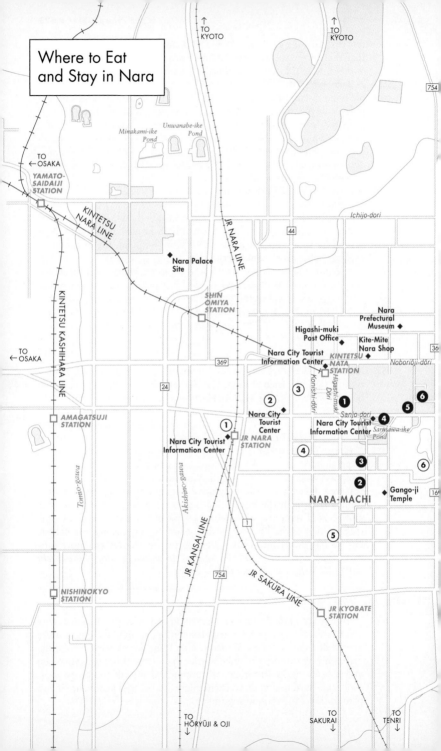

Where to Eat and Stay in Nara

TO KYOTO ↑

↑ TO KYOTO

754

Minakami-ike Pond

Unwanabe-ike Pond

Ichijo-dori

TO ←OSAKA

YAMATO-SAIDAIJI STATION

KINTETSU NARA LINE

JR NARA LINE

44

Nara Palace Site

SHIN OMIYA STATION

Nara Prefectural Museum

KINTETSU KASHIHARA LINE

TO ←OSAKA

369

Higashi-muki Post Office

Kite-Mite Nara Shop

36

Nara City Tourist Information Center

KINTETSU NARA STATION

Noboriōji-dōri

24

③

② Nara City Tourist Center

Konishi-dōri

Higashi-muki Dōri

❶

⑤ ❻

AMAGATSUJI STATION

① Nara City Tourist Information Center

JR NARA STATION

Sanjo-dori

❹

❺

Sarusawa-ike Pond

④

③

Tomio-gawa

Akishino-gawa

④

❷

❸ Gango-ji Temple

⑥

16

NARA-MACHI

⑤

JR KANSAI LINE

1

754

NISHINOKYO STATION

JR SAKURA LINE

754

JR KYOBATE STATION

TO HŌRYŪJI & OJI ↓

TO SAKURAI ↓

TO TENRI ↓

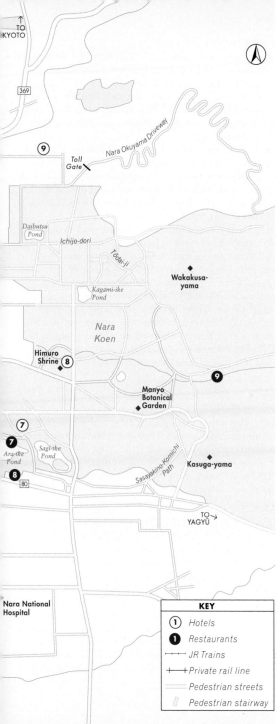

Restaurants ▼

Aji-tei Yamazakiya **1**

Harishin **2**

Hiraso **3**

Onjaku **8**

To-no-chaya **5**

Tsukihitei **9**

Uma no Me **7**

Yanagi-ja-ya **4, 6**

Hotels ▼

Edo-San **7**

Hotel Fujita Nara **2**

Hotel Nara Club **9**

Hotel Nikko Nara **1**

Kankaso **8**

Nara Hotel **6**

Ryokan Nanto **3**

Ryokan Seikanso **5**

Ryokan Tsubakiso **4**

8

KEY

① Hotels

❶ Restaurants

⊦⊦⊦ JR Trains

⊦—⊦ Private rail line

Pedestrian streets

Pedestrian stairway

NARA KOEN AREA

$$$$
B&B/INN

🏯 **Edo-San** (江戸三). Individual cottages, some with thatched roofs in the greenery of Nara Park, are what Edo-San is all about. **Pros:** perfect location in Nara Park; closest neighbors are the deer; great in-room dining. **Cons:** traffic from nearby road; English not spoken. Ⓢ *Rooms from: ¥40000* ✉ *1167 Takabatake-cho, Nara Koen* ☎ *0742/26–2662* ⊕ *www.edosan.jp* ↪ *10 Japanese-style cottages, 1 with bath* ⑪ *Some meals.*

$$
B&B/INN

🏯 **Hotel Nara Club** (奈良倶楽部). On a street of old houses with traditional gardens, this small hotel is reminiscent of a European pension. **Pros:** peaceful location; not far from main sights; home-cooked meals using local produce. **Cons:** long walk from train stations. Ⓢ *Rooms from: ¥14000* ✉ *21 Kita Mikado-cho, Nara Koen* ☎ *0742/22–3450* ⊕ *www.naraclub.com* ↪ *8 rooms* ⑪ *Some meals.*

$$$$
B&B/INN
Fodor's Choice
★

🏯 **Kankaso** (観鹿荘). At once exquisitely refined and delightfully friendly, Kankaso exemplifies the best of Japanese hospitality. **Pros:** long history of serving foreign guests; traditional architecture; convenient to Nara Koen. **Cons:** little English spoken. Ⓢ *Rooms from: ¥42000* ✉ *10 Kasugano-cho, Nara Koen* ☎ *0742/26–1128* ⊕ *www.kankaso.jp* ↪ *9 Japanese-style rooms, 5 with bath* ⑪ *Some meals.*

$$$$
HOTEL
Fodor's Choice
★

🏯 **Nara Hotel** (奈良ホテル). Built in 1909, this hotel is a beautiful synthesis of Japanese and Western architecture. **Pros:** very spacious rooms; top-class service; imperial atmosphere. **Cons:** nothing here comes cheap. Ⓢ *Rooms from: ¥30000* ✉ *1096 Takabatake-cho, Nara Koen* ☎ *0742/26–3300* ⊕ *www.narahotel.co.jp* ↪ *129 rooms, 3 suites* ⑪ *No meals.*

NARA-MACHI

$
B&B/INN

🏯 **Ryokan Seikanso** (旅館静観荘). Of the many inexpensive, small ryokan in Nara-machi, this family-run establishment is the best pick for its spotless rooms and attentive service. **Pros:** cheap and cheerful; great breakfasts; friendly service. **Cons:** rooms are getting on in years; shared bathrooms. Ⓢ *Rooms from: ¥9000* ✉ *29 Higashikitsu-ji-cho, Nara-machi* ☎ *0742/22–2670* ⊕ *www.nara-ryokanseikanso.com* ↪ *9 Japanese-style rooms, all with shared bath* ⑪ *No meals.*

CENTRAL NARA

$$$
HOTEL

🏯 **Hotel Fujita Nara** (ホテルフジタ奈良). Centrally situated between JR Nara Station and Nara Park, this modern hotel is often the best deal in town. **Pros:** central location; reasonable rates; bicycle rentals. **Cons:** it feels like a business hotel anywhere in Japan. Ⓢ *Rooms from: ¥20000* ✉ *47–1 Shimo Sanjo-cho, Central Nara* ☎ *0742/23–8111* ⊕ *www.fujita-nara.com* ↪ *114 rooms, 3 suites* ⑪ *No meals.*

$$$
HOTEL

🏯 **Hotel Nikko Nara** (ホテル日航奈良). The city's largest hotel provides plenty of creature comforts in rooms with thick carpets and large windows that let in lots of light. **Pros:** connected to JR Nara Station; near dining and shopping options; courteous staff. **Cons:** rooms and bathrooms are relatively small. Ⓢ *Rooms from: ¥21000* ✉ *8–1 Sanjo-hon-machi, Central Nara* ☎ *0742/35–8831* ⊕ *www.nikkonara.jp* ↪ *330 rooms, 1 suite* ⑪ *No meals.*

$$
B&B/INN
🏯**Ryokan Nanto** (旅館南都). The quietest ryokan on the city side of Nara Park, the Nanto has airy tatami rooms with a simplicity fit for a Zen retreat. **Pros:** family-friendly atmosphere; located between Kintetsu Nara Station and JR Nara Station. **Cons:** credit cards not accepted. Ⓢ *Rooms from: ¥16000* ✉ *29 Kamisanjo-cho, Central Nara* ☎ *0742/22–3497* ⊕ *www.ryokan-nanto.jp* ▭ *No credit cards* 🛏 *13 Japanese-style rooms, 3 with bath* ⦿ *Breakfast.*

$$$$
B&B/INN
🏯**Ryokan Tsubakiso** (旅館椿荘). Friendly service and delicious meals make for a relaxed stay in this quiet mix of old and new. **Pros:** lovely garden; central yet quiet location; vegetarian meals available upon request. **Cons:** communal bathing is not for the shy. Ⓢ *Rooms from: ¥33000* ✉ *35 Tsubaki-cho, Central Nara* ☎ *0742/22–5330* 🛏 *7 Japanese-style rooms, 3 with bath* ⦿ *Some meals.*

SHOPPING

Nara is especially known for traditional arts and crafts, including aka-hadayaki pottery, ink, and linen. Nara-machi has the highest concentration of traditional shops as well as those selling contemporary takes on the traditional. The area around Todai-ji has many touristy souvenir shops, though few that stand out. The Nara City Tourism Information Office can supply you with an English-language guide and map.

Kite-Mite Nara Shop (きてみてならショップ). For an overview of the arts and crafts of Nara Prefecture, visit the Kite-Mite Nara Shop on your way to Nara Park. A brochure in English is available. ✉ *38–1 Nobori-oji-cho, Central Nara* ☎ *0742/26–8828* ⊗ *Tues.–Sun. 10–6.*

KOBE

Kobe resonates with a cool, hip vibe, a condition of its internationalism and its position between mountains and sea. With more than 44,000 foreigners living in the city, representing more than 120 countries, Kobe may be Japan's most diverse city. It has great international cuisine, from Indonesian to French. It also has some of the best Japanese cuisine, especially the famous Kobe beef.

Kobe's diversity is largely attributable to its harbor. The port was a major center for trade with China dating back to the Nara period (710–794). Kobe's prominence increased briefly for six months in the 12th century when the capital was moved from Kyoto to Fukuhara, now western Kobe. Japan acquiesced to opening five ports, and on January 1, 1868, international ships sailed into Kobe's harbor. American and European sailors and traders soon settled in Kobe, and their culture and technology spread throughout the city. Cinema and jazz made their debut in Kobe, and that legacy is ongoing. Many original residences have survived, and the European structures contrast strikingly with the old Japanese buildings and modern high-rises.

Prior to 1995, Kobe was Japan's busiest port. But on January 17, 1995, an earthquake with a magnitude of 7.2 hit the Kobe area, killing more than 6,400 people, injuring almost 40,000, and destroying more than 100,000 homes. Communication lines were destroyed, damaged roads

8

prevented escape and relief, and fires raged throughout the city. Kobe made a remarkable and quick recovery.

The city now pulses with the activity of a modern, industrialized city. The colorful skyline reflects off the night water, adding to Kobe's reputation as a city for lovers. Don't come to Kobe looking for traditional Japan; appreciate its urban energy, savor its international cuisine, and take advantage of its shopping.

Kobe lies along the Seto Inland Sea in the center of Honshu, a little west of Osaka and several hours east of Hiroshima. Smaller than Tokyo and Osaka, Kobe is more accessible and less formidable. It is large enough, however, to keep you occupied with new attractions and events no matter how frequently you visit.

Divided into approximately 10 distinctive neighborhoods, the city extends from the business-oriented region near the harbor to the lower slopes of Mt. Rokko. Penned in by natural boundaries, Kobe expanded its territory with man-made islands in the harbor.

Rokko Island is home to numerous foreign companies and a number of shopping plazas, and is where foreigners now tend to settle. **Port Island** features conference centers and an amusement park. Port Island is linked with downtown by a fully computerized monorail—with no human conductor—that extends south to the Kobe airport.

Downtown, San-no-miya Station, in the city center, marks the heart of Kobe's entertainment and nightlife area. Every night passersby linger to hear musicians in a small park just north of the station. Moto-machi's stores are to the west, and most of the business district lies south of San-no-miya.

In Kintano-cho, Kobe's original European and American settlers built elegant residences, now known as *ijinkan*, on the city's northern slopes. Many of the preserved ijinkan have been turned into museums. Small boutiques, international cafés, and a few antiques shops seduce visitors to meander along Kitano-zaka and Pearl Street.

North of Kobe, the impressive Nunobiki Falls are surprisingly accessible from downtown, just behind the Shin-Kobe Station. Rokko-san (*san* means "mountain") is a little farther out, providing great views and cool mountain air. Arima Onsen, on the other side of Rokko-san, is one of Japan's oldest hot-springs destinations.

GETTING HERE AND AROUND

AIRPORT TRANSFERS From Kansai International Airport, ignore the train and take the comfortable limousine bus (70 minutes; ¥1,950), which drops you off in front of San-no-miya Station.

From Osaka Itami Airport, buses to San-no-miya Station leave from a stand between the airport's two terminals approximately every 20 minutes 7:45 am–9:10 pm. The trip takes about 40 minutes (¥1,050).

Kobe Airport handles mainly domestic flights, is 18 minutes from JR San-no-miya Station via the Portliner (¥330 one-way).

Airport Contact Kobe Airport (神戸空港 *Kobe Kuko*). ✉ *1 Kobe Kuko, Chuo-ku* ☎ *078/304–7777* ⊕ *www.kairport.co.jp.*

Continued on page 533

THE ART OF MONOZUKURI By Jared Lubarsky
TRADITIONAL JAPANESE CRAFTS

The Japanese take pride in their *monozukuri*: their gift for making things. And well they should, with traditions of craftsmanship centuries old to draw on, an itch for perfection, a loving respect for materials, and a profound aesthetic sense of what can be done with them.

There are really two craft traditions in Japan. In the first are the one-of-a-kind works of art—inlaid furniture and furnishings with designs in gold and mother-of-pearl, brocaded textiles, Tea Ceremony utensils, and so on—made by master artisans for wealthy patrons. These days, the descendants of these masters swell the ranks of Japan's *ningen koku-ho*, the official roster of Living National Treasures, who keep their crafts alive and set the standards of excellence. In the other are the humble charms of the *mingei* (folk craft) tradition: work in clay and bamboo, lacquer and native wood, iron and hand-forged steel—things made by nameless craftsmen for everyday use. Over the centuries the two traditions have enriched each other, and together they put Japanese craft work up among the best presents you can bring home from anywhere.

Top, clockwise: Kiyomizu pottery, ningyo doll, Darumas. Bottom: kokeshi doll

JAPANESE CERAMICS

Shopping for imari porcelain

Mashiko ware

If one Japanese folk tradition can be said to have contributed more than any other to Japan's collective cultural heritage, it must be pottery—admired by collectors and craftspeople all over the world. The tradition dates back more than 2,000 years, though pottery-making began to flourish as a real art form in the 16th century. Most Japanese pottery, apart from some porcelain and earthenware, is stoneware—formed into a wonderful variety of vases, cups, bowls, and platters and fired in climbing kilns on the slopes of hills.

Just visiting the regions where distinctive styles have developed would make a great *wanderjahr* in Japan. The village of Arita in Kyushu is famous for **imari** porcelain, with patterns of flowers and birds in bright enamel colors over blue and red underglazes. The folk pottery of **Mashiko**, in Tochigi Prefecture (northeast of Tokyo and southeast of Nikko), is admired for its rough textures and simple, warm colors. **Hagi** ware, from Western Honshu, is known for the rugged and rustic shapes of its Tea Ceremony bowls and cups. The red-brown **Bizen** ware from Okayama prefecture (also in Western Honshu)—one of the six remaining pottery centers of medieval Japan—is unglazed; every piece takes its unique colors and tones from the wood ash in the kiln. But you may also be interested in **Kyo-yaki** ceramics and porcelain from Kyoto, **Akahadayaki** pottery from Nara, or the **Jo-yachi** (glazed) pottery of Okinawa.

Hagi ware

Imari-Arita ware

Mashiko ware

Tobe ware

Kokutani ware

Bizen ware

Suzu ware

Matsushiro ware

Kutani ware

WHERE TO FIND: Most department stores in cities all over Japan have several different kinds of ceramics, though you'll find more regional specialties in the areas where they are produced. At first glance, Japanese ceramics may seem priced for a prince's table, but keep an eye out for seasonal sales; you can often find affordable pieces you will want to keep forever.

TOKYO SOURCE

Almost everyone passes through Tokyo on a trip to Japan. If you want to get an overview of traditional crafts or buy some souvenirs, the **Japan Traditional Craft Center** (⊠ *Metropolitan Plaza 1-3F, 1-11-1 Nishi-Ikebukuro* ☎ *03/5954-6066* ⊕ *www.kougei.or.jp*) is open daily 11–7 and sells crafts from all over the country, in most of the important categories from paper to tools to pottery, under its own seal of approval.

TYPES OF JAPANESE CRAFTS

Although you'll find regional craft specialties all over Japan, in every mega-metropolis and small village, the best overall selection of stores will be found in Tokyo, Kyoto, and Nara. But you can save money by looking for regional crafts closer to the source.

Hina ningyo dolls

Furoshiki

DOLLS

Traditional dolls, meant primarily for display and not as playthings, come in many different styles. **Kokeshi** dolls, which date from the Edo period, are long cylinders of wood with painted features. **Daruma** are papier-mâché dolls painted red, round as Humpty-Dumpties, representing a Buddhist priest who legend says meditated in the lotus position for so long that his arms and legs atrophied. **Hakata** dolls, from Kyushu, are ceramic figurines in traditional costume, such as geisha, samurai, or festival dancers. **Kyo-ningyo**, from Kyoto, are made of wood coated with white shell paste and then clothed in elaborate costumes.

WHERE TO FIND: Buy Kyo-ningyo in Kyoto, Hakata in Kyushu (especially in Fukuoka). Kokeshi come from the Tohoku region. Daruma can be purchased at temples all over Japan, but they come from Takasaki, north of Tokyo.

PRINTED FABRICS

Stencil-dyed fabrics were an important element of the Edo (old Tokyo) craft tradition, and survive in a range of motifs and intricate geometric designs—especially for light summer kimonos, room dividers, and cushion covers. **Furoshiki**—large cotton squares for wrapping, storing, and carrying things—make great wall hangings, as do the smaller cotton hand towels called **tenugui**, which are used as towels or as a head-covering in Kendo (Japanese sword-fighting).

WHERE TO FIND: Furoshiki and tenugui can be found all over Japan, but some stores specialize in them.

Kokeshi

Tenugui

Wajima nuri,
lacquerware

KIMONOS

Most Japanese women, unless they work in traditional restaurants, nowadays only wear kimonos rented for special occasions like weddings and coming-of-age ceremonies. A new one, in brocaded silk, can cost ¥1 million ($11,000) or more. Reluctant to pay that much for a bathrobe or a conversation piece? You might settle for a secondhand version—about ¥10,000 ($82) in a flea market, for one in decent condition—or look instead for cotton summer kimonos, called **yukata**, in a wide variety of colorful designs; you can buy one new for ¥7,000–¥10,000.

WHERE TO FIND: Kimonos are sold all over Japan, but you might want to look in Kyoto's Temple Markets for a reasonably priced, used kimono. Kyushu is also known for reasonably priced kimonos.

LACQUERWARE

For its history, diversity, and fine workmanship, lacquerware rivals ceramics as the traditional Japanese craft nonpareil. One warning: lacquerware thrives on humidity. Cheaper pieces usually have plastic rather than wood underneath, and because these won't shrink and crack in dry climates, they make safer—but no less attractive—buys.

WHERE TO FIND: Lacquerware can be found all over Japan, but it is a specialty of the Noto Peninsula (particularly Wajima). It's also very widely made in Kyushu.

Kimonos

Lacquerware being handcrafted in Wajima

Washi (Sugihara paper)

PAPER

What packs light and flat in your suitcase, won't break, doesn't cost much, and makes a great gift? The answer is **washi** (handmade paper, usually of mulberry fibers), which the Japanese craft in a myriad of colors, textures, and designs and fashion into an astonishing number of useful and decorative objects. Look for stationery, greeting cards, single sheets in color and classical motifs for gift wrapping and origami, and washi-covered jewelry boxes.

WHERE TO FIND: There are washi manufacturers all over Japan, but some of the most famous types are **Mino Washi** calligraphy paper from Gifu (see Nagoya, Ise-Shima, and the Kii Peninsula); **Tosa Washi** from Kochi (see Shikoku); and **Yama Washi** from Fukuoka (Kyushu).

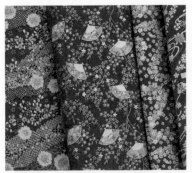

Patterned Washi

SWORDS AND KNIVES

Supple and incredibly strong, hand-forged steel was for centuries the stuff of samurai swords and armor. Genuine antique swords seldom come on the market now (imitations sold as flashy souvenirs are not really worth considering), and when they do they fetch daunting prices. But the same craftsmanship is still applied to a range of kitchen knives and cleavers, comparable in both quality and price to the best Western brands.

A set of japanese knife in a shop in Tokyo

WHERE TO FIND: You can find Japanese knives in any big-city department store, or look for them on the side streets of Kappabashi, the restaurant wholesale supply district in Tokyo. But the center for Japanese knife- and sword-making is the city of Seki, a few miles northeast of Gifu (see Nagoya, Ise-Shima, and the Kii Peninsula).

Tanto Japanese sword

SUBWAY TRAVEL Kobe's main subway line runs from Tanigami in the far north of the city, and passes through Shin-Kobe and San-no-miya stations before continuing west to the outskirts of town. Another line runs along the coast from San-no-miya and links up with the main line at Shin-Nagata Station. Fares start at ¥200 and are determined by destination. The San-no-miya–Shin-Kobe trip costs ¥210.

The Portliner was the first digitally driven monorail in the world, and departs from San-no-miya Station every six minutes from 6:05 am until 11:40 pm on its loop to and around Port Island. The ride affords a close-up view of Kobe Harbor.

TRAIN TRAVEL The Shinkansen (bullet train) stops at the Shin-Kobe Station, just north of San-no-miya. The two are connected by the Seishin-Yamate Line that extends north from San-no-miya Station to the Shin-Kobe Station. Shin-Kobe also connects to Arima.

The trip between Osaka Station and Kobe's San-no-miya Station takes 24 minutes on the JR Kobe Line rapid train, which leaves at 15-minute intervals throughout the day; without a JR Pass the fare is ¥410. The Hankyu and Hanshin private lines run between Osaka and Kobe for ¥320.

The City Loop bus starts at San-no-miya and circles through Meriken Park, Harborland, and Kitano before returning to San-no-miya. Taxis are easy to find at San-no-miya Station, but can also be found at any *noriba,* or taxi stand.

Purchase tickets from a vending machine; you surrender them on passing through the turnstile at your destination station. Fares depend on your destination.

Three rail lines, JR, Hankyu, and Hanshin, cut straight through the city from one side to the other, and converge at San-no-miya Station. Most of the city is a 10-minute walk from a train station, making trains the most convenient way to get around.

VISITOR INFORMATION

Kobe Tourist Information Center offers detailed English-language maps of all the neighborhoods, with attractions and streets clearly marked. Also pick up a "Kobe Guide" and a "Kobe Welcome Coupon," which has coupons on museums, activities, and transportation. The English-speaking staff can help book rooms, find tours, and give recommendations. The Kobe Information Center is near the West Exit of JR San-no-miya; another branch is at the JR Shin-Kobe Station. The Japan Travel Bureau can arrange for hotel reservations, train tickets, package tours, and more throughout the country.

Visitor Information Japan Travel Bureau (JTB トラベル *JTB Toraberu*). ⊠ *JR San-no-miya Station, 5–1–305 Kotono-cho* ☎ *078/231–9180.* **Kobe Information Center** (神戸市総合インフォメーションセンター). ⊠ *JR San-no-miya Station, 8 Kumoi-dori, Chuo-ku* ☎ *078/322–0220* ⊠ *Shin-Kobe Station, 1–3–1 Kanocho, Chuo-ku* ☎ *078/241–9550.*

8

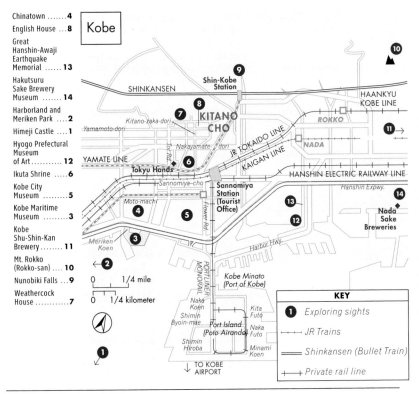

EXPLORING KOBE

DOWNTOWN KOBE

In 1868, after nearly 200 years of isolation, Kobe's port opened to the West, and Kobe became an important gateway for cultural exchange. Confined to a small area by its natural boundaries, the city has kept its industrial harbor within the city limits. The harbor's shipping cranes project incongruously against the city's sleek skyscrapers, but the overall landscape manages to blend together beautifully. The harbor is approximately a 20-minute walk southwest of the San-no-miya area.

TOP ATTRACTIONS

Fodor's Choice ★ **Great Hanshin-Awaji Earthquake Memorial** (*Hanshin Awaji Daishinsai Kinen*). In 1995, the Great Hanshin-Awaji Earthquake killed 6,433 people, leveled vast areas of the city, and destroyed much of the harbor. Using documentary footage and audio, an introductory film shows the frightening destruction of this modern city. A re-created postquake display and high-tech exhibits convey the sorrows and memories of the event. This excellent museum has English pamphlets and electronic guides, and English-speaking volunteers are on hand. It's a 10-minute walk from the South Exit of JR Nada Station, one stop east of JR San-no-miya Station. ⊠ *1–5–2 Wakinohama Kaigan-dori, Chuo-ku*

☎078/262–5050 ⊕ www.dri.ne.jp/english/index.html ☑¥600 ⏱ Tues.–Thurs. and Sun. 9:30–5:30, Fri. and Sat. 9:30–7.

Harborland and Meriken Park (ハーバーランドとメリケンパーク). No trip to Kobe is complete without a waterside visit. Within Meriken Park broken slabs of thick concrete and crooked lightposts are preserved as part of the Port of Kobe Earthquake Memorial Park. Across the grassy park the Kobe Maritime Museum's roofline of white metal poles, designed like the billowing sails of a tall ship, contrast beautifully with the crimson Port Tower. The top of the tower provides a 360-degree view of Kobe. A walkway connects to Harborland's outdoor shopping mall. Eat dinner at any of the restaurants on the waterfront and enjoy the stunning nighttime view. Nearby, a small Ferris wheel rotates lazily, the colors of its flashing lights bouncing off the sides of nearby ships. Meriken Park and Harborland are a 10-minute walk south of Moto-machi Station. ⊠ *1 Kawazaki-cho, Chuo-ku.*

Fodor's Choice ★

Hyogo Prefectural Museum of Art (兵庫県立美術館 *Hyogo Kenritsu Bijut-sukan*). This striking concrete edifice was designed by acclaimed architect Tadao Ando. Working primarily with concrete, Ando is known for his use of light and water, blending indoors and outdoors and utilizing flowing geometric paths. The permanent exhibit here features art from prominent 20th-century Japanese painters Ryohei Koiso and Heizo Kanayama, Kobe natives who specialized in Western techniques. The museum rotates its vast collection, displaying fantastic modern works from Japanese artists as well as sculptures by Henry Moore and Auguste Rodin. It also hosts international touring shows. It's a 10-minute walk from the South Exit of JR Nada Station, one stop east of JR San-no-miya Station. ⊠ *1–1–1 Wakinohama Kaigan-dori, Chuo-ku* ☎ *078/262–0901* ⊕ *www.artm.pref.hyogo.jp* ☑¥510 ⏱ *Tues.–Thurs., Sun. 10–6, Fri. and Sat. 10–8.*

Kobe City Museum (神戸市立博物館 *Kobe Shiritsu Hakubutsukan*). This museum specializes in work from the 16th and 17th centuries, focusing on reciprocal cultural influences between East and West. The first floor has a variety of displays on the West's impact on Japan in the second half of the 17th century. Other exhibits document the influence of Western hairstyles for women and the arrival of electric and gas lamps. The museum also has an impressive collection of woodcuts, maps, and archaeological artifacts, as well as Namban-style art, namely prints, silkscreens, and paintings from the late 16th to 17th century, usually depicting foreigners in Japanese settings. The historical exhibits are fascinating, but it is the artwork from this period that is the real draw.

From San-no-miya Station, walk south on Flower Road to Higashi-Yuenchi Koen. Walk through the park to the Kobe Minato post office, across the street on the west side. Then head east along the street in front of the post office toward the Oriental Hotel. Turn left at the corner in front of the hotel, and the City Museum is in the old Bank of Tokyo building at the end of the block. ⊠ *24 Kyo-machi, Chuo-ku* ☎ *078/391–0035* ☑¥200 ⏱ *Tues.–Sun. 9:30–5.*

8

WORTH NOTING

Chinatown (南京町 *Nankin-machi*). If you're heading to Meriken Park, consider a short stop in Kobe's Chinatown. The area was originally a center for Chinese immigrants, though it is now mostly popular with Japanese tourists looking for souvenirs and food. To find Nankin-machi from Moto-machi Station, walk on the port side and enter the neighborhood through the large fake-marble gate. ⊠ *Sakaemachi-dori, Chuo-ku.*

Hakutsuru Sake Brewery Museum (白鶴酒造資料館). Nada, one of Kobe's westernmost neighborhoods, is home to a number of museums and breweries—many offering free sake tasting. The most popular is the Hakutsuru Sake Brewery Museum, where at the door you'll find a sake barrel of immense proportions. Traditional tools and devices and life-size figures of traditionally clad brewers demonstrate the sake-brewing process. There are also videos in English. The tour ends with free tasting. It's a five-minute walk south from Hanshin Sumiyoshi Station. ⊠ *4–5–5 Sumiyoshiminami-machi, Higashinada-ku* ☎ 078/822–8907 ☞ *Free* ☉ *Tues.–Sun. 9:30–4:30.*

Ikuta Shrine (生田神社 *Ikuta Jinja*). Legend has it that this shrine was founded by Empress Jingu in the 3rd century, making it one of Japan's oldest. An impressive orange *torii* (gate), rebuilt after the 1995 earthquake, stands amid the bustle of modern Kobe, welcoming tourists and religious observers alike. Every year two Noh plays, *Ebira* and *Ikuta Atsumori*, at Ikuta's Autumn Festival retell parts of the 12th-century *Genpei* war. It's around the corner from Tokyu Hands department store, about 450 yards west of San-no-miya Station. ⊠ *1–2–1 Shimoyamate-dori, Chuo-ku* ⊕ *www.ikutajinja.or.jp* ☞ *Free* ☉ *Daily 7–7.*

Kobe Maritime Museum (神戸海洋博物館 *Kobe Kaiyo Hakubutsukan*). The Kobe Maritime Museum is the stunning building with a billowing roofline of metal sails. It showcases detailed ship models, opening with a 27-foot model of the HMS *Rodney,* the British flagship that led a 12-ship flotilla into Kobe Harbor on January 1, 1868. A model of the *Oshoro Maru,* one of Japan's earliest sailing ships, is adorned with pearls, rubies, gold, and silver. There are also displays of modern tankers. **Kawasaki Good Times World** is also inside the museum. High-tech displays and interactive models showcase the Kawasaki company's history. You can ride a helicopter flight simulator and see a robot work at a Rubik's Cube. Admission is included in the fee for the museum. ⊠ *2–2 Hatoba-cho, Chuo-ku* ☎ 078/327–8983 ☞ ¥600 ☉ *Tues.–Sun. 10–5.*

Kobe Shu-Shin-Kan Brewery. This is one of the few sake breweries open to tours, which should be booked the day before to ensure an English-speaking guide. All of the signage is in Japanese, but there's a fine shop. ⊠ *1–8–17 Mikagetsukamachi, Higashinada-ku* ☎ 078/841–1121 ⊕ *enjoyfukuju.com/english/our_sake/index.html* ☉ *Daily 10–6.*

KITANO-CHO

Wealthy foreigners, including Americans, English, and Germans, settled in the Kitano area in the late 19th century, bringing Western-style domestic architecture. Their homes are referred to in Kobe as *ijinkan* (pronounced "choo-eh-keh"), and the district is extremely popular with Japanese tourists, who enjoy the rare opportunity to see old-fashioned

Western houses. Some residences are still inhabited by Westerners, but more than a dozen 19th-century ijinkan in Kitano-cho are open to the public. A few of them are worth exploring, but seeing them all can be repetitious. The curious mélange of Japanese and Western Victorian and Gothic architecture makes for a good neighborhood walk. The streets are littered with small boutiques, cafés, and a few antiques shops.

To get to Kitano-cho, walk 15 minutes north along Kitano-zaka-dori from San-no-miya Station or 10 minutes west along Kitano-dori from Shin-Kobe Station. Yamamoto-dori (nicknamed Ijinkan-dori) is Kitano's main east–west street, and the ijinkan are on the small side streets ascending the hill. Tourist information centers offer detailed area maps with all attractions marked in English.

TOP ATTRACTIONS

English House (英国館 *Eikoku-kan*). This typically old-fashioned Western house (pronounced "eh-ee-ko koo-kan") was constructed in 1907 by an Englishman named Baker and served as a makeshift hospital during World War II. Now it's a house museum by day and an English pub by night. Antique baroque and Victorian furnishings dominate the interior, there are several downstairs bars, and, as if belonging to a decadent member of the royal family, a bottle of champagne rests in the bathtub. A classic black Jaguar in the driveway and an enormous moose head on the wall complete the English atmosphere. ✉ *2–3–16 Kitano-cho, Chuo-ku* ☎ *078/241–2338* 💴 *¥750* ⊗ *Museum daily 9–5; pub daily 5 pm–1 am.*

Weathercock House (風見鶏の館 *Kazamidori no Yakata*). More elaborate than any other Kobe ijinkan, this one, built by a German trader in 1910, stands out strikingly in red brick at the north end of Kitano-cho. The interior reflects various traditional German architectural styles, including that of a medieval castle. Its architecture makes this the most famous ijinkan, but the interiors are spartan, with few additional attractions. ✉ *3–13–3 Kitano-cho, Chuo-ku* ☎ *078/242–3223* 💴 *¥500* ⊗ *Daily 9–6.*

NORTH OF KOBE

Thanks to Kobe's mountain backdrop, hiking is a popular local pastime. From Shin-Kobe Station it's a short climb to the Nunobiki Falls. For a good mountain day hike, try going up Rokko-san; from Hankyu Kobe Line Rokko Station you can take a bus or taxi to Rokko Cable-Shita cable-car station ("Shita" means down or bottom). From there you can either hike all the way up the mountain or take the cable car partway. You may see wild boar—harmless unless provoked—in the forested mountains.

TOP ATTRACTIONS

Fodor'sChoice **Mt. Rokko** (六甲山 *Rokko-san*). Three cable cars scale Mt. Rokko, providing spectacular views of lush forests. If you think it's beautiful during the day, time you trip so you'll descend after dusk, when you can see the city lights twinkle against the black sea.

You can do this trip in a half day, but you may want a full day to explore the area. To get to Rokko-san, take the Hankyu Kobe Line from Hankyu San-no-miya Station to Hankyu Rokko Station (¥200). From there take a taxi or a bus to Rokko Cable-Shita Station. A

8

funicular railway travels up the mountain to Rokko-sanjo Station (¥570). You can return to Kobe by cable car or by rail. Take the Kobe Dentetsu to Tanigami Station and change for the subway back to Sanno-miya (¥900).

The Japanese were already enjoying the thermal waters at **Arima Onsen** 有馬温泉 before the 7th century. Arima is on the north slope of Rokko-san and consists of a maze of tiny streets and traditional houses. Some 30 ryokan use the curative powers of the water to attract guests. Although the water gushes up freely from springs, some ryokan charge as much as ¥10,000 for use of their baths. Go instead to the public bath, **Arima Onsen Kaikan**, in the center of the village near the bus terminal. Here ¥520

> **DISAPPEARING DOLLS**
>
> If you make it to Arima, the *Arima ningyo fude* (Arima doll brush) makes a nice souvenir. Made for calligraphy, the brushes have handles wrapped in colorful silk thread, and a little doll pops out of the handle when writing. The doll disappears when the brush is laid down. Legend has it that long ago Emperor Kotoku greatly desired a son. After he visited Arima Springs his wish was granted and a son was born. Made for more than 1,300 years, the dolls symbolize the birth of Prince Arima. The brushes are handmade locally, and their beautiful designs make them popular gift items.

gets you a soak in the steaming waters. Arima Onsen Kaikan is open daily 8 am–10 pm (closed the first and third Tuesday of the month). Take the subway north from JR Shin-Kobe Station, transferring at Tanigami and ending at Arima (¥740). ⊠ *Arima-cho, Kita-ku.*

Nunobiki Falls (布引の滝 *Nunobiki no Taki*). In the hustle and bustle of this modern city, you wouldn't think that one of Japan's most impressive waterfalls would be just behind the train station. Nunobiki Falls has four gushing cascades in the forests of Mt. Rokko. References to their beauty have appeared in Japanese literature since the 10th century. They are a 20-minute walk from Shin-Kobe Station. After the falls you can pick up the Shin-Kobe Ropeway, which stops just above the falls before continuing on to the Nunobiki Herb Park. The stopping point provides a beautiful view of the city, especially at night. The signs leading you to the falls are in Japanese, but the ANA Crowne Plaza Hotel can provide English-language hiking maps. ⊠ *Chuo-ku.*

HIMEJI

Himeji City is about 50 km (33 miles) west of Kobe and is most easily accessed via the JR Express (Sanyo Line), which will deposit you in JR Himejo Station after 40 minutes of travel time from Kobe (the trip from Kyoto on the same line takes an additional 15 minutes).

Fodor'sChoice **Himeji Castle** (*Himeji-jo*). Also known as Shirasagi-jo (White Egret Castle), Himeji Castle is visible as soon as you exit the train station. Universally beloved, it dazzles the city from atop a nearby hill. A visit to Himeji-jo could well be one of the high points of your trip to Japan, especially if you can manage to see the brilliantly lighted castle soaring above cherry blossoms or pine branches at night. Thanks to frequent

Himeji-jo, about 50 km (31 miles) west of Kobe, can be reached in about 40 minutes by train.

rail service, it should be easy to hop off, visit the castle, and jump on another train two hours later.

Himeji-jo is regarded as medieval Japan's crowning achievement of castle design and construction. It arrived at its present state of perfection after many transformations, however. It was first a fortress in the year 1333 and was transformed into a castle in 1346. Radically enlarged by Terumasa Ikeda in the period 1601–10, it has remained essentially the same ever since, surviving numerous wars and—perhaps even more miraculously—never once falling victim to the scourge of fire.

The five-story, six-floor main *donjon* (stronghold) stands more than 100 feet high and is built into a 50-foot-high stone foundation. Surrounding this main donjon are three smaller ones; all four are connected by covered passageways. Attackers would have had to cross three moats, penetrate the outer walls, and then withstand withering attack from the four towers. It was an impregnable fortress then, and its grace and grand proportions still inspire awe. Filmmaker Akira Kurosawa used Himeji-jo's exterior and the castle's grounds in his brilliant 1985 movie *Ran*.

Free guided tours in English are usually available from volunteer guides, though they cannot be booked in advance; ask when you buy your entry ticket. Tours usually take 90 minutes. From the central north exit of JR Himeji Station, the castle is a 15- to 20-minute walk or a 5-minute bus ride; also, bicycles are available free at the tourist office next door. The bus departs from the station plaza, on your left as you exit. ✉ *68 Honmachi, Himeji* ☎ *0792/85–1146* ⊕ *www.himeji-castle.gr.jp* 🎟 *¥1,000* ⊗ *Sept.–May, daily 9–4; June–Aug., daily 9–5.*

8

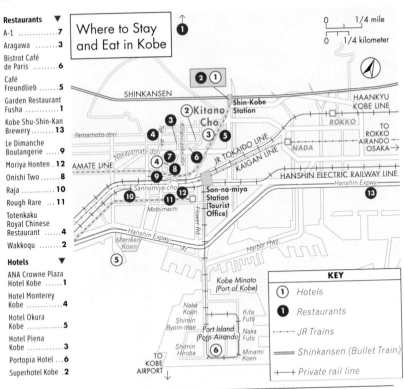

Where to Stay and Eat in Kobe

Restaurants ▼
A-1 .... **7**
Aragawa **3**
Bistrot Café
de Paris **6**
Café
Freundlieb **5**
Garden Restaurant
Fusha **1**
Kobe Shu-Shin-Kan
Brewery **13**
Le Dimanche
Boulangerie **9**
Moriya Honten . **12**
Onishi Two **8**
Raja **10**
Rough Rare ... **11**
Totenkaku
Royal Chinese
Restaurant **4**
Wakkoqu **2**

Hotels
ANA Crowne Plaza
Hotel Kobe **1**
Hotel Monterey
Kobe **4**
Hotel Okura
Kobe **5**
Hotel Piena
Kobe **3**
Portopia Hotel ... **6**
Superhotel Kobe . **2**

KEY

① Hotels

❶ Restaurants

⊢⊢⊢ JR Trains

═══ Shinkansen (Bullet Train)

⊢+⊢ Private rail line

WHERE TO EAT

Kobe is the place to find international cuisine, especially dishes from Europe and Southeast Asia. Excellent restaurants are found practically anywhere but are especially prevalent north of San-no-miya Station and in the Kitano area. For a quick snack, stop by one of the city's delicious bakeries.

$$$$
STEAKHOUSE

✕ **A-1.** With a relaxed atmosphere, A-1 is known for serving thick slices of Kobe beef. The teppanyaki steak (broiled on a hot plate) is cooked in a marinade of spices, wine, and soy and served with charcoal-grilled vegetables and crisp garlic potatoes. The "small" version is enough to fill you up, and costs ¥5,400. Four branches are scattered about town, but the main one is conveniently north of Hankyu San-no-miya Station, across from the B-Kobe hotel. ⑤ *Average main: ¥4500* ⊠ *B1F Lighthouse Bldg., 2–2–9 Shimoyamate-dori, Chuo-ku* ☎ *078/331–8676* ▭ *No credit cards.*

$$$$
STEAKHOUSE
Fodor's Choice
★

✕ **Aragawa** (あら皮). Japan's first steak house is famed for its superb, hand-fed Kobe beef from a single farm in the nearby city of Sanda. The melt-in-your-mouth *sumiyaki* (charcoal-broiled) steak is worth its weight in yen and is only served with mustard and pepper. (Don't even think about asking for other condiments.) The dining room's dark-wood paneling and lovely chandelier give it a European air. Be prepared to spend a minimum of ¥28,000 for your main course. Ⓢ *Average main: ¥30000* ✉ *2–15–18 Nakayamate-dori, Chuo-ku* ☎ *078/221–8547* ⏾ *Closed Sun.*

$$ **FRENCH**

✕**Bistrot Café de Paris** (ビストロカフェドパリ). This lively café offers delectable French cuisine that you can enjoy on an outdoor terrace—a true rarity in Japan. The menu covers all the bases, ranging from couscous to bouillabaisse. Midway up the hill on Kitano-zaka, it's great for people-watching and is a good stop while cruising the Kitano district. Lunch sets start at around ¥1,400, dinners around ¥3,000. Ⓢ *Average main: ¥1500* ✉ *1–7–21 Yamamoto-dori, Chuo-ku* ☎ *078/241–9448* ⊕ *www.cafe-de-paris.jp/.*

$$ **CAFÉ**

✕**Café Freundlieb** (カフェ フロインドリーブ). Housed in the former Kobe Union Church, this café exemplifies Kobe's relaxed beauty. High ceilings, arched windows, and white walls give the dining room a bright, airy feel. It's the perfect place to take a rest from exploring the Kitano neighborhood. The kitchen serves tasty salads and sandwiches, and the bread is baked fresh next door. Ⓢ *Average main: ¥1500* ✉ *4–6–15 Ikuta-machi, Chuo-ku* ☎ *078/231–6051* ⏾ *Closed Wed.*

$$$$ **EUROPEAN**

✕**Garden Restaurant Fusha** (ガーデンレストラン 風舎). Perfect for a romantic dinner overlooking the lights of Kobe, Fusha serves up delicious French-inspired European dishes in a relaxing, country-chic setting. The restaurant requires a 20-minute taxi ride from Shin-Kobe or Sannomiya Station, but offers a stunning night-view of the city and harbor from the candlelit outdoor tables. While the food is good, the nighttime view and atmosphere are the real draws, so be sure to reserve a table with a good view of the city. Ⓢ *Average main: ¥5000* ✉ *Kisui Golf Club, 1 Karasuharacho* ✛ *The restaurnat is difficult to get to on your own. It is best to get a taxi from Sannomiya or Shin-Kobe Station.* ☎ *078/511–2400* ⊕ *www5e.biglobe.ne.jp/~donqui/index.htm* ⏾ *Closed Tues..*

$ **CAFÉ**

✕**Le Dimanche Boulangerie.** Even among Kobe's many excellent bakeries, Le Dimanche stands out. The owners bake some of the city's best artisanal bread, seamlessly integrating Japanese and European elements. Unique specialties include the *renkon* (lotus root) tartine, crème brûlée croissant, and signature *viennois aux airelles* (Viennese cranberry roll). The second-floor café is bright and airy, with rustic hardwood floors and tables. It's the perfect spot for a light snack while browsing the many boutiques along Tor Road. Ⓢ *Average main: ¥700* ✉ *3–12–16 Kitanagasa-dori, Chuo-ku* ☎ *078/331–8760* ⊕ *le-dimanche.jp* ▭ *No credit cards* ⏾ *No dinner.*

REARED ON BEER

Around the world, Kobe beef is legendary for its succulence and taste. Cows receive daily massages, and in summer they ingest a diet of sake and beer mash. They are descended from an ancient line of *wagyu* (Japanese cows) known to be genetically predisposed to higher marbling. True Kobe beef comes from only 262 farms in the Tajima region of Hyogo Prefecture (of which Kobe is the capital), each of which raise an average of five animals. The best beef restaurants are mostly in the central Chuo-ku district, and Kobe beef is on the menu at the top hotels.

8

$$$$ STEAKHOUSE 🍴 **Moriya Honten** (モーリヤ本店). Moriya's flagship restaurant stands where the business began in 1885 as a butcher shop. Now, this cozy restaurant serves excellent grade A5 Kobe wagyu (the highest rank of Japanese beef) at reasonable prices. The atmosphere feels like being in a 19th-century home, with dark wood paneling and floors. In addition to the premium-priced Kobe beef, the restaurant also serves the excellent but less expensive Moriya beef—a great value for travelers who want to try top-grade wagyu without breaking the bank. The restaurant is popular with tourists so it is best to reserve or expect to wait if you visit during peak lunch or dinner times. [$] *Average main: ¥8000* ✉ *2–1–17 Shimoyamate-dori, Chuo-ku* ☎ *078/391–4603* 🌐 *www.mouriya.co.jp/en/head/index.html.*

$$$$ STEAKHOUSE 🍴 **Onishi Two** (大西II). Onishi has a well-deserved reputation, both with Japanese locals and longtime foreign residents, for serving fine Kobe beef. Steaks are cooked by master chefs in the middle of an enormous counter around which diners sit. Baseball players and sumo wrestlers are among the celebrity patrons. [$] *Average main: ¥6000* ✉ *3F Kitanofenikusu Bldg., 1–17–6 Nakayamate-dori, Chuo-ku* ☎ *078/332–4029* 💳 *No credit cards* 🕒 *Closed Mon. No lunch.*

$$ INDIAN 🍴 **Raja** (ラジャ). The mellow ambience at Raja is matched by the delicious Indian food. The restaurant is now in its second generation; the friendly owner/chef is the son of the reputed first Indian chef in Kobe. Among the home-style curries and samosas, vegetarians can find something *mecha oishii* (very delicious). Raja attributes the excellence of the tandoori chicken to using the highest grade charcoal available in Japan. It's on the west end of Chinatown, near Moto-machi. Dinner sets start from ¥3,200. [$] *Average main: ¥1500* ✉ *B1F Sanotatsu Bldg., 2–7–4 Sakaemachi-dori, Chuo-ku* ☎ *078/332–5253.*

$$ ECLECTIC 🍴 **Rough Rare** (ラフレア). This funky, laid-back café on two levels attracts a young, stylish clientele. Pasta, burgers, salads, and *omuraisu* (a Japanese omelet filled with ketchup-flavored rice) are served. The food isn't gourmet, but the restaurant is just plain cool. A DJ booth upstairs provides the sound track for special events. [$] *Average main: ¥1800* ✉ *18–2 Akashi-cho, near Daimaru department store, Chuo-ku* ☎ *078/333–0808* 💳 *No credit cards.*

$$$$ CHINESE 🍴 **Totenkaku Royal Chinese Restaurant** (東天閣). This place has been famous since 1945 for its Peking duck, flown in fresh from China. Built at the turn of the 20th century, Totenkaku is in one of Kobe's historic homes. With tall ceilings, red carpets, luxurious curtains, and artwork from China, the dining room itself is worth a look. You can keep the price down by ordering one of the reasonably priced noodle specialties, or by enjoying a set lunch menu for just ¥2,500. [$] *Average main: ¥10000* ✉ *3–14–18 Yamamoto-dori, Chuo-ku* ☎ *078/231–1351.*

$$$$ STEAKHOUSE Fodor's Choice ★ 🍴 **Wakkoqu** (和黒). At this elegant dining room, the excellent Kobe beef is sliced thin and cooked before you on a teppanyaki grill along with fresh vegetables and served with pepper, mustard, and soy sauce for dipping. Wakkoqu uses meat from three-year-old cows that have never been bred, which is said to be the reason for its unbelievable tenderness. Lunch set menus start at ¥3,000 and go up to ¥5,500. The pricier

option uses the highest-quality meat, a small but noticeable difference. $ *Average main: ¥5000* ✉ *Hillside Terrace Bldg. 1F, 1–22–13 Naka-yamate-dori, Chuo-ku* ☎ *078/222–0678.*

WHERE TO STAY

Kobe is an industrialized city that caters to business travelers. There are many comfortable, well-situated business hotels, almost all of which have rooms with basics like air-conditioning, private bath, and TV.

$$$$
HOTEL
Fodor's Choice
★

ANA Crowne Plaza Hotel Kobe (クラウンプラザアナ神戸). One of the tallest buildings in Kobe, this stunning luxury hotel stands out at night when its brightly lighted tower points heavenward. **Pros:** nice views of the city; connected to Shin-Kobe Station; free in-room Wi-Fi. **Cons:** one of the city's pricer options. $ *Rooms from: ¥30000* ✉ *Kitano-cho, 1-chome, 1 Kitano-cho, Chuo-ku* ☎ *078/291–1121* ⊕ *www.anacrowneplaza-kobe.jp/en* ⊅ *580 rooms, 12 suites* ❍ *No meals.*

$$$
HOTEL

Hotel Monterey Kobe (ホテルモントレー神戸). It was modeled after a monastery in Florence, so it's no surprise that the Hotel Monterey has continental furnishings in the stylish rooms and fountains gushing in the Mediterranean-style courtyard. **Pros:** European style; great location; free in-room Wi-Fi. **Cons:** not a very Japanese experience. $ *Rooms from: ¥20000* ✉ *2–11–13 Shimoyamate-dori, Chuo-ku* ☎ *078/392–7111* ⊕ *www.hotelmonterey.co.jp/kobe/* ⊅ *164 rooms* ❍ *No meals.*

$$$$
HOTEL

Hotel Okura Kobe (ホテルオークラ神戸). Rising 35 stories over Meriken Park, this is one of the city's best lodgings. **Pros:** high level of customer service; choice of Western or Japanese rooms; great views. **Cons:** the extras are pricey. $ *Rooms from: ¥35000* ✉ *Meriken Koen, 2–1 Hatoba-cho, Chuo-ku* ☎ *078/333–0111* ⊕ *www.kobe.hotelokura.co.jp* ⊅ *457 Western-style rooms, 5 Japanese-style rooms, 12 suites* ❍ *No meals.*

$$
HOTEL

Hotel Piena Kobe. With its excellent staff, comfortable rooms, and award-winning breakfasts, Hotel Piena is a step above other mid-range business hotels in downtown Kobe. **Pros:** excellent location for sightseeing in Kobe; award-winning breakfasts. **Cons:** rooms are smaller than higher-end hotels; though spotless, the rooms feel a bit dated. $ *Rooms from: ¥15000* ✉ *4–20–5 Ninomiya-cho, Chuo-ku* ☎ *078/241–1010* ⊕ *www.piena.co.jp* ⊅ *86 rooms, 4 suites* ❍ *No meals* Ⓜ *Sannomiya Station or Shin-Kobe Station.*

$$$$
HOTEL

Portopia Hotel (ポートピアホテル). A huge hotel with every imaginable amenity, the sleek Portopia Hotel rises high above the city. **Pros:** lots of facilities; sweeping views; close to the airport. **Cons:** a little dated; not convenient for downtown sightseeing. $ *Rooms from: ¥35000* ✉ *6–10–1 Minatojima Naka-machi, Chuo-ku* ☎ *078/302–1111* ⊕ *www.portopia.co.jp* ⊅ *745 rooms* ❍ *No meals.*

$
HOTEL

Superhotel Kobe (スーパーホテル神戸). This budget-friendly business hotel has just two set prices—one for singles and one for doubles. **Pros:** bargain prices; central location. **Cons:** small rooms; narrow beds. $ *Rooms from: ¥7000* ✉ *2–1–11 Kano-cho, Chuo-ku* ☎ *078/261–9000* ⊕ *www.superhoteljapan.com/en/s-hotels/kobe.html* ⊅ *87 rooms* ❍ *No meals.*

8

NIGHTLIFE

Kobe's compactness is an advantage—virtually all the best bars are within walking distance of each other. Kobe is regarded as the center of Japan's thriving jazz scene.

Booze Up Bar (ブーズアップ). This place feels like you've stepped into a Quentin Tarantino movie. Even the sound track is right: soul and funk LPs are artfully blended one to the other on dual turntables. Tasty pizzas and pastas are served up alongside good cocktails. Can ya dig it? It's northwest of Tokyu Hands department store. ⊠ *2–15–3 Shimoyamate-dori, Chuo-ku* ☎ *078/322–2873.*

Polo Dog (ポロドッグ). This place is regularly packed with foreigners, both longtime residents and travelers just passing through. It usually has live music on weekends, when the place can get loud. The bar serves burgers, salads, and excellent garlic french fries. It's arrayed with '50s and '60s Americana and is known for having the cheapest drinks in town. ⊠ *2F K Bldg., 1–3–21 San-no-miya-cho, 1 street south of Center Gai, near Flower Rd., Chuo-ku* ☎ *078/331–3945* ⊕ *www.polodog.net/contents/en/index.html.*

Sone (ソネ). The city's most famous jazz club has been run by the Sone family since 1961. There are four sets of live music every night, starting at 6:50, and the action often centers on a jazz trio with a guest vocalist. Spacious and relaxed, the place serves pizza, pasta, and salads. There's a cover charge of ¥1,140 (occasionally a bit more depending on the band). ⊠ *1–24–10 Nakayamate-dori, Chuo-ku* ☎ *078/221–2055* ⊕ *kobe-sone.com.*

SHOPPING

SHOPPING AREAS

Kobe's historic shopping area is known as **Moto-machi.** It extends west for 2 km (1 mile) from JR Moto-machi Station. Much of the district is under a covered arcade, which starts opposite the Daimaru department store and runs just north of Nankin-machi. Moto-machi is more of a functional shopping area, selling housewares (including antiques), imported foods, and electronics, with restaurants scattered between.

Nearly connected to the Moto-machi arcade, the **San-no-miya Center Gai** arcade extends from the department store Sogo to the Moto-machi area for 1 km (½ mile). Because it's next to San-no-miya Station, this is a good stop for a bite to eat. Center Gai has a hipper vibe than the Moto-machi district. Next to Sogo is a branch of the Loft department store, home to crafts and lifestyle accessories spread over four floors. The building also houses a branch of the Kinokuniya bookstore, which has a small English-language selection.

Piazza Kobe and **Motoko Town** make up the narrow shopping district running under the JR train tracks from San-no-miya to Moto-machi. The shops range from Italian leather shoes and handmade accessories to Chinese apothecaries and small electronics. Not for the claustrophobic, it is an excellent chance to see Japan living up to its reputation of making use of every last inch of space.

The Crowne Plaza Kobe is one of the tallest buildings in town.

DOLLS

Sakae-ya Doll Store (栄屋人形材料店 *Sakae-ya Ninngyo Zairyou-ten*). This store sells traditional Japanese dolls, from *kimekomi* (animals representing the zodiac calendar) to the samurai and kimono-clad ladies. There are also good examples of *oshie* (three-dimensional pictures made of silk). The tiny shop is packed with cloth for doll making, cupboards for hiding doll-making supplies, and, of course, dolls. ⊠ *5-8–5 Motomachi-dori, Chuo-ku* ☎ *078/341–1307* ☿ *Tues.–Sun. 10–5:30.*

GLASS

Tor Deco (トアデコ). This Tor Road boutique specializes in beautiful handcrafted glass items. It features the work of artisans from around the country, each with their own unique style. ⊠ *2-4–12 Nakayamate-dori, Chuo-ku* ☎ *078/322–0468* ⊕ *www.tor-deco.com* ☿ *Thurs.–Tues. 10–8.*

JEWELRY, CERAMICS, AND LACQUERWARE

Kinoshita Pearl (木下真珠). Established in 1938, this small boutique offers unique designs and quality service. Although the shop offers many classic designs, it has a range of more modern pearl jewelry as well. ⊠ *1-1–7 Yamamoto-dori, Chuo-ku* ☎ *078/221–3170* ⊕ *www.kinoshitapearl. co.jp* ☿ *Thurs.–Tues. 10–6.*

Fodor's Choice
★

Nanae (奈々重). This darling and inexpensive antiques shop in Kitano-cho has a large collection of high-quality *yukata* (lightweight summer kimonos) that you can try on. There's also a good selection of ceramics and lacquerware. Nanae, the owner, enjoys explaining the history behind the pieces. ✉ *1F Kurata Bldg., 2–14–26 Yamamoto-dori, Chuo-ku* ☎ *078/222–8565* ⊕ *www.antiquenanae.com/* ⊗ *Daily 10:30–7.*

> ## BOUTIQUE ROW
>
> Kobe's trendy crowd shops in the exclusive stores on **Tor Road**, which stretches north–south on a tree-lined slope into Kitano-cho. Fashionable boutiques selling Japanese designer brands and imported goods alternate with chic cafés and restaurants. The side streets are fun to poke about.

Naniwa-ya Shikki Store (浪花屋漆器店). This store sells excellent Japanese lacquerware at reasonable prices. It has been in operation since before World War I. ✉ *4–3–8 Motomachi-dori, Chuo-ku* ☎ *078/341–6367* ⊗ *Thurs.–Tues. 11–6.*

Tasaki Shinju (田崎真珠). This shop not only sells pearls but also exhibits astounding works of "pearl" art, including a model of the Akashi Kaikyo Bridge and a rooster with an impossibly long tail. ✉ *Tasaki Bldg., 6–3–2 Minatojima Nakamachi, Chuo-ku* ☎ *078/303–7667* ⊗ *Daily 9–6.*

MALLS

Santica Town (さんちかタウン). Santica Town is an underground shopping mall with 120 shops and 30 restaurants. It extends for several blocks beneath Flower Road south from San-no-miya Station. It's closed the third Wednesday of the month. ✉ *1–10–1 San-no-miya, Chuo-ku* ⊗ *Daily 10–8.*

WESTERN HONSHU

WELCOME TO WESTERN HONSHU

TOP REASONS TO GO

★ **Photogenic icons:** Beside Miyajima, the O-torii rises from the Inland Sea. An hour from Matsue is the austere Izumo Taisha, a Shinto shrine reputed to ensure marital happiness.

★ **Fabulous seafood:** Oysters (kaki) in Hiroshima; anago (conger eel) in Miyajima; uni-don (sea urchin over rice) in Hagi; mamakari (a sardinelike fish) in Kurashiki; and little black shijimi clams in Matsue.

★ **Lessons of the past:** Although A-Bomb Dome in Hiroshima is held in great reverence, the city has embraced the future with its energetic multinational vibe.

★ **Gardens:** Okayama is home to one of Japan's top three gardens, the spacious and lush Korakuen, which surrounds the stunning black U-jo, or "Crow Castle."

★ **The people:** Though English is not widely spoken and foreigners may draw stares, locals will go above and beyond to help puzzled tourists.

1 San-yo. San-yo comprises the sunny southern coastline of western Honshu; the region's major cities are Okayama and Hiroshima. Though the entire stretch is heavily populated and industrialized, bright spots worth a look are Kurashiki, Okayama, and Miyajima, near Hiroshima.

2 San-in. Remote as it is, a trip through the surreal landscape of San-in may come closest to providing the best of what Japan has to offer. Romantic destinations worth some extra travel time include the hidden hamlets of Hagi and Tsuwano, and the enchanting lakeside city of Matsue.

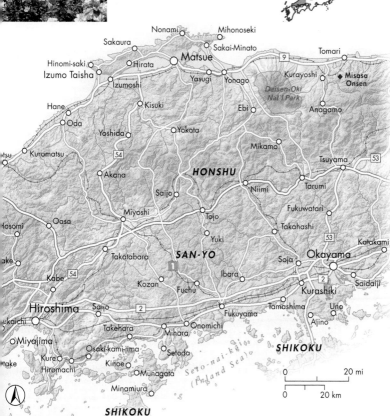

Nonami
Mihonoseki
Sakaura
Sakai-Minato
Tomari
Hinomi-saki
Izumo Taisha
Hirata
Matsue
9
Kurayoshi
Misasa Onsen
Izumoshi
Yasugi
Yonago
Daisen-Oki Nat'l Park
Hane
Kisuki
Ebi
Anagamo
Oda
Yoshida
Yokota
Mikamo
tsu
Kuromatsu
54
Tsuyama
53
Akana
Saijo
Niimi
Tarumi

HONSHU

Fukuwatari

Miyoshi
Tojo
Takahashi
osomi
Oasa
Yuki
53
Katakami
ake
Takatabara
SAN-YO
Soja
Okayama
Kabe
54
Kozan
Ibara
2
Saidaiji
Hiroshima
Saijo
Fuchu
Kurashiki
ukaichi
2
Fukuyama
Tamashima
Uno
Takehara
Onomichi
Ajino
Miyajima
Mihara
SHIKOKU
take
Osaki-kami-jima
Setoda
Kure
Kinoe
Se-to-nai-kaio
Hiromachi
Munagata
(Inland Sea)
Minamiura

9

0   20 mi

0   20 km

SHIKOKU

ka

Towa

GETTING ORIENTED

Western Honshu is bisected by a chain of picturesque, rugged mountains called the Chugoku San-chi. These mountains run east–west,

making north–south travel a difficult proposition. Keep in mind that travel along the north coast, or San-in, is incredibly slow—local trains still plod from village to village—so if you are pressed for time to get to Hagi or Tsuwano, use Yamaguchi as your base; for Matsue, Kurashiki and Okayama work best.

Updated by
Robert Morel

Like disparate siblings, the two coasts of western Honshu have distinctly different personalities. Taken together, they embody the ancient and modern—those two seemingly bipolar time frames that exist in a more profound juxtaposition in Japan than perhaps in any other country in the world.

While the southern coast, or San-yo, has basically gone along with Japan's full-steam-ahead efforts to set the pace for the developed world, you can still encounter pockets of dramatic old-world charm among the modern and shockingly new. The San-in coast, on the other hand, has largely escaped the scourge of overdevelopment, yet you may be surprised to learn that everything you'd want in a city can be found up there, concentrated in and around lovely Matsue.

Happily, neither coast is short on history, religious significance, scenic beauty, or culinary delights. Hiroshima survived one of history's most horrible events to become a lively, famously friendly, forward-looking city. Kurashiki has a remarkably preserved old-style district that can whisk you back to Edo times with a stroll down willow-draped canals and stylishly tiled warehouses. Hagi is a scenic bayside town that for 500 years has been the center of Hagi-yaki ceramics, coveted light-color and smooth-texture earthenware glazed with mysteriously translucent milky colors.

⇨ *See the glossary at the end of this book for definitions of the common Japanese words and suffixes used in this chapter.*

WESTERN HONSHU PLANNER

Travel along San-yo is easy, and the weather is usually mild. Coming from Tokyo or Osaka, Okayama and Kurashiki are natural first stops and gateways to the larger region. If you seek adventure along San-in, budget time for slow trains, layovers, incomplete or changeable information, and the like. It is possible to get from Yamaguchi up to Matsue in a harried day, but you'll have more fun if you take a couple of days or more.

WHEN TO GO

San-yo is the sunniest region in Japan, and almost any time is a good time to visit. The northern shore, or San-in, does get a strong dose of winter, but the reward is a wonderfully long, delightful spring. Like most of Japan, western Honshu gets oppressively muggy by midsummer, but the wind off the Nihon-kai cools the San-in coast. Summer festivals and autumn colors are spectacular throughout the region, and these always attract many tourists; reserve well ahead if you are traveling then.

GETTING HERE AND AROUND

AIR TRAVEL

Hiroshima Airport is the region's major airport, with many daily flights to Haneda Airport in Tokyo and direct daily flights to Kagoshima, Okinawa, Sendai, and Sapporo. Other airports in western Honshu—at Izumo, Tottori, and Yonago—have daily flights to Tokyo. ANA flies to Iwami Airport, which serves Hagi, Tsuwano, and Masuda, to Tokyo and Osaka.

BOAT AND FERRY TRAVEL

Hiroshima is a ferry hub. Setonaikai Kisen runs eight boats daily to Miyajima (¥1,850 one-way) as well as regular and high-speed ferries to Matsuyama. (regular ¥3,600; high-speed ¥7,100).

Contact Setonaikai Kisen (瀬戸内海汽船). ✉ *1–12–23 Ujinakaigan, Minami-ku* ☏ *082/253–1212* ⊕ *www.setonaikaikisen.co.jp/language/en.*

BUS TRAVEL

You won't likely need highway buses, except for making the one-hour run between Yamaguchi and Hagi (knocking three hours off the train-travel time). Two companies operate bus routes: JR and Bocho bus lines. Japan Rail Passes are only valid for use on the JR buses.

Contact Bocho Bus Center (防長バス). ☏ *0856/72–0272.*

CAR TRAVEL

All the major cities and most of the towns listed here will have at least a basic choice of car-rental outlets. If you know a little Japanese and can handle both middle-of-nowhere navigation and hectic urban traffic situations, you might consider renting a car and exploring western Honshu at your own pace—but you'll also need a good Japanese map atlas or GPS in your car.

TRAIN TRAVEL

By far the easiest way to travel to western Honshu and along its southern shore is by Shinkansen from Tokyo, Kyoto, and Osaka. Major bullet train stops are Okayama, Hiroshima, and Shin-Yamaguchi. It takes approximately four hours to travel to Hiroshima from Tokyo, and less than half that from Osaka.

JR express trains run along the San-yo and San-in coasts, making a loop beginning and ending in Kyoto. Crossing from one coast to the other in western Honshu requires traveling fairly slowly through the mountains.

Local trains and buses run between major towns on the San-in coast, but still nowhere near as often or as quickly as in San-yo. It is always advisable to reserve seats on the popular routes between big cities and to holiday destinations during peak season. Most stations now have tourist offices with English speakers that can help with this.

RESTAURANTS

Western Honshu is one of the best regions to sample local Japanese seafood, with regional specialties from the Nihon-kai (Japan Sea) and Seto Nai-kai (Inland Sea). The oysters in Hiroshima, sea eel on Miyajima, and sashimi and sushi on the San-in coast are all superb. Matsue's location means that a variety of both freshwater and saltwater fish are available. Most reasonably priced restaurants have a visual display of the menu in the window, if not photos on the menu pages. If you cannot order in Japanese and no English is spoken, you can always lead the waiter to the window display and point. If you're adventurous, it is always fun to ask, "*Osusume?*," which means "What do you recommend?"

HOTELS

Accommodations cover a broad spectrum, from pensions and *minshuku* (private residences that rent rooms) to large, modern resort hotels that have little character but all the facilities you'd expect of an international chain. Large city and resort hotels have Western and Japanese restaurants. In summer or on holiday weekends hotel reservations are necessary. Unless otherwise noted, rooms have private baths, air-conditioning, and basic TV service.

For a short course on accommodations in Japan, see Lodging in Travel Smart. Hotel reviews have been shortened. For full information, visit Fodors.com.

WHAT IT COSTS IN YEN			
	$	$$	$$$	$$$$
Restaurants	under ¥1,000	¥1,000–¥2,000	¥2,001–¥3,000	over ¥3,000
Hotels	under ¥12,000	¥12,000–¥18,000	¥18,001–¥22,000	over ¥22,000

Restaurant prices are the average cost of a main course at dinner or, if dinner is not served, at lunch. Hotel prices are the lowest cost of a standard double room in high season.

VISITOR INFORMATION

Most major towns and nowadays even the small ones have tourist information centers that offer free maps and brochures. They can also help you secure accommodations. Except for the internationally known places, though, you should not assume that extensive English is spoken.

SAN-YO REGION 山陽地方

San-yo means "sunny side of the mountain range," and the southern region along the Inland Sea is celebrated for its mild, clear climate. Although it's highly developed, to say the least, and you can't see or appreciate much of its beauty from the train or the highway, it's wonderfully easy to stop and get a closer look at it.

OKAYAMA 岡山

672 km (418 miles) west of Tokyo, 188 km (117 miles) southeast of Matsue.

The city of Okayama claims to have the most sunny days in Japan, and the disposition of the locals tends to reflect this. A beautiful black castle is set amid a spacious and luxuriant garden, justly rated among Japan's top three castles.

GETTING HERE AND AROUND

The JR Shinkansen will whisk you away from Tokyo to Okayama in 3 hours, 25 minutes (¥17,340), or from Matsue you can reach the city in 2 hours, 34 minutes by JR Yakumo Express (¥6,030).

Hop on one of the frequent streetcars plying Momotaro-dori, the main boulevard heading east from the Shinkansen Station (¥100) to get around town. To get to the castle, park, and museums ride three stops east and walk southeast. For ¥560 you can buy a combined park-castle admission ticket.

The Shinkansen Station makes Okayama an attractive base for visiting the historic charms of Kurashiki—only a 20-minute local JR train hop to the west (11 minutes by express train).

Should you need a map of Okayama or city information, head to the Tourist Information Office in the underground shopping center to the right of the JR Station's East Exit.

ESSENTIALS

Visitor Information Okayama Tourist Information Office
(岡山市観光案内所 *Okayama Kanko Annai-jo*). ⊠ *JR Station 2F, South Exit, 1–1 Ekimoto-machi* ☎ *086/222–2912.*

EXPLORING

Korakuen (後楽園 *Korakuen Garden*). One of the country's finest gardens, Korakuen has charming tea arbors, green lawns, ponds, and hills that were created at the turn of the 18th century on the banks of the Asahi-gawa. Maple, apricot, and cherry trees give the 32-acre park plenty of flowers and shade. The riverside setting, with Okayama-jo in the background, is delightful. The garden's popularity increases in peak season (April to August), but this is one of the country's largest parks, so you won't feel hemmed in by crowds. Bus 20 (¥160) from Platform 2 in front of the JR Station goes directly to Korakuen. ⊠ *1–5 Korakuen* ☎ *086/272–1148* ⊕ *www.okayama-korakuen.jp* ⊴ *¥400* ☉ *Apr.–Sept., daily 7:30–6; Oct.–Mar., daily 8–5.*

Museum of Oriental Art (岡山市立オリエント美術館 *Orient Bijutsukan*). On display at any time are at least 2,000 items from an impressive collection. Special exhibitions vary, but they generally show how Middle Eastern art reached ancient Japan via the Silk Road, and items range from Persian glass goblets to ornate mirrors to early stringed instruments. To reach the museum from the JR Station, take the streetcar (¥140) bound for Higashiyama directly north for 10 minutes. The museum is across Asahi-gawa from Korakuen (about a 10-minute

The Koraku Garden in Okayama was built in the early 18th century.

walk). ✉ *9–32 Tenjin-cho* ☎ *086/232–3636* ⊕ *www.orientmuseum.jp* 💴 *¥300* ⊘ *Tues.–Sun. 9–5.*

Okayama-jo (岡山城 *Okayama Castle*). Painted a shadowy shade of black and set off dramatically by lead tiles and contrasting white vertical-slat shutters, Okayama's castle is known locally as U-jo (Crow Castle). Though it was built in the 16th century, only the "moon-viewing" outlying tower survived World War II. A replica was painstakingly constructed in 1966. The middle floors now house objects that represent the region's history, including a collection of armor and swords and a palanquin you can climb into to have your photo taken. Unlike many other castles with great views, this one has an elevator to take you up the six floors. A five-minute walk across the bridge brings you from the South Exit of Korakuen to the castle. Boats are available for rent on the river below. ✉ *2–3–1 Marunouchi* ☎ *086/225–2096* ⊕ *www.okayama-kanko.net/ujo/index.html* 💴 *¥300* ⊘ *Daily 9–5.*

WHERE TO EAT AND STAY

$$$ ✗ **Art Dining Musashi** (アートダイニング武蔵). You'll find healthful, veg-
JAPANESE etable-laden Okayama-style cuisine at this delightful eatery. For lunch we recommend the unbeatable *bara-zushi teishoku,* or bits and pieces of sushi with vegetables, a feast for only ¥1,050. Musashi is a seven-minute walk straight out along the boulevard from the East Exit of JR Okayama Station, on the left just past 7-Eleven. ⓢ *Average main: ¥3000* ✉ *1–7–18 Nodaya-cho* ☎ *086/222–3893* ⊘ *Closed Sun.*

$$$$ 🏨 **Hotel Granvia Okayama** (ホテルグランヴィア岡山). Bright white marble
HOTEL and richly stained wood dominate the lobby at this large, luxurious hotel, a comfortable base for exploring the area. **Pros:** best location

in town; posh rooms; nice breakfast included. **Cons:** pool and other amenities cost extra; be careful with the in-room bar—don't move a thing unless you mean to buy it. $\boxed{S}$ *Rooms from: ¥30,000* ✉ *1–5 Eki-moto-machi , Kita-ku* ☎ *086/234–7000* ⤴ *323 Western-style rooms, 3 Western-style suites, 2 Japanese-style suites* ⦿ *Breakfast.*

KURASHIKI 倉敷

749 km (465 miles) west of Tokyo, 196 km (122 miles) west of Shin-Osaka.

From the 17th through the 19th century, this vital shipping port supplied Osaka with cotton, textiles, sugar, reeds, and rice. Today Kurashiki thrives on income from tourism. If your views were limited to what you see just outside the station, you'd be forgiven for thinking Kurashiki is just another overindustrialized modern Japanese city. We strongly recommend, however, walking 10 minutes southeast of the station to Bikan Chiku, a neighborhood of canals, bridges, shops, restaurants, ryokans, and museums.

You can see most of Kurashiki's sights in a day, but it's worth staying longer, perhaps in a splendid old ryokan, to fully appreciate the time-machine aspect of the place. The Bikan district is artfully lighted up at night, and a stroll down the willow-draped canals after a sumptuous meal can be an unforgettably romantic journey. The town also makes a convenient base for trips to Hiroshima (1 hour; ¥6,550) and Himeji (49 minutes; ¥4,190). Note that virtually the entire town shuts down on Monday.

GETTING HERE AND AROUND
Kurashiki is 3 hours, 50 minutes west of Tokyo or 1 hour west of Shin-Osaka by the Shinkansen and San-yo Line. In town, you can stroll leisurely through the streets taking in the scenery.

Kurashiki Tourist Information Office, outside the South Exit of the train station, has a knowledgeable staff that provides useful maps and information. There's a branch in the Bikan district a block past the Ohara Art Museum. It sells ¥300 tickets for the 20-minute canal-boat tours (summer only).

ESSENTIALS
Kurashiki Tourist Information Office (倉敷市観光案内所 *Kurashiki-shi Kanko Annnai-jo).* ✉ *Kurashiki City-Plaza 2F, 1–7–2 Achi* ☎ *086/424–1770* ◷ *Apr.–Oct., daily 9–6; Nov.–Mar., daily 9–5:15.*

EXPLORING
Kurashiki Museum of Folkcraft (倉敷民芸館 *Kurashiki Mingei-kan).* Founded in 1936, the Museum of Folkcraft highlights the beauty of traditional objects used in everyday life. Housed in a series of 18th-century storefronts, the atmosphere perfectly suits the many wooden, ceramic, and lacquerware objects on display. There are no detailed descriptions in English, but the elegance of the pieces on display speaks for itself. ✉ *1–4–11 Chuo* ☎ *086/422–1637* ⊕ *kurashiki-mingeikan. com* ⛌ *¥700* ◷ *Tues.–Sun. 9–5.*

Ohara Art Museum (大原美術館 *Ohara Bijutsukan*). In 1930, noted art collector and founder Magosaburo Ohara built this Parthenon-style building to house a collection of Western art with works by El Greco, Corot, Manet, Monet, Rodin, Gauguin, Picasso, Toulouse-Lautrec, and many others. They were shrewdly acquired for him by his friend Kojima Torajiro, a talented artist whom he dispatched to Europe for purchases. The museum is wonderfully compact and can be appreciated in a single morning or an afternoon. Two wings exhibit Japanese paintings, tapestries, wood-block prints, and pottery—including works by Shoji Hamada and Bernard Leach—as well as modern and ancient Asian art, much of it also brought home from trips made by Torajiro at Ohara's behest. The adjoining Kogei-kan (crafts hall) displays a selection of ceramic and textile art and is housed in a beautiful Edo-era storehouse. ⊠ *1–1–15 Chuo* ☎ *086/422–0005* ⊕ *www.ohara.or.jp* ⬛ *¥1,300* ⊗ *Tues.–Sun. 9–5.*

WHERE TO EAT

$$$
JAPANESE

✕**Hamayoshi** (浜吉). Three tables and a counter make up this intimate restaurant specializing in fish from the Seto Nai-kai. Sushi is one option; another is *mamakari*, a kind of vinegary sashimi sliced from a small fish caught in the Inland Sea. Other delicacies are *shako-ebi*, or mantis-shrimp, and lightly grilled *anago*, or sea eel. No English is spoken, but an English menu is available and the owner is happy to help you order and instruct you on how to enjoy the chef's delicacies. Hamayoshi is on the main street leading from the station, just before the Kurashiki Kokusai Hotel. Unlike many restaurants here, it's open on holidays. $ *Average main: ¥3000* ⊠ *2–19–30 Achi* ☎ *050/5868–7144* ⊗ *Closed Mon.*

$$$
STEAKHOUSE

✕**Kiyu-tei** (亀遊亭). For the best, and most reasonably priced grilled steak in town, come to this attractive Kurashiki-style restaurant, established in 1909. The entrance is through a nearly hidden courtyard behind a gate across the street from the entrance to the Ohara Art Museum. $ *Average main: ¥2800* ⊠ *1–2–20 Chuo* ☎ *086/422–5140* ⊗ *Closed Mon.*

$$
JAPANESE

✕**KuShuKuShu (9494)** (くしゅくしゅ). You'll be happy to find this lively little *izakaya* (traditional restaurant), a Kurashiki favorite for more than 20 years. Cool music and loud laughter can be heard from here when everything else on the street is locked up tight. Unwind to an eclectic mix of traditional white stucco, black wooden beams, bright lights, and jazz. Though the staff doesn't speak English, an English menu is available. Scores of tasty snacks, such as grilled meats or cheese and salami plates are paired with low-priced beer and sake. It's tucked along the east side of the covered Ebisu-dori shopping arcade halfway between the station and Kanryu-ji. $ *Average main: ¥1800* ⊠ *2–16–41 Achi* ☎ *086/421–0949* ▭ *No credit cards* ⊗ *No lunch.*

WHERE TO STAY

$$
HOTEL

⊡**Kurashiki Kokusai Hotel** (倉敷国際ホテル). The town's oldest Western-style hotel welcomes guests with a black-tile lobby and dramatic Japanese wood-block prints. **Pros:** location is near the good stuff; welcoming atmosphere; capable staff. **Cons:** not on the old canals; needs some renovations. $ *Rooms from: ¥18000* ⊠ *1–1–44 Chuo* ☎ *086/422–5141*

🌐 *www.kurashiki-kokusai-hotel.co.jp* 🛏 *106 Western-style rooms, 4 Japanese-style rooms* 🍴 *No meals.*

$$$$ B&B/INN Fodor's Choice ★ 🏨 **Ryokan Kurashiki** (旅館倉敷). If you're going to splurge for a luxury ryokan, this is the place. **Pros:** the feel of a luxury hotel; excellent food; lots of antiques and period pieces. **Cons:** not the "pure" ryokan experience some travelers are seeking; Kurashiki's most expensive lodging. $ *Rooms from: ¥60000* ✉ *4–1 Hon-machi* ☎ *086/422–0730* 🌐 *www.ryokan-kurashiki.jp* 🛏 *5 rooms* 🍴 *Some meals.*

$$$$ B&B/INN 🏨 **Ryori-Ryokan Tsurugata** (料理旅館鶴形). Treat yourself to a stay—or perhaps just a fantastic dinner—at this charming ryokan built in 1774. **Pros:** a great value; steeped in tradition; some rooms have private baths. **Cons:** books up quickly; a slower pace than most Westerners expect. $ *Rooms from: ¥33000* ✉ *1–3–15 Chuo* ☎ *086/424–1635* 🛏 *11 Japanese-style rooms, 3 with bath* 🍴 *Some meals.*

$ HOTEL 🏨 **Toyoko Inn Kurashiki Station South Exit** (東横イン倉敷駅南口 *Toyoko Inn Kurashiki-eki Manimi-guchi*). This reasonably priced hotel is one of Kurashiki's most popular, as it offers basic, reliably comfortable rooms at a great value. **Pros:** great location; free breakfast; free Internet. **Cons:** not directly in the old town. $ *Rooms from: ¥7500* ✉ *2–10–20 Achi* ☎ *086/430–1045* 🌐 *www.toyoko-inn.com* 🛏 *154 rooms* 🍴 *Breakfast.*

HIROSHIMA 広島

342 km (213 miles) west of Shin-Osaka, 864 km (537 miles) from Tokyo.

On August 6, 1945, at 8:15 am, a massive chunk of metal known as *Little Boy* fell from an American plane, and the sky ignited and glowed for an instant. In that brief moment, however, it became as hot as the surface of the sun in Hiroshima, until then a rather ordinary workaday city in wartime Japan. Half the city was leveled by the resulting blast, and the rest was set ablaze. Rain impregnated with radioactive fallout then fell, killing many that the fire and 1,000-mph shock wave had not. By the end of this mind-boggling disaster, more than 140,000 people died.

Modern Hiroshima's Peace Memorial Park 平和記念公園 (*Heiwa Kinen Koen*) is at the northern point of the triangle formed by two of Hiroshima's rivers, the Ota-gawa (also called Hon-kawa) and Motoyasu-gawa. Monuments to that day abound in the park, but only one original site bears witness to that enormous release of atomic energy 70 years ago: the A-Bomb Dome. Its gloomy shadows are now surrounded by a vibrant, rebuilt city. As if to show just how earnestly Hiroshima has redefined itself, only a short walk to the east is Nagarekawa-cho, the city's most raucous nightlife district.

GETTING HERE AND AROUND

The streetcar (tram) is an easy form of transport in Hiroshima. Enter the middle door and take a ticket from the automatic dispenser. Pay the driver at the front door when you leave. All fares within city limits are ¥10. A one-day pass is ¥600, available for purchase at the platform outside JR Hiroshima Station. There are seven streetcar lines; four depart from the JR Station. Stops are announced by a recording, and each stop has a sign in *romaji* (romanized Japanese) posted on the platform.

Buses also joust with the traffic on Hiroshima's hectic streets; the basic fare is ¥200. Information in English can be gathered at any of the Hiroshima Tourist Information Offices. The Hiroshima Bus Company's red-and-white Bus 24 to Heiwa Koen leaves you only a two-minute walk to the Peace Memorial Museum.

Taxis can be hailed throughout the city. Look for cabs that have the "空車" light illuminated, indicating they are ready to pick up passengers. The fare for the first 1½ km (1 mile) is ¥620, then ¥70 for every 328 yards. Special sightseeing taxis are available in front of the Shinkansen entrance of the train station. A three-hour tour runs approximately ¥13,000.

Two excellent, English-speaking Tourist Information Offices are in JR Hiroshima Station, both on the first floor at the southern and northern exits. The main tourist office, the Rest House in Peace Memorial Park, sits between the Children's Peace Monument and the Flame of Peace.

ESSENTIALS

Internet Futaba @ Café GIGA. ⊠ *Hiroshima Eki-Mae, 2–22 Matsubara-cho, Minami-ku* ☎ *082/568–4792.*

Visitor Information Hiroshima Tourist Information Office (広島観光案内所 *Hiroshima Kanko Annai-jo).* ⊠ *JR Hiroshima Station, Shinkansen Exit, 2F, 2–37 Matsubara-cho, Minami-ku* ☎ *082/263–6822.*
Rest House in Peace Memorial Park (広島市レストハウス *Hiroshima-shi resuto hausu).* ⊠ *1–1 Nakajima-cho, Naka-ku* ☎ *082/247–6738.*

TOURS

A number of sightseeing tours are available, including tours of Hiroshima and cruises on the Seto Nai-kai, in particular to Miyajima, the island with the famous tidal-basin torii.

Hiroshima Bus Company (広島バス). If you want to see the sights, a 4-hour, 40-minute tour of the city's major sights costs ¥3,500. Tours leave at 9 am and 2 pm. An eight-hour tour of both the city and Miyajima costs ¥9,470 and leaves at 9:30 am. You depart from in front of Hiroshima Station's Shinkansen entrance. All tours are in Japanese, but the sights are foreigner-friendly. ☎ *082/545–7950* ⊠ *From ¥3,500.*

EXPLORING

Fodor's Choice ★ **A-Bomb Dome** (原爆ドーム *Gembaku Domu).* This ruin is a poignant symbol of man's self-destructiveness. It was the city's old Industrial Promotion Hall, and it stands in stark contrast to the new Hiroshima, which hums along close by. Despite being directly below the bomb blast, the building did not collapse into rubble like the rest of the city. Eerie, twisted, and charred, the iron-and-concrete dome has stood darkly brooding next to the river, basically untouched since that horrible morning. The sad old building's foreboding, derelict appearance can be emotionally overwhelming. The site is just outside the official northeast boundary of Peace Memorial Park. Take Streetcar 2 or 6 from Hiroshima Station to the Gembaku-Domu-mae stop. ⊠ *North of Heiwa Kinen Koen.*

Visiting Peace Memorial Park

HISTORY

Before the atomic bomb, the area now home to Peace Park was known as the Nakajima District. Nakajima was a lively, urban center populated by around 6,500 residents. In 1949, it was decided that this area—decimated on account of being so near the bomb's hypocenter—would be reborn as a monument for peace. The park was designed by Kenzo Tange, after his design won in an international architecture competition.

THE ROUTE

The park and surrounding monuments are not structured on a grid. Visitors are welcome to make their own trail and wander off the main paths to explore. The park can be experienced in as little as an hour, with a trip to the Cenotaph, Flame of Peace, and adjoining A-Bomb Dome area, but visitors with more time should take the opportunity to walk a meandering circle around the museum. Visiting the area's nearly 60 monuments can easily fill an afternoon. The park is particularly vivid in the summer, when the oleander flowers—a gift from sister-city Honolulu—are in full bloom.

GETTING HERE

Riding the streetcar from JR Hiroshima Station is an easy way to reach Peace Park. Take the Number 1 tram bound for Hiroshima Port via Kamiyacho, disembarking at Chuden-Mae. From Chuden-Mae, it's a five-minute walk to the front of the Hiroshima Peace Memorial Museum. Riding the Number 2 or 6 tram will also take you to the Genbakudomu-mae stop (in front of the A-Bomb dome). Within the city, streetcar fares are a flat ¥160, payable when you get off.

VISITOR CENTER

The Hiroshima Peace Museum has maps and information for English speakers. International Conference Center Hiroshima, located opposite the museum in the same building, also offers assistance, in addition to English-language newspapers and magazines.

WHAT'S NEARBY

The park is surrounded by a bustling commercial area, with no shortage of restaurants. Indeed, many visitors are surprised to find a regular commercial center so close to Peace Memorial Park. There are also a few tourist-friendly eateries along the riverside, including Kakifune Kawana, a floating restaurant that boasts some of the best oysters in town.

Children's Peace Monument (原爆の子像 *Genbaku-no-ko-zo*). Many consider this the most profound memorial in Peace Memorial Park. The figure is of Sadako, a 10-year-old girl who developed leukemia as a result of exposure to the atomic radiation that lingered long after the blast. She believed that if she could fold 1,000 paper *senbazuru* (cranes)—a Japanese symbol of good fortune and longevity—her illness would be cured. She died before finishing the thousand, and it is said that her schoolmates finished the job for her. Her story has become a folktale of sorts, and it inspired a nationwide paper crane–folding effort among schoolchildren that continues to this day. The colorful chains of paper cranes—delivered daily from schools all over the world—are visually and emotionally striking. ⊠ *Heiwa Kinen Koen.*

Flame of Peace (平和の灯 *Heiwa no Tomoshibi*). Behind the Memorial Cenotaph, this flame will be extinguished only when all atomic weapons are banished. In the meantime, every August 6, the citizens of Hiroshima float paper lanterns down the city's rivers for the repose of the souls of the atomic-bomb victims. ⊠ *Heiwa Kinen Koen.*

Hiroshima Castle (広島城 *Hiroshima-jo*). Hiroshima Castle was originally built by Terumoto Mori on the Ota-gawa delta in 1589. He named the surrounding flatlands *Hiro-Shima*, meaning "wide island," and it stuck. The Imperial Japanese Army used the castle as headquarters in World War II, and with its significant depot of munitions it was one of the targets of the bomb. It was destroyed in the blast. In 1958 the five-story *donjon* (main tower) was rebuilt to its original specifications. Unlike many castles in Japan, it has lots of brown wood paneling that gives it a warm appearance, and it stands in intriguing contrast to the modern city that has evolved around it. The modern interior feels anything but castle-like, but has exhibits from Japan's feudal Edo period (17th–19th century). It's a 15-minute walk north from the A-Bomb Dome. ⊠ *21–1 Moto-machi, Naka-ku* ☎ *082/221–7512* ⊡ *¥370* ☉ *Apr.–Sept., daily 9–5:30; Oct.–Mar., daily 9–4:30.*

FAMILY **Hiroshima Children's Museum** (広島子供文化科学館 *Kodomo Bunka Kagakukan*). The city's hands-on children's museum is a good diversion for the kids. The joyful noise of excited children alleviates the somber mood of Peace Memorial Park. Kids get a kick out of conducting their own science experiments. To get here, leave the Peace Memorial Park via Aioi-bashi at the North Entrance and walk north and east, keeping the river on your left and the baseball stadium on your right. A planetarium is next door. ⊠ *5–83 Moto-machi, Naka-ku* ☎ *082/222–5346* ⊡ *Free; planetarium ¥510* ☉ *Tues.–Sun. 9–5.*

Hiroshima National Peace Memorial Hall for the Atomic Bomb Victims (原爆死没者追悼平和祈念館 *Kokuritsu Hiroshima Hibakusha Tsuito Heiwa Kinen-kan*). The memorial recounts the stories of known victims of the atomic devastation. In addition to the extensive archives of names, a collection of personal photos lends immediacy to one of the most shocking moments in history. A spiraling ramp leads downward to the Hall of Remembrance, a sobering 360-degree panorama of Hiroshima after the war. It is only up close that one sees that the photorealistic view is actually a collage of 140,000 black and white tiles, the number of people estimated to have died in the blast and in the months following. Heartbreaking firsthand accounts and memoirs of survivors are available for viewing. ⊠ *1–6 Nakajima-cho* ☎ *082/543–6271* ⊕ *www.hiro-tsuitokinenkan.go.jp* ⊡ *Free* ☉ *Mar.–July, daily 8:30–6; Aug., daily 8:30–7; Sept.–Nov., daily 8:30–6; Dec.–Feb., daily 8:30–5.*

Fodor's Choice ★ **Hiroshima Peace Memorial Museum** (平和祈念資料館 *Heiwa Kinen Shiryo-kan*). A visit here may be too intense for some, but to appreciate the horror of the bombing and the hope that made Hiroshima into the city it is today, this museum is highly recommended. Displays of models, charred fragments of clothing, melted ceramic tiles, lunch boxes, watches, and shocking photographs tell Hiroshima's story of death and destruction. The heat-ray-photographed human shadow permanently imprinted on granite steps can take you well beyond sadness, and the Dalí-esque watch forever stopped at 8:15 is chilling. Most exhibits have brief explanations in English, and more-detailed information is on the audio tour, which you can rent for ¥150. ■TIP➔ **Starting in spring 2016, the main building is under renovation, with major exhibits moved to the east building.** ✉ *1–2 Nakajima-cho, Naka-ku* ☎ *082/241–4004* ⊕ *www.pcf. city.hiroshima.jp* 🎟 *¥50* ⊙ *Mar.–Nov., daily 8:30–6; Dec.–Feb., daily 8:30–5; last admission 30 mins before museum closes.*

Hiroshima Prefectural Art Museum (広島県立美術館 *Hiroshima Kenritsu Bijutsukan*). Next to the Shukkei Garden, this museum is a visual treat. Standouts include two particularly surrealistic pieces: a typically fantastical piece by Salvador Dalí called *Dream of Venus;* and Ikuo Hirayama's much closer-to-home *Holocaust at Hiroshima*. Hirayama, who became one of Japan's most acclaimed artists, was a junior-high-school student at the time the A-bomb was dropped. The museum also holds excellent rotating exhibitions of art from classic to contemporary. ✉ *2–22 Kaminobori-cho, Naka-ku* ☎ *082/221–6246* ⊕ *www. hpam.jp* 🎟 *¥510* ⊙ *Tues.–Sun. 9–5, Sat. until 7; last entrance 30 mins before closing.*

Hon-dori (本通り). Around Hiroshima's central district are hundreds of shops. Take the tram that runs from the main station to stop T-31, or simply walk east across the north bridge out of Peace Park. The big department stores—Sogo, Fukuya, Tenmaya, and Mitsukoshi—are at the east end of the arcade near the Hatchobori streetcar stop. Many restaurants, including a big, gorgeous Andersen's, a popular bakery chain (one block down on the right from T-31), are also found here. ✉ *Hon-dori.*

Memorial Cenotaph (原爆死没者慰霊碑 *Gembaku Shibotsusha Irei-hi*). Designed by Japanese architect Kenzo Tange, the cenotaph resembles the primitive A-frame houses of Japan's earliest inhabitants. Buried inside is a chest containing the names of those who died in the destruction and aftermath of the atomic bomb. On the exterior is the inscription: "Rest in peace, for the error shall not be repeated." Looking through the Cenotaph at the Flame of Peace at night, after the sun has set and crowds have gone home, is an eerily beautiful experience. The cenotaph stands before the north side of the Heiwa Kinen Shiryokan. ✉ *Heiwa Kinen Koen.*

Shukkei-en (縮景園). Designed in 1630 by Lord Naga-akira Asano (the name means "shrunken scenery garden"), Shukkei-en resembles one once found around a famed lake in Hangzhou, China, which the *daimyo* (lord) wanted to re-create for leisurely strolls. The water is dotted with tiny rocky islets sprouting gnarled pine trees. Small bridges cross above lots of colorful carp, a fish venerated for its long and vigorous life. Shukkei-en sits east of Hiroshima Castle on the banks of the Kyo-bashi-gawa. Return to the JR Station on Streetcar 9; at the end of the line transfer to Streetcar 1, 2, or 6. ✉ *2–11 Kamiya-cho,*

Continued on page 568

Hiroshima is a city on which an atomic bomb was dropped.
Hiroshima is a city with many memorials for the lives lost.
Hiroshima is a city which continually seeks peace.

Part of a translated poem at the entrance to Hiroshima's Peace Museum

A WALK THROUGH HIROSHIMA'S
PEACE MEMORIAL PARK

By Paige Ferrari

IN FOCUS HIROSHIMA'S PEACE MEMORIAL PARK

Peace Park is both the physical and emotional center of Hiroshima. Some of the monuments here, such as the Memorial Cenotaph, have become internationally recognizable icons for peace. Others are lesser-known, but nonetheless powerful, monuments dedicated to specific groups and individuals who lost their lives on August 6, 1945. After a visit to the museum, walking through the park provides time for reflection. Like Hiroshima itself, the park honors an unhappy history while presenting an optimistic view for the future. Atomic bomb survivors—known as *Hibakusha*—and rowdy, yellow-capped groups of school kids alike visit the park throughout the year to remember the past. Though the details of the atomic bomb's impact are grim, the overwhelming message is one of hope and peace. Visitors of all backgrounds and nationalities should feel welcome here.

Paper lanterns float on the Motoyasu River during Hiroshima's annual Peace Ceremony.

STARTING FROM THE PEACE MUSEUM

As you exit the ❶ **Peace Museum** and stand under the elevated section, walk straight along the path towards the iconic A-Bomb Dome.

Framing the dome is the ❷ **Memorial Cenotaph.** The dome is shaped like a traditional Japanese house and records the names of 260,000 who ultimately perished from the initial bombing or, later, from its effects. The epitaph is translated: "Let all souls here rest in peace, for we shall not repeat the evil." Each year on August 6, thousands gather here to remember the events of past.

Continuing along the main path, which runs to the left of the Cenotaph, you'll pass by the ❸ **Pond for Peace.** Its water is intended as a symbolic offering for the victims who were unable to quench their thirst after the bomb's detonation and subsequent black rain.

At the end of the pond burns the ❹ **Flame of Peace,** first lit during the 1964 Tokyo Olympics. The structure itself resembles a pair of cupped hands. Hiroshima residents will tell you that this flame is not an eternal one. It will be extinguished the day the world is free of all nuclear weapons.

Ahead and on your left is what many visitors find to be Peace Park's most moving offering, the ❺ **Children's Peace Monument.** The statue and the cases of paper cranes behind it are dedicated to all the children who died in the blast and from radiation-related sicknesses after, including Sadako Sasaki, whose determination to fold 1,000 paper cranes before she succumbed to leukemia at age 12, is one of Hiroshima's most heartbreaking and enduring stories. Brightly colored paper cranes, on display in a series of glass

cases behind the monument, are brought from around the world but especially by groups of Japanese elementary school students.

Break off the path and walk to your left. Here, in a wooded region at the edge of the park, you'll find a cluster of specific monuments. These include the ❻ **Monument for the Korean A-Bomb Victims,** the ❼ **A-bombed Gravestone,** and the ❽ **Atomic Memorial Mound.** The mound is a particularly solemn place. Constructed on the 10-year anniversary of the bombing, it was an area once used as a crematorium and now holds the ashes of roughly 70,000 victims.

Walking towards the tip of the park, you'll come upon the ❾ **Peace Bell,** built in 1964. A map of the world without borders is carved on the bell, and all visitors are welcome to strike the bell. The bell's sound is intended to remind all who hear it of the reverberations of nuclear power. Nearby, at the narrow tip of the park near the Aioi-bashi bridge, stands the ❿ **Peace Clock Tower.** Built in 1967, the clock chimes each morning at 8:15, the moment the bomb was dropped.

Walk across the ⓫ **Aioi-bashi Bridge.** This bridge, with its characteristic T-shape, was selected as the target for the bombing. On the opposite side of the bridge you can walk around the ⓬ **A-Bomb Dome,** once the city's Industrial Promotions Hall.

To visit the bomb's nearby hypocenter, walk past the A-Bomb Dome as if you're returning to the museum. To your left, across a small street outside the park perimeter, you'll see a black temple and a white temple standing side by side, bisected by a small street. In front of the white building is a statue with a shadow permanently burned into the pedestal, a product of thermal radiation. Walk down the street between these buildings for a block, then walk half a block to your right to find yourself standing in front of what used to be ⓭ **Shima Hospital,** the bomb's hypocenter. A small plaque

(above) A couple honors the victims of the atomic bombing at the Peace Memorial Park.

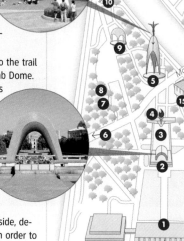

shows what the area looked like directly after the blast, but otherwise there is little to distinguish it from the surrounding commercial area.

Find your way back to the trail in front of the A-Bomb Dome. Walking back towards the museum you'll come upon the **⑭ Memorial Tower for Mobilized Students** on your left. On the day of the bombing, children as young as 12 were working outside, demolishing buildings in order to create fire-breaks that would minimize the damage from potential air attacks. Of the 8,400 students working that day, nearly 6,400 died.

As you cross the Motoyasu Bridge back onto the main park grounds, ahead on your right you'll see the **⑮ Rest House** and tourist information center. Walking back towards the museum's main building, the modern-looking building ahead of you is the **⑯ Hiroshima National Peace Memorial Hall for the Atomic Bomb Victims,** opened in 2002. Inside you can hear survivor stories and visit the research library, which houses over 100,000 memoirs written by survivors. The basement of the center provides a breathtaking artist's rendition of a 360-degree view from the hypocenter.

Walking more towards the museum itself, you'll find the **⑰ Monument dedicated to Sankichi Toge,** who was 28 at the time of the bombings. After the war, Toge protested nuclear weapons through his poetry, including the one that is on the monument. A lock of Sankichi's hair and his pen are buried on the monument, the Japanese side of which faces towards his home.

Directly in front of the museum's snack and gift store, you'll find a small, cordoned-off **⑱ Chinese Parasol Tree.** This tree is also an A-bomb survivor. Despite being scorched in the blast, new leaves started to bud and develop the next year. Today, it is a symbol for the tenacity of life and rebirth.

This is a good space to end your walk, although you should feel free to cross Heiwa Dori (Peace Boulevard) to take in some of the smaller, scattered monuments, or simply take some time to rest and reflect.

TOTAL DESTRUCTION

A-Bomb Dome today

Looking at bustling Hiroshima today, there is little evidence of the almost total destruction that visited the city on August 6, 1945. The first atomic bomb was dropped on Japan at 8:15 AM and exploded approximately 1,900 feet above the city, centered on the Shima Hospital (the actual target, the Aioi-bashi Bridge, was missed). The intial blast radius was approximately 1 square mile, and the fireball resulting from the explosion engulfed approximately 4.4 square miles; fires eventually destroyed about 69% of the buildings of Hiroshima. In the initial blast, 70,000 to 80,000 people were killed immediately, with as many as 180,000 more killed eventually by injuries sustained in the bombing or by radiation and its after-effects. The destruction in the city was almost complete in the blast- and fire-ravaged areas, and very few structures survived. The city's Industrial Promotions Hall (now better known as the **A-Bomb Dome**) was less than 500 feet from ground zero and was one of the few structures in the immediate blast radius to survive. Compared to the destruction in Nagasaki three days later, the number of dead and the amount of destruction in Hiroshima was considerably more because the city is built on a flat river plain.

Atomic bomb mushroom clouds over Hiroshima.

The A-Bomb Dome in the bomb's immediate aftermath in 1945

Ground Zero before the bombing shows a busy city; each circle is approximately 1/5 mi.

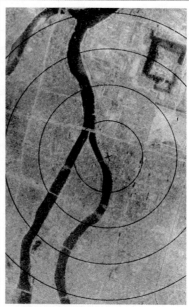

Ground Zero after the bombing (same scale). Note the almost complete lack of standing structures.

Exploring
A-Bomb Dome ... 8
Children's Peace Monument 7
Flame of Peace .. 5
Hiroshima Castle 10
Hiroshima Children's Museum 9
Hiroshima National Peace Memorial Hall 3
Hiroshima Peace Memorial Museum 2
Hiroshima Perfectural Art Museum 12
Hon-dori 6
Memorial Cenotaph 4
Peace Memorial Park 1
Shukkei-en 11

Restaurants
Kakifune Kanawa 1
Kamameshi Suishin Honten .. 5
Okonomi Mura ... 4

Hotels
ANA Crowne Plaza Hotel Hiroshima 3
Comfort Inn Hiroshima 2
Hotel Granvia Hiroshima 6

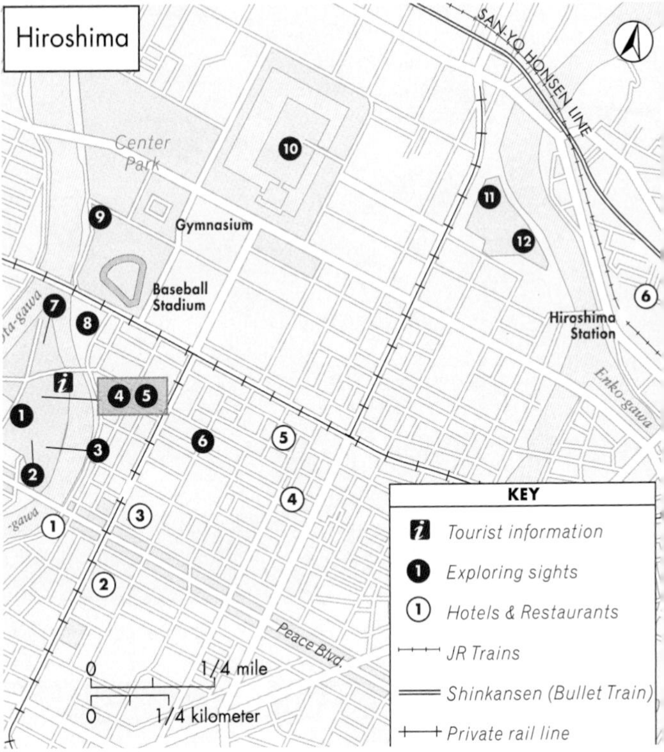

Naka-ku ☎ *082/221–3620* 🌐 *shukkeien.jp* 🎫 *¥260* 🕓 *Apr.–Sept., daily 9–6; Oct.–Mar., daily 9–5.*

WHERE TO EAT

If you don't have enough time to go out on the town for lunch or dinner, try the food court in the basement of the train station or the cluster of restaurants on the second and sixth floors of the Asse Department Store. You'll find eateries of all types, from in-and-out cheapies to elegant eateries—many are branches of famous establishments elsewhere in the city. Enter the Asse complex from the South Exit of the JR Hiroshima Station.

$$$$ SEAFOOD 🍴 **Kakifune Kanawa** (かき船かなわ *Kanawa Oyster Boat*). Hiroshima is known for its oysters, and Kanawa, on a barge moored on the Motoyasu-gawa, gets its oysters from a particularly salty area of the Inland Sea. It's believed that these waters impart the firm flesh and sweet, robust taste that loyal customers love to splurge on. It's not cheap, but the oysters are worth every yen. An English menu makes it all easy, and dining is on tatami mats, with relaxing river views. The place is an easy stroll from Peace Memorial Park. [$] *Average main: ¥8000* ✉ *3–1 Ohashi, Naka-ku* ☎ *082/241–7416* 🌐 *www.kanawa.co.jp.*

$$$$ JAPANESE 🍴 **Kamameshi Suishin Honten** (釜飯酔心). Famous for its *kamameshi*, or rice casseroles, this restaurant (part of a large chain) serves the freshest

fish from the Seto Nai-kai—*fugu*, or puffer fish, oysters, and eel, to name but a few. If you prefer your fish cooked, try the rockfish grilled with soy sauce. English menus (and Japanese-style rooms with *horiko-tatsu* pits to hang your legs in) are available. $ *Average main: ¥4000* ⊠ *6–7 Tate-machi, Naka-ku* ☎ *082/247–4411.*

$$
JAPANESE ✕ **Okonomi Mura** (お好み村 *Village of Okonomiyaki*). In this enclave 20 shops serve *okonomiyaki*, literally, "as you like it grilled." Oko-nomiyaki is best described as an everything omelet, topped with bits of shrimp, pork, squid, or chicken, cabbage, and bean sprouts. Dif-ferent areas of Japan make different okonomiyaki; in Hiroshima the ingredients are layered rather than mixed, and they throw in lots of fried noodles. Seating in these lively shops, which are generally open late, is either at a wide counter in front of a grill or at a table with its own grill. This complex is near the Hon-dori shopping area, just west of Chuo-dori. $ *Average main: ¥1500* ⊠ *Shintenchi Plaza, 2–4F, 5–13 Shintenchi, Naka-ku* ☎ *082/241–2210* ⊕ *okonomimura.jp* ▭ *No credit cards.*

WHERE TO STAY

$$
HOTEL 🛏 **ANA Crowne Plaza Hotel Hiroshima** (クラウンプラザホテル広島). One of the best in town, this reliable and popular hotel puts you close to the Peace Park and the nightlife of Nagarekawa. **Pros:** spacious dou-ble rooms; free Internet access; handy location. **Cons:** laptop rentals are expensive; one of the city's pricier hotels. $ *Rooms from: ¥18000* ⊠ *7–20 Naka-machi, Naka-ku* ☎ *082/241–1111* ⇆ *409 rooms, 1 suite* ⦿| *Breakfast.*

$
HOTEL 🛏 **Comfort Inn Hiroshima Heiwa Dori** (コンフォートイン広島平和大通り). This affordable hotel stands near Peace Memorial Park, and it's also a short walk from the happening nightspots. **Pros:** complimentary coffee available 24-hours a day; close to main attractions; free Wi-Fi. **Cons:** tiny bathrooms; spartan furnishings; thin walls. $ *Rooms from: ¥8000* ⊠ *3–17 Komachi, Naka-ku* ☎ *082/541–5555* ⊕ *www.comfortinn.com/ hotel-hiroshima-japan-JP027* ⇆ *282 Western-style rooms* ⦿| *Breakfast.*

$$$
HOTEL 🛏 **Hotel Granvia Hiroshima** (ホテルグランヴィア広島). Connected by walkways to Hiroshima's JR Station, this conveniently located hotel is welcoming to weary travelers. **Pros:** handy when you're catching a train; helpful staff; free Wi-Fi. **Cons:** far from the action; little English spoken. $ *Rooms from: ¥20000* ⊠ *1–5 Matsubara-cho, Minami-ku* ☎ *082/262–1111* ⇆ *400 rooms, 4 suites* ⦿| *No meals.*

MIYAJIMA 宮島

27 km (16 miles) southeast of Hiroshima.

Miyajima's majestic orange O-torii, or big gate, is made of several stout, rot-resistant camphor-tree trunks, and is famed for the illusion it gives of "floating" over the water. The torii is one of Japan's most enduring scenic attractions, but most of the time it actually presides over brown-ish tidal sand flats, so you will want to time your visit for when the tide is in. Ferry offices and hotels can give you a tidal forecast—don't forget to ask.

9

Behind the sea gate is the elegant shrine Itsukushima Jinja. For a few hundred yen you can walk the labyrinthine wooden boardwalks out over the tidal basin and pick your spots to snap those perfect photos.

To get to the shrine and to see the torii, go right from the pier on the path that leads through the village, which is crowded with restaurants, hotels, and souvenir shops. As you pass through the park, expect to be greeted by herds of fearless deer. Don't show or let them smell any food, or else you'll become too popular; they do have little horns, and they are known to eat most anything within reach.

GETTING HERE AND AROUND

The easiest, least expensive way to get to Miyajima is to take the train on the JR San-yo Line from Hiroshima Station to Miyajima-guchi Station. From Miyajima-guchi Station, a three-minute walk takes you to the pier where ferries depart for Miyajima. The train takes about 25 minutes (¥410) and departs from Hiroshima every 15–20 minutes. The first train leaves Hiroshima at 5:51 am; the last ferry returns from Miyajima at 10:14 pm. There are two boats, but the JR Rail Pass is only valid on the JR-operated boat (¥360 round-trip without Rail Pass). Allow a minimum of three hours for the major sights of Miyajima, or just one hour to get photos of O-torii and the shrine. Bicycle rentals are available at the Miyajima ferry terminal, offering a quick way to scoot around the island.

Inside the ferry terminal (common to both lines), tucked in the entrance to a novelty and snack shop, is the English-speaking Miyajima Tourist Association.

ESSENTIALS

Visitor Information Miyajima Tourist Association (宮島観光協会 *Miyajima Kanko Kyoukai*). ✉ *1162–18 Miyajima* ☎ *0829/44–2011* ⊕ *www.miyajima.or.jp.*

EXPLORING

Go-ju-no-to (五重の塔 *Five-Storied Pagoda*). Atop a small hill overlooking Itsukushima Jinja, this pagoda is lacquered in bright orange, like the more famous gate, and dates from 1407. At night it's beautifully illuminated. ✉ *Miyajima* ✛ *At end of Miyajima's main shopping street on way to Itsukushima Shrine.*

Itsukushima Jinja (厳島神社 *Itsukushima Shrine*). This shrine was founded in AD 593 and dedicated to the three daughters of Susano-o-no-Mikoto, the Shinto god of the moon—also of the oceans, moon-tugged as they are. It has been continually repaired and rebuilt, and the present structure is a 16th-century copy of 12th-century buildings. The orange woodwork next to the glaring white walls is surprisingly attractive, especially when complemented by a blue sky and sea. The deck has the

Miyajima's O-torii sits at the entrance to a cove and is in the water at high tide.

best frontal views of the torii. ⊠ *1–1 Miyajima-cho* ☎ *0829/44–2020* 💻 *¥300* 🕐 *Mar.–Oct., daily 6:30–6; Nov.–Feb., daily 6:30–5:30.*

Momijidani Koen (紅葉谷公園 *Momijidani Park*). Many people spend only half a day on Miyajima, but if you have more time, take a stroll through the park that is inland from Itsukushima Jinja. A steeply priced cable car goes a mile up, stopping nearly at the summit of **Misen-dake** (Mt. Misen). It's a short hike from the upper terminus to the top of the mountain, where you can look out over Seto Nai-kai and all the way to Hiroshima. ⊠ *Miyajima* ✚ *From Itsukushima Shrine, follow narrow street along river inland. Momijidani park is about a 5-min walk. Keep following street another 5 mins to get to cable-car* 💻 *Free; cable car ¥1,800 round-trip.*

O-torii (大鳥居). Miyajima's sea gate stands nearly 50 feet tall at the entrance to the cove where the ancient Shinto shrine is. This, the 18th version, was built in 1875, and has become one of the nation's most recognizable symbols. Hotels and ferry operators have tide charts so you can maximize your photo opportunities. At low tide, though, you can walk over the sand flats to admire the gate up close.

If you stay overnight on the island, and if the weather cooperates, you're guaranteed to get some photos to die for, because the gate is lighted up in spectacular fashion at night. The nearby five-story pagoda and the shrine are also illuminated. ⊠ *Miyajima.*

WHERE TO STAY

$$$$
B&B/INN
🏨 **Iwaso Ryokan** (岩惣). For traditional elegance, it's easy to like this venerable Japanese inn. **Pros:** charm to spare; great views; delicious 12-course meals. **Cons:** making reservations online requires some

YAMAGUCHI – GATEWAY TO SAN-IN

Yamaguchi (山口) is a small town, but one where you're likely to experience a disarming level of hospitality. It's also a logical base for striking out for territory hinterlands like Hagi and Tsuwano, especially if accommodations are fully booked in those romantic hideaways. The Shinkansen at nearby Shin-Yamaguchi will get you there, and—if you have the time to look around—the English-speaking Tourist Information Office will happily provide you with a map. For overnight stays, the Sunroute Hotel Yamaguchi is a basic, affordable option, about a 10-minute walk from the station.

You're likely make new friends if you duck in for a bite at favorite local restaurants or one of the many sushi bars or soba shops located in the covered shopping mall about a five-minute walk up the street from JR Yamaguchi Station.

If you're more interested in resting your travel-weary body than grabbing a meal, pop your bags in a coin locker and head one train stop over to the Yuda Onsen, where the healing sulfur baths will leave you feeling rejuvenated and ready for the next leg of your journey.

knowledge of Japanese; you'll feel like royalty—until you get the bill; the hot spring may be a bit too hot and stuffy for some. [$] *Rooms from: ¥50000* ✉ *345 Miyajima-cho* ☎ *0829/44–2233* 🌐 *www.iwaso.com* 🛏 *38 Japanese-style rooms, 33 with bath* 🍴 *Some meals.*

$$$ B&B/INN 🏨 **Ryokan Jukei-so** (聚景荘). This charming hillside ryokan has been around for more than a century, and it owes it longevity to its having the best views on the island. **Pros:** great views, inside and out; quiet hillside retreat; unobtrusive service. **Cons:** a bit boring if peace and quiet isn't your thing; staying on Miyajima is more expensive than hotels on the mainland. [$] *Rooms from: ¥20000* ✉ *50 Miyajima-cho* ☎ *0829/44–0300* 🌐 *miyajima-jukeiso.com* 🛏 *13 Japanese-style rooms* 🍴 *Some meals.*

THE SAN-IN REGION 山陰地方

If you're looking for adventure in a "real Japan" setting, you have come to the right place. Though the endless narrow ridges of steep mountains can make access from the south difficult, slow, and expensive, this hard fact of geography has kept the entire north stretch of western Honshu delightfully isolated. Any effort to explore it pays off in dividends of great scenery, precious local crafts, tasty seafood, rich history, and genuinely welcoming people.

HAGI 萩

117 km (73 miles) north of Yamaguchi.

Hagi is virtually surrounded by two branches of the Abu-gawa—the river's south channel, Hashimoto-gawa, and the river's northeast fork, Matsumoto-gawa. Rising in great semicircles behind the sleepy town are symmetrical waves of shadowy mountains, while before it stretches a sparkling blue sea.

Hagi is rich with history, and, owing to its remoteness, retains the atmosphere of a traditional castle town—though, unfortunately, its castle was a casualty of the Meiji Restoration. Turning away from feudalism to support the new order, the city was of critical importance in the 1865 to 1867 movement to restore power to the emperor. Japan's first prime minister, Hirobumi Ito (1841–1909), was a Hagi native.

Hagi is also famous for Hagi-yaki, a type of earthenware with soft colors and milky, translucent glazes ranging from beige to pink. The esteemed local ceramics industry began in the 16th century when a Mori general brought home captive Korean potters (perhaps his consolation for a failed invasion) to create pottery for their new masters. The visually soothing Hagi-yaki is second only to Raku-yaki as the most coveted pottery in Japan, and it does not come cheaply, except during the annual price-friendly Hagi-yaki Festival every May 1–5.

GETTING HERE AND AROUND

The fastest way to Hagi is by JR bus (Rail Pass accepted), crossing the mountains in just one hour for ¥1,760 from Yamaguchi City. The bus departs from the front of the train station. A JR bus also leaves from the Shinkansen Exit of Shin-Yamaguchi for an 80-minute ride for ¥2,060. Buses run hourly between 6 am and 7 pm. Some buses stop at Hagi Station, the Hagi Bus Center, or Higashi-Hagi Station; all stop at the last two. Return buses follow the same plan. The ideal way to explore Hagi is by bicycle, and you can rent a bike for between ¥800 and ¥1,000 per day near the stations or shopping arcades. A local bus system (red bus) loops around town for ¥100 a ride or ¥500 for a full day.

City information is available from English-speaking staff at the Hagi City Tourist Bureau. The Hagi City Tourist Office is downtown in Hagi City Hall.

ESSENTIALS

Visitor Information Hagi Tourist Bureau (萩市観光協会 *Hagi-shi Kanko Kyoukai*). ⊠ 3537–3 Tsubaki ☎ 0838/25–1750.

EXPLORING

If you've just arrived by bus, you won't be impressed by the run-down buildings around the Hagi Bus Center. That's okay—there's no need to linger here. Head three short blocks north, then left onto Tamachi Mall, and then west through the quaint older sections of town for 15 minutes to see the park and castle ruins. If you need to make a Tourist Info stop first, the Tourist Bureau is two doors down from the bus depot.

Akiyoshi-do (秋吉洞 *Akiyoshi Cave*). This otherworldly limestone cavern, Japan's largest, lies roughly halfway between Hagi and Yamaguchi. Although the cavern is roughly 6 miles long, only a bit less than a mile is open to the public. The path is easily accessible and lighted just enough for you to marvel at the size, but dim enough to retain a sense of wonder and mystery. Although droves of tour groups can ruin the atmosphere on weekend mornings, they have mostly cleared out by the afternoon.

The Akiyoshi Plain above the cave is a beautiful limestone karst, and makes for a pleasant spring or autumn hike. The observatory (accessible by elevator from the cave) offers impressive views in every season. If you plan to cross from the San-in to the San-yo region, stopping a couple of hours at Akiyoshi-do is highly recommended. Nine buses a day make the 40-minute, ¥1,170 trip to and from Shin Yamaguchi station, between 7:40 am and 6:55 pm. ⊠ *Hirotani Shuhocho Akiyoshi, Mine* ☎ *0837/62–0304* ⊕ *english.karusuto.com* 🖃 *¥1,200* ⊙ *Daily 8:30–6:30.*

Horiuchi (堀内). This is the old samurai section of town. From Shizuki Koen, cross the canal (on the middle bridge) to the east side, and head toward downtown. The tomb of **Tenju-in** is a memorial to Terumoto Mori, who in the early 16th century founded the tenacious clan that ruled the Choshu area for 13 generations. Next you come to the **Outer Gate of Mori**; the **Toida Masuda House Walls** are on your right as you head south. Dating from the 18th century, these are the longest mud walls in the area. At the next chance, turn right and head west to the ancient, wooden **Fukuhara Gate**. ⊠ *Hagi.*

Jo-zan Kiln (城山窯 *Jo-zan Gama*). Stop in at this pottery studio near Shizuki Koen, perhaps the best place to browse through and purchase magnificent pottery. Usually you are welcome to enter the studios and see the kilns across the street. Classes for a chance to make your own may be available. Bicycles can be rented here as well. ⊠ *31–15 Horiuchi, Horiuchi* ☎ *0838/25–1666* ⊙ *Daily 8–5.*

Shizuki Koen (指月公園). Hagi's westernmost end is bounded on three sides by the sea. This large, lovely park contains the Hagi-jo ruins and Hana-no-e Teahouse. **Hagi-jo** was one of many castles destroyed by the Meiji government around 1874 for being an embarrassing symbol of backward ways. The dramatic seaside location, with its stupendous mountain backdrop, must have made the castle a truly superb sight in its day, but alas, we can only imagine, since the walls and moats are all that remain.

The **Hana-no-e Teahouse** is a bare-bones oasis of Zen, set amid meditative gardens and judiciously pruned greenery. The attendants make the classic, slightly bitter *matcha* tea (¥500) for you while you reflect on the transient nature of life—or consider where you'd like to go next.

Mori House, south of the park, is a long narrow building once home to samurai foot soldiers in the late 18th century. The rooms are sparse and placed one next to the other. This arrangement allowed the soldiers to leap into rank-and-file assembly just outside at a moment's notice. ⊠ *1-1 Oaza Horiuchi* ☎ *0838/25–1826* 🖃 *¥210, includes admission to Hagi-jo grounds, Hana-no-e Teahouse, and Mori House* ⊙ *Apr.–Oct., daily 8–6:30; Nov.–Feb., daily 8:30–4:30; Mar., daily 8:30–6.*

Tamachi Mall (田町モール). This is the busiest street in Hagi, with some 130 shops selling local products from Yamaguchi Prefecture. The shopping mood is addictive, the wares gorgeous, and the shopkeepers friendly, so your money can go quickly. Tamachi Mall is six blocks southwest from the dated, Jetson's-style Hagi Grand Hotel, across the Matsumoto-gawa from Higashi-Hagi Station. ⊠ *Central Hagi.*

WHERE TO EAT

$$$$
JAPANESE
Fodor's Choice
★

✕ **Chiyo** (千代). Imagine a *kappo* (fine dining) course that includes squid and scallops cooked before you with butter on a sizzling-hot river stone and such goodies as *fugu*—served as sashimi or cooked tempura-style—stuffed with foie gras. Zingy homemade pickles reset your palate for each successive treat. Women beautifully dressed in formal wear serve you in a classically elegant manner, and off to the right of the intimate 10-seat counter are views of a mossy green and flowery window garden. All seating is Japanese style and no English menu is available. $ *Average main: ¥5000* ⊠ *20–4 Imafuruhagi-machi* ☎ *0838/22–1128* ⊗ *Closed Mon. No dinner Sun.*

$$
JAPANESE

✕ **Sobaho Fujita-ya** (蕎麦舗ふじたや). Colorful local characters come to this casual restaurant for beer and sake and *seiro-soba* (thin buckwheat noodles served in steaming hot baskets) and hot tempura served on fragrant handmade cypress trays. The restaurant is usually open by 11 am (or when the noodles are ready), but it closes at 6 (or when all the noodles are gone), so only a very early dinner is possible here. $ *Average main: ¥1000* ⊠ *59 Kumagaya-cho* ☎ *0838/22–1086* ⊟ *No credit cards* ⊗ *Closed Wed.*

$$$
JAPANESE

✕ **Wafu Restaurant Nakamura** (和風レストラン中村). Set-menu courses at this reliable and popular traditional restaurant typically offer a variety of fish, mountain vegetables, miso soup, and steamed rice. Nakamura has tatami and Western seating, but no English-language menu. You can select your food from the tempting window display. Reservations are accepted and recommended for larger parties. $ *Average main: ¥2500* ⊠ *394 Hijiwara* ☎ *0838/22–6619* ⊟ *No credit cards* ⊗ *No lunch mid-Aug.*

WHERE TO STAY

$$$$
B&B/INN

⌂ **Hokumon Yashiki** (北門屋敷). An elegant ryokan built upon the ruins of an old Mori clan estate, the luxurious Hokumon Yashiki pampers you in a style the ruling elite were surely accustomed to in the good old days. **Pros:** unique interior design melds traditional Japanese style with European elements; top-notch hospitality; one of the most conspicuously traditional inns in the world. **Cons:** one of the most expensive lodgings in Hagi. $ *Rooms from: ¥36000* ⊠ *210 Horiuchi* ☎ *0838/22–7251* ⊃ *42 Japanese-style rooms without bath, 5 Western-style rooms* ⦿ *Some meals.*

$
HOTEL

⌂ **Urban City Hotel Hasegawa** (ビジネスホテル長谷川). If you want a cheap, decent place to crash near the Hagi Bus Center, this business hotel is adequate—and right across the street. **Pros:** convenient to the old part of town; cheap. **Cons:** feels like you're staying in a ghost town; rooms are as minimalist as can be. $ *Rooms from: ¥8000* ⊠ *17 Karahi-machi* ☎ *0838/22–0450* ⊟ *No credit cards* ⊃ *13 Western-style rooms, 5 Japanese-style rooms* ⦿ *No meals.*

9

TSUWANO 津和野

93 km (58 miles) northeast of Hagi, 50 km (31 miles) northeast of Yamaguchi, 63 km (39 miles) northeast of Shin-Yamaguchi.

Fodor's Choice
★

This hauntingly beautiful town, tucked into a narrow north–south valley at the foot of conical Aono-yama and its attendant dormant volcanic mountain friends, may be the most picturesque hamlet in all Japan. If you catch it on a clear day, the view from the old castle ruins simply takes your breath away. Even when it's cloudy, the mist hangs romantically among the trees and ridges. The stucco-and-tile walls hearken back to ancient times, like those in Hagi and Kurashiki, and the clear, carp-filled streams running beside the streets can induce even tired, jaded travelers to take a leisurely stroll or bike ride backward through time.

It's easy to see why Tsuwano has come to be known as "Little Kyoto," and it's easier still to imagine how a gifted spirit and intellect could soar here. The towering Japanese literary figure Ogai Mori, novelist and poet, was born (in 1862) and lived here, until, at the age of 12, he went off and enrolled at Tokyo University's preparatory program in medicine.

GETTING HERE AND AROUND

Tsuwano can be reached by train: it's 2 hours, 23 minutes northeast of Hagi by JR (¥1,660); 1 hour, 8 minutes northeast of Yamaguchi by JR Yamaguchi Line (¥970); or 1 hour northeast of Shin-Yamaguchi by JR Super Oki Express (¥2,320). Though JR trains from Yamaguchi are quick and easy, JR train routes from Hagi to Tsuwano involve a change and long (80 minutes or more) stopovers in Masuda. You can also take a bus from Hagi's Bocho Bus Center directly to Tsuwano, which takes around two hours (¥2,190).

In Tsuwano all sights are within easy walking distance. You can also rent a bicycle from one of the four shops near the station plaza (two hours ¥500; all day ¥800).

Bus Contact Bocho Bus Center (防長バス). ☎ *0856/72-0272.*

VISITOR INFORMATION

The Tourist Information Office is inside the Photograph Gallery to the right of the railway station. It has free brochures, and staff members will help you reserve accommodations. As with most places in town, little English is spoken here.

Contact Tsuwano Tourist Information Office. ✉ *71-2 Ushiroda* ☎ *0856/72-1771.*

EXPLORING

Former Residence of Ogai Mori (森鴎外旧宅 *Mori Ogai Kyutaku*). While spartan, the house is worth a visit to commemorate the achievements of this gifted genius who called Tsuwano his home. Ogai Mori (1862–1922), son of the head physician to the daimyo of Shimane, became a doctor at the young age of 19 and, in spite of courting trouble for his outspoken criticism of Japan's backward ways, went on to become the author of such acclaimed novels as *The Wild Geese* and *Vita Sexualis*. He was also a prominent figure in the fledgling government behind the Meiji Restoration. From Tsuwano Station it's a 12-block

Dancers dress as white egrets in Tsuwano's Sagi-mai Shinji festival.

walk south along the main road, or take the bus and get off at Ogai Kyukyo-mae. ✉ *1–230 Machida, Kanoashi-gun* ☏ *0856/72–3210* 💴 *¥600* 🕙 *Tues.–Sun. 9–5.*

Nagomi-no-Sato (なごみの里). Tsuwano puts its geothermal gifts to good use at the spa at this hot spring. Inside and out, the tubs have great views of the surrounding gumdrop-shape volcanic peaks. It's west of everything else in town, across the river from the Washibara Hachiman-gu (a shrine where traditional horseback archery contests are held the second Sunday of April every year), but still not too far to get to by rented bike. Note that the hot springs are closed the second and fourth Thursday of the month. ✉ *256–Oaza Washibara* ☏ *0856/72–4122* 💴 *¥600* 🕙 *Daily 10–8.*

Taikodani Inari Shrine (太鼓谷稲荷神社 *Taikodani Inari Jinja*). This is one of the five most revered Inari shrines in Japan. Inari shrines are connected with the fox, a Shinto symbol of luck and cleverness. People come to pray for good fortune in business and health. A series of 1,174 red wooden gates are suspended above steps that climb up the western side of the valley to the shrine, and the journey is a nice hike with a jaw-dropping view of the valley waiting for you at the top. From the station, follow the streamside Tono-machi-dori past the Katorikku Kyokai (Catholic church), but before crossing the river turn right onto the small lane. The lane leads to the tunnel-like approach through the gates to the structure high on a cliff side. You can also take a bus that approaches by a back road; the Tsuwano Tourist Information Office can help with this. **Yasaka Jinja** is another shrine on the site, where every July 20 and 27 sees the famous Heron Dance Festival. ✉ *409 Ushiroda.*

Tsuwano Castle Ruins (津和野城跡 *Tsuwano Shiroato*). The local castle was another casualty of the Meiji Restoration in the late 19th century, but from the derelict ruins there is an awesome panoramic view of the dormant volcanic cone of Aono-yama to the east and the entire valley stretching out below. To get here you can hike a marked trail that leads from Taikodani Inari Jinja or take a chairlift from below the Taikodani Inari Jinja for ¥450 round-trip. The chairlift takes only 5 minutes, and from the top it's about a 15-minute moderate hike to the castle foundations. ✉ *477–20 Ushiroda* ⏲ *Daily 10–5.*

WHERE TO EAT AND STAY

Welcome to rural Japan, where even ATMs close for the night. No cards are accepted for the restaurants or hotels listed here, although it is possible to book and pay by credit card through a travel agency.

$$ SUSHI 🍴 **Aoki Sushi** (あおき寿司). An old-fashioned sushi restaurant with a few tables on tatami mats and a long bar counter with stools, the rustic Aoki has a cheerful staff and reasonable prices. It's also within easy walking distance of Tsuwano Station. Try the *jyo-nigiri* (deluxe sushi set); it will likely include a slice or two of tasty, chewy koi, or local carp. That and a frosty mug of beer set you back only ¥1,900. The restaurant stays open until 10 pm. [$] *Average main: ¥1500* ✉ *78–10 Ushioroda, Kanoashi-gun* ☎ *0856/72–0444* 💳 *No credit cards* ⏲ *Closed Tues.*

$$$ JAPANESE Fodor's Choice ★ 🍴 **Yuki** (遊亀). Carp dishes—yes, carp—and delectable mountain vegetables maintain Yuki's highly venerated reputation. The kitchen also serves *ayu,* or river smelt, and other specialties, but for only ¥2,800 you can get the *teishoku,* a gourmet carp course that offers a smattering of everything a fat and happy carp can become: there's chewy carp sashimi (with a wonderful lemony mustard-thyme dipping sauce); tender deep-fried carp; carp steeped so long in soy sauce, sake, and brown sugar that it is dense and even slightly dry but very delicious; and carp boiled in a tangy miso soup until it's almost flaky. This is bona-fide stamina food, and tastes way better than you might think. The dining room is chock-full of old farm implements, and there's even a stream burbling near your feet. **■ TIP→ Come early, as they close at around 7 pm, and after 3 early dinner is served by reservation only.** [$] *Average main: ¥3000* ✉ *271–4 Ushiroda* ☎ *0856/72–0162* 💳 *No credit cards.*

$ B&B/INN Fodor's Choice ★ 🏨 **Tsuwano Lodge** (津和野ロッジ). Relax and revel in style at this lodge tucked among the rice paddies and bamboo groves along the way to the Washibara Hachiman-gu Shrine. **Pros:** rooftop bath; great multicourse meals; frog-song lullabies in season. **Cons:** in a very remote place; no private baths. [$] *Rooms from: ¥10000* ✉ *Ushibara Guchi 345, Kanoashi-gun* ☎ *0856/72–1683* 💳 *No credit cards* 🛏 *8 Japanese-style rooms without bath* 🍽 *Breakfast.*

$$$ B&B/INN 🏨 **Wakasagi-no-Yado** (民宿若さぎの宿). Despite knowing little English, the family that runs this small but satisfactory inn is eager to help overseas tourists and will meet you at Tsuwano Station, an eight-minute walk away. **Pros:** nice location; heartwarming hospitality; bicycles for rent. **Cons:** small, spartan rooms; no private bathrooms. [$] *Rooms from: ¥20000* ✉ *Mori-mura ro-21* ☎ *0856/72–1146* 💳 *No credit cards* ⏲ *Closed Nov. 11–Dec. 30* 🛏 *7 Japanese-style rooms without bath* 🍽 *Breakfast.*

MATSUE 松江

194 km (121 miles) northeast of Tsuwano, 172 km (107 miles) northwest of Kurashiki.

Fodor's Choice ★ Matsue is a city blessed with so much overwhelming beauty and good food that you will wonder what to look at, what to eat, and what to do first. It's where the Shinji-ko Lake empties into the Naka-umi Lagoon, which connects directly with the Sea of Japan. This makes Matsue a seafood lover's paradise; specialties include both kinds of eel, all kinds of shrimp, shellfish, carp, sea bass, smelt, whitebait, and the famous black shijimi clams from Shinji-ko. The water also provides the city with a lovely network of canals.

Matsue also attracts and holds onto some of the country's most welcoming and interesting people, both foreign and native. This remote realm is a traveler's favorite, and once you've come here you'll surely be back—it's that kind of place. In the 1890s, the famed journalist-novelist Lafcadio Hearn came here and promptly fell in love, first with the place, and then with a local woman—a samurai's daughter, no less. In true journalistic fashion he proceeded to let the entire world know about it.

GETTING HERE AND AROUND

Japan Rail can get you to Matsue from Tsuwano (2 hours, 55 minutes northeast by JR Super Oki Express; ¥6,030) or Kurashiki, Okayama (2 hours, 17 minutes northwest by JR Yakumo Limited Express; ¥5,700). Most sights in Matsue are within walking distance of each other. Where they are not, the buses fill in. The bus station faces the train station.

ESSENTIALS

The Matsue Tourist Information Office is outside JR Matsue Station and open daily 9–6. You can collect free maps and brochures and use the Internet (also for free). The Shimane Tourist Association offers a substantial discount of 30% to 50% for foreigners at nine of its tourist attractions; the current list includes the castle and four museums. You need only present your passport or foreigner's registration card at the entrance to these places.

Visitor Information Matsue Tourist Information Office (松江市観光案内所 *Matsue-shi Kanko Annai-jo*). ⊠ *665 Asahi-machi* ☎ *0852/21–4034.*

EXPLORING

Lafcadio Hearn Memorial Museum (小泉八雲記念館 *Koizumi Yakumo Kinenkan*). The museum has a good collection of the author's manuscripts and other artifacts related to his life in Japan. One room also holds small rotating art and culture exhibitions related to Matsue. It's adjacent to Koizumi Yakumo Kyukyo, Hearn's former residence in Matsue. Two minutes from the Memorial Hall is the Hearn Kyukyo bus stop, where a bus goes back to the center of town and the station. ⊠ *322 Okudani-cho* ☎ *0852/21–2147* ⌑ *¥150* ⊙ *Apr.–Sept., daily 8:30–6:30; Oct.–Mar., daily 8:30–5.*

Lafcadio Hearn's Former Residence (小泉八雲旧宅 *Koizumi Yakumo Kyukyo*). The celebrated writer's house has remained unchanged since he left Matsue in 1891. Born of an Irish father and a Greek mother,

Lafcadio Hearn (1850–1904) spent his early years in Europe and moved to the United States to become a journalist. In 1890 he traveled to Yokohama, Japan, and made his way to Matsue, where he began teaching. There he met and married a samurai's daughter named Setsu Koizumi. He later took posts in Kumamoto, Kobe, and Tokyo. Disdainful of the materialism of the West, he was destined to be a lifelong Japanophile and resident. He became a Japanese citizen, taking the name Yakumo Koizumi. His most famous works were *Glimpses of Unfamiliar Japan* (1894) and *Japan: An Attempt at Interpretation* (1904). The house's simple elegance makes it worth a quick stop even for those unfamiliar with Hearn. ✉ *315 Kitahori-cho* ☎ *0852/23–0714* 💲 *¥150* ☉ *Mar.–Nov., daily 9–5; Dec.–Feb., daily 10–4:40.*

Lake Shinji (宍道湖 *Shinji-ko*). When dusk rolls around, you'll want to position yourself well. You won't get a better sunset than the one seen every night over the town's lake. As locals do, you can watch it from Shinji-ko Ohashi, the town's westernmost bridge, but the best spot is south of the bridge, along the road, down near water level in **Shirakata Koen,** the narrow lakeside park just west of the NHK Building. This is a great place to kick back and enjoy some tasty local microbrews and sushi. A popular *yuhi*, or sunset, spot is the patio of the Prefectural Art Museum, visible and adjacent to the park above. ✉ *Matsue.*

Matsue Castle (松江城 *Matsue-jo*). Start a tour of Matsue at the enchanting and shadowy castle and walk in the castle park, **Shiroyama Koen,** under aromatic pines. Constructed of exactly such wood, the castle was completed in 1611. Not only did it survive the Meiji upheavals intact, but it was, amazingly, never ransacked during the civil war–type turbulence of the Tokugawa Shogunate. Perhaps it's the properties of the wood, or the angles, or the mysterious tricks of light and shadows, but this castle truly feels *alive* and is a must-see sight of the region.

Built by the daimyo of Izumo, Yoshiharu Horio, for protection, Matsue-jo's *donjon* (main tower), at 98 feet, is the second tallest among originals still standing in Japan. Crouching as it does below and behind the surrounding lofty pines, Matsue-jo is slightly spooky, even in daytime. This is a fabulously preserved walk-in time capsule, with six interior levels belied by a tricky facade that suggests only five. The lower floors display an appropriately macabre collection of samurai swords and armor. The long climb to the castle's uppermost floor is definitely worth it for the view encompasses the city, Lake Shinji, the Shimane Peninsula, and—if weather conditions permit—the distant mystical snowy peak of Daisen.

The castle and park are a 1-km (½-mile) stroll northwest from Matsue Station, or take the Lakeline Bus from Terminal 7 in front of the station and get off at Otemae; the fare is ¥150. ✉ *1–5 Tono-machi* ☎ *0852/21–4030* 💲 *¥560* ☉ *Apr.–Sept., daily 8:30–6; Oct.–Mar., daily 8:30–4:30.*

Matsue English Garden (松江イングリツシユガーデン *Matsue Engurishu Gaaden*). This garden is of the same scale, arrangement, and style of any traditional English garden. There's an outdoor rest area, fountain plaza, sunken garden, indoor garden, pergola, cloister courtyard, rose

Matsue-jo is one of the most striking buildings in the region; it has been standing since its construction in 1611.

terrace, and laburnum arch. If you've covered everything else, try this place—it's quite stunning, and it was put together in only five years by a jovial English gardener named Keith Gott. The garden is on the lakeshore northwest of town, at Nishi-Hamasada. It's one stop (five minutes; get off at English Garden-mae Station) west of Matsue Shinji-ko Onsen Station by the Ichibata Railway, so it can be seen on the way to or from Izumo Taisha. ⊠ *330–1 Nishi-Hamadasa-cho* ☎ *0852/36–3030* 🖰 *Free* ⊗ *Apr.–Sept., daily 9–5; Oct.–Mar., daily 9–4.*

9

Matsue History Museum (松江歴史館 *Matsue Rekishi-kan*). This small museum gives visitors a good overview of Matsue's 400-year history. In addition to a diorama of the old castle town and scenes of daily life (including models of typical Edo-era meals), the photographs of Matsue in the Meji-era offer a rare chance to see what a provincial capital in Japan looked like at the beginning of the 20th century. English audio guides are available free of charge. The adjoining café, Kissa Kiharu, offers workshops such as making Japanese confectionery or incense among other traditional crafts. It is also a good place to relax and have coffee while looking out over the museum's Japanese garden. ⊠ *279 Tono-machi* ☎ *0852/32–1607* 🖰 *¥250.*

Meimei-an Teahouse (明々庵). Built in 1779, this is one of Japan's best-preserved teahouses. The teahouse offers views of Matsue Castle and for a small fee you can have tea and locally made sweets. To get here, leave Shiroyama Koen, the castle park, at its East Exit and follow the moat going north; at the top of the park a road leads to the right, northwest of the castle. The teahouse is a short climb up this road. Before you enter, turn around for one of the best views of Matsue's hilltop castle. ✉ *278 Kitahori-cho* ☎ *0852/21–9863* 🎫 *¥410, ¥820 with tea* 🕘 *Daily 9–5.*

Shiomi Samurai Residence (武家屋敷 *Buke Yashiki*). Built in 1730, this house belonged to the well-to-do Shiomi family, chief retainers to the daimyo. Note the separate servant quarters, a shed for the palanquin, and slats in the walls to allow cooling breezes to flow through the rooms. A few rooms have somewhat kitschy dioramas recreating scenes from household life, but they do give an idea of how Matsue samurai lived in the late Edo period. Buke Yashiki is on the main road at the base of the side street on which Meimei-an Teahouse is located (keep the castle moat on your left). ✉ *305 Kitahori-cho* ☎ *0852/22–2243* 🎫 *¥300* 🕘 *Apr.–Sept., daily 8:30–6; Oct.–Mar., daily 8:30–4:30.*

WHERE TO EAT

$$$$ JAPANESE Fodor's Choice ★

🍴 **Kawakyo** (川京). This is the best place to try the seven famous delicacies from Shinji-ko: *suzuki* (or *hosho-yaki*), sea bass wrapped in *washi* (paper) and baked over hot coals; *unagi* (freshwater eel) split, broiled, and basted in sweet soy sauce; *shirao*, a small whitefish often served as sashimi or cooked in vinegar-miso; *amasagi* (smelt), teriyaki-grilled or cooked in tempura; *shijimi*, small black-shelled clams served in miso or other soup; *koi*, string-bound, washi-wrapped, steam-baked carp; and *moroge-ebi*, steamed shrimp. Especially good is the hosho-yaki. The staff is outgoing, as is the regular crowd. Don't forget to request one of the delicious *ji-zake* (locally made sake) samplers. Try to make reservations at least a few days in advance. Kawakyo is in the block just east of the middle (Matsue Ohashi) bridge, a block north of the river. [$] *Average main: ¥5000* ✉ *65 Suetsugu Hon-machi* ☎ *0852/22–1312* 💳 *No credit cards* 🕘 *Closed Sun. No lunch.*

$$ JAPANESE

🍴 **Ohashi** (大橋). If you're pressed for time but want to grab a decent lunch, try some *warigo* soba, a local buckwheat noodle specialty. Inside the Shamine department store next to the train station, Ohashi has a filling, healthful set lunch for ¥1,000. An early dinner is also possible, since the restaurant is open until 8:15. [$] *Average main: ¥1000* ✉ *472–2 Asahi-machi* ☎ *0852/26–6551* 💳 *No credit cards* 🕘 *Closed every 3rd Tues.*

$$ JAPANESE

🍴 **Yakumo-an** (八雲庵). A colorful garden surrounds the dining area at this traditional house that serves good soba. Recommended dishes include the *sanshurui soba* (three kinds of soba) for ¥750. Add the garnishes from the top dish to each serving of soba and pour a little of the sauce on top. Drink the leftover broth, too—it's full of B vitamins and good for your metabolism. [$] *Average main: ¥1000* ✉ *308 Kitabori-cho, north of castle* ☎ *0852/22–2400* 💳 *No credit cards* 🕘 *No dinner.*

WHERE TO STAY

$$$$ B&B/INN

🏨 **Naniwa Issui** (なにわ一水). A swanky ryokan near the Matsue Shinji-ko Onsen Station (for easy access to the shrine of Izumo Taisha), Naniwa Issui is envied for its amazing views out over the big lake—and for its hot spring. **Pros:** unbeatable access to everything this city has to offer; private balcony tubs put you in the lap of luxury. **Cons:** 10-minute walk to bus stop. [$] *Rooms from: ¥30000* ✉ *63 Chidori-cho* ☎ *0852/21–4132* 🛏 *29 Japanese-style rooms* 🍽 *Some meals.*

$ B&B/INN 🏨 **Ryokan Terazuya** (旅館寺津屋). The same family has maintained a tradition of heartwarming hospitality at this charming riverside ryokan since 1893. **Pros:** high level of hospitality; train station pickup service. **Cons:** no private baths; noise from the street and nearby Shirakata Shrine. [$] *Rooms from: ¥5000* ✉ *60–3 Tenjin-machi* ☎ *0852/21–3480* 🌐 *www.mable.ne.jp/~terazuya/english* 💳 *No credit cards* 🛏 *9 Japanese-style rooms without bath* 🍴 *Some meals.*

IZUMO TAISHA

37 km (23 miles) west of Matsue.

Fodor's Choice ★ **Izumo Taisha** (出雲大社 *Izumo Grand Shrine*). The oldest of Japan's Shinto shrines, Izumo Taisha has been of tremendous cultural significance—second only to the great shrine at Ise Jingu—since the 6th century. The main building was last rebuilt in 1744. In ancient days it was the largest wooden building in the country, but since the 13th century, each time it was rebuilt, it was scaled to half its former size, and it is now *only* 78 feet tall.

Nature has arrayed a shrine of its own to compliment the ornate but somehow subdued structures: a lofty ridge of forested peaks rises behind, a boulevard of fragrant ancient pines lines the approach, and lush green lawns flank both sides. Pilgrims come here primarily to pray for success in courtship and marriage.

The *hon-den* (main building) dates from 1744 and most of the other were buildings from 1688 onward. The architectural style, with its saddled crests and ornamental roof fixtures resembling crossed swords, is said to be unique to the Izumo region, but some similarities with the main Shinto shrine on the Kii Peninsula can be noted. The taisha is dedicated to a male god, Okuninushi, the creator of the land and god of marriage and fortune. Instead of clapping twice, as at other shrines, you should clap four times—twice for yourself, and twice for your current or future partner. According to folklore, if you successfully throw a ¥5 coin so that it sticks up into the sacred hanging strands of the enormously thick 5-ton, 25 foot-long twisted straw rope, or *shimenawa*, suspended above the entrance to the main building, you will be doubly assured of good luck in marriage. It is almost impossible to do without some kind of cheating—which may say something about the difficulties of marriage.

Two rectangular buildings on either side of the compound are believed to house the visiting millions of Shinto gods during the 10th lunar month of each year. In the rest of Japan the lunar October is referred to as Kannazuki, "month without gods," while in Izumo, October is called Kamiarizuki, "month with gods." The shrine is a five-minute walk north, to the right along the main street, from Izumo Taisha-mae Station. ✉ *195 Taishocho, Izumo, Matsue* ☎ *0853/53–2298* 🎟 *Free* 🕐 *Daily 6:30 am–8 pm.*

GETTING HERE AND AROUND

The shrine is most easily seen on a day trip from Matsue, and the easiest way is to go from Matsue Shinji-ko Onsen Station. Buses run often between it and Matsue Station for ¥210. It takes one hour on the Ichibata Dentetsu (electric railway; ¥810) from Matsue Shinji-ko Onsen Station. After about 50 minutes you'll need to change trains at Kawato Station for the final 10-minute leg to Izumo Taisha-mae Station. You can also get there by taking the JR train from Matsue Station to JR Izumo Station, then transferring to the Ichibata Bus for a 30-minute ride, ¥510, to the Izumo Taisha Seimon stop.

SHIKOKU

WELCOME TO SHIKOKU

TOP REASONS TO GO

★ **Get out in nature:**
Discover Shikoku's natural charms by rafting, hiking, walking, or swimming. Best of all, bicycle across the Seto Inland Sea on a series of island-hopping bridges.

★ **Local classes:** Try a martial art, make soba noodles, dye fabrics, and learn a two-step in time for the summer dances.

★ **Frequent festivals:** Festivals mark every weekend between April and October leading up to the biggest dance festivals in the nation—Yosakoi and Awa Odori.

★ **Friendly hosts:** Encounter Shikoku's legendary hospitality firsthand in the region's ryokans and restaurants.

★ **The "real" Japan:** With its time-forgotten towns like Uchiko, unique landmarks like Dogo Onsen and Kompira-san, and acres of rice, Shikoku may well be the closest a tourist can get to "the real Japan."

1 Takamatsu and Eastern Shikoku. In Kagawa and Tokushima prefectures natural spectacles like the giant whirlpools in Tokushima and artistic attractions like Takamatsu's Ritsurin Garden and the island of Naoshima springboard you to small towns and craft workshops nearby.

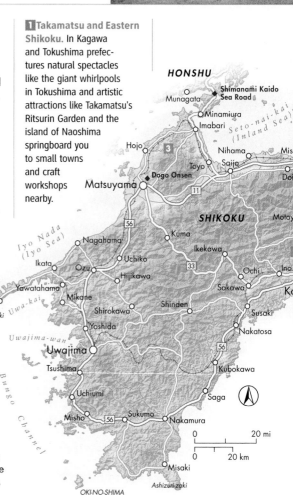

GETTING ORIENTED

Shikoku has four prefectures—Kagawa in the northeast, Tokushima to the south, Kochi along the entire Pacific coast, and Ehime in the west. This chapter is arranged as an itinerary beginning in Kagawa in Takamatsu and moving through Tokushima to the central Iya Valley, south to Kochi, and finally north toward Matsuyama, in Ehime. The reverse loop is just as practical. The advantage of finishing around Matsuyama is the easy access by bus or bicycle to Hiroshima, or by ferry to Hiroshima, Kyushu, Kobe, or Osaka—perfect for a direct link to Kansai Airport if it's time to go home.

10

2 **Kochi and Central Shikoku.** The mile-high mountains of central Shikoku are largely undeveloped—it's just too steep to build anything! Visit two great escapes: the isolated Iya Valley, with its steep gorges and mountain villages that are best explored on a rafting trip down the Yoshino River, and the rowdy, fun-loving city of Kochi, which you'll find on the sun-kissed Pacific coast.

3 **Matsuyama and Western Shikoku.** Matsuyama mixes small-town character with an exciting urban landscape. Come for Japan's best eating, fashion, and in-city sights outside of Honshu. See the superb cliff-top castle and dreamlike Dogo Onsen, the oldest hot spring in Japan, and venture into the surrounding mountain villages.

Updated by
Annamarie
Sasagawa

The smallest of Japan's four main islands, Shikoku has been a travel destination for Japanese people since the 8th century, when the Shingon Buddhist priest Kobo Daishi established an 88-temple, 870-mile pilgrimage circuit still traveled to this day. Shikoku is mountainous and mostly rural, but three of its four main cities—Matsuyama, Tokushima, and Takamatsu—have good transportation links to Honshu. They and the fourth, Kochi, are gateways to the island's smaller towns and natural getaways.

"Shikoku" means "four kingdoms" and refers to the ancient regions of Awa, Sanuki, Iyo, and Tosa, now the prefectures Tokushima, Kagawa, Ehime, and Kochi. In the Edo era, nonsamurai Japanese didn't have the right to travel freely, so going on a shogunate-approved pilgrimage to Shikoku was one of the few ways to explore the country. Visiting Shikoku no longer involves convincing the shogun of your piety, but because Shikoku's rewards lie off the beaten path, exploring it involves the challenges of a road less traveled. Public transportation is infrequent and many residents speak little or no English. What the island lacks in infrastructure and urban sophistication, though, it more than makes up for in natural wonders and cultural attractions that include ancient hot springs, mountain temples, farm villages, and summer dance festivals. Despite the language barrier, most locals are genuinely excited to socialize with visitors from abroad: you won't find a match for Shikoku hospitality elsewhere in Japan.

PLANNING

WHEN TO GO

Shikoku's unspoiled scenery offers some perfect locations in which to bask in the fleeting glories of springtime cherry blossoms and autumn foliage without the usual Honshu crowds. Summer is festival time throughout the country, but Shikoku has the best of the bunch in two epic dance festivals: Yosakoi in Kochi, held from August 9 to 12, and Tokushima's Awa Odori, held from August 12 to 15. Winter is mild on the island, but the roads into Iya can ice up, and the early autumn typhoons that batter Kochi and southern Ehime can disrupt transportation.

PLANNING YOUR TIME

A few days are enough to sample Shikoku's main pleasures, but a week on the island will allow you to discover some hidden treasures. If your time is limited, tour a major city and a rural area—Tokushima and the Iya Valley, for instance, or Takamatsu and Naoshima, or Matsuyama and the Shimanami Kaido bridges. If you have a week, add a trip to Kochi and another rural area. Express trains circle Shikoku, and the drive between most points on the island usually takes no more than four hours, so it might seem possible to cram a lot into your time. But Shikoku runs a bit slower than does mainland Japan. Ease into the same leisurely pace as the locals and take the time to linger at rural temples, chat with Buddhist pilgrims, and enjoy long lunches in the surprisingly sophisticated restaurants.

GETTING HERE AND AROUND

Depending on your route, you'll likely arrive in one of three cities. Coming by train from Kansai (often via a stopover on Naoshima), you're most likely to arrive in Takamatsu. Coming by ferry from Hiroshima or Osaka, you'll arrive in Matsuyama. If you take a bus from Kansai or an overnight ferry from Tokyo, Tokushima will be your first stop. Driving is a fantastic way to explore the countryside, and renting a car can save you time and sometimes even a little money, but be ready for challenging mountain roads. Traveling by train and bus is simpler, though service in rural areas can be infrequent and irregular. Missing a train doesn't always mean just waiting a bit for the next one: it might not arrive for hours.

AIR TRAVEL

All Nippon Airways and Japan Airlines provide domestic flights to and from Takamatsu, Kochi, Matsuyama, and Tokushima. Some low-cost airlines fly to Shikoku; the routes change frequently, but as of recently these include flights from Tokyo (Narita Airport) to Matsuyama on Jet-Star Airlines, Osaka (Kansai Airport) to Matsuyama with Peach Aviation, and Shanghai to Takamatsu on Spring Airlines.

Contacts All Nippon Airways. ☎ 800/235-9262 in U.S. and Canada, 0570/029-709 in Japan ⊕ www.ana.co.jp. **Japan Airlines.** ☎ 800/525-3663 in U.S. and Canada, 0570/025-121 in Japan ⊕ www.jal.co.jp. **JetStar Japan.** ☎ 0570/550-538 ⊕ www.jetstar.com/jp/en. **Peach Aviation.** ☎ 03/6302-8991 ⊕ www.flypeach.com. **Spring Airlines.** ☎ 0570/666-188 in Tokyo, ⊕ en.ch.com.

BOAT TRAVEL

Shikoku receives ferries from Tokyo, Osaka, Kobe, western Honshu, and Kyushu. Except for overnight ferries, reservations are rarely necessary if you don't have a vehicle, though it's a good idea to make one during the busy travel seasons of Golden Week (early May) and Obon (mid-August). Popular routes are Tokushima–Tokyo (19 hours), Toyo (near Matsuyama)–Kobe/Osaka (from 6 to 8 hours), Matsuyama–Hiroshima (3 hours by slow boat or 70 minutes by hydrofoil), Yawataham (west of Matsuyama)–Beppu (1½ hours), Naoshima to Kobe and Kobe Airport (4 hours), Takamatsu to Kobe (4½ hours), and Tokushima to Wakayama (2 hours).

BUS TRAVEL

Short-haul and overnight buses connect Shikoku's four major cities to each other and to cities on Honshu—useful when no direct train route exists. Buses also provide access to far-flung coastal and mountain regions.

CAR TRAVEL

Shikoku's narrow roads present challenges, but having your own transportation provides a priceless escape into the island's mountainous interior and secluded small towns. The rental-car service ToCoo has branches in all of Shikoku's airports and cities. You must have an international driving permit. Tourist information centers have good maps illustrating Shikoku's major roads and highways, and getting around is straightforward.

Fishing towns and rice-farming villages are all over the island. Although driving on expressways will save you a little time, if you stick to them you'll never see what life is like outside Shikoku's cities. Try the rewarding, easily navigable numbered prefectural routes. As a bonus, you'll also save on the exorbitant tolls.

■ TIP→ If you're planning to drive through the mountains, consider renting a "kei-car." These smaller vehicles, identifiable by their yellow license plates, are a bit slow on the expressways but are perfect for navigating narrow mountain roads.

Contact ToCoo. ☏ *03/4455–7850* ⊕ *www.tocoo.jp.*

TRAIN TRAVEL

Getting to Shikoku by train usually requires transferring in Okayama to a Shikoku-bound express train. Another option is the JR Sunrise Seto sleeper train from Tokyo to Takamatsu. Shikoku is belted by a single-rail track with branches into the interior. Because there is just a single track in most places, expect irregular schedules and long waits for local trains as express ones hurtle by. The Japan Rail Pass is good on all normal and express trains. Some train lines on Shikoku (mostly in rural Kochi) are not owned by Japan Railways, so you will have to pay a small extra fee to use your Japan Rail Pass on these lines. A ¥16,140 Shikoku Free Kippu ticket is good for three days of unlimited train use. In the month of your birthday you can purchase a ¥10,280 Birthday Ticket good for three days of unlimited travel for you and up to three companions. Shikoku is the rare place in Japan where a Japan Rail Pass may not save you money; price out your trip carefully to determine if the pass is worth it.

Contact Japan Rail Pass. ⊕ *www.japanrailpass.net.* **Japan Rail Shikoku.** ☏ *0570/00–4592 in Japanese only* ⊕ *shikoku-railwaytrip.com.*

ON THE MENU

Every corner of Shikoku has a special dish, cuisine, or crop. Ehime is famous for *mikan* (clementines). Between November and March you can't walk a country mile without a farmer handing you a bag of them. Ehime is also the nation's main cultivator of *tai*, or red snapper. *Tai-meshi* is rice cooked with chunks of the fish, usually in a flaming tin pot. Kagawa-ken's *sanuki-udon* is widely thought to be the nation's best udon noodle. Tokushima-ken's *Iya-soba* noodle, made from hearty

Iya Valley buckwheat flour, is even tastier if you've pounded the dough yourself at a *soba dojo*. Sand-grown at Naruto are the best *satsumaimo*, purple sweet potatoes, and *imo-taki* are popular across the island in autumn, during potato-baking parties for watching the full moon. The most renowned cuisine styles are in Kochi: *tosa-ryori* and *sawachi-ryori*, different ways of serving enormous amounts of delicious fish, particularly slices of lightly seared *katsuo* (skipjack tuna).

RESTAURANTS

Eating in Shikoku can be a surprisingly cosmopolitan experience. Matsuyama offers the widest variety of cuisines, everything from French to Indian. Takamatsu is another foodie haven, with many bistros, cafés, and izakaya pubs in and around the shopping arcades. Kochi and Tokushima have fewer foreign restaurants, but small Japanese eateries here serve local specialties. In the main cities some restaurants stay open late, but in smaller towns most places close by 8 pm.

HOTELS

Accommodations on Shikoku range from *ryokan* and *minshuku* (guest houses) in old homes to international hotels and lavish *onsen* (thermal spa) resorts. Large city and resort hotels serve Western and Japanese food. Reservations are essential during major festivals and Japanese holiday periods.

For a short course on accommodations in Japan, see Lodging in Travel Smart. Hotel reviews have been shortened. For full information, visit Fodors.com.

10

WHAT IT COSTS IN YEN			
$	**$$**	**$$$**	**$$$$**
Restaurants	under ¥1,000	¥1,000–¥2,000	¥2,001–¥3,000	over ¥3,000
Hotels	under ¥12,000	¥12,000–¥18,000	¥18,001–¥22,000	over ¥22,000

Restaurant prices are per person for a main course, set meal, or equivalent combinations of smaller dishes. Hotel prices are for a double room with private bath, excluding service and tax.

VISITOR INFORMATION

Tourist information centers in Shikoku's main cities might have the only skilled English speakers you'll meet on the island. They can help you with advice, travel reservations, and maps. Foreign tourists are still relatively rare on Shikoku, so be specific about what you're interested in, and ask a lot of questions. The website of Tourism Shikoku, based in Takamatsu, has advice and itineraries for the entire island.

Contact Tourism Shikoku. ✉ *Takamatsu Symbol Tower, 2–1 Sunport, 3rd fl., Takamatsu* ☎ *087/813–0431* ⊕ *www.tourismshikoku.org.*

TAKAMATSU AND EASTERN SHIKOKU

TAKAMATSU 高松

71 km (44 miles) south of Okayama.

If you're coming to Shikoku by train, your first stop will likely be Takamatsu, the capital of Kagawa Prefecture. Takamatsu combines urban verve with a relaxed down-home atmosphere. There is something Parisian in the air here: the locals' unwavering devotion to taking things slow, the city's wide sunlit boulevards, funky shops and cafés, and the prefectural government's dedication to funding the arts make Takamatsu the perfect place to slow down, look around, and adjust to Shikoku time.

GETTING HERE AND AROUND

It takes one hour to get to Takamatsu from Okayama by JR train. Buses from Tokyo take 10 hours, Nagoya 7 hours, Osaka 4 hours, Kyoto or Shin-Kobe 3½ hours, Sannomiya about 2½ hours, Matsuyama 2½ hours, Kochi 2 hours, and Tokushima 1½ hours. Ferries from Osaka and Kobe arrive in about 2¼ hours.

You're most likely to set off exploring from Takamatsu's northern tip, where the JR Station, bus platforms, and ferry port bracket a wide piazza around the JR Hotel Clement. At the northwest corner of the grassy Tamamo Castle park, continue straight along the park's edge toward the Kagawa Prefectural Museum and Kitahama Alley, or turn left down broad Chuo-dori to hit the city. Ten minutes on foot will bring you to the covered Hyogo-machi shopping arcade and within easy striking distance of other city sights. Takamatsu's biggest draw, Ritsurin Garden, is a 20-minute walk south.

The east-lying districts Yashima and Mure are home to two captivating attractions: the historical preserve Shikoku Mura and the Isamu Noguchi Garden Museum, a superb sculpture park. Just outside the main city, both sites are easy to access by car or local train.

VISITOR INFORMATION

The tourist information office in front of the JR Station is the place to get maps, timetables, and travel advice about Takamatsu and other Shikoku destinations. Some staffers speak English quite well. Ask about current hotel and other discounts for visitors. For local events try I-PAL Kagawa, a cultural exchange office in the central Chuo-koen. Ask for the organization's excellent city map and the latest *Kagawa Journal* newsletter.

Contacts I-PAL Kagawa. ✉ *1–11–63 Bancho* ☎ *087/837–5908* ⊕ *www. i-pal.or.jp/en.* **Takamatsu Tourist Information Office.** ✉ *1–16 Hamano-cho* ☎ *087/851–2009* ⊕ *www.takamatsu.or.jp/eng.*

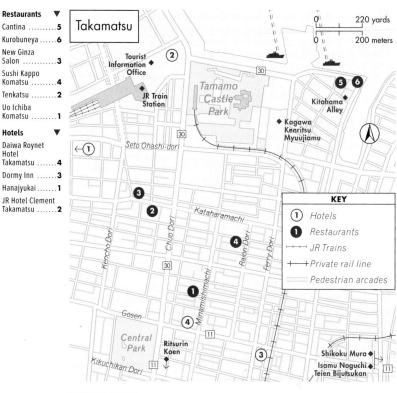

EXPLORING

Fodor'sChoice ★ **Isamu Noguchi Teien Bijutsukan** (イサムノグチ庭園博物館 *Isamu Noguchi Garden Museum*). A wonderland of indoor and outdoor sculpture both playful and profound, this facility occupies the former studio and grounds of the Japanese-American sculptor Isamu Noguchi (1904–88). The modernist artist, whose large-scale sculptures grace buildings, parks, and gardens around the world, was also known for his furniture (most notably the Noguchi table), lamps, and landscape architecture. The artist's sensitivity and expressiveness are in evidence everywhere on this site that exhibits his works in stone and other media.

Officially, visitation requires reservation by phone, fax, or email at least a week in advance, but if you call the museum you can usually gain entrance on shorter notice. One advantage to early booking, though, is that you'll have a better chance of having an English speaker accompany you as you tour. ⊠ *3519 Mure, Mure-cho ♦ 10-min taxi ride from JR Yashima Station, or 2 stops farther on Kotoden Shido Line to Kotoden Yakuri Station and take taxi or walk 20 mins* ☎ *087/870–1500* ⊕ *www. isamunoguchi.or.jp* ☞ *¥2,160* ☉ *Tues., Thurs., and Sat. at 10, 1, and 3 by appointment. Closed Aug. 13–16 and Dec. 26–Jan. 5.*

FAMILY **Kagawa Kenritsu Myuujiamu** (香川県立ミュージアム *Kagawa Prefectural Museum*). Just south of the decaying castle park, this museum contains exhibits about Kagawa's history and art. A third-floor exhibit chronicles regional history from ancient to modern times; the second floor displays art from the museum's permanent collection and presents special exhibitions; and the ground floor has an art-books library and a hands-on area where you can don a ceremonial kimono or samurai armor. (A museum staffer will even take a photo for you.) Kids can play with traditional Japanese toys. Free English audio guides are available, but you needn't know a lick of Japanese to enjoy walking inside a Neolithic hut, sitting in a 19th-century schoolroom, or crawling with a magnifying glass on the giant photo map of Kagawa. ⊠ *5–5 Tamamo-cho* ☎ *087/822–0002* ⊕ *www.pref.kagawa.lg.jp/kmuseum/foreign* ☞ *¥410* ☉ *Tues.–Sun. 9–5 (sometimes Fri. until 7:30).*

> ### CHEAP BICYCLES
>
> Take advantage of the cheap bicycle rental available at an underground garage near the JR Station and at six other locations around the city. For ¥200 a day, the whole city will open up to you. Explore out-of-the-way spots like the two skinny piers and cute lighthouses off the sun port north of the station, perfect for watching the sunset. Bikes can be returned to any rental station, a real convenience.

FAMILY

Fodor's Choice

★

Ritsurin-koen (栗林公園 *Ritsurin Garden*). Built by a feudal lord in the 17th century, this garden became public property after the 19th-century Meiji Restoration and is now a registered National Treasure. With 75 total acres, 16 of them landscaped, Ritsurin contains close to 1,000 sculpted pine trees, six carp-filled lakes, and two wooden teahouses where samurai used to gather to perform tea ceremonies and compose haiku. Give yourself at least two hours to stroll through the garden, and don't miss Kikugetsu-tei teahouse, which serves green tea and snacks daily from 9 to 4:30, with lunch also available in spring and autumn (reservation only). The garden is especially peaceful in the early morning or late afternoon. English maps are provided at the entrance. Audio guides cost ¥200, but if you book at least a week in advance you might be able to engage a free volunteer guide who speaks English. ⊠ *1–20–16 Ritsurin-cho* ✛ *10-min taxi ride from Takamatsu Station, 3-min walk from JR Ritsurinkoen Kitaguchi Station, 10-min walk from Kotoden Ritsurinkoen Station* ☎ *087/833–7411* ⊕ *www.ritsuringarden. jp* ☞ *¥410* ☉ *Daily sunrise–sunset.*

Shikoku Mura (四国村). An open-air museum east of central Takamatsu, Shikoku Mura consists of traditional houses that have been relocated from around Shikoku. The park does a fabulous job of illustrating how life on Shikoku has changed throughout the centuries. You can enter Shikoku Mura by crossing a rickety vine bridge, or play it safe and use the sidewalk detour. The route through the park is clearly marked, and the information boards in English are thoughtful and thorough. The highlights include a village Kabuki theater relocated from Shodo-shima island, thatched-roof farmhouses from mountain villages, fishermen's huts, sugarcane-pressing sheds, and lighthouse-keepers' residences.

Continued on page 600

10

THE HENRO: SHIKOKU'S 88-TEMPLE PILGRIMAGE

By Annamarie Sasagawa

On the mountainous island of Shikoku, 88 sacred temples have welcomed Buddhist pilgrims for over 1,000 years. Leave your everyday world behind, and walk in the footsteps of tradition on Shikoku's ancient pilgrimage trail.

Shikoku's 88-Temple Pilgrimage is an 870-mile Buddhist pilgrimage route encircling the island of Shikoku. The pilgrimage dates from the 9th century and is the longest of Japan's ancient pilgrimage trails.

Unlike Europe's Camino de Santiago de Campostela pilgrimage, in which pilgrims travel toward a sacred destination, all 88 temples on the Shikoku circuit are considered equally sacred; thus, there is no start- or end-point. A pilgrim completes the journey by traveling full-circle.

Although eight of the 88 temples belong to other sects of Buddhism, the Shikoku pilgrimage is a Shingon Buddhist tradition. It's unique among Japan's Buddhist pilgrimage routes in its devotion to Kobo Daishi, the founder of Shingon Buddhism. Each temple on the route, no matter which Buddhist deity it enshrines, also houses a small building dedicated to the spirit of this ancient monk.

(top left) Chikurin-ji, (top right) Byodo-ji, (bottom right) Kumatani-ji

KOCHI ONE DAY LOOP: TEMPLES 31-33

Most tourists—even those with plenty of time to spare—won't be able to travel the entire circuit. But if you have been drawn to Shikoku, you will certainly want to get a taste of the pilgrimage experience even if you don't have two full months to hike the whole route. You won't be alone; many westerners want to partake and can be seen hiking along with the other foot pilgrims (who are in short supply these days since most go on group bus tours). You don't need to don full pilgrim garb to get a taste of this experience, but you may want to buy a *Shuin-cho* (calligraphy book) to gather stamps from the various temples if you haven't already purchased one (these are available at all the larger temples). Kochi is a particularly good place to visit a few temples since there are three within reasonable walking distance. Try this one-day, 15-mile

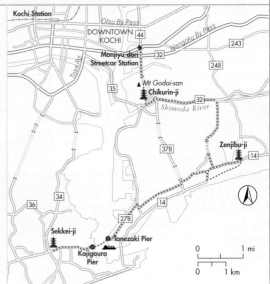

walk that takes you to the three pilgrimage temples within Kochi's city limits: **Chikurin-ji**, **Zenjibi-ji**, and **Sekkei-ji**. Allow a full day (approximately 9 hours) to complete this loop. You'll find some small shops and vending machines along the way where you can get

snacks and drinks, but be sure to pack a lunch.

From Kochi Station, take the streetcar to Monjiyu-dori station, changing at Hari-maya Bashi. (20 minutes, ¥190). Walk south from the station and cross the canal. The big hill in front of you is Mt. Godai-san.

Chikurin-ji

Chikurin-ji

Zenjibu-ji

Sekkei-ji

Turn left after the bridge, and keep an eye out for small white signs with red arrows and a stenciled silhouette of a pilgrim. Follow these signs past a shrine and up Mt. Gogai-san to **Chikurin-ji** (#31).

After visiting Chikurin-ji, follow the trail south down Mt. Godai-san. It's a steep descent. When you get to the bottom, cross the Shimoda River and turn left. Again,

look for signs that mark the pilgrim trail. After about an hour on this trail, go through the tunnel on your left. After the tunnel, you'll see a pond and **Zenjibu-ji** (#32), atop a small hill. Zenjibu-ji was also founded in 724 AD (on some road signs it's also called Mine-ji).

Walk southwest from Zenjibu-ji along the coast for about 90 minutes. When you reach the end of the pen-

insula, take the free small ferry across. **Sekkei-ji** (#33), is about 1 mi west of the ferry stop on the other side. It's a Rinzai Zen temple that was founded in AD 815.

Nagahama Shucho-jo bus stop is a 3-minute walk from Sekkei-ji. Buses run from here back to Kochi station (25 minutes, ¥440).

WHO WAS KOBO DAISHI?

Kukai, or Kobo Daishi—as he is more widely known by the honorific title bestowed after his death—was a Buddhist priest, founder of Shingon Buddhism, an esoteric form of Buddhism that focuses on rituals instead of abstract meditation. He was a scholar, calligrapher, pilgrim, and all-round adventurer.

Born to an aristocratic family in Kagawa prefecture on Shikoku in AD 774, he went to Nara in 791 to study Confucian classics, where he became interested in Buddhism. In 804, he used his family connections to join an expedition to China, where he studied esoteric Buddhism in Xi'an for two years with the Chinese master Hui-kuo.

After returning to Japan, he became the head priest of Nara's Todai-ji temple in 810. In 819, he founded the monastery town of Koya-san high in the mountains of Wakayama prefecture. For the next 16 years, Kobo Daishi traveled between Koya-san, the courts and universities of Kyoto, and pilgrimage sites around Japan. In 835, he died—or according to Shingon Buddhist tradition did not die but rather left this world to enter eternal meditation in a cave in Koya-san, where he's still believed to be.

Kobo Daishi felt a lifelong tension between academic learning and the lessons of travel that resonates with many Japanese today.

Statue of Kobo Daishi

10

HISTORY OF THE PILGRIMAGE

THE PILGRIMAGE BEGINS

The cost and difficulty of travel kept the numbers of pilgrims low until the Tokugawa era (1603–1868). Shogun **Ieyasu Tokugawa**'s rise to power in 1603 brought political stability to Japan after a century of civil war. Increased prosperity among peasants and better roads made travel possible for many who could never travel before.

Keen to prevent rural rebellion, however, the shogun quickly forbade commoners from traveling freely. The only way for a peasant to travel legally was by obtaining permission to make a pilgrimage. Shikoku was a popular destination for these "passport pilgrims." The pilgrims surged in numbers, quickly turning Shikoku's sleepy temple towns into rather lively places, and so they have remained.

A LULL IN FOOT TRAFFIC

The fun stopped when Japan entered the Meiji era (1868–1912). In the face of growing European influence in Asia, Japan's new imperial government scrambled to transform the nation into a modern power. As part of this modernization effort, Japan's ruling elite promoted a return to "pure" Japanese values, favoring Shinto, Japan's indigenous religion, over Buddhism, an import from mainland Asia.

During this period of anti-Buddhist sentiment, pilgrim numbers dropped, and six of the pilgrimage's 88 temples were destroyed, damaged, or relocated. World War II left Japan's citizens with little extra money to donate to the temples or pilgrims.

THE MODERN PILGRIMAGE

As Japan's economic recovery took hold, pilgrims once again began to arrive on Shikoku. Rising incomes and the time pressures of urban life soon created a market among would-be pilgrims for faster ways to complete the circuit. The first pilgrimage bus tours began in the 1950s, and the majority of pilgrims have traveled by car or bus ever since.

(top left) Yakuo-ji, (top middle) Ieyasu Tokugawa, (top right) Gokuraku-ji, (top bottom) Nagao-ji

WALKING THE PILGRIMAGE

It takes about two months to walk the entire 870-mile pilgrimage circuit. All 88 temples now have road access, so it's possible to do the pilgrimage by car or motorcycle in just under two weeks. By bicycle, the circuit takes about a month.

WHEN TO GO: Spring (mid-March to mid-April), brings cherry blossoms and mild weather to Shikoku and is the most popular pilgrimage season. Autumn (early October to mid-November) is also a good time to go. The rainy season (June) is best avoided; winter can be quite cold, summer hot and humid.

WHERE TO START: Although the temples are numbered, you don't have to start at #1. Start wherever is convenient and complete the circle, ideally in a clockwise fashion. However, a superstition among pilgrims says that if you travel counterclockwise (*gyaku-uchi*) you're more likely to encounter Kobo Daishi en route.

WHERE TO STAY: About a third of the 88 temples provide accommodation and meals to pilgrims for about ¥6,000 per person, but space at temple lodgings (*shukubo*) fills up fast with bus tour groups. Some temples also provide free basic accommodation in wooden sheds called *tsuyado*, which are not much more than a roof over your head. You must bring your own blankets and food. In villages near smaller temples, you'll find many *minshuku* at about the same cost as temple lodging. English isn't widely spoken on Shikoku, so some Japanese skills will make things smoother.

GEAR: To walk the pilgrimage, you'll need sturdy shoes, raingear, a warm jacket, a bilingual map, mobile phone, and enough cash to survive between major cities.

If you want to look like a Japanese pilgrim, you'll need some extra gear. A white pilgrim's overcoat (*oizuru*) indicates to the world that you're on a spiritual journey and are prepared to die en route. Black Chinese characters on a pilgrim's *oizuru* read "two people walking together" and remind lonely pilgrims that Kobo Daishi is walking with them.

You'll also need a conical straw hat, a sutra book, an embroidered stole, a set of Buddhist rosary beads, a bell, a wooden staff, and a Shuin-cho in which to collect seals from each temple (the book is not unlike the Spanish *credencial* used by pilgrims on the Camino de Santiago de Compostela) and is also available in places like Kyoto and Nara. Larger temples on Shikoku sell all these accessories, and they make good souvenirs, though they aren't at all necessary to do the walk.

TOURS: Bus tours are given in Japanese only, but the Japan-based tour operator Walk Japan (⊕ *www.walkjapan.com*) offers customized guided tours to some pilgrimage temples.

Pilgrims walking along a Shikoku beach

The prolific Osaka-born architect Tadao Ando designed the concrete-and-glass Shikoku Mura Gallery on-site. On a hill above the sugarcane-pressing shed, it looks as if shipped here from central Tokyo. Works by Renoir, Picasso, and Leonard Foujita are displayed inside, but the showstopper is the outdoor water garden. ✉ *91 Yashima-Naka-machi* ✥ *Take Kotoden Shido Line to Kotoden-Yashima Station and walk 10 mins, or JR Kotoku Line to Yashima Station and walk 15 mins; by car take Rte. 11 toward Tokushima and turn left at McDonald's on right* ☎ *087/843–3111* 🌐 *www.shikokumura.or.jp* 🎟 *¥800 to park, ¥500 to gallery, ¥1,000 combination ticket* 🕒 *Apr.–Oct., daily 8:30–6; Nov.–Mar., daily 8:30–5:30.*

NEED A BREAK?

Waraya (わら家). Locals take fierce pride in Kagawa's culinary specialty, *sanuki-udon* noodles, traveling distances that defy common sense to sample the ones served at this restored riverside house at the base of Shikoku Mura. Stop here for lunch and enjoy the rustic waterwheel. Noodles supposedly taste better if you slurp them loudly. If you're with a party of three or more, choose the family-size noodle barrel for the most bang for your slurping buck. ✉ *91 Yashima-Naka-machi* ☎ *087/843–3115.*

WHERE TO EAT

Dozens of great restaurants and stores are scattered along the central Marugame-machi arcade and the side streets lacing it to Raion-dori arcade. The city's late bedtime makes it easy to move from a meal to a nightlife spot before finding a second stop for a bite later on.

$$ MEDITERRANEAN

🍴 **Cantina.** In an old warehouse facing the waterfront, Cantina serves Mediterranean food with a Japanese twist. The tuna and cod roe pasta in cream sauce is good, as are the seafood paella and the prosciutto and mozzarella salad. Stop by for lunch, or grab a seat on the outdoor patio and watch the sun go down. Credit cards are accepted after 6 pm. [$] *Average main: ¥1975* ✉ *3–2 Kitahama-cho, Kitahama Alley* ☎ *087/811–7718.*

$$ MEXICAN

🍴 **Kurobuneya** (黒船屋). You'll find good Mexican fare alongside Japanese favorites at this second-floor establishment on Kitahama Alley. The friendly owner will happily take a break from playing jazz records, mixing fancy cocktails, and pouring beer and seasonal sake to supply delightfully quirky travel advice. [$] *Average main: ¥1980* ✉ *3–2 Kitahama-cho, Kitahama Alley C* ☎ *087/826–3636* 💳 *No credit cards* 🕒 *Closed Mon. No lunch.*

$$ JAPANESE

🍴 **New Ginza Salon** (ニューギンザサロン). The chefs at this chic little bistro transform standard Japanese ingredients into extraordinary cuisine. Antique tables and plush chairs create a sedate setting for delicious lunch plates and excellent handmade pastries. Don't worry about the Japanese-only menu—just order the daily lunch set or the best-looking dessert from the glass display case. [$] *Average main: ¥1500* ✉ *Hyogo-machi shopping arcade, 2–4–11 Hyogo-machi* ☎ *087/823–7065* 💳 *No credit cards* 🕒 *Closed Sun. No dinner.*

$$$$ JAPANESE

🍴 **Sushi Kappo Komatsu** (寿司割烹小松). Specializing in fish from the Seto Inland Sea, this intimate sushi restaurant is the place to mingle with food-loving locals or enjoy an intimate dinner for two. The ingredients

KITAHAMA ALLEY

The former warehouse town of Kitahama Alley escaped the wrecking ball, and thanks to a cohort of young entrepreneurs it now contains funky shops, craft workspaces, restaurants, cafés, and a large gallery space. The challenge is finding the place: the salt-blasted wooden and metal buildings look so derelict you might pass by without realizing it. Kitahama Alley is a 10-minute walk from Takamatsu Station. Follow the coastline east past Tamamo Koen until a canal cuts back toward the city. You'll see the warehouses on your right. Poke into stores like **Depot,** which sells funky home and kitchen items, and **Peekabooyah,** whose baby clothes are likely more fashionable than anything in your own wardrobe. For eating, try the second-floor **Juke Joint Kurobuneya** for good Mexican fare, and Cantina, a Japanese take on Mediterranean food next door.

are top-quality, and everyone here wants to make sure you enjoy your experience. Sit at the long counter and order à la carte, or dine upstairs on a prix-fixe meal in a quiet booth. There's no English menu, but some people on staff speak English. Sushi Kappo Komatsu can be hard to spot, but look for the bamboo screens and miniature rock garden out front. Reservations are recommended for the prix-fixe dinners. $ *Average main: ¥5000 ⊠ Raion-dori arcade,1F Lady Bldg., 10–16 Gobomachi ☎ 087/826–3812 ⊗ Closed Sun. No lunch.*

$$$ ✕ **Tenkatsu** (天勝). Find your favorite fish in the pool at Tenkatsu, and it
JAPANESE will be on your plate a few minutes later. You can sit close to the action at the big black countertop, or dine at tatami tables. The interior design here hardly overwhelms, but the food more than makes up for it. Plastic displays and picture menus help you choose your nonfish dishes. *Nabe* hot pots in autumn and winter are house favorites. $ *Average main: ¥2500 ⊠ 7–5 Hyogo-machi ☎ 087/821–5380.*

$$$$ ✕ **Uo Ichiba Komatsu** (魚市場小松). The simmering energy of a cantina
JAPANESE thrives in this upscale three-story restaurant. Flags and banners hang above tanks full of eels and fish waiting to be selected for your plate, and the chefs do a dazzling job preparing them. The other Japanese fare is also top-notch. Dinner is lively, but the set menus at lunch are considerably cheaper. Uo Ichiba Komatsu is across from the Kawaroku Hotel, off Marugame-machi arcade. $ *Average main: ¥3100 ⊠ 7–1 Furubaba-cho ☎ 087/826–2056 ⊗ Closed Sun. No lunch.*

WHERE TO STAY

$$ 🛏 **Daiwa Roynet Hotel Takamatsu.** An elegant hotel next to the Marugame-
HOTEL machi shopping arcade, the Daiwa offers much more than a central location. **Pros:** central location; unfailingly helpful staff; good value. **Cons:** short on local flavor. $ *Rooms from: ¥14000 ⊠ Marugame-cho 8–23 ☎ 087/811–7855 ⊕ www.daiwaroynet.jp/english/takamatsu ⤢ 175 rooms ⦿ Breakfast.*

$$$ 🛏 **Dormy Inn** (ドーミーイン). With its central location, plush decor, and
HOTEL great amenities, this branch of a national chain seems almost too good to be true in this price range. **Pros:** great value; convenient location;

10

luxurious rooftop bath. **Cons:** no in-room cots for extra guests. $ *Rooms from:* ¥21800 ⊠ *1–10–10 Kawara-machi* ☎ *087/832–5489* ⊕ *www.hotespa.net/dormyinn/en* �厂 *48 rooms* ○| *No meals.*

$$$$
B&B/INN

🏠 **Hanajyukai** (花樹海). A top choice for a luxury ryokan experience, Hanajyukai overlooks city and sea from a flower-covered mountainside. **Pros:** great service; city views; natural hot spring baths. **Cons:** away from downtown. $ *Rooms from:* ¥40000 ⊠ *3–5–10 Nishita-kara-cho* ☎ *087/861–5580, 087/834–9912* ⊕ *www.hanajyukai.jp* ▬ *No credit cards* ⤻ *40 Japanese-style rooms, 5 Western-style rooms* ○| *Some meals.*

$$$$
HOTEL

🏨 **JR Hotel Clement Takamatsu** (全日空ホテルクレメント高松). If you're inclined to indulge in Western-style luxury, this hotel next to Takamatsu Station is a good choice. **Pros:** convenient location; spacious rooms; great views. **Cons:** overpriced breakfast. $ *Rooms from:* ¥22572 ⊠ *1–1 Hamano-cho* ☎ *087/811–1111, 087/800–2222* ⊕ *www.jrclement.co.jp* ⤻ *300 rooms* ○| *No meals.*

NAOSHIMA 直島

20 km (12 miles) northeast of Takamatsu.

Fodor's Choice
★

In past centuries, pirate attacks were the biggest surprise you might encounter on the Seto Inland Sea. Now, it's the world-class art museums of Naoshima. This tiny island in the inland sea between Takamatsu and Okayama hosts three major contemporary art museums as well as an installation art project. Several surrounding islands are getting into the action, including Teshima, Inujima, Shodoshima, Megijima, and Ogijima, all of which participate in the Setouchi Triennale international art festival. If you're a contemporary art fan or even just curious, don't miss out on the cultural activity here.

It's possible to see Naoshima's major sights in one (very long) day, but staying on the island overnight allows a more leisurely pace. After the day-trippers leave on the late-afternoon ferry, Naoshima feels like a different place altogether.

GETTING HERE AND AROUND

You can reach Naoshima by taking a short ferry ride from Takamatsu or Okayama, or a longer one from Kobe. The trip from Takamatsu to Naoshima's Miyanoura Port takes 25 minutes on the passenger-only ferry and an hour on the car ferry. From Okayama, ferries depart from Uno Port, next to Uno Station, and take 15 or 20 minutes to reach Miyanoura. Ferries from Kobe take 4½ hours, departing first from the Kobe Airport ferry terminal and making a second stop to collect passengers at the Kobe city ferry terminal. There are ferries to and between Naoshima's neighboring islands, though the smaller islands might have only one or two departures a day.

Trains from Okayama to Uno Station take 50 minutes. Direct trains don't run between 8 am and 3 pm, but you can take a Kojima-bound local train and change at Chaya-machi to one headed to Naoshima. A bus to Uno Port leaves every half hour from Okayama Station (50 minutes).

The majority of the Chichu Art Museum is underground.

Get around Naoshima by bicycle, on the town bus, or in the island's one and only taxi. The town bus costs ¥100 per ride and goes to all major sights. Regular bikes are available at Miyaura Port, but you'll want a battery-assisted model to get you up the hill to Chichu Art Museum and the Benesse House Museum. Reserve a bicycle—TVC Service Rentacycle is a good option—at least one day in advance. If you rented a bike in Takamatsu, you can bring it on the ferry (¥300 each way). If you have an international driver's license, you can rent a scooter to zip around the island.

Aside from the villages of Miyanoura and Honmura, which can be covered on foot in about five minutes, Naoshima's only other major sights are its art museums.

Contacts Naoshima Taxi. ☎ 087/892–3036. **TVC Service Rentacycle.**
✉ 2249–6 Naoshima, Kagawa ☎ 090/9507–4010.

VISITOR INFORMATION
Contact Naoshima Visitor Information Center. ✉ Miyanoura Port, 2249–40 Naoshima, Kagawa-gun ☎ 087/892–2299 ⊕ www.naoshima.net/en.

EXPLORING
TOP ATTRACTIONS
Art House Project (家プロジェクト). The artists of the Art House Project have transformed seven structures or sites in the Honmura district that were abandoned as islanders departed to seek work in the city. Art, memory, and everyday life blend together as you wander through the seven "houses" (including a shrine and a former temple) while villagers around you go about their business. If you have time for only one

site, make it *Minamidera,* designed by architect Tadao Ando to hold an artwork by James Turrell. ✉ *Honmura* ☎ *087/892–3223 for Benesse House* ⊕ *www.benesse-artsite.jp/en/arthouse* ☞ *¥410 for single-site ticket except Kinza (¥510); ¥1,030 for 6 sites except Kinza* ⊗ *Tues.–Sun. 10–4:30.*

Benesse House Museum (ベネッセハウス ミュージアム). Site-specific installations can be seen from the road leading to this top-class contemporary art museum. Inside, full-length windows illuminate a rotating collection of installation pieces in natural sunlight. The museum is open later than others on the island, so if you only have a day here, save this museum for the evening. ✉ *3418 Naoshima-cho, Gotanji, Naoshima* ☎ *087/892–3223* ⊕ *www.benesse-artsite.jp/en* ☞ *¥1,030* ⊗ *Daily 8 am–9 pm.*

Chichu Bijutsukan (地中美術館 *Chichu Art Museum*). *Chichu* means "inside the earth," and this museum built into a hillside overlooking Naoshima's south coast lives up to its name. Designed by the internationally recognized architect Tadao Ando, the museum is a work of art in itself. The Chichu exhibits works by Claude Monet, Walter de Maria, James Turrell, and other major artists in natural light. The Monet gallery is breathtaking. Buy tickets at the office 50 yards down the road; during busy periods, you may have to wait to enter. ✉ *3449–1 Naoshima-cho, Naoshima* ☎ *087/892–3755* ⊕ *www.benesse-artsite. jp/en/chichu* ☞ *¥2,060* ⊗ *Mar.–Sept., Tues.–Sun. 10–6; Oct.–Feb., Tues.–Sun. 10–5.*

Naoshima Bath I ♥ Yu (直島銭湯 I ♥ 湯). Two minutes on foot from Miyanoura Port is Japan's funkiest public bath (*yu* means hot water). Created by artist Shinro Otake, the bathhouse contains, among other things, an aircraft cockpit, the bottom of a ship, and an elephant statue sourced from a museum of erotica. What's not to love? Take the plunge; you won't have another chance to bathe with art. Towels, shampoo, and soap are for sale inside; the pools themselves are gender-segregated. ✉ *2252–2 Miyanoura, Naoshima* ☎ *087/892–2626* ⊕ *www.benesse-artsite.jp/en/naoshimasento* ☞ *¥510* ⊗ *Tues.–Fri. 2–9, weekends and public holidays 10–9; closed Tues. instead of Mon. following Mon. public holiday* ⊗ *Closed Mon.*

WORTH NOTING

007 Museum (007 記念館). In contrast to the serious contemporary art elsewhere on the island, this hole-in-the-wall museum exhibits James Bond paraphernalia collected by island residents who really *really* want the movie version of *The Man with the Red Tattoo* to be filmed on Naoshima. A mishmash of kitsch and hope whose greatest appeal will be to James Bond fans, the 007 Museum is a two-minute walk northwest of Miyanoura Port. ✉ *2294 Miyanoura, Naoshima* ☎ *087/892–2299 Naoshima tourist info* ☞ *Free* ⊗ *Daily 9–5.*

Ri Ufan Bijutsukan (李禹煥美術館 *Lee Ufan Museum*). Yet another Tadao Ando creation, this museum devoted to Lee Ufan, a much-honored painter and sculptor who was born in Korea but has been based in Japan for more than a half a century, aims to encourage a "slightly out-of-the-ordinary encounter with art, architecture, and nature."

Opinions vary about how atypical the experience is, but it's definitely not a passive one. Wear comfortable shoes that are easy to remove; you'll be standing a lot and removing your shoes in parts of the museum. ✉ *1390 Azakura-ura, between Benesse House and Chichu Art Museum, Naoshima* ☎ *087/840–8285* 🌐 *www.benesse-artsite.jp/en/lee-ufan* 🎫 *¥1,030* ⏲ *Mar.–Sept., Tues.–Sun. 10–6; Oct.–Feb., Tues.–Sun. 10–5* ⏲ *Closed Mon.*

WHERE TO EAT

Naoshima cafés keep relaxed island hours, usually staying open until sundown. You need to plan ahead if your lodging doesn't provide dinner.

$ CAFÉ 🍴 **Cafe Restaurant Garden** (カフェレストランガーデン). In an old farmhouse, this café serves delicious pizza, fresh orange juice, and Naoshima apple cake. If your knees aren't up for sitting on the tatami, ask to eat in the room with plush couches and lounge chairs. [$] *Average main: ¥800* ✉ *Honmura 843–1, Naoshima-cho, Naoshima* ☎ *087/892–3301* 💳 *No credit cards* ⏲ *Closed Mon. No dinner* ✍ *Reservations not accepted.*

$$ ECLECTIC 🍴 **Café Salon Nakaoku** (カフェサロン中奥). Sandwiches, rice omelets, and coconut curry are among the eclectic fare served at this café inside a traditional house. This is a good spot for a meal, or just coffee and cake. One of the few restaurants in town open for dinner, Café Salon Nakaoku is near *Minamidera,* part of the Art House Project. [$] *Average main: ¥2000* ✉ *1167 Nakaoku, Honmura, Naoshima-cho, Naoshima* ☎ *087/892–3887* 💳 *No credit cards* ⏲ *Closed Tues.*

$$ CAFÉ 🍴 **Shioya Diner** (Shioya ダイナー). This 1950s-style café serves hot dogs, sandwiches, and whatever else the friendly owners feel like making that day. Next to the bathhouse in Miyanoura, it's a perfect stop for a post-bath beer. Shioya is sometimes closed for dinner, so in the evening it's wise to call before coming. [$] *Average main: ¥1000* ✉ *Next to Naoshima bath, 2227 Naoshima-cho, Kagawa-gun* ☎ *087/892–3290* 💳 *No credit cards* ⏲ *Closed Fri.*

WHERE TO STAY

Accommodations on Naoshima are mostly basic guesthouses, minshuku with shared facilities, and the luxury rooms at Benesse House. There aren't many mid-range options. Places fill up quickly on weekends and during holidays, so book as far in advance as possible.

$$$$ HOTEL Fodor's Choice ★ 🏨 **Hotel Benesse House** (ベネッセハウス). It's hard to say what part of a stay at the Hotel Benesse House is the most memorable: the gorgeous views of the Seto Inland Sea, special access to the artworks at the Benesse Museum, or the Tadao Ando architecture and the luxurious yet minimalist decor of the hotel rooms. **Pros:** access to art in and around the hotel; peaceful surroundings; stunning views; guests' access to a free shuttle bus to most island sights. **Cons:** restaurants are expensive; not convenient to other island dining options. [$] *Rooms from: ¥30000* ✉ *3418 Naoshima-cho, Naoshima* ☎ *087/892–3223* 🌐 *www.benesse-artsite.jp* 🛏 *65 rooms* 🍴 *No meals.*

$ B&B/INN 🏨 **Oomiyake Ryokan** (おおみやけ旅館). The owner of this small ryokan in Honmura spent decades in France and Morocco before returning to Naoshima to turn his family's 17th-century home into an inn. **Pros:**

10

traditional building; friendly owners; café next door. **Cons:** little privacy; guesthouse has the only private bathroom. $ *Rooms from: ¥9500* ⊠ *855 Naoshima, Kagawa-gun* ☎ *087/892–2328* ⊕ *www.oomiyake.jp* ▭ *No credit cards* ⇨ *3 Japanese-style rooms, 1 guesthouse* ⓧ *Some meals.*

KOTOHIRA 琴平

45 km (28 miles) south of Takamatsu.

Kotohira's draw is the Konpira Shrine, a mountaintop temple to the Shinto deity who protects seafarers. Though it's a long climb up a flight of stone steps, the shrine and its views of the Inland Sea are worth it. Other than the shrine, there's not much else in town. An evening stroll along its canal-lined streets can be pleasant, but if you have limited time on Shikoku you'll want to stay elsewhere.

GETTING HERE AND AROUND

Kotohira is one hour from Takamatsu by trains run by JR or Kotoden. Each company has its own station. If your bags will fit in station's coin lockers, stash them there; if not, someone at the shrine's gift shops will watch them for you. Before heading to the shrine, pick up a map at the information center between the two stations.

VISITOR INFORMATION

Kotohira Information Center. ⊠ *Kagawa-ken, Nakatado-gun, Kotohira-cho 811, Kagawa* ☎ *087/775–3500* ⊗ *Apr.–Sept., daily 10–5:30; Oct.–Mar., daily 10–5.*

EXPLORING

Konpira-san (金刀比羅宮 *Konpira Shrine*). According to legend, this shrine, which is also known as Kotohira-gu, was founded in the 1st century. It's stood on top of Mt. Zozu ever since, protecting sailors and seafarers. Visiting requires some effort; you'll have to climb 785 steps to the impressive main shrine and 583 more to the final lookout. It's also possible to travel by taxi to the upper gate, or even hire two sturdy locals to carry you up in a straw basket (look for them at the base of the mountain). The first half of the climb is crowded with souvenir shops, but after that the setting is more peaceful. You'll glimpse the ocean as you climb, and the noise of the town gives way to the sounds of rustling trees and birdsong. The **Treasure House,** on your right after you pass through the stone gate, displays masks used in Noh and Kabuki theater. The **Shoin,** sometimes closed for maintenance, is an Edo-period hall with artifacts and screens painted by Okyo Maruyama (1733–95), celebrated in his day and now for his realistic style. ⊠ *892–1 Kotohira-cho* ☎ *0877/75–2121* ⊑ *Shrine free, ¥800 for Treasure House, ¥800 for Shoin* ⊗ *Treasure House and Shoin usually daily 8:30–5. Shrine open all hrs.*

NEED A BREAK?	**Kinryo Sake Museum and Brewery** (金陵の郷). After climbing up to the Konpira Shrine, you may want some refreshment, or at least a diversion. When you reach the bottom, congratulate yourself with a stop at this sake museum and brewery marked by an enormous sake bottle hanging to the left of the temple stairs. You can't miss it. ⊠ *623 Kotohira-cho* ☎ *0877/73-4133* ⬚ *¥310* ⊙ *Weekdays 9–4, weekends and holidays 9–6.*

TOKUSHIMA 徳島

70 km (43 miles) southeast of Takamatsu and from Awa Ikeda.

Tokushima means "virtuous island"—ironic, considering the local residents' fondness for drinking, dancing, and hard partying. The city's annual **Awa Odori** dance festival is Japan's biggest, but there's fun to be had year-round in Tokushima and the surrounding area. Most visitors stay near the city center or in Naruto, a nearby peninsula famous for giant whirlpools that churn and thunder in the rocky straits below the cliffs. Nearby, the ambitious Otsuka Museum attracts huge crowds for its bizarre and breathtaking archive of the world's art. In surrounding hamlets you can try your hand at local crafts like indigo-dyeing or papermaking as they've been done for centuries. Back in the city proper you'll learn to dance the Awa Odori, either in a special performance hall or with the million others dancing the streets every summer during the Awa Odori Festival. Tokushima's major sights can be covered in a well-planned day or two, giving you plenty of time to move on to the mountains and gorges of Iya.

GETTING HERE AND AROUND

Tokushima is accessible by JR train: 1¼ hours from Takamatsu; 1½ hours from Awa Ikeda; 2 hours from Okayama; about 2½ hours from Kochi; 3 hours, 20 minutes from Shin-Osaka; and 3 hours, 40 minutes from Matsuyama. Buses are also an option. Highway buses depart from Takamatsu (1½ hours); Kobe (2 hours); Kochi (2 hours, 40 minutes); and Matsuyama (3 hours, 10 minutes), as well as Kyoto, Osaka, or Kansai Airport (3 hours). Overnight buses also travel here from Tokyo (10 hours), and there are ferries from Tokyo (19 hours) and Wakayama (2 hours).

Buses leave Tokushima for Naruto on the hour between 9 and 3, taking 73 minutes and costing ¥710; the return has more varied times, so check the schedule. The boat quay at Naruto Kanko-ko is a few stops before the end of the line, about an eight-minute walk from Uzu-no-michi. There are also trains to Naruto Station; catch a bus or taxi from there to the coast. Going by car from Tokushima takes roughly a half hour. Major car rental companies such as Toyota Rent a Car and Nissan Rent a Car have offices near Tokushima Station. It's always a good idea to book ahead, and you can often score discounts by booking a few weeks in advance. During busy travel seasons reservations are essential.

■ TIP→ Tokushima's best sights are far from the city center. Consider renting a car rather than relying on public transportation.

10

Contacts **Nissan Rent a Car.** ✉ *1–10 Minamidekijima-cho* ☎ *088/625–1612*
⊕ *nissan-rentacar.com/english.* **Toyota Rent a Car.** ✉ *1–18 Nakano-cho*
☎ *088/652–0100* ⊕ *rent.toyota.co.jp/eng.*

TOURS

Naruto Sightseeing Boats (鳴門観光汽船 *Naruto Kankou Kisen*). This well-regarded company offers half-hour tours of the Naruto Whirlpools on two ships: the *Wonder Naruto* (¥1,580, daily departures every 40 minutes from 9 to 4:20) and the *Aqua Eddy* (¥2,260, daily departures every half hour from 9:15 to 4:15). Reservations are required for the *Aqua Eddy.* You can book online or by phone. Both ships depart from the small pier in Kameura Port, at the southwest end of Naruto Koen Park. ✉ *Naruto Koen Kameura Kanko-ko* ☎ *088/687–0101* ⊕ *www. uzusio.com* 🎫 *From ¥1,580* ⊗ *Daily 9–4:20.*

VISITOR INFORMATION

Before hitting town, head up by glass elevator to the Clement Tower Station Building's sixth floor. Here you'll find TOPIA, the best tourist information center in western Japan. The center's fluent English speakers provide bus and train schedules, tide calendars (necessary for seeing the whirlpools at their best), and a good battle plan for tackling it all. TOPIA staff members can also advise you about travel to other Shikoku destinations.

Contact **TOPIA.** ✉ *Clement Plaza, 6F, 1–61 Terashima-Honcho Nishi*
☎ *088/656–3303* ⊕ *www.topia.ne.jp/english.*

EXPLORING

Awa Odori Kaikan (阿波踊り会館). If you miss summer's Awa Odori dance, festival you can still get a dose at this museum and theater. *Odori* means "dance," and silk-robed professionals perform the famous local step here nightly. But shine your shoes: when the troupe leader starts talking to the audience, he's looking for volunteers. Everyone will be thrilled to see you try, so stand up! Thankfully, it's an easy dance. You might get a prize for participating, and one special award goes to the biggest fool on the floor—this honor is a staple of the festival, and it's not always the foreigners who win. The best show is at 8 pm. Arrive early and browse the gift shop or treat yourself to a ropeway ride up the mountain for a lovely city view. The third floor of the building is a small museum dedicated to the Awa Odori Festival. ✉ *20 Shin-machi-bashi, 2-chome* ☎ *088/611–1611* 🎫 *Museum ¥300, afternoon dance ¥600, evening dance ¥800* ⊗ *Museum daily 9–5. Performances weekdays at 2, 3, 4, and 8, weekends at 11, 2, 3, 4, and 8 pm. Closed 2nd Wed. in Oct., Feb., and June. Closed Aug. 11–15.*

Awa Washi Dento (阿波和紙伝統産業会館 *Hall of Awa Japanese Handmade Paper*). Trek out to this paper museum also known as Washi Kaikan to make your own postcards and browse the phenomenal gift shop, which stocks everything from sheets of softer-than-silk wrapping paper to peerless parasols. The trip here by train takes one hour to Awa-Yamakawa Station, then you walk 15 minutes to the hall. It's easier to rent a car and make the one-hour drive, especially if you are continuing on to the Iya Valley. ✉ *141 Kawahigashi, Yamakawa-cho*

☎ *0883/42–6120* ⊕ *www.awagami.com/hall* ✉ *Museum ¥300, paper-making ¥500* ☉ *Tues.–Sun. 9–5.*

FAMILY **House of Indigo** (藍の館 *Ai no Yakata*). At the House of Indigo, you can try the ancient craft of dyeing cloth in cauldrons of pungent indigo. Someone at the desk will show you a price chart for items—cotton handkerchiefs cost only ¥500, silk scarves close to ¥2,000. Towels come out splendidly, but you have to ask for the separate price chart (the word is *ta-o-ru*). The dyeing process is fun, and you'll be delighted with what you make. Poke around the 400-year-old craft center when you're finished. One of the proprietors performs daily on the *shaku-hachi*, a thick-bodied wooden flute, and he'll play anytime you ask. ✉ *Aizumi-cho, Tokumei Aza Maesunishi* ✛ *From Tokushima Station take 20-min bus to Higashi Nakatomi and walk down hill behind you and follow indigo signs* ☎ *088/692–6317* ✉ *¥300* ☉ *Wed.–Mon. 9–5.*

Naruto Whirlpools (鳴門の渦潮). You can hear the thunderous roar of the giant tidal whirlpools at Naruto Kaikyo (the Naruto Straits) long before you see them. When they come into sight, the contrast between peaceful sky and furious, frothing sea is striking. The whirlpools are formed when the changing tides force a huge volume of water through the narrow, rocky bottleneck. A glass-bottom promenade called **Uzu-no-michi** overlooks the pools, but the view is even better from the deck of a tour boat. A few companies with different-size vessels offer rides that cost between ¥1,500 and ¥2,500, but all of them are exhilarating. Two of the best boats are the *Wonder Naruto* and the smaller *Aqua Eddy*, both run by Naruto Kankou Kisen. The tide table on the promenade's website shows when the pools will be at their best. ✉ *Naruto Koen* ☎ *088/683–6262* ⊕ *www.uzunomichi.jp/english* ✉ *¥510 for promenade* ☉ *Park open 24 hrs. Promenade Mar.–Sept., daily 9–6; Oct.–Feb., daily 9–5. Closed 2nd Mon. in Mar., June, Sept., and Dec.*

Otsuka Kokusai Bijutsukan (大塚国際美術館 *Otsuka Museum of Art*). On a boardwalk that rings the coastline, this museum of ceramic art is equally impressive and bewildering. Its founders commissioned more than 1,000 faithful reproductions of Western-art masterpieces on ceramic panels, the concept being that while Picasso's painting *Guernica* or Michelangelo's Sistine Chapel ceiling may fade with time, ceramic reproductions of them will live on forever. Exhibits are arranged by era, from antiquity to modern times, and it's all there, from a Pompeian banquet scene to Rembrandt's self-portraits to Warhol's *Marilyn x 100*. Cumulatively, the artworks are a bit overwhelming, though certainly not forgettable. ✉ *Naruto Park, 65–1 Fukuike Aza Tosadomari-ura, near Naruto Whirlpools, Naruto-cho* ☎ *088/687–3737* ⊕ *www.o-museum. or.jp* ✉ *¥3,240* ☉ *Tues.–Sun. 9:30–5; last entry at 4.*

10

WHERE TO EAT

Tokushima is full of slick bars and restaurants, so you'll eat well here.

$$$ ✗ **Domannaka** (どまん中). This modern izakaya-style Japanese restau-
JAPANESE rant near Tokushima Station specializes in skewers of flame-grilled chicken, beef, pork, and seafood. The vast menu also includes hot-pot stews, fresh seafood dishes, and tempura items, and there's plenty of local sake to wash it all down. Sit at the counter and chat up the

friendly chef and the regulars or, for a quieter meal, ask for a table in the back. [$] *Average main: ¥2500* ✉ *1–47 Terashima Honcho Nishi, near Agnes Hotel* ☎ *088/623–3293* 🌐 *wa-domannaka.jp* 🕑 *Closed Sun. except when Mon. is a public holiday, then closed Mon. No lunch* 💳 *No credit cards.*

$$ ECLECTIC 🍴 **YRG.** Tokushima's best spot for lunch or dinner and a favorite of the young-and-cool demographic, YRG has a laid-back atmosphere and a hip but unpretentious decor. Takao Yamasaki, the English-speaking proprietor, decides the set menus daily, aiming for nutritionally balanced yet provocative comfort food. Drink menus are inside kids' books from a dozen countries scattered on the shelves and tables. Exiting JR Station you'll see two smaller streets and one major one branch off to the left; take the middle street and walk two minutes to just before it terminates. [$] *Average main: ¥1500* ✉ *1–33–4 Terashima Honcho Higashi* ☎ *088/656–7889* 💳 *No credit cards* 🕑 *Closed Thurs.*

SAIL TOKUSHIMA

Although Tokushima best serves as a hub for accessing its surroundings, it's a charming city in its own right. Take advantage of the half-hour river tours running from Ryokoku-bashi near the Toyoko Inn. They're operated by volunteers from the Shin-Machi River Preservation Society. On weekdays from September through June, the tours run every 40 minutes from 11 to 3:40. In July and August, tours run from 11 to 7:40, and especially on weekends the accommodating volunteers will take you any time you show up. Write your name in the book and drop ¥200 in the box on the pier before boarding.

WHERE TO STAY

Expensive resorts here feel a bit worn out, and they don't deal well with guests who don't speak Japanese. A better option is the string of newer hotels by the train station.

$ HOTEL 🏨 **Agnes Hotel** (アグネスホテル). The genial atmosphere at the Agnes might derive in part from the French pastries served downstairs, all baked on premises with high-quality imported ingredients and seasonal fruit, but surely the main source is the hotel's proprietor,Takashi, gregarious in English and Japanese and dying to make your stay enjoyable. **Pros:** a minute away from the train station; bilingual manager; terrific pastries. **Cons:** no doubles, just singles and twins; spartan decor. [$] *Rooms from: ¥8000* ✉ *1–28 Terashima Honcho Nishi* ☎ *088/626–2222* 🌐 *www.agneshotel.jp* 🛏 *61 rooms* 🍽 *Breakfast.*

$ HOTEL 🏨 **The Agnes Plus** (アグネスホテルプラス). Across the street from its sister property, the Agnes Hotel, this place offers the same cheerful hospitality and comfortable, if compact, rooms. **Pros:** relaxing public bath; comfortable rooms; cheerful hospitality. **Cons:** compact rooms; no restaurant. [$] *Rooms from: ¥6000* ✉ *1–34 Terashima Honcho Nishi, Tokushima* ☎ *088/655–1212* 🌐 *www.agneshotel.jp/plus* 🛏 *46 rooms* 🍽 *Breakfast.*

$$ HOTEL 🏨 **Hotel Sunroute** (ホテルサンルート徳島). Luxurious but affordable, this hotel offers great city access—it's across from the JR Station—and excellent amenities. **Pros:** nice bathrooms; excellent location; international clientele. **Cons:** loud music. [$] *Rooms from: ¥12960* ✉ *1–5–1*

Moto-machi ☎ *088/653–8111* 🌐 *www.sunroute-tokushima.com* 🛏 *177 rooms* 🍴 *Breakfast.*

$$$ HOTEL FAMILY 🏨 **Renaissance Resort Naruto** (ルネッサンスリゾート鳴門). Stretching along a sandy beach, this resort hotel is peerless for its comfort, service, luxury, and access to the sights. **Pros:** sumptuous facilities; beachfront location; great access to Naruto. **Cons:** far from city center; beach is unsuitable for swimming. [$] *Rooms from: ¥20000* ✉ *16–45 Oge Tosadomari-ura* ☎ *088/687–2580, 088/687–2211* 🌐 *www.renaissance-naruto.com* 🛏 *167 Western-style rooms, 41 Japanese-style rooms* 🍴 *Breakfast.*

$ HOTEL 🏨 **Toyoko Inn** (東横イン). Fresh facilities and easy city access make for a pleasing stay at this comfortable chain hotel. **Pros:** two-minute walk from train station; close to dining options; reasonable rates. **Cons:** rooms could be bigger. [$] *Rooms from: ¥11000* ✉ *1–5 Ryogoku Hon-cho* ☎ *088/657–1045* 🌐 *www.toyoko-inn.com* 🛏 *139 rooms* 🍴 *No meals.*

CENTRAL SHIKOKU

IYA VALLEY AND OBOKE-KOBOKE GORGES 祖谷と大歩危小歩危

25 km (16 miles) southwest of Awa Ikeda, 105 km (65 miles) west of Tokushima, 135 km (84 miles) east of Matsuyama.

Fodor's Choice ★ In the Iya Valley, mountain villages cling to the side of improbably steep hills while turquoise rivers rush through the ravines below. This remote region was once so isolated that it became the retreat of choice for Heike clan warriors after they lost an epic battle to their Minamoto rivals in the 12th century. To get to Iya now, you don't have to string your own vine bridges across ravines like the Heike did, although some of the bridges remain. If you want to feel as though you've escaped modern Japan for a hidden world, you can't do better than here.

After some local government mergers in 2006, the villages in the Iya Valley were combined to become "Miyoshi City." Don't be fooled by the "city" moniker, though—Miyoshi City is actually a collection of rural villages administered from the small riverside town of Awa Ikeda, 32 km (20 miles) north of the Iya Valley.

Next to Iya, the Yoshino River roars through Okobe and Koboke gorges, where you'll find Japan's best white-water rafting. Try your hand at making delicious Iya soba or local crafts, or trek deeper into the valley to hike to the swordlike summit of Mt. Tsurugi.

GETTING HERE AND AROUND

Access Iya by taking the express Nampu train to Oboke Station, in the foothills of the Iya Valley. From Oboke, Yonkoh buses run to Nishi-Iya Village eight times a day from April to November, and four times a day the rest of the year (¥660). Infrequent buses also run from Awa Ikeda (1¼ hours). If you're comfortable driving on narrow mountain roads, a car offers the best way to see the valley. The closest rental-car offices are in Awa Ikeda, but renting in Tokushima and driving into the valley via Route 438/439 over Mt. Tsurugi makes sense because of the beautiful scenery, as does renting in Kochi and driving in via Route 32,

10

which follows the Yoshino River. **TIP→ Rent the smallest car possible. Mountain roads are narrow, and corners are tight!**

VISITOR INFORMATION

Miyoshi City Office of Tourism has an excellent English website with information and downloadable maps for the Iya Valley.

Contact Miyoshi City Office of Tourism. ✉ *Miyoshi City* 🌐 *www.miyoshinavi.jp/english.*

EXPLORING

Chiiori House (庵トラスト *House of the Flute*). Alex Kerr, an American artist and writer, stumbled across this dilapidated traditional farmhouse in the 1970s while traveling in Iya. He bought it and began the painstaking work of restoring its thatched roof and heavy wooden beams. Named Chiiori House, it is now the cornerstone of the activities of the Chiiori Trust, a nonprofit foundation working to preserve the region's traditional beauty while revitalizing its rural communities. You can visit the restored (thatch roof and all) Chiiori House for the day or spend the night. Reserve ahead to do either. ✉ *209 Tsurui, Higashi-Iya* ☎ *0883/88–5290* 🌐 *www.chiiori.org* 🎫 *¥500* 🕐 *Tours at noon and 2 (reservation required).*

Kazura-Bashi (かずら橋 *Vine Bridges*). Iya's most famous feature is its trio of *kazura-bashi* (vine bridges) spanning its gorges. The most popular—referred to by most signs, maps, and locals simply as "Kazura-bashi"—is 20 minutes by car from Oboke Station. A less-visited pair are closer to Mt. Tsurugi. The bridges date back 800 years, to the aftermath of the momentous Gempei War, when the defeated Heike clan fled to these valleys after losing to the rival Minamoto clan. If the refugees were attacked, they could cut the vines at a moment's notice. These days, thin steel wires reinforce the precarious planks, and fresh vines are restrung every three years, but it still feels death-defying to cross the boards over the rivers. To visit Kazura-bashi, follow sights to it from Route 32 or Route 45. If you're driving, park in the cheaper lots up the hill. The tall waterfall down the path is free, but you'll pay to cross the bridge. ✉ *Nishi-Iya Sanzon Village, Miyoshi City* ☎ *0120/404–344 Miyoshi City Tourism* 🎫 *¥550 to cross bridge* 🕐 *Daily dawn–dusk.*

WHERE TO STAY

$$$$ B&B/INN 🏨 **Iya Bijin** (祖谷美人). The private onsen bathtubs on each room's balcony here have breathtaking views of the unspoiled valley below. **Pros:** unbeatable views; in-room onsen baths. **Cons:** minimal English assistance. [$] *Rooms from: ¥40000* ✉ *9–3 Zentoku, Nishiiya Sanzon Village, Miyoshi City* ☎ *088/387–2009* 💳 *No credit cards* 🛏 *9 Japanese-style rooms* 🍴 *Some meals.*

$$$$ B&B/INN Fodor's Choice ★ 🏨 **Iya Onsen** (祖谷温泉). Perched on the edge of a steep ravine above the Iya River, this upscale hot springs inn provides absolute luxury in the middle of nowhere. **Pros:** amazing views; traditional cuisine; outdoor riverside bath. **Cons:** not much sightseeing nearby. [$] *Rooms from: ¥24990* ✉ *367–28 Matsuo Matsumoto, Tokushima-ken, Ikeda-cho* ☎ *0883/75–2311* 🌐 *www.iyaonsen.co.jp/english* 🛏 *20 rooms* 🍴 *Some meals.*

The Iya Valley's most famous attractions are its Kazura-Bashi (vine bridges).

$$$$ ⌂ **Kazuraya Ryokan** (祖谷の宿 かずらや). Iya's most cheerful family, the
B&B/INN   Hiraguris, run this traditional inn just up the road from Kazura-bashi.
FAMILY   **Pros:** traditional cooking; family hospitality; friendly vibe. **Cons:** lim-
ited English spoken. $ *Rooms from:* ¥25000 ⌂ *78 Kantei, Nishi-Iya
Sanzon Village, Miyoshi City* ☎ *0883/87–2831* ▭ *No credit cards* ⇅ *18
rooms* ⎢○⎢ *Some meals.*

$$$$ ⌂ **Mountain Lodge Chiiori** (庵トラスト). If a search for absolute serenity is
RENTAL   what brought you to Iya, head straight for Chiiori House. **Pros:** breath-
Fodor's Choice   taking views; unforgettable atmosphere; peace and quiet. **Cons:** access
★   is by winding mountain road; can be cold in winter. $ *Rooms from:*
¥38000 ⌂ *209 Tsurui, Higashi-Iya* ☎ *0883/88–5290* ⊕ *www.chiiori.
org* ⇅ *1 room* ⎢○⎢ *No meals.*

$$$$ ⌂ **Togenkyo Iya Farmhouses** (桃源郷民宿ステイ). Staying at this group
RENTAL   of farmhouses in the mountains of eastern Iya is the perfect way to
Fodor's Choice   experience traditional life here. **Pros:** traditional architecture; tasteful
★   facilities; complete privacy. **Cons:** access by winding mountain lane
can be a challenge. $ *Rooms from:* ¥30000 ⌂ *Wada 96–3, Higashi-Iya*
☎ *0883/88–2540* ⊕ *www.tougenkyo-iya.jp* ⇅ *8 houses* ⎢○⎢ *Some meals.*

SPORTS AND THE OUTDOORS

WHITE-WATER RAFTING

Fodor's Choice   **Happy Raft** (ハッピーラフト). Rafting down the wild Yoshino River's
★   rocky gorges is one of this region's great thrills, and this company is
your best bet for well-trained bilingual guides and friendly service. Half-
day trips cost ¥7,500 in high season, but you'll wish you had done the
full day for ¥15,500. You can also try a longer combination rafting-
and-canyoning trip. The staff is a great resource for travel tips about

IYA VALLEY EXPERIENCES

If a day or two spent rafting, canyoning, and bridge walking (with a night at a hot-springs resort) leaves you wanting more, venture farther into the Iya Valley. Mt. Tsurugi, the "Fufu-bashi" (so-called "husband and wife" vine bridges), and a handful of onsen-hotels and craft workshops await. Getting here isn't overly complicated—follow signs toward Higashi-Iya and Tsurugi-san—but the narrow mountain roads are challenging, and just to be sure you'll want someone to mark the way on a map. You can also take a Yonkoh bus from West Iya to Kubo, transfer to a smaller bus bound for

Mt. Tsurugi, and get off at the Kazura-bashi bus stop. Buses are infrequent, so check the schedule carefully to avoid getting stranded in the hills. The *taiken*, or "experiences," offered by local artisans are unique activities. Making delicious buckwheat soba noodles is rewarding, especially because this region is famous for its hearty strand of buckwheat, but making tofu or hiring a local Sherpa to climb Tsurugi-san with you is great fun, too. Staffers at Miyoshi City Tourist Information (⊕ *www. miyoshinavi.jp/english*) have details about the crafts workshops.

the area. ✉ *221–1 Ikadagi Otoyo-cho Nagaoka-gun, Kochi* ✛ *7½ km (4½ miles) south of Oboke Station on Rte. 32* ☎ *088/775–0500* ⊕ *en. happyraft.com* ✉ *From ¥7,500.*

KOCHI 高知

170 km (105 miles) southwest of Takamatsu, 175 km (108 miles) southwest of Tokushima, 155 km (96 miles) southeast of Matsuyama, 110 km (68 miles) northeast of Nakamura, near the southern Ehime border.

Kochi has earned a reputation for being different. The locals are rough-talking, boisterous, and social, and their spirited city has an attitude far from the Japanese norm. The famous Yosakoi Dance Festival, one of Japan's most popular summer events, is an explosion of parades and performances that fills the city for days. For weeks before and after, the streets shake with excitement, making summer the best time to visit.

GETTING HERE AND AROUND

By train, Kochi is 2 hours from Tokushima, about 2¼ hours from Takamatsu, 3½ hours from Osaka, and 4 hours from Matsuyama. By bus it is 2½ hours from Matsuyama.

Half of the city's top attractions are within striking distance of Hari-maya-bashi; the bridge is a 10-minute walk south of the train station. Getting around by bicycle is a great option; the tourist office outside the train station provides free bikes for day use.

Taxis from the train station cost about ¥550. Streetcars from the station travel just about everywhere for ¥200, and the tram lines are easily navigable. Yosakoi Gururin buses travel the city center; access farther-flung sights like Katsurahama Beach, Chikurin-ji Temple, and the Makino Botanical Garden by the My Yu bus (¥1,000), in front of Kochi Station.

VISITOR INFORMATION

The Kochi Tourist Information Booth at Kochi Station has few English speakers, but the staff will put a great effort into helping you anyway. Make sure to grab the excellent English-language city and prefecture map, as well as the *Welcome to Kochi* magazine.

Contact Kochi Tourist Information Booth. ✉ *2–10–17 Kitahonmachi ✛ Inside Tosa Terrace building in front of Kochi Station* ☎ *088/826–3337* ⊕ *www.attaka.or.jp.*

EXPLORING

DOWNTOWN

Harimaya-bashi (播磨屋橋 *Harimaya Bridge*). This arched red bridge is at the center of Kochi's best-known story, a tragic tale about a Buddhist priest caught buying a hairpin for a lover on this very spot. See what's for sale here these days, or look for bargains in the twisting, tunneled arcades and side streets. Locals come out to dine, chat, and dance (yes, dance) in parks and at outdoor cafés until the wee hours. When the stores and bars finally close, there's always a ramen cart or two doing business on the sidewalk, so pull up a stool and dig in. Kochi people won't pay you much mind until you start talking to them, but many are multilingual, affable, and easy to engage. ✉ *Harimaya-bashi.*

Hirome-ichiba (ひろめ市場 *Hirome Market*). The best place to mingle with locals is at the Hirome-ichiba Market. The busy market sells interesting pottery, jewelry, and photographs, but everyone's really here for the food. The tiny eateries and food counters have so many strange, delicious dishes that you couldn't try them all in a year. If your chosen spot doesn't have a picture menu, you can always point to someone else's plate across the broad wooden tables. The market is at the western end of the main arcade, close to the castle, about 15 minutes by foot from JR Kochi Station. Look for the mass of bicycles parked around a squat ramen stand beside the entrance, a big orange-and-green sign above the hangar-bay door, and a large crowd of well-fed locals. ✉ *2–3–1 Obiya-machi* ☎ *088/822–5287* ⊗ *Mon.–Sat. 8 am–11 pm, Sun. 7 am–11 pm. Sometimes closed Wed.*

Kochi-jo (高知城 *Kochi Castle*). West of downtown's markets and arcades you'll find barrel-chested Kochi Castle, whose feel is more rough-hewn and lived-in than that of other Japanese castles. The view from the topmost watchtower is splendid, and walking up the enormous steps or through the receiving chambers is like being transported to the Edo period. ✉ *1–2–1 Marunouchi ✛ Short bus ride or 2-km (1½-mile) walk southwest from train station; 1¾-km (1-mile) walk west from Harimaya Bridge* ☎ *088/824–5701* 🎫 *¥420* ⊗ *Daily 9–5; last entry at 4:30.*

Nichiyo-ichi Sunday Market (日曜市). Dating back to the late 17th century, this popular market offers a mile of bizarre fruits and vegetables. It's not a great place for souvenir shopping, but why not try some *yuzu-an* in a pastry pocket? This Kochi specialty replaces the red beans often found in desserts with a paste made from the sour yellow yuzu fruit grown in the prefecture. Nichiyo-ichi runs along broad, palm-lined Otetsuji-dori Street from Harimaya Bridge right up to the gates of Kochi Castle. ✉ *Otetsuji-dori* ⊗ *Sun. sunrise–sunset.*

10

White-water rafting is a popular activity in the Iya Valley.

FAMILY **Yokoyama Ryuichi Kinen Manga Kan** (横山隆一記念まんが館 *Yokoyama Memorial Manga Museum*). This playful modern facility celebrates the life and work of Japan's first great cartoonist, hometown boy Ryuichi Yokoyama. His most popular character, Fuku-chan, is still widely loved, as the crowds of schoolkids reading comics in the museum's free manga library will attest. The cartoons inspire and delight, and no language skill is required to enjoy most of the visual humor. Look through World War II propaganda cartoons (from the Japanese point of view), interactive print stations, dioramas, model railroads, and tons of comic strips. ⊠ *Kochi City Culture Plaza, 2–1 Kutanda, 3rd fl.* ⚓ *7-min walk southeast of Harimaya Bridge* ☎ *088/883–5029* ⊕ *www.bunkaplaza. or.jp/mangakan/english* 🎫 *¥410* ⊗ *Tues.–Sun. 9–6.*

OUTSIDE THE CITY CENTER

Chikurin-ji (竹林寺 *Chikurin Temple*). Buddhist pilgrims had been communing with nature in the garden of this austere mountaintop temple long before the giant ferns moved in next door at the Makino Botanical Garden. The garden, a registered National Treasure, dates from the 13th century. Its simple arrangement of ponds, rocks, and pine trees provides a soothing contrast to the vibrant foliage next door. The setting is particularly peaceful in the late afternoon. Linger at the temple a while, and you're likely to encounter white-clad Shingon Buddhist pilgrims visiting on their way around the island. ⊠ *3577 Godaisan* ☎ *088/882–3085* 🎫 *¥400 for garden* ⊗ *Daily 8:30–5.*

Katsurahama Beach (桂浜). The prefecture may be known for its great surfing and swimming beaches, but rocky Katsurahama Beach has other attractions. It's best known for its giant statue of the 19th-century political reformer Sakamoto Ryoma, Kochi's local-born hero, staring grimly out to sea from his big black pedestal. The view from a cliff-top shrine is great (moon-watching from this spot is depicted in many prints). Get here by bus (35 minutes) from Kochi Station. ⊠ *778 Urado*.

FAMILY

Fodor'sChoice

★

Makino Shokubutsuen (牧野植物園 *Makino Botanical Garden*). Planted in honor of Kochi botanist Tomitaro Makino, this Eden-like valley of flowers and trees lies hidden atop Mt. Godaisan. Different trails for each season show off the best nature has to offer. Hours can disappear as you walk through the azaleas, camellias, chrysanthemums, and thousands of other plants in this huge and lovingly tended landscape. Don't miss the giant ferns, so big you can actually sit in them. You're encouraged to leave the paths and explore on your own—as Makino wrote, "to commune with nature we need to make ourselves free and jump into her." You'll find more of his quotes, recollections, philosophy, and drawings in a fascinating museum inside the park. ⊠ *4200–6 Godaisan* ☎ *088/882–2601* ☺ *¥720* ☼ *Daily 9–5*.

OFF THE
BEATEN
PATH

Muroto Misaki (室戸岬 *Muroto Cape*). A surreal coastline awaits you at far-off Muroto. The road east from Kochi follows a rugged shoreline cut by inlets and indentations along a landscape out of Dr. Seuss, where the Pacific Black Current has shaped enormous terraces going down to the sea. A concrete promenade lets you walk the farthest tip of sea-sculpted land, where detailed signs in English explain local geography and history.

Muroto Cape is a 2½-hour drive along the coast road. To get here by public transportation, take a 1½-hour train ride to Nahari Station on the private Tosa Kuroshio train (¥1,330), and a one-hour bus ride from there (¥1,200).

Muroto Dorufin Senta. Children love the Muroto Dolphins Center, where you can swim with these intelligent mammals. The full experience costs ¥8,400 for adults and ¥5,400 for kids, though prices are discounted from November through February. If you just want to watch dolphins swim in their tanks, the fee is ¥435. The center is off Route 55 on the western side of the peninsula, a five-minute walk from Muroto Eigyosho bus stop, 50 minutes past Nahari Station. (⊠ *6810–162 Ugeihama, Muroto Misaki-cho*. ☎ *0887/22–1245*. ⊕ *www.muroto-dc.jp/en. Daily 10–4.*) ⊠ *Muroto City* ⊕ *www.muroto-geo.jp/en*.

Sakamoto Ryoma Kinenkan (坂本龍馬記念館 *Sakamoto Ryoma Memorial Museum*). During the turbulent times before the Meiji Restoration, Sakamoto Ryoma was a radical and a revolutionary. The political changes he instigated were enough to get him killed, as you'll learn in this museum jutting fabulously over the sand and surf. After seeing the blood-splashed screen from the room where he was assassinated, you'll finally know who the cowboyish samurai plastered on every street corner in Kochi is. ⊠ *830 Urado-Shiroyama* ⊹ *40-min ride on Kochi Kenkotsu bus to Ryoma Kinenkan stop* ☎ *088/841–0001* ⊕ *www. ryoma-kinenkan.jp/en* ☺ *¥500* ☼ *Daily 9–5*.

10

WHERE TO EAT

$
EUROPEAN

✕**Faust** (ファウスト). This delightful café-restaurant sits just off the main drag. Choose a table by the window and people-watch on the cobbled lane, or head indoors to the quirky third-floor dining area. The first floor looks like a diner, the second floor is more acceptable, but sitting in the funky upper level and ordering from the same inexpensive, delicious menu is having your cake and eating it, too. The cake, incidentally, is excellent. $ *Average main: ¥980* ⊠ *1–2–22 Hon-machi* ☎ *088/873–4111* ▭ *No credit cards.*

$
JAPANESE

✕**Myojin-Maru** (明神丸). Follow your nose to this place inside the Hirome-ichiba Market, and don't leave without trying the *katsuo tataki,* the regional fish specialty and the only item on the menu. Look for the orange flames erupting from this stall's window. Fresh cuts of fish are seared to perfection by a cook perilously close to being engulfed by the flames that he's feeding with big handfuls of straw. Your meal is served on a bed of rice or drizzled with a citrusy soy sauce, and you'll never eat enough of it. Myojin-Maru belongs to the captain of the largest fishing vessel in the port town Kure, where most of the restaurant's fish comes from. Locals love this place. To avoid lines, arrive early for lunch or dinner. $ *Average main: ¥975* ⊠ *Hirome-ichiba Market, 2–3–1 Obiya-machi Arcade* ☎ *088/820–5101* ▭ *No credit cards.*

$$$$
JAPANESE

✕**Tosa Ryori Tsukasa** (土佐料理 司 高知本店). Meals here range from simple bento boxes to the lavish fish platters that are a Kochi specialty. The staff will recommend the local fish called *katsuo*—in Japanese it's *sasuga Kochi,* "just as you'd expect in Kochi"—but consider the shabu-shabu meat and vegetable combinations, which your servers will teach you to cook on a special table in your private tatami room. Be careful with seating; the first floor is a bland cafeteria, so indicate that you want an upstairs room instead. $ *Average main: ¥3500* ⊠ *1–2–15 Harimaya-cho* ☎ *088/873–4351.*

WHERE TO STAY

$$
HOTEL

🛏 **7Days Hotel** (セブンデイズホテル). The 7Days and its slightly plusher annex 7Days Plus are primarily business hotels, but they stand out for their pampering service and comfortable feel. **Pros:** spacious rooms; great service; good breakfast. **Cons:** mostly twin rooms; away from entertainment. $ *Rooms from: ¥12000* ⊠ *2–13–6 and 2–13–17 Harimaya-cho* ☎ *088/884–7100, 088/884–7111* ⊕ *www.7dayshotel.com* ⤳ *170 rooms* ⦿| *No meals.*

$$$$
HOTEL

🛏 **Crown Palais Hotel Shin-Hankyu Kochi** (ホテルザ クラウンパレス新阪急高知). This Western-style luxury hotel is so spacious and modern that it almost feels out of place in gruff Kochi. **Pros:** friendly staff; good dining options; close to city center. **Cons:** slightly twee; only four double rooms among all the twins. $ *Rooms from: ¥27000* ⊠ *4–2–50 Hon-machi* ☎ *088/873–1111* ⊕ *www.crownpalais.jp/kochi/english* ⤳ *238 Western-style rooms, 4 Japanese-style rooms* ⦿| *No meals.*

$$$$
HOTEL

🛏 **Jyoseikan** (城西館). "Fit for a king" is an expression often taken for granted, but in this case it's true—Jyoseikan is where the Emperor stays when the Royal Family comes to Kochi. **Pros:** generously sized rooms; excellent service; close to the castle and market. **Cons:** not all staffers speak English. $ *Rooms from: ¥40000* ⊠ *2–5–34 Kami-machi*

☎ *088/875–0111* ⊕ *www.jyoseikan.co.jp* ⤳ *72 Japanese-style rooms* ⦿ *Some meals.*

$$ 🛏 **Richmond Hotel Kochi** (リッチモンドホテル高知). Pristine rooms, rea-

HOTEL sonable rates, and a prime location near nightlife and shopping make this hotel a superb mid-range choice. **Pros:** unbeatable location; spotless facilities; accommodating staff. **Cons:** regular-class rooms cramped. $ *Rooms from: ¥16000* ⊠ *Obiyamachi shopping arcade, 9–4 Obiyamachi* ☎ *088/820–1122* ⊕ *kochi.richmondhotel.jp* ⤳ *234 rooms* ⦿ *No meals.*

$$$$ 🛏 **UTOCO Auberge & Spa** (ウトコオーベルジュ＆スパ). This elegant spa

RESORT resort is the last thing you'd expect to find in the rough-and-tumble

Fodor's Choice fishing town of Muroto Cape. **Pros:** ocean views; superb service; luxu-

★ rious rooms. **Cons:** few sightseeing options nearby. $ *Rooms from: ¥45000* ⊠ *6969–1 Muroto-misaki-cho, Muroto City* ☎ *050/3786–0022 Hoshino Resorts main reservation* ⊕ *utocods.co.jp/en/welcome.html* ⊟ *No credit cards* ⤳ *17 rooms* ⦿ *Some meals.*

MATSUYAMA AND WESTERN SHIKOKU

MATSUYAMA 松山

160 km (100 miles) southwest of Takamatsu, 120 km (75 miles) west of Awa Ikeda, 195 km (120 miles) west of Tokushima, 155 km (95 miles) northwest of Kochi.

Shikoku's largest city, Matsuyama prides itself on a great history, friendly disposition, fantastic cultural attractions, and a love for fine food, intense fashion, and haiku. You'll be quickly captivated by the sights and feel of the city, and you can join in the fun. Bathe at Dogo Onsen—Japan's oldest hot spring—hit the fashion avenue downtown, or go restaurant crawling through the best spots on the island. Denizens say it's *sumi-yasui* (easy living) here, and you'll find Matsuyama one of the most rewarding stops along your route.

Though a large and not particularly well-organized city, Matsuyama is easy to navigate and is served by a good tram network. For visitors the action is concentrated around a few locations, the main one being the enormous central landmark, Matsuyama Castle.

10

GETTING HERE AND AROUND

BOAT TRAVEL Except for the Orange Ferry from Osaka, which docks in the town of Toyo, east of Matsuyama, all ferries to Matsuyama arrive at Matsuyama Kanko Ko Terminal. Get from here to central Matsuyama by taking a taxi (about ¥3,000; 20 minutes) or direct Iyotetsu bus (¥500; 30 minutes). There are also direct buses from Kanko Ko Terminal to Dogo Onsen (¥600; 40 minutes).

From Tokyo: Ocean Toukyu Ferry runs an overnight boat from Tokyo's Takeshiba Pier to Tokushima (19 hours; ¥10,350 for a basic tatami spot to ¥27,980 for a luxurious suite). Matsuyama is four hours by bus from Tokushima.

From Hiroshima: The Setonaikai Kisen and Ishizaki Kisen companies run hydrofoils from Hiroshima Port 14 times a day each (70 minutes), for a one-way fare of ¥6,900. The Ishizaki Kisen slow ferry from Hiroshima makes 10 trips a day (2½ hours) and costs ¥3,500 one-way.

From Kansai: The Orange Ferry runs overnight boats from Osaka to Toyo, and from Kobe to Niihama. Toyo and Niihama are east of Matsuyama. On the Orange Ferry, berths in an eight-person room go for ¥6,690; a private cabin for two starts at ¥10,800 per person. The Orange Ferry offers a 30% discount on return tickets if your return trip is in less than two weeks. Buses operated by either JR or Iyotetsu Bus Company connect Toyo Port with Matsuyama, and both ports are also near JR stations.

From Kyushu: Uwajima Unyu runs ferries between Beppu and Uwajima (three hours). Uwajima is 80 minutes by JR train from Matsuyama. Orange Ferry runs boats between Usuki and Yawatahama (2½ hours). Yawatahama is 45 minutes by JR train from Matsuyama. Kokudo Kyushu Ferry operates between Saganoseki and Misaki (70 minutes). Misaki is three hours by bus from Matsuyama.

Contacts Ishizaki Kisen. ☎ 089/953–1003 ⊕ www.ishizakikisen.co.jp. **Kokudo Kyushu Ferry.** ☎ 097/575–1020 in Saganoseki, 0894/54–0173 in Misaki ⊕ www.koku94.jp. **Orange Ferry.** ☎ 0898/64–4121 ⊕ www.orange-ferry.co.jp. **Setonaikai Kisen.** ☎ 082/253–1212 in Hiroshima, 089/953–1003 in Matsuyama ⊕ setonaikaikisen.co.jp/language/en. **Uwajima Unyu.** ☎ 0894/23–2536 ⊕ www. uwajimaunyu.co.jp.

TRAIN TRAVEL By train Matsuyama is 90 minutes from Awa Ikeda, about 2¼ hours from Takamatsu, 3 hours from Tokushima, 3 hours from Kochi, and 7 hours from Tokyo. By bus it is about 3 hours to Kochi or Tokushima. There are two main train stations in the city, JR Matsuyama Station and Matsuyama Shieki Station. JR trains and buses arrive at the JR Matsuyama Station, which is a bit far from the city center. Local buses, trams, and Iyotetsu trains go to the more central Matsuyama Shieki Station.

TRAM TRAVEL The best way to get around Matsuyama is by tram. Rides cost ¥160 per person, paid when you get off. A day-pass costs ¥500 and can be bought at stations or from the tram driver. No. 5 trams run from the JR Station to Dogo Onsen, and most of the city's best spots are along the way. The stop in the center of Matsuyama is Okaido-mae on Ichiban-cho street. ■ TIP→ If you're traveling with kids, don't miss a ride on the special Botchan steam trams that putter around the city. Botchan trains run between Shieki and Dogo Onsen 8 to 10 times a day. A one-way trip is ¥300. If you have a day pass, it's an extra ¥100.

VISITOR INFORMATION

There are tourist information offices at the JR and Shieki train stations. English maps are available even if an English speaker is not. The peerless desk staff at the Ehime Prefectural International Center (EPIC) provides advice about events, transportation, hotel reservations, and even bicycles (rentable for a refundable ¥1,000 deposit). EPIC is next to the Kenmin Bunka Kaikain, or People's Cultural Hall, off Tram 5's Minami-machi stop.

Dogo Onsen, Japan's oldest hot spring, is the biggest draw in Matsuyama.

Contacts Ehime Prefectural International Center (*EPIC*). ✉ *1–1 Dogo Ichiman* ☎ *089/917–5678* ⊕ *www.epic.or.jp/english.* **Matsuyama City Tourist Information Office.** ✉ *Matsuyama Station, 1-14-1 Minamiedo* ☎ *089/931–3914.*

EXPLORING

Dogo Onsen (道後温泉本館). Tell people you're heading to Matsuyama, and Dogo Onsen will be the first place they recommend. These hot springs have been the city's top attraction for the last millennium. Japan's oldest written text mentions it as a favorite of gods, emperors, and peasants alike, and it's still in daily use by locals and visitors. The main wooden building at present-day Dogo dates from 1894 and looks like a fairy-tale castle; the only thing that's changed significantly is the view.

Admission is ¥410, but for the real Dogo Onsen experience spend ¥840 for a bath with some frills. Head upstairs and you'll get a basket with towels and a lightweight *yukata* robe. The staff will point you to Kami-no-Yu, or the Water of the Gods. The gods apparently liked things simple: the great granite tub is plainer than modern multibath complexes, but the water feels terrific. If you want to go all out, ¥1,550 gets you into Tama-no-Yu, or Water of the Spirits, which has the same water but is usually quieter. All baths are gender segregated. Remember proper onsen etiquette: wash and rinse yourself (and your towel) before getting into the bath.

After you bathe, relax upstairs. The ¥840 ticket includes green tea and *sembei* crackers, served in a serene public tatami room. The ¥1,550 option buys you *botchan-dango* sweets in a private room, plus a quick look at the private bath reserved for the Emperor when he visits. Kicking back in the second-story tatami area is one of the great joys of coming to Dogo. Sip free tea or explore the upstairs quarters where writer Soseki Natsume stayed and worked during his time in Matsuyama. ⊠ *5–6 Yuno-machi, Dogo* ☎ *089/921–5141* ⌑ *¥410–¥1,550* ⊙ *Daily 6 am–11 pm. Last entry 1 hr before baths close.*

Ehime Museum of Art (愛媛県立美術館). The permanent collection of this museum occupying a modern city-center building isn't that big, but the selection of recent Japanese art is terrific, and the temporary exhibits are extensive. The galleries often host exhibits of works by local artists. ⊠ *Horinouchi* ☎ *089/932–0010* ⊕ *www.ehime-art.jp* ⌑ *Varies by exhibit* ⊙ *Tues.–Sun. 9:40–6.*

Fodor's Choice **Ishite-ji** (石手寺 *Ishite Temple*). A 15-minute walk from Dogo Onsen,
★ Ishite Temple is Shingon Buddhism at play. Half serene pilgrimage destination, half ancient Buddhist-themed fun park, the temple is more than worth a visit. As sprawling and elegantly unkempt as the city around it, it contains surprises that are, like the temple cats, too numerous to count.

Enter the temple by way of a stone road that's flanked by wooden stalls with vendors selling calligraphy brushes, omiyage-paper fortunes, and pilgrimage gear. Just inside the colossal temple gate you'll see a table for folding origami cranes; make one and it will be added to the heavy, colorful bunches hanging around the pillars. Past the cranes lies the main hall of worship, where you're likely to see a pilgrim or two chanting a sutra. In the surrounding area you'll also see painted panels, golden statues, a giant mandala on the stairway to the main shrine, a wooden *kami* (spirit) with a sword you can heft, and a huge bronze bell to ring (¥100).

It's serene and memorable, but the real fun at Ishite-ji Temple starts in a long, dark cave to the left of the main worship hall. It feels impossibly long, and when you finally emerge on the other side—past startling wooden statues and 88 stone Buddhas—you'll be confronted by a 100-foot statue of the priest Kobo Daishi striding across the mountains. The mountain behind the temple also holds a few surprises: a scrambling rock pathway leads up the mountain, where two spooky caves are yours to explore (even most locals don't know about them). Don't miss Ishite-ji Temple's regular festival, held on the 20th day of every month. ⊠ *2–9–21 Ishite* ☎ *089/977–0870* ⌑ *Free* ⊙ *Temple open 24 hrs. Caves open daily, usually 8–5.*

Itami Juzo Kinenkan (伊丹十三記念館 *Itami Juzo Memorial Museum*). The late Juzo Itami (1933–97) is regarded as one of Japan's most innovative and captivating film directors, known for his affectionate and absurdist portraits of Japanese life. Each film starred his wife Nobuko Miyamoto and an off-the-wall supporting character, sometimes played by Itami himself. The director's best-known films include *Tampopo* (1985), centering on a bedraggled ramen-shop owner trying to make the perfect soup, and *Ososhiki* ("The Funeral," 1984), the story of an idiosyncratic family coming together for a funeral. If you haven't seen these films, they're musts for any visitor to Japan; if you have, then you'll love the museum, curated by Miyamoto herself, showcasing video clips and objects from Itami's life. ✉ *1–6–10 Higashi Ishii* ✣ *From Shieki Station, ¥1,200 taxi ride or take Tobe-bound bus 20 mins to Amayama-bashi Bridge stop, then backtrack 2 mins on foot to museum* ☎ *089/969–1313* 🌐 *itami-kinenkan.jp* 🎫 *¥800* 🕑 *Wed.–Mon. 10–6.*

Matsuyama-jo (松山城 *Matsuyama Castle*). Mighty Matsuyama Castle stands on a 433-feet mountain in the middle of town, and the views of the city from here are stunning. Dating from 1603, it's one of the cooler castles in Japan. Inside you can watch footage of the post–World War II reconstruction; the shaping and joining of wood and the stamping out of straw wattle for the walls is astonishing. There is no concrete, no rebar, and only enough nails to hold down the floorboards. Dark-wood passageways carry the smell of old smoke from the numerous fires the castle has endured.

To get to the castle, walk uphill about 30 or 40 minutes or ride the ropeway partway up and continue on foot about 15 minutes to the castle. The station is on Ropeway Street, just north of the Okaido shopping arcade. Don't miss the lovely **Ninomaru garden** just west of the castle. ✉ *5 Maru-no-uchi* ☎ *089/921–4873* 🎫 *Castle ¥510, ropeway ¥510* 🕑 *Feb.–July, daily 9–5; Aug.–Nov., daily 9–5:30; Dec. and Jan., daily 9–4:30.*

OFF THE BEATEN PATH

Botchan Sutajiamu (坊ちゃんスタジアム *Botchan Stadium*). For an affordable taste of Japan's baseball mania, take in a game of Ehime's minor-league baseball team, the Mandarin Pirates. Even more fun at Botchan Stadium are the high-school games: Japan is nuts for high-school baseball, and the well-attended contests can get boisterous. Next door, **Ehime Ken-Budokan,** Japan's finest martial-arts stadium, stands out like a black-roof fortress: watch or try a class in any number of arts. Both venues are a short walk from JR Ichitsubo Station. ✉ *Matsuyama Chuo Koen.*

WHERE TO EAT

Matsuyama has many great restaurants. The two best streets to follow both run parallel to the main arcade. For the first, head into Okaido from the Starbucks, and go left at the first stoplight (this is Niban-cho), then take your first right to find foodie heaven. No spot on the strip is terribly expensive, and each place has a lot of character and great food. A few blocks farther east, the main artery of Yasaka-dori has many great places to eat and drink lining both sides.

10

$$$ BISTRO

🍴 **Amitie** (アミティエ). Weekend lunch and the prix-fixe dinners are outstanding—and a good value—at this special place serving French bistro–style cuisine. The food and presentation are excellent without being snooty, and the interior is funky yet not crass or grimy. Sit upstairs and strike up conversation with your neighbors; the gracious hosts and softly worn wooden interior enhance the sense of enduring conviviality. [$] *Average main: ¥2900* ✉ *6–23 Minami Horibata-cho* ✣ *Near Bijutsukan-mae tram stop, across moat from Ehime Museum of Art* ☎ *089/998–2811* 🕑 *Closed Tues. No lunch weekdays except some holidays.*

$$ ✕**Ladkey's** (ラルキー). Come here for top-quality South Asian fare per-
INDIAN sonally prepared by Ladkey, who hails from northern India. The two-
hour all-you-can-eat-and-drink meal for ¥3,240 is a closely kept secret
of Matsuyama's expat population. À la carte lunch specials start at
¥700. A picture menu will help you decide what to order. $ *Aver-
age main: ¥1100* ⊠ *5–9 Hanazono-cho, between Shieki Station and
Matsuyama Castle moat* ✛ *Follow streetcar tracks north from station
toward castle and look for yellow sign on right* ☎ *089/948–0885* ▭ *No
credit cards.*

$$$ ✕**Taihei Sushi** (大平寿司). At this totally unremarkable counter with
SUSHI totally sumptuous sushi, dinnertime is crowded and fun. A ¥2,700
or ¥3,800 combination gets you soup and up to 10 different kinds of
sushi. Not much English is spoken here, but folks are friendly and helpful; to order, just point to what looks good. $ *Average main: ¥2850*
⊠ *1–7–10 Ichiban-cho* ✛ *Look for blue-and-white sign on smaller street
1 block south of main street below castle* ☎ *089/933–7787* ⊘ *Closed
Sun. No lunch.*

$$$ ✕**Tipitina's.** Funky and unpretentious, this second-floor izakaya sits
ECLECTIC behind a faux-cowhide door. The friendly bilingual staff and the range
of delicious dishes perfectly sized for sharing will endear you to the
place. The menu is eclectic, from cheese fondue to Vietnamese spring
rolls. Try the "magical drink." $ *Average main: ¥2950* ⊠ *2–6–18
Sanban-cho* ✛ *On Yasaka-dori corner 1 block north of Sanban-cho*
☎ *089/921–7011* ▭ *No credit cards* ⊘ *No lunch.*

$ ✕**Un Petit Peu** (アン・プチ・プー). Delicious handmade custards and crepes
CAFÉ and a two-story dining area with corner views of Matsuyama's busy
night scene make this coffee-and-pastry shop a perfect part of any eve-
ning out. Extremely popular and open into the wee hours, it's a great
place to meet Matsuyamans. $ *Average main: ¥800* ⊠ *1–10–9 Niban-
cho, at Yasaka-dori* ☎ *089/931–8550* ▭ *No credit cards* ⊘ *Closed
irregularly. No lunch.*

$$ ✕**Yushoku Shunsai Mejina** (遊食旬菜 meji菜). This tiny oasis offers
JAPANESE elegant Japanese lunches and dinners impeccably served on delicate
ceramic tableware. There's no English menu, but you can't go wrong
with the set meals. Try the lunch bento box for ¥1,000, or the dinnertime omakase kaiseki set for ¥3,150 (reserve one day in advance). $ *Av-
erage main: ¥1950* ⊠ *5–6–3 Chifune-machi* ☎ *089/998–2118* ▭ *No
credit cards* ⊘ *Closed Sun.*

WHERE TO STAY

$$$ 🏨**ANA Hotel Matsuyama** (松山全日空ホテル). Downtown's biggest
HOTEL international hotel, the ANA has some great city views. **Pros:** next to
city center; easy access to sights; great views. **Cons:** somewhat generic
rooms. $ *Rooms from: ¥22000* ⊠ *3–2–1 Ichiban-cho* ☎ *089/933–5511*
⊕ *www.anahotelmatsuyama.com* ⇲ *327 rooms* ❄ *Breakfast.*

$ 🏨**Hotel Checkin Matsuyama** (チェックイン松山). At the epicenter of dining
HOTEL and nightlife in downtown Matsuyama, this reasonably priced hotel
has a hard-to-beat address. **Pros:** prime city location; plenty of parking;
hotel bath draws water from Dogo Onsen. **Cons:** lower floors get some
street noise; breakfast area can be crowded. $ *Rooms from: ¥9500*
⊠ *2–7–3 Sanban-cho* ☎ *089/998–7000* ⇲ *269 rooms* ❄ *No meals.*

$$$ ⊞ **Hotel Dogo Yaya** (ホテル道後やや). Guest rooms at this more afford-
HOTEL able alternative to Yume Kura are compact but have a modern Japanese aesthetic, and the service here is remarkable. **Pros:** close to Dogo Onsen; fashionable facilities; great breakfasts. **Cons:** staff speaks only basic English; some rooms have small windows. $ *Rooms from: ¥18600* ⊠ *6–1 Dogo Tako-cho, Dogo* ☎ *089/907–1181* ⊕ *www.yayahotel.jp* ⤳ *68 rooms* ⦿ *Breakfast.*

$$$ ⊞ **Hotel JAL City Matsuyama** (ホテルJALシティ松山). The east-facing rooms
HOTEL at this Western-style hotel near JR Station have views of Matsuyama Castle. **Pros:** friendly staff; near transportation; nice views. **Cons:** unexciting rooms; far from Dogo Onsen and downtown. $ *Rooms from: ¥21000* ⊠ *1–10–10 Ohte-machi* ☎ *089/913–2580* ⊕ *matsuyama.jalcity.co.jp* ⤳ *120 rooms* ⦿ *No meals.*

$$ ⊞ **Hotel Patio Dogo** (ホテルパティオドウゴ). It's hard to believe that a
HOTEL hotel with such nice accommodations and such an excellent location can be so affordable. **Pros:** nice bathrooms; high-quality mattresses; excellent location. **Cons:** C-class rooms are cramped. $ *Rooms from: ¥12800* ⊠ *Dogo Onsen Honkanmae, Dogo* ☎ *089/941–4128* ⊕ *www.patio-dogo.co.jp* ⤳ *101 rooms* ⦿ *No meals.*

$$$$ ⊞ **Yume Kura** (夢蔵). A splurge but absolutely worth it, this high-class
B&B/INN ryokan behind Dogo Onsen delivers the royal treatment. **Pros:** great location; elegant decor; incredible service. **Cons:** no double beds; no in-room dinner service; meals are not optional. $ *Rooms from: ¥70000* ⊠ *4–5 Dogo Yutsuki-cho, Dogo* ☎ *089/931–1180* ⊕ *www.yume-kura.jp* ⤳ *7 Japanese-style rooms* ⦿ *Some meals.*

NIGHTLIFE

Moonglow (ムーングロウ). This cozy piano bar near the Okaido shopping arcade has been hosting local and visiting jazz musicians since the 1980s. The music is as good as you'd encounter in any of Japan's major cities, and it's all the more delightful when paired with one of the bar's quirky cocktails. ⊠ *3–2–15 Sanbancho* ✛ *On Chifune-machi St., 3 buildings north of 114 Bank* ☎ *089/931–3294* ▱ *Cover ¥500; live music ¥600* ⊘ *Closed Sun.*

Salon Kitty. These compact quarters host some of Japan's biggest-name bands in intimate shows at great prices. The music leans toward rock and J-punk. ⊠ *5F, 138 Kawahara-cho* ☎ *089/945–0020.*

SHOPPING

Matsuyama is the fashion capital of Shikoku, and a stroll down its main shopping arcades, **Okaido** and **Gintengai**, will leave you reeling from the getups, which range from gorgeous to grotesque. Nowhere else outside Tokyo is fad-fashion given this high a priority. Okaido begins at the Starbucks on Ichiban-cho and goes south for a kilometer until turning right into the Gintengai; Gintengai empties out by a large Takashimaya department store and the city bus and tram terminal, Shieki Station.

Okaido, Gintengai, and Shieki complete a square adjacent to the Matsuyama Castle's moat. Inside is **Chifune-machi,** bursting with clothing stores, cafés, and other shops. You won't stumble on any hidden temples or ancient ruins, but there's plenty of good shopping.

10

UCHIKO 内子

50 km (30 miles) south of Matsuyama.

This small farming town in the mountains south of Matsuyama was a major producer of Japanese paper and wax until the early 20th century Now it's a peaceful mountain town of old merchant houses, candle and umbrella workshops, and an impressive turn-of-the-20th-century Kabuki theater. In the mid-20th century, it became famous as the hometown of the novelist Oe Kenzaburo, the second Japanese writer to win the Nobel Prize in literature.

One of Uchiko's unexpected delights is the mammoth sleeping Buddha statue inside Kosho-ji Temple. The temple was founded in the 15th century, but the Buddha statue dates from 1998. Its relative youth doesn't detract from its impressive serenity.

GETTING HERE AND AROUND

Uchiko is small enough to cover on foot, and strolling through this old town is the best way to experience it. From Uchiko Station, follow a wooden sign pointing left to the old shopping street Yokaichi, where the only change for centuries has been the height of plants against the beige-orange walls. You won't need more than a morning to poke through the fun shops full of good, cheap souvenirs: straw pinwheels, tea leaves, sour *tsukemono* pickles, and local sake.

EXPLORING

Fodor's Choice ★ **Japanese Wax Museum and Kamihaga Residence** (木蝋資料館上芳我邸 *Mokuro Shiryokan Kamihaga-tei*). The former residence of the Kamihaga family, which established the city's wax industry, is now a well-maintained museum. Exhibits here explain the rise and fall of this once-thriving industry. Comprehensive English signage and hands-on exhibits teach you more than you thought there was to know about the changing fortunes of this wax town. ✉ *2696 Uchiko* ☎ *0893/44–2771* 🖻 *¥500* ⊙ *Daily 9–4:30.*

Machiya Shiryokan (内子町立町家資料館 *Uchiko Townhouse Museum*). Just northeast of Omori's Wax Workshop, this museum is an 18th-century town house that once belonged to a wealthy family and is now open to the public. ✉ *3023 Uchiko* ☎ *0893/44–2118* 🖻 *Free* ⊙ *Daily 9–4:30.*

Omori's Wax Workshop (大森和蠟燭屋 *Omori Wa Rosokuya*). The highlight of Yokaichi Street is this shop where an elderly gentleman and his sons make distinctive candles by hand. The smaller ones are inexpensive, but the larger are surprisingly costly. This is the largest candle shop in the shopping arcade. ✉ *2214 Uchiko* ☎ *0893/43–0385* 🖻 *Free* ⊙ *Sat.–Mon., Wed., and Thurs. 9–5.*

Uchiko-za (内子座 *Uchiko Theater*). This wooden theater opened its doors in 1916, when the city was flush with cash. It has been putting on traditional Kabuki and Bunraku performances ever since. When no performances are scheduled, you can view the interior's revolving stage and trapdoors. ✉ *2102 Uchiko* ☎ *0893/44–2840* 🖻 *¥400* ⊙ *Daily 9–4:30.*

UWAJIMA 宇和島

90 km (56 miles) south of Matsuyama, 130 km (80 miles) west of Kochi.

A quiet fishing town south of Matsuyama on the Uwa Sea Uwajima has two unusual claims to fame, its sumo-style bullfights and a sex museum that's part of a Shinto fertility shrine.

GETTING HERE AND AROUND

The best way to get around Uwajima is by bicycle; you can rent bikes from Eki Rent-a-Car next to the train station for ¥100 per hour.

VISITOR INFORMATION

There's a tourist information booth inside the train station, but the main Uwajima Tourist Information office is in the ferry terminal about a 10-minute walk away. The main office sells stickers (¥50) of Uwajima's demon bull that make great souvenirs.

Contact Uwajima Tourist Information. ⊠ *1–318–16 Benten-cho* ☎ *089/522–3934.*

EXPLORING

Taga Jinja (多賀神社 *Taga Shrine*). Visitors flock to this Shinto fertility shrine not far from the train station, though not necessarily to pray: Uwajima's infamous sex museum is located here. You can tell when you've arrived—no, that sculpture is not a giant squid. Just beyond it is the museum, called **Deko Boko Jindou** (literally, a shrine honoring "things that poke out, things that go in"). The three-floor collection is astonishing. What is that samurai doing? It's best to leave the kids at the castle for this one, as they won't be admitted. ⊠ *1340 Fujie* ☎ *089/522–3444* 💴 *¥800* ⊗ *Daily 8–5.*

Togyu Bullfighting (闘牛). Two bulls literally lock horns in sumo-style contests whose origins in these parts date back at least to the 17th century. If you can make it here during one of the five annual tournaments, you can experience these generally bloodless battles of muscle and will. Uwajima's bullfighting stadium is atop Mt. Maruyama (more of a hill than a mountain), a 30-minute walk or 10-minute cab ride from Uwajima Station. ⊠ *496–2 Warei-cho* ☎ *0895/22–3934 Uwajima tourist info* 💴 *¥300 for bullfights* ⊗ *Tournaments Jan. 2, 1st Sun. in Apr., July 24, Aug. 14, and 4th Sun. in Oct.*

THE DEMON BULL

So-called "demon bulls" (*ushi-oni*) are common in Shikoku and Kansai folklore. Fearsome creatures with the bodies of bulls and the heads of demons, they will set a curse on the family of anyone who injures or angers them. Uwajima residents in particular have been traditionally wary of demon bulls and, just in case, still hold the *Ushi-oni* festival to pacify them. The event, from July 22 to 24 every year, includes fireworks, parades, concerts, and bullfighting.

10

The Tatara Ohashi Bridge is part of the Shimanami Kaido, a road-and-bridge network that connects Shikoku with western Honshu.

SHIMANAMI KAIDO しまなみ街道

Beginning in Imabari, 45 km (28 miles) north of Matsuyama.

This 60-km (37-mile) road-and-bridge route connects Imabari and Onomuchi and offers some of Japan's most pleasant cycling.

FAMILY

Fodor's Choice

★

Shimanami Kaido (しまなみ海道). By far the most scenic way to travel between Shikoku and western Honshu is the Shimanami Kaido, a 60-km (37-mile) expressway built with bicyclists in mind. The route, a series of roads and 10 long bridges, connects Imabari, just north of Matsuyama, with Onomichi, just east of Hiroshima, by way of islands in the Seto Inland Sea. Most of the islands were accessible only by ferry until the expressway was completed in 1999. By the early 2000s, the Shimanami Kaido was already one of western Japan's most popular cycling routes.

A bicycle trip across this road-and-bridge network takes in fishing villages, tangerine orchards, pearl farms, seaweed pastures, and long stretches of sparkling sea. A separate cycling track runs along each bridge, so you don't have to deal with car traffic for most of the ride. Cycling paths are clearly marked on the islands, and maps are readily available. The cycling isn't strenuous, so don't get discouraged by that first big corkscrew pathway up from Imabari to the Kurushima Ohashi Bridge. After that it's clear sailing.

Biking to Onomichi takes about six hours. If you decide you've had enough cycling along the way, you can leave your standard rental bike (as opposed to a tandem or an electric-assist bike) at any of 15 stations and complete your journey by ferry or bus. The well-informed staff members at the stations have all the schedules. Your hotel can even send your luggage ahead. ⊕ *www.go-shimanami.jp*.

GETTING HERE AND AROUND

Rental bikes, regular, tandem, and electric, are available from Sunrise Itoyama, also a lodging that's a good place to stop for the night if you've followed the route from Onomichi to Imabari.

Contact Sunrise Itoyama Rental Bike Terminal (サンライズ絲山). ⊠ *2-8-1 Sunaba-cho, Imabari* ☎ *089/841-3196* ⊕ *www.sunrise-itoyama.jp/archives/english.*

VISITOR INFORMATION

The shop employees in Imabari don't speak much English, so if you have communication problems go through the ICIEA, Imabari's helpful international-exchange association.

Contact Imabari City International Exchange Association (今治市国際交流協会 *ICIEA*). ⊠ *1-1-16 Kitahorai-cho, Imabari* ☎ *089/834-5763* ⊕ *iciea.jp/e_index.html.*

EXPLORING

Hakata Salt Company Omishima Factory (伯方塩 大三島工場). For centuries, Hakata Island has been famous for its high-quality salt, and the Hakata Salt Company offers daily free self-guided tours of its factory on Omishima Island. As you stroll along a marked visitor's path through the factory, you'll see workers turn seawater into table salt, package it up, and ship it all over Japan. There's also plenty of information, though most only in Japanese, about the history of salt. If the factory touring has you craving something salty, try the salt ice cream sold on-site. If that's not enough, you can also take a dip in the salt baths at the Mare Gracia bath complex next door. ⊠ *Omishima-cho Utena 32, Imabari-shi* ☎ *0897/82-0660* ⊕ *www.hakatanoshio.co.jp/factory/index.php* ⊙ *Self-guided tours daily 9 am–3 pm. No reservation required.*

Mare Gracia Omishima (マーレグラッシア大三島). This public bath complex is like you average friendly Japanese town bathhouse, except for one thing: the extremely salty water. One or two of the baths in the multi-bath bathing area are salted with Hakata salt from the factory next door. Islanders believe salt baths help draw out impurities and beautify your skin, but if self-pickling is not your thing you can always take a dip in the non-saltwater indoor or outdoor baths. ⊠ *Miyaura 5902, Omishima-cho* ☎ *0897/820100* 🎫 *¥500* ⊙ *Thurs.–Tues. 10 am–8:30 pm.*

Oyamazumi Jinja (大山祇神社 *Oyamazumi Shrine*). Omishima, three islands over from Imabari, is home to this expansive shrine. Founded in the 6th century, it honors the Shinto god of mountains, sea, and war. In the 8th century, victorious warriors started leaving their weaponry here after battle as thanks for divine favor. The museum on the shrine's grounds holds more than two-thirds of the nation's designated National Treasures in swords, spears, breastplates, and helmets. ⊠ *3327 Miya-ura, Oshima-cho, Omishima* ☎ *089/782-0032* 🎫 *¥1,000* ⊙ *Daily 8:30–4:30.*

10

WHERE TO STAY

$ ⬚ **Oomishima Furusato Ikoinoie** (大三島ふるさと憩の家). A former elemen-

B&B/INN tary school near the beach on Oomishima Island, two islands away

FAMILY from Imabari, has found a new identity as an "experiential lodging facility." The classrooms in the wooden school building are now tatami guest rooms, and the former sports field contains a barbecue area and a modern-art gallery. **Pros:** beach location; friendly islanders; delicious seafood meals; free Wi-Fi. **Cons:** shared baths; wooden building can be cold in winter. $ *Rooms from: ¥8000* ⊠ *5208–1 Munagata, Omishima-cho* ☏ *0897/83–1111* ⤳ *3 Japanese-style rooms with shared baths* ⦿ *Some meals* ▭ *No credit cards.*

$ ⬚ **Setoda Link Inn.** This tiny pension opened in 2012 and hosts a mix

B&B/INN of serious cyclists zipping through on racing bikes, as well as travelers cycling at a more leisurely pace. **Pros:** ocean views; free bicycle repair tools; excellent local meals. **Cons:** some guest rooms are quite small; shared bathrooms. $ *Rooms from: ¥9500* ⊠ *Setoda-machi Miyahara 2317-10, Onomichi-shi* ☏ *0845/28–0633* ⤳ *4 rooms* ⦿ *Some meals* ▭ *No credit cards.*

11

KYUSHU

WELCOME TO KYUSHU

TOP REASONS TO GO

★ **Diverse cities:** Fukuoka has vibrant nightlife, Nagasaki exudes old-world charm, Kumamoto's castle dominates the city, and Kagoshima's palm trees calm travelers.

★ **Gastronomy:** Find the sought-after Hakata ramen in Fukuoka. Nagasaki has *chanpon* (seafood and vegetable noodle soup), and Kagoshima *haskurobuta tonkatsu* (breaded pork cutlet).

★ **Volcanoes and hot springs:** Mt. Aso is notoriously active, as is Sakura-jima, across the bay from Kagoshima. Hot springs are found throughout Kyushu.

★ **Getting into the wild:** With its lava flows, outlying islands, rugged mountains, and national parks, Kyushu is an adventurer's dream. Most trails require only good shoes, water, and some time.

★ **Remote access:** Bullet trains now extend all the way to Kagoshima, and in another hour, you can be on the hot sand of Ibusuki's beaches.

1 Fukuoka. After landing at one of the world's most conveniently located airports, you can be downtown in six minutes by subway. Fabulous dining, ultramodern shopping, and humming nightlife are among the joys this vibrant city has to offer.

2 Yufuin. A delightful and popular upscale hot-springs resort, Yufuin nestles beneath the dramatic twin-peaked mountain known as Yufu-dake.

3 Nagasaki. Consistently rated by the Japanese as a favorite destination, Nagasaki has maintained its rich and colorful international past even in the face of the devastation wrought by the plutonium bomb that ended World War II. Today you'll still see the spirit of entrepreneurship that helped the city revive.

4 Kumamoto and Takachiho. Impressive and menacing, the black facade and angular aspects of Kumamoto's massive 17th-century castle give it the appearance of a sinister hideout. Suizen-ji Joju-en, a luxurious garden, is another highlight. Nearby is Takachiho, a spiritual retreat that's off the radar for most foreign visitors.

5 Aso-san (Mt. Aso). Aso National Park contains lakes, fields, and a chain of five volcanic peaks situated inside the largest caldera in the world.

6 Kagoshima. The mild climate and easygoing vibe draw comparisons to Naples, Italy, but locals fear that one day, the smoking, rumbling

GETTING ORIENTED

The gateway to the continent of Asia, Kyushu lies considerably west and south of Tokyo. A good route starts with a flight or bullet train into Fukuoka in the north, moves down to Nagasaki on the west coast by express train, then winds eastward by bus or train to the central city of Kumamoto. Take a side trip to Aso-san (Mt. Aso) or Takachiho, then head south to the city of Kagoshima. Finally you can go farther south by local train to the thermal spa resort area of Ibusuki, famous for its hot-sand baths, where you can be heat-treated on the picturesque, breezy beach.

cone of Sakura-jima out in the bay will make Pompeii a more apt analogy. Famous hot-sand baths and remote beaches are found along the southern reaches of the prefecture.

7 Kirishima-yaku Kokuritsu Koen. This mountainous national park northeast of Kagoshima rivals Takachiho as one of the most sacred places in the country.

Updated by
Chris Willson

Kyushu's landscape couldn't be more varied, with active yet accessible volcanoes, numerous thermal spas, endless fields of rice and famous potatoes, forested mountains capped by winter snows, busy harbors along lively seacoasts, and pleasant seaside retreats.

Kyushu has been inhabited and favored for human settlement for more than 10,000 years, and ruins and artifacts thousands of years old suggest that the region was the most important gateway for human contact between Japan and the rest of Asia. The most rapid anthropological changes occurred from about 300 BC to AD 300, when rice became widely cultivated and complex pottery and tools began to appear, thus conveniently framing the Yayoi period. Continuous trade with China brought prosperity and culture, and advanced ceramics were introduced—and then produced—by Korean masters who were employed and enslaved by the local fiefdoms of the 16th and 17th centuries.

It was also through Kyushu that Western knowledge, weapons, religion, and cooking methods first made their way into Japan. In the mid-1500s Nagasaki saw the arrival of fleets of enterprising and courageous European merchants and missionaries, and the resulting frenzy of trade in ideas and goods continued unabated until the Tokugawa Shogunate slammed the door shut on the whole show in the early 1600s. What brought things to a halt was a plague of panic induced by an alarming new phenomenon: Christianity.

The Portuguese and other Catholics not afraid to preach to the natives were expelled and permanently barred. The Dutch, however, were considered more money-minded, and therefore less threatening, and were permitted to stay—under scrutiny and isolation. They were housed within the enclave of Dejima, a man-made island in Nagasaki Harbor, where they were encouraged to keep bringing in coveted goods but were constantly guarded and watched. For the next 200 years, this profitable little arrangement would be the only form of contact the West would have with Japan until the arrival of Perry's forceful "Black Ship."

Today Kyushu is a fascinating mix of old and new, nature and culture. Much of the remote and rugged interior—such as that surrounding Mt.

Aso's fuming cone—is still an isolated wilderness, yet the amenities of modern life are well supplied in cities and coastal resorts.

PLANNING

WHEN TO GO

In early spring it's pleasantly warm, and the greenery is at its best. May and June usher in heavy rains, and July and August are intensely muggy. September is summery, but watch for typhoons, which can blow in at any time until late October. Autumn colors, appearing in late October or early November, are nice, particularly in the north. In January and February the mountains of central Kyushu receive a little snowfall, and that's when the Siberian cranes show up for the gentle winter the region enjoys.

PLANNING YOUR TIME

Fukuoka is a great base for exploring the northern part of Kyushu. Spend a day orienting yourself and seeing Fukuoka's sights, then take day trips to Nagasaki, Kumamoto, and Yufuin. If you have more time, it's worth getting off the beaten track to see the volcano Mt. Aso. After a day in Kagoshima, you could spend a couple of days exploring the beautiful mountainous area of Kirishima, or jump on a ferry to the island of Yakushima.

GETTING HERE AND AROUND

Travel in Kyushu is for the most part straightforward, with trains providing the bulk of the transport. Highway buses are useful for certain routes. Frequent and inexpensive ferries ply the bays and ports, linking Kyushu with offshore islands. During holiday seasons you'll want to reserve seats on express trains, but with most buses and ferries turning up 20 minutes prior to departure you should get on board with no trouble.

AIR TRAVEL

Air routes link Kyushu's major cities with Tokyo and Osaka. Fukuoka, Nagasaki, and Kagoshima have the most frequent and useful daily connections and offer some international flights. When using domestic carriers like ANA you need not enter and return from the same city: it's easy to fly into Fukuoka and out of Kagoshima, for example.

Airline Contacts All Nippon Airways (ANA). ☎ 0570/029–709 toll-free, 03/6741–1120 from mobile ⊕ www.ana.co.jp. **Japan Airlines.** ☎ 0120/747–222 toll-free, 03/5796–9345 from mobile ⊕ www.jal.co.jp/en. **Skymark Airlines.** ☎ 050/3786–0283 ⊕ www.skymark.co.jp/en.

BUS TRAVEL

Buses make useful connections around Kyushu, and if you don't have a JR Rail Pass, they are often much cheaper than the trains. For example, the bus between Nagasaki and Kumamoto is half the price and takes about the same time; plus you don't have to make any changes or wait for connections, as you do with trains. A highway bus makes a trip between Kumamoto to Yufuin, either direct or with a stopover at the

Aso-san crater. The Kyushu Express Bus Portal Site is a great way to check on bus times and prices.

Bus Contact Kyushu Express Bus. ☎ *0120/489–939 reservation line* ⊕ *www. atbus-de.com.e.jo.hp.transer.com.*

CAR TRAVEL

Renting a car is a good idea in Kyushu if you have lots of time and you will be exploring the more out-of-the-way places such as Aso-san or Takachiho. All the major rental outfits have offices in the big cities near the JR stations.

TRAIN TRAVEL

High-speed bullet trains link Fukuoka with Kagoshima. Express trains making the popular runs between Fukuoka and Nagasaki and Fukuoka and Yufuin are jammed on weekends and holidays, so book at least a day ahead.

RESTAURANTS

Fresh fish is served everywhere on Kyushu. Appetites are on the hearty side here, so there's lots of meat, too. Local specialties abound and are often reasonably priced. In the bigger cities like Fukuoka, Nagasaki, Kumamoto, and Kagoshima—and along the stylish new streets of Yufuin—you'll find plenty of Western-style restaurants.

HOTELS

You can find the usual American hotel chains, with all the familiar extras, in places like Fukuoka and Nagasaki. The rural areas surrounding Aso and Kagoshima have snug little inns with views of the surrounding peaks. In Yufuin nearly all hotels and *ryokan* (guesthouses) offer soothing thermal mineral water baths. Unless otherwise noted, all hotel rooms have private baths. Reservations are essential during the long national holidays, particularly Golden Week (from late April to early May), Obon (mid-August), and New Year's (the first week of January) when Japanese tourists flock to the island.

Hotel reviews have been shortened. For full information, visit Fodors.com

WHAT IT COSTS IN YEN			
$	**$$**	**$$$**	**$$$$**
RESTAURANTS under ¥1,000	¥1,000–¥2,000	¥2,001–¥3,000	over ¥3,000
HOTELS under ¥12,000	¥12,000–¥18,000	¥18,001–¥22,000	over ¥22,000

Restaurant prices are the average cost of a main course at dinner or, if dinner is not served, at lunch. Hotel prices are the lowest cost of a standard double room in high season.

VISITOR INFORMATION

Every major city has tourist information offices near shopping, sightseeing, and eating areas, and one or more near the high-speed train exit of each JR train station. An English speaker is usually on duty during peak travel hours. The bigger hotels generally have front-desk employees who speak and understand some English; they are good sources for information on local sights and restaurants.

ON THE MENU

The most celebrated dish in Fukuoka is *tonkotsu ramen*, a strongly flavored pork-bone-based soup with extra-thin noodles, scallions, and strips of roasted pork. Usually it gets heaps of garlic, chili pepper, and other toppings. Wherever you are on Kyushu, *ramen* can never be too far, and it's always good.

Popular in Nagasaki, *shippoku* consists of elaborately prepared dishes that blend the flavors of Asia and Europe. Served Chinese style on a revolving round tabletop and perfect for large groups, shippoku is not a solitary affair. Another Nagasaki favorite, *chanpon*, consists of Chinese-style noodles, vegetables, and shellfish in a thick soup. *Sara udon* has the chanpon ingredients fried crispy instead of boiled.

Basashi (raw horse meat) is a Kumamoto specialty. Perhaps an easier-to-swallow delicacy is *karashi renkon*, slices of lotus root stuffed with mustard and/or cayenne and deep-fried. Compared to the subdued flavors of most Japanese cuisine, these dishes attest to the region's bolder palate.

In Kagoshima, don't pass up a chance to try the famed *kurobuta tonkatsu*, or breaded fried pork cutlet from locally bred black pigs. There's also *satsuma-age*, a fried-fish cake stuffed with ingredients like garlic, cheese, meat, potato, or burdock root. *Imo-jochu*, a much-loved regional spirit distilled from sweet potatoes, helps wash down these goodies.

FUKUOKA 福岡

1,175 km (730 miles) west of Tokyo, 622 km (386 miles) west of Shin-Osaka.

Fukuoka is a good base to begin exploring Kyushu. To get a sense of the city, walk along the meandering Naka-gawa River. The stunning Canal City shopping complex, a 15-minute walk west of Hakata Station, is full of great people-watching, shops, and dining. You'll find a bit of everything, from global coffee and fast-food outlets to famous local ramen.

For night owls, there's plenty happening in the west-central downtown alleys in an area known as Tenjin at truly astounding hours. Friday nights only begin at midnight, usually with a huge and hearty bowl of *tonkotsu* (pork-bone soup) ramen—often referred to as "Hakata ramen"—a rich, tasty staple that locals seem to depend on for their legendary all-night stamina.

The Naka-gawa divides the city. Everything west of the river is known as Fukuoka, while everything east—including the station and airport—is referred to as Hakata, so trains or planes might say to or from Hakata rather than Fukuoka. But don't be confused: Hakata is just a *ku*, or district, of the whole place, which is still Fukuoka.

GETTING HERE AND AROUND

Fukuoka Airport is Kyushu's main airport. It's just two stops away—only six minutes—from Fukuoka's Hakata train station on the Kuko subway line. All Nippon Airways (ANA), Japan Airlines (JAL), and

Skymark Airlines (SKY), Jetstar, and Air Asia fly the 1 hour 50 minute route from Tokyo's Narita Airport. JAL, ANA, and Skymark also fly from Tokyo's Haneda Airport. Domestic flights also arrive from Sapporo, Nagoya, Osaka, Naha, and Ishigaki.

Expressway buses makes the 2½-hour trip between Fukuoka and Nagasaki. Buses also make the four-hour trip between Fukuoka and Kagoshima. JR Shinkansen trains travel from Tokyo (six hours) via Osaka and Hiroshima. The unreserved regular fare is ¥21,810 and trains depart every 30 minutes. Regular JR Express trains also ply this route, but are much slower.

After World War II Fukuoka was rebuilt with wide, tree-lined avenues arranged on an easy-to-navigate Western-style grid. The subway system connects the downtown attractions with a convenient extension to the international airport. The two major transportation hubs are Hakata Station and Tenjin Station. Tenjin, in the heart of downtown Fukuoka, is the terminal for both subway lines. The Kuko Line runs to Hakata Station and on to Fukuoka Airport, and the Hakozaki Line runs out toward the bay. From Fukuoka Airport to Hakata Station, the fare is ¥260. A One-Day Pass for the subway costs ¥620.

Most city buses leave from **Hakata Bus Terminal** across the street from Hakata Station, and from Tenjin Bus Center. A Downtown Fukuoka One-Day Pass costs ¥620

Airport Information Fukuoka Airport. ☎ *092/621–6059 domestic, 092/621–3003 international.*

Bus Contact Nishitetsu Bus Reservations Call Center. ☎ *092/734–2727,* ⊕ *global.atbus-de.com/route_lists/?locale=en.*

Bus Depots Hakata Bus Terminal. ⊠ *Hakata-eki Chuo-gai, Hakata-ku* ☎ *092/431–1171.* **Tenjin Bus Center.** ⊠ *2-11-2 Tenjin* ☎ *092/771–2961.*

VISITOR INFORMATION

The staff members of the Fukuoka City Tourist Information Center dispense up-to-date information about hotels, sights, restaurants, and rental cars, and have pamphlets about area attractions and businesses. Sign language assistance is also provided.

Contact Fukuoka City Tourist Information Center. ⊠ *Hakata Station, 1-1 Hakataeki-Chuo-gai* ☎ *092/431–3003.*

EXPLORING

FAMILY **Canal City** (キャナルシティ). While away the hours people-watching as you stroll around this popular shopping area. Restaurants range from takeout to upscale, and there's a huge cinema on the top floors with 3D IMAX screens. At one end of the complex is a zigzagging patio where every hour on the hour water jets spray and twirl in time to the *Indiana Jones* theme. At the other end is a futuristic half-dome structure with ingeniously tiered balconies lined with shops and cafés. The eye-catching palette of salmon pinks and pastel blues, liberal use of glass, and clever angles make this a far more interesting shopping

FAMILY **Ohori Park** (大濠公園 *Ohori Koen*). The lake in this park was once part of an impressive moat surrounding Fukuoka's castle. A leisurely 2-km (1-mile) path follows its perimeter. In early April the pink and white flowers of the park's 2,600 cherry trees present a dazzling display. Within the park is the **Fukuoka City Art Museum,** which houses a few notable works by Dalí, Miró, Chagall, and Warhol. Across from it is a traditional Japanese garden. Stop for a quick bite or a luxurious meal at Boathouse Ohori Park on the edge of the lake. ✉ *1–6 Ohorikoen, Chuo-ku* ✛ *20-min subway ride from Hakata Station to Ohori Koen Station* ☎ *092/714–6051* ⊕ *www.fukuoka-art-museum.jp* 🎟 *Park free, museum ¥200, garden ¥240* ⊙ *Museum Sept.–June, Tues.–Sun. 9:30–5:30; July and Aug., Tues.–Sun. 9:30–7:30.*

Shofuku-ji (聖福寺 *Shofuku Temple*). The monk Eisai (1141–1215) returned from a long stint in China to introduce Zen Buddhism to Japan and planted the first tea-bush seeds. Nowadays most tea is grown in other regions such as Shizuoka, but you can still buy the green tea from this region, with its legendary hue and flavor, in stores as far away as Tokyo. Eisai also established Shofuku-ji, Japan's first Zen temple, which the inscription on the main gate by Emperor Gotoba commemorates. In Zen tradition, the grounds and structure reflect the calm, austere nature of this deeply meditative philosophy. The bronze bell in the belfry was designated an Important Cultural Property. ✉ *6–1 Gokusho-machi, Hakata-ku* ✛ *15-min walk northwest from Hakata Station, or 5-min walk north of Gion Station* ☎ *092/291–0775* 🎟 *Free* ⊙ *Daily 8–5.*

WHERE TO EAT

$ ✕ **Horin** (鳳凛). To prepare for a big night in Tenjin, this is a convenient, JAPANESE delicious, and inexpensive place to grab some *tonkotsu ramen*. For ¥650 you can dive into a big bowl of thin noodles in a steamy, pork-based broth garnished with sliced pork and chopped onions. Other toppings include boiled egg and sliced *kikurage* ("tree jellyfish," or black mushrooms)—high in protein, full of vitamin B. It's near the corner, just off the south side of Kokutai-dori, two blocks west of Haruyoshi Bridge, on the way to all-night fun in the Tenjin district. $ *Average main: ¥800* ✉ *3–21–15 Haruyoshi* ☎ *092/716–6755* ▭ *No credit cards.*

$ ✕ **Ichi-ran** (一蘭). Folks in Fukuoka wait in long lines for these rectan-JAPANESE gular black boxes of extra-thin noodles swimming in pork-bone broth and topped with tasty *char-shu* (slices of roasted pork), *negi* (green onions), and sprinkles of *togarashi* (red pepper). Fill out an order form (available in English) to indicate exactly how you like it, from the amount of shredded garlic to the fat content (locals go for more fat to get that sweet flavor they adore). You then buy a ticket from the machine inside the door and place your ticket and order form on the counter. The noodles taste best when ordered slightly chewy, and the soup is flavorful even with a light fat content. There are several branches, including one in the basement of the Hakata Station, but the best one is in Canal City. $ *Average main: ¥800* ✉ *Canal City Hakata,*

B1F 1–2–22, Sumiyoshi, Hakata-ku ☎ *092/263–2201* ⊕ *www.ichiran. co.jp/english/html/q_cch.html* ▭ *No credit cards.*

WHERE TO STAY

$$$ 🏨 **Canal City Fukuoka Washington Hotel** (キャナルシテイ福岡ワシントン
HOTEL ホテル). Much classier than other members of this hotel chain, the Washington has guest rooms with views of the city or the sci-fi half-dome of Canal City. **Pros:** great value; comfortable rooms; prime window-shopping location. **Cons:** staff speaks limited English; bathroom fittings look timeworn. ⓢ *Rooms from: ¥19800* ⊠ *1–2–20 Sumiyoshi, Hakata-ku* ☎ *092/282–8800, 092/282–0757* ⊕ *www.washington-hotels.jp/fukuoka* ↩ *423 rooms* ⦿*No meals.*

$$$$ 🏨 **Grand Hyatt Fukuoka** (グランド・ハイアット・福岡). Far and away the
HOTEL best hotel in town, the sophisticated Grand Hyatt overlooks—or, rather, looks into—the Canal City shopping and entertainment complex. **Pros:** the coolest spot to base yourself. **Cons:** extra charges for spa and pool (¥2,160); could use better soundproofing. ⓢ *Rooms from: ¥33000* ⊠ *1–2–82 Sumiyoshi, Canal City, Hakata-ku* ☎ *092/282–1234, 092/282–2817* ⊕ *www.fukuoka.grand.hyatt.com* ↩ *370 rooms, 14 suites* ⦿*No meals.*

$$$$ 🏨 **Hakata Excel Hotel Tokyu** (博多エクセルホテル東急). Overlooking
HOTEL the Naka River, this upscale Western-style hotel is a short walk from Canal City. **Pros:** superb location; wide selection of rooms; speedy Internet. **Cons:**"entertainment district" close by. ⓢ *Rooms from: ¥26136* ⊠ *4–6–7 Nakasu, Hakata-ku* ☎ *092/262–0109, 092/262–5578* ⊕ *www. tokyuhotelsjapan.com/en/TE/TE_HAKAT/index.html* ▭ *No credit cards* ↩ *298 rooms, 10 suites.*

$ 🏨 **Toyoko Inn Hakata Nishi-nakasu** (東横イン博多西中洲). There are
HOTEL almost 250 Toyoko Inns scattered around Japan, and this branch offers budget-minded travelers cramped but clean accommodations, reasonable rates, and a central location near Canal City. **Pros:** near the Naka River; free breakfast; easy online booking; inexpensive. **Cons:** rooms are cramped and bland; 4 pm check-in. ⓢ *Rooms from: ¥10044* ⊠ *1–16 Nishinakasu, Chuo-ku* ☎ *092/739–1045, 092/739–1046* ⊕ *www. toyoko-inn.com/e_hotel/00044/index.html* ▭ *No credit cards* ↩ *260 rooms* ⦿*Breakfast.*

NIGHTLIFE

Fukuoka seems forever in the throes of an ongoing party—perhaps in a heroic endeavor to put off the inevitable hangover—but the surest places for memorable nightlife action are the Nakasu and Tenjin areas, which run along the Naka River. Nakasu is on the east side of the river; Tenjin is on the west. If you need sustenance, grab some ramen, yakitori, or tempura from one of the street vendors that stay open until around 2 am.

Propeller Drive (プロペラドライブ). To hang with the in crowd, drop by the bar and café known as Propeller Drive. Day or night, you are practically guaranteed to see some of the city's most stylish people. It's fancy, but there's no cover charge. All three floors have white stucco walls, and the second floor has a wonderful overhang with tables where you can sit and enjoy the view. Countless intricately framed mirrors reflect the light of crystal chandeliers. A snack you won't want to miss is the bruschetta with fresh mozzarella and basil. Kotaro, the manager, recommends the pancakes topped with cream, strawberries, and blueberries. ⊠ *1–13–30 Imaizumi* ☎ *092/715–6322* ⊕ *www.propellerdrive.jp.*

SHOPPING

Fukuoka is known for two traditional folk crafts: Hakata *ningyo* (dolls) and Hakata *obi* (kimono sashes). Made of fired clay, hand-painted with bright colors and distinctive expressions, Hakata ningyo represent children, samurais, and geisha. The obi are made of a local silk that has a slightly coarse texture; bags and purses made of this silk make excellent souvenirs.

Kyushu has a rich ceramics tradition. The shops and kilns of Arita, Karatsu, and Imari and other towns of Saga Prefecture, in particular, continue to produce fine pottery, especially a delicate-looking but surprisingly tough type of porcelain. The earthenware of Karatsu, particularly the fine tea ceremony wares, are much admired by ceramics collectors within and outside Japan.

Iwataya (岩田屋). The fifth floor of this department store carries the city's most complete selection of local merchandise, including Hakata dolls, silk, and ceramics. Also check out the impressive selection of kimono, obi, and the more inexpensive summer yukata. ⊠ *2–5–35 Tenjin* ⚓ *Take Tenjin subway station Exit W-5 and walk 2 blocks* ☎ *092/721–1111* ⊕ *www.i.iwataya-mitsukoshi.co.jp* ⊗ *Daily 10–8.*

Kawabata Shotengai (川端商店街 *Kawabata Shopping Arcade*). This aging shopping arcade runs between Nakasu Kawabata and Canal City. It has a few interesting stores selling Hakata dolls, but most locals, especially those under 60, head for the larger modern malls such as Canal City. ⊠ *Kawabata Shotengai.*

YUFUIN 湯布院

135 km (84 miles) southeast of Hakata/Fukuoka.

Southwest of the majestic twin peaks of Yufu-dake, this tranquil village resembles a checkered quilt. Forests nestle up to clusters of galleries, eclectic cafés, local crafts shops, and rustic lodgings. Most of the year, Yufuin is a relatively peaceful area, but things heat up in July and August with the arrival of national music and film festivals.

Yufuin has avoided many of the pitfalls of modern tourism, and it wasn't an accident. City planners and investors went to Europe and came back with ideas about how to set up a quaint and lovely spa town. The town has blossomed into a quiet, sedate getaway. Relatively unadorned natural baths with great views can be found here, as can a thriving arts-and-crafts industry and fantastic food.

GETTING HERE AND AROUND

The closest airport is Oita Airport. Flights from Tokyo's Haneda or Narita airports to Oita take 1½ hours. There are also direct flights from Nagoya and Osaka. Buses run from the airport to Yufuin six times a day (¥1,550; 55 minutes).

Kyushu Sanko Kotsu buses make the 3¾-hour trip between Kumamoto and Yufuin twice a day, departing at 8:04 am 12:15 pm. The one-way fare is ¥3,550.

You can reach Yufuin by train from Kumamoto by transferring at Kurume to the LTD Express Yufu (2¼ hours; ¥6,330). The LTD Express Yufu also runs between Fukuoka's Hakata Station and Yufuin Station (2 hours, 10 minutes; ¥4,040). Highway buses travel from Fukuoka Airport, via Hakata Station, to Yufuin Station (2¼ hours; ¥2,880)

Airport Information Oita Airport. ⊠ *Shimobaru, Aki-machi, Kunisaki* ☎ *0978/67–1174.*

Airport Transfer Oita Kotsu Bus Company. ☎ *097/536–3655.*

Bus Contact Kyushu Sanko Kotsu Bus. ☎ *096/325–0100* ⊕ *www.atbus-de. com.e.jo.hp.transer.com.*

Train Station Yufuin Station (由布院駅). ⊠ *8-2 Kawakita* ☎ *0977/84–2021.*

VISITOR INFORMATION

To enjoy the best of Yufuin in a day, start by picking up an English map at Yufuin Tourist Information Office. For more-detailed information, visit the Yufuin Tourist Center, a five-minute walk from the station.

Contact Yufuin Tourist Center. ⊠ *2863 Kawakami* ☎ *0977/85–4464 Japanese only.* **Yufuin Tourist Information Office.** ⊠ *Yufuin Station, 8-2 Kawakita* ☎ *0977/84–2446.*

EXPLORING

Kuso-no-Mori (空想の森). From Yufuin Station, take the five-minute taxi ride north to this collection of art galleries along the foot of Yufu-dake. ⊠ *Yufuin.*

Lake Kinrin (金麟湖 *Kinrin-ko*). In winter, steam rises from the surface of this thermal lake on the east end of town. Warm up with a dip in one of the many bathhouses along its shores. ⊠ *Yufuin.*

OFF THE BEATEN PATH

Usa Shrine (宇佐神宮 *Usa Jingu / Usa Hachimangu*). The most important Hachiman shrine in Japan, Usa Jingu has lovely ponds dotted with lotus plants. Allot an hour to see the shrine and stroll the expansive grounds. There was a long tradition in Japan of building temples and shrines in the same precinct (abolished in the Meiji period), and this is said to be the first place to do so. From Yufuin take the one-hour train to Oita, then board a 40-minute limited express train to Usa. From Usa, it's a short taxi or bus ride to the shrine. If you take the bus, get on the one bound for Yotsukaichi and get off at the stop Usa Hachiman. ⊠ *2859 Minamiusa, Usa* ☎ *0978/37–0001* 🎫 *Free* ☉ *Apr.–Sept., daily 5:30 am–9 pm; Oct.–Mar., daily 6 am–9 pm.*

There are several public bathhouses along the shores of Yufuin's Kinrin-ko thermal lake.

Yu-no-tsubo (湯の坪). Close to the train station, this neighborhood is a long shopping street lined with traditional Japanese wooden buildings. You can wander in and out of artsy craft shops and souvenir stalls, or relax in one of the many coffee shops or tearooms. ✉ *Yufuin.*

Yutaka Isozaki Gallery (由夛加磯崎ギャラリー). This gallery usually has displays of artworks in various media, including pottery and paintings. There are also small cards with inspirational messages, and illustrations such as persimmons and wildflowers that make original souvenirs. ✉ *1266–21 Kawakami* ☎ *0977/85–4750* 🕐 *Thurs.–Tues. 9–4.*

WHERE TO EAT AND STAY

$$$$ JAPANESE 🍴 **BudouYa** (葡萄屋). Part of the Yufuin Tamanoyu hotel, which until 1975 was a lodging for Zen Buddhist monks, this restaurant retains an air of solemnity. The first level has stone floors, thick wooden tables, and windows overlooking a thicket of wildflowers in the tall grass. Upstairs rooms have tatami floors and bamboo-mat ceilings. Popular dishes include salt-grilled fish, seasonal vegetables, and homemade *kabosu* (lime) sherbet. [$] *Average main: ¥9072* ✉ *Yunotsubo, Yufuin-cho, Yufu* ☎ *0977/84–2158* 🌐 *www.tamanoyu.co.jp/publicspace* 🕐 *No lunch.*

$$$$ JAPANESE FUSION 🍴 **Moustache** (レストランムスタシュ). Started by a Japanese chef who wanted to create a European atmosphere, Moustache is a café and restaurant with a flair for hearty, country-style French fare. At lunch you can order à la carte, and in the evening there is a selection of set meals. The chef recommends the rainbow trout. [$] *Average main:*

This statue of a godlike man with outstretched arms sits at the center of Nagasaki's Heiwa Koen.

¥3100 ✉ *1264–7 Kawakami, Yufuin-cho* ☎ *0977/84–5155* 🌐 *www.moustache-yufuin.com* 🕒 *Closed Mon.*

$$$$ B&B/INN **Onyado Yufu Ryochiku** (御宿由布両築). When not submerged in the mineral waters at this relaxing lodging that dates from 1925, you can toast yourself by the burning coals in the *irori* (sunken hearth) in the lobby. **Pros:** tranquil atmosphere; private mineral baths; in-town location. **Cons:** Wi-Fi only in lobby; not much except bathing going on. [$] *Rooms from: ¥48000* ✉ *1097–1 Kawakami, Yufuin-cho, Yufu, Oita-ken* ☎ *0977/85–2526, 0977/85–4466* 🌐 *www.tentacle.jp/room.html* 🛏 *8 Japanese-style rooms* 🍴 *Some meals.*

$$$$ B&B/INN Fodor's Choice ★ **Sansou Murata** (山荘無量塔). This unique and special place mixes the best of Western and Japanese accommodations. **Pros:** incredible food; marvelous staff; real taste and atmosphere. **Cons:** no wheelchair accessible rooms; expensive. [$] *Rooms from: ¥99680* ✉ *1264–2 Yufuin-cho Kawakami, Yufu* ☎ *0977/84–5000* 🌐 *www.sansou-murata.com* 🛏 *12 combination rooms* 🍴 *Some meals.*

NAGASAKI 長崎

154 km (96 miles) southwest of Fukuoka (Hakata Station).

Blessed with a breathtaking location, Nagasaki is strung together on a long series of hillocks in a scenic valley that follows the arms of the Urakami River down into a gentle harbor. Unlike Hiroshima, the city was left with no suitably intact reminders of the atomic bombing, and perhaps for this reason, there were apparently no compunctions about rebuilding the town right up to the edge of a tiny ground-zero circle with a stark steel monument at its center. Yet as relatively new as everything here is, Nagasaki's international history shows through, from lively and compact Chinatown to the European-style mansions and Catholic churches on the hillsides.

In the mid-16th century, Portuguese missionaries, including Saint Francis Xavier, came ashore to preach Christianity throughout Kyushu. This new and altruistic religion—coinciding with the arrival of firearms—threatened to spread like an epidemic through the impoverished and restive masses of the feudal system. In 1597, to give bite to a new decree by Chief Minister Toyotomi Hideyoshi to stifle worship, 26 followers were publicly crucified in Nagasaki, an act that brought condemnation from the world. This cruel and shocking display was followed not long after by Tokugawa's nationwide edict making the practice of Christianity a capital offense.

All foreigners were expelled except the Dutch, who, considered to be lacking overt propensities to convert anything but profits on trades, were sequestered on an island, Dejima. Of the local population, only merchants and prostitutes were allowed direct interactions with them. The Dutch took over the considerable trade brokering between China and Japan formerly done by the Portuguese. Though the rest of Japan was strangled by isolation and starved for foreign goods, Nagasaki continued to prosper by making use of this tiny but important offshore loophole in the Tokugawa anti-trade policy out in the harbor. This arrangement lasted until 1859, when insular Japan was forced to open up to the outside world.

Once other ports became popular, the city's status diminished. Centuries later, Mitsubishi decided to concentrate its arms manufacturing and shipbuilding capabilities here; the industrial presence and bad weather over the primary target of Kokura in northern Kyushu made Nagasaki the site of the second atomic bomb drop in 1945.

The city isn't small, but it occupies a long winding valley, so you can experience it in manageable increments. Similarities with San Francisco are frequently noted. The comparison is not far off, though the posters advertising whale-bacon and manga remind you of where you are. Most of the interesting sights, restaurants, and shopping areas are south of Nagasaki Station, but the Peace Park and the Atomic Bomb Museum are to the north, about 10 to 15 minutes by streetcar or taxi.

GETTING HERE AND AROUND

The trip from Nagasaki Airport to Nagasaki takes approximately 45 minutes by bus or car. A regular shuttle bus travels between Nagasaki Airport and Nagasaki Station and costs ¥800. All Nippon Airways and Japan Airlines fly daily from Haneda Airport in Tokyo to Nagasaki Airport (1¾ hours). There are also direct flights to Nagasaki from Okinawa, Nagoya, and Osaka.

Highway buses run from Fukuoka's Tenjin Bus Center, Hakata Bus Terminal, and Fukuoka Airport to Nagasaki Bus Terminal; the trip takes 2 hours, 30 minutes and costs ¥2,500. The Nagasaki Ken-ei Bus Company can get you to Unzen, a string of hot springs on the Shimabara

Peninsula, in 1 hour, 40 minutes (¥1,900), and direct to Kumamoto in 3 hours for ¥3,600.

From Fukuoka's Hakata Station, the JR Kamome Express train costs ¥4,380 and takes around two hours.

Nagasaki is small enough to cover on foot, and the streetcar system is the most convenient mode of transportation. Stops are posted in English, and lines extend to every attraction in town. You can purchase a one-day streetcar pass (¥500) at tourist offices and major hotels. If you don't have a pass, pay ¥120 as you get off the streetcar. If you wish to transfer from one streetcar to another, get a *norikae kippu* (transfer ticket) from the driver. Local buses are not as convenient, and the routes, timetables, and fares are complicated.

One-hour cruises of Nagasaki Harbor depart from Nagasaki-ko (Nagasaki Port) at noon and 4 pm; the cost is ¥2,000.

Airport Information Nagasaki Airport. ⊠ *Mishima-machi, Omura-city* ☎ *0957/525–555,.*

Bus Contacts Nagasaki Kenei Bus Center. ☎ *095/823–6155.*

Bus Depot Nagasaki Bus Terminal. ⊠ *3–1 Daikoku-machi* ☎ *095/826–6221.*

Train Station Nagasaki Train Station. ⊠ *1–89 Onoue-machi* ☎ *095/822–0063.*

TOURS

Nagasaki Port Pleasure Cruises. Dating back to the days when it brought in wealth and culture from across the seas, Nagasaki's greatest asset has always been its port. A short pleasure cruise around the harbor is a relaxing way to see the heart and soul of the city. ⊠ *Ferry Terminal, Nagasaki City* ☎ *095/824–0088* 🎫 *From ¥2000.*

VISITOR INFORMATION

Contacts Nagasaki Tourist Information Center. ⊠ *Nagasaki Train Station, 1–1 Onoue-machi* ☎ *095/823–3631.*

EXPLORING

TOP ATTRACTIONS

Dejima (出島). When the government deported foreigners from Japan in the mid-17th century, Dutch traders were the only Westerners allowed to remain—but they were relegated to, and confined on, this artificial island in Nagasaki Harbor. Here you can see a 450-year-old mix of Dutch housing styles that is popular among Japanese tourists. ⊠ *6–3 Dejima-machi, Nagasaki City* ✛ *Take Streetcar 1 to the Dejima stop* ☎ *095/821–7200* ⊕ *www.city.nagasaki.lg.jp/dejima/en* 🎫 *¥510* ◷ *Daily 8–6.*

Fodor's Choice **Glover Garden** (グラバー邸). This garden contains an impressive assort-
★ ment of 19th-century Western houses. Greco-Roman porticoes and arches, wooden verandas, and other random elements of European architecture adorn the structures, which are often crowned with Japanese-style roofs. The main attraction is the 1863 mansion of Thomas Glover, a prominent Scottish merchant who introduced steam locomotives and industrialized coal mining to Japan. Escalators whisk you up the steep hillside to the gardens, where you can admire the views

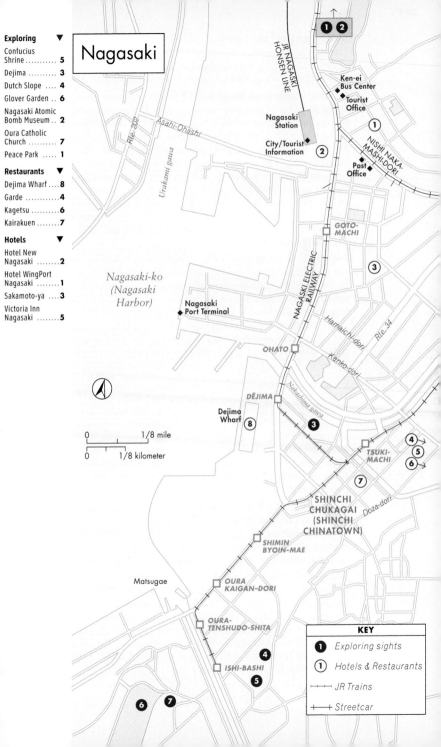

Nagasaki

JR NAGASAKI HONSEN LINE

Ken-ei
Bus Center

Tourist
Office

Nagasaki
Station

City/Tourist
Information

NISHI NAKA-
MASHI-DORI

Post
Office

Rte 202

Asahi-Ohashi

Urakami gawa

*Nagasaki-ko
(Nagasaki
Harbor)*

Nagasaki
Port Terminal

NAGASAKI ELECTRIC RAILWAY

GOTO-
MACHI

Hamaichi-dori

Rte 34

Kanko-dori

OHATO

Nakashima gawa

DEJIMA

Dejima
Wharf

TSUKI-
MACHI

SHINCHI
CHUKAGAI
(SHINCHI
CHINATOWN)

Doza-dori

SHIMIN
BYOIN-MAE

Matsugae

OURA
KAIGAN-DORI

OURA-
TENSHUDO-SHITA

ISHI-BASHI

0   1/8 mile

0   1/8 kilometer

KEY

❶ *Exploring sights*

① *Hotels & Restaurants*

＋—＋— *JR Trains*

＋—＋ *Streetcar*

of Nagasaki and the harbor. ✉ *8–1 Minami Yamate-machi, Nagasaki City* ✛ *Take Streetcar 5 to Oura Tenshudo-shita and follow signs* ☎ *095/822–8223* ⊕ *www.glover-garden.jp* 🎫 *¥610* ⊙ *Late Apr.–early May and mid-July–early Oct., daily 8 am–8:30 pm; daily 8–6 rest of yr.*

Nagasaki Atomic Bomb Museum (原爆資料館 *Genbaku Shiryokan*). The spiral staircase of this museum takes you down into a dark, thought-provoking collection of video loops, dioramas, and exhibits that demonstrate the devastating effects of the bomb detonated in Nagasaki. English audio tours are available, though what you see is already a lot to handle. The continuous, unblinking film footage is absolutely nauseating at several points, and a melted and blasted wall clock, as surreal as any Dalí painting, sears its way into your consciousness. ✉ *7–8 Hirano-machi, Nagasaki City* ✛ *Take Streetcar 1 from Nagasaki Station to Hamaguchi stop* ☎ *095/844–1231* ⊕ *www.nagasakipeace. jp* 🎫 *¥200 (optional audio guide ¥150)* ⊙ *Sept.–Apr., daily 8:30–5:30; May–Aug., daily 8:30–6:30.*

Peace Park (平和公園 *Heiwa Koen*). Nagasaki's Peace Park was built on the grounds of an old prison that was destroyed in the atomic blast. In the middle is a large statue of a godlike man sitting with one arm stretched to the sky and one to the land. A short distance down the hill, **Hypocenter Koen** marks the bomb's "hypocenter." A solitary pillar was erected to mark the exact epicenter. Curiously little distance separates the pillar from anything else. In contrast to the looming Hiroshima dome, when you come upon this spot you might not immediately recognize its significance. ✉ *Nagasaki City* ✛ *From Nagasaki Station take Streetcar 1 or 3 to Matsuya-machi stop* 🎫 *Free* ⊙ *Open 24 hrs.*

WORTH NOTING

Confucius Shrine (孔子廟 *Koshi-byo*). This bright red shrine was built in 1893 by the Chinese residents of Nagasaki. The small Historical Museum of China displays artifacts on loan from Beijing's Palace Museum of Historical Treasures and National Museum of Chinese History. ✉ *10–36 Oura-machi, Nagasaki City* ✛ *Take streetcar to Ishibashi stop and follow signs leading to shrine* ☎ *095/824–4022* 🎫 *¥600* ⊙ *Daily 8:30–5.*

Dutch Slope (オランダ坂 *Oranda-saka*). This cobblestone incline is a good place to wander on the way to Chinatown and Glover Garden. Dutch residents built the wooden houses here in the late 19th century. Many become shops and tearooms in summer. To get here, follow the street on the southeastern side of the Confucian Shrine. ✉ *Nagasaki City.*

Oura Catholic Church (大浦天主堂 *Oura Tenshu-do*). This church below the entrance to Glover Garden survived the bomb that leveled much of the city. It was constructed in 1865 to commemorate the death of 26 Christians crucified in 1597, victims of Toyotomi Hideyoshi's gruesome message of religious intolerance. It's the oldest Gothic-style building in Japan. ✉ *5–3 Minami Yamate-machi, Nagasaki City* ✛ *5-min walk from Oura Tenshu-do-shita streetcar stop* ☎ *095/823–2628* ⊕ *www1. bbiq.jp/oourahp* 🎫 *¥300* ⊙ *Daily 8–6.*

Glover Garden has a large koi pond.

WHERE TO EAT

$$ ECLECTIC INTERNATIONAL 🍴 **Dejima Wharf** (出島ワーフ). Warm evenings draw crowds to the outdoor terraces of this trendy two-story wooden complex on the pier next to Nagasaki Port. Just a short walk from the historic buildings at Dejima, you'll find a sprawl of tantalizing seafood restaurants—the oysters come highly recommended—along with Italian, Chinese, and steak restaurants. [$] *Average main: ¥1100* ✉ *Dejima Wharf, Nagasaki City* ☎ *095/828–3939.*

$$ ITALIAN 🍴 **Garde** (ガルダ). Crispy thin-crust pizza and tasty pasta dishes are the mainstays at this Italian restaurant in the Shian-bashi entertainment quarter east of Chinatown. Owner Noguchi-san started Garde in 1974 so it's pretty much a local institution. Eat in or take out. From the Shian-bashi tram stop, head two blocks north into the arcade and one block west. It's on the corner. [$] *Average main: ¥1350* ✉ *1–20 Kajiya-machi* ☎ *095/826–1302* 💳 *No credit cards* 🕘 *Closed Tues.*

$$$$ JAPANESE 🍴 **Kagetsu** (花月). Billing itself as "one of the most important historical restaurants of Japan," this quiet hilltop retreat is Nagasaki's most prestigious dining room. Dishes are served as *kaiseki* (multicourse meals) or *shippoku* (an elaborate course blending Asian and European elements). A weekday lunchtime bento box costs ¥5,400; full dinners start at about ¥14,250 and head skyward. The interior wooden beams date to 1618. Meiji Restoration leader Ryoma Sakamoto once took a chunk out of a wooden pillar with his sword during a brawl; you can still see the gashes in the main dining room. The area around Kagetsu has historically been home to many geisha, and to this day they can be booked to perform during your meal (¥27,000 per geisha for three hours). With

August 9, 1945

On August 9, 1945, three days after the blast at Hiroshima, Nagasaki fell victim to a second atomic bomb because of bad weather. The plane, named *Bockscar*, was supposed to drop the Fat Man, a new and experimental plutonium bomb, on the war industry complexes in Kokura. A delay in hooking up with *Bockscar's* B-29 escorts meant that when they reached Kokura, bad weather had rolled in and blocked their view. So they headed over to the secondary target, Nagasaki and its vital shipyards, and dropped the bomb there.

More powerful than the uranium bomb dropped on Hiroshima, the Fat Man's core of plutonium, surrounded by

TNT, imploded. The runaway fission chain reaction released the heat- and light-wave radiation of a small sun over the target, which in turn delivered a blast pressure of tons per square inch. Virtually nothing within miles of the blast was left standing, or even recognizable. Nagasaki's hilly topography and conformity to undulating river valley floors had made it a less desirable target, but it did help save a number of residential areas from total destruction. Meanwhile, 6.7 square km (2.59 square miles) were obliterated, 74,884 people were killed in the blast or died shortly thereafter, and another 74,909 were injured. The effects of radioactivity caused the deaths of an estimated 70,000 others within five years.

notice ahead of your visit, Kagetsu can provide special meals including vegetarian, nut-free, and halal. $ *Average main: ¥14256* ⌧ *2–1 Maruyama-cho, Nagasaki City* ⚓ *About 656 feet south of Shianbashi streetcar stop* ☎ *095/822–0191.*

$$ ✕ **Kairakuen** (会楽園). This ornate Chinese restaurant is a local favorite, and it's easy to see, smell, and taste why. Kairakuen serves the best *chanpon*—Nagasaki's signature dish of Chinese-style noodles, vegetables, and pork-based broth—in town. The reasonable prices are an added bonus. The restaurant is just inside the entrance to Chinatown, on the left. $ *Average main: ¥1200* ⌧ *10–16 Shinchi-machi, Nagasaki City* ⚓ *Take streetcar to Tsuki-machi and walk 2 blocks southeast along river* ☎ *095/822–4261.*

CHINESE

WHERE TO STAY

$$$$ 🏨 **Hotel New Nagasaki** (ホテルニュー長崎). Glossy marble and massive slabs of granite dominate this popular and upscale hotel. **Pros:** you can't get closer to the station; great shopping next door; spacious rooms. **Cons:** too busy for solitude seekers. $ *Rooms from: ¥28600* ⌧ *14–5 Daikoku-machi, Nagasaki City* ☎ *095/826–8000, 095/823–2000* ⊕ *www.newnaga.com* ⇲ *148 rooms* ❖ *No meals.*

HOTEL

$ 🏨 **Hotel WingPort Nagasaki** (ホテルウィングポート長崎). A business center, rental laptops, and in-room Internet connections attract corporate travelers to this hotel whose guest quarters are simple, functional, and a good value. **Pros:** spacious rooms; handy location; good value. **Cons:**

HOTEL

light sleepers beware—noises travel well here. $ *Rooms from: ¥10280* ✉ *9–2 Daikoku-machi, Nagasaki City* ☎ *095/833–2800, 095/833–2801* ⊕ *www.wingport.com/en* ⇨ *200 rooms* ⦿ *No meals.*

$$$$
B&B/INN 🛏 **Sakamoto-ya** (坂本屋). Established in 1895, this small wooden ryokan, Nagasaki's oldest lodging, seems to have changed little over time. **Pros:** lots of charm; wooden soaking tubs; private gardens; extremely personalized service. **Cons:** books up quickly. $ *Rooms from: ¥32400* ✉ *2–13 Kanaya-machi, Nagasaki City* ☎ *095/826–8211, 095/825–5944* ⊕ *www.sakamotoya.co.jp* ⇨ *11 Japanese-style rooms* ⦿ *Some meals.*

$$
HOTEL 🛏 **Victoria Inn Nagasaki** (ビクトリア イン 長崎). The vintage sofas, antique telephones, and dark oil paintings in this hotel's lobby, reminiscent of an old European drawing room, supply a dash of style and sophistication. **Pros:** comfortable stylish rooms; capable staff; great bar on the first floor. **Cons:** some single rooms have no view; limited room service. $ *Rooms from: ¥15400* ✉ *6–24 Doza-machi, Nagasaki City* ☎ *095/828–1234, 095/828–0178* ⊕ *www.victoria-inn.jp* ⇨ *87 rooms* ⦿ *No meals.*

SHOPPING

Castella sponge cake, the popular souvenir of Nagasaki, was introduced by the Portuguese in the mid-16th century. The original recipe called for just eggs, flour, and sugar, but it's been tinkered with over time. Every sweet shop and souvenir store in town has its own specially flavored recipe, but you're advised to stick with the plain old version—a delightful treat with coffee or tea.

SHOPPING AREAS

As the sun sets, everyone converges at **Amu Plaza** (Amu Puraza; アムプラーザ), which towers over Nagasaki Station. The newest shops and restaurants can be found here, along with a multiscreen movie complex. Amu Plaza is thoroughly modern, and a striking contrast to the city's old-fashioned style.

Not far from Dejima, **Hamano-machi** (浜野町) is the major shopping district in downtown Nagasaki. This covered arcade stretches over four blocks and contains numerous department stores, cake shops, cafés, pharmacies, and fashion boutiques.

Fukusaya (福砂屋). *Castella* is a simple brick-shape sponge cake first brought to Nagasaki by the Portuguese. The bakery Fukusaya has been in business since the Meiji period, so when you say "castella" in Nagasaki, most people think of this shop's cakes and their distinctive yellow packaging. There's a branch on the first floor of the Hotel New Nagasaki, next to Nagasaki Station. ✉ *Hotel New Nagasaki, 14–5 Daikoku-Machi, 1st fl., Nagasaki City* ☎ *095/822–4532.*

KUMAMOTO 熊本

118 km (73 miles) south of Fukuoka (Hakata).

Kumamoto is nearly midway along the curve of the west coast of Kyushu. From here you can go to Nagasaki to the west, Fukuoka to the north, Aso-san to the east, and Kagoshima to the south.

The town has many sights of its own, including the nationally famous Suizen-ji Garden, but the most renowned is Kumamoto Castle, a structure once deemed impregnable. Kiyomasa Kato ushered in the 17th century with the construction of a mighty fortress that was even bigger than the current replica, and he and his son held sway here until the 1630s. The Hosokawa clan then took over, and for the next few centuries Kumamoto was a center of the Tokugawa governmental authority.

In 1877, the real "Last Samurai," Saigo Takamori, brought his army of rebels here to battle untested Meiji government conscripts holed up inside. Things were looking grim. Then Takamori ordered his starving men to butcher their horses for raw and ready food. Strengthened, they did breach the castle 53 days into the siege, but reinforcements forced them to backpedal as much of the castle and compound were destroyed in a huge conflagration. It may have been the first time raw horseflesh (*ba-sashi*) was eaten in Japan, but locals continue to devour it to help their stamina.

A number of notable folks had homes that can still be seen in town, including the writers Lafcadio Hearn and Soseki Natsume, both of whom lived here for brief periods while teaching English.

In most Japanese cities the hive of activity is around the train station. However, very little of interest surrounds Kumamoto Station; the bulk of the town's attractions are to the northeast, squeezed in between the Tsuboi and Shira rivers. Most of what constitutes downtown huddles around the old castle up there.

GETTING HERE AND AROUND

The Kyushu-Sanko bus makes the one-hour run from Kumamoto Airport to JR Kumamoto Station for ¥800. Flights on ANA, JAL, and Sky Net Asia connect Tokyo's Haneda Airport with Kumamoto Airport (1¾ hours). ANA and JAL fly the hour-long route from Osaka's Itami Airport eight times a day.

The Nagasaki Ken-ei Bus (from Nagasaki Ken-ei Bus Terminal) costs ¥3,600 and takes three hours to get to Kumamoto City Kotsu Center. Kyushu-Sanko buses leaving from Kumamoto City Kotsu Center take 3½ hours to get to Kagoshima (¥3,700). There's also a Kyushu Sanko bus route linking the *onsen* (thermal baths) paradise of Yufuin and Kumamoto in 4½ hours for ¥3,550.

Shinkansen trains from Fukuoka's Hakata Station stop at Kumamoto Station and take 35 to 50 minutes (¥4,610); the 2 hour, 20 minute trip from Nagasaki (¥6,950) includes a change at Shin-Tosu. Getting from Kumamoto to Kagoshima-Chuo on the bullet train takes just 47 minutes (¥6,420).

This is one spread-out city, and buses get stuck in all the traffic, so your best bet is to hop a streetcar. Tram lines (A and B) connect the major areas of the city. The fare is a flat ¥150; pay as you get off. From the Kumamoto Eki-mae streetcar stop in front of the train station it's a 10-minute ride to downtown. One-day travel passes, good for use on streetcars and city buses, are available for ¥700 from the City Tourist Information Office. There is also a Castle Loop Bus that connects a string of sights around the castle with a stop across from the main train station and runs every 30 minutes from 8:30 to 5 daily. Tickets (¥150 single stop, or ¥400 for the day) can be bought at the tourist office in the station or at the Kotsu Center Bus Terminal near the castle.

Airport Information Kumamoto Airport. ⊠ *1802–2 Oyatsu, Mashiki-machi* ☎ *096/232–2311.*

Bus Contact Kyushu-Sanko Buses. ☎ *096/354–4845* ⊕ *www.kyusanko.co.jp/ sankobus/english.*

Bus Depot Kumamoto City Kotsu Center. ⊠ *3–10 Sakura-machi* ☎ *096/325–0100.*

Train Station Kumamoto Station. ⊠ *3–15–1 Kasuga* ☎ *050/3786–1717.*

VISITOR INFORMATION

Staffers at the Kumamoto Station Tourist Information booth provide maps and information in English. The online Kumamoto Nagomi Tourism Site has good descriptions of major sights and useful information about ATM locations, emergencies, events, etiquette in public baths, and other topics.

Contacts Kumamoto Nagomi Tourism Site. ⊠ *Kumamoto Prefecture Tourism Federation* ☎ *096/382–2660* ⊕ *kumanago.jp/en.* **Kumamoto Station Tourist Information.** ⊠ *JR Kumamoto Station, 3–15–1 Kasuga* ☎ *096/352–3743.*

EXPLORING

Former residence of Hosokawa Gyobu (旧細川刑部邸 *Kyu-Hosokawa Gyobu-tei*). This private home was built in 1646 for the Hosokawa family, who took power at the behest of Tokugawa in 1611—and whose local lineage produced Japan's former Prime Minister Morihiro Hosokawa (served 1993–94). It's an excellent example of traditional *shoin-zukuri* construction. ⊠ *3–1 Furukyo-machi* ☎ *096/352–6522* 🎫*¥300; ¥640 includes Kumamoto Castle* ⊗ *Mar.–Nov., daily 8:30–6; Dec.–Feb., daily 8:30–5.*

Fodor'sChoice ★ **Kumamoto Castle** (熊本城 *Kumamoto-jo*). The towering, ominous castle was completed in 1607, having been designed and built by Kiyomasa Kato (1562–1611), the area's feudal lord or *daimyo*. Gracefully curved, white-edged roofs rest atop the mysterious black keep. Look for slanted windows perfect for unleashing rock falls, one of many clever features to prevent intrusion. The top floor of the reconstructed castle commands an excellent view of Kumamoto, and exhibits include samurai weapons and armor arrayed to evoke images of the fearless warriors charging into battle. Volunteers conduct tours in English (¥2,000, to cover guides' transportation costs). Visit ⊕ *www.k-yokatoko.com/english* to obtain an application form. ✉ *1–1 Honmaru, Kumamoto-shi* ✛ *Take Streetcar A to Kumamoto Castle/City Hall stop* ☎ *096/352–5900* ⊕ *www.manyou-kumamoto.jp/castle* ✍ *¥500; ¥640 with Hosokawa Mansion* ⊘ *Mar.–Nov., daily 8:30–6; Dec.–Feb., daily 8:30–5.*

Suizenji Jojuen Garden (水前寺成趣園 *Suizen-ji Joju-en, Suizen-ji Park*). Created in the mid-17th century, the garden was originally part of the sprawling villa of the ruling Hosokawa family. An undulating knoll of lush green grass representing Japan—there's even a Fuji-san-like cone in about the right place—is beside a pond surrounded by a network of stone bridges. The garden is dotted with impeccably trimmed bushes and trees. For a few hundred yen you can sit on the tatami of the Kokindenju teahouse, sip green tea, and quietly contemplate the gardens. Also on the grounds is **Izumi Jinja** (Izumi Shrine), which houses the tombs of several eminent Hosokawa clan members. ✉ *8–1 Suizenji-koen* ✛ *Take Streetcar A or B east from Kumamoto Castle to Suizenji Park stop* ☎ *096/383–0074* ✍ *¥400* ⊘ *Mar.–Oct., daily 7:30–6; Nov.–Feb., daily 8:30–5.*

WHERE TO EAT

$$$
JAPANESE

✕ **Aoyagi** (青柳). The extensive menu here includes regional favorites— *basashi* (raw horse meat) and tempura-style *karashi renkon* (lotus root stuffed with fiery chili and mustard powder)—in addition to sushi and tofu dishes. You can relax in a booth or sit at the counter and admire the skilled chefs. Aoyagi is not far from the Kumamoto Castle/City Hall tram stop. Ⓢ *Average main: ¥2160* ✉ *1–2–10 Shimotori* ☎ *096/353–0311* ⊕ *aoyagi.ne.jp.*

$$$
JAPANESE

✕ **Suganoya Kamitoriten** (菅乃屋 上通店). When in Kumamoto, do as the locals do and try *basashi*—raw horse meat—at this place where it's a specialty. You can get it served in all its forms: there's a starter of raw tidbits with garlic, ginger, and assorted dunking sauces; or a finale of *hari-hari nabe,* a soup of thinly sliced delicately flavored meat and vegetables cooked in a folded-paper vessel. Ⓢ *Average main: ¥2600* ✉ *L2F Lion Parking Biru, 2–12 Joto-machi* ☎ *096/355–3558* ⊕ *service. suganoya.com/kamidori.*

$$$$
FRENCH
Fodor'sChoice
★

✕ **Tour de Chateau.** This romantic restaurant on the 11th floor of the Kumamoto Hotel Castle has stunning sunset views of Kumamoto Castle. During the day the restaurant is used for wedding receptions, but it opens to the public for dinner. The menu is French, and vegetarian options are available if requested in advance of your visit. This is a place to wine and dine in style. Ⓢ *Average main: ¥5000* ✉ *Kumamoto Hotel Castle, 4–2 Jotomachi, 11th fl.* ☎ *096/326–3311* ⊕ *www.hotel-castle. co.jp/en/restaurants.*

WHERE TO STAY

$$$
HOTEL

🛏 **Hotel New Otani Kumamoto** (ホテルニューオータニ熊本). It's not as over-the-top as its big-city counterparts, but this hotel is endowed with the same crisp service and all the right amenities. **Pros:** convenient to train station; friendly staff. **Cons:** far from castle and city restaurants; no room service. Ⓢ *Rooms from: ¥21978* ✉ *1–13–1 Kasuga*

☎ *096/326–1111, 096/326–0800* 🌐 *www.newotani-kumamoto.co.jp/eng* 🛏 *123 rooms* 🍴 *No meals.*

$$$ HOTEL 🏨 **Kumamoto Hotel Castle** (熊本ホテルキャッスル). Across from and named for the city's best-loved landmark, this hotel has great views and provides excellent service. **Pros:** great staff; eye-catching location; good restaurant. **Cons:** may be fully booked by wedding parties. [$] *Rooms from: ¥19008* ✉ *4–2 Joto-machi* ☎ *096/326–3311, 096/326–3324* 🌐 *www.hotel-castle.co.jp/en* 🛏 *179 rooms* 🍴 *No meals.*

$ HOTEL 🏨 **Toyoko Inn Kumamoto Kotsu Center Mae** (東横INN熊本交通センター前). Inexpensive but functional accommodations, a complimentary Japanese breakfast—*onigiri* (rice balls wrapped in seaweed), miso soup, and coffee—and free Internet access in the lobby are among the pluses of a stay at this member of one of the country's largest hotel chains. **Pros:** free breakfast; inexpensive; laundry facilities. **Cons:** 4 pm check-in; small rooms; sometimes noisy. [$] *Rooms from: ¥8424* ✉ *1–24 Koyaima-machi* ☎ *096/322–1045, 096/322–2045* 🌐 *www.toyoko-inn.com/e_hotel/00077/index.html* 🛏 *152 rooms* 🍴 *Breakfast.*

SHOPPING

Kumamoto's most famous product is *Higo zogan,* or Higo inlay. A unique form of metalwork originally employed in the decoration of swords, scabbards, and gunstocks of the Hosokawa clan, it consists of black steel delicately inlaid with silver and gold. It is now used to make fashionable jewelry that does not come cheap; a simple pendant can run ¥8,000, and prices for large pieces reach ¥700,000 and more. Other local products include gold paper lanterns, dolls, tops, and fine cutlery.

Kumamoto Traditional Crafts Center (*Dento Kogei-kan*). This is the best place to buy regional handicrafts. It's in a brick building across from the Akazu-mon entrance to the castle. Along with the inlaid metalwork called *Higo zogan,* check out the *kiji-uma* (which literally means "pheasant horses"), a traditional toy for boys, or the *hana-te-bako* (flower-covered boxes), a traditional present for girls. ✉ *3–35 Chiba-jo-machi* ☎ *096/324–4930* 🕓 *Tues.–Sun. 9–5.*

TAKACHIHO 高千穂

80 km (49 miles) southeast of Kumamoto.

Deep in the sacred mountains, a spiritual place full of atmosphere, is the birthplace of Japanese mythology. A visit to the Takachiho region takes you to the places where the gods first alighted on Earth, hid in caves, and created the first water spring.

More than one million Japanese visit Takachiho every year, yet few foreigners are aware of this magical and mysterious region that remains not unlike how it was generations ago. See the wonderful *Kagura* dances to the gods that have been performed since ancient times. Take a walk in the mountains, imbibe the sacred waters of mountain springs, and find your own path. You'll marvel at how the people of ancient times in these parts could create myths that so perfectly matched their environment. You'll marvel even more at the sense that these myths are still a part of everyday life in the region. An overnight stay is recommended to see the many sights and soak up the atmosphere. A day trip, while possible, doesn't really give you a full enough sense of the place.

GETTING HERE AND AROUND

Reaching Takachiho is not easy, and that has kept the town from becoming an overdeveloped tourist trap. In the most northerly part of Miyazaki Prefecture, the town is a three-hour bus ride from Kumamoto. Twice-daily buses costing ¥2,300 leave from Kumamoto Train Station, stopping at the Kumamoto Bus Station and Kumamoto Airport. You can pay on the bus or get a ticket from the vending machine in the bus terminal. Driving a rental car is much easier, and gets you there in 90 minutes. Takachiho has little public transportation, so a rental car will serve you well once you're there.

> **TAKACHIHO, THE CRADLE OF MYTH**
>
> Both Takachiho and Takachiho-no-Mine *(see Kirishima-yaku Kokuritsu Koen)* claim to be the places where the grandson of the sun goddess Amaterasu grandson descended to Earth to establish the Japanese Imperial Family. Many years ago officials from both towns went to court to argue their respective points, but the judge demurred, ruling that each town had the right to believe it was the actual place where the gods descended to Earth. Both places are very spiritual and worthy of a visit.

VISITOR INFORMATION

Get a guidebook and a map from the Takachiho Tourist Office, or download them from its website. The office can also connect you with an English-speaking guide. But go to some places by yourself to enjoy the atmosphere.

Takachiho Tourist Office. ⊠ *Takachiho* ☎ *0982/73–1213* ⊕ *takachiho-kanko.info* ⊗ *Daily 8:30–5:30.*

EXPLORING

Ama-no-Iwato Jinja (天岩戸神社 *Ama-no-Iwato Shrine*). This shrine contains the cave where the sun goddess Amaterasu hid until Ame-no-Uzume managed to lure her out. If you apply at the entrance, a Shinto priest will take you into the sacred precinct and across the valley so you can see the actual cave. ⊠ *1073–1 Iwato, Takachiho-cho, Nishiusuki-gun* ⊡ *Free* ⊗ *Dawn–dusk.*

Ama-no-Yasugawara Cave (天安河原). A dark but deeply spiritual place, this huge cave faces onto a small river. According to the myth, the gods gathered here to figure out how to get Amaterasu out of her cave. Visitors pile stones on top of each other to leave their wishes, and the place is filled with little stone piles creating an otherworldly atmosphere. ⊠ *Iwato, Takachiho-cho, Nishiusuki-gun* ⊡ *Free* ⊗ *Dawn–dusk.*

Takachiho Gorge (高千穂峡). This is an impressive ravine of the Gokase River with many waterfalls cascading into it. You can walk along a hiking path at the edge or rent a boat from the booth on the river below the parking lot (¥2,000 for up to three people). Boats are not always available, though. ✉ *Mitai, Takachiho-cho, Nishiusuki-gun* 🎫 *Free* 🕐 *For boats: Sept.–July 19, daily 8:30–4:30; July 20–Aug., daily 7:30–5:30.*

Takachiho Shrine (高千穂神社). Kagura is an ancient ritual dance to give thanks to the gods that has been performed since ancient times. These days it is performed throughout the night in homes between December and January. An excellent one-hour tourist version can be seen nightly at 8 pm at **Kagura Hozonkan,** on the grounds of Takachiho Shrine, the area's premier Shinto shrine. Nestled in a grove of old cedars, the shrine is along a path that also leads to the Takachiho Gorge. ✉ *1037 Mitai, Takachiho-cho, Nishiusuki-gun* ☎ *0982/72–2413* 🎫 *Free to shrine; ¥700 for Kagura dance* 🕐 *Kagura dance 8 pm.*

WHERE TO EAT AND STAY

$$ JAPANESE 🍴 **Nagomi** (和). This restaurant serves the famous local beef, which is cooked in the teppan style table-side. After a course of seasonal vegetables, the succulent pieces of steak are sautéed to perfection. Dessert consists of pieces of white bread fried in the meat juices and oil and then covered with sugar powder (better tasting than it sounds). [$] *Average main: ¥1400* ✉ *1099–1 Mitai* ☎ *0982/73–1109* 🕐 *Closed Wed.*

$ JAPANESE 🍴 **Sobadokoro Ten'an** (そば処天庵). For a real treat, stop for lunch at the wonderful soba shop run by Sayoko Kojima. The delicious soba and soup are served with different kinds of tempura and other dishes made with Kojima's own organic vegetables. [$] *Average main: ¥800* ✉ *1180–25 Mitai* ☎ *0982/72–3023* 💳 *No credit cards* 🕐 *No dinner.*

$$$$ B&B/INN 🏨 **Shinsen** (神仙). It is not cheap, but Shinsen just might be the best ryokan in town. **Pros:** the best in Japanese service; convenient location; great amenities; superb food. **Cons:** expensive. [$] *Rooms from: ¥64800* ✉ *1127–5 Mitai, Takachiho-cho, Nishiusuki-gun* ☎ *0982/72–2257* 🌐 *www.takachiho-shinsen.co.jp* 💳 *No credit cards* 🛏 *9 Japanese-style rooms, 4 combination rooms* 🍽 *Some meals.*

ASO-SAN (MT. ASO) 阿蘇山

Aso-san comprises the world's largest caldera—128 km (80 miles) in circumference, from 18 km to 24 km (11 to 15 miles) wide in places—formed after a massive lava-dome collapse some 100,000 years ago. Inside the crater are seven settlements, not to mention herds of cows and horses. The emerald-green grasses that nourish them thrive in the fertile volcanic soil. The crater area, officially named the Aso-Kuju (Mt. Aso National Park), contains five volcanic cones; one is the still-active Naka-dake, which sticks up out of the side of the taller Taka-dake just east of the crater's center. There's no mistaking the sulfurous stench of the mighty belches that gust freely from its mouth.

Kyushu-Sanko buses make frequent runs from Kumamoto City Kotsu Center to Aso Station and Kurokawa Onsen. The Kyushu bus continues from Kurokawa Onsen to Yufuin and Beppu. Regular buses run from Aso Station up to the base of the cable car on Mt. Aso (¥650; 40 minutes).

The JR Hohi Line runs between Kumamoto Station and JR Aso Station (¥2,240 express; ¥1,110 local). From JR Aso Station, take the bus (40 minutes; ¥650) to get to Aso-San Nishi Station. Buses run every one to two hours starting at 8:30 am; the last bus down is at 7:44 pm. From Aso-San Nishi Station you can walk 30 minutes to the crater or take the Aso Nishi Cable Car (4 minutes) to the terminus at Kako Nishi (West Crater). Aso-san makes an excellent stopover on the way to Yufuin from Kumamoto. The JR Odan Line also connects JR Aso Station to Yufuin via with a change in Oita (3 hours; ¥4,360).

If you start early, you can make Aso-san a day trip from Kumamoto. You have until 9 pm to catch the last Kumamoto-bound train, but the last bus back to distant Aso Station is at 5. If you want to spend more time in the park, stay overnight in one of the many mountain pensions clustered in the southern half.

Bus Contact Kyushu-Sanko Buses. ☎ 096/354-4845 ⊕ www.kyusanko.co.jp/sankobus/english.

Train Station JR Aso Station. ✉ 1444-2 Kurokawa, Aso-shi ☎ 0967/34-0101.

Stop by the Aso Tourist Information Office next to the train station to get your bearings and check conditions. When the volcano is producing higher than normal amounts of toxic gases, park officials close the crater-edge area.

Contact Aso Tourist Information Office. ✉ Inside JR Aso Station, 1440-2 Kurokawa, Aso-shi ☎ 0967/34-0751.

EXPLORING

Aso Volcano Museum (阿蘇火山博物館 *Aso Kazan Hakubutsukan*). Want to see what's happening inside the volcano? Two heat-impervious cameras were inserted into the most active part of the volcano, and visitors to this museum can watch what's being recorded. Another display explains that Japan sits on the busiest tectonic plate junction in the world and that these fault lines are visible from space. The museum is across from the Kusasenri parking lot and rest area. ✉ 1930 Akamizu ☎ 0967/34-2111 ⊕ www.asomuse.jp ☑ ¥860 ⊙ Daily 9-5.

Kusasenri (草千里). A 35-minute ride from the JR Aso Station on the Kyushu Sanko bus line, this bowl-shape meadow is where the region's cows and horses graze on the lush grass and wade in shallow marshes. If you have time, hike along an easy trail that goes 5½ km (3½ miles) around the base of Kijima-dake. It takes an hour or so, and provides excellent views of the otherworldly terrain. You could also march the 3 km (2 miles) straight across the rugged lava plain to the foot of Naka-dake. For several other trails in the area, pick up the "Aso Trekking Route Map" at the information center in JR Aso Station.

Fodor's Choice ★ **Naka-dake** (中岳). The caldera Nake-dake is reason enough to visit Mt. Aso National Park. Inside the crater, a churning ash-gray lake bubbles and spits scalding, reeking steam. Naka-dake's rim is a 30-minute walk from the bottom of the **Aso Nishi Cable Car** at Asosan-jo; the cable car takes you up in four minutes. You can skirt around some of the lip, but the northern reaches have been out of bounds since 1997, when toxic fumes seeped out and killed two tourists. If rumbling turns to shaking, and steam and smoke turn to sizable ash fall, know where the bunker-like shelters are located. These were built after a dozen people perished in a sudden eruption about a half century ago. ✉ *Aso-san Cable Car, 808–5 Kurokawa, Aso-gun* ☎ *0967/34–0411* 🎟 *Walk to caldera free; cable car ¥1,200 round-trip, ¥750 one-way* ⏲ *Cable car mid-Mar.–Oct., daily 8:30–6; Nov., daily 8:30–5; Dec.–mid-Mar., daily 9–5 (last return cable car 35 mins before closing)* ⏲ *Daily 8:30–5:25* ☞ *Cable car closed when volcano is producing toxic fumes.*

WHERE TO STAY

There are more than 50 lodging outfits in and around Aso National Park.

$$$$ B&B/INN 🏨 **Pension Angelica** (ペンションアンジェリカ). The main appeal of this manor in the woods is the hospitality of the Tatsuji family. **Pros:** heart-warming hosts; homemade bread; fresh air and quiet. **Cons:** have to hustle to get there early; long way to go if your stay is short; no vegetarian meals. [$] *Rooms from: ¥28000* ✉ *1800 Shirakawa, Minami-aso-mura, Aso-gun* ☎ *0967/62–2223* 🌐 *www.pensionangelica.com* 🛏 *7 rooms, 2 with bath* 🍴 *Some meals.*

$$$$ B&B/INN 🏨 **Yamaguchi Ryokan** (山口旅館). From the outdoor baths of this rustic lodge you can watch the mineral water meander down the rocky cliffs of the green mountainside. **Pros:** about as isolated as you can get in this country; awe-inspiring falls; some of the best outdoor baths. **Cons:** remote location, especially if you don't have a car; food not as stunning as the baths; no vegetarian options; Wi-Fi only in lobby. [$] *Rooms from: ¥30540* ✉ *2331 Kawayo, Aso-gun* ☎ *0967/67–0006, 0967/67–1694* 💳 🛏 *28 Japanese-style rooms* 🍴 *Some meals.*

KAGOSHIMA 鹿児島

171 km (106 miles) south of Kumamoto, 289 km (180 miles) south of Hakata/Fukuoka.

Kagoshima is a laid-back, flowery, palm-lined southern getaway on the Satsuma Peninsula with mild weather, outgoing people, and a smoking volcano out in the bay. Ancient relics believed to date back to 9,000 BC indicate that humans have been in the area a long time indeed. Kagoshima became a center of trade with Korea and China and was an important fortress town from the mid-16th century until the Meiji Restoration. Saigo Takamori and his rebel followers—reduced to a few hundred from 40,000—made their last stand in Kagoshima against the new Emperor on September 24, 1877, chased here after having sacked Kumamoto Castle. Facing 300,000 well-supplied troops, they had no chance, and Takamori was injured in the fight. Rather than face capture, he ordered one of his own men to cut off his head. Reviled and vilified during the rush to modernization, he was posthumously pardoned and honored as a national hero.

This churning, bubbling lake is found in the crater of Naka-dake in Mt. Aso National Park.

Today, the area is famous for growing the world's smallest mandarin oranges (only an inch across) and the largest white daikon radishes. Grown in the rich volcanic soil, these radishes can span 3 feet and weigh in at more than 100 pounds. There's also *kurobuta,* a special breed of black pig that locals convert into breaded, fried cutlets called *tonkatsu* (*ton* is pork; *katsu* means cutlet).

GETTING HERE AND AROUND

The flight between Tokyo's Haneda Airport and Kagoshima Airport takes 1¾ hours. There are also direct flights from Osaka, Fukuoka, Nagoya, and Okinawa. The Airport Limousine picks up passengers every 10 minutes until 9 pm at Bus Stop No. 2 outside Kagoshima Airport. From downtown, catch it in the terminal in the Nangoku Nissei Building, across the street from the East (Sakura-jima) Exit from JR Kagoshima Chuo Station. The 40-minute trip costs ¥1,250.

Frequent buses make the 4½-hour trip (¥5,450) from Fukuoka (departing from Hakata Kotsu Bus Center and Tenjin Bus Center) to Kagoshima Chuo Station. You can shrink your travel time to as little as 1½ hours by taking the Shinkansen bullet train from Hakata to Chuo Station (¥9,930).

For the past hundred years the easiest way to get around Kagoshima has been by streetcar. A ¥160 fare will take you anywhere on the trusty network. One-day travel passes for unlimited rides on streetcars and buses cost ¥600. You can buy one at the Kagoshima-Chuo Station Tourist Information Center, or on any streetcar or bus. Buses get around, but are run by five competing outfits on a complicated system.

To visit Sakura-jima, you must take a ferry from Kagoshima Port; it runs 24 hours a day. Ferries run every 15 minutes and the fare is ¥150. To get to the pier from Kagoshima Chuo Station, take Bus 5 for the short ¥150 ride.

Airport Information Kagoshima Airport. ⊠ *822 Mizobechofumoto, Kirishima* ☎ *0995/73–3638 tourist and information office.*

> **MALL BREAK**
>
> The Amu Plaza complex attached to Kagoshima Chuo Station will keep you busy with shopping and food opportunities. If you get bored, there's a cineplex. For one of the best views in town, ride the giant Ferris wheel atop the mall.

Airport Transfer Airport Limousine. ⊠ *Kagoshima* ☎ *099/247–2341.*

Bus and Train Station Kagoshima Chuo Station. ⊠ *1–1 Chuo-cho* ☎ *099/256–1585.*

Ferry Ports Kagoshima Port. ⊠ *4–1 Shin-machi, Hon-ko* ☎ *099/223–7271.*

VISITOR INFORMATION

The Kagoshima-Chuo Station Tourist Information Center is on the second floor of the station's Sakura-jima Exit. An English-speaking person is on hand to arm you with maps and advice or help you make hotel reservations.

Contact Kagoshima-Chuo Station Tourist Information Center. ⊠ *1–1 Chuo-cho* ☎ *099/253–2500.*

EXPLORING

Sakura-jima (桜島 *Sakura Island*). You can often see this volcano across Kinko Bay spewing thick plumes of dust and smoke. The last big eruption was in 1955, but the far side of the cone sometimes lets loose with explosive belching that lights the night sky red and covers the town in a blanket of ash. There are scattered lodgings and hot springs, as well as winding paths up to old lava plateaus with great views over the crater or back toward town. The ferry port is at the foot of the volcano. There are usually four ferries per hour. The one-way adult fare for the 10- to 15-minute trip is ¥160. ⊠ *Sakura-jima Port, 61–4 Yokoyama-cho, Sakura-jima* ☎ *099/293–2525.*

OFF THE BEATEN PATH

Ibusuki Tennen Sunamushi Onsen (指宿天然砂むし温泉と砂楽). This laid-back seaside resort is at the southern tip of the Satsuma Peninsula and may provide your one chance to try a therapeutic hot-sand bath. At the Sand-Bath Center Saraku, you buy your ticket and rent a *yukata*, or cotton robe—the small towel is yours to keep—on the second floor of the main hall. In the locker room you change into your robe before heading to the beach. Stand in line and wait for an assistant to call you over. You'll be buried in hot, mildly sulfur-smelling sand. Aside from providing a powerful dose of joint-penetrating heat, the stimulating, sweaty experience is guaranteed to cleanse your pores and soften your skin. This place is a highly scenic one-hour trip south of Kagoshima on the Ibusuki Nanohana local train line. Exit Ibusuki Station and follow the signs—it's a 20-minute walk or a 5-minute cab ride. ⊠ *5–25–18*

Yu-no-hama, Ibusuki ☎ *0993/23–3900* 💴 *¥920* 🕒 *Weekdays 8:30–noon and 1–9, weekends 8:30 am–9 pm.*

WHERE TO EAT AND STAY

$$ JAPANESE 🍴 **Kumaso-tei** (熊襲亭). This restaurant offers the best of Satsuma specialties in a maze of private and semiprivate Japanese-style rooms. There's an English-language menu with helpful photos of dishes like *kibinago* (raw herring), *satsuma-age* (fish cakes filled with potato or burdock root), and *kurobuta tonkotsu* (breaded, fried pork cutlets from locally bred black pigs). [$] *Average main: ¥1500* ✉ *6–10 Higashi Sengoku-cho* ✥ *From Tenmonkan-dori streetcar stop walk 4 blocks north through covered arcade and turn left* ☎ *099/222–6356* 🌐 *www.kumasotei.com.*

$$$$ HOTEL 🏨 **Shiroyama Kanko Hotel** (城山観光ホテル *Hotel Shiroyama*). On the site of the rebellious Saigo Takamori's last stand against the Emperor in 1877, this hotel sits high enough to provide enviable views but not too far away to be inconvenient. **Pros:** lofty position; great baths; free Wi-Fi. **Cons:** nothing but relaxation happening here; rooms with Sakura-jima view are expensive. [$] *Rooms from: ¥45000* ✉ *41–1 Shinshoin-cho* ☎ *099/224–2211, 099/224–2222* 🌐 *www.shiroyama-g.co.jp* 🛏 *365 rooms* 🍽 *Breakfast.*

$ HOTEL 🏨 **Sun Days Inn Kagoshima** (サンデイズイン鹿児島). This sleek business hotel offers an excellent value, a dash of style, and a convenient location. **Pros:** stylish digs; top value for the yen. **Cons:** could use a hot springs pool to compete with its rivals; meals are a bit skimpy for Westerners. [$] *Rooms from: ¥9200* ✉ *9–8 Yamanokuchi-cho* ☎ *099/227–5151, 099/227–4667* 🌐 *www.sundaysinn.com* 🛏 *351 rooms* 🍽 *No meals.*

KIRISHIMA-YAKU NATIONAL PARK 霧島屋久国立公園

43 km (106 miles) northeast of Kagoshima.

Kirishima-Yaku National Park (霧島屋久国立公園 *Kirishima-yaku Kokuritsu Koen*). According to Japanese myth, the mountainous, volcanic Kirishima is one of two possible places where Amaterasu's grandson descended to Earth. The national park, northeast of Kagoshima partly on Kyushu and partly on the offshore island Yakushima, has good hiking trails and interesting shrines in addition to the sacred mountain Takachiho-no-mine. Yakushima's spectacular flora and fauna includes the giant and ancient Japanese cedars. ✉ *Kirishima.*

GETTING HERE AND AROUND

From Kagoshima, take a local (one-hour) or express (50-minute) train to Kirishima Jingu Station. Direct buses also operate between Kagoshima Airport and the station, where you can catch a bus into the national park. It's much easier to get around, though, if you have your own wheels. Consider renting a car in Kagoshima.

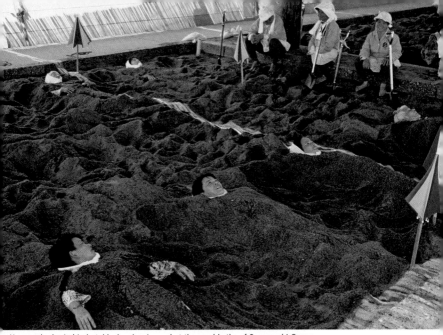

You can be buried in hot, black volcanic sand at the sand baths of Sunamushi Onsen.

EXPLORING

Kirishima Jingu (霧島神宮 *Kirishima Shrine*). The original shrine was established in the 6th century, but the present imposing structure was built under the patronage of the Shimazu clan in 1715. Wonderfully appointed and occupying an incredible setting, it has views as far away as Sakura-jima. The shrine, well worth a visit, is dedicated to Ninigi-no-mikoto, the legendary god who landed on the peak of Takachiho-no-mine nearby. ⊠ *2608–5 Kirishima-taguchi, Kirishima* ☎ *0995/57–0001* ▨ *Free* ☉ *Daily 8–6.*

Takachiho-no-mine (高千穂峰 *Mt. Takachiho*). This mountain is said to be where the goddess Amaterasu's grandson descended to Earth to establish the Japanese Imperial Family. Trouble is, the distant town of Takachiho also claims that honor. The dispute has never been settled, either legally or spiritually. Mt. Takachiho is at the southern end of the Kirishima range, and a hike to the summit takes about three hours. One a clear day, you can see the surrounding mountains in Kirishima National Park. Due to volcanic activity, particularly of Shinmoe-dake, some trails may be closed. Ask ahead of time at the Takachiho-gawara Visitor Center. ⊠ *Kirishima* ☎ *0995/57–2505 visitor center* ▨ *Free* ☉ *Visitor center daily 9–5.*

WHERE TO EAT AND STAY

$$$$ ✕**Ichi Nii San** (いちにいさん). The novel idea behind this restaurant is
JAPANESE to serve pork shabu-shabu in soba broth. The broth imparts a delicate flavor to the thinly sliced pork, which is served with seasonal vegetables.

You get to choose ramen or soba to have with the pork and broth. The dining room's honey-color wood casts a warm glow. [$] *Average main: ¥3800* ✉ *540–3 Kokubunoguchin-ishi, Kirishima* ☎ *0995/48–8123* 🌐 *ichiniisan.jp/access/kagoshima/kokubu.*

$$$$ B&B/INN Fodor's Choice ★ 🏨 **Myoken Ishiharaso** (妙見石原荘). This lodging sits alongside a river with such ferocious rapids that you might feel you're being plunged right into the drama of nature on arrival. **Pros:** modern building; beautiful hot spring; incredible food; reasonable weekday rates. **Cons:** requires transportation; very high rates on weekends and holidays. [$] *Rooms from: ¥80000* ✉ *4376–Kareigawa, Hayatocho, Kirishima* ☎ *0995/77–2111* 🌐 *www.m-ishiharaso.com/index_e.html* 🛏 *15 Japanese-style rooms, 2 Western-style rooms, 2 combination rooms* 🍴 *Some meals.*

OKINAWA

WELCOME TO OKINAWA

TOP REASONS TO GO

★ **Local flavors:** Okinawa's food, music, art, and local spirit combine powerful influences from all over Asia with funky, homegrown flavors.

★ **War memorials:** Moving memorials tell the poignant story of the chaos that ravaged this idyllic landscape during World War II's fierce final battle.

★ **Outdoor adventures:** Snorkeling, diving, trekking, sailing, fishing, whale-watching, and kayaking are in your reach in Japan's most pristine and enticing natural vistas.

★ **Dazzling reefs:** Okinawa's abundant reefs are home to varied marine life thriving in clear, warm seas. Dive with manta rays and hammerhead sharks or simply glide over gardens of hard and soft corals.

1 Okinawa Honto.
Naha's Kokusai Street and Shuri Castle are a great introduction to the area. More captivating are the war memorials on the southern peninsula, and the diving and snorkeling spots, active artisan workshops, and wild scenery to the north.

2 Kerama Islands.
Dazzling coral reefs and white beaches are only a stone's throw away from Naha's port. Though close to Okinawa's mainland, infrequent ferry times make planning ahead essential, but the vivid blue ocean makes these islands well worth the hassle.

3 Miyako Islands.
A 45-minute flight from Naha, Miyako Island has arguably the best beaches in Japan. Along with snorkeling, diving, and great waterfront accommodations, Miyako offers a whole lot of R&R.

4 Yaeyama Islands. An hour flight from Naha, Ishigaki is a great place to visit and a launch point for the surrounding sights including time-forgotten villages on Taketomi Island and the reefs and forests of untamed Iriomote. It's the perfect mixture of developed getaways and seriously off-the-map adventure.

GETTING ORIENTED

Island-hopping outside Okinawa Honto means traveling among several disparate clusters of islands; Okinawa Prefecture is a conflation of smaller archipelagos gerrymandered together, not a steady string of pearls. Traverse the long distances by plane and use ferries to get from one nearby island to another; on the islands themselves you'll enjoy the most freedom with your own transportation, but whether a bicycle or an automobile is more appropriate depends on the size of the island.

OKINAWA'S WORLD WAR II SIGHTS

The Battle of Okinawa is one of the most tragic events in modern history. Caught between two warring nations, the people of Okinawa were killed by a "Typhoon of Steel" and the brutal inhumanity of war.

(This page above) Himeyuri Peace Museum; (opposite page upper right & bottom left) Okinawa Peace Memorial Park;

By late March 1945, American forces began the assault on Okinawa, a pivotal stepping-stone to attacking the Japanese mainland. Japan's strategy was to drag out the conflict and force a war of attrition. Every sector of Okinawa's civilian population was mobilized into the front lines of the fighting. The initial bombardment by the United States was described as a "Typhoon of Steel." Artillery rained down so heavily that the bombs changed the very topography of the island. Horrific losses were followed by an awful land war. Okinawans who survived the shelling and flame-throwers succumbed to starvation, disease, suicide, or the brutality of retreating Japanese troops. The final battle of the war claimed roughly 240,000 lives—more than half of them civilian—more than a quarter of Okinawa's population. The memorials commemorating these events and the quest for world peace are Okinawa's most poignant landmarks.

THE FUTENMA ISSUE

The U.S. Marine Corps Air Station Futenma is Okinawa's most controversial U.S. military base. It is surrounded by a residential area, and locals want it closed. In 1996, the U.S. and Japanese governments agreed to close the base, but expand Camp Schwab in northern Okinawa. Many Okinawans have opposed the expansion of Schwab into Henoko Bay, citing environmental concerns.

SIGHTS IN OKINAWA HONTO

In Naha City, **Sugar Loaf Hill** was a heavily defended strategic point on General Mitsuru Ushijima's Shuri Line. American Marines made repeated frontal assaults, losing thousands of men before capturing the hill on May 18, 1945. The hill is now dwarfed by the DFS Building (Duty-Free Store) just west of Omoro-machi Monorail Station. A plaque marks the spot where so many men died.

Just south of Naha City is the **Underground Headquarters of the Japanese Imperial Navy** (236 Tomishiro, Tomishiroson). Visitors can explore the tunnels in which Imperial Navy Vice Admiral Minoru Ota lived with 4,000 men. You can see the various rooms, including the commander's office, but perhaps the most unnerving sights are the gouges in the walls and roof from grenades when the officers took their own lives.

Farther south, **Himeyuri Peace Museum** tells the tragic story of Okinawan schoolgirls who were mobilized as field nurses during the conflict. Harrowing accounts of their experiences convey the horrors of war.

Peace Memorial Park is at Mabuni Hill, and it's here where the final acts of the Battle of Okinawa took place. There are three main areas to the park. The **Peace Memorial Museum** tells the history of the Battle of Okinawa and the resulting desire of Okinawans for world peace. Outside is the **Cornerstone of Peace**, line after line of low, black, granite walls are inscribed with the names of more than 240,000 Okinawans, Japanese, Americans, Koreans, North Koreans, British, and Taiwanese who perished during the conflict. June 23 is Okinawa Memorial Day, when services, held at the Cornerstone of Peace, are usually attended by the Japanese Prime Minister. The **Peace Memorial Hall** houses a 32-foot statue of a person praying. The artist, Shinzan Yamada, began the project when he was 72, and the work took him 18 years. The statue sits on a six-petal flower representing the six continents to symbolize the global search for peace.

AN UNDERWATER MEMORIAL

One war memorial on Okinawa is far more difficult to visit. The USS *Emmons* was a U.S. destroyer that was hit by five kamikaze planes on April 6, 1945. The following day the ship was sunk before it drifted into enemy-controlled territory. In 2000, the Japanese Coast Guard discovered the wreck, and then in early 2001 it was found by local American divers. The *Emmons* lies at a depth of around 130 feet, just off Kouri Island. A few dive shops on Okinawa do offer recreational dives to view the wreck, but the depth and strong currents mean this is only an option for advanced divers.

Updated by
Chris Willson

You'll swear you've hit a different country. Let the tropical climate get you ready for sun-kissed beaches and crystal-blue waters, deserted islands ringed by rainbow-hued coral reefs, verdant jungle trails, and funky port towns full of laid-back, fun-loving islanders: it's all here welcoming you to Okinawa, Japan's most diverse and exciting destination.

Naha, Okinawa's capital, is geographically closer to Taiwan than to any of Japan's main islands, but deeper distinctions of culture and history are what really set the islands apart. Okinawa's indigenous population comprises an ethnic group independent from the mainland Japanese, and local pride lays much heavier with Okinawa's bygone Ryukyu Kingdom than it ever will with the Empire of the Rising Sun. Island culture today forms an identity around its Ryukyu roots but also reflects the centuries of cross-cultural influence brought to Okinawa on successive tides of imperialism. Ships from ancient Polynesia, Ming China, Edo Japan, and most recently wartime America brought the ravages of conquest and the joys of new tradition (snakeskin instruments, the stir-fry, and Spam). Okinawa's melting pot is sharply different from mainland Japan's commercial culture of appropriation and pastiche, touching every element of island life and lending flavor to the music, language, cuisine, architecture, arts, and lifestyle that define the archipelago.

The Okinawan archipelago spans about 700 km (435 miles) of ocean, reaching from south of Kyushu's Kagoshima Prefecture to just east of Taiwan. Of the hundreds of islands only a handful are inhabited, and even the settled ones sport more jungle and beach than they do road and city. More than 90% of the population, numbering about 1.3 million, lives on Okinawa Honto, the largest and most developed island of the chain. Honto is notorious for also housing the bulk of Japan's American military presence, though unless you're here visiting a friend in uniform, your focus will be the island's beaches, moving war memorials, natural escapes, and the World Heritage castles and monuments of the Ryukyu Kingdom.

With limited time to spend in Okinawa, we recommend you choose one of the three main island groups to explore instead of trying to cram it all in. Many travelers make the mistake of staying put on Okinawa Honto, but while its sights are terrific, you'll find more great fun, diverse adventure, and welcoming islander hospitality as you get farther away from the mainland. Okinawa rewards a traveler's intrepid spirit, so cast away your map and head out into the wild blue yonder.

12

PLANNING

WHEN TO GO

The best time to visit Okinawa will depend on your goals. Avoid mid-May to mid-June, which is the rainy season. The subtropical climate means the temperatures in winter rarely drop below 15°C (59°F), and because of this Okinawa celebrates the arrival of cherry blossoms in January. For marine sports including scuba diving, July to October is the best time since the water temperature is around 25°C–28°C (77°F–82°F) and the southerly breezes are not strong. However, July to September is also typhoon season, so the fantastic weather can be interrupted by several days of heavy rains and ferocious winds.

For those interested in Okinawan culture, try to schedule your trip to coincide with one of the many festivals, such as the Shuri Castle Festival (New Year), Naha dragon-boat races (March), Eisa festivals (August), or Naha Festival & Tug of War (October).

GETTING HERE AND AROUND

Naha is the most common entry point to Okinawa, with flights taking roughly two hours and departing regularly from most major airports in Japan. A new international terminal and a growth in tourism means there are now direct flights from nearby international hubs (including Hong Kong, Taipei, Seoul, Pusan, Shanghai, Beijing, Tenjin). Most odysseys through Okinawa begin here before moving farther into the archipelago, but there's no reason not to start farther out and work your way back: domestic flights connect directly to Miyako Airport from Osaka-Itami and Tokyo-Haneda, and to Ishigaki from Osaka-Kansai, Kobe, and Tokyo-Haneda. Flying from Naha to Miyako or Ishigaki takes around an hour. Travel agents anywhere in the country can arrange tickets for you, or via airline websites. Booking early can get you a significant discount. It is also worth checking on the prices of flight hotel packages that, if booked more than two weeks in advance, can be cheaper than the flight alone.

Public transportation in Okinawa leaves a lot to be desired. Naha is serviced by a handy monorail running from the airport through the city and terminating at Shuri Castle, taking less than an hour end-to-end with trains running about every 10 minutes. Outside the city things are less promising. The story is the same on each of the islands: yes, buses link to urban centers and popular tourist destinations, but schedules are inconvenient, hard to decipher, and confining. Budget for rental cars to make the most of your time on the larger islands.

ON THE MENU

Okinawa's famously long-lived and hearty population has made the "Okinawa Diet" a buzzword among Slow-Food enthusiasts and others interested in healthful eating. Islanders aren't sure where the secret of their longevity lies, but do your best to try it all: is it in the knobbly, green bitter *goya* (bitter melon); delicious tofu-like *fu*; salty *mozuku* seaweed; abundant tropical fruits like pineapple, mango, and papaya; conscientious consumption of every single part of the pig; *champuru* stir-fry dishes; alien-looking fish and crustaceans, sometimes still wriggling; delicious white *soki*-soba noodles, tastiest in a hot pork-stock soup with soft soki rib meat lining the bowl; Thai rice or the blindingly potent *awamori* liquor it's distilled into; aromatic, *koregusu* hot sauce, made from red chilies pickled in awamori; cloying *kokuto* black sugar; savory *umi-budo* sea grapes; purple *beni-imo* potatoes; or a mix of it all?

RESTAURANTS

Okinawa's culinary history doesn't have the same pedigree as the haute cuisine of Kyoto or Tokyo. A similar aristocratic tradition hasn't prevailed here, and prized local ingredients like soba, pork, and *mozuku* seaweed aren't necessarily expensive or hard to produce. This isn't to say that Okinawan cuisine falls short on rare delicacies or delicious cooking but simply that great, true-blue Okinawan food can be had on the cheap, anywhere. Greasy-spoon joints will have fare as traditional and as tasty as the fancy gourmet establishments, so go enjoy!

■TIP→ **One effect of the American military presence has been to increase English-language proficiency throughout Okinawa. Most restaurants and hotels will have some English-speaking staff, so feel confident about going into any establishment for a meal or to inquire about a stay.**

HOTELS

Lodgings range from no-frills beach shacks to lavish resorts. Most of the Japanese tourists visiting Okinawa have purchased packages that combine flights, a rental car, and hotel accommodation. Some choose to remain in Naha, but the majority stay at one of the large resort hotels on the west coast, many of which are on the Yomitan Peninsula or in Onna Village. The high-end resorts often have their own golf courses, fine restaurants, and even wedding chapels. However, you don't have to spend large amounts of money to find paradise. You'll get friendly service, meet interesting locals, and receive knowledgeable recommendations for tours by staying at smaller, local-run hotels and inns.

For a short course on accommodations in Japan, see Accommodations in Travel Smart. Hotel reviews have been shortened. For full information, visit Fodors.com.

WHAT IT COSTS IN YEN			
$	**$$**	**$$$**	**$$$$**
Restaurants	under ¥1,000	¥1,000–¥2,000	¥2,001–¥3,000	over ¥3,000
Hotels	under ¥12,000	¥12,000–¥18,000	¥18,001–¥22,000	over ¥22,000

Restaurant prices are the average cost of a main course at dinner or, if dinner is not served, at lunch. Hotel prices are the lowest cost of a standard double room in high season.

12

OKINAWA HONTO 沖縄本島

1,558 km (968 miles) southwest of Tokyo, 1,145 km (711 miles) southwest of Osaka. By air: 2½ hrs from Tokyo, 2 hrs from Osaka. Weekly or daily connections with most major domestic airports.

Arriving from the Japanese mainland onto Okinawa Honto brings a fresh wave of culture shock. The exciting urban landscape of Naha, the bizarre American-style strip malls, chain diners, mammoth resorts, and funky dive shops are all grafted seamlessly onto the place's laid-back, tropical vibe.

Naha's sights make for a great day or two, and some great bars and restaurants offer a good scene after dark. But rather than indulging too much in Naha's nightlife, take advantage of the early daylight to drive out to Honto's other sights. To the south, moving war memorials tell the valuable story of Okinawa's tragic history in World War II. North of Okinawa Honto, small towns sprawling up the coast are cut at intervals by resort hotels and some great treasures: active artisan enclaves, sweet diving spots, and the phenomenal Churaumi Aquarium. Beyond, the road opens out to the lush, empty northern peninsula. Scenic overviews, rocky karsts, mangrove forests, and waterfalls make for a great day trip.

If you rent a car you can see the highlights of Okinawa Honto in about three or four days: a one-night stay in Naha lets you see the city then circle the southern peninsula. Staying a night or two up north lets you hit the sights along the coast on your way there. Check out the sites of Motobu and the far north then head back to Naha for a night out before the flight or ferry to your next destination.

NAHA 那覇

Orchids growing in the airport lounges are the first sign you've come to a very different sort of place. Okinawa's capital city is the center of commerce, tourism, and youthful enterprise in the region. People here are more laid-back than elsewhere in Japan, with business suits replaced by brightly colored Kariyushi shirts, and you'll probably have an easy time feeling relaxed and energized by the city's verve as you tour the sights. Naha's appeal has a short half-life, however, and you may quickly tire of the students on school trips swarming the sidewalks, the chintzy souvenir shops and arcades, and the traffic congestion. Enjoy the wonderful sights before moving out to explore the rest of the island.

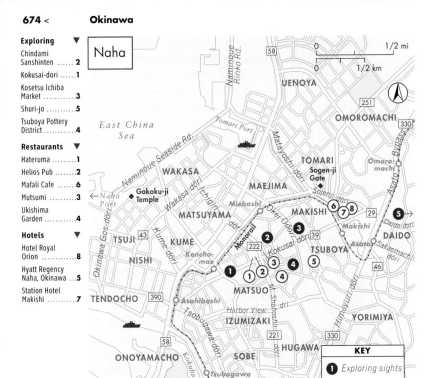

GETTING HERE AND AROUND

Japan Airlines and All Nippon Airways fly to Naha from most major Japanese destinations, with tickets usually running between ¥20,000 and ¥30,000, but discounts for booking in advance can bring the price as low as ¥9,000. Ferries between Naha and Kansai, Tokyo and southern Kyushu have fares expensive enough to make flying worthwhile, especially in light of the time you save: compare a two-hour flight from Tokyo versus a four-day boat ride with at best a ¥10,000 difference in price. Naha also has flights to Miyako, Ishigaki, and Yonaguni, all farther out in the archipelago. Several low-cost carriers fly between mainland Japan and Okinawa, including Skymark, Jetstar, and Peach Aviation.

Getting to the city is easy thanks to the clean, convenient monorail. The line begins at the airport, Naha Kuko, and weaves through the city before terminating at the castle Shuri-jo. Shopping, accommodations, and activities are all centered around bustling Kokusai Street in the middle of town. Depending on which end your hotel is closest to, you'll get off at the Kencho-mae, Miebashi, or Makishi Station. Everything you need is in within walking distance or a few monorail stops away. Trains run about every 10 minutes from 6 am until about 11:30 pm, and fares are ¥220 to ¥320 per trip.

When it's time to leave the city, ask your hotel for the closest rental-car place; Naha is denser with these than with noodle shops. It is also easy to rent a car from the airport on arrival. Most companies offer a similar selection of sensible subcompact cars, but if you want to cruise in style check out the vehicles at Celeb Rent-a-Car. You will need to show an international driver's license or a Japanese driver's license to rent a vehicle.

Airline Information ANA. ☎ *0570/029–709 toll-free* ⊕ *www.ana.co.jp.* **JAL.** ☎ *0570/025–121* ⊕ *www.jal.co.jp/en.*

Car Rentals Celeb Rent-a-Car. ✉ *Naha* ☎ *098/859–3337* ⊕ *www.celeb-r.com.* **Nippon Rent-a-Car.** ☎ *098/868–4554 Naha Branch, 03/3485–7196 English Service Desk weekdays 9–5* ⊕ *www.nipponrentacar.co.jp/english.* **ORIX Rent-A-Car.** ☎ *098/861–3900* ⊕ *www.orac.0123.ne.jp.* **OTS Rent-a-Car.** ☎ *098/856–8877* ⊕ *www.otsinternational.jp/otsrentacar/en/okinawa/.*

VISITOR INFORMATION

Before you leave the airport, equip yourself with good local maps, time schedules, and service information at the tourist information desk in the main lobby of the airport. In the city, stop by Naha City Tourist Information Center inside the Tenbusu Building on Kokusai Street.

Contacts Naha City Tourist Information Center. ✉ *Okiei-dori, 3-2-10 Makishi, Tenbusu Bldg. 1st fl.* ☎ *098/868–4887.*

EXPLORING

Chindami Sanshinten (ちんだみ 三線店). Don't leave Okinawa without hearing the unique sound of sanshin music. And you shouldn't leave Naha without taking a peek into one of the most highly regarded san-shin-maker's shops in the country. Higa-san will give you a free lesson, and several ranks of beginner-oriented sets let you choose a good arrangement if you want to take one home. (Buy one made with fake snakeskin, as real snakeskin is illegal in many countries.) Chindami Sanshinten is on the side street off Kokusai-dori. ✉ *1–2–18 Makishi* ☎ *098/869–2055* ⊗ *Daily 11–8.*

QUICK BITES

Jahana Kippan (謝花 (じゃはな) きっぱん**). Not far from Kokusai Street is a shop fit for a king. In fact, the traditional sweets that Jahana Kippan produce were once made for the royal court of the Ryukyu Kingdom. The secret recipes have been passed down from generation to generation, the ingredients are all natural, mainly based on sugarcane, winter melon, and** *kippan,* **a citrus fruit. Hisano speaks excellent English and can explain about the different delicacies. The green tea–covered sweets are popular, but the coconut-covered tougan (winter melon) is sublime.** ✉ *1–5–14 Matsuo* ☎ *098/867–3687* ⊕ *www.okinawasweets.com* ⊗ *Mon.–Sat. 9:30–7.*

Kokusai-dori (国際通り *Kokusai Street*). You're sure to get caught up in the buzzing, infectious beat of Kokusai Street, Naha's central hub for nightlife, dining, shopping, and people-watching. It's an eye-popping introduction to Okinawa's varied demographics, from the crew-cut military personnel to teenyboppers out clubbing, from street musicians to octogenarians on shopping trips. The schlock shops can be

LEGEND OF THE SHISA

Shisa, the lionlike talismans protecting doorways and adorning rooftops throughout the islands, have quite a history. It's said that during the reign of one of the ancient Ryukyu kings a terrible dragon was terrorizing Naha, destroying settlements and devouring townsfolk. When the king encountered the dragon, a local shaman and his boy gave the king some advice they had received in dreams. The boy took hold of a pendant the king wore around his neck, a lionlike figurine that had been a gift from a Chinese emissary. Held aloft toward the dragon, the figure produced a

ferocious roar, so powerful it toppled boulders from the heavens to pin the dragon to the shallow seabed, where it died and became part of the islands, now a park near Naha.

These days shisa are Okinawa's most iconic image. Homes and businesses display them in pairs, one on either side of their entranceways, the open-mouthed one scaring off evil spirits, the closed-mouth partner keeping in good spirits. These good-luck totems are popular souvenirs and come in many shapes, materials, and colors; which style you display will depend on the character of your home.

overwhelming, but those selling everything from high-proof snake liquor to pickled pig's ears carry a certain charm. Shisa figurines depicting the fantastic lion-dog creature of Okinawan legend seem to come in every shape and size, from giant ceramic sculptures to plastic trinkets. ✉ *Naha.*

NEED A BREAK?

Blue Seal. While strolling down Naha's Kokusai Street, stop by one of the Blue Seal ice-cream shops that pop up along the strip—enjoying a soft-serve swirl of vanilla and *beni imo* (purple yam) in an outdoor patio chair is the finest way to beat the heat. The shops are hard to miss, and there are several between the Kencho Mae and Makishi monorail stations. ✉ *1-3-63 Makishi* ⊕ *en.blueseal.co.jp.*

Kosetsu Ichiba Market (那覇公設市場). Three covered shopping arcades snake out from Kokusai-dori, filled with shops specializing less in trinkets and more in tasty treats. Sample deep-fried doughnuts, leaf-wrapped mochi, and tropical fruit drinks on your way to the expansive market that awaits you at the first big intersection on Ichiba Chuo Street. Passing between outdoor fruit stalls into an unassuming doorway leads you to a carnival of delightful and grotesque butcher counters, fishmongers, and pickle sellers. Pig faces stare ghoulishly down from racks displaying every other part of the animal (including some you likely never thought anyone could eat). Multicolor shellfish, neon eels, and giant crustaceans are so shockingly exotic they seem like they were pinched from Churaumi Aquarium. ✉ *Naha.*

Fodor's Choice
★

Shuri-jo (首里城 *Shuri Castle*). The sprawling, grandiose seat of the ancient Ryukyu Kingdom is far more reminiscent of Beijing's Forbidden City than Kyoto's Imperial Palace. A marvel for the eyes from the bright red walls and roof tiles to the massive gray and white walls ringing the

Kosetsu Ichiba Market is filled with produce and food stands, including this fishmonger.

vast stone courtyard, the original 15th-century castle was once part of an even more extensive property, but was mostly leveled during World War II when the Japanese Imperial Army made the complex its local headquarters. After reconstruction in 1992, Shuri Castle was named a UNESCO World Heritage Site. It's a 10-minute walk from Shuri Station, the last stop on the monorail; follow the signs from the station. Go early to beat the crowds. A gatekeeper opens the Houshinmon Gate five minutes before opening by banging a gong. ⊠ *1–2 Kinjo-cho, Shuri, Shuri* ☎ *098/886–2020* ⊕ *oki-park.jp/shurijo/* ☒ *¥820* ☉ *Apr.– June, Oct., and Nov., daily 8–7:30; July–Sept., daily 8 am–8:30 pm; Dec.–Mar., daily 8–6:30.*

Tsuboya Pottery District (壺屋焼). More than 300 years of ceramic tradition are celebrated in this area behind Kokusai-dori's main drag. More than 20 workshops produce Okinawa's distinctive pottery, ranging from cheap souvenirs to special pieces for wealthy collectors. The famous Japanese potter Shoji Hamada came here in the 1920s and left with the inspiration for his notable works, but you may be more inspired by what you find in the nearby pottery museum than what you see on sale—some of the dishes and shisa statues can be kitschy, although the bits of broken pottery whimsically accenting walls and doorways in Gaudí-esque embellishment are a lot of fun. ⊠ *Tsuboya.*

Kiyomasa Toki (清正陶器). This kiln was started by a distant forbear of the current master, Takashi Kobashikawa, himself a government-designated Master of Traditional Crafts. "The pots shapes change generation to generation with the hands of the individual potters," says Takashi, but the freewheeling geometrics and whimsical fish pattern in a unique red-and-blue glaze were perfected generations ago and are lovingly celebrated in every new piece. Mugs and tankards are around ¥4,000, cup and saucer sets from around ¥5,000, and larger bowls and platters range from affordable to astronomical. Wrapping and shipping services are available. From the Heiwa-dori arcade, head 200 yards until a small incline leads you up to the red-and-black sign. ✉ *Tsuboya 1–16–7* ☎ *098/862–3654* 🕘 *Daily 10–7.*

OKINAWA POTTERY

Walking through stalls of nearly identical terra-cotta shisa statues in the Tsuboya district, you may think that Okinawa's pottery tradition is a newfangled tourist gimmick: don't be fooled. Stop into Kiyomasa Toki for a look at 320 years of unbroken tradition. Take home a keepsake and you'll be in good company: visiting dignitaries often receive a plate as a gift from the city.

Tsuboya Pottery Museum. The small but heartfelt Tsuboya Pottery Museum has exhibits illustrating the history of the region's earthenware production, including representative pieces from all periods, and a reproduction of a traditional Okinawan house, showing Tsubo-yaki tableware and kitchen utensils. Next to the museum is an intact 19th-century climbing kiln, called a *nobori-gama*. Detailed English explanations make the experience more exciting and informative. To get to the pottery district, walk through Heiwa-dori, the left-hand arcade, until it empties out into Yachimun-dori. ✉ *1–9–32 Tsuboya* ☎ *098/862–3761* 🌐 *www.edu.city.naha.okinawa.jp/tsuboya* 🎟 *¥350* 🕘 *Daily 10–6.*

WHERE TO EAT

$$ JAPANESE 🍴 **Hateruma** (波照間). In a traditional house with a tile roof, this lively izakaya-style restaurant with a helpful picture menu also has fun music and dance shows most nights at 7:10 and 8:40. It's on Kokusai-dori a few blocks south of the Starbucks. It's open every day until midnight. [$] *Average main: ¥1000* ✉ *1–2–30 Makishi* ☎ *098/863–8859* 🌐 *hateruma.jcc-okinawa.net.*

$$ ECLECTIC 🍴 **Helios Pub** (ヘリオスパブ). This microbrewery and pub serves up five tasty home brews along with hearty snacks like Okinawan-style seafood salads and herb-seasoned bratwurst sausages. Wood floors, thick roof beams, brick pillars, and polished brass beer taps don't exactly scream, "Okinawa," but it's a great place for a hearty comfortable meal. The place is open until 11 weekdays and until midnight on weekends. It's two blocks south of Starbucks on Kokusai-dori. **■ TIP→ Smoking is still allowed in the restaurant.** [$] *Average main: ¥1000* ✉ *1–2–25 Makishi* ☎ *098/863–7227* 🌐 *helios-food-service.co.jp.*

$$ ECLECTIC 🍴 **Mafali Cafe** (マファリカフェ). Hidden on the second floor of a building behind the Makishi Station, this laid-back oasis has good food, great music, and a chill staff and clientele. A decent drink selection is backed by a surprisingly varied menu, with tacos, curry soups, and alligator steaks. Coffee and cake sets are also available. There's live music some weekends. [$] *Average main: ¥1000* ✉ *2F Asato 1–1–3* ☎ *098/894–4031* 💳 *No credit cards* 🕘 *Closed Wed.*

$ JAPANESE 🍴 **Mutsumi** (むつみ). This greasy spoon has been serving some of the island's best fare since 1958, with endearing drawings on the walls serving as a handy picture menu. Everything is twice as big and three times as filling as it looks, with soup and rice included. Walking north on Kokusai-dori one block past Starbucks, make a left onto the cobbled street just before the HAPi store's main entrance; it's the unassuming place on your left. $ *Average main: ¥750* ✉ *2–1–16 Makishi* ☎ *098/867–0862* ➡ *No credit cards* ◷ *Closed Thurs.*

$

VEGETARIAN

✕ **Ukishima Garden.** The longevity of Okinawans has gained worldwide attention. One key is a diet rich in local fruits and vegetables such as shiquasa and goya. Ukishima Garden provides the health conscious with delicious meat-free dishes and organic wines. The grain burger is tasty but on a hot summer's day the cold noodles with crunchy veggies hits the spot. $ *Average main: ¥880* ✉ *2–12–3 Matsuo* ☎ *098/943–2100* ⊕ *www.ukishima-garden.com.*

WHERE TO STAY

$$$

HOTEL

🛏 **Hotel Royal Orion** (ホテルロイヤルオリオン). You couldn't ask for a better in-town lodging than this elegant, nicely furnished hotel. **Pros:** great location; good rates. **Cons:** traffic noise from Kokusai-dori; no minibar or room service. $ *Rooms from: ¥21374* ✉ *1–2–21 Asato* ☎ *098/866–5533* ⊕ *www.royal-orion.co.jp* ➬ *209 rooms* ⌾ *No meals.*

$$$$

HOTEL

🛏 **Hyatt Regency Naha, Okinawa.** Opened July 2015, this Hyatt—the first in Okinawa—is elegant and centrally located, but without a stratospheric price tag. **Pros:** located close to Kokusai Street, but away from traffic noise; some suites have double beds. **Cons:** not as luxurious as other hotels in the Hyatt chain; far from beaches or marine sports. $ *Rooms from: ¥40000* ✉ *3–6–21 Maikishi , Naha City* ☎ *098/866–8888* ⊕ *naha.regency.hyatt.com* ➬ *280 rooms, 14 suites* ⌾ *Breakfast.*

$$

HOTEL

🛏 **Station Hotel Makishi** (ステーションホテル牧志). Located where bustling Kokusai-dori gets quieter, this high-rise hotel's white-tiled lobby leads up to improbably spacious guest rooms done up in Western style. **Pros:** large rooms; budget-friendly rates; free Wi-Fi access in every room. **Cons:** price varies depending on occupancy; some noise from Kokusai Street. $ *Rooms from: ¥14000* ✉ *1–2–25 Asato* ☎ *098/862–8001* ⊕ *www.hotel-makishi.com* ➬ *78 rooms* ⌾ *No meals.*

NIGHTLIFE

You can't visit Okinawa without hearing the entrancing, energetic sound of the sanshin, Okinawa's banjo-like string instrument. A fretless lacquered neck with three strings on a body traditionally made from snakeskin wrapped around a tight drum produces a sound at once upbeat and melancholic. Hateruma on Kokusai-dori has live shows of Okinawan music most nights.

Black Harlem. Stop here for the smooth, relaxed atmosphere, and sample some of the 10,000 soul records the owner, Takeshi, has on display behind the bar. If you're tired of hearing the sanshin and would rather chill out to Marvin Gaye and the Isley Brothers, this is your place. There's usually a cover of ¥500. ✉ *6F Cosmo Bldg., 2–7–22 Makishi* ☎ *098/866–8912* ⊕ *www.geocities.jp/soulbar_black_harlem.*

Fodor's Choice
★

Dojo Bar. Okinawa is the birthplace of karate and a place of pilgrimage for black belts from all over the world. During the day they punch, kick, and block under the tutelage of martial arts legends, then in the evening they eat and drink at the Dojo Bar. British ex-pat James Pankie-wicz started the Dojo as place where both locals and foreigners could mingle—it's got great food and atmosphere. Try a shot of goya juice. ⊠ *Asato - 1, Makishi* ✛ *About 200 yards north east of Makishi Station* ☎ *098/911–3601* ⊕ *www.dojobarnaha.com.*

Gold Disc Okinawa. In the admittedly seedier district of Matsuyama, Gold Disc Okinawa (previously Live House Kento's) has been going strong for decades with mostly '50s and '60s cover bands rocking a stage so warmly neoned out it feels like the whole bar is inside a Wurlitzer jukebox. Most nights there's an admission of ¥1,500. It's a famous spot, so anyone can point the way. Walking from Kokusai-dori, follow Ichigin-dori north until you get to the bustling Matsuyama intersection and hang a left at the Lawson convenience store. ⊠ *BF Matsu-machi Peatsuti Bldg., 1–14–19 Matsuyama* ☎ *098/868–1268* ⊕ *gold-disc.net* ✉ *¥1500.*

Rehab. On Kokusai Street, close by the Tenbusu building and information center, Rehab is a relaxing place for a few drinks at the end of your night. Come in to hear stories from Norwegian ship captains on leave, multilingual local businesspeople, the convivial barmaids, or owner Paul Patry himself, the most gregarious person within the city limits. He's also a great resource for arranging cruises, diving, kayaking, and other outdoor activities. ⊠ *3A Kakazu Bldg., 2–4–14 Makishi* ☎ *098/988–1198.*

SOUTH OF NAHA

There are at least three good reasons to explore Okinawa's southern spur. The culture park Okinawa World is an interactive trip through the islands' Ryukyu past, with restored houses, a large limestone cave, and traditional performances. More than the ancient Ryukyu culture, however, it is Okinawa's history during World War II that will resonate most with visitors. Himeyuri Peace Museum and Okinawa Peace Memorial Museum trace Okinawa's tragic story. Caught between American and Japanese militaries during the last months of the war, Okinawa suffered an astronomical toll in lost lives and resources. Like Hiroshima's Atomic Bomb Dome, these sights are important not only to local history, but also for their message teaching the value of peace to all.

GETTING HERE AND AROUND

Bus routes will take you past all the sights, but infrequent schedules will rush you or leave you bored. It's an easy drive from the city, though—every sight is on Route 331—so renting a car is highly advisable. Bus schedules change year to year.

EXPLORING

Himeyuri Peace Museum (ひめゆり平和祈念資料館 *Himeyuri heiwa kinen shiryokan*). This moving museum tells the story of 240 girls from a high school near Naha. Mobilized as field nurses in the war's final months, the girls' hellish experience tending to wounded Japanese soldiers in hidden caves near the city are retold in an intensely poignant series of dioramas, textual explanations, and displays. Photographs and journals show the girls' innocence and hope before the war, providing a moving

The sanshin is covered by snakeskin (sometimes fake).

counterpoint to the artifacts and diaries that highlight the ghastly conditions they endured during the fighting. Photographs of each girl drive home the waste and finality of the war's tragic effects. The museum is an hour from Naha via Bus 34 or 89 (¥580), with a change in Itoman to Bus 82, 107 or 108 (¥320). Buses depart hourly and continue on to the Peace Memorial. ⊠ 671–1 Aza-Ihara, Itoman ☎ 098/997–2100 ⊕ www.himeyuri.or.jp ☞ ¥310 ⊗ Daily 9–5.

Japanese Navy Underground Headquarters (Kyu Kaigun Shireibu-go). These cold, clammy tunnels are where a dramatic end came to Admiral Ota and 174 of his men on June 13, 1945. He and six of his top officers killed themselves to escape capture or death by American forces. The grenade blasts that killed the rest of Ota's men left visible shrapnel damage on the walls. An information desk has pamphlets in English, but the staff is unlikely to speak anything but Japanese. It's 25 minutes from the Naha Bus Terminal via Buses No. 33, 46, or 101. Get off at the Tomigusuku-Joshi Koen-mae (Tomigusuku Castle Park) stop, and walk 10 minutes uphill to the ticket gate. ⊠ 236 Aza Tomishiro, Tomishiro-shi, Tomishiro ☎ 098/850–4055 ⊕ kaigungou.ocvb.or.jp/top.html ☞ ¥440 ⊗ Daily 8:30–5.

Fodor's Choice ★ **Okinawa Peace Memorial Museum** (沖縄県立平和公園 Okinawa kenritsu heiwa kinen shiryokan). Rows of black granite blocks inscribed with the names of the thousands who lost their lives in World War II cover the rolling, green hills around this excellent museum. Exhibits, some designed specifically for children, provide a rare opportunity to contemplate global issues. Focusing on the brutal Battle of Okinawa. interesting exhibits highlight each side's tactical perspective and the progress of the fighting. More personal displays reveal what life was like on the ground during the chaos and include testimonies of survivors (unfortunately, only a few of these are translated). A diorama portrays life in American-occupied postwar Okinawa. The museum is 80 minutes from Naha via bus; change from Bus 89 to 82 at Itoman Terminal. The total cost is ¥1050 ⊠ *614–1 Aza-Mibuni, Itoman* ☎ *098/997–3844* ⊕ *www. peace-museum.pref.okinawa.jp/english* 🎫 ¥300 ⊙ *Daily 9–5.*

Okinawa World (おきなわワールド). It's worth spending a few hours at Okinawa World to get a quick overview of local culture. There are tropical fruit orchards and workshops for textile weaving, glassblowing, pottery, dyeing, and printing. Traditional Eisa dance performances take place several times a day. The main attraction is Gyokusendo Cave, the second-longest limestone cave in Japan. You can walk through an 890-yard cavern and marvel at the giant stalactites and stalagmites. From Naha Bus Terminal, take Bus 54 or 83 and get off at Gyokusendo-mae. ⊠ *1336 Maekawa, Nanjo City* ☎ *098/949–7421* 🎫 ¥1,650 *(includes cave)* ⊙ *Daily 9–6.*

NORTHERN OKINAWA

EXPLORING

FAMILY **Churaumi Aquarium at Okinawa Expo Park** (美ら海水族館 *Okinawa Churaumi Suizokukan*). With one of the biggest saltwater tanks in the world, the most impressive aquarium in Japan is a wonderland for the eyes. A pioneering coral-breeding experiment has tons of information about the fragile tropical ecosystem, while tanks hold dangerous sharks, freaky deep-water species, and thousands of other wondrous sea creatures. The star attraction is the 30-foot-deep tank, big enough to hold three majestic whale sharks, a dozen graceful manta rays, and schools of fish big and small from across the Pacific. Viewing the whale sharks from below is a breathtaking experience. If you haven't rented a car the easiest way to get to aquarium is Yanbaru Express bus service that runs from Naha Airport, via central Naha to the aquarium (2 hours, 20 minutes) 0980/56–5760. In addition to Churaumi Aquarium, Ocean Expo Park also houses a great Oceanic Culture Museum and the Traditional Okinawa Village Arboretum. Close by there is the Ryugujo Butterfly Garden and the charming village of Bise. ⊠ *424 Ishikawa, Motobu-cho, Kunigami-gun, Motobu* ☎ *098/048–3748* ⊕ *oki-churaumi.jp* 🎫 ¥1,850 ⊙ *Mar.–Sept., daily 8:30–7; Oct.–Feb., daily 8:30–5:30.*

Kongou Sekirinzan Boulder Park (金剛石林山). This great nature preserve lets you wander through the eerie land-before-time rock formations and gorgeous limestone spires of Japan's only tropical karst landscape. Of the three trails, the longer "Strange and Big Rocks Course" marked in yellow makes for a very interesting 1-km (½-mile) scramble. The park is all the way up Route 58 just before the road ends, about an hour from Nago. Afterward you can head to Hedo Misaki, on Okinawa's northernmost tip, for more otherworldly rock formations. ⊠ *1241 Hedo, Kunigami Village* ☎ *0980/41–8117* 🎫 ¥820 ⊙ *Apr.–Sept., daily 9–5; Oct.–Mar., daily 9–4.*

WHERE TO STAY

$$$$ HOTEL FAMILY **Hotel Orion Motobu Resort & Spa.** This hotel is an oasis on the coast of Motobu located next to Ocean Expo Park and the Churaumi Aquarium. **Pros:** all rooms have a beautiful view; walking distance to the beach and Expo Park; thermal onsen (¥1,650). **Cons:** 100 minutes from Naha Airport. [$] *Rooms from: ¥92880* ✉ *148–1 Bise, Motobu* ☎ *098/051–7300* 🌐 *www.okinawaresort-orion.com/english/* 🛏 *215 rooms, 23 suites.*

$$ HOTEL **Lue on the Beach** (オン・ザ・ビーチ・ルー). This bungalow hideaway, 15 minutes south of the Churaumi Aquarium, is a laid-back alternative to the bigger resorts. **Pros:** great location; isolated beach; good restaurant. **Cons:** slim menu; no double beds; spartan rooms. [$] *Rooms from: ¥12960* ✉ *2626–1 Sakimotobu, Motobu* ☎ *0980/47–3535* 🌐 *www.luenet.com* 🛏 *12 rooms, 12 condos* 🍴 *No meals.*

SPORTS AND THE OUTDOORS

DIVING AND SNORKELING

Happy Surfing Okinawa. Okinawa is not an easy place to surf. Because of the hidden reefs and frequently changing weather conditions, you really need to know what you're doing. Both novice and seasoned surfers should head to Danny Melhado at Happy Surfing Okinawa. Danny competed in the world championship tour, and now shares his passion for surfing and stand-up paddleboarding. Surf lessons start at ¥10,000. It is also possible to stay at his guesthouse just next to a prime surf spot (¥4,500 per person), and if you're lucky he'll fire up the pizza oven for dinner. ✉ *436 Toya, Yomitan-son* ☎ *090/1943–8654* 🌐 *happysurfingokinawa.com.*

Island Club Okinawa. This marine sports company helps time-pressed tourists fit as much adventure into their day as possible. The staffers are friendly, but have limited English ability. Courses include snorkeling, kayaking, and even a "discover scuba" class. The Island Club is near Cape Maeda on the Yomitan Peninsula. ✉ *590–1 Yamada, Onna-son* ☎ *098/963–0166.*

Natural Blue Diving Company. There are many Japanese diving shops in Okinawa, but few instructors speak English. This can make it difficult to go on fun dives, and almost impossible to do a certification course. Natural Blue Diving Company, however, is run by Yasu, a bilingual diving instructor who studied marine biology in Florida. He bases his diving and snorkeling trips around Cape Maeda, one of Okinawa's most popular dive spots. Reservations are essential. ✉ *Cape Maeda, Yomitan-son* ☎ *090/9497–7374* 🌐 *www.natural-blue.net.*

North of Nago Boat Charters. If you're an experienced diver and want to explore some of mainland Okinawa's more remote dive spots, this is a great option. One of the sites the company regularly dives is the wreck of the USS *Emmons* located near Kouri Island. It's close to 131 feet down, and there can be strong currents so this is only for advanced divers. Other spots include Ie Island, Sesoko Island, and Hedo Point. ■ **TIP→ You need to bring your own gear or rent it elsewhere.** ✉ *Motobu* ☎ *090/3790–2924* 🎫 *US$65 for a two-dive trip; US$85 for a three-dive trip.*

Reef Encounters International. Dive instructor Doug Bennett has been teaching classes on Okinawa since 1995. His shop offers NAUI certification courses at all levels. He also offers day trips to the Keramas and longer tours to Ishigaki, Iriomote, and Yonaguni. Friendly, reliable, and highly recommended, Bennett has become the guide of choice for those looking for an English-speaking dive company. ✉ *1–493 Miyagi, Chatan-cho* ☎ *098/995–9414, 090/1940–3528* ⊕ *www.reefencounters.org.*

KERAMA ISLANDS 慶良間諸島

35 km (22 miles) west of Naha by ferry.

The Kerama Islands have many pristine beaches, and divers rate the coral and clear water off their coasts highly. There are two main islands, Tokashiki and Zamami, along with many more small, uninhabited islets. You can experience the best of the Keramas in a day trip or two from Naha. Eating and drinking establishments are scattered over the two islands, so you won't lack for sustenance.

GETTING HERE AND AROUND

From Naha's Tomari Port you can catch ferries to both Tokashiki and Zamami. The daily ferry *Kerama* reaches Tokashiki-jima in 70 minutes. Marine Liner *Tokashiki* is the express ferry running twice daily. Call ahead, as the schedules change frequently.

To get to Zamami you have two choices: the high-speed *Queen Zamami* ferry reaches the island in 50 minutes, sometimes stopping at Aka-jima along the way. There are two or three departures daily. The slower *Zamami-maru* ferry reaches the island in two hours and makes only one daily run.

Once you're on one of the islands, you can rent bicycles or scooters from vendors at the piers. Zamami-jima also has car-rental agencies.

Car Rental Asagi Rent-a-Car. ☎ *098/896–4135.*

Ferry Information Tokashiki-son Renrakusho. ☎ *098/868–7541 info for Ferry Tokashiki and Marine Liner Tokashiki* ⊕ *www.tomarin.com.* **Zamami-son Renrakusho.** ☎ *098/868–4567 info for Ferry Zamami and Queen Zamami* ⊕ *www.tomarin.com.*

VISITOR INFORMATION

At Zamami's harbor you can duck into the tourist information office in the cluster of buildings to the left of the ferry exit for information in English on boat tours, bike rentals, and diving outfitters.

Contact Zamami Tourist Information Office. ✉ *1–1 Chisaki, Zamami-Town* ☎ *098/987–2277.*

TOKASHIKI-JIMA 渡嘉敷島

Tokashiki-jima. The largest of the Kerama Islands, Tokashiki gets the most tourist traffic from Naha. Two lovely beaches with clean, white sand are on the west side: Tokashiki Beach, in the center of the coast, and Aharen Beach, toward the south. ✉ *Tokashiki.*

WHO'S WHO IN OKINAWA

Encoded into islander speech are delineations for who comes from where. Ethnic Ryukyu are *shimanchu*—written with the Chinese-Japanese ideographs to literally mean island-people and pronounced in Okinawa's dialect. Ethnic Japanese by contrast are *yamatochu*, reflecting Japan's archaic name, Yamato. Everyone else in the world? *Naichu*, or mainlanders. These systems are all relative, however. More-obscure islands hold denizens of Okinawa's capital Naha to be *naichu*, while on the bigger landmasses they differentiate between *yamanchu* and *uminchu*, mountain folks and sea people. By the time you go home, Okinawa's beach life may make you a dedicated uminchu, but for the moment be happy with what you are: *tabinchu* means traveler.

ZAMAMI-JIMA 座間味島

On Zamami, late January through March is prime whale-watching season, and during those months you can join two-hour boat tours for ¥5,000. From land, the north shore gives you the best chance of seeing whale tails and fin-slapping humpback antics—bring your best binoculars. Other whale-watching tours that leave from the main island of Okinawa include Marine House Seasir (from Naha Port) and Okinawa Island Crew (from Motobu Port).

EXPLORING

Furuzamami Beach. For great snorkeling, try Furuzamami Beach, a short walk south of the harbor and village. In summer, there are snorkel rentals and showers. There's also a restaurant, and shuttle buses run to and from the pier. **Amenities:** food and drink; parking (free); showers; toilets; water sports. **Best for:** snorkeling; sunrise; swimming. ✉ *Zamami-Town.*

Marine House Seasir (マリンハウスシーサー). ✉ *2–3–13 Minato-machi, Naha* ☎ *098/869–6329* ⊕ *www.seasir.com/en/seasir-naha.htm* ☞ *Credit cards accepted.*

Okinawa Island Crew (沖縄アイランドクルー). ✉ *Sakimotobu 671–1, Motobu, Kunigami Village* ☎ *098/047–6140* ☞ *Credit cards accepted.*

Zamami Whale Watching Association. Weather permitting, from late December to early April, boats head out from Zamami port daily at 10:30 am and 12:30 pm. You can arrange these tours from Zamami Island or, more commonly and conveniently, from Tomari Port in Naha. Small boats and choppy seas can make whale-watching tough for those with weak stomachs. ☎ *098/987–2277* ⊕ *www2.vill.zamami. okinawa.jp/whale.*

MIYAKO ISLANDS 宮古諸島

300 km (186 miles) southwest of Okinawa Honto.

Some intensive beach therapy can be engaged in here. In the southwest corner of the main island, Miyako-jima, is Maehama, perhaps Japan's finest beach, and across the bridge on the adjacent tiny island of Kurima-jima lies the gorgeous Nagamahama Beach. Throughout the Miyako islands you can find bright white sand and emerald, turquoise, and cobalt waters. If you're traveling to Miyako-jima in July or August, or during a Japanese holiday, book in advance.

GETTING HERE AND AROUND
Japan TransOcean Air (part of JAL) and ANK (part of ANA) fly to Miyako-shoto from Naha (45 minutes, 13 flights daily). From the airport to Hirara, a taxi costs about ¥1,500. There are also direct flights with JTA from Tokyo Haneda and Osaka Itami.

Hirara Port, Miyako ferries make short trips to nearby, Shimoji-jima, Tarama-jima, and Minna-jima. Tickets can be bought in the ferry terminal. Irabu-jima, once only accessible by boat, is now connected to the main island by bridge.

Buses on Miyako-jima depart from two terminals in Hirara and travel the coastal roads around the island. Buses to the north of the island and Ikema-jima (35 minutes from Hirara) depart from the Yachiyo bus station. Those heading south to Maehama (25 minutes from Hirara) and Cape Higashi-henna (50 minutes from Hirara) depart from the Miyako Kyoei terminal. Buses run every couple of hours from morning to early evening.

Taxis on Miyako-jima are convenient and reasonable. A taxi for the 10-km (6-mile) trip to Maehama Beach should cost no more than ¥5,000. Most drivers speak limited English but will be able to get you to the major sights without any problems.

For car rentals, reserving in advance is advisable. Nippon Rent-a-Car and most other companies will pick you up at the airport or ferry terminal. Rates vary, beginning at around ¥36,000 per day. Another option for getting around the island is by scooter or motorbike (from around ¥2,000 for a scooter per day).

Car Rental Nippon Rent-a-Car. ☎ *0120/17–0919, 03/3485–7196 English service desk in Tokyo* ⊕ *www.nipponrentacar.co.jp/english.*

VISITOR INFORMATION
Whether you arrive by plane or ferry, stop in at the Tourist Information Desk in Hirara City for help on travel, tour, and lodging arrangements.

Contact Hirara Tourist Information Desk. ⊠ *Miyako Airport, Hirara* ☎ *098/072–0899 airport branch (limited English).*

HIRARA CITY 平良

On the main island of Miyako-jima, sprawling, unremarkable Hirara, population 48,000, doesn't have much to see but offers plenty of budget accommodations.

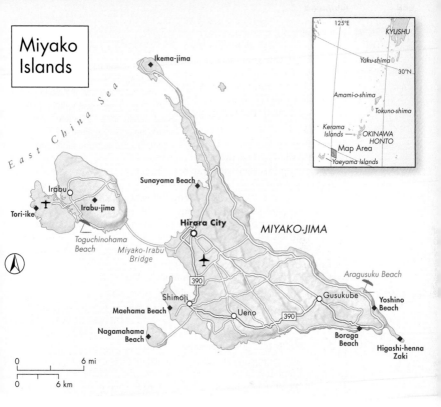

Miyako Islands

East China Sea

KYUSHU
125°E
Yaku-shima
30°N
Amami-o-shima
Tokuno-shima
Kerama Islands — OKINAWA HONTO
Map Area
Yaeyama Islands

Ikema-jima

Sunayama Beach

Irabu
Irabu-jima
Tori-ike
Toguchinohama Beach
Miyako-Irabu Bridge

Hirara City

MIYAKO-JIMA

Aragusuku Beach

390

Shimoji
Maehama Beach
Ueno
390
Gusukube
Yoshino Beach

Nagamahama Beach
Boraga Beach
Higashi-henna Zaki

| 0 | | 6 mi |
| 0 | | 6 km |

EXPLORING

OFF THE BEATEN PATH

Higashi-henna Zaki (東平安名岬 *Cape Higashi-henna*). If you have a couple of hours to spare, take a leisurely walk out to see Cape Higashi-henna's rugged landscape. A twisty, narrow road atop a spine of rock leads through a thatch of green grass out to a lonely, perfectly lovely lighthouse. The 2-km (1-mile) peninsula retains an impressive, end-of-the-earth feeling, and in spring the ground is covered with trumpet lilies. The multicolor coral can be viewed from above. Allow about one hour to walk from the Bora bus stop at Boraga Beach. If you rent a scooter in Hiraga, you can ride to the end of the road next to the lighthouse. ⊠ *Miyako*.

Ikema-jima (池間島 *Ikema Island*). Connected to the northwestern corner of Miyako-jima by a bridge, this small island, ringed by a scenic coastal road, has fine views above and below the sea. The Ikema Wetlands in the center of the island is a wildlife protection area, and home to a variety of ducks, egrets, and waders. The island is 35 minutes by bus from Hirara. ⊠ *Ikema-jima*.

Irabu-jima (伊良部島 *Irabu Island*). This small island has two more gorgeous and secluded beaches: Toguchi-no-hama and Sawada-no-hama. In 2015, it was connected to the main island by the longest toll-free bridge in Japan. ⊠ *Irabu Island, Miyako*.

Tori-ike (通り池). If you travel across one of the several small bridges from Irabu-jima to Shimoji-jima, you can check out Tori-ike, a deep, mysteriously dark cenote connected by underwater caverns to the sea. It's a justly celebrated spot for diving.

CAUTION

Although following the coastal roads is straightforward enough, driving in the interior of Miyako-jima requires time and patience, and should not be attempted after dark. Signage is confusing, and the endless sugarcane fields look identical.

BEACHES

Boraga Beach (保良泉ビーチ). On the southern shore of the island, a swimming pool filled with water from a cold natural spring sits next to a picturesque stretch of sand. Snorkel gear and kayak rentals can be arranged through the pool complex, which includes a refreshment stand. Check out the cave with the pumpkin-shape rock formation. Many of the local dive shops offer snorkeling excursions, or multisport packages that include a visit to the pumpkin-shape rock. **Amenities:** food and drink; lifeguards; parking (free); showers; toilets; water sports. **Best for:** families; snorkeling; swimming. ⊠ *Miyako*.

Fodor's Choice
★

Maehama Beach (前浜ビーチ). Maehama, or as you may see on local signs, "Yonaha Maehama," is regarded by many as Japan's best beach, and it lives up to its reputation. White sand stretches for miles on a smooth, shallow shelf extending far into the warm, clear water. In front of the Tokyu Resort there's a section of water that is netted-off to protect swimmers from jellyfish, and a lifeguard on duty from 9 to 6. Water-sports equipment rentals, showers, refreshments, toilets, and showers are available at a beach shack. Take on your friends or the locals at beach volleyball—this is an amazing place to play a game. The beach is 25 minutes from Hirara via bus. **Amenities:** food and drink; lifeguards; parking; showers; toilets; water sports. **Best for:** sunset; swimming; volleyball. ⊠ *914 Yonaha, Shimoji-aza, Miyako*.

Nagamahama Beach (長間浜ビーチ). A lovely and often deserted beach on the west side of tiny Kurima-jima, Nagamahama can be reached via the bridge just southeast of Maehama. This is a fantastic place to spend the day snorkeling and picnicking on the fine white sand. **Amenities:** parking (free). **Best for:** solitude; snorkeling; sunrise; swimming; walking; windsurfing. ⊠ *Kurima-jima, Miyako*.

Sunayama Beach (砂山ビーチ). This small beach lies behind a large sand dune (*suna-yama* means "sand mountain"), out of which juts a rugged natural stone arch. The snorkeling is good, and the beach is only a few miles by bus north of Hirara. Water-sports equipment is available for rent in the summer months. Bathrooms, showers, vending machines, and free parking are a short walk (across the dune) from the beach. **Amenities:** parking; showers; toilets; water sports. **Best for:** snorkeling. ⊠ *Nikadori, Miyako*.

Yoshino Beach (吉野ビーチ). The water here is said to have the highest concentration of colorful fish in all of Miyako-shoto; needless to say, it's an awesome spot to snorkel. The beach is just north of Higashi-henna-misaki. If Yoshino Beach is packed with busloads of tourists, try

12

Aragusuku Beach, a little farther north. Bathrooms, showers, vending machines and parking (¥500) is up on the cliff top, a shuttle bus transports visitors half a kilometer down the winding road to the beach. **Amenities:** parking (fee); showers; toilets; water sports. **Best for:** solitude; snorkeling; sunrise. ✉ *Yoshino, Miyako.*

WHERE TO EAT

$ ASIAN JAPANESE 🍴 **Chuzan** (中山). This simple tavern serves inexpensive Okinawa favorites such as *goya champuru* (a stir-fry using bitter melon); Korean-style *bibimbap,* a delicious, tangy, healthful dish of kimchi, bean sprouts, spinach, and other vegetables stirred into rice; and a plate of *katsuo* (bonito) sashimi big enough for two or three people. A couple of blocks east of the port, the place is near the junction of the Route 243 and Route 83. [$] *Average main: ¥600* ✉ *1–10 Nishizato, Hirara* ☎ *0980/73–1959* 🕒 *Closed Mon.*

$ ASIAN JAPANESE 🍴 **Goya** (郷家). The wooden walls of this rustic establishment are full of alcoves holding everything from dolls to farm implements to ancient jugs full of *awamori* (rice liquor). Partially enclosed tatami-style rooms offer intimate experiences, while the beer hall–style dining area in front of the stage makes socializing easy. There's live music nightly, and cheap, filling, delicious food. Tasty *rafute* (bacon slow-cooked in a mix of awamori, soy sauce, brown sugar, and ginger root), and *benimo* (purple potato) croquettes should be accompanied by large mugs of icy cold Orion (pronounced oh- *ree*-yon) beer. [$] *Average main: ¥600* ✉ *570–2 Nishizato, Hirara* ✥ *10 mins from downtown Hirara by taxi* ☎ *0980/74–2358* 🕒 *Closed Thurs.*

WHERE TO STAY

$$$ HOTEL 🏨 **Hotel Atoll Emerald** (ホテルアトールエメラルド). This is the nicest and most convenient hotel in downtown Hirara, and every room at this contemporary high-rise hotel next to Hirara Wharf boasts ocean views. **Pros:** friendly staff; lovely sea views; easy access to town. **Cons:** the nearby beach not one of Miyako's best; no rooms with double beds. [$] *Rooms from: ¥22000* ✉ *108–7 Shimozato, Miyako-jima, Hirara* ☎ *0980/73–9800* 🌐 *www.atollemerald.jp* 🛏 *133 Western-style rooms, 4 Japanese-style rooms* 🍽 *Breakfast.*

$$ HOTEL 🏨 **Hotel Peace Island Miyakojima.** What puts Peace Island Miyakojima a cut above the rest is the amenities: all the rooms have their own washing machine, refrigerator, and microwave. **Pros:** convenient location; great amenities; friendly staff. **Cons:** other hotels are closer to a beach. [$] *Rooms from: ¥15500* ✉ *310 Nishizato, Hirara* ☎ *0980/741–717* 🌐 *peace-k.jp/miyako* 🛏 *93 rooms* 🍽 *Breakfast.*

$$$$ RESORT Fodor's Choice ★ 🏨 **Miyakojima Tokyu Hotel & Resorts** (宮古島東急リゾート). One of Okinawa's finest resorts, the Miyakojima Tokyu Resort delivers everything you could want from a tropical vacation. **Pros:** unbeatable location; magnificent rooms; friendly staff. **Cons:** usually fully booked during high season; no double beds; no room service. [$] *Rooms from: ¥82080* ✉ *914 Yonaha, Miyako-jima, Shimoji-aza* ☎ *0980/76–2109* 🌐 *www.tokyuhotels.co.jp* 🛏 *205 Western-style rooms, 40 Japanese-style rooms, 3 Western-style suites* 🍽 *Breakfast.*

Maehama Beach on Miyako-jima may very well be Japan's best beach.

SPORTS AND THE OUTDOORS

DIVING AND SNORKELING

Penguin Divers. Fijian Joe will show you the best of underwater Miyako as you explore the beautiful reefs off the coast of Irabu-jima on either boat dives or shore dives. The company caters to both English and Japanese speakers. ✉ *1f 27 Shimosato, Hirara* ☏ *0980/79-5433, 090/8231-7161* ⊕ *diving-penguin.com* 🕿 *2-tank boat dive ¥13,000; gear rental ¥6,000.*

NIGHTLIFE

Miyako-jima has a notoriously hard-drinking nightlife and the locals love a good bottle or two of the locally distilled awamori, which is a rice liquor unique to Okinawa. There are several small bars in Hirara, especially in the blocks just east of the piers.

New York, New York. This American-style sports bar has free billiards and a friendly bar staff. It's also usually open long after all the other bars have closed and is a good option if you want to keep the party going all night long. The local Orion is always the most popular beer, although some go straight for the stronger awamori. Most locals take their awamori mixed with water and ice. They also say that a little turmeric is the key to avoiding a hangover. ■TIP➜ **Credit cards not accepted.** ✉ *575 Hirara Aza Shimozato, Miyako* ☏ *0980/72–4136.*

South Park. This place is a shrine to Americana. Posters for *Breakfast at Tiffany's, Pulp Fiction,* and *The Magnificent Seven* adorn the walls, and models of the time-traveling DeLorean from *Back to the Future* sit on the bar. South Park is a bit of a hike east of the piers, near where Route 243 crosses Route 190. ✉ *638 Shimozato, Hirara* ☏ *0980/73–7980* ⊕ *www.miyako-net.ne.jp/~south.*

YAEYAMA ISLANDS 八重山諸島

430 km (267 miles) southwest of Okinawa Honto.

This is Japan's final frontier. For a country so famous for its high-tech urban centers and overdeveloped, concreted natural vistas, Japan's farthest islands are a dramatic incongruity. The difference is like day and night, even between Ishigaki-jima, the most developed island, and Okinawa Honto. Ishigaki sports a tiny, funky port city, a few beaches, and picturesque lighthouses. Ishigaki is considered by many to be the best dive spot in Japan, and it's even possible to dive or snorkel with manta rays during the summer. The sandy lanes of its neighbor Taketomi-jima have more lion-shape shisa statues than actual people. You're unlikely to make it to Yonaguni-jima, Japan's farthest shore, to dive the bizarre underwater "ruins," but the more easily accessible Iriomote-jima promises plenty of adventure: practically the entire island is protected national parkland, from the lush jungles and mangrove-lined rivers to the glittering, shimmering coral under the waves.

ISHIGAKI-JIMA 石垣島

1 hr by plane from Naha.

A day of beachside R&R and a night in Ishigaki City's fun bars and cheap restaurants may be all it takes to make you want to move here. You wouldn't be alone: most of Ishigaki's people are either escapees seeking asylum from Japan's business-driven culture or descendants of islanders repatriating themselves into their forebears' country.

GETTING HERE AND AROUND

In 2013, Ishigaki opened a new airport around 20 km (12 miles) northeast of the city. Buses run every 15 minutes into town. The 45-minute journey costs ¥520. A taxi costs ¥3,000. Both JTA (part of JAL) and ANK (part of ANA) airlines make the 55-minute flight from Naha to Ishigaki-jima. JTA also has direct flights from Ishigaki to Nagoya, Osaka, and Tokyo. Low-cost carrier Skymark also has flights to Ishigaki from Naha and Narita.

Unless you're planning on leaving right away for Taketomi or Iriomote, it's well worth booking a rental car. From Ishigaki city, ferries connect to the surrounding islands. Only far-off Yonaguni-jima requires another flight.

Ishigaki City is small and walkable; pick up a map at your hotel or the bus center across from the port, where you'll also find pamphlets on attractions and vital ferry and bus schedules. Getting around the island by car or motor scooter is a snap—there's really no traffic and only a few roads—and rental places litter the town like sandal shops. Driving after dark can be an unnerving experience as you will probably find yourself swerving around trying to miss a wide range of frogs, crabs, snakes, and turtles as they hop, scuttle, slither, and crawl across the road.

Airline information ANA. ☎ *0570/029–709* ⊕ *www.ana.co.jp.* **JAL.** ☎ *0570/025–121, 03/6733–3062 in Tokyo* ⊕ *www.jal.co.jp/en.*

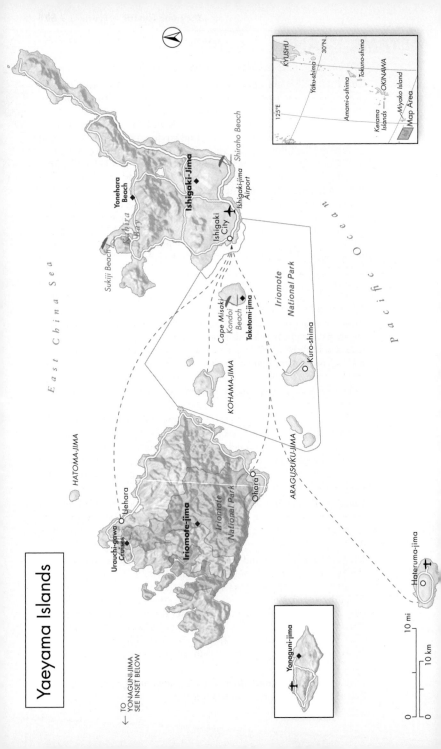

Yaeyama Islands

East China Sea

Ishira Bay

Yonehara Beach

Sukiji Beach

Ishigaki-jima

Shiraho Beach

Ishigaki-jima Airport

Ishigaki City

Pacific Ocean

Iriomote National Park

Cape Misaki
Kondoi Beach
Taketomi-jima

KOHAMA-JIMA

Kuro-shima

ARAGUSUKU-JIMA

HATOMA-JIMA

Urauchi-gawa
Cruises

Uehara

Iriomote-jima

Iriomote National Park

Ohara

Hateruma-jima

← TO
YONAGUNI-JIMA
SEE INSET BELOW

10 mi

10 km

0

Yonaguni-jima

KYUSHU

30°N

Yaku-shima

Amami-o-shima

Tokuno-shima

OKINAWA

125°E

Kerama
Islands

Miyako Island

Map Area

Car Rentals **Nippon Rent-a-Car.** ☎ 0980/82–3629 in Ishigaki, 03/3485–7196 National English Service Desk in Tokyo ⊕ www.nipponrentacar.co.jp/english. **Toyota Rent-a-Car.** ☎ 0980/82–0100 Ishigaki Airport Office ⊕ rent.toyota.co.jp/en/index.html.

Visitor Information **Ishigaki City Tourism Office.** ✉ 1–1–4 Hamasaki Town 1F, Ishigaki ☎ 0980/82–2809.

EXPLORING

Taketomi-jima (竹富島 *Taketomi Island*). It's a 10-minute ferry trip from Ishigaki City to the quaint terra-cotta-roofed cottages, sleepy lanes, and empty beaches of Taketomi Island. The cute little town is easily navigable by bicycle. Another fun option is the "old-fashioned" tour— meander between the narrow rock walls in a water buffalo–drawn cart while you're serenaded by a plonking sanshin and soaring voice of the driver. Kondoi Beach, about 15 minutes by bicycle from the center of town, has good swimming with showers and changing facilities. Hoshi-zuna Beach is famous for its star sand, which is, depending on who you ask, either the tiny exoskeletons of marine protozoa or the children of stars. ✉ *Taketomi, Ishigaki.*

Yonehara Beach (米原ビーチ). Great swimming and snorkeling are yours at the sparkling Yonehara Beach. Snorkeling here is good, but you need to watch out for strong currents during tidal changes and various types of critters that can sting or bite. There are several places to rent masks, fins, and snorkels, including the beach shack next to the main parking area. On the island's northern shore, Yonehara is about an hour from Ishigaki by bus or a half hour by car. You'll know you've found the right area when you see the giant multicolor shisas of Yoneko-yaki pottery on Route 79. **Amenities:** food and drink; parking (free); showers; toilets; water sports. **Best for:** snorkeling; swimming; walking. ✉ *Yonehara, Ishigaki.*

WHERE TO EAT AND STAY

$$ ✕ **Imagine Café.** Next to Yonehara Beach, Imagine Café is the perfect
CAFÉ place to get out of the sun for a while and have some great food. Pas-
FAMILY tas and pizzas are tasty, but the highlight is probably the passion fruit or goya smoothies made with locally grown fruit. Kaiyoko, who runs the place, used to work as a kimono designer in Kyoto, so, as you can imagine, the T-shirts sold here are far more stylish than what you'd get at the local souvenir shops. $ *Average main: ¥1200* ✉ *644–41Fukai, Ishigaki* ☎ *0980/88–2377* ▭ *No credit cards* ☉ *Closed Fri. and Dec.– Feb. except by request.*

$ ✕ **Usagi-Ya** (うさぎや). Ishigaki's finest example of Okinawan izakaya
JAPANESE cooking—where many small dishes add up to a sensational meal—is
Fodor's Choice offered here. Be sure to try something with delicious *fu*, a soft tofu-
★ like bean paste, if the crunchy pig's ears are too much for you, and curry favor with the staff by washing it down with golden Orion beer. Okinawa's proud local *awamori* is a fierce, island-made liquor dis-tilled from Thai rice. The food and drink here are terrific, but even better is the nightly floor show. At 7 and 9, performers armed with guitars and snakeskin-covered sanshin will go through every song in the archipelago's catalog, from moving traditional pieces to rock-pop

Tamatorizaki Observation Point is on Ishigaki-jima's hilly northern peninsula.

hits. Okinawan songs involve boisterous shouting and clapping from the audience, so don't be shy! After the show, see how far you can get on one of the instruments. It's just off Ishigaki's main street, close by the City Office. [$] *Average main: ¥650* ✉ *Nakamura Heights 102, 1–1 Ishigaki, Ishigaki* ☎ *0980/88–5014.*

$ HOTEL 🏨 **APA Hotel (Ishigakijima)** (アパホテル 石垣島). Unusually large beds and a central location—it's a block east of the ferry dock—make APA Hotel a great choice. **Pros:** reasonable prices; central location; all the amenities covered. **Cons:** not within walking distance of beaches. [$] *Rooms from: ¥8640* ✉ *1–2–3 Yashima-cho, Ishigaki* ☎ *0980/82–2000* 🌐 *www.apahotel.com* 🛏 *89 rooms* 🍴 *Breakfast.*

$$$$ HOTEL 🏨 **Hotel GranView Ishigaki** (ホテルグランビュー石垣). At the main intersection in Ishigaki City, the Hotel GranView Ishigaki is a short walk from the port, restaurants, and dive shops. **Pros:** in the center of town; reasonable rates. **Cons:** beaches not within walking distance; some traffic noise. [$] *Rooms from: ¥24,000* ✉ *1 Tonoshiro, Ishigaki* ☎ *0980/82–6161* 🌐 *granview.co.jp/ishigaki/index.html* 🛏 *85 rooms, 1 suite* 🍴 *No meals.*

SPORTS AND THE OUTDOORS

DIVING AND SNORKELING

The scuba-diving and snorkeling around Ishigaki-jima is superb. Trips include the coral reefs near Kabira-wan, Yonehara, and Cape Hirakubo. Lunch-inclusive outings cost around ¥13,000, plus an addition ¥4,000 for gear rental. The most famous diving spot on the island (and perhaps in Japan) is Manta Scramble, near Kabira Bay. In autumn you can sit on the ocean floor and watch manta rays circle above you.

Pushynushima. This great dive company is by the port in Ishigaki, just across the road from the Hotel GranView Ishigaki. Tanaka-san and the other dive instructors speak some English, and offer both half-day and full-day snorkeling or scuba diving tours. Diving is offered all year, but it's at its best August to October. ⊠ *2–5–6 1F, Ishigaki* ☎ *0980/88–6363* ⊕ *www.ishigaki-diving.net* ⌗ *Half-day snorkeling ¥6,200; 3-tank dive ¥17,900, plus gear rental.*

Tom Sawyer. The shop operates all year round, but ideally you want to visit in late summer so that you can see the manta rays. If you'd like to check out the ocean but don't fancy getting wet, there's also a glass-bottom- boat and a sunset cruise BBQ. Some instructors speak English. ⊠ *2–41 Tonoshiro, Ishigaki* ☎ *0980/83–4677* ⊕ *ishigaki-tomsawyer.jp.*

12

IRIOMOTE-JIMA 西表島

31 km (19 miles) west of Ishigaki-jima, 50 mins by ferry.

Surging brown rivers, dense green forests, and crystal-blue seas are Iriomote's essential draws, and there's a surprising amount of help-ful infrastructure in place to help you get the most fun out of it all. Skilled guides and tour companies make it easy and safe to explore the wilds of this pocket of primordial wilderness, and a few extremely nice lodging options let you enjoy some refined relaxation while you do. You'll want at least two nights—preferably three or four—to get the most out of Iriomote's varied environs, depending on what you want to try. It's all a blast. Returning even to two-horse Ishigaki after a few days' jungle-trekking, sea-kayaking, sailing, snorkeling, scuba diving, or river cruising will feel like reemerging into civilization. ■ TIP➜ The post office ATM may be working, but bring enough cash for your entire stay.

GETTING HERE AND AROUND

Ferries from Ishigaki-jima connect to two ports on Iriomote-jima, south-eastern Ohara (¥1800) and northern Uehara (¥2360), in just under an hour. Uehara is more convenient for Urauchi River and Hoshinosuna Beach. When seas are choppy the ferry to Uehara is canceled, but the ferry to Ohara will still run. The ferry company then provides a bus to transport passengers from Ohara to Uehara by bus. If the seas get very rough, usually during typhoons, boats will be canceled so plan your trip with some breathing room.

The long road ringing Iriomote's northern half terminates in the west at Shirahama and the east in Ohara and although infrequent buses con-nect them, all tour companies will take care of transporting you to and from your hotel or port of call at the time of your excursion. Rental scooters and cars are available, but there aren't really a lot of places to go; rely on your tour guides to get you around, and center your meals on your lodging.

WHERE TO STAY

$$$$
HOTEL
▥ **Nilaina Resort** (ニライナリゾート). "Resort" is a misnomer as this small lodge, but the Nilaina has a perfect location, wooden decks where you can kick back, and a hot tub with an ocean view. **Pros:** friendly staff; great location; plenty of outdoor activities. **Cons:** no double rooms.

[$] Rooms from: ¥23600 ✉ 10–425 Uehara, Taketomi ☎ 0980/85–6400 🌐 www.nilaina.com 🛏 4 rooms 🍴 Breakfast.

$$ HOTEL

Pension Hoshinosuna (ペンション星の砂). The exterior may be looking worn, but the rooms have possibly the best view in Japan. **Pros:** great access; diverse clientele; fantastic location. **Cons:** rooms aren't plush; no double beds. *[$] Rooms from: ¥12400 ✉ 289–1 Uehara, Taketomi-cho ☎ 0980/85–6448 🌐 www.hoshinosuna.ne.jp 🛏 11 rooms 🍴 Some meals.*

12

OFF THE BEATEN PATH

Hotel Irifune (ホテル入船). In the main village of Sonai, Yonaguni's Hotel Irifune is the place to stay for divers visiting Yonaguni. **Pros:** knowledgeable staff; clean rooms; diving instructors on-site. **Cons:** can be empty in the off-season. *[$] Rooms from: ¥14000 ✉ 59–6 Aza Yonaguni, Sonai ☎ 0980/87–2311 🌐 yonaguni.jp/en/index.html 🛏 9 Western-style rooms, 3 Japanese-style rooms without bath 🍴 Some meals.*

SPORTS AND THE OUTDOORS

BOAT TOURS

Urauchigawa Cruises. The Urauchi River, Iriomote's Amazon, is the reason many day-trippers come to the island. Boats navigate up the broad, coffee-color water that is lined by mangroves and ferns. It's a pretty magical place, almost as if you're about to enter Jurassic World. Rather than just float up and down on the river, get of the boat at the lower reaches station and then hike for an hour up to the Mariyudu and Kanbire waterfalls. Trek for another hour from the waterfalls and you are at the upper reaches station from where you can catch the boat back down the river. Kayak rentals are available if you want to go it on your own, or you can opt for a guided kayak tour. Some companies tow the kayaks upstream so you can enjoy a leisurely paddle back down. *🌐 www.urauchigawa.com 🎫 Return trip ¥1,800 ☞ 1st boat departs 9 am; last boat leaves 3:30 pm.*

DIVING

Waterman Tours. Diving instructor Tokuoka-san' takes guests to the pristine reefs around Iriomote. Two dives and a bento lunch is ¥12,600 plus ¥5,000 for full gear rental. For those without a diver's license he also offers half-day snorkeling tours for ¥7,000. Stand-up paddleboarding tours are also available. *✉ 538–1 Uehara, Taketomi-cho ☎ 0980/85–6005.*

HIKING

Fodor's Choice ★

Simamariasibi. Trekking tours through Iriomote's verdant jungle are fun and exotic, especially with a tour guide so thoroughly knowledgeable about the island's trails and conscientious about his customer's safety and enjoyment. Nagasawa-san moved to Iriomote more than a decade ago. He learned the ins and outs of Iriomote's interior by going boar-hunting with locals during the winter off-season, and leads his tours away from the regular tour spots to really let you feel immersed in nature. Along the way he'll point out a surprising amount of information about the jungle and reveal some special overlooks and locations. Nagasawa-san offers a variety of packages starting at ¥10,000 and including lunch, insurance, and transportation. **■ TIP→ Canyoning trips are particularly fun in the hot summer months.** *✉ 972 Taketomi-cho, Iriomote ☎ 0980/84–8408 🌐 www.simamariasibi.com.*

KAYAKING

FAMILY **Good Outdoor.** This company offers adults and kids a wide range of outdoor sports activities. The guides speak some English and are welcoming to foreign visitors. Spend a day or two exploring the ocean and rivers via sea kayak (from ¥10,000) or stand-up paddleboard (¥7,000), or you can go river kayaking and trekking (from ¥10,000) or kayaking and snorkeling (from ¥10,000) ✉ *607 Iriomote, Iriomote* ☎ *0980/84–8116* ⊕ *goodoutdoor.jp.*

Mansaku Tour Service. These sea kayaking tours set off where the road ends at Shirahama; from there it's into the waves. After navigating some shore points and smaller straights and islets, you'll weave in and out of the mangrove-lined estuaries along the coast. The difficulty of your tour will depend on the fitness and experience of the participants along with the weather. Your guide Mansaku-san is decently conversant in English and skilled at creating a fun atmosphere. If the weather is good you can snorkel in the crystal-clear bay. Longer camping and fishing tours are available. ✉ *10–75 Uehara #201, Iriomote* ☎ *0980/85–6222* ⊕ *www.cosmos.ne.jp/mansaku/Eindex.html.*

OFF THE
BEATEN
PATH

Yonaguni-jima. Underneath the waters off Yonaguni-jima, Japan's westernmost point, is an enormous series of ancient stone structures believed to have been a settlement that dates back to 8,000–10,000 BC, which would make it the oldest—by 5,000 years—human structure of this sort. The site has become popular among divers, especially because schools of photogenic hammerhead sharks migrate through the area in winter. Marlin fishing here is also highly rated. Yonaguni-jima is known for wonders above ground, too: unusual rock formations, the Yonaguni atlas moth, the world's largest moth species with a 24-cm (9½-inch) wingspan (don't worry, they're not scary but beautifully colored with intricate designs), and wild Yonaguni ponies. To get to Yonaguni-jima, you can fly via JTA from Ishigaki-jima or Naha. ⊕ *yonaguni.jp/en/about/index.html.*

TOHOKU

WELCOME TO TOHOKU

TOP REASONS TO GO

★ **Summer festivals:** Tohoku hosts a number of raucous, tumultuous, and exciting festivals every summer, the Tanabata Matsuri being the top draw.

★ **Coastal beauty:** Matsushima Bay's 250 islands near Sendai are beautiful, but the coast is postcard-pretty virtually anywhere.

★ **Seafood and vegetables:** The freshest seafood you'll ever eat is presented in many ways, all of them tasty. Sansai (wild mountain vegetables) are a specialty of the region.

★ **Country life:** Thatched farmhouses, rice terraces, orchards, and rugged fishing villages usher you into a world where change is slow and traditions live on.

★ **Mountain adventures:** The many fine mountain playgrounds are made all the more appealing by the relative absence of people using them.

1 Sendai. The livable, navigable city of fun-loving, stylish people within easy reach of both mountains and sea hosts the immense and colorful Tanabata Matsuri, a four-night, three-day festival that swells the town to three times its normal size.

2 Northern Tohoku. By branching out from the Shinkansen hub of Morioka, you'll come across traditional ironware teakettles, grand old castles, lovingly preserved samurai houses, sparkling lakes, and huge national parks with mountains to climb, hiking trails for all abilities, large virgin forests, and hot springs galore.

3 Tohoku's West Coast. Mountains give way to fertile plains that extend to the Sea of Japan. While you will find an occasional castle, everywhere you explore you'll encounter the best food, local women nationally celebrated for their legendary fairness of skin, mountains often buried in powder snow, and countless onsen.

13

GETTING ORIENTED

Tohoku, like the rest of Honshu, is divided by a dramatic series of densely forested mountains chains. Not only will their rugged beauty take your breath away, they can also make travel difficult. If you allow for this, you won't be overly frustrated. Tohoku is comprised of six prefectures, and stretches from Fukushima, just a short train ride from Tokyo, to the remote and rugged Aomori, the northernmost tip of Honshu, within easy striking distance of Hokkaido. This broad swath of territory encompasses mountain ranges, primitive forests, stunning seacoasts, well-preserved feudal villages, sacred glaciated peaks and secluded temples, relaxing hot springs, and bottomless lakes in the craters of volcanoes.

Updated by
Emma Parker

Tohoku translates as "east–north," and it is a path less traveled by foreign tourists. Though the recent addition of bullet trains has made getting up here easier, Tohoku is still a world away from the crowded south. The mountain villages are more remote, the forests more untamed, and the people more reserved and wary of outsiders. But don't be fooled, they are quite friendly if you show them you appreciate the pace, look, and feel of things.

Wild as the northeastern territory can be, Sendai (less than two hours away from Tokyo by bullet train) sets things in balance, right on the doorstep of the great wilderness. This attractive modern city of a million, with wide, shady boulevards, covered walkways, and shopping complexes, puts on one of Japan's biggest festivals, Tanabata, every summer in early August, in honor of an ancient legend of star-crossed lovers. It attracts more than 3 million people, and Sendai caters to them surprisingly well. Since the 2011 earthquake and tsunami, foreign visitors are particularly welcome here and throughout Tohoku.

The countryside, however, is one of Tohoku's greatest attractions. In comfort and convenience, you can ride the Tohoku Shinkansen to places like Lake Tazawa, Japan's deepest lake—a powder-blue reflection of sky that sits nestled in a caldera surrounded by virgin stands of beech trees draped in sweet-smelling vines, and steep hills studded with blue-green pines preside over all. Samurai history lives on virtually everywhere in the region, but especially in the well-preserved dwellings and warehouses that now play host to curious tourists in Kakunodate, a town also famous for its hundreds of lovely, ancient *shidare-zakura,* or dangling-branch cherry trees.

Tohoku cherishes its forever-frontier status, and has plenty of low-key cities and timeless small towns full of folks who work hard in the cool summers and somehow bide their time through the long winters, breaking the slow rhythm of rural life with countless energetic festivals. Many ski areas collect neck-high powder snow, making for great skiing and snowboarding. The fertile plains yield a bounty of treats, from the sweetest apples (Fuji apples, now found in supermarkets worldwide, originated in Tohoku) and tastiest tomatoes to the perfect rice and purest water that go into some of the best *karakuchi* (crisp, dry) sake in the land. As a bonus, you're sure never to be far from an onsen—there seems to be one in each and every municipality!

PLANNING

13

WHEN TO GO

The north and west have Japan's fiercest winters; transportation slows down significantly, even grinding to a halt during prolonged sieges of snowfall. Along the Pacific and around Sendai, however, things are decidedly milder. Fall colors in the region are fantastic, and spring brings spectacular blossoms of cherry trees. Summer is cooler with less humidity than in most of Japan.

It would be a hectic rush, but festival freaks could conceivably see all of Tohoku's big summer festivals in a single whirlwind visit, starting with Hirosaki's Neputa Matsuri (August 1–7), Aomori's Nebuta Matsuri (August 2–7), Goshogawara's Tachi Neputa (August 4–8), Akita's Kanto Matsuri (August 3–6), Yamagata's Hanagasa Festival (August 5–7), and the granddaddy of them all, Sendai's Tanabata Matsuri (August 6–8). Things do get fully booked well ahead (often as early as three to four months), so secure both your train and hotel reservations as soon as you can. Reserved seats on the Shinkansen usually sell out up to a month before the date of travel.

GETTING HERE AND AROUND

Most of the island's trains and buses ply north–south routes on either side of the mountains. Though trains are a viable means of getting around up here, in some cases a bus will save time. The most important travel routes fan out from Sendai and Morioka in the east, and from Yamagata and Tsuruoka on the Japan Sea coast in the west. Routes are often highly scenic, but there are also many tunnels and occasional boring stretches where the road or track cuts away from the coast or into a steep ravine. A journey in Tohoku is all about life at a different pace, so expect those out-of-the-way places to be hard to reach.

BUS TRAVEL

Buses take over where trains do not run, and they usually depart from and return to JR train stations. From Morioka to Hirosaki, highway buses are more convenient (and twice as fast) for getting to Akita than trains. From Tsuruoka to Yamagata, it's the same story (but it's a private bus line, not JR, and one of the terminals is in a shopping mall). Note: Overhead space is so severely limited that nothing bigger than a briefcase or handbag will fit. Store your bigger bags below.

CAR TRAVEL

Driving in Tohoku may be a good way for getting to the remote spots but presents much of the same problems as driving in other parts of Japan, and then some: absence of proper signage (especially in English); inclement weather; following tour buses on narrow, winding, one-lane roads; and getting nearly run off the highways by big trucks driven by daredevils. Although gas, tolls, and car rentals make driving expensive, some areas, such as Hachiman-tai, are more enjoyable by car.

Most rental cars are equipped with a car navigation system (which is in Japanese but with English handbooks) so navigation may not be not as difficult as you would think. However, the speeds are limited to 80 kph to 100 kph on expressways, 30 kph to 40 kph on secondary roads and in urban areas, making travel considerably slower than the Shinkansen. The approximate driving times from Tokyo (assuming you can clear the metropolitan area in 2 hours) are 6 hours to Sendai, 8–10 hours to Morioka, and 10–11 hours to Aomori.

All major towns have car-rental agencies. Nippon Rent-A-Car is the one most frequently represented. Other car-rental companies include JR Eki, Toyota, and Nissan Rent-A-Car. These outfits usually have offices near major train stations, and even smaller ones. All you need is a valid International Driver's License (available from AAA in the United States) and your home state or country's license. ■TIP➡ Note that maps are not provided by car-rental agencies; be sure to obtain bilingual maps in Tokyo or Sendai.

Contacts Nippon Rent-A-Car (ニッポンレンタカー). ☎ 03/3485–7196 English service desk ⊕ www.nipponrentacar.co.jp/english.
Toyota Rent-a-Car (トヨタレンタリース). ☎ 0800/700–0815 toll-free, 03/5954–8020 ⊕ rent.toyota.co.jp/en/index.html.

TRAIN TRAVEL
The best way to get to Tohoku from Tokyo is on the Tohoku Shinkansen trains, all of which are included in the JR Pass. The fastest Hayabusa run to Aomori, the slower Yamabiko run to Sendai and Morioka, the Tsubasa run to Yamagata, and the Komachi go to Akita. Elsewhere in Tohoku, JR local trains are slower and less frequent (every two hours rather than every hour during the day) when they cross the region's mountainous spine. Most trains and many buses are owned by Japan Railways, so a JR Rail Pass will be a worthwhile purchase. Be aware that most trains stop running before midnight. Overhead racks are adequate for small packs, but you should stow larger items in spaces at the ends of cars. In Japan no one is ever likely to touch your bags, even if left unattended.

RESTAURANTS
Tohoku is a great place for fresh food, whether from the fields, mountains, forests, or seas. Restaurants range from local sake shacks to upscale sushi bars and steak houses, and dress may be street-casual to office attire. Rarely will it be formal. Menus may not always be in English, but you can often find window displays full of plastic representations of the menu. Credit cards are fine in cities, but they are not always accepted in the countryside, so bring along enough cash. In many restaurants you'll take your shoes off at the entry and place them in a cubicle.

HOTELS

Hotels in Tohoku run the gamut from minuscule to behemoth, and often reflect local character. Make advance lodging reservations for the busy summer season, or you may find yourself paying a premium for a left-over room. Hotels and Japanese inns have the standard amenities, and, as is common in Japan, provide free toothbrushes, hair articles, robes, slippers, plentiful towels, hair dryers, and more. Most large hotels offer a choice of Japanese or Western breakfast; though it is not often included in the rates, it's seldom more than ¥1,500–¥2,000 per person.

13

Hotel reviews have been shortened. For full information, visit Fodors.com.

WHAT IT COSTS IN YEN			
$	$$	$$$	$$$$
Restaurants	under ¥1,000	¥1,000–¥2,000	¥2,000–¥3,000	over ¥3,000
Hotels	under ¥12,000	¥12,000–¥18,000	¥18,000–¥22,000	over ¥22,000

Restaurant prices are the average cost of a main course at dinner or, if dinner is not served, at lunch. Hotel prices are the lowest cost of a standard double room in high season.

SAFETY

Given the nuclear meltdowns in Fukushima Prefecture, lingering radiation in the water table and food chain is a concern. Conflicting reports about food safety differ widely depending on the source, with locals downplaying dangers. If you are concerned, ask your hotel staff about the precautions they take.

VISITOR INFORMATION

Individual towns have tourist offices that provide local information. The largest and most helpful tourist center, which provides multilingual information on all of Tohoku, is at JR Sendai Station. Within Tokyo, each prefecture has an information center with English brochures and maps. In summer the local Japan Travel Bureau can make arrangements for scenic tours by train, bus, or even taxi. The offices in Tokyo, Kyoto, and Sendai arrange tours, some in English.

Contacts Japan Travel Bureau Sendai. ⊠ *Higashi 2-Ban Cho Sq. 1F, Ichiban-chō 4–1–25, Aoba-ku* ☎ *022/221–4422.*

SENDAI 仙台

352 km (219 miles) north of Tokyo.

Sendai is Tohoku's largest city, and its 1.3 million residents enjoy the big-city amenities coupled with the easygoing vibe of a small town. Devastated by World War II, Sendai has since become a thoroughly modern and well-planned city, with wide boulevards and a surprising amount and variety of greenery. It's the economic and educational capital of the region, hosting a broad range of industries and institutions, such as prestigious Tohoku University. In recent decades the city has become a magnet for international students, teachers, and workers, and this has helped foster Sendai's energetic and affable atmosphere.

ON THE MENU

Visitors seeking culinary excellence and diversity will not be disappointed in Tohoku. Restaurants in the region serve the freshest assortment of seafood, in sushi, sashimi, grilled, broiled, and boiled versions, as well as a bounty of seaweed and generous offerings of wild mountain vegetables (*sansai*) and mushrooms (*kinoko*) in season. *Tsukemono,* or pickled vegetables, are another Tohoku specialty. *Hinaijidori,* or special local chicken, is a year-round treat and so is the marbled, exquisitely tender beef known as *Yonezawa-gyu*—very expensive, but well worth it!

In Sendai, don't be afraid to try the local delicacy—grilled or braised beef tongue, *gyutan,* which tastes like a juicy and less chewy version of well-seasoned beef jerky. In Morioka, try the *wanko soba* challenge—eat as many bowls of cold buckwheat noodles as you can. In Akita, locals are fond of *ina-niwa* udon noodles that are flatter, whiter, and more tender than the usual udon. In Kakunodate, *sakura,* or cherry blossoms, are mixed into the flour, and the result is a mildly sweet noodle, as edible as it is pink! Don't miss the truly unique *kiritanpo* (hot pot) made with chicken, local vegetables, and distinctive tubular rice cakes that have been formed and cooked onto sticks of bamboo or cedar. Yamagata has its distinctive rounded, chewy soba and incomparable beef. The local sake is uniformly excellent throughout the region, thanks to the quality rice and water.

The city's origins can largely be traced to the story of the "one-eyed dragon," local warlord Masamune Date (1567–1636). Affectionately nicknamed for both his one working eye (he was blinded in the other during a childhood bout with smallpox) and his valor in battle, Date established a dynasty in Sendai that maintained its position as one of the three most powerful *daimyo* (feudal lord) families during the shogun eras (his crescent-moon helmet is still found in popular samurai-battle imagery). In later life, his talents expanded: he engineered a canal linking two rivers, improving the transport of rice; and in an effort to further trade with Europe, he dispatched an emissary to Rome and the Vatican. He remained to his death a closet patron of Christianity, and encouraged Japanese exploration of the outside world (even after both were formally outlawed by the Tokugawa Shogunate).

GETTING HERE AND AROUND

Sendai Airport is well connected, with numerous daily flights to and from every major airport in Japan, and destinations in Asia and the Pacific as well.

But the easiest way to get to Sendai from Tokyo is the Shinkansen. From Tokyo, the Hayabusa Shinkansen rockets to Sendai in only one hour, 30 minutes, for ¥11,000.

If you have time, the JR Express bus from Tokyo to Sendai is inexpensive (¥3,000–¥6,500) and takes approximately six hours; departures leaving Tokyo from JR Shinjuku Station at midnight arrive in Sendai at 5:55 am.

Sendai's colorful Tanabata Matsuri is one of Japan's biggest festivals.

The Willer Express bus also runs from Tokyo to Sendai and takes approximately five hours in the daytime, six hours in the evening (around ¥2,500–¥6,500). Fourteen departures leave Tokyo at either JR Tokyo, Shinjuku, or Ikebukuro Station between 7:30 am and midnight. The big advantage of the Willer Express buses is their larger choice of comfortable seats. On most routes you can choose from Business class to Economy class.

Returning to Tokyo from Sendai, all night buses depart from JR Sendai Station between 10:30 pm and 12:30 am and arrive in Tokyo between 4:50 am and 8 am. Reservations are required.

Once you get to the city, take Sendai Loople, a limited-access bus that stops at Zuihoden (15 minutes from the station) and Osaki Hachiman-gu (43 minutes) and other major sights. A full-day pass costs ¥620 which gives you discounts at some sights including Zuiho-den; single rides cost ¥260. Buses depart from the West Exit of JR Sendai Station (Platform 15-3) every 15–20 minutes from 9 to 4. The Sendai subway runs roughly north–south only, and its stations are far from the most interesting sights. It's really only of use to resident commuters.

Contacts JR Express Bus (高速バス *JR Kosoku Bus*). ☏ *022/256–6646*. **Willer Express.** ☏ *050/5805–0383* ⊕ *willerexpress.com/en*.

ESSENTIALS

The Sendai City Tourist Information Center on the second floor of Sendai JR Station has English-speakers who will gladly recommend hotels and restaurants. They also provide essential maps with walking and bus routes.

Contact **Sendai City Tourist Information Center** (仙台市総合観光案内所 *Sendai-shi Sogo Kanko Annaisho*). ✉ *Sendai Station Bldg. 2F, Aoba-ku* ☎ *022/222–4069* ⊕ *www.stcb.or.jp/english/.*

EXPLORING

A convenient entry point for striking out into the region, Sendai has some interesting sights and is a fun place to spend a day poking around, shopping, and enjoying good restaurants. Walkers and people-watchers will love Sendai; it seems as if the whole city is within a quick stroll. Thousands of shops, bars, restaurants, and cafés line glittering arcades that stretch in all directions. Spiffy hotels and glitzy department stores are well located. Not far from the station, and slicing cleanly through the downtown entertainment area, are three broad avenues: Aoba-dori, Hirose-dori, and Jozen-ji-dori. There's also Chuo-dori shopping street, and all of these conveniently intersect and are linked by the wide shopping arcade of Ichiban-cho.

TOP ATTRACTIONS

OFF THE BEATEN PATH

Ginzan (銀山温泉). Ginzan Onsen is known for its unique landscape and distinguished Taisho Era (1912–26) architectural design. A flood once destroyed the village in the valley, but it sprung back up with 14 ryokans. A magnificent wooden four-story ryokan from there is depicted in Miyazaki's animated film *Spirited Away*. The Hanagasa dance shows take place Saturday evening from May to October. From JR Oishida Station, take the Hanagasa-Go bus bound for Ginzan Onsen (45 minutes). From Sendai, hop on the Yamako bus leaving Platform 22 for Shinjo and get off at Obanazawa Machi-Aijo Station, where you switch to the Hanagasa-Go bus to Ginzan Onsen stop (2 hours 15 minutes plus waiting time). ✉ *Ginzan Onsen, Obanazawa* ☎ *0237/28–2322 Ginzanso Hotel* 🏷 *¥600–¥1,000* ⏲ *Depends on ryokan.*

Sendai-jo (仙台城 *Sendai Castle*). Views of the city await those who make it to Sendai Castle, either by foot or by bus. Don't expect a fairy-tale palace, because the Japanese name is perhaps more accurately rendered as "Castle Remnants." A restored guardhouse is all that remains. The Date dynasty kept its residence here for nearly three centuries after beginning construction of the once-grand castle around 1600. Sadly, it was all pulled down during the Meiji Restoration. The Aobajo Museum, located on the grounds, displays armor and weapons used by Masamune Date, as well as a CG reconstruction of the castle in its heyday. Nearby **Gokoku Jinja** (Gokoku Shrine) is now the main feature of the area. To get here by bus, take the Sendai Loople and get off at the Sendai-jo Ato stop. ✉ *1 Kawauchi, Aoba-ku* ☎ *022/222–0218 Aobajo Museum* ⊕ *www.sentabi.jp/en/tourist/sendaijouato.html* 🏷 *Grounds free; museum ¥700* ⏲ *Grounds 24 hrs; museum: Apr. 1–Nov. 3, daily 9 am–5 pm; Nov. 4–Mar. 31, daily 9 am–4 pm.*

Fodor's Choice ★

Zuihoden (瑞鳳殿). Not your ordinary slab-of-stone memorial, the grand mausoleum of Date Masamune, the most revered *daimyo* of ancient Sendai, was made in the showy style of the Momoyama Period (16th century), where figures of people, birds, and flowers are carved and inlaid in natural colors. Looking like the world's fanciest one-story

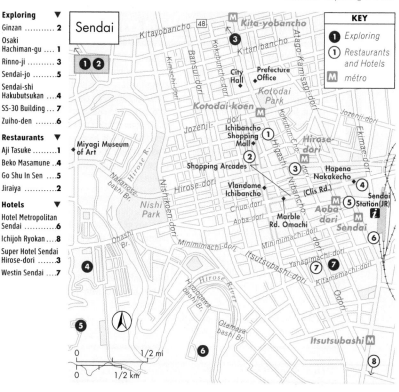

pagoda, there is so much gold leaf that in the right light it practically glows. Having burned during the firebombing in 1945, Zuihoden was reconstructed beginning in 1974. During the excavation, Date's well-preserved remains were found and have been reinterred in what appears to be a perfect replica of the original hall. The mausoleum is a 10-minute walk up hill from the Zuihoden stop; it's well worth it as it's a delightful change from other ancient architecture. ✉ 23–2 Otamaya shita, Aoba-ku ☎ 022/262–6250 ⊕ www.zuihoden.com/english/english.htm ✉ ¥550 ⊗ Feb.–Nov., daily 9–4:30; Dec.–Jan., daily 9–4.

WORTH NOTING

Osaki Hachiman-gu (大崎八幡宮 *Osaki Hachiman Shrine*). This was one of the few structures left standing in Sendai after World War II. Built in Yonezawa in 1527, the shrine pleased local *daimyo* Date Masamune so much that he had it brought to Sendai in 1607. Nestled among trees, it is indeed an elegant structure, with bright-metal ornamentation over subdued black lacquer. The main building has been designated a National Treasure. It's in the northwest section of the city, about 43 minutes from the station by the Loople and 30 minutes from the Zuihoden area. ✉ 4–6–1 Hachiman, Aoba-ku ☎ 022/234–3606 ⊕ www.oosaki-hachiman.or.jp/pop/index.html ✉ Free ⊗ Daily 24 hrs.

CLOSE UP

Tanabata Matsuri (Tanabata Festival)

Tohoku's Tanabata festival, one of the largest in Japan, is held every year from August 6 to 8 and is heralded by a massive fireworks display. The festival is believed to have evolved from a Chinese legend of a weaver girl (the star Vega in her afterlife) and her cowherd boyfriend (the star Altair, in his). As lovers tend to do, they slowly went mad, and began to spend their time idly, living as if in a dream. The jealous ruler became irate and banished them to the far sides of his kingdom (the Milky Way). But he relented, perhaps remembering some foolish love affair of his own, and allowed them to meet on one day a year: the seventh day of the seventh month.

The festival held here annually in their honor creates a great reservoir of energy. Colorful streamers flutter from every perch in town. To walk along the arcades with the endless streamers brushing down against your face, neck, and shoulders—as you bump against and smile back at other enraptured souls also seduced by the whole grand pageant—is to feel glad to be alive and in Sendai at such a wonderful time.

From 5 pm on the evening of the sixth, parades, dances, events, and demonstrations of festival spirit are held nightly through the eighth, along a short stretch of Jozen-ji-dori between Kotodai Park and Bansui-dori. The tourist information office in JR Sendai Station can help with more details, also contained in countless pamphlets.

Rinno-ji (輪王寺 *Rinno Temple*). Interested in Zen meditation? This temple, with a quintessentially Japanese garden, holds free *zazen-kai* (seated meditation class) on Saturday evenings. In June, the garden is a blaze of color; azaleas, irises, water lilies, gnarled pines, and bamboos harmonize with each other. At this season, it's best to visit in the evening when tranquillity returns after flocks of visitors leave. From JR Sendai Station, take the JR train to Kita-Sendai Station and walk 10 minutes. ✉ *1–14–1 Kitayama, Aoba-ku* ☎ *022/234–5327* 💴 *¥300* ⏲ *Daily 9–5.*

Sendai-shi Hakubutsukan (仙台市博物館 *Sendai City Museum*). The museum at the foot of the hill beneath Sendai Castle displays cultural artifacts, including pottery, paintings, and armor relating to the history of the Date family and the city. It's a three-minute walk from Hakubutsukan Kokusai Center-Mae bus stop. ✉ *26 Kawauchi, Aoba-ku* ☎ *022/225–3074* ⊕ *www.city.sendai.jp/kyouiku/museum/english* 💴 *¥400* ⏲ *Tues.–Sun. 9–4:15.*

SS-30 Building (住友生命仙台中央ビル *Sumitomo Seimei Sendai Chuo Building*). Visitors who want to get a gander of Sendai free and easily from on high can do so from the observatory deck on the top floor of this 30-story skyscraper. Bring your tourist maps and get your bearings. ✉ *4–6–1 Chuo, Aoba-ku* ☎ *022/267–8810* 💴 *Free* ⏲ *Daily 7 am–11 pm.*

WHERE TO EAT

$$
JAPANESE

✕ **Aji Tasuke** (味太助). This birthplace of Sendai's famous *gyutan* (grilled beef tongue) proudly serves excellent and inexpensive Japanese meals. A lunchtime *teishoku* (set menu) gets you three slices of grilled beef tongue and pickled cabbage, oxtail soup, and a bowl of barley mixed with rice for ¥1,500. Dinner is ¥100 extra. From the Ichiban-cho Exit of the Mitsukoshi department store, turn left, walk to the first narrow street, turn right, then go left at the next corner; Aji Tasuke is 50 yards ahead on the left. $ *Average main: ¥1600* ✉ *4-4-13 Ichiban-cho, Aoba-ku* ☎ *022/225-4641* ▭ *No credit cards* ☺ *Closed Tues.*

$$$
JAPANESE
FUSION

✕ **Beko Masamune** (べこ政宗). Fearless, meat-loving gourmets should stop here. Fatty raw beef tongue sushi and sashimi—served with a hint of wasabi—that melt smoothly in the mouth are served here. For ¥1,830 you get tongue grilled and seasoned with miso, soy sauce, or salt; a tasty bowl of oxtail soup; and a healthful mix of steamed rice and barley. Substitute skewers of chicken or sirloin for the tongue if you're less adventurous. Earthen walls, dark passages, and intimate lighting conjure up a romantic setting. It's at the entrance of the Nakaka-cho arcade, on the second floor—look for the red sign with the black cow's head. $ *Average main: ¥3000* ✉ *Nakakecho Center 2F, 1-8-32 Chuo, Aoba-ku* ☎ *022/217-1151.*

$$
SEAFOOD

✕ **Go Shu In Sen** (御酒印船). A good place for cheap seafood and sake, you can't beat the lunch deals at Go Shu In Sen. For ¥780 (even cheaper on the 5th, 15th, and 25th of the month) you get the grilled fish of the day, rice, and a bottomless cup of coffee. At dinner, your best bet is sashimi by the bucket. Go Shu In Sen is in the basement of the Shonai Bank Building, a couple of minutes from JR Sendai Station. $ *Average main: ¥1500* ✉ *3-1-24 Chuo, Aoba-ku* ☎ *022/225-6868.*

$$$$
JAPANESE

✕ **Jiraiya** (地雷也). A curtain next to a big red paper lantern leads to this inviting eatery where *kinki* (deepwater white fish) are carefully grilled on a charcoal fire. Writers, intellectuals, and celebrities often drop by to enjoy the expensive fish—it costs ¥7,000, but is big enough to be shared by two people. If you don't eat your full portion of kinki, whatever's left will be incorporated into your soup course until you are gut-bustingly full. This place is in the basement of a rundown corner building just off Ichiban-cho near Hirose Dori. $ *Average main: ¥7000* ✉ *Inomata Bldg. B1, 2-1-15 Kokubun-cho, Aoba-ku* ☎ *022/261-2164* ⊕ *www.jiraiya. com/pc/english/origin_name.htm* ☺ *Closed Sun. No lunch* ⊲ *Reservations not accepted.*

WHERE TO STAY

$$$$
HOTEL

🏨 **Hotel Metropolitan Sendai** (ホテルメトロポリタン仙台). This upscale hotel adjacent to the railway station is great value, with spacious, tastefully furnished rooms. **Pros:** unbeatably convenient; comfy rooms; discount with rail passes. **Cons:** traffic noise might disturb light sleepers; some rooms are a little dark. $ *Rooms from: ¥28000* ✉ *1-1-1 Chuo, Aoba-ku* ☎ *022/268-2525* ⊕ *www.sendaimetropolitan.jp* ⇗ *294 Western-style rooms, 1 Japanese-style room* �“❘ *No meals.*

$$$$ **B&B/INN** ⊡ **Ichijoh Ryokan** (湯主一條). The old and new are elegantly juxtaposed in this upscale ryokan, where a century-old four-story wooden building stands next to a newly built luxury lodging. **Pros:** perhaps the pinnacle of ryokan experiences; excellent meals; all rooms have a private bath. **Cons:** remote, so not much shopping or museum visiting around; you essentially need a Rail Pass to stay here; unwieldy English website for reservations and information. $ *Rooms from:* ¥54300 ⊠ *1–48 Kamasaki, Shiroishi* ✛ *Shirioshi is 27 km (17 miles) south of Sendai (about 15 mins by Shinkansen from Sendai Station)* ☎ *0224/26–2151* ⊕ *www.ichijoh.co.jp/english.html* ⤵ *14 Western-style rooms, 10 Japanese-style rooms* ⦿ *Some meals.*

$$ **HOTEL** ⊡ **Super Hotel Sendai Hirose Dori** (スーパーホテル仙台・広瀬通り). This budget hotel chain is best for on-the-go types who don't plan to spend much time in their room. **Pros:** unbeatable price; natural hot spring bath; discounts for seniors and students. **Cons:** teensy bathrooms may remind you of an airplane's lavatory; rooms somewhat spartan. $ *Rooms from:* ¥15000 ⊠ *2–9–23 Chuo, Aoba-ku* ☎ *022/224–9000* ⊕ *www.superhoteljapan.com/en* ⤵ *180 rooms* ⦿ *Breakfast.*

$$$$ **HOTEL** ⊡ **Westin Sendai** (ウェスティン仙台). An aroma of white tea hovers in the air on the 26th floor of this luxurious hotel, where the black-and-gold reception area is located. **Pros:** impeccable rooms; endless views; sky-high rooms. **Cons:** Internet access in guest rooms is expensive; feels far from the liveliness of downtown. $ *Rooms from:* ¥33900 ⊠ *1–9–1 Ichiban-cho, Aoba-ku* ☎ *022/722–1234* ⊕ *www.starwoodhotels.com* ⤵ *292 rooms* ⦿ *No meals.*

> **KOKESHI DOLLS**
>
> These simple wooden cylinders painted with striking red and green patterns, are actually an indigenous Tohoku craft, first made during the long, snowy winters, and sold to tourists at onsen resorts. You can still find them on sale there, as well as at shops selling traditional crafts; and at Hirosaki's Tsugaru-han Neputa Mura, you can even paint your own!

SHOPPING

Sendai is the unofficial capital of the Tohoku region, and you can find many well-known regional crafts of Miyagi Prefecture here: *kokeshi* dolls, *washi* handmade paper, and Sendai's Tansu chests. Heading west out of the station, follow the elevated walkways across the busy street below to where the main shopping begins in earnest. The best variety of shops can be found along the popular Clis Road arcade.

The Asa-Ichi, or Farmer's Market, is an east–west alley positioned midway in the big block that sits near the Hotel Green Well, a five-minute walk from JR Sendai Station's West Exit. It's busy from early morning to night, and you'll be able to see, hear, smell, and taste it all.

Furusato (エスパル店ふるさとコーナー). Below Sendai Station, this shopping area carries all kinds of souvenirs and will save you time if you're looking for local knickknacks. ⊠ *B1F Sendai Station, 1–1–1 Chuo, Aoba-ku* ☎ *022/267–4023* ⊙ *Daily 10–8:30.*

Shimanuki (彩りそえる しまぬき 本店). This store is tops for folk crafts from around Tohoku, such as kokeshi dolls, Nambu ironware, and cherry-bark crafts. The main branch is in Ichiban-cho near Aoba Dori, but there's another branch below Sendai Station. ⊠ *3–1–17 Ichibancho, Aoba-ku* ☎ *022/223–2370* ⊙ *Daily 10:30–7:30.*

Takasho Kanamono Honten (たかしょう(高昌) 金物本店). Need something for your favorite chef? This store carries handsome cooking knives, wasabi grinders, lacquered chopsticks, and other useful items. It also has unique pet supplies, including tea bags for cats. Why not get some for your four-legged family members, too? ⊠ *2–1–22 Chuo, Aoba-ku* ☎ *022/263–3411* ⊙ *Fri.–Wed. 10–6:30.*

13

SIDE TRIPS FROM SENDAI

MATSUSHIMA 松島

30 km (19 miles) northeast of Sendai.

Matsushima and its bay are the most popular coastal resort destinations in Tohoku. Matsushima owes this distinction to an infatuation in Japan with oddly shaped rocks, which the bay has in abundance. Hordes come to see the 250 small, pine-clad islands scattered about the bay. Long ago it was such a sublime and tranquil scene that it was fondly written of by the 17th-century haiku poet Basho. Overpopularity and a bit of pollution aside, the bay is still beautiful, and it makes for a worthwhile side trip from Sendai.

GETTING HERE AND AROUND

If you can avoid weekends or holidays and obtain a good vantage point—consider renting a bicycle from one of the shops and pedaling up into the hills—you can indeed feel your cares float away, and the islands themselves may seem to bob and sway on the gentle breeze-driven swells. The key sights are within easy walking distance of each other. To get here, take the JR from Sendai (35 minutes northeast; ¥410). For maps and info, visit the tourist office right by JR Matsushi-makaigan Station.

ESSENTIALS

Visitor Information Matsushima Tourist Information (松島町役場松島観光案内所 *Matsushima Kanko Annaisho*). ⊠ *7–1 Namiuchi-hama, Matsu-shima* ☎ *022/354–2263* ⊕ *www.matsushima-kanko.com/en.*

EXPLORING

FAMILY **Fuku-ura Jima** (福浦島 *Fuku-ura Island*). From the Godaido Temple it's a short walk across a pedestrian bridge to the islet of Fuku-ura Jima. For the ¥200 toll you can break away from the crowds to enjoy a picnic in the park with views across the bay. ⊠ *39–1 Senzui, Matsu-shima* ☎ *022/354–2263 Matsushima Tourist Information* 🎟 *¥200* ⊙ *Mar.–Oct., daily 8–5; Nov.–Feb., daily 8–4:30.*

Godaido (五大堂 *Godaido Temple*). Just to the right of the ferry pier in Matsushima is this small temple constructed in 1609 at the behest of *daimyo* Date Masamune. The temple is on a tiny islet connected to the

Matsushima's Godaido Temple is on a tiny islet connected to the mainland via two small bridges.

shore by two small arched bridges. Animals are carved in the timbers beneath the temple roof and among the complex supporting beams. ✉ *111 Azamachinai, Matsushima* ⊕ *www.matsushima-kanko.com/en/zekkei.html* ✉ *Free.*

Zuigan-ji (瑞巌寺 *Zuigan Temple*). Matsushima's main temple dates from 828, but the present structure was rebuilt to meet Date Masamune's tastes in 1609. Zuiganji is perhaps the most representative Zen temple in the Tohoku region. The main hall is currently out of bounds for a major renovation, due to end in March 2018. Instead, you can visit other parts of the temple not usually open to the public, such as the small but gorgeously decorated mausoleum of Date Masamune's grandson. The museum, filled with the temple's treasures including a statue of the warlord, is also well worth visiting. The natural caves surrounding the temple are filled with Buddhist statues that novices carved from the rock face as part of their training. ■ **TIP→ Tours in English are available if you call ahead.** ✉ *91 Matsushima Aza Chonai, Matsushima* ☎ *022/354-2023, 022/354-3218 English tours* ⊕ *www.matsushima-kanko.com/en/zekkei.html* ✉ *¥700* ⊙ *Daily: Apr.–Sept. 8–5; Oct. and Mar. 8–4:30; Dec. and Jan. 8–3:30; Nov. and Feb. 8–4.*

WHERE TO STAY

Although most travelers come to Matsushima on a day trip, spending the night is well worth the expense if you can afford the locally expensive hotel rates. There are also many good restaurants in the town, though they, too, are overpriced and often full of pushy tour-bus groups. For this reason, many people just wait to have a good meal when they return to Sendai; however, if you do stay, the hotels also have good restaurants.

$$$$ ⊞ **Hotel Ichinobo** (ホテル一の坊). This posh, expensive resort hotel has a
HOTEL   gorgeous garden that stays illuminated at night. **Pros:** luxurious touches
from top to bottom; helpful staff; panoramic views. **Cons:** tourist sites
not within walking distance; price can be prohibitive. ⓢ *Rooms from:*
¥44000 ⊠ *1–4 Hama, Takagi, Matsushima* ☎ *022/353–3333* ⊕ *www.*
ichinobo.com/matsushima/en/ ⤳ *20 Western-style rooms, 104 Japa-*
nese-style rooms ⦿ *Some meals.*

$$$$ ⊞ **Matsushima Century Hotel** (松島センチュリーホテル松島センチュリーホ
HOTEL   テル). This old-fashioned hotel sits on the island-studded bay near
tourist attractions such as Zuiganji. **Pros:** great views abound; free
pickup from station. **Cons:** busy and noisy tourist area; ocean views in
Japanese-style rooms only. ⓢ *Rooms from: ¥22460* ⊠ *8 Senzui, Mat-*
sushima-aza, Matsushima ☎ *022/354–4111* ⊕ *www.centuryhotel.co.jp/*
gaikokugo/en ⤳ *83 Japanese-style rooms, 45 Western-style rooms, 2*
suites ⦿ *No meals.*

$$$$ ⊞ **Shoan Ryokan** (松庵). This plush, sedate ryokan sits quietly on the
RESORT   edge of a peninsula called Oku-Matsushima. **Pros:** peaceful hideaway;
Fodor'sChoice   impeccable personal attention; great natural surroundings. **Cons:** very
★   expensive rates; Matsushima tourist sights are not within walking distance. ⓢ *Rooms from: ¥64000* ⊠ *1 Umeki, Tetaru* ☎ *022/354–3111*
⤳ *11 Japanese-style rooms* ⦿ *Some meals.*

YAMADERA 山寺

49 km (30 miles) west of Sendai.

If you'd like to see one of Japan's most revered—and scenic—temple
complexes, come up here on an easy day trip from Sendai or Yamagata.

GETTING HERE AND AROUND

Reach Yamadera from Sendai on the JR Senzan Line (¥842), or from
Yamagata City on the same line (¥237). Once you leave the station,
you'll find a tourist information office near the bridge, but no English
is spoken there.

EXPLORING

FAMILY   **Risshaku-ji** (山寺 宝珠山立石寺 *Risshaku Temple*). If you are expecting
Fodor'sChoice   just another mundane temple, you will certainly be surprised. Yama-
★   dera is like something conjured out of the ethereal mists of an ancient
Japanese charcoal painting. Built in the year 860, Yamadera's ambitious complex of temples is perched high on the upper slopes of Mt.
Hoju (Hoju-san), from where you can enjoy divine vistas. Belonging
to the Tendai Buddhists, who believe in the existence of "Buddha-
nature" within all living things, Yamadera attracts a steady stream of
pilgrims. Just inside the temple-complex entrance is **Konpon Chudo,**
the temple where the sacred Flame of Belief has burned constantly
for 1,100 years. Near Konpon Chudo is a statue of the Japanese poet
Matsuo Basho (1644–94), whose pithy and colorful haiku related his
extensive wanderings throughout Japan. During a visit to the temple,
he wrote, "Stillness... the sound of cicadas sinks into the rocks" and
buried the poem on the spot.

13

The path continues up many steps—nearly 1,100 of them, well tended though they be. At the summit is **Oku no In,** the hall dedicated to the temple founder, Jikaku Daishi. But if you've come this far, keep going. Of all the temples hanging out over the valley, the view from Godaido is the best. The path becomes crowded in summer and slippery in winter.

To get to the temple complex from Yamadera's JR Station, walk through the village, cross the bridge, and turn right. Allow 1 to 1½ hours for a leisurely climb up and a careful tramp down. ✉ *4456–1 Yamadera, Yamagata* ☎ *023/695–2843* 🌐 *www.jnto.go.jp/eng/location/spot/shritemp/risshakuji.html* 🎫 *¥300* 🕓 *Daily 8:30–5.*

EN ROUTE

Sakunami Onsen (作並温泉 *Sakunami Hot Spring*). If you're looking for a stopover between Yamadera and Sendai, this relaxing hot spring area (with five hotels) is five minutes by free bus from JR Sakunami Station. Sakunami is only 32 minutes (¥480) by local express from Sendai Station, close enough to be an alternative spot to spend the night. There is also a Nikka Whisky distillery here, if you're interested. ✉ *16 Sakanami Azamotoki, Aoba-ku* ☎ *022/395–2211 Iwamatsu Ryokan* 🌐 *www.sentabi.jp/en/accommodation/index3.html* 🎫 *¥1,270 weekdays, ¥1,570 weekends* 🕓 *Mon.–Sat. 11–3, Sun. 11–2 (entry closes 1 hr earlier).*

EN ROUTE

Ginzan Onsen (銀山温泉 *Ginzan Hot Spring*). Ginzan is another relaxing hot spring between Yamagata and Sendai, but this one is more isolated than Sakunami. It's about two to three hours from Sendai by bus. ✉ *Ginsan Onsen, Obanazawa.*

WHERE TO STAY

$$$$ RESORT

🏨 **Iwamatsu Ryokan** (岩松旅館). Along the Hirose River, this large ryokan has rooms that peer out over the stream and mountains. **Pros:** traditional comfort; secluded setting; free parking. **Cons:** no Western-style rooms; caters to large groups of business travelers, who can be rowdy at night. [$] *Rooms from: ¥35060* ✉ *Sakunami Onsen Motoyu, Aoba-ku* ☎ *022/395–2211* 🛏 *91 Japanese-style rooms* 🍴 *Some meals.*

HIRAIZUMI 平泉

120 km (75 miles) north of Sendai.

A culture of gold flourished in Hiraizumi in the late 11th- and 12th centuries, when the Oshu Fujiwara family, a then-powerful clan, chose to move here. Massive temple-building projects were carried out so as to create a peaceful society based on the principles of Buddhism. Hiraizumi evokes Kyoto in many ways, especially in its similar topography. In its heyday, the city served as a convenient base to transport gold, fine horses, and other materials by land and sea, and trading it made the Oshu Fujiwara family prosper. Hiraizumi, then called Mutsu, supplied much of the gold to decorate images of the Buddha and tactfully traded with the capital Kyoto and even China.

For its magnificent Golden Hall and its lovely Buddhist Jodo Garden, Hiraizumi is a worthwhile day trip from Sendai.

GETTING HERE AND AROUND

The nearest station is JR Hiraizumi Station. From Sendai, the *Yamabiko* Shinkansen rockets to Ichinoseki Station (31 minutes), then you hop on the local train one stop for Hiraizumi (¥4,100 in total). It's also accessible by local trains (two hours; ¥1,944) and by express buses (100 minutes; ¥1,700).

Tourist Information Hiraizumi Tourist Information Office. ✉ *61–7 Izumiya* ☎ *0191/46–2110* 🌐 *hiraizumi.or.jp/en.*

EXPLORING

Fodor's Choice ★ **Chuson-ji** (中尊寺 *Chuson-ji Temple*). Founded in 850, this temple's highlight is its Konjikido (Golden Hall), which was completed in 1124. The first Ou Fujiwara lord Kiyohara commissioned many temples and pagodas during his reign, perhaps as many as 40, not to mention residences for 300 priests. Nearly all were destroyed by fire except for Konjikido, and it is the only structure in Chuson-ji that remains unchanged. More than 3,000 objects have survived and are now housed in the treasure house. It's a 20-minute walk from JR Hiraizumi Station or a 10-minute bus ride. ✉ *202 Koromonoseki* ☎ *0191/46–2211* 🌐 *www.chusonji.or.jp/en/* 🎫 *¥800* ⏲ *Mar.–Oct., daily 8:30–5; Nov.–Feb., daily 8:30–4:30.*

FAMILY **Geibikei Funa-kudari** (猊鼻渓, げいび渓舟下り *Geibikei Gorge*). The surreal Geibikei Gorge is a slightly decrepit, definitely kitschy tourist attraction. You board a gondola at the local river, and your gondolier will sing in classic Japanese style as he maneuvers farther into the echoey gorge. Your destination is an upriver sandbar, where you disembark for a stroll, and for a nominal fee you can throw kiln-fired clay divots into a crack in a cliff across the river (each divot has a character on it, and if you chuck it in the hole, that fate is in store for you). Bring bread to feed the river fish—they aggressively follow the boat and jump for joy at handouts. Those fish are also available roasted and fried where you disembark. The trip takes 90 minutes. ✉ *Nagasaka Asamachi 467, Higashiyama-cho* ✥ *Take JR train from Hiraizumi to Ichinoseki (20 mins), then change to Ofunato Line to Geibikei (30 mins)* ☎ *0191/47–2341* 🌐 *www.geibikei.co.jp/wp-content/uploads/2014/04/guidance06.pdf* 🎫 *¥1,600* ⏲ *Boats leave every hr, on the hr 9:30 am–3:30.*

Motsu-ji (毛越寺 *Motsu Temple*). A World Heritage Site, Motsu Temple's main buildings were destroyed by the fire that consumed much of the area in 1226. However, its remaining Heian-Period **Jodo Garden** still provides a beautiful scenery as it was landscaped to depict the Amida Buddha's Pure Land. ✉ *Osawa 58* ☎ *0191/46–2331* 🌐 *www.motsuji.or.jp/english* 🎫 *¥500* ⏲ *Early Apr.–early Nov., daily 8:30–5; early Nov.–early Apr., daily 8:30–4:30.*

WHERE TO STAY

$$$$ B&B/INN 🏨 **Shizukatei** (しづか亭). A chorus of frogs will lull you to sleep at this stylish hot spring inn set among the rice paddies outside Hiraizumi. **Pros:** peaceful rural location; delicious, plentiful food; free pick-up from the station. **Cons:** far from town; no Wi-Fi. [$] *Rooms from: ¥45400* ✉ *10–5 Hiraizumi Nagakura* ☎ *0191/34–2211 Japanese only* 🌐 *shizukatei.com/shizukatei_english* 🛏 *10 rooms* 🍴 *Some meals.*

YAMAGATA 山形

63 km (39 miles) west of Sendai, 120 km (75 miles) southeast of Tsuruoka.

Yamagata, or Mountain Terrain, is the capital of the prefecture of the same name (and the Sister City of Boulder, Colorado). It's a community of a quarter-million souls who enjoy one of the most visually stunning locations in Japan. Everywhere you look there are arrayed lovely mountains, a play of light and shadow shifting across their sculpted flanks and lofty summits. Connoisseurs of soba and mountain vegetables will be delighted, as will fans of sweet, perfectly marbled beef. Yamagata Prefecture is the only prefecture to be 100% thermal—having at least one onsen, or hot spring, in each of its 44 municipalities. Mt. Zao is popular among foreign visitors for its "ice monsters," pillars of frozen snow shaped into mysterious forms by the blizzards, as well as its hot spring.

During the **Hanagasa Festival** (August 5–7), some 10,000 dancers from the region dance through the streets in traditional costume and *hanagasa,* hats so named for the safflowers (thistle-like orange-red flowers, locally called *benibana*) decorating them. It's based on an old ritual to promote fertility and ensure a rich harvest. Floats are interspersed among the dancers, and stalls provide food and refreshments.

GETTING HERE AND AROUND

From Sendai, you have the choice of the JR Senzan Line, which takes about one hour (¥1,144 or buy a W-ticket for ¥1,540, which allows one person to make a round-trip or two people a one-way trip from Sendai) or regular buses from the station (¥930). It's 2½ hours from Tokyo via the Tsubasa Shinkansen (¥11,000). If you're coming from Tsuruoka, you can take the non–JR bus from S-mall (two hours; ¥2,470). Yamagata is easy to navigate, so walking is the way to go unless you need to head farther afield. You can pick up free maps and brochures from the Yamagata Tourist Information Office opposite the ticket turnstiles inside Yamagata JR Station.

ESSENTIALS

Tourist Information Yamagata Tourism Information Center (やまがた観光情報センター *Yamagata Kanko Joho Center*). ✉ *Kajo Central Bldg. 1F, 1-1-1 Jonanmachi* ☎ *023/647-2333* 🌐 *yamagatakanko.com/translation/.*

WHERE TO EAT

$$ JAPANESE Fodor's Choice ★

🍴 **Maruhachi Yatarazuke** (丸八やたら漬). Housed in a converted warehouse in the Maruhachi Yatarazuke complex, the Komian Maruhachi restaurant serves traditional Yamagata dishes such as soba noodles and *imoni* potato hot pot, as well as unusual sushi made with pickles from the venerable Yatarazuke shop right next door. You can try them all in the "Three tastes of Yamagata" set (¥1,620); more elaborate set meals are also available. If you're looking for more of a snack, Tachinomi-dokoro, the standing bar on the far side of the shop, offers all the pickles you can eat for ¥300. It's a favorite with overseas directors attending the annual documentary film festival in town. [$] *Average main: ¥1620* ✉ *2-1-5 Hatagomachi* ☎ *023/623-0310* 🕒 *Restaurant: closed 1st Wed. of month; bar: closed Sun., no lunch.*

13

$$$$ ✕ **Sagoro Steakhouse** (佐五郎). If you've never indulged in some strictly
JAPANESE top-end sukiyaki or shabu-shabu—or if you have and want to feel that
way again—Sagoro will serve you a full dose of some excellent Yonezawa and Yamagata beef. The staff is polite, and the service is efficient.
This place will not only fill you up, but you may gush for days about
the beef's impossible tenderness and its impeccable marbling. Although
most dishes are pricey in this sophisticated, upscale setting, there are
some relative bargains. A simple plate of *shoga-yaki* (beef sautéed in
ginger sauce), with pickled vegetables, rice, and soup is fairly reasonable at ¥1,836. Lunchtime is even better, with prices hovering at about
¥1,500. Head three blocks east from the station and turn left. Look
for the meat shop, and you'll see the black bull on the sign above the
street. Ⓢ *Average main: ¥7000* ⌂ *1–6–10 Kasumicho* ☎ *023/631–3560*
☽ *Closed Sun.*

$$ ✕ **Shojiya** (庄司屋). Yamagata is famous for soba, and Shojiya is the old-
JAPANESE est soba restaurant in Yamagata. For lunch or a light dinner, try tempura
soba (¥1,500) or in summer, cold soba with fried tiny shrimps (*sakura-
ebi*; ¥1,320). The immediate area is as interesting as the restaurant; you
can see restored irrigation channels where five dams were built in 1623
to control flooding, and nearby are traditional kimono and green-tea
shops. The eatery is a 10-minute walk from the JR Station. Ⓢ *Average
main: ¥1500* ⌂ *Nanukamachi 2–7–6* ☎ *023/673–9639.*

WHERE TO STAY

$$$$ 🛏 **Fujiya Ryokan** (藤屋). Modern luxury permeates Fujiya Ryokan, which
B&B/INN has the ambience of an art gallery. **Pros:** excellent service; fabulous
food; perhaps the pinnacle of modern ryokan experiences. **Cons:** too
expensive and too contemporary for some; a little far from Yamagata.
Ⓢ *Rooms from: ¥64600* ⌂ *433 Shinpata, Obanazawa* ☎ *0237/28–2141*
⊕ *www.fujiya-ginzan.com/english* ⇆ *8 rooms* ⫶◯⫶ *Some meals.*

$$$ 🛏 **Hotel Metropolitan Yamagata** (ホテルメトロポリタン山形). Yamagata's
HOTEL most centrally located upscale hotel caters to many busy corporate
travelers from Tokyo and other big cities. **Pros:** central location; nice
views out front. **Cons:** breakfast is served in a room with no windows
and is rather pricey; service at reception can sometimes be a little slow.
Ⓢ *Rooms from: ¥20000* ⌂ *1–1–1 Kasumicho* ☎ *023/628–1111* ⊕ *www.
jrhotelgroup.com/eng/hotel/eng108.htm* ⇆ *116 rooms* ⫶◯⫶ *No meals.*

$$ 🛏 **Richmond Hotel Yamagata Ekimae** (リッチモンドホテル山形駅前). Two
HOTEL minutes from JR Yamagata Station, this sleek 12-story hotel offers
reasonable rates and comfortable rooms with many amenities: bath
salts, skin-care products, even special packages for kids. **Pros:** pris-
tine rooms; cheap breakfast buffet includes pancakes. **Cons:** a bit
far from downtown; a bit plain. Ⓢ *Rooms from: ¥18000* ⌂ *1–3–11
Futabacho* ☎ *023/647–6277* ⊕ *yamagata.richmondhotel.jp* ⇆ *220
rooms* ⫶◯⫶ *No meals.*

$$$$ 🛏 **Takamiya Ryokan** (深山荘高見屋 *Miyamaso Takamiya*). Foreign guests
B&B/INN favor this 300-year-old Japanese inn for the period atmosphere, the
soft thermal waters and, in winter, the chance to see Zao's famous "ice
monsters"—those fabulous frozen pillars sculpted by blizzards. **Pros:**
historic ambience; famous hot spring; close to the ski slope. **Cons:**
far from the center of Yamagata City; no elevators. Ⓢ *Rooms from:*

In summer, hiking is a popular pastime in the mountains around Yamagata, which host skiers in the winter.

¥41000 ⊠ 54 Zao Onsen ⚓ *Buses for Zao Onsen (35 mins, ¥1,000) leave from Stop 1, Yamagata Station* ☎ *023/694–9333* ⊕ *www.ryokan. or.jp/english/yado/main/09940* ⛵ *3 Japanese-style rooms, 14 Western-style rooms, 5 suites* ⦿ *Some meals.*

NORTHERN TOHOKU 北東北

MORIOKA 盛岡

184 km (114 miles) north of Sendai.

Morioka is a busy commercial and industrial city ringed by mountains, but it's more of a travel hub than a destination to visit; for that reason, a one-day (or even half-day) stopover is usually sufficient to give travelers a glimpse of the city's greenery and attractions. A nice, expansive park surrounds a ruined castle, and an ancient cherry tree has proven it belongs here by rooting itself into the crack of a huge granite slab in front of the district courthouse. But the city's major draw is the locally produced *Nanbu-tetsu*, a special type of cast iron forged into functional and highly ornamental wares. The most popular are heavy iron kettles. They are expensive, because they're specially tempered not to rust. As tea connoisseurs know, once conditioned, these pots soften the water by leeching out unwanted minerals and chemicals while adding the taste and health benefits of elemental iron. They will go on doing it forever, too, if properly cared for. Many locals are still using kettles from centuries past. Dozens of shops throughout the city sell Nanbu-tetsu, but the main shopping streets are Saien-dori and O-dori, which pass right by Iwate Koen (Iwate Park).

GETTING HERE AND AROUND

From Sendai, the quickest way to reach Morioka is the Hayabusa Shinkansen (39 minutes; ¥6,470); the cheapest way to get there is the express bus (2 hours, 40 minutes; ¥2,980). Both run many times a day from Sendai. If you want to fly from Osaka or Sapporo, Morioka (whose Hanamaki Airport is 45 minutes by bus, ¥1,400, from downtown) has two or three flights daily from Osaka's Itami Airport (1 hour, 25 minutes; ¥35,200–¥39,500) by JAL. There are also hour-long flights from Sapporo's Shin-Chitose Airport for around ¥28,000.

To get to downtown Morioka from JR Morioka Station, you can walk or take the convenient loop bus, called Denden-mushi, which goes to the shopping area on the far side of the river past the park; the bus departs every 10 to 15 minutes between the hours of 9 and 7 from Bus Stop 15 or 16 in front of JR Morioka Station (¥100 for one ride, ¥300 for the day pass).

VISITOR INFORMATION AND TOURS

The Northern Tohoku Tourist Information Center is on the second floor of JR Morioka Station, and the English-speaking staff can give you maps and other information on the three prefectures of Iwate, Akita, and Aomori. The office can also help arrange accommodations with members of a ryokan union.

Contacts Iwate Kotsu Bus Company (岩手県交通). ☎ *019/651–3355.* **Northern Tohoku Tourist Information Center** (北東北観光センター *Kita Tohoku Kanko Center*). ⊠ *JR Morioka Station 2F, Morioka Ekimae Dori 1–48* ☎ *019/625–2090.*

EXPLORING

Gozaku Store (ござ九 森九商店 *Gozaku-Moriku Shoten*). This wealthy merchant's house was built sometime between the Edo and Meiji Periods (1600–1868) and has a distinguished historical presence. It is now a miscellaneous store carrying lots of bamboo baskets and straw sandals. Behind the store is a willow tree and the river, quite a scenic view. ⊠ *1–31 Konyacho* ☎ *019/622–7129* ⊙ *Mon.–Sat. 8:30–5:30.*

OFF THE BEATEN PATH

Hanamaki Onsenkyo (花巻温泉郷 大沢温泉, 鉛温泉). Among 14 onsen that collectively make up these gorges of hot water gushers, Osawa and Namari stand out for their quality and well-kept ryokans, offering comfort and long-cherished histories. Osawa is known as poet Miyazawa Kenji's favorite, and Namari is famous for Japan's 600-year-old deepest standing bath. Osawa is 30 minutes by bus from Iwate's Hanamaki Airport, Namari 50 minutes. From Morioka, Osawa is 70 minutes, Namari 80 minutes. Arrange for a shuttle from the bus station to your ryokan. ✉ *Yuguchi Aza Osawa 181, Hanamaki* ☎ *0198/25–2021 Osawa Onsen, 0198/25–2311 Namari Onsen Fujisan Ryokan* ⊕ *www. kanko-hanamaki.ne.jp/en/spa/index. html* ✑ *¥600 for Osawa, ¥700 for Namari* ⊘ *Daily 7:30 am–9 pm (Osawa); daily 7 am–9 pm (Namari).*

Fodor's Choice **Ho-Onji** (報恩寺 五百羅漢 *Ho-On*
★ *Temple*). On the outskirts of Mt. Atagoyama is a temple district where a dozen temples are clustered. This one houses 499 statues of Buddha's disciples that were carved between 1731 and 1735, in a time of severe famine and increased religious devo-

> ## HORSING AROUND
>
> If you happen to be in town on the second Saturday in June, a small festival called **Chagu-chagu Umako**—named for the noise the big horses' bells make—features 100 locally bred and gaily decorated Nanbu-koma horses brought from nearby Takizawa Village to parade around in front of the station. The horses clomp through the streets between 9:30 and 1:30 on that day only.

tion. Each is unique, and if you look hard, you will see disciples laughing, chatting with their neighbors, eating, drinking, and even napping. Behind Ho-onji are a small cemetery and a tranquil Japanese garden. Monks ring a bell periodically; the sounds echo through the premises and the city. ✉ *31–5 Nakasugawacho* ☎ *019/641–4415* ⊕ *www.japan-iwate.info/app/ location_detail.php?lid=15* ✑ *¥300* ⊘ *Daily 9–4.*

Iwate Koen (岩手公園 *Iwate Park*). This park is large enough to get lost in, with varied landscapes, an astonishing variety of artfully placed flowers and trees, shady groves, streams, and colors in every season. It's a good place for a romantic walk. In 1597, the 26th Lord of Nambu had a fine castle built here, but all that remains are ruined walls. To reach the park from JR Morioka Station, cross Kai-un Bashi and walk straight down the middle of the three roads that meet there. ✉ *Morioka Shiroato Koen* ⊕ *www.japan-iwate.info/app/location_detail.php?lid=10* ✑ *Free.*

Kamasada Iron Casting Studio (釜足南部鉄器 *Kamasada Nanbu Tekki*). The five casters here create the fine ironwork, and their products are as authentic and beautiful as Nanbu-tekki can be. Designed by resident master caster Nobuho Miya, a saucepan with a wooden handle is elegantly traditional yet modern. Equally attractive teakettles come in all sizes and prices. If you want to place a special order, your piece will be produced in two months and can be shipped anywhere. To get to the studio, go half a block down the tiny street that extends in front of the venerable Azuma-ya soba restaurant. ✉ *2–5 Konyacho* ☎ *019/622–3911* ⊘ *Mon.–Sat. 9–5:30.*

Kogensha (光原社). Specializing in quality folk crafts like lacquerware, dyed fabrics, kites, and pottery, this shop is composed of several small buildings around a courtyard. You can walk through the charming courtyard to a small *kohi-kan* (coffee shop), where cold water is available to everyone. Along the wall to the left are poems by famous local poet Miyazawa Kenji. To get here, cross the river on Asahibashi and take the first left onto a funky little street that leads to the main shop, 50 yards down on the left. ✉ *2–18 Zaimoku-cho* ☎ *019/622–2894* ⊘ *Apr.–Dec., daily 10–6; Jan.–Mar., daily 10–5:30.*

WHERE TO EAT

$$$

JAPANESE

Fodor's Choice

★

✗ **Azuma-ya** (東家 わんこそば). Hearty soba is made from plentiful northern buckwheat, and Azuma-ya is easily Morioka's most famous place to eat these healthful noodles. The second level is devoted to the courageous and hearty of appetite, where *wanko* soba courses—all you could possibly want to eat—start at ¥2,700. Down on the first floor, popular dishes such as hand-kneaded cold tempura soba (¥1,410) and pork cutlet in a rice bowl (¥980) are speedily served. The 50 or so *maneki-neko* (decorative beckoning cats) intended to keep customers coming back, and they seem to be doing their job. Look for the traditional building with the indigo-color cloth sign outside, and note that the last order is at 8 pm. There's also a branch in front of Morioka Station. $ *Average main: ¥2700* ⊠ *1–8–3 Nakanohashi Dori* ☎ *019/622–2252* ⊕ *www.wankosoba-azumaya.co.jp/foreigner/english.*

$$$$

SEAFOOD

✗ **Banya Nagasawa** (番屋ながさわ). When you slide open the door, you may notice the two-story fish tank with piles of shells and the freezer packed with flounder, sea bream, and a frightening-looking red, pop-eyed fish that might make you recoil. But you'll instantly know what you'll be served here: all manner of seasonal grilled shellfish and fish, crisp and brown on the outside but white and tender inside. You'll be eating *warabi* (fiddle ferns) in spring, and drinking excellent local sake with friendly regulars any time of the year. It's a bit pricey, but if you're a seafood fan this won't disappoint. From JR Morioka, follow Odori to the Iwate Bank and turn right at the statue of Takuboku Ishikawa. The restaurant is 2½ blocks ahead on the right. $ *Average main: ¥6000* ⊠ *2–6–1 Saien* ☎ *019/622–2646* ☾ *Closed Sun. and mid-Aug. No lunch.*

$$$

KOREAN

✗ **Pyon Pyon Sya Morioka Ekimae Ten** (ぴょんぴょん舎盛岡駅前店). *Reimen*—a dish of clear noodles served cold with spicy kimchi, hard-boiled egg, watermelon, and a slice of beef—is a Korean delicacy that has become one of Morioka's signature dishes. It is served in a set with another Korean item such as *bibimbap* (rice in a hot stone bowl, topped with pickled vegetables, mincemeat, and egg) in this airy modern restaurant near Morioka Station. Evening meals feature meat barbecued at the table. $ *Average main: ¥3000* ⊠ *9–3 Morioka Ekimaedori* ☎ *019/606–1067.*

WHERE TO STAY

$$$$

B&B/INN

🛏 **Fujisan Ryokan** (藤三旅館). The main reason to stay here is have the opportunity to steep in the venerable Namari Onsen, which has a high ceiling and a round shape that resembles nothing so much as a giant inkwell. **Pros:** storied history; good meals; charm to spare. **Cons:** loud announcements break the peaceful moments; rather out of the way. $ *Rooms from: ¥27000* ⊠ *75–1 Namari, Hanamaki* ☎ *0198/25–2311* ⤵ *36 Japanese-style rooms, 6 with toilet* ❍ *Some meals.*

$$$

HOTEL

🛏 **Hotel Metropolitan Morioka New Wing** (ホテルメトロポリタン盛岡ニューウイング). Tastefully furnished, spacious rooms and English-speaking staff make this hotel—run by the same group as the Hotel Metropolitan Morioka (original branch)—a safe choice for visitors to Morioka. **Pros:** large, attractive rooms; various interesting packages on offer; central location. **Cons:** plumbing can be erratic; somewhat dull breakfast;

corporate feel. Ⓢ$ *Rooms from: ¥20196* ✉ *2–27 Morioka Ekimae-kita-dori* ☎ *019/625–1211* ⊕ *www.jrhotelgroup.com/eng/hotel/eng106.htm* ↩ *121 rooms* ⦿ *No meals.*

$$$$　⌂ **Morioka Grand Hotel** (盛岡グランドホテル). This pleasingly secluded
HOTEL　hotel sits near the top of a wooded hill, with a breezy view over the rolling green hills that surround the city. **Pros:** tranquillity reigns; great views; spacious modern rooms. **Cons:** dated decor; a bit far from the action. Ⓢ$ *Rooms from: ¥26000* ✉ *1–10 Atagoshita* ☎ *019/625–2111* ⊕ *www.m-grand.jp/english/index.html* ↩ *5 Japanese-style rooms, 21 Western-style rooms, 1 suite* ⦿ *No meals.*

$　⌂ **Ryokan Kumagai** (旅館熊ヶ井). This friendly and cozy Japanese inn
B&B/INN　attracts budget-minded travelers, many of them intent on hiking up nearby Mt. Iwate. **Pros:** homey atmosphere; reasonable rates; festive atmosphere. **Cons:** a bit rustic; no private baths. Ⓢ$ *Rooms from: ¥9000* ✉ *3–2–6 Osawakawara* ☎ *019/651–3020* ⊕ *www.kumagairyokan.com* ↩ *8 rooms without bath* ⦿ *No meals.*

$$$$　⌂ **Shikitei Hotel** (四季亭). A half-hour bus ride from JR Morioka Station
B&B/INN　takes you to this quiet hot spring town and upscale, traditional ryokan, which serves two meals a day in your tatami room. **Pros:** excellent meals; pure relaxation; free Internet access. **Cons:** feels a bit claustrophobic; not all rooms have a private bath. Ⓢ$ *Rooms from: ¥40000* ✉ *137 Yunotate* ☎ *019/689–2021, 019/689–2159* ⊕ *www.ryokan.or.jp/english/yado/main/92316* ↩ *22 Japanese-style rooms, 16 with bath* ⦿ *Some meals.*

TAZAWA-KO 田沢湖

40 km (25 miles) west of Morioka, 87 km (54 miles) east of Akita.

The beautiful azure waters of Tazawa-ko, an almost perfectly round crater lake, can be enjoyed from the paths along the shore, a rented paddleboat, or the motorboat trip across to the statue of Princess Tatsuko and back. Nearby are several traditional hot spring inns.

GETTING HERE AND AROUND

A 12-minute bus ride (¥360) from the JR Tazawa-ko Station gets you to the Tazawa-ko Han center on the eastern lakeshore. A small and shallow swimming area is a short distance to the northwest along the road. A 30-minute bus ride from JR Tazawa-ko Station via Tazawa-ko Han takes you to Tazawa-ko Kogen (Tazawa-ko Plateau) for ¥620. The journey offers spectacular views of the lake. Once there, you can rent your own paddleboat or rowboat. You'll want sunscreen and a hat or sunshade in summer. There's also regular bus service around the lake and bicycles available for rent (¥500 to ¥800 per hour, with two hours usually sufficient for the loop) at the Tazawa-ko Han bus terminal and at many lodgings in the area.

VISITOR INFORMATION

The Tazawa-ko Tourist Information Office to the left of the JR Tazawa-ko Station has maps and bus schedules; it's open daily from 8:30 to 6:30.

Contact Tazawa-ko Tourist Information Office
(田沢湖観光情報センター フォレイク). ✉ *JR Tazawako Station 1F, 68 Aza-Osaka, Obonai, Tazawako* ☎ *0187/43–2111* ⊕ *ohtazawako.blogspot.com.*

Tazawa-ko is the deepest lake in Japan.

EXPLORING

Tamagawa Onsen (玉川温泉 *Tamagawa Hot Spring*). The highlight is the strong, acidic water (which has a minor amount of radium): gushing out at almost 2,400 gallons per minute, it's Japan's swiftest flow from a single spring. In the vicinity is another geothermal area in a national park where many enjoy a hot-rock bath. Take worn-out T-shirts and towels because they will get stained by the waters or even the steam (be careful also of reactive jewelry, such as copper or silver). From JR Tazawa-ko Station in Akita, take the Ugokotsu bus bound for Tamagawa Onsen. The trip takes 75 minutes. ⊠ *Tazawako Tamagawa, Senboku* ☎ *0187/58–3000* ⊡ *Onsen ¥600, hot rock baths free* ⊗ *Daily 7:30–7:30.*

Tazawa-ko (田沢湖 *Lake Tazawa*). The clear waters and forested slopes of Tazawa-ko, Japan's deepest lake, create a mystical quality that greatly appeals to the Japanese. According to legend, the great beauty from Akita, Tatsuko Hime, sleeps in the water's deep, disguised as a dragon. The lake never freezes over in winter because Tatsuko Hime and her dragon husband churn the water with their passionate love-making. The less romantic, scientific reason is this: Tazawa-ko has been measured to a depth of 1,397 feet, which prevents it from freezing. Though clear enough to allow you to see a startling 300 feet or more down into it, the mineral-blue water is too acidic to support anything but a few hardy fish.

A scenic 20-km-long (12-mile-long) two-lane road is perfect for biking. Bicycles can be rented at the bus station near JR Tazawako Station. In winter, the Tazawa area is a popular downhill skiing destination, and

TOHOKU'S HINABITA ONSEN

The Tohoku region has some 650 *onsen* (thermal spas) that are mostly located or "hidden" in remote mountain villages. Traveling here (particularly in winter) is not always easy, but soaking in a relaxing onsen while you are surrounded by snow will remind you why it was worth the trouble to visit.

When you hear Japanese talk about Tohoku's onsen, there is one word you cannot miss: *hinabita*. The word means rustic, redolent of a simpler past, and for many it's this simple charm that makes the onsen here so enjoyable. Tohoku's hinabita onsen are a magnet for connoisseurs. To enjoy it fully, an overnight stay is recommended. Nearly all onsen have adjoining lodgings, and most will pick you up at a nearby train station or bus stop. Many ryokan in the region welcome not only visitors but also long-term guests, who stay for months for *toji* (therapeutic purposes). Toji has been practiced since the 17th century and is still popular, particularly among cancer patients as an alternative medicine.

the deep blue of the lake is dazzling from the lifts and trails. ✉ *Tazawako* 🌐 *www.city.semboku.akita.jp/en.*

WHERE TO STAY

$$ B&B/INN 🏨 **Kuroyu Onsen** (黒湯温泉). One of seven rustic ryokan in the Nyuto area, this one is the most cozy. **Pros:** great retreat; great service; wonderful pools. **Cons:** no private bathrooms; light sleepers may be surprised at how loud nature is at night, so bring earplugs. [$] *Rooms from: ¥12030* ✉ *2–1 Tazawa-ko Obonai, Senboku* ☎ *0187/46–2214* 🌐 *ryokan.glocal-promotion.com/ryokan/kuroyu/* 🕓 *Closed mid-Nov.–mid-Apr.* 🛏 *42 Japanese-style rooms without bath* 🍴 *Some meals.*

KAKUNODATE 角館

19 km (12 miles) southwest of Tazawa-ko, 59 km (37 miles) southwest of Morioka, 69 km (43 miles) east of Akita City.

Fodor's Choice ★ The little samurai town of Kakunodate, sometimes called "Little Kyoto," was founded in 1620 by Yoshikatsu Ashina, the local lord, who chose it for its defensible position and reliable water sources. An outpost of traditional Japan, Kakunodate is consistently regarded as one of the very best places for seeing cherry blossoms in spring. The whole town is full of *shidare-zakura* (weeping cherry trees), descended from the same trees that adorn Kyoto, and their pink flowers grace the dark-wood gates, walls, and roofs of ancient samurai houses. Along the banks of Hinokinai-gawa (Hinokinai River), these living jewel factories dangle a mile-long pink curtain. The town is also home to several samurai and merchant houses with eclectic collections of family treasures, many not at all crowded with visitors. From September 7 to 9, a loud town festival involving floats, drums, and dancing takes place here.

GETTING HERE AND AROUND

On the JR Komachi Shinkansen Line, Kakunodate can be reached from Tazawa-ko (¥1,390) or Morioka (¥2,640). Akita City is 43 minutes away on the Komachi Shinkansen Line (¥2,820). On local trains, the trip to Akita City takes 90 minutes to two hours because the trains halt at Oomagari Station for a half hour or so.

VISITOR INFORMATION

The Kakunodate Tourist Information Center is in an old *kura*-style (warehouse-like) building, adjacent to the tea shop by the station. The English-speaking staff has maps and information about the samurai houses and walks in town, and can recommend nearby lunch or dinner options. Coin lockers are also located inside.

Contact Kakunodate Tourist Information Center (観光情報センター). ✉ *Kami Sugasawa 394-2* ☎ *0187/54-2700* ⊕ *kakunodate-kanko.jp.*

> ## BARK SHOPPING
>
> Shops in Kakunodate are the best places in Tohoku to pick up the locally made *kabazaiku*, or cherry-bark veneer items—everything from warmly translucent maroon lamp shades to tiny, intricate business-card holders. If you're looking to find unique souvenirs and crafts in Japan, give Kakunodate's shops a looking-over, since anything you're likely to find in the hokey souvenir shops in the big cities will be more kitschy and overpriced.

EXPLORING

Ando House (安藤醸造 *Ando Jyozo*). A visit to this miso and soy sauce business, still located in the historic home of the Ando merchant family, is a treat for both the eyes and the taste buds. Beautiful seasonal flower arrangements and artifacts decorate the tatami mat rooms, while the unusual redbrick storehouse houses some fine painted screens. And don't miss the inner storehouse, where you can find free miso soup and pickles! ✉ *27 Shimoshinmachi, Kakunodate, Senboku* ☎ *0187/53-2008* ☜ *Free* ☽ *Daily 8:30–6.*

Aoyagi Samurai Manor Museum (青柳家 *Bukeyashiki Aoyagi-ke*). Several well-preserved samurai houses date from the founding of Kakunodate. The most renowned is Aoyagi-ke, which functions as a museum and even a bit of a shopping center (there are many restaurants and gift shops located here). The house displays an extensive collection of swords, armor, guns, and silk kimono wedding gowns as well as all kinds of historical artifacts to pore over, such as farm implements and household items. It also exhibits a large number of war documents, photos, and uniforms from the Sino-Japanese War (1894–95) to the Pacific War (1941–45). History buffs will love it, especially when you can see how much wealth these feudal bureaucrats could accumulate. The museum is a 15-minute walk northwest from JR Kakunodate Station. ✉ *3 Shimo-cho, Omote-machi* ☎ *0187/54-3257* ⊕ *www.samuraiworld.com/english* ☜ *¥500* ☽ *Apr.–Nov., daily 9–5; Dec.–Mar., daily 9–4.*

WHERE TO STAY

$$

HOTEL

🗗 **Folkloro Kakunodate** (フォルクローロ角館). Next to the station, this low-rise hotel looks to be part of the station itself. **Pros:** convenient if you need to catch an early morning train; breakfast is included; free

Wi-Fi. **Cons:** quite far from samurai houses; rooms are uninspiring; quiet neighborhood after dark. [$] *Rooms from: ¥13600* ✉ *14 Naka-suga-sawa* ☎ *0187/53–2070* 🌐 *www.folkloro-kakunodate.com/en/* 🛏 *26 rooms* 🍴 *Breakfast.*

$$ B&B/INN 🏨 **Machiyado Neko no Suzu** (町宿ねこの鈴). Smiling staff welcome you to this charming small inn that adjoins the town baths. **Pros:** local atmosphere in the baths; friendly staff; value for money. **Cons:** little soundproofing of the rooms; no individual baths. [$] *Rooms from: ¥15000* ✉ *28 Shimonakamachi, Kakunodate, Senboku* ☎ *0187/42–8105* 🛏 *13 rooms* 🍴 *No meals.*

$$$$ B&B/INN 🏨 **Tamachi Bukeyashiki Hotel** (田町武家屋敷ホテル). The fanciest ryokan in town, the Tamachi Bukeyashiki Hotel has dark wood floors, antique furnishings, glowing lanterns, and shoji screens that give the place a warm and welcoming vibe. **Pros:** genuine charm; luxurious feel; gourmet cuisine. **Cons:** a bit pricey for some; have to travel across town for a hot spring bath. [$] *Rooms from: ¥31320* ✉ *23 Tamachi Shimocho* ☎ *0187/52–1700* 🛏 *9 Western-style rooms, 3 Japanese-style rooms* 🍴 *Some meals.*

TOWADA–HACHIMANTAI NATIONAL PARK *TOWADA-HACHIMANTAI KOKURITSU KOEN* 十和田八幡平国立公園

158 km (98 miles) northwest of Morioka.

Including the windswept expanse of Hachimantai Plateau, scenic Lake Towada, beech forests, marshes of wild flowers, and many hot springs, this national park offers many opportunities to get away from it all.

GETTING HERE AND AROUND

The easiest way to reach Towada-ko by public transport is to take a JR bus from Aomori Station or Hachinohe Station. Mizuumi-Go's route travels between Aomori and Towada-ko in 2 hours, 45 minutes (¥3,090). JR Oirase-Go departs from Hachinohe Station (2 hours, 15 minutes; ¥2,670). If you don't have a Japan Rail Pass, there is a two-day pass that covers the route from Aomori to Towada (¥5,000; not available in October); it also lets you stop at other interesting sights such as Oirase Gorge. Local buses run along a network that links all the main spots, but service is frequently suspended during winter storms. There is no bus service from Morioka. If you rent a car, driving in Hachimantai is especially beautiful in early summer and fall.

EXPLORING

Hachimantai Kogen (八幡平高原 *Hachimantai Plateau*). Between Lake Tazawa and Lake Towada, the Hachimantai Plateau is a hotbed of geological activity between volcano tops. Geysers and bubbling mud pots remind you of all that goes on beneath us. There are also onsen, and any hiking you do will be rewarded by relaxing soaks in the hot springs. ✉ *Towada–Hachiman-tai National Park* ☎ *019/651–4111 tourist information at Morioka City Hall* 🌐 *www.hachimantai.jp/english-pdf/index.html.*

Nyuto (乳頭温泉郷). Inside Towada-Hachimantai National Park, Nyuto consists of seven different, albeit charming, *hinabita* onsen, characterized by their milky water and surrounded by a beech forest. Each onsen has well-managed ryokan, and you can purchase a pass (¥1,500) that gives you free shuttle transport and access to all seven. Nyuto is about 45 minutes from Tazawa-ko. From JR Tazawa-ko Station, take the Ugokotsu bus bound for Nyuto Onsen, and ask your ryokan where to get off; they will pick you up from the nearest stop. ⊠ *Tazawako Kuroyuzawa 2–1, Senboku* ☎ *0187/46–2244 for Kuroyu Onsen* ⊕ *ryokan.glocal-promotion.com/* ⊠ *¥510–¥720 (varies for each onsen)* ⊙ *Daily 11–5 (varies for each onsen).*

Oirase Gorge (奥入瀬渓流 *Oirase Keiryu*). An excellent—if a bit crowded—choice for a walk is this gorge northeast of the lake at Nenokuchi. The carefully tended trail follows a river and a series of waterfalls for a total of 9 km (5½ miles; about 2 hours 40 minutes). A two-lane road parallels the river, so if you get tired you can catch buses north to Aomori and south to Nenokuchi and Yasumiya. Be prepared for cold mist or rain, pack ample snacks and water, and find out the bus schedule before you start out. ⊠ *Towada–Hachiman-tai National Park.*

FAMILY
Fodor's Choice
★
Osore-zan (*Scary Mountain*). If you have a car, a day trip to the uppermost "hook" of the Mutsu/Shimokita Peninsula is highly recommended. A 30-minute drive north of Mutsu takes you to Osore-zan, which literally means "Scary Mountain." On the ash-gray shores of the Lake Usori caldera an other-planetary landscape awaits, with boardwalks that lead over sulfur pools and past shrines to the dead. There's even an enclosed onsen where you can shuck your clothes and bathe in the stinky water. At certain times of the year, *itako* (blind female shamans) open stalls to tell your fortune and communicate with your deceased loved ones. It's a memorable day at the end of the world. ⊠ *Mutsu* ☎ *0175/22–3825* ⊕ *www.jnto.go.jp/eng/location/spot/shritemp/osore-zan.html* ⊠ *¥500* ⊙ *May–Oct., daily 6–6.*

Fodor's Choice
★
Towada-Hachimantai National Park (十和田八幡平国立公園 *Towada Hachimantai Kokuritsu Koen*). For walking among the splendid and vast virgin beech, pine, and cedar forests deep in the heart of Tohoku, you could not pick a better destination than Towada-Hachimantai National Park. The mountains afford sweeping panoramas over the park's gorges and valleys, crystal-clear lakes like Towada-ko, gnarled and windswept trees, and volcanic cones. The park straddles Aomori, Iwate, and Akita prefectures, and sprawls over 330 square miles (855 square km). Hot springs and tiny villages lost in time are secreted here, and the fresh tree-scented air promotes a feeling of true wilderness. ⊠ *Towada–Hachiman-tai National Park* ⊕ *www.env.go.jp/ park/towada.*

Towada-ko (十和田湖 *Lake Towada*). Thanks to its famous fall colors, Lake Towada welcomes a rumbling fleet of packed tour buses when the leaves begin to change. The lake fills a volcanic crater to a depth of 1,096 feet, making it the third deepest in Japan. The crater is held aloft like a giant goblet above the surrounding topography, giving it a dramatic illusory aspect. There are boat tours that let you float by the lovely landscape. ⊠ *Towada–Hachiman-tai National Park* ☎ *0176/75–7425* ⊕ *www.towada-kankou.jp/english/laketowada.html.*

13

WHERE TO STAY

$$$$ HOTEL **Hoshino Resort Oirase Keiryu Hotel** (星野リゾート奥入瀬渓流ホテル). Once a ryokan, this resort hotel combines the best of both worlds: there are great mountain views, two meals are served each day, and yukata robes are provided (and you are encouraged to walk around in them). **Pros:** lots of activities; pleasant riverside stroll; several dining options. **Cons:** boxy rooms; fees for all the extra programs; breakfast on the terrace costs an extra ¥2,160. [$] *Rooms from: ¥57000* ✉ *231 Tochikubo, Okuse, Towada* ☎ *050/3786–0022* 🌐 *www.oirase-keiryuu.jp* 🕓 *Closed late Nov.–late Apr.* 🛏 *122 Western-style rooms, 67 Japanese-style rooms* 🍴 *Some meals.*

HIROSAKI 弘前

47 km (30 miles) south of Aomori, 230 km (143 miles) northwest of Morioka.

Fodor's Choice ★ Hirosaki is one of northern Tohoku's most attractive cities. It's most famous for its sweet apples, and its only real cultural attraction is a small but photogenic reconstructed castle. The town has a very appealing, easygoing nature, and this is suitably reflected in a local slang word, *azumashii* ("a feeling of coziness and comfort"). There's also a blue-tinged component to the light that is somehow reminiscent of Santa Fe or Taos, New Mexico.

GETTING HERE AND AROUND

The easiest way to approach Hirosaki is to take a local train from Aomori (45 minutes; ¥670). Resort Shirakami-Go is a slightly quicker option (39 minutes; ¥990). From Morioka, the fastest and cheapest way is to take the JR express highway bus (2 hours, 15 minutes; ¥5,400 round-trip).

VISITOR INFORMATION

Hirosaki is compact and walkable, but finding your bearings in this ancient castle town can prove difficult, for the streets were designed to disorient invaders before they could get to the battlements. So, by all means, pick up a map at the Hirosaki City Tourist Information Center before setting out. It's on the right side of the train station as you exit. South of the castle grounds, the Hirosaki Sightseeing Information Center displays local crafts and regional art and provides tourist information.

Contact Hirosaki City Tourist Information Center (弘前市観光案内所 *Hirosaki-shi Kanko Annaisho*). ✉ *1–1 Omotemachi, Hirosaki* ☎ *0172/26–3600* 🌐 *en.hkg.jp/infocenter.html.* **Hirosaki Municipal Tourist Center** (弘前市立観光館 *Hirosaki-shiritsu Kankokan*). ✉ *2–1 Shimo-Shiroganemachi, Hirosaki Koen Mae, Hirosaki* ☎ *0172/37–5501* 🌐 *en.hkg.jp.*

EXPLORING

Chosho-ji (長勝寺と禅林街 *Chosho Temple*). Thirty-three of the Soto Sect's Zen temples line up solemnly along a long avenue called Zenrin-gai (Zen Forest Street), at the end of which Chosho-ji temple stands with great dignity. The Tsugaru clan's family temple was originally built in Ajigasawa in 1528 but was moved here in 1610 to protect

Hirosaki Castle. You'll see a large bell dating back from the Kamakura period, an elaborate gate meant to shake off greediness and complaining, and 500 statues depicting Buddha's disciples. If you aren't full of temples yet, this area is one of the main reasons to visit Hirosaki. ✉ *1–23–8 Nishi Shigemori, Hirosaki* ☎ *0172/32–0813* ⊕ *en.hkg.jp/list.html* ✉ *¥300* ⊙ *Apr. 23–Nov., daily 9–4.*

Hirosaki-jo (弘前城 *Hirosaki Castle*). Guarded by deep moats, over which a red wooden bridge crosses in a picturesque curve, Hirosaki-jo is atop a high stone base. The original castle, completed in 1611, was set ablaze 16 years later by a lightning bolt. The present one, of

---

SHAMISEN

Shamisen literally means "three-tastes-strings," and this musical instrument sounds somewhat like the American banjo. The sound-amplification board is traditionally made of tightly stretched dog or cat skin, and it is usually played with a large comblike plectrum made of tortoiseshell or ivory. The shamisen has recently been exposed to young Japanese audiences—and to Westerners—by popular bands like the Yoshida Brothers, who forgo tradition and play the instrument with the ferocity of a rock guitar.

---

a smaller scale, dates back to 1810. In spring, the more than 5,000 *somei-yoshino* cherry trees blossom, while in fall the changing maples are even more gorgeous. A snow-lantern festival with illuminated ice sculptures is held in early February. The castle is a 30-minute walk from JR Hirosaki Station. Take the ¥100 bus from the bus pool and get off at the Shiyakusho-mae stop. ✉ *1 Shimo Shirogane-cho, Hirosaki* ☎ *0172/33–8733* ⊕ *www.hirosakipark.jp/en/* ✉ *¥310* ⊙ *Castle Apr. 23–May 5, daily 7 am–9 pm (for cherry blossoms); May 6–Nov., daily 9–5; park open 24 hrs year-round.*

FAMILY **Tsugaru-han Neputa Mura** (津軽藩ねぷた村 *Tsugaru Peninsula Neputa Village*). On the northeast corner of the castle grounds, this museum exhibits the giant drums and floats used in the annual Neputa Festival. If you miss the real thing, come here to see the 40-foot fan-shape floats as they sleep off their hangovers from the mad midsummer revelry. In the workshop you can paint your own traditional *kingyo-neputa* (bamboo-framed paper goldfish) or *kokeshi* (traditional wooden dolls) to take home as souvenirs. It has a Japanese garden with the borrowed scenery method—combining it with outer scenic objects to complete a harmony—and a food court on the premise provides inexpensive hearty Japanese meals. From mid-May to October you can rent a bicycle (¥500; need ID with address). ✉ *61 Kaminoko Machi, Hirosaki* ☎ *0172/39–1511* ⊕ *en.hkg.jp/main01.html* ✉ *¥550* ⊙ *Apr.–Nov., daily 9–5; Dec.–Mar., daily 9–4.*

WHERE TO EAT

$$$ ✕ **Anzu** (杏). Avant-garde performances of live *shamisen*—an instru-
JAPANESE ment that feels like a more serious cousin of the banjo—by promising young performers and seasoned experts are the main attraction here, more so even than the food. Jams take place every evening at 7:30 and 9:30. Arrive early to sit on cushions on the floor, in local style, and enjoy such dishes as grilled scallops. Many items on the menu are

incomprehensible to even native speakers, as they go by local names; if you are an adventurous diner, point and anticipate. **TIP→ Some of the hot pots (around ¥3,000) are big enough for two.** [$] *Average main: ¥3000* ✉ *44–1 Oyakata Machi, Hirosaki* ☎ *0172/32–6684* 🌐 *www.en-aomori.com/food-040.html* 🕒 *No lunch.*

$$$ JAPANESE 🍴 **Kikufuji** (菊富士). Tasty, healthful, and authentic dishes from the region are Kikufuji's specialty, from delicious vegetable stews like *kenoshiru* to the freshest seafood. The shellfish brought in from Mutsu Bay are superb, so try the *hotateno-kaiyakimiso* (scallops grilled in the shell). The menu (including the prices) is in Japanese, so look around at other tables to see what you might fancy. Because excellent dry, local varieties of sake are available, dinner here may be preferable over lunch. [$] *Average main: ¥2500* ✉ *1 Sakamoto-cho, Hirosaki* ☎ *0172/36–3300* 🕒 *Closed some Tues. (call to check).*

$$$$ FRENCH 🍴 **Restaurant Yamazaki** (レストラン山崎). Would you believe that people come here from all over Honshu just for a cup of soup? Scoff if you like, but try it and you'll scarf down the *ringo no reisei supu* (cold apple soup topped with crusted baked apple skins). The totally organic "miracle" apples that farmer Kimura raises and the dishes chef Yamazaki prepares keep attracting customers. In addition to apple dishes, the restaurant offers *prix-fixe* menus that always include carefully chosen ingredients that are elegantly presented. There is also a café run by the same management next door. [$] *Average main: ¥5250* ✉ *41 Oyakata Machi, Hirosaki* ☎ *0172/38–5515* 🕒 *Closed Mon.* ✍ *Reservations essential.*

$$$$ JAPANESE 🍴 **Yamauta** (山唄). Performances of traditional shamisen music, often with wailing vocals, accompany your meal here. Live shows start around 7 and 9. The restaurant serves a *teishoku* set menu and three prix-fixe menus of regional foods that usually include seaweed, grilled fish, and herring cooked with soy sauce. **TIP→ Reservations are only needed during cherry-blossom season or Neputa Matsuri.** [$] *Average main: ¥4000* ✉ *1–2–4 Omachi, Hirosaki* ☎ *0172/36–1835* 🌐 *www.en-aomori.com/food-039.html* 💳 *No credit cards* 🕒 *Closed Mon. No lunch.*

WHERE TO STAY

$$$ HOTEL 🏨 **Hotel Naqua City Hirosaki** (ホテルナクアシティ弘前). One of the most pleasant lodgings in Hirosaki, the Hotel Naqua City Hirosaki is next to the JR Hirosaki Station. **Pros:** well situated; tasty meals. **Cons:** a bit impersonal; hot water can be unreliable. [$] *Rooms from: ¥20520* ✉ *1–1–2 Omachi* ☎ *0172/37–0700* 🌐 *www.naquacity-hirosaki.com/english/index.html* 🛏 *134 rooms* 🍽 *No meals.*

$$ HOTEL 🏨 **Hotel New Castle** (ホテルニューキャッスル). The biggest advantage to this hotel is its location, a block and a half from Hirosaki Castle. **Pros:** close to the castle; free Wi-Fi. **Cons:** rooms are dated; sparse decor; some walk from JR Hirosaki Station. [$] *Rooms from: ¥13068* ✉ *24–1 Kamisayashi Machi, Hirosaki* ☎ *0172/36–1211* 🛏 *46 Western-style rooms, 3 Japanese-style rooms* 🍽 *No meals.*

Hirosaki-jo is surrounded by cherry blossoms each spring.

AOMORI 青森

37 km (23 miles) northeast of Hirosaki.

Throughout the year you can enjoy delicious seafood from Aomori Bay, including *Oma no Maguro* (tuna of Oma), as well as delicious fruits and vegetables (particularly garlic). And every summer, from August 2 to 7, the town cuts loose during the decidedly wild Nebuta Matsuri festival, a frenzied, utterly unaccountable period when normal gets thrown to the wind. People come to see illuminated floats of gigantic samurai figures paraded through the streets at night. Aomori's festival, one of Japan's largest, is said to celebrate the euphoria of post-battle victory, and is thus noisier and livelier than you may have been exposed to in other Japanese festivals. Dancers, called *heneto,* run alongside the floats, dancing and hopping crazily, and you're encouraged to join in—all you need is to buy or rent a *yukata.*

GETTING HERE AND AROUND

Despite the long winters, Aomori may return to its busier heyday since the Hayabusa Shikansen now terminates at JR Shin-Aomori Station, making the journey from Tokyo and elsewhere on Honshu an easier task. The Hayabusa Shikansen runs more or less hourly from Tokyo (three hours; ¥17,150). By JR local train it's 45 minutes (¥670) from Hirosaki.

Aomori Airport has six daily flights from Tokyo's Haneda Airport by JAL. Aomori also has three JAL flights from Osaka's Itami Airport, and two from Sapporo's Chitose Airport.

The JR highway express bus departing from Tokyo at 10:30 pm arrives at Aomori at 8:05 am (¥7,500–¥10,500 one-way).

Contact **Aomori Airport** (青森空港). ✉ *1–5 Kotani, Aomori* ☎ *017/739–2121* ⊕ *www.aomori-airport.co.jp/en.*

VISITOR INFORMATION

The Aomori City Tourist Information Center is on the south end of Aomori Station, offering English maps and brochures for the city and prefecture.

Contact **Aomori City Tourist Information Center** (青森市観光交流情報セン ター). ✉ *JR Aomori Station, 1-1-25 Shinmachi, Aomori* ☎ *017/723-4670* ⊕ *www.jnto.go.jp/eng/location/spot/tic/aomori_city.html.*

EXPLORING

Aomori Kenritsu Bijutsukan (青森県立美術館 *Aomori Museum of Art*). This contemporary arts museum houses a collection of works by Munakata Shiko (1903–75), Nara Yoshitomo (1959–), and Terayama Shuji (1935–83). Another highlight is three of Marc Chagall's backdrops created for the ballet *Aleko* (the fourth belongs to the Philadelphia Museum of Art). Unlike many museums in which gift shops are near the entrance and packed with people, the gift shop here sits quietly in a corner upstairs, seemingly asking visitors to enjoy art first before shopping. Outside, a statue of Aomori-ken (*ken* sounds like both prefecture and dog) waits in front of his food dish. ✉ *185 Chikano, Aomori* ☎ *017/783–3000* ⊕ *www.aomori-museum.jp/en* 🎟 *¥510* ⊙ *July–mid-Sept., daily 9–6; Mar.–June, daily 9:30–5; closed mid-Sept.–Feb. and 2nd and 4th Mon.*

FAMILY **Auga** (アウガ). Fish, shellfish, preserved seaweed, and fish eggs—in short, all manner of marine organisms—are hawked by hundreds of vendors in this seafood market. It's one block east of JR Aomori Station, in the basement level of a modern building with distinctive crimson pillars. ✉ *1–3–7 Shinmachi Dori, Aomori* ☎ *017/721-8000* ⊙ *Daily 5 am–6:30 pm; closed one Wed. a month (call to check).*

FAMILY **Sannai Maruyama Iseki** (三内丸山遺跡 *Sannai Maruyama Archaeological Site*). Want to know what it was like to live in this area 5,500 years ago? This, one of the country's largest archaeological sites, features a reconstruction of a Jomon settlement that lasted for roughly 1,500 years, from 3500 BC to 2000 BC. After an extensive excavation, it was opened to the public and has attracted crowds of children on school outings, people wanting to trace their roots, and, of course, archaeology buffs. Its interactive approach encourages visitors to try crafts making and cuisine. ✉ *305 Murayama, Sannai, Aomori* ☎ *017/782–9462* ⊕ *sannaimaruyama.pref.aomori.jp/english/* 🎟 *Free* ⊙ *June–Sept., daily 9–6; Oct.–Mar., daily 9–5* ☞ *Free English tours: call 017/766–8282 in advance.*

OFF THE BEATEN PATH

Sukayu Onsen (酸ヶ湯温泉 *Sukayu Hot Spring*). Milky, highly acidic water floods into the large cedar bathhouse known as a *sennin-buro,* a 1,000-person bath. Designated as a national health resort, Sukayu draws many *toji* travelers to its curative waters. It has a reputation for the best mixed-bathing in the nation—yes, men and women wearing nothing but towels. If you are a woman who prefers otherwise, take advantage of the hours that are reserved for women; men, you'll just have to deal with female onlookers. The trip is one hour from Oirase

Gorge and 70 minutes from Aomori. From JR Aomori Station, take the bus bound for Towada-ko. From Oirase Gorge, take the bus bound for JR Aomori Station and get off at the Sukayu Onsen stop. ✉ *Sukayu-zawa 50, Minamiarakawayama Kokuyurin, Arakawa* ☎ *017/738–6400* 🎫 *¥600* ⏰ *Daily 7–6; women-only 8–9 am and 8–9 pm.*

WHERE TO EAT

$$$$
SEAFOOD
✕ **Hide-zushi** (秀寿司). You're in a major seafood city, and if you want some of the best of what is available in these cold waters, this is the place to get it. Excellent service and bright surroundings, not to mention sea urchin, salmon roe, scallops, squid, tuna, and ark shell (a variety of clam) await your whetted appetite. $ *Average main: ¥4000* ✉ *1–5-12 Tsutsumi Machi, Aomori* ☎ *017/722–8888.*

$$$
SEAFOOD
✕ **Ippa-zushi** (一八寿司). What was once an early-20th-century warehouse is now a modern sushi restaurant. The fish here is fresh, and the price is right, with a price list clearly hung in the wall. The casual atmosphere makes it popular among business travelers. The fish served varies according to the season and availability, but tuna almost always appears. $ *Average main: ¥3000* ✉ *1–10–11 Shinmachi, Aomori* ☎ *017/722–2639* ⏰ *Closed 2nd and 4th Sun. of month.*

$$$
JAPANESE
✕ **Mitsu-ishi** (酒肴旬 三ッ石). Crowded with locals, Mitsu-ishi has a convivial atmosphere and dishes that appeal to everyone. Sashimi *moriawase* (assorted sashimi; from ¥820 for a one-person portion) is an excellent choice. Grilled scallops and grilled chicken with herbs are also tasty and popular. The *mitsu-ishi gozen* (¥2,055) and *hime kaiseki* (¥3,085) set menus include sashimi, tempura, grilled fish, vegetables, rice, soup, and fruit. There's an abundant sake list, too. If you're in the mood for drinks and some finger food, take a seat at the bar, where the chef sometimes hands out complimentary snacks over the counter. Look for the mood-lit white building with boxy dark roof. $ *Average main: ¥3000* ✉ *2–7-33 Yasukata, Aomori* ☎ *017/735–3314* ⏰ *Closed Sun.*

$$$
JAPANESE
✕ **Nishimura** (西むら). It would be hard to walk out of this Japanese restaurant hungry: The *danna-shu* course (¥3,240), for example, includes abalone and sea-urchin soup, seaweed and fish, a mixed hot pot, and fried eggplant. On sunny days you should come for lunch. Both the great-value *teishoku* set menus and splendid bay views from the 10th floor of the lofty ASPAM building are all yours. $ *Average main: ¥2800* ✉ *ASPAM 10F, 1–1–40 Yasukata, Aomori* ☎ *017/734–5353* ⊕ *www.en-aomori.com/shopping-001.html.*

WHERE TO STAY

$$
HOTEL
🏨 **Hotel JAL City Aomori** (ホテルジャルシテイ青森). This nine-story art deco–style hotel curves around the corner as if it belonged in 1960s Miami Beach. **Pros:** good location; comfortable rooms; free Internet. **Cons:** chain-hotel service; perhaps a bit too glitzy for some tastes. $ *Rooms from: ¥15000* ✉ *2–4–12 Yasukata, Aomori* ☎ *017/732–2580* ⊕ *www.jalhotels.com/domestic/tohoku/aomori/* 🛏 *167 rooms* 🍴 *No meals.*

$$
HOTEL
🏨 **Richmond Hotel Aomori** (リッチモンドホテル青森). A near-it-all location and comfortably furnished rooms make this moderately priced hotel a good choice in Aomori. **Pros:** great rates; comfortable rooms;

free Wi-fi Internet access. **Cons:** a long walk from JR Aomori Station; service in the restaurant can be slow. $ *Rooms from: ¥14000* ✉ *1–6–6 Nagashima, Aomori* ☎ *017/732–7655* 🌐 *aomori.richmondhotel.jp/* 🛏 *177 rooms* 🍴 *Breakfast.*

TOHOKU WEST COAST

AKITA 秋田

186 km (116 miles) southwest of Aomori City, 148 km (92 miles) southwest of Hirosaki.

In the scenic, faraway realm of Akita, the peaks of the Dewa Sanchi (Dewa Range), marked by Mt. Taihei, march off to the east, and the Sea of Japan lies at the edge of the fertile plains that extend to the west. The region's history began in the year 733, during the turbulent Nara period, with the establishment of Dewa-no-saku, a fortress built on a hill in Takashimizu by the powerful Yamato clan. The area, set up to guard trade routes, soon gained strategic importance, and during the Heian era, soldiers and their families began spreading outward. The Ando and Satake families each built major bastions in the Yuwa and Kawabe districts after the Battle of Sekigahara in 1600. These municipalities, now merged, are considered to be the foundations of modern Akita City. Today the prefectural capital (population 324,000) is a lively, likable city full of delicious food from the mountains, plain, rivers, and sea.

The countryside is devoted to producing what locals feel is the best rice in Japan, and they certainly do make good sake with it. Additionally, the fruits and vegetables grown here are unbelievably cheap and flavorful. The combination of climate, pure water, and healthful food are said to make the women of Akita the fairest in the land—a matter of prefectural, even national, pride. In the Japanese media, "scientific" studies have been trotted out since the 19th century as proof of the Akita *bijin* (Akita beauty) phenomenon.

GETTING HERE AND AROUND

ANA and JAL fly to Akita Airport four to five times daily from Tokyo's Haneda Airport (65 minutes; ¥27,890). JAL also flies twice daily from Osaka's Itami Airport and three times from Sapporo's Shin-Chitose Airport. ANA flies twice daily from Nagoya's Chubu International Airport.

If you're traveling regionally by rail, the Komachi Shinkansen from Tazawa-ko (one hour; ¥3,360); Tsugaru private line from Aomori City (two hours, 40 minutes; ¥5,600); or the Tsugaru private line from Hirosaki (two hours; ¥4,450) are the most convenient trains. From Tokyo the JR Komachi Shinkansen will spirit you off to Akita in four hours (¥17,800).

By bus, the JR Express bus Dream-Akita departs daily from JR Tokyo Station at 9:50 pm, arriving in JR Akita Station at 6:35 am (¥9,800), while the Willer Express leaves JR Tokyo Station at 10:30 pm, arriving at JR Akita Station at 8:10 am (¥5,500–¥6,400).

Airport Contact

Akita Airport (秋田空港 *Akita Kuko*). ⌧ *Aza Yamakago, Tsubakigawa, Yuwa* ☎ *018/886–3366* ⊕ *www.akita-airport.com/en.*

VISITOR INFORMATION

The Akita City Tourist Information Center is on the second floor at the station, just across from the exit from the Shinkansen tracks, and supplies many colorful English-language pamphlets and lots of friendly advice.

Contact Akita City Tourist Information Center (秋田市観光案内所 *Akita-shi Kanko Annaisho*). ⌧ *JR Akita Station 2F, 7–1–2 Naka Dori* ☎ *018/832–7941* ⊕ *www.jnto.go.jp/eng/location/spot/tic/akita_city.html.*

EXPLORING

Akita City Folklore and Performing Arts Center (民俗芸能伝承館 *Neburi Nagashikan*). If you are not in town for Akita's famous Kanto Festival, this museum is the next best thing. Try balancing one of the poles topped with paper lanterns on your palm—it's more difficult than it looks! There is also an informative video about this and other Akita festivals. Your ticket also includes entry to the former residence and kimono fabric shop of the Kaneko family, along a corridor beside the entrance. Don't miss the bats carved above the sliding doors. ⌧ *Oomachi 1–3–30, Akita City* ☎ *018/866–7091* 🎫 *¥100* ⊙ *Daily 9:30–4:30.*

Akita Museum of Art (秋田県立美術館 *Akita Kenritsu Bijutsukan*). One of the best reasons to visit this new museum is the building, designed by renowned architect Tadao Ando. Sitting in the café, you gaze across a serene pond to the castle moat and park, oblivious of the intervening road. The museum's other highlight is the enormous *Annual Events in Akita,* painted by local artist Fujita Tsuguharu (1886–1968) in just 15 days. The painting of three local festivals merged into a single scene was rendered on one of the world's largest canvases at the time, measuring 11 feet by 66 feet. The museum also hosts temporary exhibitions relating to Akita life and art. From the northwest corner of JR Akita Station, head west on Akita Chuo Dori. After four blocks the museum will be on your left, just before the Castle Hotel. ⌧ *1–4–2 Naka Dori* ☎ *018/853–8686* ⊕ *www.akita-museum-of-art.jp* 🎫 *Varies depending on exhibition* ⊙ *Daily 10–6.*

OFF THE BEATEN PATH

Shirakami Sanchi (白神山地 *Shirakami Mountains*). South of Mt. Iwaki are the Shirakami Mountains, a UNESCO World Heritage Site that is home to the world's largest virgin beech forest. The area is truly pristine and great for hiking. If you don't have a car, take the Konan bus from JR Hirosaki Station bound for Tsugaru Touge, getting off at Aqua Green Village, Anmon (90 minutes). If you want to see the Mother Tree—the forest's largest, and presumably oldest tree—get off at the last stop, Tsugaru Toge (2 hours, 10 minutes); the tree is a five-minute walk from there. Only a few buses run daily, so check the schedule in advance, and note that the road beyond Aqua Green Village only opens around July each year. ⌧ *61–1 Kanda Tashiro, Nishimeya-mura, Nakatsugarugun* ☎ *0172/85–2810 Shirakami Visitor Center* ⊕ *www.jnto.go.jp/eng/indepth/scenic/worldheritage/c_2_shirakami.html.*

WHERE TO EAT

Kawabata Dori is where people come in the evening to sample the regional hot-pot dishes, *shottsuru-nabe* (a salty fermented sandfish stew) and *kiritanpo-nabe* (a chicken stew), drink *ji-zake* (locally brewed sake), and to enjoy the lively bars. It's six blocks west of the Atorion Building, across the Asahi River and slightly south.

BIG BAMBOO

Akita's **Kanto Festival** (August 3–6) celebrates ancient fertility rites with young men balancing 36-foot-long bamboo poles (*kanto*) hung with as many as 46 lighted paper lanterns on its eight crossbars—and weighing up to 110 pounds—against a special pouched strap on their waist, hip, back, or shoulder. The lanterns represent sacks full of rice, and a bountiful harvest is fervently prayed for and celebrated in anticipation of its arrival.

$$$$ ✕ **Akita Kawabata Isariya Sakaba**
JAPANESE (秋田川反漁屋酒場). This restau-
FAMILY rant lives up to its promise of "All
Fodor's Choice of Akita in one building." Deli-
★ cious, unique regional dishes, such as the highly recommended pickle selection topped with a tiny paper scarecrow, are served on antique dishes by friendly staff. But the highlight of the evening is the arrival of a *namahage*, or monster from Akita's mountains—despite his fearsome appearance, he will happily pose for photographs! On Saturday, there is also a live performance of local folk songs. Look for the *namahage* statue outside the entrance. ⓢ *Average main: ¥4000* ⊠ *4-2-35 Omachi, Akita* ☎ *018/865-8888* ⏱ *No lunch.*

$$$$ ✕ **Inaniwa Kaiseki Omachi Sato Yosuke** (稲庭懐石大町佐藤養助). Cham-
JAPANESE pagne can't go by that name if it's produced outside a specific region, and noodles can only be called Inaniwa Udon if they are produced exclusively in Inaniwa. Established in 1860, this noodle empire has many branches across the Tohoku region, but this one is for connoisseurs who want to sample regional foods and locally brewed sake. A casual, nine-course set meal (¥3,240 to ¥5,400) comes with the signature hand-kneaded Inaniwa noodles, which have a firm texture, and fresh fruit for dessert. Make big slurps and enjoy. ⓢ *Average main: ¥4320* ⊠ *Ishidate Bldg. 2F, 5-2-13 Omachi* ☎ *018/862-3777* ⏱ *Closed Sun.* ⌕ *Reservations essential.*

WHERE TO STAY

$$$ 🏨 **Akita Castle Hotel** (秋田キャッスルホテル). Akita Castle Hotel under-
HOTEL went massive renovation in 2012, and now the bright and airy rooms overlooking the moats of Senshu Park are even more comfortable. **Pros:** good location for sightseeing; nice ambience; good views. **Cons:** a bit far from the station; impersonal feel. ⓢ *Rooms from: ¥20000* ⊠ *1-3-5 Naka Dori* ☎ *018/834-1141* ⊕ *www.castle-hotel.co.jp* ⇗ *150 rooms* ⦿ *No meals.*

$$$ 🏨 **Akita View Hotel** (秋田ビューホテル). The largest hotel in town, the
HOTEL Akita View sits beside the Seibu Department Store. **Pros:** exciting location; good value; delicious, local breakfast. **Cons:** double rooms on the small side. ⓢ *Rooms from: ¥19000* ⊠ *2-6-1 Naka Dori* ☎ *018/832-1111* ⊕ *www.viewhotels.co.jp/akita* ⇗ *192 rooms* ⦿ *No meals.*

13

$$$$ HOTEL **Hotel Metropolitan Akita** (メトロポリタンホテル秋田). Adjacent to the JR Akita Station and ALS shopping mall, this hotel's location makes it a perfect choice for shopping and exploring the sights. **Pros:** sleek and modern setting; discount for rail pass holders; elegant lounge. **Cons:** breakfast room cramped; rooms a little impersonal in style. $ *Rooms from: ¥23000* ✉ *7–2–1 Naka Dori* ☎ *018/831–2222* 🌐 *www.jrhotelgroup.com/eng/hotel/eng104.htm* *115 rooms* 🍴 *No meals.*

TSURUOKA AND DEWA-SANZAN 鶴岡と出羽三山

132 km (82 miles) south of Akita.

South of Akita along the Nihon-kai coast are small fishing villages where nets hang to dry only inches from train windows, vast plains of rice fields lead to faraway hills, rushing rivers and clear streams are full of fish, and, closer to Atsumi Onsen, you will be confronted with lofty forested mountains coming down to the endless crashing waves. Along the way is the town of Tsuruoka, once a castle stronghold of the Sakai family, which serves as a gateway to Yamagata City and the three mountains of Dewa Sanzan that are held sacred by members of the nature-loving Shugendo sect of "mountain warrior" Buddhists

GETTING HERE AND AROUND

If you are considering visiting Tsuruoka from Tokyo, the most inexpensive way is by overnight highway bus. Buses leave from various major Tokyo stations between 10 pm and midnight, and arrive in Tsuruoka in the early morning (from ¥4,000). Tsuruoka is 2½ hours south of Akita by JR Uetsu Line (¥2,270). It's easiest to get to the base of Haguro by bus (35 minutes), either from Bus Stop 2, in front of JR Tsuruoka Station, or from Stop 3, at Sho-Ko (Sho-nai Ko-tsu) Mall (it's not a JR bus); there are four departures in winter and at least hourly departures in summer. A fare of ¥820 will take you from the station to the Haguro Center village at the entrance to the peak itself. Most buses from Tsuruoka to Haguro Center continue to the summit, Haguro-sancho, which is not much farther, but the fare jumps to ¥1,180.

VISITOR INFORMATION

The Tsuruoka Tourist Information Office is just to the right from the station exit. They speak some English, though most pamphlets about Dewa-Sanzan are in Japanese, but they can help with bus schedules and lodging arrangements.

Contact Tsuruoka Tourist Information Office (鶴岡市観光案内所 *Tsuruoka-shi Kanko Annaisho*). ✉ *1–1 Suehiro Machi, Tsuruoka* ☎ *0235/25–7678* 🌐 *tsuruokakanko.com/english.*

EXPLORING

Of the three holy mountains of Dewa-Sanzan, only Haguro-san has year-round access, but you can reach the others during the summer months. In summer only, Shonai Kotsu buses also depart from Yamagata Bus Terminal, with stops at all three sacred mountains. Note that many of the bus companies conducting the trips to the mountains and towns in this area are not affiliated with JR, but they are generally not expensive.

Gas-san (月山 *Moon Mountain*). Buses leave JR Tsuruoka Station at 6 and 7 am in summer for the 90-minute trip (¥2,060) to the Gas-san Hachigo-me stop; the 10:40 and 12:55 buses also have direct connections from Haguro-san. From there you can hike three hours past the glaciers and wildflowers to the 6,500-foot summit of Gas-san, or Moon Mountain—the highest of the three mountains of Dewa district. From the top you can see the whole gorgeous gallery of mountains that is Yamagata, including one called Dewa Fuji (after Mt. Fuji) for its perfect shape. There is even a temple at the top should the spirit take you. ✉ *Mount Gassan, Haguromachi Kawadai, Tsuruoka* ⊕ *www.jnto.go.jp/ eng/location/spot/natuscen/mtgassan.html.*

Haguro-san (羽黒山). The climb up Mt. Haguro begins in Haguro Center, at the red **Zaishin Gate** (Zaishin-mon), then goes up 2,446 or so stone steps to the summit. The strenuous ascent cuts through ancient cedar trees that rise to dominate the sky. You'll pass a 14th-century pagoda sitting alone in the forest. A tea shop, open from April through November, is at a perfect stop to take in the view. The trail is just over 1.7 km (about 1 mile) in all, and it may take you an hour to reach the 1,400-foot summit with its thatch-roof shrine, **Dewa-Sanzan Jinja.** You may happen upon one of the mysterious ceremonies held there—the initiation ritual of a yama-bushi (a "mountain warrior" who seeks power from ascetic practices and close bonds to nature) lasts nine grueling days, and it is said that if an apprentice wants to complete his training he must first prove that he can engage and destroy an imaginary demon. Up to 12 buses a day make the 35-minute trip to Haguro Center from JR Tsuroka Station, many going to the summit for an extra cost (in July and August there are early-morning buses on weekdays). It is possible to stay overnight on the mountain at the temple-lodge of Sai-kan, which is attached by a long stairway to the Dewa-Sanzan Jinja. ✉ *Mount Haguro, Haguromachi Touge, Tsuruoka* ☎ *023/562–2355* ⊕ *www.jnto. go.jp/eng/location/spot/natuscen/mt-haguro.html.*

Yudono-san (湯殿山). One of a trio of Dewa peaks, 5,000-foot Yudono-san is generally the last on pilgrims' rounds. You can descend on foot in a few hours from Gas-san, but it involves interpreting signs in Japanese, a bit of exertion, and slippery metal ladders, and you'll want to check with the tourist information folks about current conditions. Buses make the 80-minute (¥1,820) run between Tsuruoka and Senin-Zawa, a trailhead for a short climb to the summit, where you must make a small monetary donation and be purified in a secret ritual that you are forbidden to photograph or tell anyone about. Once cleansed, don't miss the last bus back down to Tsuruoka, which leaves promptly at 4:30 pm. ✉ *Mount Yudono, Tamugimata, Tsuruoka* ⊕ *www.jnto. go.jp/eng/location/spot/natuscen/mtyudono.html.*

WHERE TO EAT AND STAY

If you are staying overnight in Tsuruoka, you can stay in town or up on Haguro-san itself.

$$$$ ✕ **Al-ché-cciano** (アルケチャーノ). Acclaimed executive chef and owner
ITALIAN Okuda Masayuki prepares Italian dishes that are totally original and unique. His style of Italian comes with a commitment to the freshest

This five-story wooden pagoda that can be found on Mt. Haguro was built without a single nail.

ingredients, including the produce, fish, and meat. The menu varies, but everything is reliably great. The aim here is to bring out all natural flavors and aromas of Shonai foods by using few condiments, to create a perfectly combined dish where delicate flavors are more important than heavy sauces or big portions. In winter, try risotto with turnips, truffles, and cod *milt* (sperm). A well-chosen wine list includes Italian and Japanese varietals. [$] *Average main: ¥5940* ✉ *83 Ichirizuka, Shimoyama-zoe, Tsuruoka* ✣ *20 mins by taxi or bus from JR Tsuruoka Station* ☎ *0235/78–7230* ⏲ *Closed Mon.* ✍ *Reservations essential.*

$$ B&B/INN 🏨 **Dewa Sanzan Jinja Saikan Shrine Lodge** (出羽三山神社 斉館). Really feel like roughing it? This lodge connected to Dewa-Sanzan Jinja by a long stairway allows you to enjoy the shrine and scenery at the summit after most tourists have gone home. **Pros:** healthful food; tranquil garden; easy mountain access. **Cons:** uphill walk from bus stop; all the luxuries of a monk; no privacy at night. [$] *Rooms from: ¥15120* ✉ *Haguro-machi Toge, 7 Aza-Temukai, Haguro-cho, Tsuruoka* ☎ *0235/62–2357* 🌐 *www.dewasanzan.jp* 🛏 *200 futons* 🍴 *Some meals.*

$ HOTEL 🏨 **Route Inn Tsuruoka Ekimae** (ルートイン鶴岡駅前). This hotel's location makes it a good base for visiting Dewa Sanzan or exploring other cities in Yamagata Prefecture. **Pros:** a 30-second walk from the station; complimentary breakfast; free Wi-Fi and cable Internet. **Cons:** surroundings are a bit austere; rooms boxy. [$] *Rooms from: ¥11100* ✉ *1–17 Suehiro Machi, Tsuruoka* ☎ *0235/28–2055* 🌐 *www.route-inn.co.jp/en/pref/yamagata.html* 🛏 *152 rooms* 🍴 *Breakfast.*

HOKKAIDO

WELCOME TO HOKKAIDO

TOP REASONS TO GO

★ **The beer:** Hokkaido has the Sapporo Beer brewery and local microbreweries in Otaru and Hakodate.

★ **The slopes:** Deep powder and uncrowded lift lines are hallmarks of Hokkaido's ski resorts at Niseko, Rusutsu, and Furano.

★ **The volcanoes:** Sulfur-spewing springs at Noboribetsu, Toya, Akan, and Shiretoko volcanoes burst forth into vents and craters. Check out the ash flow from the eruption of Toya's Mt. Usu.

★ **The last frontier:** Salmon-fishing bears and crested cranes, alpine flowers, and vast forests hold modern Japan at bay. Although the most convenient way to see outback Hokkaido is by car, the vistas of mountains and plains are best viewed on foot or bike.

★ **Winter wonderland:** Frigid winter nights are brightened by festivals. Out east, icebreakers cut through Arctic ice floes, and passengers spy seals and eagles.

1 Hakodate. Gateway to Hokkaido for train travelers, this bustling port and tourist city has 19th-century clapboard buildings, rattling streetcars, and the region's best public fish market.

2 Sapporo. Hokkaido's capital is modern, green, clean, and easy to navigate. At its heart is Odori Park, which hosts several popular festivals. The Susukino nightlife area is a blaze of neon and noise.

3 Otaru and Niseko.
A historic harbor town, Otaru is now popular for its gentrified canal, cafés, shops, and restaurants. Niseko has the best powder snow for skiers and snowboarders from December to April.

4 Shikotsu-Toya National Park. Soaring mountains and deep lakes offer an escape into nature two hours from Sapporo. The region includes Shikotsu, one of Japan's deepest, prettiest lakes.

GETTING ORIENTED

Hokkaido is 90 minutes north by air from Tokyo, with high (up to 7,500 feet) volcanic mountains and expansive populated and cultivated plains in between. Summers are cooler and less humid, winters colder and snowier than almost anywhere else in Japan.

14

5 Eastern Hokkaido.
The unpopulated tip of the Shiretoko Peninsula is a World Heritage Site. In the south are the Kushiro wetlands, while farther north, Ainu people at Lake Akan share their culture through song and dance.

6 Central and Northern Hokkaido. At the Daisetsu Mountains, in Hokkaido's center, cable cars lift visitors to flower-filled plateaus, and hiking trails promise panoramic views. To the far north are Rebun and Rishiri islands, friendly places with short summers, rare flowers, and creamy *uni* sea urchin.

WINTER SPORTS IN HOKKAIDO

Hokkaido is a land of wondrous winters. Ridiculous amounts of powder and great resorts delight skiers and boarders from both Japan and overseas.

(This page above) Scenic skiing at Niseko; (opposite page upper right) huge snowfalls make for great downhill skiing in Hokkaido; (opposite page bottom left) gondola lifts are numerous at Rusutsu

Hokkaido is the northernmost of Japan's four main islands. In winter, cold Siberian winds bring tons of snow for six months. For those who have to live with it, the half-year of white shroud is a curse (driving, once you've dug out your car, is slow and treacherous), but for businesses appealing to skiers and boarders it is white gold. Those used to marginal pistes in other parts of the world let out whoops of joy as they float over the deep powder. Hokkaido has a quarter of Japan's landmass, but only one-twentieth of its population. The resorts are nowhere near as crowded as on mainland Japan, and although the Hokkaido secret is out and Aussies, Chinese, and Koreans are scaling the slopes, there's more than enough powder for everybody. One of the great joys of winter sports in Japan is the special après-ski: after a long day on the slopes you can soak your aching muscles in a local *onsen* (thermal spa).

DOGSLEDDING

Although not a traditional method of transportation in Hokkaido, several dogsled races take place here during the winter months. Major events include the Japan Cup Dogsled Competition held in Wakkanai (February) and the JFSS Cup International Dogsled Race held in Sapporo (March). If you'd like to get up close and personal with man's best friend, you can give dogsledding a try at the Rusutsu resort area.

HOKKAIDO'S SKI RESORTS

More than 100 ski hills are dotted across Hokkaido. Some are small with limited facilities, and used almost exclusively by locals. Others are vast resorts that attract and cater to visitors from around the world. Hokkaido's big three are Niseko, Rusutsu, and Furano, but you can find great snow and a friendly welcome across the whole island.

FURANO

Furano, located in the center of island, is famous for its fields of purple lavender in summer, and creamy skiing in winter. Heavy snowfalls provide plenty of light powder while the local town has found a good balance between welcoming visitors and maintaining its traditional charm. Furano is about an hour from Asahikawa Airport, or three hours from Chitose Airport.

RUSUTSU

Rusutsu is a large resort stretching out over East Mountain, West Mountain, and Mount Isola. Thirty-seven courses provide everything from smooth groomed runs to steep and deep off-piste powder. Numerous gondolas, quads, and pair lifts mean you shouldn't have to wait in line. The resort also provides a whole range of other winter activities from snowshoeing to horseback riding. Rusutsu is about 90 minutes from Chitose Airport.

NISEKO

The Niseko ski area is made up of several resorts, which when combined make it arguably the best place for skiing and snowboarding in Japan. Niseko Hirafu, Niseko Higashiyama (aka Niseko Village), and Niseko Annupuri are collectively known as Niseko United and can be skied on a single pass. This gives you access to 61 official ski runs, but locals and powder hounds know many more unofficial runs that make the most of the huge snowfalls. The chairlifts at nearby Niseko Weiss closed many years ago and have been replaced by a surprisingly inexpensive snowcat service. The tracked vehicles shuttle you up the mountain and let you enjoy the powder on the way down.

Over the last decade Niseko has gone through an amazing boom, with a large increase in the number of foreign visitors. The positive side of this is that you can get by with limited or no Japanese language ability; rental equipment includes a bigger selection of large sizes; and there's a lively international scene with varied bars, accommodations, restaurants, and clientele. For those looking for a more traditional Japanese experience it is worth spending at least some time exploring the more remote corners of Hokkaido.

Updated by
Jay Farris

Hokkaido is Japan with breathing space. People here don't put on the air-conditioning in summer—they open the windows. Outside, fragrant air, wild mountains, virgin forests, pristine lakes, and surf-beaten shores are all within easy reach of cities and towns.

Hokkaido's Japanese history is, compared to the mainland, relatively short. Born during the Meiji Restoration (1868–1912), Hokkaido was developed by Japan to keep Russia from getting to it. Until then, this large northern island, comprising 20% of Japan's current landmass, had largely been left to the indigenous Ainu people, hunter-gatherers who had traded with the Japanese and Russians for centuries.

In the 1870s, after researching American and European agriculture, city design, and mining, Japan sent 63 foreign experts to harness Hokkaido's resources, introducing a soldier-farmer system to spur mainlanders north to clear and settle the land. Hokkaido was replete with coal and gold, herring shoals, and fertile soil conducive to dairy farming, potato growing, horse breeding, and even cold-climate rice planting. The legacy lives on—small holdings with silos and barns still anchor the rolling farmland, while flat landscapes with mountains on the horizon give stretches of Hokkaido a frontier flavor.

On the losing end of this colonization were the Ainu, who died by the thousands from disease, forced labor, and conflict with the Japanese. Forced assimilation and intermarriage has largely eliminated their way of life (although recent decades of activism have given the Ainu a modicum of public acceptance as Japan's only officially recognized distinct ethnic minority).

Hokkaido's people—who call themselves *Dosanko*—can be quite open-minded. Many readily come to the rescue of foreign travelers with a warmth and directness that make up for language barriers. Japanese tourists visit here for a less-traditional view of Japan, while others still settle here to seek an alternative way of life as farmers, artists, outdoor adventure guides, and guesthouse owners.

However, because Hokkaido consists more of countryside than culture-rich cities, the number of non-Japanese visitors has traditionally been small, and many locally promoted attractions—such as flower fields and dairy farms—may be of less interest to people from Western countries than the mountain scenery, wildlife, and volcanically active areas. Recently, visitors from China, Hong Kong, Taiwan, South Korea, Singapore, and Australia have started to drop by in the hundreds of thousands to enjoy the snow and escape the summer swelter.

Hokkaido remains a frontier in terms of geopolitics. In prominent places are signboards demanding the return of the southern four Kuril Islands, Japan-administered territory that the Soviet Union invaded in the final days of World War II. Japanese Self-Defense Force bases still dot the map as a Cold War–era deterrent, and travel to neighboring Russian air- and seaports is quite restricted. Nevertheless, a Russian business presence is noticeable in Hokkaido's northern and eastern fishing ports, where road signs in Wakkanai and Nemuro are in Japanese and Cyrillic; locals in Monbetsu, Abashiri, and Kushiro might first address Caucasians in Russian.

14

It's easy to romanticize Japan's Great White North as largely wild and untamed, but Hokkaido also has large cities (Sapporo's growing population is nearly 2 million, and nine other places have populations greater than 100,000), along with decent public transportation and first-world urban lifestyles. Beyond the cities, though, small-town life in Hokkaido is quiet, a tad cumbersome to explore without a car, and a bit stagnant—but for the adventurous visitor, wild beauty and open spaces abound.

The island is a geological wonderland: lava-seared mountains hide deeply carved ravines; hot springs, gushers, and steaming mud pools boil out of the ground; and crystal-clear lakes fill the seemingly bottomless cones of volcanoes. Wild, rugged coastlines hold back the sea, and all around the prefecture, islands surface offshore. Half of Hokkaido is covered in forest, home to bears, owls, hawks, cranes, foxes, and other wildlife you would have trouble finding elsewhere in Japan.

PLANNING

Hokkaido's expansiveness is daunting. The main sights—calderas, remote onsen, craggy coasts, dramatic mountains—are everywhere. Rather than rushing to see everything, consider balancing the natural with the urban, the inland with the coastal, and figure in the seasonal appropriateness of sights, activities, and available access.

WHEN TO GO

Hokkaido has Japan's most dramatic seasons. Recommended times to visit are May to September (if you are a summer person), January to March (if winter). January to March is snow, snow, snow. From late April to mid-May, Hokkaido offers Japan's last *sakura* (cherry blossoms), as well as a fireworks display of spring flowers all at once. May to September offers perfectly temperate summer weather (except for a sometimes wet July), a respite for those gasping under Asia's humidity.

However, hotel rooms can be more difficult to book in summer, and many scenic areas get crowded with tour groups and Japanese families. ■TIP→ **Avoid the middle of August, when Hokkaido celebrates Obon homecoming and travel prices spike.** Late September ushers in brief but spectacular golden foliage, peaking in early October. The periods from November to December and late March to April offer predominately chilly drizzle, so avoid these times. Winter makes travel more difficult (some minor roads and attractions are closed), but Hokkaido is no less beautiful, with snow covering everything in ever-freshened mounds of white. Early February offers the unmissable Sapporo Snow Festival.

PLANNING YOUR TIME

You'll need at least a week to experience Hokkaido, with a day or two in Sapporo and then a stay in one or two of the places recommended *below*. Distances are large, and a train or road trip across the island takes most of a day. Flying to a regional airport cuts down on unnecessary travel time. Make car and hotel reservations in advance; outside Sapporo and Hakodate, finding people who speak enough English to do bookings can be difficult. Check on access and weather for each destination when planning a winter trip, when road conditions can be unpredictable and treacherous.

GETTING HERE AND AROUND

The best way to explore Hokkaido is by train or car. Most car-rental companies allow different pickup and drop-off locations, and will meet customers at trains, ferries, and local flights. If you are staying at resort area hotels, free shuttle buses are often available.

AIR TRAVEL

Domestic carriers Japan Airlines (JAL) and All Nippon Airways (ANA), and budget carriers such as SkyMark, Jetstar, and Vanilla Air connect major Japanese airports with Sapporo (New Chitose), Asahikawa, Hakodate, Abashiri (Memanbetsu), Obihiro, and Kushiro. Flying across Hokkaido is a good way to cross the distances, particularly the far-flung eastern and northern regions. In winter, sudden changes in weather can divert or cancel flights, so plan adequate time for connections.

JAL and ANA link Hokkaido to Honshu by direct flights from Tokyo's Haneda Airport to Hakodate, Sapporo (New Chitose Airport), Asahikawa Airport, Abashiri (Memanbetsu Airport), Nemuro (Nakashibetsu Airport), and Kushiro Airport. Several direct flights a day depart from Tokyo's Narita International Airport (with many of the low-cost carriers serving Narita's no-frills Terminal 3). Other major cities on Honshu have flights to Sapporo, as do several places in the Asia and Pacific region. The cost by air from Tokyo to Sapporo can be as low as ¥10,000 compared with ¥22,430 by train. Fly-stay packages from Tokyo (subsidized by the Hokkaido government) offering excellent deals for short trips are recommended. Some air travelers arriving in Japan on European flights can, with a change of planes at Tokyo, fly at no extra charge to Sapporo. If you're flying from overseas to Sapporo via Tokyo, book the domestic portion when you buy your international ticket; otherwise, you will fork out for what is, per mile, one of the most expensive domestic tickets in the world.

Airline Information All Nippon Airways (全日空). ☎ *0570/029–709* ⊕ *www. ana.co.jp*. **Japan Airlines** (日本航空). ☎ *03/6733–3062* ⊕ *www.jal.co.jp/en*. **Skymark Airlines** (スカイマーク). ☎ *050/3786–0283* ⊕ *www.skymark.co.jp/ en*. **Vanilla Air** (バニラエア). ☎ *0570/66–6603 toll number available daily 10–6 (except public holidays)* ⊕ *www.vanilla-air.com/en/*.

BOAT AND FERRY TRAVEL

Ferries from Honshu connecting to Tomakomai, Hakodate, and Otaru offer a leisurely way to arrive, while in Hokkaido boats connect the islands of Rebun and Rishiri to the northern tip of Japan. In eastern Hokkaido, ferries offer the best bear-viewing off the Shiretoko Peninsula.

The ferries are the cheapest way to travel to Hokkaido on paper, but for roughly the same price you can fly there within two hours from the mainland. Of course, a night on the ferry does save you money on a hotel. If slow travel is your style, there are ferries from Niigata, Akita, Maizuru, and Tsuruga into Otaru, and services on the Pacific side (Nagoya, Oarai, Sendai, Hachinohe, and Aomori) connect to Hakodate or Tomakomai. Other routes include Shin Nihon-kai Ferry's Niigata to Otaru (18 hours starting at ¥6,480); Taiheiyo Ferry's Sendai to Tomakomai (14-hour service starting at ¥8,300); Shosen Mitsui's Oarai to Tomakomai (18 hours from ¥8,740); Taiheiyo Ferry's mammoth nearly 40-hour Nagoya-Sendai-Tomakomai (¥10,800); Kawasaki Kinkai Kisen's Hachinohe to Tomakomai (8 hours; ¥5,000); and Seikan Ferry's service that crosses between Aomori and Hakodate (4 hours; ¥1,690). Aside from winter, the Sea of Japan tends to be calmer than the Pacific. However, if you're worried about getting seasick, perhaps a plane or a train is a better option.

First-class is usually double the second-class price, but the extra buys you privacy and comfort, as most regular passengers stretch out on communal carpeted areas with no beds. Outside the summer holiday season, the ferries are mostly used by long-distance truck drivers and the occasional budget backpacker, cyclist, or motorcyclist.

The most budget-conscious, if you don't mind a roughly 24-hour journey, can book Shosen Mitsui's Pacific Story package. This is a bus/ferry/bus service which connects Tokyo to Sapporo for only ¥9,990, departing Tokyo mid-afternoon and reaching Sapporo the following afternoon. Reserve tickets at the Tokyo Yaesu Exit or Shinjuku Station JR Highway bus terminals.

Boat and Ferry Contacts Kawasaki Kinkai Kisen Ferry (川崎近海汽船). ☎ *03/3502–4838* ⊕ *www.silverferry.jp*. **Seikan Ferry** (青函フェリー). ☎ *017/782–3671 Aomori, 0138/42–5561 Hakodate* ⊕ *www.seikan-ferry.co.jp*. **Shin Nihon-kai Ferry** (新日本海フェリー). ☎ *06/6345–2921* ⊕ *www.snf.jp*. **Shosen Mitsui Ferry** (商船三井フェリー さんふらわあ). ☎ *0144/34–3121 Tomakomai Reservation Center, 029/267–4133 Oarai Reservation Center, 0120/489-850 free dial (domestic)* ⊕ *www.sunflower.co.jp/english/*. **Taiheiyo Ferry** (太平洋フェリー). ☎ *03/3564–4161 Tokyo, 011/281–3311 Sapporo* ⊕ *www.taiheiyo-ferry.co.jp/english*.

BUS TRAVEL

Buses cover most of the major routes through the scenic areas. There is, however, no English-language telephone service for buses in Hokkaido, so we suggest you find an interlocutor. The Sapporo International Communication Plaza opposite the clock tower will supply bus-route and schedule information and make telephone bookings if required. Alternatively, you can show up at a bus terminal and make arrangements in person.

CAR TRAVEL

Driving in Hokkaido is made easy, despite mountain bends and snow, by wide roads and English-language signage that helps guide you to wilder places. Toll highways at this writing link Sapporo only with Otaru, Asahikawa, Rumoi, and Obihiro, but nearly complete (and recently cheapened) stretches can take you close to Hakodate and Abashiri. Otherwise, two-lane roads are the norm, and untimed stoplights can slow travel.

Most major auto-rental companies have offices at Sapporo's New Chitose Airport, in major cities, and in smaller tourist areas. However, we recommend you make automotive plans around JR Sapporo Station. JR Hokkaido arranges very good value travel packages, but service is available in English only at major stations such as Sapporo and Hakodate. Car rentals, depending on the season, can cost as little as ¥6,000 per day, but budget at least ¥10,000; reservations are best made through the ToCoo website for Mazda, Nissan, Toyota, MMC, and J-Net. August is peak holiday driving season, so book early. Don't forget to request an English-language navigation system (called *car-navi*).

Japanese are cautious drivers, and Hokkaido is the best place in Japan for driving, even though wide, straight roads, treacherous winter weather conditions, and most visitors' unfamiliarity with all of the above gives Hokkaido the worst traffic fatality figures in Japan. Beware of speed traps, especially in holiday periods: in apparently rural areas a hidden village can dictate urban speed limits of 40 to 60 kph.

Rental Agencies JR Hokkaido Rent-a-Car (JR北海道レンタリース). ⊠ *1 Kita 6 Nishi 1, Kita-ku* ✢ *Just by railway overpass to east side of station across street from JR Tower Hotel* ☎ *011/742–8211* ⊕ *www.jrh-rentacar.com.* **Nippon Rent-a-Car Hokkaido.** ⊠ *Kita 6 Nishi 4, 2-13* ✢ *Go out station's north exit and turn left and it will be on your left* ☎ *011/746–0919 Sapporo Station North Exit Branch* ⊕ *www.nrh.co.jp/foreign.* **ToCoo Car Rental** (トクー!). ⊕ *www2. tocoo.jp/en.* **Toyota Rent-a-Car** (トヨタレンタリース札幌). ☎ *0123/40–0100* ⊕ *www.toyotarentacar.net/english.*

TRAIN TRAVEL

Japan Railways Hokkaido helps visitors enjoy the big country in comfort, with a three-, five-, or seven-day Hokkaido Rail Pass and good English-language information at major stations. There is also a 4-day flexible pass that can be used for a 10-day period. Although there are no Shinkasen bullet trains yet, superexpress trains connect Sapporo south to Hakodate (and on to Honshu), and north and east to Asahikawa, Kushiro, Abashiri, and Wakkanai. A three-day pass costs ¥16,500, five-day ¥22,000, seven-day ¥24,000, and the flexible pass costs ¥22,000.

Superior cars cost about ¥6,500 to ¥8,000 extra. Some JR buses are included in the pass. Train and car packages are available.

The train journey from Tokyo to Sapporo can take as little as 10 hours with good connections. This trip involves a combination of the Shinkansen train to Aomori (3 hours, 40 minutes), the northernmost point on the Tohoku Shinkansen Line, and a change to an express train for the remaining journey to Hakodate (2 hours, 20 minutes) and then on to Sapporo (3¼ hours). The JR Pass covers this route. The fancy Cassiopeia sleeper train provides greater comfort with all private rooms and eliminates the need to change trains, but the voyage takes 19 hours. The fare is ¥35,320 (¥9,500 for JR Pass holders).

Train Information **East Japan Railway Information Line.** ☎ 050/2016–1603 *information services in English, Chinese, and Korean* ⊕ *www.jreast.co.jp/e.* **JR Travel Service Center** (ツインクルプラザ南口). ⊠ *JR Sapporo Station West Exit, Kita 6 Nishi 4, Kita-ku* ☎ *011/231–9908* ⊕ *www2.jrhokkaido.co.jp/global/index.html.*

RESTAURANTS

Hokkaido's regional food includes excellent seafood, beef, lamb, corn on the cob, and potatoes. Dining out is generally much cheaper than in Tokyo and Osaka. Look for lunch and dinner *tabehodai* (all-you-can-eat) smorgasbords (called *baikingu*, from the word Viking; long story) ranging from ¥1,000 to ¥3,000. Many restaurants have picture menus or a visual display made of plastic in the window. Lead the waiter outside to the window display and point if necessary.

Outside the cities there may not be many dining choices in the evening, and many resort towns (where meals are included in hotel stays) may offer nothing but noodles and booze. Further, dinner reservations at guesthouses are required, and if you arrive without a reservation and are able to secure a room, you will generally have to eat elsewhere. Not to worry—you won't starve: There are 24-hour convenience stores (*konbini*) in any Hokkaido settlement, where you can pick up a bento box lunch, sandwiches, or just about any amenity necessary. While large hot-spring hotels often have huge buffet dinners, the smaller guesthouses excel in food that is locally caught, raised, and picked. Given the overall high quality of dining throughout Japan, you probably won't even need to leave your hotel to get a decent meal.

HOTELS

Accommodations that are easily booked in English tend to be modern, characterless hotels built for Japanese tour groups. Gorgeous lobbies and sterile, cookie-cutter rooms are the norm, although more attractive hotels are appearing as Japanese seek out lodging with more personality. Guesthouses or pensions are a cheaper and friendlier option, with welcoming owners who strive to impress guests with the catch of the day or wild vegetables on the dinner menu. Many (but not all) guesthouses have Western-style beds and regular sit-down toilets. Although booking in Japanese is the norm, simple emails via a website can work, too. Although you might not normally consider one, a youth hostel is also a decent alternative in Hokkaido, both for price and for the sense of spirit and camaraderie that you will not find in the more sterile hotels. However, some do not allow male-female couples to sleep in the same

14

room. Hostels in towns and cities are usually clean and modern, and in the national parks, although in older buildings, they can be excellent touring bases.

Outside Sapporo and Hokkaido, most hot-spring hotels (*onsen*) charge on a per-person basis and include two meals, excluding service and tax, in their rates. If you don't want meals and wish to eat convenience-store food, you can often renegotiate the price (the word in Japanese is *sudomari*). Just remember that those hot-spring hotels and guesthouses are your best bet for dinner in remote areas. Also note that with Japan's prolonged recession, some hotels may actually be cheaper than listed here. ■ TIP→ **Some onsen offer combination rooms, a Western-style room with a tatami section where you could also sleep on futon. If you're interested in trying out a Japanese-style room but still want to sleep in a Western-style bed, this is the perfect option.**

Hotel reviews have been shortened. For full information, visit Fodors.com.

WHAT IT COSTS IN YEN			
	$	**$$**	**$$$**	**$$$$**
Restaurants	under ¥1,000	¥1,000–¥2,000	¥2,001–¥3,000	over ¥3,000
Hotels	under ¥12,000	¥12,000–¥18,000	¥18,001–¥22,000	over ¥22,000

Restaurant prices are the average cost of a main course at dinner or, if dinner is not served, at lunch. Hotel prices are the lowest cost of a standard double room in high season.

BANKS AND EXCHANGE SERVICES

Outside major cities there are no foreign exchange services. Local banks in Hokkaido towns are not user-friendly for foreign visitors. Sapporo, Hakodate, Asahikawa, and Kushiro have banks with exchange counters and automatic teller machines. Banks in Sapporo are concentrated on Eki-mae Dori, the wide main street linking Sapporo Station and the Odori shopping area. Banking hours are weekdays 10 am–3 pm.

Many establishments will not take credit cards, apart from large hotels, some restaurants, and gas stations. ■ TIP→ **We recommend you get yen cash (as Japan is largely a cash-based society) from post office (yubin-kyoku 郵便局) ATMs, found in every settlement or from the increasingly abundant Seven Bank ATMs associated with 7-11s. Post offices are open until 6 pm every day and most 7-11s are open 24 hours.**

VISITOR INFORMATION

The Japan National Tourist Organization's Tourist Information Center (TIC) in Tokyo has free Hokkaido maps and brochures. It's the best place for travel information in English. In Hokkaido, pick up multilingual brochures at the Tourist Information Center found at the North Exit (*kita guchi* 北口) of JR Sapporo Station opposite Mister Donuts.

Visitor Information Hokkaido-Sapporo Food & Tourism Information Center. ✉ *1F JR Sapporo Bldg., Kita, 6 Nishi 4, Chuo-ku, Sapporo* ☎ *011/213-5088* ⊕ *www.welcome.city.sapporo.jp.*

ON THE MENU

Hokkaido is known for its seafood—the prefecture's name means "the Road to the Northern Sea." *Shakē* or *sakē* (salmon), *ika* (squid), *uni* (sea urchin), *nishin* (herring), and *kai* (shellfish) are abundant, but the real treat is the fat, sweet scallop, *kai-bashira*, collected from northernmost Wakkanai. The other great favorite is crab, which comes in three varieties: *ke-gani* (hairy crab), *taraba-gani* (king crab), and Nemuro's celebrated *hanasaki-gani* (spiny king crab)—often to be had for a reasonable price.

As for meat dishes, Hokkaido's most famous concoction, *jingisukan*, is thinly sliced mutton cooked on a dome-shape griddle. The name apparently comes from the griddle's resemblance to helmets worn by Mongolian cavalry under Genghis Khan. Vegetables—usually onions, green peppers, and cabbage—are added to the sizzling mutton, and the whole mix is dipped in a tangy brown sauce.

As for Japanese "soul food," ramen is extremely popular and inexpensive; get some *gyoza* (pot stickers) or *chahan* (fried rice) with it. Local residents favor miso ramen, which uses a less-delicate variety of fermented soybean paste than miso soup. Ramen with *shio* (salt) or *shoyu* (soy sauce) soup base is also widely available.

HAKODATE 函館

318 km (198 miles) south of Sapporo.

Facing out on two bays, Hakodate is a 19th-century port town, with clapboard buildings on sloping streets, a dockside tourist zone, streetcars, and fresh fish on every menu. In the downtown historic quarter, a mountain rises 1,100 feet above the city on the southern point of the narrow peninsula. Russians, Americans, Chinese, and Europeans have all left their mark; this was one of the first three Japanese ports the Meiji government opened up to international trade in 1859.

GETTING HERE AND AROUND

Hakodate is 3 hours south of Sapporo by express train and 2½ hours north of Aomori by JR Rapid via the Seikan Tunnel.

Streetcars cost ¥210 to ¥250, and municipal buses cost ¥210 to ¥260. The sightseeing area is hilly, so save foot power by using a one-day bus pass (¥800), a streetcar pass (¥600), or a combo pass (¥1,000), and borrow an audio walking guide (deposit ¥500) from the tourist center.

For sightseeing, hotel, and travel information in English stop at the Hakodate City Tourist Information Center inside the station building.

ESSENTIALS

Car Rental Times Car Rental (タイムズカーレンタル). ☎ 0138/27-4547 ⊕ *www.timescar-rental.com.*

Visitor Information Hakodate City Tourist Information Center (函館市観光案内所). ✉ *12–13 Wakamatsu-cho* ✛ *Located inside JR Hakodate Station.* ☎ *0138/23-5440* ⊕ *www.hakodate.travel/en.*

Hakodate

0 ——————— 1/8 mi

0 ——————— 1/8 km

Hakodate Station (JR)

Bentencho

Hakodate Harbor

Hakodate Ekimae

Waka-matsucho ❶ ❷ 279

Esan Natl. Hwy.

Omachi

Shiyakusho-mae ③

Otemachi

Hakodate City Museum of Northern Peoples

Hakodate City Museum of Literature

Meijikan

Uoichiba-dori

Suehirocho ❷ ❹

Toyo-Kawacho

British Consulate

Old Hakodate Public Hall

Motomachi ❸

Jujigai

Higashi-Kawacho

Tsugaru Kaikyo

Hakodate-Tozan Rd. ❹

Horaicho

Cable Car

▲ Mt. Hakodate

Aoyagicho

Hakodate-yama

Nijikken-zaka Rte. · *Ginza-dori* · *Kaikyo-dori* · *Seibu Loop-dori* · *Takataya-dori* · *Seibu Loop Route*

KEY
❶ Exploring sites
① Restaurants, Hotels

EXPLORING

The main sights around the foot of Mt. Hakodate can be done in a day, but the city is best appreciated with an overnight stay for the illumination in the historic area, the night views from either the mountain or the fort tower, and the fish market at dawn. City transport is easy to navigate and English information is readily available. Evening departure trains from Tokyo arrive here at dawn—perfect for fish-market breakfasts.

Asa-ichi (朝市 *Morning Market*). Bright red crabs wave giant claws from old fishing boats filled with water, squid dart furiously around restaurant tanks, and samples of dried octopus parts are piled high—it's all at Hokkaido's largest public fish market, located one block from Hakodate Station. It opens at dawn; if you can stomach it, try a fish-on-rice breakfast. Asa-ichi, which also has a fruit-and-vegetable section, stays active until mid-afternoon. ⊠ *9–19 Wakamatsu-cho.*

Harisutosu Sei Kyokai (函館ハリストス正教会 *Hakodate Russian Orthodox Church*). A green Byzantine dome and tower rise above this beautiful white Hakodate Russian Orthodox Church. The present building dates from 1916, and donations help with the upkeep of one of the city's most exotic attraction. If you're less orthodox, the Episcopal and

Catholic churches sit on either side. ⊠ *3–13 Motomachi* ☎ *0138/23–7387* ⊕ *orthodox-hakodate.jp/* ☞ *Services Sat. at 5 pm, Sun. at 10 am.*

Kanemori Akarenga (金森赤レンガ倉庫 *Kanemori Red Brick Warehouses*). On the cobbled waterfront of Motomachi, the Kanemori Red Brick Warehouses now bustle with shops, bar, and restaurants. Enjoy harbor cruises, cheer on street entertainers, or poke your head into glassblowing studios. In December there's a giant Canadian Christmas tree and nightly fireworks. The place is a 1½-km (1-mile) walk from Hakodate Station. ⊠ *14–12 Suehiro-cho* ☎ *0138/27–5530 general information* ⊕ *www.hakodate-kanemori.com/en* ⊗ *Daily 9:30–7 for shops. Bars and restaurants are open later.*

Motomachi (元町 *Motomachi Historic Area*). Overlooking the western bay at the foot of Mt. Hakodate is a 2-square-km (1-square-mile) area of wide, sloping brick- and stone-paved streets lined with the 19th-century churches, stately consulates, interesting shops, and homes of the Japanese and other nationalities who first opened up this part of Japan to commerce. Return here at night when the illuminated buildings show why Hakodate is a favorite location for romantic movies and TV shows.

The most interesting historic buildings and museums are the Victorian **Old Public Hall** (Kyu Hakodate-ku Kokaido 旧函館区公会堂), with the Emperor's Toilet; the **Old British Consulate** (Kyu Igirisu Ryojikan 旧イギリス領事館), a nice place for tea and scones; and the **Hakodate City Museum of Northern Peoples** (Hakodate Hoppo Minzoku Shiryokan 函館市北方民族資料館). They can be visited with combined tickets. To visit Motomachi, get off the streetcar at the Suehiro-cho stop. ⊠ *Hakodate* ⊕ *www.hakodate.travel/en/things-to-do/top7/motomachi* ☜ *¥300 for 1 site, ¥500 for 2, ¥720 for all 3* ⊗ *Apr.–Oct., daily 9–7; Nov.–Mar., daily 9–5.*

14

NEED A BREAK?

Kitchen and Cafe Hana (キッチンあんどカフェ華). More than 100 kimono-clad dolls watch guests with their coffees, teas, and traditional desserts in the tiny, two-room café in a house near the gates of the Old Public Hall. Look for a white two-story building with a front porch. Shoes off at the door, please, but feel free to use the variety of slippers provided. Kimonos are also available for sale. ⊠ *2-21 Funami-cho* ☎ *0138/24-4700* ⊗ *Mon.–Sun. noon–9 pm.*

WHERE TO EAT

$$$

JAPANESE FUSION

✕ **Meiji Hakodate Beer Hall** (明治はこだてビヤホール). This seaside hall serves seafood such as a sashimi set or Hakodate's speciality *ika somen* (raw squid thinly sliced and resembling noodles) as well as a huge variety of other foods from pastas to salads that can keep just about anyone satisfied. There is even a deer curry. The soaring rafters are beautiful and the atmosphere is lively. Its spaciousness and conviviality are typical of Hokkaido and, although it's in a tourist complex, even locals like the wide range of seasonal specials from a menu that changes monthly. For a beer hall, however, the choice is rather limited

Hakodate's Russian Orthodox Church dates from 1916.

with only two local Hakodate beers. $ *Average main: ¥3000* ✉ *14–12 Suehiro-cho* ☎ *0138/27–1010.*

$$ ✕ **Michi-no-Ya Shokudo** (道乃家食堂). While squid is not the only thing
JAPANESE on the menu, it is fresh—your squid is pulled flapping from the tank and might return minutes later sliced, with squid-ink black rice, delicious slivers of still-twitching flesh, soup, and pickles. You might try squid stuffed with rice (flavored with curry, soy sauce, or cheese) or with potatoes and butter (how very Hokkaido!). The restaurant has plenty of other seafood, and a picture menu for easy selection. If you've never had a crab cream croquette *(kani kurimu korokke)*, this is a good place to try it. Look for a sign with red letters on a yellow background. $ *Average main: ¥2000* ✉ *Donburi Yokocho Ichiba, Asa-ichi, 9–15 Wakamatsu-cho* ✛ *It can be entered from inside market or from outside of market at its easternmost corner near main station* ☎ *0138/22–6086* ⊘ *Closed Tues..*

WHERE TO STAY

$$$$ ⊡ **Hakodate Kokusai Hotel** (函館国際ホテル *Hokkaido International*
HOTEL *Hotel).* This bustling, modern hotel occupies three buildings a short walk from the station, the Morning Market, and the Kanemori Red Brick Warehouses. **Pros:** walking distance from train station; comfortably furnished rooms. **Cons:** modern box hotel; tour group central. $ *Rooms from: ¥27000* ✉ *5–10 Otemachi* ☎ *0138/23–0591* ⊕ *www. hakodate-kokusai.jp* ↝ *299 Western-style rooms, 6 Japanese-style rooms* ⦿ *No meals.*

$ **Pension Puppy Tail** (ペンションパピィーテール). The garlands of silk
B&B/INN flowers might be a bit overwhelming, and so might be the Fukui family's
welcoming manner. **Pros:** genuine family welcome; walking distance to
station. **Cons:** in the opposite direction from the sights; some rooms
very smalland on; some rooms have high windows with no curtains.
$ *Rooms from: ¥4100 ⊠ 30–16 Wakamatsu-cho ☎ 0138/23–5858
⊕ www.p-puppytail.com ⊟ No credit cards ⤴ 6 Western-style rooms,
13 Japanese-style rooms* ⏐❍⏐ *Some meals.*

SAPPORO 札幌

318 km (197 miles) north of Hakodate.

Fodor's Choice Modern, openhearted Sapporo is a good planning base for any trip to
★ Hokkaido's wilder regions, with plenty of English-language information and transport connections. Hokkaido's capital is also worth a few
days' stay for its major snow (February), dance (June), and beer (July
and August) festivals.

With 1.9 million inhabitants, it's four times larger than Asahikawa, the
prefecture's next-largest city, but the downtown area can be crossed on
foot in 25 minutes. Centered on the 11-block-long Odori Koen (park),
an ideal people-watching place, it has wide streets and sidewalks and
bustling shopping complexes. There is limited sightseeing, but there's
enough to fill a day or two at a holiday's start or finish. Products from
all over Hokkaido can be found, and the dining-out standards are high
and relatively cheap.

GETTING HERE AND AROUND

AIR TRAVEL Although there are no direct flights from the United States to Hokkaido, cheap international connections with All Nippon Airways
(ANA) and Japan Airlines (JAL) can add domestic discounted connections to New Chitose Airport (Shin-Chitose Kuko, the most convenient to Sapporo) via Tokyo Narita or Haneda, Osaka Kansai, or
Nagoya Centrair airports. More than 30 domestic routes link New
Chitose, 40 km (25 miles) south of the city, to the rest of Japan, and
flights from other parts of Asia are increasing through New Chitose's
new international terminal.

For those without international connections, check the budget domestic
commuter airlines such as SkyMark, Vanilla, and JetStar for the least-
expensive flights from Tokyo's Haneda or Narita airports (flights in
and out of Narita tend to be cheaper) and Nagoya, Kobe, Fukuoka,
and Sendai.

Japan Railways (JR) runs every 20 minutes or so between New Chitose
Airport and downtown Sapporo. The trip into Sapporo is usually made
by rapid-transit train (¥1,070; 40 minutes). Hokuto Bus and Chuo Bus
run shuttle buses (¥1,030) that connect the airport with downtown
hotels and JR Sapporo Station, twice every hour. The trip takes about
70 minutes but can be significantly slower in winter. Train service is
recommended. ■ TIP➔ **Don't make the mistake of getting off the train
at the suburban JR Shin-Sapporo Station.**

14

CAR TRAVEL Public transportation makes renting a car for Sapporo sightseeing unnecessary, but it's a good place to rent for setting out into the southern and western national parks. All major car companies are clustered around JR Sapporo Station, so rent your car there and take the newly opened expressways heading north, south, and east.

Car Rentals Honda Rent-a-Car Sapporo Station North Exit (ホンダレンタリース札幌北口). ✉ *Kita 10 Nishi 2 1–2, Kita-ku* ☎ *011/700–5555* ⊕ *www.hondarent.com/ver1/english*. **Toyota Rent-a-Car Sapporo Station** (トヨタレンタカーリース札幌駅前店). ✉ *Sapporo Station East, Kita 6 Nishi 1, Kita-ku* ✛ *Walk out easternmost North Exit, turn right, at 2nd block turn right again and you'll see train tracks over road. Office is in tiny building between parking structure and train tracks just east of station* ☎ *011/728–0100* ⊕ *www.toyotarentacar.net/english*.

PUBLIC TRANSIT Two circular bus routes connect many of the main sites. The Factory Line—bus stops are confusingly marked "Sapporo Walk"—connects downtown shops, the train station, the fish market, the Sapporo Factory, and the Sapporo Beer Garden. The *Sansaku* or Stroller Bus (May to October only) connects downtown with Maruyama Park and Okurayama Jump Hill. Both cost ¥200 per trip or ¥750 for a day pass. Tickets are available on the buses or from Chuo Bus counter at the JR Station or bus terminal.

Most of Sapporo's subway signs include English. There are three lines: the Namboku Line, the Tozai Line, and the Toho Line. They all intersect at Odori Station. The basic fare, covering a distance of about three stations, is ¥210. A one-day pass costing ¥1,000 provides unlimited subway rides. Tickets are available at subway stations, and the machines have English instructions. The easiest way to use all the transport is with a rechargeable IC card. JR IC cards (Suica from Tokyo or Kitaca from Sapporo) or Tokyo's Pasmo will work on subways, buses, and JR trains. The Sapporo Subway Sapica card will only work on the subway. There is a deposit for the cards that varies by type, but you can get it refunded at an appropriate ticket desk.

TAXI TRAVEL Taxi meters start at ¥640 or ¥660, depending on the company. An average fare, such as from the JR Station to Susukino, runs about ¥850, but be aware the meter ticks up fast, especially after 9 pm. In winter most taxies are fitted with ski and board roof racks, and drivers are adept at stowing even the bulkiest winter gear.

VISITOR INFORMATION

Your first stop after arriving in bustling JR Sapporo Station should be the Hokkaido-Sapporo Food and Tourism Information Center, a treasure trove of free multilingual pamphlets. The helpful staff is eager to please. Sapporo International Communication Plaza is a great place for information on sightseeing in and around Sapporo. Pick up a free copy of "What's On in Sapporo" in a salon stocked with English-language books, newspapers, and brochures that's meant to encourage socializing and also has free Wi-Fi.

EXPLORING

The name *Sapporo* is derived from a combination of Ainu words meaning "a river running along a reed-filled plain." In 1870 the governor of Hokkaido visited President Grant in the United States and requested that American advisers visit Hokkaido to help design the capital on the site of an Ainu village. As a result, Sapporo was built on a grid system with wide avenues and parks. Today, the downtown area has uncluttered streets and English signs. It's distinctly lacking in pre-Meiji historic sights. Sapporo is easy to navigate. Eki-mae Dori (Station Front Street) runs south of the station, crossed east–west by Odori Koen (Big Street Park), then continues south through the shopping district to the nightlife area Susukino and beyond to Nakajima Park.

Addresses in Sapporo take advantage of a grid pattern, laid out north (*kita*), south (*minami*), east (*higashi*), and west (*nishi*). Every address has a coordinate followed by a number (for example, Kita 1 Nishi 1) to indicate a city block. So for an address of 5-29 Kita 1 Nishi 1, look for a building with a small blue metal chip on it reading 5-29 within the North 1 West 1 city block. Downtown sights are easily covered on foot in a few hours, using Odori subway station as the center point. Underground shopping malls linking the subway station with Susukino, JR Sapporo Station, and the TV Tower are bustling thoroughfares, especially in winter.

TOP ATTRACTIONS

Fodor's Choice ★ **Hokkaido Jingu** (北海道神宮 *Hokkaido Shrine*). Follow the long gravel paths under Maruyama Park's tall cypress trees until you come to the main gate of what looks like a fortress. Before entering, wash your hands and rinse your mouth at the stone basin, then climb the stone steps to Hokkaido's loveliest Shinto shrine. Hokkaido Jingu, originally built in 1871, honors the gods of land and nature, of land development, and of healing. To this day, families with babies, anxious students facing exams, and young engaged couples seek blessings under Shinto ceremonies. In May this is the city's main viewing spot for cherry blossoms, and as the year comes to a close it's coin-tossing central for those wishing for a better future. ⊠ *474 Miyagaoka, Maruyama Koen, Chuo-ku* ✛ *15-min walk from Maruyama Koen Subway Station* ⊕ *www.hokkaidojingu.or.jp* ⊠ *Free* ☉ *Apr.–Oct., daily 6–5; Nov.–Mar., daily 7–4 though times do vary by season.*

FAMILY **Hokkaido Kaitaku no Mura** (北海道開拓の村 *Hokkaido Historical Village*). Step back into 19th-century Hokkaido and see the herring-fleet dormitory, where 60 fishermen appear to have just folded up their futons and left for a day's work, or the village clinic where a Dr. Kondo seems to have vanished, leaving his scary-looking birthing table and books behind. It's easy to spend a few hours walking in and out of 60 historic homes, shops, farms, and offices brought here from all over Hokkaido. This park museum very effectively depicts how ordinary Japanese lived and worked under Japan's policy to develop Ezo into Hokkaido before the Russians could. A ride down the main street in a horse-drawn trolley (in summer) or sleigh (in winter) costs ¥270. ■ TIP➔ Ask for the excellent free English guide at the ticket counter.

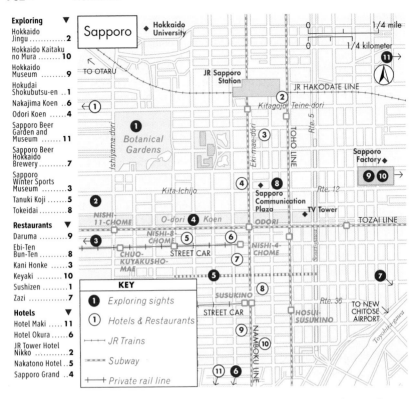

✉ *1–50–1 Konopporo, Atsubetsu-cho, Atsubetsu-ku* ✛ *About 10 km (6 miles) outside Sapporo; easiest access is via 15-min bus ride (¥210) from Shin-Sapporo Station (Bus 22 heading to Kaitakunomura) or 10-min taxi ride from same station* ☎ *011/898–2692* ⊕ *www.kaitaku.or.jp/info/info.htm* ✉ *Apr.–Nov. ¥830, Dec.–Mar. ¥680* ☉ *May–Sept., daily 9–5; Oct.–Apr., Tues.–Sun. 9–4:30.*

Fodor's Choice **Odori Koen** (大通公園 *Odori Park*). Stretching for more than a mile
★ through the center of the city, Odori Park is one of the defining land-marks of Sapporo. Buy roasted corn on the cob and potatoes from food vendors and feast on them as you watch the skateboarders and street performers. In winter, enjoy the famous Sapporo Snow Festival with its massive snow sculptures. There's the energetic and loud Yosokoi Soran Festival every spring, and for three weeks in July and August the park hosts a bacchanal called the Sapporo Beer Festival. Every block becomes a biergarten for a major Japanese beer manufacturer (the foreign and microbrews, naturally, are the farthest walk away). Last orders at 9 pm, then everyone stumbles home or out for more partying in Susukino. Not to be missed if you're in town. ✉ *Odori Nishi 2, Odori* ⊕ *www. sapporo-park.or.jp/odori/en.*

Tanuki Koji (狸小路 *Tanuki Mall*). Japanese mythology mentions the libidinous nature of the raccoon-like *tanuki* , an animal that lent its

CLOSE UP

On the Calendar

One of Japan's best-known annual events, held for a week beginning February 5 or 6, is the **Sapporo Snow Festival** (Sapporo Yuki Matsuri). More than 300 lifelike ice sculptures as large as 130 feet high by 50 feet deep by 80 feet wide are created each year by the Japanese Self Defense Forces. Memorable statues include baseball star Matsui, cavorting whales, dinosaurs, and the Taj Mahal.

The festival began in 1950 with six statues commissioned by the local government to entertain Sapporo citizens depressed by the war and the long winter nights. Now the event is so large that the sculptures are spread around three different sections of the city: Odori Koen, Susukino, and the suburban Tsudome site. You'll also find ice slides for children. One highlight is the international teams of amateur and professional ice sculptors (some from countries without snow, such as Singapore), hired by major local businesses, who spend four days sculpting their creations. Although statues are roped off, taking photographs is no problem. The festival attracts more than 2 million visitors each year, so book your stay well in advance.

During the **Yosakoi Soran Festival** every second week of June, Sapporo's streets stage Japan's version of Carnival. Based on the Kochi Festival in Shikoku, more than 40,000 performers go wild in brightly colored costumes and face paint as they run, jump, and chant *soran soran* (a Hokkaido fishermen's folk song) through the city streets. A boisterous Japanese take on hip-hop crossed with aerobics, Yosakoi is far more exciting than the traditional *bon odori* community dancing. Dance teams wave enormous flags and snap *naruko* (wooden clappers) in the wake of giant trucks, mounted with powerful sound systems and *taiko* drummers in loincloths. Ticketed seats are available in the stands along the route in Odori Koen and at an outdoor stage, but they aren't necessary—most people just perch wherever they can get a vantage point. Dance teams also perform in Susukino at night.

14

---

name to this neighborhood once frequented by prostitutes. Now a different breed of merchant in this kitschy covered arcade is eager to lighten the wallets of passersby, with small shops selling clothing, electronics, and souvenirs. Tanuki Koji has considerably lower prices than the area's department stores. It's also the place to find Hokkaido specialties, from melon confections to dried salmon and seaweed, as well as the occasional belting street performer. ■TIP➜ This is a good spot for a stroll on a rainy day. ✉ *Minami 3, extending from Nishi 1 to 7, Chuo-ku* ⊕ *www.tanukikoji.or.jp*.

WORTH NOTING

Hokkaido Museum (北海道博物館). From woolly mammoth molars to bulky 1950s home electronics, the history of Hokkaido is meticulously exhibited here in glass-topped cases—it's all a tad dry compared to the vivid history lesson at the nearby Hokkaido Historical Village, but much more thorough. The building houses an overview of Hokkaido's natural history, how Meiji-era Japan realized that this northern island had coal, fish, and agricultural opportunities ripe for the picking, and also portrays Hokkaido's story in modern times in a newly renovated building. ■**TIP**➔ **Basic audio guides are available in English.** ✉ *53–2 Konoppora, Atsubetsu-cho, Atsubetsu-ku* ☎ *011/898–0466* ⊕ *www. hm.pref.hokkaido.lg.jp/* ✍ *¥600* ⊗ *May–Sept., Tues.–Sat. 9:30–5; Oct.–Apr., Tues.–Sat. 9:30–4:30.*

Hokudai Shokubutsu-en (北海道大学植物園 *Hokkaido University Botanic Gardens*). With more than 5,000 plant varieties, these gardens are a cool summer retreat. Highlights include a small **Northern Peoples Museum** with a grisly but fascinating 13-minute film of an Ainu bear-killing ceremony in Asahikawa in 1935, and a stuffed husky sharing a room with bears and an Ezo wolf. This glassy-eyed hound in Hokkaido's oldest museum in the center of the park is Taro, one of the canine survivors abandoned in a 1958 Antarctic expedition (a story brought to non-Japanese audiences in the Disney movie *Eight Below* (2006). After his ordeal, Taro retired to Hokkaido University, died in 1970, and remains here in dusty, shaggy glory. ✉ *Kita 3 Nishi 8* ☎ *011/221–0066* ✍ *May–Oct. gardens and greenhouse ¥420; Nov.–Apr. gardens free, greenhouse ¥120* ⊗ *May–Sept., Tues.–Sat. 9–4; Oct. and Nov., Tues.–Sat. 9–3:30.*

Nakajima Koen (中島公園 *Nakajima Park*). This green oasis is a 10-minute walk beyond Susukino's lights and contains **Hoheikan,** a white-and-blue Russian-influenced 19th-century imperial guesthouse; **Hasso-an Teahouse,** an Edo-era teahouse moved here in 1919 and located in a Japanese garden; a boating lake; and the Kitara concert hall, home of the Pacific Music Festival, started in 1990 by Leonard Bernstein. It's a pleasant stroll during the day, and make-out central for youths during fleeting summer nights. ✉ *Minami 9 Nishi 4, Chuo-ku* ✛ *To get here, take Nanboku subway line to Nakajima Koen Station* ⊕ *www.sapporo-park.or.jp/nakajima/lang/english.html.*

Sapporo Beer Garden and Museum (札幌ビール園と博物館 *Sapporo Biru-en to Hakubutsukan*). Quaint brick buildings adjacent to a giant shopping mall make up the public face of Sapporo's most famous export. Here you'll find a small museum with signage mostly in Japanese that reveals the development of bottle and label designs and depicts decades of cheesecake shots from advertising posters. ■**TIP**➔ **Pick up an English-language guide at the counter for explanations of all of the different things on display in the museum.** For ¥200, you can taste any of the brews: Black Label is most popular, but the Classic and Kaitoku are only available in Hokkaido. Taste all three for ¥500. Also available are tea and soft drinks for ¥100.

In the evening the cavernous Sapporo Biergarten is filled with serious drinkers tackling the *tabe-nomi-hodai* (all-you-can-eat-and-drink) feast of lamb barbecue and beer (about ¥4,000 per person). The catch: You have to finish within 100 minutes. To get here, take a 15-minute Sapporo Walk circular bus from the train station. It's a ¥1,000 taxi ride. ✉ *Kita 7 Higashi 9, Higashi-ku* ☎ *011/742–1531 for reservations at Beer Garden* ⊕ *www.sapporobeer.jp/brewery/s_museum/* ✍ *Free* ⊗ *Museum daily 10:30–6; restaurant daily 11:30–10.*

CLOSE UP

Drinking Beer in Sapporo

Sapporo means beer to drinkers around the world, and what would a visit to the city of the same name be without a little beer research?

Head to the Sapporo Beer Museum, 2 km (1 mile) northeast of Sapporo Station for a cursory history lesson in the redbrick former factory, and then to the neighboring biergarten, where waiters in a cavernous noisy hall will rush to get a glass of the golden brew into your hands. Raise your glass— *Kampai* (Bottoms up)!

If you are in town in July and early August, join Sapporo Beer and other companies at the Sapporo Beer Garden festival in Odori Park in the city center: every night for three weeks thousands of revelers sit out under the trees with beer steins and snacks getting very lubricated. The faithful can do the factory tour and tasting at Hokkaido Brewery at Eniwa, near New Chitose Airport, where

guides (Japanese-language only) show the brewing process.

Brewmaster Seibei Nakagawa spent two years at the Berliner Brauerai studying German know-how and returned ready to put it all into practice. The first brewery was at the current Sapporo Factory shopping mall, and Sapporo *Reisi* (cold) Beer, with a red-and-black label bearing the red star symbol, first went on sale in 1877 (Sapporo's cold climate was a competitive advantage in the era before refrigeration).

Toriaezu biiru! (For the time being, beer!) is still the first order of business at parties, beer-hall barbe-cues, and campsite cookouts. Sapporo Beer dominates the market up here, but microbreweries offer interest-ing alternatives. Look for local brews, *ji-biiru,* particularly Otaru Beer (factory tour available), Hakodate, and Taisetsu.

14

Sapporo Beer Hokkaido Brewery (サッポロビール北海道工場 *Sapporo Biiru Hokkaido Kojo*). Of interest to beer meisters, the place where they actually brew the country's most famous beer offers free looks around the factory. Tours in Japanese (there is English signage) depart at 10, 11, 1, 2, 3, and 4 and give you 40 minutes of stats and sights and 20 minutes to down two free beers. Reservations are required. The brewery is served by Chuo Bus (about 70 minutes) and infrequent trains stopping at Sapporo Beer Teien Station on the JR Chitose–Sapporo Line (you might best off taking the express train toward the airport and then a local train back toward the city). Check with the JR staff). ✉ 542–1 Toiso, Eniwa City ☎ 011/748–1876 ⊕ *www.sapporobeer.jp/ brewery/hokkaido* 🎫 *Free* 🕙 *Tues.–Sun. 10–5.*

FAMILY **Sapporo Winter Sports Museum** (札幌ウィンタースポーツミュージアム *Sapporo Uintaa Supotsu Myujiamu*). Leap off a ski jump into the freez-ing air and land like a pro—or not. In this museum at the base of the Olympic Okura Jump, a realistic simulator lets you comparing jump distances. The 1972 Winter Olympics and other Japanese sporting suc-cesses in skating, curling, and many forms of skiing are celebrated with displays interesting even to nonsporting types. Outside the museum, take the chairlift to the top of the real ski jump for a chilling view of what athletes face before takeoff. It's a 15-minute bus ride from Maruyama Bus Terminal on Sapporo City Bus 円14 (¥210). ✉ *1274 Miyanomori, Chuo-ku* ☎ *011/641–8585* 🌐 *www.sapporowintersportsmuseum.com* 🎟 *¥600* ⏲ *May–Oct., daily 9–6; Nov.–Apr., daily 9:30–5.*

Tokeidai (時計台, 旧札幌農学校演武場 *Clock Tower*). For millions of Japanese, this little white-clapboard Russian-style meetinghouse defines Sapporo. Built in 1878 as the drill hall for students of Sapporo Agricultural College (now Hokkaido University), it has become the city's symbol on souvenir packaging. It even graces the label of Sapporo beer. A bit underwhelming, Tokeidai contains photographs and documents telling the region's history and a clock from Boston. ✉ *Kita 1 Nishi 2, Chuo-ku* 🌐 *www.sapporoshi-tokeidai.jp/english* 🎟 *¥200* ⏲ *Daily 8:45–5; closed the 4th Mon. and for New Year holidays.*

WHERE TO EAT

The greatest concentration of restaurants for nighttime dining is in the entertainment district of Susukino; good daytime choices are in the downtown department stores and the shopping complex around JR Sapporo Station. Hokkaido is known for its ramen, and Sapporo for its miso ramen. The city has more than 1,000 ramen shops, so it's not hard to find a noodle lunch. To track down the current ramen star shack look for the lines of enthusiastic youths outside otherwise unassuming restaurants; young Japanese use their mobile phones and the Internet to research the newest hot spot.

Soup curry—curry with more sauce than content—is currently touted domestically as a Sapporo creation, but the curry restaurants run by Indian and Nepali expats in the city are better bet.

$$$ JAPANESE

🍴 **Daruma** (だるま本店). Below the red sign depicting a roly-poly mustachioed doll, this 60-year-old establishment serves the city's freshest barbecued lamb *jingisukan* (a local delicacy, going for ¥785 a plate). It's served steaming atop heaps of vegetables. At the end of the meal you're given hot tea to mix with what's left of your dipping sauce—mixed together, they're oddly delicious! Be sure to wear your least-favorite clothes and don the paper bib that's provided. It's a chain, but this is the *honten* (main branch), so feast away until you become roly-poly yourself. [$] *Average main: ¥2500* ✉ *Crystal Bldg. 1F, Minami 5 Nishi 4, Chuo-ku* ☎ *011/552–6013* 💳 *No credit cards* ⏲ *No lunch* ✍ *Reservations not accepted.*

$$ JAPANESE

🍴 **Ebi-Ten Bun-Ten** (蛯天分店). On a narrow street near the Mitsukoshi department store, Ebi-Ten Bun-Ten is as friendly a place as you're likely to find in Hokkaido. The sliding doors behind a blue banner reveal a quiet, homey restaurant, managed for two generations by the friendly Yamada family. Taxidermy animals decorate the wood-trimmed dining room, where you'll see a bear climbing a tree. Seating is available at the counter, at tables, and in tatami rooms with cushions. Choose from many *tendon* sets (tendon is tempura on top of rice) that comes with pickles, homemade miso soup, and a big mug of tea (¥750) or the superfancy tendon set with lots of the best in seasonal seafood, soup, and pickles (¥2,700). Or put together a whole mess of tempura by

Sapporo is famous for its beer.

choosing 10 things from a large selection including crab, nori, and even parsley (¥3,500). A rudimentary English menu is available. $ *Average main: ¥1800 ⊠ Minami 2 Nishi 4, Chuo-ku ☎ 011/271–2867 ⊕ www. ebiten.co.jp/English.html ⊟ No credit cards.*

$$$$
JAPANESE
✕**Kani Honke** (かに本家). This crab-eating haven serves raw, steamed, boiled, and baked crustaceans—the waitress will tell you whether the *ke-gani* (hairy crab), *taraba-gani* (king crab), or *zuwai-kani* (snow crab) is in season. The menu is in English and has photographs, so it's easy to choose from the giant set dinners, which start at ¥6,300 or stop by for the lunch sets starting around ¥2500. Wood beams, tatami mats, and traditional decorations provide an authentic setting for the feast. Look for the building with crabs all over it and a couple of giant white signs on the roof. There's a second location near JR Sapporo Station at Kita 3 Nishi 2. $ *Average main: ¥6000 ⊠ Minami 6 Nishi 3, Susukino ☎ 011/551–0018 ⊕ www.kani-honke.jp/e.*

$
RAMEN
✕**Keyaki** (けやき). It's a mystery why a few ramen restaurants are famous and millions are not. This ordinary-looking 10-stools-at-the-plastic-counter joint in Susukino has had lines of faithful slurpers outside since the year 2000 (a lifetime for a ramen shop) and is still chopping, boiling, and serving its succinct seven-item ramen menu that includes *cha-shu* (seasoned pork) and *kaku-ni* (pressure-cooked pork). Keyaki even has a branch in the Ramen Museum in Yokohama. At the original shop you order from the vending machine at the door (there is a small guide in English with pictures on the wall by the machine, but the buttons are only in Japanese, so just ask the friendly staff for help) then wait on the bench or stand around the corner (to avoid lines, get here soon after they open at 10:30 or at least before the lunch rush). Once

you get your seat, wait for the cook to hand down a steaming bowl topped generously with vegetables from the raised and hidden kitchen. **■TIP→ If you want to keep your clothes clean, don't avoid slurping, just accept the paper bib they offer.** [$] *Average main: ¥900* ✉ *Minami 6 Nishi 3, Susukino* ☎ *011/552–4601* 💳 *No credit cards* ⏱ *No dinner.*

$$$$ SUSHI 🍴 **Sushizen** (すし善). Hokkaido sushi is famed throughout Japan, and this is probably the best of the best. It's where locals take guests when they want to impress them with a pure sushi experience. This main branch in Maruyama is the best of the four scattered around the city, while the one next to JR Sapporo Station (Daimaru 8F, Kita 5 Nishi 5) is cheaper and more welcoming to families (and you won't need reservations). [$] *Average main: ¥15000* ✉ *Kita 1 Nishi 27, Maruyama, Chuo-ku* ☎ *011/612–0068* 🌐 *www.sushizen.co.jp/en* 💳 *No credit cards* ⏱ *Closed Mon.* ✍ *Reservations essential.*

$ CAFÉ 🍴 **Zazi** (ザジ). A casual downtown coffee shop with an English menu, this hangout is popular with students and expats. Try their soups, generous pasta plates, one-pot stews, and homemade cakes. Only one busy cook works in the kitchen, so don't expect a speedy lunch. Come in when you're peckish and you'll eventually leave feeling full. Or just hang out and have a cup of coffee or tea. [$] *Average main: ¥800* ✉ *Minami 2 Nishi 5, Susukino, Chuo-ku* ☎ *011/221–0074* 💳 *No credit cards.*

WHERE TO STAY

$ B&B/INN 🏨 **Hotel Maki** (ホテル牧). Staying at Hotel Maki is a change of style from the sterility of big-city lodgings—the Inada family greets your every return with a hearty "Welcome back!" **Pros:** warm welcome and friendly family atmosphere; home cooking; good dining options nearby. **Cons:** 15-minute walk from Susukino area; not immediately to public transportation; some of the rooms have a tobacco smell. [$] *Rooms from: ¥5900* ✉ *1–20 Minami 13 Nishi 7, Chuo-ku* ☎ *011/521–1930* 💳 *No credit cards* 🛏 *15 Japanese-style rooms, 6 with bath* 🍽 *Some meals.*

$$$$ HOTEL 🏨 **Hotel Okura Sapporo** (ホテルオークラ札幌). A block from Odori Subway Station, the Hotel Okura Sapporo gets the balance between style and the personal connection just right. **Pros:** close to shopping; near public transportation; personal attention. **Cons:** limited public seating areas; a little snobby at times; some of the rooms' views are limited to the neighboring building. [$] *Rooms from: ¥26000* ✉ *Nishi 5 Minami 1, Chuo-ku* ☎ *011/221–2333* 🌐 *www.sapporo-hotelokura.co.jp* 🛏 *147 Western-style rooms* 🍽 *Breakfast.*

$$$$ HOTEL 🏨 **JR Tower Hotel Nikko Sapporo** (JRタワーホテル日航札幌). In a skyscraper looming high over the main train station, this hotel puts the city at your feet. **Pros:** part of the JR Sapporo Station complex; city views; soothing spa. **Cons:** small rooms for the price; restaurants are crowded. [$] *Rooms from: ¥33000* ✉ *JR Sapporo Station Tower, Kita 5 Nishi 2, Chuo-ku* ☎ *011/251–2222, 011/251–2510 for reservations until 8 pm* 🌐 *www.jrhotels.co.jp/tower/english* 🛏 *350 Western-style rooms* 🍽 *No meals.*

Susukino is Sapporo's busy entertainment district.

$$ 🏨 **Nakatono Hotel** (中殿ホテル). This quiet hotel one block south of
HOTEL Odori Park has been run by the Nakatono family since 1932. **Pros:**
excellent location near park; it is quiet. **Cons:** some rooms on the south
side have opaque windows; the large bath can be locked by families,
so might not always be available. $ *Rooms from: ¥12000 ✉ Minami 1
Nishi 7 ✛ A 5-min walk west from Odori Station along south side of
park* ☏ *011/231-4717* ⊕ *www.nakatono-hotel.com* ⤳ *16 Western-style
rooms, 20 Japanese-style rooms* ⵜⵓ *Breakfast.*

$$$$ 🏨 **Sapporo Grand Hotel** (札幌グランドホテル). With classic European
HOTEL style, white-gloved bellhops, and conveniences like in-room refrigera-
tors tastefully hidden away in wooden cabinets, Sapporo's grand dame
has welcomed guests since 1934. **Pros:** convenient location; long his-
tory; high-end service in a city full of business hotels. **Cons:** small win-
dows in main building; certain parts have a mall-like feel; long walk
to public areas. $ *Rooms from: ¥27000 ✉ Kita 1 Nishi 4, Chuo-ku*
☏ *011/261–3311* ⊕ *www.grand1934.com/english* ⤳ *504 Western-style
rooms* ⵜⵓ *No meals.*

NIGHTLIFE

Stretching for seven blocks in every direction, Sapporo's entertainment
district of Susukino すすきの is a mind-boggling cluster of more than
4,000 bars, nightclubs, and eateries. Bars and clubs stay open late, some
until 5 am. The seedier places are mostly west of Ekimae Dori, but all
of Susukino is safe. Susukino can be cheap, too, if you ask for a *tabe-
nomi hodai*, which might get you up to two hours of all you can eat
and drink for a reasonable sum.

SAPPORO NIGHTLIFE 101

Nightlife comes in several kinds: clubs stocked with hostesses who make small talk (¥3,000 and up per hour, proving that talk is *not* cheap); *sunakku* bars (the word sounds like "snack," which translates into fewer hostesses and expensive *odoburu*, or hors d'oeuvres); *izakaya*, for both Japanese and Western food and drink; bars with entertainment, either karaoke or live music (not to mention "soapland"), and *herusu* (health) massage parlors, which of course are not bars, and not recommended. Signs that say "no charge" only mean that there's no charge to be seated; beware of hidden extras. Many bars add on charges for peanuts, female companionship, song, cold water, hand towels, and so on. The term "free drink" refers to "drinking freely," that is, all-you-can-drink specials that cost money. So unless you want a "laddish" male-oriented environment (sunakku are not for couples) dominated by baby talk with a hostess for a high price, stick to the izakaya and live bars.

Blues Alley (ブルーズアレイ). Stop by to see the regular live music on Friday and Saturday at this casual basement bar. Have a whole set of food and an all-you-can-drink set for ¥3,500 or one with a simpler fare for ¥3,000. Alternatively, you can just hang out with a drink and a snack. Keep the hand steady for a game of darts or pool in a place where you might have a chance to hear some live music. ⊠ *B1 Miyako Bldg., Minami 3 Nishi 3, Susukino* ☎ *011/231–6166.*

Half Note Jazz Bar (三条美松ビルB1F ハーフノート). Even if you're not a fan of jazz, a night at the classy Half Note might make you into a convert. The impressive caliber of the musicians will keep you hanging on for drink after drink to see what gets played next. The cover charge and curtain time differ by night and artist, so stop by this basement spot to see if the groove going on is what you're into tonight. Wednesday nights are vocals night. ⊠ *Sanjo Mimatsu Bldg. B1, Minami 3 Nishi 5, Susukino* ✛ *You can get in from Tanuki Koji side or next street. Look for white sign with outline of a piano* ☎ *011/261–5880* ⊕ *halfnote.zero-city.com.*

Otaru Beer Leibspeise (小樽ビール ライブシュパイゼ *Otaru Biiru Raibushupaize*). One of Japan's first successful microbreweries, Otaru has made a name for itself for hiring a foreign brewmaster named Brian Dishman, formally trained in brewing techniques in Germany. Take advantage of the outdoor seating terrace in summer, but be aware that you might have to work harder to get the staff's attention. Their downtown outlet Leibspeise restaurant serves sausage, pretzels, sauerkraut, and various experimental varieties of lagers and stouts. If you're already bored with indistinguishable Japanese beers designed more to clean the palate than be an adventure for it, drop by this bar on the third floor. ⊠ *Parade Bldg. 3F, Minami 2 Nishi 3, Chuo-ku* ☎ *011/252–5807* ⊕ *www.otarubeer.com/jp/leibspeise* ☾ *Weekdays 5–midnight, weekends noon–midnight.*

Saloon Maco (サルーンマコ). The Stetson-wearing Japanese staff and patrons here sing country and pop karaoke, fortified by a *nomihodai* (all-you-can-drink plan) for ¥2,700 with beer. They have homemade bacon and sausages, which they are very proud of and use in some of their pastas. Small plates of a variety of dishes are each around ¥700. It is a bit hard to find, but look for the bright red door and a sign for Curtain Call in the middle of the block. It's on the second floor. ⊠ *2F Asano Bldg., Minami 3 Nishi 4, Chuo-ku* ☎ *011/222–4828.*

St. John's Wood (セント ジョンズ ウッド *Sento Jonzu Uddo*). Start the evening perched on a bar stool looking out on Susukino's main intersection. This friendly, pay-at-the-counter serves beer, mint juleps, whiskeys, and malts, as well as haggis, fish-and-chips, and onion rings. Their beer selection includes three beers on tap (Suntory Premium, Carlsberg, and a local microbrew black stout) and has more than 10 bottled beers from around the world. ⊠ *1F Keiai Bldg., Minami 4 Nishi 4, Susukino* ✚ *Located directly underneath 24-hr McDonald's* ☎ *011/271–0085.*

14

SHOPPING

Sapporo is known to some as Japan's largest small town, and shopping to some degree reflects that. Sapporoites aren't impressed by displays of wealth and prestige. Although you'll find a number of stores that appeal to tourists, there are no clusters of high-end boutiques as in, say, Ginza or Harajuku in Tokyo. The best shopping is along Eki-Mae Dori, between JR Sapporo Station and Susukino. Start at Stella Place, Daimaru, and Tokyu department stores around the train station, then move south to the underground shopping malls of Pole Town and Aurora Town. Surface at Odori to find decent department stores like Mitsukoshi, Parco, and Marui Imai. Walk a little farther south to find the cheap and kitschy Tanuki Koji arcade, which stretches east–west for seven blocks.

Kinokuniya (紀伊国屋). Outside Sapporo, finding English-language books and magazines is difficult, so you may want to browse in this expansive bookstore near the West Exit of Sapporo Station. Foreign magazines are with the English-language fiction, nonfiction, and language teaching books on the second floor. The children's section also has many Japanese titles in translation, and a decent selection of DVDs (although they're cheaper at Yodobashi Camera, just under the railway bridge on the same street). Kinokuniya is notorious for overcharging, so keep an eye on the prices. ⊠ *JR Sapporo Station, Kita 5 Nishi 5* ☎ *011/231–2131.*

OTARU AND NISEKO 小樽とニセコ

West of Sapporo, Meiji-era stone warehouses line a canal lighted at night by glowing lamps and filled by day with sightseers. Otaru is a medium-size port city facing the Sea of Japan. Its herring-fishing heyday between the 1870s and 1930s created the riches that built the banks, warehouses, and grand houses that give the city its historical visage.

The Niseko area lies over the mountains and extends into the hinterland, where the perfect cone of Mt. Yotei acts like the Eiffel Tower to a pastoral Paris, blessed with fertile land offering up fruit, potatoes, pumpkins, corn, and hot springs. In winter this is one of Japan's leading ski areas, and from May to October outdoor enthusiasts enjoy river rafting and hiking. Niseko is best experienced by car over two or three days. Adventure tours should be booked in advance.

OTARU 小樽

40 km (25 miles) west of Sapporo.

Otaru nets its wealth in tourists these days, but the canal where barges used to land the catch of the day is still the center of action for thousands of domestic and Asian visitors reeled in by images of a romantic weekend retreat. Visitors from countries with 19th-century stone buildings of their own may be less impressed by the tourist strip along the canal, but rent a bike or walk away from the main drag and you can explore quaint neighborhoods and interesting buildings. Otaru also makes a good base for touring around Hokkaido by car. The tourist office or your hotel can help you make reservations.

The Otaru Snow Lantern Festival (whose odd official English name is "Otaru Snow Light Path") happens around the second week of February, when thousands of snow lanterns light up the canal area and old buildings. It is a quieter concurrent alternative to the blockbuster Sapporo Snow Festival.

GETTING HERE AND AROUND

Otaru is an easy day trip from Sapporo. Trains depart every 20 minutes and take about 40 minutes (sit on the right facing forward for the best coast views); the ¥1,700 Sapporo–Otaru Welcome Pass from JR Hokkaido permits one-day travel on Sapporo subways and the JR train to and from Otaru for visitors from abroad (so you'll have to present your passport with your "temporary visitor" visa stamp) and you can pick it and other one-day deals at Sapporo Station and the JR Travel Service Center.

VISITOR INFORMATION

There is an Otaru Tourist Office inside the station, but the one at Otaru Canal Plaza directly down the street from the station has free Wi-Fi, helpful English-speaking staff, lots of guides and pamphlets, and a place to sit down and plan your stay.

Contacts Charinko Otaru. ⊠ *2–7–9 Inaho, Otaru* ☎ *0134/32–6861* ⊕ *c-otaru. sakura.ne.jp.* **Otaru Tourist Office** (小樽市観光案内, 小樽運河プラザ *Otaru-shi Kanko Annai, Otaru Unga Puraza).* ⊠ *2–1–0 Ironai, Otaru* ⚓ *Head out of station and directly down hill to canals. The newly renovated building is on left* ☎ *0134/33–1661* ⊕ *otaru.gr.jp/welcom_en/.*

EXPLORING

Kyu Aoyama Bettei (旧青山別邸と鰊御殿 *Aoyama Villa).* Gorgeous, gold-painted sliding doors and dark lacquered floors testify to the huge wealth of fishing millionaires, the Aoyamas. Teenage daughter Masae came home from a trip with another rich family in Honshu with big

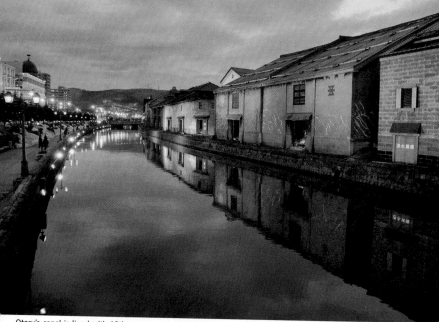

Otaru's canal is lined with 19th-century stone buildings.

ideas about how her family could spend its fortune, and in 1917 her father commissioned the chief imperial carpenter and a team of top craftsmen to create a home and garden of sumptuousness rare in Hokkaido. The modern annex also has a good restaurant serving herring-on-rice lunches. Take Bus No. 10 to Otaru Kihinkan from the station or No. 11 to the Shukutsu 3-Chome bus stop, then walk up the hill for about 1 km (½ mile). Both buses take about 20 minutes and the No. 11 is more frequent.

Next door is a real-life *Upstairs, Downstairs* (or in this case, side-by-side) with the worker's quarters in the Nishin Goten. Herring fishermen ate, slept, and dreamed of riches in this 1897 working base. On display are kitchen appliances, nets, and mislaid personal items of the men who toiled. Photographs of the Otaru coastline lined with ships, and beaches piled high with fish, reveal how the herring heydays brought riches to some—and put a serious dent in the Pacific fish stocks. ⊠ *3–63 Shukutsu, Otaru* ☎ *0134/24–0024* ⊕ *www.otaru-kihinkan.jp/eng.html* ✉ *¥1,080* ⊘ *Apr.–Dec., daily 9–5; Jan.–Mar., daily 9–4.*

Otaru Canal Area (小樽運河と栄町歴史街 *Otaru Unga*). Make a beeline to this city's most famous attraction, Otaru Canal, eight blocks downhill from JR Otaru Station. Small but charming, it runs between the ports and a contemporary shopping area called the **Sakaemachi Street Historic District,** which is even more charming: old banks and trading houses have been converted into boutiques and shops. Don't miss the music-box collection and the musical steam clock at Marchen Square on the eastern end of the district. A one-day pass (¥750) on the local bus (some of them look like old trolleys) is a useful energy-saver; during the summer, sunburned rickshaw runners offer tours.

If you feel like seeing the edge of Japan, walk to **Otaru Port** and you may see Russian, Chinese, and Korean (North as well as South) ships loaded up with used cars, bicycles, and refrigerators. If you're interested in boarding a boat yourself, summertime sightseeing boats depart from the dock just beyond the Chuo Bridge for a 25-minute trip to the Herring Mansion area. If you're ready to leave Hokkaido, there are also ferries to Akita, Niigata, Maizuru, and Tsuruga. ⊠ *Ironai and Sakaemachi, Otaru.*

FAMILY **Otaru Canal Cruise** (小樽運河クルーズ *Otaru unga kuruuzu*). Since everyone comes to Otaru for the canals, why not go out on them? When you have worn out your feet for the day, try taking a 40-minute Canal Cruise and get a nice view of Otaru's famous stone and brick warehouses from a different perspective. The cruise will take you up and down the main canal with a little jaunt under Tsukimi and Asahi bridges into the port area. The boarding platform is just over the canal from the Otaru Tourist Office at Unga Plaza. In summer the daytime cruises run 10 times per day (11 at the height of summer) and two or three at night (after 7 pm), but do check their schedule as it changes with the seasons. No cruises run between October and February (but who wants to be out on the water in winter?). At the height of the season, reservations are recommended for the night cruise. Reservations can be made by phone or at the platform. ⊠ *5–4 Minato Machi, Otaru* ☎ *0134/31–1733 for reservations* 🖃 *¥1,500; ¥1,800 at night.*

WHERE TO EAT

$ ✕ **Kita no Ice Cream** (北のアイスクリーム). Beer ice cream anyone? Maybe
CAFÉ you'd prefer cherry-blossom flavor? Or squid ink (*ikasumi*), butter potato (*jaga bata*), sea urchin (*uni*), or pumpkin (*kabocha*)? This Otaru institution serves up unconventional varieties of ice cream made from fresh ingredients in an 1892 warehouse in an alleyway one block from the canal. Single, double, and triple scoops will cost you ¥300, ¥500, or ¥700. $ *Average main: ¥500* ⊠ *1–2–18 Ironai, Otaru* ☎ *0134/23–8983* 🖃 *No credit cards* ☉ *Daily 10–7.*

$$$ ✕ **Kita Togarashi Restaurant** (小樽ジンギスカン倶楽部 北とうがらし *Otaru*
JAPANESE *Jingisukan Kurabu Kita Togarashi*). There's lamb barbecue heaven among all the sushi joints in Otaru at the easiest-to-find branch of a famous *jingisukan* restaurant. Plates of succulent lamb cost ¥780, and you cook the tender meat yourself on a dome-shape griddle with side orders of alfalfa sprouts (*moyashi*) and leeks (*negi*). If you're still hungry, pick up a crepe or a treat on your way out from one of the shops in the cute collection of buildings. Reservations are required on weekends. $ *Average main: ¥3000* ⊠ *Denuki Koji, 1–1 Ironai, Otaru* ☎ *0134/33–0015* 🖃 *No credit cards.*

$$$$ ✕ **Masazushi** (政寿司). In the middle of Otaru's famous strip of sushi
SUSHI restaurants, Masazushi serves up the morning's catch of herring, tuna, abalone, or salmon perched on quality vinegared rice. The staff will check your wasabi horseradish tolerance levels when taking your order. A good, quick lunch is the basic nine-piece-and-soup *hamanasu* set (¥1,580). The restaurant is quiet and removed from the day-tripper

crowds, and in the evening it's where local business leaders hold court in private rooms. There are English menus and some English-speaking staff. $ *Average main: ¥3150* ✉ *1–1–1 Hanazono, Otaru* ☎ *0134/23–0011, 0120/013–413 toll-free* ⊕ *www.masazushi.co.jp* ☉ *Closed Wed.*

$$
JAPANESE ✕ **Takeda Restaurant** (武田鮮魚店 *Takeda Sengyoten*). Claws emerging from a bed of fresh-cut crab and darkly gleaming red salmon eggs piled high on a bowl of rice are just two of the famous raw-fish options at this 50-year-old family restaurant in the middle of the noisy fish market. The *omakase-don* somehow gets ten kinds of fish and seafood into one bowl, although anyone hoping to still manage some sightseeing after lunch may prefer lighter dishes like oysters on the half shell (¥300 each) or a scallop grilled in its shell (around ¥350 depending on size). You can buy fresh seafood from their shop (where you can pay with a credit card) and have them serve it in their adjacent restaurant (where you must use cash). The menus have plenty of pictures and a bit of English to make ordering easier. The place is just up the steps to the left of JR Otaru Station. Look for the yellow signs with black lettering inside the market just up some stairs from the station area. $ *Average main: ¥2000* ✉ *3–10–16 Inaho, Otaru* ☎ *0134/22–9652* ⊕ *www.otaru-takeda.com* ⊟ *No credit cards.*

WHERE TO STAY

$$
HOTEL 🛏 **Authent Hotel** (オーセントホテル). This former department store in the heart of the downtown shopping area was remade into an elegant hotel. **Pros:** central location; sunset views from piano bar. **Cons:** less-expensive rooms are boxlike; crowded with tour groups. $ *Rooms from: ¥16000* ✉ *2–15–1 Inaho, Otaru* ☎ *0134/27–8100* ⊕ *www.authent. co.jp/fl/english* ⇌ *190 Western-style rooms, 5 Japanese-style rooms* ⎮⚬⎮ *No meals.*

$
HOTEL 🛏 **Grand Park Otaru** (グランドパーク小樽). Overlooking Otaru Marina, this 18-story hotel sits atop the huge WingBay shopping complex, giving easy access to outlet stores, movie theaters, and even a Ferris wheel. **Pros:** reliable service; great restaurant; shop without leaving the building. **Cons:** out-of-the-way location; shopping-mall atmosphere. $ *Rooms from: ¥9600* ✉ *11–3 Chikko, Otaru* ☎ *0134/21–3111* ⊕ *www.parkhotelgroup.com/otaru* ⇌ *296 Western-style rooms* ⎮⚬⎮ *No meals.*

$$$
HOTEL 🛏 **Otaru Furukawa Hotel** (運河の宿 小樽ふる川). Dark wooden beams, shadowy corridors, and well-chosen antiques transform a modern canal-side building into a comfortable, old-fashioned Japanese inn—a rarity in Otaru. **Pros:** old-fashioned atmosphere; beside the canal; impressive baths. **Cons:** tobacco smell in some rooms; overlooks main road. $ *Rooms from: ¥19550* ✉ *1–2–15 Ironai, Otaru* ☎ *0134/29–2345* ⊕ *www.otaru-furukawa.com/english* ⇌ *38 Western-style rooms, 5 Japanese-style room, 2 suites* ⎮⚬⎮ *Some meals.*

NISEKO ニセコ

73 km (45 miles) southwest of Otaru.

For the best skiing in Hokkaido, head for Niseko's Grand Hirafu, Annupuri, Niseko Village, and Hanazono runs. Popular with Japanese skiers in the 1970s, Niseko had another major boom three decades later when Australian tourists made this a favorite winter destination. Asia's economic downturn and the high exchange rate cut the number of foreign travelers, but now the Chinese have rediscovered the place.

GETTING HERE AND AROUND

Niseko is really a collection of villages near the town of Kutchan, a 2½-hour drive both from JR Sapporo Station and New Chitose Airport. From November to May public buses go from the airport to the Niseko ski resorts almost hourly until early afternoon. In July and August, Chuo Bus Company has two buses a day. A one-way trip costs ¥2,470, but a return ticket is ¥4,000.

From Sapporo you can drive to the Niseko area in two hours, up and over Nakayama Pass. Trains from Sapporo to Kutchan depart every 90 minutes or so; the trip takes two hours and costs ¥1,840. You will probably have to switch trains in Otaru. From Kutchan seven trains a day go to the Hirafu and Niseko villages at the heart of the scenic area. Hotels and pensions pick up guests at these two stations. Travelers with no pickup arranged should go a little farther to JR Niseko Station because Hirafu is tiny and deserted once the train has gone. In ski season there are shuttle buses connecting Kutchan, the villages, and the lift stations. Out-of-season public transport is limited.

VISITOR INFORMATION

Down the street in front of Kutchan Station (three blocks and on the left) is the excellent Michi no Eki Niseko, run by the Kutchan Tourist Association, which has information, Internet access, hotel booking help, and event listings. In Niseko go to the Niseko Hirafu Welcome Center for accommodation help, tourist information, and to stay warm while waiting for the bus. It's next to the bus arrival/departure area at the top of Hirafu village, near the Hotel Niseko Alpen.

Skiing Information Niseko United (ニセコユナイテッド). ⊕ www.niseko.ne.jp/en. **Snow Japan**. ⊕ www.snowjapan.com.

Contacts Michi no Eki Niseko View Plaza. ⊠ 77–10 Motomachi, Abuta-gun, Niseko ☎ 0136/43–2051 ⊕ www.hokkaido-michinoeki.jp/data/40/each.htm.
Niseko Hirafu Welcome Center (ニセコグランヒラフ ウェルカムセンター). ⊠ 204 Aza-Yamada, Abuta-gun, Niseko ☎ 0136/22–0109 ⊕ www.grand-hirafu.jp/.

Self-Catering Companies Hokkaido Tracks Holidays (北海道トラックスホリデーズ). ⊠ 185–6 Aza Yamada, Niseko ☎ 0136/23–3503 ⊕ www.htholidays.com/. **Vacation Niseko** (バケーションニセコ). ⊠ Niseko ☎ 0136/21–2500 ⊕ www.hanazononiseko.com/npc.

EXPLORING

Niseko. Between the skier paradise of Mt. Annupuri and gorgeous Mt. Yotei is a gentle landscape of hot springs, dairy and vegetable farms, and hiking trails. For most Western visitors the many adventure sports are the reason to visit. Australian and Canadian expats offer year-round thrills, including white-water rafting (best from April to May), backcountry skiing (December to March), mountain biking, and bungee jumping.

Thanks to the influence of young Western tourists (less likely to spend their day indoors eating), Niseko was also a major self-catering vacation destination, meaning visitors provide their own food in exchange for access to a full kitchen. With some companies staffed by English-speaking expats, this offers an unusual-in-Japan stay opportunity. The Niseko area is hands-down the best place to discover the Hokkaido countryside, and it's still relatively easy to find an English-speaking guide.

Niseko Outdoor Adventure Sports Club (*NOASC*). This activity center in Hirafu offers ski lessons in winter and leads rafting trips in the summer as well as guided backcountry tours that last between three and four hours. ⊠ *20–6 Aza Yamada, Abuta-gun, Niseko* ☎ *0136/23–1688* ⊕ *www.noasc.com.*

WHERE TO EAT

$$$
ASIAN FUSION
✕ **Izakaya Bang Bang** (居酒屋ばんばん). Sizzling *yakitori* (meat on wood skewers) and other local favorites like salmon and herring accompany imports like spareribs and tacos at this place in Hirafu Village. The folks at the nearby tables could become tomorrow's skiing or whitewater rafting buddies, and your hotel's staffers probably enjoy their evenings off here. It's open for dinner, but if you're in the area around lunchtime consider the sister restaurant Bang 2 (Deux) just next door. English translations are on the menu. $ *Average main: ¥2500* ⊠ *188–24 Aza-Yamada, Abuta-gun, Kutchan* ☎ *0136/22–4292* ⊕ *www.niseko.or.jp/bangbang.*

$$
AMERICAN
✕ **Jo-Jo's** (ジョジョズ). The platters here overflow with nourishing meals for adventurers—generous salads, juicy hamburgers, savory potato gnocchi, followed by homemade cakes. In summer they have an all-Hokkaido burger with only local ingredients. This spacious, laid-back restaurant on the second floor of Niseko Adventure Center and is busy all day with guides and their nervous or elated customers. The dining room is all soaring beams and wide windows overlooking Yotei-san. $ *Average main: ¥1500* ⊠ *179–53 Aza-Yamada, Abuta-gun, Niseko* ☎ *0136/23–2220* ⊙ *Daily 11–9* ☞ *Jo-Jo's opens at 9:30, but doesn't start serving food until 11.*

WHERE TO STAY

$$
B&B/INN
🛏 **Grand Papa** (ぐらんぱぱ). Niseko promotes itself as the St. Moritz of Asia, and this alpine-style lodging at the bottom of Hirafu Village sticks with this theme with lots of dark wood and red carpeting. **Pros:** friendly owners; casual atmosphere; home cooking. **Cons:** stairs, stairs, stairs—there's no elevator; far from the ski lifts; books up quickly. $ *Rooms from: ¥13000* ⊠ *163 Aza-Yamada, Abuta-gun, Niseko* ☎ *0136/23–2244* ⊕ *www.niseko-grandpapa.com* ⇥ *17 Western-style rooms, 3 with bath; 2 Japanese-style rooms without bath* ⍾ *Breakfast.*

$$$$
RESORT
🛏 **Hilton Niseko Village** (ヒルトンニセコビレッジ *Hiruton Niseko Birejji*). With wonderful views of Mt. Yotei and the slopes of Higashiyama, this hotel has a ski-in, ski-out location near the Niseko cable car—it's a nine-minute ride to powder heaven. **Pros:** awesome views; reasonable prices in summer; staff speaks English and Korean. **Cons:** a 20-minute shuttle bus ride to Hirafu Village; standard rooms are small for the price. $ *Rooms from: ¥35000* ⊠ *Higashiyama Onsen, Abuta-gun, Niseko* ☎ *0136/44–1111* ⊕ *www.hilton.co.uk/niseko* ⇥ *500 rooms* ⍾ *Breakfast.*

14

$$ 🏨 **Hotel Niseko Alpen** (ホテル ニセコ アルペン). At the base of the Grand
HOTEL Hirafu ski slopes sits this modern hotel with an English-speaking staff
that's happy to help you plan a Niseko stay. **Pros:** ski-in, ski-out loca-
tion; close to village life; 20 steps from the ski terminal. **Cons:** bland
rooms; crowded public areas during ski season. 💲 *Rooms from:* ¥18000
✉ *204 Aza Yamada, Abuta-gun, Kutchan* 📞 *0136/22–1105* ⊕ *www.
grand-hirafu.jp/winter/en* ↩ *78 Western-style rooms, 15 Japanese-style
rooms, 36 combination rooms* 🍴 *Some meals.*

SPORTS AND THE OUTDOORS
HIKING

Mt. Yotei (羊蹄山 *Yotei-san*). Climbing this beautiful cousin of Mt. Fuji
takes four to six hours—it's like a staircase that never ends. Two trails
lead up the mountain: the more-challenging **Hirafu Course** and the
easier but still arduous **Makkari Course.** It's a trudge without switch-
backs all the way up. Regardless of your approach, you'll find wild-
flowers in summer, and elderly Japanese racing ahead of you chomping
on bamboo shoots that grow wild on the hills. A hut at the top pro-
vides crude lodging. To get to the trails, take the bus from JR Kutchan
Station 20 minutes to Yotei Tozan Guchi (hiking trail entrance) for
the Hirafu Course, or 40 minutes to the Yotei Shinzan Koen stop for
the Makkari Course. Or you could just do what most people do and
admire it from afar.

SKIING

From November to May, skiers and snowboarders enjoy 61 courses
covering 47 km (30 miles) of powder in the Niseko area. There are five
ski resorts, but the big four are Grand Hirafu, Higashiyama, Hanazono,
and Annupuri. You can ski them all with a Niseko All-Mountain Pass
costing ¥6,400 for one day or ¥11,500 for two days. Only the very
top is above the tree line, and reaching Hirafu's big, off-trail bowl
entails a 30-minute trek above the top chairlift. Nondrivers coming
from Sapporo can buy package ski tours, including an eight-hour pass
and transportation by bus, for ¥5,800. You can book tours at almost
any city hotel. If you're driving to Niseko, check Sapporo convenience
stores for discount lift tickets.

FAMILY   **Annupuri Resort.** The wide, gently sloping runs that are kind to begin-
ners and shaky intermediates keep people coming to this quieter of
the Niseko resorts. Beginners will enjoy practicing on Niseko's famous
powder, but practiced skiers will also enjoy the more challenging runs.
Private lessons are available for children and there's a play area at the
base of the gondola. **Facilities:** 13 trails; 5¼ kilometers (3¼ miles)
of trails; 2,480-foot vertical drop; 5 lifts. ✉ *Aza Niseko 485, Niseko*
📞 *0136/58–2080* ⊕ *annupuri.info/winter/english/* 🎫 *Lift ticket* ¥5,000.

FAMILY   **Grand Hirafu.** The largest of the Niseko ski resorts has something for
everyone, though most come for the deep powder. Being the biggest,
however, does have its drawbacks and the slopes can get crowded par-
ticularly on weekends. Even with the crowds, though, who could resist
Grand Hirafu's longest run at 5½ km (3½ miles) long? The resort is
slightly more popular with skiers (than boarders), but the trails are
divided evenly between the beginner, intermediate, and advanced

courses. There's child care and an area where kids can go tubing for free (when accompanied by an adult). **Facilities:** 30 trails; 27½ km (17 miles) of trails; 3,084-foot vertical drop; 15 lifts. ✉ *204 Aza Yamada, Abuta-gun, Niseko* ☏ *0136/22–0109* ⊕ *www.grand-hirafu.jp* ⛷ *Lift ticket ¥5,100.*

Niseko Village. Situated around the Hilton Niseko Village, this resort has a superfast cable car that takes you to beautifully designed courses through the forested slopes. If you didn't get enough day skiing, the compact area is lit until 8 pm. Due to its orientation, much of the slopes stay in shadow for part of the season, keeping the powder dry and cold. There are two designated kids' play areas and a day-care center. **Facilities:** 16 trails; 9 km (5¾ miles) of trails; 2,720-foot vertical drop; 7 lifts. ✉ *Higashiyama Onsen, Abuta-gun, Niseko-cho* ☏ *0136/44–2211* ⊕ *www.niseko-village.com* ⛷ *Lift ticket ¥5,000.*

SPORTS OUTFITTERS

Niseko Adventure Centre (ニセコアドベンチャーセンター). This longtime favorite arranges guided river rafting trips, mountain biking, and winter sport outings. There's also an indoor rock-climbing wall at its village-center base. ✉ *179–53 Aza-Yamada, Niseko* ☏ *0136/23–2093* ⊕ *www.nac-web.com.*

SHIKOTSU-TOYA NATIONAL PARK 支笏洞爺国立公園

· **Shikotsuko-Toya National Park.** Mountains, forests, hot springs, caldera lakes, and volcanoes are virtually in Sapporo's backyard, less than an hour's drive away. Route 230 passes the large hot-spring village of Jozankei, then the mountains close in and the road climbs 2,742 feet to Nakayama Pass. On a clear day the view from the top is classic Hokkaido: farmland with the majestic Mt. Yotei in its midst, and on the southern horizon lie Lake Toya's volcanic crater and Noboribetsu hot springs, where the earth steams, rumbles, and erupts. ■ **TIP→ If you are unsure how to navigate Japan's bus system, rent a car to take this in.** ✉ *Shikotsu-Toya National Park.*

TOYAKO 洞爺湖

179 km (111 miles) southwest of Sapporo.

Toyako Onsen and Sobetsu Onsen (洞爺湖温泉と壮瞥温泉). World leaders met here for the G8 Summit in 2008, but Lake Toya is best known for its geothermic events. In March of 2000, Mt. Usu exploded for the first time in 23 years, shooting a 10,500-foot-high cloud of ash and smoke over the quiet resort towns of Toyako Onsen and Sobetsu Onsen. About 16,000 people were evacuated. Amazingly, by July the towns were opened for business with the still-smoking craters in their midst. Volcanic eruptions are merely an occupational hazard for residents of hot-springs towns and residents pride themselves on living with nature. ✉ *Shikotsu-Toya National Park.*

14

GETTING HERE AND AROUND

Usu-san is one of several peaks on Lake Toya's crater, a huge volcanic rim that dominates the landscape. Route 230 from Sapporo drops over the northern edge, and Route 453 from Lake Shikotsu and Noboribetsu and roads from the coast come in from the south. Volcanic activity is centered on the small town of Toyako Onsen, and a few kilometers around the lake at Showa Shin-san. A road rings the water, dotted with campsites and hot springs, and pleasure boats go out to three small islands where deer beg for snacks.

Direct buses from Sapporo to Toyako Onsen via Nakayama Toge Pass take 2½ hours (¥2,780). Donan Bus makes that Sapporo to Toyako Onsen trip four times daily and reservations can be made by phone. Toyako Onsen is accessible by JR from Sapporo. Disembark from the train at JR Toya Station for a 15-minute bus ride to the lake. The bus departs throughout the day and is ¥330. There is a ¥100 shuttle bus four times a day round the lake, nonstop takes more than an hour. Sightseeing boats leave the pier for the 20-minute crossing to the islands. Bike rentals are available near the bus station for ¥900 per hour or ¥2,000 per day, but check with your hotel or with the tourist information desk for the best deals. Some hotels have bicycles on hand for their guests. It takes about three hours to cycle the circumference of the lake.

ESSENTIALS

Bus Information Donan Bus (道南バス). ✉ *142 Toyako Onsen, Toyako-cho* ☎ *0142/75–3117, 011/865–5511 Sapporo office for reservations.*

VISITOR INFORMATION

Tourist Information, inside the bus terminal, has English-speaking staff, and although officially unable to make hotel reservations, the website has access to online booking for some hotels. Toya Guide Center provides English-speaking guides for year-round excursions such as Canadian canoeing on the lake, walking the volcano, deer spotting, and waterfall walking, but be sure to make arrangements in advance.

Tour Information Toya Guide Center (洞爺ガイドセンター *Toya gaido Sentaa*). ✉ *193-8 Toyako-cho, Abuta-gun, Toyama* ☎ *0142/82–5002* ⊕ *www. toya-guide.com.*

Visitor Information Toyako Onsen Visitor Center (洞爺湖ビジターセンター). ✉ *142-5 Toyako Onsen, Abuta-gun, Toyako* ☎ *0142/75–2555* ⊕ *www. toyako-vc.jp/en/.*

EXPLORING

FAMILY **Kazan Kagaku-kan** (火山科学館 *Volcanic Science Museum*). A rumbling sound track and shaking floors re-create the area's 1977 and 2000 volcanic eruptions in this small information center. Although there's a good explanation of the science involved in this place where eruptions happen roughly every 30 years, the museum is less useful in describing the impact on the lives of locals. This museum shares a building with the Visitor Center. ✉ *142-5 Toyako-Onsen, Toyako-cho* ☎ *0142/75–2555* ⊕ *www.toyako-vc.jp/en/volcano* 🖾 *¥600* ⊘ *Daily 9–5.*

Nishiyama Crater Trail (西山火口群散策路 *Nishiyama Kakogun San-sakuro*). A fire station, a school, and houses stand at crazy angles amid

Shikotsu-Toya National Park

KEY
JR Trains or Private Trains
Beaches

Ishikari Wan

231
275
Sassho Line
Tobetsu

Yoichi
Otaru
Sasson Line
Ishikari

Hakodate Line
Tokiwa
Okadama Airport
Ebetsu

Mt. Teine ▲
Hakodate Line
Kitahiroshima

Mt. Yoichi ▲
Sapporo
see detail map
274

393
Jozankei
Chitose Line

Mt. Ponkutosan ▲
230
Mt. Muine ▲
Mt. Sapporo ▲
453
Eniwa

Hakodate Line
Nakayama Pass
Mt. Soranuma ▲
Chitose

Kutchan
276
Kyogoku
Mt. Eniwa ▲
New Chitose Airport

Mt. Yotei ▲
Kohan
Shikotsuko Onsen
Maruyama

Kimobetsu
Lake Shikotsu
276

Mt. Shinbetsu ▲
Bifue
276
Nibutani

Rusutsu
276
Bifue Pass
Mt. Tarumae ▲
276

Mt. Nukkibetsu ▲
Otaki
Shikotsu-Toyo National Park
Tomakomai

230
453
Mt. Horohoro ▲
Shadai
Nishikioka
36
Ferry Terminal

Toyako Onsen
Nakajima Island
Lake Toya
Ainu Village
Shiraoi
FERRY TO TOKYO, SENDAI, NAGOYA, HACHINOHE

Kazan Kogaku-kan
Sobetsu Onsen
Sobetsu
Orofure Pass
Lake Kuttaru
Hagino

Toyako
Mt. Usu
Mt. Showa Shinzan
Karurusu Onsen
Takeura

Abuta
Noboribetsu Onsen

Usu
Nagawa
Muroron Line

Date
Noboribetsu

Uchiura Wan
Mareppu
Horobetsu

36
36

Muroran

FERRY TO TOKYO, SENDAI, NAGOYA, HACHINOHE

0   10 mi
0   10 km

the solidified ash flows where the 2000 eruption reached the edges of Toyako Onsen. See it all from boardwalks that wind up into the still-steaming hills. It's an impressive scene of what can happen when you live next to a volcano. As a bonus, there are views both of the lake to the north and the ocean to the south. There's also a whole series of boardwalks, mountain trails, and short stretches of roads that were cut off after the eruption. To get here from JR Toya Station, ask for the Donan Bus headed to the bus stop called Kyushoku Senta. The buses are not numbered, so check with the driver as well if you're worried. Alternatively, this can be accessed from just behind the Visitor Center at Tokyako Onsen. ✉ *3–4–5 Takashaga-dori, between Toya and Toyako Onsen, Shikotsu-Toya National Park* 🎟 *Free* 🕐 *Apr.–Nov., daily 7–6.*

Toyako Onsen (洞爺湖温泉 *Toyako Hot Spring*). Gazing up at the town-sponsored fireworks from a rooftop hot spring after a relaxing soak in the thermal waters and a pleasant dinner of local specialties—this is why thousands of Japanese come to this small lakeside town throughout the year. From April 28 to October 31, the 30-minute fireworks display is likely to be the highlight of your stay. A waterside walk in front of the wall of hotels is relaxing before the bus tours arrive in late afternoon. If you overstay your welcome in banquet areas, cleaning ladies will come in and start vacuuming. It's one reason why Hokkaido is known for top-quality food but so-so service. ✉ *Shikotsu-Toya National Park.*

OFF THE BEATEN PATH

Showa Shinzan (昭和新山). During an earthquake in 1943, Showa Shinsan rose suddenly from a farmer's wheat field. Kept secret during the Pacific War as a potentially unlucky sign, it continued growing to its present height of 1,306 feet by 1945. It's on private land, but a cable-car ride (¥1,500 round trip or ¥840 one-way) up the eastern flank of Mt. Usu provides great views of the mountain, Lake Toya, and Funka Bay. Avoid the Bear Farm near the base—a depressing tourist attraction. ✉ *184–5 Aza Showa Shinzan, Sobetsu-cho, Usu Gun, Shikotsu-Toya National Park* ☎ *0142/75–2401* 🌐 *www.wakasaresort.com/usuzan/en/index.html.*

WHERE TO EAT AND STAY

$$ EUROPEAN

🍴 **Boyotei** (望羊蹄). A European-style restaurant set in a tranquil garden, with very friendly staff, Boyotei (which literally means "View of Mt. Yotei") charms with its stone floor, low beams, long-legged tables, and family photos dating back for decades. There are English menus available, but the sizzling hamburger platters are the best choices. [$] *Average main: ¥1700* ✉ *36–12 Toyako Onsen, Abuta-gun, Shikotsu-Toya National Park* ☎ *0142/75–2311.*

$$ HOTEL

🏨 **Lakeside Spa Toya Kawanami** (湖畔の宿洞爺かわなみ). Views of the nightly fireworks and the waterfront are available from almost all rooms at this family-run hotel a 15-minute walk (1.2 km [less than a mile]) along the shore from the village. **Pros:** peaceful getaway; English-speaking owners; good deal on dinner and accommodation. **Cons:** no lake views from hot spring; no private baths in rooms. [$] *Rooms from: ¥13000* ✉ *53 Toyako Onsen, Usu-gun, Sobetsu* ☎ *0142/75–2715* 🌐 *www.kawanami.jp/en/index.html* 🛏 *30 Japanese-style rooms* 🍽 *Some meals.*

$$$$
RESORT
Fodor's Choice
★
🖻 **The Windsor Hotel Toya** (ザ・ウインザーホテル洞爺リゾート＆スパ). Visible for miles around—it looks like a giant cruise ship perched on the rim of the Toya Volcano—the Windsor is Hokkaido's best hotel for location and service. **Pros:** top service; stunning views; chance to spot Asian celebs on vacation. **Cons:** stratospheric prices; hours from major cities; some restaurants close unexpectedly during quiet season. 🖻 *Rooms from: ¥60600 ☒ Shimizu, Abuta-Gun, Toyako-cho ☎ 0120/290–500 for reservations only, 0142/73–1111 ⊕ www.windsor-hotels.co.jp ➹ 395 Western-style rooms, 3 Japanese-style rooms* ⑪ *Some meals.*

NOBORIBETSU ONSEN 登別温泉

53 km (32 miles) east of Toyako, 100 km (62 miles) south of Sapporo.

14

If you want to see how many Japanese people prefer to relax and vacation on the cheap, this is the place to go. Noboribetsu Onsen is Hokkaido's most famous spa. The town claims that some 34,300 gallons of geothermally heated water are pumped out every hour, making it the most prodigious hot spring in Asia. Not a quaint little hot-spring town, Noboribetsu caters to Japanese-style onsen tourism (i.e., soak, eat, soak, get drunk, soak, carouse, canoodle, soak), meaning services are limited once you step outside your hotel. The hotels are good, but the town is basically tourist shops; come here expecting good hot water and conveyer-belt-style Japanese service.

GETTING HERE AND AROUND

Noboribetsu City is one hour south of Sapporo by JR Limited Express. From the JR Station, a shuttle bus serves Noboribetsu Onsen. Don't confuse Noboribetsu Onsen with Noboribetsu, an industrial city that is 13 minutes by bus from its namesake spa town. If you are coming from Sapporo, arrange a tour through your hotel, JR Sapporo Station or the Sapporo International Communication Plaza.

Donan Bus travels from Sapporo to Noboribetsu Onsen; the trip takes 1 hour, 20 minutes (¥1,950; reservations advised). There are also connections to Muroran Station.

EXPLORING

FAMILY **Jigokudani** (地獄谷 *Valley of Hell*). A volcanic crater in a bow-shape valley, Jigokudani has hundreds of multicolor geysers pulsing like the heartbeat of Earth itself. Not to worry, though; the walkways to photo ops have handrails and are very safe. It's a short walk from all Noboribetsu hotels and well worth a look. There's no admission fee or formal open hours, but parking is ¥500 during the day. Prepare to explain to your kids that the strong smell came from the earth, not you. ☒ *Noboribetsu Onsen, Noboribetsu* 🖾 *Free* ☾ *Open 24 hrs.*

WHERE TO STAY

$$$$
RESORT
🖻 **Dai-ichi Takimoto-kan** (第一滝本館). Contemplate the Valley of Hell while soaking in one of the 12 different pools at Dai-ichi Takimoto-kan, a prime example of Japanese mass tourism. **Pros:** hot water to ease every known condition; crab-crazy buffets; free Wi-Fi in the main part of the hotel. **Cons:** conveyer-belt atmosphere; noisy with groups; some

rooms need sprucing up. [$] *Rooms from: ¥22830* ✉ *55 Noboribetsu Onsen, Noboribetsu* ☎ *0120/940–489* 🛏 *383 Japanese-style rooms, 12 Western-style rooms, 4 combination rooms* 🍴 *Some meals.*

$$$$ HOTEL 🏨 **Ryotei Hanayura** (旅亭花ゆら). An idyllic hot-spring hotel, the Ryotei Hanayura has floor-to-ceiling lobby windows that look out on a small canyon and river and hot springs that bubble gently among rocks and trees. **Pros:** peaceful, dignified environment; great views; bound to be a highlight of any Japan trip. **Cons:** rooms a little small; not all rooms nonsmoking; meals not optional. [$] *Rooms from: ¥60000* ✉ *100 Noboribetsu Onsen, Noboribetsu* ☎ *0143/84–2322* 🌐 *www.hanayura.com/en/index.html* 🛏 *33 Japanese-style rooms, 6 with no bath; 4 combination rooms* 🍴 *Some meals.*

NIBUTANI 二風谷

40 km (24 miles) east of Tomakomai, 115 km (71 miles) southeast of Sapporo.

Fodor's Choice ★ Nibutani is one of the last places in Hokkaido with a sizable Ainu population—or at least part Ainu, as few pure-blooded Ainu are left. The tiny village, which is nothing more than some scattered homes along a main road, has two museums and a handful of souvenir shops. It's a very long day trip from Sapporo, and if you have toured native people's centers in North America it may feel like more of the same, but it is where you can find the best, nontouristy collection of Ainu art and artifacts in Hokkaido.

GETTING HERE AND AROUND

Nibutani is hard to reach by public transport. It involves either a bus from Sapporo or a train then a change to a bus—all costing about ¥4,000 round-trip. The Tourist Office in Sapporo has information on the current public transport connections if this is your only option. Otherwise, you're better off renting a car for the day and taking the toll road (about 90 minutes). *See Sapporo section above for car rental information.*

EXPLORING

Kayano Shigeru Nibutani Ainu Archive (萱野茂 二風谷アイヌ資料館 *Kayano Shigeru Nibutani Shiryo-kan*). This important museum puts a spotlight on Ainu clothing and other items used in sacred rites, all of it collected by the late prominent Ainu activist and Nibutani resident Shigeru Kayano. Until his death in 2006, Kayano traveled extensively, and the archive contains presents to the Ainu from other indigenous peoples. The museum is across the main road from the Ainu Culture Museum. ✉ *79–4 Nibutani, Biratori* ☎ *0145/72–3215* 🎫 *¥400, ¥700 joint ticket with Nibutani Ainu Culture Museum* 🕘 *Apr. 16–Nov. 15 daily 9–5, Nov. 16–Apr. 15 by appointment.*

Fodor's Choice ★ **Nibutani Ainu Culture Museum** (二風谷アイヌ文化博物館 *Nibutani Ainu Bunka Hakubutsukan*). An excellent resource for information about the Ainu, this museum remains sadly unknown to many Japanese. Ainu artifacts, such as shoes of salmon skin, water containers made from animal bladders, and heavy blue-and-black embroidered coats, are on

CLOSE UP

Hokkaido's First Inhabitants

Once upon a time in *Ainumosir* ("human being peaceful land"), *aynu* (human beings) lived in *kotan* (villages), raising their families on a diet of *ohaw* (salmon, meat, or plants) and *sayo* (millet and other grains). They honored the god Okikurmikamu, and told *yukar* (epic poems) to remember the interwoven lives of humans and the spirit world, particularly of bears and owls. Sometimes they traded kelp, salmon, and herring with the *sisam*, the neighbors north or south.

CHANGING TIMES

Around the 15th century life changed. The southern sisam—the Japanese—began arriving in greater numbers and building trading posts along the far south coast. As the Japanese moved north and solidified their presence on the island, the aynu—regarded as "hairy people"—became forced laborers.

In 1869 the new Meiji Government lumped Ainu together with Japanese as "commoners," and the Ainu language and lifestyle were outlawed. Forced assimilation and intermarriage nearly obliterated the culture. The Hokkaido Former Aborigine Protection Law sliced up land ownership, dispossessing many Ainu of ancestral homesteads.

But the Ainu have fought back. By the 1980s Ainu were calling for basic human rights, drawing support from indigenous groups in other countries. The United Nations made 1993 the Year of Indigenous Peoples, which bolstered their efforts, and a victory was achieved in 1994 when leading activist Kayano Shigeru of Nibutani was elected the first Ainu to Japan's Parliament. In May 1997, the national government passed belated legislation acknowledging the existence of Ainu as a minority group (a landmark event in Japan's purportedly "homogeneous" society), requiring local and national governments to respect their dignity by promoting Ainu culture and traditions. The act stopped short of certifying Ainu as an indigenous ethnic group, due to concerns about aboriginal rights to land and natural resources.

THE AINU TODAY

Visitors to Hokkaido may find it hard to recognize full-blooded Ainu outside the tourist centers of Shiraoi, Nibutani, and Akan. Some 24,000 people declare themselves Ainu, although many identify as Japanese. Most Japanese have little interest in Ainu affairs, beyond buying cute wooden carvings as souvenirs. Otherwise well-informed, worldly Japanese hosts may be surprised, and a little embarrassed, by foreigners' interest in Ainu. Today, Ainu tourist parks are being revamped as cultural centers. Ainu language is taught at 14 locations, and Kayano Shoro is continuing his father's monthly Ainu radio broadcasts (FM-Pipaushi).

The best places to learn more about Ainu culture and politics are the Nibutani Ainu Culture Museum and the Kayano Shigeru Nibutani Ainu Archive; the Poroto Kotan and Ainu Museum, Shiraoi; and the Akan Ainu Kotan cultural performances.

Foundation for Research and Promotion of Ainu Culture (アイヌ文化振興・研究推進機構 *Ainu Bunka Shinko Kenkyu Sokushin Kiko*). ✉ *Presto 1.7 Bldg. 5F, Kita 1 Nishi 7, Sapporo* ☎ *011/271–4171* ⊕ *www.frpac.or.jp/english/index.html* 🎟 *Free* ⊙ *Weekdays 9–5.*

14

display, as well as implements used in *iyomante,* an Ainu ritual that sent the spirit of the bear back to the nonhuman world. There is an hour-long movie in English and a selection of tapes with traditional Ainu chants and songs. ☒ *61 Nibutani, Biatori* ☎ *0145/72–2892* ✉ *¥400, ¥700 joint ticket with Kayano Shigeru Nibutani Ainu Archive* ☉ *Apr. 16–Nov. 15, daily 9–4:30; Nov 16.–Apr. 15, Tues.–Sun. 9–4:30; closed Dec. 16–Jan. 15.*

CENTRAL HOKKAIDO

Breathtaking and often snowy Taisetsu-san is Japan's largest national park and home to Mt. Asahidake, Hokkaido's highest peak, at 7,311 feet. Roads in the region skirt through farmland and flower fields to circle the mountains north and south, and cable cars lift visitors onto mountain plateaus with steaming volcanic vents, alpine flower meadows, and awe-inspiring views. If you are a hiker, cable cars will take you to a trail that rings several mountains. Allow at least two days for reaching the area and enjoying its grandeur. Asahikawa is the largest city and the transport gateway to the park. Staying-over places are Biei and Furano for gentle countryside and Soun-kyo Gorge and Asahidake for mountain grandeur.

DAISETSUZAN NATIONAL PARK 大雪山国立公園

50 km (31 miles) east of Asahikawa.

The country's largest nature preserve, Daisetsuzan National Park contains the very essence of rugged Hokkaido: vast plains, soaring mountain peaks, hidden gorges, cascading waterfalls, thick forests, and steaming hot springs.

GETTING HERE AND AROUND

Soun-kyo village and canyon are 90 minutes east of Asahikawa by car on Route 39. The highway skirts the northern side of the park, and Soun-kyo is the gateway. You can catch a bus directly to Soun-kyo Onsen (¥2,100) from in front of Asahikawa's JR Station (bus stop #7). If you are using a JR Pass, you can save money and time by taking the train to Kamikawa Station and transferring to the Dohoku Bus for the 35-minute run to Soun-kyo. Bicycles can be rented for ¥1,000 a day in the village, and a short cycling trail along the old road by the river is a peaceful way to enjoy the gorge. From July to September a ¥440 bus ride connects the village with the Daisetsu dam and lake, but there is only one bus a day. Ask at the visitor's center.

VISITOR INFORMATION

The Soun-kyo Tourist Center, in the bus terminal, provides hiking maps and information on sightseeing and lodging. English is spoken.

Contact Soun-kyo Visitor Center (層雲峡観光協会 *Sounkyo Kanko Kyokai*). ☒ *Daisetsu-san National Park* ☎ *01658/94–400* ⊕ *www.sounkyo.net/english.*

Daisetsuzan National Park has some of Hokkaido's most rugged scenery.

EXPLORING

Fodor's Choice ★ **Daisetsuzan National Park** (大雪山国立公園 *Daisetsuzan Kokuritsu Koen*). Daisetsuzan, which means great snow mountain, refers to the park's five major peaks, whose altitudes approach 7,560 feet. They are climbable even by moderately experienced hikers, with a ring trail that is best done in summer. But you can also catch a bus or train or even drive just south of Asahikawa and simply enjoy the picturesque region.

On the park's east side is Soun-kyo, but on its unconnected west side, two **spa towns** serve as summer hiking centers and winter ski resorts. **Shirogane Onsen**, at 2,461 feet, has had especially good skiing since its mountain, Tokachi-dake, erupted in 1962 and 1988, creating a superb ski bowl. At **Asahidake Onsen** you can take a cable car (¥2,900) up Asahi-dake to an altitude of 5,250 feet and hike for two hours to the 7,513-foot summit. In late spring and early summer the slopes are carpeted with alpine flowers. Serious skiers come for Japan's longest ski season. ⊠ *Daisetsu-san National Park* ⊕ *www.asahikawa-daisetsu.jp.*

Soun-kyo (層雲峡 *Soun-kyo Gorge*). Running through a 15-mile-long ravine, Route 39 cuts through the northeast entrance of Daisetsuzan National Park. For 5 miles, sheer cliff walls rise on both sides of the canyon as the road drills into the mountains. In winter and early spring, forbidding stone spires loom as if in judgment; in other seasons they thrust through glorious foliage. On the way there are a couple of river-carved gorges called **Obako** and **Kobako**, which are pretty, but underwhelming if you've seen really gorgeous gorges before. Go see **Momijidani** (Maple Tree Valley) if you're here in autumn.

Soun-kyo Onsen village is halfway through the ravine. In summer, the pedestrian-friendly main street is lined with flower boxes, and guest-houses and souvenir shops add charm to what is basically a concrete version of an alpine village. Most activities take place outside the village, so while people are hiking through the park the village feels dead. From Late January to March, the frozen river and its ice cliffs are illuminated for the **Ice Waterfall Festival**, which is breathtaking. If you're driving, watch your gas tank, as there is no gas station in town. ⊠ *Daisetsu-san National Park* ⊕ *www.sounkyo.net/english.*

WHERE TO STAY

There's no lodging within the township of Soun-kyo Onsen if you want to stay in the northern part of the park. Because Soun-kyo's hotels are almost exclusively ryokan, where meals are included in your lodging cost, other dining opportunities in town are severely limited. A list of hotels and onsen is on the English page of the Soun-kyo Tourist Office website. Rates tend to be 20% lower in winter.

$$$$
RESORT ⊡ **Choyo Tei** (層雲峡朝陽亭). Perched on a bluff halfway up one side of the gorge, this hotel has the best views in the park. **Pros:** quality on par with other large hotels; big bathrooms. **Cons:** full of tour groups; conveyor-belt service; not the most attractive hotel. Ⓢ *Rooms from: ¥24000* ⊠ *Soun-kyo Onsen, Kamikawa* ☎ *01658/5–3241* ⊕ *en.choyotei.com* ↻ *57 Western-style rooms, 57 Japanese-style rooms, 137 combination rooms, 1 suite* ¶◯¶ *Some meals.*

$$$
B&B/INN ⊡ **Resort Pension Yamanoue** (ペンション山の上). This modern guest-house sits in the center of the village's flower-filled pedestrian area. **Pros:** in village center; expansive dinners; butterflies in late June and early July. **Cons:** must go next door for hot springs; shared bathrooms. Ⓢ *Rooms from: ¥18900* ⊠ *Soun-kyo Onsen, Kamikawa* ☎ *0165/85–3206, 0165/85–3207* ⊕ *www.p-yamanoue.com* ▭ *No credit cards* ↻ *14 Japanese-style rooms without bath* ¶◯¶ *Some meals.*

SPORTS AND THE OUTDOORS

HIKING

FAMILY **Kurodake Ropeway** (黒岳ロープウェイ *Kurodake Ropeway*). Technology helps even the most reluctant hikers up the mountains: a cable car and chairlift rise up the side of the gorge to 4,264 feet. Intrepid hikers can march one more hour to the top of Kurodake, 2,244 feet higher. From here, numerous well-marked trails lead either across volcanic gravel or shrubby plateaus. Crimson foliage sets the slopes ablaze in September. Daisetsuzan's beauty is best enjoyed slowly, as along with the breathtaking views you may encounter deer, foxes, and bears. Take care early in the season when bear cubs are being watched by their mothers. ⊠ *Soun-kyo, Kamikawa Cho, Daisetsu-san National Park* ☎ *01658/5–3031* ⊕ *www.rinyu.co.jp/modules/pico01* ▱ *¥1,950 round-trip* ◷ *June–Aug, daily 6–7; Sept.–May, daily 8–4.*

ASAHIKAWA 旭川

136 km (84 miles) northwest of Sapporo.

Asahikawa, Hokkaido's second-largest city, is the principal entrance to Daisetsuzan National Park. It is not terribly cosmopolitan; daytime life centers around a pedestrian shopping area and at night the entertainment district is raucously full of men from the farming hinterland. Travelers pass through its station, bus terminal, or airport on their way to more beautiful places, but a small Ainu museum and a winter festival in February are worthwhile if your schedule dictates a one-night stay.

14

GETTING HERE AND AROUND

Trains leave Sapporo for Asahikawa twice an hour and the journey takes about 1 hour, 30 minutes. The Hokkaido Expressway also connects the two cities and takes just under two hours to drive. Domestic airlines from Tokyo, Osaka, and Nagoya fly into Asahikawa Airport, 10 km (6 miles) from the city center, making it a good entry point for a holiday in central and eastern Hokkaido. There are car rentals at the airport and station.

VISITOR INFORMATION

Asahikawa Tourism (旭川ツアリズム *Asahikawa Tsuarizumu*). ✉ *Okuno Bldg. 5F, 7–418 Sanjo-dori* 🌐 *www.asahikawa-tourism.com.*

WHERE TO STAY

$$ HOTEL 🏨 **Washington Hotel** (藤田観光ワシントンホテル旭川 *Fujita Kanko Washington Hotel Asahikawa*). Anyone staying the night in Asahikawa can make do at this bright, busy hotel located across the street from the JR Station. **Pros:** near the train station; close to restaurants. **Cons:** small, characterless rooms; no double beds. [$] *Rooms from: ¥15000* ✉ *7 Miyashita-dori* ☎ *0166/23–7111* 🌐 *asahikawa.washington-hotels.jp* 🛏 *260 Western-style rooms* 🍴 *Breakfast.*

BIEI AND FURANO 美瑛と富良野

Biei: 23 km (15 miles) east of Asahikawa; Furano: 31 km (19 miles) farther south.

Flower fields and small farms at the base of the Daisetsuzan mountain range attract thousands of domestic and East Asian visitors hoping to get a taste of the simple country life. Although Western visitors may not be so wowed by lavender and potato fields, or by the art galleries and cutesy coffee shops that dot the region, it makes an attractive stopover area while driving to central or east Hokkaido between late May and September. Biei is a small modern village with neighboring rolling hills and a patchwork of crop fields (potato, corn, soba, sunflowers) to cycle around; Furano is a small town famous throughout Japan for its lavender farms (when in bloom) and its ski resort.

GETTING HERE AND AROUND

Trains from Asahikawa depart every hour and reach Biei in 30 minutes and Furano in 70 minutes. In July and August there are special trains, sightseeing buses, and bus or train packages from Sapporo, which combine Biei and Furano flowers with a popular zoo at Asahikawa.

VISITOR INFORMATION

Outside Furano Station, flower farm information, shuttle buses, and help with hotel searches are available at the Furano Tourist Association.

Contact Furano-Biei Tourism Center (富良野美瑛広域観光センター *Furano Biei Koiki Kanko Center*). ⊠ *JR Furano Station, Hinode Machi 1–30, Furano* ☎ *0167/23–3388* ⊕ *www.furanotourism.com/en.*

EXPLORING

Farm Tomita (ファーム富田 *Faamu Tomita*). In Japanese eyes, lavender is one of the favorite souvenirs Hokkaido, and this is the farm where it all started—back in 1903. Now thousands of visitors come to see fields of lavender, poppies, cosmos, herbs, and marigolds. *Irodori* is the field with flowers planted in seven strips, each a different color. Lavender peak season is early July to early August. During this time, the JR Lavender Batake Station—seven minutes closer than JR Nakafurano Station—is open. This is worth a look if you're a flower aficionado. ⊠ *Hokusei, Sorachi-gun, Nakafurano-cho* ☎ *0167/39–3939* ⊕ *www.farm-tomita.co.jp/en/* ⊡ *Free* ⊘ *Daily 8:30–5.*

EASTERN HOKKAIDO 道東

Bears and eagles rule the mountains of Shiretoko National Park. Farther inland are the mysterious lakes of Akan National Park, where Ainu people hold on to their pre-Japanese culture with spirit worship, music, and dance. South, around Kushiro, are the vast wetland breeding grounds of the striking *tancho-zuru* (red-crested crane). On the eastern coast flowers carpet the land in the short summer, while in winter creaking ice floes nudge against the shore, providing a temporary home to seals and seabirds. Unfortunately, the ice is getting thinner and the viewing season shorter—this is the front line of global warming.

Japan's last frontier is also a hotbed of international politics. Japan and Russia are engaged in bitter disputes over islands, fishing, and mineral rights. Russian sailors hang around fishing ports, and signboards across the region proclaim, "Return the Northern Territories!" This is Japan's campaign to reclaim the Kuril Islands, some just kilometers off its eastern shore, that were occupied by the Soviets in the closing days of World War II.

There are regional airports in Kushiro and Memanbetsu, and express trains reach Abashiri and Kushiro. The largest city is Kushiro, famous for its morning fish market, but more beautiful touring bases include Akan Onsen and Abashiri, and the small fishing town of Utoro, halfway up the Shiretoko Peninsula.

ABASHIRI 網走

517 km (321 miles) east of Sapporo.

A good touring base for eastern Hokkaido, Abashiri is a small town in the shadow of Tento-san. On the town outskirts are shallow coastal lakes with flowers and seabirds. Bicycles can be rented for slow sightseeing. The whaling fleet sets out from here on "research" trips ("research" is the official word, common parlance would call it "hunting") under Japan's interpretation of IWC rules, which keeps Japan at loggerheads with conservationists. Winters are harsh: visitors bundle up for boat tours through the *ryuhyo* (ice floes) that jam up on its shores and stretch out to sea as far as the eye can see.

GETTING HERE AND AROUND

The significant distance from Sapporo to Abashiri makes it advisable to take either the expressway or one of the four daily so-called express trains. This is a four- or five-hour trip, with the train sometimes chugging along at almost walking speeds through the northern Daisetsu mountain area, then a dead-end turn at Engaru, where passengers must stand and turn the seats to face forward again.

Abashiri has enough sights for a day or more as you set out to cycle the 27-km (17-mile) lakeside cycling road or the equally easy 40-km (25-mile) one-way cycle along Lake Notoro to Tokoro town. There are six buses a day from the station, circling the sights on Tento-san; a day pass costs ¥800. The tourist office staff will keep bags for ¥300 per item. After taking in Abashiri's sights, take your car or go by bus to the Shiretoko, Akan, or Kushiro Marsh areas.

VISITOR INFORMATION

Some staff members at the Abashiri Tourist Association, adjoining the JR Station, speak English. This is where to find information about transportation and lodging in the area.

Contacts Abashiri City Tourism Association (網走市役所観光課 *Abashiri Shiyakusho Kanko-ka*). ⊠ *Minami 6 Higashi 4, Abashiri* ☎ *0152/44–6111* ⊕ *abashiri.jp/tabinavi/en/index.html.*

EXPLORING

FAMILY **Abashiri Prison Museum** (網走監獄博物館 *Abashiri Kangoku Hakubutsukan*). Spartan cells line the central corridors in five wooden prison blocks, showing how the convicts who built much of early Hokkaido lived out their years. Used between 1912 and 1984, the prison is now a museum with cell blocks, watchtowers, and farm buildings. Only the most heinous criminals were banished to this forbidding northern outpost, the Alcatraz of Japan. English information is entertainingly lost in translation, but anguished-looking mannequins illustrate the grimness of life behind bars, and how for those who did escape it could be even worse. If you're in the mood, try out a prison meal—a tray with a bowl of rice, a piece of fish, miso soup, and a few pickles. ⊠ *1–1 Yobito, Abashiri* ☎ *0152/45–2411* ⊕ *www.kangoku.jp/world* ☜ *¥1,080* ⊗ *Apr.–Oct., daily 8–6; Nov.–Mar., daily 9–5.*

Fodor's Choice **Hokkaido Museum of Northern Peoples** (北海道北方民族博物館 *Hoppo Minzoku Hakubutsukan*). Hokkaido is the southernmost point of the ★ northern community of the Ainu. This museum's delightful exhibits link the polar indigenous people, such as the Ainu, Inuits, and Sami (or Lapps) in a way that shows surprising similarities over wide spaces. Displays compare and contrast the kitchen implements, clothing, and hunting tools of various cultures from northern Japan, the neighboring Russian island of Sakhalin, and the northern parts of America and Eurasia. English-language pamphlets are available. Of particular interest are videos depicting life in the frozen north, such as building igloos. The museum is 5 km (3 miles) from JR Abashiri Station on Tento-san. By bus from the station, take the KankoShisetsu Meguri to the Hoppo Minzoku Hakubutsukan Mae stop, whcih is right in front of the museum. ✉ *309–1 Shiomi, Abashiri* ☎ *0152/45–3888* 🌐 *www.hoppohm.org/english/index.htm* 🎫 *¥550* 🕒 *July–Sept., daily 9–5; Oct.–June, Tues.–Sun. 9:30–4:30.*

SIGHTSEEING CRUISES

Aurora Icebreakers (流氷観光砕氷船おーろら号運航 *Ryuhyo Kanko Saihyosen O-rora-go Unko*). If you really want to break the ice in future conversations about Hokkaido and you're in Abashiri between late January and early April, take in some *ryuhyo* ocean drift icebergs (with some bird- and seal-watching). Weather permitting, icebreakers *Aurora 1* and *Aurora 2* sail from Aurora Terminal at the east end of Abashiri Port for ¥3,300, letting you inspect winter *ryuhyo* (drift ice) at close range. Drift ice is unpredictable, so check local conditions before you sail.

If that sounds too cold, try summer, when between late April and late October you can board the same boats from Utoro Port (50 miles away from Abashiri) for a sail around the uninhabited peninsula of Shiretoko National Park. ■ **TIP→ Travel agencies in Tokyo and Sapporo offer package tours for both seasons.** ✉ *Aurora Port, Minami 3 Nishi 4, Abashiri* ☎ *0152/24–2147 summer, 0152/43–6000 winter* 🌐 *ms-aurora.com/abashiri/en.*

WHERE TO EAT AND STAY

$$$$ JAPANESE 🍴 **Nakazushi** (中鮨). Rotarian Kanio Nakano presides over the catch of the day in a small restaurant, run for 50 years by the same family. Depending on the season, Nakano-san offers you salmon roe on rice, sea urchin, and plump, juicy local scallops. *Tsuchi-kujira* (Baird's beaked whale) is also sometimes on the menu, but Nakano-san can make substitutions if you let him know your no-whale preference (say "no *kujira*"). [$] *Average main: ¥4000* ✉ *Minami 2 Nishi 2, near Abashiri Central Hotel, Abashiri* ☎ *0152/43–3447.*

$$ HOTEL 🏨 **Abashiri Central Hotel** (網走セントラルホテル *Abashiri Hotel*). Creature comforts await you at this downtown hotel, which seems a world away from rugged outback seaport city Abashiri. **Pros:** in the town center; caters to foreign visitors. **Cons:** cookie-cutter hotel design; boring views. [$] *Rooms from: ¥15000* ✉ *Minami 2 Nishi 3–7, Abashiri* ☎ *0152/44–5151* 🌐 *www.abashirich.com* 🛏 *96 Western-style rooms, 2 Japanese-style rooms, 6 combination rooms* 🍽 *Some meals.*

$$$$ RESORT 🏨 **Hotel Abashiriko So** (ホテル網走湖荘). Waterbirds drift by the windows of the big but friendly hotel on the shore of Lake Abashiri, a few miles from town. **Pros:** lakeside location; ideal for bird-watching; impressive menu. **Cons:** out of town; popular with tour groups. [$] *Rooms from: ¥25000* ✉ *78 Yobito, Abashiri* ☎ *0152/48–2245* 🌐 *www.abashirikoso.com/world/eng/index.html* 🛏 *37 Western rooms, 20 Japanese rooms, 100 hybrid rooms* 🍽 *All-inclusive.*

SHIRETOKO NATIONAL PARK 知床国立公園

A highlight of any trip to Hokkaido, the spectacular and miraculously uninhabited Shiretoko National Park is a UNESCO World Heritage Site.

GETTING HERE AND AROUND

From Sapporo to Abashiri it's a five-hour express train, then a local train to Shari, and finally a 55-minute bus ride to Utoro. With connections the trip takes seven hours. Depending on the season, about seven daily bus connections go from Shari to Utoro. Buses from Abashiri and the airports in Kushiro and Memanbetsu also connect to Utoro. Coming from Kushiro it's a two-hour drive to the ugly fishing village of Rausu on the south side of the peninsula, and then a 30-minute drive over the Shiretoko Pass (closed November–April) to Utoro.

From Sapporo the daily overnight Eagle Liner bus takes seven hours (¥15,430 round-trip to Utoro), departing Sapporo Chuo Bus Terminal at 11:15 pm (the return trip leaves Utoro Bus Terminal at 9:20 am). Reservations with Chuo Bus are necessary and can be made at the terminal behind the TV Tower in Sapporo, where the bus departs. Utoro and Shiretoko Shari JR Station are also connected by six buses daily in summer.

From the end of April to the end of October, shuttle-bus trips link Utoro Bus Terminal with the Nature Center and Shiretoko Five Lakes between 8:30 and 4:30 (¥960–¥1,980 round-trip depending on distance). If you are coming by car, park at the Nature Center and board the shuttle. The 12-km (7-mile) dirt road to Kamuiwakka Onsen waterfall is open to shuttle buses only between July 13 and September 20 (closed in winter). Be careful of wildlife when driving; Shiretoko is full of grazing deer that favor cleared roadside verges and are largely unperturbed by vehicles.

Apart from hiking, a boat is the best way to see the wildest parts. From late April to October, several boat companies in Utoro harbor offer one- to three-hour trips (¥5,000–¥10,000) out along the peninsula, beneath soaring 600-foot cliffs to the tip of the cape. Early-morning and late-afternoon trips on a small boat offer the best chances to see bears come down to the beaches to forage. On the Rausu side, boats head out into the Nemuro Straits along Russia's Kunashiri Island, and summer is the best time for whale-watching. A stay of at least one night is recommended for hiking, hot springs, wildlife spotting, and silence. Look for the green sign with white lettering. Shiretoko Nature Cruise is a mom-and-pop operation offering summer and winter cruises from the Rausu side of Shiretoko Peninsula.

Shiretoko Naturalist's Association is a nonprofit offering nature walks, guided tours, and lots of local lore.

ESSENTIALS

BOAT TOURS **CafeFox Cruises.** Cafe Fox offers three-hour Shiretoko World Heritage Cruises along the coast two times a day (9:20 and 2 pm). Guidance is in Japanese. ⊠ *Utoro Higashi 96–5, Utoro* ☎ *0152/24–2656* ⊕ *www. hitcolour.com/cafefox/cruise.*

Shiretoko Nature Cruise. Contact this company for sea cruises to see whales, sea lions, and birds along the coast. ☎ *0153/87–4002* ⊕ *www.e-shiretoko.com.*

TOUR INFORMATION **Shiretoko Naturalist's Association** (知床ナチュラリスト協会 *Shiretoko Nachurarisuto Kyokai*). The association's guides lead guided walks around Shiretoko Five Lakes, but everything is in Japanese. ⊠ *Utoro Higashi 284, Shari* ☎ *0152/22–5522* ⊕ *shinra.or.jp.*

Fodor's Choice ★ **Shiretoko National Park Nature Center** (知床自然センター *Shiretoko Shizen Center*). Crowds swarm to this nature center for film screenings, souvenir shopping, and dining, but you might be more interested in the latest information about animal sightings. The mile-long trail behind the center offers a peaceful trek to the Furepe Waterfall that's even better because the day-trippers hardly venture here. Bears have been spotted on this trail in the early morning. The Nature Center is about 4 km (2 miles) from Utoro. ■TIP→ In summer ask about the shuttle bus from here to Kamuiwakka Falls. ⊠ *531 Iwaobetsu, Utoro* ☎ *0152/24–2114* ⊕ *center.shiretoko.or.jp/en* ⊙ *Apr. 20–Oct. 20, daily 8–5:40; Oct. 21–Apr. 19, daily 9–4.*

VISITOR INFORMATION

In Utoro, pick up information about the park, its sights, and access at Utoro-Shiretoko Michi no Eki, a two-minute walk from the bus terminal on the waterfront. On the Rausu side, information can be found at the Rausu Visitor Center. Don't forget to check out the hourly 26-foot-high geyser in the woods out back.

Contacts Rausu Visitor Center (羅臼ビジターセンター). ⊠ *6–27 Yunosawa, Rausu* ☎ *0153/87–2828.* **Utoro-Shiretoko Michi no Eki** (ウトロ知床道の駅 *Utoro-Shiretoko Road Station*). ⊠ *186 Banchi 8, Utoro Nishi* ☎ *0152/22–5000.*

EXPLORING

Fodor's Choice ★ **Shiretoko National Park** (知床国立公園 *Shiretoko Kokuritsu Koen*). On the Shiretoko Peninsula, Shiretoko National Park is worlds away from modern Japan: brown bears hook salmon out of tumbling rivers; Blackiston's fish owls and Steller's sea eagles glide through the skies; and a steaming hot spring river tumbles to the sea at Kamuiwakka.

With the park's protected status came mass tourism. Efforts to preserve the area's natural beauty have resulted in strict rules, and limited shuttle-bus access to the last few kilometers of peninsula road—no longer close to Kamuiwakka—makes the experience more challenging. But it's worth the effort: the charming Ezo-shika deer stare at you with as much wonder as you do them. If you visit outside the summer crush—June and September are good times—Shiretoko is a remarkable, untouched pocket of wilderness in a heavily industrialized and technologically advanced nation.

Most tour buses whisk you in and out of 24 hours—with an overnight stay in a resort, quick photo stops along the way, and maybe a boat tour. If you're traveling on your own, it's best to visit the popular destinations at noon or at the end of the day when buses are headed out. Shiretoko is lovely, but the weather, even in summer, is fickle. A Shiretoko stay (and

Kamuiwakka Onsen is filled by a series of waterfalls.

hiking plans) can be marred by mists and rain. ✉ *Utoro* ☎ *0152/22–6226* ⊕ *www.shiretoko.asia/world/index.html.*

Kamuiwakka Onsen (カムイワッカ温泉). *Kamui* means "spirit" or "god" in the Ainu language, and there's something wondrous, almost otherworldly, about this tumbling hot waterfall on the north shore under Io-zan (Mt. Io, as in Sulphur Mountain). Hot water rushes down the mountain through a series of multicolor falls and pools. Wear shoes that can get wet as you will scramble up over slippery rocks to a couple of pools higher upstream; the park staff is there to help you up down and caution you not to go much farther than the roped-off third pool. Access is by car or bus only (at certain times of the year) from July to mid-October. ✉ *Shiretoko National Park.*

Rausu-dake (羅臼岳岩尾別温泉熊ノ湯 *Mt. Rausu*). Towering 5,448 feet along the spine of the peninsula, Mt. Rausu is snow-covered from October to June. The most accessible trailhead is 5 km (3 miles) east of Utoro behind the Hotel Chi-no-hate; if you are a fast hiker, you can walk for one hour, 20 minutes to a 1,920-foot rocky outcrop, then another two hours to the top. From there trails head west (two hours) to meet the Utoro-Rausu highway at Shiretoko Pass, or go over the ridge and down to Rausu (three hours). Check weather conditions before hiking, sign the trailhead books, and fix a bear bell to your backpack.

Aching muscles can be soaked in open-air hot springs waiting at the end of the hike: **Iwaobetsu Onsen**, just below the Hotel Chi-no-hate parking lot, has four steaming rocky pools where there's a strong likelihood of sitting naked with strangers. Near the trailhead and campsite on the Rausu side, look for **Kuma-no-yu**, two boiling pools areas for men and women separated by some unfortunate concrete and rusty pipes, but fenced in for privacy. ✉ *Shiretoko National Park.*

FAMILY Fodor's Choice ★ **Shiretoko Goko** (知床五湖 *Shiretoko Five Lakes*). A stop for every tour bus route in the region, this collection of small lakes sits on a forested precipice above the ocean. It takes just over an hour to walk around all five lakes on boardwalk paths, and there are some newer boardwalks for the city slickers who don't want to get their shoes dusty. The lakes are lovely reflecting pools for the mountains, but crowds do disturb the idyll a bit. Luckily, most tour groups only circle the first two lakes. Park at the Nature Center, and get bus tickets for the 20-minute drive Shiretoko Goko and beyond. Guided tours off the boardwalk paths are also available depending on the season. Check their website for available guides. During certain times (bear season or times when the ecosystem is particularly sensitive), you might have to pay for a guide or pay to attend a lecture before setting out. ✉ *Shiretoko National Park* ☎ *0152/24–2125 Shiretoko Shari Tourist Association* 🌐 *www.goko.go.jp/english* 🎫 *¥410 per car for parking* 🕐 *Late Apr.–Nov., daily 7:30–6.*

SMELT FISHING

Lake Akan in winter is dotted with ice holes. Fishermen crouch in subzero temperatures to hook *wakasagi* (pond smelt) from the depths. Visitors can slide across the lake and try their luck, fortified with *amasaké*, a delicious—and slightly alcoholic—drink made from sweetened brown rice. The successful can head back to the shore where stall holders are on hand to mince the catch for a raw meal or fry or grill it. Grilled wakasagi often appears on the winter menus of Hokkaido izakaya. Wakasagi fishing costs ¥1,500 per person at Ice Land Akan, including a chair and your own personal ice hole.

WHERE TO EAT

$$ JAPANESE 🍴 **Matsui Suisan - Shiretoko Tabi no Eki** (松田水産 知床旅の駅 *Shiretoko Station of Journey*). This bustling village eatery serves steaming crab curry, golden sea urchin on rice, and anything else they can make out of the morning's catch. They often give customers free crab legs to suck on while they wait. It's near the harbor down from the Shiretoko Grand Hotel and across the street from the 7-11; picture menus are available for easy ordering. [$] *Average main: ¥2000* ✉ *Utoro Higashi 151, Shari* ☎ *0152/24–2910* 💳 *No credit cards.*

WHERE TO STAY

$ HOTEL 🏨 **Iruka Hotel** (いるかホテル). Owned by a diver/wildlife photographer (*iruka* means dolphin), this hotel guesthouse sits by the water in Utoro. **Pros:** personal welcome; great food; nature-spotting advice. **Cons:** slow to respond to email reservation inquiries; small rooms. [$] *Rooms from: ¥10400* ✉ *Utoro Nishi 5, Shari* ☎ *0152/24–2888* 🌐 *www.iruka-hotel.com* 🛏 *13 rooms* 🍽 *Some meals.*

$$ RESORT **Shiretoko Daiichi Hotel** (知床第一ホテル). Beneath vast ceiling murals, replica antique furniture stands toe-deep in plush carpets decorated with regional flowers—as far as Japanese resort hotels go, it doesn't get much better than this. **Pros:** luxurious digs; best place for sunset view; delicious dining. **Cons:** Western rooms are plain and boxy; nature can oddly feel a bit distant; tour group frenzy in the lobby. [$] *Rooms from: ¥18000* ✉ *306 Utoro Onsen, Shari* ☎ *0152/24–2334* 🌐 *www.shiretoko-1.com/en/index.html* 🛏 *178 Japanese rooms, 41 Western rooms, 19 combination rooms* 🍴 *Some meals.*

AKAN NATIONAL PARK 阿寒国立公園

58 km (36 miles) southeast of Abashiri.

This national park is sometimes overlooked in favor of Daisetsu and Shiretoko, but offers great fishing and hiking opportunuties.

GETTING HERE AND AROUND

There are about six buses (¥2,700; 90 minutes) a day to Akanko from Kushiro Airport and station. You can also catch a bus from Akanko to Abashiri if you change buses in Bihoro. Two buses a day also connects Akan to Soun-kyo.

Akan Bus Co. has escorted bus tours (in Japanese only) from May to the end of October, departing from Kushiro Station for Akanko, Lake Mashuko, and Kawayu Onsen. Since there are so few options to see this part of Japan, such tours may be unavoidable for those who don't want to drive themselves. Reservations are required.

EXPLORING

Akan National Park (阿寒国立公園 *Akan Kokuritsu Koen*). Volcanoes rise from primeval forests and lakeside beaches bubble with hot springs in this national park, unfairly overshadowed by neighboring Daisetsu and Shiretoko. In Akan's northern forests, strange, cylindrical algae called *marimo* bob to the surface of the namesake lake. Elsewhere Ainu men pluck and blow eerie music from traditional instruments, while women dancers duck and weave in honor of the red-crested *tancho* white cranes that fly in every winter, breeding on the wetland on the park's southern border. In summer, it's a hiker's heaven of trails and hot springs; in winter, the lakes freeze over and ice festivals spill out onto the frozen expanses. ✉ *2–6–20 Akanko Onsen, Akan-cho* ☎ *0154/67–3200* 🌐 *www.lake-akan.com/en/.*

Akanko Onsen (阿寒湖温泉). A major stop on bus tours, this small town on the lakeshore has giant hotels blocking the views from the main road. Kitschy souvenir shops sell endless rows of carved Ainu-style bears, and bottles of *marimo* algae balls line the shelves like eyeless pets waiting for adoption. It's a bit much. At the western end of the town is the one cobbled street of the Ainu village, lined by shops and restaurants and home to a small museum and a performance center. ✉ *4–1 Chuo 1, Akan-cho* 🌐 *www.lake-akan.com/en.*

Smelt-fishing through holes chopped in the ice is a popular wintertime activity at Lake Akan.

Akanko Ainu Theatre Ikor. From May to October there are excellent traditional dance performances or puppet shows four or five times a day starting at 11 am and lasting about 30 minutes. The venue's seating faces a wall that's open to the outside, which gives the performances a dynamic natural background. The 9 pm show includes fire performances from the *Iomante* (a traditional ceremonial bear sacrifice that was once a part of Ainu village life—an actual bear is no longer sacrificed). Performances cost ¥1,080. ⊠ *4–7–84 Akanko Onsen, Akan-cho, Kushiro* ☎ *0154/67–2727* ⊕ *www.akanainu.jp.*

Akan Nature Center (阿寒ネイチャーセンター). Between May and October you can enjoy the lake from a canoe with the help of the Akan Nature Center, which offers two- or eight-person Canadian canoes for a 45-minute beginner course (¥2,100), a two-hour adventure course (¥5,300), or an early morning private tour (starting at ¥14,700 for two people). Reserve at least one day in advance. The center is in Akanko Han, near the Ainu village and next to Spa Inn Yamaguchi on the north end of the main town street. Ask about their camping and mountain climbing trips, as well. If you are impervious to cold, it also has winter programs. ⊠ *Akanko Onsen 5–3–3, Akan-cho* ☎ *0154/67–2801* ⊕ *www.akan.co.jp.*

FAMILY **Ice Land Akan** (あいすランド阿寒). Between January and March, Ice Land (which becomes Fishing Land May through November) occupies the southern corner of Lake Akan and is used for a variety of outdoor activities such as ice skating, Nordic skiing, and ice fishing; activities are run by the tourist agency Koudai. There are four access points to Ice Land from around the hot spring area: one on either side of Hotel Gozensui (the access point on the western side is the dock used during fishing season), one through an outdoor passage under the New Akan Hotel, and one just to the northeast of Akan no Mori Tsuruga Resort Hanayuuka. ■**TIP→ The agency has no English-speaking staff, so your best bet is to have your hotel arrange your activities; communication shouldn't be an issue during the activity.** ⊠ *Akanko Onsen 2, Akan-cho, Kushiro* ☎ *0154/67–2057* ⊕ *www.koudai-akan.net/iceland.html.*

Kushiro-Shitsugen National Park (釧路湿原 *Kushiro-Shitsugen Kokuritsu Koen*). Graceful red-crested cranes preen and breed in protected Kushiro Wetlands, which constitutes 60% of Japan's remaining marshes. These rare cranes, whose feathers were thought to bring good luck, were ruthlessly hunted at the beginning of the 20th century and were even believed to be extinct until a handful of survivors were discovered in 1924. They now number about 650. The crane—long-legged and long-billed, with a white body trimmed in black and a scarlet cap—is a symbol of long life and happiness. Legends hold that the birds live 1,000 years, and indeed, in captivity some have made it to a rather impressive 80 years of age. They pair for life, making them the symbol of an ideal couple and are frequently alluded to in Japanese wedding speeches.

■**TIP→ November to March is the best season for wild-crane watching.** This is when the birds fly in from Russia, China, and Korea and gather at feeding stations such as Tsurumidai, off Route 53. In summer, nesting birds retreat deep into the swamps to raise their chicks and can only be spotted with binoculars.

Canoe paddlers on the Kushiro River have a chance to see cranes and other birds: canoe rental companies are at Lake Toro, off Route 391, and by the Norroko-go, a slow sightseeing train from Kushiro (July and August only). The marshland comprises 71 square miles (184 square km) and viewing areas with wooden walkways and observation towers are located off Routes 53 and 359. ⊠ *Kushiro* ⊕ *www.lake-akan.com/en/eastern/kushiro.*

Lake Akan (阿寒湖 *Akan-ko*). Chugging tour boats with noisy Japanese commentaries and even speedboats disturb the waters between the smoking volcanoes Me-Akandake and O-Akandake (He-Akan and She-Akan). But out on Churui Island, silence is green among Akanko's strangest inhabitants, *marimo*, as they nestle peacefully in display tanks. Marimo are spherical colonies of green algae that may be as small as a Ping-Pong ball or as large as a soccer ball (the latter taking up to 500 years to form). Rare life forms, *marimo* can only be found in Lake Yamanaka, near Fuji-san, and in a few lakes in North America, Siberia, and Switzerland. These strange algae act much like submarines, bobbing to the lake surface when bright sunshine increases their photosynthesis, then diving below during inclement weather when light levels drop. Nearby shops offer them in bottles.

While you're in the area, take a look at **Mashu-ko** one of the world's clearest lakes, visible only from afar (if at all, as it's often shrouded in fog). **Kussharo-ko** is less impressive, but you can enjoy a hot sand bath on the lakeshore just north of Ikenoyu Onsen. Japanese travelers often take in all three lakes on the same trip. ⊠ *Shiretoko National Park* ⊕ *www.lake-akan.com/en/.*

Tancho no Sato Crane Park (あかんランド丹頂の里 *Akan Rando Tancho no Sato Akai Berei*). Try out some miniature golf, dine at a crane-themed restaurant, or experience a bit of agriculture at this onsen tourist stop with a small hotel and camping facilities. Across the street is the Akan International Crane Center where, for ¥470, you watch eggs hatching, baby chicks taking their first steps, and staffers providing medical care for these stately creatures. When the crowds are mostly gone in winter, you can watch the preening cranes strut. The facilities are about 45 minutes south of Lake Akan by car. ✉ *23–36 Akan-cho, Shiretoko National Park* ☎ *0154/66–2330* 🌐 *www.akan.jp*.

WHERE TO STAY

$ B&B/INN **Onsen Minshuku Yamaguchi** (民宿山口 *Spa House Yamaguchi*). A mynah bird named Taro may screech a welcome as you enter this small home, which is just past the Ainu village end of the town. **Pros:** good value; friendly service; great food. **Cons:** well-worn rooms; thin walls; no lake views. [$] *Rooms from: ¥10020* ✉ *5–3–2 Akanko Onsen, Akan-cho* ☎ *0154/67–2555* 🌐 *www.goodinns.com/yamaguchi* 💳 *No credit cards* 🛏 *10 Japanese-style rooms without bath* 🍴 *Some meals.*

NORTHERN HOKKAIDO 道北

Travelers with more time might trek north to Soya Misaki, Japan's northernmost cape, for the stark beauty of the Rebun and Rishiri islands. Wakkanai, the regional center, is a rather unpleasant fishing town 396 km (246 miles) north of Sapporo. Use it as the jumping-off point to the islands and to the coastal grasslands to the south. The best season is late May to early September.

THE NORTHERN CAPE AND ISLANDS

Wakkanai is 396 km (246 miles) north of Sapporo.

Japan's northernmost point is windy and empty. In the short summer season, tiny alpine flowers bloom in coastal grasslands and on rocky outcrops overlooking the sea. In winter, little happens as people batten down the hatches. Come here only when you've already seen Daisetsu and Shiretoko. Visitors journey here for the hiking, flowers, bragging rights of having seen Japan's northernmost extremity, and the solitude found in such edge-of-the-world places.

GETTING HERE AND AROUND

From June through August, ANA flies from Shin-Chitose Airport directly to Rishiri Airport (45 minutes) on Rishiri and Hokkaido Air Systems flies two flights a day from Sapporo's slightly inconvenient Okadama Airport. There are also buses year-round from Sapporo to Wakkanai (six hours), and then ferry connections to both Rishiri and Rebun islands.

Heart Land Ferry has boats that make the daily two-hour crossing to Rebuno and the 100-minute crossing to Rishirio. In summer there are four or five daily ferries, two daily in winter. One-way fares to Rebun are ¥2,370, and to Rishiri they're ¥2,140. A ferry between the two islands costs ¥850 (or you can pay about twice the price and spend your journey in the upper-level lounge rather than in a seat).

ESSENTIALS

Ferry Information Heart Land Ferry (ハートランドフェリー). ⊠ 2-7-1 Kai-un, Wakkanai ☎ 0162/23-8010 ⊕ www.heartlandferry.jp/english.

EXPLORING

Rebun-to (礼文島 Rebun Island). Created by an upward thrust of Earth's crust, Rebun-to is the older of the two main islands in the Sea of Japan. Many travelers flock here when they're bored of package tours, and summer on Rebun is a year's worth of energy squeezed into three months. Along the east coast are numerous villages anchoring fleets of fishing boats just offshore; prickly *uni* sea urchins are spotted through bottomless boxes held over the side of the boat and then raked in. On the west coast, civilization holds on, sheltered from relentless winter winds.

14

Visible on a hiking trail that takes about eight hours to navigate, Rebun has cliffs that stave off the surging waters of the Sea of Japan. Inland, more than 300 species of wildflowers blanket the mountain meadows—by mid-June in such profusion that each step seems to crush a dozen of the delicate blossoms. Don't tread on the white-pointed *usuyuki-so* (roughly meaning "dusting of snow"), found only on Rebun. Views of Sakhalin at the northernmost point available on clear days. ☎ 0163/86–2655 ⊕ www.rebun-island.jp/en.

Rishiri-to (利尻島 Rishiri Island). If you're driving along the western side of Hokkaido, the coastal road offers you a view of Mt. Rishiri for an hour or two. This Mt. Fuji clone is the result of an underwater volcano whose cone now rises 5,646 feet out of the water. The scenery is wilder than on Rebun, and though it's a larger island, Rishiri has fewer inhabitants. The rugged terrain makes it harder to support life and warrants hardier climbing. The intermediate **Kutsugata Course** (four hours for the fittest hikers) on the west side of the island takes you past patches of wildflowers—including the buttercup-like *botan kimbai* and the vibrant purple *hakusan chidori*—and numerous bird species. Cycling around the island is also an option (four hours of flat coastal road if the weather is not too windy). ☎ 0163/84–2349 ⊕ www.town. rishiri.hokkaido.jp/kankou-annai/.

Soya Misaki (宗谷岬 Cape Soya). This is the end of Japan. Ahead of you, across the frigid waters, is Russia's Sakhalin Island (sometimes visible). This lonely but significant spot is the site of several monuments marking the border of Japan's territory. A public bus makes the hour-long run between Wakkanai and Cape Soya six times a day. Ask about buses back, too, so you can plan properly. It's worth going to if you've come up this far, just to say you've done it. ⊠ Cape Soya, Wakkanai.

WHERE TO STAY

$ B&B/INN 🏠 **Maruzen Pension Rera Mosir** (マルゼンペンション レラモシリ *Maruzen Penshon Rera Moshiri*). Although it is a bit removed from town and the ferry landing, the pension is very close to where nature really starts and that is why most people are here on Rishiri Island. **Pros:** beautiful scenery all around. **Cons:** the nearby school might get loud at times. [$] *Rooms from: ¥11950* ✉ *227–5 Sakaemachi, Rishiri* ☎ *0163/82–2295* 🛏 *10 Western-style rooms, 2 Japanese-style rooms* 🍴 *Some meals* 💳 *No credit cards.*

$ B&B/INN 🏠 **Pension Uni** (ペンションうーにー). This sky-blue building sits atop the cliffs above Rebun's ferry terminal and can be seen from the ferry. **Pros:** good views; tasty seafood. **Cons:** no English spoken; steep climb up from the harbor. [$] *Rooms from: ¥11880* ✉ *Kafuka Irifune, Rebun-cho, Rebun-to* ☎ *0163/86–1541* 💳 *No credit cards* 🛏 *9 Western-style rooms, 1 Japanese-style room* 🍴 *Some meals.*

UNDERSTANDING JAPAN

BOOKS AND MOVIES

ABOUT JAPANESE

ESSENTIAL PHRASES

MENU GUIDE

BOOKS AND MOVIES

Books

Among the acclaimed novelists at work in Japan today is Haruki Murakami, whose *1Q84, Hard-Boiled Wonderland and the End of the World,* and numerous short stories are often bizarre and humorous blends of magical realism and science fiction. Banana Yoshimotos's *Kitchen* and *Goodbye Tsugumi* are escapist fun. Nobel Prize winner Kenzaburo Oe's *A Personal Matter* is a compelling novelistic coming to terms with his relationship with his handicapped son. *Grotesque,* by one of Japan's leading mystery writers, Natsuo Kirino, is dark and psychologically complex, and is illuminating about Japanese culture. Meanwhile, Western authors Richard Flanagan (*The Narrow Road to the Deep North,* winner of the 2014 Man Booker Prize and not to be confused with Basho's *haiku* anthology) and David Mitchell (*The Thousand Autumns of Jacob de Zoet*) are garnering acclaim for their novels based on Japanese history.

Haiku, the 5-7-5 syllable form that the monk Matsuo Basho honed in the 17th century, especially in his *The Narrow Road to the Deep North,* is perhaps the best known genre of Japanese poetry; two fine small collections of poems by Basho and other haiku masters are the beautifully illustrated *Monkey's Raincoat* and *A Net of Fireflies.* *One Hundred Leaves* by Frank Watsonis is a new annotated translation of the classic anthology *Hyakunin Isshu.*

History and Society. Andrew Gordon's *A Modern History of Japan: From Tokugawa Times to the Present* includes the March 2011 disasters and their political fallout. Oliver Statler's *Japanese Inn* uses one family enterprise to trace 400 years of social change. Tomiko Higa and Dorothy Britton's *The Girl with the White Flag* illustrates war in Okinawa from the perspective of a seven-year-old girl, and is replete with vivid details.

Yamamoto Tsunetomo's *Hagakure* is an 18th-century guide to the Way of the Samurai. In *Confessions of a Yakuza,* Dr.

Junichi Saga records his conversations with a dying gangster.

A fine study of the Japanese mind is to be found in Roger J. Davies and Osamu Ikeno's *The Japanese Mind: Understanding Contemporary Japanese Culture.* Karel van Wolferen's *The Enigma of Japanese Power,* R. Taggart Murphy's *Japan and the Shackles of the Past,* and *Dogs and Demons* by Alex Kerr, the first foreigner to win the Shincho Gakugei literature prize, shed light on the Japanese sociopolitical system.

Religion. The classic gateways to this subject are Suzuki Daisetsu's seminal *Introduction to Zen Buddhism* and *Zen and Japanese Culture.* Shinto master Yamakage Motohisa introduces Japan's ancient religion to Western readers in *The Essence of Shinto.*

Art, Architecture, and Crafts. *Japanese Art* by Joan Stanley-Baker surveys the whole of Japanese art history. Nishi Kazuo and Hozumi Kazuo's *What Is Japanese Architecture?* treats the subject historically and has examples of buildings you will actually see on your travels. Philip Jodidio's *Ando: Complete Works 1975–2014,* Kenneth Frampton's *Kengo Kuma: Complete Works,* Kenzo Tange's *Tange by Tange,* and Toyo Ito's *Toyo Ito* illustrate four postwar Japanese architects' work.

Movies

Western viewers have typically encountered Japanese cinema in the work of directors Mizoguchi Kenji, Ozu Yasujiro, and Kurosawa Akira. Three of Mizoguchi's finest films explore the role of women in feudal Japan: *The Life of Oharu* (1952), *Ugetsu* (1953), and *Sansho the Bailiff* (1954). Ozu's films—among them *Late Spring* (1949), *Early Summer* (1951), and *Tokyo Story* (1953)—explore traditional Japanese values in the everyday lives and relationships of middle-class families. Kurosawa's *Rashomon* (1950), a 12th-century murder story told by four different narrators, inspired a worldwide interest in Japanese cinema. Among his other classics are period films *Seven Samurai* (1954), and *Ran* (1985), but *To Live* (1952), the story of a bureaucrat trying to make his last days meaningful, is perhaps his most moving film.

The next wave of postwar filmmakers include Ichikawa Kon, who directed two powerful antiwar movies, *The Burmese Harp* (1956) and *Fires on the Plain* (1959), but is probably best known for *Tokyo Olympiad* (1965); Teshigahara Hiroshi, whose allegorical *Woman in the Dunes* (1964) is based on the novel by Abe Kobo; and Imamura Shohei, who made *The Ballad of Narayama* (1983), about life and death in an Edo-period mountain village, and *Black Rain* (1989), based on a novel by Ibuse Masuji, which deals with the atomic bombing of Hiroshima.

More recent Japanese filmmakers who have won acclaim abroad include Itami Juzo and Suo Masayuki. Itami's work includes *Tampopo* (1985), a highly original comedy about food; and *Minbo* (1992), which dissects the world of Japanese gangsters. Suo's *Shall We Dance?* (1996) is a bittersweet comedy about a married businessman who escapes his daily routine by taking ballroom dance lessons. More recent Japanese dramas winning acclaim abroad are Takita Yojiro's *Departures* (2008), which received an Academy Award for its humorous look at the cultural divide between city and countryside, and *Like Father Like Son* (2013), directed by Hirokazu Koreeda. Its thoughtful depiction of contemporary Japanese families moves beyond its babies-switched-at-birth trope and won it the *prix du jury* award at Cannes. Kimizuka Ryoichi's *Reunion* (2012) takes an oblique look at the human impact of the 2011 tsunami in the story of a volunteer preparing the bodies of victims for burial.

Though Japanese gangster flicks date back to such Kurosawa classics as *Drunken Angel* (1948) and *Stray Dog* (1949), an edgy gangster genre emerged in the 1990s led by Takeshi Kitano. His films *Fireworks* (1997) and *Zatoichi* (2003) have won awards at the Venice Film Festival. There are many, many Japanese gangster films, including a whole exploitative subset that mixes extreme violence with basically soft-core porn. Like gangsters films, the popularity of the samurai movie is enduring in Japan. Based on best-selling manga, *Rurouni-Kenshin* (2012), directed by Keishi Ohtomo, is indicative of the new kind of samurai-action movie gaining popularity in recent years.

Those interested in Japanese anime should start with the Academy Award–winning picture *Spirited Away* (2001) by Hayao Miyazaki. Other modern anime pioneers include Osamu Tezuka, Mamoru Oshii, Satsoshi Kon, Hideki Anno, and Katsuhiro Otomo.

Japanese horror focuses more on psychological terror than on blood-spurting special effects, but some can be quite gruesome, such as the hair-raising *Audition* (1999), directed by cult favorite Miike Takashi; *Infection/Kansen* (Ochiai Masayuki, 2004); and *Dark Water* (Hideo Nakata, 2002). More commonly, films hinge on foreboding and inescapable doom; they typically involve ghosts (usually women in white dresses and long hair) or poltergeists seeking revenge. The horror hits *Ringu/Ring* (Hideo Nakata, 1998) and *Ju-on: The Grudge* (Takashi Shimizu, 2002) are representative of this genre; both have been remade by American directors for wider audiences.

ABOUT JAPANESE

To read and write Japanese you need a command of some 2,000 *kanji* (ideogram characters derived from Chinese) and two syllabic alphabets, called *hiragana* and *katakana*. The pronunciation of all the *kanji* and their various inflections can be rendered in either alphabet, although *katakana* is normally used for the spelling of foreign loan-words, making it the most immediately useful for visitors.

The alphabets are made up of four types of syllables: the single vowels *a, i, u, e,* and *o* (pronounced ah, ee, ooh, eh, and oh); vowel-consonant pairs like *ka, ni, hu,* or *ro*; the single consonant *n* (which punctuates, for example, the upbeats of the word for bullet train, *Shinkansen: shee-*n*- ka-*n*- se-*n); and compounds like *kya, chu,* and *ryo*—also each one syllable. Thus Tokyo, the capital city, has only two syllables—*tō* and *kyō*—not three. Likewise pronounce Kyōto *kyō-to*, not *kee-oh-to*. The Japanese *r* is rolled so that it sounds like a bounced *d*. There is no *l*-sound in the language, and the Japanese have great difficulty in distinguishing *l* from *r*, whether spoken or written.

No diphthongs. Paired vowels in Japanese words are not slurred together, as in the English *brain* or *stein*. The Japanese separate them, as in *mae* (*ma*-eh), which means "in front of"; *kōen* (*ko*-en); and *tokei* (to- *keh*-ee), which means "clock" or "watch."

Macrons. Many Japanese words, when rendered in *romaji* (Roman letters) use a macron, or bar, over certain vowels to indicate whether it is pronounced long or short. The macrons in *Tokyo*, for example, direct you to double the length of the *o*: *to-*o*- kyo-*o. Likewise, when you see double consonants, as in the city name Nikkō, double up on the *k*s—as you would with "bookkeeper"—and elongate the *o*. (Note, however, that macrons are often omitted recently.)

Emphasis. Some books state that the Japanese emphasize all syllables in their words equally. This is not true. Take the words *sayōnara* and *Hiroshima*. Americans are likely to stress the downbeats: *sa*-yo-*na*-ra and *hi*-ro- *shi*-ma. The Japanese actually emphasize the second beat in each case: sa- *yō*-na-ra (note the macron) and hi- *ro*-shi-ma. Metaphorically speaking, the Japanese don't so much stress syllables as pause over them or race past them: emphasis is more a question of speed than weight. In the vocabulary below, we indicate emphasis by italicizing the syllable that you should stress.

Note also the unstressed pronunciations. The word *desu* roughly means "is." It looks like it has two syllables, but the Japanese race past the final *u* and just say "dess." Likewise, some verbs end in *-masu*, which is pronounced "mahss." Similarly, the character *shi* is often quickly pronounced "sh," as in the phrase meaning "pleased to meet you": *ha*-ji-me- *mash(i)*-te.

Hyphens. Throughout this book we have hyphenated certain words to help you recognize meaningful patterns and vocabulary elements. This isn't conventional; it is practical. Seeing *Eki-mae-dōri* (literally "Station Front Avenue) this way instead of run together in a single word, for example, makes it easier to register the terms for "station" and "avenue" for use elsewhere. You'll also run across a number of sight names that end in *-jingu* or *-jinja* or *-taisha*, all of which mean "Shinto shrine."

Structure. Japanese sentences are structured quite differently, subject-object-verb, instead of subject-verb-object as in English. "I am going to Tokyo" would translate literally in Japanese as "Tokyo to I'm going."

Note: placing an "o" before words like *tera* (*otera*) and *shiro* (*oshiro*) makes the word honorific. The meaning is clear enough without it, but omitting the polite form would be exceedingly un-Japanese.

ESSENTIAL PHRASES

ENGLISH	PRONUNCIATION	JAPANESE

BASICS

ENGLISH	PRONUNCIATION	JAPANESE
Yes/No	ha-i / ii-e	はい / いいえ
Please	o-ne-gai shi-masu	お願いします
Thank you (very much).	(dō-mo) a-ri-ga-tō go-zai-ma su	（どうも）ありがとうございます
You're welcome.	dō i-ta-shi-mashi-te	どういたしまして
Excuse me.	su-mi-ma-sen	すみません
Sorry	go-men na-sai	ごめんなさい
Good morning.	o-ha-yō go-zai-ma-su	おはようございます
Good day/afternoon.	kon-ni-chi-wa	こんにちは
Good evening.	kom-ban-wa	こんばんは
Good night.	o-ya-su-mi na-sai	おやすみなさい
Good-bye	sa-yō-na-ra	さようなら
Mr./Mrs./Miss	-san	〜さん
Pleased to meet you.	ha-ji-me-mashi-te	はじめまして
How do you do?	dō-zo yo-ro-shi-ku o-ne-gai shi-masu	どうぞよろしくお願いします

NUMBERS

The first reading is used for reading numbers, as in telephone numbers, and the second is often used for counting things.

1	i-chi / hi-to-tsu	一 / 一つ
2	ni / fu-ta-tsu	二 / 二つ
3	san / mit-tsu	三 / 三つ
4	yon (shi) / yot-tsu	四 / 四つ
5	go / i-tsu-tsu	五 / 五つ
6	ro-ku / mut-tsu	六 / 六つ
7	na-na (shi-chi)/ na-na-tsu	七 / 七つ
8	ha-chi / yat-tsu	八 / 八つ
9	kyū / ko-ko-no-tsu	九 / 九つ
19	jū-kyū	十九
20	ni-jū	二十

ENGLISH	PRONUNCIATION	JAPANESE
21	*ni*-jū-i-chi	二十一
30	*san*-jū	三十
40	*yon*-jū	四十
50	*go*-jū	五十
60	*ro*-ku-jū	六十

DAYS OF THE WEEK

Sunday	*ni*-chi yō-bi	日曜日
Monday	*ge*-tsu yō-bi	月曜日
Tuesday	*ka* yō-bi	火曜日
Wednesday	*su*-i yō-bi	水曜日
Thursday	*mo*-ku yō-bi	木曜日
Friday	*kin* yō-bi	金曜日
Saturday	*dō* yō-bi	土曜日
weekday	*hei*-ji-tsu	平日
weekend	*shū*-ma-tsu	週末

MONTHS

January	*i*-chi *ga*-tsu	一月
February	*ni* ga-tsu	二月
March	*san* ga-tsu	三月
April	*shi* ga-tsu	四月
May	*go* ga-tsu	五月
June	*ro*-ku *ga*-tsu	六月
July	*shi*-chi *ga*-tsu	七月
August	*ha*-chi *ga*-tsu	八月
September	*ku* ga-tsu	九月
October	*jū* ga-tsu	十月
November	*jū*-i-chi *ga*-tsu	十一月
December	*jū*-ni *ga*-tsu	十二月

ENGLISH	PRONUNCIATION	JAPANESE

USEFUL EXPRESSIONS, QUESTIONS, AND ANSWERS

ENGLISH	PRONUNCIATION	JAPANESE
Do you speak English?	*ei*-go ga wa- *ka*-ri-ma-su *ka*	英語がわかりますか。
I don't speak Japanese.	ni- *hon*-go ga wa- *ka*-ri-ma- *sen*	日本語がわかりません。
I don't understand.	wa- *ka*-ri-ma- *sen*	わかりません。
I understand.	wa- *ka*-ri-ma-shi- *ta*	わかりました。
I don't know.	*shi*-ri-ma- *sen*	知りません。
I'm American (British).	wa- *ta*-shi wa a- *me*-ri-ka (i- *gi*-ri-su) jin *desu*	私はアメリカ（イギリス）人です。
What's your name?	o- *na*-ma-e wa *nan* desu *ka*	お名前はなんですか。
My name is [name].	[name] to *mo*-shi- *ma*-su	〜と申します。
What time is it?	i-ma *nan*-ji desu *ka*	今何時ですか。
How?	*dō* yat-te	どうやって。
When?	*i*-tsu	いつ。
yesterday/today/tomorrow	ki- *nō* /kyō/ *ashi*-ta	昨日 / 今日 / 明日
this morning	*ke*-sa	けさ
this afternoon	*kyō* no *go*-go	今日の午後
tonight	*kom*-ban	今晩
Excuse me, what?	su- *mi*-ma- *sen*, *nan* desu *ka*	すみません、何ですか。
What is this/that?	*ko*-re/ *so*-re wa *nan* desu *ka*	これ / それは何ですか。
Why?	*na*-ze desu *ka*	なぜですか。
Who?	*da*-re desu *ka*	だれですか。
I am lost.	*mi*-chi ni ma-yo-i- *mashi*-ta	道に迷いました。
Where is the [place]	[place] wa *do*-ko desu *ka*	はどこですか
.. train station?	e-ki	駅
.. subway station?	chi- *ka*-te-tsu-no eki	地下鉄の駅
.. bus stop?	*ba*-su *no*-ri- *ba*	バス乗り場

ENGLISH	PRONUNCIATION	JAPANESE
.. taxi stand?	*ta*-ku-shi-i *no*-ri- *ba*	タクシー乗り場
.. airport?	*kū*-kō	空港
.. post office?	*yū*-bin- *kyo*-ku	郵便局
.. bank?	*gin*-kō	銀行
.. [name] hotel?	[name] ho- *te*-ru	ホテル
.. elevator?	e-re- *bē*-tā	エレベーター
Where are the restrooms?	*to*-i-re wa *do*-ko desu *ka*	トイレはどこですか。
here/there/over there	*ko*-ko/ *so*-ko/ *a*-so-ko	ここ / そこ / あそこ
left/right	hi- *da*-ri/ *mi*-gi	左 / 右
straight ahead	mas- *su*-gu	まっすぐ
Is it near (far)?	chi- *ka*-i (*tō*-i) desu *ka*	近い (遠い) ですか。
Are there any rooms?	*he*-ya ga a-ri- *ma*-su *ka*	部屋がありますか。
I'd like [item].	[item] ga ho- *shi*-i no desu ga	がほしいのですが。
.. newspaper	*shim*-bun	新聞
.. stamp	*kit*-te	切手
.. key	*ka*-gi	鍵
I'd like to buy [item].	[item] o kai- *ta*-i no desu ga	を買いたいのですが。
.. a ticket to [destination].	[destination] *ma*-de no *kip*-pu	までの切符
map	*chi*-zu	地図
How much is it?	i- *ku*-ra desu *ka*	いくらですか。
It's expensive (cheap).	ta- *ka*-i (ya- *su*-i) de su *ne*	高い (安い) ですね。
a little (a lot)	su- *ko*-shi (*ta*-ku-san)	少し (たくさん)
more/less	*mot*-to ō-ku/ su-ku-na-ku	もっと多く / 少なく
enough/too much	*jū*-bun/ō- *su*-gi-ru	十分 / 多すぎる
I'd like to exchange	*ryō*-ga e shi-te i- *ta*-da-ke-masu *ka*	両替していただけますか。
.. dollars to yen	*do*-ru o *en* ni	ドルを円に

ENGLISH	PRONUNCIATION	JAPANESE
.. pounds to yen	*pon*-do o *en* ni	ポンドを円に
How do you say [word] in Japanese?	ni- *hon*-go de wa [word] wa *dō i*-i-masu *ka*	日本語で.はどう言いますか。
I am ill/sick.	wa- *ta*-shi wa *byō*-ki desu	私は病気です。
Please call a doctor/an ambulance.	*i*-sha/kyū-kyū-sha o *yon*-de ku-da- *sa*-i	医者/救急車を呼んでください。
Please call the police.	*ke*-i-sa-tsu o *yon*-de ku-da- *sa*-i	警察を呼んでください。
Help!	*ta*-su- *ke*-te	助けて!

USEFUL WORDS

airport	*kū*-kō	空港
bay	wan	湾
beach	*ha*-ma	浜
behind	*u*-shi-ro	後ろ
bridge	*ha*-shi or - *ba*-shi	橋
bullet train, literally "new trunk line"	*Shin*-kan-sen	新幹線
castle	o- *shi*-ro or -jō	城
cherry blossoms	*sa*-kura	桜
city or municipality	-shi	市
department store	de- *pā*-to	デパート
district	-gun	郡
east	hi- *ga*-shi	東
exit	*de*-guchi or -guchi	出口
festival	*ma*-tsuri	祭
foreigner	*gai*-jin (more politely: gai- *ko*-ku-jin)	外人
garden	*ni*-wa	庭
gate	mon or torii	門 / 鳥居
hill	oka	丘
hot-spring spa	*on*-sen	温泉

ENGLISH	PRONUNCIATION	JAPANESE
in front of	*ma*-e	前
island	shima or -jima/-tō	島
Japanese words rendered in roman letters	*rō*maji	ローマ字
lake	*mi*-zu- *u*-mi or -ko	湖
main road	*kai*-dō or *kō*-dō	街道 / 公道
morning market	asa- *i*-chi	朝市
mountain	yama or –san	山
museum	bi- *ju*-tsu-kan for art; haku- *bu*-tsu-kan for natural history, etc.	美術館・博物館
north	kita	北
park	*kō*-en	公園
peninsula	-hantō	半島
plateau	*kō*-gen	高原
pond	ike or -ike	池
prefecture	-ken/-fu	県 / 府
pub (Japanese-style)	iza- *ka*-ya	居酒屋
river	kawa or -gawa	川 / 河
sea	*u*-mi or -kai	海
section or ward	-ku	区
shop	*mi*-se or -ya	店 / 屋
shrine	jinja or -gu	神社 / 宮
south	mi- *na*-mi	南
street	michi or -dō	道
subway	chi- *ka*-tetsu	地下鉄
temple	tera or -ji/-in	寺 / 院
town	*ma*-chi	町
train	*den*-sha	電車
train station	eki	駅
valley	*ta*-ni	谷
west	*ni*-shi	西

MENU GUIDE

ENGLISH	PRONUNCIATION	JAPANESE
BASICS AND USEFUL EXPRESSIONS		
a bottle of	*ip*-pon	一本
a glass/cup of	*ip*-pai	一杯
ashtray	*ha*-i- *za*-ra	灰皿
bill/check	kan- *jō*	勘定
bread	pan	パン
breakfast	*chō*-sho-ku	朝食
butter	ba- *tā*	バター
cheers!	kam- *pai*	乾杯!
chopsticks	*ha*-shi	箸
cocktail	*ka*-ku- *te*-ru	カクテル
Does that include dinner?	*Yū*-sho-ku *ga*tsu-ki- *ma*-su-ka	夕食が付きますか。
fork	*fō*-ku	フォーク
I am diabetic.	wa- *ta*-shi wa tō-*nyō*-byō de su	私は糖尿病です。
I am dieting.	*da*-i-et-to *chū* desu	ダイエット中です。
I am a vegetarian.	*saisho*-ku shu- *gi*-sha/ beji- *tari*-an de-su	菜食主義者 / ベジタリアンです。
I cannot eat [item].	[item] wa *ta*-be-ra- *re*-ma- *sen*	は食べられません。
I'd like to order.	*chū*-mon o shi- *tai* desu	注文をしたいです。
I'd like [item].	[item] o o-ne- *gai*-shi-ma su	をお願いします。
I'm hungry.	o-na-ka ga *su*-i-te i- *ma*-su	お腹が空いています。
I'm thirsty.	*no*-do ga ka- *wa*-i-te i- *ma*-su	喉が渇いています。
It's tasty.	*o*-i-shi-i (ma- *zu*-i) desu	おいしい (まずい) です。
knife	*na*-i-fu	ナイフ
lunch	*chū*-sho-ku	昼食
menu	me-nyū	メニュー
napkin	*na*-pu- *kin*	ナプキン

ENGLISH	PRONUNCIATION	JAPANESE
pepper	ko-*shō*	こしょう
plate	*sa*-ra	皿
Please give me [item].	[item] o ku-da-*sa*-i	をください。
salt	*shi*-o	塩
set menu	*te*-i-sho-ku	定食
spoon	su-*pūn*	スプーン
sugar	sa-tō	砂糖
wine list	*wa*-i-n *ri*-su-to	ワインリスト
What do you recommend?	*o*-su-su-me *ryō*-ri wa *nan* desu *ka*	おすすめ料理は何ですか。

MEAT DISHES

gyō-za	minced pork spiced with ginger and garlic in a Chinese wrapper and fried or steamed	ギョウザ
hayashi *rai*-su	beef flavored with tomato and brown sauce with onions and peas over rice	ハヤシライス
kara-*a*-ge	deep-fried chicken	から揚げ
karē-*rai*-su	curried rice: thick curry gravy typically containing beef over white rice	カレーライス
katsu-*ka*-rē	curried rice with tonkatsu	カツカレー
niku-*ja*-ga	beef and potatoes stewed together with sweetened soy sauce	肉じゃが
okonomi-*ya*-ki	a Japanese pancake made from a batter of flour, egg, cabbage, and meat or seafood, griddle-cooked and sprinkled with green onions and a Worcester-shire-soy-based sauce	お好み焼き

o-yako- *dom*-buri (*o*-yako-don)	literally, "mother and child bowl": cooked chicken and egg in broth over rice	親子どんぶり（親子丼）
rōru *kya*-betsu	rolled cabbage; beef or pork rolled in cabbage and cooked	ロールキャベツ
shabu-shabu	thin slices of beef swirled for an instant in boiling water flavored with soup stock and then dipped into a thin sauce	しゃぶしゃぶ
shō-ga-yaki	pork cooked with ginger	しょうが焼き
shū-mai	shrimp or pork wrapped in a light dough and steamed (originally Chinese)	シュウマイ
su- *bu*-ta	sweet-and-sour pork, originally a Chinese dish	酢豚
suki- *ya*-ki	one-pot meal of thinly sliced beef, green onions, mushrooms, thin noodles, and tofu simmered in a mixture of soy sauce, mirin, and a little sugar	すき焼き
su- *tē*-ki	steak	ステーキ
tanin- *dom*-buri (*ta*-nin-don)	literally, "strangers in a bowl": similar to oyako-domburi, but with beef instead of chicken	他人どんぶり（他人丼）
ton- *ka*-tsu	breaded deep-fried pork cutlets	トンカツ
yaki- *ni*-ku	thin slices of beef marinated then barbecued over an open fire at the table	焼き肉

| yaki- *to*-ri | bits of chicken on skewers with green onions, marinated in sweet soy sauce and grilled | 焼き鳥 |

SEAFOOD DISHES

a-ge- *za*-kana	deep-fried fish	揚げ魚
a-ji	horse mackerel	あじ
a- *sa*-ri no *sa*-kamushi	clams steamed with rice wine	あさりの酒蒸し
bu-ri	yellowtail	ぶり
do- *jō* no yana- *ga*-wa-nabe	loach cooked with burdock root and egg in an earthen dish	どじょうの柳川鍋
ebi fu- *ra*-i	deep-fried breaded prawns	海老フライ
ika	squid	イカ
i- *wa*-shi	sardines	いわし
karei fu- *ra*-i	deep-fried breaded flounder	かれいフライ
ka-tsuo no ta- *ta*-ki	bonito lightly braised, eaten with chopped ginger and scallions and thin soy sauce	かつおのたたき
ma-guro	tuna	まぐろ
ni- *za*-kana	soy-simmered fish	煮魚
sa-ba no *mi*-so-ni	mackerel stewed with soybean paste	さばの味噌煮
sam-ma	saury pike	さんま
sa-shimi	fresh raw fish served sliced thin on a bed of white radish with a saucer of soy sauce and horseradish	刺身
sa- *wa*-ra	Spanish mackerel	さわら
sha-ke / *sā*-mon	salmon	しゃけ / サーモン
shime- *sa*-ba	mackerel marinated in vinegar	しめさば

shio- *ya*-ki	fish sprinkled with salt and broiled until crisp	塩焼き
tako	octopus	たこ
ten-jū	deep-fried prawns served over rice with sauce	天重
teri- *ya*-ki	fish basted in soy sauce and broiled	照り焼き
u-na-jū	eel marinated in a slightly sweet soy sauce, charcoal-broiled, and served over rice	うな重
yaki- *za*-kana	broiled fish	焼き魚

SUSHI

a-ji	horse mackerel	あじ
ama- *e*-bi	sweet shrimp	甘えび
a-nago	conger eel	あなご
ao- *ya*-gi	round clam	あおやぎ
chirashi *zu*-shi	a variety of seafood arranged on the top of a bowl of rice	ちらし寿司
e-bi	shrimp	えび
futo- *ma*-ki	big roll with egg and pickled vegetables	太巻き
hamachi	yellowtail	はまち
hirame	flounder	ひらめ
ho- *ta*-te-gai	scallop	ほたて貝
ika	squid	いか
i-kura	salmon roe	いくら
ka-ni	crab	かに
kappa- *ma*-ki	cucumber roll	かっぱ巻き
kariforunia- *ma*-ki	California roll, with crabmeat and avocado (originally American)	カリフォルニア巻き
ka-zuno- *ko*	herring roe	数の子
ko- *ha*-da	shad	こはだ

ma-guro	tuna	まぐろ
ma-ki *zu*-shi	raw fish, vegetables, or other ingredients rolled in sushi rice and wrapped in dried seaweed	巻き寿司
mi-ru-gai	giant clam	みる貝
nigiri *zu*-shi	rice shaped by hand into bite-size cakes and topped with raw or cooked fish or other ingredients	にぎり寿司
sa-ba	mackerel	さば
sha-ke / *sā*-mon	salmon	しゃけ / サーモン
shinko- *ma*-ki	a type of pickle rolled in rice and wrapped in seaweed	新香巻き
tai	red snapper	たい
tako	octopus	たこ
ta-mago	egg	玉子
tekka- *ma*-ki	small bits of tuna rolled in rice and wrapped in seaweed	鉄火巻き
to-ro	fatty tuna	とろ
u-ni	sea urchin	うに

VEGETABLE DISHES

ae- *mo*-no	vegetables dressed with sauces	和えもの
daigaku *i*-mo	fried yams in a sweet syrup	大学いも
go-bō	burdock root	ごぼう
hō- *ren*-so	spinach	ほうれん草
ka-bocha	pumpkin	かぼちゃ
kim-pira *go*-bō	carrots and burdock root, fried with soy sauce	きんぴらごぼう
kyū-ri	cucumber	きゅうり

ne-gi	green onions	ねぎ
ni- *mo*-no	vegetables simmered in a soy- and sake-based sauce	煮物
o- *den*	street food of various types of fish cakes, vegetables, and boiled eggs simmered in a soy fish stock	おでん
o-hi- *ta*-shi	boiled vegetables with soy sauce and dried shaved bonito or sesame seeds	おひたし
ren-kon	lotus root	れんこん
sato- *i*-mo	taro root	さといも
su-no- *mo*-no	vegetables seasoned with vinegar	酢の物
ta-kenoko	bamboo shoots	タケノコ
tem-pura	vegetables, shrimp, or fish deep-fried in a light batter and dipped into a thin sauce with grated white radish	天ぷら
tsuke- *mo*-no	Japanese pickles made from white radish, eggplant, or other vegetables	漬け物
ya- *sai* i- *ta*-me	stir-fried vegetables	野菜炒め

EGG DISHES

cha-wan *mu*-shi	vegetables, shrimp, etc., steamed in egg custard	茶碗蒸し
medama- *ya*-ki	fried eggs, sunny-side up	目玉焼き
omu- *rai*-su	omelet with rice inside	オムライス
yude *ta*-mago	boiled eggs	ゆで卵

TOFU DISHES

agedashi *dō*-fu	deep-fried plain tofu garnished with spring onions, dipped in hot broth	揚げだし豆腐
hiya- *yak*-ko	cold tofu with soy sauce and grated ginger	冷やっこ
mābō *dō*-fu	tofu and ground pork in a spicy sauce (originally Chinese)	マーボー豆腐
tō-fu no *den*-gaku	tofu broiled on skewers and flavored with miso	豆腐の田楽
yu- *dō*-fu	boiled tofu with green onions	湯豆腐

RICE DISHES

chā-han	fried rice with vegetables and pork	チャーハン（炒飯）
chi- *ma*-ki	sticky rice wrapped in bamboo skin	ちまき
gohan	steamed white rice	ご飯
o- *ka*-yu	rice porridge	お粥
oni- *gi*-ri	triangular balls of rice with fish or vegetables inside and wrapped in sheets of dry seaweed	おにぎり

SOUPS

miso *shi*-ru	thin broth containing tofu, mushrooms, or other ingredients in a soup flavored with miso or soybean paste	みそ汁
sui- *mo*-no	clear broth, often including fish and tofu	吸い物
ton- *ji*-ru	pork soup with vegetables	豚汁

NOODLES

hiya- *mu*-gi	similar to sōmen, but thicker	ひやむぎ

rā-men	Chinese noodles in soy sauce, miso, or salt-flavored broth, often with chāshū (roast pork)	ラーメン
so-ba	buckwheat noodles served in a broth or, during the summer, cold on a bamboo mesh (called *za*-ru soba)	そば
sō-men	summer dish of very thin wheat noodles, usually served cold with a tsuyu or thin sauce	そうめん
u-don	broad flour noodles that can be lunch in a light broth, or a meal (nabe- *ya*-ki *u*-don) when meat, chicken, egg, and vegetables are added	うどん
yaki- *so*-ba	noodles fried with beef and cabbage, garnished with pickled ginger and vegetables	焼きそば

FRUIT

an-zu	apricot	あんず
bu- *dō*	grapes	ぶどう
i-chigo	strawberries	いちご
ichi- *ji*-ku	figs	いちじく
kaki	persimmon	柿
kuri	chestnuts	栗
ku-rumi	walnuts	くるみ
mi- *kan*	tangerine (mandarin orange)	みかん
mo-mo	peach	桃
nashi	Japanese pear	梨
ringo	apple	リンゴ
saku- *ram*-bo	cherry	さくらんぼ
sui-ka	watermelon	西瓜

DESSERT

aisu	ice cream	アイス
kōhii *ze*-rii	coffee-flavored gelatin	コーヒーゼリー
pu-rin	caramel pudding	プリン
wa- *ga*-shi	sweet bean-paste confection	和菓子
yō-kan	sweet bean-paste jelly	ようかん

DRINKS

Alcoholic

bii-ru	beer	ビール
chū-hai	shōchū mixed with soda water, lemon juice, or other flavoring	チューハイ
nama *bii*-ru	draft beer	生ビール
sa-ke	rice wine, also called Ni- *hon*-shu, which can be semi-sec (*a*-makuchi) or dry (*ka*-rakuchi), usually served warm (atsukan), although purists prefer it cold	酒, 日本酒
shō-chū	spirit distilled from potatoes	焼酎

Nonalcoholic

ja-sumin cha	jasmine tea	ジャスミン茶
jū-su	juice, but can also mean any soft drink	ジュース
kō-cha	black tea	紅茶
kōhii	coffee	コーヒー
ni- *hon* cha	Japanese green tea, also called simply o-cha	日本茶
ū-ron cha	Oolong tea	ウーロン茶

TRAVEL SMART
JAPAN

GETTING HERE AND AROUND

■ AIR TRAVEL

Flying time to Japan is 14 hours from New York, 13 hours from Chicago, and 10 hours from Los Angeles. Your trip east, because of tailwinds, can be about 45 minutes shorter.

You can fly nonstop to Tokyo from most major U.S. airports. While some airports offer nonstop flights to Osaka, many route through Tokyo or another Asian hub city. Fares to Japan usually run around $1,200 (more during peak travel times) but in the off-season there are often good deals to be found.

Both of Japan's major carriers offer reduced prices for flights within the country, which are real cost- and time-savers if your trip includes destinations such as Kyushu or Hokkaido, though tickets must be booked outside Japan and there are restrictions on use in peak times. JAL offers the Yokoso Visit Japan Fare; ANA has the Experience Japan Fare.

Air Pass Information Visit Japan Fare.
☎ 800/235–9262 ⊕ www.anaskyweb.com.
Yokoso Visit Japan Fare. ☎ 877/875–2526 ⊕ www.jal.co.jp/yokosojapan.

TRAVEL TIMES FROM TOKYO			
To	By Air	By Car or Bus	By Train
Osaka	1¼ hours	7–8 hours	2½ hours
Hiroshima	1½ hours	10 hours	5 hours
Kyoto	1¼ hours	7 hours	2 hours
Fukuoka	2 hours	14 hours	5 hours
Sapporo	1½ hours	15 hours	10 hours
Naha (Okinawa)	3 hours	NA	NA

■ TIP➜ Ask the local tourist board about hotel and local transportation packages that include tickets to major museum exhibits or other special events.

AIRPORTS

The major gateway to Japan is Tokyo's Narita Airport (NRT), 80 km (50 miles) northeast of the city. The Haneda Airport International Terminal, which opened in 2010, offers flights to major international cities and is only 20 km (12 miles) south of central Tokyo. The newer Centrair Airport (NGO) near Nagoya opened to take the strain off Narita. International flights also use Kansai International Airport (KIX) outside Osaka to serve the Kansai region, which includes Kobe, Kyoto, Nara, and Osaka. Fares are generally cheapest into Narita, however. A few international flights use Fukuoka Airport, on the island of Kyushu; these include Continental flights from Guam, JAL from Honolulu, and flights from other Asian destinations. New Chitose Airport, outside Sapporo on the northern island of Hokkaido, handles some international flights, mostly to Asian destinations such as Seoul and Shanghai. Most domestic flights to and from Tokyo are out of Haneda Airport.

Terminals 1 and 2 at Tokyo's Narita Airport are for international flights while Terminal 3 is for low-cost carriers. Terminal 2 has two adjoining wings, north and south. When you arrive, your first task should be to convert your money into yen; you need it for transportation into Tokyo. In both wings ATMs and money-exchange counters are in the wall between the customs inspection area and the arrival lobby. Both terminals have a Japan National Tourism Organization tourist information center, where you can get free maps, brochures, and other visitor information. Directly across from the customs-area exits at both terminals are the ticket counters for airport limousine buses to Tokyo.

If you have a flight delay at Narita, take a local Keisei Line train into Narita town 15 minutes away, where a traditional shopping street and the beautiful Narita-san Shinsho-ji Temple are a peaceful escape from airport noise.

Flying into Haneda provides visitors with quicker access to downtown Tokyo, which is a short monorail ride away. Stop by the currency exchange and Tourist Information Desk in the second-floor arrival lobby before taking a train into the city. There are also numerous jade-uniformed concierge staff on hand to help passengers with any questions.

If you plan to skip Tokyo and center your trip on Kyoto or central or western Honshu, Kansai International Airport (KIX) is the airport to use. Built on reclaimed land in Osaka Bay, it's laid out vertically. The first floor is for international arrivals; the second floor is for domestic departures and arrivals; the third floor has shops and restaurants; and the fourth floor is for international departures. A small tourist information center on the first floor of the passenger terminal building is open daily 9–5. Major carriers are Air Canada, Japan Airlines, and Delta Airlines. The trip from KIX to Kyoto takes 75 minutes by JR train; to Osaka it takes 45–70 minutes.

Airport Information **Centrair Airport (NGO)** (中部国際空港セントレア). ☎ *0569/38–1195* ⊕ *www.centrair.jp.* **Fukuoka Airport (FUK)** (福岡空港). ☎ *092/621–0303* ⊕ *www.fuk-ab. co.jp.* **Haneda Airport (HND)** (羽田空港). ☎ *03/6428–0888* ⊕ *www.haneda-airport. jp/inter/en.* **Kansai International Airport (KIX).** ☎ *072/455–2500* ⊕ *www.kansai-airport.or.jp/en/index.asp.* **Narita Airport (NRT)** (成田空港). ☎ *0476/34–8000* ⊕ *www. narita-airport.jp.* **New Chitose Airport (CTS)** (新千歳空港). ☎ *0123/23–0111* ⊕ *www. new-chitose-airport.jp.*

GROUND TRANSPORTATION

Known as "The Gateway to Japan," Narita is the easiest airport to use if you are traveling to Tokyo. It takes about 90 minutes—a time very dependent on city traffic—by taxi or bus. The *Keisei Skyliner* and *Japan Railways NEX* are the easiest ways to get into the city. If you are

arriving with a Japan Rail Pass and staying in Tokyo for a few days, it is best to pay for the transfer into the city and activate the Rail Pass for travel beyond Tokyo.

Directly across from the customs-area exits at both terminals are the ticket counters for buses to Tokyo. Buses leave from platforms just outside terminal exits, exactly on schedule; the departure time is on the ticket. The Airport Limousine offer shuttle-bus service from Narita to Tokyo.

Japan Railways trains stop at Narita Airport terminals 1 and 2. The fastest and most comfortable is the Narita Limited Express (NEX), which makes 23 runs a day in each direction. Trains from the airport go directly to the central Tokyo Station in just under an hour, then continue to Yokohama and Ofuna. Daily departures begin at 7:44 am; the last train is at 9:44 pm. In addition to regular seats, there is a first-class Green Car and private, four-person compartments. All seats are reserved, and you'll need to reserve one for yourself in advance, as this train fills quickly.

The Keisei Skyliner train runs every 20–30 minutes between the airport terminals and Keisei-Ueno Station. The trip takes around 40 minutes. The first Skyliner leaves Narita for Ueno at 7:28 am, the last at 10:30 pm. From Ueno to Narita the first Skyliner is at 5:58 am, the last at 6:20 pm. There's also an early train from the airport, called the Morning Liner, which leaves at 7:49 am and costs ¥1,400.

Contacts **Japan Railways** (JR東日本). ☎ *050/2016–1603.* **Keisei Railway** (京成電鉄). ☎ *03/3831–0131 Ueno information counter, 0476/32–8505 Narita Airport counter.*

TRANSFERS BETWEEN AIRPORTS

Transfer between Narita and Haneda, the international and domestic airports, is easiest by the Friendly Limousine Bus, which should take 75 minutes and costs ¥3,000. The Keisei Access Express runs between the two airports but requires a transfer at Aoto Station.

TRAVEL TIMES FROM TOKYO

From Narita	To	Fares	Times	Notes
Airport Limousine (buses)	Various $$$$ hotels in Tokyo and JR Tokyo and Shinjuku train stations	¥3,100	Every hr until 9:00 pm	70–90 mins, can be longer in traffic
Airport Limousine (buses)	Tokyo City Air Terminal (TCAT)	¥2,900	Every 10–20 mins from 6:55 am to 11 pm	
Narita Limited Express (NEX)	Central Tokyo Station, then continue to Yokohama and Ofuna	One-way fare ¥3,020; Green Car ¥4,560	Daily departures begin at 7:40 am; the last train is at 9:44 pm	All seats are reserved
Keisei Skyliner train	Keisei-Ueno Station	¥2,470	Every 20–30 mins, 7:28 am–10:30 pm	All seats are reserved
Taxi	Central Tokyo	¥20,000 or more		
From Haneda	**To**	**Fares**	**Times**	**Notes**
Tokyo Monorail	Central Tokyo	¥490	Every 20 mins, 5:13 am–midnight	Trip takes 25–30 mins. Connect to other major stations via the Yamanote Line at Hamamatsucho Station
Taxi	Central Tokyo	¥5,000–¥6,000		

Contacts Friendly Airport Limousine. ☎ 03/3665-7232 ⊕ www.limousinebus.co.jp/en/.

FLIGHTS

Japan Airlines (JAL) and United Airlines are the major carriers between North America and Narita Airport in Tokyo; American Airlines, Delta Airlines, and All Nippon Airways (ANA) also link North American cities with Tokyo's Haneda and Narita airports. Most of these airlines also fly into and out of Japan's two other international airports, Kansai International Airport, located south of Osaka, and Centrair, near Nagoya.

Airline Contacts All Nippon Airways. ☎ 800/235-9262 in U.S., 03/6741-1120 in Japan ⊕ www.ana.co.jp. **American Airlines.** ☎ 800/433-7300 in U.S., 03/3298-7677 in Japan ⊕ www.aa.com. **Delta Airlines.** ☎ 800/241-4141 in U.S., 0570/077-733 in Japan ⊕ www.delta.com. **Japan Airlines.** ☎ 800/525-3663, 03/6733-3062 in Japan ⊕ www.jal.co.jp. **United Airlines.** ☎ 800/864-8331 in U.S., 03/732-5011 in Japan ⊕ www.united.com.

▌ BOAT TRAVEL

Ferries connect most of the islands of Japan. Some of the more-popular routes are from Tokyo to Tomakomai or Kushiro in Hokkaido; from Tokyo to Shikoku; and from Tokyo or Osaka to Kyushu. You can purchase ferry tickets in advance from travel agencies or before boarding. The ferries are inexpensive and are a pleasant, if slow, way of traveling. Private cabins are available, but it's more fun to travel in the economy class, where everyone sleeps on the carpeted floor in one large room. Passengers eat, drink, and enjoy themselves in a convivial atmosphere. There is little English information for local ferries, apart from three companies serving the Inland Sea between Osaka/Kobe and Kyushu. *For information on local ferries, see the Essentials sections for individual towns within each chapter.*

Information Ferry Sunflower (フェリーさんふらわあ). ⊕ www.ferry-sunflower.co.jp. **Hankyu Ferry** (阪九フェリー). ⊕ www.han9f.co.jp. **Meimon Taiyo Ferry** (名門大洋フェリー). ⊕ www.cityline.co.jp.

▌ BUS TRAVEL

Japan Railways (JR) offers a number of long-distance buses that are comfortable and inexpensive. You can use Japan Rail Passes on some, but not all, of these buses. Routes and schedules are constantly changing, but tourist information offices will have up-to-date details. It's now possible to travel from Osaka to Tokyo for as little as ¥5,000 one-way. Buses are nonsmoking, generally modern, and very comfortable, though overnight journeys still mean sleeping in your seat. Foreign travelers are not often seen on these buses, and they remain one of the country's best-kept travel secrets. Japan Rail Passes are not accepted by private bus companies. City buses outside Tokyo are quite convenient, but be sure of your route and destination, because the bus driver probably won't speak English.

Local buses have a set cost, anywhere from ¥100 to ¥200, depending on the route and municipality, in which case you board at the front of the bus and pay as you get on. On other buses cost is determined by the distance you travel. You take a ticket when you board at the rear door of the bus; it bears the number of the stop at which you boarded. Your fare depends on your destination and is indicated by a board at the front of the bus. Japan Railways also runs buses in some areas that have limited rail service.

These buses are covered by the JR Pass, even if some reservation clerks tell you otherwise. Bus schedules can be hard to fathom if you don't read Japanese, however, so it's best to ask for help at a tourist information office. The Nihon Bus Association has information about routes and which companies have English information online.

Reservations are not always essential, except at peak holiday times and on the most popular routes, like Tokyo–Osaka.

Bus Information JR Kanto Bus (JRバス関東). ⊕ www.kanto-bus.co.jp/english/guide/nightway.html. **Nihon Bus Association** (日本バス協会). ⊕ www.bus.or.jp/en. **Willer Express.** ☎ 050/5805–0383 ⊕ willerexpress.com.

▌ CAR TRAVEL

You need an international driving permit (IDP) to drive in Japan. IDPs are available from the American Automobile Association. These international permits, valid only in conjunction with your regular driver's license, are universally recognized; having one may prevent problems with the local authorities. By law, car seats must be installed if the driver is traveling with a child under six.

Major roads in Japan are sufficiently marked in roman type, and on country roads there's usually someone to ask for help. However, it's a good idea to have a detailed map with town names written in *kanji* (Japanese characters) and *romaji* (romanized Japanese).

Car travel along the Tokyo–Kyoto–Hiroshima corridor and in other built-up areas of Japan is not as convenient as the trains. Roads are congested, gas is expensive (about ¥160 per liter), and highway tolls are exorbitant (tolls between Tokyo and Kyoto amount to ¥10,550). In major cities, with the exception of main arteries, English signs are few and far between, one-way streets often lead you off the track, and parking is often hard to find.

That said, a car can be the best means for exploring cities outside the metropolitan areas and the rural parts of Japan, especially Kyushu and Hokkaido. Consider taking a train to those areas where exploring the countryside will be most interesting and renting a car locally for a day or even half a day. Book ahead in holiday seasons. Car rental rates in Tokyo begin at ¥6,300 a day and ¥37,800 a week, including tax, for an economy car with unlimited mileage.

Major Agencies Avis. ☎ *0210/31–1911* ⊕ *www.avis-japan.com.* **Budget.** ☎ *800/472–3325* ⊕ *www.budgetrentacar.com.* **Hertz.** ☎ *800/654–3001* ⊕ *www.hertz.com.* **National Car Rental.** ☎ *800/227–7368* ⊕ *www.nationalcar.com.*

GASOLINE

Gas stations are plentiful along Japan's toll roads, and prices are fairly uniform across the country. Credit cards are accepted everywhere and are even encouraged—there are discounts for them at some places. Many stations offer both full and self-service and may offer a discount for pumping your own gas. Often you pay after putting in the gas, but there are also machines where you put money in first and then use the receipt to get change back. The staff will offer to take away trash and clean car windows. Tipping is not customary.

PARKING

There is little on-street parking in Japan. Parking is usually in staffed parking lots or inside large buildings. Expect to pay upward of ¥300 per hour. Parking regulations are strictly enforced, and illegally parked vehicles are towed away. Recovery fees start at ¥30,000 and increase hourly.

ROAD CONDITIONS

Roads in Japan are often narrower than those in the United States, but they're usually well maintained. Driving in cities can be troublesome, as there are many narrow, one-way streets and little in the way of English signage except on major arteries. Japanese drivers stick to the speed limit, but widely ignore bans on mobile phone use and dashboard televisions. Wild boars are not uncommon in rural districts, and have been known to block roads and ram into cars in the mountainous city of Kobe and in Kyushu, especially at night. From December to April northern and mountainous areas are often snowy.

ROADSIDE EMERGENCIES

Emergency telephones along highways can be used to contact the authorities. A nonprofit service, JHelp.com, offers a free, 24-hour emergency assistance hotline. Car-rental agencies generally offer roadside assistance services. Mobile phones are now so widespread that local drivers can call for help from the middle of nowhere.

Emergency Services Fire and Ambulance. ☎ *119.* **Police.** ☎ *110.*

RULES OF THE ROAD

In Japan people drive on the left. Speed limits vary, but generally the limit is 80 kph (50 mph) on highways, 40 kph (25 mph) in cities. Penalties for speeding are severe. By law, car seats must be installed if the driver is traveling with a child under six, while the driver and all passengers in cars must wear seat belts at all times. Driving while using handheld phones is illegal.

Many smaller streets lack sidewalks, so cars, bicycles, and pedestrians share the same space. Fortunately, considering the narrowness of the streets and the volume of traffic, most Japanese drivers are technically skilled. However, they may not allow quite as much distance between cars as you're used to. Be prepared for sudden lane changes by other drivers. When waiting at intersections after dark, many drivers, as a courtesy to other drivers, turn off their main headlights to prevent glare.

Japan has a zero-tolerance policy when it comes to drinking and driving, so it's wisest to avoid alcohol entirely if you plan to drive.

▌ TAXI TRAVEL

Taxis are an expensive way of getting around cities in Japan, though nascent deregulation moves are easing the market a little. In Tokyo, for instance, the first 2 km (1 mile) costs ¥730 and it's ¥90 for every additional 280 meters (400 yards). Between 10 pm and 5 am there is a 20% service charge. If possible, avoid using taxis during rush hours (7:30 am–9:30 am and 5 pm–7 pm).

In general, it's easy to hail a cab: do not shout or wave wildly—simply raise your hand. Japanese taxis have automatic door-opening systems, so do not try to open the taxi door. Stand back when the cab comes to a stop—if you are too close, the door may slam into you. Only the curbside rear door opens. A red light on the dashboard (visible through the front window) indicates an available taxi, and a green light indicates an occupied taxi.

Drivers are for the most part courteous, though not necessarily chatty. Unless you're going to a well-known destination such as a major hotel, it's advisable to have a Japanese person write out your destination in Japanese. Your hotel concierge will do this for you. Remember, there is no need to tip.

▌ TRAIN TRAVEL

Riding Japanese trains is one of the pleasures of travel in the country. Efficient and convenient, trains run frequently and on schedule. The Shinkansen (bullet train), one of the fastest trains in the world, connects major cities north and south of Tokyo. It is slightly less expensive than flying, and is in many ways more convenient because train stations are more centrally located than airports. If you have a Japan Rail Pass, it's also extremely affordable.

Other trains, though not as fast as the Shinkansen, are just as convenient and substantially cheaper. There are three types of train services: *futsu* (local service), *tokkyu* (limited express service), and *kyuko* (express service). Both the tokkyu and the kyuko offer a first-class compartment known as the Green Car. Smoking is allowed only in designated carriages on long-distance and Shinkansen trains. Local and commuter trains are entirely no-smoking.

Because there are no porters or carts at train stations, it's a good idea to travel light when getting around by train. Savvy travelers often have their main luggage sent ahead to a hotel that they plan to reach later in their wanderings. It's also good to know that every train station, however small, has luggage lockers, which cost about ¥300 for 24 hours.

If you plan on traveling by rail, consider a Japan Rail Pass, which offers unlimited travel on Japan Railways (JR) trains. You can purchase one-, two-, or three-week passes. A one-week pass is less expensive than a regular round-trip ticket from Tokyo to Kyoto on the Shinkansen. You must obtain a rail pass voucher prior to departure for Japan (you cannot buy them in Japan), and the pass must be used within three months of purchase. The pass is available only to people with tourist visas, as opposed to business, student, and diplomatic visas.

When you arrive in Japan, you must exchange your voucher for the Japan Rail Pass. You can do this at the Japan Railways desk in the arrivals hall at Narita Airport or at JR stations in major cities. When you make this exchange, you determine the day that you want the rail pass to begin, and, accordingly, when it ends. You do not have to begin travel on the day you make the exchange; instead, pick the starting date to maximize use. The Japan Rail Pass allows you to travel on all JR-operated trains (which cover most destinations in Japan) but not lines owned by other companies.

The JR Pass is also valid on buses operated by Japan Railways. You can make seat reservations without paying a fee on all trains that have reserved-seat coaches, usually long-distance trains. The Japan Rail Pass does not cover the cost of sleeping compartments on overnight trains (called blue trains), nor does it cover the newest and fastest of the Shinkansen trains, the *Nozomi,* which make only one or two stops on longer runs. The pass covers only the *Hikari* Shinkansen, which make a few more stops than the *Nozomi,* and the *Kodama* Shinkansen, which stop at every station along the Shinkansen routes. However, it can be used on all the Yamagata, Tohoku, Joetsu, and Hokuriku Shinkansen trains.

Japan Rail Passes are available in coach class and first class, and as the difference in price between the two is relatively small, it's worth the splurge for first class, for real luxury, especially on the Shinkansen. A one-week pass costs ¥29,110 coach class, ¥38,800 first class; a two-week pass costs ¥46,390 coach class, ¥62,950 first class; and a three-week pass costs ¥59,350 coach class, ¥81,870 first class. Travelers under 18 pay lower rates. The pass pays for itself after one Tokyo–Kyoto round-trip Shinkansen ride. Contact a travel agent or Japan Airlines to purchase the pass.

Many travelers assume that rail passes guarantee them seats on the trains they wish to ride. Not so. If you're using a rail pass, there's no need to buy individual tickets, but you should book seats ahead. You can reserve up to two weeks in advance or just minutes before the train departs. If you fail to make a train, there's no penalty, and you can reserve again.

Seat reservations for any JR route may be made at any JR station except those in the tiniest villages. The reservation windows or offices, *midori-no-madoguchi,* have green signs in English. If you're traveling without a Japan Rail Pass, there's a surcharge of approximately ¥500 (depending upon distance traveled) for seat reservations, and if you miss the train you'll have to pay for another reservation. All JR trains are nonsmoking, although the Shinkansen have a few small, enclosed compartments that allow smoking. Your reservation ticket shows the date and departure time of your train as well as your car and seat number. Notice the markings painted on the platform or on little signs above the platform; ask someone which markings correspond to car numbers. If you don't have a reservation, ask which cars are unreserved. Unreserved tickets can be purchased at regular ticket windows. There are no reservations for local service trains. For traveling short distances, tickets are usually sold at vending machines. A platform ticket is required if you go through the wicket gate onto the platform to meet someone coming off a train. The charge is between ¥120 and ¥160 depending on the station.

Most clerks at train stations know a few basic words of English and can read roman script. They are invariably helpful in plotting your route. The complete railway timetable is a mammoth book written only in Japanese; however, you can get an English-language train schedule from the Japan National Tourism Organization that covers the Shinkansen and a few of the major JR Limited Express trains. JNTO's booklet *The Tourist's Language Handbook* provides helpful information about purchasing tickets in Japan. The Jorudan Route Finder is a good online source for searching train times and prices.

Information Japan Rail Pass. ⊕ *www.japanrailpass.net.* **Jorudan Route Finder** (ジョルダン). ⊕ *www.jorudan.co.jp/english.*

ESSENTIALS

■ ACCOMMODATIONS

Overnight accommodations in Japan run from ultramodern luxury hotels to *ryokan* (traditional inns). Western-style rooms with private bathrooms are widely available in large cities, but in smaller, out-of-the-way towns it may be necessary to stay in a Japanese-style room—an experience that can only enhance your stay. Japanese-style rooms generally have tatami flooring and a futon instead of a bed. Rarely do they have a private bath or shower; guests bathe in communal baths, following a particular etiquette, and baths are frequently only open a few hours a day. Large chain and business hotels usually quote prices based on rooms and occupancy. Traditional *minshuku* (Japanese bed-and-breakfasts) and ryokan prices are generally per-person and include dinner and breakfast. If you do not want dinner at your hotel, it is usually possible to renegotiate the price. Stipulate, too, whether you wish to have Japanese or Western breakfasts.

A travel agent based in Japan can help you make reservations and other travel arrangements, and this is a particularly useful service since some hotels and ryokan do not have English-language websites. Japan Hotel.net, J-Reserve, Rakuten Travel, and Tabiplaza, an offshoot of Nippon Travel Agency, offer a wide range of accommodations from big-city luxury to out-of-the-way family guesthouses. Budget Japan Hotels offers big discounts on cheaper rooms at major hotels.

Japan Travel Agents IACE Travel. ✉ *Minato-ku* ☎ *03/5282–1522 in Japan, 877/489–4223 in North America* ⊕ *www.iace-usa.com.* **JTB (Japan Travel Bureau).** ✉ *2–3–11 Higashi-Shinagawa, Shinagawa-ku* ☎ *03/5796–5454 in Japan, 800/700–1540 in North America* ⊕ *www.jtbcorp.jp/en.* **Nippon Travel Agency.** ✉ *Shinbashi Eki-mae Bldg. 1, 2–20–15 Shinbashi, Minato-ku* ☎ *310/768–0017 in U.S., 03/3572–8161 in Japan* ⊕ *www.ntainbound.com.*

Online Accommodations Jalan. ⊕ *www.jalan.net.* **Rakuten Travel.** ⊕ *www.travel.rakuten.com.*

APARTMENT AND HOUSE RENTALS

English-language newspapers and magazines such as the *Japan Times, Metropolis, Kansai Scene,* or *Tokyo Weekender* may be helpful in locating a rental property. Note that renting apartments or houses in Japan is not a common way to spend a vacation, and weekly studio-apartment rentals may be fully booked by local business travelers.

The range of online booking services for Japan is expanding, although most of the accommodation booked this way is large and impersonal and staff in the hotel may not speak any English. Also check the location carefully to avoid incurring unforeseen extra costs and hassles in trying to reach the sights from a suburban hotel.

Contacts Arc Corporate Housing. ☎ *03/5414–7070, 03/5575–3232* ⊕ *www.arc-corporate-housing.com.* **Flexstay Hotel Management.** ⊕ *corporate.mystays.com/e.* **Sakura House—Apartments.** ☎ *03/5330–5250* ⊕ *www.sakura-house.com.*

Rental Listings Kansai Scene. ⊕ *www.kansaiscene.com.* **Metropolis.** ⊕ *www.metropolis.co.jp.*

HOME VISITS

Through the home visit system travelers can get a sense of domestic life in Japan by visiting a local family in their home. The program is voluntary on the homeowner's part, and there's no charge for a visit. The system is active in many cities throughout the country, including Tokyo, Yokohama, Nagoya, Kyoto, Osaka, Hiroshima, Nagasaki, and Sapporo. To make a reservation, apply in writing for a home visit at least a day in advance to the local tourist information office of the place you are visiting. Contact the Japan National Tourism Organization *(Visitor Information, below)* before leaving for Japan for more information on the program.

INEXPENSIVE ACCOMMODATIONS

JNTO publishes a listing of some 700 accommodations that are reasonably priced. To be listed, properties must meet Japanese fire codes and charge less than ¥8,000 per person without meals. For the most part, the properties charge ¥5,000 to ¥6,000. These properties welcome foreigners (some Japanese hotels and ryokan prefer not to have foreign guests because they might not be familiar with traditional-inn etiquette). Properties include business hotels, simple ryokan and minshuku, and pensions. It's the luck of the draw whether you choose a good or less-than-good property. In most cases rooms are clean but very small. Except in business hotels, shared baths are the norm, and you are expected to have your room lights out by 10 pm.

Many reasonably priced accommodations can be reserved through the nonprofit organization Welcome Inn Reservation Center. Reservation forms are available from your nearest JNTO office *(Visitor Information, below)*. The Japanese Inn Group, which provides reasonable accommodations for foreign visitors, can be reserved through this same service. The center must receive reservation requests at least one week before your departure to allow processing time. If you are already in Japan, the Tourist Information Centers (TICs) at Narita Airport and Kansai International Airport and in downtown Tokyo and Kyoto can make immediate reservations for you at these Welcome Inns. Telephone reservations are not accepted.

Contacts Japan Hotels and Ryokans Search. ⊕ *www.jnto.go.jp/ja-search/eng/index.php.* **Japanese Inn Group.** ☎ *06/6225–3611* ⊕ *www.japaneseinngroup.com.*

TEMPLES

You can also arrange accommodations in Buddhist temples, known as *shukubo*. JNTO has lists of temples that accept guests and you can arrange for your stay here as well. A stay at a temple generally costs ¥3,000 to ¥9,000 per night, including two meals. Some temples offer instruction in meditation or allow you to observe their religious practices, while others simply offer rooms. The Japanese-style accommodations are very simple, and range from beautiful, quiet havens to not-so-comfortable, basic cubicles. For specific information on temple lodging in the Kii Mountain range in southern Japan, try contacting the Shukubo Temple Lodging Cooperative.

Contacts Shukubo Temple Lodging Cooperative. ☎ *0736/56–2616* ⊕ *www.shukubo.net.*

■ ADDRESSES

The simplest way to decipher a Japanese address is to break it into parts. For example: 6-chome 8–19, Chu o-ku, Fukuoka-shi, Fukuoka-ken. In this address the "chome" indicates a precise area (a block, for example), and the numbers following chome indicate the building within the area. Note that buildings aren't always numbered sequentially; numbers are often assigned as buildings are erected. Only local police officers and mail carriers in Japan seem to be familiar with the area defined by the chome. Sometimes, instead of chome, "machi" (town) is used. Written addresses in Japan also have the opposite order of those in the West, with the city coming before the street. "Ku" refers to a district of a city, "shi" refers to a city name, and "ken" indicates a prefecture, which is roughly equivalent to a state in the United States. It's not unusual for the prefecture and the city to have the same name. There are a few geographic areas in Japan that are not called ken. One is greater Tokyo, which is called Tokyo-to. Other exceptions Kyoto and Osaka, which are followed by the suffix "-fu"— Kyoto-fu, Osaka-fu. Hokkaido, Japan's northernmost island, is also not considered a ken.

Not all addresses conform exactly to the above format. Rural addresses, for example, might use "gun" (county) where city addresses have "ku" (district). Even Japanese people cannot find a building based on the address alone. If you get in a taxi with a written address, do not assume the driver will be able to find your destination. Usually, people provide very detailed instructions or maps to explain their exact locations. It's always good to know the location of your destination in relation to a major building or department store.

■ COMMUNICATIONS

INTERNET

Except for some traditional ryokan and minshiku, nearly all hotels have high-speed Internet access. Wireless Internet access (Wi-Fi) is increasingly available for free at coffee shops and in hotel lobbies across the country, however there are still a number of hotels that do not offer in-room Wi-Fi. There are Internet cafés in many cities, but they tend to be dark, cavelike halls focused more on *manga* (comic book) and computer games than checking email. Although free Wi-Fi is not as widespread as in the United States, there are some free services that allow tourists to access a number of hot spots around the country. Two of the most useful are Travel Japan Wi-Fi (throughout Japan) and Free Wi-Fi Japan (mostly Tokyo and the surrounding tourist sites).

Contacts Free Wi-Fi Japan. ⊕ *flets.com/freewifi/index.html.* **PuPuRu Mobile Phone Rental.** ⊕ *www.pupuru.com/en.*

Travel Japan Wi-Fi. Wi-Fi access at up to 200,000 hot spots throughout Japan using iOS or Android devices. Requires online registration. ⊕ *wi2.co.jp/tjw/english.html.*

PHONES

The country code for Japan is 81. When dialing a Japanese number from outside Japan, drop the initial "0" from the local area code. The country code for the United States is 1.

CALLING WITHIN JAPAN

Public telephones are a dying species in cell-phone-happy Japan. But there are sometimes public telephones near convenience stores, train and bus stations, and, of course, in hotel lobbies. Phones accept ¥100 coins as well as prepaid telephone cards. Domestic long-distance rates are reduced as much as 50% after 9 pm (40% after 7 pm). Telephone cards, sold in vending machines, hotels, and a variety of stores, are tremendously convenient.

Operator assistance at 104 is in Japanese only. Weekdays 9–5 (except national holidays) English-speaking operators can help you at the toll-free NTT Information Customer Service Centre.

Contacts Directory Assistance. ☎ *104.* **NTT Information Customer Service Centre.** ☎ *0120/36-4463.*

CALLING OUTSIDE JAPAN

With pay phones that can be used for international calls becoming more of a rarity, and high rates calling from hotels, the best way to call abroad is to use an Internet-based service like Skype or Google Voice. There are still a few telephone cards that can be used to call out of Japan such as the KDDI Super World Card. Each card has different access codes so follow the included instructions. Major U.S. cellular carriers also offer international voice and data plans. Check with your carrier for details.

Japan has several telephone companies for international calls, so make a note of all the possible access code numbers to use to connect to your U.S. server before departure.

Access Codes AT&T Direct. ⊕ *www.att.com/esupport/traveler.jsp.* **MCI WorldPhone.** ☎ *800/955-0925* ⊕ *consumer.mci.com/international/english/resources/accessnos.jsp.* **Sprint International Access.** ☎ *800/866-7509* ⊕ *shop.sprint.com/mysprint/services_solutions/index.jsp#!/.*

CALLING CARDS

Telephone cards for ¥1,000 can be bought at station kiosks or convenience stores and can be used in virtually all public telephones. For international calls, look for phones that accept KDDI prepaid cards valued between ¥1,000 and ¥7,000. Cards are available from convenience stores.

MOBILE PHONES

Japan is the world leader in mobile-phone technology, but overseas visitors cannot easily use their handsets in Japan because it is a non-GSM country. It's best to rent a phone from one of the many outlets at Narita, Kansai, and Nagoya airports. Softbank sells SIM cards so you can use your own number in Japan. Most company rental rates start at ¥525 a day.

Contacts JALABC Rental Phone. ⊕ *www. jalabc.com/english/index3.html.* **Softbank.** ⊕ *www.softbank-rental.jp.*

■ CUSTOMS AND DUTIES

Japan has strict regulations about bringing firearms, pornography, and narcotics into the country. Anyone caught with drugs is liable to be detained, refused reentry into Japan, and deported. Certain fresh fruits, vegetables, plants, and animals are also illegal. Nonresidents are allowed to bring in duty-free: (1) 400 cigarettes or 100 cigars or 500 grams of tobacco; (2) three 760-milliliter bottles of alcohol; (3) 2 ounces of perfume; (4) other goods up to ¥200,000 value.

Getting through customs at a Japanese airport goes more smoothly if you are well dressed, clean-shaven, and as conventional-looking as possible. Visitors arriving off flights from other Asian countries are particularly scrutinized for narcotics. Note that visitors must have a written prescription for any prescription medicine brought into Japan and that some over-the-counter medicines from the United States are not legal in Japan.

Contacts Ministry of Finance, Customs and Tariff Bureau. ☎ *03/3581–4111* ⊕ *www. customs.go.jp.* **U.S. Customs and Border Protection.** ⊕ *www.cbp.gov.*

■ DAY TOURS AND GUIDES

The Japan National Tourism Organization (JNTO) sponsors a Goodwill Guide program in which local citizens volunteer to show visitors around; this is a great way to meet Japanese people. These are not professional guides; they usually volunteer both because they enjoy welcoming foreigners to their town and because they want to practice their English. You will have to negotiate the itinerary with the guide. The services of Goodwill Guides are free, but you should pay for their travel costs, their admission fees, and any meals you eat with them while you are together. To participate in this program, make arrangements for a Goodwill Guide in advance through JNTO in the United States or through the tourist office in the area where you want the guide to meet you. The program operates in 75 towns and cities, including Tokyo, Kyoto, Nara, Nagoya, Osaka, and Hiroshima. Bookings can be done through the website.

The Japan National Tourism Organization can also put you in touch with various local volunteer groups that conduct tours in English; you need only to pay for the guide's travel expenses, admission fees to cultural sites, and meals if you eat together. Assume that the fee will be ¥25,000 to ¥30,000 for a full eight-hour day.

Contacts Goodwill Guides. ⊕ *www. jnto.go.jp/eng/arrange/travel/guide/list_ volunteerGuides.php.* **Japan Guide Association.** ☎ *03/3863–2895* ⊕ *www.jga21c.or.jp.* **Japan National Tourism Organization.** ⊕ *www.jnto.go.jp/eng.*

■ ELECTRICITY

The electrical current in Japan is 100 volts, 50 cycles alternating current (AC) in eastern Japan, and 100 volts, 60 cycles in western Japan. The United States runs on 110-volt, 60-cycle AC current. Wall outlets in Japan accept plugs with two flat prongs, as in the United States, but do not accept U.S. three-prong plugs.

Consider making a small investment in a universal adapter, which has several types of plugs in one lightweight, compact unit. Most laptops and mobile phone chargers are dual voltage (i.e., they operate equally well on 110 and 220 volts), so require only an adapter. These days the same is true of small appliances such as hair dryers. Always check labels and manufacturers' instructions to be sure. Don't use 110-volt outlets marked for shavers only for high-wattage appliances such as hair dryers.

▌EMERGENCIES

The following embassy and consulate is open weekdays, with one- to two-hour closings for lunch. Call for exact hours.

General Emergency Contacts Ambulance and Fire. ☎ *119.* **Police.** ☎ *110.* **U.S. Embassy and Consulate.** ✉ *1–10–5 Akasaka, Minato-ku, Minato-ku* ☎ *03/3224–5000* ⊕ *japan.usembassy.gov* Ⓜ *Namboku Line, Tameike-Sanno Station (Exit 13).*

▌HEALTH

Japan is a safe, clean country for travelers with drinkable water and no major water- or insect-borne diseases. Condoms are sold widely, but they may not have the brands you're used to. Speak with your physician and/or check the CDC or World Health Organization websites for health alerts, particularly if you're pregnant or traveling with children or have a chronic illness.

SPECIFIC ISSUES IN JAPAN

Tap water is safe everywhere in Japan. Medical treatment varies from highly skilled and professional at major hospitals to somewhat less advanced in small neighborhood clinics. At larger hospitals you have a good chance of encountering English-speaking doctors.

Mosquitoes can be a minor irritation during the rainy season, though you are never at risk of contracting anything serious. If you're staying in a ryokan or any place without air-conditioning, anti-mosquito coils or an electric-powered spray are provided. Dehydration and heatstroke could be concerns if you spend a long time outside during the summer months, but sports drinks are readily available from the nation's ubiquitous vending machines.

General Information and Warnings U.S. Department of State. ⊕ *www.travel.state.gov.*

OVER-THE-COUNTER REMEDIES

Medication can only be bought at pharmacies in Japan, but every neighborhood seems to have at least one. Ask for the *yakyoku* (薬局). Pharmacists in Japan are usually able to manage at least a few words of English, and certainly are able to read some, so have a pen and some paper ready, just in case. In Japanese, aspirin is *asupirin* and Tylenol is *Tairenoru.* Following national regulations, Japanese drugs often contain less potent ingredients than foreign brands, so the effects can be disappointing; check advised dosages carefully.

Drugs and medications are widely available at drugstores, although the brand names and use instructions will be in Japanese, so if you're on regular medication, take along enough supplies to cover the trip. As with any international travel, be sure to bring your prescription or a doctor's note just in case.

▌HOURS OF OPERATION

General business hours in Japan are weekdays 9 to 5. Many offices also open at least half the day on Saturday, but are generally closed Sunday.

Banks are open weekdays from 9 until 4 or 5. As with shops, there's a trend toward longer and later opening hours.

Gas stations follow usual shop hours, though 24-hour stations can be found near major highways.

Museums generally close Monday and the day following national holidays. They are also closed the day following special exhibits and during the weeklong New Year's celebrations.

Department stores are usually open 10 to 7, but close one day a week, varying from store to store. Other shops are open from 10 or 11 to 8 or 9. There's a trend toward longer and later opening hours in major cities, and 24-hour convenience stores, many of which now have ATM facilities, can be found across the entire country.

HOLIDAYS

As elsewhere, peak times for travel in Japan tend to fall around holiday periods. Avoid traveling during the few days before and after New Year's; during Golden Week, which follows Greenery Day (April 29); and in mid-July and mid-August, at the time of Obon festivals, when many Japanese return to their hometowns (Obon festivals are celebrated July or August 13–16, depending on the location). Note that when a holiday falls on a Sunday, the following Monday is a holiday.

Japan's national holidays are January 1 (*Ganjitsu*, New Year's Day); the second Monday in January (*Senjin-no-hi*, Coming of Age Day); February 11 (*Kenkoku Kinen-bi*, National Foundation Day); March 20 or 21 (*Shumbun-no-hi*, Vernal Equinox); April 29 (*Showa-no-hi*, Showa Day); May 3 (*Kempo Kinen-bi*, Constitution Memorial Day); May 4 (*Midori-no-hi*, Greenery Day); May 5 (*Kodomo-no-hi*, Children's Day); the third Monday in July (*Umi-no-hi*, Marine Day); the third Monday in September (*Keiro-no-hi*, Respect for the Aged Day); September 23 or 24 (*Shubun-no-hi*, Autumnal Equinox); the second Monday in October (*Taiiku-no-hi*, Sports Day); November 3 (*Bunka-no-hi*, Culture Day); November 23 (*Kinro Kansha-no-hi*, Labor Thanksgiving Day); December 23 (*Tenno Tanjobi*, Emperor's Birthday).

▌ MAIL

The Japanese postal service is very efficient. Airmail between Japan and the United States takes between five and eight days. Express service (known as EMS) is also available through post offices.

Although there are numerous post offices in every city, it's probably best to use the central post office near the main train station, because the workers often speak English and can handle foreign mail. Some of the smaller post offices are not equipped to send packages. Post offices are open weekdays 9 to 5 and Saturday 9 to noon. Some central post offices have longer hours, such as the one in Tokyo, near Tokyo Station, which is open 24 hours year-round. Most hotels and many convenience stores also sell stamps.

The Japanese postal service has implemented the use of three-numeral-plus-four postal codes, but its policy is similar to that in the United States regarding zip-plus-fours; that is, addresses with the three-numeral code will still arrive at their destination, albeit perhaps one or two days later. Mail to rural towns may take longer.

It costs ¥110 to send a letter by air to North America. An airmail postcard costs ¥70. Aerograms cost ¥90.

To get mail, have parcels and letters sent "poste restante" to the central post office in major cities; unclaimed mail is returned after 30 days.

SHIPPING PACKAGES

FedEx has drop-off locations at branches of Kinko's in all major cities. A 1-kilogram (2.20-pound) package from central Tokyo to Washington, DC, would cost about ¥10,000, and be delivered within four days. Two-day shipping is available at a higher rate.

The Japanese postal service is very efficient, and domestic mail rarely goes astray. To ship a 5-kilogram (11.02-pound) parcel to the United States costs ¥10,150 if sent by airmail, ¥7,300 by SAL (economy airmail), and ¥4,000 by sea.

Allow a week for airmail, two to three weeks for SAL, and up to two months for packages sent by sea. Large shops usually ship domestically, but not overseas. Express Mail Service (EMS), at ¥7,300, is usually the best option.

Contacts FedEx. ☎ *0120/003–200 toll-free, 043/298–1919* ⊕ *www.fedex.com/jp_english.*

▌MONEY

Japan can be expensive, but there are ways to cut costs. This requires, to some extent, an adventurous spirit and the courage to stray from the standard tourist paths. One good way to hold down expenses is to avoid taxis (they tend to get stuck in traffic anyway) and use the inexpensive, efficient subway and bus systems. Instead of dining at restaurants with menus in English and Western-style food, head to places where you can rely on your good old index finger to point to the dish you want, and try food that locals favor.

ITEM	AVERAGE COST
Cup of Coffee	¥250–¥600
Glass of Wine	¥600–¥1,000
Glass of Beer	¥500–¥800
Sandwich (convenience store)	¥300
One-Mile Taxi Ride in Capital City	¥700
Museum Admission	¥1,000

ATMS AND BANKS

The easiest way to withdraw money is at convenience-store ATMs. 7-11 stores and 7 Bank ATMs accept most internationally branded cards. ATMs at many Japanese banks do not accept foreign-issue debit or credit cards. UFJ and Shinsei banks are members of the Plus network, as are some convenience store cash machines. ATMs at post offices and major convenience stores accept Visa, MasterCard, American Express, Diners Club, and Cirrus cards. In more-rural areas, it can be difficult to find suitable ATMs so it is best to get cash before heading out into the countryside.

PIN codes in Japan are comprised of four digits. In Japanese an ATM is commonly referred to by its English acronym, while a PIN is *ansho bango*. If you need assistance, contact the bank staff by using the phone next to the ATM. Many machines also have English on-screen instructions.

CREDIT CARDS

MasterCard and Visa are the most widely accepted credit cards in Japan. When you use a credit card you'll be asked if you intend to pay in one installment as most locals do, say *hai-ikkai* (Yes, one time) just to fit in, even if you plan differently once you get home. Many vendors don't accept American Express. Cash is still king in Japan, especially at smaller businesses—even in large cities like Osaka and Tokyo.

Reporting Lost Cards American Express. ☎ *03/3220–6100 in Japan* ⊕ *www. americanexpress.com.* **Diners Club.** ☎ *0120/074–024 in Japan* ⊕ *www.dinersclub. com.* **MasterCard.** ☎ *00531/113–886 in Japan* ⊕ *www.mastercard.us.* **Visa.** ☎ *00531/111–555 in Japan* ⊕ *www.visa.com.*

CURRENCY AND EXCHANGE

The unit of currency in Japan is the yen (¥). There are bills of ¥10,000, ¥5,000, ¥2,000, and ¥1,000. Coins are ¥500, ¥100, ¥50, ¥10, ¥5, and ¥1. Japanese currency floats on the international monetary exchange, so changes can be dramatic.

▌**TIP**➜ **Even if a currency-exchange booth has a sign promising no commission, rest assured that there's some kind of huge, hidden fee. And as for rates, you're almost always better off getting foreign currency at an ATM or exchanging money at a bank.**

▌PACKING

Pack light, because porters can be hard to find and storage space in hotel rooms may be tiny. What you pack depends more on the time of year than on any dress code.

For travel in the cities, pack as you would for any American or European city. At more expensive restaurants and nightclubs men usually need to wear a jacket and tie. Wear conservative-color clothing at business meetings. Casual clothes are fine for sightseeing. Jeans are as popular in Japan as they are in the United States, and are perfectly acceptable for informal dining and sightseeing.

Although there are no strict dress codes for visiting temples and shrines, you will be out of place in immodest outfits. For sightseeing leave sandals and open-toe shoes behind; you'll need sturdy walking shoes for the gravel pathways that surround temples and fill parks. Make sure to bring comfortable clothing to wear in traditional Japanese restaurants, where you may need to sit on tatami-matted floors. For beach and mountain resorts pack informal clothes for both day and evening wear. Central and southern Japan are hot and humid June to September, so pack cotton clothing. Winter daytime temperatures in northern Japan hover around freezing, so gloves and hats are necessary, and clip-on shoe spikes can be bought locally.

Japanese do not wear shoes in private homes or in any temples or traditional inns. Having shoes you can quickly slip in and out of is a decided advantage. Take wool socks (checking first for holes!) to help you through those shoeless occasions in winter.

All lodgings provide a thermos of hot water and bags of green tea in every room. For coffee you can call room service, buy very sweet coffee in a can from a vending machine, or purchase packets of instant coffee at local convenience stores. If you're staying in a Japanese inn, they probably won't have coffee.

▮ PASSPORTS

Hotels in Japan require foreign guests to show passports at check-in, but police are unlikely to ask foreign visitors for on-the-spot identification, although crime crackdowns on nightlife areas of big cities and political tensions with neighboring countries can alter local circumstances in some areas.

U.S. Passport Information U.S. Department of State. ☎ 877/487–2778 ⊕ travel.state.gov/passport.

▮ SAFETY

Even in its major cities Japan is a very safe country, with one of the lowest crime rates in the world. You should, however, keep an eye out for pickpockets and avoid unlighted roads at night like anywhere else. ▮TIP➔ **Distribute your cash, credit cards, IDs, and other valuables between a deep front pocket, an inside jacket or vest pocket, and a hidden money pouch. Don't reach for the money pouch once you're in public.**

The greatest danger is being caught in an earthquake and its resulting tsunami. Earthquake information is broadcast (in Japanese) as news flashes on television within minutes, and during major disasters national broadcaster N.H.K. broadcasts information in English on radio and television. Minor tremors occur every month, and sometimes train service is temporarily halted. Check emergency routes at hotels and higher ground if staying near coastal areas.

▮ TAXES

An 8% national consumption tax is added to all hotel bills. Another 3% local tax is added to the bill if it exceeds ¥15,000. You may save money by paying for your hotel meals separately rather than charging them to your bill.

At luxury hotels, a 10% service charge is added to the bill in place of individual tipping. At more expensive ryokan, where individualized maid service is offered, the service charge is usually 15%. At business hotels and other budget lodgings, no service charge is added to the bill.

There's an across-the-board, nonrefundable 8% consumption tax levied on all sales, which is included in the ticket price. Authorized tax-free shops will knock the tax off purchases over ¥10,000 if you show your passport and a valid tourist visa. A large sign is displayed at such shops.

An 8% tax is also added to all restaurant bills. Another 3% local tax is added to the bill if it exceeds ¥7,500. At more expensive restaurants a 10% to 15% service charge is added to the bill. Tipping is not customary.

▍TIME

All of Japan is in the same time zone, which is 14 hours ahead of New York, and 17 hours ahead of San Francisco. Daylight saving time is not observed.

▍TIPPING

Tipping is not common in Japan. It's not necessary to tip in taxis, hair salons, barbershops, bars, or nightclubs. A chauffeur for a hired car usually receives a tip of ¥500 for a half-day excursion and ¥1,000 for a full-day trip. Porters charge fees of ¥250 to ¥300 per bag at railroad stations and ¥200 per piece at airports. It's not customary to tip employees of hotels, even porters, unless a special service has been rendered. In such cases, a gratuity of ¥2,000 to ¥3,000 should be placed in an envelope and handed to the staff member discreetly.

▍TOURS

Japan is daunting for first-time visitors, so a package tour is a great way to get into the country and find your feet. However, beware of expensive optional tours such as tea ceremonies, theater tours, and night views. Local tourist offices can tell you how to have the same experience without emptying your wallet.

The country can be quite a culture shock, so resist the temptation to book tours that pack in too much sightseeing. Opt for those that include half days of freedom, because just stepping outside the hotel into the local streets is likely to provide some unimagined sights and experiences.

Tokyo and Kyoto feature on almost every tour of Japan, while Hiroshima, Nara, and Nikko are normally the secondary destinations.

RECOMMENDED COMPANIES

Alexander & Roberts. Alexander & Roberts' mix of fully guided and freestyle tours lets travelers choose how much guidance they want during their trip. While tours generally focus on the main Tokyo-Kyoto-Hiroshima tourist route, there are optional side trips that take travelers a bit off the beaten track. ☎ 800/221–2216 ⊕ *www.alexanderroberts.com* ✉ *$600 (4-day Kyoto tour)–$6,000 (11-day Tour across Japan).*

Explorient Travel Services. Explorient offers private, customizable tours with a focus on luxury travel. Aimed at travelers who want every last detail taken care of, Explorient tours cover both major tourist destinations like Kyoto and Tokyo as well as more out-of-the-way sights such as the inland sea or Japan's UNESCO World Heritage Sites. ☎ 800/785–1233 ⊕ *www. explorient.com* ✉ *$3,500–$6,000.*

Kintetsu. With the motto "You dream. We plan," Kintetsu is a good choice for travelers who do not need a guide, but want someone to take care of all the logistics of their trip. Kintetsu offers package and guided tours but focuses on planning custom vacations, offering expert advice and planning ideas to fit any budget. ☎ 212/259–9600 ⊕ *www.kintetsu.com* ✉ *$500 (a short Tokyo Trip)–$5,000 (10-plus days across Japan).*

Smithsonian Journeys. Smithsonian offers small group tours covering Japan's major tourist sites making them a good choice for travelers looking for the comfort and camaraderie of a group. Although less customizable than private tours, they are generally more affordable. There are also some cruise tours for those interest in traversing the Pacific by boat rather than plane.

Tour prices include transportation from the United States. ☏ *855/530–1542* ⊕ *www. smithsonianjourneys.org* ✉ *$6,000.*

SPECIAL-INTEREST TOURS

ART

Japan is overflowing with art—from pottery and painting to the precise skills of flower arranging and calligraphy. Many tours include museums and art galleries, but only some get you right into artist studios with English-language help to understand their skills and the chance to try your hand.

Absolute Travel. Absolute Travel's "Artistic Traditions of Japan" tour offers visitors a chance to experience and learn about the country's long history of art and fine craftsmanship. Tours cover major tourist cities like Kyoto and Tokyo as well as the "art island" Naoshima. All tours are private and customizable with the finest luxury dining and accommodation. ☏ *212/627–1950* ⊕ *www.absolutetravel. com* ✉ *$15,000.*

CYCLING

Cycling is popular in Japan, but local bike-rental shops may not have frames large enough for non-Japanese cyclists. For more information on cycling in Japan see the *Japan Cycling Navigator.*

Aloha Bike. Aloha Bike's experienced cycling guides take the uncertainty out of cycling across Japan. While clients need to be fit, Aloha offers a range of tours of varying routes and difficulties. With everything from 2-day trips around the Mt. Fuji Five Lakes area, to 11-day treks from coast to coast, it is easy to add a short cycling tour to an otherwise self-planned trip. ☏ *0558/22–1516* ⊕ *www. alohabike.com* ✉ *$400 (2-day tour)–$3,000 (11-day tour).*

Japan Cycling Navigator. A must for travelers planning a self-guided cycling trip, *Japan Cycling Navigator* offers information and on cycling routes throughout the country. ⊕ *www.japancycling.org.*

DIVING

Okinawa, Kyushu, and the islands and peninsula south of Tokyo are all popular diving areas. If you are a novice diver, make sure that a dive leader's "English spoken" means real communication skills. Dive Japan has lists of dive services and locations.

Dive Japan. Although rarely updated, the Dive Japan website is still the best English-language resource for information on dive sites around the country. ⊕ *www. divejapan.com.*

ECOTOURS

Whales, monkeys, bears, and cranes—Japan does have fauna and flora to appreciate slowly, but English-language tours are limited. Naturalist Mark Brazil, who writes extensively about wild Japan, leads ecotours through Zegrahm Eco Expeditions.

One Life Japan. With a range of cycling, hiking, and ecotours, One Life Japan gives travelers an inside look at life in rural Japan. A small, independent outfit, it offers a level of personal interaction and community involvement that larger tours have difficulty matching. Focusing on active, challenging, and sustainable travel it is a good choice for those looking for an adventure and a look into everyday life far from the big city. ☏ *090/3337–3248* ⊕ *www.onelifejapan.com* ✉ *$2,000.*

Zegrahm Eco Expeditions. Bridging the luxury and ecotour markets, Zegrahm offers tours to off-the-beaten-track locations while pampering clients with top-class dining and accommodation. While it may not offer a look into daily life in the countryside, it is an excellent way to see some of the country's most stunning nature while still being able to sleep and dine in style. ☏ *864/264–0821* ⊕ *www. zeco.com* ✉ *$14,000 (15-day tour).*

GOLF

Japan's love affair with golf does not make it any easier for non-Japanese-speaking visitors to reserve a game unless introduced by a club member. Japan

Golf Tours takes guided groups from the United States, and Golf in Japan, put together by golfing expats, helpfully lists more than 2,000 courses that welcome foreign golfers.

Golf in Japan. For golfers, this website offers extensive information on golf courses and clubs throughout the country, including costs, access, and how to reserve time on the green. ⊕ *www.golf-in-japan.com.*

HIKING

Japan has well-marked trails, bus-train connections to trailheads, and hidden sights to be discovered. Millions of Japanese are avid and well-equipped hikers. English information is growing, so check local tourist offices for details. Visit Outdoor Japan's website for all outdoor activities. Quest Japan, run by an experienced British hiker, has a range of tours in all seasons.

Outdoor Japan. Outdoor Japan is the first place to look for information on nearly any kind of outdoor activity, from hiking to snowboarding, to kayaking, ⊕ *www.outdoorjapan.com.*

Quest Japan. Quest Japan offers hiking tours ranging from 10 days to more than two weeks. Not for the inexperienced, these hikes offer a look at some of the country's most stunning mountains and historic trails. ⊕ *www.questjapan.co.jp* ✉ *$2,000.*

LANGUAGE PROGRAMS

There is no better way to learn the language than to immerse yourself by studying Japanese in Japan, with classes, a homestay, and cultural tours on which to put the newfound skills into action. Japanese Information and Culture Center (JICC) has good links to schools and procedures for study-abroad programs.

Japan Information and Culture Center (JICC). JICC has a wealth of information about various language programs in Japan. ☎ *202/238–6900* ⊕ *www.us.emb-japan.go.jp/jicc.*

MOTORCYCLE TOURS

For bikers, a motorcycle tour is by far the best way to see Japan's unique countryside. The roads are excellent and Japan has a thriving motorcycle tour culture. Though road signs are often marked in English, this isn't often the case in rural areas. The Japan Biker FAQ has information on riding in Japan, and Sasa Trails offers customized motorcycle tours throughout the country.

Japan Biker FAQ. The Japan Biker FAQ has everything you need to know about traveling around Japan by motorcycle. ⊕ *www.thejapanfaq.com/bikerfaq-toc.html.*

▌VISITOR INFORMATION

The Tourist Information Center (TIC) near Tokyo Station has a wealth of information for visitors, as do the more than 140 tourist information offices around the country certified by JNTO. Look for the sign showing a red question mark and the word "information" at train stations and city centers.

Contacts Tourist Information Center (TIC). ✉ *Shin Tokyo Bldg. 1F, 3–3–1 Marunouchi, Chiyoda-ku* ☎ *03/3201–3331* ⊕ *www.jnto.go.jp/eng.*

ONLINE TRAVEL TOOLS

Online cultural resources and travel-planning tools abound for travelers to Japan. Aside from the expected information about regions, hotels, and festivals, Web Japan has offbeat info such as the location of bargain-filled ¥100 shops in Tokyo and buildings designed by famous architects. Another good source for all-Japan information and regional sights and events is Japan-guide.com. Hyperdia has excellent information about train travel, as does the "train route finder" by Jorudan. Urban Rail has an excellent map of the Tokyo and Osaka subways system.

Urban Rail maintains a useful subway navigator, which includes the subway systems in Tokyo and the surrounding areas. The Metropolitan Government website is an excellent source of information on sightseeing and current events in Tokyo.

Check out the websites of Japan's three major English-language daily newspapers: the *Asahi Shimbun, Daily Yomiuri,* and the *Japan Times.* Both *Metropolis* and *Time Out Tokyo* have up-to-date event, dining, and arts listings.

All About Japan Web Japan. ⊕ *web-jpn.org.*

English-Language Media Sources
Asahi Shimbun. ⊕ *ajw.asahi.com.*
The Japan News. ⊕ *the-japan-news.com.*
Japan Times. ⊕ *www.japantimes.co.jp.*
Kansai Scene. ⊕ *www.kansaiscene.com.*
Metropolis. ⊕ *www.metropolisjapan.com.*
Time Out Tokyo. ⊕ *www.timeout.jp.*

Currency Conversion XE.com. ⊕ *www.xe.com.*

Transportation Hyperdia. ⊕ *www.hyperdia. com.* **Jorudan.** ⊕ *www.jorudan.co.jp/english.* **Urban Rail.** ⊕ *www.urbanrail.net.*

INDEX

PHOTO CREDITS

Front cover: Sepavo | Dreamstime.com [Description: Kyoto, Japan gardens at Heian Shrine]. 1, Gavin Hellier/age fotostock. 2-3, JTB Photo/age fotostock. 5, Steve Vidler / age fotostock. Chapter 1: Experience Japan: 8-9, DatacraftUIG / age fotostock. 16 (left), Wikimedia Commons. 16 (top right), JNTO. 16 (bottom right), Tibor Bognar/age fotostock. 17 (top left), Chi King/Flickr. 17 (bottom left), Thomas La Mela/Shutterstock. 17 (right), Imre Cikajlo/iStockphoto. 27 (top), Yasufumi Nishi/ JNTO. 27 (bottom), Gavin Hellier/age fotostock. 46, Javier Larrea / age fotostock. 47, Steve Vidler / age fotostock. 48 (top left), 663highland/Wikimedia Commons. 48 (bottom left), Public domain. 48 (right), Javier Larrea / age fotostock. 49 (top left), Fedor Selivanov/Shutterstock. 49 (bottom left), Razvan Radu-Razvan Photography/iStockphoto. 49 (center), Rachelle Burnside/Shutterstock. 49 (right), CAN BALCIOGLU/Shutterstock. 50 (left), Neale Cousland/Shutterstock. 50 (top right), Ilya D. Gridnev/Shutterstock. 50 (bottom right), Wikimedia Commons. 51 (left), Yasufumi Nishi/JNTO. 51 (top right), Dr_Flash/Shutterstock. 51 (bottom right), Tataroko/Wikimedia Commons. 52 (top left), tci/age fotostock. 52 (bottom left), Tibor Bognar / age fotostock. 52 (right), Jochen Tack / age fotostock. Chapter 2: A Japanese Culture Primer: 53, Sergii Rudiuk / Shutterstock. 54, thinboyfatter/Flickr. 55, Kagawa Prefecture/JNTO. 55 (inset), sevenke/Shutterstock. 56–57, JNTO. 57 (bottom right), Payless Images/Shutterstock. 58 (top), JNTO. 58 (bottom), Saga Prefecture/JNTO. 59 (all), Hokkaido Tourism Organization/JNTO. 60 (top and bottom), Nagano Prefecture/JNTO. 61 (top), JNTO. 61 (bottom), Jill Battaglia/iStockphoto. 62 (top), Tondo Soesanto Soegondo/Shutterstock. 62 (bottom), svry/Shutterstock. 63, Kanazawa City/JNTO. 64 and 65`(top), JNTO. 65 (bottom), Photo Japan / age fotostock. 66, Okinawa Convention & Visitors Bureau/JNTO. 67, Ishikawa Prefecture / JNTO. 68, Ishikawa Prefecture Tourist Association and Kanazawa Convention Bureau/ JNTO. 69 (left), su.bo/Flickr. 69 (right), Nagano Prefecture/ JNTO. 70, Jim Epler/iStockphoto. 71, Iwate Prefecture/JNTO. 72, Iain Masterton / age fotostock. 73 (bottom left), JNTO. 73 (top right), Nagano Prefecture/ JNTO. 74, Christophe Boisvieux / age fotostock. 75, chrisho/iStockphoto. 76, John Warburton-Lee Photography / Alamy. 77 (bottom left), Juri Pozzi/iStockphoto. 77 (top right), Japan Ryokan Association/ JNTO. 78, ton koene/age fotostock. 79 (bottom left), Lukas Kurtz/Flickr. 79 (top right), luisvilla/Flickr. 80, Steve Silver / age fotostock. 81 (bottom left), FOTOSEARCH RM / age fotostock. 81 (top right), _Yuki_K /Flickr. 82, Steve Silver / age fotostock. 83 (bottom left), Kodokan/ JNTO. 83 (top right), Steve Silver / age fotostock. 84, Kevin O'Hara/age fotostock. 85 (bottom left), strikeael/Flickr. 85 (top right), Oote Boe/age fotostock. 86, Kanazawa City/JNTO. 87 (bottom left), simonhn/Flickr. 87 (top right), jonrawlinson/Flickr. 88, Mitchell Coster /age fotostock. 89 (bottom left), Okayama Prefecture/JNTO. 89 (top right), Noriko Kitano. 90 and 91 (bottom), Yasufumi Nishi/ JNTO. 91 (top), thinboyfatter/Shutterstock. 92, Y.Shimizu/ JNTO. 93 (bottom left), Yasufumi Nishi/ JNTO. 93, (top right), JNTO. 94, PSno7/Shutterstock. 95, Yasufumi Nishi/JNTO. 96, Christopher Heschong/Flickr. Chapter 3: Tokyo: 97, JNTO. 98, Cheng Chang/iStockphoto. 99 (top left), Lluís Casas/Flickr. 99 (bottom right), Akira Okada/ JNTO. 100, Christian Kober/age fotostock. 101 (bottom left), Karl Baron/Flickr. 101 (top right), jetalone/Flickr. 102, Y. Shimizu. 110, Tibor Bognar/age fotostock. 118, Cristian Baitg/iStockphoto. 124, MeeRok/Shutterstock. 130, Tifonimages/Shutterstock. 135, MIKI Yoshihito/Flickr. 146, Sylvain Grandadam/age fotostock. 150, Iain Masterton/age fotostock. 185, José Fuste Raga/age fotostock. 199, José Fuste Raga/age fotostock. 209, JNTO. 210 (top left), ton koene / age fotostock. 210 (bottom left), idealisms/Flickr. 210 (top right), Andrew Currie/Flickr. 210 (bottom right), JTB Photo / age fotostock. 211 (center left), robcocquyt/Shutterstock. 211 (top), Sylvain Grandadam / age fotostock. 211 (bottom left), Mie Prefecture, JNTO. 211 (right), bptakoma/Flickr. 212, Kimtaro/Flickr. 213 (top), JNTO. 213 (bottom), dichohecho/Flickr. 214 (top left), Ron Koeberer / age fotostock. 214 (bottom), SeanPavonePhoto / iStockphoto, 214 (top right), ton koene / age fotostock. 215, Boaz Rottem / age fotostock. 216 (top), LIMI feu SS 2010 collection. 216 (center), N.HOOLYWOOD. 216 (bottom), Somarta. 226, ehnmark/Flickr. Chapter 4: Side Trips from Tokyo: 231, Yujiro | Dreamstime.com, 232 (top) and 233 (top left), Aschaf/Flickr. 233 (top right), Yasufumi Nishi/ JNTO. 233 (bottom), H.L.I.T./Flickr. 234, ototadana/Flickr. 238-39, JTB Photo / age fotostock. 238 (bottom), Banzai Hiroaki/Flickr. 239 (top and bottom), flickr.com/diloz. 240 (top and bottom), Wikimedia Commons. 241 (top), Vidler Steve / age fotostock. 241 (bottom), Odakyu Electric Railway/JNTO. 242 (top left, right 3, and right 4), jetalone/Hajime NAKANO/Flickr. 242 (bottom left), flickr.com/diloz. 242 (right 2), imgdive/Banzai Hiroaki/Flickr. 242 (top right), skyseeker/Flickr. 243, Azlan DuPree/Flickr. 244 (top), flickr.com/diloz. 244 (center), jetalone/Hajime NAKANO/Flickr. 244 (bottom), By imgdive/Banzai Hiroaki/Flickr. 245, JTB Photo / age fotostock. 259 and 268, JTB Photo/age fotostock. 270, Vladimir Khirman/iStockphoto. 273, Imre Cikajlo/iStockphoto. 275, Tony Waltham/age fotostock. 282, 288 and 290, Aschaf/Flickr. 297, Yasufumi Nishi/ JNTO. 300, matteusus/iStockphoto. Chapter 5: Nagoya, Ise-Shima, and the Kii Peninsula: 305, Christian Goupi / age fotostock. 307 (top left), 663highland/Wikimedia Commons. 307 (bottom right), ThorstenS/Wikimedia

Commons. 308-09, TOYOTA MOTOR CORPORATION. 310, brytta/iStockphoto. 317, and 327, UTB Photo / age fotostock. 332, Sepavo | Dreamstime.com. 338, Christophe Boisvieux / age fotostock. Chapter 6: The Japan Alps and the North Chubu Coast: 341, Tearswept | Dreamstime.com. 343 (top left), Gunma prefecture/ JNTO. 343 (bottom right), Justin Lancaster/Shutterstock. 344 and 345 (bottom left), JNTO. 345 (top right), microstock8/Shutterstock. 346, rumpleteaser/Flickr. 353, Nagano Prefecture/ JNTO. 356, David Poole/ age fotostock. 362, Hiro1775 | Dreamstime.com. 365, Tibor Bognar / age fotostock. 374, 663highland/Wikimedia Commons. 379 and 382, JTB Photo / age fotostock. 386, Paolo Negri / age fotostock. Chapter 7: Kyoto: 389, Atlantide SNC / age fotostock. 390, Salawin Chanthapan/Shutterstock. 392, Aschaf/Flickr. 397, Sylvain Grandadam / age fotostock. 403, Matt Comeaux/iStockphoto. 406, MShades/Chris Gladis/Flickr. 407, Christian Goupi / age fotostock. 408 (top), rudiuk/Shutterstock. 408 (bottom), PlusMinus/Wikimedia Commons. 409 (top left), RachelH_/Flickr. 409 (bottom left), Wikimedia Commons. 409 (top right), whitefi eld_d/whity/Flickr. 409 (bottom right), rudiuk/Shutterstock. 410 (top left), Lonnie Duka / age fotostock. 410 (bottom left), JTB Photo / age fotostock. 410 (top right), John Weiss/Flickr. 410 (bottom right), shisho_1975/Shinji WATANABE/Flickr. 411, Christophe Boisvieux/age fotostock. 420, Richard T Nowitz / age fotostock. 429, Fg2/Wikimedia Commons. 433, Iain Masterton / age fotostock. 434, Tibor Bognar / age fotostock. 442, José Fuste Raga /age fotostock. 460, Klaus-Werner Friedric / age fotostock. 463, Klaus-Werner Friedric / age fotostock. 467, Atlantide SNC / age fotostock. Chapter 8: The Kansai Region: 473, JTB Photo / age fotostock. 474, Bernard Gagnon/Wikimedia Commons. 475 (top left), Martin Mette/Shutterstock. 475 (bottom right), Neale Cousland/Shutterstock. 476, Fred Hsu/Flickr. 477 (bottom left), DoNotLick/Flickr. 477 (top right), blogefl /Flickr. 478, Iain Masterton / age fotostock. 479 (bottom left), Hokkaido Tourism Organization/ JNTO. 479 (top right), beggs/Flickr. 480, Aschaf/Flickr. 488, RinzeWind/Flickr. 491, coward_lion / iStockphoto. 493, José Fuste Raga / age fotostock. 512, Cowardlion | Dreamstime.com. 517, Javier Larrea / age fotostock. 527 (left), Kyoto Convention Bureau / JNTO. 527 (top right), tehcheesiong/Shutterstock. 527 (bottom right), glimmerous/Eve/Flickr. 527, (bottom center), Claudia van Dijk/Shutterstock. 528 (top), JTB Photo / age fotostock. 528 (bottom), Naoto Takai/Flickr. 529 (top left), Wikimedia Commons. 529 (middle left), Ehime Prefecture/JNTO. 529 (bottom left), Ishikawa Prefecture Tourist Association and Kanazawa Convention Bureau/JNTO. 529 (top center), Saga Prefecture/JNTO. 529 (middle center), Ishikawa Prefecture Tourist Association and Kanazawa Convention Bureau/JNTO. 529 (bottom center), Nagano Prefecture/JNTO. 529 (top right), Naoto Takai/Flickr. 529 (middle right), Okayama-ken Kanko Renmei/JNTO. 529 (bottom right), Japan Convention Services, Inc./JNTO. 530 (top left), Naomi Hasegawa/Shutterstock. 530 (bottom left), Craig Hanson/Shutterstock. 530 (top right), Friedensreich Hundertwasser/Wikimedia Commons. 530 (bottom right), ma_shimaro/Flickr. 531 (top left), NH/Shutterstock. 531 (bottom left), takayuki/Shutterstock. 531 (top right and bottom right), JTB Photo / age fotostock. 532 (top left), Tomomarusan/WIkimedia Commons. 532 (bottom left), DKPugh/Shutterstock. 532 (top right), willem!/Wikimedia Commons. 532 (bottom right), maxstockphoto/Shutterstock. 539, Tibor Bognar / age fotostock. 545, Crowne Plaza Kobe. Chapter 9: Western Honshu: 547, JNTO. 548, shrk/Flickr. 549 (top), NASAblueshift/Flickr. 549 (bottom), jfeuchter/Flickr. 550, JNTO. 554, Okayama-ken Kanko Renmei/JNTO. 562-63, JNTO. 564, Brent Winebrenner / age fotostock. 565 (all), JNTO. 566 (top), JNTO. 566 (bottom), Ewing Galloway/age fotostock. 567 (top), FOTOSEARCH RM / age fotostock. 567 (bottom left and bottom right), Wikimedia Commons. 571, Dave Collins / age fotostock. 577, JTB Photo / age fotostock. 581, JNTO. Chapter 10: Shikoku: 585, JTB Photo / age fotostock. 586 (top) highland/Wikimedia Commons. 587 (top), JNTO. 587 (bottom), yosakoigraffiti/Flickr. 588, Randym/Shutterstock. 595 (left), JTB Photo / age fotostock. 595 (top right), Reggaeman/Wikimedia Commons. 595 (bottom right), Wikimedia Commons. 596 (left and right), 663highland/Wikimedia Commons. 597 (top left and top right), Reggaeman/Wikimedia Commons. 597 (bottom), PHGCOM/Wikimedia Commons. 598 (left), (top right, and bottom right), Reggaeman/Wikimedia Commons. 598 (top center), Wikimedia Commons. 599, Ehime Prefecture/JNTO. 603, Edmund SumnerVIEW / age fotostock. 613, Mike Crane/stockstudioX/iStockphoto. 616, Mark Treston/HappyRaft. 621, Tibor Bognar / age fotostock. 628, JTB MEDIA CREATION, Inc. / Alamy. Chapter 11: Kyushu: 631, Kagoshima Prefectural Tourist Federation/ JNTO. 632, Paolo Gianti/Shutterstock. 633, Hourin. 634, Jordan Austin/Flickr. 643, JTB Photo / age fotostock. 644, Burak Demir/iStockphoto. 649, Lukas Kurtz/Flickr. 660, Igorberger/Wikimedia Commons. 663, JNTO. Chapter 12: Okinawa: 665, Nancy Kennedy/Shutterstock. 666, Ippei Naoi/iStockphoto. 667 (top), Sam DCruz/Shutterstock. 667 (bottom), Sharon Kennedy/Shutterstock. 668, Okinawa Convention & Visitors Bureau. 669 (bottom), Okinawa Convention & Visitors Bureau. 669 (top), mdid/Flickr. 670, Simamariasibi. 677, Okinawa Convention & Visitors Bureau. 681, Photo Japan / Alamy. 690, Okinawa Convention & Visitors Bureau. 694, JTB Photo / age fotostock. 696, Chris Willson / Alamy. Chapter 13: Tohoku: 699, Yasufumi Nishi/ JNTO. 700, Yasuf-

NOTES

NOTES

NOTES

ABOUT OUR WRITERS

 Kyoto updater Judith Clancy has lived in the city for over 40 years, and has made a 130-year-old renovated weaving studio her home. She is the author of *Exploring Kyoto*; *Kyoto Machiya Restaurant Guide*; *Kyoto: City of Zen*; and *Kyoto Gardens: Masterworks of the Japanese Gardener's Art.*

 Jay Farris has spent 15 years getting acquainted with Japan and now calls Tokyo home after a few years of living in Yamagata. He works as a translator and, having graduated from the University of Tokyo with a master's degree in urban engineering, as a guide for curious tourists who are interested in urban history and Tokyo's rich backstory. Jay updated the Hokkaido chapter.

Rob Goss has been based in Tokyo since 1999. Rob's writing has appeared in almost 100 publications around the globe, including *Time*, *National Geographic Traveler*, and the in-flight magazines of Delta, US Airways, KLM, and others. He is also the author of four books on Japan with Tuttle Publishing, with three more currently on the way. Rob updated the Nagoya, Ise-Shima, and the Kii Peninsula chapter, as well as parts of the Tokyo chapter

Robert Morel has been exploring Japan since 2003 and still thinks the best way to get from Hokkaido to Okinawa is by bicycle. He currently writes about, photographs, and lives in Tokyo's historic Yanaka neighborhood. He updated the Side Trips Tokyo, Kansai, Western Honshu, and Travel Smart chapters, as well as parts of the Tokyo chapter.

 Tohoku updater Emma Parker spent five years in Tohoku before moving to Tokyo and working in the field of international cultural relations. She now lives in rural Niigata, where she is active as a writer, translator, and tour guide. She is interested in developing authentic tourism based on local customs and traditions.

Annamarie Sasagawa grew up in the wilds of northern British Columbia and now lives in Tokyo's Shinjuku ward. After years on the road as a tour leader in Japan, she hung up her backpack to get a PhD in cultural anthropology at the University of Tokyo. Annamarie updated our Experience, Japanese Cultural Primer, Japan Alps and the North Chubu Coast, and Shikoku chapters.

 Chris Willson is a travel writer and photographer who lives in Okinawa. His website is ⊕ *www.travel67.com*. He updated the Okinawa and Kyushu chapters.

Our coverage of Tokyo was updated by Brett Bull, Rob Goss, Misha Janette, Noriko Kitano, Robert Morel, and Yukari Sakamoto.